Visser's Annotated European Patent Convention

Visser's Annotated European Patent Convention

2025 Edition
updated until 01.04.2025

Kaisa Suominen
Nina Ferara
Peter de Lange
Andrew John Rudge

Wolters Kluwer

Published by:
Kluwer Law International B.V.
PO Box 316
2400 AH Alphen aan den Rijn
The Netherlands
E-mail: international-sales@wolterskluwer.com
Website: www.wolterskluwer.com/en/solutions/kluwerlawinternational

Sold and distributed by:
Wolters Kluwer Legal & Regulatory U.S.
920 Links Avenue
Landisville, PA 17538
United States of America
Email: customer.service@wolterskluwer.com

ISBN: 978-940-352-299-9
e-Book ISBN: 978-940-352-349-1
web-PDF ISBN: 978-940-352-359-0

Introduction

Visser's Annotated European Patent Convention reproduces the complete text of the European Patent Convention, the Implementing Regulations, two Protocols and the Rules relating to Fees in the form in which they are in force on 1 April 2025. It also includes the Rules relating to Unitary Patent Protection and the Rules relating to Fees for Unitary Patent Protection. Note that for situations where the EPC articles and rules apply mutatis mutandis to prosecution of UP requests and UP's at the EPO, notes to the UPR and RfeesUPP do not repeat those notes.

The notes to each individual article and rule of the Convention provide a commentary on the text of the law, explaining the interpretation of each paragraph. The notes give a short indication of important issues having a bearing on the interpretation of the law. They include references to case law up to 1 April 2025 and the Guidelines for Examination in the European Patent Office, edition April 2025.

The book is intended as a reference book, providing a quick grasp of the essentials of the law both for the patent attorney and the trainee. The detail in the notes reflects the detail required for daily practice and for answering questions posed in the European qualifying examinations of the last few years. Note, that the complete text of the Arrangement for Deposit Accounts and the Arrangements for Automatic Debiting is not included in the book; however, the notes to Rfees5 give a summary. Trainees preparing for the examinations should note, that they must know the law and its interpretation on 31 October of the year prior to the examination (OJ 2017 A88).

Cross-references in the notes to articles and rules aim at giving an insight into the structure of the Convention. The abbreviation 'EPC' is only added to a reference where its absence could cause confusion. Cross-references from provisions in EPC2000 to EPC1973 provide quick access to the text of the old provisions. A cross-reference table links EPC1973 provisions to those of EPC2000. The reader is referred to the 14th edition (2006) of this book for provisions of EPC1973 which may still be applicable to specific cases; EPC1973 is not included in this book.

Numerous references to case law and the April 2025 edition of the Guidelines allow the user to consult the sources of the information contained in the notes and give a quick access to important case law. The notes do not provide all possible references to the Guidelines but mainly those where the Guidelines are the main or only source of information and where they emphasise that case law is being followed by the departments of first instance. References in the notes to the EPC and case law have been highlighted to facilitate looking up the references.

A case law table provides a cross-reference between decisions of the boards of appeal and paragraphs of the book. A table with brief summaries of the decisions of the Enlarged Board of Appeal cited in the book is also included.

In spite of all due care taken during the compilation of the notes, the authors do not accept any responsibility for errors. The contributors and the publisher wish to express their gratitude to readers who provided comments. Any comments on inaccuracies or suggestions for improvement are welcomed. Please send them to Mrs Anja Kramer at anja.kramer@wolterskluwer.com.

Turku, 15 April 2025

Previous Editions

The Annotated European Patent Convention was founded by Derk Visser, who updated the work annually up to and including the 25th edition, published in 2017. Editions published as from 2018 are written by an author team and include the year of publication in the title.

Contributors to the 2025 edition

Kaisa Suominen, MSc (Eng.), Editor
European and Finnish patent attorney at Laine IP Oy
Art. 1-51, 92, 94-98, 164-178

Nina Ferara, MSc
European patent attorney at United Kingdom Atomic Energy Authority (UKAEA)
Art. 58-74, 93, 99-112a, 119, 133-134a and 150-153

Peter de Lange, MSc, LLM
European and Dutch patent attorney at V.O. Patents & Trademarks
Art. 75-86, 90, 123-125, 127-132 Rfees, UPR and RfeesUPP

Andrew Rudge, MA, PhD
European and Chartered (UK) patent attorney at Pfizer Limited
Art. 52-57, 87-89, 113-118, 120-122 and 135-149a

Revision note

A vertical line in the right-hand margin of a page indicates text amended or newly introduced on account of publications in the Official Journal of the EPO and on the EPO website as from 1 April 2025 or on account of a new insight of the authors.

The following important amendments have been made since March 2024:

- new **R.36(5)**, **R.39(2a)** and **R.160(3)** (entry into force 16.12.2025);
- the text of the rules that have been amended to be gender neutral (entry into force 01.04.2025);
- updated notes on **Art.52**, **Art.53**, **Art.54**, **Art.55**, **Art.56**, **Art.57**, **Art.87**, **Art.88**, **Art.89**, **R.25**, **R.26**, **R.27**, **R.28**, **R.29**, **R.52**, **R.53** and **R.54**;
- updated notes on infringement under the UPCA (see **Art.64**);
- the Lao People's Democratic Republic became a validation state (see **Art.79**);
- updates reflecting the April 2025 edition of the Guidelines for Examination in the EPO, the Guidelines for Search and Examination at the EPO as PCT Authority and the Unitary Patent Guidelines; and
- a new brief introduction to the EPC for readers new in the field (see **Introduction to the EPC**).

Notation

The book uses the following abbreviations for terms and references. A reference placed before a full stop at the end of a sentence refers only to that sentence; a reference placed after the last full stop of a paragraph refers to the entire paragraph.

AAD.3	Point 3 of the Arrangements for the Automatic Debiting procedure; see **Rfees5(2):3**
ADA.14	Point 14 of the Arrangements for Deposit Accounts; see **Rfees5(2):2**
AG-IP §243	WIPO publication, *PCT Applicant's Guide*, International Phase, paragraph 243
Ante Art.52	Document preceding Art.52 and containing information on than one document, here on Part II of the EPC
Art.2	Article 2 of the EPC
Art.2 PCT	Article 2 of the PCT
Art.14(2):3	Article 14, paragraph 2 of the EPC, note 3 in this book
A-X,7.5.5	EPO publication, *Guidelines for Examination in the European Patent Office*, part A, chapter X, section 7.5.5
CLBA	EPO publication, *Case Law of the Boards of Appeal of the EPO*, 10th edition, July 2022
CA/PL 17/06	Explanatory remarks of the EPO to amendments of the Implementing Regulations EPC2000, dated 07.08.2006
CA/PL 29/06	Explanatory remarks of the EPO to amendments of the Implementing Regulations EPC2000, document Add. 1 dated 27.10.2006
CA/65/17	Administrative Council document 65 of 2017
Dec. Pres.	Decision of the President of the EPO
D1/92	Decision of the Disciplinary Board of Appeal
Empel	M. van Empel, *The Granting of European Patents* (Sijthoff, Leiden 1975)
EPC	European Patent Convention as revised by the diplomatic conference of November 2000 (EPC2000)
EPC1973	European Patent Convention of 05.10.1973
GL/PCT-EPO A-IV,1.1	EPO publication, *Guidelines for Search and Examination at the EPO as PCT Authority*, part A, chapter IV, section 1.1
G1/93 hn.1, r.16	Decision of the Enlarged Board of Appeal in referral 1 of the year 1993, headnote 1 and point 16 of the reasons for the decision
IPREE2018	Implementing provisions to the Regulation on the European qualifying examination of 01.01.2019
J27/94	Decision of the Legal Board of Appeal
MR/2/00	Basic proposal for the revision of the EPC1973, dated 13.10.2000
MR/24/00	Proceedings of the Diplomatic Conference of 20 to 29 November 2000, document of 15.07.2003

NatLaw	EPO publication, *National law relating to the* EPC, 23rd edition
Not. EPO	Notice of the EPO
OJ 1995 p.9	Official Journal of the European Patent Office, year 1995, page 9 (format until December 2013)
OJ 2007 se4 EN	Official Journal of the European Patent Office, year 2007, special edition 4, English version
OJ 2014 A12	Official Journal of the European Patent Office, year 2014, article 12 (format as from January 2014)
OJ 2014 sp4	Official Journal of the European Patent Office, year 2014, Supplementary Publication 4
P:4.2	Preamble of the EPC, note 4.2
PC	Paris Convention
PCT	Patent Cooperation Treaty
PLT	Patent Law Treaty
Prot. Rec. Art.1(2)	Article 1(2) of the Protocol on Jurisdiction and the Recognition of Decisions in respect of the Right to the Grant of a European patent
REE2009	Regulation on the European qualifying examination of 01.01.2009
RoP	Rules of Procedure of the UPC
RPBA	Rules of Procedure of the Boards of Appeal (OJ 2024 A15)
RPBA2007	Rules of Procedure of the Boards of Appeal which entered into force on 13.12.2007 (OJ 2007 p.536)
RPEBA	Rules of Procedure of the Enlarged Board of Appeal (see R.12c(2))
Rfees2	Article 2 of the Rules relating to Fees
RfeesUPP.2	Article 2 of the Rules relating to Fees for Unitary Patent Protection
R1/08	Decision of the Enlarged Board of Appeal on a petition for review under Art.112a
R.88	Rule 88 of the EPC
R.88 PCT	Rule 88 of the PCT
Singer Art.56 note 10	Singer / Stauder / Luginbühl, *Europäisches Patentübereinkommen*, 9th edition (Wolters Kluwer, 2023), Article 56, marginal note 10
T54/89	Decision of a Technical Board of Appeal
UP-1.5.2	EPO publication, *Unitary Patent Guidelines*, section 1.5.2
UPCA	Agreement on a Unified Patent Court
UPR.6	Rule 6 of the Rules relating to Unitary Patent Protection

Introduction to the EPC

This chapter provides a high-level overview of the EPC, summarising some of the basic features and omitting many details and exceptions that can be found in the detailed notes to each provision.

1 Structure of the EPC

The EPC deals first with the organisation of the EPO and the languages that may be used in EPO proceedings (**Art.1** to **51**), before setting out the requirements for patentability (Art. **52** to **57**), other aspects of substantive patent law (Art.**58** to **74**) and the formal requirements that apply to patent applications (Art.**75** to **85**). Thereafter, the patent procedures are specified: firstly, the grant procedure (Art.**90** to **98**); secondly, the opposition procedures (Art.**99** to **105**); and, lastly, the appeal procedure (Art.**106** to **112a**). These are followed by provisions relating to all procedures before the EPO and provisions governing the interface between the EPC and other patent laws (Art.**113** to **178**). The Implementing Regulations (rules) are organised according to the same structure: for example, the grant procedure is dealt with in **R.35** to **74**, the opposition procedure in **R.75** to **96** and the appeal procedure in **R.97** to **103**.

2 From filing to grant

When first studying the EPC, it may be convenient to begin by following the path taken by a European patent application, starting with the receipt of the application and its initial examination (**Art. 90**). At this stage, some formal requirements are examined, and certain fees must be paid (**Art.78**). Next, the EPO carries out a search to find out what was known about the claimed invention before the application was filed (**Art.92**) and carries out a preliminary assessment of patentability. The main patentability requirements are novelty and inventive step (**Art.52(1)**, **54** and **56**) and the claimed invention must also fall outside the scope of certain excluded categories (**Art.52(2)** and **Art.53**). The claimed invention must be novel over everything made available to the public before the filing date and over other European patent applications having an earlier filing date. The application itself must also meet certain requirements; for example, the description must sufficiently disclose the invention (**Art.83**) and the claims must be clear (**Art.84**).

The application is published by the EPO (**Art.93**) and, if the applicant wishes to proceed further, a thorough substantive examination is carried out (**Art.94**), which results in either the grant of the European patent or the refusal of the application (**Art.97**). If the application is refused, the applicant can file an appeal (**Art.106**). Before refusing the application, the EPO must give the applicant an opportunity to comment (**Art.113(1)**) and hold oral proceedings if requested (**Art.116**).

If the patent is granted, third parties can file an opposition against it, seeking revocation of the patent (**Art.99**). It is also possible for the proprietor to voluntarily limit the patent after the grant (**Art.105a**).

3 Effect of a granted European patent

A European patent gives the proprietor the right to prevent others from using the invention commercially without the proprietor's consent. These rights are not specified in the EPC itself but are found instead in the national laws of the contracting states and the Unified Patent Court Agreement (UPCA) (**Art.64(3)**). In relation to the latter agreement, the proprietor's right to exclude others from using the invention is set out in Art.25 to 29 UPCA.

A granted European patent does not automatically remain in force in all contracting states. Some contracting states require the filing of a full or partial translation of the patent into an official language of that state shortly after grant (**Art.65**), and renewal fees are payable. The patent may also be registered as a unitary patent in respect of a number of participating EU member states (**UPR.5**).

4 **Claiming priority of earlier application**
In principle, the filing date of the application (**Art.80**) is the cut-off date for prior art. The invention claimed in the application must be novel and inventive over prior art that was made available to the public before that cut-off date. However, the application may claim the priority of another application filed at most twelve months earlier (priority application). The filing date of that priority application is referred to as the priority date and becomes the cut-off date for the prior art instead of the filing date (**Art.87**).

5 **Filing through PCT**
It is also possible to file a European patent application as an international patent application under the PCT (Euro-PCT application). The applicant can initiate the procedure before the EPO based on the international application at any time up to 31 months from the priority date (**Art.153, R.159**). The first steps of the procedure under the PCT and when entering the EPO regional phase differ from those of a European application filed directly at the EPO. From substantive examination onwards, the procedure is the same.

6 **Unity of invention and divisional applications**
The claims of a patent application should not be directed to two or more different inventions, in other words, the application must have unity of invention (**Art.82**). If the patent application concerns multiple inventions, the applicant can file one or more divisional applications for the second and further inventions (**Art.76**). Divisional applications can also be filed in other cases, for example, to prosecute narrow and broad claims for the same invention in separate applications.

7 **Renewal fees**
Beginning two years after the application is filed, a yearly renewal fee must be paid. The renewal fee is paid to the EPO up to the grant of the patent (**Art.86**). After the grant, a renewal fee must be paid to the patent office of each state where the proprietor wishes to maintain the patent in force (**Art.141**) or, in the case of a unitary patent, to the EPO (**UPR.13**).

8 **Languages**
The official languages of the EPO are English, French and German (**Art.14**). Details of which language a party can use in oral and written proceedings before the EPO are specified in **Art.14** and **R.3** to **6**. In certain cases, in written proceedings, a party may initially use an official language of an EPC state and file a translation into an official language of the EPO later (**Art.14(4)**). In such a case, a fee reduction may apply (**R.7a(1)**).

9 **Departments of the EPO**
The Receiving Section carries out the initial examination of formal requirements (**Art.16**), the search is carried out by a search division (**Art.17**), and the subsequent examination up to grant is carried out by an examining division (**Art.18**). If an opposition is filed, an opposition division examines the opposition (**Art.19**). Appeals are heard by the boards of appeal (**Art.21**).

The Legal Division handles requests to register assignments of patent applications and other matters in the European Patent Register (**Art.20**).

A board of appeal can refer a legal question to the Enlarged Board of Appeal (**Art.22, Art.112**). The Enlarged Board also hears petitions for review of decisions of the boards of appeal (**Art.112a**).

The President of the EPO is responsible for managing the EPO (**Art.10**).

List of Contents

Convention on the Grant of European Patents

(EUROPEAN PATENT CONVENTION)

of 5 October 1973
as revised by the Act revising Article 63 EPC of 17 December 1991
and the Act revising the EPC of 29 November 2000

text as adopted by decision of
the Administrative Council of 28 June 2001

PREAMBLE

The Contracting States,

DESIRING to strengthen co-operation between the States of Europe in respect of the protection of inventions,

DESIRING that such protection may be obtained in those States by a single procedure for the grant of patents and by the establishment of certain standard rules governing patents so granted,

DESIRING, for this purpose, to conclude a Convention which establishes a European Patent Organisation and which constitutes a special agreement within the meaning of Article 19 of the Convention for the Protection of Industrial Property, signed in Paris on 20 March 1883 and last revised on 14 July 1967, and a regional patent treaty within the meaning of Article 45, paragraph 1, of the Patent Cooperation Treaty of 19 June 1970,

HAVE AGREED on the following provisions:

1 **General**

The considerations in the Preamble should be considered as guidelines for interpreting the EPC.

The EPC consists of the Preamble, Articles, Rules, and five protocols. The Rules relating to Fees are not part of the EPC and were adopted later. See **Art.164**.

2 **Interpretation of the EPC**

2.1 RULES FOR INTERPRETATION IN THE EPC

The following rules of interpretation of the provisions of the EPC are given in the EPC itself:

Preamble: relation with Paris Convention (PC) and PCT
Protocol on the interpretation of **Art.69**
Art.125: Reference to general principles of national law
Art.150: Application of the provisions of the PCT
Art.164: Order of prevalence between treaties, protocols and rules
Art.177: Three equally authoritative texts
R.26(1): Interpretation of **Art.53**.

2.2 THE VIENNA CONVENTION ON THE LAW OF TREATIES

The EPC is an international treaty and must be interpreted according to the rules of international law. Basic rules for interpretation of treaties are given in the Vienna Convention on the Law of Treaties of 23 May 1969, reprinted in part in OJ 1984 p.193. The Vienna Convention entered into force on 27 January 1980, whereas the EPC entered into force on 7 October 1977 (see **Art.169**). Even though the Vienna Convention does not have a retroactive effect (Art.4 Vienna Convention), the EPO has decided that the rules for interpretation in the Vienna Convention also apply to the EPC. It is well recognised that Art.31 and 32 of the Vienna Convention about the interpretation of treaties codified already existing rules of public international law. (**G5/83** r.1-4)

2.2.1 *General rule of interpretation and good faith*

Art.31(1) of the Vienna Convention states that a treaty shall be interpreted in good faith in accordance with the ordinary meaning to be given to the terms of the treaty in their context and in the light of its object and purpose.

This general rule of interpretation is a single rule of interpretation. It requires several methods of interpretation, in particular the grammatical, systematic and teleological methods, to be applied in a holistic manner (**J5/23** r.2.3). The grammatical method of interpretation involves analysing the linguistic meaning of the terms, using e.g. dictionaries, in the three languages of the EPC (**Art.177**). The systematic method involves the interpretation of a provision in the context of the EPC as a whole, using factors such as how the same and similar terms are used in other provisions of the EPC, the effect of the possible interpretations on any related provisions in the EPC, and the division of the EPC into parts and chapters. Under the teleological method, the purpose of the provision is considered. Applying these methods of interpretation in a holistic manner means that the methods should be applied in combination, without a fixed hierarchy between them. For example, the systematic and teleological interpretation of the term 'any person' outweighed the grammatical interpretation in **G9/93**.

The rule that a treaty must be interpreted in good faith forms the basis of the principle of good faith and the principle of protection of legitimate expectations as applied by the EPO. The application of these principles is set out in **Art.125:2**.

2.2.2 *Additional matter to be considered*

Later agreements between the contracting states regarding the interpretation of the treaty or the application of its provisions can also be taken into account in the interpretation of the EPC according to Art.31(3) of the Vienna Convention, as well as any subsequent practice in the application of the treaty which establishes the agreement of the contracting states regarding its interpretation. An amendment of the Implementing Regulations can be regarded as a subsequent agreement or practice (**G2/12**, r.vii.4) and can justify a dynamic interpretation of the EPC (**G3/19**, r.xxvi.7).

Additionally, the preparatory work and circumstances at the time of drafting the treaty can be used to confirm an interpretation resulting from the application of Art.31 of the Vienna Convention or to determine the interpretation when the above rules give ambiguous or conflicting results (Art.32 Vienna Convention, **G5/83** r.5). The preparatory documents are often extensively analysed by the boards when interpreting a provision of the EPC (see e.g. **G1/86**).

Art.32 of the Vienna Convention permits the use of further supplementary means of interpretation. For instance, general legal principles can also help to interpret the EPC (**G1/86** r.12).

2.2.3 *Publication of preparatory documents*

The preparatory documents for EPC1973 ('travaux préparatoires') are published on the EPO website, organised chronologically and as extensive collections of the relevant documents for each article and rule. The collection of documents is virtually complete and includes both minutes of meetings and draft texts. However, some documents are only available in German and French because the UK was initially not involved in the project as it was not a member of the EU then.

Preparatory documents for EPC2000 have also been published on the EPO website.

Decisions of the Administrative Council amending the Implementing Regulations and preparatory documents of such amendments are also published on the EPO website since 2012 in the section "Transparency portal".

2.3 HARMONISATION
The interpretation of the EPC must take into account the goal of harmonisation of national and international patent law, an aspect not dealt with by the Vienna Convention. The harmonisation requires a consistent interpretation of the EPC and the national provisions, many of which have been adopted from the EPC. Therefore, the Boards of Appeal must take into account national interpretations of the provisions of the EPC. (**G5/83 r.6**)

3 **Paris Convention and PCT**
The PC is mentioned twice in the EPC, once in the Preamble and once in **Art.87(1)**. As stated in the Preamble, the EPC constitutes a special agreement within the meaning of Article 19 of the PC. Such agreements may not contravene the provisions of the PC (Article 19 of the PC).

The provisions of the EPC contain no cross-references to articles of the PC to avoid that provisions would apply which were subject to differences of interpretation. In line with this policy, the provisions of the PC about priority (Art.4A(1)), which contains an unclarity, have not been adopted in the EPC. Rather, the EPC contains a complete set of rules on priority (**Art.87-89, R.52, 53**). This set of rules agrees with the general understanding of Article 4 of the PC in the contracting states of the EPC. Thus, the EPC does not contravene the provisions of the PC and complies with Article 19 of the PC. (**J15/80**)

As stated in the preamble, the EPC is a regional patent treaty under Art.45(1) PCT. Therefore, the EPC must permit the filing of European patent applications to all persons who are entitled to file international applications under the PCT (see **Art.58**). For the precedence of the PCT over the EPC in case of conflicting provisions, see **Art.150(2)**.

4 **Amendments and revisions of the EPC**
The Convention may only be revised by a diplomatic conference according to **Art.172**. The Administrative Council has a limited competence to amend the Convention and is competent to amend the Implementing Regulations (**Art.33(1)**). The notes to the cited articles give an overview of the revisions and amendments.

4.1 EFFECT OF AMENDMENT AND REVISION
New legislation, introduced by amendment or revision, usually applies to pending cases unless its non-application is expressly provided for in the transitional provisions of the new legislation. As a corollary, new legislation normally does not apply retrospectively and, in order to safeguard interests based on the former state of the law, an express provision for retrospective effect is necessary before it will be judicially acknowledged. (**T315/03 r.5.9**)

The principle of legitimate expectations does not apply in case of changes in legislation (**T315/03 r.5.11**). Most amendments and revisions of the EPC contain detailed transitional provisions to provide some legal certainty for pending cases. See e.g. OJ 2022 A101 Art.2.

4.2 DEVELOPMENT OF A COMMON EU PATENT SYSTEM

On 17.12.2012 the member states of the European Union and the European Parliament laid the grounds for unitary patent protection in the EU by signing two Regulations, one setting up a unitary patent and the other establishing a translation regimen. The unitary patent is a European patent, granted by the EPO under the rules and procedures of the EPC, which has a unitary effect for the participating member states. The applicant may choose between either a national patent, a European patent with unitary effect, a European patent taking effect in one or more of the EPC contracting states or a European patent with unitary effect validated in addition in one or more other EPC contracting states not being participating member states. The Regulations were adopted by all EU member states except Spain because of the language hurdle. Croatia joined the EU in 2013 and has not adopted the Regulations. The Regulation setting up a unitary patent is a special agreement within the meaning of **Art.142.**

The third element of the legal framework for unitary patent protection, the Agreement on a Unified Patent Court (UPC Agreement, UPCA), sets up a single patent jurisdiction. The Agreement entered into force on 01.06.2023 and is open for ratification and accession. The two Regulations thus apply as of that date (OJ 2013 p.110). The ratification progress can be found on https://www.epo.org/en/applying/european/unitary.

The text of the Regulations is reproduced in OJ 2013 p.111 and p.132 and the text of the Agreement and the statute of the court in OJ 2013 p.286 and p.345. The rules governing the EPO when carrying out its tasks under the Regulations (as amended on 23.03.2022) are published in OJ 2022 A41 and A42. The budgetary and financial rules are published in OJ 2016 A41.

The Rules relating to Unitary Patent Protection (UPR) and Rules relating to Fees for Unitary Patent Protection (RfeesUPP) can be found in the Annex.

In order to obtain a European patent with unitary effect, the applicant must file a request for unitary effect at the EPO, within one month of the publication of the mention of the grant in the Bulletin. Thereafter, renewal fees for the European patent with unitary effect are to be paid yearly to the EPO. The request for unitary effect can only be filed for European patents having the same set of claims for all participating member states (**R.138**).

After entry into force of the Unified Patent Court, all European patents (and supplementary protection certificates) are subject to revocation and infringement proceedings before it, for the participating member states. However, during a transitional period, currently set to last seven years with an option to extend it to a further seven years, it is possible to opt out from the Unified Patent Court, i.e., to indicate that the European patent validated nationally in the participating member states is to be subject to national revocation and infringement proceedings. It is not possible to opt out a European patent with unitary effect.

PART I GENERAL AND INSTITUTIONAL PROVISIONS

Chapter I *General Provisions*

Art. 1 European law for the grant of patents

A system of law, common to the Contracting States, for the grant of patents for invention is established by this Convention.

1 **Principles of the EPC**
The four principles of the European Patent Convention are:
- a law for granting patents (**Art.1**);
- called European patents (**Art.2(1)**);
- designating one or more states (**Art.3**);
- having the effect of a national patent in each state (**Art.2(2)**).

The EPC is self-executing and is independent of national laws for its implementation (**J15/80**).

Art. 2 European patent

Art. 2(1) Patents granted under this Convention shall be called European patents.

Art. 2(2) The European patent shall, in each of the Contracting States for which it is granted, have the effect of and be subject to the same conditions as a national patent granted by that State, unless this Convention provides otherwise.

1 **Effect of European patent**
A European patent does not completely fall apart into a bundle of national patents. It retains its special character after the grant: the EPC overrules national law if EPC provisions relating to European patents are at variance with national law. The desire for the harmonisation of rules governing patents has been expressed in the Preamble. The main EPC provisions relating to European patents are:
- the protection of a process patent extends to the direct products of the process (**Art.64(2)**);
- the term of the patent is 20 years (**Art.63(1)**), possibly extended on the grounds of **Art.63(2)**;
- the text of the European patent in the language of the proceedings is the authentic text (**Art.70(1)**);

- a European patent may only be revoked in a national procedure on the grounds given in **Art.138**;
- the scope of protection is determined by the claims, the description and the drawings may be used for interpreting the claims (**Art.69** and protocol);
- the bundle of national patents is subject to the centralised opposition procedure of the EPC (**Art.99**) and the centralised limitation and revocation procedure of **Art.105a-c**;
- revocation in an opposition procedure has retroactive effect (**Art.68**);
- a review of a board of appeal decision under **Art.112a** may affect a European patent; and
- the minimum period for payment of the first renewal fee for a granted patent to a national patent office is set by **Art.141**.

The EPC allows a wide interpretation of patentability, including, for instance, pharmaceuticals and chemical products.

2 **Relationship with the unitary patent**
On 17.12.2012 the member states of the European Union and the European Parliament laid the grounds for unitary patent protection in the EU. The unitary patent (UP) is a European patent, granted by the EPO under the rules and procedures of the EPC, which has a unitary effect for the participating member states.

To obtain a UP, the applicant must file a request for unitary effect at the EPO within one month of the publication of the mention of the grant in the Bulletin. Thereafter, renewal fees for the European patent with unitary effect are to be paid yearly to the EPO (**UPR.13(1)**). The request for unitary effect can only be filed for European patents having the same set of claims for all participating member states (**UPR.5(2)**).

The Agreement on a Unified Patent Court (UPC Agreement, UPCA) sets up a single patent jurisdiction. After entry into force of the Unified Patent Court on 01.06.2023, all European patents (and supplementary protection certificates) will be subject to revocation and infringement proceedings before it for the participating member states. However, during a transitional period, currently set to last seven years with an option to extend it to a further seven years, it will be possible to opt out of the Unified Patent Court, i.e., to indicate that the European patent validated nationally in the participating member states is to be subject to national revocation and infringement proceedings.

Art. 3 Territorial effect

The grant of a European patent may be requested for one or more of the Contracting States.

1 **Patent for one or more contracting states**
It was the intention of the drafters of EPC1973 to introduce a community patent. As this turned out to be impossible, the scope was reduced to a system for the grant of patents for one or more states (see **J7/90** r.6.1). A list of contracting states is given in **Art.169:1**.

Under Art.79 EPC1973 contracting states could be designated when filing the patent application. EPC2000 changed the designation system and all contracting states are designated on filing (**Art.79(1)**). The selection of contracting states in which protection is desired is now made after grant by validating the patent in countries of interest; validation requires the filing of any translation required under **Art.65(1)** and payment of renewal fees under **Art.141** and any special fee due under **Art.65(2)** for publication of the translation (see NatLaw table IV).

The advent of a community patent is one step closer with the entry into force of the Unified Patent Court Agreement (UPCA) on 01.06.2023, since it will allow to streamline revocation and infringement proceedings for the participating member states. For such member states, the proprietor of a European patent has the option to request unitary effect, resulting in a supranational unitary patent (UP) instead of a bundle of national European patents (**UPR.6(1)**).

Art. 4 European Patent Organisation

Art. 4(1) A European Patent Organisation, hereinafter referred to as the Organisation, is established by this Convention. It shall have administrative and financial autonomy.

Art. 4(2) The organs of the Organisation shall be:
(a) the European Patent Office;
(b) the Administrative Council.

1 **Organisation versus Office**
The 'European Patent Office' is abbreviated as 'EPO' in the notes of this book, whereas the 'European Patent Organisation' is written in full.

2 **Governance of the European Patent Organisation**
The European Patent Organisation is self-governing and is based on the principle of separation of powers such that the legislature, the executive and the judiciary are not concentrated in any one body (**G3/08** r.7.2):
- The Administrative Council has limited legislative powers 'restricted to lower-ranking rules' including amending the Implementing Regulations and time limits in the EPC (**Art.33(1)**; **G3/08** r.7.2.1). A Diplomatic Conference of the Contracting States is required to amend the EPC (**Art.172(1)**).
- The European Patent Office is an organ of the European Patent Organisation and has executive power to grant patents (**Art.4(3)**). The President has executive power to manage the European Patent Office in organisational respects (**Art.10**).
- The Boards of Appeal are structurally integrated departments of the European Patent Office and not an independent organ of the European Patent Organisation (**Art.15**). Nonetheless, the Boards of Appeal are assigned the role of an independent judiciary and in taking their decisions they comply only with the provisions of the EPC (**Art.23**). The interpretation of the EPC is primarily the responsibility of the Boards of Appeal (**G3/08** r.7.2.5).

3 **Academy of the European Patent Organisation**
By a decision of 17.06.2004 the Administrative Council set up a European Patent Academy for education and training in the field of European and international patent law, including the preparation of candidates for the European qualifying examination. The Academy is an institution of the European Patent Organisation and is managed by the European Patent Office. The Regulations of the Academy are published in OJ 2004 p.362.

4 **Employees of the EPO**
The EPO has approximately 6300 employees (EPO Social Report 2023), who remain citizens of their contracting state of origin. An EPO salary is only subject to a low, internally levied tax.

Art. 4(3) The task of the Organisation shall be to grant European patents. This shall be carried out by the European Patent Office supervised by the Administrative Council.

Art. 4a Conference of ministers of the Contracting States

A conference of ministers of the Contracting States responsible for patent matters shall meet at least every five years to discuss issues pertaining to the Organisation and to the European patent system.

1 **General**
This provision was introduced by EPC2000 and aims to set up a conference of ministers responsible for patent matters of the contracting states. The conference is a permanent body within the framework of the EPC but is not an organ of the Organisation. The conference cannot take any decision which has a legally binding effect on the Organisation. The function of the conference is of a purely political nature; it can set objectives for the Organisation and initiate co-operation between contracting states extending beyond the scope of the EPC. The model for the conference of ministers is the Intergovernmental Conferences of 1999 and 2000; during the latter the London Agreement was established (see **Art.65(1):2**). (OJ 2007 se4 EN p.6)

The conference cannot amend the EPC and is not a diplomatic conference in the sense of **Art.172.**

No conference of ministers has been held since the entry into force of EPC2000.

Chapter II *The European Patent Organisation*

Art. 5 Legal status

Art. 5(1) The Organisation shall have legal personality.

Art. 5(2) In each of the Contracting States, the Organisation shall enjoy the most extensive legal capacity accorded to legal persons under the national law of that State; it may in particular acquire or dispose of movable and immovable property and may be a party to legal proceedings.

1 **Legal capacity of the European Patent Organisation**
The Organisation can take part in legal actions and in economic transactions because it has legal personality.

Art. 5(3) The President of the European Patent Office shall represent the Organisation.

1 **Representation of the Organisation**
The President may, according to this provision, represent the European Patent Organisation. This is one of the President's functions but not one of the President's powers. The President may only represent the Organisation by performing a legal act, such as the signing of an agreement, if the President has the power to perform that act. The President's powers are governed by the EPC in articles other than **Art.5(3)**, such as **Art.10** and **Art.33(4)**. (**G5/88** hn.I, r.2.2-4, see also **Art.10:1**)

Art. 6 Headquarters

Art. 6(1) The Organisation shall have its headquarters in Munich.

Art. 6(2) The European Patent Office shall be located in Munich. It shall have a branch at The Hague.

1 **Branch of the EPO in The Hague**
The EPO set up a branch at The Hague to avail itself of the search facilities of the Institut International des Brevets (IIB) in The Hague, which had an excellent search department (OJ 1978 p.202). When the Netherlands started to provide protection for inventions in 1912, they could avoid the deficiencies of the search systems already set up in France and Germany. They devised a new system and had sufficient funds to copy the entire French and German patent documentation. Before the institution of the EPO, France already cooperated with the Netherlands in the IIB, because of the disorganised system in France. The IIB was incorporated into the EPO in 1978.

It should be noted that in 1973, at the time of drafting the Convention, the offices of the IIB that were to become the EPO branch were located in The Hague. When the EPO started its activities in 1978, the offices had been set up in Rijswijk, a city neighbouring The Hague. There has never been any EPO office in The Hague. The revision of the EPC in 2000 did not change the location of the branch. The 2006 Agreement between the Netherlands and the EPO corresponding to the Protocol on Privileges and Immunities defines that the branch of the EPO is at 'The Hague (Rijswijk)'.

2 **Sub-office of the EPO in Berlin**
Under the Protocol on Centralisation, Section I(3)(a), a sub-office was created in Berlin in 1978 for searching European patent applications under the direction of The Hague (OJ 1978 p.195, p.245). The Protocol is part of the EPC according to **Art.164(1)**. The Berlin sub-office was set up to give West Berlin, at that time an exclave in East Germany, more ties to West Germany. Although the ties are no longer necessary after the reunification of East and West Germany in 1990, the relatively small sub-office is maintained because of its low operational costs.

Since 1989 the Berlin sub-office is also a filing office in the sense of **Art.75(1)(a)** (Dec. of Pres. OJ 1989 p.218).

3 **Location of the EPO in Haar**
On 09.10.2017 the Boards of Appeal Unit was relocated from the EPO headquarters in Munich to Haar, a municipality neighbouring Munich. The relocation was part of the reform of the boards of appeal to strengthen the perception of their independence (see **R.12a:1**). The office in Haar is not a filing office.

Holding oral proceedings in Haar instead of Munich does not violate the EPC even though Haar is not mentioned in **Art.6(2)**, because it does not violate the right of parties to be heard and the development of the notion of independence of the boards has made a spatial separation between the administrative bodies of the EPO in Munich and the boards necessary (**G2/19** r.IV).

Art. 7 Sub-offices of the European Patent Office

By decision of the Administrative Council, sub-offices of the European Patent Office may be created, if need be, for the purpose of information and liaison, in the Contracting States and with intergovernmental organisations in the field of industrial property, subject to the approval of the Contracting State or organisation concerned.

1 **Sub-offices**
Following a decision by the Administrative Council taken in 1992, a sub-office was opened in Brussels for liaison with the European Union to support industry and ensure the competitiveness of the European economy (OJ 1993 p.404; OJ 2004 p.88). The bureau in Brussels is not a filing office (A-II,1.1).

In 1990 the International Patent Documentation Centre (INPADOC) in Vienna was integrated into the EPO as a sub-office (OJ 1990 p.492). The sub-office is in charge of the EPO's bibliographic databases and is tasked with providing public access to patent information. Note that the Vienna sub-office is not a filing office of the EPO (OJ 2007 se3 A1 Art.1(2)).

Art. 8 Privileges and immunities

The Protocol on Privileges and Immunities annexed to this Convention shall define the conditions under which the Organisation, the members of the Administrative Council, the employees of the European Patent Office, and such other persons specified in that Protocol as take part in the work of the Organisation, shall enjoy, in each Contracting State, the privileges and immunities necessary for the performance of their duties.

1 **Protocol on Privileges and Immunities**
The Protocol on Privileges and Immunities is an integral part of the EPC (Art.164(1)). The Protocol defines the inviolability of the premises of the Organisation and the immunity of the people working in the Organisation. It ensures that the Organisation is not restricted in the execution of its tasks by national laws. The protocol also applies to members of the epi having specific duties (OJ 2009 p.28). The text of the Protocol has not been reproduced in this book.

Art. 9 Liability

Art. 9(1) The contractual liability of the Organisation shall be governed by the law applicable to the contract in question.

The will of the parties as laid down in contracts is, in principle, decisive.

Art. 9(2) The non-contractual liability of the Organisation in respect of any damage caused by it or by the employees of the European Patent Office in the performance of their duties shall be governed by the law of the Federal Republic of Germany. Where the damage is caused by the branch at The Hague or a sub-office or employees attached thereto, the law of the Contracting State in which such branch or sub-office is located shall apply.

1 **Indemnities**
The board of appeal is not competent to decide on indemnities for loss or damage allegedly caused by the EPO in the course of proceedings (J14/87). A Board of Appeal has no power to make an order against the EPO to pay costs incurred by parties due to proceedings unjustifiably delayed by the EPO (T315/03 r.15.8; ten years to dispose of first instance opposition proceedings).

Employees of the EPO cannot be tried for neglect of duty (Art.14(a) Protocol on privileges and immunities); any claim must be made against the EPO.

Art. 9(3) The personal liability of the employees of the European Patent Office towards the Organisation shall be governed by their Service Regulations or conditions of employment.

1 **Personal liability of employees of the EPO**
The EPO can recover damages in whole or in part from an employee that has wilfully caused harm or has been seriously negligent. No recovery of damages is possible in respect of harm caused by a decision of the board of appeal or the Enlarged Board of Appeal.

Art. 9(4) The courts with jurisdiction to settle disputes under paragraphs 1 and 2 shall be:
(a) for disputes under paragraph 1, the courts of the Federal Republic of Germany, unless the contract concluded between the parties designates a court of another State;
(b) for disputes under paragraph 2, the courts of the Federal Republic of Germany, or of the State in which the branch or sub-office is located.

Chapter III *The European Patent Office*

Art. 10 Management

1 **Powers of the President**
The President directs the EPO according to **Art.10(1)**, which is to be interpreted in its context, in particular having regard to **Art.10(2)** and **Art.5(3)**. **Art.10(2)** contains a list of functions and powers of the President essentially concerned with internal matters of the EPO. It is not clear to what extent the President can direct the EPO in any external activity not directly related to one of the powers and functions listed in **Art.10(2)** without the supervision of the Administrative Council. However, it is clear that concluding an agreement with another patent office which has no connection with the functioning of the EPO and merely serves to satisfy political interests of that office is not within the President's power. Such an agreement requires authorisation and approval from the Administrative Council under **Art.33(4)**. Hence, an agreement of the President with the German patent office on mail intended for the EPO but erroneously addressed to the German patent office in Berlin at a time the EPO did not yet have a filing office in Berlin (OJ 1981 p.381) was beyond the powers of the President. See also **Art.23(1):2**. (**G5/88** hn.II, r.2, **G7/88** and **G8/88**)

The President has issued, pursuant to **Art.10(2)(a)**, internal instructions such as the Guidelines for Examination in the European Patent Office (**Art.10(2):1**) and instructions concerning the processing of personal data in EPO proceedings (Dec. Pres. OJ 2021 A98, some changes relating to publication of the list of professional representatives in its Annex published in Dec. Pres. OJ 2024 A108).

The functions and powers specified in sub-paragraphs (b) to (i) of **Art.10(2)** are essentially concerned with the internal operations of the EPO (**G5/88** r.1.2).

Art. 10(1) The European Patent Office shall be managed by the President, who shall be responsible for its activities to the Administrative Council.

Art. 10(2) To this end, the President shall have in particular the following functions and powers:
- **(a) he shall take all necessary steps to ensure the functioning of the European Patent Office, including the adoption of internal administrative instructions and information to the public;**
- **(b) unless this Convention provides otherwise, he shall prescribe which acts are to be performed at the European Patent Office in Munich and its branch at The Hague respectively;**
- **(c) he may submit to the Administrative Council any proposal for amending this Convention, for general regulations, or for decisions which come within the competence of the Administrative Council;**
- **(d) he shall prepare and implement the budget and any amending or supplementary budget;**
- **(e) he shall submit a management report to the Administrative Council each year;**
- **(f) he shall exercise supervisory authority over the staff;**
- **(g) subject to Article 11, he shall appoint the employees and decide on their promotion;**

(h) he shall exercise disciplinary authority over the employees other than those referred to in Article 11, and may propose disciplinary action to the Administrative Council with regard to employees referred to in Article 11, paragraphs 2 and 3;

(i) he may delegate his functions and powers.

1 **Guidelines for Examination in the EPO (Art.10(2)(a))**
The President has issued under sub-paragraph (a) the *Guidelines for Examination in the European Patent Office* and *Guidelines for Search and Examination at the EPO as PCT Authority* to ensure a proper functioning of the EPO. The Guidelines contain general instructions as to the practice and procedure within the EPO. The examiners in departments of first instance act as a general rule in accordance with the Guidelines and may depart from these instructions only in exceptional cases. The EPO has a policy of annually revising the Guidelines to keep them in line with legal and procedural developments. A new version comes into force on the first of March every year.

Art. 10(3) The President shall be assisted by a number of Vice-Presidents. If the President is absent or indisposed, one of the Vice-Presidents shall take his place in accordance with the procedure laid down by the Administrative Council.

1 **Vice-Presidents**
There are three Vice-Presidents, one for each Directorate-General. See the decision of the Administrative Council on deputisation for the President of the EPO (OJ 1978 p.326).

Art. 11 Appointment of senior employees

This article sets out the appointment of the President and higher personnel and lays down the powers of the President in the latter.

Art. 11(1) The President of the European Patent Office shall be appointed by the Administrative Council.

Art. 11(2) The Vice-Presidents shall be appointed by the Administrative Council after the President of the European Patent Office has been consulted.

Art. 11(3) The members, including the Chairmen, of the Boards of Appeal and of the Enlarged Board of Appeal shall be appointed by the Administrative Council on a proposal from the President of the European Patent Office. They may be re-appointed by the Administrative Council after the President of the European Patent Office has been consulted.

1 **Appointment of members of boards of appeal**
The powers of the president of the EPO under **Art.11(3)** have been delegated to the president of the Boards of Appeal under **R.12d(2)**. The persons to be appointed as members of boards of appeal are proposed by the president of the BoA on merit and appointed by the Administrative Council under **Art.11(3)**. Once appointed, a member cannot be removed by a decision of the president of the BoA alone.

The board members are appointed for a term of five years according to **Art.23(1)**, after which they may be re-appointed by the Administrative Council after consultation of the president of the BoA.

Art. 11(4) The Administrative Council shall exercise disciplinary authority over the employees referred to in paragraphs 1 to 3.

Art. 11(5) The Administrative Council, after consulting the President of the European Patent Office, may also appoint as members of the Enlarged Board of Appeal legally qualified members of the national courts or quasi-judicial authorities of the Contracting States, who may continue their judicial activities at the national level. They shall be appointed for a term of three years and may be re-appointed.

1 **External legally and technically qualified members**
The participation of external legally qualified members from the EPC contracting states in proceedings before the Enlarged Board of Appeal has proved to be a success. It is expected that the involvement of national judges will further the harmonisation of patent case law in Europe. (OJ 2007 se4 EN p.12)

EPC2000 no longer allows the appointment of external technically and legally qualified members to the technical and legal boards of appeal, because sufficient expertise is available in house. (OJ 2007 se4 EN p.12)

Art. 12 Duties of office

Employees of the European Patent Office shall be bound, even after the termination of their employment, neither to disclose nor to make use of information which by its nature is a professional secret.

Art. 13 Disputes between the Organisation and the employees of the European Patent Office

Art. 13(1) Employees and former employees of the European Patent Office or their successors in title may apply to the Administrative Tribunal of the International Labour Organization in the case of disputes with the European Patent Organisation, in accordance with the Statute of the Tribunal and within the limits and subject to the conditions laid down in the Service Regulations for permanent employees or the Pension Scheme Regulations or arising from the conditions of employment of other employees.

Art. 13(2) An appeal shall only be admissible if the person concerned has exhausted such other means of appeal as are available to him under the Service Regulations, the Pension Scheme Regulations or the conditions of employment.

Art. 14 Languages of the European Patent Office, European patent applications and other documents

Implemented by:
R.3 Language in written proceedings
R.4 Language in oral proceedings
R.5 Certification of translations
R.6 Filing of translations
R.7 Legal authenticity of the translation of the European patent application

R.7a Reduction of fees
R.7b Declaration of eligibility for a reduction of fees
R.36(2) Language of divisional application

1 **Transitional provision EPC2000**

The revised **Art.14(1)** and (2) applies to European patent applications filed after entry into force of EPC2000 (OJ 2007 se4 EN p.217, Art.7(1)). Hence, a filing date was accorded for a European application filed in any language only if the application has a filing date on or after the date of entry into force of EPC2000.

The revised **Art.14(3)** to (6) shall apply to European patent applications pending at the time of entry into force of EPC2000 and to European patents already granted at that time (OJ 2007 se4 EN p.219, Art.1(1)).

2 **Language restrictions**

The framework of language restrictions in the EPC is based on three categories of languages:

1 The three official languages of the EPO, i.e. English, French and German (**Art.14(1)**, first sentence).
2 The official languages of the EPC contracting states other than English, French or German (**Art.14(4)**, first sentence). These languages are also called 'admissible non-EPO languages'.
3 All other languages.

For the purpose of according a date of filing, a European patent application may be filed in any language (see **R.40**), thereby implementing Art.5(2) of the Patent Law Treaty. For the prosecution of an application by the EPO, the application must be available in one of the official EPO languages (**Art.14(2)**, first sentence). If the application was initially filed in an another language, it must be translated into one of the official EPO languages (**Art.14(2)**, first sentence), the choice of the official EPO language being left to the applicant. The official EPO language of filing or translation becomes the language of the proceedings (**Art.14(3)**). In all proceedings before the EPO a party must use the language of the proceedings. However, another official EPO language may be used in written and oral proceedings, provided a translation or interpretation is provided where required by **R.3** and **R.4**.

R.7a(1) provides a reduction of fees where an admissible non-EPO language is used for filing patent applications to compensate for the burden of providing a translation into an official EPO language. **Art.14(4)** and **R.7a(2)** restrict the fee reduction to certain persons.

Art. 14(1) The official languages of the European Patent Office shall be English, French and German.

Art. 14(2) A European patent application shall be filed in one of the official languages or, if filed in any other language, translated into one of the official languages in accordance with the Implementing Regulations. Throughout the proceedings before the European Patent Office, such translation may be brought into conformity with the application as filed. If a required translation is not filed in due time, the application shall be deemed to be withdrawn.

1 **Language of the patent application**
The requirements for obtaining a date of filing for a European patent application in **R.40(1)** do not contain any restriction concerning language. Hence, the application may be filed in any language, such as Chinese, Dutch or Latin. This is supported by the words 'any other language' in **Art.14(2)**. The documents of the application need not all be in the same language (A-VII,1.1; EPO practice changed in 2014, see Guidelines edition November 2014).

Art.14(2) imposes requirements to be met after accordance of a date of filing, to be examined during the formalities examination under **Art.90(3)** and **R.57(a)**. Hence, compliance with these requirements is not necessary for according a date of filing.

A European patent application may be filed with a national authority according to **Art.75(1)(b)** and **(2)**. Some national authorities impose language restrictions. The languages admitted by national authorities are given in NatLaw table II, note 3 and further requirements are set out in note 5. At present (April 2025), most contracting states that allow European patent applications to be filed with their national authority permit such applications to be filed in any language according to **Art.14(2)**, with some additionally requiring partial or full translations. The exceptions are Bulgaria, Cyprus, North Macedonia and Spain, which only allow such applications to be filed either in an official language of the EPO or in their respective local official language.

Note that the choice of filing office may be restricted by national security requirements as set out in **Art.75(2):1** (see NatLaw table II, note 2).

Use of an admissible non-EPO language (see **Art.14(4):2**) for the application may entitle the applicant to a reduction of the filing fee (**G6/91** r.18-21). See **R.7a(1)** and notes thereto for entitlement requirements, also for a reduction of the examination fee.

2 **Translation of the patent application**
If the application is filed in any other language than one of the official EPO languages English, French or German, a translation into one of the official languages must be filed according to **Art.14(2)**, first sentence. A translation in more than one language, e.g. partly in German and partly in English, does not comply with the 'into one of the official languages' of **Art.14(2)**.

The meaning of 'any other language' in **Art.14(2)** is ambiguous. It could mean any language other than the three official EPO languages or any language other than one of the official languages. The latter meaning is preferred, because it covers all cases other than a patent application filed in one of the official languages. It therefore covers the case of an application filed in two languages. Such an application is not in 'one of the official languages' but in two; since the case of two languages can be regarded as covered by 'any other language', the application must be translated into one of the official languages.

When an application is filed by reference to a previously filed application as permitted by **R.40(1)(c)**, this previously filed application must also be translated into an official EPO language if it is not in an official EPO language according to the parallel provision **R.40(3)**. For divisional applications see **R.36(2):2**.

Where an application filed in an official EPO language is a translation of an earlier application which is not in an EPO language and from which it claims priority, **Art.14(2)**, second sentence, cannot be used to correct the translation. It might be possible to include translated parts of the earlier application under **R.56(3)** as missing parts for correcting the translation. The EPO has not yet confirmed that this is permitted.

3 **Filing the translation**

Any translation of the patent application must be filed within two months of filing the application (**R.6(1)**). When the application was filed by reference to a previously filed application, any translation must also be filed within two months of filing (**R.40(3)**). The translation must be presented in the same form as application documents (**R.49(1)**).

The procedure for examination of the filing of the translation is set out in A-III,14. The filing of a translation will not be examined when according a date of filing, because the language of the patent application is not a requirement for according a date of filing (**R.40(1)**). The EPO will check the filing of the translation only during the examination as to formal requirements under **R.57(a)** and, if it was not filed within the two-month period of **R.6(1)**, **R.36(2)** or **R.40(3)**, invite the applicant to correct this deficiency under **R.58** within two months from invitation. Thus, the applicant has at least four months to file the translation (CA/PL29/06 Add.1). During this relatively long period the EPO cannot carry out the examination as to formal requirements under **R.57** which prepares the application for publication and the search, which makes it difficult to achieve the timely publication of an application which takes advantage of the full 12-month priority period.

Failure to file the translation within the period of **R.58** results in the application being deemed withdrawn according to **Art.14(2)**, last sentence, the loss of rights being notified under **R.112(1)**. If applicable, the applicant can prove within two months of the notification that they did file the translation in due time (**R.112(2)**). The two-month periods of **R.6(1)**, **R.36(2)** and **R.58** are excluded from further processing (**R.135(2)**) but re-establishment according to **Art.122** and **R.136(3)** in these periods is possible if 'all due care' can be proven.

Some contracting states allow conversion of the deemed withdrawn European application to a national application under **Art.135**.

4 **Correction of translation**

An applicant or proprietor may correct the translation to bring it into conformity with the original text throughout any proceedings before the EPO (**Art.14(2)**, second sentence; **Art.70(2):1** and A-VII,7). A correction of the translation in opposition or limitation proceedings is not allowable if it offends against **Art.123(3)** (A-VII,7; T2845/19). It is irrelevant whether the applicant or proprietor is a national or resident of an EPC contracting state or of any other state.

The ability to correct applies both to an application filed in a non-EPO language, to a divisional application filed in a non-EPO language where the parent was filed in this language (**R.36(2)**), and to an application filed by reference to a previously filed application in a non-EPO language under **R.40(1)(c)**. In all cases the translation may subsequently be brought into conformity with the original, earlier or previous application. (A-VII,7)

See **R.159(1)(a):2** for correction of the translation of a Euro-PCT application.

When assessing whether an amendment complies with **Art.123(2)**, the EPO assumes that the originally filed translation is in conformity with the text in the original language (A-VII,7). However, the basis for the assessment of an amendment is the text in the original language (**Art.70(2)**). An applicant should inform the EPO of any translation error.

5 **Relevance of the translation**
The text of the application in an official EPO language, either as filed directly or as translated, is the authentic text in any proceedings before the EPO (**Art.70(1)**). However, when the application is not filed in an official EPO language, the original text will be the 'application as filed' (**Art.70(2)**) for the purpose of determining extension of subject-matter in the sense of **Art.123(2)**. The EPO assumes for this purpose that the translation conforms to the original text of the application (**R.7**). If there is doubt about the accuracy of the translation, the EPO may request the filing of a certificate that the translation corresponds to the original text (**R.5**).

The content of a European prior right, i.e. a prior art document under **Art.54(3)**, is determined by the original text as filed, not by any translation into an official EPO language (A-VII,7).

It is in principle possible to file a computer translation if there is not sufficient time to prepare a proper translation within the time limit of **R.58** and to correct the translation subsequently. However, this may cause the search to be based on an incorrect translation or the issuance of a declaration that a meaningful search was not possible, affecting the following proceedings. The EPO may ask for a certificate of translation under **R.5** if it has doubts as to the accuracy of the translation.

Art. 14(3) The official language of the European Patent Office in which the European patent application is filed or into which it is translated shall be used as the language of the proceedings in all proceedings before the European Patent Office, unless the Implementing Regulations provide otherwise.

1 **Language of the proceedings**
The official EPO language in which the application is filed or into which it is translated becomes the language of the proceedings. The language of the proceedings cannot be changed during the proceedings concerning an application or the resulting patent, because this is not provided for in the EPC. If a translation is required, the EPO will send an invitation to file it in English, and update the language of the proceedings on receipt of the translation, if applicable (A-VII,2).

The language of the proceedings must be used in all proceedings before the EPO (**Art.14(3)**). Hence, in written proceedings all documents should be filed in the language of the proceedings. Derogations for written proceedings are provided in **R.3**, which allows that documents may be filed in any official EPO language (**R.3(1)**), except for amendments of the application or patent, which must be in the language of the proceedings (**R.3(2)**). Documents to be filed within a time limit may also be submitted in an admissible non-EPO language and subsequently translated into an official EPO language (**Art.14(4)**). Documentary evidence may be filed in any language (**R.3(3)**).

In oral proceedings the default language is the language of the proceedings (**Art.14(3)**), but any official language of the EPO or a contracting state may be used, provided the provisions for interpretation in **R.4** are observed.

A request for unitary effect can only be filed in the language of the proceedings (**UPR.6(2)**).

Art. 14(4) Natural or legal persons having their residence or principal place of business within a Contracting State having a language other than English, French or German as an official language, and nationals of that State who are resident abroad, may file documents which have to be filed within a time limit in an official language of that State. They shall, however, file a translation in an official language of the European Patent Office in accordance with the Implementing Regulations. If any document, other than those documents making up the European patent application, is not filed in the prescribed language, or if any required translation is not filed in due time, the document shall be deemed not to have been filed.

1 **Language of further documents and translation**

Documents filed subsequent to the filing of the patent application, also called 'further documents', must be filed in the language of the proceedings (**Art.14(3)**). By way of exception, a further document may also be filed in another official EPO language (**R.3(1)**). When the further document concerns amendments of the patent application, it must be filed in the language of the proceedings (**R.3(2)**).

Art.14(4), first sentence, allows a restricted class of persons to file further documents in an official language of an EPC contracting state. These documents must subsequently be translated into an official EPO language (**Art.14(4)**, second sentence) in accordance with **R.3**: for most documents into any official EPO language (**R.3(1)**), for those documents which concern amendments, into the language of the proceedings (**R.3(2)**).

Art.14(4) defines the persons that may file those further documents that have to be filed within a time limit in an official language of a contracting state. A translation in any official EPO language must normally be filed within one month of filing the document (**R.6(2)**).

Whereas a mistake in the translation of a patent application can be corrected using **Art.14(2)** second sentence, a mistake in the translation of a further document can only be corrected as an error under **R.139** (**G6/91** r.10).

2 **Admissible non-EPO language**

The official languages of contracting states in which further documents in the meaning of **Art.14(4)** may be filed with the EPO are referred to in this book as 'admissible non-EPO languages', or 'admissible languages' if the latter does not cause confusion (see A-X,9.3.1(b)). The terms 'authorised language' and 'allowed language' sometimes occur in case law.

The official languages of the contracting states are listed in NatLaw table II, note 4. A few special cases of official languages:

- Belgium: Dutch, French and German;
- Finland: Finnish and Swedish;
- Ireland: Irish and English;
- Liechtenstein: German;
- Luxembourg: French, German and Luxembourgish; and
- Switzerland: German, French and Italian.

Where a contracting state has several official languages, the choice of language is up to the party concerned. A party who has several nationalities may choose between the official languages of the contracting states of nationality and the contracting state of residence (Münchner Gemeinschaftskommentar, K. Haertel (Heymanns) Art.14, p.15, Randnummer 18 und 22). For example, a Swiss party may choose Italian as language for the fee reduction of **R.7a(1)**, even though that party's own language is German or French.

3 **Entitled persons**

Under **Art.14(4)**, first sentence, natural or legal persons are entitled to use an admissible non-EPO language if:

- they have their residence within the territory of the state;
- they have their place of business within the territory of the state; or
- they are a national of the state and resident abroad, inside or outside a contracting state.

In the case of several applicants or proprietors, an admissible non-EPO language may be used if at least one of them is entitled to use this language (A-X,9.3.1). For example, German and Dutch joint applicants are entitled under **Art.14(4)** to request examination in Dutch (**J4/18**).

If the admissible language is used by a natural person, their residence and nationality determine the admissible languages. If the admissible language is used by a legal person, the place of business determines the admissible languages (**T149/85**).The nationality or residence of applicants is decisive, not that of their representative (**T149/85**). See **Art.133(2):1** for the interpretation of 'principal' in the first sentence of **Art.14(4)**.

Note that the admissible language depends on nationality, residence or place of business, whereas compulsory representation before the EPO (**Art.133(2)**) depends on the residence or place of business only: the EPO needs a postal address within Europe for acts performed after filing.

4 **Further documents to be filed within a time limit**

Art.14(4) restricts the use of an admissible non-EPO language to documents to be filed within a time limit. An example of such a document is the response to a communication of the EPO under **Art.94(3)**, inviting the applicant to correct deficiencies in the application and usually specifying a period of four months. Other examples are a request for examination and a notice of opposition.

A document containing observations filed by a third party under **Art.115** is an example of a document which need not be filed within a time limit. Hence, the provision of **Art.14(4)** does not apply and the observations must be filed in one of the official languages of the EPO according to **Art.14(1)**, as explicitly provided in **R.114(1)**. Note that **R.3(1)**, first sentence is not applicable, because the third person is not a party to the proceedings.

Although the filing of a request for revocation or limitation under **Art.105a** is not subject to any time limit, the request may nonetheless be filed in an admissible non-EPO language (D-X,2.1(iv)), because **R.6(2)** referring to the request acts as a lex specialis.

5 **Period for filing translation**

The period for filing the translation is fixed by **R.6(2)**. The period is normally one month of filing the document. If the translation is not filed in due time, the document will be deemed not to have been filed (**Art.14(4)**, third sentence) or disregarded (**R.3(3)**). This sanction applies not only to non-filed translations of documents filed in an admissible non-EPO language but also to non-filed translations in the language of proceedings of amendments of the patent application that have been filed in another official EPO language (consequence of 'any document' in **Art.14(4)**, third sentence). The fate of the document is set out in the next section.

Non-observance of the period may be remedied using further processing (**Art.121** and **R.135(2)**) by paying the further processing fee and filing the translation within two months from notification of the loss of rights. Re-establishment is ruled out by **R.136(3)**.

6 **Wrong language of further document**
A document filed in a wrong language or a document filed in an admissible non-EPO language for which no translation is filed in due time will be deemed not to have been filed (**Art.14(4)**, last sentence). The EPO notifies the person who filed the document. Such documents are put in the file and are open to public inspection according to **Art.128(4)**; third party observations and notices of opposition in an inadmissible language are communicated to the applicant or proprietor. (A-VII,5)

Examples of documents filed in an inadmissible language are: a reply to an invitation under **Art.94(3)** in Russian, a request for re-establishment in Italian filed by a Greek living in Greece, third party observations under **Art.115** filed in Polish, an opposition filed in Dutch by the Dutch representative of a German opponent who is resident in Germany, and a notice of appeal filed in Japanese.

An accompanying document, such as a cover letter, relating to the performance of a procedural act within a time limit and filed in a wrong language, is put in the file and the procedural act is regarded as being performed, but any other content of the accompanying document is ignored. Examples of such procedural acts are the filing of the designation of the inventor (**R.19**), the filing of a certified copy of an earlier application from which priority is claimed (**R.53(1)**), and the filing of the translation of an earlier application from which priority is claimed (**R.53(3)**). (A-VII,5)

The party cannot rely on the translation as a document filed in a permitted language and within the time limit, e.g. simultaneously with the original, because a translation cannot become the original. Whatever the date on which it is filed it remains a translation, with all ensuing legal consequences. (**G6/91** r.10; **T41/09** r.2.2)

Art. 14(5) European patent applications shall be published in the language of the proceedings.

See **Art.93** for the publication of the application and **Art.14(3)** for the language of the proceedings.

Art. 14(6) Specifications of European patents shall be published in the language of the proceedings and shall include a translation of the claims in the other two official languages of the European Patent Office.

1 **Language of publication of the specification**
See **Art.98** for the publication of the specification of the patent.

The translations of the claims must be filed on invitation by the EPO under **R.71(3)**. The EPO does not check the correctness of the translations.

Art. 14(7) The following shall be published in the three official languages of the European Patent Office:
(a) the European Patent Bulletin;
(b) the Official Journal of the European Patent Office.

See **Art.129** for the publication of the Bulletin and the OJ.

Art. 14(8) Entries in the European Patent Register shall be made in the three official languages of the European Patent Office. In cases of doubt, the entry in the language of the proceedings shall be authentic.

Art.14(3) Language of the proceedings

Art.127 European Patent Register

Art. 15 Departments entrusted with the procedure

To carry out the procedures laid down in this Convention, the following shall be set up within the European Patent Office:

(a) a Receiving Section;
(b) Search Divisions;
(c) Examining Divisions;
(d) Opposition Divisions;
(e) a Legal Division;
(f) Boards of Appeal;
(g) an Enlarged Board of Appeal.

Implemented by:
Art.16 Receiving Section
Art.17 Search Divisions
Art.18 Examining Divisions
Art.19 Opposition Divisions
Art.20 Legal Division
Art.21 Boards of Appeal
Art.22 Enlarged Board of Appeal
Art.23 Independence of the members of the boards
Art.24 Exclusion and objection
R.9-13 Organisation of the European Patent Office

1 **Reorganisations of the EPO**
The departments of the EPO mentioned in **Art.15** are grouped in Directorates-General (**R.9(1)**). Three reorganisations have changed the grouping from five Directorates-General to three and changed locations of the departments.

In 1990 the EPO started the BEST project (Bringing Examination and Search Together), which aims at improving quality and efficiency of search and examination. Before BEST, the search and the examination were performed by two different persons, a searcher in the Hague and an examiner in Munich. Under BEST both the search and the examination are performed by the same examiner, who may be located in the Hague, Berlin or Munich (OJ 1990 p.333 and EPO Annual Reports). The search examiner is also the first member in the examining division (OJ 2003 p.206 §1; B-I,2). The BEST project was completed in 2006. The distinction between search divisions and examining divisions has not yet been removed in **Art.15**, because there was insufficient preparation time for the diplomatic conference to include such a change in EPC2000; such an amendment will likely to considered by the next Diplomatic Conference.

In 2016 the departments of second instance, the Boards of Appeal and the Enlarged Board of Appeal, formerly Directorate-General 3, became part of the Boards of Appeal Unit, a separate organisational unit underlining their independence. The Boards of Appeal Unit has moved from the city of Munich to Haar. See **R.12a** and CA/43/16 Rev. 1.

In 2017 a further reorganisation combined the former Directorates-General DG1 (search, examination and opposition) and DG2 (patent administration) to have the entire patent granting process in one Directorate-General (CA/65/17). The proposed renumbering of DG4 and DG5 to DG2 and DG3 has not yet been implemented (situation April 2020, see e.g. OJ 2020 A45 which refers to the vice president of DG5).

2 Administrative structure of the EPO

Since 2017 the EPO is divided administratively into three Directorates-General, to which the departments of **Art.15(a) - (e)** are assigned (**R.9(1)**), and a Board of Appeal Unit to which the departments (f) and (g) are assigned.

The examiners, forming the search, examining and opposition divisions, are part of Directorate-General 1 (DG1), which is divided into three principal directorates according to technology. About the same number of examiners should be located in Munich and in the Hague (see the Protocol on the Staff Complement of EPC2000, reproduced in OJ 2001 se1 p.45). The examiners are assigned to a separate search division and examining division set up for each patent application filed; similarly, they are assigned to a separate opposition division set up for each patent for which a notice of opposition is filed. The Receiving Section is also part of DG1.

Each principal directorate of DG1 includes formalities officers, who are responsible for examination on filing and examination as to formal requirements, tasks the EPC has allocated to the Receiving Section (**Art.16** and **R.10(1)**).

Directorate-General 4 (DG4) is Corporate Services, comprising human resources, general administration, central procurement and finance.

Directorate-General 5 (DG5) comprises the Legal Division and legal and international affairs, located in Munich. Members of the Legal Division are entrusted with the tasks of the Unitary Patent Protection Division (Dec. Pres. OJ 2022 A69, Part I, **Art.20:1**).

Departments (a) to (e) are departments of first instance; departments (f) and (g) are departments of second instance.

Although the EPC distinguishes the Receiving Section, search divisions, examining divisions, opposition divisions and the Legal Division as departments of the EPO, they are no longer indicated as separate organisational units in the Organisational Structure of the EPO. To ensure greater flexibility in allocating specific tasks, EPC2000 has removed several references to the Receiving Section and search divisions and replaced wording such as 'the Receiving Section shall ...' by 'the EPO shall ...' (compare **Art.90(1)**, **Art.92**, **Art.93(1)**).

Responsibility for a case is transferred from one department to another when a relevant procedural act is carried out, e.g. when the request for examination is filed (see e.g. **R.10**). The department to which the case is transferred becomes competent to handle the case.

The Ombuds Office service can be used to address difficulties between users and the EPO that cannot be otherwise resolved (https://www.epo.org/en/about-us/services-and-activities/ombuds-office). The service can handle any issue arising from activities of the EPO and is independent from formal processes. It does not address matters that concern the boards of appeal. The service is meant as an informal, impartial and confidential venue and can be contacted via ombuds@epo.org. For example, the Ombuds Office handles cases that fall into the following categories: information needs, healthy working relationships and clarity of publicly available records. Most cases get resolved within a month. While the cases themselves are confidential, the insights gained from them can be shared within the EPO, e.g. to improve quality and services.

Art. 16 Receiving Section

The Receiving Section shall be responsible for the examination on filing and the examination as to formal requirements of European patent applications.

Implemented by:
R.10(1) Limitation in time of responsibility of Receiving Section

1 **Responsibilities of the Receiving Section**
According to **Art.16** the Receiving Section is responsible for the examination on filing, i.e. whether a filed application can be accorded a filing date (**Art.90(1), R.55**) and the examination as to formal requirements (**Art.90(3), R.56-60**); according to A-VI,2.1, it also takes care of the publication of the application (**Art.93, R.67-69**). The Receiving Section is composed entirely of formalities officers (**G1/02**, r.6.1).

The Receiving Section is not competent to decide on a request for an amendment or correction of an application that requires a technical examination; the decision on such a matter must wait until the case has been transferred to the examining division, because the latter is competent in such matters (J4/85).

The transfer of responsibility from the Receiving Section to an examining division is governed by **R.10(1)**. The search division carries out the search while the case lies with the Receiving Section (consequence of **R.10(1)**; B-IV,1.2).

The Receiving Section of the EPO should not be confused with the receiving Office which accepts international applications under the PCT (**Art.151**).

Art. 17 Search Divisions

The Search Divisions shall be responsible for drawing up European search reports.

1 **Responsibilities of the search divisions**
According to **Art.17** the search division is responsible for carrying out the search and drawing up the European search report for an application (**Art.92, R.61-65**). The 'European search report' should be interpreted as 'extended European search report' in the meaning of **R.62**, including the search report proper and the search opinion on patentability (B-II,4). The drawing up of any supplementary search report under **Art.153(7)** for a Euro-PCT application is also the responsibility of the search division (J6/83). The search division determines the definitive content of the abstract (**R.66**; F-II,2.2). A search division normally consists of one search examiner (B-I,2.2).

The search division starts the prior art search for a patent application after the application has been accorded a date of filing, the filing fee and search fee have been paid, claims have been filed and any translation of the application has been filed. The search is carried out in parallel with the formalities examination (B-IV,1.2).

The search division uses the international patent classification (**R.8**, B-V,1). A decision of the President on a classification of an application is not appealable (**Art.106(1)**).

The search report and the abstract are published (A-VI,1.3) and transmitted to the applicant (B-X,12; F-II,2.6) and the examining division (B-X,11.1).

2 **Composition of a search division**
The search division to which the search of an application is entrusted consists usually of one examiner, who is also the first member of the examining division for that application. However, all 'search actions' (e.g. search reports and written opinions) are endorsed by the other two members of the examining division. (B-I,2)

Art. 18 Examining Divisions

Art. 18(1) The Examining Divisions shall be responsible for the examination of European patent applications.

Implemented by:
R.10(2)-4 Start of responsibility of examining division
R.91 Responsibility for limitation and revocation proceedings

1 **Responsibilities of the examining divisions**
When the Receiving Section ceases to be responsible for a European patent application, an examining division becomes responsible according to **R.10**. The passing of competence has been laid down in the Implementing Regulations to ensure flexibility.

The examining division is responsible for the substantive examination of the application (**Art.18(1)**) using the procedure prescribed in **Art.94(3)**, for the grant of the patent or the refusal of the application (**Art.97**) and the publication of the patent under **Art.98**. The examining division is also competent for the substantive examination of Euro-PCT applications and for searches under **R.164(2)**.

The responsibility of the examining division ends with the notification that the application is deemed to be withdrawn under **Art.94(4)** or with the notification of the decision to grant the patent or refuse the application (**Art.97**). The examining division is, however, competent for requests for correction of decisions taken by it under **R.140**.

According to **R.91** the examining division is also responsible for decisions on requests for limitation or revocation under **Art.105a**. The examining division is furthermore responsible for issuing technical opinions under **Art.25**.

Art. 18(2) An Examining Division shall consist of three technically qualified examiners. However, before a decision is taken on a European patent application, its examination shall, as a general rule, be entrusted to one member of the Examining Division. Oral proceedings shall be before the Examining Division itself. If the Examining Division considers that the nature of the decision so requires, it shall be enlarged by the addition of a legally qualified examiner. In the event of parity of votes, the vote of the Chairman of the Examining Division shall be decisive.

1 **Composition of an examining division**
An examining division consists of a chairman, a first member and a second member, who are all technically qualified examiners. In exceptional cases, a legally qualified member is added.

The major part of the work of the examining division is, as a general rule, carried out by the first member, previously called primary examiner. However, oral proceedings are before the entire examining division of three or four examiners. Likewise, decisions are taken by the entire examining division. The chairperson of the division checks the substance of the decision, and the second member carries out formal checks. **Art.18(2)** clarifies that each decision, whether final or not, is taken by the entire examining division.

The EPC has opted for the relatively costly principle of collegiate decision-making to increase the quality of the decisions taken, thereby reducing the number of appeals. Another reason for collegiate decision-making was to avoid that decisions were influenced by the national background of individual examiners in the early days when the EPC was still new. (Empel no. 443)

No use has been made of the possibility to decide that in certain categories of cases the examining division consists of one technically qualified examiner only (**Art.33(3)**).

Examiners must be impartial. If examiners are suspected of partiality, they may be objected to, as set out in **Art.24:2**.

Art. 19 Opposition Divisions

Art. 19(1) The Opposition Divisions shall be responsible for the examination of oppositions against any European patent.

Art. 19(2) An Opposition Division shall consist of three technically qualified examiners, at least two of whom shall not have taken part in the proceedings for grant of the patent to which the opposition relates. An examiner who has taken part in the proceedings for the grant of the European patent may not be the Chairman. Before a decision is taken on the opposition, the Opposition Division may entrust the examination of the opposition to one of its members. Oral proceedings shall be before the Opposition Division itself. If the Opposition Division considers that the nature of the decision so requires, it shall be enlarged by the addition of a legally qualified examiner who shall not have taken part in the proceedings for grant of the patent. In the event of parity of votes, the vote of the Chairman of the Opposition Division shall be decisive.

1 Composition of opposition division

Art.19(2) establishes the collegiate nature of an opposition division. The presence of one member who may have taken part in the grant proceedings is a compromise. On the one hand, the purpose of an opposition is the examination of new facts and/or arguments brought forward by the opponent; there is no reason to deprive the opposition division of an examiner with knowledge of the patent in order to fairly assess such facts and arguments. On the other hand, the members of the opposition division should be unbiased as in appeal proceedings and an examiner who granted the patent may be biased towards finding it valid. The possibly biased member is always in a minority position. (Empel no. 465)

If the composition of an opposition division does not comply with **Art.19(2), this** is a substantial procedural violation in the sense of **R.103(1)(a)** (**T251/88; T382/92; G5/91** r.5).

Examiners must be impartial. If examiners are suspected of partiality, they may be objected to as set out in **Art.24:2**. Taking part in grant proceedings for a family member (e.g. a parent or a priority application) of the opposed patent is not considered as "participating" in grant proceedings and would not be counted as such for the purposes of **Art.19(2)**. (D-II, 2.1)

Art. 20 Legal Division

Art. 20(1) The Legal Division shall be responsible for decisions in respect of entries in the Register of European Patents and in respect of registration on, and deletion from, the list of professional representatives.

1 **Duties of Legal Division**

The Legal Division has responsibility for the following duties regarding the European Patent Register (see **Art.127** for the terminology): entitlement procedures (**Art.61(1)** and **Art.99(4)**), interruption of proceedings (**R.142**), registration of licences and other rights (**R.23** and **R.24**), registration of transfers of rights and changes of name (**R.22**), and rectification of the designation of the inventor (**R.21**). (OJ 2013 p.600)

Whilst OJ 2013 p.600 states that 'sole' responsibility for these duties lie with the Legal Division, according to subsequent case law, the Legal Division does not have exclusive jurisdiction over the question of interruption (**T854/12** r.1.2; **T54/17** r.1.4).

The registration of transfers of rights and changes of name and the rectification of the designation of the inventor are entrusted to formalities officers if the request can be granted directly (OJ 2013 p.601).

The Legal Division also has the sole responsibility for entries, registrations and deletions in the list of professional representatives (**Art.134(1)**) and for assessment of the legal incapacity of a professional representative (**J901/86** hn.3) (OJ 2013 p.600).

Members of the Legal Division are also entrusted with the tasks of the Unitary Patent Protection Division (**UPR.1(1)** and Dec. Pres. OJ 2022 A69, Part I). These tasks are listed in Art.9 of EU regulation 1257/2012 and comprise various administrative actions like maintaining the Register for unitary patent protection.

Art. 20(2) Decisions of the Legal Division shall be taken by one legally qualified member.

1 **Decisions of the Legal Division**

Decisions of the Legal Division can be appealed before the Legal Board of Appeal (**Art.106(1)** and **Art.21(2)**, see **J1/78** as an example). If a decision of the Legal Division deals with multiple applications, only a single appeal need be filed (**J1/16** hn.1).

Art. 21 Boards of Appeal

Implemented by:
R.12a Boards of Appeal Unit and President of Boards of Appeal
R.12b Presidium of the Boards of Appeal
R.12c Boards of Appeal Committee and Rules of Procedure
R.12d (Re-)appointment of members of boards

1 A board of appeal has the status of an internationally recognised judicial authority, because its members are only bound by the EPC (**Art.23(3)**), they are appointed for a fixed term (**Art.23(1)**), their impartiality is safeguarded (**Art.24**), at least one of the members is legally qualified (**Art.21**), they have their own rules of procedure (**R.12c(2)**) and they issue written, reasoned decisions (**R.102**) (**G1/97** r.5(c)).

Duties are allocated to the departments of second instance by the Presidium of **R.12b(4)**, and not by the President. The Administrative Council can delegate disciplinary matters concerning a professional representative to an existing board of appeal (**R.12b(6)**). However, until now these matters have been dealt with by a separate board. The Rules of Procedure for the Boards of Appeal are adopted by the Boards of Appeal Committee (**R.12c(2)**).

The boards of appeal have an independent oversight mechanism for the processing of personal data (OJ 2025 A2).

2 **Competence of boards of appeal**

Art.21 governs the competence of the boards of appeal. The boards are responsible for the examination of appeals from decisions of first instance departments and have jurisdiction to interpret the EPC. The boards have also jurisdiction to refuse enforcement of legislation which has been defectively enacted, for example if passed by an insufficient number of contracting states or delegations of the Administrative Council, or enforcement of a Rule which conflicts with an Article in the sense of **Art.164(2)** (**T315/03** r.5.8).

Cases from examining divisions not handled by technical boards of appeal as specified in paragraphs (3a) and (3b) of **Art.21** are normally handled by the Legal Board of Appeal (paragraph (3c)), e.g. a decision from an examining division consisting of fewer than four members and not relating to the refusal of a patent application, the grant, limitation or revocation of a patent, but for example to re-establishment (**G2/90** r.3.2, adapted to the revised wording of **Art.21(3)(a)**). See **Art.21(3):1.2** for an exception.

Art. 21(1) The Boards of Appeal shall be responsible for the examination of appeals from decisions of the Receiving Section, the Examining Divisions and Opposition Divisions, and the Legal Division.

1 **Competence to examine appeals**

The search division does not issue decisions. Hence, an opinion of the search division, e.g. on lack of unity of invention, cannot be appealed. There is also no possibility to appeal a decision of the President or a decision of a board of appeal, because these decisions are not comprised in the exhaustive list of **Art.106(1)**.

Art. 21(2) For appeals from decisions of the Receiving Section or the Legal Division, a Board of Appeal shall consist of three legally qualified members.

Art. 21(3) For appeals from a decision of an Examining Division, a Board of Appeal shall consist of:

(a) two technically qualified members and one legally qualified member, when the decision concerns the refusal of a European patent application or the grant, limitation or revocation of a European patent, and was taken by an Examining Division consisting of less than four members;

(b) three technically and two legally qualified members, when the decision was taken by an Examining Division consisting of four members, or when the Board of Appeal considers that the nature of the appeal so requires;
(c) three legally qualified members in all other cases.

1 **Board competent to decide on appeal from decision of an examining division**
The intention of the **Art.21(3)** is that appeal cases in which the emphasis is on technical problems are dealt with by the technical boards of appeal (**Art.21(3)(a)**) and appeal cases in which the emphasis is on legal questions are dealt with by the Legal Board of Appeal (**Art.21(3)(c)**) (**T850/95** r.3.3; **G1/11** r.9). The formulation of **Art.21(3)** in terms of procedure instead of expertise has resulted in a complicated provision including gaps (**G1/11** r.13), the interpretation of which has required a large number of decisions of boards of appeal.

Appeals from a decision of an opposition division are always dealt with by a technical board of appeal, independent of the emphasis of the case (**Art.21(4)**).

1.1 DECISIONS BY TECHNICAL BOARD OF APPEAL (ART.21(3)(A) AND (B))
The decisions under paragraphs (a) and (b) are taken by a technical board of appeal and indicated by a T number. The composition of the technical board depends on the composition of the examining division as set out in **Art.18(2)**. A technical board includes at least one legally qualified member to ensure that expertise on legal matters is always available (**J21/09** r.21).

The examining division usually consists of three technical members and may be enlarged by a legal member if the case so requires (**Art.18(2)**). **Art.21(3)(b)** refers to such a four-member division.

1.2 DECISIONS BY LEGAL BOARD OF APPEAL (ART.21(3)(C))
The decisions mentioned under paragraph (c) are taken by the Legal Board of Appeal and indicated by a J number (from the German 'Juristische Beschwerdekammer').

The Legal Board of Appeal is competent to hear appeals under **Art.21(2)** and appeals against decisions taken by an examining division consisting of fewer than four members when the decision does not concern the refusal of an application or the grant of a patent, but e.g. the refund of the examination fee under **Rfees11** (**J9/10**). In all other cases, i.e. those covered by **Art.21(3)(a)**, **(3)(b)** and **(4)**, the technical board of appeal is competent. (**G2/90** hn.I)

Since **Art.21(3)(a)** does not apply to an interlocutory decision of an examining division which is concerned solely with the refusal of a request for refund of a search fee under **R.64(2)**, the case should be handled by a Legal Board according to **Art.21(3)(c)**. However, that is inappropriate because of the technical character of the matter. The EBoA decided that there is a gap in **Art.21(3)** and, in view of the objective of the provision, that such a case must be decided by a technical board. (**G1/11** hn)

2 **Decisions on requests for correction of a patent**
A decision of an examining division refusing a correction of the decision to grant (**R.140**) concerns the grant within the meaning of **Art.21(3)(a)**, in that it relates to the text in which the patent has been granted. An appeal from such a decision is to be decided by a technical board of appeal (**G8/95** hn, r.4). However, the description, claims and drawings of a European patent cannot be corrected using **R.140** (**G1/10** r.3, 5).

3 **Decisions concerning request for limitation or revocation**
Requests for limitation or revocation of European patents under **Art.105a-105c** will entail ex parte proceedings requiring a decision by an examining division. Since limitation proceedings will focus in particular on compliance with **Art.84** (clarity of the claims) and **Art.123(2)** and (3) (added subject-matter, extended scope), appeals against the resulting decisions should be heard by the technical boards, as set out in **Art.21(3)(a)**. (OJ 2007 se4 EN p.22)

Art. 21(4) For appeals from a decision of an Opposition Division, a Board of Appeal shall consist of:
(a) two technically qualified members and one legally qualified member, when the decision was taken by an Opposition Division consisting of three members;
(b) three technically and two legally qualified members, when the decision was taken by an Opposition Division consisting of four members, or when the Board of Appeal considers that the nature of the appeal so requires.

1 **Board competent to decide on appeal from decision of an opposition division**
Paragraph (4) does not include the phrase 'three legally qualified members in all other cases' of paragraph (3)(c). Therefore, the technical board of appeal is exclusively competent to hear all appeals against decisions of the opposition divisions. The Legal Board of Appeal is not competent to handle appeals against decisions of the opposition divisions.

Hence, an appeal against a decision issued by a formalities officer in opposition proceedings, e.g. revoking a patent for not filing a translation of the amended claims under **R.82(3)**, must also be heard by a technical board of appeal. Since a formalities officer may only take decisions involving no legal difficulties, there is no reason why the three-member Legal Board should be competent to hear the appeal. (**G2/90**)

If the Legal Division has taken an adverse decision during opposition proceedings, e.g. relating to a transfer, the Legal Board of appeal is competent to hear the appeal against this decision (see for example **T553/90** r.2.2).

Art. 22 Enlarged Board of Appeal

Implemented by:
R.13 Business distribution scheme for the Enlarged Board of Appeal and adoption of its Rules of Procedure

1 **General**
The Enlarged Board of Appeal is in general not a further instance, but a special department ensuring the uniform application of the EPC. However, it is a further instance for review of decisions of the boards of appeal under **Art.112a.** Its decisions and opinions are given a G number (from the German 'Grosse Beschwerdekammer'), its decisions on a petition for review an R number.

Art. 22(1) The Enlarged Board of Appeal shall be responsible for:
(a) deciding on points of law referred to it by Boards of Appeal under Article 112;
(b) giving opinions on points of law referred to it by the President of the European Patent Office under Article 112.
(c) deciding on petitions for review of decisions of the Boards of Appeal under Article 112a.

Art.112 Referral to the Enlarged Board of Appeal
Art.112a Petition for review

Art. 22(2) In proceedings under paragraph 1(a) and (b), the Enlarged Board of Appeal shall consist of five legally and two technically qualified members. In proceedings under paragraph 1(c), the Enlarged Board of Appeal shall consist of three or five members as laid down in the Implementing Regulations. In all proceedings, a legally qualified member shall be the Chairman.

Implemented by:
R.109(2) Composition EBoA for examining petitions for review

1 **Composition for petitions for review**
The measures laid down in **Art.22(2)** and **R.109(2)** have been established in order to avoid the EBoA being overwhelmed by petitions for review. First, a three-member panel filters out the clearly inadmissible and clearly unallowable petitions for review. Second, admitted petitions will be examined by a five-member Enlarged Board of Appeal. (OJ 2007 se4 EN p.24)

Art. 23 Independence of the members of the Boards

Art. 23(1) The members of the Enlarged Board of Appeal and of the Boards of Appeal shall be appointed for a term of five years and may not be removed from office during this term, except if there are serious grounds for such removal and if the Administrative Council, on a proposal from the Enlarged Board of Appeal, takes a decision to this effect. Notwithstanding sentence 1, the term of office of members of the Boards shall end if they resign or are retired in accordance with the Service Regulations for permanent employees of the European Patent Office.

1 **Term of appointment**
A board member is appointed for a term of five years according to **Art.23(1)** with the possibility of re-appointment for a subsequent term (**Art.11(3)**). The legislator limited the term to five years, because it could not be excluded, when drafting the EPC1973, that the workload of the boards would decrease after some time (Singer, 1st ed., Art.11, note 3). If board members are not re-appointed, they are assigned to another position in the office (Service Regulations Art.41).

The independence of the members of the boards of appeal requires that the executive authorities cannot exert pressure on them and that they do not have to fear for their position if they take decisions disagreeable to those authorities. For that reason, it is of vital importance that the members of the boards cannot be dismissed. The five-year term of **Art.23(1)** conflicts with that independence, because it gives the AC a possibility to dismiss a member by denying him a re-appointment. See also **R.12a:2**.

2 **Removal of board member**

A member of the Enlarged Board of Appeal (EBoA) or a board of appeal may only be removed from office on serious grounds. The Administrative Council (AC) must request the EBoA to make a proposal to remove the board member and then take a decision to this effect based on the proposal. The procedure before the EBoA is laid down in RPEBA Art.12a and Art.2(2) and (5).

In a disciplinary case against a board member the judicial independence of the Enlarged Board of Appeal according to **Art.23(3)** was fundamentally violated. In December 2014 the President ordered a 'house ban' on a member of the boards of appeal because of alleged misconduct (see **G2301/16**). Note, that according to **Art.10(2)(h)**, the President may only propose disciplinary actions to the AC with regard to board members (situation prior to the reform of the BoA in 2016, see **R.12a:1**) and that the AC has disciplinary power over these members under Art.11(4). Nevertheless, the AC confirmed the suspension and requested the EBoA to make a proposal to remove the member from office.

During the proceedings dealing with the request in June 2016, the President of the EPO, who was not a party to the proceedings, intervened and instructed the EBoA not to carry out an investigation of the alleged facts, contrary to Art.12(7) RPEBA, and not to conduct the oral proceedings in public, contrary to the order of the EBoA and Art.12(9) RPEBA, and threatened the members of the EBoA with disciplinary measures (**G2301/16** r.40). See the following section for the disciplinary measures. Since the intervention of the President violated the judicial independence of the EBoA and the AC as party to the proceedings did not distance itself sufficiently from the President's position, the board decided not to make the requested proposal.

The publication of decision **G2301/16** was held back by the above President of the EPO but was published in 2018 after the next President of the EPO took up office.

3 **Term and disciplinary measure**

Since 2015, the finite term has become an actual threat to the independence of the board members. The removal of a board member from office on serious grounds is normally preceded by a suspension until the AC has received a proposal from the EBoA and takes a decision to remove the member. The Service Regulations of the EPO (available on the EPO website), amended and approved by the AC in 2015, allow the AC to suspend board members to the end of their five-year term under **Art.23(1)**. Upon expiry of the five-year term, the AC can deny re-appointment without a proper **Art.23(1)** proposal from the EBoA. Hence, any board member can be suspended indefinitely by a mere decision of the AC, which affects the independence of the boards. (**G2301/16** r.9-13)

The board member who was given a 'house ban' was removed from the boards of appeal at the end of December 2017, the expiry of his five-year term, without a proposal from the EBoA and without any reasons being published.

Art. 23(2) The members of the Boards may not be members of the Receiving Section, Examining Divisions, Opposition Divisions or Legal Division.

1 **Exclusions of membership**
The search divisions are not mentioned in this provision, because they cannot take appealable decisions and, hence, a conflict with the separation of instances is not possible.

Art. 23(3) In their decisions the members of the Boards shall not be bound by any instructions and shall comply only with the provisions of this Convention.

1 **Binding of board of appeal**
The boards are not bound by instructions such as those referred to in **Art.10(2)(a)**, i.e. the Guidelines (followed by **T162/82** hn.1) and by decisions of national courts (see e.g. **T885/02** r.3.3) though decisions and opinions given by national courts may be taken into consideration in interpreting the EPC (**G3/19** r.xiv.1). Neither do decisions of the Administrative Council on the interpretation of EPC provisions bind the boards; such decisions may nevertheless be taken into account for purposes of interpretation (**J16/96** r.2).

Art. 23(4) The Rules of Procedure of the Boards of Appeal and the Enlarged Board of Appeal shall be adopted in accordance with the Implementing Regulations. They shall be subject to the approval of the Administrative Council.

1 **Rules of Procedure of the Boards of Appeal**
See **R.12c(2)** for Rules of Procedure of the Boards of Appeal and of the Enlarged Board of Appeal. The Rules of Procedure are binding on the Boards of Appeal and the Enlarged Board of Appeal (Art.23 RPBA and Art.19 RPEBA).

Art.23(4) is directed to the process by which the Rules of Procedure are adopted; it does not require that the Rules of Procedure should always comply with the current version of the Implementing Regulations. Although the Implementing Regulations of the EPC should not be amended so as to cause a conflict with an already existing Rule of Procedure, if a conflict does arise, the amended rule will not be applicable to the boards of appeal and the RPBA will be regarded as a provision 'otherwise provided' as stated in **R.100(1)** (**G6/95**).

The RPBA can be used in interpreting the EPC but cannot give the boards powers that the EPC did not (**T1914/12** r.7.2.3).

Art. 24 Exclusion and objection

1 **General**
All parties are entitled to have their cases decided in an objective way by unprejudiced, impartial judges. This legal principle is laid down in the EPC in **Art.24**, which allows members of boards of appeal and the Enlarged Board of Appeal to be objected to and excluded from proceedings. There are no comparable provisions for members of the departments of first instance; case law has provided corresponding rules (see below).

Specific grounds for objection are given in **Art.24(1)**. A member of a board may ask to be excluded from an appeal for any reason (**Art.24(2)**); a party may also request the exclusion of a member of a board for a reason stated in the law (**Art.24(3)**). **Art.24(4)** relates to the procedure used to decide on the objection.

2 **Partiality in departments of first instance**
The EPC has no provisions for exclusion of a member of a department of first instance from participation because of suspected partiality, in contrast with the provision for the members of second instance departments (**Art.24**). The Enlarged Board of Appeal has decided that the basic requirement of impartiality also applies to employees of the departments of first instance, albeit less strictly than stipulated in **Art.24(1)** (**G5/91**). For instance, one member of an opposition division may have taken part in the proceedings for grant of the patent to which the opposition relates (**Art.19(2)**, in contrast with **Art.24(1)**). The fact that an examiner and a party hold different views on issues relevant to the case is not in itself indicative of partiality, and can be remedied in appeal proceedings (**T261/88**). Examiners may be suspected of partiality if they are former employees of a party. The length of time between the examiners' last action for their former employer and their first action as examiner in a case to which this employer is a party may be important when assessing partiality, since any residual bias due to this employment would gradually fade away with time; 21 months is regarded as sufficiently long (**T261/88**).

Any challenge to impartiality must be submitted to the division, which will forward it to the responsible superior of the members of the division, usually a Director of a department of first instance. A decision of the superior rejecting an objection to a member cannot be appealed separately. However, the decision regarding the objection may be challenged in an appeal against the final decision of the division. The decision of the responsible superior should be annexed to the final decision, so that a board of appeal can take it into account when evaluating the case (**T727/19**, r. 2.4). According to the Enlarged Board of Appeal, it would also be possible for the opposition division itself to decide on the objection by means of an appealable interlocutory decision, but this is not the current practice as set out in the Guidelines. (**G5/91**; E-XI)

Partiality of a member of the first instance constitutes a substantial procedural violation in the sense of **R.103(1)(a)** (**T261/88** r.2.1). Where a decision by a first-instance department is set aside because of a substantial procedural violation, and a party has reasonable grounds to suspect that the same composition of the department would be tainted by the previous decision and therefore partial, the case will be reheard before a different composition of the department at the request of the party (**T433/93** hn. II).

Participation of a member in a decision of a board of appeal in breach of **Art.24(1)** or despite being excluded by a decision under **Art.24(4)** is a ground for review (**Art.112a(2)(a)**). Suspicion of partiality under **Art.24(3)** is only a ground for review if proven and decided by the board (preliminary decision of 15.06.2009 in case **G2/08** r.1.3).

Art. 24(1) Members of the Boards of Appeal or of the Enlarged Board of Appeal may not take part in a case in which they have any personal interest, or if they have previously been involved as representatives of one of the parties, or if they participated in the decision under appeal.

1 **Partiality in departments of second instance**
Members of a board of appeal may be objected to if there is a suspicion of partiality, so the members are prevented from being influenced in their decision-making by extraneous considerations, i.e. considerations other than the arguments that are factually and legally relevant to the case (preliminary decision of 07.12.2006 in case **G1/05**).

Partiality for objective reasons is a prejudice or apparent bias, i.e. a preconceived judgment regarding substantive issues on how a case should be decided. A preconceived judgment of a member of a board may be caused by participation in a previous decision on the case; such a judgment may result from the laudable desire of the member to be logical and coherent in successive decisions (**T1028/96** r.6.1).

Partiality for subjective reasons is to willingly favour a party by granting it rights to which it is not entitled or by intentionally disregarding the rights of another party (**T843/91** hn. IV). Partiality for subjective reasons is related to persons, whereas partiality for objective reasons is related to subject-matter (see also E-X).

Art.24(1) contains three specific reasons for objection to members of the boards of appeal to safeguard parties from prejudice and partiality:

1 A member may not have a personal interest in the appeal.
2 A member may not have been involved previously as representative of one of the parties. The German and French version of the provision make clear that the exclusion must be limited to members that have previously been involved as representatives of one of the parties in this particular case; otherwise, a former representative of a company would be excluded from all cases of this company.
3 A member of a board of appeal or the Enlarged Board of Appeal may not have participated in the decision under appeal. The 'decision under appeal' is the decision of a department of first instance, not the decision of the board of appeal referring to the Enlarged Board of Appeal.

The first two reasons relate mainly to partiality for subjective reasons (see e.g. **T843/91** r.6.3), the third reason to partiality for objective reasons.

The exclusion does not apply to a member of a board deciding on a patent in opposition appeal who was also a member of a board deciding on the grant of the same patent, because the latter decision is not 'the decision under appeal'. However, participation of the member in the opposition appeal may be objected to under **Art.24(3)** on the ground of prejudice if the opposition appeal concerns the same or comparable crucial issue as the decision in grant, e.g. sufficiency of disclosure (**T1028/96** hn. I, r.6.2, 6.5).

2 **Partiality in Enlarged Board of Appeal**
Participation of members of the Enlarged Board of Appeal in the referring decision of the board of appeal is not governed by **Art.24(2)** but by the Rules of Procedure of the Enlarged Board of Appeal. **Art.2(4)** of these Rules requires that at least four of the members of the Enlarged Board shall not have taken part in the proceedings referring the point of law (even stricter in the preliminary decision of 07.12.2006 in case **G1/05** r.26).

Art. 24(2) If, for one of the reasons mentioned in paragraph 1, or for any other reason, a member of a Board of Appeal or of the Enlarged Board of Appeal considers that he should not take part in any appeal, he shall inform the Board accordingly.

1 **Withdrawal of member**
If a member of a board of appeal or the Enlarged Board of Appeal considers, for a reason mentioned in paragraph 1 or for any other reason, that they should not take part in an appeal, they must inform the board accordingly (**Art.24(2)**). An example of any other reason is a close family relationship with a party, e.g. a party being represented by a law firm in which the EBoA member's husband and son are partners (preliminary decision of 07.12.2006 in case **G1/05** r.3, 4).

The requirement of impartiality in proceedings before the boards of appeal and the Enlarged Board of Appeal must be very strictly observed in view of their judicial functions at supreme level within the European system of patent law (**G5/91** r.3). **Art.24(2)** serves to safeguard this principle by obliging members to inform the board if they consider that they should not take part in the appeal for any reason. This avoids that such reason comes up later and affects the proceedings. Hence, a ground put forward in a notice of withdrawal by a member should normally be respected by the decision on replacement. (preliminary decision of 07.12.2006 in case **G1/05** r.5-7)

However, a member cannot withdraw from the proceedings at will, i.e. for reasons not related to the protection of a party from the possible partiality of the member. On the other hand, it should also be avoided that board members have to sit in cases where they are convinced or fear that they might not be able to be impartial. If no party raises an objection to the withdrawal, the board will decide to replace the member. (preliminary decision of 07.12.2006 in case **G1/05** r.8-11)

Art. 24(3) Members of a Board of Appeal or of the Enlarged Board of Appeal may be objected to by any party for one of the reasons mentioned in paragraph 1, or if suspected of partiality. An objection shall not be admissible if, while being aware of a reason for objection, the party has taken a procedural step. An objection may not be based upon the nationality of members.

1 **Objections to members of board of appeal**
Members of a board of appeal may be objected to (**Art.24(3)**):
- for taking part in a case in which they have any personal interest; or
- if they have previously been involved in this case as representatives of one of the parties; or
- if they participated in the decision under appeal; or
- if suspected of partiality.

Nationality of a member cannot be used as a reason for objection.

In the first two cases partiality is presumed, in the fourth case partiality is suspected. For example, a former representative of a party that did not act in the case in suit is not presumed to be partial under **Art.24(1)** but may be suspected of partiality under **Art.24(3)**.

Participation of a member of the Enlarged Board of Appeal in a technical or legal board of appeal is not a ground for exclusion or objection, because the legislator has deliberately provided this structure. Otherwise, this fact would have been a ground for exclusion or objection. (**R19/12** r.13.3)

An objection of partiality cannot be based alone on the participation of a member of the Enlarged Board of Appeal in a decision referred to the Enlarged Board of Appeal. There may be a ground for objection if there is a reason to believe that the prior decision was the result of a preconceived attitude, or if the member has expressed outspoken, extreme or unbalanced views on the matter. (preliminary decision of 07.12.2006 in case **G1/05** r.20-27)

The president of the boards of appeal, who is chair of the Enlarged Board of Appeal by force of habit, has resigned some management functions in response to a partiality objection in order to avoid a possible conflict of interests as manager and chairman (**R19/12**).

A suspicion may be based on views expressed on other occasions. However, the suspicion must be substantiated in mentioning the member involved, stating concrete remarks and circumstances and the relation to the present case. A view on the issue to be decided expressed by a member on a previous occasion is insufficient to suspect partiality. There may be partiality if members have expressed that they would never change their mind on a certain question. (preliminary decision of 16.10.2009 in case **G3/08** r.2)

When parties become aware of a reason for objection, they must raise the objection before they take a procedural step. Raising an objection is not regarded as a procedural step in the sense of **Art.24(3)**.

Whereas the reasons for exclusion in **Art.24(1)** may be put forward by anyone (preliminary decision of 15.06.2009 in case **G2/08** r.1.2), a suspicion of partiality may only be put forward by a party to the proceedings under **Art.24(3)**. However, a suspicion of partiality raised by a third person, not party to the proceedings, may be taken into account under Art.4(1) RPEBA (and similarly, under Art. 3(1) RPBA) (preliminary decision of 16.10.2009 in case **G3/08** r.1). When a third person files objections, the board should assess whether they amount to abuse of procedure (preliminary decision of 15.06.2009 in case **G2/08** r.2.3).

Art. 24(4) The Boards of Appeal and the Enlarged Board of Appeal shall decide as to the action to be taken in the cases specified in paragraphs 2 and 3, without the participation of the member concerned. For the purposes of taking this decision the member objected to shall be replaced by his alternate.

1 **Procedure**

An objection to one or more members of a board of appeal can only be made in the course of an appeal pending before that board of appeal (**T843/91**). The procedure to assess objections under **Art.24(1)** and (3) comprises a first step of determining the admissibility of the objection and a second step of examining the objection substantively. The first step prevents abuse to delay the proceedings.

The admissibility is assessed by the board in its original composition (**T1028/96** hn. II). The three formal conditions for admissibility are:

1 the party may not have taken a procedural step while being aware of a reason for objection (**Art.24(3)**); hence, the request should be filed as soon as there is a suspicion of partiality;
2 the objection may not be based upon the nationality of the members (**Art.24(3)**); and
3 the objection must be reasoned, indicating facts and arguments to support the objection (**T1028/96** r.2).

The first condition reduces the chances that a party makes the objection only because an adverse decision is expected. The membership of the boards of appeal as designated according to **R.12b(4)** is published annually in the first issue of the OJ and the actual composition of the board competent for a specific case is given in the summons to the oral proceedings.

If the objection is admissible, the second step in the assessment of the objection, i.e. the examination, starts with the appointment of the alternate(s) of the member(s) objected to. In its new composition the board decides on the objection and as to the action to be taken according to **Art.24(4)**. The issue is not whether the member was in fact partial but whether reasons exist to suspect the member of partiality (**T1028/96** r.6.1).

Proceedings in the case may only continue after the decision on objection has been taken (Art.3(3) RPBA). Documents in a file relating to the exclusion of or objections to members of the boards of appeal or of the Enlarged Board of Appeal are excluded from public inspection (**R.144(a)**).

Art. 25 Technical opinion

At the request of the competent national court hearing an infringement or revocation action, the European Patent Office shall be obliged, on payment of an appropriate fee, to give a technical opinion concerning the European patent which is the subject of the action. The Examining Division shall be responsible for issuing such opinions.

1 **Formal and substantive issues**

The fee for a technical opinion is fixed in **Rfees2(1)20**. If the request for an opinion is withdrawn before the EPO has done any substantive work, 75% of the fee will be refunded (**Rfees10**).

The responsible examining division will give a technical opinion on any question which is similar to those normally dealt with in substantive examination work; it does not give an opinion on the scope of protection and does not make specific statements on the question whether or not a patent is valid or is infringed, because these matters are for the national courts to decide (E-XIII,2). An individual cannot obtain a technical opinion from the EPO; only national courts have this privilege (**Art.25**).

Chapter IV *The Administrative Council*

Art. 26 Membership

Art. 26(1) The Administrative Council shall be composed of the Representatives and the alternate Representatives of the Contracting States. Each Contracting State shall be entitled to appoint one Representative and one alternate Representative to the Administrative Council.

1 **Representative in Administrative Council**
The appointed representative of a contracting state in the Administrative Council is usually the president of the national patent office. The composition of the Administrative Council is published on the EPO website (OJ 2024 A110).

2 **Role of Administrative Council**
The Administrative Council is an organ of the European Patent Organisation (**Art.4(2)**). Its task is the supervision of the European Patent Office (**Art.4(3)**). The competence of the Administrative Council is set out in **Art.33**. Many Council decisions and preparatory documents are published on the EPO website since 2012 and can be found under 'Administrative Council documents' in the 'Transparency portal'.

Art. 26(2) The members of the Administrative Council may, in accordance with the Rules of Procedure of the Administrative Council, be assisted by advisers or experts.

Art. 27 Chairmanship

Art. 27(1) The Administrative Council shall elect a Chairman and a Deputy Chairman from among the Representatives and alternate Representatives of the Contracting States. The Deputy Chairman shall ex officio replace the Chairman if he is prevented from carrying out his duties.

Art. 27(2) The terms of office of the Chairman and the Deputy Chairman shall be three years. They may be re-elected.

Art. 28 Board

1 **Setting up of the Board**
By decision of the Administrative Council of 05.06.2003, which entered into force on 01.07.2003, a Board of the Administrative Council has been set up to assist the Chairman in preparing and ensuring the continuity of the work of the Council (OJ 2003 p.333 and 579).

Art. 28(1) When there are at least eight Contracting States, the Administrative Council may set up a Board composed of five of its members.

Art. 28(2) The Chairman and the Deputy Chairman of the Administrative Council shall be members of the Board ex officio; the other three members shall be elected by the Administrative Council.

Art. 28(3) The term of office of the members elected by the Administrative Council shall be three years. They may not be re-elected.

Art. 28(4) The Board shall perform the duties assigned to it by the Administrative Council in accordance with the Rules of Procedure.

Art. 29 Meetings

Art. 29(1) Meetings of the Administrative Council shall be convened by its Chairman.

Art. 29(2) The President of the European Patent Office shall take part in the deliberations of the Administrative Council.

Art. 29(3) The Administrative Council shall hold an ordinary meeting once each year. In addition, it shall meet on the initiative of its Chairman or at the request of one-third of the Contracting States.

Art. 29(4) The deliberations of the Administrative Council shall be based on an agenda, and shall be held in accordance with its Rules of Procedure.

Art. 29(5) The provisional agenda shall contain any question whose inclusion is requested by any Contracting State in accordance with the Rules of Procedure.

Art. 30 Attendance of observers

Art. 30(1) The World Intellectual Property Organization shall be represented at the meetings of the Administrative Council, in accordance with an agreement between the Organisation and the World Intellectual Property Organization.

Art. 30(2) Other intergovernmental organisations entrusted with carrying out international procedures in the field of patents, with which the Organisation has concluded an agreement, shall be represented at the meetings of the Administrative Council, in accordance with such agreement.

Art. 30(3) Any other intergovernmental and international non-governmental organisations carrying out an activity of interest to the Organisation may be invited by the Administrative Council to be represented at its meetings during any discussion of matters of mutual interest.

Art. 31 Languages of the Administrative Council

Art. 31(1) The languages used in the deliberations of the Administrative Council shall be English, French and German.

Art. 31(2) Documents submitted to the Administrative Council, and the minutes of its deliberations, shall be drawn up in the three languages specified in paragraph 1.

Art. 32 Staff, premises and equipment

The European Patent Office shall place at the disposal of the Administrative Council, and of any committee established by it, such staff, premises and equipment as may be necessary for the performance of their duties.

Art. 33 Competence of the Administrative Council in certain cases

Fields of competence of the Administrative Council as provided in some other articles of the EPC: **Art.4(3), 11(3), 23(1)** and the articles mentioned in **Art.35(2)**.

Art. 33(1) The Administrative Council shall be competent to amend:
(a) the time limits laid down in this Convention;
(b) Parts II to VIII and Part X of this Convention, to bring them into line with an international treaty relating to patents or European Community legislation relating to patents;
(c) the Implementing Regulations.

Part II-VII Art.52-141
Part X Art.150-153

1 **Amendment of the EPC**
The Convention can in principle only be amended by a Revision Conference (**Art.172**). **Art.33(1)** is an exception intended to allow the Organisation to respond quickly to changing circumstances. The Implementing regulations can be amended by the Administrative Council (Art.33(1)(c)). Amendments are prepared by DG1 and DG5 in consultation with a.o. the epi (Art.134a(1)(a)). Since 2012 users of the patent system have been consulted through the EPO website (OJ 2012 p.643).

2 **Amendment of time limits in the Convention** (**Art.33(1)(a)**)
Paragraph 1(a) allows the Administrative Council to amend the time limits in the Convention. These time limits are, in the sense of **Art.120**, periods within which a party has to perform an act before the EPO. Six such time limits have been amended in EPC1973 over about 30 years. Since the term of the patent in **Art.63** is not such a time limit, a revision of the term requires an amendment under **Art.33(1)(b)** or a Revision Conference according to **Art.172** (see **Art.63(2):1**).

3 **Amendment of the Convention in view of international treaties (Art.33(1)(b))**
The Administrative Council may bring the parts of the Convention relating to patent law and procedural law in line with international treaties or European Community legislation relating to patents under **Art.33(1)(b)**. It is understood that the Administrative Council can exercise this competence in the case of any treaty, convention or Community text containing provisions relating to patent law (for example, the provisions of Part II, Section 5 of Annex 1C (the TRIPS Agreement) to the Agreement Establishing the World Trade Organization of 15 April 1994). Any consensus already achieved at EU, WIPO or WTO level can be directly echoed in the EPC, avoiding the need to

convene a revision conference and dispensing with national ratification procedures of uncertain duration and outcome. (OJ 2007 se4 EN p.32)

It may only do so once the international treaty or EU legislation has entered into force or after expiry of the period for implementation if such period has been laid down in the EU legislation (**Art.33(5)**). A decision on amendment requires unanimity of the contracting states and representation of all of them (**Art.35(3)**). A decision on amendment will not take effect if a contracting state declares within twelve months of the date of the decision that it does not wish to be bound by that decision (**Art.35(3)**).

These conditions, introduced to accommodate the misgivings of contracting states about a transfer of sovereign rights to the European Patent Organisation, have made the provision so restrictive that it will be barely applicable in practice.

4 **Amendment of the Implementing Regulations (Art.33(1)(c))**
The Implementing Regulations can be amended under **Art.33(1)(c)** by a decision of the Administrative Council. Over the past years the Implementing Regulations have been amended approximately twice a year.

The amendments may relate to procedural and substantive issues and are only limited by **Art.164(2)** (G2/07 r.2.2, distinguishing **J11/91** r.2.3.4).

Art. 33(2) The Administrative Council shall be competent, in conformity with this Convention, to adopt or amend:
(a) the Financial Regulations;
(b) the Service Regulations for permanent employees and the conditions of employment of other employees of the European Patent Office, the salary scales of the said permanent and other employees, and also the nature of any supplementary benefits and the rules for granting them;
(c) the Pension Scheme Regulations and any appropriate increases in existing pensions to correspond to increases in salaries;
(d) the Rules relating to Fees;
(e) its Rules of Procedure.

1 **Service Regulations**
The Service Regulations are available on the EPO website; search for 'EPO' and 'Service Regulations'.

Art. 33(3) Notwithstanding Article 18, paragraph 2, the Administrative Council shall be competent to decide, in the light of experience, that in certain categories of cases Examining Divisions shall consist of one technically qualified examiner only. Such decision may be rescinded.

Art.18(2) Composition of examining divisions
No use has been made of this possibility.

Art. 33(4) The Administrative Council shall be competent to authorise the President of the European Patent Office to negotiate and, subject to its approval, to conclude agreements on behalf of the European Patent Organisation with States, with intergovernmental organisations and with documentation centres set up on the basis of agreements with such organisations.

1 **Agreements concluded by the President**
Examples of such agreements are: agreements regarding the seat of the EPO in Munich and the branch in The Hague, the integration of the IIB and INPADOC into the EPO (see **Art.6(2)**), and the agreement between the EPO and WIPO regarding the PCT (**Art.152**).

Art. 33(5) The Administrative Council may not take a decision under paragraph 1(b):
- **concerning an international treaty, before its entry into force;**
- **concerning European Community legislation, before its entry into force or, where that legislation lays down a period for its implementation, before the expiry of that period.**

Art.33(1)(b) Amendment to align EPC with international treaties

Art. 34 Voting rights

Art. 34(1) The right to vote in the Administrative Council shall be restricted to the Contracting States.

Art. 34(2) Each Contracting State shall have one vote, except where Article 36 applies.

Art.36 Weighting of votes

Art. 35 Voting rules

Art. 35(1) The Administrative Council shall take its decisions, other than those referred to in paragraphs 2 and 3, by a simple majority of the Contracting States represented and voting.

Art. 35(2) A majority of three-quarters of the votes of the Contracting States represented and voting shall be required for the decisions which the Administrative Council is empowered to take under Article 7, Article 11, paragraph 1, Article 33, paragraphs 1(a) and (c), and 2 to 4, Article 39, paragraph 1, Article 40, paragraphs 2 and 4, Article 46, Article 134a, Article 149a, paragraph 2, Article 152, Article 153, paragraph 7, Article 166 and Article 172.

Art.7 Sub-offices of the EPO
Art.11(1) Appointment of senior employees
Art.33(1)(a) Amendment of Convention time limits
Art.33(1)(c) Amendment of the Implementing Regulations
Art.33(2) Amendment to the Financial Regulations, Service Regulations, Pension Scheme Regulations, Rules relating to Fees and Rules of Procedure of the Administrative Council
Art.33(3) Composition of Examining Divisions
Art.33(4) Authorisation of the President to conclude agreements
Art.39(1) Payment of proportion of renewal fees for a patent to the EPO
Art.40(2) Contribution by contracting states if EPO has insufficient income
Art.40(4) Decision on scale position of contracting state
Art.46 Preparation and adoption of the budget

Art.134a Provisions governing epi, admission to and conduct of the European qualifying examination, disciplinary power over representatives, obligation of confidentiality and non-disclosure privilege
Art.149a(2) Serving of members of the (E)BoA on a European patent court
Art.152 The EPO as ISA or IPEA
Art.153(7) Dispensing with supplementary search report or reduction of the search fee there for
Art.166 Accession to the Convention
Art.172 Revision of the Convention

Art. 35(3) Unanimity of the Contracting States voting shall be required for the decisions which the Administrative Council is empowered to take under Article 33, paragraph 1(b). The Administrative Council shall take such decisions only if all the Contracting States are represented. A decision taken on the basis of Article 33, paragraph 1(b), shall not take effect if a Contracting State declares, within twelve months of the date of the decision, that it does not wish to be bound by that decision.

Art.33(1)(b) Amendment to align EPC with international treaties

1 **Conditions for amending EPC in view of international treaties**

Art.35(3) is introduced in response to the need to lay down a special provision governing the adoption and entry into force of a decision of the Administrative Council under **Art.33(1)(b)** modifying the EPC.

Three guarantees are laid down in **Art.35(3)**:

- An Administrative Council decision under **Art.33(1)(b)** requires unanimity among the voting Contracting States (**Art.35(3)**, first sentence).
- All the Contracting States must be represented when votes are being cast (**Art.35(3)**, second sentence).
- Each Contracting State has a period of twelve months from the time the decision is adopted by the Administrative Council in which to declare that it does not wish to be bound by the decision, thus preventing the decision's entry into force. This period allows representatives of the Contracting States on the Administrative Council to confer with the national legislative bodies to ensure that the change is acceptable (**Art.35(3)**, third sentence).

However, the guarantees offered by **Art.35(3)** differ from those in **Art.172** in one fundamental respect: whereas **Art.172(4)** obliges a Contracting State to cease to be a party to the EPC if it has not ratified a revised text of the EPC in due time, a state exercising its right to declare its opposition to the entry into force of an Administrative Council decision under **Art.33(1)(b)** does not incur any sanction. The alternative under **Art.172(4)** - between ratifying in due time and ceasing to be a party to the EPC - is therefore supplemented by the genuine possibility of intervention by national legislative bodies. (OJ 2007 se4 EN p.34)

Art. 35(4) Abstentions shall not be considered as votes.

Art. 36 Weighting of votes

Art. 36(1) In respect of the adoption or amendment of the Rules relating to Fees and, if the financial contribution to be made by the Contracting States would thereby be increased, the adoption of the budget of the Organisation and of any amending or supplementary budget, any Contracting State may require, following a first ballot in which each Contracting State shall have one vote, and whatever the result of this ballot, that a second ballot be taken immediately, in which votes shall be given to the States in accordance with paragraph 2. The decision shall be determined by the result of this second ballot.

Art. 36(2) The number of votes that each Contracting State shall have in the second ballot shall be calculated as follows:
- (a) the percentage obtained for each Contracting State in respect of the scale for the special financial contributions, pursuant to Article 40, paragraphs 3 and 4, shall be multiplied by the number of Contracting States and divided by five;
- (b) the number of votes thus given shall be rounded upwards to the next whole number;
- (c) five additional votes shall be added to this number;
- (d) nevertheless, no Contracting State shall have more than 30 votes.

Art.40(3), (4) Level of fees and payments - Special financial contributions

Chapter V *Financial Provisions*

Art. 37 Budgetary funding

The budget of the Organisation shall be financed:
(a) by the Organisation's own resources;
(b) by payments made by the Contracting States in respect of renewal fees for European patents levied in these States;
(c) where necessary, by special financial contributions made by the Contracting States;
(d) where appropriate, by the revenue provided for in Article 146;
(e) where appropriate, and for tangible assets only, by third-party borrowings secured on land or buildings;
(f) where appropriate, by third-party funding for specific projects.

Art.146 Cover for expenditure for carrying out special tasks

Art. 38 The Organisation's own resources

The Organisation's own resources shall comprise:
(a) all income from fees and other sources and also the reserves of the Organisation;
(b) the resources of the Pension Reserve Fund, which shall be treated as a special class of asset of the Organisation, designed to support the Organisation's pension scheme by providing the appropriate reserves.

Art. 39 Payments by the Contracting States in respect of renewal fees for European patents

Art. 39(1) Each Contracting State shall pay to the Organisation in respect of each renewal fee received for a European patent in that State an amount equal to a proportion of that fee, to be fixed by the Administrative Council; the proportion shall not exceed 75% and shall be the same for all Contracting States. However, if the said proportion corresponds to an amount which is less than a uniform minimum amount fixed by the Administrative Council, the Contracting State shall pay that minimum to the Organisation.

1 **Renewal fee payment of contracting states**
At present a contracting state remits 50% of the renewal fee it has received for a European patent to the EPO (OJ 1984 p.296).

Art. 39(2) Each Contracting State shall communicate to the Organisation such information as the Administrative Council considers to be necessary to determine the amount of these payments.

Art. 39(3) The due dates for these payments shall be determined by the Administrative Council.

Art. 39(4) If a payment is not remitted fully by the due date, the Contracting State shall pay interest from the due date on the amount remaining unpaid.

Art. 40 Level of fees and payments – Special financial contributions

Art. 40(1) The amounts of the fees referred to in Article 38 and the proportion referred to in Article 39 shall be fixed at such a level as to ensure that the revenue in respect thereof is sufficient for the budget of the Organisation to be balanced.

> Art.38 The organisation's own resources
> Art.39 Payments by the Contracting States in respect of renewal fees for European patents

Art. 40(2) However, if the Organisation is unable to balance its budget under the conditions laid down in paragraph 1, the Contracting States shall remit to the Organisation special financial contributions, the amount of which shall be determined by the Administrative Council for the accounting period in question.

Art. 40(3) These special financial contributions shall be determined in respect of any Contracting State on the basis of the number of patent applications filed in the last year but one prior to that of entry into force of this Convention, and calculated in the following manner:
- (a) one half in proportion to the number of patent applications filed in that Contracting State;
- (b) one half in proportion to the second highest number of patent applications filed in the other Contracting States by natural or legal persons having their residence or principal place of business in that Contracting State.

However, the amounts to be contributed by States in which the number of patent applications filed exceeds 25 000 shall then be taken as a whole and a new scale drawn up in proportion to the total number of patent applications filed in these States.

Art. 40(4) Where the scale position of any Contracting State cannot be established in accordance with paragraph 3, the Administrative Council shall, with the consent of that State, decide its scale position.

Art. 40(5) Article 39, paragraphs 3 and 4, shall apply mutatis mutandis to the special financial contributions.

> Art.39(3), (4) Payments by the Contracting States in respect of renewal fees for European patents

Art. 40(6) The special financial contributions shall be repaid with interest at a rate which shall be the same for all Contracting States. Repayments shall be made in so far as it is possible to provide for this purpose in the budget; the amount thus provided shall be distributed among the Contracting States in accordance with the scale referred to in paragraphs 3 and 4.

Art. 40(7) The special financial contributions remitted in any accounting period shall be repaid in full before any such contributions or parts thereof remitted in any subsequent accounting period are repaid.

Art. 41 Advances

Art. 41(1) At the request of the President of the European Patent Office, the Contracting States shall grant advances to the Organisation, on account of their payments and contributions, within the limit of the amount fixed by the Administrative Council. The amount of such advances shall be determined in proportion to the amounts due from the Contracting States for the accounting period in question.

Art. 41(2) Article 39, paragraphs 3 and 4, shall apply mutatis mutandis to the advances.

Art.39(3), (4) Payments by the Contracting States in respect of renewal fees for European patents

Art. 42 Budget

Art. 42(1) The budget of the Organisation shall be balanced. It shall be drawn up in accordance with the generally accepted accounting principles laid down in the Financial Regulations. If necessary, there may be amending or supplementary budgets.

Art. 42(2) The budget shall be drawn up in the unit of account fixed in the Financial Regulations.

Art. 43 Authorisation for expenditure

Art. 43(1) The expenditure entered in the budget shall be authorised for the duration of one accounting period, unless the Financial Regulations provide otherwise.

Art. 43(2) In accordance with the Financial Regulations, any appropriations, other than those relating to staff costs, which are unexpended at the end of the accounting period may be carried forward, but not beyond the end of the following accounting period.

Art. 43(3) Appropriations shall be set out under different headings according to type and purpose of the expenditure and subdivided, as far as necessary, in accordance with the Financial Regulations.

Art. 44 Appropriations for unforeseeable expenditure

Art. 44(1) The budget of the Organisation may contain appropriations for unforeseeable expenditure.

Art. 44(2) The employment of these appropriations by the Organisation shall be subject to the prior approval of the Administrative Council.

Art. 45 Accounting period

The accounting period shall commence on 1 January and end on 31 December.

Art. 46 Preparation and adoption of the budget

Art. 46(1) The President of the European Patent Office shall submit the draft budget to the Administrative Council no later than the date prescribed in the Financial Regulations.

Art. 46(2) The budget and any amending or supplementary budget shall be adopted by the Administrative Council.

Art. 47 Provisional budget

Art. 47(1) If, at the beginning of the accounting period, the budget has not been adopted by the Administrative Council, expenditures may be effected on a monthly basis per heading or other division of the budget, in accordance with the Financial Regulations, up to one-twelfth of the budget appropriations for the preceding accounting period, provided that the appropriations thus made available to the President of the European Patent Office shall not exceed one-twelfth of those provided for in the draft budget.

Art. 47(2) The Administrative Council may, subject to the observance of the other provisions laid down in paragraph 1, authorise expenditure in excess of one-twelfth of the appropriations.

Art. 47(3) The payments referred to in Article 37(b) shall continue to be made, on a provisional basis, under the conditions determined under Article 39 for the year preceding that to which the draft budget relates.

> Art.37(b) Financing of budget by renewal fee payments by contracting states
> Art.39 Payments by the contracting states in respect of renewal fees for European patents

Art. 47(4) The Contracting States shall pay each month, on a provisional basis and in accordance with the scale referred to in Article 40, paragraphs 3 and 4, any special financial contributions necessary to ensure implementation of paragraphs 1 and 2. Article 39, paragraph 4, shall apply mutatis mutandis to these contributions.

> Art.40(3), (4) Level of fees and payments, special financial contributions
> Art.39(4) Interest on payments

Art. 48 Budget implementation

Art. 48(1) The President of the European Patent Office shall implement the budget and any amending or supplementary budget on his own responsibility and within the limits of the allocated appropriations.

Art. 48(2) Within the budget, the President of the European Patent Office may, in accordance with the Financial Regulations, transfer funds between the various headings or sub-headings.

Art. 49 Auditing of accounts

Art. 49(1) The income and expenditure account and a balance sheet of the Organisation shall be examined by auditors whose independence is beyond doubt, appointed by the Administrative Council for a period of five years, which shall be renewable or extensible.

Art. 49(2) The audit shall be based on vouchers and shall take place, if necessary, in situ. The audit shall ascertain whether all income has been received and all expenditure effected in a lawful and proper manner and whether the financial management is sound. The auditors shall draw up a report containing a signed audit opinion after the end of each accounting period.

Art. 49(3) The President of the European Patent Office shall annually submit to the Administrative Council the accounts of the preceding accounting period in respect of the budget and the balance sheet showing the assets and liabilities of the Organisation together with the report of the auditors.

Art. 49(4) The Administrative Council shall approve the annual accounts together with the report of the auditors and shall discharge the President of the European Patent Office in respect of the implementation of the budget.

Art. 50 Financial Regulations

The Financial Regulations shall lay down in particular:

- (a) the arrangements relating to the establishment and implementation of the budget and for the rendering and auditing of accounts;
- (b) the method and procedure whereby the payments and contributions provided for in Article 37 and the advances provided for in Article 41 are to be made available to the Organisation by the Contracting States;
- (c) the rules concerning the responsibilities of authorising and accounting officers and the arrangements for their supervision;
- (d) the rates of interest provided for in Articles 39, 40 and 47;
- (e) the method of calculating the contributions payable by virtue of Article 146;
- (f) the composition of and duties to be assigned to a Budget and Finance Committee which should be set up by the Administrative Council;
- (g) the generally accepted accounting principles on which the budget and the annual financial statements shall be based.

Art.37 Budgetary funding
Art.39 Payments by the contracting states in respect of renewal fees for European patents
Art.40 Level of fees and payments-Special financial contributions

Art.41 Advances to the Organisation
Art.47 Provisional budget
Art.146 Cover for expenditure for carrying out special tasks

Art. 51 Fees

1 **General**

This provision provides the basis for a coherent and systematic fee system:

- **Art.51(1)** provides a general clause enabling the EPO to levy fees.
- There are two types of fees: those provided for in the Convention itself, in which case the legal consequences of failure to pay in due time are mentioned in the Convention; and those provided for in the Implementing Regulations, in which case the Implementing Regulations also lay down the consequences of failure to pay (new **Art.51(3)**). As an exception, the designation fee is provided in **Art.79(2)** and the consequences of failure to pay in **R.39(2)**, which allowed straightforward amendment of the law when the designation fee for each contracting state was replaced by a flat designation fee for all contracting states.
- The time limits for payment are given in the Implementing Regulations with three exceptions: the time limits for payment of the opposition and appeal fees (**Art.99** and **Art.108**) and the time limit for payment of the first renewal fee for a European patent (**Art.141(2)**) are in the Convention.
- The amounts of the fees and the manner of payment are provided in the Rules relating to Fees (**Art.51(4)**).

(OJ 2007 se4 EN p.46)

2 **Right of Organisation to payment**

Rfees1 defines what fees are: fees to be paid to the EPO and provided for in the Articles and Rules, and fees fixed by the President for special services.

A party to proceedings before the EPO is free to decide whether to pay any fee that falls due. The procedural fees prescribed under the EPC are generally due before the EPO performs the act for which the fee is charged. The sanction for failure to pay is generally either a total or partial loss of rights. If the procedural act is not performed, the fee ceases to be due to the EPO. If a party does not pay certain fees, associated procedural acts will not be carried out, e.g. the examination fee (**Art.94(1)**), the opposition fee (**Art.99(1)**), and the appeal fee (**Art.108**). In other cases the application will be regarded as withdrawn, e.g. when the filing fee or the search fee is not paid timely (**Art.78(2)**).

The Organisation is entitled to the fees fixed by the President in accordance with **Rfees3** for services rendered, such as delivery of periodicals. The termination of financial obligations relating to these fees is laid down in **Rfees13**.

3 **Right of party to refund**

A party is entitled to refund of a fee if the payment lacks a legal basis (see **Rfees9**).

An example is the reimbursement of the fee for further processing or re-establishment when the request for further processing or re-establishment appeared to be necessary at one time, but later it turned out that no loss of rights had occurred. Another example is a renewal fee paid during an appeal procedure examining whether or not the application was correctly deemed to be withdrawn; if it is found that the application was indeed deemed withdrawn, the fee is refunded. Another example is the reimbursement of the appeal fee according to **R.103(1)**.

A refusal by a department of the EPO to reimburse may be appealed. A refusal by the President can only be opposed by filing grievances against the EPO under **Art.9**. See **Art.104(3)** for a provision for the recovery of costs in an opposition procedure through a civil court in a contracting state.

Art. 51(1) The European Patent Office may levy fees for any official task or procedure carried out under this Convention.

Art. 51(2) Time limits for the payment of fees other than those fixed by this Convention shall be laid down in the Implementing Regulations.

1 **Legal basis for payments**
The legal basis for payment of most fees is provided in the Convention, i.e. the Articles, whereas the time limit for payment is usually fixed in the Implementing Regulations. The obligation to pay a fee within a specified period is therefore usually governed by both an article and a rule; e.g. **Art.94(1)** and **R.70(1)** for the examination fee.

Exceptionally, the time limits for paying the opposition fee (**Art.99**) and the appeal fee (**Art.108**) are fixed in the Convention.

Art. 51(3) Where the Implementing Regulations provide that a fee shall be paid, they shall also lay down the legal consequences of failure to pay such fee in due time.

Art. 51(4) The Rules relating to Fees shall determine in particular the amounts of the fees and the ways in which they are to be paid.

1 **Rules relating to Fees**
Whereas the Convention and Implementing Regulations lay down what fees are to be paid and the associated period for payment, the Rules relating to Fees (Rfees) fix the amounts due and the allowable methods of payment. The Rfees do not form part of the Convention (see **Art.164(1)**).

PART II SUBSTANTIVE PATENT LAW

Chapter I *Patentability*

1 Requirements for patentability

The EPC allows for the grant of patents for inventions in all fields of technology (including, for example, computer-implemented inventions, chemical products, food products and pharmaceuticals) as long as the invention claimed in the patent meets clear patentability criteria (including absolute novelty, inventive step and industrial applicability). The Treaty of Strasbourg, which was signed in 1963 and took effect in 1980, was used as the basis for the substantive requirements for patentability. The Treaty of Strasbourg is part of the legal framework of the Council of Europe and has led to the harmonisation of patentability criteria across Europe.

The order of the provisions in this chapter of the EPC is somewhat unusual. The relationship between these provisions may be clarified by arranging them in a different order. In the scheme below, the text of each provision is only a short-hand for the actual provision it refers to.

The scheme indicates four essential requirements for patentability (§2.1.1(a) - (d)), which are expanded in §2.2 - 2.6. The first requirement, that an invention is claimed, is different from the third requirement, that the invention involves an inventive step. An invention is regarded as the result of a mental activity and need not necessarily be novel or associated with an inventive step (T384/91 r.5 §4). The definition of the state of the art in §2.3 below has been separated from the EPC provisions on novelty (**Art.54**), as the state of the art is important not only for the assessment of novelty but also for the assessment of inventive step.

2 Overview of requirements

2.1 PATENTABLE INVENTIONS

1 European patents shall be granted for:
(a) any inventions, in all fields of technology, provided they are
(b) new,
(c) involve an inventive step and
(d) are susceptible of industrial application. (**Art.52(1)**)

2 An invention is not patentable if:
(a) it is contrary to morality (**Art.53(a)**);
(b) it relates to a plant or animal variety or a biological process for the production of plants or animals (**Art.53(b)**); or
(c) it relates to a method of medical treatment or a medical diagnostic method practised on the body (**Art.53(c)**).

2.2 INVENTIONS

1 An invention is not:
(a) a discovery, scientific theory or mathematical method;

(b) an aesthetic creation;
(c) a scheme, rule or method for performing a mental act, playing a game or doing business, or a computer program; or
(d) a presentation of information. (**Art.52(2)**)

2 Subject-matter or activities referred to in paragraph 1 are not patentable to the extent to which a European patent application or European patent relates to such subject-matter or activities as such. (**Art.52(3)**)

2.3 STATE OF THE ART

1 The state of the art of a European patent application comprises everything made available to the public before the date of filing of the European patent application. (**Art.54(2)**)

2 The state of the art also comprises European prior rights, for novelty only. (**Art.54(3); Art.56**)

3 The state of the art does not, however, comprise a disclosure made no earlier than six months before the date of filing of the European patent application if that disclosure was due to, or in consequence of:
(a) an evident abuse in relation to the applicant (**Art.55(1)(a)**), or
(b) a display by the applicant at an international exhibition (**Art.55(1)(b)**).

4 A substance, forming part of the state of the art, is not excluded from patentability if claimed for use in a medical treatment or a medical diagnostic method, provided its use for any medical treatment or medical diagnostic method is not comprised in the state of the art. (**Art.54(4)**)

5 A substance is also patentable if claimed for a specific use in a medical treatment or medical diagnostic method, provided that such specific use does not form part of the state of the art. (**Art.54(5)**)

2.4 NOVELTY

An invention is new if it does not form part of the state of the art. (**Art.54(1)**)

2.5 INVENTIVE STEP

An invention involves an inventive step if it is not obvious to a person skilled in the art having regard to the state of the art. Prior rights are not to be considered in deciding on inventive step. (**Art.56**)

2.6 INDUSTRIAL APPLICATION

An invention is susceptible of industrial application if it can be made or used in industry. (**Art.57**)

Art. 52 Patentable inventions

Art. 52(1) European patents shall be granted for any inventions, in all fields of technology, provided that they are new, involve an inventive step and are susceptible of industrial application.

1 **Requirements for patentability**

Art.52(1) indicates four essential requirements for the patentability of claimed subject-matter to be recognised: (1) it must amount to an invention, (2) it must be new, (3) it must involve an inventive step and (4) it must be susceptible of industrial application. Requirement (1) implies that the claimed subject-matter must have a technical character (G-I,1).

The wording of **Art.52(1)** clearly indicates that patent protection is reserved for creations in a field of technology. In order to be patentable, the subject-matter claimed must therefore have a 'technical character' or – to be more precise – involve a 'technical teaching', i.e. an instruction addressed to a skilled person on how to solve a particular technical problem using particular technical means. It is on this understanding of the term 'invention' that the patent granting practice of the EPO and the jurisprudence of the boards of appeal are based. The same considerations apply to the assessment of computer programs. (OJ 2007 se4 EN p.48)

Thus, the EPO must determine whether subject-matter claimed as an invention has a technical character and develop further the concept of an invention in an appropriate manner in light of technical developments and the state of knowledge (OJ 2007 se4 EN p.48).

An invention must involve a human intervention which brings about a desired result by utilising the forces of nature. One definition, which is in conformity with the concept of 'invention' under the EPC, taken from German case law, is: a technical teaching, i.e. a teaching to methodically utilise controllable natural forces to achieve a causal, perceivable result (**G2/07** r.6.4.2.1). The 'causal, perceivable' provides the causal link between the characterising features of an invention and the technical effect of the invention, necessary for an inventive step under **Art.56**.

An invention must relate to a physical entity or a physical activity (**G2/88**). An invention need not be tangible; hence, an electrical signal is not barred from patentability (**T533/09** hn).

Inventions which are contrary to morality, which relate to plant and animal varieties, or which relate to medical treatments or medical diagnostic methods are excluded from patentability according to **Art.53**.

In principle, any invention is patentable; hence, an exception to this rule, such as in **Art.52(2)**, must be interpreted narrowly (**G5/83**). However, the principle according to which exclusions from patentability laid down in the EPC are to be construed in a restrictive manner does not apply without exception (**G1/04** r.6)

All technical fields are encompassed by **Art.52**, including biochemistry and genetic technology. The EPC provides for the absolute protection of substances in all fields of industry and technology. To be technical, an invention must have a technical character or involve a technical teaching. An invention as claimed must encompass aspects that impart technical character to essentially all ways of performing the invention. If the claims encompass entirely non-technical embodiments, the invention is not technical (**T619/02** r.2.2). The phrase 'in all fields of technology' excludes non-technical subject-matter from patentability.

The industrial applicability of an invention need not be specified in the application – other than in the special case of gene sequences (**R.29**) – but the advantages of the invention over the state of the art, to be mentioned according to **R.42(1)(c)**, are likely to imply industrial applicability.

The term 'invention' in the EPC should generally be construed to mean the subject-matter of a claim, i.e. the combination of technical features defined in a claim (**G2/98** r.2); it is the patentability of the invention defined in this way that should be assessed (**T169/20**). The teachings of the description can, however, be considered, at least when applying the exclusions of **Art.53** and when assessing inventive step (**G2/21**).

Art. 52(2) The following in particular shall not be regarded as inventions within the meaning of paragraph 1:
(a) discoveries, scientific theories and mathematical methods;
(b) aesthetic creations;

(c) schemes, rules and methods for performing mental acts, playing games or doing business, and programs for computers;
(d) presentations of information.

1 **Definition of invention**

When the EPC was being drafted, no agreement could be reached on a positive definition of an invention. As a result, the EPC only tells us what is not considered to be an invention (**Art.52(2)**). The following two positive requirements may nevertheless be derived from the EPC:

1 the invention must be such that it can be carried out by a skilled person (**Art.83**);
2 the invention must be of both a concrete and a technical character (G-II,1; **T854/90** hn1), and must not merely provide a direction for the human mind.

According to **Art.52(1)**, an invention must lie in a field of technology, which results in the requirement under **R.42(1)(a)** that the description must state the technical field to which the invention relates. The invention must concern a technical problem (**R.42(1)(c)**), and it must have technical features in terms of which the matter for which protection is sought can be defined in a claim (**R.43(1)**) (G-I,2(ii)). If there are no technical means and no technical effect, there is no invention (**T51/84** hn.II). See **Art.52(1):1** for the definition of the term 'technical'.

A 'technical character' is essential for the presence of an invention; the determination of whether an invention exists is separate from the other requirements of **Art.52** (**T154/04**).

The EPC does not require the invention to entail technical progress or any useful effect in order to have technical character. However, any advantageous effects should be stated in the description (**R.42(1)(c)**); advantageous effects are often important in determining inventive step (G-I,2).

According to **Art.52(2)** subject-matter (including the 'activities' mentioned in **Art.52(3)**) which is abstract (e.g. discoveries, scientific theories) or non-technical (e.g. aesthetic creations or presentations of information) shall not be regarded as an invention. Subject-matter is not considered to be an invention only to the extent that it relates to an excluded category as such (**Art.52(3)**). Hence, a claimed invention having features relating to both technical subject-matter and abstract or non-technical subject-matter is not excluded from patentability; however, if the claims encompass entirely non-technical embodiments, the invention is not patentable (**T619/02**).

The limitations of **Art.52(2)** must be interpreted narrowly, as they restrict patentability. However, in view of the phrase 'in particular' in **Art.52(2)**, the list of subject-matters excluded from patentability is not exhaustive, and the exclusion might arguably be generalised to subject-matter which is essentially abstract in character, which is non-physical and therefore not characterised by technical features in the sense of **R.43(1)**. (**T163/85** r.2)

When assessing patentability of inventions according to **Art.52**, the EPO may use the so-called 'two-hurdle approach', particularly in the case of computer-implemented inventions (**G1/19** r.37). The non-exhaustive list of exclusions of **Art.52(2)** is used for each of the two hurdles in different ways. The first hurdle, sometimes referred to as **Art.52** hurdle or patent eligibility hurdle, consists of determining whether the claimed invention falls under one of the exclusions of **Art.52(2)** 'as such', i.e. according to **Art.52(3)**. As long as at least one feature of the claim possesses technical character, the first hurdle is cleared. Note that the first hurdle does not include any novelty or inventive step assessment, i.e. it is done without considering any prior art. (G-II 2)

Case law, in particular **T931/95** and **T258/03**, has interpreted **Art.52(2)** to mean that a claim embodies an invention if it comprises at least one technical feature. The EPO thereby applies the 'any technical means' or 'any hardware' approach when considering the first hurdle (**G1/19** r.28). Since most claims containing non-technical features have at least one technical feature, exclusion will be more the exception than the rule. The determination of the patentability of claims including technical and non-technical features has moved from an assessment under **Art.52(2)** (under the former 'contribution approach', which required the distinguishing features to be technical) to an assessment of inventive step under **Art.56** or the second hurdle of the two-hurdle approach (**T258/03** r.4.6; **G1/19** r.38). Importantly, inventive step can be based only on the technical features defined in the claim. Non-technical features do not provide a technical contribution and are thus ignored in assessing inventive step, unless such features interact with the technical subject-matter of the claim in solving a technical problem and thereby make a technical contribution (**G1/19** r.30(f)). See **Art.56:4** for more details on the second hurdle.

2 **Discoveries (Art.52(2)(a))**

Finding a new property of a known material is a mere discovery and unpatentable. If that property is put to practical use, however, a patentable invention may have been made. For example, the discovery that a known material is able to withstand mechanical shock is a discovery as such but a railway sleeper made from that material is an invention (G-II,3.1). Equally, a claim defining a new use of a known compound based on an unknown property may be allowable, because, on proper interpretation of the claim, the attaining of the new technical effect which underlies the new use is a technical feature of the claimed invention (**G2/88** r.2.3, 8, 9).

However, the explanation of a property of a known substance occurring in a known use in terms of a new technical effect is a mere discovery and will not make a claim directed to the use of the compound based on this effect novel (**T892/94** hn.II).

To find a substance freely occurring in nature is a mere discovery. However, if the substance found in nature has first to be isolated from its surroundings and a process for obtaining it is developed, that process is patentable. Moreover, if the substance can be properly characterised by either its structure, by the process by which it is obtained or by other parameters, is new in the sense of having no previously recognised existence, and is associated with a technical effect, then the substance per se may be patentable. For example, the discovery of a gene that exists in nature may amount to a patentable invention if the gene is associated with a technical effect such as its use in making a certain polypeptide or its use in gene therapy. (Decision of the opposition division published in OJ 1995 p.388, hn.II; G-II,3.1)

3 **Mathematical methods (Art.52(2)(a))**

The exclusion relating to mathematical methods is applied narrowly. For example, the exclusion applies if a claim is directed to a method of performing a specific algorithm on abstract data and the claim does not require any technical means. However, if a claim specifies technical means such as a computer for carrying out the method, then it has technical character and is not excluded under Art.52(2)(a).

A mathematical method performed on technical data without technical means may still be excluded from patentability as a method for performing mental acts (see **Art.52(2):5**).

Once technical character has been established, the claim is assessed for novelty and inventive step. In the analysis of inventive step, a mathematical method may contribute to producing a technical effect that serves a technical purpose through its application to a field of technology and/or by being adapted to a specific technical implementation.

A technical purpose through application to a field of technology must be a specific one, for example controlling a specific technical system such as a car braking system, or encoding data for efficient storage such as image compression. Additional examples are given in G-II,3.3.

A generic purpose such as 'controlling a technical system' does not confer technical character to a mathematical method. Further, a claim involving a mathematical method needs to be functionally limited to a technical purpose, rather than merely being suitable for application to a technical purpose. This can be achieved by establishing a sufficient link between the technical purpose and the mathematical method steps; a detailed example is given in G-VII,5.4.2.4.

A claim to a mathematical method may also contribute to the technical character of an invention if the claim is directed to a specific technical implementation of the mathematical method and the mathematical method is particularly adapted for that implementation in that its design is motivated by technical considerations of the internal functioning of the computer (**T1358/09** r5.5). For example, the adaptation of an algorithm to exploit a hardware feature of the computer processor (namely, using word size shifts in a polynomial reduction algorithm that are matched to the word size of the processor) can contribute to producing a technical effect in terms of the efficient implementation of the algorithm by the hardware (G-II,3.3).

A mathematical method that is algorithmically more efficient than prior art methods does not contribute to technical character and is not taken into account when assessing inventive step. However, if the mathematical method is applied to a field of technology and/or is adapted to a specific technical implementation thereby producing a technical effect, the computational efficiency of steps affecting this technical effect is taken into account when assessing inventive step. (G-II,3.3)

Inventions in the fields of artificial intelligence (AI) and machine learning (ML) may be considered to be mathematical methods. Technical character is not necessarily conferred to such inventions merely by the use of terms like 'neural network' or 'support vector machine', because these terms may refer to abstract mathematical models. Patentability of such inventions may depend on the underlying technical field. For example, image classification or audio processing via AI/ML algorithms are often considered inherently technical whereas AI-enhanced natural language processing or logistics are typically considered inherently non-technical. (G-II 3.3.1, **T0912/05**, r.3)

The field of reinforcement learning is not considered inherently technical (**T1952/21** r.19-23).

4 Aesthetic creations (Art.52(2)(b))

The attribute 'aesthetic' is usually used to refer to beauty or the appreciation of beauty. In the context of the EPC, it refers more generally to creations having – as opposed to a technical character – an appearance or effect intended to evoke impressions as apprehended or perceived by the human senses, including the sense of smell. (**T619/02** r.2.4.1)

An aesthetic creation thus relates to an article the appreciation of which is mainly subjective. Such an article defined solely in terms of its aesthetic effect is not patentable. If an aesthetic effect is obtained by technical means, although the aesthetic effect itself is not patentable, the means of obtaining it may be. A process for producing an aesthetic creation may comprise a technical innovation and may thus be patentable. (G-II,3.4)

An example of a feature excluded from patentability is a colour which merely provides an aesthetic effect by making fingerprints less visible on an object or which facilitates classification of an object, the latter being a form of presentation of information (**T119/88**). See G-II,3.4 for more examples.

5 **Mental acts (Art.52(2)(c))**

A subconscious process which takes place in the human mind (such as perception of odours) is not to be considered a mental act (**T619/02**, r.2.1). From this it may be deduced that a mental act must be a conscious process.

The complexity of a method does not exclude it from being considered a mental act (**T914/02**). However, a claim to a method is not excluded as a mental act under Art.52(2)(c) if it comprises technical means, such as a computer, to carry out at least one of its steps or if it provides a physical entity as the resulting product. Such a claim may also include steps which are to be carried out mentally by the user of the method. These mental steps contribute to the technical character of the method only if, in the context of the invention, they contribute to producing a technical effect serving a technical purpose. (G-II,3.5.1).

6 **Computer programs (Art.52(2)(c))**

The Diplomatic Conference for revision of the EPC in 2000 debated the removal of computer programs from **Art.52(2)(c)**, with the argument being put forward that this exclusion was obsolete in view of existing EPO practice (MR/2/00). However, the removal of the exclusion could have had unforeseen consequences with regard to potential change of practice. Moreover, the Conference did not want to anticipate an EU directive on computer programs which was being discussed at the time. It was therefore agreed to leave the exclusion as it stood, and to defer any consideration of amendment to a future conference.

A method involving technical means is an invention within the meaning of **Art.52(1)**. Hence a claim directed to a computer-implemented invention avoids the exclusion merely by referring to the use of a computer, a computer-readable storage medium or other technical means (**G1/19** r.28,29; **T258/03**; **G3/08** r.10.13). A technical feature may be described at a high level of abstraction or functionally, and it may be implicitly evident that a certain claimed method is computer-implemented and hence technical (**T697/17**). On the other hand, the mere possibility of making use of an unspecified computer for performing a claimed method is not enough to establish the use of technical means (**T388/04**). Hence, claims directed to a computer-implemented method, a computer-readable storage medium or a device cannot be objected to under **Art.52(2)(c)** (G-II,3.6).

Computer programs are in principle excluded from patentability by **Art.52(2)(c)** if claimed as such (i.e. not as a computer-implemented method or computer readable storage medium). However, the exclusion does not apply to computer programs having a technical character. In order to have a technical character, and thus not be excluded from patentability, a computer program must produce a 'further technical effect' when run on a computer. A 'further technical effect' is a technical effect going beyond the 'normal' physical interactions between the program (software) and the computer (hardware) on which it is run. The normal physical effects of the execution of a program, e.g. the circulation of electrical currents in the computer, are not in themselves sufficient to confer technical character to a computer program. Examples of further technical effects which confer technical character to a computer program are the control of a technical process and control of the internal functioning of the computer itself or its interfaces. (**T1173/97**; **G3/08**; G-II,3.6)

A computer program (a sequence of computer-executable instructions) and a corresponding computer-implemented method are distinct from each other. Only the former is excluded under **Art.52(2)(c)** in the cases discussed above. (G-II,3.6)

Programming a computer, i.e. the intellectual activity of working out what are the steps to be included in a computer program, may involve technical considerations since it is concerned with defining a method which can be carried out by a machine. However, such technical considerations are not enough to give a technical character to the program; the programmer must have had technical considerations beyond 'merely' finding a computer algorithm to carry out some procedure. (**G3/08** r.13.5)

Examples of sets of claims defining a computer implemented invention are given in F-IV,3.9.

7 **Rules for playing games (Art.52(2)(c))**

The exclusion of rules and methods for playing games covers games including table-top games and video games. Generally, rules for table-top games, such as the dealing of cards and ranking of hands in poker, are perceived by players and are only meaningful in the context of the game. Hence game rules are of an abstract, purely mental nature and therefore excluded from patentability (**T336/07**). Video games may include interactive elements and storylines in a virtual game world. As these elements are conceptual in nature, they are considered to relate to abstract, non-technical schemes (**T12/08**).

A claim that includes technical means for implementing game rules has technical character and so is not excluded under **Art.52(2)(c)**. For example, if a game is won by matching two random numbers, the use of a pair of dice or a computer to generate the two random numbers imparts technical character. (G-II,3.5.2)

Video games such as virtual reality games typically involve technical means for sensing user input, processing the game state and outputting visual, audio and haptic feedback. Such features may be assessed as presentation of information (see **Art.52(2):9**). For example, displaying the current score in a game is regarded as the presentation of non-technical information.

Rules for games may have a psychological effect of amusing, surprising and entertaining players. In some cases, game rules lead to balanced or rewarding gameplay, e.g. matching gamers in a competitive video game based on each player's skill level. However, such effects do not qualify as technical effects. (G-II,3.5.2)

8 **Methods of doing business (Art.52(2)(c))**

A method of doing business is any subject-matter which is of financial, commercial, administrative or organisational nature (G-II,3.5.3).

Its patentability is assessed in the same way as the patentability of computer programs as set out in the previous section: the method must be an invention and, therefore, must have technical character to be patentable. The technical character may be imparted by steps solving a technical problem or achieving a technical effect (see e.g. **T38/86** hn.4).

Earlier decisions such as **T931/95** (Pension benefit systems) found that the mere use of technical means in a method claim does not necessarily confer a technical character on such a claim. Examples of such mere use are the step of using data processing means for a purely non-technical purpose, e.g. for controlling a pension benefits system, and amounting to no more than the general teaching to use data processing means and the step of processing and producing information having purely administrative, actuarial and/or financial character (**T931/95** r.3). A technical character may be conferred if a step solves a technical problem or achieves a technical effect, the use of the data processing means requires technical considerations, or the information being processed relates to a physical entity. However, these decisions have been superseded by **T258/03** (Dutch auction) which criticises **T931/95** for qualifying the relevance of technical features in determining the technical character of a method. Such qualification involves remnants of the contribution approach by implying an evaluation in the light of the available prior art or common general knowledge (r.4.3). According to **T258/03** a method involving technical means is an invention within the meaning of **Art.52(1)**.

In contrast with a method of doing business, an apparatus for carrying out a method of doing business can never be excluded from patentability. Whereas the exclusion of the method is justified by the wording of **Art.52(2)(c)**, an apparatus in the sense of a physical entity or concrete product is not mentioned in **Art.52(2)**. The implied physical features of such an apparatus give it a technical character; hence, the apparatus is an invention in the sense of **Art.52(1)** (**T931/95** r.5, confirmed by **T258/03** r.3.7). However, the implied use of unspecified technical means to carry out a claimed method does not in itself provide technical character and does not take the claims beyond a business method as such; rather, only specified technical means will provide technical character to the method (**T388/04**, r.3).

A few examples of methods of doing business:

- A traffic control system for a city is not patentable, because it is a business-like ruling activity (**T16/83**).
- A method relating to the activity of checking authorisations of people by using cards and a card reader is essentially a business operation; it does not have technical character and is therefore not patentable (**T854/90** hn.2).
- A computer system for controlling an improved pension benefit system is not patentable if the only improvement is in a field excluded by **Art.52(2)** (**T931/95**).
- A method of doing business is not excluded from patentability if the invention does not reside in an abstract method as such but relates to technical means such as a computer network to carry out the method and the invention solves a technical problem in a non-obvious way. For example, the rules of an automatic auction method using a computer network are excluded per se, but an auction system implementing those rules has technical character (**T688/05**).

The mere aim of financial gain or commercial success does not mean that an invention is inevitably a method of doing business (**T619/02** r.2.1).

A claim relating to a business method which includes technical features is not excluded from patentability under **Art.52(2)**; however, when an inventive step is assessed under **Art.56**, all non-technical features will be disregarded in defining the objective technical problem (see **Art.56:4**).

9 Presentation of information (Art.52(2)(d))

Presentation of information is the conveying of information, e.g. visual, audio or haptic information, directly to a human user. It concerns both the 'cognitive content' of the information, i.e. what is being conveyed, and the manner of its presentation (**T1194/97** r.3.7.3; **T1143/06**; **T1741/08**; G-II,3.7). The patentability of information presented directly to a user is assessed differently under **Art.52(2)(d)** from data conveyed to a technical system.

Data conveyed to a technical system that are defined in terms which inherently comprise the technical features of the system are considered to be 'functional data'. Functional data are found, for example, in data encoding schemes, data structures and electronic communication protocols. Functional data are not regarded as presentations of information in the sense of **Art.52(2)(d)**.

For example, a claim to a television signal adapted to generate a picture is allowed if it is defined in terms of the technical features of the television system such as aspect ratio and active-video portion (**T163/85**). Likewise, a claim to a record carrier on which data is recorded in a specified data structure, e.g. including picture line synchronisations, line numbers and addresses, is not excluded from patentability if the data structure is defined in terms of the technical features of the system that the record carrier is used in (**T1194/97** r.3.4).

A claim relating to a method of presenting information to a user containing at least one technical feature for presenting the information, e.g. a computer display or a speaker, has technical character and will not be excluded from patentability under **Art.52(2)(d)** (see **Art.52(3):1**). Likewise, a claim directed to a physical object that is labelled with information, e.g. printed instructions, does not fall under the exclusion of **Art.52(2)(d)** (**T553/02** r.1.2.3; **T1252/16** r.3).

Once technical character has been established, the claim is assessed for novelty and inventive step. In the examination of inventive step, features relating to the presentation of information are disregarded if they do not contribute to producing a technical effect (see **Art.56:4**). Whether a technical effect is involved is determined by considering what information is presented, why it is presented and how it is presented.

9.1 WHAT INFORMATION IS PRESENTED AND WHY IT IS PRESENTED

Information presented to a user may contribute to a technical effect if the information credibly assists the user in performing a technical task (**T336/14**; **T1802/13**). For example, **T1214/09** holds that searching and retrieval of an image by a user from a set of images presented on a display is not a technical task, and therefore the layout of the images has no technical effect.

Similarly, display of data in a colour-coded format to make it easier for a user to understand is not considered a credible technical effect because this choice is only concerned with the way in which information is processed by a human mind (**T1567/05**). Likewise, providing a predictive text input which may lower the cognitive burden on the user is not considered as making a technical contribution (**T1741/08**).

If what is presented to the user relates to static or predetermined information about an internal state of a device that assists the user with a non-technical task using the device, it does not make a technical contribution even though the device is technical. For example, displaying a button sequence that enables a user to configure a device without needing to learn the sequence of buttons is not a credible technical effect (**T1073/13**). On the other hand, information about an internal state of a device that may dynamically change and is automatically detected has a technical effect if it enables a user to properly operate the device. For example, the presentation of information that prompts a user to interact with a device to prevent a technical malfunction has a technical effect.

Information presented to users for their subjective evaluation or non-technical decision making is not considered technical (**T756/06** r.13). For example, the state of a casino computer game is not considered technical information and so cannot contribute to a technical effect.

If information is presented to a user to cause a physiological reaction which can be measured when assessing a medical condition, such a presentation of information may be considered to produce a technical effect. An example is an audio stimulus for assessing hearing impairment. However, the choice of where to put a notification on a display to minimise information overload for the user is not considered to qualify as a technical effect because this is not a physiological reaction (**T862/10**).

9.2 HOW THE INFORMATION IS PRESENTED

How information is presented generally relates to the form in which the information is presented, the arrangement of the information or the timing of its presentation to a user (G-II,3.7). How the information is presented to a user may contribute to a technical effect if it facilitates a continued human-machine interaction or enables the user to perform a technical task.

For example, a continued human-machine interaction was found to be facilitated in a football video game by indicating the location of the nearest off-screen teammate using a guide mark on the edge of the screen. This was found to resolve the conflicting technical requirements of displaying a zoomed-in area when the limited display area may be too small to show a complete area of interest. (**T928/03**)

A technical effect may also arise if information is presented in a proactive and timely manner to enable the user to perform a technical task in a more efficient or precise manner. For example, in a visual aid for a surgeon, displaying the orientation of a ball joint implant which enables the surgeon to position the implant accurately is considered to provide a technical effect.

In **T643/00** the search and retrieval of images by a user was facilitated by changing the resolution of displayed images when an image is selected by the user, leading to a continued human-machine interaction.

However, the display of a diagram or layout is considered non-technical, even if the diagram or layout conveys information in a way that is appealing, lucid or logical to a viewer (**T125/04**).

9.3 USER INPUT

Features of a user interface that provide a mechanism for user input, e.g. entering text, making a selection or submitting a command, are usually considered to make a technical contribution because user input requires compatibility with a predetermined protocol of a machine (G-II,3.7.1).

Methods of enabling user input, e.g. gestures or key strokes, may be considered to make a technical contribution if a physical ergonomic advantage can be objectively established. Performance-oriented improvements to the detection of input, such as allowing faster or more accurate gesture recognition or reducing the processing load of the device when performing recognition, can also make a technical contribution (G-II,3.7.1).

Features concerning the graphic design of a menu, such as its look and feel, that are determined by aesthetic considerations, subjective user preferences or administrative rules, do not contribute to the technical character of a menu-based user interface (**T1143/06**; G-II,3.7.1).

Art. 52(3) Paragraph 2 shall exclude the patentability of the subject-matter or activities referred to therein only to the extent to which a European patent application or European patent relates to such subject-matter or activities as such.

1 **Exclusion of subject-matter 'as such'**
A claimed invention is not patentable only to the extent that it relates to subject-matter not regarded as an invention according to **Art.52(2)** as such. A claimed invention relating to both technical subject-matter and abstract or non-technical subject-matter is not excluded from patentability, because the mixture of technical and non-technical features in combination is regarded as an invention in the sense of the EPC.

The mixture of features must involve technical means to solve a technical problem to be patentable (**T603/89**). Whereas the discovery of steam power is not patentable because of **Art.52(2)(a)**, technical means in the form of a steam engine using steam power is not excluded from patentability. The test to be met is whether the invention relates to excluded subject-matter as such, and not whether the invention has practical utility (**T388/04**, r.4).

The examination as to whether there is an invention is separate and distinct from the examination as to whether the claimed invention is susceptible of industrial application, is new and involves an inventive step. The EPO is free to consider whether a claimed invention is excluded from patentability before it examines whether it involves an inventive step (**T388/04**, hn I). It is irrelevant whether the feature or features giving a claim a technical character are new or known from the prior art. The formerly applied contribution approach, according to which there was no invention if the contribution made over the prior art, i.e. the one or more new, characterising features, did not have a technical character, has no basis in the EPC (**T931/95** r.6; G-II,2).

Art. 53 Exceptions to patentability

European patents shall not be granted in respect of:
(a) inventions the commercial exploitation of which would be contrary to "ordre public" or morality; such exploitation shall not be deemed to be so contrary merely because it is prohibited by law or regulation in some or all of the Contracting States;
(b) plant or animal varieties or essentially biological processes for the production of plants or animals; this provision shall not apply to microbiological processes or the products thereof;
(c) methods for treatment of the human or animal body by surgery or therapy and diagnostic methods practised on the human or animal body; this provision shall not apply to products, in particular substances or compositions, for use in any of these methods.

Implemented by:
(a) **R.28** Exceptions to patentability
R.29 The body and its elements
(b) **R.26** General and definitions
R.27 Patentable biotechnological inventions
R.28 Exceptions to patentability
R.29 The body and its elements

1 Exclusion based on ordre public and morality (Art.53(a))

Art.53(a) excludes from patentability inventions the commercial exploitation of which would be contrary to 'ordre public' or morality. The provision is in line with both Article 27.2 of the TRIPS agreement and with Article 6.1 of Directive 98/44/EC relating to the legal protection of biotechnology inventions. The TRIPS agreement and the EU directive exclude from patentability only those inventions that must be barred from 'commercial exploitation' to protect public order or morality. (OJ 2007 se4 EN p.51)

1.1 ORDRE PUBLIC AND MORALITY

The concept of 'ordre public' covers the protection of public security and the physical integrity of individuals as part of society. It also encompasses the protection of the environment. In general, 'ordre public' is formed by the ethically based constitutional or other rules, usually backed up by penal provisions, that reflect the basic values prevailing in society and trade (**T866/01** r.6.9). Accordingly, inventions the commercial exploitation of which is likely to breach public peace or social order or to prejudice the environment seriously are to be excluded from patentability as being contrary to 'ordre public' (**T356/93** r.5).

The concept of morality is related to the belief that some behaviour is right and acceptable whereas other behaviour is wrong; this belief is founded on the totality of the accepted norms which are deeply rooted in a particular culture. For the purposes of the EPC, the culture in question is the culture inherent in European society and civilisation. Accordingly, inventions the exploitation of which is not in conformity with the conventionally accepted standards of conduct pertaining to this culture are to be excluded from patentability as being contrary to morality (**T356/93** r.6; **T866/01** r.6.12).

Since **Art.53(a)** raises only the question of whether the commercial exploitation of an invention is contrary to 'ordre public' or morality, any other questions of 'ordre public' and morality, such as the morality of patenting animals or genetically modifying a mouse, cannot be considered under **Art.53(a)** (**T315/03** r.4.2). The provision refers only to commercial exploitation of the invention, not of the patent; the EPO is not obliged to consider the effect of granting patent rights on ordre public as distinct from the effect of commercialising the invention. Where the invention was made using biological samples obtained from patients, demonstration of informed consent for use of such samples is not required for ordre public to be satisfied (**T1213/05**).

In **R.28(1)** the EPC explicitly excludes the patentability of processes for cloning or modifying the genetic identity of human beings, the industrial or commercial use of human embryos and the genetic modification of animals which causes them suffering without any substantial medical benefit to humans or animals. The human body and the simple discovery of any of its elements, including the (partial) sequence of a gene, is not patentable according to **R.29(1)**. However, an element isolated from the human body or produced by a technical process is patentable, even if the structure of that element is identical to that of a natural element (**R.29(2)**).

G2/06 held that inventions (here, human embryonic stem cell cultures) which, at the time of filing the application, require the destruction of human embryos for their performance are excluded from patentability under **R.28(1)(c)**, which prohibits the granting of patents concerning the use of human embryos for commercial purposes, and falls within the scope of **Art.53(a)**. For further details, see the discussion at **R.28(1)(c)**.

1.2 **TESTS FOR EXCLUSION UNDER ART.53(A)**

The qualification in the second half-sentence of **Art.53(a)** clarifies that the assessment of whether or not particular subject-matter is to be considered contrary to 'ordre public' or morality is not dependent upon any national laws or regulations. Conversely, particular subject-matter is not automatically regarded as complying with the requirements of **Art.53(a)** merely because its exploitation is permitted in some or all of the contracting states (**T356/93** r.7).

T356/93 r.8 derives from the travaux préparatoires of the EPC that **Art.53(a)** must be narrowly construed, in particular in respect of plant and animal varieties.

A fair test for raising an objection under **Art.53(a)** is to consider whether it is probable that the public in general would regard the invention as so abhorrent that the grant of patent rights would be inconceivable (G-II,4.1). Note however that **T1213/05** makes clear that the effect of the patent as such is not relevant, only the commercial exploitation of the invention must be considered. Further, the commercial exploitation of the invention may go beyond what is recited in the claims (**G2/06**, relating to human embryonic stem cells). It is important to consider the use of the invention indicated in the application rather than all possible uses: an anti-personnel mine is excluded; a method to blow a safe is not excluded (G-II,4.1.2). A letter bomb would not be excluded since there is no commercial market in letter bombs, such that there can be no commercial exploitation. In decision **T866/01** r.6 and 9 a composition for the euthanasia of lower mammals was not considered to be excluded under the morality provisions of **Art.53(a)**, since the euthanasia of mammals is a conventional part of the veterinary practitioner's professional work. This was in spite of the argument made that the composition was not solely useful for the euthanasia of lower mammals and could also be used to euthanise higher mammals and humans.

Being contrary to 'ordre public' and being contrary to morality are two separate objections to patentability either or both of which can be raised in a particular case (**T315/03** r.10.2).

Decision **T315/03** developed a three-step test for considering the exclusion of a claim relating to genetically modified animals from patentability under **Art.53(a)** (see r.10 and its application to two requests in r.12 and 13). The first step is to consider pursuant to **R.28(1)(d)** whether the genetic modification according to the invention is likely to cause the animals suffering, whether there is likely to be a substantial medical benefit to humans or animals and what the balance between the suffering and benefit is likely to be. A claim to a process of genetically modifying an animal causing suffering without corresponding benefit fails the balancing test of **R.28(1)(d)** and must be excluded under **Art.53(a)**. Details of the test are given in **R.28(1)**:3; an example can be found in **T315/03** r.13.2.1-4.

A claim that has passed this first test must be subjected to the second test, formulated in decision **T19/90** r.5: the suffering of animals and possible risks to the environment must be balanced against the usefulness of the invention to mankind. This test can be used in all 'ordre public' and morality cases (**T315/03** r.10.5) involving suffering caused to animals, even if the animals are not genetically modified (**T1553/15**). The second test is broader than the first test and allows criteria different from the first test to be taken into account (**T315/03** hn.VI.2). These criteria may include the possible use of non-animal alternatives to obtain the benefit of the invention (**T315/03** r.10.6 and 13.2.7) and threats to the environment (r.13.2.8-9). Although the degree of suffering may be used as criterion in the second test, it is regarded as effectively impossible to make a distinction between acceptable and unacceptable suffering; accordingly, the degree of suffering is of no assistance in applying the test (**T315/03** r.13.2.6). An example of the application of the test to a mouse genetically modified by insertion of an activated oncogene can be found in **T19/90** r.6 and **T315/03** r.13.2.5-9. In decision **T606/03** a claim to a transgenic mouse was rejected, bearing in mind the potential for suffering, on the basis that only some of the mutant animals would be of medical benefit to humans. However, claims were allowed to transgenic mice of a particular category which would not be expected to suffer.

A claim that has passed the second test must be subjected to a third test in which arguments can be considered relating to morality or 'ordre public' under **Art.53(a)** other than those regarded in the second test (**T315/03** r.10.7). Morality objections may include a possible threat to evolution or the use of the genetically modified animals in research being morally unacceptable to the public (see the example in **T315/03** r.13.2.10). In decision **T315/03** nothing before the board was found to suggest that the use of animals in medical research is considered to be contrary to morality in European culture (r.13.2.21).

The arguments put forward in applying the three tests can only be considered when supported by evidence (**T315/03** r.10.10). However, the EPO may give allegations made without evidence some weight if they are well-known and/or easily verified (**T315/03** r.13.2.14). Opinion poll evidence is of very limited value for establishing that subject-matter is contrary to 'ordre public' or morality (**T356/93** r.15; **T315/03** r.10.4). Since the **Art.53(a)** objection is made as of the effective date of the claim, evidence arising after that date may be taken into account only if it is directed to the position at the effective date (**T315/03** r.10.10). Technical developments concerning the use of the invention which occur after the filing date and have a potential bearing on the issue of ordre public should not be considered; an innocuous way of carrying out the invention which becomes available after the filing date is not relevant. (**G2/06** r.33).

2 Exclusion of plant and animal varieties and biological processes (Art.53(b))

In principle, plants and animals and methods of producing plants and animals are patentable under the EPC. However, a number of exceptions are laid down in **Art.53(b)**. A first exception is that plant and animal varieties are not patentable. A second exception is that methods of producing plants and animals which are essentially biological in nature are not patentable. Moreover, **Art.53(b)** is interpreted such that claims directed to plants, plant material or animals are also not allowable if the claimed product is exclusively obtained by means of an essentially biological process or if the process features of a product-by-process claim define an essentially biological process (**R.28(2)**; **G3/19**).

Art.53(b) expressly states that the exclusion does not apply to microbiological processes and their products.

2.1 PLANT AND ANIMAL VARIETIES

Art.53(b) provides that plant and animal varieties are not patentable. The background to this exception is that several of the EPC contracting states have developed special legal protection for plant breeding at national and international level, specially adapted to meet the interests of plant breeders and farmers. The protection available under the 'International Union for the Protection Of new Varieties of plants' (UPOV = Union Internationale pour la Protection des Obtentions Végétales) is limited to plant varieties, i.e. the specific products which are used in farming and gardening. To avoid double protection by plant breeders' rights and patents, the EPC could have excluded from patent protection only those plants already covered by plant breeders' rights. However, taking this approach, given that plant breeders' rights vary between the contracting states, would have been contrary to the principle of uniform patent protection (**Art.118**). For this reason, the EPC excludes all plant varieties from patent protection. (**G1/98** r.3.4-3.7)

A plant variety is a multiplicity of plants which are largely the same in their characteristics (i.e. homogeneous) and remain substantially the same after every propagation cycle (i.e. stable). The precise definition of a plant variety is given in **R.26(4)**, which follows the wording of the concept of variety in the UPOV Convention (see also **T320/87** r.12 and **T356/93** r.23). Plants that are not stable cannot be classified as plant varieties and, therefore, are patentable (**T320/87** r.14).

Seeds chemically treated to make them resistant to herbicides are patentable. The treatment does not cause genetic modification of the seed, and the effect of the treatment is not transmissible to future generations. (**T49/83**)

G1/98 decided that a claim wherein specific plant varieties are not individually claimed, may still be patentable under **Art.53(b)** even though it may embrace plant varieties. Hence, a distinction must be made between a claim in respect of or encompassing plant varieties, which is not excluded, and a claim directed to one or more specific plant varieties, which is excluded from patentability (**G1/98** r.3.10). Two steps can be distinguished in the development of a genetically modified plant variety: a first step in which a genetic engineer provides tools to bestow a desired property on plants by inserting a gene into the genome of those plants, and a second step in which the breeder develops a plant variety having not only the desired property, but also homogeneity and stability by inserting the gene into a specific plant. The first, more technical step cannot be protected by plant breeders' rights as it is not directed to a plant variety; it can be implemented in an indefinite number of plant varieties and should be protected by a patent. The second, more biological step should be protected by plant breeders' rights (**G1/98** r.3.8, 3.10).

Whether or not a plant is a plant variety and therefore excluded from patentability depends only on whether or not it meets the criteria set out in **R.26(4)**. It is irrelevant for the exclusion whether the method for its production is recombinant gene technology or a classical plant breeding process (**G1/98** hn.III; **T1854/07** r.10.4; G-II,5.4.1).

The principle of **G1/98** should also be followed in the case of animals: the exclusion of animal varieties in **Art.53(b)** applies to claims that define an animal variety or varieties but does not apply to claims that (might) embrace one or more animal varieties, which is certainly true for a claim directed to a taxonomic category of animals higher than varieties (**T315/03** Oncomouse hn.7.1, r.11.4, 11.7 and **G1/98** r.3.10, last sentence).

2.2 BIOLOGICAL PROCESSES AND PRODUCTS

The Implementing Regulations were adapted in 1999 to the Directive of the European Union relating to the legal protection of biotechnological inventions by inserting **R.26** to **R.29** (see **R.26(1):1**). **R.28(2)** was added in 2017 (OJ 2017 A56).

Art.53(b) excludes essentially biological processes for the production of plants or animals from patentability. This exclusion also covers product and product-by-process claims directed to plants, plant material or animals if the claimed product is exclusively obtained by means of an essentially biological process or if the process features recited in the claim define an essentially biological process (**R.28(2)** and **G3/19** hn, reversing **G2/12** and **G2/13**).

R.26(5) provides a definition of the term 'essentially biological' which, however, does not give any useful guidance on how to interpret the term (G2/07 r.4.5, r.5). The EBoA has therefore determined the meaning of the term in the case of processes for the production of plants, based on the legislative history, context and purpose of **Art.53(b)**. The exclusion of plant breeding processes from patentability was introduced to avoid dual protection by the EPC and the UPOV Convention. Such processes were conventional methods for the breeding of plant varieties at the time the law was drafted (~1961), which included in particular the sexual crossing of plants, i.e. of their whole genomes, and subsequent selection of the plants having the desired trait(s). These traits were determined by the natural phenomenon of meiosis, a special type of cell division in which genes are mixed, which occurs in sexual reproduction. Conventional methods may also include steps taken to assist the breeding process. (G2/07 = G1/08 r.6.4.2.2-3)

The EBoA has therefore excluded conventional plant breeding methods from patentability by interpreting 'essentially biological' in a process for the production of plants in **Art.53(b)** as relating to sexual crossing and selection where changes in the genes are only caused by meiosis. Processes changing the genome by technical means, such as irradiation, should therefore be patentable.

The EBoA has defined the extent of the exclusion of processes for the production of plants or animals (in G2/07 for plants; extended to animals in G-II,5.4.2), as follows:

- A non-microbiological process for the production of plants based on sexually crossing the whole genomes of plants and subsequently selecting desirable plants is in principle excluded from patentability as being 'essentially biological' within the meaning of **Art.53(b)** (G2/07 hn.1; T315/03 distinguished). Hence, a method of breeding plants (or animals) by crossing specific plants (or animals) and selecting offspring with the desired traits is excluded from patentability. On the other hand, a process for treating plants or animals to improve properties such as yield or growth, e.g. a method of pruning a tree or treating soil to promote growth, is not excluded because the process does not include the steps of sexual crossing and selection.
- Any technical step that enables or assists the process, as a further step or as part of the steps of crossing or selection, does not make the process patentable (G2/07 hn.2). It is irrelevant whether such a technical step is new or known, whether or not it occurs in nature or whether the essence of the invention lies in it (G2/07 hn.4; T320/87 and T356/93 overruled). The technical step may be patentable per se. For example, the technical step of using a special greenhouse or genetic molecular markers to assist in breeding does not make the breeding process patentable but the greenhouse, markers and their use may be patentable per se.
- However, a process is not excluded from patentability if it includes in the crossing and selection steps an additional technical step which introduces a trait into the genome or modifies a trait in the genome of the plant produced, the introduction or modification not being the result of the mixing of genes of the plants chosen for sexual crossing (G2/07 hn.3). The additional step in such a rare process must modify the crossing and selection steps.
- An additional step changing the genes which is not part of the crossing and selection steps but is applied before or after the sexual crossing and selection steps is to be ignored for assessment of the exclusion. Such a step can be patented per se under **R.27(c)**, without including explicitly or implicitly a sexual crossing and selection process. (G2/07 r.6.4.2.3)

In **G2/12** and **G2/13** (now overruled), the EBoA held that the exclusion from patentability of essentially biological processes for the production of plants in **Art.53(b)** does not extend to the plants or plant material produced by such processes. The EBoA abandoned this interpretation of **Art.53(b)** in **G3/19** on account of developments that occurred after decisions **G2/12** and **G2/13** were taken. One such development was the introduction of **R.28(2)**, showing the clear legislative intent of the Contracting States to exclude such plants and animals from patentability (**G3/19** r.xxvi.7). **G3/19** decided that product claims and product-by-process claims directed to plants, plant material or animals are not allowable if:

- the claimed product is exclusively obtained by means of an essentially biological process; or
- the process features recited in the claim define an essentially biological process.

R.28(2) and **G3/19** both provide a legal basis for this exclusion of plants and animals exclusively obtained by means of an essentially biological process.

See G-II,5.4 and 5.4.2 for examples of essentially biological processes and products thereof.

In order to protect the legitimate expectations of patent proprietors and applicants, the new interpretation of **Art.53(b)** given in **G3/19** has no retroactive effect on European patents granted before 01.07.2017 and European patent applications which have a date of filing, or if priority has been claimed, a priority date, before 01.07.2017 and which were still pending on 14.05.2020 (**G3/19** hn, r.xxix).

Transgenic plants and mutants produced using technical means, e.g. using CRISPR/Cas, are patentable, while the products of conventional breeding processes are not (G-II,5.4). The term 'exclusively obtained' in **R.28(2)** and **G3/19** indicates that a plant or animal originating from a production process involving a technical intervention in the genome is not excluded from patentability even if the production process additionally involves steps of crossing and selection (G-II,5.4). If a technical feature of a claimed plant or animal might be the result of either a technical intervention or an essentially biological process, a disclaimer is necessary to exclude the product of an essentially biological process from the claimed subject-matter (G-II,5.4) and the description should not describe such essentially biological processes as alternative methods to obtain the claimed plant or animal (G-II,5.4).

A biotechnological invention is patentable if it concerns biological material isolated from its natural environment or produced by a technical process, even if it previously occurred in nature (**R.27(a)**). Such material is new, because it was previously not available to the public. **R.27** provides a demarcation between invention and discovery under patent law for biotechnological inventions (OJ 1999 p.573).

2.3 MICROBIOLOGICAL PROCESSES AND PRODUCTS

Microbiological processes and the products thereof are patentable (**Art.53(b)**). A microbiological process is a process involving or performed upon or resulting in microbiological material (**R.26(6)**). Neither the EPC nor the Directive define 'microbiological material'. **T356/93** r.34 and 35 defines 'microbiological' as relating to technical activities in which direct use is made of micro-organisms and 'micro-organisms' as generally unicellular organisms with dimensions beneath the limits of vision which can be propagated and manipulated in a laboratory. The EPC defines biological material as material containing genetic information and capable of reproducing itself or being reproduced in a biological system (**R.26(3)**). A microbiological process refers to a process in which micro-organisms are used to make or to modify products or in which new micro-organisms are developed for specific uses. Consequently, the products thereof encompass products which are made or modified by micro-organisms as well as new micro-organisms themselves (**T356/93** hn.V). An application for an invention which is a biological process or its product may require the deposit of a sample of biological material with a depositary institution under **R.31(1)**.

The propagation of a micro-organism is regarded as a microbiological process (G-II,5.5.1). Micro-organisms, including moulds, bacteria, actinomycetes, yeasts, viruses, plasmids and genes are also patentable (**T162/86**, **T281/86**, **T292/85**, G-II,5.5.1). Plant cells as such are not considered to be plants but microbiological products (**T356/93** hn.III).

3 **Exclusion of medical treatment** (Art.53(c))

Although therapeutic, surgical and diagnostic methods constitute inventions, they are in general not patentable under the EPC. The exclusion from patentability under **Art.53(c)** is based on socio-ethical and public health considerations, according to the travaux préparatoires of EPC1973 and EPC2000 (**T385/86** r.3.1; **T24/91** r.2.4; OJ 2007 se4 EN p.50). The exclusion is allowed by Article 27(3)(a) TRIPS. The intention is to ensure that nobody who wants to use one of the methods specified in **Art.53(c)** as part of the medical treatment of humans or animals should be prevented from doing so by patents (see **T116/85** r.3.7 and **T24/91** r.2.4). In other words, the exclusion of **Art.53(c)** intends to protect patients and those treating them.

However, in the travaux préparatoires of EPC2000 the EPO admitted that the purpose of the provision, to keep medical practice free from patent law restrictions, was not in fact achieved in practice (CA/PL/PV9 §30; see also **T1020/03** r.46).

In EPC1973, methods of medical treatment were not to be regarded as inventions which are susceptible of industrial application by way of a legal fiction. Such methods therefore did not comply with the requirements of **Art.52(1)** and were not patentable. EPC2000 removes this fiction and instead merely excludes such methods from patentability. As a result, the exclusion has been moved from previous Art.52(4) EPC1973 to **Art.53(c)** EPC2000, to group it with the other public policy exclusions, and to bring the law into line with TRIPS Art.27.3(a). Under EPC2000, any medical or veterinary activity should be free from restraint by patents, whether or not the activity is commercial or industrial. However, **G1/04** r.10, 11 held that the scope of the exclusion for diagnostic methods remained valid when EPC2000 entered into force.

Art.53(c) distinguishes three different methods of medical treatment which are excluded from patentability: methods for treatment by surgery, methods for treatment by therapy and diagnostic methods. The interpretation of each of these methods is discussed in the following sections. The interpretation in each case must take into account the overriding intention of the exclusion, i.e. to provide sufficient freedom from patent legislation for anyone practising medicine.

On the other hand, to the extent possible, **Art.53(c)** must be construed narrowly, as must any exclusion to patentability (**G5/83** r.22; **T385/86** r.3.1, 3.2).

The exception under **Art.53(c)** does not extend to new products, particularly substances or compositions, for use in any of these three different types of treatment or diagnosis. Novelty for a substance or composition that is already known may be established by a new medical use in accordance with **Art.54(4)-(5)** (see **Art.54(4):2** and **Art.54(5):2**).

3.1 TREATMENT

The treatments mentioned in **Art.53(c)** are by their nature medical treatments, which include curative and non-curative treatments. A curative treatment has a therapeutic purpose. A non-curative treatment is not directed to the health of the body; it includes e.g. a cosmetic treatment, the termination of pregnancy, castration, sterilisation, artificial insemination, embryo transplantation, treatments for experimental and research purposes, and the removal of organs, skin or bone marrow from a living donor. (**T182/90** r. 2.2)

Since the travaux préparatoires state that the aim of **Art.53(c)** is merely to exclude curative treatments, the exclusion should only extend to treatments that are suitable or potentially suitable for maintaining or restoring the health, physical integrity or physical well-being of a human being or an animal or preventing disease (**T383/03** r.3.2-3.4, following **T144/83** r.3 and **T329/94** r.5; see **T182/90** r.2.4, 2.5.2 for an opposite opinion). Hence, cosmetic treatments do not fall within the exclusion (**T383/03** r.4.2).

The rearing of livestock is a part of agriculture and therefore an industrial activity according to **Art.57**. Hence, treatment of animals in order to achieve improved growth, meat quality (G-II,4.2.1) or wool or milk production (**T774/89**) should be patentable, as also expressed by the Munich Diplomatic Conference of 1973 (Empel no. 120). The medical treatment of animals, being part of rearing, may also be regarded as an industrial activity. Hence, a treatment to cure or immunise one or more animals is both a therapeutic treatment and an industrial activity. Such a treatment is excluded from patentability under **Art.53(c)** in spite of its industrial applicability, because **Art.53(c)** takes precedence over **Art.57** (**T116/85** r.3.5, 4.1). See below for methods having both therapeutic and non-therapeutic effects.

The exclusion from patentability of **Art.53(c)** applies irrespective of the person carrying out the method. This has been confirmed by several decisions. It is impossible to draw a distinction between a therapeutic treatment of an animal carried out by a farmer and the same treatment as carried out by a veterinarian (**T116/85** r.4.3). A medical treatment need not necessarily be carried out by a physician (**T182/90** r.2.2; **T329/94** r.5). The medical competence of the person carrying out a step of a method or under whose supervision the step is carried out may be, at first sight, a useful indication as to whether the method falls under **Art.53(c)** or not; however the purpose and inevitable effect of the step are much more important (**T329/94** r.5).

The opinion **G1/04** held that the qualification of an activity as having a diagnostic character may not depend on who is involved. The wording of **Art.53(c)** is unequivocal in that the exclusion relates only to the method and not to the person carrying out the method (**G1/04** r.6.3). When this is applied mutatis mutandis to treatments, the person carrying out a method of treatment is irrelevant for the exclusion of a method of treatment from patentability. Previous decisions **T24/91** and **T385/86** (holding that a diagnostic or therapeutic method is one which has to be carried out by a specialist medical practitioner) are overruled as far as the relevance of the person carrying out the method is concerned.

3.2 TREATMENT BY SURGERY

G1/07 hn.1 specifies that the exclusion of methods of treatment of the body by surgery in **Art.53(c)** includes methods in which, when carried out, maintaining the life and health of the subject is important and which comprise or encompass an invasive step representing a substantial physical intervention on the body which requires professional medical expertise to be carried out and which entails a substantial health risk even when carried out with the required professional care and expertise.

The exclusion is not confined to surgical methods pursuing a therapeutic purpose (**G1/07** r.3.3.10). Methods of treatment by surgery e.g. for cosmetic purposes, organ transplantation or embryo transfer are hence also excluded from patentability (**G1/07** r.3.3.7; G-II,4.2.1.1).

The definition in **G1/07** hn.1 is not exhaustive. An intervention may be considered to be surgical even if the intervention is not invasive and no tissues are penetrated, e.g. repositioning body limbs and catheterisation can be regarded as surgical (**G1/07** r.3.4.2.5; **T5/04**). Factors other than the required medical expertise and the health risk involved may also determine that a physical intervention on the body constitutes treatment by surgery (**G1/07** r.3.4.2.4).

Invasive techniques of a routine character which are performed on uncritical body parts and generally carried out in a non-medical, commercial environment are not excluded from patentability; this is generally the case for tattooing, piercing, hair removal by optical radiation and micro-abrasion of the skin (**G1/07** r.3.4.2.2). Similarly, routine interventions in the medical field do not fall under the exception if they are uncritical methods involving only a minor intervention and no substantial health risks (**G1/07** r.3.4.2.2; G-II,4.2.1.1; **T2699/17**). For example, an intravenous injection that can be delegated to a paramedical professional may be considered as representing a minor routine intervention which does not imply a substantial health risk when carried out with the required care and skill (**T663/02**). On the other hand, an injection into the heart represents a treatment by surgery (**G1/07** r.3.4.2.7).

The Enlarged Board in **G1/07** did not give an authoritative, once and for all definition of what 'treatment by surgery' may comprise (**G1/07** r.3.4.2.5). The scope of the term may change with time and in light of new technical developments (**G1/07** r.3.4.2.5; **T182/90**). Accordingly, the departments of first instance and the boards of appeal are better suited to define 'treatment by surgery' based on the technical reality of the individual cases before them (**G1/07** r.3.4.2.4).

Computer-assisted surgical methods do not avoid **Art.53(c)** merely by being computer-assisted (G-II,4.2.1.1).

No distinction is to be made between humans and animals when the scope of the exclusion is interpreted (**G1/07** r.3.3.7).

A claim which comprises a step encompassing an embodiment which is a method for treatment of the body by surgery cannot be left to encompass that embodiment. The embodiment may be disclaimed, provided the disclaimer complies with the requirements of **G1/03** and **G2/03**. (**G1/07** hn.2)

The surgical step may only be omitted from the claim if the omission is compatible with **Art.84** in that the step is not an essential feature defining the invention (see **G1/07** hn.2). Omission is possible for a method relating to operating a device without any functional link between the claimed method and the effects of the device on the body (**G1/07** r.4.3.2). However, if a step is essential for a claimed method but not specified, the step must be read into the claim when assessing whether the claim falls under **Art.53(c)** (**T2612/19** r.1.3).

The health risk of a surgical method may be assessed using a risk matrix combining levels of likelihood and the health impact of a complication associated with a medical act (**T663/02** hn. II).

See decisions **T836/08** and **T923/08** for the effect of claim category on the exclusion.

3.3 TREATMENT BY THERAPY

3.3.1 *Therapy*

The meaning of the term 'treatment' is explained in **Art.53:3.1** above. 'Therapy' is concerned with bringing a body from a pathological state back to its normal, healthy state or with preventing a pathological state (**T774/89** r.2.3.4; G-II,4.2.1.2). Treatment by therapy is defined as any treatment which is designed to cure, alleviate, remove or lessen the symptoms of, or prevent or reduce the possibility of contracting any disorder or malfunction of the human or animal body (**T24/91** r.2.27).

The concept of therapy should not be construed narrowly. As an example, the relief of pain, discomfort or incapacity is to be construed as therapy in the sense of **Art.53(c)**, irrespective of its origin. The symptoms caused by natural circumstances (e.g. menstruation, pregnancy or age), or by reaction to the environment (e.g. atmospheric conditions provoking tiredness, headaches) overlap with and are often indistinguishable from symptoms of a disease or an injury. Moreover, the biochemical effects and mechanisms which medicaments generate in order to restore the normal, capable and painless state of the body are often very similar or identical in these instances, irrespective of the nature of the real cause. It would be impossible and undesirable to distinguish between causal and symptomatic therapy, i.e. healing or cure and mere relief. Therefore, a method for relieving menstrual discomfort by administering a chemical composition is a therapy excluded under **Art.53(c)** and a first medical use of the composition should be pursued if the composition is not yet known as medicament. (**T81/84** r.3, 4)

In contrast, the use of a compound for reducing the perception of fatigue before or after physical exercise is regarded as a non-therapeutic treatment. Since the manifestations of fatigue induced by the natural circumstance of exercises do not overlap with symptoms of a disease or injury, this case must be distinguished from **T81/84**. The condition of fatigue is not comparable to a pathological state. Whereas a therapeutic treatment starts from a pathological state, a non-therapeutic treatment starts from a normal, healthy state. (**T469/94** r.4.2 and **T774/89** r.2.3.4)

Art.53(c) does not mention prophylactic treatment. The Munich Diplomatic Conference preferred to leave it to case law to clarify whether prophylactic treatment was excluded, because the industrial nature of a particular treatment, particularly when applied to animals, might justify the grant of a patent (Empel no. 119). Case law has established that prophylactic treatment is therapeutic in nature, because prophylactic and curative treatments are directed to the same objective, i.e. the maintenance or restoration of health (**T19/86** r.7; **T182/90** r.2.2; **T820/92** r.5.2).

The prevention of pregnancy is not in general a therapy according to **Art.53(c)**, because pregnancy is not an illness (**T74/93** r.2.2.3). Such a method may be susceptible of industrial application, provided the requirements of **Art.57** have been fulfilled. These are not fulfilled for a method of contraception which is to be applied by women themselves in the private and personal sphere (**T74/93** r.2.2.4).

T1635/09 held that use of a composition as a contraceptive in which concentrations of substances were selected to avoid side-effects is a medical method because such prevention is therapeutic; the use is therefore excluded from patentability (r.3.1). Note that this reasoning potentially makes the cosmetic use of any composition a therapeutic treatment because all cosmetic products try to prevent side-effects. 'Prevention of a side-effect' should not be regarded as therapeutic treatment, as prevention is not a treatment of the side-effect. For the same reason, 'prevention' cannot be regarded as prophylaxis, the latter being the preventive treatment of a disease.

The removal of the symptoms of myopia, hyperopia and astigmatism of the eye is a therapeutic treatment (**T24/91** r.2.7).

The treatment of an implant secured to the body is regarded as treatment of the body in the sense of **Art.53(c)** if the treatment has a direct therapeutic effect, e.g. laser ablation of an implanted cornea in a patient's eye, which directly changes the refractive power of the patient's eye (**T24/91** r.2.6). The manufacture of prostheses, e.g. limbs or teeth, outside the body as well as taking measurements therefor on the body is patentable; however, making a prosthetic tooth inside the mouth is excluded under **Art.53(c)** (G-II,4.2; **T775/97** r.2.6).

A claim is not allowable if it includes at least one feature defining a physical activity or action which constitutes a method for treatment of the human body by therapy, for instance the measurement of a pressure value in the body which has a functional link with the therapeutic treatment applied (**T82/93** r.1.4, following **T820/92**). The exclusion of **Art.53(c)** applies to multi-step methods which comprise or encompass at least one therapeutic step (**G1/07** r.3.2.3.2; G-II,4.2.1.2). An undisclosed disclaimer can be permitted under **Art.123(2)** to exclude the therapeutic step (**G1/03** hn.2.1). However, any amendment to a granted patent must comply with **Art.123(3)**.

A claim containing nothing but technical features directed to a technical operation performed on a technical object and a subsequent technical operation performed on a body is not allowable under **Art.53(c)** if it defines a method for treatment of the body by therapy or surgery (**T82/93** r.1.1, method for operating a cardiac pacer). A method of measuring the flow of small quantities of liquid in an implanted drug dosimeter providing a reading characterising the capacity of the pump of the dosimeter is not a treatment under **Art.53(c)** if there is no functional link and hence no physical causality between the steps of the method and the therapeutic effect produced on the body by the dosimeter, i.e. determining when a certain volume of drug is administered. Such a method does not hinder the doctor in carrying out a therapeutic or surgical treatment. (**T245/87** r.3.2.2, 3.2.3)

3.3.2 Combination of therapeutic and non-therapeutic indications

A method may have both a therapeutic and a non-therapeutic effect. Its patentability depends on the wording of the claim and the disclosure of the effects in the description of the application.

If the non-therapeutic effect and the therapeutic effect of a step in a method of treatment are inextricably linked, a claim including the non-therapeutic effect would necessarily include the therapeutic effect and would be excluded. It is not relevant for the purpose of **Art.53(c)** whether the main or even the only reason for carrying out the claimed method is non-therapeutic. Even the addition of a non-therapeutic purpose to the claim is of no avail. In **T820/92** the method concerned the administration of two substances to prevent pregnancy. Whereas the first substance produced the preventive effect, which was non-therapeutic, the second substance had a prophylactic effect avoiding the ill consequences of the use of the first substance. Since one step of the claimed method had a therapeutic effect, the method claim fell under the prohibition of **Art.53(c)**. (**T820/92** r.5.2; **T82/93** hn.I)

A method of incurring loss of body weight by administering a certain compound can have a therapeutic and a non-therapeutic effect. The two effects are not inseparably linked but are distinguishable because they involve two distinct groups of people. Application of the method to people not suffering from obesity would not be beneficial to the health of those people but improve their bodily appearance (cosmetic treatment). However, application of the method to people suffering from obesity would be beneficial to their health (therapeutic treatment). The cosmetic treatment is not rendered unpatentable by the fact that the compound has both a cosmetic and therapeutic effect, however difficult it might be to distinguish between the two effects. Hence, a claim is not excluded from patentability if its wording is chosen to cover the cosmetic treatment only (**T144/83** r.3, 4, see also **T464/94**). This does not apply to surgery – a cosmetic surgical method is still a surgical method and excluded from patentability (**T1172/03**).

A method of removing plaque from teeth has the cosmetic effect of improving the appearance of the teeth but also inevitably involves a therapeutic effect by preventing caries, as was acknowledged in the description of the patent application in case **T290/86** (r.3.2). The two effects are inseparably linked and the claimed method was therefore found to be excluded under **Art.53(c)**.

If the patent disclosure reveals that the intention of the claimed method is to obtain both a therapeutic effect (remedying scours in animals) and a linked non-therapeutic effect (weight increase of the animal being bred) at the same time, a claim directed to the non-therapeutic effect is excluded (**T438/91**). A method to increase the production of meat is not patentable when the increase is a consequence of the improvement of the animal's health due to therapeutic treatment; the increase is a secondary effect of the treatment (**T780/89**).

A claim directed to thenoyl peroxide for use in a method of therapeutic treatment of the human or animal body (first medical indication) and a claim directed to the use of thenoyl peroxide as a cosmetic product were both allowed. Thenoyl peroxide in the same preparation can be used in the treatment of acne and in the cleansing of the skin. Hence, the cosmetic treatment may also incidentally involve a medical treatment. The term 'cosmetic' in the claim was regarded as sufficient to distinguish from therapeutic treatment. (**T36/83** r. 6)

The term 'non-therapeutic' in a claim relating to the use of a medication to increase milk production in cows served as a disclaimer of any therapeutic use in case **T774/89** (r.2.3.4). The non-therapeutic treatment was found to be independent of the state of health of the animal.

3.4 DIAGNOSTIC METHODS

3.4.1 *Diagnosis and diagnostic methods*

Diagnosis is the determination of the nature of a medical or veterinary medicinal condition intended to identify or uncover a pathology (**G1/04** r.5.1).

According to opinion **G1/04** a claim relating to a diagnostic method is excluded from patentability under **Art.53(c)** if it includes all of the following phases:

1. the examination phase, involving the collection of data;
2. the comparison of these data with standard values;
3. the finding of any significant deviation, i.e. a symptom, during the comparison; and
4. the attribution of the deviation to a particular clinical picture, i.e. the deductive medical or veterinary decision phase (diagnosis for curative purposes *stricto sensu*).

The above four phases are an interpretation in G-II,4.2.1.3 of the less-intelligible three steps in the headnote 1 of **G1/04**.

Hence, a claim relates to a diagnostic method only if it includes all four of these phases. If one phase is omitted, there is no diagnostic method but merely an intermediate finding of diagnostic relevance (**G1/04** r.6.2.2, 6.2.3). Further, for the diagnostic method as a whole to be 'practised on the human or animal body' each method step of a technical nature must be practiced on the human or animal body.

The Enlarged Board of Appeal followed the established case law based on **T385/86** and overruled **T964/99** concerning the scope of the exclusion. This narrow interpretation of **Art.53(c)** is based on the principle that exclusions from patentability in the EPC are to be construed in a restrictive manner (**G1/04** r.6) and on the fact that a narrow interpretation provides more legal certainty. In the Enlarged Board's opinion, the importance of legal certainty was found to outweigh the importance of protecting medical and veterinary practitioners. According to the EBoA, the protection of medical practitioners can be achieved on a national level by introducing a right to use the methods in question (**G1/04** r.6.1, 6.3). It should be noted, however, that the TRIPS Agreement does not allow such immunity as an exception to the rights conferred by a patent (all EPC contracting states except Monaco are bound by TRIPS).

The exclusion cannot be circumvented by omitting one of the above features from a claim if its essential nature can be inferred from the patent application or patent as a whole, because such a claim would not then comply with the requirements of **Art.84**. The clarity requirement of **Art.84** means that an independent claim within the meaning of **R.43** should explicitly specify all of the essential features needed to define the invention. Hence, a claim that focusses on one step of a diagnostic method while omitting other steps essential to that method (cf. **T965/99**) does not meet the requirement of **Art.84**. (**G1/04** r.6.2, 6.2.3)

Preparatory or intermediate steps in addition to the steps describing phases 1-4 are irrelevant for determining the diagnostic character of a method claim (G-II,4.2.1.3).

Although the EBoA held that phases 1-3 should comply with the criterion 'practised on the human or animal body', in most cases only phase 1 must comply. The criterion implies an interaction with the human or animal body but direct physical contact is not necessary. The criterion is fulfilled if the method step concerned requires the presence of the body. (G-II,4.2.1.3)

The clinical picture in phase 4 need not be an underlying disease; a pathology suffices (**T125/02**).

In the assessment of the diagnostic character of a method, the presence or absence of a medical practitioner is not relevant. In this context, no distinction is to be made between essential method steps having diagnostic character and non-essential method steps lacking it (**G1/04** hn.2).

In **T330/03** a method for measuring a parameter of a biological sample using illumination with light was regarded patentable, because the method did not enable a decision to be made on the treatment necessary and was therefore not a diagnostic method in the sense of **Art.53(c)**. Similarly, in **T504/03** a data processing method for an X-ray tomography device was not excluded from patentability.

An imaging method is not excluded as a treatment by surgery merely because the image data obtained by the method during a surgical intervention immediately allows a surgeon to decide on the course of action to be taken during the surgical intervention. (**G1/07** hn.3, r.5)

3.4.2 *Method practised 'on the body'*

Art.53(c) specifies that excluded diagnostic methods must be 'practised on the human or animal body'. The qualification was added because interested circles had objected to the exclusion of diagnostic methods as such, which would have led to the exclusion of diagnostic methods which were not of a specifically medical nature, such as the use of equipment to determine the blood group of a patient (Empel no.121). The intention was therefore to exclude from patent protection only methods practised on the body, whereas, for instance, extra-corporal laboratory tests were intended to be patentable

(**T964/99** r.4.3). The undesirable consequence of the qualification is that a doctor carrying out a diagnosis that includes an essential laboratory test may be inhibited by a patent from carrying out this test, which is contrary to the intention of **Art.53(c)**. As an example, a quick, reliable laboratory blood test for the diagnosis of colon cancer, where early detection is of immense importance for the chances of survival, was regarded as patentable (**T435/88** r.3).

Opinion **G1/04** ruled that in a diagnostic method under **Art.53(c)** all method steps of a technical nature belonging to the preceding steps which are constitutive for making the diagnosis for curative purposes stricto sensu must satisfy the criterion 'practised on the human or animal body'. A specific type or intensity of interaction is not required; any preceding step of a technical nature thus satisfies the criterion if its performance implies any interaction with the human or animal body, necessitating the presence of the latter. (**G1/04** hn3, 4)

The criterion is to be considered only in respect of method steps of a technical nature. Hence, it does not apply to the deductive phase and to method steps of a non-technical nature, such as comparing data collected in the examination phase with standard values (**G1/04** r.6.4.1). Only those phases identified above are to be considered when determining whether a method is a diagnostic method. Additional steps are not relevant, even if these are practised on the body (**T1197/02**). Data processing steps are typically neither part of the data collection phase, nor of the comparison phase (**T143/04** hn).

This narrow interpretation of 'practised on the human or animal body' makes a claim relating to a diagnostic method patentable if it comprises at least one technical method step without interaction with the body, such as processing or displaying data.

A diagnostic method having a step in which an object is inserted into the body may also be excluded from patentability on the ground of the surgical character of the step. For example, a method for blood extraction used in a diagnostic method was regarded not patentable in **T329/94** r.4 (see also **T964/99** r.6.1). However, in view of the more recent decision **G1/07** hn.1, the insertion of an object into the body may not always be regarded as a surgical step.

3.4.3 *Method carried out by medical or technical staff*

Art.53(c) does not specify which persons have to carry out a diagnostic method for it to be excluded from patentability. It accords with the socio-ethical and public health considerations on which **Art.53(c)** is based: the provision protects patients such that they can be diagnosed and receive the necessary treatment without infringing a patent, whether the necessary methods are carried out by a medical professional, a technician or a layman. The provision does not primarily intend to protect medical professionals in the exercise of their profession.

Since **Art.53(c)** relates only to the method and not to the person carrying out the method, whether a method is a diagnostic method cannot depend on the participation of a medical or veterinary practitioner. It is irrelevant whether such a person is present or not, whether such a person bears any responsibility or not, and whether the method steps can also, or only, be practised by medical or technical support staff, the patients themselves or an automated system (opinion **G1/04** hn.2). In coming to this conclusion the EBoA followed **T116/85**, **T182/90**, **T329/94** and **T964/99** and overruled **T385/86** r.3.5, **T24/91** r.2.4, **T655/92** r.5.3, **T964/99** r.6.2 as far as these decisions relate to the relevance of the person carrying out the method.

3.5 PRODUCTS FOR USE IN MEDICAL METHODS

The second clause of **Art.53(c)**states that products for use in a medical method, in particular substances and compositions, are not excluded from patentability by the first clause of **Art.53(c)**. Hence, products used in medical methods, such as medicines for use in methods of treatment, tools for use in methods of surgery and devices for performing measurements in diagnostic methods, are in principle patentable. Claims directed to substances and compositions for use in a medical method may derive novelty from the medical use recited in the claim, even if the substance or composition as such is not novel (**Art.54**(4) or (5)).

The effect of **Art.53(c)**, second part sentence, is that the manufacture, distribution and sale of medicaments and medical devices may be restricted by patents on such products. A justification for this restriction is that the decision to purchase medical products is usually taken long before their actual use, at a moment when due consideration can be given to any extra costs that arise from the patenting of such products (see Benkard, *Europäisches Patentübereinkommen*, 3rd edition (Beck, 2019), Art.53 note 181). Moreover, the patentability of medical products gives industry an impetus to make further technical advances in this field. On the one hand, **Art.53(c)**, first part sentence, protects the freedom of medical and veterinary practitioners to use the best available treatments for the benefit of their patients, uninhibited by any concern that a particular treatment might be covered by a patent (**G1/07** r.3.2.3, 3.3.6). On the other hand, medical and veterinary practitioners are restricted in the treatments they use to the extent that any, possibly patented, medicaments and tools must be acquired (**T1731/12** r.19). As a consequence, the best available treatment may be prohibitively expensive if a patented medicament or device is to be used in the treatment.

3.6 MEDICAL DEVICES

The features of a medical device may be defined functionally in terms of the manner in which the device is operated in relation to the body of the patient. Such a functional feature does not itself transform the device claim into a method claim and does not exclude the device from patentability under **Art.53(c)** (**T1798/08** r.3.2). However, **Art.53(c)** does exclude devices which are defined by a functional feature that can only be obtained by carrying out a surgical or therapeutic step (**T1731/12** hn; **T775/97** r.2.8).

A method which is only concerned with the operation of a (medical) device, without any functional link between the claimed method and the medical effects produced by the device on the body, is not a method for treatment excluded under **Art.53(c)**. For example, a claim directed to a method for controlling pulse energy in a pacemaker to prolong battery life is patentable if none of the steps of controlling the pulse energy has a therapeutic effect (**T789/96**). On the other hand, if there is such a functional link, the method is excluded from patentability (**G1/07** r.4.3.2).

As a practical recommendation, a patent directed to a method of operating a medical device should also include a claim directed to the device itself. If a granted method claim is considered to be excluded from patentability under **Art.53(c)** in opposition proceedings, rewriting the method claim as a device claim may otherwise violate **Art.123(3)** by extending the protection conferred (see H-V,7.3 for cases where such an amendment was allowed).

Art. 54 Novelty

Art. 54(1) An invention shall be considered to be new if it does not form part of the state of the art.

1 **Novelty**

The purpose of **Art.54(1)** is to prevent the state of the art from being patented again (**T12/81 r.5**). The state of the art is defined in **Art.54(2)** as everything that has been made available to the public (see **Art.54(2):1**). In order to examine the novelty of a claim it is necessary to first determine the effective date of the claim (or of the embodiment under examination in case of partial priority, see **Art.87:5 and Art.88(3)**), then identify the state of the art, i.e. relevant subject-matter made available to the public before the effective date and, lastly, compare the features of the claim with the disclosure of the state of the art.

The subject-matter of a claim is novel over a cited prior art document if it includes at least one technical feature which distinguishes it from the disclosure of that document (**G2/88 r.7**). On the other hand, a claim is not novel if the skilled person would directly and unambiguously derive an embodiment falling within the ambit of the claim from a cited prior art document (**T890/17 r.1.2**), and the prior art document provides an enabling disclosure. The concept of disclosure, i.e. that the embodiment must be directly and unambiguously derivable, is the same for novelty and for **Art.123(2)** (**G2/10 r.4.6, hn.1a**). Hence, the embodiment must be directly and unambiguously derivable from the cited document for the skilled person using only common general knowledge; the disclosure can be explicit or implicit. This rule applies not only to prior art documents but also to other types of prior art, such as public prior use.

Any element of subjectivity must be excluded in applying the concept of novelty (**G1/92 r.2.1**). A lack of novelty can only be established by citing prior art as evidence; the personal knowledge of the examiner plays no role (**T21/83**). Moreover, the citing of documents is an essential element of the substantiated reasoning required by B-XI,3.2 (search opinion), **R.71(2)** (communication issued by the examining division) and **R.111(2)** (decision of the examining division).

For assessing novelty, prior art must be evaluated as of the date it became available to the public (G-VI,3). A prior art document must be read in light of the common general knowledge that the skilled person had on the date that the document was made available. This avoids taking into account any knowledge of later developments, which is only to be taken into account in the assessment of inventive step. Prior rights under **Art.54(3)** must be interpreted using common general knowledge as of the date of filing or, where appropriate, the priority date of the prior right.

2 **Single disclosure**

In order to destroy the novelty of a claim, the prior art must disclose the claimed features in combination. Generally, this means that the disclosure of a document must be considered in isolation when assessing novelty (**T153/85 hn.III**) though common general knowledge may be taken into account. The exceptional case in which the disclosures of more than one document may be combined in the assessment of novelty is discussed below in note 3.

Even if the elements of a claimed invention are all disclosed in one document, the combination of those elements is nevertheless new if the elements are disclosed separately. It is not permissible to pull together features separately disclosed in a single document, e.g. a catalogue, and thus assemble something not specifically disclosed in that document. (**T305/87**)

The disclosure of a prior art patent consists not only of the invention disclosed in that patent but also extends to statements made concerning the prior art. The disclosure made may therefore include a combination of features relating to the invention and features contained in a statement relating to the prior art, provided that statement is unambiguously disclosed as forming part of the invention (**T333/02** r.6). However, when a statement is no more than a general description of the state of the art, care must be taken in combining the statement with the teaching of the invention (**T291/85** r.9).

3 **Cross-reference in document**

Although a document must be considered in isolation in the assessment of novelty, the disclosure of a document may, under certain limited circumstances, be supplemented by the disclosure of a second document that is referenced in the first document.

The incorporation is allowed if the first document contains a specific reference to the second document in relation to specific features, for example, where the first document discloses a chemical compound and states that it can be prepared using a specific method disclosed in the second document (**T153/85** hn.4, r.4.2; G-IV,8). Only the features of the second document that are specifically referred to in the first document are incorporated (**T422/92** r.2.3.1). The mere statement 'incorporated by reference' does not amount to a specific reference.

For the relevance of referenced documents in a patent application to sufficiency of disclosure, see **Art.83:2.1.2.** With regard to the content of the application as filed for assessing extension of subject-matter, see **Art.123(2):1.1.**

Even in the absence of a cross-reference, when interpreting a prior art document, it is necessary to read it having the common general knowledge of the skilled person in mind. For this purpose, it is allowable to look at representative technical literature as an aid to the correct interpretation of any particular term in the prior art document. For example, a prior art disclosure of the use of rubber where its elastic properties are used, even if not explicitly stated, takes away the novelty of the use of an elastic material. (G-VI,2; **T288/90** r.4.4)

4 **Requirement for a direct and unambiguous disclosure**

An invention lacks novelty if there is a direct and unambiguous disclosure of all the features of the claimed invention in a single prior art document (G-VI,2). A strict approach is taken when assessing novelty, and in cases of doubt, a prior art document is interpreted narrowly (see, for example, **T988/95**).

There is an important distinction between information which can be derived directly and unambiguously from a document, and generally known equivalents of the disclosed subject-matter that are not mentioned. The latter may not be taken into account when assessing novelty (G-VI,2), although they may be considered when assessing obviousness (**T167/84**). This strict approach to the assessment of novelty is justified in order to reduce the risk of self-collision between European patent applications and patents under **Art.54(3)** (**T167/84**; see also **Art.54(3):1**).

Novelty may only be denied if the prior art disclosure is enabling (see **Art.54(2):4.3**).

5 **Assessment of novelty**

A mere difference in wording is insufficient to establish novelty (**T114/86** hn.2, **T198/84** r.4). For a lack of novelty, it is not necessary for a prior art document to explicitly mention all the features of a claim. It is sufficient that an embodiment falling under the scope of the claim is directly and unambiguously derivable from the prior art document (**T1599/18** hn). In other words, in order for novelty to be denied, there must be a direct and unambiguous disclosure in the state of the art which inevitably leads the skilled person to subject-matter falling within the scope of what is claimed (**T1654/19** r.9).

A substance disclosed in a prior art patent is prejudicial to the novelty of a patent application claiming the same substance in a better-defined form (**T12/81**).

The disclosure of a process for making a product makes available the direct product of that process, even if the product is not named or was not actually manufactured (**T181/82** r.7; **T12/81**).

Before deciding on the novelty of a claim, a basic initial consideration is to construe the claim in order to determine its technical features (**G2/88** r.7). The claim should be interpreted in a technically sensible manner and be given the broadest, technically reasonable interpretation. In this step, **Art.69** and its Protocol are not relevant (**T223/05** hn, **T1705/17** r.1.2), but see pending referral **G1/24**.

5.1 **INTENDED USE FEATURE**

In the assessment of the novelty of a product claim, a particular intended use which is a feature of the claim ('Object X for use Y…'; Apparatus X for carrying out process Y) must be disregarded, unless the use referred to implies that the product (object X, apparatus X) is in some way different from its known form, i.e. the term 'for' must be interpreted as meaning 'suitable for'. Thus, a product which otherwise possesses all of the features specified in a claim, but which would be unsuitable for the stated purpose, should not normally be considered as prejudicial to the novelty of the claim. For example, a known ice cube tray made of plastic is not prejudicial to the novelty of a claim referring to 'a mould for molten steel', because the low melting point of the plastic material makes it unsuitable for the claimed purpose. However, a tray possessing all the features of the mould and having a sufficiently high melting point would be novelty-destroying, even if the use of the tray as a mould for molten steel was not disclosed. (F-IV,4.13)

The same should hold true for a method claim in which an object is defined functionally as being 'for' a certain purpose: the object feature should be construed to include anything which is suitable for achieving the stated purpose.

Exceptions to the general rule that an intended purpose is irrelevant to the novelty of a product claim are expressly provided for by **Art.54**(4) and **Art.54**(5) (first and second medical use claims - see note 5.2 below).

A means-plus-function feature ('means for') is usually interpreted in the same way as a 'for use' feature, i.e. any prior art feature suitable for carrying out the function of the means-plus-function feature will anticipate it. As an exception, means-plus-function features carried out by a computer are interpreted as means adapted to carry out the relevant functions, rather than merely means suitable for carrying them out (**T410/96**; F-IV,4.13.2). In this way, such a feature provides novelty over an unprogrammed data processing apparatus or a data processing apparatus programmed to perform a different function (**T208/84** hn.2, F-IV,3.9.1).

In relation to a process or method claim qualified by a stated purpose ('Process for'; 'Method for'), a distinction must be made between a purpose relating to the reason for using the process or method and a purpose relating to an effect arising from the use of the process or method. In the former case, the specific application of the process or method stated may imply the presence of additional steps which impart novelty (e.g. **T843/93**, 'Method for remelting galvanic layers' includes a functional feature implying the layers are actually melted; **T1931/14**, 'Process for producing oxygen for fuelling a power generating plant' includes a functional feature implying that such a plant is fuelled). Equally, in the case of a claim directed to a method for manufacturing product X, the actual preparation of product X is a limiting feature of the claim (**T268/13**). However, if the 'for' feature defines a technical effect which inevitably arises when carrying out the remaining steps of the claimed process or method, this feature does not limit the claim (e.g. **T304/08**, 'Method for reducing malodor' means method 'suitable' for reducing malodor. (F-IV,4.13.3)

See **Art.84:1.9** for the effect of a use feature on the clarity of a claim.

5.2 MEDICAL USES

Claims may be granted relating to a known substance or composition when it is for use in a new surgical, therapeutic or diagnostic method of the kind referred to in **Art.53(c)** (G-II,4.2). The novelty of such a claim, which takes the form: 'substance X for use as a medicament', is recognised as a kind of legal fiction under **Art.54(4)**. Such a claim is known as a 'first medical use' claim.

In addition, even when the first medical use of a substance or composition is known, the novelty of a claim directed to a second (or further) medical use of the substance or composition may be recognised under **Art.54(5)** if the second (or further) use is novel. Such a claim is known as a 'second medical use' claim.

Examples of claims for first and second medical uses are given in **Art.54(4):2**, **Art.54(5):2** and **Art.54(5):3**.

6 Selection inventions

The term 'selection invention' refers to the claiming of a specific embodiment of a known generic class. A typical selection invention involves the identification of a sub-range of subject-matter from a larger known range or the identification of a specific compound falling within a generic chemical formula. The novelty of a selection invention is to be judged according to the rule that a disclosure of a genus does not take away the novelty of a species falling within that genus, whereas the disclosure of a species always takes away the novelty of a genus. Hence, the prior disclosure of copper takes away the novelty of metal whereas the prior disclosure of metal does not take away the novelty of copper (G-VI,4). Similarly, the novelty of a range is destroyed if the prior art discloses an example which falls within that range (**T188/83** hn.I).

The recognition of the novelty of selection inventions is consistent with the fact that a general concept in an application as filed cannot be considered as a basis under **Art.123(2)** for a limiting amendment to a particular embodiment of that general concept (**G1/03** r.2.2.2). The way in which disclosure is considered should be uniform under **Art.54** and **Art.123(2)**.

An inventive step for a selection invention is based on a particular technical effect that is achieved by the selection and that is not achieved by other embodiments of the generic area selected from (G-VII,12).

6.1 SELECTION OF INDIVIDUAL ENTITIES FROM A GROUP

An individual entity or a sub-group selected from a known group of elements is novel if the selected entity or sub-group is not disclosed in an individualised form in the prior art (**T12/81**). An entity selected from a single list of specifically disclosed entities is not novel. A selection from two or more known lists of some length to arrive at a specific combination of features is novel, provided this selection is not specifically disclosed in the prior art (**T12/81 r.13**). A list is usually considered to have sufficient length if it has at least two or three elements (G-VI,7). An example of the two-list principle is the identification of an individual chemical compound by selecting specific substituents from two or more lists of substituents given for a generic formula (which is often referred to as a 'Markush' formula). (G-VI,7(ii)(a))

6.2 SELECTION OF SUB-RANGE FROM A NUMERICAL RANGE

A claimed range lacks novelty if the prior art discloses a single value that falls within it; such a single value could be the endpoint of a different range or a specific embodiment (G-VI,7(i)(b)).

A sub-range selected from a broader numerical range in the prior art is not considered novel merely because it has no overlap with the endpoints of the broader range, instead each of the following two requirements must be satisfied:

1. the selected sub-range is narrow compared to the known range; and
2. the selected sub-range is sufficiently far removed from any specific examples disclosed in the prior art.

These requirements are set out in G-VI,7(i), citing **T261/15**, which modified the original test of **T279/89**.

The meaning of 'narrow' and 'sufficiently far removed' must be decided on a case-by-case basis (G-VI,7(i)).

Note that the relative terms 'narrow' and 'far removed' appear incompatible with the disclosure test (see **G2/10** r.4.6). The board in **T1688/20** was convinced that these two criteria do not always need to be assessed when examining the novelty of a sub-range (r.3.3). The board concluded that in cases where applying the 'gold standard' disclosure test of **G2/10**, it could be established whether or not the skilled person, using common general knowledge, can directly and unambiguously derive a claimed sub-range from a particular disclosed range of the prior art, no supporting tests or criteria are necessary to reach a conclusion. Thus none of the criteria set out in **T279/89** needs to be applied (r.3.4). The board found the claimed range of 56 to 59 to be novel over the prior art range of 55 to 60.

The test as originally set out in **T279/89** included as a third requirement that the selected sub-range is not an arbitrary specimen of the prior art but another invention (purposive selection, new technical effect). However, under current case law, considerations of this kind are only considered to be relevant to the determination of inventive step (see e.g. **T230/07**, **T1137/20**).

When considering the terms 'narrow' and 'far removed', it may to relevant to consider whether or not the person skilled in the art would, in the light of the technical facts, seriously contemplate applying the technical teaching of the prior art document in the claimed sub-range. If it can be fairly assumed that the skilled person would do so, it can be concluded that the claim is not novel (G-VI,7(i)(b); **T26/85** hn, **T1543/21**). For this reason, it may not be sufficient to exclude specific values disclosed in the prior art document from the claim. If a prior art document contains a reasoned statement dissuading the use of a part of the claimed range, the skilled person would not seriously contemplate working in that range (**T26/85** hn). One board has found that a range of 0.3 to 0.7, selected from a prior art range of 0.1 to 1.0, cannot be considered to be narrow simply because it covers approximately 50% of the prior art range (**T1375/22**).

If a claim specifies multiple ranges for different parameters, a prior art document disclosing a range having an endpoint in the claimed range for each individual parameter does not anticipate the claim if the specific combination of the endpoints for the different parameters is not disclosed (G-VI,7(ii)(b)).

7 Use claims

7.1 USE CLAIM VS. product and process claims

A claim directed to a product, i.e. a physical entity, confers absolute protection upon that product, i.e. the claim covers the product wherever it exists and whatever the context. Such a claim therefore covers all uses of the product, whether known or unknown. If the product is known in the prior art, then a claim to the product as such lacks novelty. On the other hand, a claim to a particular use of a known product is in effect a claim to that product only when it is being used in the particular manner claimed, this being an additional technical feature of the claim. Such a claim therefore confers narrower protection than a claim to the product per se. A use claim relates to the use of a particular physical entity to achieve an effect. In general, a use claim is therefore not a process claim within the meaning of **Art.64(2)**, and does not cover products produced by the use. (**G2/88** r.5)

7.2 USE CLAIMS

A claim relating to a new use of a known product to attain a new technical effect is novel. This is true even if the means used to realise the new technical effect (i.e. the steps necessary to practise the invention) are identical to the means used in a known use of the product. In such a case the novelty of the use resides only in the new purpose, based on the new technical effect. The attaining of the technical effect must be considered as a novel functional technical feature of the claim (**G2/88**, Friction reducing additive; **G6/88**, Plant growth regulating agent). Hence, the intentional and purposive application of a known substance for a new use is novel. For example, a claim directed to the use of a known substance as an additive in oil for reducing friction based on the newly discovered friction-reducing effects of the substance is novel in spite of the known use of the same substance as an additive in oil for inhibiting rust (**T59/87**). Similarly, the new purpose of controlling fungi on plants makes the use of a substance for that purpose new despite its known use as a growth regulator, even if both uses require the same treatment of spraying the plants (**T231/85**). The two uses relate to the application of the substance in distinctly different situations, depending on the desired effect.

Thus, the technical effect may make the invention novel, although both the technical realisation and the substance are known. The new effect may even have occurred inherently when the prior art use was employed, but remained unrecognised, and therefore hidden and unavailable to the public (**G2/88**, **G6/88**). Even if the technical realisation is known, the new effect is nonetheless not available to the public if it is not revealed so clearly when carrying out the prior art use as to disclose the invention's essential character to a skilled person (**T208/88** hn; **T59/87** hn).

A claim directed to the use of a known substance for a *known* non-medical purpose to attain a new technical effect related to the known use is not novel. The mere explanation of an effect obtained when using a known substance in a known way does not confer novelty to a known use if the skilled person was aware of the occurrence of the desired effect. (**T892/94** hn.II)

For the use feature to confer novelty, as recognised by **G2/88** and **G6/88**, a second non-medical use claim must be directed to the 'use of a known compound' and cannot be directed to the 'use of a process' (**T684/02** hn). In the latter case, the claimed use amounts to no more than the carrying out of the known process.

The determination of infringement in the case of a claim having only a new purpose as the characterising feature is difficult as the performance of the invention does not, in general, indicate the purpose; the purpose is merely in the mind of the user. The Enlarged Board has left the problem of determining infringement to national courts. Such a claim should at least prevent competitors from advertising their products as suitable for the claimed use.

Art. 54(2) The state of the art shall be held to comprise everything made available to the public by means of a written or oral description, by use, or in any other way, before the date of filing of the European patent application.

1 Absolute state of the art

The novelty of a claim is assessed in view of the state of the art as defined in **Art.54(2)** and **(3)**. The EPC uses the so-called 'absolute state of the art' criterion, codified in **Art.54(2)**. This is sometimes called 'absolute novelty', but since the state of the art under **Art.54(2)** is relevant for both novelty and inventive step, it is more appropriate to use the term 'absolute state of the art' (see e.g. **T107/82** r.11). The absolute character of the state of the art is reflected in the fact that the EPC contains no restriction as to the means of disclosure, no restriction in time, no geographical restriction and no restriction as to the public to whom the art has been made available (Empel no. 76-82). There is only one exception to the absolute state of the art: certain non-prejudicial disclosures, although made available to the public, are not taken into consideration (**Art.55**).

The state of the art is supplemented (for novelty only) by prior European rights which are published after the effective date of the claim concerned but which have an earlier filing or priority date (**Art.54(3)**, **Art.89**).

The following sections deal with the issues of availability, means of disclosure and extent of disclosure. See also Guidelines G-IV.

2 Availability

2.1 GENERAL

Availability of information to the public for the purpose of **Art.54(2)** requires only the possibility that the public had access to the information; it is not necessary that a person actually accessed it (**T444/88**, **T381/87**). The language of the information is irrelevant, because the skilled person is considered to be proficient in all languages (**T920/92** r.2.4). The EPO provides machine translations for patent documents on its website. A machine translation of a document may be used in proceedings unless the quality of the translation is questioned with substantiated reasoning (**T991/01**; G-IV,4.1).

Subject-matter is available to the public if one person could have gained knowledge of it without a breach of confidentiality (G-IV,7.2.1; **T482/89** hn.3). If a product is sold without any conditions being imposed on the sale, its full structure and contents are disclosed from the time of availability, even if knowledge of these elements would require destruction of the product and/or time consuming investigation (see **Art.54(2):2.4**).

A printed document sent by post is available to the public not at the time of posting it, but at the time of delivery. A document is available in a library if a member of the public can consult the document, regardless of whether it has been entered in a catalogue. A doctoral thesis is not public if not entered in a catalogue and held in a publicly inaccessible archive of the library. On the other hand, the latest edition of a periodical is available to the public from the point at which it may be requested and consulted in a library, even if it has not been entered into the library catalogue at that point. A journal may also, of course, be made available online. (T381/87; see also **T1057/09**)

The issue of accessibility of information is frequently encountered in the assessment of public prior use. In particular, the examination of a component or property of a device or compound may require a significant effort or advanced analysis (see **Art.54(2):3.6** below).

The EPO must in general establish the state of the art by carrying out its own independent search. An acknowledgement of prior art in the patent or patent application under examination cannot be relied upon if the applicant or proprietor resiles from it (**T691/94**; **T1898/20**).

2.2 DATE

According to **Art.54(2)** the state of the art comprises everything made available before the date of filing of the European patent application, the date of priority counting as the date of filing where priority has been validly claimed (**Art.89**). This defines a day as the minimum unit of time. Anything made available on the date of filing or priority itself is not included in the state of the art. The EPC does not take into account time zones, which may affect the date on which information becomes available. For example, a document published in Amsterdam at 00h30 and immediately transmitted to London is available in London the previous day at 23h30. Whereas in times past the location of publication was important, modern means of communication, such as the internet, allow a nearly instantaneous world-wide publication. There is no case law of the boards of appeal on this issue yet.

A document with a vague publication date ('ca 1960') will still qualify as prior art if the date is sufficiently far in advance of the date of filing of a patent in suit (**T267/03** hn.1).

Instructions for the use and installation of kitchen appliances are usually made available together with the product to be installed and proof is therefore required to establish the date on which such instructions are made available in the same way as for public use; a printing date in the instructions is not an adequate indication of the date of availability (**T511/02** r.4). However, a copyright notice in a television manual stating a year creates a presumption that the manual was published in that year; facts in a copyright notice are presumed to be correct (**T861/04** r.2.5).

A document published before the filing date is direct evidence of the state of the art, being an instance of what has been made available to the public before the filing date. Its status as part of the state of the art can only be challenged by reference to its authenticity. A post-published document is self-evidently not part of the state of the art but can be used to draw an inference about the state of the art or common general knowledge as of the relevant date. The plausibility of such an inference may be challenged but the automatic rejection of such a document as evidence of prior art is not justified. (**T1110/03** r.2)

2.3 **PUBLIC**

Art.54(2) requires that the information must have been made available to the public. The use of the term 'public' emphasises that the qualifications of the recipient of the information are irrelevant to the question of whether the information forms part of the state of the art or not (Empel no. 82). Information need not have been made available to a skilled person to be regarded as state of the art.

At least one member of the public must have had access to the information. The sale of an article to one person not bound by confidentiality makes the article available to the public (T482/89). The public need not have a certain level of education (T165/96 r.1.1.1.3). However, where a disclosure is given orally, it has been held that the person receiving the information must be a skilled person in order to be able to understand the information and distribute it further (see e.g. obiter dictum in T877/90 r.2.1.6).

2.4 **SECRECY**

The availability of information implies the absence of any obligation to maintain its secrecy. Information communicated to a person bound by an obligation of confidentiality is not made available in the sense of Art.54(2). Information shared at a meeting that was understood by the parties to be secret, even if that understanding is tacit and a non-disclosure agreement has not been signed, is not publicly disclosed (T830/90).

If something is disclosed publicly in spite of a non-disclosure agreement, the matter is part of the state of the art, unless the exception of Art.55(1) applies.

Something does not automatically become public because of a demonstration on factory premises (G-IV,7.2.1 and 7.2.3).

A secret document, e.g. a document for licensees only, is not public, even if the distribution is large in comparison with the total number of people skilled in the art, since part of the public is excluded from access (T300/86 r.2).

A document, the contents of which may not be disseminated to third parties, may still be available to the public, provided third parties can buy the document themselves in order to obtain knowledge of its contents. Such a restriction may serve merely to protect the interests of the content provider. (T50/02 r.2.4, 2.5)

The contents of an EPO file are secret before publication of the application and publicly available thereafter (Art.128(4)).

There is a *prima facie* assumption that any person involved in medicine is obliged to maintain confidentiality where there is a need for patient confidentiality or a need to protect the development and testing of prototype devices (T152/03 r.3.4).

3 Means of disclosure

3.1 **WRITTEN DISCLOSURE**

Written disclosure of technical information is usually in the form of patent documents and articles in scientific or technical journals. However, a written disclosure may be in any accessible form, even in a small-ad newspaper distributed in a small geographical area (T165/96). Technical documents originating from companies should be carefully examined to distinguish between secret company papers and publicly available documents (T37/96). The same applies to correspondence between different companies and between companies and clients. The price of a document is not relevant to its availability; the price of technical information is usually adapted to the market (T50/02 r.2.3.5, document of $ 6000).

Something can also be made public by advertising it or otherwise showing it on television.

3.2 DRAWINGS

The drawings form part of the disclosure of a patent application and are as much a part of the disclosure as the description (**T169/83** r.3.2).

A feature solely shown in a drawing belongs to the state of the art only if a skilled person can derive a technical teaching from it in the absence of any other description (**T204/83**). Dimensions which can only be obtained from a measurement in a schematic drawing are not part of the disclosure unless it is a construction drawing drawn to scale (**T204/83**). The fact that one dimension is larger than another dimension may in particular circumstances be derivable from a drawing merely by visual inspection (**T1943/15** r.4.5). In contrast with a drawing, a photo is a reproduction of an object and thus will normally be regarded as an exact representation of the object from which dimensions may be taken (**T857/91** r.3.2; however, see **T1943/15** r.8.2).

A document must be assessed in its entirety by the skilled person. It is not legitimate to arbitrarily isolate parts of a document in order to derive technical information in an acontextual manner which is distinct from or even in contradiction with the teaching of the document as a whole. Thus, a technical feature which is derived from or based on dimensions obtained from a diagrammatic representation and which is contradicted by the teaching of the description, does not form part of the disclosure of the document. (**T56/87**)

A summary of case law until 2019 on dimensions taken from drawings is given in **T1943/15** r.4.

3.3 ORAL DISCLOSURE

An oral disclosure, such as a lecture or an account of a prior use, is valid prior art if the date and content of the disclosure and its availability to the public can be ascertained (**T406/92** r.6, 7). It may be difficult to prove what was actually disclosed during a lecture, as was the case in **T86/95** r.3 and **T1212/97** r.1-11. The standard of proof for ascertaining the contents of an oral disclosure is a high one (G-IV,7.3.4).

An oral disclosure is not part of the state of the art if the lecture was only accessible to persons bound by confidentiality or if the disclosure was an evident abuse and the requirements of **Art.55(1)(a)** are met (G-IV,7.3.2).

An oral disclosure will only be cited as prior art in grant proceedings or taken into account in opposition proceedings if the EPO has sufficient proof concerning the content of the disclosure and the fact that it took place. A written document describing the oral disclosure, even if published after the date of the oral disclosure, may be used as proof (B-VI,2). However, if the applicant or proprietor can give good reasons why the written account cannot be relied upon then the oral disclosure should not be used as prior art and the matter should not be pursued further (G-IV,7.4). Caution must be exercised since neither evidence from a person who attended the lecture nor a script from which the lecturer purportedly read necessarily reflects the actual content that was delivered.

3.4 DISPLAY

Where an object is displayed to the public, e.g. at an exhibition, only its visible features are made available (**T1085/92**). However, non-visible features may be disclosed in oral or written explanations provided at the same time. When a device is displayed in operation, the visible changes may implicitly disclose the internal features of the device. However, a disclosure of this kind may not be taken into account if the object concerned was displayed at a recognised international exhibition under **Art.55(1)(b)** and the applicant complies with the requirements of **Art.55(2)**.

3.5 INTERNET DISCLOSURE

As a matter of principle, disclosures on the internet form part of the state of the art according to **Art.54(2)**. Information disclosed on the internet or in online databases is considered to be publicly available as of the date the information was publicly posted (G-IV,7.5). The usual standard of proof applies in establishing the content and publication date of an internet disclosure, namely the 'balance of probabilities'. (**T1711/11**; G-IV,7.5.2)

The relevant web pages must in principle be available without any condition of confidentiality being attached to them. A requirement to pay for access (analogous to purchasing a book) or access to a limited circle of people (e.g. by password protection) is as such no bar to availability, provided that the content is not confidential. (G-IV,7.5.1)

The EPO generally considers an explicit publication date in an internet disclosure to be reliable. The burden of proof is on the applicant or proprietor to show otherwise; the more reliable a disclosure and its source, the harder it will be to prove that the publication date is incorrect (G-IV,7.5.3). The reliability of online technical journals made available by scientific publishers is the same as that of traditional paper journals, i.e. very high (G-IV,7.5.3.1). Publishers of newspapers or periodicals, television or radio stations, academic institutions, international organisations, public organisations and standardisation bodies are generally deemed to provide reliable publication dates for web pages (G-IV,7.5.3.2; **T1469/10** hn).

The date marked on an internet disclosure that has previously been published on paper, such as a manual for a software product, or a handbook for a physical product, can be taken as a date of publication. (G-IV,7.5.3.2)

The EPO assumes that the content of web pages has not been manipulated unless there are specific indications to the contrary (G-IV,7.5.1). Computer-generated timestamps, such as the 'last modified' date, are considered to be reliable publication dates in the absence of such contrary indications (G-IV,7.5.4). However, a 'last modified' date that was not updated when uploading new information may suggest an earlier date of publication than the actual date. Furthermore, the date on a document may be the date of production of the document rather than the publication date.

Where a relevant internet disclosure is not associated with a date or a given date is shown to be unreliable, further evidence may be obtained from internet archiving services, such as www.archive.org, or by indexing dates assigned to the web page by search engines (**T1961/13**). (G-IV,7.5.4)

If no date can be obtained, the disclosure cannot be used as prior art. The disclosure may be cited as an 'L' document in the search report. The disclosure is citable against future applications using the date of retrieval from the internet by the EPO as the date of publication. (G-IV,7.5.4)

3.6 PUBLIC USE

3.6.1 *General*

Public prior use is the term used to refer to the availability of an actual product or method to the public (as opposed to a description of it in a document) before the date of filing of the application. Demonstrating disclosure by public use commonly requires the provision of extensive evidence. The assessment of the content of a written disclosure is a matter of interpreting text, while the assessment of a public prior use often requires the analysis of a product (G-IV,7.2.1)..

A product or method disclosed by prior public use is regarded as part of the state of the art if the following matters in relation to the alleged use are proved: When, What, How, Where and by Whom (G-IV,7.2; **T93/89** r.8.1, **T194/86**). If sufficient specific details relating to these matters are provided, the public prior use is substantiated. If the alleged public prior use is substantiated, contested by the proprietor, and relevant for the outcome of the opposition proceedings, the opposition division may need to take further evidence (e.g. by hearing witnesses or performing an inspection) in relation to those facts which are relevant to the case and which cannot yet be considered proven on the basis of the evidence already on file (G-IV,7.2).

In those public prior use cases where practically all the evidence in support of the public prior use lies within the power and knowledge of an opponent, i.e. in the majority of cases, the prior use must be proven up to the hilt, i.e. beyond all reasonable doubt (**T472/92** hn. I).

A single sale is sufficient to render the article sold available to the public, provided the buyer is not bound by an obligation to maintain confidentiality (**T482/89**).)

3.6.2 Accessibility and analysability

Opinion **G1/92** deals with various aspects of public prior use. The composition or internal structure of a product, whether chemical or other, forms part of the state of the art when the product as such is available to the public and can be analysed and reproduced by the skilled person, irrespective of whether or not particular reasons can be identified for such analysis. This position is consistent with **Art.54(2)**, which does not make any distinction between different means for making available information (r.1.2) and on the fact that the possibility of access to information makes it public, irrespective of whether there is any reason to search for it (r.2). Characteristics which are only revealed when the product is exposed to interaction with specific outside conditions, e.g. reactants or the like, in order to prove a particular effect or result or to discover potential results or capabilities, go beyond what is disclosed by the product per se as they are dependent on deliberate choices being made. Typical examples of such characteristics are the application of a known substance as a pharmaceutical and the use of a known compound for a particular purpose based on a new technical effect (**G2/88**). Thus, such characteristics cannot be considered as having already been made available to the public (r.3). (**G1/92**, overruling **T93/89** (adhesive on paper; only available if there is reason for analysis) and **T461/88** r.6.3 (program on microchip too expensive to analyse), broadening **T406/86** (available only if analysis is simple).

G1/92 shifts the emphasis in the assessment of public prior use from the existence of the product to the technical teaching that may be directly and unambiguously derived from the product. Teaching that cannot be derived does not form state of the art. Hence, it is possible for an existing, publicly available product to be patented (as a product claim) based on a new teaching relating to the product. For example, a commercially available polymer is not part of the state of the art if no known method exists for its manufacture and an analysis of the polymer does not reveal the chemical process by which it was made. Similarly, a microbiological product does not belong to the state of the art if there is a high probability of variation upon attempted reproduction of the product microbiologically and a skilled person cannot establish the identity of the reproduced product with the prior art product because intrinsic or extrinsic features of those products are not accessible (**T977/93**).

Opinion **G1/92** states, in relation to a product which has been placed on the market, that 'Where it is possible for the skilled person to discover the composition or the internal structure of the product and to reproduce it without undue burden, then both the product and its composition or internal structure become state of the art'. This could be interpreted to mean that a commercial product only becomes state of the art if the product itself can be reproduced without undue burden. This would mean that if the product can't be reproduced without due burden then no information that can be derived by analysing it enters the state of the art either.

This interpretation was not followed in decision **T952/92**. According to this decision, the degree of burden involved in analysing a product is in principle irrelevant to the determination of what constitutes the state of the art (**T952/92** r.2.2, interpreting **G1/92** r.1.4). Thus it is not necessary that a prior art product can be completely analysed, enabling it to be exactly reproduced, in order for it to be novelty-destroying prior art (**T952/92** r.2.3 last par., interpreting **G1/92** r.1.4). Information concerning the composition and internal structure of a product which is state of the art is made available if direct and unambiguous access to such information is possible by means of known analytical techniques which were available for use by a skilled person before the relevant filing date (**T952/92** r.4.3).

More recent decision **T1833/14**, on the other hand, interpreted **G1/92** r.1.4 differently from **T952/92**, and found that a commercially available product was not made available to the public as the skilled person could not reproduce it without undue burden. Therefore, the alleged public prior use did not amount to an enabling disclosure. (**T1833/14** r.1.9; G-IV,7.2.1)

The divergence that has become apparent in this and other case law is being addressed by referral **G1/23**. The board in case **T438/19** has asked the EBoA whether a product that was put on the market before the filing date of a European patent application should be excluded from the state of the art within the meaning of **Art.54(2)** for the sole reason that its composition or internal structure could not be analysed and reproduced without undue burden by the skilled person before that date. The referring decision discusses the relevant case law in detail.

4 Extent of disclosure

4.1 GENERAL

The concept of disclosure is the same for the purposes of **Art.54** and **Art.123(2)**, in that the disclosure of the document (prior art document or application as filed) is the subject-matter that a skilled person would derive directly and unambiguously from it using common general knowledge (**G2/10** r.4.6, hn.1a).

In determining novelty, a prior-art document is to be read as it would have been read by a person skilled in the art on the date of its publication or, where **Art.54(3)** applies, its filing date or priority date (G-VI,3). The understanding of the skilled person must not be supplemented by knowledge which might have been obtained between the date at which the prior art is to be assessed and the filing or priority date of the patent at issue.

4.2 IMPLICIT DISCLOSURE

A document discloses subject-matter derivable directly and unambiguously from that document, including any features which are implicit in what is expressly mentioned in the document. For example, a disclosure of the use of rubber in circumstances where its elastic properties are used, even if this is not explicitly stated, takes away the novelty of a claim requiring the use of an elastic material. (G-VI,2)

The state of the art also includes any feature which is implicit in a document in the sense that, in carrying out the teaching of the document, the skilled person would inevitably arrive at that feature. A document describing a process, which would inevitably result in a product not explicitly referred to, implicitly discloses that product (**T666/89**).

If a claim is directed to a product defined by an unusual parameter and a known product is identical to the claimed product in all other respects (which is to be expected if, for example, the starting materials and the manufacturing processes are identical), then in the first place an objection of lack of novelty arises and the burden of proof for an alleged distinguishing feature lies with the applicant (G-VI,6; **T1764/06**).

A document does not disclose well-known equivalents not mentioned in the document (G-VI,2).

A claim defining a compound by reference to a certain level of purity lacks novelty over a prior art document describing the same compound only if the prior art document discloses the compound at the claimed level of purity in an enabling manner. Such a disclosure could be implicit if the document discloses a method of preparing the compound which inevitably results in the level of purity claimed. Such a claim does not lack novelty if the disclosure of the prior art document needs to be supplemented to arrive at the claimed purity, for example by providing suitable (further) purification methods (**T1085/13**; G-VI,6).

4.3 ENABLING DISCLOSURE

In order to take away the novelty of a claimed invention, a disclosure of that invention in the prior art needs to be enabling, i.e. the invention must be disclosed sufficiently clearly and completely that it can be carried out by a skilled person using no more than common general knowledge. A document that does not provide an enabling disclosure, i.e. a disclosure which is insufficient in the sense of **Art.83**, does not form part of the state of the art (**T206/83** r.2, **T26/85** hn.I; G-IV,2).

A disclosure of a compound and the process steps for its manufacture is not enabling if it is not clear from either the disclosure itself or the common general knowledge how to obtain necessary starting or intermediate materials. In such a case neither the compound nor the process is part of the state of the art (**T206/83** r.2).

4.4 EXCLUDED SUBJECT-MATTER

Under **Art.54**, the disclosure contained in a document includes explicitly disclaimed subject-matter with the exception of disclaimers for unworkable embodiments (G-IV,5.1(i) and G-VI,1). An embodiment is unworkable if it is insufficiently disclosed; such an embodiment is not novelty-destroying (**T206/83** r.12). A prior art document disclosing a range of values for a parameter and containing a reasoned statement dissuading a skilled person from using part of the range does not make that part of the range available to the public (**T26/85** hn.II).

4.5 ERRONEOUS DISCLOSURE

If a prior art document contains an error, it is read as corrected if the skilled person can directly and unambiguously derive from the prior art document that it contains an error and what the only possible correction should be. If the skilled person can detect the error but identifies more than one possible correction, the passage at issue is disregarded. If the skilled person cannot directly and unambiguously derive from the prior art document that an error has occurred, the literal disclosure is taken into account as is. (G-IV,9)

Where the literal disclosure of a document is clearly erroneous and does not represent the intended technical meaning, such an erroneous disclosure should not be considered as part of the state of the art (T77/87 hn.1). Similarly, published matter may be excluded from the state of the art if it is so implausible in the eyes of skilled readers that they would reject it as erroneous (**T412/91** r.4.6).

An abstract, e.g. of a Japanese patent application or in a chemical journal, intended to reflect the contents of the original document, should be interpreted in the light of that original document if the latter is available. If the abstract diverges from the content of the original document, its contents should not be considered as part of the state of the art (T77/87 hn II; **T1080/99** r.4).

A numerical error in a disclosure does not affect the validity of the disclosure if the skilled person can easily correct it on the basis of common general knowledge and without any extensive research (T171/84).

Art. 54(3) Additionally, the content of European patent applications as filed, the dates of filing of which are prior to the date referred to in paragraph 2 and which were published on or after that date, shall be considered as comprised in the state of the art.

1 **Prior rights**

In most patent systems, including the European patent system, a patent application is not open to public inspection during the period between filing and publication. Only on publication are the contents of an application therefore 'made available to the public' in the sense of **Art.54(2)**. This raises the potential for conflict with a later filed application for the same or a similar invention. In the case of such conflict, the earlier application is often referred to as a prior right. Double patenting - i.e. allowing two successive patents for the same subject-matter - is avoided by taking the earlier application into account when assessing the patentability of the later application. How this is done varies from one patent system to another. Historically, there are two common approaches: the 'prior claim' approach and the 'whole contents' approach. In the 'prior claim' approach only the claims of the prior right are taken into account. The claims of the later application may not overlap with the granted claims of the earlier application. Switzerland and Liechtenstein used the 'prior claim' approach for national applications until 2008. In the 'whole contents' approach, the whole content of the earlier application, i.e. not only the subject-matter claimed but also the subject matter disclosed, is regarded as state of the art for the later application (see the historical overview in **G1/03** r.2.1.1, see also **Art.139:1**).

The EPC employs the whole contents approach, whereby the entire disclosure of a European prior right becomes part of the state of the art from the date of filing or, where applicable, the priority date of the prior right, provided that the application is published later (**Art.54(3)** and **Art.89**; see also **Art.60(2)**). The harsh effect of the whole contents approach is mitigated by confining its application to novelty and disregarding prior rights for the assessment of inventive step (**Art.56**, last sentence).

It follows that for the assessment of novelty, an applicant's own earlier European patent application may form relevant prior art for their later European patent applications for the examination of novelty. This is sometimes known as 'self-collision'. However, the risk of this is reduced by the EPO's strict approach to the assessment of novelty (see **Art.54(1):4**). Moreover, an undisclosed disclaimer can be used to restore novelty over a prior right without violating **Art.123(2)** (**G1/03**).

The content of the application as filed is relevant in case of **Art.54(3)**. Any errors in a subsequent translation of the application under **Art.14(2)** have no effect. If subject-matter is erroneously omitted from a translation into the language of the proceedings and not published under **Art.93**, the content of the application as filed for the purpose of **Art.54(3)** is still determined by the original text in the non-official language. (G-IV,5.1)

The content of the application within the meaning of **Art.54(3)** includes any parts added pursuant to **R.56** or **R.56a** or, for Euro-PCT applications pursuant to R.20.5, R.20.5bis or R.20.6 PCT. In addition, any erroneously filed application documents or parts remain in the application under **R.56a(4)** and R.20.5bis(d) PCT (G-IV,5.1). Note, the EPO as designated or elected office does not recognise an incorporation by reference that was allowed by the receiving Office under R.20.5bis(d) PCT for PCT applications filed before 01.11.2022 and such incorporation should not be effective under **Art.54(3)** either (OJ 2020 A81).

The content of a European prior right does not include the abstract (**Art.85**) or any priority document (G-IV,5.1). Any subject-matter disclosed in both a European patent application and a priority application from which priority is validly claimed enters the state of the art under **Art.54(3)** as of the priority date. Any subject-matter disclosed in a priority application but omitted in a European patent application claiming its priority does not enter the state of the art under **Art.54(3)** at all.

If an application specifically refers to a document, the relevant part of the document referred to is considered to form part of the content of the application for the purpose of **Art.54(3)** (F-III,8).

If an applicant files two European patent applications on the same day for the same invention, the applicant must withdraw one of them or amend one or both of them in such a manner that the subject-matter of the claims of the applications is not identical (prohibition on double patenting; G-IV,5.4; **G4/19**; **Art.97(2):2**). Should two applications with the same effective date be filed by different applicants, each must be allowed to proceed as though the other did not exist (see **Art.60(2)**; G-IV,5.4).

National prior rights do not form part of the state of the art within the meaning of **Art.54(3)** (**T550/88** hn.1). However, an applicant or proprietor can inform the EPO of a national prior right in an EPC contracting state and then file a separate set of claims for that state (**R.138**). National prior rights can also be considered during national revocation proceedings and revocation proceedings before the UPC according to **Art.138(1)** and **Art.139(2)**.

The effect of a prior European right in a state to which a European application has been extended is dealt with in **Art.139:1**.

2 Requirements for prior rights

Art.54(3) recognises only European applications as prior rights. A Euro-PCT application can also become a prior right under **Art.54(3)** if the filing fee of **R.159(1)(c)** is paid to the EPO as designated or elected Office and, if the international application is published in a language that is not an official language of the EPO, an English, French or German translation is filed (**Art.153(5)**; **R.165**).

The date of filing of a European prior right under **Art.54(3)** must be before the date of filing of the application under examination. Where the earlier application claims priority, the filing date is replaced by the priority date (**Art.89**), provided that the priority is valid; in case of partial priority, the priority must be valid for the subject-matter that is used in the novelty attack. The validity of the priority claim is assessed on the day the prior European right is published; later changes have no effect (see below).

The earlier application must be published under **Art.93** on or after the filing date of the application under examination (**Art.54(3)**). Moreover, the publication must be valid in the sense that the application must still be pending on the publication date (J5/81 r.3). If the published application is not a valid publication under **Art.93** because the application was withdrawn before the publication date but too late to prevent its publication, the application will not enter the state of the art under **Art.54(3)** at all. It will, however, enter the state of the art under **Art.54(2)** as of its publication date (J5/81).

An withdrawal of a priority claim or a loss of priority taking effect before the publication date results in the filing date rather than the priority date of the earlier application being the effective date of the prior right. (G-IV,5.1.1). However, for reasons of legal certainty, the prior right effect of an application is not affected by changes taking effect after the publication date of the application; if a priority claim is withdrawn or the right to priority is lost after the publication of the application, the priority date is still the effective date of the prior right under **Art.54(3)** (G-IV,5.1.1; F-VI,3.4). Note that it could be argued that this conclusion in F-VI,3.4 is in conflict with **Art.60(2)**. A priority right is lost e.g. if a priority document required under **R.53(1)** or a translation of the priority document required under **R.53(3)** is not filed in due time.

3 **Establishment of prior right for applications filed under EPC1973**

For applications with a filing date before 13.12.2007 (date of entry into force of EPC2000) and any patents granted on such applications, Art.54(4) EPC1973 continues to apply. It stated that: '*[Art.54(3)] shall be applied only in so far as a Contracting State designated in respect of the later application, was also designated in respect of the earlier application as published.*'

Hence for a patent application under examination having a filing date before 13.12.2007, the prior right effect under **Art.54(3)** of an earlier European patent application is limited to those designated states of the patent application under examination that were also designated in the earlier application. Note that the current automatic designation of all states with one designation fee was only introduced in 2009.

Art.54(4) EPC1973 is still applicable to European patent applications filed before 13.12.2007, as well as to any patents granted on such applications, for the entire patent term (Dec. Administrative Council OJ 2007 se1 p.197; OJ 2007 se4 EN p.52; D-VII,8). Therefore, Art.54(4) EPC1973 remains relevant until at least December 2027 and indeed beyond that date in the case of supplementary protection granted pursuant to **Art.63(2)**.

The filing date of the application or patent under examination determines whether Art.54(4) EPC1973 still applies; the priority date of the application or granted patent under examination is not relevant (Not. EPO OJ 2007 p.505). The relevant date of a Euro-PCT application is the international filing date, not the date of entry into the European phase. The filing date of the prior right is not relevant.

For divisional applications, the date of filing of the parent application is the relevant date (**T116/18 of 11.10.2021** r.10.1). Note that the EPO published a document on its website in 2007 stating that the date of receipt of a divisional application at the EPO determines whether Art.54(4) EPC1973 is applicable and not the date of filing of the parent application attributed to the divisional application. The EPO stated that therefore a parent and divisional application may be treated differently as regards the application of Art.54(4) EPC1973 (§10.1 of the document 'Implementation of the Decision of the Administrative Council of 28 June 2001 on the transitional provisions under Article 7 of the Act revising the European Patent Convention of 29

November 2000', available on the EPO website and mentioned in OJ 2007 p.507). However, this document has no formal legal status.

If Art.54(4) EPC1973 applies, R.23a EPC1973 and R.87 EPC1973 also apply, as well as Art.60(2) EPC1973 (H-III,4.2; OJ 2003 se1 p.202).

R.23a EPC1973 provided that: '*A European patent application shall be considered as comprised in the state of the art under Article 54, paragraphs 3 and 4 [EPC1973], only if the designation fees under Article 79, paragraph 2 [EPC1973], have been validly paid.*'

R.23a EPC1973 thus provides that a European patent application has a prior right effect only for those states for which the designation fee is paid. The fees could be paid after the publication of the application from 1997 onwards. Therefore, the indication of a state as designated state on the front page of the published European prior right is not sufficient (OJ 1997 p.13, p.113). Because a designation fee had to be paid for each designated state for applications filed before 01.04.2009, applicants often only designated a few states. Hence, Art.54(4) EPC1973 can provide a significant limitation of the prior right effect (see **Rfees2(2)** for the old designation fee structure).

The assessment of patentability may hence differ between designated states due to the effect of European prior rights under Art.54(4) EPC1973. An application may accordingly contain two or more sets of claims in such cases, one set of claims for the designated states in which the earlier application is effective as a prior right and another set for the other designated states (as permitted by R.87 EPC1973). An applicant can also withdraw the designation of the states in which the earlier application is effective as a prior right (**Art.79(3)**).

For applications with a filing date before 13.12.2007 and any patents granted on such applications, an international application with an earlier effective date is only regarded as a prior right under **Art.54(3)** if the additional requirements of Art.158(2) EPC1973 are met (Art.158(1) EPC1973). According to that provision, it is necessary to file a translation of the international application in an EPO official language (if it was not published in such a language) and pay a national fee to the EPO in the regional phase. This national fee consisted of the filing fee and a designation fee which had to be paid for each designated state (R.106 EPC1973). Hence, the prior right effect extends only to those states for which the designation fee was validly paid upon entry into the European phase (OJ 1997 p.114).

Art. 54(4) Paragraphs 2 and 3 shall not exclude the patentability of any substance or composition, comprised in the state of the art, for use in a method referred to in Article 53(c), provided that its use for any such method is not comprised in the state of the art.

Art.53(c) Methods of treatment of the human or animal body by surgery or therapy and diagnostic methods

1 **Transitional provision EPC2000**

The revised **Art.54(4)** is applicable to European patents already granted at the time of EPC2000 entry into force (13.12.2007) and to European patent applications pending at, or filed on or after that time (OJ 2007 se4 EN p.52).

2 **First medical use**

The invention of a new use for a known product can be protected in the form of a use claim: 'The use of [known product] for [new use]'; a product claim in the form: '[Known product] for [new use]' is in general not novel under **Art.54(1)**, because a use feature cannot usually impart novelty to a known product (see e.g. F-IV,4.13). When the invention is a new use of a known substance or composition in a medical treatment or diagnostic method, protection cannot be obtained in the form of a use claim, because a claim in the form 'The use of [known substance or composition] for [method of treatment or diagnosis]' is considered to be equivalent to a medical method, which is excluded from patentability under **Art.53(c)**, first sentence (**G5/83**).

By way of compensation for the exclusion of such methods and uses, **Art.54(4)** deems known substances and compositions to be new, provided they are used for the first time in an excluded medical method (OJ 2007 se4 EN p.54). The patentability of an invention of this kind is not derived from the substance or composition as such but from the claimed purpose, namely from its intended use (**G2/08** r.5.10.9). The use feature is regarded as a technical feature that, by way of exception for this type of claim, makes the claim novel (**T9/81** r.7).

A broad wording is allowed for a first medical use claim under **Art.54(4)**, e.g. 'substance X for use as a medicament' (see **T128/82**; **T36/83**). Even if only one specific therapeutic application is disclosed in an enabling way in the application, such a claim is sufficiently disclosed under **Art.83** and has basis under **Art.123(2)** and **Art.87(1)** (**T419/16**). This broad purpose-limited product protection for the first medical use is confirmed by the EBoA in **G5/83** r.15 and **G2/08** r.5.8. Based on this practice, the inventor of the first use of a substance or composition in an excluded medical method should receive broad protection covering any use in such a method. This corresponds to the contribution to the art, namely opening up the field of medical use for the substance or composition concerned (OJ 2007 se4 EN p.54).

The format of a first medical use claim can be used not only in the case of therapeutic treatments but also for substances and compositions for use in treatments by surgery and for use in diagnostic methods (**T1252/20**). See **Art.54(5):3** for an example of a set of claims protecting the medical use of a substance.

The novelty of a broad first medical use claim is not only destroyed by a previous disclosure of the specific therapeutic effect mentioned in the description but also by a previous disclosure of any other therapeutic application (see **T128/82** r.13).

The novelty of a first or second medical use claim can only be recognised under **Art.54(4)** or **(5)** if the claim is directed to the medical use of a 'substance' or 'composition' (**T1252/20**). These provisions do not apply when the invention is a new use for a medical device such as a surgical instrument. A substance is a species of matter of definite chemical composition. A composition is the combination or union of several things; a combination, aggregate, mixture. A claim directed to two substances presented side-by-side, that can be applied simultaneously, separately or at intervals to a body is regarded as a claim for a composition in the sense of **Art.54(4)** and **(5)** (**T9/81** r.9, so-called 'kit-of-parts'). Note that a compound is a substance composed chemically of two or more elements in definite proportions, as opposed to a mixture (definitions from the Oxford English Dictionary).

A device usually does not qualify as a 'substance or composition' because a device is not normally denoted as a chemical entity (**T2003/08** r.16).

A product has usually been held to qualify as a 'substance or composition' in the sense of **Art.54(4)** or **(5)** if it is the active ingredient in the specific medical use and if the therapeutic effect can be ascribed to its chemical properties, i.e. a use of a chemically inert substance (e.g. a filler) cannot benefit from **Art.54(4)** and **(5)** (**G5/83** r.23; **T1758/15** r.5.2, 7.2.4; G-VI,6.1.1). However, the board in **T1252/20** disagreed with **T1758/15** and found that a solution is a composition because it is a shapeless liquid defined without any device-like features, even if the solution transforms inside the patient's body into a hydrogel that acts like a device, i.e. the therapeutic effect can be ascribed to the mechanical properties of the hydrogel.

Art. 54(5) Paragraphs 2 and 3 shall also not exclude the patentability of any substance or composition referred to in paragraph 4 for any specific use in a method referred to in Article 53(c), provided that such use is not comprised in the state of the art.

Art.53(c) Methods of treatment of the human or animal body by surgery or therapy and diagnostic methods

1 **Transitional provision EPC2000**

Revised **Art.54(5)** applies to European patent applications pending on 13.12.2007 (entry into force of EPC2000), in so far as a decision on the grant of the patent has not yet been taken and to European patent applications filed on or after the time of EPC2000 entry into force. (OJ 2007 se4 EN p.54)

2 **Second medical use**

A second medical use is a new medical use of a substance or composition for which a first medical use is already known. **Art.54(5)** confers notional novelty on a known substance or composition by virtue of the new medical use. It permits purpose-related product protection for each further new medical use and is formulated as a substance or composition for a specific new medical use. (**G2/08** r.5.9-10)

The form of a second medical use claim should thus be 'Substance or composition X for use in' followed by the specific therapeutic, surgical or diagnostic method falling within the terms of **Art.53(c)**, e.g. 'a method for treating disease Y' (G-II,4.2). If the claim does not use the proper wording, the claim is read as directed to the substance or composition 'suitable for' the recited use and is not novel if the substance or composition is already known (G-VI,6.1.2). The same applies if the claim specifies a use that is non-medical (e.g. **T815/22**) or a use that encompasses medical and non-medical uses (**T1186/16**; see generally G-VI,6.1.2).

The form of a second medical use claim can also be used if the recited use is, in fact, the first medical use of the substance but the use of such a format in the case of a first medical use is unnecessarily restrictive. Indeed, in such a case, it is possible to include both a first medical use claim and a second medical use claim in the patent application (see **Art.54(5):3** below).

A disclosure in a prior art document destroys the novelty of a claimed invention only if it is an enabling disclosure (**T206/83**). The disclosure of a medical treatment in a prior art document is only enabled if the prior art document makes it credible that the therapeutic effect on which the disclosed treatment relies can be achieved (**T699/19** r.26).

2.1 SPECIFIC USE

The EPC does not provide any further clarification of what is meant in **Art.54(5)** by the term 'any specific use in a method referred to in **Art.53(c)**'. The term includes the treatment of another disease than in the already known medical use of the substance but is not limited thereto. The recited use may also be a new way of treating a particular disease where the use of the substance or composition for the treatment of that disease is already known. The requirement of a 'specific use' must be construed as contrasting with the generic broad protection conferred by a first medical use claim ('for use as a medicament'). The recited use must pertain to a use that is a non-patentable medical use in the sense of **Art.53(c)**. (**G2/08** r.5.10)

The Enlarged Board cited with approval the following examples of patentable second medical use inventions based on a new manner of treating the same disease with the same substance or composition (**G2/08** r.5.10.7):

- The treatment of a novel group of subjects (patients), distinguished from the known group by the physiological or pathological status of the subjects (e.g. **T19/86**: treatment of sero-positive pigs where treatment of sero-negative pigs is known; **T893/90**: controlling bleeding in non-haemophilic mammals whereas controlling haemophilic bleeding in haemophilic mammals is known). Newer case law also acknowledges novelty on the basis of specifying a new sub-group of subjects to be treated (e.g. **T1399/04**: specific genotype of a virus; **T694/16**: patients exhibiting specific biomarkers).
- The use of a new route or mode of administration (e.g. **T51/93** r.3.1: subcutaneous injection where intramuscular injection is known; **T138/95**: intrapulmonary adsorption where aerosol delivery is known).
- The use of a new dosage regimen (e.g. **T1020/03**; **G2/08** hn, r.6.1).
- The exploitation of a different technical effect underlying a new application (e.g. **T290/86**: use of a salt solution for removing plaque from teeth where the use of the salt solution for depressing the solubility of tooth enamel in organic acids is known).

However, as is also the case with second non-medical use claims, an invention which is based on the mere explanation of a known technical effect underlying a known medical use is not considered to be novel (**T254/93** hn.II, cited with approval in **G2/08**).

Therapeutic uses of a substance may hence be based not only on the treatment of a different disease but also on the treatment of the same disease by a different therapeutic method differing, for example, in the dosage, administration regime, group of subjects treated, or route of administration (G-VI,6.1.2).

There is no requirement for a second medical use claim under **Art.54(5)** to recite a specific disease or pathological condition; the claim may specify the use in more general terms encompassing a range of diseases (e.g. 'for use as an anti-inflammatory medicament') (G-VI,6.1; **T752/17**). The claim may even recite 'for use as a medicament', without limitation in terms of the disease, and still be directed to a 'specific use' as required by **Art.54(5)** provided that another aspect of the medical use is specified in the claim, e.g. 'wherein the medicament is administered orally' (**T295/22**; overruling G-VI,6.1.2 Example 2).

2.2 PATENTABILITY ISSUES

The EPO will apply the whole body of jurisprudence relating to the assessment of novelty and inventive step when considering the patentability of a second medical use claim. The claimed second medical use must reflect a different technical teaching from known medical uses. For example, a claimed dosage regimen that falls within the scope of a broader prior art teaching must fulfil the requirements for novelty applying to selection inventions. (G2/08 r.6.3)

The following decisions help to clarify when a second medical use invention may be considered to be novel: **T290/86; T1020/03; T836/01; T1074/06.** Any new technical effect underlying the distinguishing feature of a second medical use claim must be considered when examining inventive step under **Art.56.** (G2/08 r.6.3)

In order for an application claiming a new second medical use to comply with **Art.83**, it is necessary that information in the application makes it credible that the therapeutic agent is suitable for the therapeutic application specified in the claim. A lack in this respect cannot be remedied by post-published evidence. (**G2/21** r.77)

Clinical data may not be required if the application provides information in the form of pre-clinical experimental results showing an effect that, for the skilled person, directly and unambiguously reflects the therapeutic application (**T752/17**). Such results may have been generated in in vitro tests or using animal models. Indeed, no experimental results of any kind may be necessary if the claimed therapeutic use is credible based on the common general knowledge or a plausible technical concept disclosed in the application (**T699/19** r.30). These principles also apply to a therapeutic indication underlying a first medical use claim.

The infringement of a second medical use claim can often be demonstrated by reference to the use and dosage information in the product information leaflet that manufacturers provide for prescription medicines. In some cases, however, it is possible for manufacturers to deliberately omit information of this kind in an attempt to avoid patent infringement.

2.3 SWISS-TYPE CLAIM AND PURPOSE-RELATED PRODUCT CLAIM

Purpose-related product protection for a second medical use invention under **Art.54(5)** was not available before the entry into force of EPC2000. EPC1973 only had a provision for the patentability of the first medical use in the form of a purpose-related product claim (Art.54(5) EPC1973). A product claim for a second medical use was not patentable. The Enlarged Board of Appeal allowed protection in the form of a claim directed to the use of a substance or composition for the manufacture of a medicament for a specified new and inventive therapeutic application. Such a claim avoids both the lack of novelty of the substance per se and the prohibition on claiming a method of treatment. (**G5/83** r.23)

The manufacture of the medicament derives its novelty from the new therapeutic use. Hence, the claim should preferably be directed to the 'use of a substance or composition for the manufacture of a medicament for [new and inventive therapeutic application]' (**G5/83; G1/83** and **G6/83** deal with the same issues but with different parties; see also OJ 1984 p.581). This claim format is called a Swiss-type second medical use claim because it originated in the practice of the Swiss patent office.

Decision **G5/83** was not followed by the courts of all contracting states. To eliminate any legal uncertainty concerning the patentability of further medical uses, EPC2000 introduced new **Art.54(5)**, which allows a purpose-related product claim for each further new medical use of a substance or composition already known as a medicine. (OJ 2007 se4 EN p.54)

Since the introduction of EPC2000 removed the need for a Swiss-type claim approach, a claim deriving its novelty only from a new therapeutic use of a medicament may not have the format of a Swiss-type claim unless the application has a filing date or priority date before 29.01.2011. (**G2/08** r.7)

3 **Medical use claims and unity**

The following independent claims are possible for a novel substance X having a therapeutic application in the treatment of diseases Y and Z:

1 Substance X.
2 Pharmaceutical composition comprising substance X.
3 Substance X for use as a medicament.
4 Substance X for use in the treatment of Y.
5 Substance X for use in the treatment of Z.

If substance X is novel, all claims 1-5 have unity of invention (**Art.82**).

If substance X *per se* turns out to be known in a non-medical field, claim 2 in the form of a pharmaceutical composition claim and claim 3 in the form of a first medical indication form the broadest possible fallback positions. In such a case, claims 4 and 5 will generally be considered as having unity of invention. In particular, an application disclosing for the first time several medical uses for a known substance may have (independent) claims for the uses; as a general rule, no *a priori* lack of unity objection will be raised (G-VI,6.1).

If a therapeutic application of substance X turns out to be known, claims 4 and 5 in the form of second and further medical use claims may still be patentable. However, these different treatments must have a single general inventive concept to avoid a non-unity objection (G-VI,6.1).

Art. 55 Non-prejudicial disclosures

1 **General**

According to **Art.55**, a disclosure that has been made available to the public is disregarded in the assessment of patentability in two specific situations. No other non-prejudicial disclosures are recognised under the EPC (G-V). In particular, the EPC does not provide for a general grace period for the filing of a patent application after the inventor has publicly disclosed the invention.

Art. 55(1) For the application of Article 54, a disclosure of the invention shall not be taken into consideration if it occurred no earlier than six months preceding the filing of the European patent application and if it was due to, or in consequence of:

(a) an evident abuse in relation to the applicant or his legal predecessor, or

(b) the fact that the applicant or his legal predecessor has displayed the invention at an official, or officially recognised, international exhibition falling within the terms of the Convention on international exhibitions signed at Paris on 22 November 1928 and last revised on 30 November 1972.

Art.54 Novelty

1 **Time limit and nature of disclosure**

The intention of **Art.55** is to protect an applicant in two specific situations. In the first situation, one of the applicant's inventions is disclosed by a third party in circumstances that amount to an evident abuse. In the second situation, the applicant discloses an invention at a recognised international exhibition. In such cases, the disclosure is not taken into account when assessing novelty and inventive step if the applicant files a European patent application in a timely manner.

The relevant date for calculating whether the six-month condition referred to in **Art.55(1)** is met or not is the date of the actual filing of the European patent application; the date of priority is not to be taken into account of in this calculation (**G3/98** hn). See also **Art.80:4** on the difference between 'filing of the application' and 'date of filing'.

An abusive disclosure or disclosure at an international exhibition will not be regarded as state of the art if it occurred no earlier than six months preceding the filing of the applicant's application with the EPO and, in the case of an exhibition, the applicant complies with the requirements of **Art.55(2)**. A later filing will make the disclosure prejudicial. If the applicant files a national application first, the subsequent priority claiming European application must nevertheless comply with the six-month condition. Alternatively, an international application may be filed complying with the six-month condition because an international application is deemed to be a European application (**Art.153(2)**). Note that the requirement that the disclosure occurs no earlier than six months prior to the filing date is a condition which must be met and not a time limit in the sense of **Art.120**. Hence, neither the extensions available under **R.134** nor any other provision relating to time limits is applicable.

Note that the term 'disclosure' in **Art.55(1)** means making something 'available to the public' in the sense of **Art.54(2)**. This interpretation of 'disclosure' is supported by Article 4(4) of the Strasbourg Convention (1963), to which **Art.55(1)** should correspond according to the travaux préparatoires EPC1973 and which uses the term 'made public'.

The publication of a European patent application can be disregarded under **Art.55(1)** if its filing was due to, or the result of, an evident abuse; the publication by the EPO is then a consequence of the evident abuse. Accordingly, the rightful applicant is protected in two ways, firstly if the publication of the abusive application constitutes prior art under **Art.54(2)** and secondly, if the abusive application has an earlier effective date and is published on or after the filing date of the application under examination. In the second case, the abusive application is not a European prior right because, according to **Art.54(3)**, only earlier applications that are published on or after the effective date of the application under examination are prior rights, which requirement is not met if the publication is disregarded under **Art.55(1)** (see also G-V,3).

Precisely in order to afford protection against such a European patent application having an earlier effective date, **Art.55(1)** uses the phrase 'no earlier than six months' instead of 'within six months'. Hence, the provision can be used to disregard the publication of an abusive European patent application that occurs after the filing date of the application under examination for the purpose of **Art.54(3)** (Empel §88). In practice, European patent applications with an earlier effective date are published at most about eighteen months after the filing date of the application under examination.

A Euro-PCT application which would constitute a prior right under **R.165** can be similarly disregarded.

If the application under examination is filed claiming priority and, subsequent to the priority date, a European patent application is published which was filed by a third party, results from evident abuse, and has a priority or filing date that is earlier than the priority date of the application under examination, the third parties' European patent application can only be disregarded as a prior right under **Art.55** if the application under examination has a filing date no later than six months after said publication (**G3/98**) (G-VI,3).

If the earlier European application was filed by a non-entitled applicant, the inventor or successor in title of the inventor may also begin an entitlement action under **Art.61**.

Note that the safeguard of **Art.55(1)** applies only to the applicant who has suffered from an evident abuse or displayed the invention at an exhibition; other applicants cannot invoke the provision.

2 **Abusive disclosure** (**Art.55(1)(a)**)

The evident abuse must be an act (or failure to act) that harmed the applicant or a legal predecessor of the applicant; i.e. the evident abuse can be invoked only by the harmed person or the successor in title of the harmed person.

The word 'abuse' in **Art.55(1)(a)** was interpreted in **T585/92** r.6 to imply a requirement of actual intent to harm or actual knowledge that harm would or could be expected; the harm can be e.g. commercial damage. This interpretation is followed in G-V,3 which adds that constructive knowledge that harm would or could ensue is sufficient. The decision does not regard a disclosure that is the result of an inadvertent mistake as an 'abuse'. An erroneous publication by the Brazilian patent office was considered to be an inadvertent mistake rather than an abuse because of the lack of any personal or contractual relationship between the patent office and the applicant. The decision does not give any particular legal basis for its interpretation. **T436/92** r.5.2 follows this decision and holds that mere negligence or breach of confidentiality without intention to harm is not evident abuse.

Another decision, **T173/83** r.6, not followed by the Guidelines, holds that 'abuse' does not require the intention to harm; a disclosure by a person not authorised to disclose the invention is evident abuse not only when the person acts with an intention to harm when disclosing the invention, but also when the person discloses the invention in breach of confidentiality, or when the person, knowing full well that disclosure is not permitted, discloses the invention in such a way as to risk causing harm to the inventor.

An abusive disclosure is often one that is in breach of a secrecy agreement. A condition of confidentiality is often tacit and derived from a relationship of good faith or trust. A parent company-subsidiary relationship, a joint venture, or the delivery of test specimens may also imply a tacit agreement to maintain confidentiality.

However, even if there is a tacit understanding concerning confidentiality between two parties, a specific piece of correspondence sent from one party to the other might not be subject to this understanding if the nature of the correspondence suggests otherwise, e.g. if the correspondence is a brochure intended for use in advertising. In these circumstances, the publication of the brochure by the party receiving the correspondence might not be an evident abuse in relation to the party sending the correspondence (**T173/83**).

In terms of proving that a particular disclosure was abusive, the boards of appeal has taken the view in at least one decision that the use of the adjective 'evident' in **Art.55(1)(a)** indicates that the standard of proof is a high one (**T291/97** r.13).

The legal predecessor of the applicant mentioned in **Art.55(1)** is often the inventor.

3 **Procedure in the case of an abusive disclosure**
If the abusive disclosure of an invention takes place, the injured party must ensure that a European patent application is filed early enough so that the date of the disclosure is no more than than six months before the filing of that application. If a first application for the disclosed invention has already been filed, the European patent application may claim the priority of that first application but the condition that the disclosure is no more than than six months before the filing of the European patent application must still be complied with for **Art.55(1)** to apply. Naturally, if the priority date is before the date of an abusive disclosure that is state of the art under **Art.54(2)**, it may not be necessary to exclude the disclosure under **Art.55(1)**.

An applicant can challenge whether an abusive disclosure should be taken into consideration in a first substantive response in grant proceedings. The examining division will investigate the matter (B-VI,5.5) and if it regards the proof that the publication is abusive as sufficient, it will not take the abusive disclosure into consideration.

If the abusive disclosure is the publication of a European patent application, the applicant can start an **Art.61** procedure against the non-entitled person that filed the application.

4 **Exhibition (Art.55(1)(b))**
The few exhibitions to which this provision applies are registered by the International Exhibitions Bureau under the Convention relating to International Exhibitions and are listed, for information, each year in the OJ under *International Treaties* (OJ 2024 A53 Table II.1.2). Recent and upcoming international exhibitions are:

02.10.2023 – 28.03.2024	Expo 2023	Doha, Qatar
13.04.2025 – 13.10.2025	Expo 2025	Osaka, Japan
19.03.2027 – 26.09.2027	Expo 2027	Yokohama, Japan
01.10.2030 – 31.03.2031	Expo 2030	Riyadh, Saudi Arabia

5 **Procedure in the case of display at an international exhibition**
An applicant desiring protection for an invention displayed at an international exhibition must file a European patent application early enough so that the date of the first disclosure of the invention at the exhibition is no more than six months before the filing of that application. If a first application for the disclosed invention has already been filed, the European patent application may claim the priority of that first application but the condition that the disclosure is no more than six months before the filing of the European patent application must still be complied with. Naturally, if the priority date is before the date of the exhibition then it may not be necessary to exclude the disclosure under **Art.55(1)**.

Art. 55(2) In the case of paragraph 1(b), paragraph 1 shall apply only if the applicant states, when filing the European patent application, that the invention has been so displayed and files a supporting certificate within the time limit and under the conditions laid down in the Implementing Regulations.

Implemented by:
R.25 Certificate of exhibition

1 **Statement and certificate**

In order to ensure that a disclosure is not taken into consideration under **Art.55(1)(b)**, the applicant must also file a statement according to **Art.55(2)**. The statement must be filed on the date of filing the European patent application (A-IV,3.1). If the statement is omitted when filing the application, the only remedy available is to refile the application with the missing statement. In particular, there is no time limit for filing the application and none of the remedies associated with missed time limits (e.g. **Art.121** and **Art.122**) can be used.

A supporting certificate must also be filed within four months of the filing of the application (**Art.55(2)** and **R.25**). The certificate must comprise an authenticated identification of the invention (**R.25(d)**). The Receiving Section acknowledges receipt of the certificate and draws the applicant's attention to any manifest defects if rectification is still possible within the four-month period (A-IV,3.2).

If the required statement is filed with the application but the certificate is not filed in due time, the EPO notifies the applicant of a loss of rights (**R.112(1)** and **Art.55(1)**). If the EPO has made a mistake concerning the filing of the certificate, the loss of rights can be contested in the usual way (**R.112(2)**). In other cases, further processing can be requested under **Art.121** and **R.135**. (A-IV,3.2)

The corresponding procedure for a Euro-PCT application is set out in **R.159(1):9**.

The examining division will investigate whether the claimed invention is the same as the displayed invention identified in the certificate (B-VI,5.5).

If the European patent application is filed too late to comply with the six-month condition of **Art.55(1)**, a statement is omitted on filing, or a certificate is not filed in time or is deficient, the disclosure at the exhibition is taken into account and may be prejudicial to the patentability of the claimed invention.

The EPC does not recognise a priority claim based on the disclosure of an invention at an exhibition, but national law may do so (**T382/07** r.8.2).

Art. 56 Inventive step

An invention shall be considered as involving an inventive step if, having regard to the state of the art, it is not obvious to a person skilled in the art. If the state of the art also includes documents within the meaning of Article 54, paragraph 3, these documents shall not be considered in deciding whether there has been an inventive step.

Art.54(3) European prior rights

1 **Overview**

For an invention to be patentable it must be both new in the sense of **Art.54** and involve an inventive step in the sense of **Art.56**. These are two separate requirements. An invention is new if it does not form part of the state of the art (**Art.54(1)**), i.e. if there is a difference between the invention and the state of the art. The nature of this difference, and in particular whether the skilled person would have been motivated to add the missing feature(s) in the expectation of achieving the technical effects that arise from this difference, determines whether there is an inventive step. If there is no difference between the invention and the state of the art there can be no inventive step, i.e. the question of inventive step only arises if there is novelty (G-VII,1; note that the state of the art that is relevant here is the state of the art according to **Art.54(2)** only).

If the skilled person was motivated by the prior art to combine the features of the claimed invention, and hence to make the invention without any special insight, the invention is considered to be obvious and consequently to lack an inventive step. An invention is obvious if it follows plainly or logically from the prior art (G-VII,4). In considering obviousness, it may be necessary to consider whether the skilled person would have bridged the gap between the prior art and the invention by routine research. Alternatively, the difference between the prior art and the invention may be found in a second piece of prior art and it may be necessary to consider whether it would have occurred to the skilled person to combine these different pieces of prior art. The fact that different pieces of prior art can be combined when considering obviousness is an important difference with respect to the assessment of novelty, in which each piece of prior art is evaluated individually.

The assessment of whether an invention is obvious is to some extent subjective and the conclusion reached may vary from one individual to another, depending on that person's level of knowledge and outlook. The relevant individual for the purposes of **Art.56**, is the notional 'person skilled in art'. It is self-evident that closely defining the characteristics of this fictional person is an important factor in making the assessment under **Art.56** objective and consistent.

As a further aid to consistency, the EPO conducts the assessment of inventive step within the framework of a structured assessment called the problem-solution approach (G-VII,5; see also **G1/19** r.26 and **G2/21** r.24). The problem-solution approach comprises the steps of determining the closest prior art made available under **Art.54(2)**; defining an objective technical problem solved by the claimed invention, on the basis of the effects achieved by the novel features of the invention vis-à-vis this closest prior art; and considering whether the claimed invention is an obvious solution to this problem or not based on the prior art as a whole. This approach attaches importance to the effects achieved by the novel features of the claimed invention vis-à-vis the closest prior art disclosure. Obviousness is more a matter of whether the skilled person would have been motivated to use the novel features of the invention to solve the objective technical problem rather than whether the skilled person would have simply considered using the novel features per se.

The assessment of inventive step is carried out by taking into account 'the state of the art', i.e. everything made available to the public up until the end of the day before the filing or priority date to which the claimed invention is entitled (**Art.54(2)**; Empel §96; **T107/82** r.11). Thus, the state of the art for the purpose of **Art.56** is as set out in **Art.54(2)** and notes thereto. To take such documents citable under **Art.54(3)** (European prior rights) into account would only exacerbate the already harsh effect of the whole contents approach (see **Art.54(3):1**). Prior art citable under **Art.54(3)** is therefore explicitly excluded when assessing inventive step.

2 Person skilled in the art

Since the assessment of obviousness in the final step of the problem-solution approach is to be carried out through the eyes of a 'person skilled in the art' (see **Art.56:3.3** below), it is necessary to identify this fictional person. Relevant characteristics are the level of skill, attitude and knowledge of the person skilled in the art. A person skilled in the art is also commonly referred to as a 'skilled person'.

Depending on the field of technology concerned, the skilled 'person' may be a single individual or a team of individuals (G-VII,3). For example, for a particular invention in the field of computing, the skilled person was considered to be either an electronics engineer with a knowledge of programming or else a team comprising an electronics engineer and a computer programmer (**T164/92**). The skilled person has likewise been found to consist of a software project team (**T172/03**), a team comprising an expert in mail processing and a weighing expert (**T986/96**) and a team comprising a PhD researcher with experience in gene technology and two laboratory technicians (**T412/93**).

2.1 LEVEL OF SKILL AND EXPERIENCE OF THE SKILLED PERSON

The skilled person is considered to be a skilled practitioner in the field of technology with which invention is concerned (G-VII,3) and has neither the level of knowledge of the average member of the public at large (Empel §95) nor that of an advanced senior scientist (**T500/91** r.2.2). The skilled person resembles an ordinary practitioner having average ability and has the normal means and capacity for routine work and experimentation (G-VII,3).

The skilled person is considered to lack the inventive imagination necessary to solve problems for which routine solutions do not yet exist (**T223/92** r.5.5). In a similar vein, the skilled person is only capable of following normal design procedures and is not capable of creative thinking (**T455/91** r.5.1.3.8). The skilled person is competent but self-evidently does not have inventive capability (**T39/93** r.7.8.4).

The skilled person can only be expected to carry out experimental work by routine means within the framework of the normal practice of filling gaps in knowledge by the application of existing knowledge (**T530/95** r.9).

Nationality makes no difference. For instance, there is no difference between a European and an American skilled person; knowledge is accessible everywhere (**T124/85**).

2.2 ATTITUDE AND OUTLOOK OF THE SKILLED PERSON

The skilled person is oriented towards practicalities (**T5/81**). The skilled person is constantly occupied in developing the relevant technical field (G-VII,3) and seeks to eliminate deficiencies, overcome drawbacks and improve known devices and products (**T15/81** r.3; **T195/84** r.8.1). However, the skilled person is not expected to solve technical problems by performing scientific research in areas that are not yet explored (**T500/91** r.2.2).

The skilled person is purpose-driven by the goal of solving a technical problem. The skilled person will not act out of idle curiosity but rather with a specific technical purpose in mind (**T939/92**). The skilled person will not carry out frivolous or random research and has no desire to know how things work; such research is more characteristic of the approach taken by an inventor rather than that taken by a skilled person.

The skilled person is conservative by nature and a captive of established prejudices in the relevant field (**T455/91** r.5.1.3.3).

2.3 KNOWLEDGE POSSESSED BY THE SKILLED PERSON – COMMON GENERAL KNOWLEDGE

The skilled person is presumed to have access to everything in the state of the art (G-VII,3). This is reflected in **Art.56** itself, which states that an invention involves an inventive step if it is not obvious 'having regard to the state of the art'. This body of disclosures that make up the state of the art is commonly referred to as the 'prior art'. It is therefore legitimate, when assessing inventive step, to consider every disclosure in the state of the art as a potential starting point for the skilled person.

However, whilst the skilled person has access to the whole state of the art, the skilled person only has an active knowledge of a certain subset of this knowledge, known as the common general knowledge. Common general knowledge is knowledge in the field of the invention of which the skilled person has immediate possession (**T206/83** r.5). When assessing inventive step, it is regarded as obvious for the skilled person to combine the teachings of a specific prior art disclosure with the common general knowledge.

Common general knowledge is the knowledge an experienced person in the relevant field is expected to have, or knowledge that the skilled person is at least expected to be aware of and can easily find (**T766/91** r.8.2). Common general knowledge is therefore only a subset of the total knowledge in a technical field and is usually found in basic handbooks and textbooks (**T206/83** r.5). Since the common general knowledge available to the skilled person is part of the prior art, its extent must be evaluated on the day before the date of filing or, where appropriate, the date of priority of the invention.

Common general knowledge need not be in writing and may be part of the unwritten mental furniture of the skilled person, in which case written or oral evidence from an actual skilled person may be required (**T939/92** r.2.3). Proof of an allegation that something is part of the common general knowledge is only required if the allegation is challenged by another party or the EPO (see e.g. **T1877/07** r.5). This approach is procedurally efficient and is justified because the parties can be presumed not to be taken by surprise by anything that is common general knowledge in the particular field concerned (**T766/91** r.8.1).

Information in writing is only common general knowledge when it complies with each of the following three requirements, which are common to all cases: the skilled person must be able to (a) select the right reference book, (b) identify the appropriate section of the book without undue effort and (c) derive the correct information from that section without further investigation (**T890/02** r.3, giving a summary of the case law):

(a) Common general knowledge is normally represented by the contents of reference books (**T890/02** r.3). These include basic handbooks and textbooks on the subject of interest (**T20/81** r.5; **T206/83** r.5; **T171/84** r.5; F-II,4.1). Subject-matter appears in such books because it is already common general knowledge; it does not become common general knowledge by being published (**T766/91** r.8.2). A handbook or textbook describing a basic general technical theory or methodology may also represent common general knowledge, even if it only provides specific applications in technical fields different from the field of interest (**T426/88** hn.I). The language of a book is irrelevant to its status as a general reference book (**T426/88**). The contents of patent documents normally do not belong to the common general knowledge (**T171/84** r.5). The same applies to scientific papers (**T893/98** r.2.5). On the other hand, when a field of research is so new that textbooks are not yet available, a skilled person may derive common general knowledge from sources such as patents (**T51/87** r.9) and scientific papers (**T772/89** r.3.3). A scientific study is, exceptionally, also regarded as common general knowledge if the skilled person would try and obtain the most recent and best information which, for practical reasons, is not immediately available from textbooks (**T676/94** r.10(iii)).

(b) A skilled person must be able to identify the appropriate section(s) of the reference book without any significant effort. A search of the literature covering nearly the whole state of the art is regarded as an undue effort (**T171/84** r.12). Therefore, searching a database such as Chemical Abstracts or Biological Abstracts, covering virtually the complete state of the art and in total representing much more than the skilled person's common general knowledge, is an unacceptable burden (**T206/83** r.6; **T890/02** r.12). In contrast, some nucleotide sequence databases, set up as a handbooks or encyclopaedias, are regarded as common general knowledge because they do not require sophisticated search strategies and allow the extraction of unambiguous and straightforward information about an enzyme without undue effort simply by providing its name (**T890/02** r.8, 9).

(c) The relevant section(s) of the reference book must provide the correct information or unambiguous data that can be used without further research (**T890/02** r.3(c)). Such section(s) may alternatively refer the skilled person to articles describing specifically what to do or at least giving a generally applicable and unambiguous method for the relevant purpose (**T206/83** r.5).

Common general knowledge is not just an important concept under **Art.56**. It is also important in the assessment of novelty under **Art.54(1)**, since it may be used to cure a lack of enablement in a prior art disclosure, e.g. by enabling the skilled person to identify suitable starting materials in order to put into effect a process for making a specific chemical compound (see **Art.54(2):4.3** for a discussion of enabling disclosure). Furthermore, an invention is sufficiently disclosed in the sense of **Art.83**, if the disclosure of a European patent application allows the skilled person, using the common general knowledge, to carry out the invention. Common general knowledge also plays a role in determining whether or not an error in an application can be corrected under **R.139**.

For the purposes of **Art.56** and **Art.83** the same level of skill is attributed to the person skilled in the art (G-VII,3). However, for the assessment of inventive step the skilled person only has knowledge of the prior art; for evaluating sufficiency, the skilled person has knowledge of both the prior art and the invention disclosed in the patent application or patent under consideration (**T694/92** r.7). Hence, the knowledge possessed by the skilled person is different for the purposes of **Art.56** and **Art.83**.

2.4 TECHNICAL FIELD IN WHICH THE SKILLED PERSON IS KNOWLEDGEABLE

The person skilled in the art is knowledgeable in the technical field of the invention. The word 'art' should not be construed as referring to technology in general but as referring to the specific field of technology with which the invention is concerned. The relevant field must be technical. If the invention relates to the use of computing in the field of business, for example, the skilled person will be skilled in software engineering rather than in business. Hence, the skilled person in the context of a management system for order placement was regarded as a software project team. Such a team would not include any business expert but would have knowledge of the business-related features of the order management method in the form of a requirements specification. (**T172/03** r.6, 16)

The specific technical field in which the skilled person is knowledgeable is defined by the technical problem to be solved (**T422/93** hn.1). If that problem prompts the skilled person to seek a solution in another technical field, that other field is the relevant specific technical field (**T26/98**; G-VII,3). For example, if the problem to be solved is the prevention of wear in a metal scraper on a conveyor belt, the skilled person for the assessment of inventive step is skilled in the field of materials, not in the field of conveyor belts (**T32/81** Conveyor belt; r.4.2).

Where the technical fields relating to the problem addressed by the invention and solution provided by the invention are different, the skilled person is an expert in the field of the problem, not in the field of the solution (**T422/93** hn.2, established case law).

In some cases, a team of skilled persons from different specific technical fields is required, in particular where different parts of the problem relate to different technical fields (**T141/87** r.3.7; **T986/96** r.3.1.1). For example, a person skilled in electronics may consult a computer programmer if confronted with a program listing (**T164/92** hn. II).

When the skilled person's own knowledge is insufficient to solve the problem, the skilled person may be expected to look for solutions in relevant neighbouring technical fields and broader general technical fields (**T176/84**; **T195/84**). However, the skilled person will not consult prior art in remote technical fields (**T11/81**) unless specifically prompted to do so (**T560/89**; G-VII,3).

3 Problem-solution approach

The EPO assesses whether an invention involves an inventive step using the problem-solution approach (sometimes also known as the problem and solution approach). This approach may be derived, in part, from the requirement in **R.42(1)(c)** that the invention must be disclosed in terms of a technical problem and its solution. Although the use of the problem-solution approach is not mandatory, it is very unusual for the EPO to take any other approach. If, exceptionally, some other method is adopted, the reasons for not using the problem-solution approach should be stated (CLBA I. D.2).

In decision **T465/92** the board of appeal used such an alternative approach. The board in **T188/09** agreed that an alternative approach could sometimes be justified, provided that one of the situations specified in **T465/92** applies: either there is no close prior art because the invention breaks new ground or there are several equally close relevant citations. Moreover, the alternative approach must provide the same result as the problem-solution approach. (**T188/09** r.1-9)

Note that the objectivity and predictability of the assessment of inventive step under **Art.56** is in part based on the consistent use of the problem-solution approach (**G1/19** r.26; G-VII,5). Different methods are unlikely to give the same result in all situations. Correct use of the problem-solution approach assesses the actual objective contribution to the art made by the inventor rather than the subjective contribution the inventor believes has been made (**T24/81** hn) and at the same time tries to avoid any hindsight analysis based on knowledge of the invention which would be unfair to the inventor (**T645/92** r.2.1).

The problem-solution approach comprises three main steps (G-VII,5; see also **G1/19** r.26 and **G2/21** r.24):

1 Identifying the closest prior art (G-VII,5.1).

2 Establishing the objective technical problem addressed by the claimed invention in view of the closest prior art. The objective technical problem is established by considering the technical effects achieved by using the distinguishing feature or features of the claimed invention compared to the closest prior art (G-VII,5.2).

3 Considering whether the solution to this problem (i.e. the claimed invention) would have been obvious to the skilled person when starting from the closest prior art and trying to solve the objective technical problem. The first instance departments of the EPO commonly answer this question by considering whether a prior art teaching 'would' (rather than 'could') have prompted the skilled person to make the invention (G-VII,5.3).

A possible implementation of the problem-solution approach in the case of a simple mechanical invention lacking an inventive step could comprise the following steps:

1 identifying the document that is the closest prior art;

2 formulating the objective technical problem by:
   (a) identifying those features of the claimed invention which are anticipated by the closest prior art, i.e. are found in combination in the closest prior art;
   (b) identifying the remaining feature(s) as the distinguishing feature(s) of the claim;
   (c) identifying the technical effect(s) achieved by the distinguishing feature(s) over the closest prior art;
   (d) formulating the objective technical problem as 'how to modify the closest prior art to achieve these technical effect(s)';

3 assessing whether the subject-matter of the claim is obvious as a solution to the objective technical problem by:
   (a) showing that the skilled person, trying to solve the objective technical problem, would consult a particular second document, e.g. because it is in the same, a neighbouring, or a general technical field;
   (b) showing that the second document teaches the distinguishing feature(s);
   (c) showing that the second document provides a motivation to apply the distinguishing feature(s) to solve the objective technical problem;
   (d) showing that the teaching of the second document is compatible with the teaching of the closest prior art, such that the skilled person combining these teachings arrives at something falling within the claimed subject-matter;
   (e) concluding that the skilled person (not merely could, but) *would* have applied the distinguishing feature to solve the technical problem and that the claimed subject-matter is therefore obvious and lacks an inventive step.

3.1 CLOSEST PRIOR ART

According to the problem-solution approach, the assessment of inventive step is simplified by choosing the most promising starting point for the skilled person in making the claimed invention and assessing obviousness solely in relation to this closest prior art document. If the invention is not obvious starting from the closest prior art, it is unlikely that it will be obvious starting from more remote prior art.

To identify the closest prior art, it is necessary to first define the state of the art from which this document is to be chosen by establishing the effective date of the invention. This effective date is the filing date of the European patent application or patent whose patentability or validity is being considered (**Art.54(2)**) or, if appropriate, the priority date to which the claimed invention is entitled (**Art.89**). The state of the art includes everything made available to the public within the meaning of **Art.54(2)** up until the end of the day preceding the effective date (**T4/81** hn.2; Empel §97). The state of the art under **Art.54(3)** is not taken into account (**Art.56**). The relevant state of the art therefore includes information made available in writing, orally, by use or in any other way, including common general knowledge which may not have been set out in writing (G-VII,2; **T939/92**). Knowledge known only by the applicant is not prior art (**T181/95**).

The closest prior art disclosure is that which, in one single reference, discloses the combination of features which constitutes the most promising starting point for a development leading to the invention (**T432/92**; G-VII,5.1). The primary consideration in the selection of the closest prior art is that it should be conceived for a similar purpose or aim at the same objective as the invention and have the most relevant technical features in common, i.e. require the minimum of structural modification (CLBA I.D.3.1). A further criterion may be the similarity of the technical problem addressed (**T495/91**). An objective assessment of the closest prior art using these criteria helps to avoid any ex post facto analysis being applied (**T730/96**, r.2.1).

The most important criterion is that the closest prior art should be conceived for a similar purpose, i.e. directed to the same purpose or effect as the claimed invention (e.g. **T1148/15** r.4.2). The number of structural and functional features that are shared with the claimed invention is a second criterion. A document cannot qualify as the closest prior art merely because it discloses something having a close structural similarity with the claimed invention (**T273/92** r.3; **T506/95** r.4.1).

If there are a number of close prior art documents and the choice of the closest prior art is not unambiguous, the problem-solution approach should be repeated for each of these prior art documents. If the invention is obvious based on the choice of at least one of these documents as a starting point, the invention lacks an inventive step, and the choice of starting point needs no specific justification. (**T1742/12** r.6.5, 6.6; G-VII,5.1)

However, in opposition proceedings, applying the problem-solution approach from different starting points is only permitted if it has been convincingly shown that these documents are equally valid springboards (G-VII,5.1). Accordingly, various attacks starting from different prior art documents cannot be freely developed by the opponent (**T320/15** r.1.1.2). The advantages of this approach to the EPO in terms of procedural efficiency are evident.

The starting point for the assessment of inventive step is usually a specific prior art embodiment, e.g. a known device, product or method. It can also be a public prior use (**T1464/05**). It should not be a speculative disclosure of what might be possible (**T1764/09**). The age of the closest prior art document is in principle not relevant (**T1408/04** r.2 – 45-year-old document selected) but may be one factor taken into account, particularly if the document's disclosure is associated with well-known disadvantages that would discourage the skilled person (**T1000/92** r.4.3).

The closest prior art for an invention relating to a medical use of a compound should be a document disclosing the treatment of the same therapeutic indication according to **T2571/12**. The closest prior art for an invention relating to a process for manufacturing a chemical compound, on the other hand, should be a known process for making that compound rather than an alternative use of the same process (e.g. **T961/96** r.5.1).

3.2 OBJECTIVE TECHNICAL PROBLEM

In the second step of the problem-solution approach, the claimed invention is compared with the closest prior art, and the distinguishing feature or features of the invention over the closest prior art are identified. A distinguishing feature may have one or more technical effects associated with it. Such effects may be disclosed in the application, known from the common general knowledge or demonstrated by evidence submitted in the proceedings. The objective technical problem is the task faced by the skilled person in trying to modify the closest prior art to achieve these technical effects (G-VII,5.2; **T1019/99**). Examples of technical effects that may be associated with the distinguishing feature of an invention are the improved control of an electric motor, the reduced weight of a gearbox, the greater potency of a pharmaceutical compound and the higher yield of a chemical process.

The objective technical problem need not be the same as the problem stated in the application as filed (the 'subjective technical problem') though this is the correct place to start. For instance, it may be found that the invention does not solve the problem alleged to have been solved in the application or does not solve it across the scope of the claim. In such a case the relevant effect underlying the problem can no longer be taken into account. Equally, closer prior art unknown to the applicant may be found, which already discloses the feature on which the original problem was based – the objective technical problem may only be based on the technical effects associated with distinguishing features. In these cases, reformulation of the problem may be necessary, possibly to meet a less ambitious goal (**T246/91**). However, a reformulation of the objective technical problem may also take into account additional technical effects and the result may be that a more ambitious problem has been solved. Any effect provided by a distinguishing feature of the invention and derivable from the application as filed may be used as a basis for the reformulation (**T386/89**), provided all the information necessary to achieve the effect is at the disposal of the skilled person (**T1639/07** r.2.5).

New effects submitted by the applicant during the proceedings may, in principle, also be used, even if they are not explicitly stated in the application as filed. However, an applicant or proprietor may only rely upon a technical effect that the skilled person, having the common general knowledge in mind, and based on the application as originally filed, would derive as being encompassed by the technical teaching of the application and embodied by the same originally disclosed invention (**G2/21** hn.2). This refers to what the skilled person understands at the filing date from the application as originally filed as the technical teaching of the invention (**G2/21** r.93). A technical effect relied upon later in the procedure needs to be encompassed by that technical teaching and to embody the same invention; if these requirements are met, such an effect does not change the nature of the claimed invention (adapted from r.93). In principle, a technical effect can be based on evidence submitted by the applicant in the course of the proceedings before the EPO (**T20/81**), even if that evidence did not yet exist or was not public at the priority or filing date of the application ('post-published evidence') (**G2/21** hn.1).

The two requirements for relying on a new technical effect developed in **G2/21** ('encompassed by the technical teaching'; 'embodied by the same originally disclosed invention') are cumulative, separate requirements according to **T116/18** and **T314/20**. The purpose of these requirements is to prevent the filing of applications for speculative inventions – the invention should have been made at the time of filing and properly disclosed in the application. In **T116/18**, the board considered that the first requirement was met if the new technical effect was conceptually comprised by the broadest technical teaching in the application (no need for literal disclosure) and the second requirement was met if the skilled person would have no legitimate reason to doubt, based on the application and the applicable common general knowledge, that the new technical effect could be achieved (r.11.10-11.11). In **T314/20**, however, the board found this latter requirement to be equivalent to an ab initio implausibility standard which was not adopted by **G2/21** and hesitated to apply it (r.6.13.8-6.13.11). In any case, the board in **T314/20** found that the new technical effect could not be taken into account since it contradicted the teaching of the application (the skilled person would have expected the claimed combinations to have a similar effect to other disclosed combinations rather than an enhanced effect).

The applicant or proprietor has the burden to properly demonstrate that the purported advantages of the claimed invention have successfully been achieved (**G2/21** r.26). Furthermore, substantially all claimed embodiments must demonstrate the technical effect relied on (G-VII,5.2). For example, if a class of compounds is claimed, the applicant or proprietor must make it credible that substantially all the claimed compounds demonstrate the asserted technical effect (**T939/92** r.2.6). Alleged advantages or improvements to which the proprietor or applicant merely refers, without offering sufficient evidence that they are achieved, cannot be taken into consideration when formulating the objective technical problem (**T20/81** hn, r.3; **T2044/09**).

The problem must be a technical problem which the skilled person in the particular technical field might have been asked to solve at the relevant date without any knowledge of the claimed invention.

The problem must be formulated so that it does not contain pointers to the solution since the inclusion of elements of the invention in the objective technical problem necessarily results in hindsight (**T229/85**; G-VII,5.4.1). An exception arises when a claim feature refers to an aim to be achieved in a non-technical field – such a feature may legitimately appear as part of the objective technical problem (**T641/00** (Comvik) hn.1, hn.2; **G1/19** r.31; see **Art.56:4** below for further comments on computer-related inventions). On the other hand, a problem should not be formulated so generally as to circumvent indications in a prior art document towards the claimed solution (**T1019/99** r.3.3). Generally, the objective technical problem should be based precisely on the technical effects arising from the distinguishing features of the claim; it should be as specific as it can be whilst avoiding any elements of the solution or pointers towards the solution. The objective technical problem must always be based on the effects achieved by the claimed invention in comparison with the closest prior art. The effects underlying any technical progress made by the claimed invention in comparison with a marketed product are not relevant if this product is not the closest prior art (**T164/83**, **T181/82**).

The objective technical problem may be to provide an alternative solution to a known problem. (T92/92). Hence, the technical problem addressed does not have to involve any improvement over the closest prior art (T588/93; G-VII,5.2). Furthermore, an improvement in one property may be used to show an inventive step even if other properties are no better or even worse as compared to the closest prior art, at least as long as the other properties are maintained at a reasonable level so that the improvement is not completely offset by disadvantages in other respects (T254/86 hn). Even very small improvements can be relied upon in some cases, e.g. a 0.5% increase in the yield of a commercial process (T38/84).

3.3 OBVIOUSNESS

In the third step of the problem-solution approach, it is necessary to determine whether or not the claimed invention, starting from the closest prior art and bearing in mind the objective technical problem, would have been obvious to the skilled person.

The disclosure of the closest prior art document must be considered in the light of all knowledge that has become available to the skilled person up to and including the day before the filing or priority date that applies (G-VII,4). Note that this is different from the position in relation to novelty, according to which a prior art document must be evaluated on the date the document became available to the public, precisely in order to avoid such further development of its subject-matter in the mind of the skilled person (G-VI,3).

3.3.1 *Could-would approach*

According to the Guidelines, the question to be asked in the final step of the problem-solution approach is whether there is any teaching in the prior art as a whole that would (not simply could, but would) have prompted the skilled person, faced with the objective technical problem, to modify or adapt the closest prior art while taking account of that teaching, thereby arriving at something falling within the terms of the claims, and thus achieving what the invention achieves (G-VII,5.3).

This approach is based on the case law. Obviousness is not to be assessed by considering what the skilled person could have done but by considering what the skilled person would have done in the expectation of solving the objective technical problem or in the expectation of achieving some improvement or advantage (T2/83; T7/86; T414/98). If the problem solved by the claimed invention was not appreciated in the prior art (e.g. a known tablet was said to have good performance), the skilled person would not have modified this known tablet (e.g. by incorporating a barrier layer to improve performance) because the prior art provides no prompt or motivation to do so (T2/83 r.7). Equally, if the problem solved by the claimed invention was the reduction of load on a processor in a set-top box, and the common general knowledge taught that, in general terms, processor load could be reduced by using two separate processors instead of one, the addition of an additional processor is something the skilled person would have been motivated to try (T1148/15 r.6.4). This so-called 'could-would approach' reduces the risk of an ex post facto analysis wrongly suggesting that an invention is obvious (T564/89).

The invention is obvious if a pointer in the prior art as a whole would have prompted the skilled person to make the modification leading to the invention (T1317/08). In coming to the conclusion that the skilled person would have been prompted to make the invention, tangible evidence must be adduced (T1014/07). The incentive or prompt to apply certain measures need not be explicit. It may, for example, arise from a statement in the prior art that a certain feature avoids conditions known to be a cause of the problem solved by the patent (**T257/98; T35/04**; G-VII,5.3).

If a product can be envisaged and is desirable, but no obvious method exists for its manufacture, it may be claimed per se if it is made available for the first time (**T268/98** r.4.3; **T595/90** hn.2). In such a case, the skilled person would not have arrived at the invention and indeed could not have done so.

3.3.2 Combination of teachings

When assessing inventive step, the combination of different prior art teachings must be considered (G-VII,6), including the combination of the closest prior art with common general knowledge, the combination of different passages of the closest prior art, the combination of the closest prior art with a different document and the combination the closest prior art with a different kind of prior art (e.g. the combination of a prior use and the teaching of a document). Often, the claimed invention results from combining the features of the closest prior art with one or more features in a single further prior art teaching. It is always considered obvious for the skilled person to combine the teaching of the closest prior art with common general knowledge (G-VII,6); in other cases, a detailed assessment is necessary.

In principle, when assessing inventive step, combinations of three or more teachings may be considered. However, if it is necessary to combine the closest prior art teaching with two or more further prior art teachings to arrive at the claimed invention, then that fact alone may already be a sign that there is an inventive step if the invention is more than an aggregation of different features solving partial problems (G-VII,6; see **Art.56:3.4** for partial problems).

In deciding whether it would be obvious to combine prior art teachings, it must be considered whether the second teaching is in the same technical field, a neighbouring technical field, a general technical field or a remote technical field; whether the second teaching provides any motivation to add the feature(s) missing in the closest prior art; and whether the second teaching is compatible with the teaching in the closest prior art or whether any modification is necessary in order to combine the features (G-VII,6).

It is more likely to be obvious to combine a second teaching with the closest prior art if:

- The second prior art teaching is in the same technical field, a neighbouring technical field or a broader general technical field.
- The second prior art teaching includes a pointer in the form of a reference to solving the technical problem. The reference need not be explicit but may be implicit. An example of an implicit indication is that preferred features contribute to avoiding conditions known to be a cause of the problem. (**T716/07** r.4.3; G-VII,5.3)
- One of the two prior art teachings contains a clear and unmistakable reference to the other – it is generally obvious for the skilled person to combine two documents when one contains a clear reference to the other (G-VII,6(iii)). The combination of two parts of the same prior art disclosure, e.g. disclosing different embodiments, is obvious if there is a reasonable basis for associating these parts with one another (**T95/90**; G-VII,6(iii)).

On the other hand, it is unlikely to be obvious to combine a second teaching with the closest prior art if the second teaching is in a remote technical field and there is no explicit reference linking the disclosures or there is an inherent incompatibility between the two disclosures in features essential to the invention (G-VII,6(i)).

The combination of two prior art teachings will be obvious if the skilled person has a pointer that guides the skilled person from the first teaching to the second. Such a pointer is usually linked to the problem to be solved. For example, a prior art device might suffer from the known drawback that it consumes too much energy. When a second prior art document discloses features that are described as reducing energy consumption, then the reduction of energy consumption is a pointer that guides the skilled person from the first prior art document to the features in the second document. A solution in the form of the combination of the teachings of the two prior art documents is therefore obvious.

The skilled person will take into account the prior art in a neighbouring field where the same or similar problems occur (**T176/84** hn), but only to the extent that the skilled person can be expected to be aware that such problems occur in that field. Neighbouring fields must be sufficiently similar from a technical perspective so that methods and products from one field will be regarded as an obvious application in the other. If the connection from one field to another can only be made via a broader general field, the two fields are not neighbouring fields (**T176/84** r.5.3.2).

Examples of neighbouring fields include:

- gas chromatography and absorption spectral analysis (**T454/87**);
- moulding technology in dentistry and prosthodontics (**T358/90**);
- pharmaceuticals and cosmetics (**T838/95**);
- automotive electronics and aviation electronics (**T1910/11**).

Likewise, the skilled person will look in a non-specific, broader, general technical field if the same or similar problems occur in that field and the skilled person can be expected to be aware of them (**T195/84** hn). The IPC class in which a document is classified is less relevant to the status of a broader general technical field than the presence of the same or similar problems **T195/84** r.8.4). For example, a skilled person in the field of ophthalmic lenses who is confronted with the technical problems of adhesion and abrasion resistance in relation to a coating on the surface of the lens, will also refer to the state of the art in the more general field of coated plastic sheets, in which the same problems relating to the adhesion and abrasion resistance of coatings arise and of which the skilled person is aware (**T891/91** r.4.1.6). Similarly, the skilled person faced with a problem relating to the wrapping of hay bales would consult the broader general field of packaging methods relating to large diameter objects (**T189/92** r.6.1.4).

The skilled person will not look for a solution to the objective technical problem in a remote field because the skilled person would not expect to find a solution in such a field to a problem relating to different products and methods (**T11/81** r.3).

Examples of remote fields include:

- wigs and carpets (**T767/89**);
- closures for means of transporting money and bulk goods packaging, because of the different security risks (**T675/92**);
- doors for computer cabinets and doors for aeroplane hangars (**T9/82**);
- pencil sharpeners with automatically closing containers and saving boxes having comparable automatic closing means (**T176/84** r.5.3).

If an application in suit refers to a remote technical field, the reference does not make that remote field a neighbouring field (**T28/87** r.5.4). Such a pointer in the application is representative of the way the inventor was thinking when the invention was made and not of the way the skilled person would think based on the prior art.

Nevertheless, a skilled person will look for a solution in a remote technical field if prompted to do so, for example by a statement in the prior art document about a relationship between materials used in the field of that document and in a remote field (**T560/89** hn, r.5.2; G-VII,3).

A number of examples are listed in G-VII, Annex 1 of inventions that lack an inventive step because they are combinations of the closest prior art with common general knowledge. If, for example, the invention relates to a particular building structure made of aluminium and the closest prior art discloses the same building structure and says that it should be made of a light-weight metal, then the invention is obvious since the skilled person knows from common general knowledge that aluminium is a light-weight metal. Such an invention may be described as the use of a known material (e.g. aluminium) on the basis of its known properties (e.g. as a lightweight building material) in a known manner (e.g. to make a building structure) – 'similar use', **T130/89.** In the absence of any unexpected effect, the mere substitution of an element by another element known to have a relevant equivalent property is not inventive (**T213/87**). In deciding whether a new use of a measure in a specific field is obvious, where another use of the measure is known in the same field, the problems to be solved by the use of this measure, both in the case to be decided and in the known case, must be taken into account (**T39/82** hn). If there is no fundamental difference between the two problems, there is no inventive step (**T142/84** r.8.2).

An example is given in G-VIII, Annex 1 of an invention involving an inventive step, the features of which result from the combination of a second prior art teaching with the closest prior art. The closest prior art is a known gas holder. The invention involves the use of a device with the gas holder that allows it to rise and fall without the need for an external guiding framework. A similar device was already known to be of use for supporting a floating dock. However, the device needed to be specifically modified in order to overcome unexpected difficulties encountered in its use with a gas holder. It seems from the way this example is presented that the use of the device with a floating dock would be seen as a use in a neighbouring technical field and the invention might have been obvious were it not the case that the two teachings were not compatible. An example of a routine combination of prior art teachings is one in which the yield of a chemical process is increased by employing a modification which is known to increase yield (**T199/84, T132/86**).

Two examples are given in G-VII, Annex 2 of inventions involving the combination of a second prior art teaching with the closest prior art, one being obvious and the other non-obvious. In the first case, the invention relates to a machine that makes sausages in a single step by using a mincing machine and a filling machine side by side. The closest prior art is the mincing machine and the second prior art document discloses the filling machine. The invention is obvious since the two machines are compatible and are merely carrying out their known functions individually. In the second case, the invention is a painkilling drug comprising a compound known to be a painkiller and a compound known to be a sedative. The use of the sedative makes the painkilling compound more effective. The closest prior art is the known painkiller and the second prior art document discloses the sedative. The combination is not obvious since the skilled person, seeking to enhance the activity of the painkiller, would not combine it with a second compound not known to have any painkilling activity.

3.3.3 *Routine work and optimisation*

The skilled person is in possession of the means and the capacity for routine work and experimentation (G-VII,3). Such expertise can be derived from the common general knowledge. If an invention arises from the routine development or optimisation of the closest prior art, then it will lack an inventive step. However, the skilled person will only carry out routine work or experimentation if there is a reasonable expectation of some improvement or advantage (**T2/83**; CLBA I.D.7.1).

Routine work includes workshop modifications, such as a simple extrapolation from known data, choosing parameter values from a limited range of possibilities by routine experimentation and the application of normal design procedures. An example of routine optimisation is the optimisation of two parameters in a device by simultaneously solving two known equations in order to find an acceptable compromise (**T36/82**). Conducting routine experiments such as trial-and-error experimentation within the limits of the common general knowledge cannot lead to an invention (**T104/92**, varying proportions of polymers in laminate). See G-VII, Annex 3.1(ii) and (iii) for examples of obvious design procedures and extrapolation.

The recognition of a problem while conducting routine experiments does not contribute to inventive step (**T532/88** r.3.2, established case law).

Starting from the amorphous form of a pharmaceutically active compound as prior art, it is obvious to try and make a crystalline form of the same compound because the skilled person in the field of pharmaceutical drug development will routinely screen for polymorphs (**T777/08** hn). An inventive step can only be acknowledged if a prejudice has been overcome or if the claimed crystalline form has unexpected properties.

The determination of the optimum dosage regimen required to achieve a known therapeutic effect can sometimes be considered to be routine experimentation (**T237/15** r.4.6.1).

The skilled person will only carry out experiments over a range of parameter values if there is a reasonable expectation of some specific improvement or advantage. For example, a chemical manufacturing process may be known to have an increasing yield for temperatures in a range from 20 °C to 120 °C. The skilled person facing the problem of selecting a temperature providing a high yield will select a temperature near 120 °C. The skilled person will not carry out experiments to determine the yield over the temperature range, because the skilled person does not have a reasonable expectation of a higher yield other than at the highest temperature. Hence, the skilled person will not find any sub-range having an unexpectedly high yield unless there is a pointer toward such a sub-range.

The routine optimisation of the value of a parameter is a standard task for a skilled person. The result of such optimisation is obvious (G-VII, Annex 3.1(iii)) unless an unexpected effect is produced (G-VII, Annex 3.2(i)). Hence, it was obvious to optimise the value of a physical parameter to achieve a compromise acceptable for the intended use, where two effects had contrary dependence on the value (**T410/87** r.3.4). Similarly, the simultaneous optimisation of a number of lens properties leading to a quality formula was obvious (**T263/86**). The concurrent optimisation of two parameters by the simultaneous solution of two known equations expressing the parameters was obvious for the skilled person in a case where the prior art suggested that this calculation might give favourable results (**T36/82**).

3.3.4 Selection invention

Whether or not it is regarded as obvious to make a certain selection from a known set or a range depends on the presence of an unexpected technical effect associated with the selection, i.e. the selection must be associated with a particular technical effect and there must be no hint to lead the skilled person to make that selection (**T2623/11** r.4.2). In the absence of such an unexpected effect, the selection is obvious to a skilled person. In a case in which the invention results from a selection among a number of known and equally likely possibilities, the could-would approach does not normally apply, and a separate pointer is not required (**T894/19**).

For example, if an invention resides in selecting a specific compound from a known genus of compounds, the selection will be obvious if the selected compound only has properties which were already known to apply to the genus as a whole (G-VII, Annex 3.1(iv)). Such a selection from a set of known suitable compounds amounts to an arbitrary choice and does not involve an inventive step (**T939/92** r.2.5.3; **T967/97** hn). However, the selection is not obvious if the selected compound has unexpected advantages; a skilled person has no pointer to such a compound (see G-VII, Annex 3.2(ii) for an example).

The selection of a sub-range of values from a known range of values for a parameter in a process or device is within the normal abilities of the skilled person if the properties associated with the sub-range are expected based on the prior art (see G-VII, Annex 3.1(ii) for an example). However, if the properties associated with the sub-range are unexpected, the skilled person will not be guided to this sub-range. In that case, the selection of the sub-range is not obvious (see G-VII, Annex 3.2(i) for an example).

The criterion of 'seriously contemplating' in relation to the novelty test for overlapping ranges (see **Art.54(1):6**) should not be confused with the criteria applied in the assessment of inventive step. The former criterion is based on technical feasibility, whereas the presence of an inventive step depends on whether the skilled person would have selected the sub-range claimed in the expectation of some improvement or advantage. (G-VII,12)

3.3.5 Surprising effect – bonus effect

A surprising effect can be regarded as an indication of an inventive step (**T181/82** hn.I) and this is commonly encountered in the field of chemistry (see **Art.56:5**).

However, a surprising effect does not justify the recognition of an inventive step if the skilled person would have been motivated to make the invention because another advantageous effect could be achieved by combining prior art teachings in a straightforward manner or because the skilled person was in any case obliged to adopt a certain solution (**T21/81**; **T69/83**). In these cases, the surprising effect is merely a bonus effect. For example, if the state of the art already recommends a specific measure to improve the resistance to wear of an electric relay, an additional advantageous effect (e.g. that the measure causes the relay to produce a chatter before the end of its life) will not make the measure inventive (**T21/81**). This is the case even if the new effect is unforeseen in the prior art.

An enhanced effect cannot be relied upon as evidence of an inventive step if it is observed when conducting obvious tests (**T296/87** r.8.4, obvious to test which enantiomer in a racemate is more active).

Similarly, an additional, surprising effect occurring in a 'one-way street' situation is not an indication of an inventive step (**T192/82** hn.2; G-VII,10.2). In a 'one-way street' situation the skilled person has only one available approach for modifying the closest prior art to choose from.

3.3.6 *Teaching away*

The skilled person is subject to prejudices. A prejudice that might have diverted the skilled person away from an alleged invention may indicate the presence of an inventive step in relation to an invention that rejects such a prejudice. Applicants frequently argue that the skilled person would have been subject to a prejudice which teaches away from a claimed invention, but such arguments are often unsuccessful (see CLBA I. D.10.2).

A prejudice must reflect the common thinking in the relevant technical field. A single opinion should not be taken in isolation; the whole of the relevant prior art should be taken into consideration to gauge the common thinking. A single statement in a prior art patent, stating that a claimed invention is not realisable, does not create a prejudice (**T206/83**). Such a statement is not necessarily representative of the general thinking in the field and the disclosure of the prior art patent may be based on special premises or on the idiosyncratic view of the drafter (**T19/81**). A prejudice may, however, sometimes be based on a significant scientific publication (**T148/83**) or a specialised manual (**T18/81** r.8). A standard textbook is also accepted as representing the opinion of the skilled person (**T19/81**, **T104/83**). See G-VII, Annex 4 for an example of a prejudice.

A party who wishes to rely on a prejudice has the onus of demonstrating its existence (**T119/82** r.14; **T48/86** r.4.2.3). A high standard of proof is required (**T1989/08**).

3.3.7 *Hindsight*

When assessing obviousness under **Art.56**, the use of hindsight (sometimes referred to as an ex post facto analysis) is to be avoided wherever possible.

Avoiding hindsight is most crucial when assessing obviousness in the last step of the problem-solution approach. There is always a risk that, having used the disclosure of the application as a starting point to identify documents disclosing the features of the invention, it will seem obvious in hindsight that a skilled person could have made the invention by combining the features disclosed in these documents (**T564/89**, r.5.5). This is particularly the case when the means used to solve the objective technical problem are straightforward.

To avoid a hindsight view, the could-would approach insists that there must be a motivation in the prior art that justifies the fact that the skilled person would indeed have combined relevant features to make the invention (G-VII,5.3; **T414/98** r.6.1). If an invention is associated with a technical advantage which was not appreciated in the prior art and is related to the use of one of the distinguishing features of the claim, any finding of obviousness could well be biased by a hindsight view (G-VII,8). Furthermore, the prior art must be read in an objective manner and technical terms must be given their normal meaning without being influenced by the invention concerned (**T645/92**; **T970/00** hn). The interpretation of prior art documents should not be influenced by the problem solved by the invention if that problem was not appreciated in those documents (**T5/81** r.11).

Obviousness under **Art.56** is to be assessed on the basis of the state of the art, including everything known up until the end of the day before the effective date of the claimed invention. Nothing that was made available to the public on or after the effective date is to be taken into account. In particular, the disclosure of the patent application or patent under examination and any data filed by the applicant or proprietor in proceedings before the EPO is to be ignored. Thus, obviousness is to be considered without the use of any hindsight (G-VII,8).

Using knowledge of the invention in the first step of the problem-solution approach is, however, unavoidable (**T1087/15**). The disclosure of the application as filed and the features and effects of the claimed invention must be used to identify the relevant prior art and, in particular, the closest prior art. The use of hindsight at this point is nevertheless minimised by making an objective assessment of the closest prior art and giving more weight to prior art embodiments that were conceived for the same purpose as the claimed invention rather than embodiments simply having the most features in common (**T730/96**, r.2.1; **T870/96** r.4,1).

Hindsight must also be avoided in the second step of the problem-solution approach. The objective technical problem must be formulated so as not to contain any pointer to the claimed solution (see **Art.56:3.2**).

3.4 PARTIAL PROBLEMS

Sometimes, it is not appropriate to use the problem-solution approach to assess the obviousness of a claimed invention as a whole; it is more appropriate to conduct a problem-solution analysis for each of several distinguishing features separately. In such as case, a number of partial problems are derived and assessed independently.

An invention is based on partial problems if it contains two or more sets of features conferring novelty over the closest prior art, each relating to a solution to a different problem, without any interaction between these two sets of features that brings about a technical effect in excess of the sum of their individual effects, the said sets of features being merely juxtaposed (**T389/86** r.4.2; G-VII,5.2, G-VII,6, G-VII,7).

For example, consider an invention concerning a door comprising a profile surrounded on all sides with PVC skin foam. A first partial problem may be to reinforce the edges of the foam, a second partial problem may be to improve the aesthetic appearance of the door. If the two sets of features in the claim solving these two partial problems (applying a strong cover layer on the edges and imprinting a wood-like profile on the foam) do not have any functional reciprocity then they are merely juxtaposed and may be considered separately (**T130/89**). Another example is presented in **T552/89**, in which the objective problem comprised two partial problems, the first partial problem being solved by combining the closest prior art with a second document and the second partial problem being solved by combining the closest prior art with a workshop modification of the teaching of a third document; the invention was therefore obvious.

In these cases, the assessment of inventive step involves carrying out the problem-solution approach twice, once for each partial problem, and a different piece of prior art can be combined with the closest prior art in each case (**T389/86**; G-VII,6). The invention is not obvious if the solution to at least one of these partial problems involves an inventive step (**T130/89**).

Partial problems may also arise in opposition proceedings when a claim covers different embodiments that do not have unity of invention (**T314/99**). It is not possible to object under **Art.82** that a patent lacks unity of invention (**G1/91**). In such a case, the problem-solution approach may need to be applied separately to each embodiment.

4 Mixed-type inventions

Inventions including a mixture of technical and non-technical features can be referred to as mixed or mixed-type inventions (**G1/19** r.30(f), G-VII,5.4). In particular, computer-implemented inventions are often mixed-type inventions (see **Art.52(2):6**). Non-technical features are those that would be considered excluded from patentability under **Art.52(2)** (G-II,2). In general, only features that contribute to the technical character of the invention may be taken into account when assessing inventive step. Non-technical features do not contribute to the technical character of the invention unless such features contribute to producing a technical effect serving a technical purpose in the context of the invention. Therefore, non-technical features, to the extent that they do not interact with the technical subject-matter of the claim to solve a technical problem, are ignored in assessing inventive step (**G1/19** r.30(f)). In particular, where a claim refers to an aim to be achieved in a non-technical field, this aim may legitimately appear in the formulation of the problem as part of the framework of the objective technical problem (**T641/00** Comvik r.7).

Assessment of patentability of mixed-type inventions can be done via the so-called two-hurdle approach (**G1/19** r.37, G-II,2). The first hurdle is whether the claimed subject-matter can be considered an invention in the sense of **Art.52(2)**, this is the so-called patent eligibility hurdle (**Art.52(2):1**). The second hurdle considers inventive step of the claim as a whole, typically by applying the 'Comvik approach' set out in and named after **T641/00**. This approach is a particular implementation of the problem-solution approach originally proposed for evaluation of inventive step of computer-implemented inventions (**G1/19** r.34). Comvik approach has proved to be popular, and is currently used for most mixed-type inventions. The non-technical aim of the invention is used as a constraint (**T641/00** Comvik hn.1, 2; **G1/19** r.31) and the non-technical features are used as a requirements specification for the skilled person (**T1082/13** hn. 2, 3). A requirements specification can be understood as the non-technical instruction that the skilled person receives when they are tasked with solving the objective technical problem.

4.1 COMVIK APPROACH

According to the Comvik approach, any non-technical features of a claim may be incorporated into an aim to be achieved in a non-technical field, unless the features interact with technical features of the claim in a way that they produce a further technical effect (**T641/00**). Subsequently, this aim, including the non-technical features of the claim, is presented to the skilled person in the form of a requirements specification, and the skilled person is charged with the task and objective technical problem of implementing a technical solution that would achieve the stated aim. Consequently, the question of whether the skilled person would arrive at the non-technical features while solving the technical problem does not arise. The relevant question for obviousness is whether it would be obvious for the skilled person to implement a technical solution corresponding to the claimed subject-matter (**T351/19**).

The Guidelines propose the following steps for implementing the problem-solution approach in case of claims involving non-technical features, following the Comvik approach (G-VII,5.4):

i) Prima facie assessment of the technical character of each claim feature (see e.g. **T172/03** r.11). If there are no features possessing technical character, then there is no invention within the meaning of **Art.52(1)**, i.e. the claim fails the first patentability hurdle. In practice, this step often translates to identifying any technical means used as part of the claim features.
ii) Selection of the closest prior art based on the claim features possessing technical character as identified in step (i).
iii) Identification of the difference(s), that is, claim features differing from the closest prior art and the associated technical effects in the context of the entire claim.

Care should be taken to avoid missing any feature that might contribute to the technical character of the claim, for example by loosely paraphrasing the wording of the claim (**T756/06** r.6). A non-technical feature may interact with other features so as to produce a technical effect (**T154/04** r.13). The more thorough assessment of the technical contribution of features carried out in step (iii) may reveal that a feature considered in step (i) to be prima facie not contributing to the technical character of the invention, does in fact make such a contribution, or vice versa. In such cases, the selection of the closest prior art in step (ii) may have to be revised.

The outcome of step (iii) is one of the following:

(a) There are no differences compared to the prior art and a novelty objection is raised. Note, that the Guidelines suggest that a non-technical feature can make a claim novel. However, some case law holds that novelty can only be established on the basis of a technical feature of an invention (**T154/04** r.14, 15; **G1/19** r.30(f)).

(b) The difference(s) does not make a technical contribution (in practice, this would amount to the difference(s) not giving rise to any technical effect) and an inventive step objection is raised.

(c) The difference(s) makes a technical contribution. Any identified technical effect must be derivable from the application as filed when considered in the light of the closest prior art and must be achieved over the whole scope of the claim, i.e. by substantially all embodiments encompassed by the claim (G-VII,5.4.1).

In the case of outcome (c), the objective technical problem is formulated based on the technical effect(s) of the difference(s). Any distinguishing feature that does not make a technical contribution and any non-technical effect achieved by the claimed features as a whole may be used in the formulation of the problem, as part of what is 'given' to the skilled person. This is not considered hindsight because the rule of not including features of the solution in the problem applies only to features that make a technical contribution (**T641/00** hn.2; **T1461/12**; G-VII,5.4.1).

Some examples of applying the Comvik approach are provided in G-VII,5.4.2, as well as in the discussion under **Art.56:4.4**.

Once the objective technical problem is formulated, the Comvik approach generally follows the standard problem-solution approach. That is, there is a consideration of whether the skilled person, faced with the formulated problem, would arrive at the claimed solution in an obvious manner.

For example, in **T1225/19**, the invention was a computer-implemented method of reminding a user about a task that required the presence of another person when that other person was nearby the user, using a location-sharing service. The board essentially analysed that the following purely administrative business scheme is given to a software programmer as the technically skilled person to implement on a mobile device (smartphone): 'please remind the user of an action when a contact which is involved in the action is or will be close to the user, to realise the action'. Having this business scheme in hand, the software programmer has to solve the objective technical problem of providing the computer implementation and automation of this business scheme in the device. The board found that the technical solution as defined in the claim, including the use of a location-sharing service, neither called for a particular technical implementation nor provided a further technical effect beyond the straightforward computer implementation. Hence, the claim was not inventive.

As a further example, in **T505/18**, the invention pertained to a navigation system for a vehicle with a display for showing advertisements. The distinguishing feature of 'stopping output of an advertisement while a vehicle is moving close to an intersection' was considered to give rise to a technical effect of improved safety in a vehicle navigation system. The objective technical problem was then formulated as adapting the navigation system of the closest prior art document to improve driving safety. The closest prior art document was considered to teach away from the stated goal because its aim was to provide advertisements at any point during the vehicle operation. In particular, safety was not considered at all. Therefore, the claim was inventive.

4.2 BUSINESS METHODS

Inventive step of claims directed towards business methods or problems in the fields of doing business may be assessed without directly using the Comvik approach. Instead, one may take the business scenario corresponding to the non-technical features as the starting point for the problem-solution approach (**T1049/19**). For example, in **T912/05**, the board agreed with the applicant that explicitly separating claim features possessing technical character from those that do not is not necessary for inventive step assessment. Instead, the board considered the features of the claim directly contributing to the non-technical object to be achieved (i.e. notifying a recipient of the availability of a mail piece and receiving instructions concerning its delivery) as the task to be implemented by the skilled person. This approach has been further formalised in **T1463/11**, where the notional business person was introduced by the board as a counterpart to the skilled person. Whereas the skilled person is a fictional expert in a particular technical field (e.g. an engineer or a scientist), the notional business person is a fictional expert in the underlying business field (e.g. an accountant or a business consultant). Although the notional business person is not an expert in any technical field, the extent of their general knowledge should not be artificially restricted. Particularly, the notional business person knows that the business-related requirements specification can be implemented on a computer system, including a distributed one (**T1082/13** r.4.8). Collaboration between the notional business person and the skilled person is not seen as necessary to automate a particular business process (**T1902/13** r.3.3).

The areas of expertise and therefore the tasks of the notional business person and the skilled person do not overlap, since otherwise the skilled person would be providing input in the non-technical area. Therefore, the notional business person provides a complete business specification to be implemented by the skilled person. Reframing the non-technical features of the claim as business constraints can be a useful approach to ensure that the entire technical contribution of the invention is considered for establishing inventive step. While a problem of the type 'implement the business requirement' will normally never lead to an allowable claim on its own, this formulation can help to establish what is to be implemented by the skilled person. If this implementation is found to have at least one technical effect, the problem can be reformulated as 'achieving said technical effect of the implementation'. (**T144/11** r.2.7-2.8)

Correctly separating the features associated with the tasks of the notional business person and those of the skilled person is critical for inventive step assessment, since the former can be used as part of the problem formulation, while the latter contribute to inventive step. This analysis can lead to positive inventive step assessment even for inventions concerned with a purpose in a non-technical field. For example, the underlying invention of **T2314/16** was about reward distribution to influencers in an affiliate marketing scheme, which lies in a non-technical field of marketing. However, the claim in question included features concerning allocation of influencers to partial image areas of an advertisement display area on a webpage. This task required knowledge of website design and was considered to be within the scope of the skilled person's work and was therefore part of the solution to the technical problem of implementation of the reward distribution. The claims were subsequently deemed to involve an inventive step.

Caution should be exercised to not conflate features implemented by the skilled person with features that automatically give rise to a technical effect. Even though a ' technical expert' might be responsible for devising certain features of the invention, this is only a necessary condition for considering whether those features could give rise to a technical effect, but not a sufficient one (**T1998/22**, r.11.6).

4.3 TECHNICAL EFFECTS OF MIXED-TYPE INVENTIONS

Any effect that is technical and goes beyond the normal electrical interactions within the computer on which a computer-implemented method is carried out may be considered when assessing inventive step (**G1/19** r.51). How such effects are to be distinguished from normal interactions with the computer is discussed extensively in G-II,3.6.1 to 3.6.4. See also discussion under **Art.52(2):6**.

Processor load balancing and database technology are generally considered to be technical (G-II,3.6.4); software programming and pure linguistics are generally considered to be non-technical (**T817/16** r.3.13).

The boards of appeal have identified a few arguments used by applicants that are typically unsuccessful (so-called fallacies):

- The broken technical chain fallacy: a final technical effect in a chain of technical effects cannot be used to establish an overall technical effect if it is conditional on actions, preferences or mental activities of a user. In other words, a chain of technicality is broken by a non-technical element, that is, the user. This fallacy can be prevalent in inventions related to graphical user interfaces (GUIs) since they often involve human-computer interaction. (**T1741/08**; **T1670/07**).
- The non-technical prejudice fallacy: attempts to argue the presence of inventive step based on an asserted prejudice in the prior art against the non-technical features of the claim. Such prejudice cannot be invoked because the non-technical features are integrated into the formulation of the objective technical problem under the Comvik approach (**T1670/07**).
- The technical leakage fallacy: defending inventive step based on the implementation of non-technical method features by technical means. This 'leakage' of the technical elements into the non-technical aim or purpose of the claim is not sufficient to imbue technicality onto the entire method (**T1670/07**).
- The software implementation fallacy: the argument that modifying software causes a modified behaviour of the computer. However, modifying software does not automatically lead to a 'further' technical effect, and more often than not corresponds to the normal functioning of the computer (**T1755/10**).

Features pertaining to a mathematical method (algorithm) may make a technical contribution if the mathematical method is applied to a particular technical aim or use case and/or is adapted to a specific technical implementation (e.g. specific hardware) in the context of the claim. If steps of a mathematical method are used to derive or predict the physical state of an existing real object based on the measurement of physical properties of that object, as in the case of indirect measurements, those steps make a technical contribution regardless of what use is made of the results (G-II,3.3 includes examples of technical contributions made by mathematical methods). Technical effects may be harder to come by for algorithms aimed at natural language processing. For example, suggesting query terms that are semantically close to different meanings of an input term was deemed a cognitive or linguistic issue and did not give rise to a credible technical effect (**T2418/12** r.3.2).

Credible technical effects should be objective and not user-dependent (as they would otherwise lead to the broken technical chain fallacy). For example, a single-drag gesture enabling specific actions on a touchscreen (i.e. dragging without lifting the finger) could simplify a user's operations. This simplification is in principle a technical effect, but its usefulness depends on subjective user preferences. Such an effect was not deemed credible and objective and was therefore not used as basis for an objective technical problem. (**T1958/13** r.2.2.5)

An inventive step can also be based on features pertaining to the calculation of the state of a virtual game world if the features concern the internal functioning of the computer system (G-II,3.5.2). For example, using contact determination points on the player character that overlapped with an object was considered to be a computationally effective and efficient approach to determine the collision direction (**T1225/10** r.6.2.2). The technical effect was in the specific way of determining a display state based on selected data, and not an inevitable result of programming the game rules per se.

The assessment of inventive step in the field of computer-implemented simulations according to the Comvik approach was considered in **G1/19**. Such methods can, for the purpose of assessing inventive step, solve a technical problem by producing a technical effect going beyond the simulation's implementation on a computer. For that assessment, it is not a sufficient condition that the simulation is based, in whole or in part, on technical principles underlying the simulated system or process (**G1/19** hn.1, hn.2; G-II,3.3.2). Calculated numerical data reflecting the physical behaviour of a system modelled in a computer cannot usually establish the technical character of an invention even if the calculated behaviour adequately reflects the behaviour of a real system underlying the simulation. Only in exceptional cases may such calculated effects be considered implied technical effects (**G1/19** r.128). If a claimed process results in a set of numerical values, it depends on the further use of such data whether a technical effect resulting from that further use can be considered in the assessment of inventive step. If such further use is not, at least implicitly, specified in the claim, it will be disregarded for this purpose (**G1/19** r.124).

4.4 EXAMPLES OF MIXED-TYPE INVENTIONS

G-VII,5.4.2 provides several examples illustrating the Comvik approach. **T931/95** considered a claim relating to a conventional computer system for controlling an improved pension benefits plan. The only novel feature in the claim was an improvement of the pension plan. The improvement of the pension plan could not contribute to an inventive step because the improvement lay in the non-technical field of economics. The only technical contribution was the programming of the computer system. The inventive step was assessed from the point of view of a programmer as the skilled person, having knowledge of the desired improved pension benefits plan and the underlying schemes of information processing. The claim did not involve an inventive step, since the technical features of the apparatus claimed were functionally defined by known steps of information processing and the use of computer systems was known in the economic sector. (**T931/95** r.8)

Additionally, G-II,3 considers exclusions from patentability under **Art.52(2)** and (3) and discusses technical contributions of excluded features within inventive step assessment. Some particularly relevant examples of mixed-type inventions, e.g. those concerned with mathematical methods, machine learning and simulations, are provided in section G-II,3.3 and its two subsections. Care should be taken when citing those examples because some do not include any underlying case law (either as a way to simplify them conceptually or as plausible examples without specific existing case law). For example, **T1741/22** disagrees with the example 'providing a medical diagnosis by an automated system processing physiological measurements' listed in section G-II,3.3 as providing a technical contribution. CLBA I.D.9.2 is an extensive section dealing with the problem-solution approach when applied to mixed-type inventions and including many examples directly backed by case law.

5 **Inventions in the fields of chemistry and biotechnology**

Inventions in the fields of chemistry and biotechnology often concern new compounds, be they small organic compounds or large biopolymers such as proteins and nucleic acids. A structural difference in a compound compared to the prior art has no intrinsic value or significance for the assessment of inventive step if it does not manifest itself in a valuable property in the widest sense, i.e. an effect or an increase in the potency of an effect (**T22/82** r.6). Compounds must therefore have some activity to be patentable. This activity, e.g. a biological activity as a pharmaceutical or an agrochemical, will correlate with the structural features of the compound. When the structure of a prior art compound is modified, it is not possible a priori to predict what the effect of that structural change will be on activity. Inventions in these fields also often involve new uses of known compounds, for instance the use of a compound known to be useful in the treatment of a disease X in the treatment of a different disease Y.

In the case of a new compound having a specific activity or effect underlying the objective technical problem solved, it is therefore necessary to identify the closest known compound having the same or a similar effect and ask whether the skilled person would have expected the claimed compound to have that activity or effect in view of the structural changes made (**T20/83**). Such an expectation can only arise if there is a teaching in the closest prior art, the common general knowledge or a second document that the structural differences are so small that they would have no bearing on the properties underlying the technical problem (**T852/91** r.8.2). General concepts of bioisosterism are not sufficient to deny an inventive step; there must be a specific teaching relevant to the class of compounds concerned (**T643/96** r.4.2.3.5). The activity on which an inventive step is based may be the same activity found in the closest prior art (provision of a further compound with the same activity) or a higher level of activity (provision of a more potent compound). A higher level of activity must be demonstrated by comparative tests and must be shown convincingly to have its origin in the characterising feature(s) of the invention (**T181/82** r.3; **T197/86**; G-VII,10.2). This means that the comparative data must be generated using the most structurally similar embodiment in the prior art – such an embodiment must be specifically rather than notionally disclosed (**T181/82** hn.2). Furthermore, such comparative data must be reproducible on the basis of information supplied by the party concerned so that other parties can verify its accuracy (**T494/99** and other decisions cited in CLBA I.D.4.3.2).

If a class of chemical compounds is being claimed, the variance of structure and function must also be taken into account in assessing whether the alleged technical problem has been solved or not: it must be credible that substantially all the claimed compounds have the technical effect relied upon (**T939/92** hn.II, r.2.6). This usually means that a range of compounds falling across the scope of the claim must be shown to be active. The provision of further compounds without any activity is not considered to be inventive.

A claim to a new compound or composition that is useful in therapy does not have to be limited to its use in specific indications, even though as a rule only certain specific activities are taught in the description (**T128/82** r.10). The compound can be claimed per se. Accordingly, an inventive step for a compound or composition claim cannot be denied on the ground that only certain specific uses are taught in the description; similarly no objection of lack of support under **Art.84** can be raised on this basis.

Biological systems are complicated and it is often difficult to predict whether a particular approach in the field of biotechnology will be successful. In assessing the obviousness of such inventions, the question is often posed as to whether the skilled person would have had a reasonable expectation of success when trying to solve the objective technical problem using the claimed invention (CLBA I.D.7.1 and cases cited therein, particularly **T60/89**). If the skilled person must make non-trivial decisions and apply technical skill to reach the claimed solution, the skilled person does not have a reasonable expectation of success (G-VII,13). A reasonable expectation of success may exist even if the results are not clearly predictable (strong incentive to try, **T149/93**). On the other hand, a reasonable expectation of success should not be confused with an understandable 'hope to succeed' (**T296/93**). Whether there is an expectation of success must be considered by scientifically evaluating the facts at hand (**T207/94**).

In certain situations, however, when there was at least no reason to expect failure, the boards have declined to take into account whether a reasonable expectation of success existed and instead considered that the skilled person would adopt a 'try and see' attitude (see CLBA I.D.7.2). This is particularly the case when the invention is based on the application of a known technique, without modification, in a similar situation (e.g. **T333/97**, application of a known anti-sense technique in plant cells; **T377/95**, use of a protein known to generate an immunological response as a protective vaccine; **T1045/98**, testing of a known antibody in an in vitro mouse model on the basis of promising in vitro results). However, the boards have found that such a 'try and see' approach is not usually appropriate when testing on human beings in the context of clinical trials is concerned (e.g. **T1011/17**).

An inventive step for a combination of two known compounds having a biological activity is usually assessed on the basis of whether the combination produces an unpredicted synergistic effect rather than an expected additive effect (**T1814/11**).

Inventions in the field of chemistry frequently concern processes for making compounds. Such a process may be inventive on the basis of new process steps when the product is already known (inventive process) or may be inventive on the basis that the product is new and inventive (analogy process). New intermediates that form part of an inventive process for the preparation of a known compound involve an inventive step if they contribute to the surprising effects achieved by the process (**T22/82** hn.I; 'process effect'). The mere novelty of the intermediate may not be sufficient to impart inventive step; however, an inventive step may be acknowledged when the preparation of the intermediate or the further processing of the intermediate in the context of the process as a whole is inventive (**T163/84** hn; **T18/88**; **T648/88**).

T65/82 required that the intermediates in a non-inventive analogy process must provide a structural contribution to the end product and must be non-obvious when compared with both prior art close to the intermediates themselves and prior art close to the final products of the process.

6 Secondary indicators of inventive step

The EPO has identified secondary indicators (also known as indicia or indications) which can point to the presence of an inventive step. They can be used to strengthen or weaken arguments developed using the problem-solution approach. As their name indicates, their importance is secondary. The assessment of inventive step must primarily involve an assessment of the prior art through the eyes of a skilled person. Secondary indicators alone do not suffice to demonstrate the presence of an inventive step, though they may be one factor taken into account (**T24/81** r.15; **T181/82**; **T330/87** r.8.3). An overview of secondary indicators is given in CLBA I.D.10.

6.1 LONG-FELT NEED

If the closest prior art is very old, and there has been a long period of inactivity in the development of the art, this may be an indication of inventive step, provided that during this time an urgent need for solving the problem demonstrably existed (**T79/82** r.4; **T109/82** r.5.5; G-VII,10.3).

For example, if a long standing method is modified to become more expensive but less environmentally damaging, then the fact that the method has existed for a long time is no indication of inventive step if the new method was not used previously because of its cost and became attractive only recently in view of stricter environmental regulations (**T24/81**, steel production using carbon dioxide as a blowing gas instead of oxygen). An example of a long-felt need is the need to reduce the risk of an explosion in the mass manufacture of ethylene oxide (**T41/84**).

A fingertip-sized piece of waffle on a waffle with outer glazing solved a long-felt need to avoid smudgy fingers; the solution was simple but unprecedented (**T330/87**).

Overcoming a known disadvantage of a product that has been commercially successful for 20 years, in spite of its disadvantages, is an indication of inventive step (**T271/84** hn; **T165/85** r.8.7).

Seven years is regarded as a long period for a strongly felt need relating to health problems (**T106/84** r.8.6). Six years is regarded as a long time for a strongly felt need in a quickly developing technological field (**T145/84**). CLBA I.D.10.4 gives some examples in which periods of 11 to 80 years between publication of the prior art document and the filing of the application were regarded as secondary indicia in support of inventive step.

6.2 COMMERCIAL SUCCESS

Commercial success alone is not an indicator of inventive step but may become so when coupled with a long-felt need and evidence that the commercial success derives from technical progress underlying the invention rather than one or more other factors such as selling techniques and advertising (G-VII,10.3). Commercial success may play a larger role where an objective evaluation of the prior art has not provided a clear answer (**T1212/01** Viagra) and can reinforce a positive conclusion already reached through an analysis of the prior art (**T335/86**).

Commercial success therefore plays, at best, a minor role in the analysis of inventive step (**T91/83**, **T69/82**, **T270/84**). Examples of cases in which commercial success was taken into account as a secondary indicator of inventive step are **T677/91** and **T626/96**.

6.3 SIMPLE SOLUTION

Where a simple solution to a long-standing problem is developed without any sacrifice of quality, and it has escaped those working in the field in spite of considerable activity, the very simplicity of the invention may be a secondary indication of the presence of an inventive step (**T106/84** hn.2; **T229/85** r.7).

An example of a major improvement brought about by a simple innovation concerned a paper fastener in the form of an elongated hollow profile strip having a slit along its underside; a sheet of paper inserted into the slit was captured by glass spheres inside the hollow strip; the invention was the surface roughening of the glass spheres to improve the suspension of sheets of heavy paper (**T349/95**).

7 Problem inventions

A problem invention is based on the discovery of an unrecognised problem. The discovery may give rise to an inventive step even if the claimed solution is, once the problem has been identified, trivial and obvious (**T2/83** hn.I). A minimum requirement for a problem invention is that the problem must be clearly and unambiguously disclosed in the application as filed (**T971/92** r.3.7.1).

However, posing a problem does not represent a contribution to the inventive merits of the solution if the problem could have been posed by a skilled person (**T109/82** hn.I). The skilled person is assumed to be constantly occupied with the elimination of deficiencies and the achievement of improvements; such aims are inherently obvious (**T15/81** r.3). Problem inventions are therefore rarely recognised by the boards of appeal (see CLBA I.D.9.12) and as of 2010 they are no longer mentioned in the Guidelines (formerly in G-VII,9). **T764/12** and **T2321/15** are examples of decisions acknowledging an inventive step based on the discovery of a yet unrecognised problem.

The unrecognised problem cannot be used as the objective technical problem, because the unrecognised problem contains pointers to the solution, which is incompatible with the problem-solution approach. Instead, a broader objective technical problem should be formulated. For example, the objective technical problem can be to improve the reliable functioning of a device, where the unrecognised problem is that the malfunctioning is caused by a specific component of the device. When drafting the patent application, the previously unrecognised problem should be presented as part of the invention rather than being discussed in the section dealing with the prior art.

8 Interpretation of prior art documents

The technical disclosure in a prior art document should be considered in its entirety. It is not justified to isolate arbitrarily parts of such a document from their context in order to derive therefrom technical information which would be distinct from, or even in contradiction with, the integral teaching of the document (**T56/87** hn).

Prior art documents may contain errors which the skilled person may be able to interpret or ignore. When assessing the relevance of a document with a potential error, the following criteria can be applied:

1 If the skilled person can directly and unambiguously derive from the prior art document both that an error exists and that a single correction is applicable, the document is considered to contain the correction (**T591/90** modified by G-IV,9).

2 If the skilled person can directly and unambiguously derive from the prior art document that an error exists but is able to identify more than one possible correction, the part of the document containing the error is not taken into account (T422/07 r.5.2.2 modified by G-IV,9).

3 If the skilled person cannot directly and unambiguously derive from the prior art document that an error exists, the literal disclosure is taken into account (G-IV,9).

Art. 57 Industrial application

An invention shall be considered as susceptible of industrial application if it can be made or used in any kind of industry, including agriculture.

1 **Industry**

'Industry' should be understood in a broad sense as including any physical activity having a technical character (G-III,1). The concept of 'industry' implies that an activity is carried out continuously, independently and for financial gain (**T144/83** r.5). Industrial application does not include application in a private and personal sphere (see e.g. **T74/93**, method of contraception to be used in the private sphere). However, if a method can be carried out as a paid service then it is industrially applicable (see **T1165/97** hn, distinguishing **T74/93** on the facts). Neither does industrial application include a commercial or financial application (**T953/94**). It should be noted, nevertheless, that a product for use in a non-industrial application, such as a paint brush for use in creating art, may be industrially manufactured and hence is susceptible of industrial application.

Under EPC1973, medical treatments were considered to lack industrial applicability under Art.52(4) EPC1973. Under EPC2000 this legal fiction no longer applies, and these activities are now considered industrially applicable but excluded from patentability on socio-ethical grounds under **Art.53(c)**.

Agriculture is specifically mentioned in **Art.57** to clarify the position of the EPC in view of diverging national laws at the time the Convention was drafted (Empel §116).

2 **Manufacturability and industrial application**

Industrial applicability requires that the invention can be manufactured or used, which entails that the invention is sufficiently disclosed (**Art.83**) and does not violate physical laws. A claim which includes perpetual motion as the intended function or purpose of the invention is not industrially applicable since it violates physical laws and will be objected to under **Art.83** and **Art.57**. However, a perpetual motion machine claimed merely as a device having a particular construction is only objectionable under **Art.83** according to G-III,1 (see also **T85/82** and F-III,3).

A perpetual motion machine is an example of an invention based on an erroneous physical theory. Patentability requires that where an invention is based on a specific theory, the theory must be valid or, where validity has not yet been proven, it must have a reasonable prospect of being proven to be valid. Acknowledgement of the theory by the scientific community at large may be regarded as such proof.

The mere fact that a claimed substance (e.g. a polypeptide or protein) can be produced in industry does not necessarily mean that the requirements of **Art.57** are fulfilled. An additional requirement is that there is some profitable use for which the substance can be employed (**T870/04** hn). The practical exploitation of the substance, if not self-evident, must be directly derivable from the application (**T898/05** hn.1) as understood by the skilled person at the filing date (**T1109/10** r.2). The indication of how to exploit the substance must have a sound and concrete technical basis and speculative indications of possible objectives that might be achievable by carrying out further research with the substance are insufficient (**T898/05** r.5; **T870/04** r.21).

The industrial application of an invention must be stated in the application if this is not obvious (**R.42(1)(f)**). The industrial application of a gene sequence is not regarded as self-evident and must be disclosed in the application (**R.29(3)**; F-II,4.9; G-III,4). A gene sequence is not a patentable invention in the absence of an indication of its function (G-III,4). The indication of the function must be substantial, specific and credible; a speculative use does not suffice (decision of the opposition division published in OJ 2002 p.293 r.11(ii)). See also **R.29(3):1**.

Although industrial applicability and the requirement for technical character are intimately related (**T854/90** r.2.1; G-III,1), they are not synonymous and constitute two distinct, non-equivalent requirements for a patentable invention under the EPC (**T953/94** r.3.11; **T619/02** r.2.6.2).

Chapter II *Persons entitled to apply for and obtain a European patent - Mention of the inventor*

Art. 58 Entitlement to file a European patent application

A European patent application may be filed by any natural or legal person, or any body equivalent to a legal person by virtue of the law governing it.

1 **Open filing system**
The EPC is an open filing system. Any person may file a European patent application, irrespective of their nationality and whether they have a residence or place of business in an EPC contracting state. In contrast, the PCT is a closed system (Art.9 PCT). For example, Argentinians living in Argentina may file a European patent application, whereas they may not file an international patent application, because Argentina is not a contracting state of the PCT. Because there is no such limitation under the EPC, the EPO can act as a designated office under the PCT giving EPC contracting states (especially those without substantive examination by the national patent office) the possibility of closing the 'national route' under the PCT (Art.45 PCT). The point was controversial during the drafting of the EPC (Empel §142)

A European patent application may be filed by any natural person (i.e. a human person) or legal person. What constitutes a legal person is a matter of national law. Even a natural person who has no legal capacity to act (for example due to age or illness) can file an application; the following steps must then be taken by a representative or guardian. The entitlement to the grant of the patent is governed by **Art.60(1)** and the requirement that certain applicants must be represented by a professional representative in the further procedure is governed by **Art.133**.

Art. 59 Multiple applicants

A European patent application may also be filed either by joint applicants or by two or more applicants designating different Contracting States.

1 **Multiple applicants**
A European application may be filed by one or more applicants according to **Art.58** and **Art.59**, respectively.

Art.59 distinguishes between joint applicants and applicants designating different contracting states. This implies that joint applicants are applicants designating the same contracting states (e.g. A and B are both an applicant for all contracting states). The possibility of filing an application by two or more applicants designating different contracting states (i.e., different applicants are listed for different contracting states) is in line with **Art.71**, which allows the transfer of an application for individual contracting states.

Art.59 requires that applicants designating the same contracting states act as joint applicants. Similarly, **Art.118** states that applicants designating different contracting states are regarded as joint applicants. Hence, in all cases in which there are two or more applicants, they are regarded as joint applicants.

Joint applicants have the procedural status of a single applicant and must act in common to maintain the unitary character of both the application and the procedure before the EPO (see **Art.118:1**). They cannot acquire a procedural status different from that of a single applicant because otherwise each of them could perform different and contradictory procedural acts (**J2/01** r.2.5.1). There will be one, uniform text of the application for the designated states resulting in uniform patent protection (see **Art.118:2** for exceptions).

The joint applicants may appoint one applicant or a representative as the common representative in the Request for Grant form (**R.41(3)**). Otherwise, the EPO applies **R.151** to appoint one of the applicants or a representative of an applicant as the common representative. The common representative is the single point of contact for the EPO.

When different applicants are specified for different designated states, **R.72** provides that the patent is granted for each designated state to the applicant(s) registered in respect of that state. See EP 0 166 725 for an example. However, any resulting unitary patent can only be transferred in respect of all the states in which the unitary patent has effect (Art.3(2) EU Regulation 1257/2012).

The order of naming the applicants in an application on the filing date may have certain consequences for any resulting unitary patent (**Ante UPR:4**).

Art. 60 Right to a European patent

1 **General**
The right to a patent belongs to the person who made the invention or to the successor in title of that person (**Art.60(1)**). When two or more persons independently make the same invention and file a patent application for it, the right to a patent belongs to the person who filed the first application (**Art.60(2)**). In proceedings before the EPO the applicant, who is not necessarily the person entitled to be granted a patent under **Art.60(1)**, is regarded as the entitled person (**Art.60(3)**).

Art. 60(1) The right to a European patent shall belong to the inventor or his successor in title. If the inventor is an employee, the right to a European patent shall be determined in accordance with the law of the State in which the employee is mainly employed; if the State in which the employee is mainly employed cannot be determined, the law to be applied shall be that of the State in which the employer has the place of business to which the employee is attached.

1 **Inventor**
Art.60(1) lays down as substantive law that the inventor or the successor in title of the inventor has the right to a European patent. If a patent application is filed by a person not having the right to a European patent for the invention, the entitled person (the inventor or the inventor's successor in title) can use the two-step procedure of **Art.61** as a remedy before the grant of the patent and any remedies under national law after grant (see also **Art.138(1)(e)**). The first step of the procedure is for the entitled person to begin an action in a court of a contracting stage. If successful, the judgment can be used in the second step to seek a remedy before the EPO under **Art.61**.

The concept of 'inventor' is a concept established by the EPC which must be interpreted uniformly and autonomously, i.e. uniformly for all EPC contracting states and not on the basis of national law. This is in line with the first sentence of **Art.60(1)**, which does not refer to national law (see **J8/20** r.4.2.2). On the other hand, **G3/92** r.3.4 suggested that the competent national court will apply one national law to settle a case concerning a claim to entitlement. Under both approaches, the court decision will have the same outcome for all EPC contracting states and serve as the basis for the further procedure before the EPO under **Art.61** if the national court judges the claimant to be entitled.

According to **J8/20**, an inventor must be a natural person (i.e. a human) and cannot be a machine having artificial intelligence. The EPO verifies that the inventor designated by the applicant is a natural person (A-III,5.1).

When the inventor is an employee, **Art.60(1)** states that the right to a patent must be determined in accordance with the law of the state in which the inventor is mainly employed or, if this state cannot be determined, in accordance with the law of the state in which the employer has the place of business to which the employee is attached. Hence, the law of an EPC state or non-EPC state may apply. Whether the employer or employee has the right to a patent is determined under the relevant national law. Where the inventor is an employee, Prot. Rec. **Art.4** and **Art.5** give specific rules to determine which court (or other authority of a contracting state) has jurisdiction to determine entitlement to the grant of a patent.

What constitutes a successor in title is not defined in the EPC. National law governs the question of whether a transfer (e.g., an assignment) of the right of **Art.60(1)** is valid or has occurred by operation of a contract, inheritance or other rule of law. A national court deciding on the issue will identify the applicable law according to their domestic provisions (**J8/20** r.4.2.2). The successor in title may be an employer, an assignee or an heir.

The moral right of the inventor to be acknowledged is established by **Art.62** and realised in **Art.81**, first sentence, **R.19** and **R.20**. If the applicant is not the inventor or is not the sole inventor, the applicant must indicate how the right to the European patent under **Art.60(1)** was obtained (**Art.81**, second sentence).

If two or more inventors jointly made an invention, each of them has the right to be mentioned under **Art.81** and each of them, or their successor in title, is entitled under **Art.60(1)** to become a co-applicant (using the procedure of **Art.61**) or a co-proprietor (using a procedure under national law). If the co-applicants do not appoint a common representative, the EPO will appoint a common representative under **R.151(2)** (see **Art.99(4)** for opposition proceedings). The co-applicants can arrange their internal legal arrangements themselves or a court can decide on these. National law may regulate the position of the co-proprietors in each designated state after the grant of the patent. For the case of an entitlement dispute concerning a patent application disclosing multiple inventions (e.g. embodiments) with different inventors, see **R.18**.

The EPO does not examine whether the applicant is entitled to the patent under **Art.60(1)** (**Art.60(3)**).

The entitlement to the patent under **Art.60(1)** and the property right in the application under **Art.71** are, in principle, distinct rights, with corresponding procedures under **Art.61** and **R.22**, respectively. For example, an applicant who lacks the entitlement to the patent may still assign the application (if there is no stay). Moreover, **Art.61** appears not directly applicable in case of a dispute about the validity of an assignment (see **R.22(3)**:2). However, a party who successfully claims entitlement in a national procedure and takes over the application under **Art.61(1)(a)** also becomes the owner of the application.

If the inventor has also filed a European patent application for the invention, the inventor may be able to invoke **Art.55** against any disclosures made and any prior rights filed by the non-entitled party.

Art. 60(2) If two or more persons have made an invention independently of each other, the right to a European patent therefor shall belong to the person whose European patent application has the earliest date of filing, provided that this first application has been published.

Art.93 Publication of a European patent application

1 **Transitional provision EPC2000**
The revised **Art.60** is applicable to applications filed on or after 13.12.2007, the date of entry into force of EPC2000 (OJ 2007 se4 EN p.58). See **Art.54(3):3**.

2 **First-to-file principle**
The provision reflects the first-to-file principle and is implemented by **Art.54(3)**. If two or more persons independently make the same invention and file a patent application for it, as a matter of principle, patent laws generally specify that only one patent can be granted, even if all applications are otherwise allowable. The EPC resolves this conflict between applications in **Art.54(3)** and **Art.60(2)**: the person who first files an application has the right to a patent and the later filed application must be novel over the first filed application, provided that the first filed application is published. Although this first-to-file principle puts an administrative burden on the inventor in having to file the application as soon as possible, the resulting patent system is less complex, gives more legal certainty and results in fewer cases of double patenting than a patent system based on the first-to-invent principle.

The person who files first will have the right to a patent only if the application is validly published under **Art.93**. If the application is withdrawn shortly before publication and is nevertheless published invalidly, it does not form a prior right under **Art.54(3)** (see **J5/81**).

The date of filing for the purposes of **Art.60(2)** is the priority date for applications validly claiming priority (**Art.89**).

Note that **Art.54(3)** also applies to multiple applications filed by the same applicant and to applications having the same inventor.

Two applications relating to the same subject-matter, with different applicants and filed on the same date, must be allowed to proceed as though the other does not exist (G-IV,5.4). See **Art.97(2):2** if the applications are filed by the same applicant.

Art. 60(3) In proceedings before the European Patent Office, the applicant shall be deemed to be entitled to exercise the right to a European patent.

1 **Assessment of the entitlement to the patent**
According to **Art.60(3)** the EPO assumes by way of a legal fiction that the applicant is entitled to exercise the right to a patent, i.e. the right mentioned in **Art.60(1)**; **Art.61** provides an exception if a national court decides that another person is entitled. Lack of entitlement is therefore neither a ground for refusal nor a ground for opposition.

The applicant on the filing date is the person identified in the Request for Grant form as the applicant (**R.41(2)(c)**; **Art.81**, second sentence); in the subsequent procedure the applicant is the applicant as indicated in the Register. Joint applicants are assumed to be entitled to exercise the right to a patent in common (**J2/01** r.2.5.1; see also **Art.59:1**).

The EPC attributes the entitlement to exercise the right to a patent to the applicant who may not necessarily be the person having the substantive right to the patent; note that the applicant is not mentioned in **Art.60(1)**. Even though, as a consequence of the legal fiction contained in **Art.60(3)**, a European patent application may as a matter of fact be filed by a person other than the inventor or the inventor's successor in title, contrary to the legal right of the latter, as a matter of law only the inventor or the inventor's successor in title is entitled to the grant of a European patent (**G3/92** r.2). The inventor or the inventor's successor in title can initiate national court proceedings, followed by the procedure of **Art.61** as a remedy.

According to **J2/01** r.2.6, the right to a patent in **Art.60(3)** is a formal, procedural right, which derives from the status of being the registered applicant, in contrast with the right to the patent in **Art.60(1)**, which is a substantive right. The distinction between the procedural right and the substantive right is deliberate and allows the EPO to disregard questions of entitlement in terms of substantive law. In fact, the EPO has no power to determine disputes regarding substantive entitlement (**G3/92** r.3). **Art.60(3)** allows the EPO to decide questions relating to procedural rights, such as the right to file a divisional application, by reference to the Register.

The legal fiction of **Art.60(3)** relieves the EPO from the need to investigate the substantive entitlement to the grant of a patent. When a person referred to in **Art.60(1)**, other than the applicant, successfully disputes the entitlement to a patent before a national court, the procedural status of the application at the EPO may be changed under the conditions provided in **Art.61**. (**J18/93** r.1)

Whilst having no jurisdiction to investigate entitlement, the EPO nevertheless may consider the question of party status in various scenarios. For example, the EPO may need to investigate whether party status has passed from one person to another as the result of a universal succession, e.g. as a result of the death of a natural person or the merger of two companies. The EPO may also have to consider whether to register a purported transfer of an application from one person to another. However, these are purely evidentiary matters and do not relate to entitlement in the sense of **Art.60(1)**.

Art. 61 European patent applications filed by non-entitled persons

1 General

Art.61 deals with the remedies available when a person other than the applicant is held by a national court to be the person entitled to the grant of a European patent. **R.14** and **R.16** specify a number of conditions which must be met for such remedies to become available. **R.16** also makes reference to the Protocol on Recognition, which lays down in Art.1(1) that the courts of the contracting states have jurisdiction to decide on entitlement disputes. The Protocol on Recognition also governs in Art.9(1) the recognition of the final decision of a court of a contracting state in the other contracting states.

Art. 61(1) If by a final decision it is adjudged that a person other than the applicant is entitled to the grant of the European patent, that person may, in accordance with the Implementing Regulations:

(a) prosecute the European patent application as his own application in place of the applicant;

(b) file a new European patent application in respect of the same invention; or

(c) request that the European patent application be refused.

Implementation:
R.14 Stay of proceedings
R.15 Limitation on withdrawals
R.16 Procedure under Art.61(1)
R.17 Filing a new application
R.18 Partial transfer of right
R.51(6) Renewal fee for a new application

1 **Entitlement procedure**

If a person is of the opinion that they are entitled to the grant of a European patent instead of the person whom the EPO has registered as applicant, that person can only obtain rights in the application by contesting entitlement before a national court. The choice of the court and the recognition of its decision by the other contracting states designated in the application is set out in the Protocol on Recognition. The EPO will stay grant proceedings according to **R.14(1)** after the entitled person has provided it with proof that proceedings before the national court have been opened. The proceedings will only be stayed after the publication of the application. The stay prevents the application from being amended to the detriment of the entitled person. **R.15** prohibits withdrawal of the application or any designation. **R.14** and **R.15** secure the rights of the entitled person until the national court reaches a final decision. After the final decision of the court has been issued, the entitled person may exercise the rights granted by **Art.61(1)**. The entitled person has three options: to continue with the prosecution of the pending application as applicant, to file a new application or to request refusal of the application. These three options will be discussed in the following sections. See also **R.16(1):1** for details on the procedure under **Art.61(1)**.

Art.99(4) provides the procedure under which an entitled person may exercise the right as proprietor of the patent to defend the patent in pending opposition proceedings.

2 **Prosecute application (Art.61(1)(a))**

The new applicant must inform the EPO in writing of its intention to prosecute the application; the new applicant then takes the place of the original applicant and continues the grant procedure (A-IV,2.4).

Options (a) and (b) of **Art.61(1)** each have their advantages: option (a) does not require payment of several fees, whereas option (b) allows the applicant to start grant proceedings afresh and, for example, to pursue subject-matter which may have been abandoned by the original applicant.

Option (a) is, in principle, only open for a third party who has become entitled to the entire subject-matter of the application. If the third party is adjudged to be entitled to only a part of the subject-matter, the third party can file a new application for that part under option (b), see below).

Option (a) may also be used if the third party is entitled to part of the subject-matter of the application and the application cannot be properly divided according to **R.18**. The third party can then use option (a) to become an additional applicant. (Singer Art. 61, note 22)

A court may also decide that a person is entitled to become a co-applicant (e.g. **J1/23**). It is recommended that the court also decides on the appointment of the common representative (**R.151**).

3 **File new application (Art.61(1)(b))**
The rules for filing a new application are set out in **R.17**. The new application is treated in the same way as a divisional application in many respects (**Art.61(2)** and notes thereto). The original application is deemed to be withdrawn at the filing date of the new application (**R.17(1)**).

If the third party is adjudged to be entitled to only a part of the subject-matter, the third party must file a new application for that part under (b) (see also **R.18(1)**). The original application can remain pending but must be confined to the subject-matter to which the original applicant remains entitled.

If the judgement is effective for only some designated states under Art.9 Protocol on Recognition and the third party files a new application for those states, the original application must be confined only with respect to those states and may have different claims for the other states (**R.18(2)**; C-IX,2.3)

4 **Refusal of application (Art.61(1)(c))**
The EPO must accede to the request to refuse the original application; the decision on the request is open to appeal (**Art.106(1)**; A-IV,2.6).

Art. 61(2) Article 76, paragraph 1, shall apply mutatis mutandis to a new European patent application filed under paragraph 1(b).

Art.76(1) European divisional applications

1 **Similarities between new application and divisional application (same legal basis)**
A new application filed under **Art.61(1)(b)** is treated in many respects in the same way as a divisional application because of the reference in **Art.61(2)** to **Art.76(1)**. Hence, the provisions of **Art.76(1)** for a divisional application apply also to a new application. In particular, since **Art.76(1)** refers to the Implementing Regulations for filing a divisional application, these rules should also be applied to a new application in so far as the Implementing Regulations do not specifically provide otherwise. **Art.61(1)** provides a basis for those specific rules that relate to the filing of a replacement application. The requirements for a new application and a divisional application are the same in respect of the following issues:

- The new application must be filed with a filing office of the EPO (**Art.76(1)**, **R.36(2)**; A-IV,2.5).
- The language of the new application must be the language of the proceedings of the original application or the language of the original application as filed if that was not an official EPO language (**Art.76(1)**, **R.36(2)**; A-VII,1.3).
- The new application has the same filing and priority date as the earlier application, provided the content of the new application does not extend beyond the subject-matter of the earlier application (**Art.76(1)**, **G3/92** r.5.4, see also **Art.100(c)**).
- The designation of inventor is governed by **R.60(2)**.

2 **Similarities between new application and divisional application (different legal basis)**

Art.61(1) refers to the Implementing Regulations for the filing of a new application. These rules should be applied instead of equivalent rules for filing a divisional application as referred to in **Art.61(2)** and **Art.76(1)**, since the former rules form leges speciali. Several rules specific to a new application lay down the same procedure as the rules for a divisional application:

- The application number of the earlier application must be given in the Request for Grant form (**R.41(2)(f)**).
- The filing fee, search fee and designation fee must be paid in accordance with **R.17(2)** and (3).

3 **Differences between new application and divisional application**

In the following cases, a new application and a divisional application are treated differently:

- The renewal fees for a new application are only due in respect of the years following the year of its filing (**R.51(6)**). In contrast, for a divisional application, they are due from the filing date of the parent application (**R.51(3)**).
- A new application can be filed even if the earlier application is no longer pending (**G3/92** r.5.5, 5.6). In contrast, a divisional application can only be filed when the earlier application is pending (**R.36(1)**). Decision **G3/92** was taken under EPC1973, in which Art.61(2) EPC1973 did not refer to Art.76(3) EPC1973, which included a reference to the Implementing Regulations. Hence, under EPC1973, a new application was bound by its own provisions (R.15 and R.16 EPC1973) and not by the Implementing Regulations relating to filing divisional applications. Under EPC1973 a new application was therefore not bound by R.25 EPC1973 (**R.36** EPC2000), which stated that a divisional application could only be filed during the pendency of the parent application; hence, a new application could be filed even if the earlier application was no longer pending (**G3/92** r.5.5, 5.6). In EPC2000, the reference to the procedure for filing a divisional application was merged into **Art.76(1)**. Hence, the reference in **Art.61(2)** to **Art.76(1)** in EPC2000 introduced an indirect reference to **R.36(1)**, which requires the parent application to be pending. This change in the EPC appeared to have created a conflict with the reasoning underlying **G3/92**, causing uncertainty about whether a new application can still be filed when the earlier application is no longer pending. Nevertheless, the legislator's intention was to maintain the applicability of **G3/92**. Hence, the Guidelines permit filing a new application also if the earlier application is no longer pending (A-IV,2.1 and C-IX,2.2). It may also be noted that **R.16(1)** only excludes the remedies of **Art.61(1)** in the case that the European patent has been granted and not in the more general case where the application has ceased to be pending.
- **Art.61(2)** does not refer to **Art.76(2)** because the national entitlement decision may have effect in only some designated states under certain circumstances (see **R.16(2)**).

Art. 62 Right of the inventor to be mentioned

The inventor shall have the right, vis-à-vis the applicant for or proprietor of a European patent, to be mentioned as such before the European Patent Office.

Implemented by:

R.19 Designation of the inventor
R.20 Publication of the mention of the inventor
R.21 Rectification of the designation of an inventor

1 **Moral right of inventor**
The moral right of the inventor to be mentioned, as expressed in **Art.62** is realised by **Art.81**, which requires that the inventor is designated in the European patent application.

Chapter III *Effects of the European patent and the European patent application*

1 **General**
Art.2(2) provides that a European patent shall, in each contracting state for which it is granted, have the same effect as a national patent, unless otherwise provided. This chapter contains some provisions providing certain rights relating to European patent applications and patents which are binding on the contracting states and some provisions which allow national law to influence the effect of European patent applications and patents. See Nat-Law tables III, IV, V and IX for the specific provisions of the contracting states affecting European patent applications and patents.

The provisional protection conferred by a published application is governed by **Art.67**. This provisional protection is deemed not to have existed if the application does not lead to a patent (**Art.67(4)**). If the application does lead to a patent, the provisional protection is replaced by the normal protection conferred by the patent under **Art.64** on the date of grant. The limitation or revocation of the patent in subsequent opposition proceedings or the limitation or revocation of the patent under **Art.105a** has the result that the provisional and normal protection are deemed never to have existed, either in full or in part (**Art.68**). The lapse of a patent when a renewal fee remains unpaid or on expiry of the patent term leads to the protection afforded by the patent ceasing at a certain point in time, but this does not affect the patent protection in existence up to the point at which the lapse occurs. Surrender of a patent generally has no retro-active effect (i.e. patent protection ceases on the date of surrender) but may have retro-active effect depending on national law (e.g. in NL surrender has retro-active effect) (D-VII,5.1). The extent of the provisional and normal protection is a matter of national law.

Art. 63 Term of the European patent

Art. 63(1) The term of the European patent shall be 20 years from the date of filing of the application.

1 **Term of patent**
A European patent has a uniform term of 20 years for all contracting states. The finite 20-year term seeks to balance the benefits of the patent system in encouraging and rewarding innovation on the one hand and the cost to society of excluding free access to technology on the other.

The relevant date for calculation of the 20-year term of the patent is the date of filing and not the priority date, in conformity with Art.4bis(5) of the Paris Convention.

The EPC does not set out how the expiry of the 20-year term is to be calculated; **R.131** defines the calculation of 'periods' and not 'terms'. It is also silent on whether or not the day of filing is to be included in the patent term. This has led to a divergence between contracting states in calculating the point at which the patent expires. A difference of a day in the date of lapse may have commercial implications for the proprietor; it is also important because an application for a Supplementary Protection Certificate under **Art.63(2)** has to be filed while the patent is in force.

Some contracting states include the day of filing in the patent term, in this case 'from the date of filing' in **Art.63(1)** is interpreted as in **R.14(4)** and **R.142(4)**. Other contracting states regard the following day as the first day of the term. The 20 years may be calculated as 'full years'. According to this approach, if the day of filing is 26.11.2009, the last day of validity of the patent will be 25.11.2029 if the day of filing is used as starting point and 26.11.2029 if the next day is used as starting point. Alternatively, the 20 years may be calculated according to **R.131(3)** with the day of filing as the day of the relevant event or the first day of validity as the day of relevant event in the sense of **R.131(2)**. In that case, the last day of validity will be 26.11.2029 or 27.11.2029.

UPR.14(1) defines the patent term for unitary patents as '20 years after the date of filing of the European patent application'; **R.131** applies (**UPR.20(2)**).

Note, that the term is not extended under **R.134** on account of non-working days at the EPO.

After expiry of the term, each designated state informs the EPO of the date of lapse of the patent for its territory, which information is entered in the Register (**R.143(1)(p)**) during the opposition period and any opposition proceedings and in a special section of the Register thereafter. The date of lapse is not defined in the EPC. Some contracting states define it as the date of expiry of the term, i.e. the last day of validity of the patent; other states define it as the day after the last day of validity.

The consequences of not having proper definitions for the patent term and the date of lapse are visible in national registers. For example, European patent EP 1 255 752 B1 has a filing date on the Register of 15.02.2001. Its expiry date is given as 14.02.2021 in the national registers of CH, GB and IE and as 15.02.2021 in the national registers of BE, NL and LU. In order to accurately determine the lapse of a specific patent in a specific contracting state, the national register should be inspected and the national patent office should be consulted. However, the information provided by national patent offices is not always consistent.

Harmonisation of the patent term is difficult, because differences in interpretation have been enshrined in national practice and law. One way forward would be dispute resolution under **Art.173**.

Art. 63(2) Nothing in the preceding paragraph shall limit the right of a Contracting State to extend the term of a European patent, or to grant corresponding protection which follows immediately on expiry of the term of the patent, under the same conditions as those applying to national patents:

(a) in order to take account of a state of war or similar emergency conditions affecting that State;

(b) if the subject-matter of the European patent is a product or a process for manufacturing a product or a use of a product which has to undergo an administrative authorisation procedure required by law before it can be put on the market in that State.

1 **Extended term of patent**

Any state using or intending to make use of **Art.63(2)(b)** must inform the EPO of the duration of any extension of term or corresponding protection and the conditions under which it will be granted, in order to permit an exchange of views within the Administrative Council (Act revising Art.63, Resolution on mutual information, OJ 1992 p.1).

Art.63(2)(b) gives a proprietor of a patent compensation in the form of an extended patent term for delayed commercialisation due to a lengthy administrative authorisation procedure, as is common for pharmaceuticals. Whereas the time from the conception of the invention to market is usually between 5 and 8 years for an electronic device, it is in general more than 12 years for a new drug. All EU states, and EEA states Norway and Iceland, must provide such Supplementary Protection Certificates for medicinal products under EU Regulation 469/2009. Switzerland and the UK also have corresponding national provisions. An extension of up to 5 years is available. In all of these states a further six months of additional protection is possible if agreed paediatric studies are completed in a timely manner.

According to EU regulation 1610/96 which entered into force on 08.02.1997, EU states must also grant supplementary protection certificates for plant protection products. The certificate provides for the extension of patent protection by up to 5 years in the same way as a certificate for a medicinal product. (OJ 1997 p.77)

Art. 63(3) Paragraph 2 shall apply mutatis mutandis to European patents granted jointly for a group of Contracting States in accordance with Article 142.

Art.142 Unitary patent for group of states

Art. 63(4) A Contracting State which makes provision for extension of the term or corresponding protection under paragraph 2(b) may, in accordance with an agreement concluded with the Organisation, entrust to the European Patent Office tasks associated with implementation of the relevant provisions.

Art. 64 Rights conferred by a European patent

Based on the general principle of equivalence between European and national patents set out in **Art.2(2)**, this provision establishes that a granted European patent confers on its proprietor the same rights in each contracting state as would be conferred by a national patent.

Art. 64(1) A European patent shall, subject to the provisions of paragraph 2, confer on its proprietor from the date on which the mention of its grant is published in the European Patent Bulletin, in each Contracting State in respect of which it is granted, the same rights as would be conferred by a national patent granted in that State.

1 **Rights conferred by patent**

The rights conferred by a national patent, and therefore by a European patent, represent the extent to which the proprietor may prevent others from using the patented invention, i.e. which acts constitute infringement and what remedies are available in respect of any infringement.

Many EPC states have made the maintenance of rights dependent on the filing of a translation of the specification (see **Art.65**). A European patent confers rights on its proprietor immediately on publication of the mention of the grant, but these rights are deemed void ab initio if the national requirements relating to translation are not complied with in a timely manner (NatLaw table IV, note 2). See also the comments on the London Agreement under **Art.65(1)**.

Art. 64(2) If the subject-matter of the European patent is a process, the protection conferred by the patent shall extend to the products directly obtained by such process.

1 **Protection of product directly obtained by a process**
Art.64(2) extends the protection conferred by a process patent to the products obtained directly by the process, even if those products are not patentable per se. Art.25(c) UPCA implements this rule for European patents with and without unitary effect in the UPC states.

Only the directly obtained product is protected. Defining the boundary between direct and indirect products is a matter of case law of the national courts and the UPC. However, in EU states, if the patented process is for the production of biological material possessing specific characteristics, the protection extends to further generations of biological material obtained by propagation or multiplication that still possesses those characteristics (Art.8(2) EU Directive 94/88/EC; see **R.26(3)** for the definition of biological material).

The protection may extend to a known product (not patentable under **Art.52(1)**) or a plant variety (not patentable under **Art.53(b)**). The fact that the product is not patentable does not affect the validity of the process claim, because **Art.64** is not a provision relating to patentability (**Art.52-57**) but a provision concerning the protection conferred by the patent in infringement proceedings before a national court (**G1/98** r.4).

Historically, **Art.64(2)** was particularly important in some contracting states that had made a reservation under Art.167(2) EPC1973 to exclude patent protection for certain inventions: Greece did not allow patents for pharmaceutical products, and Spain did not allow patents for chemical and pharmaceutical products. These reservations expired in 1992.

The effect of **Art.64(2)** is not to make the product of the process novel (**T248/85** hn.1). Equally if the product of the process is not inventive, it may not be claimed in the form of a product claim or even in the form of a product-by-process claim (**T150/82** r.10).

The protection of products directly obtained by means of a patented process is especially useful if a third party manufactures such a product using the patented process in a country where no patent protection for the process exists, and the product is imported into a state in which a European patent for the process is in force.

Obtaining proof that the product has been made according to the patented process may be difficult, especially when the process has been carried out in a country where the process is not protected, and no court-ordered access to the production facilities is possible. In some cases, the presence of impurities and other characteristics of the product may point toward the use of the patented process.

Under most national laws and Art.55(1) UPCA, if the patented process results in a new product, any manufacture of that product by a third party is assumed to have used the patented process unless the third party provides proof to the contrary.

2 **Product-by-process claim**
The extension of the protection of a process claim to the product directly obtained by the process under **Art.64(2)** should be distinguished from the protection provided by a product-by-process claim. The protection under **Art.64(2)** extends to products which are not patentable per se, and covers known products, but it is limited to products which are directly obtained by the patented process (**Art.64(2)**).

A product-by-process claim is a product claim that defines the product in terms of a manufacturing process (F-IV,4.12). It covers the product when it is made by any process and gives the broadest possible protection. However, the product itself must be patentable, and, therefore, the claim may not cover known products. (**G1/98** r.4; **T150/82**)

A product-by-process claim is generally only allowable when it is not possible to define the product in any other way. A product-by-process claim is only patentable if the product itself is patentable, i.e. complies with the provisions of **Art.52** to **Art.57**, and there is no other information available in the application which could enable the applicant to define the product satisfactorily by reference to its structure, composition or any testable parameter. (**T150/82**, **T248/85**, **T664/90**; **T1242/06** r.45)

As an example, the boards of appeal have allowed the limitation of a range in a product claim by means of a process feature, because the alternative, a feature in the form of a desired property, would not have been allowable in some contracting states (**T129/88** r.2.2.3/4). An improved product quality alone is not generally considered to be the kind of structural feature in a product-by-process claim which can establish novelty or inventive step (**T394/03**).

Art. 64(3) Any infringement of a European patent shall be dealt with by national law.

1 **Infringement**

Even prior to the creation of the Unified Patent Court, with its supranational jurisdiction over European and unitary patents, the result of infringement proceedings in one EU state could have effects in other EU states based on the Brussels I Regulation (EU regulation 1215/2012 on jurisdiction of courts and the recognition and enforcement of judgements in civil and commercial matters, and its predecessors), e.g. as the result of a cross-border injunction.

The EPC imposes only two restrictions concerning the substantive law to be applied during national infringement proceedings, which relate to the manner in which the scope of protection of the patent must be determined (**Art.69**) and the extension of the protection of a process claim to the direct product of the process (**Art.64(2)**). In an infringement procedure the EPO is only competent to provide, on request of a national court, a technical opinion (**Art.25**). All other questions must be answered by national courts under national law, which includes the UPCA if applicable.

The authentic text of the patent specification in national infringement proceedings is determined by **Art.70**.

A third party can start a procedure for obtaining a ruling on infringement after the mention of the grant of the patent, because rights under the patent are conferred on the proprietor at that moment (**Art.64(1)**). If, during opposition proceedings before the EPO, an action for infringement is brought before a national court, the alleged infringer can intervene in the opposition procedure (**Art.105**). National law determines whether or not the national court will postpone taking a decision in the infringement proceedings until the opposition proceedings are complete.

2 **Unified Patent Court Agreement**

For the contracting states that have ratified the UPCA, the European patent falls under the jurisdiction of the UPC. The UPC applies the substantive provisions of the UPCA on patent infringement (Art.24-29 UPCA) in the proceedings before it as well as the procedural provisions of the UPA and the implementing Rules of Procedure (RoP).

The UPCA is an international treaty between a number of EPC contracting states and, at the same time, equivalent to national law in the sense of **Art.64(3)** (see also **Art.149a(1)**, which permits such treaties).

The text of the UPCA can be found on the EPO website and was published in OJ 2013 p.287-364.

The UPC has competence in respect of (Art.32(1) UPCA):

(a) actions for actual or threatened infringements of patents and supplementary protection certificates and related defences, including counterclaims concerning licences;
(b) actions for declarations of non-infringement of patents and supplementary protection certificates;
(c) actions for provisional and protective measures and injunctions;
(d) actions for revocation of patents and for declaration of invalidity of supplementary protection certificates;
(e) counterclaims for revocation of patents and for declaration of invalidity of supplementary protection certificates;
(f) actions for damages or compensation derived from the provisional protection conferred by a published European patent application;
(g) actions relating to the use of the invention prior to the granting of the patent or to the right based on prior use of the invention;
(h) actions for compensation for licences on the basis of Art.8 of EU regulation 1257/2012 (see **UPR.12**); and
(i) actions concerning decisions of the European Patent Office in carrying out the tasks referred to in Art.9 of EU regulation 1257/2012 (see **UPR.20:2**).

2.1 OPT-OUT

During a transitional period until 01.06.2030 (which can be extended by the Administrative Committee of the UPC), a proprietor or applicant can file an application to opt-out from the jurisdiction of the UPC a European patent without unitary effect; an opt-out can no longer be filed once an action before the UPC has started (see the list of actions in Art.32 UPC), irrespective of whether the action is still pending at the time of the opt-out (Art.83(3) UPCA; Art.2(1(e) UPCA; R.5(6) RoP). An opt-out can be filed before or after the grant of the European patent. In the following, the term 'proprietor' also refers to the applicant.

The opt-out must be filed with the Registry of the UPC, not with the EPO (R.5(1) RoP). Where the patent has two or more proprietors, all proprietors must file the opt-out; the proprietors in all designated EPC contracting states must be considered, possibly only in the states where the patent was validated (R.5(1)(b) RoP). If the party filing the opt-out is a proprietor but is not registered as such in the national patent register, the party must file a declaration that they are entitled to be registered in the national patent register (R.5(1)(a), R.5(3)(e) RoP). The opt-out must contain information such as the name and address of the proprietor, the representative or other person filing the opt-out on behalf of the proprietor, and details of the patent (including the EP publication number); hence an opt-out can only be filed for one or more specific patents (R.5.3 RoP). No fee needs to be paid. Representation is not required (R.5(4) RoP).

Any natural person can file an opt-out on behalf of a proprietor, but if the person is not a UPC representative as defined in Art.48 UPC, a mandate (power of attorney) signed by the proprietor must be submitted with the opt-out (R.5(3)(b)(ii) RoP). European patent attorneys can only be UPC representatives if they have certain additional qualifications and are entered on a list of representatives kept by the UPC (Art.48 UPC). If an unauthorised opt-out is filed (e.g. by mistake), the proprietor may file a request to remove the opt-out from the register (R.5A RoP).

The opt-out must be filed using the electronic systems of the UPC (R.4(1) RoP), namely the CMS website or the API system for the automatic exchange of documents. The document must be filed as a pdf file and be electronically signed in a specific way. In practice, a special type of smart card is necessary to use those systems and sign the documents.

A European patent application can also be opted out, provided that the EP publication number is available (R.5(1),(3) RoP) A PCT publication number is insufficient (UPC FAQ). The opt-out will also apply to any patent which is subsequently granted. If an application is opted out, unitary effect can still be registered after grant; the opt-out will then be deemed to be withdrawn (R.5(9) RoP).

The Registrar of the UPC registers the opt-out after having performed a number of automatic checks and without any substantive examination (R.5(5) RoP). The UPC keeps a public register of opt-outs and informs the EPO of the opt-out (R5(11) RoP). If the opt-out is registered in spite of the fact that it fails to meet one or more requirements, a correction can be filed. The opt-out will be effective from the date of correction, implying that an opt-out can be ineffective even though it was registered (R.5(5)).

The opt-out extends to any supplementary protection certificate (e.g. for a medicament) based on the patent (R.5(2) RoP).

An opt-out can be withdrawn by filing an application to withdraw, but not in the event an action has started concerning the patent before a national court of a UPC state (R.5(7),(8) RoP). The withdrawal cannot be reversed.

The intention is that an opt-out is effective for the entire duration of the patent (UPC Q&A Opt-out published in 2015).

2.2 RIGHT TO PREVENT DIRECT USE OF THE INVENTION

According to Art.25 UPCA, a European patent (with or without unitary effect) confers on its proprietor the right to prevent any third party not having the proprietor's consent from carrying out any of the following acts:

(a) making, offering, placing on the market or using a product which is the subject-matter of the patent, or importing or storing the product for those purposes;

(b) using a process which is the subject-matter of the patent or, where the third party knows, or should have known, that the use of the process is prohibited without the consent of the patent proprietor, offering the process for use within the territory of UPC states in which that patent has effect;

(c) offering, placing on the market, or using, a product obtained directly by a process which is the subject-matter of the patent, and importing or storing such a product for those purposes.

The phrase ‘placing on the market’ refers to acts of commercialization such as sale, rent (to let), and lease.

Art.5 of EU regulation 1257/2012, concerning the right of the proprietor to prevent third parties from infringing a patent, refers indirectly to Art.25-29 UPCA for the definition of what acts infringe a unitary patent. The reason for using an indirect reference is to limit the possibilities for the CJEU to interpret the provisions of the UPCA relating to substantive patent law (Luginbühl/Hütterman, Einheitspatentsystem, 2024, p.48).

For all EU states, the protection conferred by a European patent on a product containing or consisting of genetic information extends to any material in which the product is incorporated and in which the genetic information is contained and performs its function (Art.9 EU Directive 94/88/EC). Hence, importing soy meal containing a patented gene sequence was not patent infringement, because the patented DNA sequence could not perform its function in soy meal, which is dead material (Court of Justice EU C-428/08).

If a patented product is sold by the proprietor or with their consent within the EU, the patent is 'exhausted' for that specific product (physical object), and the proprietor cannot object to the use and further sale of the product as patent infringement; see Art.29 UPCA and note 2.6 below.

2.3 RIGHT TO PREVENT INDIRECT USE OF THE INVENTION

According to Art.26(1) UPCA, a European patent (with or without unitary effect) confers on its proprietor the right to prevent any third party not having the proprietor's consent from supplying or offering to supply, within the territory of the Contracting Member States in which that patent has effect, any person other than a party entitled to exploit the patented invention, with means, relating to an essential element of that invention, for putting it into effect therein, when the third party knows, or should have known, that those means are suitable and intended for putting that invention into effect.

This provision does not apply when the means are commercial staple products (everyday products), except where the supplier induces the recipient of the products to perform any of the patent-infringing acts prohibited by Art.25 UPCA (Art.26(2) UPCA).

Persons who carry out an act that is covered by one of the limitations of Art.27(a) to (e) UPCA are not considered to be parties entitled to exploit the invention within the meaning of Art.26(1) UPCA (Art.26(3) UPCA). For example, supplying means relating to an essential element of the invention to a consumer who uses the invention privately for non-commercial purposes (Art.27(a) UPCA) is still a patent-infringing indirect use of the invention.

2.4 LIMITATIONS ON THE EFFECT OF A PATENT

Art.27 UPCA lists a number of activities that do not constitute an infringement of a European patent or unitary patent. Only a brief summary of each item in the list is given here. Detailed comments can be found e.g. in Luginbühl/Hütterman, Einheitspatentsystem, 2024).

- Art.27(a): Acts done privately and for non-commercial purposes, e.g. use of a patented device by a consumer. Selling the device to the consumer can still be patent infringement (see Art.26(3) UPCA).
- Art.27(b): Acts done for experimental purposes relating to the subject-matter of the patented invention. Note that the use of a patented device as a research tool (e.g. a microscope) can still infringe the patent.
- Art.27(c): Use of plant material for plant breeding (developing new plant varieties).
- Art.27(d): Use of a patented pharmaceutical compound for carrying out clinical trials for registering a human or veterinary medicine in the EU.
- Art.27(e): The 'extemporaneous' preparation of a medicine by a pharmacy in an individual case (i.e. not for stocking), in accordance with a medical prescription, and use of the prepared medicine.

- Art.27(f): Use of a patented device on a ship or vessel, provided that the ship enters the waters of a UPC state temporarily or accidentally and provided that the ship is a foreign ship (i.e. registered in a non-UPC state that is a contracting state of the Paris Convention or WTO member or in a UPC state in which the patent is not in force). The device must be used in the body, machine, tackle, gear or other accessories of the ship.
- Art.27(g): Use of the patented invention in the construction or operation of aircraft or land vehicles or other means of transport, with similar limitations as for (f).
- Art.27(h): Entry or landing of aircraft of a foreign country (similar as in (f)), and storage, use and installation of spare equipment of such aircraft. The foreign country must be bound by the Convention on International Civil Aviation (i.e., all UN member states).
- Art.27(i): This clarifies the application of the 'exhaustion' rule to harvested products, see note 2.6 below.
- Art.27(j): This clarifies the application of the 'exhaustion' rule to animal livestock, see note 2.6 below.
- Art.27(k): This clarifies the application of the 'exhaustion' rule to software, see note 2.6 below.
- Art.27(l): This clarifies the application of the 'exhaustion' rule to biological material.

Supplying means relating to an essential element of the invention is not patent infringement if these means are used in any of the activities of, specifically, items (f) to (l) (Art.26(3) UPCA). For items (a) to (l), it must be considered to what extent the exception itself covers obtaining the necessary equipment and starting materials.

2.5 RIGHTS BASED ON PRIOR USE OR PRIOR POSSESSION OF THE INVENTION

Art.28 UPCA provides that any person, who, if a national patent had been granted in respect of an invention, would have had, in a UPC state, a right based on prior use of that invention or a right of personal possession of that invention, enjoys, in that state, the same rights in respect of a European patent (with or without unitary effect) for the same invention.

If a third party already commercially used the invention before the priority date (secretly), the national laws of the UPC states give the third party a right to continue the use without infringing the patent, within certain limits and under certain conditions defined in national law. Typically, the prior use must be in the same state. A few UPC states also give such a right to a third party who possessed the invention before the priority date or filing date of the patent, without a requirement that the third party put the invention to commercial use (e.g., France). Hence, the right based on prior use (or prior possession) of the third party to which Art.28 UPCA refers, is a right of the third party to continue the use of the invention without infringing the patent.

For European patents with and without unitary effect, the extent and conditions of any right based on prior use and prior possession are defined under national law, to which Art.28 UPCA simply refers. Hence, the question of whether such a right exists in a certain case must be answered for each UPC state separately.

For further details, see e.g. Tilmann/Plassmann, Unified Patent Protection in Europe, 2018, notes to Art.28 UPCA.

2.6 EXHAUSTION OF THE RIGHTS CONFERRED BY A PATENT

Art.29 UPCA provides that the rights conferred by a European patent (i.e. without unitary effect, see the definition in Art.2I UPCA) do not extend to acts concerning a product covered by that patent after that product has been placed on the market in the European Union (e.g. sold within the EU) by the patent proprietor or with their consent (e.g. by a licensee) unless there are legitimate grounds for the patent proprietor to oppose further commercialisation of the product.

This rule reflects the principle of exhaustion: the rights under a patent are said to be exhausted for a particular article covered by the patent when that the article is sold by the proprietor (or otherwise placed on the market by the proprietor, e.g. by lease), and the proprietor cannot use the patent to object to the further sale and use of that specific article (i.e. of the physical object that was sold) unless there are legitimate grounds for the patent proprietor to oppose the further commercialisation of the product.

The UPC will have to establish through case law what factors constitute legitimate grounds for the patent proprietor to oppose further commercialisation of the product under Art.29 UPCA.

Under Art.29 UPCA, a sale (or similar act) by the proprietor (or with their consent) in any EU member state causes the exhaustion of the patent right. The same applies in the case of a sale or similar act in a non-EU member state of the European Economic Area (i.e. Norway, Iceland, and Liechtenstein) (Luginbühl/Hütterman, Einheitspatentsystem, 2024, p.49). A sale in other states does not cause exhaustion. It does not matter if the European patent is in force in the EU member state where the article is sold by the proprietor. A sale of the product by a person other than the proprietor in a state where a European patent is not in force does not cause the exhaustion rule to apply.

Art.6 of EU Regulation 1257/2012 confirms that the exhaustion rule applies to unitary patents.

The exhaustion rule of Art.29 UPCA allows the owner of a patented object to repair it but does not allow the owner to replicate it. The UPC will have to define the boundary between repairing a patented object and making a new object in its case law (Luginbühl/Hütterman, Einheitspatentsystem, 2024, p.451).

The question of whether and how Art.29 UPCA applies to process patents is not straightforward because a patent granted with only process or method claims does not unambiguously cover a product. See, e.g., Luginbühl/Hütterman, Einheitspatentsystem, 2024, p.448.

2.6.1 Exhaustion and biological material

The exhaustion rule of Art.29 UPCA does not permit the owner of a patented object or material to replicate the object or produce more of a patented material.

However, in the case of biological material as the patented product, the patent protection does not extend to any biological material that is obtained by propagation or multiplication of the product if the product was placed on the market in the EU by the patent proprietor or with their consent and the application for which the product was marketed involves that propagation or multiplication (Art.27(l) UPCA). See **R.26**(3) for the definition of biological material. For instance, if the proprietor sells seeds with a patented genomic trait for sowing to a farmer, the farmer can sell the harvested plants. However, Art.27(l) UPCA does not permit using the obtained biological material subsequently for other propagation or multiplication (Art.27(l) UPCA), e.g. does not permit sowing harvested seeds. To partially address this, Art.27(i) UPCA allows a farmer to use the product of their harvest (e.g. harvested seeds) for propagation or multiplication by them on their own holding, within certain limits and conditions. Art.27(j) provides a similar exception for animal livestock, breeding stock and other animal reproductive material. Furthermore, developing new plant varieties (plant breeding) involves growing multiple generations of plants and is exempt under Art.27(c).

2.6.2 *Exhaustion and software*
The exhaustion rule of Art.29 UPCA does not permit the owner of a patented product to make copies of it. To not hinder the normal use of software, Art.27(k) UPCA specifies that the patent protection does not cover reproducing software as far as necessary for the use of a computer program by the lawful acquirer in accordance with the intended purpose of the computer program and permits the making of necessary back-up copies by persons having the right to use the computer program.

Art. 65 Translation of the European patent

1 **Validation of the European patent**
The steps to be carried out to maintain the effect of a European patent in a designated contracting state after grant of the patent are often referred to as the validation of the patent. This validation of a patent should be distinguished from the validation of the patent in a non-contracting state during grant proceedings as set out in **Art.79(2):2.2**, which is equivalent to the designation of a contracting state.

The requirements for validation are different for different contracting states and are set out in the brochure NatLaw table IV, the html version on the EPO website being often more up to date than the pdf version. The steps may include:

- The filing of a translation of the claims or the entire specification in an official language of a state if the patent is not granted in an official language of that state (**Art.65(1)**). Several states have limited their translation requirements by becoming party to the London Agreement (see **Art.65(1):2**).
- The appointment of a professional representative authorised to act before the national office.
- The payment of a fee for publishing the translation (**Art.65(2)**).
- The use of a prescribed form for filing the translation.

The payment of national renewal fees is also necessary to keep the patent in force after grant (**Art.141**).

For most contracting states the filing of the translation must be carried out within three months from the publication of the mention of the grant. A few states have a longer period. However, a proprietor may have to act sooner if a renewal fee falls due. If a national renewal fee falls due within two months of publication of the mention of the grant, it must be paid before expiry of those two months (**Art.141(2)**). It is unfortunate that the legislator has chosen different periods for filing the translations and paying national renewal fees. Note, that the invitation to pay a national renewal fee will be sent to the proprietor and not to the representative if no different address for service has been recorded with the national office. A proprietor may regard such an invitation as a scam and fail to take action (see OJ 2014 A42).

Several states that have acceded to the London Agreement have no requirements for filing a translation and paying a fee for publishing it. When a European patent is granted, it becomes automatically and immediately a validated patent in these countries. Such a patent will only lapse if a national renewal fee is not paid (see **Art.141**). The automatic validation may have consequences for co-pending national patents under **Art.139(3)**. If e.g. the proprietor has prosecuted a national GB application to grant and a co-pending European application claiming priority from the GB application is also granted with the same scope of protection, the GB patent will be revoked on expiry of the opposition period or, if an opposition is filed, on closure of the opposition proceedings if the European patent is maintained. The proprietor can avoid the loss of the GB patent by ensuring that the patents have different scopes of protection, by withdrawing the GB designation before grant of the European patent or by surrendering the EP(GB) patent before the GB patent is revoked.

States that do require the filing of a translation and the payment of a fee for publishing may consider the European patent to be void ab initio in that state if the requirements are not complied with (**Art.65(3)**). In this case, there will be no consequences for a co-pending national patent.

2 Translation of the patent

The EPO publishes a European patent in the language of the proceedings but includes claims in all three official EPO languages (**Art.14(6)** and **R.71(3)**). Since a patent may have a considerable effect on commercial activities, a state may require under **Art.65(1)** that a translation is filed in one of its official languages in order to improve the public's understanding of the patent. A contracting state may require that such a translation is filed both after grant when the patent is validated for that state and after amendment or limitation in opposition or limitation proceedings. A contracting state that has acceded to the London Agreement has either no right or a limited right to request a translation, thereby relaxing the translation requirements for the patent proprietor.

A country demanding a translation may publish the translation and require that the proprietor pays at least part of the cost of publication (**Art.65(2)**). When the proprietor does not file the translation or pay any fee for publishing for a contracting state, the patent may be deemed void ab initio in that state (**Art.65(3)**).

3 European patent with unitary effect

Following the entry into force of the Unified Patent Court Agreement (UPCA), the proprietor of a European patent has the option, for those participating EU member states that have ratified the UPCA, to request unitary effect, resulting in a supranational unitary patent (UP) instead of a bundle of national European patents (Art.2(a), Art.3(1) and Art.18(1) of EU regulation 1257/2012). This unitary patent can only be litigated as a whole at the Unified Patent Court (Art.3 UPCA). Unitary effect is only possible where the European patent has the same set of claims in all the participating EU member states, regardless of how many of them have actually ratified the UPCA at the time (Art.3(1) of EU regulation 1257/2012 and **UPR.5(2)**). A request for unitary effect must be filed at the EPO within one month of the publication of the mention of grant of the patent (Art.9(1)(g) of EU regulation 1257/2012 and **UPR.6(1)**) and is dealt with by the Unitary Patent Protection Division (**UPR.4**). No fee is payable for requesting unitary effect and, eventually, no translation will need to be filed. However, for a period of time until machine translations are considered to be of a suitable standard, a single translation of the patent is required, in English if the language of the proceedings is

French or German, or in any other official language of the EU where the language of the proceedings is English (Art.6 of EU regulation 1260/2012 and **UPR.6(2)**). Once unitary effect has been registered by the EPO, the European patent cannot have any effect nationally in any of the contracting states to which unitary effect extends (no double protection, Art.4(2) of EU regulation 1257/2012) and no national validation is therefore necessary or possible.

Art. 65(1) Any Contracting State may, if the European patent as granted, amended or limited by the European Patent Office is not drawn up in one of its official languages, prescribe that the proprietor of the patent shall supply to its central industrial property office a translation of the patent as granted, amended or limited in one of its official languages at his option or, where that State has prescribed the use of one specific official language, in that language. The period for supplying the translation shall end three months after the date on which the mention of the grant, maintenance in amended form or limitation of the European patent is published in the European Patent Bulletin, unless the State concerned prescribes a longer period.

Relevant provisions:
Art.97(3) Publication of the mention of the grant
Art.98 Content of specification (no abstract)
Art.103 Publication of a patent maintained in amended form
R.71(3) Invitation to approve text to be granted

1 **Translation of patent in language of contracting state**

Art.65(1) allows a contracting state to request a translation of the European patent when it is not drawn up in one of its official languages. A group of states has reduced the need for translation by acceding to the London Agreement (see next section).

The translation requirements for each contracting state and extension state can be found in the regularly updated html version of NatLaw table IV on the EPO website. The pdf version of NatLaw is often outdated. NatLaw also provides details relating to the appointment of a national representative, the period for filing the translation and any extension, the manner in which the translation may be filed and the payment of fees (which are relatively high for some states).

A required translation must be of the patent as granted or as amended in opposition (**R.82(2)**) or limitation (**R.95(3)**) proceedings. All contracting states allow correction of the translation under the conditions of **Art.70(3)** and (4). Whereas a contracting state may require a translation of the whole patent under **Art.65(1)**, it may only require a translation of the claims of a patent application for the purposes of obtaining provisional protection under **Art.67**.

According to **Art.65(1)** the proprietor has at least three months from the publication of the mention of the grant to file a translation of the patent in an official language of a designated state. Contracting states are free to provide a longer period if they wish and Iceland and San Marino provide periods of four and six months respectively. Note that the translation of the claims of the patent in the two official EPO languages other than the language of the proceedings must be filed earlier, i.e. within the time limit for responding to the **R.71(3)** communication, requesting the applicant to approve of the text intended for grant.

2 **London Agreement**

The optional 'Agreement on the application of Article 65 EPC' or 'London Agreement' has the objective of reducing the cost of obtaining a European patent by at least partly waiving the translation requirements of **Art.65(1)** (OJ 2001 p.550). It has a legal basis in **Art.149a** and entered into force on 01.05.2008 (OJ 2008 p.123). Information on the contracting states bound by the agreement and their translation requirements is available in the html version of NatLaw on the EPO website. A list of contracting states to the agreement is provided in **Art.169:1.1.**

A state party to the London Agreement having English, German or French as an official language may not require any translation of a European patent under **Art.65(1)**.

A state not having English, German or French as official language may not require a translation of the whole patent in its official language if the patent is granted in the official EPO language prescribed by that state. However, such a state may always require that the claims are translated in one of its official languages. Note, that requesting a translation of the claims departs from the literal wording of **Art.65(1)**, which merely provides for requesting 'a translation of the patent'. See the EPO website for the implementation of the London Agreement for each participating state.

A party to the London Agreement may prescribe that in the case of a dispute the proprietor must supply at the request of an infringer or a court a translation of the whole patent in an official language of the state concerned.

Art. 65(2) Any Contracting State which has adopted provisions pursuant to paragraph 1 may prescribe that the proprietor of the patent must pay all or part of the costs of publication of such translation within a period laid down by that State.

1 **Fee for publishing**

A state that prescribes that a translation of a European patent must be supplied, may also demand payment of a fee for publishing the translation. NatLaw table IV indicates for each state requiring a translation whether the payment of the fee is required.

The fee for publishing does not have a well-defined name. The following names are also used: fee for publication, special fee, publication fee, national validation fee. The fee of **Art.65(2)** should not be confused with the validation fee required for extending the effect of a European patent application and patent to a non-contracting state (see **Art.79(2):2.2**).

Art. 65(3) Any Contracting State may prescribe that in the event of failure to observe the provisions adopted in accordance with paragraphs 1 and 2, the European patent shall be deemed to be void ab initio in that State.

1 **Failure to provide translation**

All states that require a translation have made use of this provision (NatLaw introduction to table IV, note 2). Re-establishment in the case of late filing cannot be granted under **Art.122**, because the time limit is not one that must be observed vis-à-vis the EPO (**Art.122(6)**); a remedy may be available under national law.

The Court of Justice of the European Union has ruled in its decision C-44/98 of 21.09.1999 that the right of a contracting state to prescribe the filing of a translation does not contravene the principle of free movements of goods under EU law.

Art. 66 Equivalence of European filing with national filing

A European patent application which has been accorded a date of filing shall, in the designated Contracting States, be equivalent to a regular national filing, where appropriate with the priority claimed for the European patent application.

1 **European filing equivalent to national filing**
This provision firstly serves to ensure that all states that are party to the Paris Convention (PC) recognise a right of priority generated by the filing of a European patent application, by stating that a European patent application, which has been accorded a filing date, is equivalent to a regular national filing in the designated contracting states; these states are PC countries (Art.4A(1), (2) PC).

The equivalence with a national patent application also forms the basis for the conversion of a European application into a national application, maintaining its priority claim where applicable (**Art.135**). In view of **Art.140**, a European patent application is also equivalent to a national utility model and a utility certificate, and conversion into a national utility model or certificate is also possible.

The equivalence between a European patent application and a national patent application moreover supports the minimum level of provisional protection of **Art.67(2)**.

A date of filing is accorded to a European patent application when the Receiving Section concludes that the application fulfils the requirements of **Art.80** (**Art.90(1)**).

Art. 67 Rights conferred by a European patent application after publication

Art. 67(1) A European patent application shall, from the date of its publication, provisionally confer upon the applicant the protection provided for by Article 64, in the Contracting States designated in the application.

Art.64 Rights conferred by a European patent

1 **Provisional rights conferred by application**
This provision states as a general principle that a European patent application on publication gives the applicant the same rights in a designated contracting state as a granted patent gives its proprietor (**Art.2(2)**), albeit provisionally. The extent of protection is defined in **Art.69(2)**. However, **Art.67(2)** allows states to derogate from this far-reaching provision by providing a reduced level of protection if they so wish. The level of protection accorded by each EPC state is set out in NatLaw table III.A, note 2.

Since a published European patent application usually designates all contracting states, the applicant enjoys uniform provisional protection. However, this effect is deemed never to have occurred if the relevant designation is withdrawn or deemed to be withdrawn (**Art.79(3)**).

The provisional protection starts on the day that the application is published. It is immaterial whether or not the search report or the mention of the publication in the Patent Bulletin is published at the same time (**Art.127, R.143(1), Art.129(a)**). A third party can start an opposition or revocation procedure only after the grant of the patent. The applicant is informed of the intended publication date in a communication from the EPO issued about 4 weeks before publication takes place (see **R.67(2):1**).

A European patent application which has been withdrawn before it is published does not give rise to provisional protection (**Art.67(4)**). This may happen if the application is withdrawn before the date of publication but too late to prevent publication.

The provisional protection associated with a published European patent application is also applicable in extension states according to the Extension Ordinances, Art.4 (OJ 1994 p.80) and may also apply in validation states depending on the terms of the validation agreement (OJ 2016 A5). See Art.29 PCT for the provisional protection conferred by an international application.

Art. 67(2) Any Contracting State may prescribe that a European patent application shall not confer such protection as is conferred by Article 64. However, the protection attached to the publication of the European patent application may not be less than that which the laws of the State concerned attach to the compulsory publication of unexamined national patent applications. In any event, each State shall ensure at least that, from the date of publication of a European patent application, the applicant can claim compensation reasonable in the circumstances from any person who has used the invention in that State in circumstances where that person would be liable under national law for infringement of a national patent.

1 **Minimum rights conferred by application**

All contracting states provide an equivalent degree of provisional protection to a European application and a national application. See NatLaw table III.A for the different provisions for each state: all states have provided for either compensation reasonable in the circumstances or damages.

Art. 67(3) Any Contracting State which does not have as an official language the language of the proceedings may prescribe that provisional protection in accordance with paragraphs 1 and 2 above shall not be effective until such time as a translation of the claims in one of its official languages at the option of the applicant or, where that State has prescribed the use of one specific official language, in that language:

(a) has been made available to the public in the manner prescribed by national law, or

(b) has been communicated to the person using the invention in the said State.

1 **Translation for provisional protection**

A state that does not have the language of the proceedings as an official language may make the provisional protection dependent on the filing of a translation of the claims in one of its official languages. NatLaw table III.B indicates which states have made use of this provision. The table indicates for each state whether the appointment of a national representative is required, whether any fee is payable and the languages which are permitted.

All states, except Malta and Switzerland, require a translation of the claims under **Art.67(3)** if the language of proceedings is not an official language of that state (NatLaw table III.A, note 3). The translation is made available to the public by inspection, by mention in a bulletin, by publication, or by entry in the national patent register.

The translations required for obtaining provisional rights are not governed by the London Agreement, which relates only to translations after grant (**Art.65(1):2**). For example, when the language of proceedings is English, France requires a French translation of the claims for provisional protection but does not require a translation of the granted patent specification. Note that the granted claims are always available in the three EPO languages, (**Art.14(6)**) whereas the claims in the published application are only available in the language of the proceedings.

There is no time limit for filing the translation. However, provisional protection is only effective when the translation is published (**Art.67(3)(a)**) or communicated to the person using the invention (**Art.67(3)(b)**). See NatLaw table III.A, note 4 for the way in which provisional protection becomes effective each state. Most states use provision (a) and about a fifth of them in addition use provision (b). As an exception, provisional protection in the Netherlands begins 30 days after the user of the invention has been notified of the applicant's rights by a so-called writ accompanied by a translation of the claims in Dutch or an indication that the translation has been entered in the patent register.

The EPO provides information on the requirements of **Art.67(3)** in a communication sent about four weeks prior to the publication of the patent application, in which it also informs the applicant of the intended publication date (OJ 1991 p.224; see **R.67(1):1**).

Provisional protection also applies to Euro-PCT applications after their publication (**Art.153(2)**, **Art.93**, **Art.67**). If the international application is not published in an official language of the EPO, the provisional protection under **Art.67** starts only after publication of a translation into an official language by the EPO (**Art.153(4)**). For example, where the international application is published in Japanese and an English translation is published by the EPO under **Art.153(4)**, the protection for Great Britain starts on the date of publication of the English translation (**Art.67(1)**) but the protection for Germany starts only after a translation of the claims in German has been published or sent to the user of the invention (**Art.67(3)**).

Art. 67(4) The European patent application shall be deemed never to have had the effects set out in paragraphs 1 and 2 when it has been withdrawn, deemed to be withdrawn or finally refused. The same shall apply in respect of the effects of the European patent application in a Contracting State the designation of which is withdrawn or deemed to be withdrawn.

1 **Retroactive effect of withdrawal and refusal of application**
The application is finally refused at the end of the period for filing an appeal following a decision to refuse, or, if the decision to refuse is appealed, when the appeal is rejected (see **Art.106(1):3**).

The provisional protection associated with a published European patent application ends the day before the day of publication of the grant of the patent. It is then replaced by the rights conferred by the patent.

Art. 68 Effect of revocation or limitation of the European patent

The European patent application and the resulting European patent shall be deemed not to have had, from the outset, the effects specified in Articles 64 and 67, to the extent that the patent has been revoked or limited in opposition, limitation or revocation proceedings.

Art.64 Rights conferred by a European patent
Art.67 Rights conferred by a European patent application after publication

1 **Retroactive effect of limitation and revocation of patent**
Art.68 establishes the retroactive effect of limitation and revocation in all post-grant proceedings. A European patent application and patent are deemed not to have conferred any rights from the outset (*ex tunc*) in the designated contracting states to the extent that the patent is revoked or limited in opposition proceedings according to **Art.101(2)** and (3), limitation or revocation proceedings under **Art.105a** or national revocation proceedings. The equivalent provision relating to pre-grant proceedings is **Art.67(4)** which provides that the preliminary protection accorded by a published European patent application is deemed never to have existed when the application is withdrawn, deemed withdrawn or finally refused. The inclusion of national revocation proceedings in **Art.68** harmonises the retroactive effect of limitation and revocation in all proceedings before the EPO and the contracting states. (OJ 2007 se4 EN p.68)

Since a European patent has the effect of a national patent (**Art.64(1)** and **Art.2(2)**), the retroactive loss of the rights according to the EPC is binding on all designated contracting states, including those states having different national provisions.

A European patent with unitary effect remains a European patent and **Art.68** therefore applies equally to any unitary part of the patent.

The revoked patent remains valid prior art. Renewal fees cannot be refunded. Whether licence fees are to be refunded or not depends on the provisions of the relevant licence contract and the applicable national law. Infringers may still be liable for the payment of compensation if the proprietor has won a case against them before the date of revocation, depending on national law.

Art. 69 Extent of protection

1 **General**
The extent of protection conferred by a patent may determine the outcome of infringement proceedings and thereby the actual value of the patent. Since a European patent confers the same rights as a national patent (**Art.64(1)**) on the proprietor and infringement of a European patent is dealt with by national law (**Art.2(2)** and **64(3)**), it is accepted that a European patent may confer a different extent of protection in different contracting states. **Art.69(1)** tries to limit this divergence by giving guidance to national courts on the extent of protection conferred by a European patent or European patent application in an attempt to harmonise varying national approaches. A unified interpretation of the European patent and a uniform determination of the extent of protection in accordance with **Art.69** would give the proprietor more legal certainty. To provide more clarity, a Protocol on the Interpretation of **Art.69** has been added by the legislator. The proto-

col aims to prevent an expansive approach to determining the scope of protection which focuses on the general inventive concept, as has been traditional in Germany; it also aims to prevent a narrow approach to determining the scope of protection which adheres to the exact wording of the claims, as has been traditional in the United Kingdom. The overview of national case law in Singer Art.69 note 35 ff. illustrates the degree of harmonisation that has been achieved.

A question on whether **Art.69(1)**, second sentence and **Prot.Rec.Art.1** are to be applied on the interpretation of claims when assessing the patentability of an invention is pending as G1/24. Other questions referred to the EBoA relate to the use of description and figures for interpretation of the claims, and to use of a definition of a term given in the description, and if yes, in which cases.

Note that the extent of protection conferred by a European patent need not be the same in all designated contracting states as a result of European or national prior rights (**R.138**), reservations under former Art.167(2) EPC1973, or a partial transfer of rights following an entitlement dispute (**R.18**).

Art. 69(1) The extent of the protection conferred by a European patent or a European patent application shall be determined by the claims. Nevertheless, the description and drawings shall be used to interpret the claims.

Implemented by:
Protocol on the interpretation of Art.69 of the Convention

1 **Extent of protection determined by claims**

Pursuant to **Art.69(1)**, the extent of protection conferred by a patent or a patent application is primarily determined by the claims. Nevertheless, the description and drawings should be used to interpret those claims (see also **Art.84, R.43-45**).

Note that under EPC1973 the English version of Art.69(1) referred to the 'terms of the claims', pointing to the literal meaning, whereas the German and French versions referred to 'Inhalt' and 'teneur', suggesting a broader interpretation. **Art.69(1)** EPC2000 refers only to the claims as such, not their terms.

According to German case law, interpretation of the claims according to **Art.69** and its protocol serves not only to resolve any ambiguities in the claims but also to clarify the technical terms used therein, as well as to clarify the significance and scope of the invention. The interpretation must be made through the eyes of the skilled person, not through the eyes of a philologist. Terms in the claims and description must therefore be construed as they would be by the skilled person in view of the overall content of the specification, according to the idea behind the invention and having regard to the problem and solution as derived from the patent (see **R.42(1)(c)**). (German Federal Court of Justice, OJ 2001 p.259)

Where the description states that a feature is necessary for practicing the invention, the claims can be interpreted to contain this feature, even if it is not explicitly present (**T416/87**). The drawings can have a comparable function (**T169/83**).

According to German case law, if applicants declare during grant proceedings that they do not seek protection for a particular embodiment, they may not broaden the extent of protection of their patent to cover this embodiment. The principle of good faith requires them to adhere to their declaration. (German Federal Court of Justice, OJ 1998 p.141)

Art. 69(2) For the period up to grant of the European patent, the extent of the protection conferred by the European patent application shall be determined by the claims contained in the application as published. However, the European patent as granted or as amended in opposition, limitation or revocation proceedings shall determine retroactively the protection conferred by the application, in so far as such protection is not thereby extended.

1 **Extent of protection before and after grant**
The extent of the protection conferred by a European patent application before grant is determined by the latest filed claims contained in the publication of the application (**Art.69(2)**). This is either a European patent application published under **Art.93** or a Euro-PCT application published pursuant to **Art.153(3)** (WO publication) or **Art.153(4)** (translation published by EPO). Since **Art.69(2)**, second sentence, refers to opposition, limitation and revocation proceedings, a limitation of the patent in any of these proceedings retroactively limits the extent of protection conferred by the application. (OJ 2007 se4 EN p.68)

Applicants may amend the claims after receipt of the search report (**Art.123** and **R.137(1)**). If they make use of this opportunity before the end of the technical preparations for publication (**R.67(1)**, five weeks before publication), the application will be published including the claims as filed and the amended claims (**R.68(4)**); the amended claims determine the extent of the provisional protection. Amendment as of right is only possible together with the first substantive response (**R.137(2)**).

The extent of the protection conferred by a European patent after grant is determined by the claims as granted or as amended in opposition, limitation or national revocation proceedings (**Art.69(1)** and **Art.68**). Any amendment of the claims during opposition or limitation proceedings may not extend the protection conferred by the patent (**Art.123(3)**). The claims as granted or as amended in opposition, limitation or national revocation proceedings also determine retroactively the provisional protection conferred by the published application provided this protection is not thereby extended compared with the protection conferred by the claims of the published application (**Art.69(2)**, second sentence).

In other words, even if the claims of the patent as granted are broader than those of the application as published, which may be the case provided there is a basis for such a broadening in the application as filed, third parties' rights are not affected by such broadening during the period up to the grant of the patent; if on the other hand, the claims of the patent as granted are narrower than those of the application as published, third parties benefit from the narrowing retroactively. (**G1/93** r.10)

When a patent is maintained in opposition, limitation, or national revocation proceedings with a limited scope of protection which retroactively removes the grounds on which an infringement action is based, any compensation or damages already paid may be subject to reimbursement, depending on national law. If the patent is never granted or is revoked in opposition or revocation proceedings, no rights are considered to have ever existed (**Art.67(4)**, **Art.68**); this retroactively negates any right to compensation, at least in so far as pending or future claims to compensation are concerned.

Art. 70 Authentic text of a European patent application or European patent

1 **General**
This provision specifies the authentic text of a European patent application and patent. It indicates the importance of the language of the proceedings when interpreting the disclosure of the application and patent before the EPO and before authorities in each contracting state.

Art. 70(1) The text of a European patent application or a European patent in the language of the proceedings shall be the authentic text in any proceedings before the European Patent Office and in any Contracting State.

1 **Authentic text of application and patent in proceedings**
The language of the proceedings is the official language of the EPO in which the application is filed or into which the application is translated (**Art.14(3)**). The wording of the claims of a European patent in the other official EPO languages as filed under **R.71(3)** carries no legal weight (A-VII,8).

Mistakes in the published specification of a European patent (**Art.98**) arising in the course of its production have no legal significance. The published specification is for information purposes only and has no legally binding character. It is the text on which the decision to grant the patent is based (**Art.97(1)** and **R.71a(1)**) that is decisive. (C-V,10)

Art. 70(2) If, however, the European patent application has been filed in a language which is not an official language of the European Patent Office, that text shall be the application as filed within the meaning of this Convention.

Implemented by:
R.7 Legal authenticity of the translation of the European patent application

1 **Authentic text of the application as filed**
Art.70(2) establishes that if a European patent application is filed in a language which is not an official language of the EPO, that text is the 'application as filed' for the purposes of:

- **Art.14(2)**: bringing the translation into conformity with application as filed;
- **Art.54(3)**: establishing content of a European prior right (A-VII,7; G-IV,5.1);
- **Art.61(1)(b)** and **(2)**: assessing any extension of subject-matter for a new application filed after an entitlement dispute;
- **Art.76(1)**: assessing any extension of subject-matter for a divisional application;
- **Art.100(c)**: assessing any extension of subject-matter for a patent in opposition proceedings;
- **Art.123(2)**: assessing any extension of subject-matter when amending a patent application; and
- **Art.138(1)(c)**: assessing any extension of subject-matter in national revocation proceedings. (OJ 2007 se4 EN p.168)

The EPO need not investigate the correctness of the translation of its own motion; it may assume the translation is correct (**R.7**, which is a lex specialis of **Art.114**, D-V,6.1) unless someone provides proof to the contrary. Although the EPO is not obliged to check the correctness of the translation, it may do so anyway if it suspects that there are inaccuracies in it.

If the translation into an official EPO language or an amendment made during prosecution has potentially extended the subject-matter of the application, **Art.70(2)** prescribes the use of the original text in the non-EPO language as the basis for determining whether such an extension has occurred. The extension of subject-matter is a ground for opposition (**Art.100(c)**) and a ground for revocation (**Art.138(1)(c)**).

Art.70(2) applies equally to a Euro-PCT application which is filed in a language other than English, French or German – see **R.159(1):2.1**.

Note that a correction of a translation during opposition proceedings will not be allowed if it extends the protection conferred by the patent, thereby contravening **Art.123(3)** (A-VII,7).

Art. 70(3) Any Contracting State may provide that a translation into one of its official languages, as prescribed by it according to this Convention, shall in that State be regarded as authentic, except for revocation proceedings, in the event of the European patent application or European patent in the language of the translation conferring protection which is narrower than that conferred by it in the language of the proceedings.

1 **Authentic text in the case of narrow translation**

Contracting states may require the filing of a translation of the claims of a European patent application for provisional protection to be recognised (**Art.67(3)**) and the filing of a translation of a European patent for the patent to be valid (**Art.65(1)**). Such a translation can become the authentic text under **Art.70(3)** in the case that the translation provides a narrower scope of protection than the text in the language of the proceedings. As an exception, the broader text in the language of the proceedings remains authentic in revocation proceedings.

Belgium and Germany have not made use of **Art.70(3)** and the authentic text is always the text in the language of the proceedings (see NatLaw table V).

Art. 70(4) Any Contracting State which adopts a provision under paragraph 3:

(a) shall allow the applicant for or proprietor of the patent to file a corrected translation of the European patent application or European patent. Such corrected translation shall not have any legal effect until any conditions established by the Contracting State under Article 65, paragraph 2, or Article 67, paragraph 3, have been complied with;

(b) may prescribe that any person who, in that State, in good faith has used or has made effective and serious preparations for using an invention the use of which would not constitute infringement of the application or patent in the original translation, may, after the corrected translation takes effect, continue such use in the course of his business or for the needs thereof without payment.

Art.65(2) Payment for publication of the translation of the patent in an official language of a state

Art.67(3) Publication of the translation of the claims of the application in an official language of a contracting state

1 **Correction of narrow translation**

All countries that regard a translation with a narrower scope of protection as the authentic text have provisions pursuant to paragraph (b). See NatLaw table V, note 2. See OJ 2011 p.398 for an example of the legal effect of a translation error in a patent.

See **Art.122(5)** for a right of continued use after re-establishment of rights equivalent to the right of paragraph (b).

Chapter IV *The European patent application as an object of property*

1 **Transfer and licencing**

A European patent application may have a considerable economic value and provision must be made allowing it to be transferred or licensed in each contracting state. The treatment of national applications and patents as objects of property is provided for in national law. As a European patent application has effects extending over several states, some property questions must be settled in the EPC. Therefore, the EPC provides uniform provisions allowing for the transfer and licensing of European patent applications and the registration of such transactions in the European Patent Register. The grant of other rights may also be registered (**R.23(1)**).

Changes in the name of an applicant or proprietor, not involving a transfer of a right, are entered in the Register on production of supporting evidence (E-XIV,5).

The transfer of an application before the EPO takes place as the result of either a legal act (**Art.72**), e.g. a sale, a gift or a will, or the action of a law, e.g. an inheritance. The requirements relating to the act of transferring a European patent application are laid down in **Art.72**. The EPC has no special provisions for the establishment of rights, apart from license rights (**Art.73**). Such rights must be established in conformity with national law (**Art.74**). The transfer of a European patent application is recognised by the EPO only after payment of the appropriate fee and entry of the transfer in the European Patent Register (**R.22(1), (2)**).

2 **Competence**

The EPC provisions relating to the transfer of patent applications and patents primarily aim at ensuring that the EPO is aware of the identity of the applicant or proprietor during proceedings before it. The EPC does not have explicit provisions governing the competence of the EPO and the national offices in the case of a transfer or the national legal effects of a transfer registered with the EPO. The following reasoning supports the view that competence passes from the EPO to national offices at the date of mention of the grant. The reasoning is in line with the decisions of national courts published in OJ 1984 p.276 and OJ 1987 p.438.

The EPC is a system of law, common to the contracting states, for the grant of patents (**Art.1**). Hence, the EPO is competent in all matters provided for in the EPC relating to a European patent application, such as the according of a filing date, the designation of inventor and the registration of transfers. Therefore, **Art.71-73** and **R.22-24** pertaining to transfers and licensing are binding on the contracting states. In consequence, most contracting states have no provisions in their national law for registering the transfer of a European patent application other than by duplicating information taken from the European Patent Register and transmitted by the EPO. Thus, the registration of the transfer of an application before the EPO must have legal effect in the designated contracting states. As a consequence, national offices are not competent to register the transfer of a European patent application. Legal matters relating to the European patent application as a property right not provided for in the EPC follow national law (**Art.74**). Entitlement disputes in relation to an application, for example, can only be decided by national courts (see **Art.61(1)** and Prot. Rec.)

Art.2(2) and **Art.97(3)** delimit the periods during which the EPO and the national offices, respectively, are competent to decide on requests for the registration of transfers and licences. The European patent is subject to national law in matters of transfer according to **Art.2(2)**, because the EPC does not provide otherwise. Hence, after publication of the mention of the grant (**Art.97(3)**), the European Patent Register is for registration purposes only, and registration of a transfer as required by **R.85** has no national legal effects. **R.85** merely enables the EPO to keep the Register updated until the end of the opposition period or until any opposition proceedings are disposed of and it should not take precedence over national provisions for the transfer of patents. The national offices alone are competent to register the transfer of a European patent with national legal effect. This applies also during the opposition period and during opposition proceedings. Several states recognise under special conditions a transfer registered by the EPO under **R.85** (NatLaw table IX, note 6). The national requirements for registering the transfer of a European patent in the national patent registers are given in NatLaw table IX.

If, for example, a person to whom a European patent has been transferred wants to sue an infringer, the person must have the transfer registered with the national office of the contracting state in which the infringer is domiciled; the registration of the transfer of the patent with the EPO does not suffice.

According to Art.7 of EU regulation 1257/2012, a unitary patent as an object of property will be treated as the national patent of the participating state in which the applicant had a residence or place of business at the filing date or, if such a state does not exist, as a German national patent. Any transfer of the unitary patent or license concerning it will be recorded in the Register for unitary patent protection held by the EPO, on payment of an administrative fee (**UPR.20(2)**), and will have effect in all participating states.

Art. 71 Transfer and constitution of rights

A European patent application may be transferred or give rise to rights for one or more of the designated Contracting States.

Implemented by:
R.22 Registration of transfers
R.23 Registration of licenses and other rights
R.85 Transfer of the European patent

1 **Transfers and licences**

A European patent application has a unitary character in proceedings before the EPO (**Art.118**). This does not, however, preclude the transfer of the European patent from one applicant to another, in part or in full, but requires instead that different applicants act in common (see **R.151**) and on the basis of a single text (**R.138**). Hence, an application may be transferred either as a whole or in respect of one or more states (**Art.71**). This is in accordance with **Art.59**, which allows different applicants for different states. The transfer of the application and the associated rights applies to the whole territory of a contracting state (**Art.71**), whereas a license can be granted also for only a part of the territory of a contracting state (**Art.73**). An application can also be transferred for a share; transfer of rights to particular subject-matter does not seem possible but a license can be given for a part of the patent application's subject-matter (**Art.73**). A transfer may occur by way of assignment (**Art.72**) or universal succession, e.g. in case of merger of companies.

The procedure and requirements for registering the transfer of a patent application before the EPO are provided in **R.22**. The transfer becomes effective vis-à-vis the EPO when the required documents have been filed and the fee has been paid, with an exception for cases of universal succession (**R.22(3)**).

Although **Art.71** is only applicable to the transfer of an application, according to **R.85** the transfer of a patent during the opposition period or while opposition proceedings or any subsequent appeal proceedings are pending (**R.100(1)**) must also be entered in the Register in the same way as the transfer of an application, as prescribed in **R.22**, to become effective vis-à-vis the EPO. Such registration is necessary for the EPO to be able to establish the identity of the proprietor in opposition proceedings.

A unitary patent can only be transferred in respect of all the states in which it has effect (Art.3(2) EU Regulation 1257/2012).

2 **Other rights**

The grant or transfer of a right in rem in respect of a European patent application and any legal means of execution affecting the application may also be registered at the EPO (**R.23(1)**). The grant of a right in rem includes the grant of a security interest such as a lien (the right to keep possession of property until a debt is discharged) or the grant of a usufruct (the right to use property without payment). An example of a legal means of execution is the seizure of an application as an item of property.

Art. 72 Assignment

An assignment of a European patent application shall be made in writing and shall require the signature of the parties to the contract.

1 **Requirements for assignment**

An assignment is a legal transfer (Dutch: rechtsgeldige overdracht, German: rechtsgeschäftliche Übertragung). A European patent application may only be assigned in writing and cannot be assigned by means of an oral agreement. The written document must be signed by all the parties to the contract according to **Art.72** (E-XIV,3). The EPO will not accept a declaration of transfer signed only by the assignor (E-XIV,3). Representatives may sign an assignment only if they are authorised to do so. In the case where a document is signed on behalf of a legal person, the EPO may require evidence of the signatory's entitlement to sign.

The rights in an application owned by one of two joint applicants may be assigned without the consent of the other applicant, provided that this is consistent with any contractual obligations that exist and the relevant provisions of national law.

National laws may prescribe different requirements for the transfer of a national application, such as, for example, notarisation of the agreement, recordal of the transfer in a patent register and publication of the assignment (see e.g. **J16/05** r.2.1). In contrast, the assignment of a European patent application complying with **Art.72** and **R.22** will be effective vis-à-vis the EPO and have legal effect in all the contracting states (see **Art.74:1**).

In general, the EPO does not require the filing of the instrument of transfer but only of a document providing evidence that the transfer has taken place (**R.22(1)**). It is recommended to use the Form 5055 to make such a declaration. Whatever evidence is used, the requirement that it be signed by both parties remains. See **R.22(1):1** for accepted signatures. In case of doubt, the EPO may request the filing of a certified copy of the instrument of transfer.

Art. 73 Contractual licensing

A European patent application may be licensed in whole or in part for the whole or part of the territories of the designated Contracting States.

Implemented by:
R.22 Registering a transfer
R.23 Registering of licences and other rights
R.24 Special entries for licence registrations

1 **Registering of licences**
Licences are entered in the Register according to **R.23** in the same way as transfers; see **R.143(1)(w)**. Before entry, a fee must be paid, and evidence of the existence of the licence must be provided (**R.23(1)**, referring to **R.22(1)**, (2)).

However, **Art.73** only applies to European patent applications and does not apply to European patents (see **R.85**). So, licences in respect of a patent cannot be registered with the EPO, not even during the opposition period, as the EPC makes no provision for it (see **R.23:1**). A licence granted in respect of a European patent must therefore be registered separately at each national office and satisfy national requirements. Licenses granted in respect of unitary patents are, however, recorded in the Register for unitary patent protection by the EPO upon request (**UPR.20(2)**, applying **R.23** EPC, and **UPR.16(1)(j)**).

Art. 74 Law applicable

Unless this Convention provides otherwise, the European patent application as an object of property shall, in each designated Contracting State and with effect for such State, be subject to the law applicable in that State to national patent applications.

1 **Application of national law**
Art.74 is one of the provisions of the EPC, together with **Art.66** (equivalence of European filing with national filing) and **Art.67** (rights conferred by a European patent application after publication), that makes a choice between harmonising the law across the contracting states and allowing individual national laws to prevail. Providing a uniform provision governing the European patent application as object of property turned out not to be possible. The present compromise can cause difficulties in certain cases; see e.g. **J4/10**.

Art.71-73 and **R.22-24**, **R.85** are examples of the EPC providing 'otherwise'; these EPC provisions overrule national law.

Art.148 allows a group of contracting states to specify a set of uniform property rules which harmonise national law across the group. These rules may deviate from **Art.71-73**. This allows the group to move towards a unified European patent application that can only be transferred, mortgaged or subjected to any legal means of execution collectively for all states in the group.

The EPO registers the transfer of a European patent application (**Art.71**, **Art.72**) only if its validity is clear. Because transfers often involve complex aspects of international civil law, the assessment of the validity of the transfer by the EPO is kept within sensible bounds according to **R.22(1)**.

The competence of applicants to perform legal acts in relation to the property rights represented by their European patent applications and patents must be decided by national law, in view of **Art.74** (**J900/85** r.9, sometimes referred to as JXX/XX).

PART III THE EUROPEAN PATENT APPLICATION

Chapter I *Filing and requirements of the European patent application*

1 **General**
Applicants have, in general, the choice of filing their European patent application with the EPO or with a national authority of a contracting state (**Art.75(1)**). However, national law may restrict the choice by prescribing that the applicant must file the European patent application with a national authority for reasons of national security (**Art.75(2)**). A European divisional application and a new application under **Art.61** must always be filed directly with the EPO (**Art.61(2)** and **Art.76(1)**).

Art. 75(1) A European patent application may be filed:
(a) with the European Patent Office, or
(b) if the law of a Contracting State so permits, and subject to Article 76, paragraph 1, with the central industrial property office or other competent authority of that State. Any application filed in this way shall have the same effect as if it had been filed on the same date with the European Patent Office.

Art.76(1) European divisional applications
Implemented by:
R.35 Filing of the patent application

1 **EPO filing offices (Art.75(1)(a))**
Applicants may, subject to national security provisions under **Art.75(2)**, file their European patent applications directly with the EPO. The filing offices of the EPO for paper applications are specified in **R.35(1)**. The reference to **Art.76(1)** in subparagraph (b) is a reminder that a divisional application must be filed directly with the EPO.

Promptly after receipt of the application, the EPO issues a receipt to the applicant stating the application number and the date of receipt of the documents making up the application (**R.35(2)**). Subsequently, the Receiving Section carries out the examination on filing according to **Art.90**, determining amongst other things, whether the requirements for according a date of filing are satisfied.

A European patent application filed directly with the EPO must be filed using a method of filing permitted by **R.2**. The date of filing accorded to the application will be the date of receipt by a filing office of the EPO permitted by **R.35(1)** in a form allowed by **R.2**, provided the requirements of **Art.80** are met. An application filed on paper at a location of the EPO other than the ones mentioned in **R.35(1)** may be forwarded by that office to an EPO filing office as a courtesy service and will be accorded as date of receipt, the date on which the application arrives at the EPO filing office.

2 **National filing offices (Art.75(1)(b))**
Most contracting states allow applicants to choose between filing their European patent applications with a filing office of the EPO (see **R.35**) and with their national authorities (NatLaw table II, note 1). The exceptions are BE, NL and SM, where European applications must be filed with the EPO unless, for BE and NL, the application may be relevant to national security.

Several contracting states do not give applicants a choice and require that European patent applications be filed with their national authorities for reasons of national security (see **Art.75(2)**; NatLaw table II, note 2).

Filing with a national authority may restrict the languages in which the European patent application may be filed. NatLaw table II, note 3 gives the languages in which a European application must or may be filed with a national office. See **Art.14(2):1**. Some contracting states impose translation requirements for parts of or all of a European patent application when filing the application with its national office in a language that is not an official language of that state. For example, PL requires that a translation of the application accompanies the filing. CY, ES, IT, MT and PT also have specific translation requirements (see NatLaw table II, note 5).

Promptly after receipt of the application, the national authority issues a receipt to the applicant stating the application number and the date of receipt (**R.35(2)**) and informs the EPO of the same data (**R.35(3)**). Most national authorities examine whether the subject-matter of the application must be kept secret. The national authority forwards those applications evidently not subject to secrecy requirements to the EPO within six weeks of filing, or, where further examination concerning the need for secrecy is required, within four months of filing or, if priority has been claimed, fourteen months of the date of priority (**Art.77**, **R.37(1)**). The EPO notifies the applicant under **R.35(4)** of the receipt of the application forwarded by the national authority and starts the examination on filing according to **Art.90**.

Before receipt of the communication under **R.35(4)** from the EPO, the applicant may send further documents relating to the application to the national authority. The national authorities accept (automatic) debit orders for deposit accounts according to ADA.12.1-12.3, notes to AAD.4 in ADA Annex A.2 and A-II,1.6. Payment of the filing, search and claims fees other than by debit order should not be made to national offices. After the applicant has received the communication under **R.35(4)**, further documents must be sent directly to the EPO (A-II,3.2). A document nevertheless sent to a national authority may be forwarded by that authority to the EPO as a courtesy service, but the date of receipt accorded to it will be the date on which the document arrives at the EPO (see, inter alia, OJ 2005 p.445).

When filing a European application with a national office, the applicant can use the (electronic) filing methods as permitted by that national office (see NatLaw table II, note 5).

3 **Form of documents**
The form of the application documents is prescribed under **R.49**.

Art. 75(2) Paragraph 1 shall not preclude the application of legislative or regulatory provisions which, in any Contracting State:
(a) govern inventions which, owing to the nature of their subject-matter, may not be communicated abroad without the prior authorisation of the competent authorities of that State, or

(b) prescribe that any application is to be filed initially with a national authority, or make direct filing with another authority subject to prior authorisation.

1 **National security and requirement to file first with national office**
The EPC has no provisions for handling applications that should be kept secret in the interest of national security. **Art.75(2)** allows the contracting states to apply national provisions regarding secrecy to European applications, using one of the following two options.

The first option is governed by **Art.75(2)(a)**. Applicants themselves decide whether the subject-matter of their European application is relevant for national security. If so, they must file the application with the national authority. If the national authority confirms that the application is relevant for national security, it does not forward the application to the EPO (**Art.77(2)**) and subjects it to the national procedure for secret applications; otherwise, it will forward the application to the EPO (**Art.77(1)**). An applicant who regards the subject-matter as not being relevant for national security, may file the application directly with a filing office of the EPO. Some contracting states may on request authorise applicants in doubt to file their application directly with the EPO.

The second option is laid down in **Art.75(2)(b)**. A contracting state may require that each European application concerning an invention made in that state and / or for which the applicant is a resident of that state is filed initially with its national authority, allowing a check on subject-matter that must be kept secret. Alternatively, a contracting state may allow direct filing with the EPO only after prior authorisation. Such authorisation can sometimes be obtained from a national office within a few hours. Usually contracting states permit applicants to file directly with the EPO if they have filed a first application from which priority is claimed with its national authority. For example, a Greek applicant must file a European patent application in Greece if it does not claim the priority of an earlier Greek application.

The provisions of each contracting state under both paragraph (a) and (b) can be found in NatLaw table II, note 2. Limited information on other states can be found in Section B1 of the PCT Applicant's Guide.

Where two or more states require the same European application to be filed first with their national authorities, the applicant should apply for a foreign filing licence from the most lenient state or states and make the first filing with the national authority of the least lenient state. In case the first filing has been made with the USPTO, the applicant must request the USPTO to issue a licence for foreign filing of the subsequent application abroad, i.e. outside the USA.

Art. 76 European divisional applications

1 **Transitional provision EPC2000**
Revised **Art.76** is applicable to divisional applications received at the EPO on or after the date of entry into force of EPC2000 (13.12.2007), regardless of whether the parent application was filed under EPC1973 or EPC2000. (OJ 2007 se4 EN p.78)

See the transitional provisions of **Art.54(3)** for extent of the prior art for the divisional application.

2 **General**

An applicant may file one or more divisional applications ('divisionals') on the basis of a pending European application (A-IV,1.1). A divisional may serve as the basis for a further divisional application in turn (**G1/06** r.10.2; see also **R.36(1):1**).

A divisional may be filed of the applicant's own volition (voluntary division) or at the request of the EPO to meet an objection under **Art.82** that the application lacks unity (mandatory division).

A divisional is regarded as a new European patent application and its procedure is in principle independent from the procedure of the parent (**G4/98** r.5). Hence, the provisions in the EPC for a European patent application should be applied mutatis mutandis, unless otherwise provided (see e.g. **Art.76** and **R.36**). The 'otherwise provided' relates to the date of filing, designations, periods for payment of fees and extension of subject-matter beyond the content of the parent application.

Another consequence of the independence of the divisional is that the fate of the parent after the filing of the divisional cannot affect it (**G1/06** r.12.2, case consolidated with **G1/05**). For example, examination of the divisional will not be stayed, either on request or by the EPO of its own motion, due to pending opposition or appeal proceedings concerning the parent (C-IX,1.1).

Art. 76(1) A European divisional application shall be filed directly with the European Patent Office in accordance with the Implementing Regulations. It may be filed only in respect of subject-matter which does not extend beyond the content of the earlier application as filed; in so far as this requirement is complied with, the divisional application shall be deemed to have been filed on the date of filing of the earlier application and shall enjoy any right of priority.

Implemented by:
R.36 Provisions for filing divisional application

1 **Filing of divisional application**

A divisional is based on an earlier application and is entitled to the effective date of that earlier application (**Art.76(1)**). The earlier application may be any European patent application. The earlier application may be a divisional, since a divisional is treated as an ordinary application and a divisional is included in 'any pending application' of **R.36(1)** (**G1/06** r.10.2).

A divisional must be filed directly with the EPO (**Art.76(1)**, first sentence). **R.36(2)** specifies the offices in Munich, The Hague and Berlin as filing offices. National offices are not competent to receive divisionals, since this would cause too much delay to allow for a prompt publication. A divisional filed with a national office may, as a courtesy service, be forwarded to the EPO. However, the documents are only allocated a date of receipt when they arrive at the EPO. (A-IV,1.3.1)

A divisional must be filed using a method of filing permitted by **R.2(1)**.

A divisional may be filed by reference to the parent following **R.40(1)(c)**. (A-IV,1.3.1; see also **R.36(2):2**)

The claims may be filed after the date of filing of the divisional as a consequence of **R.40(1)**, even if the parent is no longer pending at the date of filing the claims (A-IV,1.2.1).

The Request for Grant form should be used (**R.41(1)**) and the box for a divisional (**R.41(2)(e)**) ticked.

At the time of filing the divisional and up to compliance with the requirements of **R.40(1)**, the parent must still be pending, i.e. not granted, withdrawn, deemed to be withdrawn or finally refused (**R.36(1)**). See **R.36(3)** and (4) for the filing, search, and designation fee to be paid when filing a divisional, **R.38(3)** and (4) for any page fee and divisional fee, **R.45(1)** for the claims fees and **R.51(3)** for the renewal fees.

When a divisional meets the requirements of **Art.80** and **R.40(1)**, it will be accorded the same date of filing as the parent (A-IV,1.2.1). The date it meets the requirements of **R.40(1)** will be regarded as the date of receipt for the purpose of **R.36(1)**; although this has not been stated explicitly in the Guidelines, it is tacitly assumed. The requirement of **Art.76(1)** restricting the content of the divisional to subject-matter contained in the parent is assessed during substantive examination (A-IV,1.2.1). See **Art.76(1):6** for the procedure after filing.

A divisional that does not meet the requirements of **Art.80** and **R.40(1)**, even after correction, will not be dealt with as a divisional application (**Art.90(2)**).

Note, that the Guidelines regard **R.40** as applicable to divisionals (A-IV,1.2.1 and 1.3.1), whereas the travaux préparatoires of EPC2000 state: 'As no individual filing date is accorded to a divisional, **R.40** is not applicable to divisionals' (OJ 2003 se1 p.159).

The reason for the impedimental wording of **Art.76(1)** is given in **G1/06** point VIII and reason 2.

2 Applicant

The issue of who is entitled to file a divisional is not raised in **Art.76**, because it was regarded self-evident that Art.4G Paris Convention applies, which states that 'the applicant may divide the application'. Hence, the applicant of the parent is entitled to file a divisional, as confirmed by **R.36(1)**. (**J2/01** r.2.4)

The right to file a divisional is a procedural right that derives from the applicant's status as applicant for the earlier application (**J2/01**, r.5.1). As a consequence of **Art.60(3)**, dealing with the procedural status of the applicant, the applicant named in the Register is regarded as entitled to file a divisional. However, where universal succession occurs, the new owner is entitled to file a divisional, even if they are not registered at the EPO as the applicant for the parent application (**J7/21**).

Multiple applicants are joint applicants, each of which can only exercise their party rights in common with the other applicant(s) (see **Art.59:1**). Hence, if the parent application has multiple applicants at the time a divisional application is filed, the divisional application must be filed by the same multiple applicants jointly. If this requirement is not complied with, the application will not acquire divisional status (**J2/01** r.12 and point III of Summary of facts and submissions). Neither can the application be dealt with as an independent application with the date of its receipt as filing date (**G1/06** r.11.1). Any substantive rights of applicants to part of the subject-matter of the parent under **Art.60(1)** are not relevant for the procedural status of the applicant, because **Art.60(1)** does not refer to 'the applicant'. (**J2/01** r.6)

Representatives may act on the basis of an individual authorisation in respect of the parent only if it expressly empowers them to file divisionals (A-IV,1.6). See **R.152(6)** for the consequences of not filing an authorisation if requested to do so.

The designation of the inventor for a divisional is preferably contained in the Request for Grant form (**R.19(1)**). If not made in the Request for Grant form, the EPO will invite the applicant to make the designation within a period to be specified (**R.60(2)**) of at least two months. If a divisional relates to only a part of the subject-matter of the parent, only those inventors designated in the parent who contributed to that part of the subject-matter need be designated in the divisional.

3 **Transfer of application**

R.36(1) lays down that only the applicants of the parent or their successors in title entered in the Register (**R.143(1)(f)**) may file a divisional. In the case of a transfer the new applicant may file a divisional only on or after the date that the transfer of the parent was duly registered with the EPO under **R.22** (A-IV,1.1.3). A representative that must file an authorisation may only act on the basis of the authorisation filed in respect of the parent if it expressly empowers the filing of divisionals (A-IV,1.6).

Where the parent is filed by joint applicants, the divisional should also be filed by the same joint applicants. There are two possibilities to reduce the number of applicants for the divisional. Suppose the parent disclosing a first and a second invention is filed by a first and second applicant. The divisional relates only to the second invention, in which the first applicant is not interested and in which the second applicant has a substantive right. The second applicant can file the divisional as sole applicant only if the first applicant has notified the EPO under **R.22** before the filing of the divisional. The **R.22** notification can take the form of a transfer of the right to the second invention from the first applicant to the second applicant, or an agreement of the first applicant that the divisional is being prosecuted further in the sole name of the second applicant (J2/01, r.8). Alternatively, both applicants can file the divisional and the first applicant can subsequently notify the EPO under **R.22** as above and withdraw as applicant.

4 **Language**

A divisional must, according to **R.36(2)**, be filed in the language of the proceedings of the parent or the language in which the parent was filed if that language was not an official EPO language (A-IV,1.3.3).

5 **Priority**

If the parent claims priority from one or more earlier applications, then the divisional retains any such priority according to **Art.76(1)**, last sentence, even though the date the divisional was filed is well outside the priority year. A declaration of priority need not be filed a second time, as the right of priority is granted automatically for a divisional, provided the priority claim of the parent is valid on the date the divisional is filed. A priority right may be withdrawn or else lost according to **Art.90(5)** or **R.53(3)**. Priority documents also need not be filed again; the EPO places them in the file of the divisional. If the priority documents have not yet been filed for the parent, they must be filed for both the parent and divisional to the extent the applicant wants to enjoy a right of priority for these applications. (A-IV,1.2.2; see also **R.53(1):1** and **(2):1**)

If the priority claim of the parent has been withdrawn before the filing of a divisional, the divisional is not entitled to that priority. However, the withdrawal of the priority claim of the parent after the filing of the divisional does not affect the priority of the divisional. Equally, the withdrawal of a priority claim in respect of the divisional does not affect the priority claim of the parent. (A-IV,1.2.2)

An example: The priority application P1 has a filing date D1: 02.01.2008 and contains subject-matter A and B. A subsequent application P2 is filed at date D2: 20.12.2008 with subject-matter A, B, C and D, claiming priority of P1 for A and B. Non-unity is noticed between A-C and B-D. On 01.06.2010 P2 is divided and a divisional P3 with subject-matter A and C is filed, automatically obtaining the priority of P1. The effective date for subject-matter A in P3 is D1 and for C D2.

6 **Examination on filing, search and publication**

The divisional will in principle be dealt with as a new, independent application (**G4/98** r.5). It will be treated in the same manner as ordinary applications and subject to the same requirements, unless specific provisions of the EPC, in particular those of **Art.76** or **R.36**, require something different (**G1/06** r.3.1, 9.1).

After filing, the divisional is searched, published and examined in the same way as other European patent applications (A-IV,1.8). During substantive examination, compliance with the requirement of **Art.76(1)**, second sentence, will also be assessed, i.e. whether the subject-matter of the divisional does not extend beyond the content of the parent (C-IX,1.4). If complied with, the divisional is accorded the date of filing of the parent. Any amendment of the divisional after filing is assessed for extension of subject-matter beyond the content of the divisional as filed (**Art.123(2)**).

The filing and search fee (**R.36(3)**) and any page fee or divisional fee (**R.38(3), (4)**) must be paid within one month of filing. Any claims fees must be paid within one month of filing the first set of claims (**R.45(2)**). The designation fee must be paid within six months of the mention of the publication of the search report for the divisional (**R.36(4)**). Examination must be requested within the same six-month period (**R.70(1)**).

The EPO has not provided guidance on the time of publication of the divisional. In practice, the divisional will be published two to four months after its filing, assuming that the parent has already been published. If the claims are filed later than the application and are not available by this time, the publication will be postponed until they are available (see **Art.93(1):1**). The publication will include a search report if available at the completion of the technical preparations for publication. If not available, the search report will be published later.

7 **Scope of claims**

Applicants are free to determine the scope of protection they desire by including or excluding specific subject-matter disclosed in the description (**G2/10** r.4.5.5). A divisional may disclaim subject-matter disclosed positively in the parent (**G2/10** r.4.6).

The claims of a divisional as filed need not be limited to the subject-matter already claimed in the parent. The applicant may obtain a patent for a preferred embodiment in the parent and pursue more general claims in the divisional application (**G2/10** r.4.5.5).

However, the subject-matter of the claims of the divisional may not extend beyond the content of the parent as filed (**Art.76(1)**). (C-IX,1.4; see the following section for the extent of the subject-matter)

The claims of the divisional may be amended after its filing to aspects of the parent disclosed in the divisional as filed but not encompassed by the claims of the divisional as filed (**G1/06** r.9.2). The amendment may not extend the subject-matter of the divisional (not the parent!) as filed because of **Art.123(2)**. (**T441/92** r.4.2)

The parent and divisional must not contain claims directed to the same subject-matter in order to avoid double patenting (**G4/19**). However, one application may claim its own subject-matter in combination with that of the other application; e.g. if the parent and divisional claim separate and distinct elements A and B, respectively, which may operate in combination, one of the two applications may also include a claim directed to A plus B. (C-IX,1.6 in view of G-IV,5.4; see **Art.97(2)**:2)

An independent claim in the parent may include all the features of an independent claim in the divisional combined with an additional feature (**T587/98** hn).

An independent claim of a divisional may be restricted to only a part of the subject-matter claimed in the parent, if this part is directly and unambiguously derivable from the parent as being a separate part or entity, i.e. one which can even be used outside the context of the invention of the parent (**T545/92**; C-IX,1.4).

As an exception to the prohibition of identical claims, the claims of a divisional may have the same scope as that of the parent, provided that, by the time the claims of the divisional are submitted, the parent (without being granted) has ceased to exist. In that case the question of double patenting does not arise. (**T441/92** r.2.2; see also **G1/06** r.13.4, 13.5)

A decision in appeal for a parent case is binding for the same subject-matter in a divisional case, and claims refused on appeal for the parent case cannot be pursued on appeal in the divisional case (**T51/08**).

The practice of filing a sequence of substantially identical divisionals to keep rights pending for up to twenty years for strategic reasons was regarded unsatisfactory by the Enlarged Board of Appeal (**G1/06** r.13.5).

8 Subject-matter of divisional application

The subject-matter of a divisional may not extend beyond the content of the parent, according to **Art.76(1)**. The content of the parent is the total technical information content of the disclosure, including the description, claims and drawings (**G1/06** r.9.2; **T1409/05** r.3.1.2). The content of the parent does not include the abstract (**Art.85** and **T246/86** applied analogously).

The same test as for extension of subject-matter under **Art.123(2)**, i.e. the disclosure test, must be used for assessment under **Art.76(1)** (**G1/06** r.5.1 and **G2/10** r.4.3, 4.6). The subject-matter of a divisional must be objectively and unambiguously derivable from the parent (**T423/03**). The divisional will be accorded the filing date of the parent including any priority claim only if its subject-matter does not extend beyond the content of the parent (**Art.76(1)**, second sentence).

The subject-matter of the divisional must be disclosed in the parent as filed and not be unequivocally and definitively abandoned by the time of filing the divisional (**G1/06** r.11.2). Subject-matter deleted from an application, e.g. on grounds of non-unity, may be filed as a divisional. When deleting subject-matter, the applicant should avoid any statements which could be interpreted as abandonment (C-IX,1.3). Explicitly abandoned subject-matter cannot be used for a divisional because such subject-matter is regarded as dedicated to the public (**J15/85**, r.4, 5; **J2/01** r.6). As an exception, an expressly declared abandonment of claims may be revoked later in order to reinstate claims in a divisional, provided this was the real intention of the party when deleting the claims (**T910/92**).

Material in the pending parent only relevant for the invention of the divisional should be removed from the parent, as being irrelevant matter in the sense of **R.48(1)(c)** (F-V,11.1). Likewise, material in the divisional unrelated to or inconsistent with the invention of the divisional should be removed where necessary (C-IX,1.5).

Amendment of the divisional after its filing is subject to the restrictions of **Art.123(2)** (**G1/06** r.9.2) with respect to the divisional as filed, not with respect to the parent as filed (**T441/92** r.4.2). After the filing of the divisional, no interchange of subject-matter between the parent and divisionals is possible.

9 **Correction of extension of subject-matter**

If the subject-matter of the divisional as filed extends beyond that of the parent, the examining division will ask the applicant to remove the added matter. If the added matter is not deleted, the divisional will be refused under **Art.97(2)** (C-IX,1.4). An interpretation of the second sentence of **Art.76(1)** that a divisional containing subject-matter extending beyond the content of the parent on the date of filing of the divisional is invalid is not correct (**G1/05** r.2.9, consolidated with **G1/06**). Since a divisional must be treated in the same manner as an ordinary application and be subject to the same requirements, the applicant has a right to amend in order to overcome the deficiency after filing according to **Art.123(1)** (**G1/06** r.3.1 and 3.4), even during opposition proceedings (**G1/06** r.3.6). The proceedings of **G3/06** relating to correction of extension of subject-matter during opposition proceedings were terminated, because all appeals in the referring case were withdrawn (OJ 2007 p.312). Pendency of the parent at the time of the amendment is not relevant (**G1/06** r.8.2). If the added matter is not removed, the divisional will be refused under **Art.97(2)** as not meeting the requirements of **Art.76(1)** (**G1/06** r.2.4).

It is not possible to convert a divisional into an application with its own filing date, because the EPC does not provide for it (**T555/00** hn.3, r.1.6; **G1/06** r.11.1, overturning **T904/97** r.4.1.2). Neither is it allowable to file a divisional containing subject-matter added to the parent application and claiming as filing date the date on which that subject-matter was added (**G1/06** r.11.1). Any content in the parent omitted on filing a divisional cannot be re-introduced in that divisional or in any further divisional based on that divisional (**G1/06** r.11.2).

A divisional divided from a divisional is examined applying **Art.76(1)** mutatis mutandis, i.e. by regarding the first-generation divisional as the earlier application out of which the second-generation divisional has been divided. If the first-generation divisional does not comply with the requirements of **Art.76(1)**, the second-generation divisional is likewise invalid (**T1158/01** hn).

Once the divisional has been filed and the conditions of **Art.76(1)** have been met, the divisional is treated quite separately from the parent and must itself comply independently with all requirements of the EPC. Hence, in view of **Art.123(2)**, amendments after filing of the divisional may not extend the subject-matter beyond the contents of the divisional as filed. Note that the requirement of **Art.76(1)** is separate from that of **Art.123(2)** and that a divisional must meet both requirements; i.e. the divisional must neither contain subject-matter extending beyond the content of the parent nor be amended after its filing in such a way that it contains subject-matter extending beyond the content of the divisional as filed. (**T441/92** r.4.1-4.2)

The following is an example of the application of both requirements. The parent discloses only subject-matter A+B. The divisional on filing discloses only A. The EPO regards the broadening as extension of subject-matter beyond the content of the parent and requests the applicant to amend the divisional to A+B to comply with **Art.76(1)**. However, the introduction of B in the divisional would violate **Art.123(2)** by extending the subject-matter of the divisional beyond its content on filing. Hence, the two requirements may form an inescapable trap.

It is therefore recommended to include all subject-matter of the parent in a divisional; if the divisional includes amended claims, the claims of the parent should be included in the description of the divisional, e.g. as clauses. The divisional is preferably filed in the language of filing of the parent if the parent was not filed in an official EPO language, thereby making it possible to correct translation errors in the divisional (see **R.36(2):1**).

Extension of subject-matter beyond either the content of the parent or beyond the content of the divisional as filed is a ground for opposition (**Art.100(c)**). Since the EPO will keep the file of the parent for at least the same time as the file of the divisional (**R.147(5)**), it will be available for inspection to assess any extension, even if the parent has been withdrawn before publication (**Art.128(3)**) or abandoned later on.

Art. 76(2) All the Contracting States designated in the earlier application at the time of filing of a European divisional application shall be deemed to be designated in the divisional application.

1 **Designation of contracting states**

All contracting states designated in the parent, i.e. not withdrawn or deemed withdrawn, at the time of filing a divisional are deemed designated in the divisional (**Art.76(2)**; A-IV,1.3.4; see also **G4/98** r.5). The reference to the 'time' of filing the divisional application ensures that in case of the withdrawal or deemed withdrawal of a designation of a contracting state, only the contracting states which remain designated in the earlier application at that point in time are deemed to be designated in the divisional application (MR/2/00).

Similarly, all extension states and validation states designated in the parent at the time of filing a divisional are deemed designated in the divisional (A-IV,1.3.5).

The designation fee for the divisional must be paid in accordance with **R.36(4)**. If the designation fee is not paid in due time, the divisional application will be deemed withdrawn (**R.39(2)**).

Art. 77 Forwarding of European patent applications

Art. 77(1) The central industrial property office of a Contracting State shall forward to the European Patent Office any European patent application filed with it or any other competent authority in that State, in accordance with the Implementing Regulations.

Implemented by:
R.37 Forwarding of patent applications by national authorities

Art. 77(2) A European patent application the subject of which has been made secret shall not be forwarded to the European Patent Office.

Art. 77(3) A European patent application not forwarded to the European Patent Office in due time shall be deemed to be withdrawn.

1 **Failure to forward application to EPO**
When a European application is filed at a national office, the national office will inform the EPO of the filing (**R.35(3)**); this may occur before the national office forwards the application to the EPO (A-II,3.2). If the application does not reach the EPO within fourteen months after filing or, where priority has been claimed, after priority (**R.37(2)**, the EPO notifies the applicant under **R.112** that the application is deemed to be withdrawn. The period is extended in case of an interruption in the delivery of mail (**R.134(2)**, last sentence; A-II,1.6). All fees paid in respect of the application are refunded (A-II,3.2). Hence, as well as the filing fee, page fee and search fee, the claims fees, designation fee and examination fee are also refunded (**R.37(2)**, last sentence).

Re-establishment of rights under **Art.122(1)** is not possible, because the non-observance of the fourteen-month period is not the fault of the applicant (J3/80). However, a request for conversion into a national patent application under **Art.135(1)(a)** may be filed (A-II,1.6). See **Art.135(2)** for special provisions relating to this conversion.

Art. 78 Requirements of a European patent application

1 **Meaning of 'application'**
In the EPC, the word 'application' can have different meanings. In some contexts, 'application' means a set of documents, making up the European patent application. In other contexts, 'application' can mean the European patent application itself, i.e. description, claims, abstract and drawings. The word 'application' can also refer to the manner in which something is used, e.g. in 'industrial application' in **Art.57**. Attention must be paid to the meaning the word has in these different contexts. **Art.78**, for instance, uses the first, broad meaning, whereas **Art.83** uses the second, narrow meaning of 'application'. In **Art.71-74**, the term 'application' is used to refer to a right, i.e. the application as an object of property.

Art. 78(1) A European patent application shall contain:
(a) a request for the grant of a European patent;
(b) a description of the invention;
(c) one or more claims;
(d) any drawings referred to in the description or the claims;
(e) an abstract,
and satisfy the requirements laid down in the Implementing Regulations.

Implemented by:
(a) **R.41** Request for grant
(b) **R.42** Contents of the description
  R.30 Requirements relating to nucleotide and amino-acid sequences
  R.31 Deposit of biological material
  R.32 Expert solution
  R.33 Availability of biological material
  R.34 New deposit of biological material
(c) **R.43** Form and content of claims
  R.44 Unity of invention
(d) **R.49(2)** Form of the drawings
(e) **R.47** Form and content of the abstract
General:
  R.48 Prohibited matter
  R.49 Presentation of application documents

R.50 Documents filed subsequently

1 **Request for Grant form**
The use of the EPO Request for Grant form 1001 is not necessary for obtaining a date of filing. However, use of the form is a formal requirement for an application (**R.41(1)**). When not provided on filing, the EPO will invite the applicant to remedy the deficiency. If the form is still not provided in the set period, the application will be refused (**Art.90(5)**).

2 **Description**
If an application discloses a nucleotide or amino acid sequence, a sequence listing must be provided in an annex to the description. The sequence listing must be filed in a specific format according to **R.30**.

An application for an invention relating to biological material that is not publicly available and which cannot be put into effect without access to that material requires the deposit of the biological material with a depositary institution under **R.31** for sufficient disclosure as prescribed in **Art.83**. The availability of a sample of the material is governed by **R.32** and **33**.

3 **Drawings**
Art.78(1) does not state that drawings are necessary; the necessity is to be determined by the applicant, heeding **Art.83** (sufficiency of disclosure). Formulas are not drawings, and need not comply with the requirements for drawings. It should be noted that the USA requires drawings for all features of the claims that can be illustrated by such means.

If drawings referred to in the description are missing, the Receiving Section will proceed according to **Art.90(4)** and **R.56**, which may result in redating of the application. Serious deficiencies in the drawings must be corrected under **Art.90(4)** and **R.58**. The presentation requirements of the drawings are specified on the basis of **R.49**.

4 **Examination**
Compliance with parts a) and b) is verified during the examination of **Art.90(1)** for accordance of a date of filing (**Art.80**). Compliance with all parts a) to e), i.e. with respect to all documents making up the application, is verified during the subsequent formalities examination (**Art.90(3)**). The method of filing the application must be in accordance with **R.2(1)**.

Art. 78(2) A European patent application shall be subject to the payment of the filing fee and the search fee. If the filing fee or the search fee is not paid in due time, the application shall be deemed to be withdrawn.

Implemented by:
R.38 Period for payment of filing fee, search fee and page fee
R.45 Claims fees, period for payment and sanction on non-payment
Rfees2(1)1 Amount of filing fee
Rfees2(1)1a Amount of page fee
Rfees2(1)1b Amount of divisional fee
Rfees2(1)2 Amount of search fee
Rfees2(1)15 Amount of claims fee

1 **Filing fee and search fee**
The filing fee and the search fee must be paid within one month of filing the application, according to **R.38(1)**.

Payment of the filing fee and search fee for divisional applications is dealt with in **Art.76(1)** and **R.36(3)**, for new applications in **Art.61(1)** and **R.17(2)**, and for Euro-PCT applications in **Art.153(1)** and **R.159(1)**.

See **Rfees9** and notes thereto for any refund of the filing and search fee and **R.7a(3):2** for a reduction of the filing and search fee for certain applicants.

The page fee due under **R.38(2)** as part of the filing fee must be paid within the later of one month of filing the application, the first set of claims or the certified copy of the previously filed application. See **R.38(3):1** for the consequences of not paying the fee in due time and **Rfees2(1)1a** for the amount of the fee.

The divisional fee due under **R.38(4)** as part of the filing fee must be paid within one month of filing a divisional application; the amount is given in **Rfees2(1)1b**.

2 **Other fees payable at filing**
Any claims fees for an application due under **R.45(1)** must be paid within one month of filing the first set of claims (**R.45(2)**, **Rfees2(1)15**). When the claims are filed together with the application, any claims fees must be paid within the same one-month period as the filing and search fee. See **R.45** for the consequences of not paying the claims fees.

3 **Missing filing fee or search fee**
Payment of the filing fee and search fee is verified under **Art.90(3)** and **R.57(e)**. If payment of either of these fees has not been made, the application is deemed withdrawn (**Art.78(2)**, second sentence. The loss of rights ensues on expiry of the one-month period, not at expiry of the period for requesting further processing (A-III,16.2). The applicant will be notified of any loss of rights (**R.112(1)**). Further processing under **Art.121** and **R.135** is possible and must be requested within two months from the notification of the loss of rights. Re-establishment in the one-month period is excluded under **R.136(3)**, but re-establishment is available for the two-month period for requesting further processing. A possible remedy, if applicable, is to prove within two months after notification of the loss of rights that the payment was actually made in due time (**R.112(2)**).

Another remedy is to re-file the application and claim priority from the failed application and any earlier application, if still possible. Such refiling does not require the payment of the further processing fee at the cost of a later date of filing.

After deemed withdrawal it is sometimes possible to convert to a national application under **Art.135**. See NatLaw table VII.

Art. 79 Designation of Contracting States

1 **Historical background of the designation system**
A European patent is not necessarily granted for all contracting states to the EPC, but only for those contracting states to the EPC that are designated in the application (designated states), more precisely for those states that are designated states at the time of the grant. The patent can additionally be granted for some states that are not a contracting state to the EPC, namely the validation states and extension states.

Historically, the applicant had to specify one or more of the contracting states as designated states when filing the patent application and had to pay a designation fee for each designated state within, essentially, one month from filing (Art.79 and Art.80 EPC1973 in the original version). This system was quite harsh and prone to mistakes by applicants. The designation system was gradually simplified by providing for the default designation of all contracting states in the request for grant form, extending the period for paying the designation fees until after the receipt of the search report, and setting a cap on the designation fee. Under the current system, introduced in 2009, the designation fee is a flat fee (**R.39**). Moreover, all contracting states to the EPC are deemed to be designated on filing and remain so until the grant unless the applicant withdraws the designation of a state (see **Art.79(3)**) or unless the designation of those contracting states that are member states of the EU is deemed to be withdrawn under **R.39(2a)**. Only states that are contracting states to the EPC on the filing date of the patent application are deemed to be designated.

Remnants of the former system of paying a designation fee per designated state can still be found in **Rfees2(2)** and can be observed in connection with prior rights for older patents and applications (**Art.54(3):3**). A description of the old system can still be found in A-III,11.3. The old system remains applicable to European patent applications filed before 01.04.2009 and to Euro-PCT applications that have entered the European phase before said date.

The system of validation states (**Art.169:6**) is still based on the old designation fee system and requires the payment of a fee for each validation state where patent protection is desired. The fee must be paid early in the procedure (well before the grant of the patent). The same applies to extension states (**Art.169:5**).

Under the current system, proprietors can decide in which contracting states they desire to obtain protection before the grant by withdrawing a designation of a contracting state if desired for some reason (**Art.79(3)**) and after the grant by paying renewal fees only in the desired states and, for those states that require the filing of a translation after the grant of the patent, by deciding whether or not to validate the patent in such a stage (see **Art.65:1**).

Art. 79(1) All the Contracting States party to this Convention at the time of filing of the European patent application shall be deemed to be designated in the request for grant of a European patent.

1 **Designation of contracting states**

All states that are contracting states of the EPC at the filing date of the application are deemed to be designated according to **Art.79(1)**; for divisional applications, see **Art.76(2)** (A-III,11.1). The applicant can generally withdraw the designation of a contracting state if desired (**Art.79(3)**). See **Art.169(1):1,2** for the effect of the designation of a state for which the EPC enters into force shortly after the filing of the application.

Where two or more applicants file an application, the applicants may designate different contracting states according to **Art.59**. In other words, an application may specify different applicants for different contracting states.

The publication of the application indicates the designated contracting states (**R.68(3)**) and the patent specification indicates the designated states for which the patent is granted (**R.73(3)**).

Art. 79(2) The designation of a Contracting State may be subject to the payment of a designation fee.

Implemented by:
R.17(3) Designation fee for a new application
R.36(4) Designation fee for a divisional application
R.39 Designation fee, period for payment, and sanction
R.159(1)(d) Designation fee for a Euro-PCT application
Rfees2(1)3 Amount of designation fee

1 Designation fee

1.1 AMOUNT OF DESIGNATION FEE AND PERIOD FOR PAYMENT

Art.79(2) enables the EPO to require the payment of a designation fee; **R.39(1)** specifies the requirement.

A single designation fee must be paid for the designation of all contracting states (**Rfees2(1)3**). The designation fee does not cover extension states and validation states. A reduction of the designation fee is available for certain applicants (**R.7a(3)**).

The designation fee becomes due on the date the Bulletin mentions the publication of the search report under **Art.92** (according to A-X,5.2.2) and must be paid within six months of that date (**R.39(1)**). The period for payment expires on the same date as the period for filing the request for examination, i.e. for paying the examination fee (**R.70(1)**). The designation fee, hence, has the character of a non-refundable surcharge on the examination fee.

Applicants are reminded of the expiry of the six-month period in the communication of **R.69(1)** informing them of the publication date of the search report. The period may be extended under **R.134** due to non-working days. The search report allows applicants to make an adequate assessment of the prospects of their application, following which they can decide whether to continue the procedure or terminate it by not paying the designation fee. The period of six months from the mention of the publication of the search report for paying the designation fee also applies to a new application (**R.17(3)**) and a divisional application (**R.36(4)**). The period for Euro-PCT applications is specified in **R.159(1)(d)**.

The designation of all contracting states remains valid until the expiry of the period for paying the designation fee, even if the fee is not paid. This can be relevant when filing a divisional application during that period (**R.39(1)**; A-IV,1.3.4).

1.2 EFFECT OF NON-PAYMENT OF DESIGNATION FEE AND REMEDIES

The EPO checks the payment of the designation fee under **Art.90(3)** (C-II,4). The application is deemed withdrawn if the designation fee is not paid in due time (**R.39(2)**). The EPO notifies the applicant of the loss of rights under **R.112(1)**.

If applicable, the applicant may prove within two months from the notification of the loss of rights under **R.112(1)** that the designation fee was in fact paid on time (**R.112(2)**).

The applicant may use further processing according to **Art.121** and **R.135** to remedy the loss of rights by paying the designation fee and the further processing fee within two months of notification of the communication. Re-establishment is possible if the period for paying the designation fee with further processing is missed.

The loss of the application ensues on the expiry of the normal period of **R.39(1)** and not at the expiry of the two-month period for requesting further processing (A-III,11.2.3, applying **G4/98** r.7.2 mutatis mutandis).

2 Extension to and validation in states not party to the EPC

2.1 EXTENSION OF PATENT TO NON-CONTRACTING STATE

In addition to the designated EPC contracting states, the application can be extended to non-EPC contracting states which have concluded an Extension Agreement with the EPO. The box in the Request for Grant form for extending the application to all extension states is pre-crossed; hence, the form is deemed a request to extend the application to all non-contracting states which have an Extension Agreement on the filing date of the application. See **Art.169:5** for the list of extension states and the provisions of the Extension Agreements (only one extension state remains). The extension to a state takes effect only if the extension fee for that state is paid within the period for payment of the designation fee.

An extension fee is payable for each extension state where protection is desired. See **Art.169:2** for the Extension Ordinance. The amount of the extension fee for each extension state is EUR 102 as laid down in Art.3 of the Extension Ordinance (OJ 1994 p.82; the original DEM 200 converts to EUR 102 at the exchange rate fixed when the Deutsche Mark was replaced by the Euro; see also Schedule of fees OJ 2024 sp4 p.27). The extension fees must be paid within the same period as the designation fee as laid down in **R.39(1)** and **R.159(1)(d)** (OJ 1997 p.215, point 12). Under the automatic debiting system, extension fees will only be debited for those extension states for which the applicant indicates in the Request for Grant form that it intends to pay the extension fee (ADA Annex A.2, point 3 note I.10).

The Register and Bulletin will mention the extension states for which the extension fees have been paid (OJ 1997 p.479, point 7).

2.2 VALIDATION OF PATENT IN NON-CONTRACTING STATES

Applicants can also validate their European patent applications and patents for a state that is not an EPC contracting state. The patent will confer essentially the same protection in that state as a patent granted by the EPO for the EPC contracting states. See **Art.169:6** for the list of validation states and the Validation Agreements.

Applicants may mark in the Request for Grant form the non-contracting states for which, at the time of filing, they intend to have their application and patent validated and to pay the validation fees.

The validation fee for validating a non-contracting state must be paid to the EPO within six months from the publication of the search report. The amount of the fee depends on the validation state:

Cambodia	KH	EUR 180	(OJ 2018 A15)
Georgia	GE	EUR 200	(OJ 2023 A104)
Lao People's Democratic Republic	LA	EUR 180	(OJ 2025 A24)
Moldova	MD	EUR 200	(OJ 2015 A84)
Morocco	MA	EUR 240	(OJ 2015 A18)
Tunisia	TN	EUR 180	(OJ 2017 A84)

The period for payment and the remedy in the event of non-payment is the same as for payment of an extension fee (see the following section).

If the validation fee is not paid in due time, the request for validation is deemed withdrawn. (OJ 2018 A15)

2.3 **NON-PAYMENT OF EXTENSION AND VALIDATION FEES AND REMEDIES**

If an extension fee or validation fee is not paid in due time, the corresponding extension or validation is deemed withdrawn. The following two remedies are available if the basic period of **R.39(1)** or **R.159(1)(d)** has not been observed.

An extension or validation fee not paid in the basic period may still be paid with a 50% surcharge in a grace period of two months from the expiry of the basic period (OJ 2015 A19). The grace period is an aggregate period (**R.131(2):3**).

The EPO will not issue a loss of rights communication for unpaid extension or validation fees. In the particular case that the designation fee is not paid, the application is deemed withdrawn, and the EPO will issue a loss of rights communication for the designation fee. The applicant can then pay the designation fee and any extension or validation fee using further processing. See A-III,12.2 for the conditions.

EPC remedies not explicitly referred to in the Extension Agreements do not apply to actions taken by the EPO under the extension or validation procedure (J22/10 r.3.3.3; A-III,12.1). Hence, re-establishment of rights under **Art.122** and **R.136** is not available to remedy non-payment of the extension and validation fees. (OJ 2015 A19; A-III,12.2)

Art. 79(3) The designation of a Contracting State may be withdrawn at any time up to the grant of the European patent.

1 **Withdrawal of a designation**

The applicant may withdraw a designation of a contracting state at any time up to the grant of the patent (**Art.79(3)**). The patent is then not granted for that state. This can be used, for example, to avoid collision in a contracting state between a European patent application or patent and a national application or patent of the same family (**Art.139(3)**).

If the designation of all contracting states is withdrawn, the application is deemed to be withdrawn (**R.39(2)**).

If the applicant withdraws the designation of a contracting state that is a participating member state of EU regulation 1257/2012 (on the unitary patent), it is not possible to request unitary effect after the grant of the patent (**UPR.5(2)**).

Withdrawal of a designation is not possible from the date a third party provides evidence to the EPO that proceedings concerning entitlement have been instituted until the resumption of the grant proceedings (**R.15**).

Art. 80 Date of filing

The date of filing of a European patent application shall be the date on which the requirements laid down in the Implementing Regulations are fulfilled.

Implemented by:
R.40 Requirements for date of filing
R.55 Redating after remedy of deficiencies
R.56 Redating after late filing of missing parts or drawings
R.56a Redating after late filing of correct application documents or parts

1 **General**

The requirements for the accordance of a date of filing laid down in **R.40** reflect the worldwide standard laid down in Art.5 of the Patent Law Treaty (PLT).

In view of the many details contained in Art.5 PLT, it was regarded appropriate to consolidate the EPO provisions on the accordance of a filing date in the Implementing Regulations. (OJ 2007 se4 EN p.84)

R.55 provides the applicant with a chance to remedy deficiencies preventing the allocation of a filing date under **R.40. R.56** allows an applicant to add missing parts of the description or missing drawings after accordance of the date of filing with a re-dating of the application in certain cases. **R.56a** allows an applicant to file correct application documents or parts after the filing date with a re-dating of the application in certain cases.

2 **Transitional provision EPC2000**

The revised **Art.80** is applicable to European patent applications filed on or after 13.12.2007. This also applies to **R.55** and **R.56**, which implement **Art.80.** (OJ 2007 se4 EN p.84; for **R.56** see **J10/07** r.1.3)

3 **Legal effects of date of filing**

The date of filing of an application is the date of receipt of application documents complying with the requirements of **Art.80**, by one of the offices referred to in **Art.75(1)** using a method permitted by **R.2(1)**. A valid date of filing has various legal effects, discussed below (see **T1409/05** r.3.2.6).

The following effects will ensue immediately when the filing date has been accorded:

- a European patent application is pending as of that date (**Art.80** in conjunction with **Art.90(1)**, (2));
- applicants can formally claim to have deposited their invention with the EPO on the filing date as notional date, from which their right to the patent arises under **Art.60(2)**;
- a European patent application gives rise to a right of priority for subsequent European, national or international patent applications as from the date of filing (**Art.87(2)**);
- the state of the art and hence the extent of search and examination is defined by the filing date (**Art.54(2)** and (3)).

Upon publication the following legal effect of the date of filing will unfold:

- the application will count as prior right under **Art.54(3)** for other applications as from its date of filing.

The date of filing an application will be replaced by the date of filing of an earlier application for the purposes of **Art.54** to the extent that a priority claim is valid (**Art.89**).

4 **Requirements and examination**

The EPC makes a distinction between the terms 'filing (of) the application' in **Art.55, 76, 79, 133, R.6, 17, 25, 36 - 38, 50 - 53, 152, 157,** and 'date of filing (of the application)' in e.g. **Art.54, 63, 76, 80, 87, 89.** The German version of the EPC uses a clearer terminology 'Einreichung der Anmeldung' and 'Anmeldetag der Anmeldung', the former being the act of filing performed by the applicant or the date on which the act is performed, the latter a date accorded to an application by the EPO. The confusion in the English version would have been avoided had the legislator used the term 'date of the application' instead of 'date of filing' because this 'date of filing' is accorded by the EPO and may not be the same as the date on which the applicant filed the application, for example in case of filing a patent application on paper by post.

Upon receipt of application documents, the EPO will examine under **Art.90(1)** whether they satisfy the requirements of **R.40** for accordance of a date of filing. If the requirements are met, the date on which the application documents were received is considered the 'filing of the application' and the EPO accords this as the 'date of filing' (**Art.80**). The EPO does not notify the applicant of the date of filing.

If no date of filing can be accorded, the EPO will invite the applicant to remedy the deficiencies that exist within two months under **Art.90(4)** and **R.55**. If the applicant does not remedy each deficiency or provides an insufficient remedy, no filing date will be accorded and the application will not be dealt with as a European patent application (**Art.90(2)**). After receipt of a sufficient remedy, the date on which the remedy was received is considered the 'filing of the application' and the EPO will accord this as the 'date of filing'. The EPO informs the applicant of this date (**R.55**; see **R.40(3)** for an exception).

Once the application documents satisfy the requirements of **R.40**, the 'filing the application' date is fixed and does not change anymore (see A-II,4.1.5).

The 'date of filing' is usually identical with the 'filing the application' date. However, they need not be the same; the 'date of filing' may change by a re-dating of the application, e.g. due to late filing of drawings under **R.56(2)**. Re-dating does not affect the 'filing of the application' date but does change the 'date of filing'. Hence, re-dating will change periods triggered by the 'date of filing', such as the priority period of **Art.87(1)** and the due date for renewal fees of **R.51(1)**, but will not change periods triggered by 'filing the application', such as the one-month period of **R.38(1)**. (G3/98 r.2.2)

Art. 81 Designation of the inventor

The European patent application shall designate the inventor. If the applicant is not the inventor or is not the sole inventor, the designation shall contain a statement indicating the origin of the right to the European patent.

Implemented by:
R.19 Filing the designation of inventor
R.20 Publication of the mention of the inventor
R.21 Rectification of the designation of an inventor
R.60 Subsequent designation of the inventor

1 **Designation of the inventor**

Art.81 realises the right of inventors according to **Art.62** to be mentioned before the EPO. Inventors are also mentioned in published applications and patents; they may waive this right according to **R.20(1)**.

Co-inventors should be mentioned in the application in the order indicated by the applicant. The order may be based on the contribution of the inventors to the subject-matter of the application; being mentioned first can be regarded in such a case as a moral right of the main inventor.

Where the inventor and applicant differ, a statement under the second sentence of **Art.81** must be included in the designation. The statement must identify the applicant as the employer or the successor in title of the inventor (J8/20 r.4.2.2). If the statement is not filed, the application is refused.

R.19 gives the requirements for designating an inventor. **R.21** governs the rectification of the designation of the inventor. See also A-III,5.

2 **Missing or deficient designation**
If the designation of the inventor is not filed at the date of filing or is deficient, e.g. the name or country and place of residence is missing, or is not signed by the applicant, the EPO will invite the applicant to remedy the deficiency as set out in **R.57(f)** and A-III,5.4 and 5.5. Not complying with **Art.81** results in refusal of the application (**R.60(1)**). The procedure for correction is set out in **R.57:7**.

Corrections of the designation made at the instigation of the inventor or applicant can be made at any time (A-III,5.5).

Art. 82 Unity of invention

The European patent application shall relate to one invention only or to a group of inventions so linked as to form a single general inventive concept.

Implemented by:
R.44 Unity of invention
R.64 European search report where the invention lacks unity
R.137(5) Amendment of claims to unsearched subject-matter lacking unity
R.164 Unity of invention and further searches of a Euro-PCT application

1 **General**
Art.82 has a regulatory function and seeks to ensure a rational procedure by preventing non-related inventions being lumped together by applicants for the purpose of saving fees. (**T110/82** r.5)

2 **Unity of invention**
Art.82 specifies that a European patent application shall relate to one invention only or to a group of inventions so linked as to form a single general inventive concept. **R.44** defines a single general inventive concept as a technical relationship among inventions involving one or more of the same or corresponding special technical features. The special technical features are features that define a contribution that each of the inventions considered as a whole makes over the prior art. See **R.44(1):1**.

An application can be refused if the claims do not comply with **Art.82**; see **R.48(1)(c)** for non-unitary subject-matter in the description. **Art.82** uses the term 'invention' in the sense of subject-matter. Hence, a group of inventions may exist as a plurality of independent claims in the same or in different categories, or a plurality of alternative embodiments defined in a single independent claim (F-V,2; see **R.43(2):1**). A group of inventions may also exist in the form of a plurality of dependent claims. If a group of inventions is claimed, the requirement is that the inventions in this group are so linked as to form a single general concept(F-V,2). A dependent claim and the higher-ranking claim on which it depends cannot be considered to lack unity of invention (F-V,2.1; F-V,3.2.3).

Lack of unity should neither be raised nor insisted upon on the basis of a narrow, literal or academic approach. This is particularly so during search when the possible lack of unity does not necessitate a further search. (F-V,2.2)

3 **Assessment of unity**
Unity of invention is assessed by both the search division (see **R.64(1):2**) and the examining division (see **R.64(1):3**). Lack of unity may be noticed a priori, i.e. before the prior art search, or a posteriori, i.e. after prior art is taken into account (F-V,2.2).

The requirement of unity of invention also applies when a Euro-PCT application enters the European phase. **R.164** sets out the procedure for conducting further searches and if unity of invention is lacking then further search fees have to be paid to have all claims searched. During proceedings before the EPO, unity of invention is also important in determining whether an amendment of the claims introduces unsearched, non-unitary subject-matter which is prohibited by **R.137(5)**.

Lack of unity is not a ground for opposition (**Art.100; T162/85** r.9) or revocation in national proceedings (**Art.138(1)**). In opposition proceedings it is irrelevant that the patent as granted or amended does not meet the requirement of unity (**G1/91** hn). Thus, after an opposition procedure, a patent maintained in amended form need not meet the requirement of unity (**G1/91** hn).

Art. 83 Disclosure of the invention

The European patent application shall disclose the invention in a manner sufficiently clear and complete for it to be carried out by a person skilled in the art.

Implemented by:
R.30 Requirements relating to nucleotide and amino acid sequences
R.31 Requirements relating to biological material
R.34 New deposit of biological material
R.42 Contents of the description

1 **Principle of disclosure**
Art.83 is one of the basic provisions of patent law. The general principle of the law is that in return for a monopoly protecting an invention, the applicant must provide a complete disclosure of that invention, thereby enabling the public to practice the invention at the latest after the expiry of the patent term. **Art.83** governs the adequacy of the teaching in the disclosure. An insufficient disclosure may result in refusal of the application under **Art.97(2)**; it is also a ground for opposition (**Art.100(b)**) and revocation (**Art.138(1)(b)**). See **Art.84:4** for the relationship between **Art.83** and **Art.84**.

2 **Sufficiency of disclosure**
The disclosure of the patent application must be sufficient for the skilled person to be able to practice the invention as defined in the claims, taking into account common general knowledge and the literature referred to in the description.

When assessing sufficiency of disclosure, a feature of an embodiment must be given an interpretation that is meaningful for the function the feature is expected to perform; the skilled person will exclude other interpretations as being irrelevant for working the invention. (**T521/12** r.9)

An objection of lack of sufficiency of disclosure presupposes that there are serious doubts, substantiated by verifiable facts; the evidence available in each particular case determines whether or not a claimed invention can be considered as enabled on the basis of the disclosure of one worked example (**T409/91**; **T694/92**; F-III, 1). The EPO seldom raises an objection of insufficient disclosure. When raised, it is often based on the claims being unduly broad, an essential feature of the invention not being disclosed, or the presence of inconsistencies. Insufficiency is more often raised in opposition and national proceedings.

2.1 CONTENT OF THE DISCLOSURE

Sufficiency of disclosure must be judged on the basis of the application as a whole, including the description and the claims (**T14/83** r.3).

Any sequence listing filed under **R.30** and relevant information regarding biological material deposited under **R.31** or **R.34** must be taken into account when assessing sufficiency.

The decisive date for fulfilling the sufficiency requirement is the date of filing (**G1/03** r.2.5.3). Insufficient disclosure in the priority application, using common general knowledge at the priority date, leads to invalidity of the claimed priority (**T193/95** r.3.1; **T107/09** r.17).

2.1.1 Common general knowledge

The skilled person may use common general knowledge to cure insufficiencies or errors in the disclosure and enable the carrying out of the invention (**T206/83** hn, r.5). The required research or experiments should not involve an undue effort on the part of the skilled person (**T171/84** r.12). Documents neither belonging to the common general knowledge nor referred to in the application as filed cannot be used to supplement the sufficiency of the disclosure (**T580/88** r.2.3). The scope of the common general knowledge has been set out in **Art.56:2.3**.

An error in the description is immaterial to the sufficiency of the disclosure if the skilled person could recognise and rectify it without undue effort using the common general knowledge in the specific technical field (**T171/84** hn, r.12).

Applicants are well-advised not to be unduly influenced by their excessive experience in the field to which the invention relates, thereby neglecting to provide all the detailed instructions in the specification which are necessary for carrying out the invention without difficulties and relying immoderately on the possibility of using common general knowledge to fill gaps and to rectify any deficiency in the disclosure (**T171/84** r.13).

2.1.2 Referenced document

The disclosure of a patent application may be supplemented by the disclosure of a document it refers to. The requirement that the application must enable the skilled person to work the invention without undue effort is complied with if the teaching is completed by reference to a document cited in the application as filed (**T611/89** r.3.1; **T267/91** r.2). The language of the document referred to is irrelevant (**T920/92** r.2).

The reference document must be available to the public. It will only be considered if it was publicly available on the date of filing of the application or, if this was not the case, it was available on or before the filing date to the EPO and also available to the public on or before the date of publication of the application (e.g. by being present in the file of the application) (**T737/90**).

A feature from a referenced document relating to an essential feature of the invention is not only important for sufficiency of disclosure but also for the definition of the invention. Since a patent application must itself identify all the features of the invention for which protection is sought, such a feature may not merely be referred to but must be included in the claim by amendment (**T689/90** r.1.4; F-III,8). The rules for inclusion by amendment are stricter than the above rules for considering sufficiency of disclosure, because in such a case the feature must be regarded as being part of the content of the application as filed according to **Art.123(2)**. These rules are discussed in **Art.123(2):1.1.**

2.2 SUFFICIENCY

Sufficiency of disclosure requires that the teaching of the application enables the skilled person to carry out the claimed subject-matter over the whole scope of the claims, without undue burden. A broad claim generally requires the disclosure of several alternatives over the range of the claim; one embodiment may nevertheless suffice where the skilled person can perform the invention over the whole claimed range (F-III,1; F-IV,6.3; **T435/91** r.2.2.3). If the only embodiment disclosed does not have the technical advantages of the invention as stated in the application, it cannot be the basis for generalisation over the range of the claim; therefore, the disclosure is insufficient (**T1173/00** r.3.1).

If a claim includes non-working embodiments, the disclosure is still sufficient if there is a large number of conceivable alternatives and the specification contains sufficient information on the relevant criteria for finding appropriate alternatives over the claimed range with reasonable effort (**G1/03** r.2.5.2)

The disclosure of a composition defined by its function must comprise the technical teaching to make the composition (**T435/91**).

Although the skilled person for the purpose of **Art.56** and **Art.83** has the same level of skill, the knowledge for both purposes is different (**T60/89**). The skilled person when assessing inventive step is aware of the common general knowledge in the art at the relevant date and has access to all prior art in the relevant technical field (G-VII,3). The skilled person when assessing sufficiency of disclosure of a patent has knowledge of the patent specification and is aware of documents cited in the patent and the common general knowledge in the art (**T171/84**; **T377/17**).

Sufficiency requires that it must be possible to reproduce claimed living matter (e.g. plants, animals or micro-organisms) in such a way that it has exactly the same technical features before and after reproduction. Reproducibility can be demonstrated by, for example:

1 a deposit of biological material from which the invention can be reproduced without undue burden (see **R.31** and **R.34**); or
2 disclosing in the application as filed the sequence responsible for the claimed trait with instructions on how to introduce the sequence in a target organism reproducibly. (G-II,5.4)

3 Insufficient disclosure

An insufficient disclosure cannot be remedied later than the filing date by adding further examples or features because of **Art.123(2)**. If no embodiment is sufficiently disclosed in order to avoid easy copying of the invention and the missing information is not available from the general knowledge of a skilled person, the application will be refused (**T219/85**). This is rather unlikely to happen. If some embodiments are insufficiently disclosed, the claims must be restricted to the sufficiently disclosed embodiments, the other embodiments being deleted. (F-III,2)

There can be a fundamental insufficiency in the invention, as shown in the following examples, which is irreparable (F-III,3).

A first example is where the successful performance depends on chance, i.e. results are unrepeatable or success in achieving these results is unreliable, e.g. in a micro-biological process involving mutations. The description or the knowledge of the skilled person must then suffice to identify the desired or erroneous product and/or show how to correct the process. In the absence of such information, reliance on chance events amounts to undue burden. (**T14/83**, **T226/85**, **T727/95** r.11)

A second example of a fundamental insufficiency is an invention violating established physical laws, e.g. a device having a specified construction and alleged to operate as a perpetuum mobile. A claim to a perpetuum mobile relating merely to its structure does not comply with **Art.83**. Since the structure does not solve the problem, i.e. achieve a perpetuum mobile, there is also an inventive step problem under **Art.56**. If a claim to a perpetuum mobile is directed to its function and not merely to its structure, it will be objected to under **Art.83** and also **Art.57** as not being industrially applicable (e.g. **T541/96**, Cold nuclear fusion). (F-III,3, G-III,1)

A third example is an invention defined in terms of a functional feature where the actual implementation of the feature is an undue burden for the skilled person (**T1063/06** hn.II; see **Art.84:1.6**).

Time-consuming and ethically questionable tests, e.g. to establish whether a particular product has a claimed pharmaceutical effect, are unreasonable if the claim could have been defined by features making the tests superfluous; such a claim does not comply with **Art.83** (**T1635/09** r.7.3).

If there is an error in the description (e.g. a wrong number), this is immaterial for the sufficiency of the disclosure, if the skilled person can recognise and correct it using the common general knowledge (**T171/84**). An erroneous disclosure that cannot be corrected using common general knowledge should not be considered part of the state of the art under **Art.54(2)** (**T77/87** hn1).

3.1 INSUFFICIENCY AND INVENTIVE STEP

Lack of reproducibility of a claimed invention may become relevant for sufficiency of disclosure or inventive step, depending on the way the invention is claimed. If a technical effect expressed as a functional feature in the claim is not achieved, the claimed invention will be regarded as insufficiently disclosed. Since the technical effect is presented as part of the solution, it cannot be part of the problem to be solved. If a technical effect is not expressed in the claim but is part of the objective technical problem, not achieving the technical effect is an inventive step issue. (**G1/03** r.2.5.2; **T5/06** r.7; **T380/05** r.7.2; F-III,12)

Art. 84 Claims

The claims shall define the matter for which protection is sought. They shall be clear and concise and be supported by the description.

Implemented by:
R.43 Form and content of claims
R.62a Plurality of independent claims during search
R.63 Incomplete search due to not clear subject-matter

1 Clarity and interpretation of claims

Art.84 in combination with **R.43(1)** stipulates that the claims shall be clear and define the matter for which protection is sought in terms of the technical features of the invention. These requirements serve two purposes, both ensuring that the public is not left in any doubt as to which subject-matter is covered by a particular claim and delimiting the claimed subject-matter from the prior art in order to provide clarity regarding the technical contribution to the art it provides. (**T728/98** r.3.1)

The clarity of the claims is of utmost importance, as the claims define the scope of the matter for which protection is sought. The clarity requirement applies to independent and dependent claims alike and to the claims as a whole (F-IV,4.1; **G3/14** r.49). The words used in the claims should have their ordinary meaning; if a specific meaning has been given, this must be clear from the wording; this is important, as only the claims of the European patent will be translated into the other official languages.

A patent may be its own dictionary and may define technical terms and determine how a skilled person has to interpret a specific word when used in the description or in the claims. This will not be necessary if the patent does not depart from the meaning a word normally has in the respective technical field and which a skilled person would attribute to it. If, however, it is intended to use a word which is known in the art in an unconventional way, the description may give this word a special, overriding meaning by explicit definition. (**T500/01** r.6)

Complexity of a claim is not tantamount to lack of clarity. The simplicity of a claim is not a criterion for the granting of a patent. (**T1020/98** hn. I)

Art.84 requires that the claims must be clear in themselves, without including any knowledge derived from the description of the patent application. The description is mentioned in **Art.84** only for the requirement of support. (**T988/02** r.3.3.1)

Art.69(1) should not be invoked to interpret the claims in terms of the description for the purpose of **Art.84**, because **Art.69** concerns only the extent of protection and **Art.84** the definition of the matter to be protected by a claim (**T1129/97**; established case law, confirmed in **T56/04**).

1.1 INCONSISTENCIES

Inconsistencies between the claims and the description may cast doubt on the extent of protection. Inconsistencies may render the claims objectionable under Art.84, first sentence, or unclear or unsupported under Art.84, second sentence. The examining division may request that the description is amended to accord with the claims in order to resolve any such inconsistencies (H-V,2.7).

A first type of inconsistency is a simple verbal inconsistency. For example, the description does not emphasise a feature, while the claims are limited to the inclusion of the feature, or vice versa. The description should be limited or the claims broadened. (F-IV,4.3(i))

A second type is an inconsistency regarding apparently essential features. For example, an independent claim does not mention a feature which is essential to the invention according to the general knowledge or according to the description. The claim is then unclear, as Art.84 and R.43(1) require not only that the claim must be technically comprehensible, but must also clearly define the object of the invention, i.e. indicate all the essential features thereof (**T32/82** r.15; F-IV,4.3(ii)). The claim need not be amended if the applicant can show that the feature is not essential. In another example, features required by the independent claims are described as optional in the description. The description should be amended so that the features are not described as optional (F-IV,4.3(iii)).

A third type of inconsistency is when part of the subject-matter of the description and/or drawings is not covered by the claims. Embodiments in the description which are not covered by the independent claims should be deleted or marked as not being covered by the claims (F-IV,4.3(iii); **T1808/06** r.2). For example, the claims specify a vehicle propelled by an electric motor, but an embodiment in the description also shows a vehicle propelled by an internal combustion engine. The description should be amended to either remove the internal combustion engine embodiment, or prominently mark it as not being covered by the claimed invention. A dissenting decision, **T1989/18**, found that no amendment was required in respect of this kind of inconsistency, considering that the clarity of the claims under **Art.84** was unaffected if the description disclosed unclaimed subject-matter and there was no other legal basis that would require amendment. Decisions **T1444/20** and **T2194/19** similarly concluded that embodiments in the description extending beyond the scope of the claims need not be deleted as long as they do not affect the clarity of the claims, nor result in contradictions with them. However, the majority of recent decisions on this topic support the interpretation that the description should be amended to be in line with the claims (**T1024/18**, **T0121/20**, **T2766/17**, **T2293/18**, **T1516/20**, **T1968/18**, **T3097/19**, **T438/22**). Decision **T3097/19** summarises some of the previous decisions and lays out the case for the description to be strictly in line with the claims to ensure legal certainty (r.25-37). Decision **T438/22** provides **Art.84**, **Art. 94(3)**, **R.42**, **R.48** and **R.71(1)** as legal basis that the BoA considers as justification for deleting or disclaiming embodiments outside the scope of the claims in the description (r.5.5.3). Decision **T56/21** looked set to refer the question of description amendments to the Enlarged Board of Appeal , but instead provided its own interpretation of the matter. In this case, the board found that there is no legal basis in the EPC (and particularly not in **Art.84**, **R.42**, **R.43** and **R.48**) for requiring an adaptation of description according to the allowed claims. The somewhat related question of claim interpretation based on the description has been referred to the Enlarged Board of Appeal via an interlocutory decision **T439/22** (G1/24). While not directly linked to the matter of description amendments, the reasoning of the EBoA in this case may shed some light on the debate on adaptation of description as well.

Note that, inconsistencies between the claims and the description present at grant cannot be revisited in opposition, since **Art. 84** is not a ground of opposition. Only inconsistencies introduced by amendments to the claims during opposition may be invoked. (**T 2391/18**)

A fourth type of inconsistency arises from claim-like clauses. For example, a divisional application includes the claims of the parent appended to the description as clauses (see **Art.76(1):8**). These clauses should be deleted prior to grant as they may lead to a lack of clarity over the scope of protection in contravention of **Art.84**, and may be an irrelevant and unnecessary duplication of subject-matter prohibited under **R.48(1)(c)**. (F-IV,4.4) In decisions **T1444/20** and **T1426/21**, however, the boards of appeal have found that there is no basis in the EPC requiring the deletion of such clauses, as long as there are no inconsistencies between the claim-like clauses and the claims.

General statements in the description which imply an expanded extent of the protection in vague terms, e.g. to everything covered by the spirit of the invention or, if the invention relates to a combination of features, to the separate features, are objected to (F-IV,4.4).

1.2 ESSENTIAL FEATURES

An independent claim must specify all essential features needed to define the invention (**T133/85** r.2) except in so far as such features are implied by the generic terms used, e.g. a bicycle implies the presence of wheels. The essential features should in particular comprise those features which distinguish the invention from the closest prior art (**T1055/92** hn.III). This implies that it is not always necessary for a claim to identify technical features or steps in detail (r.4). It is sufficient if a claim modifying a known product clearly identifies the product and states the modifications. There is an inconsistency and lack of clarity if a claimed process does not lead to the desired product. Such an objection could be raised based on common general knowledge or the teaching of the description.

There is a large amount of case-specific case law on essential features, where the discussion concentrates on a specific technical question. If the EPO raises an objection based on the lack of an essential feature in an independent claim, the applicant must argue why the features present in said claim achieve the claimed effect and solve the technical problem.

If a non-technical feature is regarded as constitutive for defining an invention, it must be included as an essential feature in the independent claim. An example is a method step of making a deductive decision about a pathology in a diagnostic method: if the essential nature of this feature is unambiguously inferable from the patent or patent application, it is to be included in the independent claim. (**G1/04** r.6.2.4).

1.3 RELATIVE TERMS

A claim is not clear in the sense of **Art.84** if it comprises an unclear technical feature for which no unequivocal, generally accepted meaning exists in the relevant art (**T728/98** hn.I). Examples of these features are relative terms as 'thin', 'wide' or 'strong'. Such a feature should be replaced by a more precise wording from the description. If there is no such basis and the term is not essential to the invention, it should be retained to avoid an extension of subject-matter. In opposition proceedings, a replacement may enlarge the scope of the claim, which is not allowed according to **Art.123(3)**. If the relative term is essential for the definition of the invention, it is not allowed in the claim. Such a term may not be used to distinguish from the prior art. The words 'about', 'approximately' and 'substantially' may be applied mainly to numerical values and only if they do not prevent an unambiguous distinction from the prior art and the skilled person knows within which tolerance a certain effect can be obtained. (F-IV,4.6 and 4.7; see also **G2/88** r.2.5)

A vague term can be made slightly more acceptable by adding 'in practical circumstances'; the skilled person may then understand the meaning.

The provision of **Art.69(1)** according to which the description and the drawings shall be used to interpret the claims, applies also to the clarity requirement of **Art.84**, provided that the claims are not self-contradictory. Where a claim specifies an undefined, relative quality, e.g. a product should be 'water-soluble', it is not normally necessary to identify any method for its determination. The claim is clear in the sense of **Art.84**, if the quality has a sufficiently precise meaning to the skilled person taking into account the common general knowledge and having regard to its context in the light of the description. (**T860/93**, criticising the broad statements in **T454/89**)

Where a claim is self-contradictory in that it has mutually incompatible features, it is not permissible to rely on the description to resolve the contradiction. (**T860/93** r.5.7; **T454/89**)

1.4 UNCLEAR EXPRESSIONS

Expressions like 'preferably', 'for example', 'such as', 'more particularly' in a claim may introduce ambiguity and give rise to a clarity objection. The feature following the expression is entirely optional and can be ignored when assessing the scope of the claim (F-IV,4.9).

In an expression such as 'about 200 C' or 'approximately 200 C' the value is interpreted as being as accurate within the range of the method used to measure it or as having an error margin specified in the application or, if no error margin is specified, as having a margin determined by rounding off to the last decimal place. The Guidelines do not indicate when to use which interpretation. (F-IV,4.7.1)

A term such as 'substantially' or 'approximately' applied to a structural unit, e.g. a tray plate with a substantially circular circumference, is interpreted as a feature of the unit being produced within the tolerance of the method used to manufacture it. (F-IV,4.7.1)

Unclear expressions will be objected to if the application suggests that they extend the interval beyond the above-mentioned error margins or manufacturing tolerance. (F-IV,4.7.2)

Use of the word 'in' to define a relationship between entities and/or activities in a claim may cause ambiguity in the scope of the claim. Examples are: cylinder head in an engine; in a telephone apparatus including a dial-tone detector, the dial-tone detector including ...; in a device for ..., the improvement consisting of ... It is essential to define the scope clearly; therefore, the use of the word 'in' for defining relationships should normally be avoided. (F-IV,4.15)

Use of brackets in a claim defining a feature may lack clarity. For example, it is unclear whether or not a '(concrete) moulded brick' is limited to concrete. Use of brackets with a generally accepted meaning is allowable, such as in '(meth)acrylate', meaning 'acrylate' and 'methacrylate', and in formulae. (F-IV,4.18)

Trademarks and the like are only allowed if they are unavoidable and have a precise meaning (see e.g. **T480/98** (unclear) and **T623/91** (clear)).

Claims defining the invention by the result to be achieved should not be allowed, unless the invention can only be defined in such terms and the result can be verified by described tests involving nothing more than trial and error.

1.5 PARAMETER FEATURES

A parameter in a claim which depends on the mode of operation of a device such as the adjustable pulse time of a laser, i.e. on a human factor irrelevant to the device per se, makes the extent of protection ambiguous and indefinite. Such a claim lacks clarity under **Art.84**. (**T227/91** r.3)

A claim for a product characterised by parameters related to its physical structure is allowed, provided the parameters can be clearly and reliably determined in an objective manner by a method for measuring (**T94/82**). This applies analogously to process-related features characterised by parameters.

The requirements of **Art.84** with respect to features defined by parameters are summarised in **T849/11** r.1.1 (F-IV,4.11):

1 the claims must be clear in themselves when read by the skilled person (not including knowledge derived from the description);
2 the method for measuring a parameter (or at least a reference thereto) must appear completely in the claim itself; and

3 an applicant who chooses to define the scope of the claim by parameters needs to ensure that the skilled person can easily and unambiguously verify whether the skilled person is working inside or outside the scope of the claim.

If explicit inclusion of the measurement method to meet requirement 2 would make the claim unclear through complexity or lack of conciseness, a reference to the description under **R.43(6)** may instead be made. Alternatively, requirement 2 can be fulfilled if the measurement method to be used belongs to common general knowledge, or all known methods yield the same result within the limits of experimental accuracy (**T1156/01** r.2.3; F-IV,4.11).

An opponent alleging that the measurement of a parameter is unclear must provide proof that a skilled person is unable to determine the value of the parameter (**T525/99**, r.3.1.2: a party making an allegation must prove the correctness of the allegation).

1.6 DEFINITION IN TERMS OF EFFECT

A claim must be defined in terms of technical features according to **R.43(1)**. A technical feature is a feature that can be read by a skilled person as an instruction as to the technical procedure to be followed to achieve a given result. Such an instruction may be explicit or functional, i.e. defined in terms of an effect. (**T68/85** r.8.4.1)

A definition in terms of effect is often chosen to provide a broader scope of protection. The Guidelines distinguish between two types of definition in terms of effect: a functional feature and a result to be achieved. The requirements for allowing these two types of definition are different (F-IV,4.10)

1.6.1 Functional features

A functional feature in a claim is a feature defined in terms of function rather than structure. A functional feature is a feature known to the skilled person. It is often in the form of means-plus-function which defines its function without reference to other features ('means for mixing powder') or with reference to another feature ('means for transmitting the signal to an input port').

A functional feature has a scope extending to all means providing the same effect, where structurally disclosed means within that scope only represent examples. Accordingly, a means-plus-function feature is anticipated by any prior art feature suitable for carrying out its function. Note that the EPO sometimes makes a prior art document relevant in the assessment of patentability by giving a 'means for' feature in the document the function it has in the patent application although the feature in the document has a different function but can, unintentionally, perform the function of the patent application.

As an exception, means-plus-function features carried out by a computer are interpreted as means adapted to carry out the relevant functions, rather than merely means suitable for carrying them out (F-IV,4.13.2; **T410/96**).

A functional definition is acceptable if the broad scope cannot be obtained easily with a definition in structural terms, the skilled person can provide some means of performing this function without undue burden (F-IV,2.1) and the skilled person would appreciate that means other than those disclosed in the description could be used for the same function (F-IV,6.5).

A functional feature is sufficiently disclosed if the examples given in the description allow a skilled person to implement other embodiments. For example, the feature 'terminal position detecting means' supported only by a limit switch can obviously also be realised by a photoelectric cell or a strain gauge. The EPO may require limitation of the scope of a functional feature if the description shows only one particular way of implementing the feature and alternatives are not obvious. (F-IV,6.5)

A medicament claim may define the illness to be treated in a functional way, e.g. an illness that requires as treatment the selective occupation of a specific receptor, provided the skilled person has instructions either from the application or from common general knowledge to recognise which medical conditions fall within this definition (**T241/95** r.3.1.1; F-IV,4.21)

Functional features are less common in chemistry than in other technical fields. **Art.83** requires that a claim defining a chemical compound using a functional feature is allowable provided the feature can be reduced to practice without undue burden (**T1063/06**, r.5). This requirement is met if the number of alternative compounds covered is finite (**T1063/06**, r.5.5). However, if the number of alternatives is infinite and includes compounds not yet structurally defined on the priority date, the burden is undue (**T1063/06**, r.3.2). This is the case for a claim defining a compound having a specific medical effect, the compound to be selected by testing every conceivable compound with a newly discovered screening method. Such a compound claim is not patentable, although a claim relating to the screening method as such could be patentable. The compound claim is an example of a 'reach-through' claim, having a scope broader than the applicant's actual contribution to the art and claiming unexplored fields of research.

1.6.2 Result to be achieved

The second type of definition in terms of effect consists of a feature defining the invention by a result to be achieved (F-IV,4.10). For example, a claim relating to an agent for selective weed control contains as feature a specified compound 'in an amount producing a synergistic herbicidal effect' (**T68/85** r.2), or to a device having flanges 'so dimensioned as to enable the device to be moved by facial muscles and to hold it firmly in the speaking position' (**T204/90**).

The result to be achieved is often related to the technical problem solved by the invention and is normally not part of the state of the art, in contrast with the above functional feature. It is therefore important that the description or common general knowledge provides tests and criteria to allow the skilled person to assess whether the desired result is achieved (**T241/95** hn.II). As a general rule, claims which attempt to define the invention by a result to be achieved should not be allowed, in particular if they only amount to claiming the underlying technical problem (F-IV,4.10). A claim that defines a result to be achieved that essentially corresponds to the problem to be solved must include all features necessary to achieve the result (**T809/12** r.2.8).

A definition in terms of a result to be achieved is allowable if all of the following requirements are met:

1 the feature cannot otherwise be defined more precisely without restricting the scope;
2 the feature provides instructions sufficiently clear to be reduced to practice without undue burden, if necessary with reasonable experiments; the result can be verified directly and positively; and
3 the state of the art does not stand in the way of using such functional and therefore general and broad terminology. (**T204/90** r.3.2, following **T68/85** hn, r.8.4.1-3; F-IV,4.10)

1.7 **DISCLAIMERS**

Generally, the subject-matter of a claim is defined in terms of positive features. However, in special circumstances the extent of a claim may be limited by a negative feature. Negative limitations may be used only if adding positive features to the claim either would not define more clearly and concisely the patentable subject-matter still protectable or would unduly limit the scope of the claim. It has to be clear what is excluded by means of the negative feature. (F-IV,4.19)

A negative feature may be included already in the original claims, or be introduced in a claim by way of amendment under **Art.123(2)**. The conditions for allowance of such an amendment, i.e. a disclaimer, are discussed in **Art.123(2):2.4**.

1.8 **PRODUCT-BY-PROCESS CLAIMS**

Claims for products defined in terms of a process are allowed only if the product is patentable (new and inventive) and the product cannot be defined in a better way. A product is not novel because of a novel process (**T150/82**). However, a novel process step can establish the novelty of a claimed product if it causes the product to have different properties from prior art products (CLBA I.C.5.2.7).

According to **T20/94** hn.2 it is immaterial whether the claim uses the words 'product X obtainable by process Y', 'obtained by' or 'directly obtained by' (F-IV,4.12). Since courts and patent offices other than the EPO may interpret words differently, it is recommended to use the broadest term 'obtainable' when drafting a patent application.

1.9 **USE FEATURES**

1.9.1 Apparatus and products stating a use

A claim commencing with, e.g. 'product X for use in application Y' or 'device for mixing powders' is interpreted as 'suitable for the use' and limits the scope of the claim only to the extent of suitability for the specified use (F-IV,4.13.1; **T304/08**).

As an exception, a claim to a known substance or composition for use in a medical method is interpreted as limited to that use (F-IV,4.13.1; see also **Art.54(4):2** and **Art.54(5):2**).

Lack of clarity can result if a claim for a first entity specifies the relationship of the first entity to a second entity related to it through use but not included in the scope of the claim. For example, clarity is lacking in a claim relating to a plug for fitting in a wall, the length of the plug being related to the thickness of the wall. There is no lack of clarity, if the features of the second entity are standardised ('a box for storing audio cassettes which project out of the box for easy removal') or are usual in the art ('a cover sheet for a hay bale, the size of the sheet being related to the dimensions of the bale' **T455/92**). Initially, such a claim is interpreted as not including the second entity or its features and the first entity is limited to being suitable for use with the second entity. If the claim is without any doubt directed to a combination of the first and second entities or where the use leads to a lack of clarity, the claim must be reworded to define the combination, e.g. by changing 'connectable' to 'connected'. (F-IV,4.14)

Use features are common in distributed inventions, where the invention relates to an improvement in two separate but inter-related products which may be sold separately, but each carry out the same inventive idea, such as an electric plug and socket or transmitter and receiver (F-IV,3.2). The use feature in such an invention relates the two independent claims in respect of each of the products and causes a co-operative functionality between them. This effect of the use feature must be taken into account when assessing the clarity of the claims (**T1194/97** r.2.4). For example, the independent claims relate to a reading device and a record medium for use in the device, on which digital data is recorded in a specified data structure. The reference to the reading device explains the data structure and thus clarifies the subject-matter for which protection is sought. The claim is limited in so far as the 'for use' excludes interpretations which would be incompatible with this use (**T1194/97** r.2.2).

'Use of the substance X as insecticide' is not a claim directed to the substance X, but is equivalent to the process claim 'the process of killing insects using substance X'. 'Use of a transistor in an amplifying circuit' is a process claim for the process of amplification using a circuit with a transistor, and not a claim for an amplifying circuit comprising a transistor, nor a claim for the process of using the transistor in building such a circuit. (F-IV,4.16)

See **Art.54(1):5.1** for more information concerning the assessment of novelty when product/apparatus claims include a use feature.

1.9.2 *Methods stating a use*

Two different types of stated purpose are possible for a method, those that define the use of a method, and those that define an effect arising from the steps of the method (F-IV,4.13.3; **T1931/14** r.2.2.4).

Where the stated purpose of a method defines the use of the method, e.g. 'method for storing data', the purpose is considered a step in the method so that the method achieves its stated purpose. For a 'method of manufacturing a product', the fact that the method results in the product is treated as an integral method step.

Where the stated purpose of the method is a technical effect that inevitably arises from carrying out the steps of the method, e.g. 'method for reducing friction', the technical effect is not limiting on the claim because it is inherent in the steps. Such a method is not novel in view of prior art disclosing the method even if it does not mention the stated purpose. (F-IV,4.13.3)

1.10 COMPRISING VS. **consisting**

The terms 'comprising' and 'consisting' have a specific meaning in patents that deviates from everyday language. 'Comprising' is not limiting; 'consisting' is limiting. Hence, a claim directed to a compound comprising components A and B does not exclude the presence of other components. However, a claim directed to a compound consisting of components A and B does not include other components. The expression 'consisting essentially of' or 'consisting substantially of' may be used to indicate the presence of other components that do not materially affect the essential characteristics of the claimed components. (F-IV,4.20)

2 Conciseness

Single claims as well as the totality of the claims must be concise (F-IV,5). A large number of claims does not meet the requirement of clarity and conciseness of **Art.84** and **R.43(5)** (**T246/91** r.7). The number of independent claims in the same category is also limited by **R.43(2)**.

A Markush formula is the most concise means of defining a class of chemical compounds (**T1020/98** hn.II).

The EPO tries to force applicants to comply with **Art.84** before it carries out the search. It levies claims fees, increasing with the number of claims, on filing (**R.45**; see in particular **R.45(1):2** for reduction of claims fees). The EPO will ask an applicant to indicate the independent claims to be searched if a plurality of independent claims in the application does not comply with the requirements of **R.43(2)** (**R.62a**). If the application is not sufficiently clear for a search to be carried out, the applicant will be requested to indicate the subject-matter to be searched (**R.63**). Any unsearched subject-matter may not be used for amendment of claims during prosecution of the application (**R.137(5)**).

3 Support in the description

The claims must be supported by the description according to **Art.84**. This means that there must be a basis in the description for the subject-matter of every claim and that the scope of the claims must not be broader than is justified by the extent of the description and drawings and also the contribution of the invention to the art (**T409/91** r.3.3; F-IV,6.1).

Support by the description is generally assumed, unless exceptionally there are reasons to believe that the skilled person would be unable to practice the invention across the scope of the claims using routine methods. The support must be of a technical character. Examiners should only raise an objection of non-support if they have well-founded reasons, preferably supported by a published document. (F-IV,6.3)

An embodiment presented in the application as filed as not being part of the invention but e.g. as belonging to the state of the art or as a comparative example cannot be claimed (**G2/10** r.4.5).

Subject-matter disclosed only in a claim may later be added to the description. Where the claim is dependent, it may suffice if the description mentions that the claim represents a particular embodiment of the invention. (F-IV,6.6)

3.1 BROAD CLAIMS

Most claims are generalisations of one or more examples. A claim should not be so broad that it goes beyond the disclosed invention nor yet so narrow as to deprive applicants of a just reward for disclosing their invention. An invention in a new field permits wider claims than an advance in a known field. The applicant should be allowed to cover all obvious modifications, equivalents to and uses of the invention.

A claim may broadly define a feature in terms of its function, even when it is supported by only one example, provided that example enables the skilled person to select alternatives. If the description suggests that the function should be carried out in a particular way and other ways appear inappropriate, the claim must be restricted to this particular way. (see F-IV,4.22)

A broad claim concerning a group of chemical compounds per se does not lack support for the sole reason that the description does not make it sufficiently credible that an alleged technical effect (which is not, however, part of the claim) is obtained by all compounds. 'Supported by the description' means that the technical features stated in the description as being essential features of the described invention must be present in the claims (**T409/91** r.3.2). The question of whether a technical effect is achieved by all the claimed compounds arises under **Art.56**, if this effect is the sole reason for the alleged inventiveness of the compounds. (**T939/92** hn.I, II, r.2.2.2)

3.2 BROAD CLAIM IN OPPOSITION

Art.84 is not a ground for opposition. If a very broad claim has been granted, it cannot be opposed based on **Art.84**. However, lack of support can imply that the disclosure is also insufficient under **Art.83**, which can be used as ground for opposition. Although **Art.83** and **Art.84** relate to different parts of the application, they give effect to the same legal principle that the patent monopoly should be justified by the technical contribution to the art. The claims should not extend to subject-matter which, after reading the description, would not be at the disposal of the skilled person. Covetously monopolising a technical area extending well beyond the actual technical contribution to the art would be contrary to the requirement of support in **Art.84**. Hence, all essential features must be included in the main claim. The disclosure of the invention is only sufficient if it enables the skilled person to obtain substantially all embodiments falling within the ambit of the claims (**T226/85** r.2). The disclosure of only a single way of performing the invention is only sufficient if it allows the skilled person to perform the invention in the whole range that is claimed. (**T409/91** hn, r.3; see also **T595/90** hn. II)

3.3 AMENDMENT OF CLAIMS

The scope of the claims may be extended during the examination of the application, provided there is support for the extension in the description. After grant, e.g. during opposition proceedings, extension is not allowed any more (**Art.123(3)**). It is not usually permitted under **Art.123(2)** to delete a feature from an independent claim if the application as filed presents the feature as essential (**T260/85**).

4 Relation between Art.83 and 84

T94/82 provided an explanation of the relationship between the requirements of **Art.83** and **Art.84** in case of a claim defining a product in terms of parameters relating to its physical structure. The requirement of **Art.83** is fulfilled if the description enables the skilled person to obtain the product; the requirement of **Art.84** is met if the parameters in the claim can be clearly and reliably determined by objective procedures. However, there are situations where these requirements overlap. This is relevant for examination: the requirements of both **Art.83** and **Art.84** will be examined during grant proceedings; during opposition proceedings compliance with **Art.83** will be examined without restriction, but compliance with **Art.84** will be examined only in relation to an amendment of the patent (**G3/14**; see **Art.100:2** and **Art.101(3):1**).

4.1 LACK OF SUPPORT

Each of the requirements for sufficiency and support gives effect to the same legal principle that the patent monopoly should be justified by the technical contribution to the art (**T409/91** hn). The protection conferred by the claims of a patent should correspond to the technical contribution to the art set out in the disclosure, ensuring that the patent monopoly does not extend to subject-matter which, after reading the patent specification, would not be at the disposal of the skilled person (**T435/91** r.2.2.1; F-IV,6.1).

An objection under **Art.83** relating to the non-availability of some embodiments and the requirement that the skilled person can carry out the invention across its scope may lead to an objection under **Art.84** that the claims are not properly supported. It has to be decided on a case by case basis whether broad functional terminology in the claims is the only possible way to define the invention to provide fair protection. (**T292/85** r.3)

Only if the whole scope of a claim is affected by an ambiguity such that it is impossible to carry out the invention at all, should an objection under **Art.83** be raised. Otherwise an objection under **Art.84** is appropriate (**T608/07**; F-III,11).

4.2 LACK OF CLARITY
The EPO has no uniform way of handling clarity objections relating to parameters. A claim using parameters that are not defined or for which a measuring method is not provided in the application may be objected to under **Art.83** or **Art.84**. Normally, an ambiguity in a claim will lead to an objection under **Art.83** only if the whole scope of the claim is affected, in the sense that it is impossible to carry out at all the invention defined therein. Otherwise an objection under **Art.84** is appropriate.

Where a claim contains an ill-defined parameter and where, as a consequence, a person skilled in the art would not know whether they were working within or outside of the scope of the claim, this, by itself, is not a reason to deny sufficiency of disclosure as required by **Art.83**. Nor is such a lack of clear definition necessarily a matter for objection under **Art.84** only. What is decisive for establishing insufficiency within the meaning of **Art.83** is whether the parameter, in the specific case, is so ill-defined that a person skilled in the art is not able, on the basis of the disclosure as a whole and using common general knowledge, to identify (without undue burden) the technical measures necessary to solve the problem underlying the application at issue (**T593/09**; CLBA II.C.8.2.2.2.a). Care has to be taken in opposition that an insufficiency objection is not merely a hidden objection under **Art.84**, especially in the case of ambiguities in the claims. (F-III,11)

Art. 85 Abstract

The abstract shall serve the purpose of technical information only; it may not be taken into account for any other purpose, in particular for interpreting the scope of the protection sought or applying Article 54, paragraph 3.

Art.54(3) Prior rights
Implemented by:
R.47 Form and content of the abstract
R.66 Definitive content of the abstract

1 **Informative character of abstract**
An application must contain an abstract (**Art.78(1)(e)**). The purpose of the abstract is to inform the public about the invention disclosed in the application. It is therefore included in the publication of the application (**R.68**). The contents of the abstract as published are determined by the search division (**R.66**). The abstract should also assist the EPO in finding the published patent application as prior art when conducting a search on a later application (**R.47(5)**).

The informative character of the abstract means that it cannot be regarded as part of the content of the application as filed in the sense of **Art.123(2)** (**T246/86**) or **Art.54(3)** (**Art.85**). After publication under **Art.93(2)** the abstract is available to the public in the sense of **Art.54(2)** and may be used as state of the art for assessing both novelty and inventive step (**T160/92** hn.I). However, as for abstracts in general, if the abstract and the original document (the patent application) contain conflicting teachings, the disclosure of the abstract should be interpreted by reference to the original document; if the disclosure of the abstract is erroneous, it should not be considered as part of the state of the art (**T77/87** hn.2).

2 **Missing abstract**
If the abstract is lacking in the application documents, this is a formal deficiency. The Receiving Section will notify the applicant (**Art.90(3)**, **R.57(d)**) and invite correction of the deficiency within a period of two months (**R.58**). If not filed in time, the application will be refused (**Art.90(5)**). Re-establishment is available as a remedy; the abstract can also be filed if the decision is appealed (J11/20).

Art. 86 Renewal fees for the European patent application

1 **Character of renewal fees**
Art.86 governs the payment of renewal fees for patent applications which are pending after two years from the date of filing of the application. Renewal fees differ from most of the other EPO fees in that their payment is not in respect of any particular service rendered. The requirement to pay renewal fees is a generally accepted fund-raising provision for patent offices which makes it possible to keep the initial costs of patenting in the form of filing, search and examination fees below the break-even level and reduce the financial hurdle at the start of the patenting process. The annually recurring renewal fees are also a stimulus for an applicant or proprietor to allow patent rights to lapse as soon as protection is no longer desired (T1402/13 r.4.4.3).

The renewal fees to be paid to the EPO under **Art.86(1)** relate only to patent applications. After grant, renewal fees must be paid to the national offices of contracting states in order to keep the patent in force (**Art.86(2)**), respectively to the EPO for unitary patents (**UPR.13**). Part of the revenue from renewal fees received by the national offices for European patents is paid to the EPO under **Art.39(1)**.

Art.86 and **R.51** provide a self-contained set of rules relating to the payment of renewal fees, aimed at providing a simple system of administration for the EPO (J4/91 r.2.4.2). The payment of renewal fees has several unique aspects compared to the payment of other fees at the EPO.

Most fees can only be paid validly within a normal period running from the due date (see **Rfees4** for the meaning of 'due date'). A payment before the due date is invalid. In contrast, a renewal fee that falls due under **R.51(1)** must be paid on a specific date, the due date, and not within a period running from the due date. The due date is the last day of the month containing the anniversary of the date of filing. Hence, a renewal fee may be paid up to three or six months before the due date (**R.51(1)**), depending on the year of pendency for which the fee is being paid.

In some special cases, renewal fees are indeed to be paid during a period running from the due date, as for other fees. Special provisions establish a four-month period for the payment of certain renewal fees for a divisional application (**R.51(3)**), in the case of re-establishment of rights under **Art.122** (**R.51(4)**) and in the case of a successful petition for review under **Art.112a** (**R.51(5)**); **R.159** specifies a special rule for Euro-PCT applications entering the European phase.

Furthermore, for most fees payable to the EPO, lack of payment within the relevant period leads to an immediate loss of rights (commonly the deemed withdrawal of the application) which can be remedied by payment with a surcharge during an additional period (commonly using further processing). A renewal fee may also be paid during an additional period of six months from the due date, provided an additional fee ('surcharge') is paid (**R.51(2)**). However, the loss of right only occurs at the end of this six-month grace period and not at the due date (**Art.86(1)** and **R.51(2)**). As a further complication, the six-month period is not calculated under **R.131(4)** but according to the special provisions of **J4/91**, except for certain cases under **R.159**, and under **R.51(3)**, **R.51(4)** and **R.51(5)**.

Art. 86(1) Renewal fees for the European patent application shall be paid to the European Patent Office in accordance with the Implementing Regulations. These fees shall be due in respect of the third year and each subsequent year, calculated from the date of filing of the application. If a renewal fee is not paid in due time, the application shall be deemed to be withdrawn.

Implemented by:
R.51 Date for payment of renewal fees
Rfees2(1)4 Amount of renewal fee
Rfees2(1)5 Additional fee

1 **Patent years**
No renewal fee is due for an application in respect of the first two years of pendency. The first renewal fee to be paid to the EPO is due in respect of the third year of pendency (**Art.86(1)**). The last renewal fee to be paid to the EPO is due in respect of the year of pendency in which the mention of the grant is published (**Art.86(2)**). The renewal fees for the European patent in respect of the subsequent years of pendency must be paid to the national offices (**Art.141(1)**). If the mention of grant is published in the first or second year of pendency, no renewal fees are paid to the EPO.

A year of pendency runs from the day after the anniversary of the filing date until the next anniversary of the filing date (based on **R.131(2)**, first sentence). These years are counted from the date of filing, not from the priority date, because **Art.89** does not refer to **Art.86(1)**. However, a renewal fee in respect of the coming year is due not on the anniversary of the filing date but on the last day of the month containing the anniversary of the date of filing (**R.51(1)**). (A-X,5.2.4)

An example: an application is filed on 04.06.2018, the anniversary of the filing date is 04.06, the first year of pendency runs from 04.06.2018 to 04.06.2019 (based on **R.131(3)**), the second patent year from 05.06.2019 to 04.06.2020 and the third patent year from 05.06.2020 to 04.06.2021. The first renewal fee payable, i.e. the renewal fee in respect of the third year, is due on 30.06.2020. There is no renewal fee due under **Art.86** if the mention of the grant is published on or before 04.06.2020; renewal fees are due to national patent offices after the grant. The renewal fee in respect of the third year is due if the mention is published on or after 05.06.2020. See A-X,5.2.4 for more examples.

2 **Payment of renewal fee**
The renewal fee must be paid at the latest on the due date and may be paid up to three or six months before this date (**R.51(1)**). If the renewal fee has not been paid on the due date, the renewal fee plus an additional fee (**Rfees2(1)5**) can be paid within an additional period of six months of the due date (**R.51(2)**).

The amount of the fee is determined by **Rfees2(1)4** as valid at the date the payment is considered to have been made to the EPO pursuant to **Rfees7** (A-X,5.1.2 and for example OJ 2022 A2 Art.4.1). An increase in fee can be avoided by an early payment up to three or six months before the due date (**R.51(1)**; OJ 1987 p.4). A reduction of the fee is available for certain applicants (**R.7a(3)**).

3 **Notification of non-payment of renewal fee**

If the renewal fee has not been paid on or before the due date, the EPO informs the applicant as soon as possible, as a courtesy service, of the possibility of payment with additional fee in the already running six-month period from the due date (A-X,5.2.4). The EPO is not compelled to send this notice. Hence, the applicant cannot derive rights from the omission of such a reminder (**J1/89** hn.I.2). Re-establishment under **Art.122** cannot be based on the absence of such a notice (**J12/84** hn.2). Where the EPO does send the notice, the applicant can rely on its accuracy; a payment made late due to a misleading notice will be regarded as made in due time (**J1/89**).

If the renewal fee and additional fee are not paid within the six-month period, the EPO will send a communication under **R.112(1)**, notifying the applicant of the loss of rights. In contrast with the courtesy service, the EPO is obliged to send the communication under **R.112(1)**.

4 **Effect of non-payment**

Non-payment of the renewal fee by the due date does not result in the loss of the application. If the renewal fee and the additional fee have not been paid within the six-month period, the application will be deemed withdrawn upon expiry of the six-month period (**Art.86(1)**, second sentence, and **R.51(2)**, second sentence). Hence, a divisional application can be validly filed in the six-month period, even if the renewal fee and additional fee for the parent application are not paid before the expiry of the six-month period.

Note, that the fact that the loss of rights takes place at the end of the six-month period departs from the principle that deemed withdrawal usually takes effect on expiry of the normal period and not on the expiry of a grace period (**J4/86**, endorsed by **G4/98** r.7). The rules relating to the payment of renewal fees for a European patent with unitary effect are different in that the patent will lapse on the date the renewal fee was due if the renewal fee and any additional fee are not paid in due time (**UPR.14(2)**).

5 **Remedy**

Failure to pay the renewal fee before or on the due date may be redressed by paying the renewal fee with additional fee within the six-month additional period of **R.51(2)**. Further processing and re-establishment are excluded, because the due date is not a time limit in the sense of **Art.121(1)** and **Art.122(1)** but simply a condition to be met. Moreover, there is no actual loss of rights if the payment is not made on or before the due date.

Failure to pay the renewal fee and additional fee within the six-month additional period cannot be redressed using further processing because the period is excluded in **R.135(2)**. Because of this exclusion, re-establishment under **Art.122** and **R.136** is possible (**R.136(3)**). The period of one year within which the request for re-establishment must be filed starts running at the expiry of the six-month additional period (**R.136(1)**). Re-establishment must be requested within two months from the removal of the cause of non-compliance. The fee for re-establishment, the renewal fee and the additional fee must be paid and all due care must be proven.

6 **Refund of renewal fee**

Renewal fees paid for an application which is no longer pending on the due date are refunded (A-X,10.1.1). If the payment is prepared or made using Central fee payment (CFP, the payment will be rejected (see **Rfees5**). Payments of renewal fees that are not due by debit order or by bank transfer (which can happen if the payer does not use CFP for the payment) are repaid to the deposit account or bank account used for the payment (OJ 2024 A82).

If the anniversary is e.g. on 15.07.2018, then a renewal fee is due on 31.07.2018. A payment made on 10.07.2018, i.e. before the due date, is a pre-payment, which will be refunded as having no basis if the application is withdrawn or becomes deemed to be withdrawn on or before the due date, i.e. on or before 31.07.2018.

Art. 86(2) The obligation to pay renewal fees shall terminate with the payment of the renewal fee due in respect of the year in which the mention of the grant of the European patent is published in the European Patent Bulletin.

1 **Last renewal fee for EPO**
The last renewal fee payable to the EPO is the renewal fee in respect of the patent year in which the mention of the grant is published; the patent year runs from the day after the anniversary of the filing date until the next anniversary of the filing date (see **Art.86(1):1**). Renewal fees for the following patent years are to be paid to the national offices and to the EPO for unitary patents (A-X,5.2.4, Example 1).

The payment of this last renewal fee is verified by the EPO before it will grant the patent (**Art.97(1)** and **R.71a(4)**).

2 **Anniversary and projected publication date in the same month**
If, at the time the EPO can issue the decision to grant (i.e. when the technical preparations for the publication of the patent specification are completed, OJ 2006 p.409), the projected publication date for the mention of the grant falls in the same month as the anniversary of the filing date, it may happen that the next renewal fee is to be paid to the EPO under **Art.86(2)** yet does not become due before the projected publication date. This is the case if the projected publication date (which is four weeks after the date of the decision to grant; OJ 2006 p.409) is in the part of the month after the anniversary of the filing date (e.g.: anniversary date: 02.01, projected publication date of the mention of the grant: 10.01, end of the month: 31.01). The reason is that **Art.86(2)** refers to patent years, i.e. to the anniversary of the filing date (A-X,5.2.4), but a renewal fee becomes due only at the end of the month (**R.51(1)**). The applicant could then pay the renewal fee already before the due date but is not obliged to do so. National patent offices may not require the payment of the renewal fee for the patent year at issue (**Art.141(1)**). To prevent this unclear legal situation, the EPO avoids the situation that the publication of the mention of the grant falls in the part of the month after the anniversary date by postponing the decision to grant until the projected publication date falls in the next month (A-X,5.2.4, Example 1). The postponed publication date then becomes the next possible date for publication, the renewal fee becomes due before that next possible date for publication, and the EPO awaits the payment of the renewal fee before it issues the decision to grant (**R.71a(4)**).

Chapter II *Priority*

1 General

The Paris Convention (PC) is the basis upon which the concept of priority in the international patent system rests and all contracting states to the EPC are also states to which the PC applies. Art.19 PC recognises the right of such states to make separate agreements between themselves concerning the protection of industrial property and the EPC and the PCT are examples of such agreements (see EPC Preamble). However, Art.19 PC also imposes the obligation that agreements such as the EPC and the PCT must not contravene any provision of the PC.

The PCT recognises compliance with the PC by explicitly stating in Art.8 PCT that the conditions necessary to establish a valid priority claim and the effect of such a priority claim are governed by Art.4 of the PC. In contrast, the EPC does not apply the PC directly but instead has its own complete, self-contained set of rules on priority in **Art.87-Art.89**. Nevertheless, in view of the reference to Art.19 PC in the EPC Preamble, it is clear that this self-contained set of rules in the EPC is intended to comply with the basic principles concerning priority laid down in the PC (**G1/93** r.4, **G2/98** r.3, **G1/22** r.25). In its decisions concerning the interpretation of Art.87-Art.89 EPC, notably **G1/93**, **G2/98** and **G1/22**, the Enlarged Board has taken this into account.

The PC establishes a set of minimum requirements which signatory states are expected to comply with. As long as these requirements are met, PC states are free to adopt their own additional regulations concerning priority. In particular, the PC only regulates external priority, i.e. the right to claim priority in country X have first filed an application in country Y (Art.4A(1) PC, 'in the other countries'). It does not regulate the effect of an internal priority claim (i.e. the right to claim priority in country X having first filed an application in country X). The EPC also allows internal priority rights and thereby extends beyond the minimum rights guaranteed by the PC. The PC is ambiguous as to whether a patent application can claim the priority of an industrial design or a trademark, but the case law of the legal board of appeal has clarified that this is not allowed. (**J15/80**; A-III,6.1)

Art.87 deals with the main substantive aspects of claiming priority and in particular the kind of application from which priority may be claimed. **Art.88** is mainly concerned with the procedural and formal aspects of claiming priority but also deals with further substantive aspects. **Art.89** deals with the effect of a valid priority claim: the right of priority has the effect that the date of filing of a European patent application will be replaced by the date of filing of an earlier application for certain purposes.

The rules on priority in the EPC apply not only to direct European applications but also to Euro-PCT applications that have entered the European phase (see **Art.150(2):2**).

Art. 87 Priority right

1 **General**

Art.87 provides for the recognition of priority rights under the EPC and the first four paragraphs of this provision correspond to Art.4A(1)-(3) and Art.4C(1), (2) and (4) of the Paris Convention (PC). However, **Art.87(1)** goes beyond the minimum rights necessary to comply with Art.4A(1) of the PC and also provides, in alignment with Art.2 of the TRIPS Agreement, for the recognition of a priority right based on a first filing made in a member of the WTO.

Note that **Art.87(2)** and (4) still only refer to a state (party to the PC) and not to a member (of the WTO). This seems to be inadvertent. In the original proposal for the amendment of **Art.87, Art.87(1)** referred to a person who has filed an application in or for 'any State party to the Paris Convention for the Protection of Industrial Property or the Agreement Establishing the World Trade Organization'. Using this wording, in which the filing always took place in a state of one kind or another, no consequential amendment of **Art.87(2)** or (4) was necessary. However, a further amendment to **Art.87(1)**, proposed by the Irish delegation, was adopted during the conference (see EPC2000 travaux préparatoires, document MR/12/00). The amendment removed the reference to a 'state' party to the WTO agreement and replaced it with a reference to a WTO 'member', in order to avoid excluding e.g. Hong Kong or Taiwan. However, the need to further amend **Art.87(2)** and (4) in order to refer to both states and members was apparently overlooked. This could be rectified by a future Diplomatic Conference.

Art.87(1) also goes beyond the minimum rights necessary to comply with Art.4A(1) of the PC by recognising internal as well as external priority (see **Art.87(1):1**).

Art.87(5) provides a basis for recognising a right of priority based on a first filing made with an industrial property authority of a state which is neither a party to the PC nor a member of the WTO agreement, but this provision has not been used.

Art. 87(1) Any person who has duly filed, in or for
(a) any State party to the Paris Convention for the Protection of Industrial Property or
(b) any Member of the World Trade Organization,
an application for a patent, a utility model or a utility certificate, or his successor in title, shall enjoy, for the purpose of filing a European patent application in respect of the same invention, a right of priority during a period of twelve months from the date of filing of the first application.

1 **'Duly filed in or for any state'**

According to **Art.87(1)**, the first application used as the basis for a priority claim must be 'duly filed'. The word 'duly' refers to the requirement that the first application must be filed in such a way that a date of filing is accorded, giving the application the status of a regular national filing according to **Art.87(3)**. According to **Art.87(2)**, only a regular national filing gives rise to a right of priority.

The first application must be filed in or for any state party to the PC or a member of the WTO. Therefore, an application not filed in or for a PC state or WTO member cannot serve as a basis for claiming a right of priority (subject to **Art.87(5)**). The language 'Member of the World Trade Organization' was chosen carefully to avoid the use of the word 'State' (see **Art.87:1**). A list of the PC states and a list of the WTO members can be found in OJ 2024 A53.

The first application may be a national application filed with the national authorities of a state or member ('filed *in* a state') or an international or regional application in which the state or member is designated ('filed *for* a state'). Hence, the priority of an earlier national, European or PCT application may be claimed (F-VI,1.3).

The state in or for which a first application is filed may be designated in the subsequent priority claiming European application (internal priority) because **Art.87(1)** has no restrictions on the state in or for which the first application is filed ('any') and **Art.3** allows the designation of any contracting state. The PC only provides for external priority, i.e. the filing of a first application in PC state A and the claiming of the priority of that application in state B (see Art.4A(1) PC: 'for the purpose of filing in the other countries'). The PC neither provides for nor prohibits the recognition of internal priority. Under the PCT (see Art.8(2)(b) PCT), internal priority is regulated by national law.

2 **'An application'**

The application must be for a patent, a utility model, or a utility certificate. The list is exhaustive. Hence, a priority claim based on the deposit of an industrial design is not recognised (**J15/80**).

3 **A person or their successor in title**

Only the person who has duly filed a patent application or a successor in title of that person enjoys the right of priority (**Art.87(1)**). The priority right, therefore, initially belongs to the applicant for the priority application; the inventorship is of no consequence (**T5/05**; **T844/18** r.108).

In order for a priority claim to be valid, it is necessary that the applicant for the priority-claiming European patent application (the subsequent applicant) is the applicant for the priority application (the priority applicant), or has obtained the right to claim priority (the priority right) from the priority applicant by a transfer of that right. The EPO may examine whether this requirement has been met in grant and opposition proceedings, and opponents may challenge the validity of the priority right on this basis (**G1/22**, consolidated with G2/22, hn, r.91,112,117,129). However, if the subsequent applicant and the priority applicant are different, the subsequent applicant is presumed to be entitled to claim priority if the priority claim was made in accordance with the formal requirements of **Art.88(1)** and **R.52** and **R.53** (filing of a priority declaration and a priority document) or in accordance with the corresponding provisions of the PCT (**G1/22** hn). This presumption also applies if, in the case of joint applicants, the subsequent applicants differ from the priority applicants and even if there is no overlap between the applicants (hn, r.107,137). The presumption is based on the reasoning that filing the subsequent application and, in particular, the priority document typically requires the cooperation of the priority applicant.

This presumption is rebuttable to take into account rare cases in which the claiming of priority by the subsequent applicant appears to be unjustified, e.g. in case of bad faith behaviour on the side of the subsequent applicant (**G1/22** r.108,131). The presumption is strong, and a party seeking to rebut it must bring forth specific facts supporting serious doubts about the subsequent applicant's entitlement to priority (r.110). Note, however, that a party cannot be expected to prove a negative fact (**T2037/18**); a declaration from the priority applicant that consent to the subsequent filing was not given will probably be sufficient as a rebuttal.

Moreover, although a transfer of the priority right is necessary if the subsequent applicant is not the same as the priority applicant, there are no formal requirements dictating how the transfer must occur. An implied or informal agreement is sufficient for a valid transfer of the priority right (**G1/22** r.122). If the priority applicant A allows the subsequent applicant B to rely on the priority, this is sufficient to form an implied or informal agreement to transfer the priority (**G1/22** r.122).

If a PCT application is filed that lists party A as the applicant for one or more states and party B for one or more other states (as is permitted by R.4.5(d) PCT), there is a rebuttable presumption of consent by A and a corresponding implied agreement to transfer the priority right (**G1/22** r.123,124, fourth sentence of the headnote). This presumption can be rebutted e.g. by showing that party B acted in bad faith (**G1/22** r.126). The interpretation of a joint filing of a PCT application (i.e., a joint filing with the informed involvement of A) as sufficient proof for an implied agreement on the (joint) use of the priority right by B applies independently from the rebuttable presumption that is based on the timely filing of the priority document and meeting the other formal requirements for claiming priority (**G1/22** r.138).

This rule for PCT applications is particularly useful for PCT applications filed before 2011 that claim the priority of a US patent application filed in the name of the inventors and mention the inventor as the applicant for the USA only and a company as the applicant for all other states (**G1/22** r.37).

The right to claim priority may be concretely transferred by means of a written assignment, or by operation of law (e.g. by the merger of companies), or by an informal or implicit agreement. An assignment need not be in writing and need not be signed by the parties (**G1/22** r.99,100,122). The reason is that priority rights that are claimed for the benefit of European patent applications are autonomous rights under the EPC (even though the priority application may be a national patent application), such that the transfer of a priority right must be assessed only in the context of the EPC, essentially without reference to national law (**G1/22** r.85,86,130). Moreover, the EPC does not impose formal requirements for transferring the priority right by agreement (**G1/22** r.86). Note that **G1/22** overruled earlier decisions that applied formal requirements set under national law to assignments of priority rights. Whether or not an implied agreement exists must be assessed under the autonomous law of the EPC (**G1/22** r.126).

G1/22 leaves open the question of whether an agreement to transfer the right to priority can be retroactive or must be concluded before the filing date of the subsequent application (**G1/22** r.100). Instead, the Enlarged Board comes to the conclusion that the presumption of entitlement renders such questions largely irrelevant. The presumption of entitlement exists on the date on which the priority is claimed, which can be after the filing date because the priority declaration under **R.52** can be filed separately after the filing of the application. The rebuttal of the presumption must also relate to the circumstances on the date when the priority declaration is filed; later developments cannot affect the rebuttable presumption (**G1/22** r.109). Older case law held that the transfer of the priority right was to be concluded before the filing date of the subsequent European or Euro-PCT patent application or on the same date but before the moment of filing (**T577/11** hn.3; **T1946/21**).

In the event that the rebuttable presumption is rebutted, and the applicant cannot demonstrate that the priority right was properly transferred, the priority claim is invalid.

The headnote of **G1/22** can be easier understood by grouping its four sentences as follows: A) the EPO is competent to assess entitlement to priority, B) there is a rebuttable presumption that the applicant is entitled to priority if **Art.88(1)** is complied with; this presumption also applies if the applicants differ, and C) in the case of a PCT application filed by multiple applicants, an agreement between the applicants may be implied in certain situations.

The rules given in **G1/22** apply in the context of a priority right that is claimed *for* a European patent application or patent (**Art.87**). This applies regardless of whether the validity of the priority claim is relevant to the effective date of a claim in an application or patent whose patentability or validity is being considered or whether the validity of the priority claim is relevant to the question of whether a European prior right is prior art or not under **Art.54(3)** (**G1/22** r.35, **T521/18**). However, the validity of a priority right claimed for a national application or patent is another matter. Other patent offices may apply different rules for assessing the priority of a national patent application or patent, even if priority is claimed *from* a European patent application. Moreover, it cannot be assumed that the national courts of the EPC states or the UPC will assess entitlement to priority in the same way as the EPO, even when considering the validity of a European patent (see **G1/22** r.115).

3.1 RIGHTS ARISING FROM A FIRST APPLICATION

The filing of a first application in or for a state creates two distinguishable rights for the applicant. The first one is the right to pursue the grant of a patent having effect in that state. The second one is the right to claim priority from this application in a subsequent application filed in or for a state that recognises the first filing as giving rise to a right of priority. When, for instance, the first filing is made in a state party to the PC, other states party to the PC must recognise a claim to priority based on this first application. The priority right is in fact a bundle of rights, one for each state (and each regional patent office) where a subsequent application can be filed, and can be transferred separately for different states (see **G1/22** r.83 and Wieczorek, *Die Unionspriorität im Patentrecht*, Köln, 1975, p.139).

A strict distinction should be made between the priority right claimed for the benefit of a European patent application (**Art.87**), which arises from the filing of the first application, and the entitlement to a European patent, which arises from making an invention (**Art.60(1)**) (**G1/22** r.129).

4 'A European patent application in respect of the same invention'

The EPC does not explicitly define the meaning of the term 'the same invention'. Opinion **G2/98** has ruled that a narrow or strict interpretation is appropriate, equating it with 'the same subject-matter' referred to in **Art.87(4)**. Consequently, a priority right is only valid if the claim defining the invention, i.e. the specific combination of features present in the claim, is specifically disclosed in the first application as a whole, either explicitly or implicitly (**G2/98** r.2). Whether or not a feature is related to the function and effect of the invention is irrelevant (**G2/98** r.8.3). The requirement is that the subject-matter of the claim, i.e. all its features in combination, must be derivable directly and unambiguously from the first application, as seen from the perspective of the skilled person using common general knowledge. This disclosure test is the same as the 'gold standard' test for judging the compliance of an amendment made to an application with the requirement of **Art.123(2)** (**G2/98** r.1 and 2; **G2/10**, F-VI,2.2). However, there are some differences in the way the test is applied under **Art.87(1)** and **Art.123(2)**: the disclosure in the first application must also be enabling for priority to be valid (**G1/15** hn) and priority may be valid for only parts of the claim under examination (partial priority). See **Art.88(4):2** for further details of the extent to which the subject-matter of the claimed invention must be disclosed in the first application.

This strict interpretation of the term 'the same invention' is consistent with Art.4 PC and other provisions in the EPC, in particular **Art.87(4)** and **Art.88(2)-(4)** (**G2/98** r.5, 6.8). A broader interpretation of the term 'the same invention' would be one that recognises the priority of a claim, including a feature not disclosed in the priority document and not related to the function and effect of the invention (see e.g. **T73/88**). Such an interpretation is inappropriate because it is at variance with the principle that the right to the patent should be associated with the application that first discloses the claimed subject-matter (**G2/98** r.8.1), it leads to an inconsistency between the term 'the same invention' in **Art.87(1)** and the term 'the same subject-matter' in **Art.87(4)** (**G2/98** r.8.2), and it results in legal uncertainty because the question of whether a claimed feature is related to the effect and function of the invention depends on the prior art that happens to be found (**G2/98** r.8.3).

If the first application discloses embodiments falling within the subject-matter of the claim under examination, the claim is entitled to priority only for the part of the subject-matter that is disclosed in the first application (partial priority), see **G1/15** and **Art.88(3)**.

The wording of **Art.87(1)** is open to different interpretations regarding the possible exhaustion of the priority right in the sense of whether or not the same priority right may be validly claimed in more than one European patent application. Case law has endorsed the interpretation that priority is not exhausted when it is claimed for the first time, i.e. the same priority right may be claimed for more than one European patent application (**T15/01** hn.1, r.33, 34; **T5/05**). An earlier decision **T998/99**. which adopted the alternative interpretation, should not be followed as it is an 'exception' (**T15/01** r.40).

5 **'During a period of twelve months'**

A European patent application claiming priority must be filed within a period of twelve months from the date of filing of the first application (**Art.87(1)**; see **R.131(4)** for the computation of the period).

This twelve-month priority period is extended if it expires on a non-working day (**R.134(1)**), if the delivery of mail is interrupted (**R.134(2)**) and such interruption is recognised by the EPO (**R.134(4)**) or if the EPO is on strike (**R.134(1)**). Note that the priority period of **Art.87(1)** is also extended in order to account for days on which national offices are not open for business if the European application is filed at such an office (see **R.134(3)** and notes thereto).

There are only limited remedies for failing to meet the twelve-month period for claiming priority. Further processing cannot be used because the period is excluded under **Art.121(4)**. The application of re-establishment is permitted according to **Art.122**, but the request must be filed within two months of the expiry of the twelve-month priority period (**R.136(1)**). The application may also be regarded as having been received within the priority period, even if it is actually received after the expiry of that period, provided the conditions of **R.133** or the conditions of **R.134(5)** are met.

If the Receiving Section notices that a European patent application has been filed later than the expiry of the relevant priority period, it notifies the applicant that the claim to priority will be considered invalid unless either (1) a corrected date is indicated in accordance with **R.52(3)** within four months of the filing date of the application or sixteen months from the priority date; or (2) re-establishment is requested in accordance with **Art.122** and **R.136(1)** within two months from expiry of the priority period (A-III,6.6). The date of filing accorded to a European patent application can be later than the date on which the application was received by the EPO, e.g. if drawings have been added later (**R.56**).

A priority claim which relates to a first application filed on the same day as the priority claiming European application will be disregarded, because the priority period starts on the day following the date of filing of the first application (Art.4C(2) PC; **R.131(2)**), (A-III,6.1).

6 'The first application'

6.1 PRIORITY MAY ONLY BE CLAIMED FROM A FIRST FILING

The application from which priority is claimed must be a 'first application' in the sense that it must be the application in which the applicant describes for the first time the subject-matter in respect of which the priority claim is asserted. This principle is expressed in the EPC by the use of the ordinal number 'first' in **Art.87(1)** interpreted in view of its further use in **Art.87(4)**. It should be noted that the word 'first' in **Art.87(1)** appears prima facie be a reference to the 'duly filed application' in the same provision, merely distinguishing between the 'duly filed application' and the 'subsequent, priority claiming application'. However, **Art.87(4)** confirms the 'first application' requirement by providing a limited exception thereto.

If the subject-matter has been disclosed in a still earlier application originating from the same applicant or the same applicant's predecessor in title, the priority claim does not comply with the requirements of **Art.87(1)** and the priority right for the earlier described subject-matter is invalid (Wieczorek, *Die Unionspriorität im Patentrecht*, Köln, 1975, p.28). This is to prevent applicants from filing a cascade of applications at regular intervals and deciding at some opportune moment which one to claim priority from.

Still earlier applications of other applicants describing the same subject-matter are not detrimental to the right of priority (F-VI,1.4; **T788/05** r.2, also discussing the case of co-applicants of the still earlier application).

By way of exception, a subsequent application will be considered as a first application, in spite of a previous first application relating to the same subject-matter having been filed by the same applicant or the applicant's predecessor in title, if the requirements of **Art.87(4)** have been fulfilled.

6.2 LACK OF FULL EQUIVALENCE BETWEEN PARIS CONVENTION STATES AND WTO MEMBERS

The question arises, following the amendment to **Art.87(1)** to refer to both PC states and WTO members, as to whether these states and members should be treated equivalently when determining the first filing of subject matter for which priority is claimed. On the one hand, **Art.87(1)** seems to introduce an equivalence between a filing in a PC state and a filing in a member of the WTO and it could be assumed that priority should now only be recognised if based on a first filing in all of these states and members in combination. On the other hand, any interpretation of **Art.87(1)** must still remain compliant with the corresponding provisions of the PC, which make no mention of WTO members. The PC specifically recognises the validity of a priority claim based on a first filing in a PC state.

This situation can only be reconciled in a satisfactory manner by distinguishing between PC states and WTO members and not treating them equivalently in all situations. Importantly, priority should always be recognised based on a first filing in a PC state, regardless of whether there has been an earlier filing in a WTO member. This is a prerequisite for compliance of the EPC with the PC.

It seems that the legislator intended the 'first filing' principle that results from the interplay between **Art.87(1)** and **Art.87(4)** to also apply to WTO members. Even though **Art.87(4)** does not refer to WTO members, this seems to have been the result of an oversight rather than a deliberate choice (see **Art.87:1**). Hence, priority should only be recognised from the first filing in a member of WTO member and not from a second filing. If there is an earlier filing for the same subject matter in a WTO country, and the principles of **Art.87(4)** do not apply, the priority claim should be considered to be invalid. It is less clear whether priority should be denied based on a WTO member filing if there is an earlier filing for the same subject matter in a PC state but there seems no reason in principle not to apply this rule.

The result of these considerations is that PC states and WTO members should be considered equivalent when deciding on the first filing of any particular subject matter with the one important exception that the validity of a priority claim based on a first filing in a PC state must be recognised regardless of whether there has been an earlier filing in a WTO member.

6.3 PARTIAL PRIORITY

The EPC applies the priority right at the level of the subject-matter of the claims of the patent application claiming priority, as implied by **Art.88(2)-(4)**. The principle of partial priority applies by analogy (see **Art.88(3):2**). Hence, the right to priority of the subject-matter of a claim of an application can only be based on a first application, i.e. an earlier application specifically disclosing for the first time the subject-matter of that claim. If the earlier application is not the first application describing the subject-matter because a part of the subject-matter of the claim (e.g. an embodiment) has been described in a still earlier application originating from the same applicant or the applicant's predecessor in title, the priority right for that part of the subject-matter of the claim is invalid, unless the exception of **Art.87(4)** applies. The effective date of that part of the subject-matter is the date of filing of the application. The claim will then not be novel if the still earlier application was published prior to the filing date of the application (**Art.54(2)**), if the still earlier application is a European application published on or after the filing date of the application (**Art.54(3)**), and also if other relevant prior art is published prior to the filing date of the application. The priority right is valid for the part of the subject-matter of the claim that is not disclosed in the still earlier application and that is disclosed for the first time in the earlier application. Hence, the 'first application' requirement may lead to the claim having partial priority in cases wherein the still earlier application discloses an embodiment falling within the claim, which has the result that the priority is invalid for the embodiments of the claim that are already disclosed in the still earlier application (**G1/15, T282/12**; F-VI,1.5).

As an example, if the claim under examination and the earlier application specify 'gold or silver' and a still earlier application discloses 'gold', the priority is invalid for the embodiment 'gold' but valid for the embodiment 'silver'. Similarly, if the claim under examination and the earlier application specify 'metal' and the still earlier application discloses 'gold', the priority is invalid for the embodiment 'gold' even if that embodiment is not specifically mentioned in the claim under examination or in the earlier application. If the still earlier application was published prior to the filing date of the application under examination, this publication anticipates the embodiment 'gold' and the claim as a whole lacks novelty. The remainder of the claim (metal with the exception of gold) is still entitled to priority.

Art. 87(2) Every filing that is equivalent to a regular national filing under the national law of the State where it was made or under bilateral or multilateral agreements, including this Convention, shall be recognised as giving rise to a right of priority.

1 **Claiming priority from a regular national filing**
A European patent application may claim the priority of a regular national filing in or for a state (see **Art.87(1):2**). A filing 'for' a state can be under a bilateral or multilateral treaty, such as the EPC or PCT. A European filing having a filing date according to the EPC (**Art.80**) is equivalent to a regular national filing in the designated contracting states (**Art.66**) and is therefore filed 'for' those designated states. A European patent application may therefore claim the priority of an earlier European patent application.

The term 'regular national filing' is defined in **Art.87(3)**.

Although **Art.87(2)** only refers to a 'State' and does not mention a member of the WTO, it does not appear that the legislator intended to distinguish between the two (see **Art.87:1**). It must therefore be assumed that a national filing under the national law of a WTO member must also be a 'regular' filing in order to give rise to a right of priority.

Art. 87(3) A regular national filing shall mean any filing that is sufficient to establish the date on which the application was filed, whatever the outcome of the application may be.

1 **Regular national filing**
The requirements that must be fulfilled in order to establish a filing date at a national office are governed by national law. For instance, Norway requires one or more claims as a minimum requirement for obtaining a filing date for a national patent application.

The final clause of **Art.87(3)** ('whatever the outcome of the application may be') has the effect that the withdrawal, deemed withdrawal or refusal of the first application after its filing does not affect the right to priority that it has created. For example, if the filing fee for a European first application is not paid, the application will be deemed withdrawn upon expiry of the period of **R.38(1)** (**Art.78(2)**). This will have no effect on the validity of the priority right created by the accordance of a filing date, whether a subsequent application claiming its priority is filed before or after the deemed withdrawal. The need to comply with the PC was one reason why the Enlarged Board found, under EPC1973, that non-payment of the designation fees and the consequent deemed withdrawal of the designations of the contracting states could not have the retrospective effect that filing date was lost (**G4/98** r.5).

It is possible to file a so-called 'provisional application for patent' in the US. The EPO regards such a provisional application as a duly filed national application in the sense of **Art.87(3)** which gives rise to a right of priority within the meaning of **Art.87(1)**. (OJ 1996 p.81)

Art. 87(4) A subsequent application in respect of the same subject-matter as a previous first application and filed in or for the same State shall be considered as the first application for the purposes of determining priority, provided that, at the date of filing the subsequent application, the previous application has been withdrawn, abandoned or refused, without being open to public inspection and without leaving any rights outstanding, and has not served as a basis for claiming a right of priority. The previous application may not thereafter serve as a basis for claiming a right of priority.

1 **Priority claim from a first application**

The purpose of this provision is to give the applicant the possibility of changing the application from which priority may validly be claimed for any particular subject matter by replacing a previous application (which was the original first filing) by a subsequent application (which is then regarded as the new first filing). It may be that the original first filing was filed too early, before research into the invention was complete, and does not adequately or completely describe the invention. **Art.87(4)** allows the applicant to file a subsequent, improved application which will be regarded as a first filing from which priority can validly be claimed. The priority period is restarted and within twelve months from the filing of this new application, the applicant can file an application validly claiming its priority.

The text of the provision implies that the right of priority according to **Art.87(1)** may only be based on a first application, i.e. the application in which the applicant has disclosed the subject-matter for the first time. This requirement is consistent with the interpretation of the term 'first application' in **Art.87(1):6.**

See **Art.87(1):4** for the interpretation of the phrase 'the same subject-matter' in **Art.87(4).**

2 **Requirements for regarding a subsequent application a first application**

Each of the following conditions contained in **Art.87(4)** must be met, for a subsequent application for the same subject-matter as the previous application to be regarded as a first application for priority purposes (F-VI,1.4.1):

1 The previous and subsequent applications must have been filed in or for the same state. Although **Art.87(4)** does not refer explicitly to a member of the WTO, this seems to have been advertent (see **Art.87:1**). The provision should therefore be read to mean that the previous and subsequent applications must have been filed in or for the same PC state or WTO member.

The fact that a previous application that has not left any rights outstanding, was not filed in or for the same state or member as the subsequent application may only be revealed during a file inspection in the applicant's office, as might be carried out in a discovery procedure under national law.

2 At the filing date of the subsequent application, the previous application must have been withdrawn, abandoned or refused. The previous application may not have been open for public inspection on or before the filing date of the subsequent application (see also the German text of **Art.87(4)**). Hence, a publication after the filing date of the subsequent application is not an obstacle to the subsequent application being regarded as a first application. Furthermore, the previous application may not leave any rights outstanding. Using an application as a basis for filing by reference under **R.40(1)(c)**, without claiming its priority, does not as such generate outstanding rights (F-VI,1.4.1).

3 The previous application may not have served as a basis for claiming a right of priority before the filing date of the subsequent application. Furthermore, after the filing date of the subsequent application, the previous application may no longer serve as a valid basis for claiming a right of priority. The last sentence of **Art.87(4)** is an implementation of the requirement in the same provision that the previous application does not leave any rights outstanding. After the replacement of a previous application by a subsequent application, priority on the basis of the previous application may no longer be recognised (Bodenhausen, *Guide to the Ap-*

plication of the Paris Convention for the Protection of Industrial Property, BIRPI 1969, commentary on the identical sentence in Art.4C(4) PC). This has the effect that at any one moment, there is only ever one application from which priority may validity be claimed.

4 The applications must have been filed by the same applicant or the first applicant's successor in title. Although this condition is not explicitly stated in **Art.87(4)**, it is a consequence of **Art.87(1)**, which states that only the applicant or the applicant's successor in title enjoys the right to claim priority. Hence, an applicant can only claim priority from a first application that has been filed by the same applicant or the applicant's predecessor in title. Only such first applications are relevant for the application of **Art.87(4)**. Applications not filed by the same applicant or the applicant's successor in title are not detrimental to the first application requirement of **Art.87(1)**. (**T5/05** r.4)

If any one of these requirements is not fulfilled, the subsequent application will not be regarded as a first application, and a priority claim based on the subsequent application will be invalid in so far as it relates to subject-matter already described in the previous application. The EPO will consider this issue only if there is evidence of the existence of a previous application and the priority is relevant in view of cited prior art. Where appropriate, the EPO will request the applicant to provide evidence, usually from a patent office, that the requirements of **Art.87(4)** are complied with (F-VI,1.4.1). A priority claim based on a US continuation-in-part is evidence for the existence of an earlier application; priority may only validly be claimed for the subject-matter first disclosed in the continuation in part since the earlier US application must necessarily have been pending when the continuation-in-part was filed (and was therefore not 'withdrawn, abandoned or refused'). A priority claim based on a US continuation or a divisional application is always invalid for all the subject matter disclosed because of the existence of an earlier application pending at the date of filing and the fact that no subject-matter may been added when filing a continuation or divisional.

3 **Example**

The effect of **Art.87(4)** is aptly demonstrated by the facts underlying decision **T1056/01**. Application A was filed with the UK patent office on 08.04.1991 and withdrawn in favour of application B, filed with the UK patent office on 07.04.1992. Application A came to light because the UK patent office published, as part of its normal procedure, the title of the application, the name of the applicant and the fact that application A was withdrawn before publication. European application C was filed on 07.04.1993 claiming priority from application B. The applicant could not prove to the satisfaction of the EPO that application A had been withdrawn on the filing date of application B, as required under of **Art.87(4)**. As the UK patent office had destroyed the file of application A five years after the withdrawal, it could not provide evidence of the actual date of withdrawal. Since applications A and B disclosed the same invention, application B was not the first application in the sense of **Art.87(1)** and the priority claim was invalid. A publication on 16.02.1993 was therefore prior art and destroyed the novelty of the main claim of European application C.

Art. 87(5) If the first filing has been made with an industrial property authority which is not subject to the Paris Convention for the Protection of Industrial Property or the Agreement Establishing the World Trade Organization, paragraphs 1 to 4 shall apply if that authority, according to a communication issued by the President of the European Patent Office, recognises that a first filing made with the European Pat-

ent Office gives rise to a right of priority under conditions and with effects equivalent to those laid down in the Paris Convention.

1 **Recognition of priority from a state not party to Paris Convention and not WTO member**
Art.87(5) enables the President to issue a communication that the patent office of a state not party to the PC and not a member of the WTO recognises that a first filing made with the EPO gives rise to a priority effect according to the PC in that state. The effect of issuing such a communication is that a first filing made with that patent office will be recognised as a first filing according to **Art.87(1)** to (4); hence, the EPO will recognise that such a first filing gives rise to a right of priority under the EPC.

The President has not yet issued any communication under **Art.87(5)** (A-III,6.2).

Art. 88 Claiming priority

1 **General**
Art.88 contains a first paragraph relating to the procedural requirements for claiming priority and three subsequent paragraphs relating to substantive requirements for claiming priority. In the following notes, the term 'previous application' will be used to refer to the application whose priority is claimed, following the usage in **Art.88(4)**. The application whose priority is claimed is also often referred to as the 'priority application' (see e.g. **G2/98**).

2 **Effect of priority claim and its withdrawal on time limits**
The priority date is the starting point for the calculation of certain periods, such as the period for designating the inventor (sixteen months, **R.60(1)**) and the period that must expire before the application is published (eighteen months, **Art.93(1)**). In the case of multiple priority claims, the earliest claimed priority date is decisive (**Art.88(2)**). Furthermore, the priority date is important for determining the state of the art under **Art.54(2)** and (3) (**Art.89**).

An applicant can withdraw a priority claim in order to extend a period that is calculated by reference to the priority date (E-VIII,8.2). The withdrawal has no effect on periods that have already expired (A-III,6.11; E-VIII,1.5).

An applicant can also withdraw a priority claim in order to delay publication of the application. However, if the withdrawal takes place after the technical preparations for publication have been completed (**R.67(2)**), the application will still be published when eighteen months from the priority date have elapsed; it will be a normal publication under **Art.54(2)**, with effect under **Art.54(3)** from the filing date and not from the priority date. (F-VI,3.5; G-IV,5.1.1)

The priority claim can be withdrawn for a European application even after the application is published.

In all these cases, the withdrawal of the earliest priority claim may have the effect that state of the art is determined at a later date, which may negatively affect the patentability of the claimed invention.

3 Invalid priority claim

If the applicant does not file a declaration of priority within sixteen months from the earliest priority date claimed, there is no priority claim for the European application under examination (**Art.88(1), R.52(2)**). A late-filed declaration of priority is invalid unless it is permitted as the correction of an error (**R.139:3.1.1**) or a request for re-establishment is allowed (**Art.122**). The essential elements of a declaration of priority are the date of the previous application and the state in or for which the previous application was filed (A-III,6.5.3) – the number of the previous application can be supplied later (**R.59**).

A priority claim for a European patent application is invalid from the outset if:

- the applicant for the European patent application is neither the applicant for the previous application nor the successor in title thereof (**Art.87(1)**);
- the European application is not filed within the twelve-month period of **Art.87(1)**, extended where appropriate according **R.134(1)-(4)**, unless re-establishment is allowed (**Art.122; R.136(1)**);
- the previous application is for an industrial property right that is not mentioned in **Art.87(1)**;
- the previous application was neither filed in or for a contracting state of the Paris Convention (PC) nor in or for a member of the WTO (**Art.87(1)**).

A priority claim may also be invalid from the outset if there is a mistake in the declaration of priority which is not corrected in a timely manner (**R.52(3), R.139**).

A priority claim for a European patent application may be invalid in respect of certain subject-matter if:

- the previous application is not the first application in the sense of **Art.87(1)** for the subject-matter at issue, and the exception of **Art.87(4)** does not apply;
- the subject-matter at issue is not implicitly or explicitly disclosed in the previous application (**Art.88(4):2** and **Art.87(1):4**);
- the previous application does not contain an enabling disclosure of the subject-matter at issue (**T193/95** r.3.1, **G1/15** hn; see **Art.88(4):2**).

4 Loss of priority right

The right of priority is lost (A-III,6.10) where:

- the certified copy of the previous application (priority document) is not filed in due time (**R.53(1), R.59**);
- the application number of the previous application is not stated in due time (**R.52(1), R.59**);
- a requested translation of the previous application is not filed in due time (**R.53(3)**).

The applicant is notified (**R.112(1)**) of any non-entitlement to or loss of priority (**Art.90(5)**). Any period that runs from the priority date and has not yet expired when priority is lost is recalculated to take the loss of priority into account.

Art. 88(1) An applicant desiring to take advantage of the priority of a previous application shall file a declaration of priority and any other document required, in accordance with the Implementing Regulations.

Implemented by:
R.52 Declaration of priority
R.53 Priority documents

R.54 Issuing priority documents

1 **Formalities for claiming priority**
Art.88(1) governs the formal requirements for claiming priority by requiring the filing of a declaration of priority and any other document as set out in the Implementing Regulations.

The application will only have the benefit of the priority of a previous application if the applicant fulfils the following three requirements:

1 The applicant must file a declaration of priority stating the date of the previous application, the state or WTO member in or for which it was made and the file number (**R.52(1)**). See **R.52(2), (3)** for the time limit and correction of errors. Later addition or correction of a declaration of priority may also be possible under **R.139** in certain circumstances (A-III,6.5.2).
2 The applicant must file a certified copy of the previous application (**R.53(1)**). See **R.53(1)** for the time limit and **R.53(2)** for cases in which a copy need not be filed.
3 The applicant must file a translation of the previous application, or a declaration that the application and the previous application are identical, if the previous application is not in an official EPO language and the validity of the priority claim is relevant to patentability (**R.53(3)**). See **R.53(3)** for the time limit and correction of errors.

The information in the declaration of priority is included on the front page of the published patent application and the published patent specification (**R.52(5)**).

Art. 88(2) Multiple priorities may be claimed in respect of a European patent application, notwithstanding the fact that they originated in different countries. Where appropriate, multiple priorities may be claimed for any one claim. Where multiple priorities are claimed, time limits which run from the date of priority shall run from the earliest date of priority.

1 **Multiple priorities**
The first sentence of **Art.88(2)** allows the claiming of multiple priorities and corresponds in substance to the first part of the first sentence of Art.4F PC. The second sentence allows multiple priorities to be claimed for a single claim and is further discussed hereinafter. Finally, the third sentence provides that any periods that run from the priority date (e.g. the period that must elapse before publication of the application, **Art.93(1)(a)**) run from the earliest claimed priority date (see **Art.88:2**).

A claim will be entitled to multiple priority dates when different embodiments falling within the scope of the claim have been disclosed for the first time in different priority applications. This is an example of 'partial priority', which is also encountered when only part of a claim is entitled to priority, with the other part having the filing date as its effective date (see **Art.88(3):2** below).

2 **Effective dates of a claim with multiple priorities**
The following example relates to a device which may comprise one or more of the different features A, B and C.

A first French national application, having filing date P1, describes three embodiments: the device, the device comprising feature A and the device comprising feature B. There is no disclosure of feature C.

A second German national application, having filing date P2, includes the disclosure of the French application and also describes the device comprising feature C and the device comprising both features B and C.

A third European application, having filing date F, claims the priority of both previous applications and is filed within twelve months of the filing of the French application.

Claim 1 of the European application defines the device itself.

Claim 2 of the European application depends on Claim 1 and adds features 'A or C'.

Claim 3 of the European application depends on Claim 1 or 2 and adds feature 'B'.

The effective date of Claim 1 is P1. Claim 2 defines two embodiments of the invention; the embodiment including A has an effective dateP1; the embodiment including C has an effective date P2. Claim 3 defines three embodiments. The first embodiment, resulting from its dependence on Claim 1, includes only B and has an effective date P1. The second embodiment, resulting from its dependence on Claim 2, includes the combination of A and B and has an effective date F, since neither the first nor second application describes this combination of features. The third embodiment, also resulting from its dependence on Claim 2, includes the combination of B and C and has an effective date P2. For the European application, any time limit calculated based on the priority date runs from the earliest date of priority, i.e. from P1 (**Art.88(2)**, last sentence). (See also F-VI,1.5)

Art. 88(3) If one or more priorities are claimed in respect of a European patent application, the right of priority shall cover only those elements of the European patent application which are included in the application or applications whose priority is claimed.

1 **Element**

The term 'elements' in **Art.88(3)** is used in the sense of 'subject-matter', not in the sense of single features (**G2/98** r.5.1.2). Hence, the right of priority is only valid for claimed subject-matter that is included, i.e. disclosed, in the priority application. The right of priority is invalid for claimed subject-matter that is not disclosed in the priority application (**G1/15** hn).

An application claiming priority from a previous application can itself serve as a basis for priority for a later application in as far as the application contains subject-matter that is not included (i.e. is not disclosed) in the previous application (**G1/15** r.5.1.2, see also Art.4F, second paragraph, PC).

2 **Partial priority**

A partial priority is a situation in which only a part of the subject-matter of a claim is entitled to the priority date of a previous application. The remaining subject-matter of the claim may be entitled to a different priority date or may only be entitled to the filing date of the application concerned. Partial entitlement to priority is frequently encountered when the subject-matter of a patent application is extended beyond that of an earlier application from which priority is claimed, for example by introducing a generalisation of a more specific disclosure in the priority application.

Partial priority arises when a claim can be split into different embodiments, e.g. in the case of an 'OR' claim (see **G2/98** r.6.1-6.7 discussing the travaux préparatoires of the EPC and distinguishing between 'AND' and 'OR' claims). Where a first priority application discloses a feature A and a second priority application discloses a feature B for use together with A (i.e. the second priority application discloses A+B), then an 'AND' claim directed to A+B cannot enjoy priority from the first priority date, because the invention A+B was disclosed only at the date of the second priority application. Hence, multiple priorities cannot be claimed for an 'AND' claim (**G2/98** r.6.6). However, where a first priority application discloses a feature A and a second priority application discloses a feature B as an alternative to feature A, then an 'OR' claim directed to A or B (i.e. a claim reciting 'A or B') can enjoy the first priority for part A of the claim and the second priority for part B of the claim (**G2/98** r.6.7). It is also acceptable to claim two different priorities for a claim directed to C, if the feature C, either in the form of a generic term or formula, or otherwise (a generic 'OR' claim), encompasses feature A as well as feature B (**G2/98** r.6.7).

Decision **G1/15** reconsidered the validity of partial priority in the context of a generic 'OR' claim. **G1/15** r6.4 gave a two-step test for assessing whether a generic 'OR' claim may enjoy partial priority. The first step is to determine the subject-matter disclosed in the priority application using the disclosure test of **G2/98**. In the second step, it is determined whether this subject-matter is encompassed by the generic 'OR' claim of the subsequent application. If so, the claim is conceptually divided into a first part corresponding to the invention disclosed in the priority application and enjoying priority, and a remaining second part not enjoying this priority. The priority application must disclose the subject-matter of the first part directly and unambiguously, implicitly or explicitly, and in an enabling manner, and must also be the 'first application' for that subject-matter in the sense of **Art.87(1)** (**G1/15** hn).

For example, when a priority application discloses an embodiment using iron and the claim of the subsequent application refers generally to embodiments using metal, the embodiment using iron is entitled to priority, but the embodiments using other metals do not enjoy that priority. See also F-VI,1.5 and **T260/14** r.2 for examples.

Art.88(3) expressly refers to the case of multiple priorities. In such a case, the remaining second part of the subject-matter as identified in the two-step test may be entitled e.g. to a second priority date or to the filing date of the application or may involve partial priority in turn, as the case may be. For example, when a first priority application discloses iron and a later second priority application discloses metal, a claim specifying metal enjoys the first priority only for the embodiment with iron and the second priority date for the other embodiments.

T1519/15 considered that a generic 'OR' claim can also result from the absence of a feature in the claim of the subsequent application. It applied **G1/15** to a case in which the priority application disclosed a circuit having four sensing capacitors and seven transistors and the claim of the subsequent application related to a circuit having at least two sensing capacitors (the presence or absence of transistors being unspecified). Since the claim permits any number of transistors, it encompasses the specific embodiment including seven transistors. The four sensing capacitors are also encompassed by the at least two sensing capacitors in the claim. Hence, the claim enjoys a partial priority for the embodiment of the priority application, but not for the remaining embodiments covered by the claim, for example embodiments including three or five sensing capacitors, since these embodiments are not disclosed in the priority application.

G1/15 made it clear that poisonous priority applications (e.g. **T571/10**) and toxic divisional applications (e.g. **T557/13**) are not possible when the EPC is interpreted properly.

Art. 88(4) If certain elements of the invention for which priority is claimed do not appear among the claims formulated in the previous application, priority may nonetheless be granted, provided that the documents of the previous application as a whole specifically disclose such elements.

1 **Disclosure in application as a whole**

The term 'elements' in **Art.88(4)** refers to subject-matter defined by a claim of the European application or patent being examined (**G2/98** r.6.2). For a priority claim to be valid, that subject-matter must be specifically disclosed in the priority application as a whole, either explicitly or implicitly (**G2/98** r.2). According to **Art.88(4)**, it is irrelevant whether the subject-matter appears in the claims or in any other part of the priority application. Since drawings are an integral part of an application, a feature may also be disclosed in a drawing (**T169/83**).

According to the Guidelines, no account should be taken, when determining the validity of a priority claim, of subject-matter solely found in that part of the description of the earlier application referring to prior art or in an explicit disclaimer (F-VI,2.2). Note, however, that for the assessment of novelty, the disclosure of a prior art document does include prior art explicitly described and any matter explicitly disclaimed (G-IV,5.1).

2 **Specific disclosure**

The specific disclosure required by **Art.88(4)** means that the subject-matter of a claim, i.e. all its features, must be derivable directly and unambiguously from the disclosure of the invention in the priority application. This disclosure test should be the same as the test for compliance of an amendment to an application with the requirement of **Art.123(2)** (**G2/98** r.1 and 2; F-VI,2.2; **Art.123(2):1.2**). Hence, the test is the same as the 'gold standard' test of **G2/10** r.4.3, 4.6 (see **Art.87(1):4**).

Specific disclosure includes features which a skilled person regards as implicit in what is expressly mentioned in the document (F-VI,2.2).

Conversely, the need for a specific disclosure means that it is not sufficient if the disclosure refers merely in broad and general terms to a detailed feature of the claim (F-VI,2.2; e.g. **T409/90**). Exact literal correspondence of features is not required. It suffices if, on a reasonable assessment, there is in substance a disclosure of the same subject-matter of the claim (F-VI,2.2).

A later application may disclaim subject-matter disclosed as a positive feature in the priority application provided the requirements of **G2/98** are met (**G2/10** r.4.6). Moreover, a disclaimer which is permitted under **G1/03** can be introduced when filing a subsequent European patent application without affecting the right to priority from the first application not containing the disclaimer (F-VI,2.2)

The priority document must provide an enabling disclosure of the subject-matter for which priority is claimed (**G1/15** hn; **T193/95** r.3.1). For example, a priority document disclosing a new chemical compound without a reproducible method for its preparation, the method not being part of the common general knowledge, does not give rise to a right of priority for the compound.

The disclosure of the priority application is to be read through the eyes of the skilled person and bearing in mind the common general knowledge (**G2/98** r.9). However, such a manner of reading only serves to interpret the meaning of the technical disclosure and place it in context; the common general knowledge of the skilled person cannot be used to complete an otherwise incomplete technical disclosure (**T744/99**). The common general knowledge may be used to interpret implicit features in the disclosure but not to introduce equivalents, which are not relevant for priority but only for the assessment of inventive step.

When drafting a subsequent application, it is recommended to take the literal text of the priority application as a starting point and to add any subject-matter as needed to avoid introducing unnecessary differences between the two texts that could jeopardise the validity of the priority claim.

3 **Effect of intermediate document on claims not entitled to priority**
A document published during the priority interval, the technical contents of which corresponds to that of the priority application, constitutes prior art against an application claiming priority from that application, to the extent such priority is not validly claimed, e.g. because the claim under consideration is a generalisation of the disclosure in the priority application (G3/93). Note that this holding applies for any document published in the priority interval if the priority is invalid.

Suppose an applicant files an application P1 disclosing features A+B. One month later, a document D is published disclosing features A+B. A month after this publication, the same applicant files an application P2 disclosing features A+B+C. Finally, on the anniversary of the filing of P1, the same applicant files a European patent application with claim 1 containing the features A+B and a claim 2 containing the features A+B+C and priority is claimed from P1 and P2. Claim 1 is entitled to the priority of the first application P1 and claim 2 is entitled to the priority of the second application P2. Since claim 2 is not entitled to the priority of application P1 (**Art.87(1)**), document D is prior art under **Art.54(2)** for claim 2. (**G3/93**)

Art. 89 Effect of priority right

The right of priority shall have the effect that the date of priority shall count as the date of filing of the European patent application for the purposes of Article 54, paragraphs 2 and 3, and Article 60, paragraph 2.

Art.54(2) State of the art
Art.54(3) European prior rights
Art.60(2) Right to a European patent

1 **General**
Art.89 provides that, if priority is validly claimed, the date of priority replaces the date of filing when determining the date on which the state of the art is assessed under **Art.54(2)** and **Art.54(3)**, the date at which prior European rights enter the state of the art under **Art.54(3)** and the right to a European patent under **Art.60(2)**.

The nature of the articles referred to in **Art.89** makes it clear that the provision applies only to substantive patent law.

Several procedural provisions under the EPC also specifically provide that a claimed priority date will replace the filing date. However, in these provisions, the priority date replaces the filing date as long as priority has been 'claimed' and has not been lost under **Art.90(5)** or **R.53(3)**, whether it is substantively valid or not. Where several priority dates are claimed, the earliest prevails (**Art.88(2)**).

2 **Procedural provisions in which the filing date is replaced by the priority date**

A claimed priority date may replace the filing date in the following provisions:

- **Art.93(1)** Publication of the European patent application
- **R.31(2)(a)** Statement of depositary institution and file number of culture
- **R.37(2)** Forwarding of applications to the EPO by national offices
- **R.60(1)** Designation of the inventor
- **R.155(3)** Transmission of a request for conversion to a national application
- **R.157(3)** Forwarding of Euro-PCT application to EPO as receiving Office
- **R.159(1)** Entry of Euro-PCT application in regional phase

Furthermore, in **R.37(1)(b)**, a period of four months from the filing of the application is replaced by a period of fourteen months from the priority date if priority has been claimed; this concerns the period allowed for a national office to forward a European patent application to the EPO.

3 **Provisions in which the filing date is NOT replaced by the priority date**

A claimed priority date may not replace the filing date in the following provisions:

- **Art.55** Non-prejudicial disclosures
- **Art.63(1)** Term of the patent
- **Art.83** Disclosure of the invention
- **Art.86(1)** Payment of renewal fees
- **Art.123(2)** Extension of subject-matter beyond application as filed
- **R.31(1)(a)** Deposit of biological material
- **R.38** Payment of filing and search fee
- **R.56(2)** Correction of parts or drawings missing from application
- **R.56a** Correction of erroneously filed application documents

However, note that in the case of **Art.83**, the priority application must also disclose the invention in a manner sufficiently clear and complete for it to be carried out by a person skilled in the art for priority to be recognised (enabling disclosure) and that in the case of **R.31(1)(a)** this may mean that a deposit of biological material must be made before the priority date.

4 **Effect of priority right on state of the art**

A valid priority claim has the effect that a document published on or after the priority date but before the filing date of the application claiming priority does not belong to the state of the art under **Art.54(2)**. Likewise, a European application filed on or after the priority date but before the filing date of the application claiming priority and published on or after the filing date does not belong to the state of the art under **Art.54(3)**. A European application filed before the priority date and published between the priority date and the filing date is state of the art under **Art.54(3)** but not state of the art under **Art.54(2)** (J21/82 r.3).

The EPO does not usually investigate the validity of a right to priority unless it is important to do so because there is intervening prior art with an effective date between the filing and priority dates of the application or patent under examination. The validity of a claimed priority right is important if there is relevant prior art (**Art.54(2)**) published on or after the priority date and before the date of filing, or a relevant second European application (**Art.54(3)**) which has a publication date after the filing date and a filing/priority date on or after the priority date and before the date of filing.

The manner in which valid rights of priority determine how the state of the art is assessed is decisive for determining the right to a patent when several applicants independently file an application for the same invention (**Art.60(2)**).

Art.89 does not refer to **Art.55** (see **Art.55(1):1**).

PART IV PROCEDURE UP TO GRANT

1 **Examination of the patent application**

The examination of a European patent application can be divided into three stages: examination on filing, examination as to formal requirements and substantive examination.

1 The first examination after receipt of the application documents is the examination on filing according to **Art.90(1)**. The Receiving Section examines whether the application meets the requirements of **Art.80** for accordance of a date of filing. Non-compliance results in the application not being dealt with as a European patent application (**Art.90(2)**).

2 The second stage is the examination as to formal requirements according to **Art.90(3)** by the Receiving Section and by the examining division once the application has been transferred to the latter (A-I,2). The procedure and the objects of the second stage are clearly separated from the first stage to avoid that the results of the examination in the second stage influence the conclusion of the examination on filing (**J22/03** r.3.2).

The second stage starts only after the application has been accorded a date of filing (**Art.90(3)**). The Receiving Section checks amongst others the representation of the applicant, the correctness of the Request for Grant form and, where appropriate, the priority claim, the presence of the abstract, designation of inventor and drawings, and the layout of the application documents. Non-compliance with the requirements most often results in the application being refused. The Receiving Section also examines whether the filing and search fee have been paid in time and any translation required under **Art.14(2)** has been filed. Non-compliance results with these requirements results in the application being deemed withdrawn. An application which passes the examination as to formal requirements is ready for publication under **Art.93**.

The search is carried out in parallel with the formalities examination (B-IV,1.2). The search division will draw up the search report (**Art.92(1)**) accompanied by the search opinion on patentability (**R.62(1)**).

3 In the substantive examination under **Art.94** an examining division assesses whether the application and the invention to which it relates meet the requirements of the EPC, in particular whether the invention is patentable in the sense of **Art.52(1)**, i.e. whether the invention is new, involves an inventive step and is susceptible of industrial application. If the applicant does not reply in time to an invitation from the examining division to file observations, the application will be deemed to be withdrawn. The EPO may take decisions on specific issues prior to the decision terminating the grant procedure. If the application or invention does not meet the requirements of the EPC, the application will be refused. Otherwise a patent will be granted.

2 **Possible negative outcomes of the examination**
If deficiencies in the application are noted and are not corrected during the examination proceedings, the application is not dealt with as a European patent application, is refused or is deemed to be withdrawn. A refusal is an appealable decision of the EPO based on the documents on file. A withdrawal is a decision of the applicant, actively withdrawing the application. A finding that the application is 'deemed to be withdrawn' is an observation made by the EPO after the failure of an applicant to respond in due time. The legal consequences can normally be remedied using further processing or re-establishment. The observation that the application is deemed withdrawn becomes an appealable decision only after a request for a decision by the applicant (**R.112(2)**).

Art. 90 Examination on filing and examination as to formal requirements

1 **Patent Law Treaty**
The Patent Law Treaty (PLT) entered into force on 28.04.2005 and aims to harmonise and streamline formal procedures. The implementation of the PLT in EPC2000 has modified the procedures before the EPO. Firstly, it has harmonised the various remedies that are available. Secondly, it has made the requirements for according a date of filing more lenient and has broadened considerably the possibilities for correcting deficiencies in the application after filing. The applicant has more options available at the expense of a more complex remedial system and increased legal uncertainty.

The EPO has implemented all options of the PLT because it intends to become party to the PLT. If a more restricted version had been adopted in EPC2000, a widening later on would have been more difficult. The EPO can tailor various requirements to its needs as it gains experience with the procedures. The PCT, in contrast, could only implement a subset of the PLT provisions, because the articles of the PCT have not been appropriately amended.

2 **Options on filing**
Many options on filing introduced by the implementation of the PLT are remedial in character; see in particular **R.40** on filing an application without claims, **R.52** on late filing of the declaration of priority, and **R.56** on adding missing parts to the application after its filing. Because of this remedial character, the various options open to the applicant are intended to be used sparingly to correct deficiencies and cope with special circumstances.

The option of filing by reference (**R.40(1)(c)**) may be useful if there is not sufficient time to prepare a complete application or for filing a divisional application, having the same description and drawings as the parent application.

Late filing of missing parts of the description or drawings under **R.56** should be used for remedying an incorrect transmission of the application documents or if incomplete documents are submitted.

Filing without claims as allowed by **R.40(1)** can be used, provided that the description is suitable to provide basis under **Art.123(2)** for the later filed claims, e.g. by including claim-like clauses in the description upon filing.

Art. 90(1) The European Patent Office shall examine, in accordance with the Implementing Regulations, whether the application satisfies the requirements for the accordance of a date of filing.

Implemented by:
R.55 Correction of deficiencies on filing

1 **Procedure on filing**

After filing of the application documents with the EPO, the EPO (or the national authority when filed according to **Art.75(1)(b)**) marks the documents with the date of receipt, checks the nature and number of the received documents and issues a receipt to the applicant stating the date of receipt of the documents making up the application (**R.35(2)**).

If the documents have been filed with a national authority, this authority immediately issues a receipt to the applicant (**R.35(2)**) and informs the EPO of the receipt of the documents (**R.35(3)**, see also A-II,3.2). Applications not liable to secrecy must be forwarded to the EPO within six weeks after filing (**R.37(1)(a)**), extendable to four months after filing or, where priority has been claimed, to fourteen months after the date of priority, where further examination as to liability to secrecy is necessary (**R.37(1)(b)**). Applications received by the EPO later than fourteen months from filing or, where priority has been claimed, from the date of priority are regarded as withdrawn (**R.37(2)**). When the EPO has received the application, it informs the applicant accordingly (**R.35(4)**).

The Receiving Section is competent to examine the application documents and determine whether they satisfy the requirements for the accordance of a date of filing as set out in **Art.80** and **R.40** according to **Art.90(1)** (**Art.16**; see also A-II,4.1). A national authority with which an application is filed is not competent to carry out this examination. Hence, a possible re-dating of a deficient application under **R.55** will be substantially later when the application is filed with a national authority than when it is filed directly with the EPO.

2 **Examination on filing, correction and sanction**

The examination on filing distinguishes between five different types of requirements: those mentioned in **R.55**, the identification of the applicant (**R.40(1)(b)**), the filing of a certified copy of a previous application (**R.40(3)**, first sentence), the filing of a translation of a previous application (**R.40(3)**, second sentence), and dealing with missing parts (**R.56**), each having its own correction procedure and sanction on non-compliance, as set out in the notes to **R.40**.

The invitation under **Art.90(4)** and **R.55** to correct the application documents should always precede a communication under **R.112(1)** that the application is deemed withdrawn because of non-payment of the filing and search fees (**J18/96** r.3.2-3). If the filing date accorded following an invitation under **R.55** is the date on which a correction is filed, all periods running from the date of filing run from this date of requesting correction. The application will not be dealt with as a European patent application if the deficiencies are not duly remedied (**R.55**).

Certain errors in the application documents, for instance, an erroneous identification of the applicant, may be corrected under **R.139** (**J7/90** hn.I). Such a correction has a retroactive effect and, hence, does not result in redating of the application (**J4/85**).

3 **According of date of filing**
The date of filing accorded will be the date of receipt of the application documents if they meet the requirements of **R.40** or else the date on which deficiencies are rectified (A-II,4.1.5). As an exception, where the application is filed by reference to a previously filed application and the applicant files the certified copy only within two months of invitation under **R.55**, the application maintains its original date of filing (A-II,4.1.5). The application may be re-dated if the applicant inserts parts of the description or drawings after the date of filing (see **R.56**) or submits correct parts (**R.56a**).

If the application documents meet the requirements of **R.40** on the date of receipt of the application documents and the date of filing accorded is the date of receipt, the EPO does *not* specifically inform the applicant of the date of filing. However, if the application is redated, the applicant is informed of the new date of filing (**R.55**, last sentence; **R.56(2)**, last sentence; **R.56a(3)** and **R.56a(6)**).

The EPO does not take a decision when a date of filing is accorded. The question of compliance with the requirements of **R.40** may be raised at any time during the grant proceedings. Correspondingly, the EPC does indicate when the EPO must send a **R.55** communication informing the applicant of a new date of filing after the correction of the application documents. The communication may be issued even after the formalities examination of **Art.90(3)**, despite the order of the two stages of examination set in **Art.90(3)**. The EPO is not negligent when the communication is issued half a year after the filing of the application. Hence, an applicant may not rely on having received a date of filing when this communication has not been received. (J22/03 r.2, 3)

See **Art.169:1.2** for the date of filing of an application filed just before the coming into force of the EPC in a state.

Art. 90(2) If a date of filing cannot be accorded following the examination under paragraph 1, the application shall not be dealt with as a European patent application.

1 **No date of filing accorded**
If the applicant does not provide an indication that a European patent is sought, or a description or reference to a previously filed application, the requirements of **R.40(1)(a)**, respectively **(c)**, are not met. The procedure of **R.55** is followed, and the application may be accorded a filing date later than the date on which the first documents were received (see **R.55:1**) (A-II,4.1.4).

If no information is provided identifying the applicant or allowing the applicant to be contacted (see A-II,4.1.2), the requirement of **R.40(1)(b)** is not fulfilled. Since **R.55** does not refer to **R.40(1)(b)**, no invitation for correction will be sent; the EPO cannot send a communication informing the applicant of the deficiency because no contact information has been provided. If the applicant corrects the deficiency within two months from the date of receipt of the original application documents at the EPO, then the date of filing is the date on which all the requirements of **R.40** are met. If the deficiency is not remedied within two months from the date of receipt of the original application documents, no date of filing will be accorded and the application will not be dealt with as a European patent application (**Art.90(2)**). (A-II,4.1.4)

If no date of filing is accorded, the application does not give rise to a right of priority (**Art.87(3)**, Art.4A(3) Paris Convention) and cannot serve as a basis for filing a divisional application (**R.36**) or for conversion into a national application (**Art.135**). The application does not constitute a first filing rendering the priority of a later application invalid under **Art.87(4)** either. All fees paid in connection with the filing are refunded. The applicant can request a decision under **R.112(2)** which can be appealed. (A-II,4.1.4)

Art. 90(3) If the European patent application has been accorded a date of filing, the European Patent Office shall examine, in accordance with the Implementing Regulations, whether the requirements in Articles 14, 78 and 81, and, where applicable, Article 88, paragraph 1, and Article 133, paragraph 2, as well as any other requirement laid down in the Implementing Regulations, have been satisfied.

Art.14 Languages
Art.78 Requirements of an application
Art.81 Designation of the inventor
Art.88(1) Declaration of priority
Art.133(2) Compulsory representation
Implemented by:
R.57 Examination as to formal requirements

1 **Examination as to formal requirements**

The purpose of the examination of **Art.90(3)** is to make the application ready for publication under **Art.93**. The examination is carried out by the Receiving Section (**Art.16**) after the application has been accorded a date of filing (**Art.90(3)**).

The issues to be examined, the action taken if deficiencies are noted, sanctions and remedies are set out in the notes to **R.57**.

Art. 90(4) Where the European Patent Office in carrying out the examination under paragraphs 1 or 3 notes that there are deficiencies which may be corrected, it shall give the applicant an opportunity to correct them.

Implemented by:
R.55 Correction of deficiencies on filing
R.56 Missing parts of description or missing drawings
R.58 Correction of deficiencies in the application documents
R.59 Deficiencies in claiming priority
R.60 Subsequent designation of the inventor

1 **Correction of deficiencies on filing and formal deficiencies**

The provision gives an applicant an opportunity to correct any deficiencies in the application. There are two different procedures for correcting deficiencies: a first procedure for deficiencies noted during the examination on filing under **Art.90(1)** and a second procedure for deficiencies noted during the formalities examination under **Art.90(3)**.

Details of the examination on filing are dealt with in **Art.90(1):1** and **R.40**. The procedure for correction of deficiencies under **Art.90(4)** is set out in **Art.90(1):1**, **R.55** and **R.56**. The sanction on not correcting the deficiencies in due time is provided in **Art.90(2)**.

The examination as to formalities is provided in **Art.90(3)** and **R.57**. Deficiencies noted during this examination can be corrected according to the procedure of **Art.90(4)** in conjunction with **R.58** to **60**. The examination, invitation and sanction for each formal requirement are set out in the notes to **R.57**. **Art.90(5)** is the general provision for the sanction on not correcting formal deficiencies.

Art. 90(5) If any deficiency noted in the examination under paragraph 3 is not corrected, the European patent application shall be refused unless a different legal consequence is provided for by this Convention. Where the deficiency concerns the right of priority, this right shall be lost for the application.

1 **Effect of non-corrected deficiencies**

The legal effect of any deficiencies established by the EPO and not corrected by the applicant is provided by **Art.90(5)**. All deficiencies concern obligations that must, in principle, be fulfilled on filing. (OJ 2007 se4 EN p.92)

The default sanction of **Art.90(5)** on not correcting formal deficiencies noted in the examination as to formalities under **Art.90(3)** is the refusal of the application. The EPC may provide different legal consequences, such as the application being deemed withdrawn when the requirements of **R.57(a)** or **(e)** are not complied with. The notes to **R.57** for the different formal requirements indicate the appropriate sanctions.

After a deemed withdrawal, it is sometimes permitted to convert the European application to a national application under **Art.135**. See NatLaw table VII. Another remedy is to file a new European application and, if possible, claim the priority of an earlier application or of the deemed withdrawn or refused application, which must have received a date of filing to give rise to a right of priority.

A refusal decision under **Art.90(5)** can be appealed and the deficiency can be corrected at the appeal stage (**J18/08**; **J11/20** hn.2). Interlocutory revision under **Art.109** is granted if the deficiency is corrected with the statement of grounds and the grounds for refusal are overcome (E-XII,7.4.4).

2 **Date on which sanction takes effect**

As a rule, a sanction for not complying with a requirement takes effect upon expiry of the normal period set for complying with the requirement and not upon expiry of any subsequent remedial period, such as the two-month period of **R.135(1)** for requesting further processing. For example, failure to pay the filing or search fee results in the application being deemed withdrawn on the expiry of the one-month period of **R.38** (A-III,16.2). Any act performed after the loss of the application is without legal consequence. Hence, a divisional application should be filed before the sanction takes effect.

Non-observance of the two-month period of **R.58** for correction of deficiencies in the application may lead to the application being refused under **Art.90(5)** or being deemed withdrawn. The deemed withdrawal takes effect at the expiry of the two-month period (**G4/98** r.7); the refusal becomes final two months after notification of the decision to refuse (**G1/09** r.4.2).

Art. 91 (deleted)

Art. 92 Drawing up of the European search report

The European Patent Office shall, in accordance with the Implementing Regulations, draw up and publish a European search report in respect of the European patent application on the basis of the claims, with due regard to the description and any drawings.

Implemented by:
R.61 Content of the European search report
R.62 Extended European search report
R.62a Plurality of independent claims
R.63 Incomplete search
R.64 Search report where the invention lacks unity
R.65 Transmittal of the search report to the applicant
R.66 Definitive content of the abstract
R.68 Form of the publication of the search report
R.69 Information about publication of the search report

1 **General**

The provision obliges the EPO to draw up a search report in respect of a European patent application. The search is an important element of the grant procedure, determining the state of the art for the application. The assessment of the patentability of the invention by the EPO is based on the documents mentioned in the search report (see **R.61(1)**).

The reference in **Art.92** to 'the European patent application' implies that a search is only performed on an application which has a filing date (otherwise it is not a European patent application, see **Art.90(2)**) and is pending when the search is performed (OJ 2007 se4 EN p.98).

2 **Start of the search**

Generally, the search is carried out after the formalities examination under **Art.90(3)** (B-IV,1.2). Since the EPO usually only renders a service after payment of the corresponding fee, the search will only start after payment of the filing fee and search fee. Where the application is not filed in an official EPO language, the search will not start before receipt of a translation into one of those languages (see **R.6(1)**). The date on which the search starts is recorded in the file (B-IV,1). This date is important since the search fee will be refunded if the application is (deemed) withdrawn or refused before the search starts (**Rfees9(1)**).

The search can only start if the application documents on filing are complete enough for the search to be performed (E-VIII,4.1). Since the search must be based on the claims according to **Art.92**, the search can only start after the claims and any translation have been filed (see **R.57:2** and **4**). It should be noted that in certain cases the translation may be filed as late as about one month before publication of the application, making it difficult to publish the search report together with the application.

If the search division has despatched a communication under **R.62a** (multiple independent claims) or **R.63** (unsearchable subject-matter) the search can only proceed after receipt of the applicant's response or expiry of the period for response. (E-VIII,4.1; OJ 2015 A93)

3 **Drawing up of the European search report and the opinion**

The search report for a European patent application will be drawn up by a search division (**Art.17**). A search division consists normally of one search examiner; for inventions covering several fields a division may consist of two or three search examiners. However, all 'search actions' are endorsed by the two other members of the examining division. (B-I,2)

At the same time as the search division draws up the search report, it also determines the definitive content of the abstract according to **R.66** and F-II,2.2.

Telephone conversations and informal interviews are normally only possible during substantive examination (B-II,1.1, also giving exceptions for the search).

The search examiner will also be the first member of the examining division in the substantive examination of the patent application (see **Art.15:1**). For increased efficiency the examiner prepares, already at the search stage, an opinion as to whether the application and the invention to which it relates seem to meet the requirements of the EPC, also called the opinion on patentability. The search report and the opinion are issued together to the applicant in the form of an extended European search report. The content of the search report is specified in **R.61**. Details of the opinion are given in **R.62**.

4 **Basis and extent of search**

The search will be based on the claims with due regard to the description and any drawings (**Art.92**). Hence, the search is not restricted by the literal wording of the claims (B-III,3.2). The search is based on the application as filed, including any missing parts filed under **R.56(3)**. In case of erroneously filed documents, if both the erroneously filed documents and the correct documents are part of the application as filed (**R.56a**(4)), the search is unaffected. The search examiner also checks the 'completely contained' criterion and in case the conclusion of the Receiving Section is believed to be incorrect, the search is widened to documents relevant in case the application is later redated. The same procedure applies to missing parts or elements filed under R.20.6 PCT for Euro-PCT applications. (B-III,3.3.1)

The search division has the discretionary power to make a complete search of the invention, even if essential features are not defined in the claims but only in the description or drawings (**T708/00** r.4). The search examiner must also anticipate amendments and should cover subject-matter to which claims might reasonably be amended during prosecution (B-III,3.5, **R.137(5)**). However, a single broad claim in the application as filed without dependent claims does not entitle the applicant to a search extending to all the features of a large number of disclosed embodiments covered by the claim (**T1679/10** r.4.2; B-III,3.5).

If the application contains a plurality of independent claims not complying with **R.43(2)**, the search division will ask the applicant to indicate the independent claims to be searched (**R.62a**).

If the search division considers that a complete search is not possible because the application does not sufficiently comply with the EPC or relates to subject-matter excluded from patentability, it will ask the applicant to indicate the subject-matter to be searched; in such a case the search division may carry out a partial search or no search at all (see **R.63**).

If the search division considers that an application lacks unity, it invites the applicant to pay further search fees to search the further inventions and informs the applicant that only the part of the application that relates to the inventions for which search fees have been paid will be searched (see **R.64(1):2**). Any unsearched non-unitary subject-matter may not be used for amendment of claims during prosecution of the application if the restriction of the search is justified (**G2/92**; see also **R.64(1):3**; H-II,6.2).

Claims above the number of fifteen for which no claims fees have been paid will not be searched (**R.45(3)** and B-III,3.4).

The extent of the search in terms of publication dates is given in **R.61(3):1**. In general, the examiner accepts the validity of any priority claimed by the application being searched. However, if the examiner finds prior art under **Art.54(2)** published on or after the priority date and before the date of filing or a prior right under **Art.54(3)** filed on or after the priority date and before the filing date, the examiner will allocate effective dates to the claims of the application being searched, depending on the presumed validity of the priority claim. If the prior right also claims priority, effective dates will also be allocated to the parts of the prior right. (F-VI,2.1)

Since the applicant is not allowed under **R.137(1)** to amend the claims before receiving the search report, the search is based on the claims as filed on the date of filing or filed later of the applicant's own volition or as correction under **R.57(c)** and **R.58** (B-III,3.3). See **R.63(1)** for an exception.

5 Transmittal and publication of the search report

The search report provides a basis on which the applicant can decide whether to continue prosecution of the application. Hence, the period for requesting examination expires six months after the mention of the publication of the search report (**R.70(1)**). When the search report has been drawn up, it will be transmitted to the applicant under **R.65**. Voluntary amendments can be submitted together with the first substantive response to the search report (**R.137(2)**).

The search report is also important for third parties, in particular for competitors, as it gives an indication of the scope of protection that a patent granted for the application may have. The law has always provided for publication of the search report in **Art.92** because the accessibility of the published document provided legal certainty for third parties before online inspection became available, informing them about the search results and the start of the period for requesting examination.

The EPO informs the applicant of the date on which the Bulletin will mention the publication of the search report (**R.69(1)**). This communication is despatched immediately after the publication of the search report.

The EPO publishes the search report together with the application if the former is available before termination of the technical preparations for publication (A-VI,1.3). If not available, the search report is published separately (**R.68(1)**; A-VI,1.5). The form of the publication is governed by **R.68**. The search opinion (**R.62(2)**) and the search strategy (OJ 2017 A106 §4(d)) are not published but are available via file inspection under **Art.128** (A-VI,1.3).

6 Top-up search

When the examiner carries out the search, the search documentation will usually not be complete. Prior art under **Art.54(3)**, so-called European prior rights, are available to the examiner and can be searched. However, they may only be cited after they have been published because of **Art.128(1)**. A European patent application only becomes prior art under **Art.54(3)** when it is published eighteen months after its priority or filing date. Only when examiners have ascertained that another European patent application has been published, will they cite it as prior art under **Art.54(3)**. The latest citable European prior right is an application filed the day before the filing date of the application being examined and published eighteen months later. (C-IV,7.1)

A PCT application may also constitute prior art under **Art.54(3)** (**Art.153(5)** and **R.165**). If the EPO does not handle the PCT application in the international phase, the application will become available to the examiner only after publication (the EPO has not made use of Art.13(1) PCT). Hence, examiners can only search for such prior rights after eighteen months from the filing or priority date. If they consider the application being examined to be novel in view of such a prior right, they can continue the examination and even issue a **R.71(3)** communication, without waiting for any translation or an effective entry of the prior international application into the European phase. (**T1849/12** r.3.3) See C-IV,7.1 for details how PCT applications are handled during the top-up search.

Hence, the examiner usually carries out a top-up search at the earliest eighteen months after the priority or filing date of the application being examined. The top-up search is usually the first step of the substantive examination (**Art.94(3):3**). If the priority claim of the application being examined is valid for the whole content of the application, the top-up search may be carried out at the earliest eighteen months from the priority date. (C-IV,7.1 and **T1849/12** r.3.2)

The top-up search also takes into consideration potentially relevant prior art cited by other patent offices in respect of applications in the same family and therefore needs to be performed at the start and end of examination (C-IV,7.1).

The results of the top-up search may be included in the search report or in the first **Art.94(3)** communication. If not yet available by that time, the examiner must ensure that the top-up search is completed before the application is reported to be in order for grant. In the rare case the prosecution is accelerated and the top-up search is not yet completed before the application is considered ready for grant, the communication of the intention to grant under **R.71(3)** is postponed until the top-up search can be completed. (C-IV,7.1)

A top-up search is performed for any file at the start and end of examination (C-IV,7.1).

The top-up search at the beginning of examination is also the beginning of the substantive examination in the sense of **Rfees11** concerning the (partial) refund of the examination fee.

The EPO also carries out a top-up search to find any relevant national prior rights under **Art.139(2)** at the end of the grant proceedings and informs the applicant of the outcome in the **R.71(3)** communication (C-IV,7.2).

7 **Completion of the search**

The EPO always performs an accelerated search for directly filed European patent applications; no PACE request is needed. The EPO strives to issue the search report within six months from the date of filing the application, provided that the application documents are complete (E-VIII,4).

For supplementary European searches for PCT applications entering the European phase, the EPO strives to issue the search report within six months from the expiry of the **R.161(2)** period even if acceleration has been requested under PACE. In order for the supplementary European search to start sooner, the applicant can expressly waive the period or any remaining part of the period and pay any claims fees due (E-VIII,4, OJ 2015 A93).

If the search report has not been issued within six months from the date of filing and the applicant files an enquiry about the status of the file using Form 1012 (see **Art.94(1):6**), the EPO will issue the search report within one month from receipt of the enquiry. (E-VIII,7)

8 **Legal effect of publication of the search report**
The mention of the publication of the search report in the Bulletin has the following legal implications for direct European applications:
- **R.39(1)**: The mention triggers the six-month period for payment of the designation fee. Extension and validation fees must be paid within the same period.
- **R.70(1)**: The mention triggers the six-month period for filing the request for examination, paying the examination fee and, where appropriate, filing comments on the search opinion attached to the search report under **R.70a**. If the request for examination was filed before the EPO transmitted the search report to the applicant, the applicant is invited to confirm the request for examination (**R.70(2)**). After the filing of the request for examination or receipt of the confirmation thereof, the examining division can start the examination of the application (**Art.18(1)** and **R.10**).

For Euro-PCT applications, see **R.159**.

Art. 93 Publication of the European patent application

1 **General**
In return for patent protection, the invention is made public to foster innovation. Publication of patent applications allows before grant allows for provisional protection (**Art.67**) and allows third parties to consider pending applications in freedom-to-operate analyses. Third parties may also benefit from technologies disclosed in applications that are published but do not proceed to grant. The EPO normally issues search reports within five months of filing a European application (European Patent Guide 5.2.009) such that the applicant can decide whether to let the application become public based on a thorough assessment of the prior art.

Art.93 is the basis for the publication of the application. The publication of the search report is governed by **Art.92**. The application and the search report are preferably published together. If the search division cannot complete the search report in time for it to be published together with the application, the application is published in a timely manner in the interests of the public and the search report is published later (**R.68(1)**).

Art. 93(1) The European Patent Office shall publish the European patent application as soon as possible
(a) after the expiry of a period of eighteen months from the date of filing or, if priority has been claimed, from the date of priority, or
(b) at the request of the applicant, before the expiry of that period.

Implemented by:
R.67 Technical preparations for publication
R.68 Form of the publication of the patent application

1 **Form and date of publication**

The publication of a patent application contains a front page, the description, claims and any drawings as filed, the abstract, and the search report if available (**R.68(1)**). The form of the publication is determined by **R.68(1)**. The application is published in the language of the proceedings (**Art.14(5)**). The front page mentions bibliographic data, the designated states (**R.68(3)**) and the abstract.

Timely filed new or amended claims will be included in the publication in addition to the claims as filed (**R.68(4)**), which can be important for the scope of the provisional protection (**Art.69(2)**). Even if claims are deemed abandoned because of non-payment of the claims fees under **R.45(3)**, the complete first set of claims as filed by the applicant will be included in the publication. The publication will indicate if the claims were filed after the date of filing (**R.68(4)**). Since the publication must include the claims (**R.68(1)**), the publication will be postponed if the first set of claims is filed after the date of filing and is not yet available (see also **Art.69(2)**, first sentence).

Any timely requested and allowed correction under **R.139** is incorporated in the publication. If a decision is pending on such a correction, a warning is printed on the first page if the correction could be detrimental to the rights of third parties, e.g. in the case of a correction of a priority claim. (A-VI,1.3)

The EPO informs the applicant of the completion of the technical preparations for publication under **R.67(1)**) and of the publication number and the date on which it intends to publish the patent application (A-VI,1.1). This communication is despatched about four weeks before the intended date of publication, i.e. after the completion of the technical preparations.

The publication date is a Wednesday (OJ 1997 p.542), usually the first Wednesday after the expiry of the eighteen-month period of **Art.93(1)(a)**, irrespective of whether this day is a public holiday or not. At the publication date, an entry is made in the Register (**R.143(1)(a)-(i)** and (**2**)) in the three EPO languages (**Art.14(8)**). The European Patent Bulletin also mentions the date of publication of the search report and, if published earlier, also the date of publication of the application, together with bibliographic data (**Art.129(a)**).

2 **Early publication on request**

The application can be published before the expiry of the eighteen months at the request of the applicant, provided that the filing fee and search fee have been paid (A-VI,1.1). The applicant may desire an early publication to obtain rights under **Art.67** with respect to third parties or to prevent a third party from coming too close to the subject-matter of the applicant's application with the third party's own later filed application: the third party's application only needs to be novel over a not-yet-published application, but needs to have an inventive step over a published application.

3 **Deferred publication**

If a priority claim is withdrawn, the publication is deferred until eighteen months after the date of the earliest existing priority claim or the date of filing, as the case may be, provided the notification of the withdrawal reaches the EPO before termination of the technical preparations for publication (**R.67(2)**). If received later, the publication will not be deferred, and the withdrawal of the priority claim will be published in the Bulletin. The same procedure applies if the priority right is lost under **Art.90(5)**. (A-VI,1.1)

4 **Invalid publication**

The application will not be published if it has been finally refused or withdrawn or is deemed to be withdrawn before the termination of the technical preparations for publication (**R.67(2)**). The application is, however, published if, upon said termination, a request for a decision under **R.112(2)** has been received but no decision has yet been taken or if there is a pending request for re-establishment (A-VI,1.2). If after said termination of the technical preparations the application is withdrawn to avoid publication, non-publication cannot be guaranteed and the application may still be published (see **R.67(2):1**). Such a publication of the application is not according to **Art.93** and is sometimes referred to as an invalid publication. If applicants want to have the option of continuing with prosecution if the application is still published after a late withdrawal of the application, they should make the withdrawal conditional on prevention of the publication (see **R.67(2):3**).

An invalid publication has the following legal implications:

- **Art.54(2)**: the content of the publication may be used as prior art;
- **Art.54(3)**: since the publication is not valid, the application does not have the effect of a European prior right;
- **Art.67(4)**: the application is deemed never to have conferred provisional protection under **Art.67(1)**;
- **Art.128(4)**: the publication does not give rise to the possibility of inspecting the files (OJ 1993 p.56);
- **Art.139(1)**: the publication does not give rise to a national prior right effect (J5/81 r.3).

5 **Legal effect of publication of the patent application**

The publication of the application triggers certain legal changes and provides the opportunity to undertake certain actions:

- **Art.54(2)**: the published application forms part of the state of the art;
- **Art.54(3)**: the prior right effect comes into force;
- **Art.67**: applicants can exercise their rights of the provisional protection;
- **Art.115**: third parties may file observations to be considered during examination;
- **Art.127**: data of the application is entered in the Register;
- **Art.128(4)**: the file of the application becomes open for public inspection.

See **Art.92:8** for the legal effect of the publication of the search report.

Art. 93(2) The European patent application shall be published at the same time as the specification of the European patent when the decision to grant the patent becomes effective before the expiry of the period referred to in paragraph 1(a).

1 **Early publication after early grant**

The application will be published before expiry of the eighteen months from the filing or priority date in the exceptional case that the patent is granted earlier. The application and the patent will then be published simultaneously (**Art.93(2)**; A-VI,1.1). However, it is not possible for the EPO to fully determine the state of the art under **Art.54(3)** when a patent is granted so early.

The examiner carries out a top-up search for European prior rights after eighteen months has elapsed from the filing or priority date (see **Art.92:6**). PCT applications should also be considered as potential prior rights; only if they enter the European phase, usually 31 months after the filing or priority date, will they become European prior rights. If the EPO does not act as an international authority for a PCT application, the application is not available to the EPO until its publication. In practice, it is therefore understood that European patents are not granted before expiry of the eighteen-month period of **Art.93(1)(a)** so that the complete state of the art can be taken into consideration.

Art. 94 Examination of the European patent application

1 **General**
Art.94 deals with the initiation of the examination (paragraphs (1) and (2)) as well as the conduct of the examination procedure (paragraphs (3) and (4)).

Art. 94(1) The European Patent Office shall, in accordance with the Implementing Regulations, examine on request whether the European patent application and the invention to which it relates meet the requirements of this Convention. The request shall not be deemed to be filed until the examination fee has been paid.

Implemented by:
R.7a(1) Reduction of examination fee on account of language
R.70 Request for examination
R.70a Response to extended search report
R.142(4) Interruption of period because of interruption of proceedings
R.159(1) Period for requesting examination for Euro-PCT application
Rfees2(1)6 Amount of the examination fee
Rfees14(1) Amount of reduction of examination fee

1 **Examination on request**
The substantive examination of the application is the second stage of the grant procedure, which follows the formalities examination of **Art.90(3)**. The substantive examination will only be carried out if the applicant has filed a request for examination under **R.70**. The requirement for examination to be requested allows the applicant to stop the grant procedure after the first stage, possibly because prejudicial prior art has been identified in the search, thereby relieving the applicant of the need to pay an examination fee.

Since **Art.94(1)** does not refer to a written request, the Implementing Regulations may provide in the future for filing the request by means other than in writing (OJ 2007 se4 EN p.100). They may permit a deferred examination, e.g. to cope with an excessive workload or to provide flexibility for applicants. Since **Art.94(1)** does not state who may file the request, a system of deferred examination may be combined with the option of allowing a third party to request the examination (OJ 2007 se4 EN p.102).

The examining division which will carry out the examination takes over competence from the Receiving Section on receipt of the request for examination, when the request is filed after transmission of the search report (**R.10(2)**), or on receipt of the confirmation of the request for examination upon invitation under **R.70(2)** when the request has been filed before transmission of the search report (**R.10(3)**). When the request for examination has been filed before transmission of the search report and the applicant has waived the invitation under **R.70(2)**, the examining division becomes competent on the day the search report is transmitted to the applicant (**R.10(4)**).

2 **Filing the request for examination**

The filing of a request for examination entails the performance of two acts according to **Art.94(1)**. The first act is the filing of the written request for examination ('request' in **Art.94(1)**); the second act is the payment of the examination fee (**Art.94(1)**, last sentence). The request is valid only if both the filing of the written request and the payment of the fee have been carried out in due time (**Art.94(1)**, last sentence).

A written request for examination is included in the Request for Grant form with the relevant box already ticked. The Request for Grant form is mandatory when filing a European patent application (**R.41(1)**) but an omission can be corrected under **R.58**. The written request for examination is thus always filed together with the Request for Grant form. Hence, no separate filing of the written request is necessary. An applicant who must be represented under **Art.133(2)** may file the Request for Grant directly, without a representative (**Art.133(2)**) and, hence, also the written request for examination.

The examination fee is due when the request for examination is filed (see **Rfees4(1):1**). Since the request is included in the Request for Grant form, the examination fee can be paid as from the date of filing the Request for Grant form.

The examination fee must be paid within the period of **R.70(1)**, i.e. within six months from the publication of the search report. Since the written request has been filed together with the application, the payment of the examination fee is the only act still to be performed within the period of **R.70(1)**. The applicant can base the decision to pay the examination fee on the results of the search and the accompanying opinion. If the results do not justify continuing with prosecuting the application, the applicant can terminate the procedure by not paying the examination fee (**Art.94(2)**).

Anybody may pay the examination fee (see **Rfees6(1):1**). See the notes to **Art.94(2)** and to **R.70** for details of filing the request for examination, the consequence of failure to file it in due time and remedies.

Where the search opinion states that there are deficiencies in the application, which is usually the case, the applicant must not only pay the examination fee but also file a response to these objections before the expiry of the period of **R.70(1)** (**R.70a**). Moreover, the period for filing the designation fee (**R.39**) expires on the same day as the period for paying the examination fee.

3 **Examination fee, reduction and refund**

The amount of the examination fee is laid down in **Rfees2(1)6**.

The examination fee is reduced by 30% if an entitled applicant files the request for examination in an admissible non-EPO language (see **R.7a(1):3** for entitlement) (**G6/91** r.21). Only the request for examination must be filed in an admissible non-EPO language for to the reduction of the examination fee. Whether or not the description and the claims of the application or responses to communications from the EPO are in an admissible non-EPO language is irrelevant. See **R.7a(1):3** for the filing of the request. The examination fee is also reduced for certain applicants, see **R.7a(3)**. See **Rfees14(2)** for a reduction of the examination fee for a Euro-PCT application.

The examination fee will be refunded in part or in total if the EPO does not carry out a substantive examination. The amount of the refund depends on the time the procedure terminates, either due to refusal by the EPO, the application becoming deemed to be withdrawn or withdrawal of the application by the applicant. See **Rfees11** for details of the conditions applying to such a refund.

4 Acceleration of examination

The examination of a direct European application can be accelerated in several ways, such as omitting procedural steps and reducing the response time of the EPO. See Not. EPO OJ 2015 A94 for a summary.

If the examination fee is paid on filing of the application and the invitation under **R.70(2)** is waived, examination is requested unconditionally, irrespective of the results of the search (see **R.70(2):3**). A communication under **Art.94(3)** will be sent to the applicant instead of the search opinion under **R.62(1)**, together with or shortly after the search report.

The examination can be further accelerated by filing a PACE request (see **Art.94(1):4.1**). After receipt of the request, the examining division will strive to issue a communication within three months from receipt of a response from the applicant. The applicant must respond to the communication within the period set and should deal with all the points raised in the communication and cooperate with the EPO. The EPO aims to respond within three months. (E-VIII,4.2)

The applicant can request the EPO to use the Patent Prosecution Highway, which expedites the grant procedure by allowing the EPO to use the work already conducted by another patent office (see **Art.94(1):4.2**).

The grant can also be accelerated as set out in **Art.97(1):2**.

See **R.159:4** for accelerating the processing of a Euro-PCT application.

Following substantiated, non-anonymous third-party observations, the EPO will aim to issue the next communication within three months of the receipt of the observations (OJ 2017 A86 §5.1; E-VI,3). See **R.114(2):1**.

4.1 PACE REQUEST

The programme for accelerated prosecution of European patent applications (PACE) enables a faster processing of applications during examination (Not. EPO OJ 2015 A93).

An applicant can apply for accelerated examination by filing a PACE request. The EPO may restrict the number of requests allowed depending on the technical field and the applicant. The PACE request for acceleration must be filed online using Form 1005. The EPO will acknowledge receipt promptly. A request not filed online or not using Form 1005 will not be processed. The request must be filed for one application at a time. It will not be published and will be excluded from file inspection. (OJ 2015 A93 §1-3, 6)

It should be noted that the request is a 'document' in the sense of **R.2** the filing of which is governed by the Decisions of the President taken under **R.2**. A Notice of the EPO making it mandatory to file a PACE request online appears to violate **R.2**.

PACE may be requested to accelerate a search. However, the search procedure is always accelerated, and so there is no benefit to be gained by filing such a request (see **Art.92:7**).

Accelerated examination can only be requested after the examining division has become responsible for the application according to **R.10** (see **R.70(1):1**; **R.70(2):1** and C-II,1). Hence, a PACE request filed during the search will not accelerate examination. The EPO enters the date on which responsibility for an application passes to the examining division in the Register. (OJ 2015 A93 §12)

When accelerated examination has been requested, the examining division strives to issue a communication within three months from receipt of the PACE request or the applicant's response to a previous communication, whichever is the latest (OJ 2015 A93 §14, 15). The applicant can enquire with the EPO customer services as to the status of an application for which a PACE request has been filed (OJ 2015 A93 §7). However, only a status enquiry filed online using Form 1012 will result in the next communication being issued within one month if the EPO has not met the three-month commitment (E-VIII,7).

The examination will no longer be accelerated if the applicant withdraws the PACE request or requests an extension of a period, or if the application has been refused, withdrawn, or deemed withdrawn. Since a PACE request may be filed only once during each stage of the procedure, the removal of an application from the PACE programme cannot be undone by refiling the PACE request. Hence, an allowed request for further processing will continue the proceedings but without accelerated examination. (OJ 2015 A93 §2, 4)

Accelerated examination will be suspended if a renewal fee is not paid by the due date (OJ 2015 A93 §5). After payment, accelerated prosecution will resume.

4.2 PATENT PROSECUTION HIGHWAY

The Patent Prosecution Highway (PPH) programme permits a patent office to accelerate prosecution of a patent application by using positive results of a previous examination by another patent office. If an applicant has obtained a positive examination result for one patent office and wants to have the same or similar claims granted for another patent office, a PPH request with the latter office will accelerate the prosecution.

The EPO has PPH agreements with several patent offices. At present (April 2025), these are:

AU	OJ 2022 A58	KR	OJ 2022 A115
BH	OJ 2025 A19	MX	OJ 2020 A21
BR	OJ 2024 A99	MY	OJ 2020 A82
CA	OJ 2020 A137	NZ	OJ 2024 A98
CL	OJ 2024 A56	PE	OJ 2022 A116
CN	OJ 2022 A115	PH	OJ 2020 A83
CO	OJ 2022 A88	RU*	OJ 2020 A11
EA*	OJ 2020 A114	SA	OJ 2022 A59
IL	OJ 2020 A125	SG	OJ 2020 A138
JP	OJ 2022 A115	US	OJ 2022 A115

* = suspended as of 25.04.2022 (OJ 2022 A44 and A45).

Applicants can request PPH for a European application if they want to use the results of the examination of a corresponding application carried out by one of the participating offices to accelerate examination at the EPO. The European application and the corresponding application must have the same earliest date, whether this be the priority or filing date. The corresponding application may be a national application or a PCT application. Hence, the results of the examination may be the results of an examination by a national office or a written opinion of the ISA or an international preliminary examination report drawn up by one of the participating offices as IPEA. An exhaustive list of possible combinations of national and PCT applications and first filings and priority-claiming applications that can be used for PPH is given in OJ 2020 A21 Annex 1 and 2. See also E-VIII,4.3. See OJ 2022 A115 for the IP5 PPH program with JP, KR, CN and US.

The results of the examination by the other office must indicate that at least one claim is patentable or allowable. The claims in the EP application must sufficiently correspond to the patentable or allowable claim(s), i.e. be of the same or a similar scope or narrower and be in the same category. Substantive examination of the EP application must not yet have begun when the PPH request is filed. The examination starting date is visible for an unpublished EP application by file inspection using the MyEPO and for a published EP application in the Register.

For participation in the PPH pilot programme, the applicant must file a request using Form 1009 and file a series of documents as listed in Section II.C of the OJ notice for that office mentioned in the table above. There is no fee for requesting PPH at the EPO. In practice, a PPH request will not be published and will be excluded from file inspection. It is presumed that this exclusion is based on the application, mutatis mutandis, of the Dec. Pres. OJ 2007 se3 p.125 Art.1(1) to exclude PACE requests from file inspection.

Once the request is granted, the application will be processed in an accelerated manner. The conditions of the PACE programme (**Art.94(1):4.1**) apply by analogy to applications under PPH (OJ 2020 A21). For example, the application will be removed from PPH if the applicant requests extension of a period. As the EPO assesses patentability of the application in an independent manner, use of the results of the earlier examination does not guarantee allowance of the EP application. Applicants desiring only accelerated processing at the EPO are recommended to use PACE, which does not require an allowable corresponding application or the filing of associated documents and which can be filed after the substantive examination has started.

Similarly, the results of the examination by the EPO can be used in another office with which the EPO has a PPH agreement. It is strongly recommended to check any restrictions offices may apply during PPH prosecution, such as prohibiting the amendment of claims by including features from the description.

4.3 STATUS ENQUIRY

A party to proceedings may contact the EPO to enquire about the progress of a file. The enquiry must be filed online using Form 1012 (OJ 2016 A66; C-VII,2.1; E-VIII,7). The EPO will acknowledge receipt of the form. Enquiries and responses will be entered in the file and are open to public inspection.

The response of the EPO indicates the period within which it intends to issue the next communication. Although Form 1012 is not a PACE request, it will speed up processing in certain cases: if a communication has not been issued within the committed period, and additionally the application is processed under PACE or a previous enquiry has been filed, the next communication will be issued within one month from receipt of the enquiry. (OJ 2016 A66; E-VIII,7)

5 Deferral of examination

The EPC has a fixed period for requesting examination in **R.70(1)**. A deferred examination, of interest to applicants whose inventions take a long time to reach the market, is currently not available. At the moment, an applicant can extend the duration of patent prosecution by requesting the extension of periods set by the EPO and by using the remedy of further processing (**Art.121**) to extend each period for response by approximately three months.

Art. 94(2) If no request for examination has been made in due time, the application shall be deemed to be withdrawn.

Implemented by:
R.70(1) Six-month period for requesting examination

1 **Effect of non-payment of the examination fee**
The request for examination must be filed 'in due time', i.e. within the period laid down in **R.70(1)**. If the request for examination is not made within a six-month period of mention of publication of the search report (**R.70(1)**), the application is deemed withdrawn under **Art.94(2)** (A-VI,2.3). See **R.70(1):2** for further processing according to **Art.121** and **R.135** as remedy.

The two-month period for requesting further processing according to **Art.121** and **R.135** is not an extension of the six-month period but a remedy with retrospective effect (**J4/86** r.4 applied mutatis mutandis, equating the grace period of **R.85b** EPC1973 with that of the two-month period of **R.135(1)** EPC2000). Hence, when the request is not filed during the normal period and further processing is not used to remedy the defect, the application remains deemed withdrawn as of the end of the six-month period.

As a consequence, a renewal fee which becomes due after expiry of the normal six-month period must be refunded if the request for examination is not filed (**J4/86** hn, mutatis mutandis). Likewise, a divisional application filed after expiry of the six-month period will only be regarded as a divisional application if further processing is granted (see **R.36(1):2.1.3**). The fiction of **Art.94(2)** has the effect that the application is deemed never to have conferred the rights provided for in **Art.67** (**Art.67(4)**).

Art. 94(3) If the examination reveals that the application or the invention to which it relates does not meet the requirements of this Convention, the Examining Division shall invite the applicant, as often as necessary, to file his observations and, subject to Article 123, paragraph 1, to amend the application.

Art.123(1) Amendments
Implemented by:
R.71(1) Invitation to correct deficiencies
R.71(2) Content of communication

1 **General**
Details of the procedure can be found in
- **R.71:** Examination procedure
- **R.112:** Noting of loss of rights
- **R.113:** Signature, name and seal on notices and communications
- Guidelines Part C, in particular C-III to C-V

The examination procedure should be concluded in a timely manner. If an applicant does not cooperate, the examiner may refuse the application (**T84/82**). See **Art.94(1):4** for acceleration of the examination.

A response filed by the applicant during examination may be in an admissible non-EPO language (with a subsequent translation) if the response has to be filed within a time limit (**Art.14(4)**), but must be in an official EPO language in other cases (**R.3(1)**).

2 Substantive examination

The EPO will invite the applicant to file observations in respect of all deficiencies found in the application and to amend the application. The first substantive assessment is carried out by the search division together with the search, i.e. before the request for examination must be filed, and the outcome is issued as an opinion annexed to the search report (**R.62(1)**). The applicant must respond to any objections raised in the opinion within the period for filing the request for examination (**R.70a**). Subsequently, deficiencies are noted in communications of the examining division under **Art.94(3)**. Although the search opinion has similar content as a communication under **Art.94(3)**, it is not an invitation within the meaning of this article.

The applicant is the master of the examination procedure according to **Art.113(2)**: the EPO is bound to the text filed or approved by the applicant. However, the examining division may propose amendments.

The burden of proposing amendments to enable progress in the examination procedure lies with the applicant (**T300/89** r.9.1).

When the examiner challenges the unity of the claims, the applicant need not file both amended claims and an amended description in reply to the communication. First, the question of unity must be settled in relation to the claims and only after that should the examiner request the applicant to amend the description. (**T544/88**)

An amendment of the application will be objected to by the examiner if it contravenes a provision of the EPC, e.g. by introducing a lack of clarity or extending the subject-matter of the application beyond the content of the application as filed. See H-IV,2 and **Art.123(2)** for extension of subject-matter.

An amendment introducing further information regarding prior art which is relevant will normally not be objected to and is often required under **R.42(1)(b),(c)** (H-IV,2.2.7; F-II,4.3). An amendment removing a lack of clarity will normally not be objected to, provided that the change does not extend beyond the disclosure of the application as originally filed (H-IV,2.2.8).

Later filed statements of advantages and additional examples or explanations, which cannot be included in the application by amendment without contravening **Art.123(2)**, may be taken into account for assessing patentability, e.g. inventive step or sufficiency of disclosure. This material will be added to the file which is public, thus becoming part of the state of the art. The presence of such material will be mentioned on the cover page of the patent specification (H-V,2.2).

3 Start of examination

Once the request for examination has been filed, and the examining division has assumed responsibility under **R.10**, the substantive examination of the application will start.

One of the first steps is a top-up search for additional prior art as set out in **Art.92:6**. The date on which substantive examination begins is recorded in the file (C-IV,7.1). This date is relevant for calculating any possible refund of the examination fee if the application is (deemed) withdrawn or refused (**Rfees11**).

The examiner will consider the results of the top-up search and any arguments and amendments filed by the applicant under **R.70a** for a direct European application or under **R.159(1)(b)** or **161(1)** for a Euro-PCT application when drafting the first communication.

4 **First communication**

The first communication of the EPO in the examination phase should cover, where appropriate, all objections to the application (**R.71(2)**), including not only substantive matters but also formal matters, e.g. matters regarding the requirements of **R.41-43, 46, 48, 49** and **50**. The communication must contain a reasoned statement covering, where appropriate, all grounds against the grant of a patent (**R.71(2)**). The communication must state clearly and unequivocally what response is required from the applicant, e.g. the justification of an inventive step, a deletion or limitation of the scope of a claim, or a division of the application because of a lack of unity (**J13/84**). Apart from objections, a first communication may also include positive statements on patentability and suggestions on overcoming objections (C-III,4.1.2). The communication must state the period for reply, generally between two and four months from notification of the communication (**R.132**). The first communication may consist of the minutes of a telephone conversation with the applicant (C-VII,2.5).

At least one substantive communication under **Art.94(3)** is required before a decision to refuse the application on a substantive ground can be issued (unless a summons to oral proceedings is the first action in examination). Only if a prior communication sets out the essential legal and factual reasoning to support a finding that a requirement of the EPC has not been met can a decision based on such a finding be issued without contravening **Art.113(1)** (**T17/22**). Accordingly, the examining division issues at least one substantive communication under **Art.94(3)** if deficiencies persist in the application after the applicant's response to the search opinion (C-III,4). Some communications issued by the examining division do not count as a substantive communication, e.g. an invitation to indicate the basis of amended claims under **R.137(4)**. A list of such communications can be found in C-III,4.

The first communication may also be a summons for oral proceedings. This happens only in exceptional cases where, despite the applicant's reply to the search opinion, no possibility of a grant can be envisaged. All objections to the application must be covered and substantiated in the annex to the summons by giving the essential legal and factual reasons; this annex may not include any new objections or cite new documents. In addition, the summons will justify why it has been issued as a first action. For divisional applications, the examining division can exceptionally issue summons as first action if, essentially, the parent was refused or withdrawn, there is no prospect of a grant for the divisional application, and the essential objections were raised before against the parent application or in the search report. (C-III,5)

The oral proceedings may be cancelled or postponed if the applicant genuinely tries to overcome the objections stated in the summons (C-III,5). Therefore, it is recommended to file auxiliary requests and arrange a consultation with the examiner (see **Art.116:3**).

5 **Response, further communication and immediate refusal**

The communication under **Art.94(3)** will state the period within which the applicant must file a response (**R.71(1)**). The consequences of failure to observe the period are dealt with in **Art.94(4)**.

In the reply to the first communication, the applicant may put forward any arguments (both legal and technical) against the objections raised by the examining division, in support of the text of the application as filed or already amended.

Normally, the applicant will have tried to deal with all the objections in response to the first communication from the examining division. If the only outstanding objection is the need to amend the description, the examiner will invite the applicant to amend the description.

If examination of the applicant's reply to a communication under **Art.94(3)** shows that objections persist, the examiner will consider recommending to the other members of the examining division that the application be refused, provided that there is no outstanding request for oral proceedings (**Art.116**) and provided that the decision can be based on the grounds of which the applicant was already notified in a prior communication (**Art.113(1)**). (C-IV,3)

Where there is a reasonable prospect that an additional invitation to overcome the objection(s) could lead to a grant, the examiner will send a further written communication or contact the applicants by telephone. The examiner may also make suggestions on how to overcome the raised objections. If the examination of the applicant's reply shows that the applicant has not addressed all the main objections, it may be appropriate to draw the deficiencies to the applicant's attention, e.g. by telephone. But if no positive reaction is expected, the examiner should consider recommending to the other members of the examining division that the application be refused immediately, provided the requirements mentioned earlier are met. (C-IV,3)

It is established case law that the examining division may send an immediate refusal after a first communication, provided the decision to refuse complies with **Art.113(1)**; a prior warning is not required (**T1002/03** r.5). Such an immediate refusal is in principle allowable when the decision to refuse is based solely on grounds on which the applicant has had an opportunity to comment (**T201/98**; C-IV,3). In **T1002/03** the first communication raised objections concerning the lack of clarity of claim 1 and the lack of an inventive step for claims 1 and 5; in response, the applicant filed an amended claim 1 to meet the clarity objection and provided three pages of arguments concerning inventive step; since the examining division did not regard the arguments as convincing, it refused the application. The applicant can only continue prosecution after a refusal by filing an appeal.

The risk of an immediate refusal can be avoided by requesting oral proceedings in the response to the first communication under **Art.94(3)** (**T300/89** r.9.2) or to the search opinion (see **R.70a(1):1**). Since such a request may not be ignored (**Art.116(1)**) and since the appointment of oral proceedings involves a substantial amount of work for the EPO, the examiner will usually send a second communication.

If, in response to an unfavourable communication, the applicant decides not to continue with a European application, it is recommended not to answer the communication and let the case be deemed withdrawn. A response to the communication may result in a refusal, which decision may have a negative bearing on the prosecution of the case before other patent offices or courts. The applicant may withdraw the application in response to the first communication to obtain a partial refund of the examination fee (**Rfees11(b)**).

6 Auxiliary requests

Where an applicant is uncertain about the patentability of a set of claims, filing one set of claims as a main request and one or more alternative sets of claims as auxiliary requests may clarify the procedural position and expedite the procedure without requiring the applicant to abandon the preferred position. It allows the applicant to have the patentability of a narrower request recognised without abandoning a higher-ranking request which is not regarded as allowable. An applicant may have a refused request re-examined by a board of appeal. The following requirements for and the examination of such requests are set out in H-III,3.3.

Auxiliary requests will be admitted, provided they are in a clear order, their content is clear, they relate to one invention, they do not re-introduce unallowable subject-matter already abandoned by the applicant and the text of the claims is clear (**R14/10**; H-III,3.1.1; 3.3.2.1). If the auxiliary requests are filed late, they must additionally conform to a convergent approach, in that the most broadly worded set of claims is filed as main request and sequentially narrower sets of claims as auxiliary requests (H-III,3.3.2.2; **T1685/07** r.6.5-6.6).

Identical claims in auxiliary requests may be replaced by references. The number of requests should not be excessive (**T907/91**). The examining division examines the requests in the order presented by the applicant. If it considers an auxiliary request patentable, it will propose this request for grant in a communication under **Art.94**(3) or a communication under **R.71**(3) or, where appropriate, during oral proceedings, and state why the higher ranking requests, including the main request, are not acceptable. Requests ranking lower than the allowable request will not be examined.

The procedure for grant in the case of auxiliary requests has been set out in **R.71**(3):5.1 and **R.71**(6):5.

In appeal, new auxiliary requests are often not admitted (Art.12 RPBA; see **Art.114**(2):2). Therefore, applicants should endeavour to file all possible auxiliary requests during examination.

7 Request for a decision

An applicant wishing to close the debate may request a decision according to the state of the file (C-V,15). If, in response to such a request, the application is refused, the refusal may be appealed under **Art.106**(1). A request for a refusal according to the state of the file qualifies as a sufficient reply to avoid the application becoming deemed to be withdrawn (**Art.94**(4); C-IV,3).

A request for a decision according to the state of the file is in effect a waiver of the applicant's right to comment on the raised objections under **Art.113**(1) (**T685/98** r.3.2). The request should be explicit and unambiguous (C-V,15.1). If there is a pending request for oral proceedings at the time a decision is requested, the examining division interprets the request for a decision as a withdrawal of the request for oral proceedings (**T2704/16** r.1; C-V,15.1).

The applicant may submit new arguments with a request for a decision. The examining division must consider these newly-presented arguments and issue a reasoned decision to refuse, a further communication under **Art.94**(3), or a summons to oral proceedings, as appropriate in view of **Art.113**(1). (**T123/14**; C-V,15.2, 15.3, 15.4).

A refusal decision according to the state of the file is taken by a standard form which refers to one earlier communication, or exceptionally to more than one earlier communication. Such a decision taken by means of a standard form contains no reasoning of its own (C-V,15.2). In certain cases, the examining division can refuse the application after a request for a decision according to state of the file but must issue a self-contained decision, e.g. if the applicant filed amendments or arguments after the referenced earlier communication, or if the earlier communication is not sufficiently reasoned, or if not all the objections in the earlier communication still apply (C-V,15.2, 15.3). In other cases, the examining division must issue a new communication so as to avoid violating **Art.113**(1), e.g. to avoid raising new objections in the refusal decision or violating the requirement that decisions be reasoned (**R.111**(2)) (C-V,15.4).

Art. 94(4) If the applicant fails to reply in due time to any communication from the Examining Division, the application shall be deemed to be withdrawn.

1 **Period for responding**

The period for response to the communication under paragraph 3 is normally between two and four months from notification of the communication and can be extended to a total period of six months by request, according to **R.132**; the request must be filed before the expiry of the period (E-VIII,1.6.1). See **R.132(2):2** for details of the extension. The examiner is not expected to issue a new communication within any particular time frame following a response from the applicant. Such an expectation does exist, however, if the prosecution is accelerated (see **Art.94(1):4**).

A reply from the applicant does not have to be substantively complete or cogent to qualify as a reply within the meaning of **Art.94(4)**. For the application not to be deemed withdrawn, it is enough for the applicant to comment on, even incompletely, or to file amendments in reply to at least one of the objections raised in the communication under **Art.94(3)**. In contrast, purely formal requests, such as a request for an extension of the time limit, for a consultation or oral proceedings, do not qualify as replies under **Art.94(4)**. However, a request for a decision according to the state of the file qualifies as a reply meeting **Art.94(4)**.

A reply devoid of any substantive content and which cannot be understood as a waiver, express or implied, of the rest of the period set for reply is not a response within the meaning of **Art.94(4)**, and the examining division may not take any further action until the end of the period. (**T685/98**)

2 **Sanction on late filing and remedies**

If a response to the invitation of **Art.94(3)** is not filed within the period specified in the invitation, including any possible extension, the application is deemed withdrawn under **Art.94(4)** and the EPO notifies the applicant of the loss of rights according to **R.112(1)**. In practice, the **R.112(1)** communication is despatched about one month after expiry of the period. Within two months from the notification under **R.112(1)** the applicant can request further processing (**Art.121** and **R.135**) by paying the fee for further processing and filing a response. A request for further processing thus extends the period for reply, including any possible extension according to **R.134**, by three to four months at the expense of paying the moderate further processing fee (**Rfees2(1)12**).

Instead of or in addition to a request for further processing the applicant can, within two months from the **R.112(1)** notification, apply for an appealable decision according to **R.112(2)** if the applicant is of the opinion that the EPO did receive a response in due time. (see **R.112(2):1**)

Failure to meet the two-month period of **R.135(1)** or **R.112(2)** can only be remedied by requesting re-establishment in respect of that two-month period according to **Art.122** and **R.136**: the applicant must file the request for re-establishment, prove all due care was taken, pay the re-establishment fee and complete the omitted act, all within two months from removal of the cause of non-compliance but not later than one year from expiry of the period in which re-establishment is requested.

Art. 95 (deleted)

Art. 96 (deleted)

Art. 97 Grant or refusal

Art. 97(1) If the Examining Division is of the opinion that the European patent application and the invention to which it relates meet the requirements of this Convention, it shall decide to grant a European patent, provided that the conditions laid down in the Implementing Regulations are fulfilled.

Implemented by:
R.71 Examination procedure
(3) Communication of text to be granted
(4) Additional claims fees
(5) Approval of text to be granted
(6) Filing of amendments or corrections
(7) Sanction
R.71a Conclusion of the grant procedure
(1) Decision to grant
(2) Resumption of examination
(5) Crediting of already paid fees
(6) Refund of fee for grant and publishing
R.72 Grant of the European patent to different applicants
R.140 Correction of errors in decisions

1 **Intention to grant the patent**
If the examining division considers that the text of the patent application and the invention to which it relates meet the requirements of the EPC, it must establish that several further requirements are met before it can decide to grant the patent.

The requirements to be met for grant are given in:
- **R.71(3)**, filing translations of the claims in the official EPO languages other than the language of the proceedings and paying the fee for grant and publishing; by carrying out these acts the applicant is deemed to approve the text of the application;
- **R.71(4)**, payment of any additional claims fees;
- **R.71a(3)**, payment of the designation fee if not yet paid;
- **R.71a(4)**, payment of any renewal fee due.

The examining division will issue a **R.71(3)** communication informing the applicant of the text it intends to grant the patent in and inviting the applicant to comply with the relevant requirements. The requirements stated in **R.71(3)** and, where applicable, **R.71(4)** must be complied with within a period of four months from notification of the **R.71(3)** communication. Non-observance results in the application being deemed withdrawn under **R.71(7)**. **R.71(6)** gives the applicant the possibility to file reasoned amendments or corrections instead of carrying out the acts specified in **R.71(3)**. The examining division will examine the amended text.

2 **Acceleration of the grant**

The **R.71(3)** communication will be issued within tight deadlines if accelerated examination has been requested (see **Art.94(1):5**). The subsequent steps in the grant procedure can only be accelerated by promptly responding to EPO communications.

An applicant can accelerate the grant of the patent by complying with all outstanding requirements immediately after receipt of the **R.71(3)** communication, i.e. by filing the translations of the claims and paying all necessary fees (fee for grant and publishing (**R.71(3)**); any claims fees (**R.71(4)**); any designation fee (**R.71a(3)**); and any renewal fee (**R.71a(4)**). It is recommended to pay the next renewal fee if the response is filed less than three months before the renewal fee due date; the fee will be reimbursed if the mention of the grant is published in the current patent year.

Note that applicants using the automatic debiting procedure may have to pay the above fees separately to ensure rapid grant. The applicant is informed of this situation in the **R.71(3)** communication.

3 **Disapproval of the text to be granted**

Art.97(1) does not provide for the case in which an applicant disapproves the text proposed by the examining division for grant. In such a case, the examining division can no longer decide upon the proposed text, because the applicant has not approved the text as required under **Art.113(2)**. The procedures developed for the case where disapproval is expressed are set out in **R.71(6)** and notes thereto.

Explicit disapproval of the text to be granted occurs mainly in cases where a main request and one or more auxiliary requests are pending (see **R.71(6):5**).

In the common case where only one set of claims is pending, an explicit disapproval of the text proposed for grant is usually accompanied by a request for amendment. The examining division will not decide upon the text it proposed but will examine the amended text (**R.71(6):3, 4**).

4 **Decision to grant**

When the relevant requirements have been complied with in due time, the examining division will decide to grant the patent and start the preparations for publication of the patent specification under **Art.98**. The written decision under **Art.97(1)** states which text forms the basis for the grant (**R.71a(1)**, last sentence) by referring to the **R.71(3)** communication. It also states the designated contracting states and the projected date of publication of the mention of the grant in the Bulletin. The patent will be granted for the contracting states that are designated states at the date of grant (see **Art.79**). The decision draws attention to the requirements for translations of the specification or claims in official languages of certain contracting states under **Art.65(1)** (C-V,10). The decision is notified to the applicant when the technical preparations for publication of the patent specification have been completed (C-V,10; OJ 2006 p.409).

The decision takes effect on the date of publication of the mention of the grant in the Bulletin (**Art.97(3)**), i.e. it does not take effect on the date the decision is taken. In practice, the mention of the grant is published four weeks after the issue of the decision (OJ 2006 p.409). The date of the publication of the mention is entered in the Register (**R.143(1)(o)**). From the date of publication of the mention of the grant, the rights associated with the patent are conferred on its proprietor (**Art.64(1)**). The EPO publishes the patent specification in practice on the same day as the mention of the grant (**Art.98**). Promptly after the publication of the specification the EPO sends a patent certificate to the proprietor in electronic form (**R.74**). Certified copies of the certificate with the specification annexed are issued on paper upon request and payment of an administrative fee (OJ 2021 A95).

After the decision has been taken, both the EPO and the applicant are bound by the decision as far as the text of the patent to be granted is concerned (**R.140:3.1**). See **R.140:3.2** for correcting the published specification of the patent where it does not conform to the text as granted.

The publication of the mention of the grant can be retracted by the EPO, for instance, if a stay under **R.14** is retroactively declared. The retraction is published in the Bulletin (see e.g. Bulletin 2019-26 p.6169 under II.12(12)).

Applicants may withdraw their application up to the day before the date of publication of the mention of the grant. Where necessary, the publication of the mention of the grant is retracted (E-VIII,8.1).

After the publication of the mention of the grant, the proprietor may have to file translations of the specification or claims in contracting states in order to 'validate' the patent for those states (**Art.65**) and has to pay renewal fees to national patent offices (**Art.141**). For a unitary patent, a request and a translation have to be filed with the EPO and renewal fees are to be paid to the EPO. Third parties may file an opposition against the patent within nine months from the publication of the mention of the grant (**Art.99**).

5 **Appealability of decision to grant**

The decision to grant is, in principle, appealable. However, since applicants are deemed to have given their approval under **R.71(5)** for the text to be granted, situations in which the applicant is adversely affected by the decision are rare (**Art.107**). An example of such a situation is where the decision is not based on the text approved. This may happen if the examining division grants the patent despite a request of the applicant to disregard an earlier approval and amend the application (see e.g. **T1093/05** hn). An appeal filed with the object of amending the patent as granted will be inadmissible because the applicant is not adversely affected by the decision to grant (**J12/83** r.3). A discrepancy between the published specification of the patent and the text as approved does not give rise to a right to appeal. The published specification can be corrected on request at any time (C-V,10).

If the examiner issues a communication under **R.71(3)** for a set of claims filed as an auxiliary request, the applicant will be asked to approve the grant based on this set of claims and abandon the higher-ranking requests. A decision to grant based on the remaining approved request is not appealable because the applicant is not adversely affected. If the applicant wants to obtain the patent for a higher-ranking request, the text proposed by the examiner should not be approved, and the higher-ranking request should be maintained; as a consequence, the application will be refused, and the decision to refuse can be appealed. Subsequently, the applicant can defend the higher-ranking request in appeal proceedings. In opposition proceedings, proprietors are not requested to withdraw higher-ranking requests before a decision is taken that a patent can be maintained in amended form. Instead, a single decision is taken on all requests. The decision states which requests have been rejected and which request is allowed. The proprietor can appeal this decision if the highest-ranking request (main request), pending at the time the opposition division takes its decision, is not allowed. See **R.71(6):5** and **R.81(3):1** for details of handling auxiliary requests.

Art. 97(2) If the Examining Division is of the opinion that the European patent application or the invention to which it relates does not meet the requirements of this Convention, it shall refuse the application unless this Convention provides for a different legal consequence.

1 **Refusal of the application**

An application will be refused if it does not meet the formal and/or substantive requirements of the EPC (**Art.97(2)**).

The application is refused in its entirety without making any exception for any patentable matter in it (**T5/81**). For example, when the examiner considers one of the claims unallowable and the applicant does not amend this claim, the entire application is refused. An interlocutory decision on the non-allowable claim, which can be appealed separately from the allowable claims, will not be issued. Any appeal against the refusal of the application should include a main request, which includes the allowable and non-allowable claims, and an auxiliary request for only the allowable claims. The board of appeal will examine all requests, including a request considered allowable by the examining division, with the risk of a final refusal (**G10/93** hn). A safer but costly way of securing rights in the allowable claims is to remove the non-allowable claim and have the patent granted; the prosecution of the non-allowable claim can be continued by filing a divisional application for that claim in due time (**Art.76, R.36(1)**).

The decision to refuse the application must be reasoned (**R.111(2)**) and be based on grounds and evidence known to the applicant and on which the applicant has had an opportunity to comment **Art.113(1)**). The omission of reasoning is a substantial procedural violation, which entitles the applicant to reimbursement of the appeal fee (**R.103**). The same applies to a violation of the applicant's right to be heard under **Art.113(1)**.

If the applicant appeals the refusal, the examining division can revise its decision in the light of the statement of grounds under **Art.109(1)**. If the examining division does not revise its decision, the case will be remitted to the board of appeal. After the board has taken a decision, it can remit the case back to the same examining division for further prosecution (**Art.111(2)**).

An example of 'a different legal consequence' as mentioned in **Art.97(2)** is the deemed withdrawal of the application, for example when a renewal fee is not paid (**Art.86(1)**), a response to a communication is not filed in time (**Art.94(4)**), the fee for grant and publishing is not paid, a claims fee is not paid or the translations of the claims under **R.71(7)** are not filed.

2 **Double patenting as a ground for refusal**

A European patent application is to be refused under **Art.97(2)** and **Art.125** if it claims the same subject-matter as a European patent which has been granted to the same applicant and which does not form part of the state of the art under **Art.54(2)** and (3) for the patent application under examination. In such cases, the patent application is refused under the prohibition of double patenting (**G4/19** hn.1, r.78). The existence of overlapping designated contracting states under **Art.79** is an additional condition for the prohibition to apply (**G4/19** r.5, r.80). The Enlarged Board confirmed the established practice of the EPO regarding double patenting objections in **G4/19** in view of a clear remark in the travaux préparatoires to the EPC1973 that the prohibition of double patenting was a generally recognised principle of procedural law according to a majority (r.55). The Enlarged Board did so without addressing the criteria of the same applicant and same invention. Moreover, there is no established case law about when an applicant and a proprietor are the same for the prohibition of double patenting.

The application can be refused on the ground of double patenting if it has the same effective date (filing date or priority date) as the granted European patent, which can be the case e.g. if the application was filed on the same day as the European patent application leading to the already granted European patent, or claims the same priority date (G-IV,5.4). Therefore, a patent application can be refused on the ground of double patenting if it is the parent from which the granted patent was divided, a divisional of the granted patent, an application from which the granted patent claims the priority or an application which claims the priority of the granted patent. Note that only European patent applications form prior rights under **Art.54(3)**, not granted patents; the first headnote of **G4/19** is imprecise. Furthermore, a patent application should not be refused for double patenting if the application under examination forms part of the state of the art for the patent under **Art.54(2)** or (3). In case of a priority application and priority-claiming application with claims directed to the same subject-matter and both being European applications, the applicant should ensure that the priority-claiming application is granted first because the patent term of that application expires later.

Two claims are not directed to the same subject matter for the purposes of **G4/19** if they differ by at least one feature (**T943/17** r.3.2). Accordingly, if the claims of the applications are merely partially overlapping, there is no impermissible double patenting (**T877/06**). **G2/10** r.4.5.5 acknowledged that an applicant might have a legitimate interest in obtaining rapid protection for a preferred embodiment in a first application and then pursuing broader claims in a divisional application (G-IV,5.4). **T2907/19** held that it is permissible that an independent claim of a divisional application corresponds to a dependent claim of the granted parent application. On the other hand, **T1128/19** held that it is not permissible if an independent claim of a divisional application is directed to the same subject-matter as an embodiment of a claim of the granted parent application.

Should two applications with the same effective date be received from two different applicants, each must be allowed to proceed as though the other did not exist (G-IV,5.4).

See **Art.139(3)** for double patenting between a European patent and a national patent with the same effective date.

Art. 97(3) The decision to grant a European patent shall take effect on the date on which the mention of the grant is published in the European Patent Bulletin.

Implemented by:
R.71a Conclusion of the grant procedure
(3) Designation fee
(4) Renewal fee

1 **Publication of decision to grant**

The communication notifying the decision to grant informs the applicant of the date of the publication of the mention of the grant. The communication is sent to the applicant when the technical preparations for publishing the patent specification have been completed (C-V,10). The scheduled date of publication in the Bulletin (**Art.129**) is four weeks after the issuance of the decision to grant (OJ 2006 p.409).

The mention of the grant will not be published until the designation fee or any due renewal fee have been paid (**R.71a**(3) and (4)).

If the decision to grant has been notified to the applicant, but the mention of the grant has not yet been published, the applicant can still withdraw the designation of states because the decision to grant is not effective at that time (**Art.97(3)**, **J7/96** r.6.3).

The patent specification is published as soon as possible after the publication of the mention of the grant and in practice on the same date (**Art.98**). The effect of the grant is that it confers the rights of **Art.64(1)** on the proprietor. A deficiency in the publication of the mention of the grant does not necessarily render the decision to grant ineffective (**J14/87**). See also **Art.98:1**.

The European patent has, in each designated state, the effect of a national patent from the date of publication of the mention of the grant (**Art.2(2)**, **Art.64(1)**). Many contracting states require translation of the granted patent or part of it under **Art.65(1)**, which gives the applicant at least three months after the publication of the mention of the grant for filing any such translation. The EPO does not inform the applicant about the states that require translation; the information is available on the EPO website.

In rare cases, the EPO can retract the mention of the grant by a subsequent notice in the Bulletin, which states that the mention of the grant is deleted, e.g. if the proceedings have been stayed or the application is withdrawn shortly before the publication of the mention of the grant.

A granted patent is subject to national law unless otherwise provided (**Art.2(2)**). The opposition procedure is an example of the 'otherwise provided', where the patent is still bound by the EPC; another example is **Art.138**.

2 **Legal effect of the publication of the mention of the grant**

- **Art.2(2)** the European patent has the effect of a national patent unless the EPC provides otherwise;
- **Art.64(1)** the European patent confers the same right as a national patent;
- **Art.65(1)** requirement to file translations of the European patent;
- **Art.99(1)** the 9-month opposition period begins;
- **Art.105a** centralised limitation and revocation possible;
- **Art.141** renewal fees must be paid to the national patent offices;
- **UPR.6** period for filing a request for unitary effect.

Art. 98 Publication of the specification of the European patent

The European Patent Office shall publish the specification of the European patent as soon as possible after the mention of the grant of the European patent has been published in the European Patent Bulletin.

Implemented by:
R.73 Content and form of the specification
R.74 Certificate for a European patent

1 **Publication of the specification**

The specification of the granted patent will be published as soon as possible after the publication of the mention of the grant (**Art.97(3)**), which in practice is on the same day. The purpose of the publication is to inform the public of the grant of the patent and its content; the published specification has no binding character (**R.140:3.2**).

Applicants are informed of the date of publication of the mention of the grant in the decision to grant, which is sent to them after the completion of the technical preparations for publishing the patent (C-V,10).

The mention of the grant of the patent is published in the European Patent Bulletin (**Art.97(3)**).

The form and contents of the published patent specification are governed by **R.73**.

After the publication of the specification, the EPO sends the proprietor a certificate (**R.74**). If no notice of opposition is filed within nine months of the grant of the patent, the proprietor is informed, and an appropriate entry is published in the Bulletin (C-V,13).

The means by which errors in the published specification can be corrected are dealt with in **R.140:3.2**.

PART V OPPOSITION AND LIMITATION PROCEDURE

Art. 99 Opposition

Art. 99(1) Within nine months of the publication of the mention of the grant of the European patent in the European Patent Bulletin, any person may give notice to the European Patent Office of opposition to that patent, in accordance with the Implementing Regulations. Notice of opposition shall not be deemed to have been filed until the opposition fee has been paid.

Implemented by:
R.75 Opposition to lapsed or surrendered patent
R.76 Content of the notice of opposition

1 **General**

The EPC provides for an opposition procedure after grant in order to improve the quality of European patents by allowing other parties to bring forward facts and evidence prejudicial to maintaining granted patents. Such facts can include those not usually available to examiners, such as oral disclosures and public prior uses. The opposition procedure has the character of a centralised revocation procedure affecting all national rights originating from a European patent.

Revocation of the patent in opposition proceedings has an effect ex tunc in that the patent is deemed never to have conferred the rights of **Art.64** (**Art.68**). The opposition procedure and its effects are an exception to the rule that European patent is subject to national law after grant (see **Art.2(2)**).

An overview of the opposition procedure is published in OJ 2016 A42. Opposition proceedings may be accelerated in the case of a pending infringement action (see **Art.101(1):4**).

2 **Person entitled to oppose**

2.1 ADMITTED PERSONS

Any person has the right to file an opposition according to **Art.99(1)**. Since the filing of an opposition is not only in the interests of the opponent, but also in the interests of the public, restricting the filing of oppositions is undesirable. 'Any person' must be construed in line with **Art.58** as meaning: (a) any natural person, (b) any legal person or (c) any body equivalent to a legal person by virtue of the law governing it (**G3/99** r.9). A fictional person, i.e. a person having no legal existence, cannot validly file an opposition (**T1165/03**). If an opposition is filed by a body that may lack legal personality under national law (such as a UK partnership) and if no evidence in support of the status of that body as a legal person can be produced, the EPO will treat the opposition as being filed by several persons acting in common (**T482/02** of 09.02.2005 hn).

A (single) notice of opposition may also be filed by several persons acting in common (**R.151(1)**, last sentence). Such persons are filing only one opposition, need to pay only one opposition fee, and are joint opponents (or common opponents) throughout the proceedings. The joint opponents must act through a common representative (see **R.151(1):2**). The common representative is either appointed by the persons filing the opposition or by the EPO according to **R.151** (**G3/99** r.14). Each of the persons must be of the type (a), (b) or (c) mentioned above. (**G3/99** r.3, 9, 10)

A party filing two notices of opposition to the same patent acquires party status as opponent only once (**T9/00**).

Multiple oppositions against the same patent are dealt with in a single procedure. Prior art filed as part of an inadmissible opposition may be taken into account by the opposition division under **Art.114(1)** if an admissible opposition has also been filed and the prior art is considered relevant (**T966/02** r.2.4).

The identity of the opponent must be clear before the end of the opposition period (**T25/85**). See **R.76(2):2.2** for correction of the identity of the opponent.

The fact that, according to **Art.99(1)**, an opposition may be filed by any person is incompatible with a requirement that the opponent must have a commercial or other interest in the opposition (**G1/84** r.3, **G3/97** r.3.2). Opponents can, for example, seek unfettered access to the patented invention out of mere curiosity or to supplement their professional training (**T798/93** hn.I).

An opposition is not inadmissible because the opponent is a licensee of the patent, even if the licence agreement includes a no-challenge provision (**G3/97** r.3.3.2).

2.2 OPPOSITION BY STRAW PERSON

Straw persons in opposition proceedings are persons who file an opposition in their own name but are acting on behalf of a usually unnamed principal. Opponents may resort to the use of a straw person to hide their identity from the proprietor, e.g. to avoid showing an interest in the patented technology or to attack a patent while conducting negotiations with the proprietor. Some companies offer the service of acting as a straw person in opposition; the professional representative will represent such a company before the EPO instead of the principal; see e.g. **T616/08**.

The EPO accepts a straw person as opponent since decision **G3/97**, provided that the use of a straw person does not circumvent the law.

The status of the opponent is a procedural status. Hence, the opponent is the person who fulfils the requirements of the EPC for filing an opposition; in particular, the person must be identifiable (see **R.76(2)(a)**). The status of the opponent is similar to that of an applicant, who is 'deemed' to be entitled to the patent (**Art.60(3)**). It is irrelevant for the opposition proceedings whether the opponent is a nominal opponent, also called a straw person, acting on behalf of a, possibly unnamed, principal. Hence, an opposition is not inadmissible only because it is filed by a straw person. (**G3/97** r.2.1; case consolidated with **G4/97**; overturning **T10/82**, **T219/86** hn.1, **T635/88**, **T798/93** hn.2)

However, an opposition is inadmissible if the action of a straw person is to be regarded as a circumvention of the law by abuse of process. This is the case if a straw person represents the proprietor's interests, because proprietors are not entitled to oppose their own patents (see below). Neither may a straw person be used to circumvent the requirements relating to representation. This is the case if a person not entitled to act as a professional representative files an opposition in their own name on behalf of a client, in the context of activities which, taken as a whole, are typically associated with professional representatives. (**G3/97** r.4)

A challenge to the admissibility of an opposition based on the opponent's identity may be raised before the departments of first and second instance by the patent proprietor or the EPO of its own motion (**G3/97** r.5). The burden of proof is borne by the person raising the issue and clear and convincing evidence is required. As a rule, the EPO will not know that a straw person has filed an opposition on the proprietor's behalf, and the admissibility of the opposition will not be questioned. There may be an indication that an opponent is acting as a straw person on behalf of the proprietor where the opponent is bound by the proprietor's instructions as a subsidiary company within a large group or as an employee of the proprietor (**G3/97** r.5.1.1). An indication that a straw person is being used to circumvent the provisions on representation is where a person, not being a professional representative, regularly acts as an opponent, creating the impression that these activities in opposition proceedings are part of the person's normal professional activities (**G3/97** r.5.1.2). However, the law is not circumvented when a professional representative files an opposition on behalf of a client, specifying the representative as opponent, or when an opponent having either a residence or place of business in one of the contracting states, acts on behalf of a principal who does not meet these requirements (**G3/97** r.4.2).

2.3 SELF-OPPOSITION

Under EPC1973 patent proprietors were able for a time to oppose their own patents ('self-opposition') allowing amendment of the granted patent in a central procedure before the EPO. Decision **G1/84** allowed such self-opposition. However, later decision **G9/93** overruled the earlier decision and forbade self-opposition. Hence, despite the term 'any person' in **Art.99(1)**, proprietors may not oppose their own patents. However, an opposition can be filed by an inventor who is not a proprietor (**T3/06** r.2).

In order to provide a central procedure for amending a patent after grant, EPC2000 has introduced the limitation procedure of **Art.105a-c**.

2.4 TRANSFER OF THE OPPOSITION

According to general principles of procedural law, a party to proceedings does not have the discretion to transfer its party status to another person. The EPC contains exceptions for the transfer of the status of applicant and proprietor in **Art.71** and **R.85**. The only exceptions for opponents are **R.84(2)**, which implicitly allows the transfer of party status to the opponent's heirs, and certain cases recognised in the case law. Hence, the status as an opponent cannot be freely transferred. The public interest in the speedy conclusion of opposition proceedings does not allow for the time-consuming examination of contested questions arising as a result of frequent transfers or the lengthening of the procedure caused by the introduction of new lines of attack by a new party. (**G2/04**, r.2.1.2, r.2.2.2, hn.Ia; see also **G3/97**, r.2.2)

The EPO has the duty to consider the status of the opponent at all stages of the procedure. The validity of a transfer of opponent status may therefore be raised at all stages during the proceedings, even for the first time in appeal. If alleged opponents file an appeal, their status as opponent is not protected by the prohibition on reformatio in peius. If the board denies the validity of the transfer, the opposition procedure has to be conducted afresh from the time of the transfer, this time with an entitled opponent. (**T1178/04**)

Opponent status may be transferred by universal succession from a deceased opponent to an heir, in the case of a natural person, and from one legal person to another in the case where companies are incorporated and merged (**T355/86; T349/86; T475/88**). **G4/88** also allows the transfer of opponent status to a third party in a case where a company files an opposition in the interests of a part of the company without legal personality and subsequently transfers the assets of that part of the company to the third party. The opposition, which is an inseparable part of the assets, must be regarded as transferable when the assets are transferred in accordance with the principle that an accessory object follows the principal object. Hence, an opposition may be transferred as part of the opponent's assets together with the assets in the interest of which the opposition was filed. However, party status is not automatically transferred in this situation (see for example **T234/18** and **T7/17**) and evidence must be produced showing that it was the intention of the parties to transfer the party status along with the business assets. In **T74/00**, it was held that a transfer arising from the death of the opponent need not be accompanied by any specific assets of the deceased. The new opponent gains its status purely from being the heir of the previous opponent.

G2/04 forbids the transfer of opponent status to a third party where a company files an opposition in the interests of one of its subsidiaries having legal personality and subsequently transfers the assets of the subsidiary to a third party. Since the company in **G4/88** was the sole legal entity and could not file an opposition in the name of a part of the company, whereas the company in **G2/04** could file an opposition in the name of its subsidiary, the Board concluded that the two cases are essentially different. The Board decided to interpret **G4/88** restrictively and not to extend its rationale to other situations because there was no overriding interest for the parties or the public. (**G2/04 r.2.2**).

Party status may be transferred within the above bounds at any stage of the opposition and opposition appeal procedures; the right to lodge an appeal may also be transferred (**T563/89 r.1.1**). The transfer must be substantiated (**T670/95**). The previous party retains its rights until the required proof has been provided (**R.22(3); T870/92**). If a purported notice of appeal does not indicate how a transfer of status has taken place, it is not the duty of the Board of Appeal to investigate further (for example, by examination of appropriate trade registers) to substantiate the transfer (**T428/08**). A transfer of opposition may be to one successor party only, to avoid other persons becoming party to the proceedings after expiry of the relevant time limits (**T298/97 r.7.6**).

The following precautions can be taken to avoid problems with a transfer:

- File the opposition in the name of both the company and the subsidiary if the latter has legal personality; the company can withdraw from the opposition after the transfer (**G2/04 r.2.1.2**). See **T960/08 r.3.1** for necessary conditions and **T9/00** for a failed variant of this precaution.
- If it is not clear who will have the right to appeal, file the appeal in the name of the company as a main request and in the name of the subsidiary as an auxiliary request (**G2/04 r.3.2**; see e.g. **T1877/08 r.1**).

- Ask the EPO for advice before filing the opposition or appeal, noting date and persons contacted for later proof. If the advice of the EPO is followed but turns out to be wrong, the principle of good faith may be invoked to correct the name of the opponent (see **Art.125:2**).
- File the opposition through a straw person as legally accepted by **G3/97**, because any change of the straw person's principal is irrelevant.

Formal requirements have to be fulfilled for the opponent status to be considered transferred, namely submitting a duly substantiated request and evidence in the opposition proceedings; no fee is due (**T960/08** r.2.2.).

2.5 WITHDRAWAL OF THE OPPOSITION

Withdrawal of an opposition does not directly end the opposition procedure, as the opposition division may continue the proceedings of its own motion in the public interest (**Art.114(1)** and **R.84(2)**). Moreover, the Division must take a decision which is entered in the Register (**R.143(1)(r)**). (**T197/88**)

The opposition proceedings are also continued if one or more common opponents withdraw from the opposition, since otherwise a single one of the common opponents, not being the common representative, could of its own motion end the opposition (**G3/99** r.13). The common representative should notify the EPO of any withdrawal. A withdrawal of the common representative should also be communicated to the EPO; the new common representative must be appointed either by the remaining common opponents or by application of **R.151**. See also **R.151(1):2**.

See also **R.84** for surrender of the patent, death of the opponent and withdrawal of the opposition during first instance proceedings and **Art.110:9** for withdrawal in opposition appeal.

3 Filing

3.1 PERIOD FOR FILING

Opposition can only be filed against a granted patent within nine months from the publication of the mention of the grant under **Art.97(3)** (**Art.99(1)**). The date of the publication of the patent specification under **Art.98** is not relevant. An opposition filed before the mention of the publication of grant of the patent is not regarded as an opposition. In that case the opposition documents become part of the public file and the opposition fee is refunded (D-IV,1.1).

Since the nine-month period and the payment of the opposition fee are regarded as essential requirements, they are provided in the Convention rather than the Implementing Regulations.

3.2 FORMAL REQUIREMENTS

The notice of opposition must be filed in writing (**R.76(1)**) and signed (**R.76(3)**, **R.50(3)**, D-III,3.4). It must be filed with an EPO filing office using a method permitted under **R.2(1)**. The notice may be filed e.g. electronically (R.2(1):5).

The notice of opposition must be in one of the three official languages of the EPO, not necessarily the language of the proceedings (**R.3(1)**). Since the notice of opposition is a document to be filed within a time limit, it may also be filed in an official language of a contracting state according to **Art.14** if the opponent (not the representative, **T149/85**) has a residence or place of business in that state or is a national of that state. In that case a translation in one of the three official EPO languages must be filed within the later of one month from filing the notice of opposition and the end of the opposition period (**R.6(2)**). If the time limit for filing the translation is not complied with, neither **Art.121** nor **Art.122** is available, because the opponent is not an applicant or proprietor (**T702/89**).

3.3 OPPOSITION FEE AND LATE FILING

The opposition is not deemed to have been filed until the opposition fee has been paid (**Art.99(1)**, second sentence). The amount of the opposition fee is fixed in **Rfees2(1)10.** A single opposition filed by two or more persons acting in common is admissible on payment of only one opposition fee (**G3/99** r.10). The late filing of the notice of opposition or the late payment of the opposition fee cannot be remedied with **Art.121, Art.122** or **R.139,** because an opponent is not an applicant or proprietor as required by **Art.121** and **Art.122** and the acts of late filing and payment are not errors or mistakes in documents as required by **R.139.** (**T702/89** r.3, **T323/87** r.5, **T128/87** r.2)

4 Notice of opposition deemed (not) to have been filed

On receipt of a notice of opposition the EPO assesses whether the opposition is regarded as filed on the basis of the documents received (D-IV,1.2.1). Only after the opposition is considered filed will the EPO assess the admissibility of the opposition under **Art.101.** All cases where a notice of opposition is regarded as not filed can be derived directly from the EPC. See **T765/08**, r. 9-11 for the legal status of a document deemed not to have been received.

An opposition will be regarded as not filed if:

- The opposition fee is not paid in due time (**Art.99(1)**), causing the opposition to be deemed not to have been filed.
- The notice of opposition has no signature (**R.76(3)** in conjunction with **R.50(3)**), and the signature is not provided in due time, causing the notice being deemed not to have been filed (D-IV,1.2.1(ii)). Further processing and re-establishment are not available for the opponent. If, after invitation by the formalities officer, the signature is provided in due time, the notice retains its date of filing (**R.50(3)**).
- The opponent is represented and an authorisation is not filed on invitation by the EPO within the time set (**R.152(2)**). The act of filing is deemed not to have been carried out (**R.152(6)**).
- The notice of opposition is not in an official language of the EPO according to **R.3(1)** nor in an admissible non-EPO language according to **Art.14(4)**, e.g. in Japanese. The opposition will be regarded as not filed, unless the opposition is filed in an admissible language before the end of the opposition period (**Art.14(4)**). **R.6(2)** does not apply to an opposition filed in Japanese, because the opposition is not filed in an admissible non-EPO language according to **Art.14(4)**.
- The notice of opposition is filed in an official language of a contracting state but the opponent is not entitled to use the language according to **Art.14(4)**. Hence, a notice of opposition in Dutch filed by a German opponent is deemed not to have been filed, even if the opponent is represented by a Dutch representative (**Art.14(4); T149/85**).
- The notice of opposition is filed in an admissible non-EPO language but the translation of the notice required under **Art.14(4)** is not filed within the later of one month after filing the notice or the end of the opposition period (**R.6(2)**). Hence, the notice is regarded as not received (this applies to all further documents filed at the EPO) (**Art.14(4)**). (**T193/87**; D-IV,1.2.1(iv))

5 **Procedure after filing**

An opposition division is the competent department of the EPO to deal with the notice of opposition (**Art.19(1)**). It first assesses whether the notice of opposition is deemed to have been filed or not, next it examines the admissibility of the opposition (**Art.101(1)** and **R.77**) and finally it examines the allowability of the opposition, i.e. whether the invoked grounds for opposition prejudice the maintenance of the patent (**Art.101(1)**).

The following four cases may arise following the filing an opposition:

- No opposition exists, because the notice of opposition is deemed not to have been filed, e.g. due to late filing of the notice of opposition or late payment of the opposition fee. An already paid opposition fee will be refunded. See **Art.101(1):1** and D-IV,1.4.1.
- An opposition has been filed but there are major errors in the notice of opposition. The errors must be remedied according to **R.77(1)** within the opposition time limit, otherwise the opposition is inadmissible. The fee paid for an inadmissible opposition is not refunded. See **R.77(1):1** and D-IV,1.2.2.1.
- An opposition has been filed but there are small errors in the notice of opposition. The errors must be corrected according to **R.77(2)** within a period to be set by the EPO (normally two months) (D-IV,1.3.2, 1.4.2), otherwise the notice is inadmissible. See **R.77(2)** and D-IV,1.2.2.2.
- An admissible opposition and been filed and the opposition will be examined according to **Art.101**.

Art. 99(2) The opposition shall apply to the European patent in all the Contracting States in which that patent has effect.

1 **Territorial extent of opposition**

The opposition is in respect of all designated states. An opposition filed in respect of only some of the designated states is treated as if it were filed in respect of all designated states (D-I,3). The outcome of the opposition proceedings also applies to the extension states and validation states, based on their national law (see **Art.169:4** and e.g. OJ 2016 A5 §17 for Morocco).

The patent in opposition proceedings may have different claims, description and drawings for different designated states because of national prior rights (**R.138**), European prior rights under EPC1973 (see **Art.54(3):3**), or a transfer of the patent to an entitled third party for some but not all designated states (**R.18(2)**; **R.78(2)**).

Art. 99(3) Opponents shall be parties to the opposition proceedings as well as the proprietor of the patent.

1 **Parties to opposition proceedings**

The proprietor is not involved in the formal examination of the notice of opposition by the formalities officer to assess whether the opposition is deemed filed and admissible. This part of the examination is in fact ex parte (D-IV,3; Empel no. 472). The subsequent substantive examination is inter partes.

If an opposition is withdrawn or finally rejected as inadmissible, the opponent is no longer a party in the proceedings (D-I,6). An assumed infringer who intervenes according to **Art.105** becomes party to the opposition proceedings. A third person who has filed observations according to **Art.115** is not a party to the proceedings.

Art. 99(4) Where a person provides evidence that in a Contracting State, following a final decision, he has been entered in the patent register of such State instead of the previous proprietor, such person shall, at his request, replace the previous proprietor in respect of such State. Notwithstanding Article 118, the previous proprietor and the person making the request shall not be regarded as joint proprietors unless both so request.

Art.118 Unity of patent
Implemented by:
R.78 Procedure where the proprietor is not entitled

1 **Opposition and entitlement procedure**
If during the opposition period or the opposition procedure third parties provide proof to the EPO that they have started court proceedings seeking a judgement that they are entitled to the patent, the opposition procedure will be stayed, unless they consent to continuation of the opposition procedure (**R.78(1)**).

The Protocol on Recognition, according to which entitlement decisions of national courts must be recognised in all EPC Contracting States, applies only to patent applications and not to patents. Therefore, a national decision on entitlement to a patent is not recognised by the other states designated in the patent on the basis of the Protocol. However, such a decision can be recognised in the EU based on EU regulation 1215/2012 and in most EFTA countries based on the Lugano Convention.

When the entitled person has replaced the first proprietor for some but not all designated states and the entitled person and first proprietor do not request to become joint proprietors, there will be two opposition procedures running at the same time before the same opposition division. This allows new proprietors to independently defend the part of the patent transferred to them. In such a case, the outcome of the opposition can be different for the respective states (see **R.78(2)**).

Art. 100 Grounds for opposition

Opposition may only be filed on the grounds that:

(a) the subject-matter of the European patent is not patentable under Articles 52 to 57;

(b) the European patent does not disclose the invention in a manner sufficiently clear and complete for it to be carried out by a person skilled in the art;

(c) the subject-matter of the European patent extends beyond the content of the application as filed, or, if the patent was granted on a divisional application or on a new application filed under Article 61, beyond the content of the earlier application as filed.

Art.52 Patentable inventions
Art.53 Exceptions to patentability
Art.54 Novelty
Art.55 Non-prejudicial disclosures
Art.56 Inventive step
Art.57 Industrial application
Art.61 Application filed by non-entitled person

1 **Grounds for opposition**

The list of grounds for opposition in **Art.100** is exhaustive in view of the word 'only' in **Art.100**.

The grounds for opposition must, in principle, be set out in the notice of opposition. The EPO has restricted the possibilities for introducing new grounds during the opposition procedure, i.e. after expiry of the 9-month opposition period (see **R.76(2):4.3.1**). See **R.76(2):4.3.3** for a discussion of what grounds are regarded as separate grounds.

1.1 PATENTABILITY (ART.100(A))

The ground of **Art.100(a)** applies if the subject-matter of the claims of the patent as granted is not considered to be an invention under **Art.52**, if it falls under one of the exceptions to patentability (**Art.53**), if it is not new (**Art.54**), if it does not involve an inventive step (**Art.56**) or if it is not susceptible of industrial application (**Art.57**). The opposition procedure is especially suitable for demonstrating a lack of patentability in view of an oral disclosure or prior use.

A notice of opposition based solely on the ground of lack of novelty in view of a national prior right is inadmissible, because a national prior right is not prior art within the meaning of **Art.54(3)** and cannot, therefore, support the ground of **Art.100(a)** (D-III,5; **T550/88** hn1 and hn2). Nevertheless, during the opposition proceedings the patent may be amended in view of national prior rights (**R.138**, H-II,3.3, see also **R.80**).

1.2 DISCLOSURE (ART.100(B))

Art.100(b) relates to lack of compliance with the requirement of sufficiency of disclosure of **Art.83**.

If an embodiment of the invention is not sufficiently disclosed, that embodiment should be deleted from the patent. If the proprietor does not remove it, the embodiment itself cannot be revoked, because the EPO can only decide on the patent in the text submitted or approved by the proprietor (**Art.113(2)**); in this case the entire patent has to be revoked.

1.3 EXTENSION (ART.100(C))

Art.100(c) corresponds to **Art.123(2)** and provides a sanction in case the claims of the patent lack basis in the application as filed, and for a patent granted on a divisional application also in case the claims as granted lack basis in the earlier application as filed (**Art.76(1)**).

If the application as filed is in a non-EPO language, the claims as granted must have a basis in the application as filed in the non-EPO language (**Art.70(2)**). The opposition division may assume that the translation of the application filed during the grant procedure is correct (**R.7**), unless evidence to the contrary is provided, for example by the opponent (D-V,6.1).

2 **Invalid grounds for opposition**

Grounds other than those of **Art.100** cannot be used in the notice of opposition. Examples of invalid grounds:

- The granted claims do not comply with the unity requirement of **Art.82** (**T162/85** r.9; see **Art.82:3**).
- The granted claims are not clear and concise in the sense of **Art.84** (see **Art.84:4** and **T409/91** for the relation between **Art.83** and **Art.84**). **Art.84** was not included as ground of opposition, because the other grounds for opposition were regarded adequate to deal with the issues concerned and allowing clarity objections would delay the opposition proceedings too much (travaux préparatoires EPC1973, see **G3/14** r.69).

The check of **Art.84** is only made if the claims are amended in the opposition procedure; claims unclear from the outset can be maintained (**T23/86; G3/14**). Clearness and conciseness are only relevant in as far as they can influence decisions on issues under **Art.100** (for example by leading to a broader claim interpretation) or arise in amendments in consequence of these issues (**T127/85; T23/86**). See also **Art.101(3):1.**

- A claim is not divided in preamble and characterising part as required by **R.43(1)**. This is merely a matter for the grant procedure (**T99/85**).
- Inadequate acknowledgement of the state of the art in the patent (**T220/85** r.3).
- A re-establishment of rights during the grant procedure is unfounded (**Art.122**).
- A mere allegation that a priority claim is invalid. However, this may introduce relevant state of the art supporting one of the grounds of **Art.100(a)**.
- Double patenting (**T98/19**) See also **Art.97(2):2**).
- For a patent granted on a divisional application, an objection that the parent was not pending when the divisional application was filed (**T1316/20**).

Moreover, an opponent cannot argue that the priority of the patent is invalid on the ground that the patent application was filed after the priority year and the decision of the Receiving Section (or examining division) to grant re-establishment was unjustified (**T1482/21**).

Art. 101 Examination of the opposition – Revocation or maintenance of the European patent

1 **Opposition division**

The examination of the opposition is carried out by an opposition division, which consists of three technically qualified examiners. At least two of the technically qualified examiners, one of which is the chair of the division, must not have taken part in the grant procedure (**Art.19(2)**, D-II,2). If necessary, the division is enlarged with one legally qualified examiner (D-II,2.2). All decisions are taken by and oral proceedings conducted before all three or four examiners. An outline of the opposition procedure is given in OJ 2016 A42.

Art. 101(1) If the opposition is admissible, the Opposition Division shall examine, in accordance with the Implementing Regulations, whether at least one ground for opposition under Article 100 prejudices the maintenance of the European patent. During this examination, the Opposition Division shall invite the parties, as often as necessary, to file observations on communications from another party or issued by itself.

Implemented by:
R.77 Rejection of the opposition as inadmissible
R.79 Preparation for the examination of the opposition
R.80 Amendment of the patent
R.81 Examination of the opposition
R.83 Request for documents
R.84 Continuation of the proceedings by the EPO of its own motion
R.85 Transfer of the patent
R.86 Documents in opposition proceedings
R.142 Interruption of proceedings

1 **Procedure prior to assessment of admissibility**

As soon as the EPO receives an opposition, it enters the filing date in the Register, publishes the filing date in the Bulletin (D-I,8) and sends a copy of the opposition to the proprietor for information (D-IV,1.1).

If the formalities officer notes deficiencies which may cause the notice of opposition being deemed not to have been filed (see **Art.99(1):4**) and which can still be remedied, the formalities officer may, as a courtesy, invite the opponent to remedy them within the appropriate time limit (D-IV,1.3.3). Notification of a missing signature is not a matter of discretion; this notification must be carried out according to **R.50(3)**.

If the deficiencies are not remedied in time, the formalities officer will notify the opponent that the opposition is deemed not to have been filed (**Art.119, R.112(1)**); the opponent can request the opposition division to take an appealable decision on this matter under **R.112(2)**. If such a decision is not requested within two months after notification, and if there is no other valid opposition pending, the proceedings are closed and the parties are informed accordingly. The documents submitted with the notice of opposition become part of the file, and are regarded as observations under **Art.115**. The opposition fee is refunded in this case, as there is no legal basis for the payment (D-IV,1.4.1, **T193/87** hn). Since no opposition exists, the assessment of admissibility under **R.77** will not be carried out.

2 **Assessment of admissibility**

When the opposition is regarded as filed, the admissibility of the opposition will subsequently be assessed according to **R.77** on the basis of the contents of the notice of opposition as filed and any correction filed within the opposition period (**T522/94** hn. II). Serious deficiencies must be corrected before expiry of the opposition period (**R.77(1)**), whereas minor deficiencies can be corrected within a period set by the EPO, which may expire after the end of the opposition period (**R.77(2)**). The formalities officer may, as a courtesy, notify the opponent of deficiencies under **R.77(1)** which can still be remedied; in contrast, the formalities officer must notify deficiencies as required by **R.77(2)** (D-IV,1.3.3). These notifications may be made together with any courtesy notification in respect of **R.77(1)**. See **R.77** and notes thereto for deficiencies and the procedure for remedy. If the deficiencies are corrected in due time, the opposition will be regarded as admissible.

If the opposition is regarded as inadmissible and the opponent's right to be heard has been respected, the formalities officer will take a decision to reject the notice of opposition as inadmissible, which decision is also communicated to the proprietor under **R.77(3)** (D-IV,1.4.2). Where the inadmissibility relates to facts, evidence or arguments, the file is submitted to the opposition division to take the decision (D-IV,1.4.2; D-IV,3). There is no refund of opposition fee if the opposition is inadmissible because the fee was paid with legal basis. The opposition proceedings have in fact started and a substantial amount of work has already been done. The opposition division will not consider the substance of an inadmissible notice of opposition (**T925/91**), although provided at least one admissible opposition has also been filed, the division may consider of its own motion any relevant art cited in an inadmissible opposition (**T966/02** r.2.4).

The question of admissibility may be raised all through the opposition procedure, even in opposition appeal proceedings (**T289/91**). The EPO must check admissibility ex officio in every phase of the opposition and ensuing appeal (**T522/94** r.3). The EPO or the proprietor may challenge admissibility, e.g. on lack of facts, evidence or arguments (**T222/85**; D-IV,5.1). The decision on admissibility is normally taken together with the final decision.

3 **Preparation of the examination**

If the opposition is regarded as admissible, the formalities officer will invite proprietor to file observations and any amendments to the patent (**R.79(1)**). The amendments must comply with **R.80**. The EPO forwards the response of the proprietor to the opponents and invites them to reply, if considered expedient (**R.79(3)**). The dossier is subsequently forwarded to the opposition division. During the examination of the opposition the opposition division may invite parties to comment on specific issues (**R.81(2), (3)**).

The usual period for responding to communications under **R.79** and **81** is four months for matters of substance and two months for other matters. These periods may be extended exceptionally following a reasoned request (see **R.132(2)**:2; E-VIII,1.6.1).

4 **Acceleration of the procedure**

The total time needed for a decision in straightforward cases is fifteen months from expiry of the opposition period (OJ 2016 A43).

The processing of the opposition will be accelerated if an infringement or revocation action is pending before the Unified Court or a national court of a contracting state and a party to the opposition proceedings files a reasoned request with the EPO. Acceleration is also possible if the EPO is informed by the Unified Patent Court, the national court, or the competent authority of a contracting state that there are pending infringement or revocations actions.

The EPO will make every effort to issue the next procedural step within three months from the request. The parties should cooperate in making their submissions promptly and in full. Extension of periods above the normal four months will be granted only in exceptional, duly substantiated cases. (OJ 2023 A99)

Acceleration measures depend on when the EPO is informed of parallel court proceedings. These measures include inviting the proprietor to comment on the opposition within three months, issuing the summons within two months of the proprietor's reply and with minimum notice, rescheduling oral proceedings to the earliest possible date, and providing the decision and minutes within one month of the oral proceedings. (E-VIII,5)Further reasons for acceleration are given in D-VII,1.2, e.g. where the opposition proceedings are of a considerably longer duration than usual. The PACE program is not applicable in opposition (OJ 2015 A94 §9).

5 **Extent of substantive examination**

The extent of the substantive examination is restricted by the extent of the opposition stated in the notice of opposition according to **R.76(2)(c)**. The grounds given in the notice of opposition define the legal framework of the examination. Addition of grounds during the procedure is restricted as set out in **R.76(2)**:4. Facts and evidence should be provided in the notice of opposition (**R.76(2)(c)**). If filed later, they may be disregarded (**Art.114(2)**; **R.76(2)**:4.3). Amendments of the patent made during the opposition procedure are open to a range of objections according to **Art.101(3)**.

The opposition division is not obliged to consider all the grounds for opposition referred to in **Art.100**. The examination of grounds for opposition is guided by a set of principles developed by the Enlarged Board. The opposition division is obliged to examine only those grounds for opposition listed in the opponent's statement under **R.76(2)(c)**. In addition to this, the opposition division may in accordance with **Art.114(1)** examine of its own motion any ground for opposition under **Art.100** not invoked by the opponent where said ground is relevant and prejudices the maintenance of the European patent. (**G10/91** hn.2; **R.81(1)**)

The practice of the office is to primarily consider the grounds set out in the notice of opposition, following **G10/91** and as laid down in **Art.101(1)** and **R.81(1)**. However, the opposition division tends to admit new grounds at any stage of the proceedings if they are prima facie relevant (D-V,2.2; E-VI,2).

6 Substantive examination of the opposition

The substantive examination of the opposition must be carried out in accordance with **R.81**. Chapter D-V of the Guidelines gives details of the examination of the grounds of **Art.100**.

The patent may be amended only when the amendments are occasioned by grounds of **Art.100** (**R.80**). The amendment may not extend the subject-matter of the patent beyond the original disclosure (**Art.123(2)**) nor extend the protection conferred (**Art.123(3)**). It is permissible to replace a granted single independent claim by two or more independent claims, if this is the most appropriate response to the grounds of opposition (**T263/05**). Subject-matter in the description of the application which was deleted during prosecution as no longer relevant to the claimed invention may not generally be reinstated during opposition (**T684/02**).

If the parties in an opposition procedure take different views, the burden of proof is on the opponent (**T219/83**). If the opponent proves that the teaching of the patent does not lead to the claimed result and the opposition division shares this view, the proprietor must prove to the contrary (F-III,4).

According to **Art.101(1)** and **R.79(1)**, the proprietor has a right to file observations on a notice of opposition. Any further observations of parties are only admissible if the opposition division deems them necessary and expedient. This is in the interest of the efficient conduct of the opposition proceedings. The parties must follow the guidance of the opposition division, and not proceed of their own motion. (**T295/87**)

The opposition division may invite parties to file further observations to clarify issues. All communications and replies thereto are communicated to all parties (**R.81(2)**). The proprietor will be invited, where appropriate, to file amendments to the patent (**R.81(3)**). To comply with the requirement of **Art.113(1)**, any communication to the proprietor will contain a reasoned statement, covering all grounds against maintenance of the patent, where necessary (**R.81(3)**). Oral evidence may be taken (**Art.117**, **R.117**, D-VI,1; E-IV,1.2 and 1.4) or an additional search may be carried out, where necessary (D-VI,5).

The format of documents sent to the EPO must comply with **R.35-50** according to **R.86**; for example documents must be signed (**R.50(3)**).

The period for filing the observations is normally fixed at four months (D-VI,3.1 and E-VIII,1.2(ii)), which may be extended on request to six months in exceptional, duly substantiated cases (E-VIII,1.6). No direct loss of rights occurs upon failure to comply with a time limit fixed for filing observations in opposition proceedings (**G1/90** r.8). The EPO regards submissions and requests from parties as received in time when they have been filed before closure of the proceedings (see **G12/91** hn); however, facts and evidence may be disregarded under **Art.114(2)** when not filed in due time (E-VIII,1.8, similar to **R.83**, second sentence).

Oral proceedings are held if requested by a party or considered expedient by the opposition division (**Art.116(1)**). The parties are summoned in accordance with **R.115(1)** and their attention is drawn to the points to be discussed (**R.116**). The conduct of oral proceedings is set out in **Art.116:3**.

Art. 101(2) If the Opposition Division is of the opinion that at least one ground for opposition prejudices the maintenance of the European patent, it shall revoke the patent. Otherwise, it shall reject the opposition.

1 **Decision to revoke the patent by the EPO**

After the proprietor has been given the chance to comment, the opposition division is in a position to decide the case. The proprietor can avoid the risk of an unexpected decision revoking the patent by asking for oral proceedings, thereby deferring any decision.

The revocation can be on any of the grounds mentioned in **Art.100**, not necessarily those put forward by the opponent. The opposition division may of its own motion add grounds to those relied on by the opponent which are prima facie prejudicial to the maintenance of the patent (**R.81(1)**, second sentence; **G10/91** hn1). If the opposition division adds new grounds of its own motion, the parties can expect to be given an opportunity to comment on those grounds (**T515/05**). See **R.76(2):4.3** for adding grounds during the procedure.

For the European patent to be revoked, it is sufficient for one of the grounds for opposition to prejudice its maintenance. The patent is maintained where none of the grounds for opposition prejudices its maintenance. (OJ 2007 se4 EN p.110)

2 **Revocation of the patent at the proprietor's request**

A proprietor has several options for having the patent revoked by the EPO whilst avoiding any substantive reasoning on patentability in the decision revoking the patent. Such reasoning could otherwise affect proceedings relating to other patents in the same patent family before other patent offices or courts.

Traditionally, a proprietor who wishes the patent to be revoked by the opposition division proceeds by stating that they no longer approve the text in which the patent was granted and do not submit an amended text. The patent is then revoked in view of **Art.113(2)** (D-VI,2.2; D-VIII,1.2.5; **T73/84**). The opposition division also revokes the patent if the proprietor simply requests that the patent be revoked in the opposition procedure (D-VI,2.2).

If the proprietor unambiguously surrenders, abandons or renounces the patent, this is interpreted as a request that the patent be revoked (D-VIII,1.2.5). Generally, a statement by the proprietor making it unambiguously clear that it is no longer desired that the patent be maintained is considered to be a request for revocation, irrespective of the wording used (**T237/86**, hn; D-VII,5.1).

In the case that the opposition division has found that an amended form of the patent meets the requirements of the EPC, the proprietor can also effect the revocation of the patent by refraining from filing translations of the amended claims, leading to the revocation under **R.82(3)**.

Note that a proprietor cannot request the EPO to terminate the opposition procedure without a decision. Even if the patent has been surrendered before the national offices of all states, **R.84(1)** gives the opponent the right to continue the opposition proceedings.

A request to revoke the patent during opposition proceedings should be distinguished from a request for revocation under **Art.105a(1)**. The former request will be dealt with in the inter-partes opposition procedure, whereas the latter request normally starts an ex parte revocation procedure based on **Art.105a**. However, a request for revocation under **Art.105a(1)** filed during pending opposition proceedings is not admissible (**Art.105a(2)**). Conversely, if an opposition is filed while revocation proceedings under **Art.105a(1)** are pending, the revocation will take precedence (**R.93(2):1**).

Art. 101(3) If the Opposition Division is of the opinion that, taking into consideration the amendments made by the proprietor of the European patent during the opposition proceedings, the patent and the invention to which it relates
(a) meet the requirements of this Convention, it shall decide to maintain the patent as amended, provided that the conditions laid down in the Implementing Regulations are fulfilled;
(b) do not meet the requirements of this Convention, it shall revoke the patent.

Implemented by:
R.82 Maintenance of the European patent in amended form

1 **Maintenance of patent in amended form**
As long as the patent remains unamended, **Art.101(2)** limits the jurisdiction of the EPO during opposition proceedings to a consideration of the grounds for opposition mentioned in **Art.100**. In contrast, when the patent has been amended, **Art.101(3)** confers jurisdiction on the EPO to decide upon the patent in the light of the requirements of the EPC as a whole. However, objections based upon articles other than **Art.100** are not allowed if the objections do not arise out of the amendments made (**T301/87** hn.1).

The claims of an amended patent may be examined for compliance with the requirements of **Art.84**, such as clarity, only when, and then only to the extent that, an amendment introduces non-compliance with **Art.84**. Hence, an amendment of the patent does not open the door for a general assessment of the patent for compliance with all requirements of the EPC. A dormant lack of clarity in the patent as granted that does not arise directly from an amendment made by the proprietor does not give rise to a clarity examination. Similarly, the combination of an independent claim and a dependent claim does not introduce a new claim and should therefore not be assessed for clarity. However, a claim must be examined for compliance with **Art.84** if a feature from a dependent claim as granted is introduced into an independent claim as granted and the introduction disconnects this feature from other features of that dependent claim and causes an alleged lack of compliance with **Art.84**. (**G3/14**; see D-V,5 for more clarity examples)

Unity is not a ground for opposition, because **Art.100** does not refer to **Art.82**. Neither must a patent being maintained in amended form under **Art.101(3)** comply with the unity requirements of **Art.82** (**G1/91**). **T263/05** extends **G1/91** such that other requirements of the EPC only apply where it is reasonable that they do so. In particular, once an amendment is considered to be necessary and appropriate, purely administrative provisions of the EPC do not apply.

See **R.82** for the procedure for maintenance in amended form. If the proprietor does not approve the text and does not submit a new text, the patent is to be revoked (**T73/84**).

The subject-matter of the amended patent may not extend beyond the content of the application as filed, and the protection conferred by the patent may not be extended by any amendment (**Art.123(2), (3)**). The opposition division does not assess independent claims which are not opposed; however, where a process claim is opposed, a product-by-process claim referring to the process is considered to be implicitly covered by the extent of opposition (**G9/91**; D-V,2.1).

2 **Revocation of the patent**
The patent will still be revoked, in spite of the opposition division's favourable opinion, if:
- the translations of the amended claims in the other two languages of the EPO are not filed within the three-month period set by the opposition division (**R.82(2)**), and are furthermore not filed within two months of notification (**R.82(3)**);
- no new representative is appointed within a two-month period set by the EPO, after an interruption of the proceedings because of death or legal incapacity of the former representative (**R.142(1)(c)**), while representation is necessary according to **Art.133(2)**. (**R.142(3)(a)**)

The proprietor can remedy failure to meet the above time limits with re-establishment (**Art.122**). Further processing is not available because the periods do not relate to a patent application but to a patent.

Art. 102 (deleted)

Art. 103 Publication of a new specification of the European patent

If the European patent is maintained as amended under Article 101, paragraph 3(a), the European Patent Office shall publish a new specification of the European patent as soon as possible after the mention of the opposition decision has been published in the European Patent Bulletin.

Art.101(3)(a) Maintenance of the patent in amended form
Implemented by:
R.87 Content and form of the new specification

1 **Publication**
The words 'as soon as possible' in the provision indicate that it is not always technically possible to publish the new specification on the same day as the mention of the opposition decision is published in the Bulletin (OJ 2007 se4 EN p.112). The new specification is published in electronic form (**R.87** referring to **R.73(2)**).

Art. 104 Costs

1 **General**
Each party to proceedings pays its own costs unless the opposition division orders a different apportionment of costs (**Art.104(1)**), where one party has to pay some or all of the costs incurred by another party. For example, the division may order an opponent to pay to the proprietor the costs incurred by the proprietor in attending oral proceedings. An apportionment of costs is ordered where reasons of equity demand it, i.e. for reasons of fairness. Since different apportionments are the only exception in the EPC to the principle that each party pays its own costs, there is no room for a practice where the losing party reimburses the costs of the winning party.

See also **R.122** for the costs of hearing witnesses and taking evidence by the EPO.

Art. 104(1) Each party to the opposition proceedings shall bear the costs it has incurred, unless the Opposition Division, for reasons of equity, orders, in accordance with the Implementing Regulations, a different apportionment of costs.

Implemented by:
R.88(1) Procedure for apportionment of costs

1 **Reasons for apportionment**

A decision to apportion costs differently requires special circumstances, such as improper behaviour, which make it equitable to award costs against one of the parties (**T170/83**). An apportionment of costs is ordered when the conduct of a party is not in keeping with the care required to assure the effective exercise of the rights involved or in response to culpable actions of an irresponsible or even malicious nature (**T765/89**). Since the apportionment of costs is a matter of equity, no absolute rules can be given for when a cost apportionment is justified or not. Costs may even be apportioned against the winning party, e.g. in the case where a prior art document is filed late by the opponent without justification and the revocation of the patent is based on that document, a cost apportionment may be given against the opponent.

Art.16(1) RPBA gives a few examples where a different apportionment of costs may be ordered in appeal proceedings: amendment of a party's case, extension of a period, acts or omissions prejudicing the timely and efficient conduct of oral proceedings, failure to comply with a direction of the board, abuse of procedure. In all cases, the equity requirement of **Art.104** must be complied with.

Examples from the Guidelines and case law:

- The proprietor requests revocation of the patent (see **Art.99(3):1**) just before the oral proceedings and it was already clear that the proprietor had no case when the summons was issued. The unnecessary costs involved in preparing for the oral proceedings incurred by the opponent may be charged to the proprietor. (see D-IX,1.4)
- Relevant facts and evidence, including prior art, are submitted at a late stage without a good reason (**T117/86**); the same applies for requests.
- Notification just prior to the oral proceedings that a party will not appear and the non-attendance renders the oral proceedings unnecessary (**T937/04** r.5.2). A different apportionment may not be appropriate, however, in cases such as those involving sudden serious illness. Parties summoned to oral proceedings have the equitable obligation to inform the EPO as soon as they know that they will not be attending (**T212/07**).
- Culpably making inaccurate or false statements, thereby requiring the other party to incur costs in gathering further evidence (**T952/00**).

Apportionment of costs cannot be based on the withdrawal of an appeal, because such withdrawal is an absolute right. Based on the principle of free party disposition, this right may not be restricted, not even implicitly, by the threat of cost apportionment (**T490/05**). The Board can decide on apportionment of costs even after withdrawal of the (sole) appeal (**T765/89**).

Art. 104(2) The procedure for fixing costs shall be laid down in the Implementing Regulations.

Implemented by:
R.88(2) Procedure for fixing costs

1 **Procedure**

The procedure for fixing costs is set out below for the opposition division. Boards of appeal can also apportion costs according to **Art.104(1)** and also directly fix the costs under **Art.104(2)** in appeal (see e.g. **T930/92** r.4.1 and **T934/91** hn1). They derive such power from **Art.111(1)**, second sentence. A decision of a board fixing the costs cannot be appealed (**T934/91** hn.2).

The procedure for apportioning and fixing costs involves the following three steps:

1 The first step in a cost apportionment is a decision taken by the opposition division under **Art.104(1)** which orders an apportionment of costs different from the one where each party pays its own costs (**R.88(1)**). The EPO may take such a decision of its own motion or on request of a party (D-IX,1.2). The decision states which costs are differently apportioned. See **R.88(1)** for the kind of costs that can be taken into consideration. The costs ordered to be paid may be all or part of the costs incurred by the party, e.g. 75% of the opponent's costs for attending oral proceedings. The actual amounts are determined in the second step. A board may express the costs ordered directly as a specific amount (Art.16(2) RPBA). The decision apportioning costs cannot be the sole subject of an appeal (**R.97(1)**; **Art.106(3)**). Hence, a decision apportioning costs, or refusing a request for cost apportionment, cannot be appealed by a party who is not adversely affected by the main decision on the patent (**Art.107**), even if that party must pay the apportioned costs. Neither can such a party challenge the cost apportionment as a respondent in an appeal of the other party (**T1237/05**). Furthermore, an appeal relating to apportionment of costs is inadmissible if the appeal relating to the decision on the patent is inadmissible for lack of substantiation, with the possible exception of a case involving a substantial procedural violation (**T154/90**, hn.I, II).

2 In the second step, at least one party requests the opposition division to fix the actual amount of the costs to be paid under the above decision apportioning them (**R.88(2)**). The request may only be filed after the decision apportioning the costs has become final (**R.88(2)**), i.e. after the expiry of the appeal period or after any appeal, or directly if the decision cannot be appealed under **R.97(1)**. The request must be accompanied by a bill of costs and supporting evidence (**R.88(2)**). A formalities officer with specialist knowledge examines the credibility of the costs (**R.88(2)**), fixes the costs and notifies the parties (D-IX,2.1). In the case of costs apportioned by the Board, the Board directly fixes the costs upon request (**T2165/08**).

3 The third step provides the possibility for a review by the opposition division of the costs fixed by the formalities officer. The party desiring such a review must file a reasoned request for a decision by the opposition division and pay the prescribed fee within one month of the communication on the fixing of costs (**R.88(3)**). The opposition division takes its decision without oral proceedings (**R.88(4)**). The decision is appealable, but only if the amount of the costs exceeds the amount of the appeal fee (**R.97(2)**). It is not clear whether the amount of the costs relates to the total amount to be paid by a party or the amount which is in dispute.

Art. 104(3) Any final decision of the European Patent Office fixing the amount of costs shall be dealt with, for the purpose of enforcement in the Contracting States, in the same way as a final decision given by a civil court of the State in which enforcement is to take place. Verification of such decision shall be limited to its authenticity.

1 **Enforcing payment**
Art.104(3) provides means to enforce payment of the apportioned costs. Since the EPO cannot enforce payment from an unwilling party, the final decision by the EPO is given the same status as a national decision, allowing enforcement under national law. The decision referred to also covers the final fixing of the costs by the opposition division, according to D-IX,3. A party that wishes to enforce payment under national law should request a review of the fixing of the costs because only such a review results in a decision that will have national effect.

Art. 105 Intervention of the assumed infringer

1 **General**
The purpose of **Art.105** is to safeguard an assumed infringer as far as possible against costly and time-consuming revocation proceedings before various national courts by providing a route into the centralised opposition procedure before the EPO as long as it is within the competence of the EPO to deal with the question of validity of the patent concerned. Because the nine-month opposition period of **Art.99(1)** has often lapsed before infringement court proceedings are started, **Art.105** gives the assumed infringer a period to intervene in a pending opposition procedure or pending opposition appeal procedure concerning the patent (**G1/94**); after a valid intervention the intervener is treated as an opponent.

The intervention may be based on any ground for opposition under **Art.100**, even a new ground (**G1/94**). A new ground raised by an intervention during appeal proceedings may cause the case to be remitted to the first instance (**G1/94** r.13). The intervener cannot challenge any board of appeal decision taken in the opposition which has become final at the time of the intervention (**T694/01** hn, **T689/19** r. 4).

Art. 105(1) Any third party may, in accordance with the Implementing Regulations, intervene in opposition proceedings after the opposition period has expired, if the third party proves that
(a) proceedings for infringement of the same patent have been instituted against him, or
(b) following a request of the proprietor of the patent to cease alleged infringement, the third party has instituted proceedings for a ruling that he is not infringing the patent.

Implemented by:
R.89 Filing of notice of intervention

1 **Person and time limit for intervention**
Alleged infringers must file the notice of intervention within three months (**R.89(1)**) from the institution of the first action between them and the proprietor, and pay the opposition fee in the same period (**R.89(2)**).The first action is either proceedings for infringement instituted by the proprietor or proceedings for a ruling on non-infringement instituted by the alleged infringer (**Art.105(1)**(a) and (**b**); **T296/93** hn). The proceedings must be directed to establishing infringement or non-infringement as a final outcome; proceedings directed to the preservation of evidence to enable a party to initiate separate infringement proceedings are not sufficient (**T439/17** hn.1; D-VII,6(i)).

In the former case the serving of a writ under national law, making the alleged infringer aware of the proceedings, is regarded as the institution of the proceedings from which the three-month period runs (**T694/01** r.2.3). Likewise, for an interim injunction granted in ex parte proceedings, i.e. without the alleged infringer being involved, the date the order is served on the intervener is regarded as the trigger for the period, on the basis that the intervener is not aware of the ex parte proceedings until service of the order (**T452/05** r.1.2). As long as relevant court proceedings have been instituted, it makes no difference whether the court action has been later withdrawn or not – an intervention is still admissible even if the action has been withdrawn when the notice of intervention is filed (**T1809/22**).

Under **Art.105(1)(b)**, interveners must show both that they have received a 'request' of the proprietor and that this demands the intervener to 'cease' infringement. A criminal complaint against the alleged infringer may also be accepted as a trigger (**T1713/11** r.2). Mere warnings of infringement and threats of legal action are however insufficient (**T887/04** r.2.1). National law determines whether the proceedings for a non-infringement ruling are to be instituted before a court or before another body (OJ 2007 se4 EN p.114).

1.1 INTERVENTION DURING OPPOSITION PROCEEDINGS

According to **Art.105(1)** a third party may intervene 'in opposition proceedings'; hence, opposition proceedings must be in existence at the time of filing the intervention (**G4/91** hn1). The intervener must pay the opposition fee (**R.89(2)**).

An intervention filed before expiry of the nine-month opposition period will be regarded as a normal opposition according to **Art.99**.

After interveners have complied with all requirements of **Art.105**, their status corresponds to that of an opponent under **Art.99**. In particular, they are entitled to file an appeal under **Art.107**, first sentence, or participate in an appeal as party as of right under **Art.107**, second sentence. The valid filing of the appeal requires that the intervener pays the appeal fee as required under **Art.108**. (**G3/04** r.4, 10, 11)

The above intervener has an independent right to continue the proceedings in case all other oppositions are withdrawn. Interveners who have filed an appeal also have the right to continue the appeal proceedings on their own when the other appellants have withdrawn their appeals. (**G3/04** r.10)

1.2 INTERVENTION DURING TWO-MONTH APPEAL PERIOD

If the intervention is made after the decision terminating the opposition proceedings has been issued by the opposition division but before the expiry of the two-month appeal period, and the decision is not appealed, then the intervention is inadmissible because there are no pending proceedings as required by **Art.105(1)** (**G4/91** hn. IV). The decision is regarded as issued in written proceedings on the day the decision is handed over to the EPO postal service (**T631/94**, **G12/91**, **R.111(1)**:4). An intervention filed after the announcement of the decision of the Opposition Division in oral proceedings, but before the notification of the written decision, was held in **T791/06** to be filed in the appeal proceedings, not in the opposition proceedings. If the decision is appealed, opposition proceedings are still pending and the intervention is admissible (**G4/91** r.6; D-VII,6).

1.3 INTERVENTION DURING APPEAL PROCEEDINGS

An intervention filed during pending appeal proceedings is admissible, as the term 'opposition proceedings' in **Art.105(1)** also includes subsequent appeal proceedings (**G1/94**, following **T338/89**, overruling **T390/90**).

According to **Art.107**, the entitlement to appeal is restricted to parties to the first instance proceedings that led to the decision under appeal. A party that intervenes during the appeal proceedings was not a party to the first instance proceedings, and, hence, has no right to appeal; such an intervener becomes a party as of right in the appeal proceedings. If the sole, or each, appeal is withdrawn, an intervener having this status may not continue the proceedings and the appeal proceedings are terminated for all parties as regard the substantive issues, including any new grounds raised by the intervener (**G3/04** r.6, 10). However, the question of whether an intervener at the appeal stage may continue an appeal after the withdrawal of all appeals has been referred to the Enlarged Board of Appeal in G2/24.

The question of the independent right to continue was also referred in **G4/03**, but the proceedings were terminated because of the withdrawal of the remaining intervention in the referring decision (OJ 2004 p.542).

If the precise time of filing on the same day of the sole appellant's notice of withdrawal of appeal and a notice of intervention can be established, their chronological order must be taken into account (**T517/97**). Withdrawal of an appeal is a procedural act which has immediate effect; its effect is not postponed to midnight of the date of filing (**T517/97** r.4).

Art. 105(2) An admissible intervention shall be treated as an opposition.

1 **Formal requirements for notice of intervention**

A valid intervention requires the filing of a notice of intervention including the proof of institution of proceedings (**Art.105(1)**), the filing of an admissible, i.e. written and reasoned, notice of opposition and payment of the opposition fee (**R.89(2)**), all before the end of the three-month period (**R.89(1)**). Re-establishment after non-compliance with this period is not possible, because re-establishment is in principle only available for an applicant and proprietor, not for an intervener.

When the intervention is filed during pending appeal proceedings, no appeal fee need be paid, because the EPC has no provisions requiring this (**G3/04** r.11; overruling **T1011/92** and **T517/97** r.2). Note, that **R.89(2)** does require payment of the opposition fee in such a case (**G3/04** r.5). The intervener becomes party as of right in the appeal proceedings (**G3/04** r.6).

Although the intervention is treated as an opposition, as an exception the opposition division may dispense with forwarding some communications and invitations to the intervener (**R.79(4)**, D-IV,5.6). The intervener can obtain copies of these documents by file inspection.

Art. 105a Request for limitation or revocation

1 **General**

Art.105a-c provide for the centralised limitation and revocation of European patents by an administrative procedure before the EPO. An important reason to introduce the limitation procedure in EPC2000 was the impossibility of a centralised limitation of the patent by the proprietor after self-opposition was prohibited by **G9/93**. The examining division is competent to take decisions in these limitation and revocation procedures (**R.91**).

Art.105a–c are applicable to European patents already granted at the date of entry into force of EPC2000 and to European patents granted in respect of European patent applications pending at, or filed on or after that date. (OJ 2007 se4 EN p.118)

The limitation procedure is designed to avoid costly and duplicative national disputes over the validity of a European patent and to enhance legal certainty. The procedure may be useful where relevant prior art is discovered after grant of the patent, or the patent is granted with too broad a scope. A request for limitation must include amended claims that constitute a limitation vis-à-vis the claims as granted or as amended in opposition or limitation proceedings (**R.95(2)**). The limitation may relate to a dependent claim only (D-X,4.3.1).

Whilst limited claims may be tailored to products that have come on the market, only amendments which limit one of the claims or which are necessary in view of such a limitation are allowed. It is not permissible to introduce non-limiting amendments in the description or in the claims that are not a consequence of the limitation of the claims, e.g. by tidying up unclear claims, making amendments to improve the patent or making cosmetic changes. Adding dependent claims is also impermissible if not directly caused by the limitation of the claims. (D-X,4.3.1)

Centralised revocation is also possible. The revocation has ex tunc effect. Revocation may be useful when the proprietor owns a controversial patent in a field of technology that attracts a good deal of public interest, thereby limiting damage to the proprietor's reputation. Centralised revocation may also be used to minimise the cost of defending numerous national proceedings.

Art. 105a(1) At the request of the proprietor, the European patent may be revoked or be limited by an amendment of the claims. The request shall be filed with the European Patent Office in accordance with the Implementing Regulations. It shall not be deemed to have been filed until the limitation or revocation fee has been paid.

Implemented by:
R.90 Subject of proceedings
R.91 Competence of the examining division
R.92 Requirements of the request
Rfees2(1)10a Limitation and revocation fee

1 Requirements of the request

Under **Art.105a(1)** a European patent may be revoked or limited (by an amendment of the claims) at the request of the proprietor, subject to payment of a fee. **R.92** sets out the criteria for admissibility. The request must be filed in writing (**R.92(1)**). Electronic filing is possible (see **R.2(1):5**).

The request must include details of the patent proprietor (**R.92(2)(a)**). Where a patent is owned by different proprietors in different states, details of these proprietors and evidence that the requester is entitled to act on their behalf must also be included (**R.92(2)(c)**).

The patent number must be identified, and a list of the contracting states in which the patent has effect must be provided (**R.92(2)(b)**).

Amended claims, and where appropriate an amended description and drawings, must be filed (**R.92(2)(d)**).

R.90 makes clear that only the patent as granted or amended by the EPO may be the subject of limitation or revocation proceedings. Amendments made before national courts or patent offices will not be taken into account, although the proprietor may of course request limitation before the EPO in order to bring the European patent into line with amendments made nationally.

The request is deemed not filed until the limitation or revocation fee has been paid (**Art.105a(1)**). The amount of the limitation and revocation fees is fixed in **Rfees2(1)10a.**

A request for revocation or limitation may be withdrawn at any time (D-X,9).

Art. 105a(2) The request may not be filed while opposition proceedings in respect of the European patent are pending.

Implemented by:
R.93 Precedence of opposition proceedings

1 **Precedence of opposition proceedings**
Art.105a(2) governs the relation between the limitation procedure and opposition proceedings. The priority it gives to opposition proceedings prevents a request for limitation or revocation from being filed when opposition proceedings are already pending. In this case, the request for limitation or revocation is deemed not to have been filed (**R.93(1)**). A proprietor who wants the patent to be revoked can request so in the opposition procedure; the patent will then be revoked by the opposition division with a decision that contains no comments on the patentability of the invention (**Art.101(2):2**).

Where an opposition is filed while limitation proceedings are pending, the limitation proceedings are terminated and the limitation fee is refunded (**R.93(2)**). However, if revocation proceedings are pending when an opposition is filed, the revocation proceedings continue.

The European limitation procedure does not, however, take precedence over national proceedings (national revocation proceedings in particular). Where parallel cases do occur, the national proceedings can be stayed or continued in accordance with the provisions of the relevant national law. Where national proceedings resulting in limitation have already been concluded, the limitation can be extended to further contracting states via limitation proceedings before the EPO. It must also be emphasised that the limitation of a European patent in proceedings before the EPO does not preclude a further limitation in national proceedings. (OJ 2007 se4 EN p.116)

Art. 105b Limitation or revocation of the European patent

Art. 105b(1) The European Patent Office shall examine whether the requirements laid down in the Implementing Regulations for limiting or revoking the European patent have been met.

Implemented by:
R.94 Rejection of the request as inadmissible

1 **Examination of the request**
Under **R.94** the requirements of the request for limitation or revocation set out in **R.92** are examined, and any deficiencies noted. The requester will be notified and invited to correct any such deficiencies within a period to be fixed by the EPO. If the deficiencies are not corrected, the request will be rejected as inadmissible. If the request is admissible, the proceedings progress to the next stage.

The limitation procedure requires the EPO to examine whether the requirements laid down in **R.95** for a requested limitation or revocation have been met. With limitation, this means in particular establishing whether the requested amendment of the claims actually limits the patent, and whether the requirements of **Art.84, Art.123(2)** and **Art.123(3)** are met. The EPO does not examine whether the aim of the limitation - e.g. delimitation with respect to a particular prior art - is achieved, or whether the subject-matter of the limited patent is patentable under **Art.52-57** EPC.

In the event that the requirements of **R.95** are not met, the examining division will offer one opportunity to correct deficiencies and to offer further amendments to the claims (and description and drawings, if appropriate). The time limit is to be specified by the division (**R.95(2)**).

Art. 105b(2) If the European Patent Office considers that the request for limitation or revocation of the European patent meets these requirements, it shall decide to limit or revoke the European patent in accordance with the Implementing Regulations. Otherwise, it shall reject the request.

Implemented by:
R.95 Decision on the request

1 **Allowance or rejection of the request**
After examination of the request under **Art.105b(1)** is concluded, the examining division is required to limit or revoke the European patent, provided the requirements of **Art.105b(1)** are met. Otherwise the request must be rejected. Limitation should be based on the revised version of the claims submitted by the proprietor. The communication notifying the patent proprietor that the request for limitation can be allowed will invite the proprietor to file a translation of the amended claims (**R.95(3)**). The proprietor thus has an opportunity to check the amended version of the patent before the decision to limit is taken. Any obvious mistakes or typing errors may be rectified on request. On the other hand, substantive amendments to the claims may no longer be made, as the request for limitation has already been examined and allowed. If no response to this communication is submitted, the request will be rejected (**R.95(4)**). Decisions of the examining division in limitation proceedings are subject to appeal in accordance with **Art.106**. (OJ 2007 se4 EN p.118)

Art. 105b(3) The decision to limit or revoke the European patent shall apply to the European patent in all the Contracting States in respect of which it has been granted. It shall take effect on the date on which the mention of the decision is published in the European Patent Bulletin.

1 **Effect of decision**
When the decision to revoke or limit the European patent in accordance with **Art.105b(3)** is published, the effects of the European patent are cancelled ab initio (see **Art.68**) in full or in part in respect of all the contracting states in which it is or was valid. (OJ 2007 se4 EN p.118)

The decision may include different sets of claims for different contracting states. Such a situation can arise where the limitation takes into account one or more national prior rights. The requester must inform the EPO of the existence of such national prior rights under **R.138**, without which a request for limitation including different sets of claims will be refused. Different sets of claims may only be based on European prior rights under **Art.54(3)** where the patent was granted in respect of an application filed before the date of entry into force of EPC2000 (13.12.2007) (see **Art.54(3):3** for the transitional provisions). R.87 EPC1973 remains applicable to such patents. (D-X,10.1)

The limitation may also be different for different contracting states because the claims forming the basis of the limitation procedure were different in different contracting states. This situation can occur where the patent has different claims for different contracting states because of national prior rights or European prior rights under **Art.54(3)** (taking into account the above transitional provisions), or where a partial transfer of rights has taken place (**Art.61** and **R.18(2)**). (D-X,10.2)

It is possible for a European patent to be limited differently in proceedings before the EPO and in proceedings before a national office. For example, a patent may first be limited in Germany in national proceedings and then limited differently at the EPO under **Art.105a.** If the limitation made before the EPO is narrower than the limitation made in Germany then the central limitation will apply equally in all states including Germany (**Art.105b(3)**). However, if the limitation made before the EPO is broader than the limitation made in Germany it would seem that the narrower scope should still apply in Germany regardless of the central limitation, particularly bearing in mind **Art.123(3)** EPC.

Once the decision has been taken, the limitation will become effective in the designated contracting states. If any translation requirements under **Art.65** are not met or any required fees are not paid to the national offices, a contracting state may prescribe that the patent is void ab initio (**Art.65(3)**).

Art. 105c Publication of the amended specification of the European patent

If the European patent is limited under Article 105b, paragraph 2, the European Patent Office shall publish the amended specification of the European patent as soon as possible after the mention of the limitation has been published in the European Patent Bulletin.

Implemented by:
R.96 Content and form of the amended specification

1 **Publication of amended specification**

Under **Art.105c**, when the EPO publishes the decision to limit the European patent, it will publish an amended European patent specification containing, in accordance with **R.96**, the new version of the claims, a translation thereof into the two other official languages of the EPO and the description and drawings (including any amendments made). The patent in the amended form has retroactive effect (**Art.68**).

Contracting states may require the filing of a translation of the amended specification under **Art.65** in the same way as for a granted European patent (OJ 2007 se4 EN p.118; see NatLaw table IV, note 2 for the requirements of each state).

PART VI APPEALS PROCEDURE

Art. 106 Decisions subject to appeal

Art. 106(1) An appeal shall lie from decisions of the Receiving Section, Examining Divisions, Opposition Divisions and the Legal Division. It shall have suspensive effect.

Implemented by:
R.98 Appeal against surrendered or lapsed patent

1 **Second instance**

The appeal procedure entails the judicial review of a decision taken by a department of first instance, such as an examining or opposition division. The boards of appeal are responsible for conducting appeal proceedings (**Art.21(1)**). Whether an appeal is handled by a technical board of appeal or the Legal Board of Appeal is governed by **Art.21**.

To ensure a uniform application of the law, a board of appeal or the President of the Office may refer questions on important points of law to the Enlarged Board of Appeal.

Selected decisions of the boards are included in the Guidelines for examination (see **Art.10(2):1**). Since the Guidelines constitute administrative instructions and are not part of the EPC, the boards are not bound by them (**Art.23(3)**).

2 **Appealable decisions**

The Boards of Appeal are responsible for examining appeals (**Art.21(1)**). The competence and composition of the Technical and Legal Boards of Appeal are governed by **Art.21(2)-(4)**.

The list of appealable decisions in **Art.106(1)** is exhaustive: a decision taken by any other body or individual is not appealable to the Boards. The search divisions are not included in **Art.106(1)** because search divisions do not issue decisions; instead, they issue opinions that are not appealable. Hence, the search division's opinion on lack of unity (**R.64(1)**) is not appealable until it is incorporated in a decision of the examining division (see **R.64(1):3**). A decision on a request for limitation or revocation is appealable because it is taken by an examining division (**R.91**; see also OJ 2007 se4 EN p.118).

A notice of loss of rights under **R.112(1)** is not a decision and is not appealable (**J13/83 r.4**). If applicants disagree with the findings in the notification, they must ask for a decision of the EPO under **R.112(2)**. The decision is appealable. If they do not ask for a decision within two months from the notification, the loss of rights ceases to be contestable.

Decisions of the boards of appeal are themselves not subject to appeal. A decision of the board of appeal taken under **R.112(2)**, e.g. after failure to reply to an invitation of the board of appeal during grant proceedings (**R.100(3)**), cannot be appealed, because the decision was not taken by a department mentioned in **Art.106(1)**. Likewise, a decision of the President, e.g. on the classification of a patent (**R.11(1)**) or on a request for exemption from the requirements for becoming a professional representative (**Art.134(7)**), cannot be appealed because the President is not mentioned in **Art.106(1)**. A separate appeal is not possible against a decision taken by a director of a department on an objection to a member of an opposition division on the ground of suspected partiality under **Art.24**; the decision may be challenged in an appeal against a final decision of the division or an interlocutory decision allowing separate appeal (**G5/91** hn.II).

Only decisions are appealable, not statements reflecting a preliminary opinion. Whether or not a document issued by the EPO constitutes a decision or a communication depends on the substance of its contents, not upon its form (**J8/81**). The decisive question is whether the document at issue, when objectively interpreted in its context, can be understood by its addressee as a final (i.e. not merely preliminary) and binding determination of substantive or procedural issues in a case by the department of the EPO issuing the document (**J12/19**). Hence, even if a document issued in a case is not called a decision by the EPO, it may still be an appealable decision (see e.g. **T1181/04** r.2.4).

Note that although the Unitary Patent Protection Division of the EPO (**UPR.3**) is made up of members of the Legal Division, its decisions concerning unitary effect and other related matters are not decisions taken by the Legal Division and appeals against these decisions are not therefore heard by a Board of Appeal. Instead, an appeal against one of these decisions must be brought before the Unified Patent Court (Art. 32(1) UPCA).

3 **Suspensive effect**

An appeal has a suspensive effect, according to **Art.106(1)**, second sentence. Suspensive effect means that the consequences of a decision are suspended; it prevents the impugned decision from having any legal consequences until the decision in appeal is taken (**T1/92** r.3.1). The following actions are not taken in view of this suspensive effect: entry in the Register, mention in the Bulletin, and, where appropriate, publication of a new patent specification (E-XII,1). Renewal fees must be paid during appeal proceedings against a decision to refuse an application (see e.g. **T395/16**). Renewal fees must also be paid to national patent offices during appeal proceedings against a decision of an opposition division to revoke a patent.

The suspensive effect does not cancel the appealed decision. Only the final decision in appeal can either set aside the impugned decision or confirm the impugned decision and so terminate its pending status. (**J28/03** r.12, 13)

An appeal against the refusal of a patent application allows for validly filing a divisional application during the appeal procedure, independently of the outcome of the appeal, even if the refusal is confirmed. (**J28/03** r.10, 11; Not. EPO OJ 2002 p.112; see also **R.36(1):2.1.2**). A divisional application can also be filed in the two-month appeal period following a refusal decision; this possibility does not depend on the suspensive effect of a possible appeal (**G1/09** r.3 and 4; see also **R.36(1):2**).

An appeal has no suspensive effect if it is filed by a third party or relates to a subject not open to appeal and is, therefore, clearly inadmissible. An example is an appeal by a third party against a decision to grant a patent, which appeal relates to the lack of clarity of the granted claims (**G2/19** r.B.II.9). Generally, an appeal that is clearly inadmissible or deemed not to have been filed has no suspensive effect (Singer Art.106, note 15).

If re-establishment is granted following the late filing of a notice of appeal, the suspensive effect should become effective with the grant of the re-establishment (Singer Art.106, note 18).

The following is an example of the effect of an appeal confirming a decision under **R.112(2)**. A loss of rights arising by operation of law, without a decision, and notified under **R.112(1)** takes effect on the expiry of the unobserved period, e.g. the deemed withdrawal of an application after failure to reply to a communication under **Art.94(3)**. If the decision under **R.112(2)** is confirmed in appeal, the deemed withdrawal has still taken effect on the expiry of the unobserved period. Therefore, any divisional application should have been filed before the expiry of the unobserved period.

Art. 106(2) A decision which does not terminate proceedings as regards one of the parties can only be appealed together with the final decision, unless the decision allows a separate appeal.

1 **Interlocutory decision**

An interlocutory decision is a decision that does not terminate the proceedings for any party. For example, in a first-instance opposition procedure, at the end of oral proceedings, the decision that a patent in amended form meets the requirements of the EPC is taken as an interlocutory decision according to EPO practice (**R.82(1):2**). Such a decision is interlocutory because the opposition division issues the final decision to maintain the patent in amended form only later, after any appeal proceedings, when the proprietor has filed the translated claims and paid the prescribed fee (**R.82(1):1**). Interlocutory decisions are exceptional during other first instance proceedings and are usually given only if the duration or cost of the proceedings as a whole is thereby reduced (E-X,3). A department taking an interlocutory decision on an issue has no power thereafter to continue the examination of that issue; any further submissions of parties relating to that issue are inadmissible (**T390/86**).

Some examples of interlocutory decisions are a decision refusing the refund of additional search fees (**T2526/17**; **R.64**), a decision refusing an extension of a period (**J37/89**), a decision taken by an opposition division that an opposition is admissible (see e.g. **T376/90**), decisions concerning the exclusion of and objection to members of any department (**G5/91** hn.II; **G1/05**, preliminary decision of 07.12.2006), and decisions of boards of appeal referring questions to the Enlarged Board of Appeal under **Art.112(1)(a)**.

2 **Appealability of interlocutory decision**

An interlocutory decision may or may not be made separately appealable. An interlocutory decision of an opposition division that a patent in amended form meets the requirements of the EPC is always made appealable, according to EPO practice (**R.82(1):1**). Otherwise, an interlocutory decision will be made separately appealable, for instance, if the continuation of the proceedings depends on a ruling in appeal on a fundamental point of law (E-X,3). If an interlocutory decision allows for a separate appeal, as permitted by **Art.106(2)**, the requirements for an admissible appeal must still be complied with, e.g. the decision must be taken by a department mentioned in **Art.106(1)** (see **Art.106(1):2** above). The first instance proceedings must be suspended until the appealable interlocutory decision has become final, i.e. during any appeal against it (E-X,3).

An interlocutory decision that allows separate appeal will indicate that it is subject to appeal in the order of the decision and will be issued in writing and be reasoned; if no separate appeal is allowed, reasons may be given in the final decision (E-X,3).

If no appeal is filed against an appealable interlocutory decision, the decision becomes *res judicata* and can no longer be impugned in an appeal against the final decision (**T55/90** r.2.3). Any decision of a board remitting an opposition to the opposition division with the order to maintain the patent in amended form (after the filing of the translated claims and payment of the fee) cannot be challenged later, either before the opposition division or in a later appeal against the final decision (**T55/90** r.2.4). In such a case, an appeal against the final decision to maintain a patent in amended form can only concern the formalities of **R.82(2)** (**T55/90** r.2.6).

If no separate appeal is allowed, the interlocutory decision can be contested with the final decision, irrespective of the outcome of the procedure, e.g. also if the final decision is to grant the patent (**J37/89**, r.4.2-4.3).

Art. 106(3) The right to file an appeal against decisions relating to the apportionment or fixing of costs in opposition proceedings may be restricted in the Implementing Regulations.

Implemented by:
R.97 Appeal against apportionment and fixing of cost

1 **Decision apportioning costs**

A decision apportioning costs cannot be the sole subject of an appeal (**R.97(1)**). A decision fixing the amount of the cost cannot be appealed unless the amount exceeds that of the fee for appeal (**R.97(2)**).

If costs are apportioned to be paid by a victorious party, that party cannot appeal the apportionment because it is not adversely affected by the decision on substantive matters and hence cannot appeal on any other grounds (**Art.107**). Where a valid appeal has been filed by the losing party, the victor cannot separately appeal against the apportionment of costs (**T1237/05**).

When a party has lost an opposition and is ordered to pay part of the costs of another party in accordance with **Art.104(1)**, the losing party can appeal the apportionment by simultaneously appealing the substantive decision of the opposition division. The appeal does not have to be based on convincing substantive grounds for the apportionment of costs to be considered. In this way, a party can circumvent **Art.106(3)**. However, if the substantive aspect of the appeal is rejected as inadmissible, e.g. because of lack of grounds, then the remaining subject of the appeal, i.e. the apportionment, becomes the sole subject, which according to **R.97(1)** must fail (**T154/90** r.1.3).

Art. 107 Persons entitled to appeal and to be parties to appeal proceedings

Any party to proceedings adversely affected by a decision may appeal. Any other parties to the proceedings shall be parties to the appeal proceedings as of right.

1 **Persons entitled to appeal**

Appeal is open to any party adversely affected by a decision (**Art.107**, first sentence). The party must have been party to the first instance proceedings which led to the decision under appeal. The German and French versions of **Art.107** make this clearer than the English version and state that 'any party to the proceedings that led to a decision may appeal the decision in so far as the party is adversely affected by the decision' (**T656/98** r.1). A 'party' is confined to the parties entered in the Register in the first instance proceedings. A successor in title based on an assignment becomes party only after having been duly recorded in the Register (see **R.22**). When a transfer of a patent takes place during the appeal period and an appeal is filed in the name of the new proprietor, evidence of this transfer must be given to the EPO before the expiry of the appeal period for the appeal to be considered admissible (**T956/03** r.7). To overcome this, an appeal may be filed naming the original proprietor as a main request, and the new proprietor as an auxiliary request (**G2/04**).

If a party consists of a plurality of persons, an appeal against a decision which adversely affects this party has to be filed on behalf of all these persons (**T755/09** r.1). An appeal filed in common by several persons must be filed by the common representative, which applies both to joint opponents (**G3/99** r.18), joint proprietors (**T1154/06** r.1), and joint applicants.

Where the validity of an opponent's status after the alleged transfer of an opposition is disputed in appeal, the appeal of the opponent is admissible - a 'party' is someone who took part in the first instance proceedings; however, the opponent's procedural status up to the decision in appeal is limited to the issue of its entitlement; should opponent status be revoked on appeal, it is no longer entitled to take part in the proceedings, but it is not the case that the opponent never assumed party status (**T1178/04**).

When a party ceases to exist, its universal successor in law immediately acquires party status (**T15/01** r.11, 12). The existence of a legal entity is determined by national law (**G1/13** r.5.1). National law is not followed when it confers procedural rights contrary to the EPC, such as transfer of an opposition before the EPO (**G1/13** r.8). When a party ceases to exist during proceedings before the EPO, for example because the company is dissolved, and is restored with retroactive effect under national law, the EPO will recognise the retroactive effect (**G1/13** hn). See **R.101(2):1** for correction of an incorrect name or address of an appellant.

A person who was not a party to opposition proceedings can, as an exception, become party to the opposition appeal (as a party of right) by intervening under **Art.105** (**G1/94**, **G3/04**).

Appeal is open only to the parties to proceedings which led to the appealed decision (**Art.107**). The party in grant proceedings is the applicant. Parties in opposition proceedings are the proprietor and the one or more opponents, as well as any intervener (**Art.105**). Both the requester and the applicant or proprietor are parties in respect of decisions on a request for correction of the mention of the inventor (**R.21**), for stay (or resumption) of the proceedings (**R.14**), for registering of a transfer or licence (**R.22**, 23), or for inspection of files (**Art.128**, **J27/87**). The proprietor is the party in limitation or revocation proceedings under **Art.105a**. A person who has filed observations under **Art.115** is a 'third party' and is not a party to the proceedings. The EPO or its employees are never party to appeal proceedings under **Art.106**.

The boards check the requirements of **Art.107**. If not complied with, the appeal is rejected as inadmissible (**R.101(1)**).

2 **Adversely affected**

Parties may file an appeal only if they are adversely affected (**Art.107**, first sentence, see also **G1/99** r.6.3). Parties are only adversely affected if a decision does not agree with their explicit request (**J12/85**). The relevant issue in this respect is the difference between the formally-submitted requests and the order of the appealed decision. Whether a party is adversely affected, has to be assessed by comparing the final requests submitted at the first-instance proceedings with the substance of the decision under appeal (**T466/20**).

An applicant is adversely affected by a decision to refuse a patent application. On the other hand, the applicant is rarely adversely affected by a decision to grant a patent. In principle, an applicant can appeal a decision to grant a patent if the applicant has not agreed to the text of the application as granted, in view of **Art.113(2)**. However, an applicant is deemed to have approved the text intended for grant when the applicant pays the fee for grant and files the translated claims (**R.71(5)**). An appeal against a decision to grant can exceptionally be considered admissible if the documents communicated to the applicant under **R.71(3)** did not correspond to the text in which the examining division intended to grant the patent (**T408/21 and T1823/23**, departing from **T265/20**).

A proprietor is generally adversely affected by a decision to revoke a patent unless the proprietor requested the revocation or disapproved of the text of the patent (**Art.101(2):2**). A proprietor is adversely affected if the opposition division decides to maintain the patent in amended form and thereby does not accede to the proprietor's main request, or to auxiliary requests ranking higher than the allowed auxiliary request. This is not the case if the proprietor withdraws the main request and the higher ranking auxiliary requests (**T506/91**, CLBA V.A.2.4.2.a). In such a case, the allowed auxiliary request was the proprietor's *de facto* main request when the opposition division took the decision. Note that opposition divisions usually announce the decision only at the end of oral proceedings. Any 'conclusions' on requests announced during oral proceedings are irrelevant under **Art.107** because such conclusions have no binding character and are not interlocutory decisions (see e.g. **T611/15** r.1.1.4).

An opponent is generally adversely affected by a decision to reject the opposition or to maintain the patent in amended form. However, if the opponent requested only partial revocation during the first instance proceedings (i.e. the opponent limited the extent of the opposition), the opponent is only adversely affected to the extent that this request for partial revocation is not granted (**T299/89** r.3; see **R.76(2):4.2**). However, if the patent is maintained in an amended form with claims that the opponent explicitly agreed with, the opponent is not adversely affected (**T156/90**). In the rare case that an invitation under **R.82(1)** is issued before a patent is maintained in amended form, the opponent can still appeal even if no observations are filed in response to the invitation (**G1/88**).

An opponent is not adversely affected by a decision to revoke a patent, even if the decision contains reasoning favourable to the proprietor (e.g. if the granted claims were held to be novel but not inventive).

An appeal is inadmissible if the grounds on which it is based have been taken away before the start of the appeal, e.g. where inspection of the file of a not-yet-published application has been refused by the Receiving Section but the application has been published before the appeal proceedings have started, thereby removing the adverse effect of the decision (**J27/87**).

3 Party as of right

3.1 GENERAL

Parties to the proceedings that have led to the appealed decision and which have not appealed are party to the appeal proceedings as of right (**Art.107**, second sentence). For example, a proprietor or one or more opponents that have not filed an appeal are parties as of right in opposition appeal proceedings.

A party whose appeal is found to be inadmissible or is deemed not to have been filed also becomes a party as of right in appeal proceedings based on an admissible appeal filed by another party. The same applies to a party that withdraws its appeal. An opponent who withdraws its opposition during appeal proceedings ceases to be a party as far as the substantive issues are concerned.

In appeal proceedings, an appealing party is referred to as the appellant and a party as of right opposing the appellant is referred to as the respondent.

The rights of a party as of right are restricted compared with those of an appellant. In particular, a party as of right has no right to continue the proceedings if the sole appellant withdraws its appeal. If there are several appellants and one withdraws its appeal, the further appellants have the right to continue the appeal, and the appeal fees they have paid are not reimbursed unless **R.103** applies. (**G2/91**, see also **Art.110:11**)

3.2 REFORMATIO IN PEIUS

The boards of appeal have introduced the principle of the 'prohibition of reformatio in peius', i.e. the principle that a sole appellant should not end up in a worse position as the result of filing an appeal. The principle prevents the boards from going beyond a request of a sole appellant, putting that party in a worse position than it was in before it appealed (**T60/91** r.7). The prohibition does not apply to an applicant appealing a decision to refuse a patent application because the appeal cannot put the appellant in a worse position (**G10/93** r.2, 3). The board of appeal has the power to examine in such an appeal whether the application meets all requirements of the EPC, even if some requirements have not been considered by the examining division or were regarded as having been met (**G10/93** hn; see **Art.114(1)** and notes thereto).

The prohibition of reformatio in peius is applied in inter partes proceedings where either the proprietor or the opponent is not appellant. This is the case if one of the parties has withdrawn from the proceedings or one of the parties is a party as of right. A party as of right is not contesting the decision of the first instance, and, therefore, a request by it which goes beyond the appellant's original appeal request is not admissible. A party as of right may only make requests in the appeal proceedings which defend the results obtained before the first instance (**G9/92** r.11; case consolidated with **G4/93**). The following points in opposition appeals emerge.

3.2.1 *Opponent as party as of right*

If the patent proprietor is the sole appellant against an interlocutory decision maintaining the patent in amended form, neither the board of appeal nor the non-appealing opponent may challenge the maintenance of the patent as amended in accordance with the interlocutory decision (**G9/92** hn. I). If a set of claims in appeal contains claims held allowable by the opposition division and additional independent claims, the board may examine only the additional claims if the proprietor is the sole appellant (**T345/21**).

3.2.2 *Proprietor as party as of right*

If the opponent is the sole appellant against an interlocutory decision maintaining a patent in amended form, the patent proprietor is primarily restricted during the appeal proceedings to defending the patent in the form in which it was maintained by the opposition division in its interlocutory decision (or in a more limited form). Amendments proposed by the proprietor as a party as of right may be rejected as inadmissible if they are neither appropriate nor necessary (**G9/92** hn.II). Thus, the rights of the appellant outweigh the principle of ex officio examination under **Art.114(1)** (**G9/92** r.2-6). **G9/92** follows **T369/91** and overrules **T576/89** and **T123/85**. Although the scope of amendment available to the proprietor is restricted, this does not give the appellant/opponent the right to dictate the form of such amendments; this is still a matter for the proprietor (**T23/04** r.2.5.3).

In this case, the claims of the patent may in principle not be amended beyond the scope of the claims maintained by the opposition division since this would put the opponent and sole appellant in a worse position than if it had not appealed. As an exception, based on equity, such an amendment may be allowed in order to meet an objection made by an opponent or the board of appeal during appeal proceedings if the patent would otherwise have to be revoked as a direct consequence of an inadmissible or unallowable amendment that was regarded allowable in the impugned decision of the opposition division, e.g. if an added feature violates **Art.123(2)** (**G1/99** hn, r.13.1, 13.2) or if the added feature renders the claim unclear or renders the claimed invention insufficiently disclosed. The exception applies not only in case of an error of judgment of the opposition division but also in case the factual and/or legal basis on which the proprietor added the feature changes, since the proprietor would otherwise be prevented from adequately defending its patent against new facts and objections introduced into the proceedings at the appeal stage (**T1843/09**).

The nature and order of the requests to be filed by the proprietor to benefit from the exception (see **G1/99** hn) can be summarised as follows: (1) introduce a further limiting feature (i.e. reduce the scope of the patent further to avoid any reformatio in peius), (2) only if this is not possible, introduce a feature which extends the scope of the claims held allowable by the opposition division (i.e. replace the feature at issue with another feature), (3) finally, if such amendments are not possible, delete the feature; provided that each request complies with **Art.123(2)** and (3). Hence deleting the feature objected to is only allowable if the amendments under (1) and (2) cannot be made, e.g. because the application as filed discloses neither more specific nor more general embodiments of the feature objected to.

The prohibition applies in principle until the final settlement of the opposition, including any continued opposition proceedings after a remittal (**T1843/09** hn).

3.2.3 *Extent of prohibition*

Where the proprietor is the sole appellant, the prohibition of reformatio in peius prevents the opponent or Board of Appeal from objecting to the claims upheld by the opposition division. However, the prohibition of reformatio in peius does not apply to requests not allowed by the opposition division or to any request made for the first time in appeal (**T226/98** r.9.2). For example, if a request in appeal includes a claim not comprised in the set of claims allowed by the opposition division or a claim amended in view of such a set, the prohibition does not apply and the board of appeal has the power and duty pursuant to **Art.111(1)** and **R.82** to assess the patentability of this claim. If the board regards the claim as unallowable, it will dismiss the entire request despite the presence of claims allowed by the opposition division (see e.g. **T226/98** r.12.11). This is a consequence of the fact that a request can only be decided on as a whole (**T303/94** r.2; **T401/95** r.2). A proprietor as appellant desiring to rely on the prohibition of reformatio in peius must file at least one request before the board of appeal that contains only claims allowed by the opposition division.

The prohibition of reformatio in peius is not applicable to separate points decided by the opposition division; it applies only to an allowed request as a whole (**T372/92** r.1.2; **T401/95** r.2; **T266/98** r.9). For example, if an appeal is lodged against a decision of the first instance to refuse the main request, then the whole of that main request is before the board of appeal and within its jurisdiction. If the opposition division has decided that a claim of this main request was novel but lacked inventive step, the board is nevertheless empowered to examine novelty and decide that the claim is not novel (**T303/94** r.2; **T583/95** r.2; **T1341/04** r.1.4).

According to **T1178/04**, the prohibition of reformatio in peius does not apply to the question of whether an opposition is admissible; the EPO has a duty to examine this at any stage of the proceedings. According to this view, if an application was upheld in amended form by the opposition division and only the opponent appealed, the proprietor could nevertheless challenge the admissibility of the opposition at the appeal stage and, if successful, have the decision set aside and the patent maintained as granted. This approach was, however, not followed by the board in decision **T882/17**. According to this later decision, admissibility of the opposition may indeed be reconsidered at the appeal stage but a finding of inadmissibility at this stage cannot lead to the interlocutory decision of the opposition division being set aside because this would be contrary to the prohibition of reformatio in peius. Such a finding at the appeal stage can only lead to the opponent's appeal being rejected.

3.3 CHOICE BETWEEN PARTY AND PARTY AS OF RIGHT

Parties as of right are rather restricted in appeal proceedings: they cannot continue the appeal after the sole appellant has withdrawn its appeal and they are restricted primarily to defending the results obtained before the first instance (see also **T239/96** r.2-6). Hence, it is generally disadvantageous to be merely party as of right. It is possible for a party to become appellant when there is an appeal and at the same time not lose the appeal fee if another party does not lodge an appeal. The party should file a notice of appeal and pay the appeal fee within the two-month period for appeal. If it turns out that no other party has filed an appeal, the appeal can be withdrawn before the expiry of the four-month period for filing grounds and the appeal fee will be fully reimbursed under **R.103(1)(b)**. If another party has filed an appeal, the party can instead file its statement of grounds and become an appellant in the appeal proceedings.

Art. 108 Time limit and form

Notice of appeal shall be filed, in accordance with the Implementing Regulations, at the European Patent Office within two months of notification of the decision. Notice of appeal shall not be deemed to have been filed until the fee for appeal has been paid. Within four months of notification of the decision, a statement setting out the grounds of appeal shall be filed in accordance with the Implementing Regulations.

Implemented by:
R.99 Content of the notice of appeal and the statement of grounds

1 **Filing an appeal**
The filing of an appeal against a decision of a department of first instance involves three acts to be performed in two steps. The first step includes the acts of filing a notice of appeal and paying the appeal fee, both within two months from the date of notification of the impugned decision. The second step is the act of filing a statement setting out the grounds of appeal ('statement of grounds') within four months from the date of notification. The procedure for the assessment of the acts is set out in **Art.110:2** and **3**.

The notice of appeal and the statement of grounds must be in writing (**R.1**), in an official EPO language or an admissible non-EPO language (**R.3(1)**), and comply with **R.50** (form of subsequently filed documents). They must be filed with a filing office of the EPO using a means of communication allowed under **R.2(1)**.

A party as of right becomes party to the appeal proceedings under **Art.107** and does not have to comply with the requirements of **Art.108** (**T864/02**).

If several parties file an appeal, each of them must pay the appeal fee and each of them becomes appellant. Appeal fees are not reimbursed simply because several parties have validly filed an appeal against the same decision. (**G2/91**)

An appeal may not be conditional (see **R.101(1):1.3**).

2 **Periods**
The two- and four-month periods of **Art.108** provide, respectively, an early warning to other parties and the public that an appeal is being filed and sufficient time for the appellant to prepare its grounds of appeal. Both periods are calculated from the date of notification of the decision which is being appealed. The pronouncement of a decision during oral proceedings does not trigger either period (see **R.111(1):2**). However, an appeal can be validly lodged immediately after the pronouncement of the decision during oral proceedings, well before the notification of the decision (**T389/86**).

3 **Notice of appeal**
The notice of appeal informs the public and any other parties that the impugned decision will be appealed. Its content is governed by **R.99(1)**: name and address of the appellant, an indication of the impugned decision and a request defining the subject of the appeal.

4 **Appeal fee**
A notice of appeal is not deemed to have been filed unless the appeal fee is paid within two months of notification of the impugned decision (**Art.108**, first and second sentence; **G1/18**). The appellant may use the fail-safe arrangement of **Rfees7(3)** for a payment that is only credited to an EPO account after the expiry of the time limit.

The amount of the appeal fee is fixed in **Rfees2(1)11**. The amount is lower for certain appellants such as natural persons and SME's (see **Rfees2(1):11**). If the amount paid falls short by a small amount (see **Rfees8**) the appeal fee is regarded as validly paid if the circumstances justify overlooking the amount lacking (**T130/82**).

The appeal fee will be refunded in full if the notice of appeal is deemed not filed (see **Art.108:6** below) and either in full or in part in the situations set out in **R.103**.

5 **Statement of grounds of appeal**

The statement of grounds of appeal must state the legal and factual reasons why the impugned decision should be set aside. See **R.99(2)** for the requirements that the statement of grounds must meet in order for the appeal to be admissible. Additional requirements for the statement of grounds are provided in Art.12 RPBA (see **Art.108:7**).

6 **Sanctions and remedies**

The EPC has two sanctions for non-compliance with the requirements for filing an appeal: the appeal is either deemed not to have been filed (**Art.108**, second sentence) or is inadmissible (**R.101**). If the appeal is deemed not to have been filed, no appeal proceedings have been initiated and any appeal fee that has been paid will be reimbursed. If the appeal is inadmissible, appeal proceedings have been initiated but end prematurely and the appeal fee is not reimbursed. An inadmissible appeal filed in grant proceedings provides a possibility to file a divisional application (see **R.36(1):2.1.2**). The following sub-sections set out the situations in which the two sanctions apply.

6.1 NOTICE OF APPEAL

Where no notice of appeal is filed and the appeal fee is paid within or after the two-month period, there is no appeal and the appeal fee will be reimbursed (**G1/18** hn.3). See also **R.99(1):2**.

Where the notice of appeal is filed after the two-month period, the appeal is deemed not filed. Any appeal fee, paid within or after the two-month period, will be reimbursed. (**G1/18** hn.1(b),(c),2)

If the content of the notice of appeal does not comply with **R.99(1)**, the appeal will either be rejected as inadmissible (**R.101(1)**) or deemed not filed (**R.101(1):2**), depending on the nature of the deficiency.

6.2 APPEAL FEE

Where no appeal fee is paid and the notice of appeal is filed within or after the two-month period, the notice of appeal is deemed not filed (**Art.108**, second sentence).

Where the appeal fee is paid after the two-month period and the notice of appeal is filed within or after the two-month period, the appeal is deemed not filed (**G1/18** hn.1(a),(b)).

The appeal fee will be reimbursed if the appeal is deemed not filed (**G1/18** hn.2).

6.3 STATEMENT OF GROUNDS

Where the statement of grounds is not filed or is filed after the four-month period, the appeal is inadmissible (**R.101(1):1.3**).

If the content of the statement of grounds does not comply with **R.99(2)**, the appeal is inadmissible (**R.101(1)**). A board has no discretionary power to hold an appeal admissible when the requirements of **R.99(2)** are not met (e.g. **T2222/19**). The admissibility of an appeal can only be considered as a whole; there is no notion of partial (in)admissibility of an appeal under **R.99(2)** (**T509/07**; CLBA V.A.2.6.8). However, parts of the statement of grounds can be held inadmissible under Art.12 RPBA.

6.4 **REMEDIES**

An applicant or proprietor can remedy a failure to file the notice of appeal and/or pay the appeal fee within the two-month period or file the grounds of appeal within the four-month period by requesting re-establishment (**Art.122**). An opponent can in general not use re-establishment (**Art.122, T210/89** hn.1). As an exception, an opponent as appellant can request re-establishment in the four-month period for filing the statement of grounds (**G1/86; T210/89** hn.2; E-VIII,3.1.2). The same applies to an appealing intervener, who is considered to be an opponent. Since a decision on re-establishment is taken by the board, it cannot be appealed (**Art.106(1)**).

See **R.101(1):3** for remedying deficiencies in the contents of the notice of appeal and the statement of grounds.

7 **Requirements in the RPBA**

Art.12 RPBA provides requirements for the statement of grounds, which apply in addition to **R.99(2)**. The statement of grounds of appeal must contain the party's complete appeal case. The statement must set out clearly and concisely the reasons why it is requested that the decision under appeal be reversed or amended, and should specify expressly all requests, facts, objections, arguments, and evidence relied on (Art.12(3) RPBA). The same requirements apply to any response to the appeal filed by a respondent (Art.12(1)(c) RPBA and Art.12(3) RPBA).

The board has discretion not to admit any part of the statement of grounds which does not meet the requirements of Art.12(3) RPBA (Art.12(5) RPBA). The board can, for example, hold inadmissible any set of claims that is filed together with the statement of grounds without substantiation. Furthermore, the requirement in Art.12(3) RPBA to 'expressly' specify the requests, facts, objections, arguments, and evidence in the grounds of appeal or reply means that the board may disregard, for example, parts merely referring to submissions presented in first instance proceedings (explanatory remarks to Art.12(5) RPBA in OJ 2020 sp2). The sanction that applies if the appellant does not set out its complete case in the statement of grounds is that later submissions completing the case can be held inadmissible (Art.13 RPBA). The same sanction applies if a respondent's response does not comply with Art.12(3) RPBA.

Notably, whereas the sanction of Art.12(5) RPBA provides discretion for the board, a board has no discretionary power to hold an appeal admissible when the requirements of **R.99(2)** are not met (e.g. **T2222/19**). Moreover, the admissibility of an appeal can only be considered as a whole, which is not the case for the inadmissibility of parts of the appeal as specified in Art.12(5) RPBA (CLBA V.A.2.6.8). The requirement of Art.12(3) RPBA is accordingly independent of the requirement of **R.99(2)**.

The boards furthermore have a discretionary power whether or not to admit any part of a party's appeal case, even if filed as part of the grounds of appeal, or any part of the reply of the respondent, even if filed within the period set, which is not directed to the requests, facts, objections, arguments, and evidence on which the appealed decision was based, unless the party demonstrates that the part at issue was admissibly raised and maintained in the proceedings leading to the decision under appeal (Art.12(4) RPBA 2020). This provision applies to appeal cases wherein the statement of grounds was filed on or after 01.01.2020 (Art.25(2) RPBA). If documents are not admitted under Art.12(4) RPBA, this has no effect on the admissibility of the appeal (explanatory remarks to Art.12(4) RBPA in OJ 2020 sp2).

The board will generally not admit requests, facts, objections or evidence which were held inadmissible or were withdrawn or withheld at first instance, even if resubmitted with the statement of grounds (Art.12(6) RPBA).

For late-filed submissions in appeal, generally see **Art.1(2):2**.

Art. 109 Interlocutory revision

1 General

Interlocutory revision is a procedure in which an allowable appeal is handled and decided on by the department of first instance that took the contested decision rather than by a board of appeal. The procedure is substantially faster than the procedure before a board of appeal. The department of first instance will grant interlocutory revision when it considers the appeal to be admissible and allowable within three months from receipt of the statement of grounds. If the appeal is not regarded as allowable, no interlocutory revision will be granted and the appeal will be remitted to a board of appeal without comments as to its merit. Appellants will know that interlocutory revision has not been allowed if they receive a communication informing them of the commencement of proceedings before the board of appeal and of the number of the appeal.

The appeal is well founded and suitable for interlocutory revision if the grounds of appeal and main request clearly meet the objections on which the refusal of the application was based (**T139/87**). If, for example, an application is refused on the ground of lack of novelty and the amended claims filed with the appeal are clearly novel, interlocutory revision should be granted, the decision to refuse should be set aside, and the examining division should continue the grant proceedings by examining inventive step. If the independent claims clearly do not meet the requirements of **Art.123(2)** or do not overcome other objections raised by the examining division earlier in the procedure and referenced in the decision, no interlocutory revision will be granted (E-XII,7.4.2). However, **T1060/13** r.4 and **T682/22** consider these remarks in E-XII,7.4.2 to be inconsistent with the established case law.

The department of first instance will rectify its decision if the applicant amends the wording of the claims in accordance with a proposal made by the examiner that the applicant has previously rejected, or if it has made an error, e.g. not taking into account important evidence or disregarding a request for oral proceedings. If a substantial procedural violation has occurred, interlocutory revision must be granted even if new objections arise (E-XII,7.4.2(a); E-XII,7.4.1); the new objections should be dealt with in continued examination proceedings. Interlocutory revision will also be granted where a new argument or new evidence overcomes the objections in the decision under appeal (E-XII,7.1).

The appellant may file amended claims. Interlocutory revision will be granted if the amendments are substantial (**T47/90**) and clearly overcome the grounds for the refusal, even if further new objections arise; the appellant is entitled to have the new objections examined by two instances (**T219/93**). Other grounds against the grant of a patent should not prevent the granting of the interlocutory revision; they can be dealt with in the continued procedure before the first instance (**T139/87**). For example, if a refusal is based on lack of novelty and inventive step has not been discussed, interlocutory revision should be granted if the claimed invention is novel but does not involve an inventive step (E-XII,7.4.2(b)).

Interlocutory revision is never possible on the basis of an auxiliary request since applicants have the right to have their main request examined by a board of appeal (**T919/95**; E-XII,7.4.3).

If re-establishment in the time limit of **Art.108** has been requested, the first instance will allow interlocutory revision only if it can take the decision on re-establishment within the three-month time limit of **Art.109(2)** for remittance to a board of appeal and the conditions for granting interlocutory revision are fulfilled. In all other cases the appeal and the application for re-establishment will be remitted to a board of appeal. (E-VIII,3.3)

Interlocutory revision does not automatically result in reimbursement of the appeal fee. Even if the examining division grants interlocutory revision, there is no obligation for it to reimburse the appeal fee. The proper interpretation of **R.103** is that a substantial procedural violation must have taken place in the proceedings leading to the contested decision in order for the appeal fee to be reimbursed in the case of interlocutory revision. (**T79/91** r.4.2)

A department of first instance is not competent to refuse a request for reimbursement of the appeal fee in an interlocutory revision, because a decision in interlocutory revision may not adversely affect the appellant (**G3/03** hn.I, r.2). If the requirements for interlocutory revision are fulfilled but the request for reimbursement of the appeal fee is not considered allowable, the department of first instance must grant the interlocutory revision and remit the request for reimbursement to a board of appeal, which will give a decision solely on reimbursement. The board of appeal would have been competent to deal with the substantive issues if no interlocutory revision had been granted is competent to decide on the request for reimbursement (**G3/03** hn.II). If the appeal is no longer pending at the time of a request for reimbursement (for example, because the department of first instance has already dealt with the appeal by interlocutory revision), then there is no basis for refunding the appeal fee (**T21/02** hn).

Art. 109(1) If the department whose decision is contested considers the appeal to be admissible and well founded, it shall rectify its decision. This shall not apply where the appellant is opposed by another party to the proceedings.

1 **Rectification of decision**

In grant proceedings, the interlocutory revision of a decision to refuse a European patent application is always possible since the appellant (applicant or joint applicants) is never opposed by another party. In opposition proceedings, interlocutory revision is only possible in special cases, e.g. if all oppositions are withdrawn and the proprietor appeals. An interlocutory revision is not possible for decisions regarding mention of the inventor (**R.21**), stay of the proceedings (**R.14**) or registering a transfer (**R.22**), because there are opposing parties. If interlocutory revision is not possible under **Art.109(1)**, last sentence, the first instance department remits the appeal immediately to the board of appeal.

See **Art.110:3** on the assessment of admissibility of the appeal. When considering the admissibility of the appeal for the purposes of applying **Art.109(1)**, the admissibility of any new claim requests is not be to taken into account (**T682/22** r.2.4.1).

An appeal is considered well founded e.g. if the grounds of the appeal contain an amendment to the application which meets the objections on which the contested decision of the examining division was based. In that case the department that issued the decision should rectify that decision by granting interlocutory revision. (**T139/87**)

A decision granting interlocutory revision is not appealable because it does not adversely affect a party (**Art.107**) and/or does not terminate the procedure (**Art.106(2)**).

Art. 109(2) If the appeal is not allowed within three months of receipt of the statement of grounds, it shall be remitted to the Board of Appeal without delay, and without comment as to its merit.

1 **Remittal to board of appeal**
On expiry of the three-month period, the board of appeal becomes responsible for the case. The department of first instance loses jurisdiction and interlocutory revision is no longer possible. (**T778/06**)

The first instance department remits the appeal to the board of appeal without comment as to the merit of the appeal, according to **Art.109(2)**. Since the reasons underlying the first instance's exercise of discretion are therefore not apparent, it has been suggested that even when the board of appeal considers that interlocutory revision would have been justified, it is not open to the board to criticise the first instance (**T704/05** r.5.3). However, many boards of appeal do in fact make such criticisms.

Art. 110 Examination of appeals

If the appeal is admissible, the Board of Appeal shall examine whether the appeal is allowable. The examination of the appeal shall be conducted in accordance with the Implementing Regulations.

Implemented by:
R.100 Examination procedure
R.101 Rejection of the appeal as inadmissible

1 **Rules of Procedure of the Boards of Appeal**
The Rules of Procedure of the Boards of Appeal (RPBA), published in OJ 2024 A15, form an important part of the procedural framework governing appeal proceedings. Additional procedural rules for appeals are given in Art.**106-111** and **R.97-103**. Furthermore, the common procedural provisions of **Art.113-125** also apply in appeal, including the right to be heard, the right to oral proceedings, and the power of the EPO to hold inadmissible late-filed facts and evidence. The rules for the first instance proceedings apply also to the appeal proceedings unless otherwise provided (**R.100(1)**), e.g. **R.80** applies to amendments made in opposition appeal proceedings.

The RPBA are binding upon the boards, provided that the rules do not lead to a situation that would be incompatible with the spirit and purpose of the EPC (Art.23 RPBA). The RPBA can help in clarifying and interpreting the EPC but they cannot confer on the boards any powers that the EPC does not give them (**T1914/12** r.7.2.3). The RPBA may deviate from the EPC provisions governing first instance procedure, but not from those governing procedure before the boards; **R.116(1)** is an example of the former (**G6/95**).

A revised version of the RPBA entered into force on 01.01.2020 ('RPBA'; see OJ 2019 A63). Extensive official explanatory notes to the RPBA can be found in OJ 2020 sp2. The RPBA were subsequently amended by inserting Art.15a RPBA regarding videoconference oral proceedings, which entered into force on 01.04.2021 (OJ 2021 A19). Further amendments to Art.13(2), R.15(1) and R.15(9)(b) RPBA entered into force on 01.01.2024 (OJ 2023 A103). The amended provisions apply to all appeal proceedings pending on or after 01.01 2024.

The previous version of the RPBA was published in OJ 2007 p.536 ('RPBA2007') and continues to apply in part for appeal cases already pending on 01.01.2020. In particular, even though the RPBA apply to all appeals pending on or filed after 01.01.2020 (Art.25 RPBA), Art.12(4) RPBA2007 continues to apply to any statement of grounds filed before 01.01.2020 and any reply thereto filed in due time, instead of Art.12(4)-(6) RPBA (Art.25(2) RPBA). Moreover, where a summons to oral proceedings or a communication under **R.100(2)** was notified before 01.01.2020, Art.13 RPBA2007 continues to apply instead of Art.13(2) RPBA (Art.25(3) RPBA).

The 2020 revision of the RPBA aimed to increase the efficiency, predictability for the parties, and the harmonisation of appeals (CA/3/19). However, the effect of the 2020 revision to the RPBA on first and second instance proceedings may in some cases decrease efficiency for parties. For example, parties must endeavour to include all requests, evidence and arguments in first instance proceedings as the boards will generally not admit any such submissions that are not part of the impugned decision (Art.12 RPBA; see **Art.110:5**).

According to the new RPBA, the boards will no longer remit cases back to first instance for further prosecution, unless there are special reasons for doing so (Art.11 RPBA). This could have had the effect of disadvantaging parties by removing the possibility of two instances of review, e.g. if a ground, such as inventive step, was heard for the first time in appeal. However, the boards have not interpreted the new provision in this manner and regard the need for two instances of review as a 'special reason' justifying remittal. This is indeed consistent with Art.12(2) RPBA which states that the primary object of appeal proceedings is to review the decision under appeal in a judicial manner – to examine matters going beyond the scope of the decision would not be in line with this primary purpose.

To make the work of the boards transparent and predictable, a list of cases in which the boards are likely to take substantive action, for example by holding oral proceedings, is published annually on the EPO website (Art.1(2) RPBA).

The procedure for amending the RPBA is laid down in **R.12c**.

2 **Assessment on filing of the notice of appeal**

A notice of appeal is assessed on filing in a similar manner to a notice of opposition, which is apparent from the equivalence of **Art.101(1)**, **R.77** and **R.79** on the one hand and **Art.110**, **R.100** and **R.101** on the other. The procedural aspects of appeal proceedings are not discussed in detail in the Guidelines, because the boards of appeal are not bound by the Guidelines but only by the EPC (**Art.23(3)**).

If the board notes deficiencies which may cause the notice of appeal being deemed not to have been filed (see **Art.108:6**) and which can still be remedied, it may, as a courtesy, invite the appellant to remedy them within the two-month period of **Art.108** (similar to D-IV,1.3.3; see also **Art.125:2** on good faith). Notification of a missing signature is not at the board's discretion; this notification must always be made according to **R.50(3)**.

If not remedied in time, the board (in particular the registrar of the board) will notify the appellant that the appeal is deemed not to have been filed (**Art.119**, **R.112(1)**); the appellant can apply for a decision on the matter according to **R.112(2)**. Since such a decision under **R.112(2)** is taken by the board, it cannot be appealed (**Art.106(1)**). Any documents submitted with a notice of appeal that is deemed not filed will be added to the file and regarded as observations under **Art.115**. Since an appeal is not in existence, there will be no examination for its admissibility under **R.101** and the appeal fee will be reimbursed.

In appeals in ex parte proceedings, the department of first instance has a power to grant interlocutory revision under **Art.109**. This this is the case e.g. in an appeal against the refusal of a patent application. The first assessment of the appeal is therefore not carried out by a board of appeal but by the department of first instance. The department of first instance will forward the case to the boards if it does not grant interlocutory revision.

3 **Assessment of admissibility**

Once the notice of appeal is regarded as filed, the admissibility of the appeal will subsequently be assessed (**G1/18**). An appeal is admissible if it does not contain any of the deficiencies listed in **R.101**. In simple cases the department of first instance that took the impugned decision may decide that the appeal is admissible when granting interlocutory revision (**T473/91**). Major deficiencies in the notice and grounds must be corrected before expiry of the relevant period of **Art.108** (**R.101(1)**). Minor deficiencies may be corrected in response to an invitation from the EPO (**R.101(2)**).

The admissibility of an appeal must be checked ex officio in every phase of the appeal proceedings (**T15/01** r.1). A decision concerning admissibility is normally taken together with the final decision. There is no refund of the appeal fee when a decision is taken that an appeal is inadmissible because the appeal proceedings have started and a substantial amount of work has already been done (**T89/84**), a partial refund is still possible if no oral proceedings are held (**R.103**).

4 **Examination of allowability**

When examining whether an appeal is 'allowable' under **Art.110**, a board of appeal examines whether the grounds on which the appeal is based warrant a rectification of the impugned decision, as can be inferred from the French text of the provision. See also the German text of **Art.109(2)** as compared with the English text. The examination of allowability is implemented by **R.100**. The examination is carried out by the first instance under **Art.109** in ex parte proceedings where the appeal can be allowed immediately on the basis of the grounds of appeal themselves; the second instance has exclusive jurisdiction in other cases (**T473/91**).

5 **Extent of examination**

The primary object of appeal proceedings is to review the impugned decision in a judicial manner (Art.12(2) RPBA). Accordingly, a party's appeal case must be directed to the requests, facts, objections, arguments and evidence on which the impugned decision was based (Art.12(2) RPBA) and a party's ability to deviate from the requests and submissions made at first instance is highly restricted under the RPBA (see **Art.110:6**).

In opposition appeal proceedings, the main purpose of the appeal procedure is to give the losing party a possibility to challenge the decision of the opposition division on its merits in a judicial procedure (**G9/91**, r.18) and the board itself is also limited to an extent in terms of the scope of its examination. The board may not examine subject-matter, i.e. claims, not covered by the extent of opposition as stated in the notice of opposition (**G9/91** r.11). See **R.76(2):4** for details of the extent of the opposition.

The board may furthermore consider only the grounds for opposition on which the appealed decision is based, unless the proprietor agrees to the introduction of an additional ground into the proceedings (**G10/91** hn.3). A ground for opposition put forward in the notice of opposition, but subsequently not maintained at oral proceedings, is considered a fresh ground if reintroduced on appeal (**T376/04** r.1.1). This applies also to further appeal proceedings after an initial remittal to the opposition division. Any ground raised in the first opposition proceedings, but not relied on in the second, will be considered a fresh ground of opposition if reintroduced to the proceedings in the further appeal (**T986/04**). If an opposition division holds a late-filed ground inadmissible, the board can admit the ground if the opposition division exercised its discretion in accordance with the wrong principles, without taking the right principles into account, or in an arbitrary or unreasonable way, even without the consent of the proprietor (**T842/22; T1286/14**). Which grounds are regarded as separate grounds for opposition is discussed in **Art.100:1.**

In grant appeal proceedings, however, the board has the power to examine whether the application meets the requirements of the EPC, including any requirements the examining division did not consider or regarded as having been met (**G10/93** hn, following **J4/80** hn.I and **T105/87** r.1). The board is not limited to reviewing the decision under appeal, even if this is the primary object of the appeal proceedings (Art.12(2) RPBA). Boards therefore frequently raise added matter objections and clarity objections which were not noted in the decision.

6 Amendment of case pursued at first instance in appeal proceedings

The primary objective of appeal proceedings is to review the first instance decision under appeal. As a result, the board is only obliged to take into account those parts of a party's appeal case that (a) are directed to the requests, facts, objections, arguments and evidence on which the decision is based, or (b) were admissibly raised and maintained in the first instance proceedings even though not discussed in the decision (Art.12(2) and Art.12(4) RPBA). Furthermore, the party's case must be fully substantiated in the statement of grounds when the party is the appellant or in the reply thereto when the party is the respondent (Art.12(3) RPBA; see **Art.110:7** below). Any aspect of a party's case which does not meet either criteria (a) or (b) is an amendment of that party's case and will be considered at the discretion of the board following a consideration of admissibility. The need to assess whether a part of a party's case was admissibly raised, even though not dealt with in the appealed decision, can arise, for example, when a patent is maintained as granted by an opposition division and auxiliary requests filed by the proprietor are not therefore addressed in its decision.

An aspect of a party's case that is filed as early as possible in the first instance proceedings should generally be considered to have been admissibly raised in those proceedings and hence should be taken into account by a board of appeal. For example, a document filed by an opponent within the nine-month opposition period should generally be admitted, and any auxiliary request filed by the proprietor within the time limit set under **R.79(1)** should also generally be admitted. However, according to **T364/20**, an auxiliary request cannot automatically be deemed to have been admissibly raised just because it was filed at the earliest possible opportunity – there may be exceptional circumstances in which an auxiliary request, even when filed at this stage, could be considered an abuse of the proceedings in view of the unjustified number or divergence of the requests filed. According to this decision, in order to assess whether an auxiliary request was admissibly raised, the board must decide whether the first instance department should have admitted the auxiliary request had a decision on admissibility been required. Requests filed after the expiry of the time limit set under **R.79(1)** must be considered to have been late filed unless submitted as a direct and timely response to a change in the proceedings, e.g. in response to a negative finding on an objection raised for the first time in the provisional opinion of the opposition division or the filing of a new piece of prior art by the opponent. The admissibility of a late filed request must be assessed, bearing in mind that the patent proprietor should be given more freedom to redefine its fallback positions in the proceedings before the opposition division than in appeal. The Board in **T246/22** provides another approach to assess whether auxiliary requests have been admissibly raised. In this Board's view, "carry-over requests" that were not discussed in the first instance proceedings may be regarded as admissibly raised by a party if said party shows that they were filed in due time and that the reason for filing those auxiliary requests within the first instance proceedings (i.e. their purpose) was clear. The latter condition may be satisfied by the party submitting arguments in support of the patentability of the auxiliary requests together with said requests during the first instance proceedings.

If a party wishes to pursue on appeal something which is an amendment of its case at first instance, it must identify the amendment when filing its grounds of appeal, or response thereto, and provide reasons for submitting it for the first time on appeal. If the amendment is an amendment of a patent application or patent, the applicant or proprietor, respectively, must also indicate the basis for the amendment in the application as filed and the reasons why the amendment overcomes an objection which has been raised (Art.12(4) RPBA; see, for example, **T1731/19**). If such justification is not provided at the first opportunity, the amendment is less likely to be admitted by the board since the justification itself will then amount to a further amendment of the party's case made during the appeal proceedings (Art.12(3) and Art.12(5) RPBA).

With respect to an amendment to a party's case, relative to first instance proceedings, the board will not admit requests, facts, objections or evidence which should have been submitted or which were no longer maintained in those proceedings, unless the circumstances of the appeal case justify their admittance (Art.12(6) RPBA). Furthermore, the board will not admit requests, facts, objections or evidence which were held inadmissible in the first instance proceedings unless it can be argued that the decision not to admit them suffered from an error or that the circumstances of the appeal case justify their admittance (Art.12(6) RPBA).

In exercising its discretion to admit an amendment of a party's case, the board will consider the complexity of the amendment, the suitability of the amendment to address the issues which led to the decision under appeal, and the need for procedural economy (Art.12(4) RPBA). When considering the admissibility of an objection or request which was not admitted by the first instance department, the board should only overrule the way in which the first instance department exercised its discretion if it comes to the conclusion that the wrong principles were applied or discretion was exercised in an unreasonable way (**G7/93** r.2.6). Since holding part of a party's case inadmissible means that that part is disregarded, Art.12(6) RPBA does not apply if a submission was analysed in depth in the impugned decision before being formally held inadmissible (**T1525/17**). According to **T618/20**, whilst prima facie allowability is an important factor to be taken into account by the first instance department in relation to a new claim request, the need for procedural economy must be given an increasing amount of weight during oral proceedings.

When considering whether an amendment to an appellant's case should have been filed during the first instance proceedings, the board will pay attention to whether the amendment addresses a late development in the proceedings (e.g. in oral proceedings) which the party did not have the opportunity to address at the time. For instance, if new claims are filed by the proprietor during oral proceedings before the opposition division, the patent is maintained on this basis, and the opponent appeals, it may be appropriate for the opponent to file a new document with its grounds of appeal that is relevant to the new claims but was not relevant to the previously pending claims (e.g. **T573/21**). Alternatively, if the opposition division admits a new document as the closest prior art that was only filed shortly before oral proceedings, it may be appropriate for the proprietor to file new evidence of a technical effect with its grounds of appeal or response thereto in order to demonstrate an inventive step over this document (e.g. **T757/21**).

On the other hand, if the examining division raises an objection under **Art.123(2)** or **Art.84** during oral proceedings and invites the applicant to file a new request to address this issue, the applicant cannot decline this opportunity and expect the new request to be admitted by the board of appeal (e.g. **T2322/22**). The same applies to a proprietor faced with an objection under **Art.123(2)** in oral proceedings before the opposition division (e.g. **T1441/21**). Equally, a board may decide not allow an opponent to introduce a new document into appeal proceedings if it is simply further evidence to support its case. Neither the fact that the evidence on file was insufficient to convince the opposition division nor the potential relevance of the new document are sufficient in themselves to justify the late filing (e.g. **T114/21**).

Generally speaking, new arguments concerning the way in which the law should be interpreted and references to board of appeal decisions supporting such an interpretation are not regarded as an amendment to a party's case and are automatically admissible at any stage of the appeal proceedings (e.g. **T2988/18**). However, if a party's arguments extend to an analysis of the facts underlying a particular case and their similarity to the case in hand then this may amount to an allegation of fact that represents an amendment to the party's case (e.g. **T116/18 of 28.07.2023**).

A board has the discretion to admit on appeal a document or request which was held inadmissible by a first instance department. However, it is not generally possible for an appellant to contest the decision of a first instance department to admit a document or request on which the impugned decision is based. For instance, the board in **T446/19** saw no legal basis for excluding an auxiliary request filed by the proprietor during oral proceedings before the opposition division, the request having been admitted and decided upon. If the party concerned requested the first instance department to allow additional time or an adjournment in order to deal with the document or request, and this was denied, it is possible that the party's right to be heard was violated and the decision could be set aside by the board on this basis.

7 Requirement for appeal case to be substantiated

According to Art.12(3) RPBA, the statement of grounds of appeal and the reply thereto must contain each party's complete appeal case. This is interpreted to mean that if any part of a party's case is not set out in a sufficiently complete manner in the statement of grounds or reply thereto, it does not have to be taken into account by the board.

For instance, if an auxiliary request is filed by an applicant or proprietor, but the relevant basis under **Art.123(2)** is not indicated, or the reasons according to which the auxiliary request overcomes an alleged problem with a higher-ranking request is not indicated, the board may decide not to take that auxiliary request into account. In **T1268/10**, auxiliary requests were not taken into account since the respondent did not indicate in its response to the grounds of appeal how the new features of the claims would address a later finding that the main request lacked an inventive step (see also **T312/22** for another similar example).

Equally, if an objection is made by an opponent against one of the proprietor's requests, the board may decide not to take that objection into account if it is not substantiated in sufficient detail. As an example, an inventive step attack was held to be insufficiently substantiated in **T2117/18** since it merely referred to the combination of the teaching of two documents without providing any specific reasoning. Equally, an objection under **Art.123(3)** EPC was not considered by the board in **T1914/19** since it did not address the reasoning of the opposition division finding that the main request complied with **Art.123(3)**.

A mere reference to arguments or requests filed during the first instance proceedings, or a mere repetition of arguments used in first instance proceedings, does not usually amount to sufficient substantiation: a party must also explain why any relevant aspect of the reasoning in the impugned decision is wrong (**T2117/18**). For example, in **T552/22**, three auxiliary requests that had been filed before the opposition division were filed once more in response to the opponent's appeal. No reasons were given explaining how the amendments made overcame the opponent's objections under **Art.56** and **Art.83** other than a general reference to arguments made in the response to the opposition. The requests were not admitted.

8 Amendment of appeal case after the grounds of appeal and response have been filed

According to Art.13(1) and Art.13(2) RPBA, an amendment to a party's appeal case is only admissible under certain circumstances. When considering the admissibility of further appeal submissions, the board will therefore conduct an analysis in two stages (e.g. **T22/21** and decisions cited therein). The board will first consider whether the further submissions represent an amendment of the party's appeal case. Only if this preliminary question is answered in the affirmative will admissibility criteria be applied.

It is therefore necessary to consider the meaning of the word "amendment". It would clearly be an amendment of an opponent's appeal case to raise a new ground of opposition (though this is subject to the more stringent admissibility criteria established in **G10/91**) or file a new document. However, the meaning of "amendment" goes much further than this. It would also be an amendment of an opponent's appeal case to base an inventive step attack on a different document as closest prior art, or even on a different passage of the same document, or to raise an objection under **Art.123(2)** on the basis of a claim feature which had not previously been objected to. For instance, in **T2866/18** the opponent based part of its appeal case on a lack of novelty in view of a specific document and indicated it would only comment on lack of inventive step over the same document if the board found the claimed invention to be novel. When, in oral proceedings, the board recognised the novelty of the claim, the opponent's inventive step attack was found to be an amendment of its case and was not admitted. In **J14/19**, the board found that the use of a new document as the closest prior art or the use of a new passage within the established closest prior art as a starting point in an inventive step attack (new factual element in same legal context) or the use of an already cited passage in a document to support a different ground of appeal (same factual element in new legal context) goes beyond the mere refinement of an existing line of argument and constitutes an amendment to an appeal case. On the other hand, the board considered that statements not containing any factual element and merely concerning the interpretation of the EPC were not new arguments which could be considered to be an amendment of an appeal case.

In the case of an applicant or a proprietor, it would clearly be an amendment of such a party's appeal case to seek to introduce new evidence relating to a technical effect or the common general knowledge. However, most frequently the applicant or proprietor seeks to introduce a new set of claims to deal with an objection which is upheld by the board. If, as a result, this leads to the claiming of a new combination of features, the appeal case has clearly been amended. Where the case law diverges is on the question of whether the mere deletion of a claim, or an alternative within a claim, results in an amended appeal case. In many cases the board has found that such an amendment to the claims must always been seen as an amendment of the appeal case (e.g. **T494/18**, deletion of product claims; **T22/21** and decisions cited therein) but in other cases the board has considered that such an amendment to the claims only amounts to an amendment of the appeal case if it changes the factual and legal framework of the case (e.g. **T2243/18**, deletion of product claims; **T2091/18**). In **T494/18**, the board emphasised the need for a party to file its complete appeal case at the earliest stage (Art.12(3) RPBA) and that this leads to an expectation that all requests should be "specified expressly" at this point. In **T2243/18**, on the other hand, the board considered that the amendment made to the claims limited the appeal case without amending it.

In **T184/18** it was found that an amendment restricting to claims that were held allowable by the opposition division and not challenged by any party during the appeal proceedings was not an amendment for the purposes of the RPBA.

It should be noted that a party's appeal case does not include the case that it made at first instance (see **Art.110:7**). It should also be noted that the point in time at which an objection or request is considered to have been filed during the appeal proceedings is not necessarily the first time that it is alluded to. Some boards have found that an objection or request can only be considered to have been validly filed when it has also been sufficiently substantiated (e.g. **T1732/10**). This may mean, for instance, that the admissibility of an objection filed with grounds of appeal, but only substantiated later in the appeal proceedings, may need to be considered under Art.13(1) or Art.13(2) RPBA rather than under Art.12(6) RPBA (e.g. **T2117/18**). However, this approach was questioned in **T1220/21**.

One area in which the case law currently diverges is the question of whether a new procedural request is an amendment of a party's case which is subject to Art.13(1) and Art.13(2) RPBA. According to **T1006/21** (which was followed by **T139/20**), a procedural request is not an amendment of a party's case and must be considered by the board whenever raised. According to the board, procedural requests include a request for remittal to the first instance, a request for a referral to the Enlarged Board, a request that the appeal be held inadmissible, a request that a claim request, an allegation of fact or evidence be admitted or held inadmissible, a request for the interruption of proceedings, a request for the exclusion of a board member, a request for the appointment of oral proceedings, a request for the rescheduling of oral proceedings, a request for the acceleration of proceedings and a request for a stay of proceedings. However, this distinction between procedural requests and other requests was rejected by the board in **T1774/21** which found that a request for non-admission of an objection did indeed represent an amendment to a party's case if not filed as early as possible and hence was governed by Art.13(2) RPBA. The board cited **T18/21** and **T755/16** in favour of this alternative interpretation.

8.1 ADMISSIBILITY CRITERIA TO BE APPLIED BETWEEN FILING OF GROUNDS/REPLY THERETO AND EXPIRY OF PERIOD SET FOR FILING WRITTEN OBSERVATIONS UNDER R.100(2) OR, WHERE NO SUCH COMMUNICATION IS ISSUED, NOTIFICATION OF A COMMUNICATION UNDER ART.15(1) RPBA

According to Art.13(1) RPBA, any amendment to a party's appeal case after it has filed its grounds of appeal or reply thereto must be justified and its admission into the appeal proceedings is subject to the discretion of the board of appeal. The party concerned must provide reasons that justify the timing of the amendment, i.e. explain why it could not have been made earlier, either in the first instance proceedings or in the appeal proceedings. For instance, if a proprietor files a new claim request with its response to the opponent's grounds of appeal, it is advisable for the opponent to raise any new objection immediately, in a further written response (the board may not issue its preliminary opinion on matters to be discussed at oral proceedings until at least one month has elapsed from the filing of any response to the grounds of appeal according to Art.15(1) RPBA).

Since Art.12(4)-(6) RBPA apply mutatis mutandis (Art.13(1) RPBA), a party must identify any amendment of its case and provide reasons justifying its admissibility – in the case of an amendment to the text of an application or patent both basis for the amendment and an explanation of how it overcomes an objection must be provided.

In exercising its discretion, the board may apply any of the criteria of Art.12(4) RPBA (complexity of amendment, suitability of amendment to address a relevant issue, need for procedural economy) as well as the taking note of the state of the proceedings and considering whether the amendment is not just suitable to address a relevant issue but whether it actually, prima facie, overcomes that issue and whether or not it gives rise to new objections (Art.13(1) RPBA).

Regardless of the position of the board, any other party to the proceedings must also be given the chance to contest admissibility (Art.13(3) RPBA).

8.2 ADMISSIBILITY CRITERIA TO BE APPLIED AFTER EXPIRY OF PERIOD SET FOR FILING WRITTEN OBSERVATIONS UNDER R.100(2) OR, WHERE NO SUCH COMMUNICATION IS ISSUED, NOTIFICATION OF A COMMUNICATION UNDER ART.15(1) RPBA

According to Art.13(2) RPBA, an amendment to a party's appeal case at this late stage of the proceedings shall, in principle, not be taken into account unless there are exceptional circumstances which have been justified with cogent reasons by the party concerned. This provision was amended as of 01.01.2024 (OJ 2023 A103) to refer to an amendment of a party's case made after notification of a communication under Art.15(1) RPBA (drawing attention to significant matters to be discussed and often containing a preliminary opinion) rather than after notification of a summons to oral proceedings.

Exceptional circumstances may occur, for example, when the board of appeal raises new objections in its preliminary opinion or during oral proceedings that have not been previously raised or admits new objections made for the first time by a party: the proprietor should be allowed to file a new request that overcomes these objections. For instance, in **T1440/17**, the board adopted a new claim interpretation in its preliminary opinion which justified the subsequent filing of an auxiliary request. Equally, in **T360/21**, the board adopted a certain interpretation of technical terms in its preliminary opinion that justified the admittance of a document representing common general knowledge. In **T2353/19**, the board explained that the newly raised issue must underlie the final conclusion of the board in order to justify the admission of a late-filed request. In this case the board found a lack of novelty based on arguments already in the proceedings before the issuance of its preliminary opinion and the late-filed request was therefore not justified even though filed in reaction to a further novelty objection raised in that opinion.

However, exceptional circumstances can exist even if there has not been a late development in the proceedings – the exceptional circumstances demanded by Art.13(2) RPBA do not themselves have to lead to the filing of the amendment. Exceptional circumstances may exist simply because the amendment concerned is not detrimental to procedural economy or the legitimate interests of any party to the proceedings. For instance, in **T602/21**, a new auxiliary request filed in advance of oral proceedings was admitted because the subject matter of the auxiliary request was already pending (the amendment made merely involved the deletion of two claims), other auxiliary requests were withdrawn (maintaining a convergent approach) and the remaining claims had not before been objected to by the opponent (see also **T908/18** and **T2920/18**, involving the deletion of claims). In an ex parte appeal, when other parties are not involved, only procedural economy needs to be taken into account (e.g. **T1294/16**) and boards are usually more inclined to exercise discretion favourably (see also **T1623/20**). For instance, in **T1790/17**, the board admitted a new request filed during oral proceedings on the basis that it was a direct reaction to the exchange or arguments that had taken place and overcame the grounds on which the contested decision was based.

Furthermore, the board in **T1906/19** observed that the term 'in principle' in Art.13(2) RPBA leaves some leeway for the boards to admit an amendment to a party's appeal case even if there are no exceptional circumstances, in particular if the amendment is not detrimental to procedural economy.

When exercising its discretion under Article 13(2) RPBA, the board may also rely on the criteria set out in Article 13(1) RPBA (see, for example, **T1440/17** and cases cited therein).

Regardless of the position of the board, any other party to the proceedings must also be given the chance to contest admissibility (Art.13(3) RPBA).

9 Closure of debate in oral proceedings

The appeal procedure is in principle in writing, but can include oral proceedings if requested by a party or deemed expedient by the board of appeal (**Art.116**). The board can reject a request for further oral proceedings (**Art.116(1)**). In the summons to oral proceedings, the board may indicate issues which are important for the decision or questions that have to be settled (see **R.116(1):3**). In general, oral proceedings are concluded by a final decision and form the end of the appeal procedure.

During oral proceedings, a party may make submissions until the chair closes the debate, after which the board deliberates and then issues its decision on the matter under discussion (**G12/91** r.3). The announcement of a negative decision often takes parties by surprise; had they expected a negative decision, they would have filed a further request. The inability to file a further request is a commonly used ground in petitions for review, the inability being regarded as a fundamental violation of **Art.113**. These petitions are usually rejected as unallowable.

The uncertainty in oral proceedings frequently prompts applicants to file a divisional application prior to oral proceedings, pay the fees after a negative decision, and continue prosecution with the divisional application. If the facts and objection in the case of the divisional are the same and the previous board has already dealt with the objection, a new board has no power to examine the objection again (**T51/08** r.3, 4).

The last moment in time a party can file a further request in oral proceedings is the moment the chair declares the debate closed for deliberation. The party must then request that the debate be re-opened and file its request. (**R10/08** r.8)

10 **Accelerated processing**

A board may accelerate appeal proceedings of its own motion or on request by a party, a court (including the UPC) or competent authority of a contracting state (Art.10(3) to (6) RPBA). The request of a party must contain reasons justifying the acceleration and be supported by documentary evidence where appropriate.

Valid reasons for acceleration include pending infringement proceedings (OJ 2024 sp1, IV.1). However, a board is not required to accelerate appeal proceedings even if the reason provided would in principle justify acceleration. Exceptionally, the board may accelerate appeal proceedings *ex* officio, e.g. if the case concerns important legal questions (**T1063/18**), or because of substantial delays in the first instance proceedings (**T2707/16**).

11 **Termination of proceedings and withdrawal of appeal**

Appellants can withdraw their appeal (**T674/03** r.3). When the sole appellant withdraws the appeal, appeal proceedings are terminated, both in ex parte and in inter partes proceedings, in so far as the substantive issues settled by the contested decision at first instance are concerned (**G8/91** hn). If an appeal has been withdrawn, the board may decide to continue with issues related to the appeal, such as a request for reimbursement of the appeal fee (**T41/82**) or for apportionment of the costs pursuant to **Art.104** (**T117/86**). If the appealed decision was an interlocutory decision, the procedure before the opposition division will continue, e.g. with the filing of translated claims under **R.82**.

Withdrawal of the opposition by an opponent who is the sole appellant is regarded as withdrawal of the appeal (**G8/93**). The board is not allowed to continue opposition appeal proceedings of its own motion, as might have been expected from **R.84(2)** in conjunction with **R.100(1)**, because opposition proceedings and opposition appeal proceedings are of a different nature (**G7/91** r.7). In contrast to the purely administrative character of the opposition procedure, the appeal procedure is to be considered as a judicial procedure, which is by its nature less investigative than an administrative procedure. (**G7/91, G8/91, T357/89, T695/89**)

As a consequence, appeal proceedings are terminated after the opponent, as the sole appellant, withdraws its opposition, irrespective of whether the proprietor agrees to termination and even if, in the board's view, the requirements under the EPC for maintaining the patent are not satisfied (**G8/93** hn; see also **G7/91** r.10, 11).

When an opponent who is a party as of right in the appeal (in particular, respondent) withdraws its opposition, the appeal procedure continues with the examination of the appeal of the proprietor. The board must dismiss the appeal if the proprietor/appellant cannot convince the board that the decision of the opposition division is incorrect (see e.g. **T1262/19**). The opponent ceases to be a party to the proceedings as far as the substantive issues are concerned (**T340/05**). Evidence submitted prior to withdrawal can still be used in the appeal. Moreover, the opponent remains a party to the proceedings for any apportionment of costs under **Art.104**. (**T789/89**)

In special cases, a partial withdrawal of an appeal is also possible, namely if the withdrawn part relates to a special issue dealt with separately in the appealed decision (**J19/82**).

As sole appellant, it is possible to withdraw an appeal before a final decision is announced in oral proceedings to avoid a decision being published which may contain reasoning adverse to the appellant's interests. However, once a decision has been announced in oral proceedings, the appeal proceedings are terminated and the board is obliged to issue a reasoned decision. Withdrawal of the appeal after a decision is announced is therefore without any legal effect (**T1008/19**). Note, the boards often announce one or more conclusions in the course of the oral proceedings and ask the parties to confirm their final requests before the board announces the decision at the end of the oral proceedings. Withdrawal of an appeal is possible after the board has announced one or more conclusions and before the board announces the decision.

Art. 111 Decision in respect of appeals

1 **General**
The board of appeal reviews the impugned decision and decides on the appeal. If the board sets aside the impugned decision, it may exercise any power within the competence of the department of first instance that took the decision or remit the case to that department for further prosecution (**Art.111(1)**). After remittal the department of first instance is bound by the decision of the board (**Art.111(2)**). The content of the decision, such as the reasons and signature, are governed by **R.102**. The form of the decision must comply with **R.111(2)**.

All decisions of the boards are published in the language of the proceedings on the EPO website unless excluded from file inspection under **Art.128(1)**. Some decisions are also published in all three official languages of the EPO in the OJ. The date of a decision in appeal finally refusing a patent application is published in the European Patent Bulletin and Register according to **Art.127, 129, R.143(1)(n)**.

Art. 111(1) Following the examination as to the allowability of the appeal, the Board of Appeal shall decide on the appeal. The Board of Appeal may either exercise any power within the competence of the department which was responsible for the decision appealed or remit the case to that department for further prosecution.

Implemented by:
R.102 Form of decision of the Board of Appeal
R.103 Reimbursement of appeal fees

1 **Decision in appeal proceedings**
The board of appeal may take an interlocutory decision, which does not terminate proceedings, or a final decision, which does (see e.g. **Art.106(2)**). The word 'final' is also used in a different sense in the expression 'a decision has become final', where it has the different meaning of 'a decision has become res judicata', i.e. the decision is no longer open to appeal (see the section below).

The investigative powers of the boards of appeal pursuant to **Art.114(1)** are limited in inter partes proceedings to the extent of the initial requests of the parties (**G9/91** r.1, see also **G10/91; G9/92; R.76(2):4.2** and **R.99(2)**).

If the appellant has filed an admissible set of auxiliary claims, the board of appeal will first decide on the main set of claims, and, if not acceptable, on the auxiliary set of claims (**T156/87**). When the board of appeal decides to grant a patent, the case will be remitted to the department of first instance with instructions on the exact scope of the claims to be granted, so the first instance can then take care of the administrative procedure necessary for grant as set out in **R.71** and **R.71a** (the description having been adapted where necessary).

A decision of the board of appeal must comply with the requirements of **R.102**. A decision will be based on the request of a party. Hence, a request in oral proceedings is not a mere basis for a discussion, but a procedural declaration to the board for a decision to be made on that basis. A request for the grant of a patent includes the applicant's approval of the text in the sense of **Art.113(2)**. (**J8/98**)

2 **Remittal to first instance**

According to **Art.111(1)** a board of appeal may remit a case to the department of first instance whose decision was appealed. The board will only remit a case for further prosecution, i.e. for the department of first instance to decide on the allowability of the claims, if there are special reasons for doing so (Art.11 RPBA). In contrast, a remittal with the order to grant or maintain a patent on the basis of a set of claims found allowable by the board does not require special reasons. The aim in restricting remittal is to prevent undue prolongation of the proceedings.

A fundamental deficiency apparent in the proceedings at first instance is normally a special reason for remittal (Art.11 RPBA). A fundamental deficiency is not caused by any procedural violation but rather by a substantial procedural violation in the sense of **R.103(1)(a)** (**T689/05** r.4.2; **T996/09** r.21). However, even if there was a substantial procedural violation, a board may decide not to remit the case if the remittal would only unnecessarily delay the proceedings (**J8/18** r.2).

Art.11 RPBA must be read in conjunction with Art.12(2) RPBA which provides that it is the primary object of the appeal proceedings to review the decision under appeal in a judicial manner. Consequently, a board setting aside a decision under appeal should remit the case if a full assessment for compliance with the EPC has not yet been carried out. Otherwise, the board would effectively be taking the place of the first instance division rather than reviewing the contested decision in a judicial manner. (**T731/17**; **T1966/16**; **T1621/17**; **T1616/18**)

The principles of the following cases decided under RPBA 2007 appear to still hold true under the 2020 revision to the RPBA. A case will usually be remitted if new facts or evidence admitted into the proceedings significantly alter the legal and factual framework, resulting in a fresh case (**T340/12** r.3.1). Remittal can also be appropriate if amended claims filed and admitted in appeal make it necessary to decide on grounds of opposition that were not the subject of the appealed decision and the appeal proceedings (**T648/10** r.7). Cases are also normally remitted if the appealed decision is based solely upon a particular issue, leaving other essential issues outstanding, and the appeal on the particular issue is allowed (**T389/12** r.3.1). For instance, in the event that the opposition division revokes a patent on the sole ground of lack of novelty and the board finds the claims to be novel, the decision under appeal can be set aside and the case is normally remitted for further prosecution (**T389/12**).

The first instance department to which a case is remitted is generally bound by the reasoning given in the decision of the board of appeal (**Art.111(2)**).

3 **Res judicata effect of board of appeal decision**
A decision of the board of appeal becomes formally res judicata as soon as it is issued, i.e. it is not open to appeal (**G1/97** r.2a). The principle of res judicata is based on public policy considerations that see the need for an end to litigation (**T167/93** r.2.7). This applies both to interlocutory and final decisions. A decision taken by a board of appeal can only be set aside by the Enlarged Board of Appeal hearing a petition for review based on one of the limited grounds set out in **Art.112a(2)**. **T167/93** r.2.5 lists six criteria a decision must comply with for res judicata to apply.

The substance of a board of appeal decision is binding both on the board and on the parties to the proceedings (substantive res judicata). If the same parties in new or the same proceedings before the EPO dispute the same issue, the EPO is bound by the substance of the earlier decision. This could arise, for example, when the refusal of a divisional application is being reviewed by a board of appeal, the divisional having identical claims to those rejected by the board of appeal that reviewed the refusal of the parent application. If proceedings are resumed before the same board following an interlocutory decision that has become final, the board must take the substance of its decision as the basis for its subsequent decision. Thus, for example, when the novelty of a set of claims is acknowledged by a board of appeal and the application is remitted for further examination, the board of appeal reviewing a subsequent decision to refuse the application for lack of inventive step cannot challenge the previous decision on novelty. (**T694/01** r.2.10)

An example of res judicata is a case remitted by the board with an order to maintain a patent on the basis of amended claims: neither the wording nor the patentability of these claims may be further challenged in subsequent proceedings before the EPO (**T843/91**).

The principle of res judicata and that of the binding effect of the ratio decidendi pursuant to **Art.111(2)** are not mutually exclusive but complement each other. The binding effect of the ratio decidendi extends to matter which has not become res judicata, but it only applies in so far as the facts are the same. On the other hand, a matter which has become res judicata is not open for reconsideration following a remittal for further prosecution, not even in case of a change of the facts, e.g. by introduction of new documents (**T449/15**).

Art. 111(2) If the Board of Appeal remits the case for further prosecution to the department whose decision was appealed, that department shall be bound by the ratio decidendi of the Board of Appeal, in so far as the facts are the same. If the decision under appeal was taken by the Receiving Section, the Examining Division shall also be bound by the ratio decidendi of the Board of Appeal.

1 **Binding effect of board of appeal decision**
The binding effect of a decision applies only to the extent determined by the nature of the proceedings and the provision of the law.

According to **Art.111(2)**, first sentence, a department to which a case is remitted is bound by the ratio decidendi of the decision of the board of appeal, in so far as the facts are the same. For example, if a board of appeal has rejected certain claims and has remitted the case for further prosecution of the remaining claims, the examination of the rejected claims cannot thereafter be reopened, either by the examining division or by the board of appeal in any subsequent appeal proceedings (**T79/89**). The competence of the latter board of appeal is restricted in the same way as that of the first instance department after the remittal (CLBA V.A.10.4). **Art.111(2)**, first sentence, also applies in opposition proceedings.

An appeal decision for a parent case is binding for the same subject-matter in a divisional application, and claims refused on appeal for the parent application cannot be pursued on appeal in the divisional application (**T51/08**, **T790/10**).

1.1 BINDING EFFECT IN SAME CASE

The binding effect of **Art.111(2)** does not extend to a department other than the one that took the contested decision. For example, a decision of a board of appeal taken during grant proceedings has no binding effect in subsequent opposition proceedings or on appeal therefrom, not only because different parties are involved but also because the EPC does not extend the binding effect of a decision in this manner (**T167/93** hn, r.2.10; E-X,4; CLBA V.A.10.3).

By way of exception, according to **Art.111(2)**, second sentence, the examining division is bound by the assessment of the Legal Board of Appeal considering a decision taken by the Receiving Section. In this way, procedural questions settled for the first instance by the Legal Board of Appeal cannot be reopened by the examining division. There is no need for such an exception for the opposition division, as most procedural questions relate to the grant procedure, and the opposition division need only assess the grounds of opposition of **Art.100**, which are not procedural but substantive in nature.

A decision is not only binding on the outcome of the assessment of individual claims but also on all the findings of fact which led to that decision. For example, if the board decides that a document is novelty destroying by disclosing certain features, the proprietor cannot contest that the document discloses these features in connection with inventive step of an auxiliary request (T956/19 r.42-44).

Art.111(2) refers only to the ratio decidendi, i.e. the essential reasoning on which the outcome of the case depends (**T843/91**), and not to obiter dicta, i.e. findings that do not support the order of the decision. Therefore, the binding effect of a board of appeal decision does not apply to obiter dicta.

1.2 BINDING EFFECT ON OTHER CASES

A decision of a board of appeal has a binding effect only in the individual case which the board has remitted to the department of first instance. It has no binding effect on other cases but may serve as a guiding principle. In general, the departments of first instance follow the decisions of the boards of appeal in order to maintain a consistent practice and to avoid unnecessary appeals. There is, however, no principle in the EPC preventing the first instance from having a question, already decided by a board, reconsidered in another case by the same or another board. This may, in appropriate cases, contribute to the development of the law. (**J27/94** r.4)

A party may legitimately expect that first instance departments will not deviate from established case law if this case law has become part of the consistent practice of the department of first instance, in particular if this practice has been included in the Guidelines or a Notice from the EPO. (**J27/94** r.5)

If there is no solid body of consistent case law on the interpretation of a substantive provision governing patentability but only a very limited number of individual decisions, there can be no legitimate expectation that the EBoA will not overrule that interpretation (**G2/07** r.2.5).

Art.20 RPBA stipulates that, where a board departs from an earlier decision on a point of law, the board must explain its departure in the reasons for the decision and inform the President. The President may decide to refer the point of law to the EBoA (**Art.112(1)(b)**). Should a board consider it necessary to deviate from an interpretation or explanation of the EPC given in an earlier opinion or decision of the EBoA, the question must be referred to the EBoA (**Art.21** RPBA).

Decisions of the EPO taken by first instance departments and boards of appeal have no substantive res judicata effect for national courts in revocation proceedings pursuant to **Art.138**, even if the same parties are involved (**T694/01** r.2.12). Hence, the assessment of prior art by the EPO has no binding effect in national revocation proceedings. In Germany, decisions of the EPO are regarded as expert opinions which must be acknowledged but which are without further legal effect (OJ 1999 p.322; OJ 2010 p.622).

Art. 112 Decision or opinion of the Enlarged Board of Appeal

1 **Competence and composition of Enlarged Board of Appeal**

One of the functions of the Enlarged Board of Appeal (EBoA) is to ensure a uniform application of the law and to resolve important points of the law (**Art.112(1)**). Therefore, it has the competence according to **Art.22(1)** to give decisions on points of law referred to it by the boards of appeal (BoAs) and to give opinions on points of law referred to it by the President. The EBoA also has competence under **Art.22(1)(c)** to conduct a judicial review of a board of appeal decision when deciding on a petition for review. See **Art.112a** and notes.

In early drafts of the EPC a European Patent Court was to have jurisdiction to hear appeals from decisions of the boards of appeal in grant proceedings. However, during the negotiations leading to EPC1973, no agreement could be reached on the creation of such a court. Hence, it was decided that a decision of a BoA is final and cannot be appealed further under EPC1973 (Empel §521). **Art.112a** EPC2000 later added the limited possibility of having a decision of a BoA reviewed for procedural errors.

When a BoA refers a point of law to the EBoA, the EBoA will take a decision on this point alone and will not decide on any other issue in the appeal case. The final decision in the case is then always taken by the BoA, applying the interpretation of the law given by the EBoA.

The wording of **Art.112(1)** is modelled on old German law. The legislator has given the EBoA a limited power in order to achieve a consistent application of the EPC. The right of the President to refer questions to the EBoA is very limited; since the President is in an executive position (**Art.10**), the President should not have too much legislative influence.

According to **Art.112(1)**, the EBoA has jurisdiction only over referrals by BoAs and the President. The EBoA may not investigate legal issues of its own motion. Moreover, the legislator decided to restrict the number of referrals further by including several conditions in **Art.112(1)**, to be discussed below. As a consequence, some lack of uniformity in the application of the law has arisen, leading to a degree of legal uncertainty for users of the European patent system.

The EBoA comprises about thirty members, who are appointed by the Administrative Council under **Art.11(3)**. They are drawn from the members of the BoAs, who for their part, according to **Art.23(2)**, may not be members of the departments of first instance. Under **Art.11(5)** the Administrative Council may appoint legally qualified members of the national courts of the EPC states as members of the EBoA. The aim is to further the harmonisation of patent law.

The Rules of Procedure of the EBoA (RPEBA) are adopted by the Boards of Appeal Committee of the Administrative Council under **R.12c** and are subject to the approval of the Administrative Council (**Art.23(4)**). The current version of the RPEBA is published in OJ 2024 sp1 p.34.

For each referral under **Art.112(1)**, the EBoA consists of seven members drawn from the above list, five of whom are legally qualified and two of whom are technically qualified, as governed by **Art.22(2)**. At least four members must not have taken part in the proceedings before the BoA referring the point of law (Art.2(4) RPEBA) to avoid members of the referring board having a majority in the EBoA. Partiality of the EBoA's members is dealt with by **Art.24(3)**.

Art. 112(1) In order to ensure uniform application of the law, or if a point of law of fundamental importance arises:

(a) the Board of Appeal shall, during proceedings on a case and either of its own motion or following a request from a party to the appeal, refer any question to the Enlarged Board of Appeal if it considers that a decision is required for the above purposes. If the Board of Appeal rejects the request, it shall give the reasons in its final decision;

(b) the President of the European Patent Office may refer a point of law to the Enlarged Board of Appeal where two Boards of Appeal have given different decisions on that question.

1 **Conditions for referral by a board of appeal** (**Art.112(1)(a)**)

A BoA may only refer a question to the EBoA under **Art.112(1)(a)** if the following two conditions are met:

- the question must relate to ensuring uniform application of the law or to a point of law of fundamental importance; and
- the board must consider that a decision is required.

A BoA will refuse a request for referral if either of these conditions is not met. Under EPC1973, the condition for referral was if an 'important point of law' arises; it remains to be seen whether the change to refer only to points of law 'of fundamental importance' has any impact. The conditions limit considerably the number of cases referred by the boards of appeal, as shown in the following examples.

A referral presupposes an admissible appeal; this does not apply when the referral concerns the admissibility of an appeal (**G2/04**, r.1.2).

The EBoA itself, when reviewing a petition for review under **Art.112a**, is not a board of appeal in the meaning of **Art.112(1)(a)**, and cannot refer a point of law to the EBoA for a decision (**R7/08**).

The question must be of a legal, not of a factual nature (**T118/89**). Hence, a technical question, such as the extent of the abilities of a skilled person (**T181/82** r.14) or a question relating to appreciation of evidence in a concrete case (**T845/90** r.4.1) will not be referred to the EBoA. Note, that the English text of the provision uses 'point of law' and 'question' in the same sense, whereas the French and German texts use only 'question de droit' and 'Rechtsfrage'.

A referral to ensure uniform application of the law is not necessary if there is no contradictory case law and earlier decisions can be followed (see e.g. **J47/92** r.5). Two decisions are not contradictory if they are based on different circumstances (**T143/91** r.5.9.5; **T248/88** r.3.3). There is no contradictory case law if an isolated decision deviates from established case law (**T248/88** r.3.3), nor if EPO case law diverges from national jurisprudence (**T154/04**). See also **Art.111(2):1.2.**

There is no important point of law if there is no general interest in clarifying a specific issue, e.g. if the question is geared essentially to the specific facts of the case to hand (**T601/92** r.5; **T939/92** r.4.1). An important point of law is normally derived from the essential reasoning on which a decision is based; however, obiter dicta may also concern important points of law that can give rise to legal uncertainty and can justify a referral (**G3/93** r.2; **G3/08** hn.5).

Most requests for a referral by a party are refused for non-compliance with the second condition, i.e. the necessity for a decision. This necessity is generally determined in view of the functioning of the EPO, not in view of legal certainty for the public. If a BoA can answer an important point of law beyond doubt by reference to the EPC, the question need not be referred to the EBoA (**J5/81** hn.2). A decision is not required either if the appeal would have to be dismissed for reasons not related to the question to be referred (**J16/90** r.1.2). A referral is ruled out if the question does not arise in the case under appeal (**J14/91** r.5.2; **T26/88**). When a BoA intends to take a favourable decision on an issue for which a party has requested a referral, there is no need anymore for a referral and the BoA will refuse any request for referral (**T461/88** r.10; **T301/87** r.4.9).

The attitude of the boards of appeal towards the necessity of referral in the case of contradictory decisions does not appear to be consistent, a subject on which Van Empel raised concerns as early as 1975 (Empel, §523). The following examples will make this clear. The board of **T998/99** took a decision relating to the exhaustion of a priority right which contradicted the uniform practice of the EPO; the decision was published in the OJ. It deemed that a referral was not required, because 'it is first and foremost for the boards of appeal to decide on this question', without reference to the conditions of **Art.112(1)** (r.6). On the other hand, in an earlier case an isolated decision **J22/95** interpreted the notion of the effective designation of a contracting state in a way that conflicted with standing practice of the EPO. In order not to increase legal uncertainty, publication of this decision in the OJ was delayed until the President's referral of the case to the EBoA was published (OJ 1998 p.569). The decision **T15/01** contradicted the earlier decision **T998/99** based on similar facts. The BoA deemed that a referral for ensuring uniform application of the law was not required, because the first and second instance practice of the EPO was uniform, with the exception of this earlier decision (**T15/01** r.40). Such a practice of refusing requests for referral creates legal uncertainty until a sufficient number of contradictory cases have been decided. Reference is made to notes on **Art.53(c)** on the patentability of diagnostic methods, where a considerable body of contradictory case law accumulated over more than fifteen years before the President made a referral to the EBoA (**G1/04**). The decision **J15/98**, published in the OJ, on the language requirement for according a date of filing was contrary to the practice of the office; the issue of referral was not mentioned. In a later, similar case in which neither the appellant nor the BoA referred to **J15/98**, the practice of the office was implicitly endorsed (**J9/01**, not published in the OJ). Due to the fact that the Guidelines referred only to the unpublished decision **J9/01**, the public was supposed to know that the EPO did not follow **J15/98**. Similarly, CLBA, 6th edition, I.D.3 informs the public that decision **T465/92** on use of the problem-solution approach in the assessment of inventive step is a 'one-off' decision; however, the 7th to 9th editions no longer mention the 'one-off' character of this decision. Decisions of the EBoA could have created more legal certainty in these cases.

2 Procedure in the case of referral by a board of appeal

During appeal proceedings, a BoA may refer a question to the EBoA either of its own motion or following a request from a party to the appeal (**Art.112(1)(a)**). The board has the discretion to grant or refuse such a request from a party. If the BoA rejects the request, it must give the reasons in its final decision (**Art.112(1)(a)** last sentence). The referral is in the form of an interlocutory decision.

When a BoA refers a question, the proceedings which gave rise to the question will be stayed and will be continued after the EBoA has given its decision, which is binding on the board of appeal (**Art.112(3)**). The parties to the appeal proceedings remain parties to the proceedings before the EBoA (**Art.112(2)**). Any third party may send its views on the referred question in a written statement (an *amicus curiae* brief) to the EBoA, which may then take it into account (Art.10 RPEBA). The EBoA may publish an invitation in the OJ under Art.10(2) RPEBA inviting the submission of such statements (see e.g. OJ 2019 A50).

If oral proceedings take place before the EBoA, the decision of the EBoA is not usually pronounced at the end of the oral proceedings but is instead handed down in writing afterwards.

If two or more points of law have been referred that relate to the same or a similar question, the EBoA may consider them in consolidated proceedings (Art.8 RPEBA, see e.g. **G2/99** and **G3/99**). Where proceedings before the BoA referring a question to the EBoA are terminated whilst the question is pending before the EBoA, e.g. if the sole appellant withdraws its appeal, the proceedings before the EBoA are also terminated for want of legal basis (see e.g. OJ 2007 p.312).

Art.20(1) RPBA requires that a board gives the grounds for deviating from an earlier decision of a BoA, unless the grounds are in accordance with an earlier decision or opinion of the EBoA, and that the BoA informs the President of its decision. If, in its decision, a BoA gives an interpretation of the EPC that is different to that given in the Guidelines, the BoA may state its grounds for doing so (Art.20(2) RPBA). Where a BoA considers it necessary to deviate from an interpretation or explanation of the EPC in an earlier opinion or decision of the EBoA, the question must be referred to the EBoA (Art.21 RPBA, see e.g. **T301/95**).

3 Conditions for referral by the President (Art.112(1)(b))

The President of the EPO may refer a point of law to the EBoA under **Art.112(1)(b)**, i.e. may refer a question of law (see the German and French text), provided the following two conditions are met:

- the question of law must relate to ensuring uniform application of the law or it must be of fundamental importance; and
- two boards of appeal must have given different decisions on that question.

These conditions limit the freedom of the President to refer points of law to the EBoA. The first condition has already been discussed above.

The term 'different decisions' in **Art.112(1)(b)** must be interpreted in view of the purpose of the provision in establishing uniformity in the way in which the law is applied and is to be understood restrictively in the sense of 'conflicting decisions' (**G3/08** hn.3). In both **G3/95** and **G3/08** the EBoA decided that the referral was inadmissible because it found that the decisions referred by the President were not in conflict.

A difference between two decisions caused by a change in thinking over time cannot on its own form the basis for a referral (**G3/08** hn.4). The EBoA regarded a period of seven years between the two decisions as compatible with the notion of the development of the case law (**G3/08** r.10.9). The EBoA did not address the resulting legal uncertainty for the users of the system.

A change in thinking may include moral considerations, such as an increasing sensitivity to partiality. Such changing concepts require a dynamic interpretation of the law and, hence, changes in case law over time. (**R19/12** r.23; **G3/98** r.2.5)

A restrictive interpretation of the condition that the decisions must stem from two boards of appeal would unduly restrict the power of the President, since it would not allow referral in the case of two conflicting decisions of the Legal BoA. In accordance with the purpose of **Art.112**, to ensure a uniform application of the law, the condition that two different boards must be involved is deemed met if the two decisions were given by the same board in a different composition. (**G4/98** r.1.2; **G3/08** hn.2)

A reason for not referring contradicting decisions to the EBoA can be that the practice of the EPO is uniform, in spite of a one-off decision (e.g. **T465/92, J15/98**), or that the question is not regarded as an important point of law. Views on what constitutes an important point may differ between the EPO and the users of the EPC, i.e. applicants, proprietors and patent attorneys. Whereas the EPO regarded the competence of a department to reimburse the appeal fee (**G3/03**) as an important point of law, users regarded the exhaustion of a priority right (**T15/01**) as being of vital importance. The users can inform the President of the importance they attach to a point of law and request referral, as happened in cases **G4/98** and **G1/04**.

4 **Procedure in the case of referral by the President**

A BoA must inform the President if it takes a decision deviating from earlier decisions. When the President has decided to refer a case to the EBoA, the President delegates the drafting of the questions and the justification for the referral to DG5, the legal directorate of the EPO. The procedure before the EBoA when giving an opinion on a referral by the President is similar to the procedure when giving a decision on a referral by a BoA, as described above. However, there are no parties to the proceedings; in particular, the President is not a party. Any person may submit views on the referral in a written statement (an *amicus curiae* brief), which may be taken into account (Art.10(1) RPEBA).

When the President refers a point of law to the EBoA, the EBoA issues an opinion, not a decision (**Art.22(1)(b)**). The opinion has no bearing on the decisions that have given rise to the referral, because the proceedings which led to the contradictory decisions are already closed.

Art. 112(2) In the cases referred to in paragraph 1(a) the parties to the appeal proceedings shall be parties to the proceedings before the Enlarged Board of Appeal.

Art. 112(3) The decision of the Enlarged Board of Appeal referred to in paragraph 1(a) shall be binding on the Board of Appeal in respect of the appeal in question.

1 **Binding effect of decision of Enlarged Board of Appeal**
A decision of the EBoA on a question is binding on the board of appeal which referred the question (**Art.112(3)**). The binding effect applies to the order of the decision and to the supporting reasons; it does not apply to any obiter dicta of the EBoA (**T389/95** r.2.6-2.9; see also **Art.111(2)** for the similar binding effect of a decision of a BoA).

A decision or opinion of the EBoA has no effect on decisions which have already become final. The decision or opinion may affect the opinion of the BoA in pending cases.

A decision or opinion of the EBoA does not bind a BoA in future cases. However, if a BoA considers it necessary to deviate from a decision or opinion of the EBoA, it must refer a question to the EBoA according to Art.21 RPBA (see e.g. **T788/90**, decision taken in 1994). The EBoA is not bound by its own decisions either (e.g. **G9/93** overruling **G1/84**).

When a decision or opinion of the EBoA changes the interpretation of the EPC, parties are entitled to expect that the EPO applies its previous interpretation up to the date on which the decision or opinion was made available to the public (**G5/93** r.2.3). A decision can be considered to be made public when published on the EPO website. The EBoA may also prescribe transitional provisions itself (see e.g. **G2/08** r.7; **G3/19** hn.)

The EPC does not provide that a department of first instance is bound by a decision or opinion of the EBoA but the departments of first instance tend to follow established case law. If a decision of such a department deviates from a decision or opinion of the EBoA and is appealed, the BoA will usually set the decision aside but it may in exceptional cases refer the matter again to the EBoA.

2 **Effect of referral on pending cases**
A board usually stays appeal proceedings if the outcome of those proceedings depends on the answers the EBoA will give to questions of law referred to it (**T1145/09** r.3).

First instance proceedings will be stayed by the department of first instance or on request of a party if a referral to the EBoA is pending and the outcome of the examination or opposition proceedings depends entirely on the decision of the EBoA (E-VII,3). For specific cases the President may decide to stay ex officio all first instance substantive proceedings the outcome of which depends entirely on the outcome of the EBoA decision (see e.g. Not. EPO OJ 2022 A27 in relation to G1/22 and G2/22, entitlement to priority).

3 **Pending referrals to the Enlarged Board of Appeal**
A list of decisions and opinions of the EBoA is given in the case law index of this book. The following cases are pending on 01.04.2024:

- **G1/23** Availability to the public, the referring decision is **T438/19**;
- **G1/24** Interpretation of the claims, the referring decision is **T439/22**;
- **G2/24** Appellant status for an intervener, the referring decision is **T1286/23**.

4 **Overruled decisions of the Enlarged Board of Appeal**
The following decisions of the EBoA were overruled in part or entirely by a subsequent decision of the EBoA or a change in the law:

- **G1/83**, **G5/83**, **G6/83** Swiss-type claim, overruled by **G2/08** r.7;
- **G1/84** self-opposition, overruled by **G9/93**;

- **G2/12, G2/13** plants or animals exclusively obtained by means of an essentially biological process; abandoned in view of **R.28(2)** by **G3/19** r. xxvi.8.

The following decisions of the EBoA were overruled in part or entirely by EPC2000:

- **G3/91** re-establishment on entry into European phase;
- **G5/92, G6/92** re-establishment in period for requesting examination;
- **G1/97** hn.I no revision of final decision of a board of appeal.

Art. 112a Petition for review by the Enlarged Board of Appeal

1 **General**

It was noted in decision G1/97 that under EPC1973 there was no possibility of having a final decision of a board of appeal reviewed, whereas the review of a corresponding court decision was possible in the contracting states. In response, EPC2000 provides a limited judicial review of decisions of the boards of appeal by virtue of **Art.112a** (OJ 2007 se4 EN p.126). **Art.112a** makes the EBoA a further instance, but with a limited scope.

Art. 112a(1) Any party to appeal proceedings adversely affected by the decision of the Board of Appeal may file a petition for review of the decision by the Enlarged Board of Appeal.

1 **Entitlement to file petition**

Under **Art.112a(1)**, a party adversely affected by the decision in appeal proceedings may file a petition for review. For a discussion of adverse effect, see **Art.107:2**.

A petition for review cannot be validly requested for interlocutory decisions that do not terminate proceedings. Petitions for review are intended as an extraordinary legal remedy and are therefore only available for interlocutory or final decisions that terminate proceedings for the affected party. (**R5/23**, r.5.2, 6, 7.5)

Art. 112a(2) The petition may only be filed on the grounds that:

(a) a member of the Board of Appeal took part in the decision in breach of Article 24, paragraph 1, or despite being excluded pursuant to a decision under Article 24, paragraph 4;

(b) the Board of Appeal included a person not appointed as a member of the Boards of Appeal;

(c) a fundamental violation of Article 113 occurred;

(d) any other fundamental procedural defect defined in the Implementing Regulations occurred in the appeal proceedings; or

(e) a criminal act established under the conditions laid down in the Implementing Regulations may have had an impact on the decision.

Art.24(1) Exclusion and objection
Art.24(4) Decision on exclusion and objection
Art.113 Right to be heard and basis of decisions
Implemented by:
R.104 Further fundamental procedural defects
R.105 Criminal acts
R.106 Obligation to raise objections

1 **Grounds for filing petition**

Under **Art.112a(2)** a petition for review may only be based on a small number of specific grounds. These are, on the one hand, fundamental procedural defects in appeal proceedings, and, on the other hand, a criminal act which may have had an impact on the decision.

Fundamental procedural defects are, in the first place, the deficiencies defined in **Art.112a(2)(a)** to **(c)**, i.e. a breach of **Art.24** governing the exclusion of and objection to members of a Board of Appeal, the participation of a person not appointed as a member of the Boards of Appeal, and a fundamental violation of **Art.113**. **Art.112a(2)(d)** refers to further fundamental procedural defects defined in **R.104**. These defects include, for example, a fundamental procedural defect arising from failure to take into account a request made by a party.

The examples in **Art.112a(2)(a)** to **(c)** and particularly the wording of **Art.112a(2)(d)** make it clear that only fundamental (and not minor) procedural defects can be the basis for a petition for review. Under no circumstances may the petition for review be a means to review the application of substantive law. This restriction is justified because the function of the petition for review is to remedy intolerable deficiencies occurring in individual appeal proceedings, not to further the development of EPO procedural practice or to ensure the uniform application of the law.

To succeed on the basis of a fundamental violation of **Art.113**, petitioners must show both that the decision under review was based on grounds or evidence on which they had no opportunity to comment and that there is a causal link between the defect and the decision. In the absence of such a link, the violation cannot be considered fundamental (**R1/08**).

The right to be heard of **Art. 113** does not impose an obligation on a board of appeal to disclose in advance to the parties how and why it will come to its conclusion on the basis of the decisive issues under discussion. This is part of the reasoning given in the written decision. (**R24/22** r.20)

Petition **R7/09** was successful on the basis that the proprietor's right to be heard under **Art.113** was fundamentally violated when the EPO did not forward the opponent's appeal to the proprietor, and a decision on the appeal was taken without further correspondence. The EBoA confirmed that a proprietor or professional representative has no obligation to monitor the online file of a case to ensure that they are aware of all developments.

The EBoA is competent to consider violations of the Rules of Procedure of the Boards of Appeal to determine whether they have led to a fundamental violation of **Art.113** (**R2/08**).

A decision to hold a claim request inadmissible can be reviewed if it is arbitrary or manifestly illegal (**R10/11** r.5.2).

It is not yet clear if misapplying the rules for referring questions to the EBoA is a fundamental procedural defect that can be used as a ground for a petition for review.

R.106 provides that a petition for review shall only be admissible if the defect was objected to during the appeal proceedings and the objection was rejected by the board of appeal, unless the objection could not have been raised during the appeal proceedings. Case **R1/08** found a petition admissible on the basis that, although the petitioner did not object during the appeal proceedings, the board of appeal revoked the patent at oral proceedings directly after deliberation, and the written decision was based on grounds and arguments of which the petitioner was not aware. Hence, an objection could not have been raised during the appeal proceedings.

One of the most serious defects from which a decision might suffer is that criminal behaviour had an impact on the decision. In these cases, the possibility of review by the Enlarged Board of Appeal exists. However, the EPO has no power to establish whether certain behaviour was an offence within the meaning of criminal law. Thus **R.105** states that a petition may be based on a decision by a competent court or authority that a criminal act has occurred; a conviction is not necessary.

If criminal proceedings against the person concerned are not possible, in particular in the event of the death of this person, no petition for review is possible: any examination of the issue of whether a criminal act occurred must fail because the boards are subject only to the EPC and have no international penal code at hand suitable as a yardstick in order to assess criminal behaviour.

In view of national differences relating to the definition of behaviour which is 'criminal' within the meaning of penal law, the definition of what constitutes a 'criminal act' within the meaning of **Art.112a(2)(e)** is left to the case law of the Enlarged Board of Appeal. (OJ 2007 se4)

The list of **Art.112a** and **R.104** is exhaustive. Only a revision of the EPC or an amendment made to the implementing regulations by the Administrative Council may add violations to the list.

2 **Evidence ofprocedural violation**

The occurrence of a procedural violation may be proven by statements from witnesses who attended oral proceedings or by the minutes of the oral proceedings drafted under **R.124**. However, the minutes are rarely useful as evidence because they are typically very brief. See also **R.105:1, 106** and **124**. The EBoA noted in petitions **R7/08** and **R10/08** that the petitioner may reasonably be expected to object to minutes that do not indicate evidence of a procedural violation if such a violation did indeed occur.

Art. 112a(3) The petition for review shall not have suspensive effect.

1 **Lack of suspensive effect**

Art.112a(3) makes clear that a petition for review is an extraordinary legal remedy, the filing of which does not affect the res judicata quality of the decision under attack. It necessarily follows that a decision of the board of appeal has legal effect until a successful petition for review results in a decision of the EBoA which sets the decision of the board of appeal aside, i.e. overturns its res judicata effect, and re-opens appeal proceedings. This is further clarified in **Art.112a(5)**. (OJ 2007 se4)

Note the difference between the filing of an appeal, which does have suspensive effect (**Art.106(1)**), and the filing of a petition for review, which does not.

Art. 112a(4) The petition for review shall be filed in a reasoned statement, in accordance with the Implementing Regulations. If based on paragraph 2(a) to (d), the petition shall be filed within two months of notification of the decision of the Board of Appeal. If based on paragraph 2(e), the petition shall be filed within two months of the date on which the criminal act has been established and in any event no later than five years from notification of the decision of the Board of Appeal. The petition shall not be deemed to have been filed until after the prescribed fee has been paid.

Implemented by:
R.107 Contents of the petition for review

1 **Filing of petition for review**

Art.112a(4) specifies the form in which a petition for review must be filed, the time limits which apply to its filing and the accompanying fee which must be paid. The contents of the statement setting out the grounds for the petition for review are further defined in **R.107**. This provides that the petition for review shall contain:

1 the name and address of the petitioner as provided in **R.41(2)(c)**;
2 a statement identifying the decision to be reviewed;
3 a statement setting out the grounds on which the petition is based as well as an indication of the facts, evidence and arguments presented in support of these grounds.

The possibility of filing a petition for review must not cause long-lasting legal uncertainty for third parties. The outcome of the new appeal proceedings following a successful review might be that a revoked patent or refused patent application is revived so that protection that has been lost is re-established. Thus, it is important that the period for filing such petitions is short.

As with opposition and appeal proceedings, the statement of grounds must indicate the reasons for the petition, and must allow the EBoA (and third parties) to understand immediately why the decision concerned suffers from a fundamental procedural violation (**R5/08**).

The short time limit under **Art.112a(4)**, second sentence, i.e. two months after the notification of the decision of the Board of Appeal, would make it nearly impossible to base a petition for review on criminal behaviour. In these exceptional and particularly serious cases, the period therefore starts when the relevant court decision becomes final. The need to protect a party adversely affected by criminal behaviour prevails over legal certainty for third parties. However, there is an absolute time limit of five years after the expiry of which no petition for review is admissible. This period should be sufficient to obtain a national decision on a criminal act.

The periods under **Art.112a(4)** are excluded from further processing under **Art.121(4)**. Re-establishment according to **Art.122** and **R.136** is available to applicants and proprietors. Whether it is also available to opponents by application of the principles established in **G1/86** is yet to be decided. An absolute period of two months rather than the usual twelve months applies according to **R.136(1)**.

A substantial fee is payable for a petition for review (**Rfees2(1)11a**). However, **R.110** provides that the fee for the petition for review shall be reimbursed if the Enlarged Board re-opens proceedings before the Board of Appeal, unless reimbursement is not considered equitable.

The filing of a petition for review is entered in the European Patent Register. (OJ 2007 se4)

Art. 112a(5) The Enlarged Board of Appeal shall examine the petition for review in accordance with the Implementing Regulations. If the petition is allowable, the Enlarged Board of Appeal shall set aside the decision and shall re-open proceedings before the Boards of Appeal in accordance with the Implementing Regulations.

Implemented by:
R.108 Examination of the petition
R.109 Procedure in dealing with petitions for review
R.110 Reimbursement of the fee for petitions for review

1 **Examination of petition for review**

Examination of the petition is governed by the provisions of **R.108** to **R.110**. These note that:

1 The petition for review shall be rejected as inadmissible if:
(a) it is not filed by a party adversely affected by the contested decision;
(b) it is not filed in due time;
(c) the reasoned statement setting out the grounds for the petition does not sufficiently substantiate the reasons why the decision under attack should be set aside;
(d) the alleged procedural defect was not objected to as prescribed in **R.106** (see notes **Art.112a(2):1**); or
(e) the alleged criminal act is not established as provided for in **R.105** (see notes **Art.112a(2):1**).

2 If the petition for review is admissible, the Enlarged Board of Appeal shall examine whether the alleged procedural defect occurred in appeal proceedings or whether the established criminal act might have had an impact on the decision.

3 If the petition for review is allowable, the Enlarged Board of Appeal shall set aside the contested decision and re-open appeal proceedings before the Board of Appeal which rendered the decision. If appropriate the Enlarged Board of Appeal may order that the Board of Appeal be composed differently. In exceptional cases, the Enlarged Board of Appeal may re-open appeal proceedings before another Board of Appeal.

R.109(1) provides that in deciding on a petition for review, the provisions relating to proceedings before the Boards of Appeal shall apply, unless otherwise provided.

Each alleged procedural deficiency in the decision is to be considered separately by the EBoA for admissibility and allowability (**R3/08**).

In **R12/20**, the EBoA deemed the petition for review to be inadmissible after the underlying opposition proceedings concluded and no appeal was filed. The issuance of a final and legally valid decision by the opposition division meant the loss of the applicant's legal interest in the proceedings.

The EBoA examines a petition for review in a two-stage procedure as set out in **R.109(3):1**. See also the RPEBA (OJ 2015 A35), especially Art. 11, Art. 12, and Art. 17.

If the petition for review is allowed, the consequence shall be that the decision of the board of appeal is set aside and appeal proceedings reopened before the boards of appeal. This decision overturns the res judicata effect of the previous decision. The result of the second appeal proceedings may be the same as in the first appeal proceedings, or different. (OJ 2007 se4)

Art. 112a(6) Any person who, in a designated Contracting State, has in good faith used or made effective and serious preparations for using an invention which is the subject of a published European patent application or a European patent in the period between the decision of the Board of Appeal and publication in the European Patent Bulletin of the mention of the decision of the Enlarged Board of Appeal on the petition, may without payment continue such use in the course of his business or for the needs thereof.

1 **Third party right to continue use**

The revival of lost patent protection may prejudice third-party interests. Thus, provision must be made for intervening rights concerning the continued use of the invention. **Art.112a(6)** governs this issue in terms similar to those of **Art.122(5)** concerning the protection of third-party interests in the case of re-establishment of rights after non-observance of a time limit despite all due care having been taken. The requirement of good faith guarantees that no rights can be acquired in an abusive way. (OJ 2007 se4)

2 **Renewal fees**

The EPC2000 Diplomatic Conference decided that payment of renewal fees in the Contracting States for a European patent during review proceedings is a matter of national law. The lack of a uniform procedure has caused uncertainty about the fate of a patent after a review procedure. In particular, the EPC does not stipulate that retroactive payment of renewal fees after grant must be possible in the contracting states if a patent is revoked by a decision of a board in opposition appeal proceedings (or the board dismisses an appeal against a decision to revoke the patent by the opposition division) and the EBoA allows the petition for review and sets aside the decision of the board.

For unitary patents, **UPR.13(6)** provides that the renewal fees can be paid within a period from the decision of the EBoA.

National patent offices should either require no payment of the renewal fees during the procedure before the EBoA or permit the payment of the fees within a period after the decision of the EBoA that allows the petition for review (cf. **UPR.13(6)**) or accept the payment of renewal fees during the procedure before the EBoA. Any approach under national law wherein a patent inevitably lapses, even if the petition for review is allowed, is to be rejected as incompatible with **Art.112a** from a systematic and teleological point of view (see **P:2.2**).

PART VII COMMON PROVISIONS

Chapter I *Common provisions governing procedure*

1 **Applicability of provisions**
All provisions in this Part are applicable to any procedure before the EPO, unless stated otherwise.

Art. 113 Right to be heard and basis of decisions

Implemented by:
R.111 Form of decisions
R.112 Noting of loss of rights
R.113 Signature, name, seal

Art. 113(1) The decisions of the European Patent Office may only be based on grounds or evidence on which the parties concerned have had an opportunity to present their comments.

1 **Opportunity to comment**
The provision lays down the principle that the EPO may base its decisions only on grounds or evidence on which a party has had an opportunity to comment. Parties cannot be surprised by negative decisions. The opportunities to comment have been worked out in the provisions for written or oral comment, time limits, the remedy of deficiencies, and the taking of evidence. The EPO must discuss the arguments of the parties. All evidence used for the decision must be or become public. Minutes of oral proceedings may demonstrate that the right to be heard of the parties was complied with (C-III,10.3).

The term 'grounds' refers to the legal and factual reasons leading to the decision, e.g. to the refusal of the application, and not in the narrow sense of a legal requirement of the EPC (**T233/18**).

There is a substantial procedural violation if the parties' arguments are not discussed or if not enough time has been provided for a reply. For example, when parties announce the filing of further evidence, and the EPO does not give them a reasonable period for filing, there is a substantial procedural violation (J4/82). This also applies to the late filing of a new ground of opposition or new amendments (E-VI,2.2.4). See **R.115(2):1** for the right to be heard in oral proceedings where a party is absent.

In case of late-filed facts, evidence and requests, the decision must include the reasons for the decision on their admissibility, and these reasons must not surprise the party or parties. In examination, reasons are however only required in case of non-admittance of the late-filed facts, evidence or requests. (E-VI,2.2.4)

The opposition division must give the parties an opportunity to present observations after a board of appeal remits the case for further prosecution on the basis of new evidence filed and admitted in appeal, even if submissions concerning the new evidence had already been made during the appeal proceedings. Immediate termination of the opposition proceedings after remittal constitutes a substantial procedural violation in the sense of **R.103**. (**T892/92**)

Parties and their representatives have no duty under **Art.113(1)** to monitor the proceedings by regularly inspecting the online file (**R7/09**). Hence, the mere fact that a document was visible in the online file does not mean that a party had an opportunity to comment on it.

The first instance departments may not take an adverse decision while a period for filing a reply or remedying a deficiency is still running; otherwise, the party's right to be heard is violated unless the party unequivocally waived its right (**T663/99**; **J8/20**; CLBA III. B.2.5.2).

A decision against a party who has been duly summoned but who fails to appear at oral proceedings may not be based on facts put forward for the first time during those oral proceedings. In these circumstances, new evidence may not be considered unless it has been previously notified and it merely supports the assertions of the party who submits it. On the other hand, new arguments may in principle be used to support the reasons for the decision. (**G4/92**)

Art. 113(2) The European Patent Office shall examine, and decide upon, the European patent application or the European patent only in the text submitted to it, or agreed, by the applicant or the proprietor of the patent.

1 **Consent of party to text**

Applicants and proprietors control the text of the application or patent which the EPO considers during grant and opposition proceedings, both in first and second instance. They decide the text under discussion and its amendments under **Art.123**. The EPO can only propose amendments. An implementation of **Art.113(2)** is the approval of the text to be granted under **R.71(5)**. The board of appeal and the first instance are not competent to grant a patent in a version different from that submitted or agreed by the applicant (**T32/82**).

If an applicant agrees with only part of the text in an opposition or appeal procedure, and does not provide an amended text, the department can only revoke the entire patent. However, in a national revocation procedure it may be possible to revoke the patent in part (**Art.138(2)**).

Art. 114 Examination by the European Patent Office of its own motion

Art. 114(1) In proceedings before it, the European Patent Office shall examine the facts of its own motion; it shall not be restricted in this examination to the facts, evidence and arguments provided by the parties and the relief sought.

1 **Examination of own motion**

The basic principle of examination of its own motion, also called ex officio examination, applies in principle to all procedures before the EPO, from the Receiving Section to the Enlarged Board of Appeal. However, the application of ex officio examination in opposition procedures in first and second instance is restricted.

The opposition procedure under the EPC resembles a national revocation procedure, and, consequently, the opposition proceedings under the EPC must likewise be considered as contentious proceedings between two parties normally representing opposite interests, who should be given equally fair treatment (**G9/91** r.2). **Art.114(1)** must be applied in an even more restrictive manner in the appeal procedure in opposition, which is to be considered as a judicial procedure (**G1/99** r.6.6).

An ex officio examination in opposition proceedings might be interpreted as favouring one party. The EPO will therefore mainly examine the objections as formulated in the notice of opposition. **R.81(1)** specifies that grounds for opposition not invoked by the opponent may be examined by the opposition division of its own motion if they would prejudice the maintenance of the European patent.

Examples of restrictions on the ex officio examination can be found below and in **R.76(2):4**.

2 **Examination of facts and evidence**

The ex officio examination has its major impact in the exact determination of the state of the art used in the examination.

The EPO may carry out a top-up search providing facts to complement the state of the art given in the application and the search report (B-XI,3.9).

Applicants cannot leave the fact-finding to the EPO; they must cooperate. They must e.g. formulate proposals for claims, and look for patentable matter outside the claims. The EPO stops the examination of its own motion if the necessary cooperation of a party is lacking, e.g. if a party claiming prior public use withdraws from the proceedings and the facts are difficult to establish without the party's cooperation (**T129/88**). When two parties in an opposition procedure assert opposite facts without proper evidence, and the EPO cannot provide the evidence of its own motion, then this disadvantage is put on the opponent (**T219/83**).

The opposition division or the board of appeal may introduce documents from the search report in the proceedings if they regard them to be relevant (**Art.114(1)**), although it is not their duty to redo the examination for grant (**T387/89**). Documents cited in the opposed patent are not automatically part of the opposition proceedings; however, the most relevant state of the art on which the patent is based, is part of the proceedings (**T536/88**).

Art.114(1) does not mean that a board of appeal must conduct a rehearsing of the first instance proceedings without regard to how late submissions were made. If in first instance a late-filed submission is not taken into account, the second instance need neither take it into account. (**T97/90**)

The board of appeal decides on reimbursement of appeal fees of its own motion (**J7/82**).

3 **Examination of grounds**

In an appeal from a grant refusal the board of appeal has the power to examine whether the application meets the requirements of the EPC, including requirements the examining division did not consider or regarded as having been met (**G10/93** hn; see e.g. **T1158/01**, r.2).

The extent of opposition as indicated according to **Art.101** and **R.76(2)(c)** may not be widened by using **Art.114(1)**, because **Art.114(1)** is subject to **Art.101** with **R.76(2)(c)** as far as the extent is concerned (**G9/91**, confirming **T9/87** hn). Note, that this limitation of the applicability of an Article by a Rule has a strained relation with **Art.164(2)**.

During opposition proceedings new grounds for opposition may be added to those indicated in the notice of opposition under **R.76(2)(c)** but only when deemed prima facie relevant; new grounds are not allowed in appeal proceedings, unless the proprietor agrees to it (**G10/91**, overruling **T493/88**).

In so far as the substantive issues settled by the contested decision at first instance are concerned, appeal proceedings are terminated, in ex parte and inter partes proceedings alike, when the sole appellant withdraws the appeal. (**G8/91** hn)

Art. 114(2) The European Patent Office may disregard facts or evidence which are not submitted in due time by the parties concerned.

1 Late-filed submissions in first instance

The EPO may disregard late-filed facts or evidence according to **Art.114(2)**. It allows a normal course of the proceedings and makes tactical abuse of late submission of facts impossible (**T273/84**). The admissibility of late submitted facts and evidence is determined by their importance for the case, the state of the proceedings and the reasons for the late submission (E-VI,2). Because 'arguments' are not mentioned in paragraph 2, a late submission of new arguments is allowed, being indispensable for oral proceedings. However, if a new argument changes a case substantially, the argument may be disregarded (**T124/87** hn3). The late filing of amendments is covered by **Art.123(1)**, not by **Art.114(2)**. The admissibility of a late-filed amendment in grant proceedings is a matter of discretion of the examining division according to **R.137(3)** (see also **R.71(6):2**).

In opposition proceedings, facts or evidence not indicated in the notice of opposition and filed after the expiry of the opposition period are considered late-filed unless they are due to a change in the subject of the proceedings (D-VI,1; see also **R.76(2):4**). Late-filed amendments in opposition proceedings may be refused if the examination of the opposition is substantially complete (**T406/86** hn.2).

1.1 GROUNDS FOR CONSIDERING LATE-FILED SUBMISSIONS

Summary of the grounds for deciding to act of its own motion, especially with respect to late submissions of facts and evidence:

1 basis for the examination of its own motion is that the EPO is obliged to the public not to grant patents of which it is certain that they have no legal basis;

2 the EPO must check the relevance of late submissions and communicate the result;

3 in contrast to timely submitted facts and evidence, late submission may be rejected without extensive reasoning;

4 something will only be considered as being late submitted if a careful preparation of the case would have given rise to an earlier submission. (**T156/84**)

The check as to relevance is not required if the late submission could have been filed earlier and forms an abuse of procedure; a department may refuse such a document without assessing its relevance (**T951/91** r.5.9, **T534/89** hn2).

The grounds for admitting late-filed grounds, facts and evidence are given in **R.76(2):4**.

2 Late-filed submissions in appeal

For appeals under RPBA2007, 'everything' (i.e. requests, facts, objections, arguments and evidence) presented in the grounds of appeal or reply is taken into account (Art.12(4) RPBA2007). Requests, facts or evidence filed after the period for filing the grounds of appeal or reply may be not be admitted by the board. If a new argument changes a case substantially, the case may be referred to first instance with an apportionment of costs (**T97/90** hn.2).

Under the 2020 revision of the RPBA, the 'due time' of **Art.114(2)** for filing submissions is, in effect for most cases, before the decision in first instance proceedings; even if presented in the grounds of appeal or reply, a board may disregard facts, evidence, requests, objections or arguments on which the impugned decision was not based (Art.12(4) RPBA). See also **Art.110:5**.

2.1 GROUNDS FOR CONSIDERING LATE FILED SUBMISSIONS

The board may admit late-filed submissions, i.e. amendments to the appeal case, on consideration of inter alia their complexity, their suitability to address the issues which led to the decision under appeal, and the need for procedural economy (Art.12(4) and 13(1) RPBA).

Requests, facts or evidence which were not admitted at first instance may be admitted by the board if the decision not to admit them suffered from an error in the use of discretion, or if the circumstances of the appeal case justify their admittance. Furthermore, the board should admit claim requests that were not admitted in first instance only on substantive grounds to avail the applicant or proprietor a full judicial review of the decision (**T1816/11** r.2.6; **T1159/13** r.5.4). However, the board will generally not admit requests, facts, objections or evidence which were withdrawn or withheld at first instance. (Art.12(6) RPBA)

Examples of decisions regarding late-filed submissions prior to the 2020 revision of the RPBA are given in **Art.114(2):3.2** below.

3 Examples

3.1 EXAMPLES RELATING TO FIRST INSTANCE PROCEEDINGS

If an alleged prior public use is not adequately substantiated, it is immaterial and, if the substantiation is not submitted in due time, may be disregarded under **Art.114(2)** (**T93/89**).

An alleged prior public use deliberately filed late in order to abuse the procedure may be disregarded irrespective of its potential relevance (**T534/89**). Even an assertion of prior public use based on the opponent's own activities which is filed after the expiry of the opposition period without good reasons is an abuse of the proceedings and a breach of the principle of good faith; such an assertion should be disregarded irrespective of its potential relevance (**T17/91**).

If the parties to opposition proceedings make contrary assertions which they cannot substantiate and the EPO is unable to establish the facts of its own motion, the patent proprietor is given the benefit of the doubt (**T219/83**).

3.2 EXAMPLES RELATING TO APPEAL PROCEEDINGS PRIOR TO THE 2020 REVISION OF THE RPBA

Where late-filed evidence or arguments in appeal raise a case substantially different from that decided in first instance, the case will be remitted to the first instance with an award of costs against the tardy filer. A late-filed new ground of objection in an opposition appeal should only be referred to the first instance where it might result in the revocation of the patent. Where the maintenance of the patent is not at risk, the Board can either refuse to admit the new ground or admit it in the proceedings and decide it against the opponent (**T97/90**).

A relevant document for the first time submitted in an opposition appeal often incites the board of appeal to remit the case to the opposition division (**Art.111(1)**).

Evidence of common general knowledge may introduce new facts and thereby change the framework of the appeal. If filed only with the notice of appeal, the Board is empowered to disregard such evidence, even though a document indicating common general knowledge merely serves to confirm what is already commonly known in the field. (**T85/93** hn, r.1)

Supporting evidence for a restatement of the problem of a patent application is regarded as submitted in due time if submitted together with the grounds of appeal (**T1/80** hn.II). An allegation of insufficient disclosure made for the first time during oral proceedings in opposition appeal is in general rejected because of its late submission (**T294/85** r.4). The delay in the proceedings must be weighed against the requirement of examination of its own motion. An alleged prior use submitted for the first time in the notice of appeal was regarded as inadmissible although close to the subject-matter of the impugned patent, because it was submitted too late in view of the uncertainty in the result and duration of the taking of the evidence (there was no proof that the object claimed was indeed identical with the object asserted to have been sold) (**T262/85**).

Art. 115 Observations by third parties

In proceedings before the European Patent Office, following the publication of the European patent application, any third party may, in accordance with the Implementing Regulations, present observations concerning the patentability of the invention to which the application or patent relates. That person shall not be a party to the proceedings.

Implemented by:
R.114 Filing and communication of observations

1 General

Art.115 gives a third party the possibility to file observations on a case pending before the EPO and have them examined. Although observations usually contain arguments against patentability, they may also give arguments in favour of patentability. Such observations help to avoid the grant of invalid patents. It is an easily accessible route, because there are no fees to be paid (OJ 2017 A86 §1), in contrast with the opposition procedure.

Observations can be filed during pending proceedings but only after publication of the application. Filing is possible both in grant and opposition proceedings because **Art.115** refers to 'application' and 'patent'. They will be taken into account during first and second instance proceedings.

Details of the filing and subsequent procedure are provided in **R.114.** The EPO prefers online filing of third party observations using a structured online form to facilitate and promote their use because of the proven usefulness of the observations in examination (OJ 2011 p.418 and p.420).

2 **Third party**

The title of the article is confusing in that 'parties' are not 'parties to the proceedings'. The French and German texts of the article are clearer.

Since only a 'third party' may file observations, the applicant or any other party to proceedings may not file observations under **Art.115** (E-VI,3). It is not clear whether a third party not living or working in or being a national of a contracting state must be represented in view of **Art.133(2)** for filing observations.

The language requirements and procedure are laid down in **R.114.**

Observations may be filed anonymously with departments of first instance (OJ 2017 A86 §3.2). See e.g. the observations dated 12.05.1998 and 07.12.1999 in the case EP 0451216 filed by the cartoon character Buzz Lightyear.

The boards of appeal have not reached a unanimous view on considering anonymous observations. They may be considered in ex parte appeal cases (**T1336/09** r.2.2). Whereas in opposition appeal, the board in **T735/04** r.2 did consider an anonymous observation, the board in **T1439/09** r.1.7 regarded an anonymous observation as not filed if not signed after a **R.50(3)** invitation. The latter board held that an anonymous observation could be used by a party for late submissions in opposition proceedings to avoid apportionment of cost. However, this is not a sound reason, because even if the board can identify a third party that sent an observation, it will not know whether the third party was instructed by a party to the proceedings. The Enlarged Board of Appeal does not consider anonymous statements (**G1/03**, Summary of facts and submissions VI(3)).

3 **Issues to be raised**

Only patentability questions can be raised according to **Art.115**. Since 'Patentability' is the title of the chapter of the EPC containing **Art.52-57**, the questions could be interpreted to relate only to these provisions. The EPO notice OJ 2017 A86 §3.4 restricts observations to 'substantive requirements of the EPC, e.g. Articles 52-57'. However, the Guidelines use a broader interpretation (E-VI,3). The case law on which the interpretation is based, uses the broad interpretation usually without giving any grounds.

The EPO considers also clarity objections under **Art.84** (see e.g. **T598/97** r.3) and insufficient disclosure under **Art.83** (see e.g. **T918/94** r.9). Hence, lack of unity (**Art.82**) could also be considered. The EPO also accepts observations relating to non-technical subject-matter under **Art.52(2)** and **(3)**, exclusions under **Art.53**, industrially not applicable according to **Art.57** and unallowable amendments under **Art.76(1)** and **123(2)** (E-VI,3). Formal issues, such as the validity of an authorisation or the allowability of a request for re-establishment, will not be considered. Non-entitlement of the proprietor to the patent can only be raised in a national procedure (**Art.138(1)(e)**). During opposition, non-unity issues will not be considered (**Art.100:2**) and clarity issues only if relating to amendments (**Art.101(3):1**).

4 **Period for filing**

There is no provision in the EPC explicitly defining circumstances during pending proceedings wherein the information filed under **Art.115** should not be taken into account as being filed too late. In grant proceedings, third party observations filed between the dispatch of an R.71(3) communication and the handing over of the decision to grant to the EPO postal service will be considered. Later filed third party observations are not considered (E-VI,3).

An opposition division may consider a ground of opposition raised in third party observations if there are clear reasons to believe that such grounds are prejudicial to the maintenance of the European patent (**G10/91**, r.16).

In **T667/92** a new ground raised in an **Art.115** submission during opposition appeal was not admitted because of the restricted applicability of **Art.114(1)** to opposition appeals.

A submission under **Art.115** putting forward public prior use should give all required evidence as to what, who and where, because the EPO will not invite the third party to provide this information (**T908/95** r.4.1; E-VI,3).

Art. 116 Oral proceedings

Implemented by:
R.4 Language in oral proceedings,
R.111(1) Form of the decision in oral proceedings,
R.115 Summons to oral proceedings,
R.116 Preparation of oral proceedings,
R.124 Minutes of oral proceedings

1 **Oral proceedings**

Although the procedure before the EPO is in principle in writing, the parties are by way of exception entitled to oral proceedings, as they may speed up the procedure. In some situations, a consultation by telephone or videoconference may be useful (see **Art.116:3** below).

An examining division will generally send at least one **Art.94(3)** communication before considering to issue summons to oral proceedings. It should be noted that a search opinion, a supplementary search or an opinion or report from the PCT procedure is not an **Art.94(3)** communication. (C-VIII,5.1)

As of 01.01.2023, oral proceedings before examining divisions, opposition divisions, the Legal Division and the Receiving Section are held by videoconference (Dec. Pres. OJ 2022 A103). Oral proceedings by videoconference first became possible before examining divisions, at the discretion of the division, followed by a pilot project for oral proceedings before opposition divisions. During the COVID-19 pandemic, oral proceedings by videoconference were extended to the Legal Division and the Receiving Section, before being made the rule rather than an exception.

In case oral proceedings are held on the premises of the EPO, they will in general be held in the place where the relevant department of the EPO is located (**T1012/03** r.37). Since the question of venue of oral proceedings is a matter of organisational nature belonging to the management of the EPO pursuant to **Art.10(2)**, an examining division is not competent to decide on a request to change the venue and such a request is therefore not allowable (**T1012/03**; **T1142/12** hn; E-III,2). **G2/19** confirmed that holding appeal oral proceedings in Haar does not violate the EPC.

Oral proceedings before a board of appeal are held as scheduled on the premises of the EPO or by videoconference (Art.15a RPBA), the choice of the format being at the discretion of the board. If a party cannot attend oral proceedings held on the premises of the EPO, for example due to pandemic-related travel restrictions, it must request a change of date under Art.15(2) RPBA. The location and start time of oral proceedings may also change on short notice, but the EPO will not, as a rule, issue a communication informing parties of such changes. Instead, parties must monitor the 'Oral proceedings calendar' on the EPO website for any changes. (OJ 2020 A103). Up-to-date information is available on the EPO website, in the part dedicated to boards of appeal.

A calendar of public oral proceedings is available on the EPO website for any interested person to follow such oral proceedings, see **Art.116(4):1** below. See Art.134(1):2 for submissions by accompanying persons during oral proceedings.

2 **Oral proceedings by videoconference**

As of 01.01.2023, oral proceedings before examining divisions, opposition divisions, the Legal Division and the Receiving Section are held by videoconference (Dec. Pres. OJ 2022 A103). If there are serious reasons against holding oral proceedings by videoconference, they may be held in-person on the premises of the EPO on request of the applicant or instigation of the division or section. The serious reasons must foreseeably persist on the day of the oral proceeding. Serious reasons include impediments which prevent the applicant or its representative participating in a videoconference. As a rule, the non-availability of videoconferencing equipment or objections against the reliability of videoconferencing technology are not regarded as serious reasons. A request to hold oral proceedings on the premises of the EPO should be filed as early as possible, preferably when requesting oral proceedings. If this request is not allowed, the EPO will give reasons for the refusal of the request. A decision to refuse in-person oral proceedings is not separately appealable; the decision may be challenged in appeal against a final decision (**Art.106(2)**). (Dec. Pres. OJ 2022 A103 Art.1(2), Not. EPO OJ 2022 A106 §4-6).

Parties and their representatives may connect to a videoconference oral proceeding from different locations. The members of the division or section may also connect to the videoconference oral proceeding from different locations and establish a separate videoconference to deliberate and vote among themselves. The venue of oral proceedings by videoconference is deemed to be the location of the division or section. (Dec. Pres. OJ 2022 A103 Art.2, Not. EPO OJ 2022 A106 §12-13)

Summons issued for videoconference oral proceedings include a request for an e-mail address to which the EPO will send a calendar appointment for the oral proceedings with a videoconference meeting link. As of 01.10.2021, all oral proceedings are held only on Zoom. This also applies to videoconference oral proceedings before the boards according to the EPO website. The Zoom web client is not suitable to attend oral proceedings requiring simultaneous interpretation due to its limited functionality. For detailed technical information, see EPO website, 'Oral proceedings held as a videoconference – technical guidelines'. It is recommended to arrange a test videoconference with the EPO by e-mailing serviceline@epo.org.

At the beginning of videoconference oral proceedings, the EPO will check the identity of a representative or authorised employee of each party, unless the person is known. The identity of other persons is not controlled beyond oral confirmation by the person whose identity has been checked or is known, unless there are serious reasons for doing so. However, the identity of anyone giving evidence is checked. See E-III,8.3.1 for ways of proving identity.

During videoconference oral proceedings, parties must file documents by e-mail using the e-mail address indicated by the division, section or board and thus should ensure to have access to e-mail. In inter partes videoconferences, parties should copy in the other parties (OJ 2020 A71, OJ 2022 A106 §15; see **R.2(1):6.1**). Additional technical and procedural information is provided on the EPO website under 'FAQ – Oral proceedings held by videoconference'. Recording or retransmission of oral proceedings by videoconference is not allowed (Not. EPO OJ 2022 A106 §14). Screen sharing for illustrating an argument may be allowed but does not mean that the document shown has been submitted (E-III,8.5.2).

In case of technical problems that cannot be overcome during the oral proceedings, a new date is set by the division or section. A party not connecting for another reason is deemed not to have appeared, and the oral proceedings may be continued. (Dec. Pres. OJ 2022 A103 Art.5)

A new date is also set if the oral proceedings need to be adjourned due to a lack of time. In such a case, the summons must indicate points to be discussed, and may indicate the division's provisional opinion on those points or indicate points that are closed. In case the new date is such that the parties will not have time to receive the new summons, the parties must expressly waive their right to the new summons. (E-III,8.11.2)

Oral proceedings before the Unitary Patent Protection Division are held in the same manner as before first instance divisions of the EPO (OJ 2023 sp3 p.2-4).

2.1 ORAL PROCEEDINGS BY VIDEOCONFERENCE IN APPEAL

Art.15a RPBA provides for videoconference oral proceedings in appeal and entered into force on 01.04.2021 (OJ 2021 A19). A board may decide to hold oral proceedings by videoconference (Art.15a(1) RPBA). Consent by the parties is not required, but parties may submit reasons for their preference on the type of oral proceedings. Should a party have a clear preference for oral proceedings in either in person or by videoconference, it may be preferable to file a reasoned request already together with the grounds of appeal or the first reply to appeal. The practice of the boards is to hold proceedings by videoconference without the parties' consent since 01.01.2021 and Art.15a RPBA codifies this practice (CA/5/21 §5, §7).

In case of oral proceedings held on the premises of the EPO, a party, representative or accompanying person may be allowed to attend by videoconference upon request of that person (Art.15a(2) RPBA). The chair and other members of the board may also participate by videoconference, regardless of whether the oral proceedings are held on the premises of the EPO or by videoconference (Art.15a(3) RPBA).

G1/21 hn. held that the conduct of oral proceedings before the boards of appeal in the form of a videoconference is compatible with the EPC, even without the consent of all parties to the proceedings, during a general emergency impairing the parties' possibilities to attend in-person oral proceedings at the EPO premises. The Enlarged Board concluded that oral proceedings in the form of a videoconference are oral proceedings within the meaning of **Art.116** (r.30) and, although not fully equivalent to oral proceedings held in person, normally do not infringe a party's right to be heard or the right to fair proceedings (r.44). Nevertheless, in-person hearings should be the default option. Parties can only be denied this option for good reasons (r.45). A decision not to hold the oral proceedings in person must be justified by circumstances specific to the case. These circumstances should relate to limitations and impairments affecting the parties' ability to attend oral proceedings in person on the premises of the EPO (r.49). If in a particular case a videoconference is not suitable, the oral proceedings must be held in person (r.48). The decision whether good reasons justify a deviation from the preference of a party to hold the oral proceedings in person is a discretionary decision of the board (r.50). The Enlarged Board limited the scope of its answer to periods of general emergencies and to appeal proceedings only (r.16), thereby giving no express view on videoconference oral proceedings beyond this limited scope. The referring decision **T1807/15** was taken 12.03.2021 and the Enlarged Board did not comment on Art.15a RPBA, which entered into force on 01.04.2021, in **G1/21** of 16.07.2021. **T245/18** found that Art.15a RPBA is compatible with the EPC in view of **G1/21**.

3 **Consultations**

A consultation is an informal discussion between an applicant and an examiner or formalities officer and not a kind of oral proceedings; it may speed up grant proceedings but it is not part of the formal procedure. Moreover, statements made by the examiner during a consultation are not binding on the division and no final decision can be taken during the consultation (C-VII,2.3; **T160/92** r.3.3). The grant of a request for a consultation is a discretionary matter for the examiner based on whether the consultation would serve a useful purpose (C-VII,2.1); its refusal is not a procedural violation (**T951/92** r.3(ix)), provided the applicant's right to be heard is not violated when a decision is taken (**Art.113(1)**). Consultations during the search stage are usually not permitted (B-II,1.1). Consultations in inter partes proceedings are usually refused, because of the contentious character of such proceedings (E-III,1.1). Whereas oral proceedings are always held before the complete examining division, a consultation is usually only attended by the first member.

A consultation is preferably held by videoconference (see **Art.116:2** above). It is advisable to agree on a date and time for a consultation, e.g. by e-mail, so both the party and the examiner have an opportunity to prepare. Consultations allow for a free and rapid exchange of views so that both the examiner and applicant can indicate what subject matter they consider allowable and address each other's concerns in order to work towards a result acceptable to both. In this way a satisfactory decision is often reached more quickly than in written proceedings. The EPO draws up minutes of the consultation, places them in the file and sends a copy to the party. The minutes include any documents filed by e-mail during the consultation as annexes and include information on the next required action. (C-VII,2.4)

A shared area in MyEPO may be used for documents to be discussed or under discussion during a consultation. Both the applicant and the EPO can upload documents in docx-format and make amendments to them confidentially in real time. The documents in the shared area are informal and must be later formally submitted by the applicant or issued as part of an official communication (e.g. as part of a communication under **R.71(3)**). (Dec. Pres. OJ 2024 A20; C-VII,2.6)

4 **Conduct of oral proceedings**

The EPO summons the parties for oral proceedings at the request of a party or where the EPO considers it expedient (**Art.116(1)**). The invitation may contain an opinion and an indication of points of view of the parties and items to be discussed (E-III,5). Parties attending in-person oral proceedings must take into account the time required for the security inspection of persons entering the premises of the EPO and items they carry (OJ 2017 A6).

The oral proceedings start with a formal part, including identification of the parties (E-III,8.3.1). The substantive part of the proceedings begins with submissions of the parties; in opposition cases first the opponent(s) and then the proprietor (E-III,8.5). Late filed submissions may cause adjournment of the proceedings if it is of crucial importance and the parties cannot reasonably be expected to familiarise themselves in the time available with the new facts or evidence or the proposed amendments (E-VI,2.2). Submissions during oral proceedings may be typed or handwritten (E-III,8.5; 8.7; **R.82(2):3**).

The following discussion is intended to clarify facts for the EPO. If the department intends to depart from a previous legal assessment of the situation or from a prevailing legal opinion, or if facts are seen in a different light, causing the case to take a significant turn, the parties should be so informed (E-III,8.9).

After deliberation, the department closes the oral proceedings by pronouncing the decision or by announcing that the procedure will be continued in writing (E-III,8.11). The reasoning of the decision need not be made at this time; the subsequently notified written decision must contain the reasoning (**R.111**; E-III,9). The decision is usually notified two to six months after the date of the oral proceedings; however, the notification may be more than 20 months after the oral proceedings (see e.g. **T307/03**).

A party desiring to contest a decision taken by a department of first instance in oral proceedings must file the notice of appeal within two months after the date of notification of the decision (**Art.108**), not after the date the decision is delivered in oral proceedings. The form of the decision is determined by **R.111**, while signatures are required by **R.113** and by **R.102** for decisions of the board of appeal. Any fact submitted to the department of first instance after a decision in oral proceedings has been pronounced is not taken into account anymore. Such facts must be put forward in an appeal. If the department considers timely filed facts relevant, it might revise its decision under **Art.109**.

The EPO aims that oral proceedings do not exceed eight working hours, unless it is likely that a conclusion is imminent. In case it is necessary to continue the oral proceedings another day, a new summons is issued with at least two months' notice, unless the parties agree to a shorter period. Minutes of the oral proceedings should be sent to the parties before the new oral proceedings, preferably together with the summons. No new date for making submissions under **R.116** is fixed, unless the subject of the proceedings has changed. (E-III,8.11.2)

Art. 116(1) Oral proceedings shall take place either at the instance of the European Patent Office if it considers this to be expedient or at the request of any party to the proceedings. However, the European Patent Office may reject a request for further oral proceedings before the same department where the parties and the subject of the proceedings are the same.

1 **Right to oral proceedings**
A request for oral proceedings of a party is not assessed on expediency; exceptions are a further request (**Art.116(1)**) and a request to the Receiving Section (**Art.116(2)**). A first request for oral proceedings may not be refused by the EPO (**T19/87**) subject to **Art.116(2)**. The request must be granted even if filed after the issue of the **R.71(3)** communication but before the termination of the proceedings, which occurs three days prior to the date stamped on the decision (**G12/91** r.9.1). Not granting oral proceedings requested by a party having a right to it is a substantial procedural violation (**T93/88**) that may give rise to reimbursement of the appeal fee under **R.103**; a decision taken after an unjustified refusal to hold oral proceedings must be set aside (**T556/95** r.7). To avoid unnecessary oral proceedings, a request for oral proceedings should be filed on condition that the case put forward is not allowed. If the department considers oral proceedings requested by a party as inexpedient, it will consult the party (E-III,2). A request for further oral proceedings with the same parties and the same subject is usually rejected (E-III,3).

The EPO will in general offer new oral proceedings after a change in composition of an Opposition Division after oral proceedings (**T862/98** hn, r.2.3; **T315/03** r.15.2).

An appellant who was not a party to the foregoing proceedings or who invokes a grievance which is not appealable, has no right to oral proceedings. An example is a third party appealing a decision to grant a patent based on the objection that the granted claims are unclear. (**G2/19** r.B.II.8)

Art. 116(2) Nevertheless, oral proceedings shall take place before the Receiving Section at the request of the applicant only where the Receiving Section considers this to be expedient or where it intends to refuse the European patent application.

1 **Oral proceedings before Receiving Section**
The right to oral proceedings before the Receiving Section is restricted in the interest of procedure economy. Oral proceedings will take place at the request of the applicant if the Receiving Section intends to refuse the application, e.g. if the application is not rectified after invitation to do so (**Art.90(5)**, **R.58**). Oral proceedings will also take place at the request of the applicant if the Receiving Section considers it expedient. Oral proceedings are expedient if they can clarify questions which speed up the procedure; they are not expedient when they only delay without providing clarification, e.g. if a deficiency cannot be corrected. Oral proceedings may be expedient if a loss of rights will occur because of a deficiency of the application, e.g. when during the examination on filing or the examination as to formal requirements the application may be refused under **Art.90(5)**, first sentence, deemed withdrawn under **R.37(2)** or **R.39(2)**; or when the right of priority may be lost (**Art.90(5)**, second sentence), or the missing parts are not regarded as completely contained in the sense of **R.56(3)**.

Art. 116(3) Oral proceedings before the Receiving Section, the Examining Divisions and the Legal Division shall not be public.

Art. 116(4) Oral proceedings, including delivery of the decision, shall be public, as regards the Boards of Appeal and the Enlarged Board of Appeal, after publication of the European patent application, and also before the Opposition Divisions, in so far as the department before which the proceedings are taking place does not decide otherwise in cases where admission of the public could have serious and unjustified disadvantages, in particular for a party to the proceedings.

1 **Publicly accessible oral proceedings**
Oral proceedings are in principle publicly accessible to allow the public to verify that justice is done. This applies in particular to boards of appeal, which operate like courts. As an exception, oral proceedings before the boards of appeal prior to publication of the application are not public, analogous to **Art.128**.

Oral proceedings before departments of first instance may be public only in proceedings after grant.

Members of the public can attend opposition oral proceedings held by videoconference by giving prior notice by requesting a meeting link by email at least three working days prior to the proceedings. The email is to be sent to support@epo.org and indicate the application number, the date of the oral proceedings, as well as the name and email address of the requester. The Not. EPO OJ 2022 A106 §21-26 and its annex as well as the EPO website under 'Information about access to oral proceedings by videoconference before opposition divisions' provide more details and conditions for attendance of the public.

2 **Not-publicly accessible proceedings**
According to **Art.116(3)** oral proceedings before the Receiving Section, examining divisions and the Legal Division are not public.

Oral proceedings before the Disciplinary Board of Appeal are in general not public (see e.g. **D20/99**). Oral proceedings relating to partiality are in general not public in view of **R.144(a)** (see e.g. **T190/03**, F&S VII).

Oral proceedings in opposition proceedings in cases relating to genetically modified products are often not publicly accessible in view of the antipathy the subject-matter arouses in the public.

Art. 117 Means and taking of evidence

Implemented by:
R.117 Decision on taking of evidence
R.118 Summons to give evidence
R.119 Taking of evidence
R. 120 Hearing of a witness by a national court
R. 121 Commissioning of experts
R. 122 Costs of taking of evidence
R. 123 Conservation of evidence
R. 124 Minutes of taking of evidence

1 **General**
Many articles and rules of the EPC state that the EPO gives opinions, which a party may prove to be not true. In principle, no absolutely certain proof is required, which is most often not possible either, but a declaration of probability to make the fact credible. If a declaration by the EPO is equivocal, the advantage is for the applicant or the proprietor. The reliability of an item of evidence determines its weight; e.g. an unsigned statement by an unknown and unnamed person has minimal weight (**T750/94** hn. II r.8).

Thus, decisions on evidence brought forward in opposition proceedings must be arrived at on the basis of the overall balance of probability, as distinct from 'beyond all reasonable doubt', 'up to the hilt' or 'absolute conviction'. Each of the parties must therefore seek to prove facts alleged by it to that degree of proof. (**T270/90**). However, it is the established practice of the boards of appeal to apply the criterion of 'absolute conviction' rather than the 'balance of probabilities' in cases of prior public use for which the evidence lies entirely within the sphere of the opponent (**T738/04** r.3.4).

The more serious the issue, e.g. refusal or revocation, the more convincing must be the evidence, for example in a case of alleged prior publication or public prior use (**T750/94** hn. I, **T472/92** hn. I).

Art.117 and **R.117** to 124 set out the procedure for formal taking of evidence. The procedure involves as a first step and as a precondition for its use a decision to take evidence in the sense of Art.117 (R.117); such a decision must set out all matters prescribed in **R.117**. (**G4/95** r.8(a))

Art. 117(1) In proceedings before the European Patent Office the means of giving or obtaining evidence shall include the following:
(a) hearing the parties;
(b) requests for information;
(c) production of documents;
(d) hearing witnesses;
(e) opinions by experts;
(f) inspection;
(g) sworn statements in writing.

1 **Departments**
In proceedings before the EPO, the following EPO departments have the power to take evidence: the Receiving Section (see **J20/85**), the examining divisions, the opposition divisions, the legal division, the boards of appeal and the Enlarged Board of Appeal (see also **Art.112a**). (OJ 2007 se4 EN p.134)

Evidence before the Receiving Section may relate to proof of timely payment of fees, proof that **Rfees7(3)** applies for a late payment, use of due care (**Art.122(1)**), requirements for corrections under **R.139** (**J20/85**).

2 **Means of giving evidence**
The list of means of taking evidence is not exhaustive but shows merely examples (**G2/21** r.40). The EPO is not able to compel persons to provide information. Hence, if the EPO cannot obtain the information, it may request a national court according to **R.120** to obtain the information under legal force, e.g. to compel a witness to testify before the court. The national courts of the EPC states are obliged to cooperate under **Art.131(2)**.

The hearing of parties under **Art.117(1)(a)** is used to allow a party to formally give evidence about a contested fact, similar to a hearing of a witness, while the hearing of parties in regular oral proceedings is to clarify facts and opinions.

An example of a request for information under **Art.117(1)(b)** is that the EPO asks the publisher of a book about the date of publication. See e.g. **T750/94**.

Any document is allowed under the production of documents of **Art.117(1)(c)**. The probative value of any such documents depends on the particular circumstances (**T482/89**).

A witness being heard under **Art.117(1)(d)** cannot be a party to the proceedings, see **Art.117(1)(a)**. The witness cannot be heard under oath by the EPO, but a national court may re-examine the testimony under oath at the request of the EPO (**R.119(2)**). A person summoned as a witness may request to be heard by a national court of the person's country of residence (**R.120**). Witnesses are entitled to compensation of costs and lost earnings (**R.122**). The decision to hear a witness may be made conditional upon the party who requested the hearing making a deposit for the costs with the EPO (**R.122**). The minutes of a witness hearing are normally an extensive or even literal transcript (**R.124**). The witness hearings can be conducted in the form of a videoconference; a witness may also request so (**R.117**, **R.118(2)(c)**, OJ 2020 A135 §13). In case of a witness hearing in opposition, the opposition division usually is extended by a legal member (E-IV,1.6.1).

Art.117(1) and **Art.113(1)** embody a basic procedural right to give evidence in an appropriate form and to have that evidence heard. If the taking of evidence is timely requested (e.g. a request to hear a witness), as proof of a fact that is contested and that is decisive for the outcome of the case, and the evidence is relevant and hence could be decisive for whether the fact is considered to be proven or not, the body hearing the case must, as a rule, order the requested taking of evidence. Hence, all appropriate offers of evidence made by the parties, i.e. requests to take evidence, should be taken up by the EPO (**G2/21** r.41-42). A refusal of a timely and appropriate request to hear a witness can be a substantial procedural violation. This applies both to a request made by an opponent to corroborate its case when that case is contested by the proprietor (**T1738/21**) and to a request made by a proprietor to contest an alleged public prior use by hearing a witness offered by the opponent (**T778/21**).

Parties have no obligation to announce in their offer of a witness how exactly the witness will be able to corroborate the alleged facts. It is not common to inform the witness before the hearing about the questions they will be asked, nor does the party offering the witness have to guess and answer these questions in advance already in their offer of the witness in order to substantiate why the witness is to be heard. (**T2517/22** r.6)

Under **Art.117(1)(e)**, an opinion of an expert may be used as evidence. Only the opinions of experts that are formally appointed by the EPO under **R.121** are opinions according to **Art.117(1)(e)**. Equally, the hearing of an expert under **R.117** requires a formal decision to do so (E-IV,1.6.1). Opinions of experts submitted by parties are, however, admissible as other evidence. Moreover, a technical expert may be allowed to speak as an accompanying person during oral proceedings (**G4/95**).

Experts are persons who, based on their expertise, can pronounce empirical theses (in German, 'Erfahrungssätze'), which are normally used to draw conclusions from facts. A person pronouncing facts for the observation of which special expertise is required is not an expert but an expert witness and, hence, a witness in the sense of **Art.117(1)(d)**.

A party may request the appointment of an expert; however, the EPO rarely does so because it is usually not necessary because of the specialised technical knowledge of the examiners (D-VI,1). If the EPO appoints an expert, the procedure is set out in **R.121** and the compensation of costs in **R.122.** Usually, the appointed expert submits a written opinion and is formally heard under **R.117.**

An inspection under **Art.117(1)(f)** is the direct (visual) observation of an object, usually on the premises of the EPO. It may involve the demonstration of a product or process during oral proceedings or a separate taking of evidence. Taking of evidence by inspection can be conducted in the form of a videoconference (OJ 2020 A135 §14). In some cases, the EPO must inspect an object in person, i.e. not through a videoconference (**T2011/21**, complex three-dimensional object).

A sworn statement under **Art.117(1)(g)** is known in English as an affidavit. It is a written declaration under oath, made before a competent person who takes the oath and indicates the consequences of a false declaration (e.g. up to three years imprisonment in Germany). As the EPC does not contain any indication of the probative value of such a document, the principle of free evaluation of evidence applies (**T482/89**). It is not proper for the EPO to request the filing of statements under oath with content suggested by a department of the EPO because this involves the risk of leading witnesses and could seriously undermine the probative value of such statements (**T804/92**).

Unsworn statements can also be submitted as evidence, e.g., as a signed declaration. If a fact alleged and substantiated in a written declaration submitted by a party in opposition is contested by the other party, and if the contested fact is relevant to the decision to be taken, the person making the declaration is generally to be heard as a witness if the party offers the witness. The ensuing hearing of the witness allows the opposition division and the parties to question the witness. It thus enables the opposition division to establish the facts based on that person's testimony. If the person is not offered as a witness, the opposition division generally cannot rely on the declaration as evidence of the contested fact. (E-IV,1.2; **T474/04** hn)

Third parties may request that the EPO takes evidence even before the start of opposition proceedings, e.g. between the publication of a patent application and the grant of the patent, if it is likely that the evidence will be difficult or even impossible to obtain later (**R.123**).

3 Language of evidence

The languages of evidence that can be used in written and oral proceedings are given in **R.3(3), R.4(3),(5),(6).**

When producing documents (**Art.117(1)(c)**) any language can be used, provided a translation in an official language of the EPO is filed on invitation within a period to be specified (**R.3(3)**). The EPO may disregard such a document if no translation has been filed in due time (**R.3(3)**), which an applicant can remedy using further processing (**Art.121 and R.135**) or a proprietor using re-establishment (**Art.122** and **R.136**).

When hearing parties, witnesses or experts, any language may be used by the person being heard, provided the party requesting the taking of evidence makes provisions for interpretation into an EPO language as permitted under **R.4(3)**.

Statements made during oral proceedings in an official language of the EPO are entered in the minutes of the hearing in that language. Statements made in another language are entered in the official EPO language into which they have been translated (**R.4(6)**).

4 **Evaluation of evidence**

Proceedings before the EPO follow the principle of the free evaluation of evidence. This means that there are no firm rules defining the extent to which certain types of evidence are, or are not, convincing. Instead, the question of whether a fact can be regarded as proven has to be assessed on the basis of all the relevant evidence that is not held inadmissible on formal grounds (**G3/97** r.5).

The EPO has to decide according to its own discretion and its own conviction, by taking account of the entire content of the parties' submissions and, where appropriate, any evidence admissibly submitted or taken, without observing formal rules, whether a contested factual assertion is to be regarded as true or false. The EPO must assess the evidence comprehensively and dutifully. The only decisive factor is whether the members of the division or board are personally convinced of the truth of the factual allegation, i.e. how credible they classify a piece of evidence. Note, case law may specify a high standard of proof in certain cases. The decision must set out the reasons why a contested fact is considered to be proven or not. (**G2/21** r.30-31)

Disregarding evidence that is admissibly submitted and relied upon by a party to support a contested fact, and that can be decisive for the final decision, is a substantial procedural violation (based on **G2/21** r.32).

Art. 117(2) The procedure for taking such evidence shall be laid down in the Implementing Regulations.

Implemented by:
R.118 Summons to give evidence before the EPO
R.119 Examination of evidence before the EPO
R.120 Hearing by a competent national court
R.121 Commissioning of experts
R.122 Costs of taking of evidence
R.123 Conservation of evidence
R.124 Minutes of oral proceedings and of taking of evidence

Art. 118 Unity of the European patent application or European patent

Where the applicants for or proprietors of a European patent are not the same in respect of different designated Contracting States, they shall be regarded as joint applicants or proprietors for the purposes of proceedings before the European Patent Office. The unity of the application or patent in these proceedings shall not be affected; in particular the text of the application or patent shall be uniform for all designated Contracting States, unless this Convention provides otherwise.

Implemented by:
R.138 Different claims for different states
R.151 Common representative

1 **Unity of application and patent**

The unity of application, procedure and patent is a basic principle of the EPC: a single procedure for granting a single European patent (as mentioned in the Preamble). In particular, a patent cannot have different claims for different designated states unless an exception applies (see below). This principle is mentioned in the second sentence of **Art.118**. It applies in all proceedings before the EPO, not only in the specific case of an application with different applicants for different states of the first sentence of **Art.118** but also to applications with joint applicants (co-applicants for all states) or a single applicant.

The first sentence provides that in case of an application having different applicants for different designated states (see **Art.59**, e.g. applicant A for DE and applicant B for all other states), the applicants are deemed joint applicants. Therefore, they must act jointly and exclusively through a common representative, as in the case of joint applicants (see **R.151**).

The principle of unity also applies to European patents in opposition proceedings, i.e. a patent can only be maintained in amended form with a single text for all designated states unless an exception applies. If the patent has multiple proprietors, these must act jointly, with one exception as set out in **Art.99(4)**.

The principle of unity of the application is distinct from the requirement of unity of invention of **Art.82**. Moreover, it does not prohibit transferring an application to a new applicant for some, but not all, designated states (**Art.71**).

The unitary character of a patent in proceedings before the EPO and the unitary character of a unitary patent under Art.3(2) EU regulation 1257/2012 are two distinct legal concepts. However, a unitary patent can only be granted for a European patent that has been granted for all participating Member States with the same set of claims (**UPR.5(2)**).

2 **Exceptions from unity**

The 'unless otherwise provided' in **Art.118** allows a deviation from the unity of application or patent. Hence, an application or patent can have a different set of claims for different designated states if one of the following exceptions applies:

1 In the case of a national prior right, different claims may be filed for the state concerned and, if necessary, a different description and drawings (**R.138**). The different claims may only be submitted after the EPO has noted the existence of the prior right.

2 A third party adjudged to be entitled to a patent for some but not all designated states during opposition may replace the proprietor for those states and independently amend the patent for those states (**Art.99(4)**, **R.78(2)**). Furthermore, if a third party is adjudged to be entitled to a part of the subject-matter of an application, the judgement exceptionally has effect in some, but not all, EPC states, and the third party files a new application under **Art.61(1)(b)** for those states, the original applicant may file two sets of claims for the original application: a first, restricted, set of claims for the states concerned by the judgement and second set of claims for the other designated states (**R.18(2)**).

3 Applications filed before 13.12.2007, i.e. the date of entry into force of EPC2000, follow EPC1973 in respect of European prior rights, which are effective only for validly designated contracting states (see **Art.54(3):3**). Hence, such applications may have different claims for different states and, if necessary, also a different description and drawings in the case of European prior rights (R.87 EPC1973). The different claims may only be submitted after the EPO has noted the existence of the prior rights. Under EPC2000, European prior rights are effective in all contracting states. Hence, it is not allowed to file different claims for different states for applications filed on or after 13.12.2007 in the case of European prior rights.

4 Historically, an application filed on or before 07.10.1992 in which a state (e.g. Greece or Spain) was designated which made a reservation under former Art.167(2)(a) EPC1973 could have different claims for those states. (H-III,4.4)

The claims fee (**R.45**) for an application with multiple sets of claims is calculated only for the set with the highest number of claims (A-III,9). All sets of claims must be translated into the two official EPO languages other than the language of the proceedings under **R.71(3)**.

Art. 119 Notification

Decisions, summonses, notices and communications shall be notified by the European Patent Office of its own motion in accordance with the Implementing Regulations. Notification may, where exceptional circumstances so require, be effected through the intermediary of the central industrial property offices of the Contracting States.

Implemented by:
R.125 General provisions on notification
R.126 Notification by post
R.127 Notification by technical means of communication
R.128 Notification by delivery by hand
R.129 Public notification
R.130 Notification to representatives

1 **Notification**

Notification is the act by which the addressee is given the opportunity to take notice of a communication sent by the EPO in the way prescribed by the EPC. Notification is of special importance for the calculation of periods under **Art.120**.

R.125 prescribes the means of communication that may be used by the EPO when communicating with a party. The means of communication that may be used by a party when communicating with the EPO are governed by **R.2**.

2 **Receipt theory**

The date on which documents are received is of key importance when the EPO communicates with parties. When a party has to file a document, the date of receipt by the EPO is the relevant event for determining whether a time limit has been met (**T702/89** r.2.2; Not. EPO OJ 2005 p.44 §5). Similarly, when the EPO despatches a communication from which a time limit is reckoned, the date of receipt by the party is important in calculating the time limit (seven-day rule) even if it is the date of the document itself (the deemed notification date of **R.126(2)** and **R.127(2)**) from which the beginning of the time limit is calculated (**R.131(2)**).

3 **Documents to be notified**

The following documents must be notified (**R.125**):

1 decisions, even if the decision has already been pronounced in oral proceedings (**R.111(1)**); the notification of the decision in writing triggers the period for appeal (**Art.108**);
2 summonses, e.g. for oral proceedings (**R.115(1)**) and for the taking of evidence (**R.118(1)**);

3 notices and communications triggering a period, e.g.
   (a) a communication from the Receiving Section under **R.55** (compliance with the requirements for according a date of filing); **R.56** (addition of missing parts); **R.58** (rectification of deficiencies in the application documents); or **R.60** (subsequent identification of the inventor);
   (b) the notification of the search report by the search division under **R.65**;
   (c) communications from the examining division under **Art.94** and **R.71**;
   (d) communications from the opposition division under **Art.101** ff and **R.81** ff;
   (e) communications from the board of appeal under **Art.110** and **R.100** ff;
   (f) the notification of loss of rights under **R.112(1)** by departments of all instances;

4 notices and communications required by other provisions of the EPC;

5 notices and communications required by the President; up to now the President has not prescribed such notifications.

Notification can be made through a national patent authority if, in an important case, delivery by post is unsuccessful and public notification is not expected to be successful. See **R.125(3)**.

Art. 120 Time limits

The Implementing Regulations shall specify:

(a) the time limits which are to be observed in proceedings before the European Patent Office and are not fixed by this Convention;

(b) the manner of computation of time limits and the conditions under which time limits may be extended;

(c) the minima and maxima for time limits to be determined by the European Patent Office.

Implemented by:
R.131 Calculation of periods
R.132 Periods specified by the EPO
R.133 Late receipt of documents
R.134 Automatic extension of periods when:
(1) the EPO is closed
(2) general dislocation in the postal delivery or transmission
(3) a national office is closed for receipt of a patent application
(4) publication of period of dislocation
(5) local dislocation in the postal delivery or transmission
R.142 Interruption of proceedings

1 **General**

R.132(1) of the Implementing Regulations specifies the duration of periods not fixed in the Articles or Rules (**Art.120(a)**), **R.131** and **R.134** the computation and extension of periods (**Art.120(b)**), and **R.132(2)** the minimum and maximum duration of periods to be determined by the EPO (**Art.120(c)**).

2 **Terminology**

A period having a well-defined start and end is called a 'period', 'Frist' and 'délai' in the English, German and French version of the EPC, respectively. However, the English version also uses the term 'time limit' for the same notion. This is undesirable from a legal point of view, where terminology should be unequivocal. Moreover, **R.131** defines the calculation of periods, whereas the EPC does not define the calculation of time limits.

Decision **J18/04** r.21, 26 recognised this confusing terminology and decided that the term 'time limit' is an equivalent of 'period' in EPC1973. (E-VIII,1.1)

EPC2000 has addressed this issue and uses 'time limit' in the more English meaning of 'a fixed point in time beyond which something ceases to be possible or allowable' (Oxford English Dictionary). In the terminology of EPC2000 'a time limit is the expiry of a period'. Hence, the legislator has for the sake of consistency replaced the term 'time limit' in the Rules of EPC2000 by 'period' wherever possible (OJ 2003 se1 p.159, Introduction). The replacement has no legal consequences (**J19/10** r.7.1). The 'time limit' in **R.50(3)** still used in the meaning of 'period' is probably an oversight.

It should be noted that this correction has not been made in the earlier drafted Articles of the Convention of EPC2000. Therefore, the Articles frequently refer to 'time limit' where the corresponding Rules refer to 'period'. In recent amendments of the Rules the legislator appears to have lapsed back into the pre-EPC2000 terminology, which is still the common terminology within the EPO (see e.g. **R.125(1)**).

3 Periods

The periods used in the provisions of the EPC can be divided in two classes.

The first class contains the periods of a legally indicated length fixed for carrying out a particular procedural act (**J24/03** hn. I). In EPC1973 such periods were called 'time limits'. Examples are the one-month period for payment of the filing fee and search fee (**R.38**), the two-month period of **R.58** for correcting formal deficiencies in the application, the period to be specified for correcting substantive errors under **R.71(1)**, the twelve-month period for claiming priority (**Art.87(1)**), the period for responding to a communication from an examiner (**Art.94(3)**) and the opposition period (**Art.99(1)**). The period is not necessarily equal to the period during which the procedural act may be validly performed. In many cases the EPC allows applicants to perform acts even before the period starts to run (**J18/04** r.30).

The second class contains periods within which a party need not perform an act before the EPO and internal periods of the EPO. Examples are the term of a patent (**Art.63(1)**), the patent years for the payment of renewal fees in **Art.86** (OJ 1984 p.272), the eighteen-month period of **Art.93(1)(a)** (see e.g. **J32/89** r.3), internal periods as in **Art.109(2)** and the 'negative' periods of six months in **Art.55(1)** and two and five weeks in **R.67** (see e.g. **J32/89** r.3)

Art.120 deals with time limits, i.e. the expiry of periods of the first class. Their triggering and computation are governed by **R.131**. Some periods may be extended upon request under **R.132** and periods will be extended automatically under **R.134(1)-(3)**. **R.133** and **R.134(5)** provide a legal fiction that a late received document may be deemed received in due time. In special cases a period may be interrupted (**R.14(4)**, **R.142(4)**).

Periods calculated from the priority date must be calculated anew from the filing date if the priority claim has been withdrawn before the expiry of the period as calculated from the priority date (A-III,6.11). Failure to observe a period of the first class can be remedied using either further processing or re-establishment. Time limits or periods of the second class are not open for the legal remedies of further processing and re-establishment.

A condition that must be complied with for carrying out an act cannot be equated with a period; for the former the duration is determined by the occurrence of the condition, whereas for the latter the duration is predetermined from the outset. E.g. the filing of a divisional requires compliance with the condition of pendency of the parent application (**R.36(1)**); the last day on which the divisional can be filed, i.e. the last day of pendency of the parent application, is not predetermined from the outset but determined by occurrence of the condition of pendency. Therefore, **R.36(1)** does not impose any time limit for filing a divisional application but rather sets a condition. (J24/03 hn.II, III)

The computation of periods of the second class is not explicitly provided for in the EPC. It is generally accepted to apply mutatis mutandis the computation of the periods of the first class as set out in **R.131**; however, the extensions under **R.132** and **R.134** are not applicable.

4 **Convention period and office period**

The EPC distinguishes two types of periods: convention periods and office periods.

A convention period is a period of which the duration is fixed in the Articles or Rules of the EPC, such as the periods for the payment of filing and search fee (**R.38**), for the filing of the request for examination (**R.70(1)**) and for filing the notice of appeal (**Art.108**). A convention period cannot be extended on request under **R.132**.

An office period is a period the duration of which is not fixed by the EPC but by the EPO in each specific case as set out in **R.132**. Examples are the period for responding to a communication of an examiner under **Art.94(3)** and the period of **R.70(2)** inviting applicants to indicate whether they desire to proceed further. An office period may be extended on request under **R.132**.

5 **Non-observance of period**

Possible consequences of not observing a time limit or period:

- the application will not be dealt with as a European patent application (**Art.90(2)**);
- the application is refused or the right of priority is lost (**Art.90(5)**);
- the application is deemed withdrawn (**Art.94(2), 94(4)**);
- the patent is revoked (**R.82(3)**).

If non-observance leads to a direct loss of rights, the affected party is notified according to **R.112(1)**.

Art. 121 Further processing of the European patent application

1 **Remedy**

Further processing is the main remedy for non-observance of a time limit vis-à-vis the EPO in the grant procedure and related ex parte appeal proceedings. It allows further processing of the application merely by paying a fee; no written request is necessary. If further processing is possible, re-establishment according to **Art.122** is not possible (**R.136(3)**). Further processing is a reliable remedy. In contrast, re-establishment is not reliable (see **Art.122:1**; OJ 2007 se4 EN p.140), because it requires the applicant to prove exercise of all due care. A summary of the requirements for further processing are given in **Art.121(2):1**.

Art. 121(1) If an applicant fails to observe a time limit vis-à-vis the European Patent Office, he may request further processing of the European patent application.

1 **Applicability**

The reference in **Art.121(1)** to 'applicant' restricts the application of further processing to patent applications; patents are excluded. Hence, further processing can be used in grant proceedings and subsequent ex parte appeal proceedings but not in opposition proceedings.

Since **Art.121(1)** allows only the applicant to request further processing, an applicant to whom the application has been transferred may only request further processing after the transfer has been registered at the EPO (**R.22(3)**).

Further processing is available both for Convention periods, i.e. periods fixed by the EPC, such as the one-month period of **R.38** for paying the filing and search fee, and for office periods, i.e. periods fixed by the EPO, such as the period of **R.50(3)** for redressing an unsigned document. Further processing is excluded for the periods mentioned in **Art.121(4)** and **R.135(2)**.

The applicability of further processing does not depend on the sanction on failing a time limit. It is irrelevant whether the sanction is a deemed withdrawal of the application, a total loss of rights such as refusal of the application (see e.g. **R.30(3):1** and **R.60(1):2**) or a partial loss of rights such as loss of a priority claim.

A refusal of an application under **Art.97(2)** cannot be remedied using further processing, because the refusal does not follow a failure to observe a time limit, as required by **Art.121(1)**. A refusal is a consequence of the fact that the application itself does not meet the requirements of the EPC. The only remedy is to appeal the refusal.

2 **PCT**

Further processing can be applied to Euro-PCT applications, in particular to the period for entering the regional phase before the EPO (see **R.160**). When the receiving Office declares in the international phase the application as withdrawn, further processing may be possible before the EPO in connection with the review and excuse procedure (see R. 159:4).

Art. 121(2) The European Patent Office shall grant the request, provided that the requirements laid down in the Implementing Regulations are met. Otherwise, it shall reject the request.

Implemented by:
R.135(1) Requirements for request
R.135(3) Department competent to decide

1 **Requirements for further processing**

The requirements for an allowable request for further processing as provided in **Art.121** and **R.135** are:

1 The request must be filed by an applicant (**Art.121(1)**). A request filed by any other party, such as a proprietor or an opponent, is not allowable.
2 The request must relate to a failed time limit (**Art.121(1)**). A loss of rights due to any other cause cannot be remedied using further processing.
3 The time limit must be vis-à-vis the EPO (**Art.121(1)**). **Art.121** is not applicable to a time limit vis-à-vis a national office, e.g. for filing a translation of a European patent under **Art.65(1)**.
4 The period is not excluded from further processing under **Art.121(4)** and **R.135(2)**.
5 The fee for further processing must be paid (**R.135(1)**, **Rfees2(1)12**).
6 The omitted act must be completed (**R.135(1)**). The omitted act may relate to a payment, the filing of a document, or both.
7 The payment of the fee and the completion of the omitted act must be carried out within two months from notification of the communication concerning the failed time limit (**R.135(1)**).

More details of the requirements are set out in the cited provisions. The requirements do not include a written request. A failed fee payment can therefore be remedied by merely paying the omitted fee and the fee for further processing.

If the requirements are met, the EPO will grant the request for further processing (**Art.121(2)**). The requirements to be met are merely formal in nature; hence, compliance is simple, making further processing a reliable remedy. The request will be decided on by the department competent to decide on the omitted act (**R.135(3)**).

2 **Rejection of request for further processing**
If the requirements for requesting further processing have not been met, the EPO will reject the request (**Art.121(2)**, second sentence). After rejection of the request or not requesting further processing, the legal consequence of not observing the time limit takes effect at expiry of the unobserved, normal period, not at the end of the two-month period for requesting further processing (the Guidelines apply **G4/98** r.7 mutatis mutandis, see A-III,11.2.3).

Art. 121(3) If the request is granted, the legal consequences of the failure to observe the time limit shall be deemed not to have ensued.

1 **Grant of request for further processing**
If a request for further processing is granted, the European patent application must be treated as if the non-observance of the time limit had not happened and has been pending throughout. If the request is refused, the loss of rights will have occurred on expiry of the relevant period and the application ceased to be pending then (J4/11 r.22; A-IV,1.1.1).

Art. 121(4) Further processing shall be ruled out in respect of the time limits in Article 87, paragraph 1, Article 108 and Article 112a, paragraph 4, as well as the time limits for requesting further processing or re-establishment of rights. The Implementing Regulations may rule out further processing for other time limits.

Art.87(1) Priority period
Art.108 Periods for filing appeal
Art.112a(4) Periods for filing petition for review
Implemented by:
R.135(2) Exclusion of other periods from further processing

1 **Periods excluded from further processing**
The EPC excludes several periods from further processing. The more important periods, the non-observance of which affects third parties most, are laid down in **Art.121(4)**. Other periods, mainly relating to periods that have a remedial character, are contained in the easier amendable Rules (see R.135(2):1).

Art.121(4) explicitly excludes several periods from further processing: the priority period under **Art.87(1)**, the two periods for appeal in **Art.108**, the periods for petition for review in **Art.112a(4)**, and the periods for requesting further processing in R.135(1) and re-establishment of rights in R.136(1). Instead, re-establishment is available as a remedy for all but the period for requesting re-establishment (see Art.122(4):1 and R.136(3):1 for reasons to allow only re-establishment). The remedy of failing these important periods should be based on specific grounds, as required by re-establishment, and should not be possible by the easy further processing.

The exclusion of the periods for requesting further processing and re-establishment prevents chaining of remedies. Note that further processing is not possible for the period for requesting re-establishment, whereas re-establishment is possible for the period for requesting further processing (see **R.136(3):1**).

Further exceptions to the applicability of further processing have been provided for in **R.135(2)**. This affords the flexibility needed to adapt the scope of application of **Art.121** to changing practical requirements and new periods. It is not the purpose of the second sentence of **Art.121(4)** to enable the scope of application of further processing to be generally restricted. Only if an adequate legal remedy is already provided by the law will it be possible to rule out application of **Art.121.** (MR/24/00)

Art. 122 Re-establishment of rights

1 **Remedy**

The remedy of re-establishment can restore applicants or proprietors in their rights lost after non-observance of a time limit. The remedy causes true party intention to prevail over procedural certainty about loss of rights; therefore, precise limited circumstances and conditions are defined to avoid legal uncertainty for third parties (**T824/00** r.6). Re-establishment requires that the requester has exercised all due care, which must be proven convincingly. The required proof makes re-establishment an unreliable remedy. This is supported by the fact that the prevention of hardship ensuing from the application of **Art.122** was the whole point of introducing **R.133** and **134** (**J13/05** r.3.2).

The requirements for re-establishment conform to Art.12(1) of the Patent Law Treaty (PLT). This article offers a choice between 'all due care' and 'unintentional delay', the latter requirement being used by the USPTO, because no agreement could be reached on a single requirement. The EPO decided not to use the more party-friendly 'unintentional delay', because they were more familiar with the 'all due care' criterion.

Other provisions to avert the consequences of non-observance of time limits are given in **Art.121** (further processing), **R.51(2)** (additional period for renewal fee), **R.132(2)** (extension of time limit upon request), **R.133** (excuse of late receipt), **R.134** (automatic extension of periods), **R.142** (interruption of proceedings), **Rfees7(3)** (late payment) and **Rfees8** (small amount missing). It is strongly recommended to use, where possible, these remedies instead of re-establishment, because they are reliable for not requiring proof of all due care and do not give rise to third parties' rights as in **Art.122(5)**.

Art. 122(1) An applicant for or proprietor of a European patent who, in spite of all due care required by the circumstances having been taken, was unable to observe a time limit vis-à-vis the European Patent Office shall have his rights re-established upon request if the non-observance of this time limit has the direct consequence of causing the refusal of the European patent application or of a request, or the deeming of the application to have been withdrawn, or the revocation of the European patent, or the loss of any other right or means of redress.

1 **Entitled person**

According to the wording of the provision both an applicant and a proprietor may apply for re-establishment. Third parties have been excluded from re-establishment, because they have national remedies available, which are not available to the applicant and proprietor.

Exceptionally, an appellant already known as opponent, who has validly filed a notice of appeal, may request re-establishment of rights for filing the grounds of appeal within the four-month time limit (**G1/86**). The extension of the applicability is based on the principle of equal treatment of parties to judicial proceedings. The decision **G1/86** must be interpreted narrowly: an appellant known as opponent cannot apply re-establishment to the two-month time limit for filing an appeal (**T210/89**). If the application has been transferred, the new owner may request re-establishment only after the EPO has received the transfer documents referred to in **R.22(1)**.

Re-establishment can be requested by the applicant of a Euro-PCT application in the transitional phase and the regional phase because of the fiction of **Art.153(2)**. For the procedure in the transitional phase on the review and excuse procedure, see R.159:4. Re-establishment can be used for time limits not excluded under Art.122(4) and R.136(3).

2 **Failed period**

Re-establishment is only applicable to a loss of rights due to non-observance of a time limit according to **Art.122(1)**. The period defining the time limit must have a starting date and a duration; time restrictions imposed by the EPO but not having these elements are not regarded as time limits for the purposes of **Art.122** (**J18/04** hn. II).

The time limit is defined as the expiry of a period of a legally indicated length fixed for carrying out a particular procedural act. In procedural law, an act to be carried out within a time limit is different from a conditional act, which can only be validly carried out during the circumstances forming the condition; the circumstances are not created to carry out the act, whereas the period of specified duration is created to carry out the act. Hence, as an example, the condition of pendency of the earlier application in **R.36(1)** for filing a divisional application is not a time limit in this sense and therefore not open to re-establishment. Note that these decisions do not use EPC2000 definition of 'time limit' as the expiry of a period. (**J24/03**, hn. I, r.4; **J18/04** r.7-11)

Similarly, re-establishment of rights is not possible for failure to be present on the date appointed for oral proceedings (E-VIII, 3.1.1).

No re-establishment is possible in a non-observed time limit that does not give rise to one of the consequences of **Art.122(1)**. An example is the period for the submission of the observations by the proprietor on a statement of another party to the opposition proceedings or on communications from the opposition division (**R.79(1)**). Also excluded are periods to be observed by third parties before the EPO, e.g. by the opponent or intervener (**Art.99, 105**). As an exception, the four-month time limit for filing grounds by an opponent in the appeal procedure is not excluded (**G1/86**). The national authorities that must forward the application within fourteen months (**Art.77**) are also third parties for whose failures re-establishment does not apply.

Art.122(4) and **R.136(3)** exclude from re-establishment the period for requesting re-establishment and the periods for which further processing is available. Hence, re-establishment is not applicable for most periods in the grant procedure, where further processing is the main remedy.

Re-establishment in the priority period of **Art.87(1)**, implementation of which is required by Art.13 PLT, and the period for filing a petition for review under **Art.112a(4)** is explicitly allowed in **R.136(1)**.

The principle of proportionality, which makes a sanction proportional to the number of days a time limit was missed, cannot be relied on. Although older case law does use the principle, more recent case law holds that only the conduct before expiry of the period is decisive, not the length of the ensuing delay (see **T439/06** r.15).

3 **Loss of rights**

The loss of rights to be remedied can be any total loss of an application or a patent as expressly stated in the provision. The loss may relate to 'any other right', i.e. a partial loss of rights, such as the right of priority and the right of designating states. The loss may also concern 'any means of redress', such as the right to request further processing.

Art.122(1) requires that the loss of rights must be the 'direct consequence' of the non-observance of a time limit. The 'direct consequence' means that the non-observed time limit must have been a time limit which was explicitly and specifically provided by the EPC for the performance of the procedural act in question (**J18/04** r.12).

Non-observance of the priority period of **Art.87(1)** has the direct consequence of causing the loss of priority, a partial loss of rights, by virtue of **Art.90(5)**. Non-observance of the period for requesting further processing during the grant procedure has the direct consequence of the loss of the right to file such a request under **Art.121(1)**. In opposition, non-observance of the time limit for filing a translation of amended claims has the direct consequence of revocation of the patent (**R.82(3)**).

Re-establishment is not available for a loss of rights that is not the direct consequence of the non-observance of a time limit. An example of an indirect loss of rights is where the applicant fails to observe the twelve-month priority period, resulting in lack of novelty because of intermediate prior art. The refusal of the application cannot be remedied using re-establishment, because it is not a direct consequence of the failure to meet the twelve-month priority period. See **J18/04** r.13 for another example.

4 **All due care**

Re-establishment of rights will only be allowed if the party can prove that all due care required by the circumstances has been taken, in other words, that the party has been diligent and careful and the delay was caused by unforeseeable factors; errors of law, however, do not constitute grounds for re-establishment (**D6/82**). All due care usually requires proof that the non-observance was caused by a one-time error in an otherwise properly working system, involving an exhaustive description of the time limit monitoring system employed.

All due care requires the presence of a system for monitoring time limits and, for larger offices, at least one effective cross-check (**T428/98** r.3.5). An isolated procedural mistake of an otherwise properly functioning administration is an admissible ground for re-establishment (**J2/86**).

If a professional representative runs a one-person office, appropriate provisions should be made so that, in the case of an absence through illness, the observance of time limits can be ensured with the help of other persons (**J41/92** r.4.4).

The requirement of all due care by the applicants or proprietors extend to their representative and to the personnel of the representative (**J5/80**). The extent of the due care depends on the person concerned. The representative is responsible for the instruction and supervision of the personnel and the heaviness of the delegated tasks. The personnel must have been selected, trained and supervised properly, and be up to the delegated tasks (**J5/80**); the same applies to temporary personnel.

A culpable error of an assistant is not to be imputed to the representative, if the latter has exercised all due care. The extent of the due care depends on the specific circumstances according to **Art.122(1)**. It always includes the above-mentioned instruction and supervision. However, the kind of time limit that needs to be observed and the legal consequences of missing it has also to be taken into consideration. Hence, time limits without further ordinary remedy require more care than other time limits. Representatives must therefore verify the calculation of time limits such as those for filing an appeal once the file has been handed over to them. (**T439/06**)

All due care may be proven in the case of natural events and inevitable circumstances (force majeure) (**J18/82** r.11). Workload and long-lasting illness are not sufficient grounds, but a sudden illness is (**T525/91** hn). A human error occurring for the first time, due to pressure and not to negligence, may be regarded as an isolated mistake (**T111/92** r.4). Unexpectedly long delivery times are valid grounds (**T81/83** r.3, see also **T777/98** hn). An incorrect interpretation of the EPC by the party is not a valid ground (**D6/82** hn4). Shortness of money is a valid ground for re-establishment, provided the shortness was due to circumstances beyond the control of the applicant and they have exercised all due care in seeking financial assistance (**J22/88**). Reliance on a courtesy service such as the EPO's reminder for payment of a renewal fee (A-X,5.2.4) is no exercise of due care (**J12/84** hn2).

5 **Examples**

A few examples of cases where re-establishment is possible:

- payment of a renewal fee plus additional fee (**R.51(2)**);
- filing of a priority claiming patent application within the priority period (**Art.87(1)**);
- filing a notice of appeal (**Art.108**);
- filing a translation of an application (**R.6(1)**);
- filing a request for further processing (**Art.121**).

Art. 122(2) The European Patent Office shall grant the request, provided that the conditions of paragraph 1 and any other requirements laid down in the Implementing Regulations are met. Otherwise, it shall reject the request.

Implemented by:
R.136(1) Requirements for filing request
R.136(2) Grounds and facts, completion of omitted act
R.136(4) Competent department

1 **Requirements for re-establishment**

The requirements for an allowable request for re-establishment as provided in **Art.122** and **R.136** are:

1. The request must be filed by an applicant or proprietor (**Art.122(1)**). A request filed by any other party, such as an opponent, is in principle not allowable. See **Art.122(1):1** for an exception.
2. The request must relate to a failed time limit (**Art.122(1)**). A loss of rights due to any other cause cannot be remedied using re-establishment.
3. The time limit must be vis-à-vis the EPO (**Art.122(1)**). **Art.122** is not applicable to a time limit vis-à-vis a national office, e.g. for filing a translation of a European patent under **Art.65(1)**.
4. The time limit is not excluded from re-establishment under **Art.122(4)** and **R.136(3)**.
5. The written request must be filed and the fee for re-establishment must be paid (**R.136(1)**, **Rfees2(1)13**).
6. The omitted act must be completed (**R.136(2)**). The omitted act may relate to a payment, the filing of a document, or both.
7. The filing of the request, payment of the fee and the completion of the omitted act must be carried out within two months from removal of the cause of non-compliance and within one year from expiry of the unobserved period (**R.136(1)**, note the two exceptions therein).

More details of the requirements are set out in the cited provisions. If the requirements are met, the EPO will grant the request for re-establishment (**Art.122(2)**) and the legal consequences of the failure to observe the time limit shall be deemed not to have ensued (**Art.122(3)**).

2 **Rejection of request for re-establishment**

If the requirements for requesting re-establishment have not been met, the EPO will reject the request (**Art.122(2)**, second sentence). The decision will state the grounds for the rejection (**R.111(2)**, E-VIII,3.3).

After rejection of the request or not requesting re-establishment, the legal consequence of not observing the time limit takes effect at expiry of the unobserved, normal period, not at the end of the two-month period for requesting re-establishment (similar application of the principle set out in A-III,11.2.3 for further processing, applying **G4/98** r.7 mutatis mutandis). Any fees paid to complete the omitted act are reimbursed (**J16/82, T1426/14**).

Any decision to reject a request for re-establishment taken by a first instance department is subject to appeal (**Art.106(1)**). A decision to reject a request for re-establishment taken by a board of appeal is not subject to further appeal and can only be contested in specific circumstances by filing a petition for review according to **Art.112a(1)**.

3 **Grant of request for re-establishment and review thereof**

A decision to grant a request for re-establishment taken by the Receiving Section or an examining division is not subject to appeal, since the applicant is not adversely affected, and becomes final as soon as it is taken. According to **T1482/21** r.2.2.8 such a decision is also binding on other departments of the EPO and cannot be reviewed by an opposition division or board of appeal in later proceedings.

Art. 122(3) If the request is granted, the legal consequences of the failure to observe the time limit shall be deemed not to have ensued.

1 **Effect of grant of request**

Art.122(3) states the principle underlying the re-establishment of rights, i.e. that the consequences of failure to observe a time limit will be deemed not to have ensued where a request for re-establishment of rights is granted.

The grounds of the decision need only be stated in case the request is not granted. However, in opposition proceedings the grounds must always be given, as the opponents are party to the re-establishment proceedings. (E-VIII, 3.3)

Art. 122(4) Re-establishment of rights shall be ruled out in respect of the time limit for requesting re-establishment of rights. The Implementing Regulations may rule out re-establishment for other time limits.

Implemented by:
R.136(3) Other periods excluded from re-establishment of rights

1 **Periods excluded from re-establishment of rights**

Art.122(4) rules out re-establishment in the period for requesting re-establishment to avoid chaining of remedies.

Other periods are ruled out by **R.136(3)**. Periods excluded from re-establishment for other reasons are given in **Art.122(1)**:2.

Art. 122(5) Any person who, in a designated Contracting State, has in good faith used or made effective and serious preparations for using an invention which is the subject of a published European patent application or a European patent in the period between the loss of rights referred to in paragraph 1 and publication in the European Patent Bulletin of the mention of re-establishment of those rights, may without payment continue such use in the course of his business or for the needs thereof.

1 **Right to continue use**

Since the request for re-establishment of rights does not have a suspensive effect on the proceedings, the legal consequences of the failure to meet a time limit will remain in force until re-establishment is allowed. Therefore, any person may use the invention to the extent rights to its subject-matter have been lost.

The right of continued use of an invention after allowance of re-establishment is equivalent to the right of continued use in the case of an incorrect translation according to **Art.70(4)(b)**. The meaning of 'use' is determined by national law. The use must have been made in good faith. Use includes preparations for use. There is no equivalent rule for further processing.

A loss of rights and subsequent re-establishment before the publication of the application, i.e. before provisional protection has commenced, does not give a third party rights to continue use of the invention, because such a right can only arise after the publication of the application and a granted request for re-establishment. (J5/79)

Art. 122(6) Nothing in this Article shall limit the right of a Contracting State to grant re-establishment of rights in respect of time limits provided for in this Convention and to be observed vis-à-vis the authorities of such State.

1 **Re-establishment before national offices**

The EPC contains a few time limits which a party has to observe before a national office, e.g. filing of a translation of the patent (**Art.65**), filing of a request for conversion (**Art.135(2)**), payment of renewal fees for European patents (**Art.141**). **Art.122(1)** restricts the application of re-establishment by the EPO to non-observed time limits vis-à-vis the EPO. **Art.122(6)** allows national authorities to apply re-establishment in the case of non-observance of EPC time limits vis-à-vis national authorities.

Art. 123 Amendments

1 **General**

The right to amend an application or patent as provided in **Art.123** is important for meeting objections made by the EPO in grant proceedings, for dealing with the grounds raised by opponents in opposition proceedings and for adjusting the desired scope of protection. During the grant procedure, and any opposition procedure that follows, a more complete view of the state of the art is obtained, which often necessitates amendment of the text of the application or patent. Amendments are most usually made to the claims of an application, in order to meet objections relating to patentability and clarity and then sometimes to the description in order to remove resulting inconsistencies. An amendment may result in an addition, replacement or deletion.

The first paragraph of **Art.123** restricts the number of opportunities the applicant or proprietor has for making amendments, the second paragraph limits the freedom that the applicant or proprietor has in amending a patent application or a patent and the third paragraph further limits the freedom that the proprietor has in amending a granted patent.

Art. 123(1) The European patent application or European patent may be amended in proceedings before the European Patent Office, in accordance with the Implementing Regulations. In any event, the applicant shall be given at least one opportunity to amend the application of his own volition.

Implemented by:
R.50(1) Form of amendments
R.80 Amendment of the European patent
R.137 Opportunities for amendment
R.138 Different claims, description and drawings for different states
R.139 Correction of errors in documents filed with the EPO
R.140 Correction of errors in decisions

1 **Opportunity to amend**

Art.123(1) provides the basic right to amend the application and, where applicable, the patent. The provision establishes that the conditions under which amendments may be made (**R.137-140**) and also the form that amendments must take (**R.50(1)**, first sentence) are laid down in the Implementing Regulations.

The right of applicants in **Art.123(1)**, second sentence, to amend at least once of their own volition and its implementation in **R.137** restrict the right to amend and strike a balance between the interest of the applicant in obtaining a granted patent and the interest of the EPO in conducting an efficient procedure. The applicant is given a single opportunity at the start of the substantive examination to file voluntary amendments; any further amendment requires consent of the EPO. This restricts the 'at least one' in **Art.123(1)** to 'only one as of right'. Later amendments must be admitted in the procedure if they are an appropriate and timely response to an objection of the examining division, so as to respect the right to be heard of the applicant (**Art.113(1)**).

The exceptional case of an amendment leading to different claims, a different description and different drawings for different states is governed by **R.138** (relating to national prior rights). Whereas **Art.123** deals with the amendment of the application and patent, **R.139** and **140** deal with the correction of mistakes in documents filed with the EPO and in decisions of the EPO, bringing them into line with what was intended at the time of filing or issuance. See **R.139:1** for a discussion of the relationship between amendment and correction.

Art. 123(2) The European patent application or European patent may not be amended in such a way that it contains subject-matter which extends beyond the content of the application as filed.

1 Extension beyond the application as filed

The underlying idea of **Art.123(2)** is that applicants and proprietors should not be allowed to improve their position by amendments to the application or patent that add subject-matter not disclosed in the application as filed, as this would give them an unwarranted advantage and could be damaging to the legal security of third parties relying on the content of the original application (**G1/93** r.9).

The applicant does not have the benefit of the doubt under **Art.123(2)**. Where the content of the application relating to a requested amendment is essentially speculative, the amendment is not allowable. (**T400/94**)

A reformulation of a phrase in an application is in principle allowed but is not recommended because of the inherent danger of extension of subject-matter. Reformulation should only be used to remove inconsistencies.

Art.123(2) uses the phrase 'subject-matter which extends beyond the content of the application as filed'. It is to be noted that also amendments restricting the scope of the claims can extend beyond the content of the application as filed. For **Art.123(2)**, it does not matter whether the amendment broadens or limits the scope of the claim. In contrast, **Art.123(3)** specifies that the patent may not be amended in such a way as to extend the protection it confers. This provision applies only after the grant of the patent.

Note that the terms 'disclosed in' and 'having a basis in' are used for **Art.123(2)** and **R.137(4)**; the terms 'having support in' and 'supported by' for **Art.84** (see also **G2/10** r.3.7). In other words, an amended claim must have basis in the application as filed under **Art.123(2)**.

1.1 CONTENT OF THE APPLICATION AS FILED

Whether an amendment extends the subject-matter of an application must be assessed with respect to the content of the application as filed. The content of the application as filed does not include the abstract (as a consequence of **Art.85**; **T246/86**). The title of the application given in the Request for grant form is not part of the content of the application as filed (**R.41(2)(b)**; H-V,8). A title or heading included in the description is part of the content (**T1437/07** r.3).

An application from which priority is claimed does not form part of the application as filed, even if a copy of it is filed together with the application (**T260/85**). It is therefore not generally possible to amend an application by adding matter which is only present in a priority document. As an exception, missing drawings and missing parts of the description may be taken from a priority document and inserted in the application as filed without re-dating of the application, provided the conditions of **R.56(3)** are complied with. These missing parts are then considered to be part of the application as filed (H-IV,2.2.2). It is also possible to correct erroneously filed application documents based on the content of the priority document without a re-dating of the application if the conditions of **R.56a(4)** are met. In such cases, the corrected parts are considered to be a part of the application as filed. Furthermore, any erroneously filed parts that remain in the application pursuant to **R.56a(4)** are also considered to be a part of the application as filed (H-IV,2.2.3). These opportunities under **R.56(3)** and **R.56a(4)** are only available at the filing stage of the application and cannot be applied at later stages.

Amendment of a divisional application after its filing is subject to the restrictions of **Art.123(2)** with respect to the divisional application as filed (**T441/92** r.4.2) and cumulatively with the restriction of **Art.76** with respect to the parent application(s).

If the application is filed in a non-EPO language, the original text in that language constitutes the basis for determining compliance with **Art.123(2)** and not the translation filed under **Art.14(2)** (**Art.70(2)**). The EPO assumes that the translation conforms to the original text unless evidence is submitted to the contrary, e.g. by an opponent (**R.7**). (A-VII,7)

For a Euro-PCT application the application 'as originally filed' is the PCT application as originally filed (B-VIII,6). This includes missing parts filed or incorporated under R.20.5 PCT and, for PCT applications filed on or after 01.11.2022, corrected elements submitted under R.20.5bis PCT. The corrected elements and the original erroneously filed elements are both treated as a part of the application as filed (C-III,1.3). For PCT applications filed between 01.07.2020 and 31.10.2022, in cases where the applicant used R.20.5bis PCT in the international phase, see C-III,1.3 and OJ 2020 A81.

Features only described in a cross-referenced document are prima facie not part of the content of the application. By way of exception, such features may be introduced into a claim by amendment without violating **Art.123(2)** if the description of the application as filed leaves no doubt to the skilled reader that (**T689/90**.r.2.2; case law summarised in H-IV,2.2.1):

1 protection is or may be sought for such features;
2 such features contribute to solving the problem of the invention;
3 such features at least implicitly belong to the description of the invention as filed; and
4 such features are precisely defined and identifiable in the reference document.

All essential features in the reference document which belong together must be incorporated into the claim; it is not permissible to single out a particular one (**T6/84** hn). See **T1819/07**.r.3.4 for an insufficiently defined feature: a claimed particle size range was regarded as unclear because no method for measuring the size of the particles was specified; a reference in the description to a document disclosing both a method of making and of measuring the particles was of no avail because the reference actually only disclosed the method of making the particles.

The reference document must be available to the public. This condition will only be met if the document was publicly available on the date of filing of the application or, if this is not the case, it was available on or before the filing date to the EPO or to the receiving Office of a Euro-PCT application that was not filed with the EPO, and also available to the public on or before the date of publication of the application (e.g. by being present in the file of the application) (H-IV,2.2.1).

1.2 DISCLOSURE TEST FOR EXTENSION OF SUBJECT-MATTER

The EPO uses the so-called disclosure test (also referred to as the 'gold standard') for determining whether an amendment extends the subject-matter beyond the content of the application as filed: an amendment is not allowable if the overall change in content of the application, seen objectively and relative to the date of filing, results in the skilled person being presented with new technical information which is not directly and unambiguously derivable, from the whole content of the application as filed, even when account is taken of matter which is implicit to a person skilled in the art using common general knowledge (**G3/89** r.2; **G2/10** r.4.3, r.4.5.1; H-IV,2.2).

Other conditions (e.g. the 'two-list principle', see **Art.123(2):2.4.4**) are not additional or alternative to the disclosure test but a possible way to verify that the amendment passes the disclosure test (**T1255/18** r.3.2).

A disclosure may be explicit or implicit. An implicit disclosure is a clear and unambiguous consequence of what is explicitly disclosed. Hence, a literal basis for an amendment is not required by the wording of **Art.123(2)** (**T667/08** r.4.1.4). An implicit disclosure is part of the technical content of the application that is not explicitly mentioned in the application but is clearly and unambiguously derivable by the skilled person from matter explicitly mentioned in the application. The common general knowledge of the skilled person in the technical field at the filing date is taken into account in deciding what is clearly and unambiguously implied by the explicit disclosure of the application. An implicit disclosure is *not* technical information that the disclosure of the application renders obvious for the skilled person in view of the common general knowledge; such technical information does not belong to the disclosure of the application. (**T823/96** r.4.5)

The Guidelines emphasise that a patent application is directed to a technical audience and that its disclosure must be appreciated through the eyes of a skilled person without a disproportionate focus on the structure of the claims. (H-IV,2.2; **T2619/11** and **T1363/12** hn)

The disclosure test is the generally accepted test for any amendment (**G2/10** r.4.3). This test is also used to assess the identity of invention when claiming priority (**G2/98** r.9), to assess extension of subject-matter in a divisional application (**G1/06** r.5.1 and **G2/10** r.4.3) and to assess the allowability of a correction under **R.139**, second sentence (**G3/89** hn.I). The uniform application of the disclosure test preserves the structural relationship established in the EPC, based on the first-to-file system, between the provisions defining the prior art and their impact on patentability, the substantive requirements for validly claiming priority and for filing divisional applications and the right to amend the application (**G2/10** r.4.6).

Historically, the disclosure test was first expressed in **G3/89** hn.I about corrections of errors, confirmed in **G2/98** about priority, and identified as generally accepted and referred to as the 'gold standard' in **G2/10.**

For the assessment of the identity of invention when claiming priority (**G2/98**), the disclosure test can be considered as an implementation of the requirement that the priority application as a whole must specifically disclose the subject-matter of the claim under examination (**Art.88(4)** based on Art.4H PC; see T77/97).

The Enlarged Board of Appeal has allowed a departure from the disclosure test only in two specific cases, where addition of an undisclosed feature is necessary to exclude subject-matter for legal reasons and where the feature does not provide a technical contribution to the claimed invention (**G2/10** r.4.3). Firstly, an undisclosed disclaimer may be added to a claim under specific conditions (**G1/03** r.2). Secondly, in rare cases it may be possible to escape from the **Art.123(2)-(3)** trap, by maintaining an undisclosed feature in a patent claim that does not provide a technical contribution to the invention (**G1/93** hn.II, r.16, see **Art.123(3):3**).

An amendment that does not introduce new technical information does not contravene **Art.123(2)**, e.g. deleting an expression from a claim that has no technical meaning (**T781/22:** deleting the expression 'premium class' in a claim directed to a seating arrangement in an aircraft; T433/22).

It is incorrect to say that an amendment complies with **Art.123(2)** if it does not generate novel subject-matter. For instance, a claim directed to 'metal' is not novel over an application mentioning 'copper', yet the mention of 'copper' does not provide a basis for such a claim (**T194/84**).

If the application as filed discloses both a general and a preferred range, an amendment specifying a range that is the combination of the preferred disclosed narrower range and one of the part ranges lying within the disclosed overall range on either side of the narrower range meets the disclosure test (established case law, see **T925/98** and **T760/22**).

A feature on which the amendment is based and that is taken from a drawing must not be accidental but be disclosed as a deliberate measure directed to the solution of the technical problem. The skilled person must be able to clearly and unmistakably recognise from the drawings, in the context of the whole description, that the feature in the drawing is the deliberate result of technical considerations directed to the solution of the technical problem involved. (**T398/00** r.3.4; H-V,6).

Features only shown in drawings may be used in the amendment of claims, provided such features are clearly, unmistakably and fully derivable from the drawings in terms of structure and function by a person skilled in the art and so understood in relation to the content of the description as a whole as to be manifestly part of the invention (**T169/83** hn).

Adding a feature derived from a measurement in a drawing is not generally allowed since drawings are usually schematic and not drawn to scale (**T204/83**).

2 Amendment of the claims

2.1 DELETION OF A FEATURE

A specific feature may not be replaced by a disclosed general expression, when such an expression introduces implicit features which were not originally disclosed in combination with the other features of the claim (**T416/86**). It is not allowed to delete features from an independent claim that are presented as essential in the description (**T260/85**). A feature described in the application as optional and which later-on has become essential to delimit the invention from prior art found after the filing date, may be introduced into a claim, provided that the resulting combination of features still corresponds to the teaching of the application (**T583/93** r.4.5). In general, introduction into a claim of a feature described as non-essential is not ruled out by **Art.123(2)** (**T583/93** hn.II).

Extending the scope of a claim by deleting a technical feature does not contravene **Art.123(2)** if, according to the disclosure test, the application as originally filed (including the description and drawings) directly and unambiguously discloses the subject-matter of the amended claim (**T80/21** r.2.2; see also **T66/85**).

A different test which can be applied when considering the allowability of replacing a feature in a claim or deleting a feature from a claim is the three-point essentiality test (**T331/87** modified by H-V,3.1). According to this test, the amendment contravenes **Art.123(2)** if it fails one or more of the following conditions:

1. the feature was not explained as essential in the originally filed disclosure;
2. the skilled person would directly and unambiguously recognise that the feature is not, as such, indispensable for the function of the invention in the light of the technical problem it serves to solve; and
3. the skilled person would recognise that the replacement or removal of the feature requires no modification of one or more of the features to compensate for the change, i.e. it does not in itself alter the invention.

However, even if the amendment is not unallowable on either of these criteria, it may still fail to meet the requirement of **Art.123(2)**, namely if it does not comply with the general requirement of a direct and unambiguous disclosure as set out in **G2/10** (H-V,3.1). Hence, the three-point essentiality test is only a necessary but not a sufficient condition (**T80/21** r.2.2).

The removal from a claim of a feature which 'does not provide a technical contribution to the subject-matter of the claimed invention' within the meaning of **G1/93**, the removal of which broadens the protection of the claim, does not contravene **Art.123(2)** (**T802/92**, ohmic contacts on a photovoltaic cell, all embodiments showing the contacts). The latter decision shows less regard for the wording of the claims in favour of an increased emphasis on the general inventive concept and might not be tenable in view of **G2/98** (see also Protocol on **Art.69**).

The deletion of alternatives from a single list is allowed if the alternatives have been explicitly disclosed. Deletion of alternatives from more than one list is allowable if it does not create new technical information not directly and unambiguously derivable from the application as originally filed. (H-V,3.3)

The deletion of alternatives from several lists in a claim is a common amendment in the chemical field in which a group of compounds may be defined by means of a general formula with several independently variable substituents (often referred to as a Markush formula). The case law in this area has generally allowed such a limiting amendment if the remaining generic group of compounds differs from the original group of compounds only by its smaller size and the amendment does not single out a new subclass of compounds either not previously disclosed or associated with a new technical contribution. As noted in decision **T795/21**, these criteria are subordinate to the gold standard disclosure test and represent considerations which may arise when applying that disclosure test in order to support the conclusion reached.

Whether deletion or limitation of a claim is regarded as substantive abandonment of the subject-matter removed, negating the possibility of pursuing protection for such subject matter in a divisional application, depends on the circumstances and wording of the request for amendment (**J15/85**; **G1/05**; **G1/06**). An express and unambiguous abandonment of a claim and the corresponding parts of the description is a substantive abandonment (**T61/85**). A declaration of abandonment must be interpreted taking into account all the circumstances: if the party's real intention is to meet an objection rather than to abandon subject-matter, the later pursuit of protection for that subject matter is permitted without violating the legal security of third parties (**T910/92**).

2.2 REPLACEMENT OF A FEATURE

The three-point test discussed above in **Art.123(2):2.1** also applies to the replacement of a feature in a claim.

2.2.1 Replacement of a specific feature

A generalisation in the form of an amendment which replaces a disclosed specific feature either by its undisclosed function or by a more general undisclosed term and thus incorporates undisclosed equivalents into the content of the application as filed is not allowable under **Art.123(2)** (**T416/86**; **T284/94** r.2.1.6; CLBA II.E.1.8.1). In general, a species may not be replaced by an undisclosed genus as such an amendment contravenes the disclosure test. However, a specific expression in a claim which does not properly describe a feature present in the cited state of the art and in the invention may possibly be replaced by a more general expression which is more accurate without extending the subject-matter (T52/82, still cited in CLBA).

A genus may not be replaced by a species if this species is not disclosed in the application as filed. See **Art.54(1):6** on selection inventions.

An error in a claim or in the description which is the result of an inaccurate calculation, the correction of which is not obvious, may be corrected according to **Art.123(2)** if the amendment follows unequivocally for a skilled reader from the application as filed. (T13/83, T784/96)

See **Art.123(3):2** for amendments changing the category of a claim.

It is permissible to add a first medical use claim to an application (a compound for use as a medicament, **Art.54(4)**) even if the application as filed discloses only a specific medical use for the compound concerned and does not explicitly mention the generalised use of the compound 'as a medicament' (T419/16).

2.2.2 *Replacement of a range*

Claims originally directed to a wide range may also be amended to recite a narrower range if there is basis for such an amendment.

End points of disclosed ranges may also be combined even if the resulting range has not been disclosed explicitly in the application as filed. Thus, the combination of a preferred range and part of a more general range lying on one or the other side the preferred range is allowed (T2/81). Note that the boards of appeal consider this to be established case law (see CLBA II. E.1.5.1) while the Guidelines H-V,3.5 are more equivocal, stating that such a combination 'can usually' be derivable from the original disclosure.

In **T612/09**, an end point of a preferred disclosed range was combined with an end point of another disclosed range. In **T201/83**, an end point of a disclosed range was amended based on a value given in an example of the application as originally filed, since the skilled person could readily recognise the value as not being the decisive element for achieving the technical effect of the embodiment of the example. Another consideration when assessing the allowability of such an amendment is whether a clearly recognisable functional or structural relationship exists between the value in question and the other features of the claim (T570/05).

2.3 ADDITION OF A FEATURE

A technical feature from an embodiment of the description or drawings may be added to a claim.

See **Art.83:2.1.2** for adding a feature from a cross-referenced document.

When a feature taken in isolation from an embodiment in the description is added to a claim, the amended claim forms an intermediate generalisation, i.e. a generalisation of the embodiment which is intermediate in scope between the scope of the original claim as filed and the scope of the embodiment. Such an intermediate generalisation does not extend beyond the subject-matter of the application as filed if the feature is not related or inextricably linked to the other features of the embodiment and the overall disclosure justifies the generalising isolation of the feature and its introduction into the claim. The amended claim should not be a particular combination created artificially from individual features pertaining to separate embodiments; the application is not a reservoir from which any features can be combined. (H-V,3.2.1)

An intermediate generalisation reducing the scope of a claim does not contravene **Art.123(2)** if the new combination of features solves a problem unambiguously derivable from the application in isolation from any other element of the embodiment not included in the claim (T17/86; followed by T284/94 hn. I; T470/05 r.2.4; established case law).

It should be noted that the rejection of a claim under **Art.123(2)** because a limiting amendment has created an inadmissible intermediate generalisation has no strong legal basis in the EPC. It makes the clear concept of extension of subject-matter dependent on the definition of the problem, which may change over time (see also **G2/98** r.8.3). **Art.123(2)** is not related to the problem-solution approach of **Art.56** but relates to extension of disclosed subject-matter. When the set of features in a claim includes features added in isolation from an embodiment in the description, compliance with **Art.123(2)** should not depend on whether or not the set of features solves a specific problem. Hence, if a claim contains a selection of features from a specific disclosed context caused by adding an isolated feature from that context to the claim, which selection does not serve any meaningful technical purpose, the requirements of **Art.123(2)** should be regarded as being complied with, and in the subsequent assessment of inventive step the lack of technical purpose should result in rejection of the claim under **Art.56**.

Examples of intermediate generalisation are given in H-V,3.2.1.

2.4 ADDITION OF A DISCLAIMER

A claim may be amended by the addition of a disclaimer. A disclaimer is a negative technical feature that excludes specific subject-matter from the scope of the claim. The excluded subject-matter may be one or more specific embodiments, a subgroup or an area. Since a disclaimer can be either present in a claim of an application as filed or added as an amendment during prosecution, a disclaimer should not be defined as a specific type of amendment as in **G2/10** r.2.2, which definition is not consistent with r.2.1 of the decision either. Instead, a disclaimer should be simply viewed as a negative feature.

The amended claim including the disclaimer must meet all the requirements of the EPC. The insertion of a disclaimer in a claim must comply with the clarity requirement of **Art.84**; it may be allowable if the claimed subject-matter cannot be defined more clearly and concisely in terms of positive features (see F-IV,4.19 and **Art.84:1.7**). The excluded subject-matter cannot be taken into account for the assessment of clarity, conciseness and support (**Art.84**), sufficiency of disclosure (**Art.83**) and inventive step (**Art.56**). In respect of inventive step, a relevant question is whether an advantageous effect is demonstrated by the remaining subject-matter and can be deduced from the application as filed. (**G1/03** hn.2.4; **G2/10** r.4.5.5)

The allowability of an amendment adding a disclaimer depends on whether or not the disclaimer or the subject-matter excluded by it has a basis in the application as filed. The following three cases can be distinguished:

- A 'disclosed disclaimer', in which the negative feature is disclosed in the application as filed. For example, the disclaimer is 'not A', and 'not A' is disclosed.
- A 'disclaimer excluding disclosed subject-matter', where the subject-matter of the disclaimer is disclosed as a positive feature but the disclaimer as such is not disclosed. For example, the disclaimer is 'not A', and 'A' is disclosed but 'not A' is not disclosed.
- An 'undisclosed disclaimer', where neither the disclaimer nor the excluded subject-matter is disclosed. For example, the disclaimer is 'not A', and neither 'A' nor 'not A' are disclosed.

2.4.1 *Disclosed disclaimer*

A disclaimer based on a negative feature disclosed in the application as filed may be inserted in a claim by way of amendment. The negative feature may be disclosed in an explicit way (**T245/91** r.3.2; **T255/91** r.2.1.7) or in an implicit way (**T278/88** r.3).

2.4.2 *Disclaimer excluding disclosed subject-matter*

Subject-matter originally disclosed in the application as a positive feature of the invention may be excluded from the scope of a claim by inserting a disclaimer in the claim.

The applicant is free to disclaim subject matter disclosed in the application as part of the invention as long as the requirements of **Art.123(2)** are met. The applicant may be interested, for example, in obtaining a first patent for a preferred embodiment and then a second patent for the general teaching and may need to introduce a disclaimer for the preferred embodiment in the second patent to avoid double patenting. A desire to license part of the subject matter of the invention could be another reason for pursuing different embodiments in different patents. (**G2/10** r.4.5.5, overturning **T1102/00**)

The insertion of a disclaimer excluding disclosed subject-matter may violate **Art.123(2)** by adding subject-matter and, like any amendment of an application or patent, must pass the disclosure test. Since the disclaimer does not as such define a feature of the claimed invention, the test must be applied to the subject-matter remaining in the claim after amendment. Hence, the inclusion of the disclaimer infringes **Art.123(2)** if the remaining subject-matter presents the skilled person with technical information which is not directly and unambiguously derivable from the application as filed, the information being neither explicitly nor implicitly disclosed for a skilled person using common general knowledge. (**G2/10** hn.1a, r.4.5.2; confirming **T4/80** and **T1107/06**)

The test requires an assessment of the relationship between the excluded subject-matter and the remaining subject-matter. The skilled person will not usually be presented with new technical information in the case of a disclaimer excluding one specific embodiment from an invention disclosed in general terms including different embodiments. However, the insertion of a disclaimer that restricts the remaining subject-matter to a subgroup or intermediate generalisation that is not disclosed in the application as filed, or singles out any hitherto not disclosed individual compound or group of compounds, or leads to a particular undisclosed meaning applying to the remaining subject-matter contravenes **Art.123(2)**. (**G2/10** hn.1b, r.4.5.4, following **T615/95** hn.1)

Note, that the so-called rules of logic do not apply: if the application discloses an embodiment or smaller region B within a broad region A, it is not the case that A-B is logically and inevitably disclosed. As a consequence, a claim to A disclaiming B does not inevitably comply with **Art.123(2)**. On the other hand, a reasoning solely suggesting that the introduction of the disclaimer modifies the subject-matter would be insufficient to motivate an objection under **Art.123(2)**. (**G2/10** r.4.5.3)

The requirements set out in **G1/03** are only applicable to an undisclosed disclaimer and not to a disclaimer excluding disclosed subject-matter (**G2/10** r.3; overturning **T1050/99**, **T1102/00**, **T868/04**, **T795/05** and **T1559/05**). If the remaining subject-matter after addition of a disclaimer excluding disclosed subject-matter extends the subject-matter of the application as filed, the amendment is not allowable; the strict requirements of **G1/03** should not be applied for determining the allowability of the amendment (**G2/10** r.4.7).

2.4.3 *Undisclosed disclaimer, allowability*

In specific cases an undisclosed disclaimer, where neither the disclaimer per se nor the excluded subject-matter is disclosed in the application as filed, may be inserted in a claim by way of amendment under **Art.123(2)**. The allowability of such undisclosed disclaimers has been analysed in **G1/03** using the test for extension of subject-matter developed in **G1/93** (see also H-V,4.2). The EBoA concluded that an amendment to a claim by the insertion of a disclaimer may not be refused under **Art.123(2)** for the sole reason that neither the disclaimer nor the subject-matter excluded by it from the scope of the claim have a basis in the application as filed (**G1/03** hn. I, case consolidated with **G2/03**).

The allowability of an undisclosed disclaimer according to **G1/03** may be considered in the following different cases, as confirmed by **G1/16**:

1 A claim is not novel over prior art under **Art.54(3)**. An undisclosed disclaimer may be used to restore novelty over a European prior right. The purpose of **Art.54(3)** is to avoid double patenting. The delimitation of a claim from the disclosure of an earlier application by means of a disclaimer achieves this purpose by splitting the subject-matter of the invention in two parts: a part identical with the first application, the right to which is preserved for the first applicant, and the rest, disclosed for the first time in the second application, the right to which belongs the applicant of the second application. Such a disclaimer excludes subject-matter for legal reasons and has no bearing on the technical information in the application. Its insertion is therefore not in contradiction to **Art.123(2)**. (**G1/03** hn. II.1 and r.2.1, **G1/16** r.37 and r.45)

2 A claim is not novel over an accidental anticipation under **Art.54(2)**. An undisclosed disclaimer may be added to the claim to restore novelty over such an anticipation.

An anticipation is accidental if it is so unrelated to and remote from the claimed invention that the person skilled in the art would never have taken it into consideration when working on the invention. Accidental anticipation often occurs in the fields of chemistry and biotechnology. For example, a claim might relate to a large group of chemical compounds with certain properties which are advantageous for a specific use. Prior art which discloses a single member of the group but for a completely different use constitutes an accidental anticipation. It would be unfair if such a disclosure represented a bar to patenting the entire group in the absence of a basis for a disclaimer of the known compound in the application as filed. Since an accidental anticipation has nothing to do with the teaching of the claimed invention, a disclaimer excluding the subject-matter of the anticipation does not change the technical information relating to the invention and therefore does not contravene **Art.123(2)**. (**G1/03** hn. II.1 and r.2.2, **G1/16** r.37 and r.45)

3 A claim is not novel in view of an anticipation under **Art.54(2)** that is not accidental. The Enlarged Board of Appeal ruled that an undisclosed disclaimer may not be used to restore novelty in such a case. This prohibition avoids the unrestricted use of disclaimers. An applicant could otherwise wait for the state of the art to be revealed by the EPO and tailor the patent to it using disclaimers, thereby reducing the importance of a detailed description. For example, the applicant could claim a broad class of compounds with yet unknown properties, disclaim those which turn out to be known and test the rest for advantageous properties in order to demonstrate an inventive step. (**G1/03** r.2.3)

4 A claim includes subject-matter excluded from patentability, e.g. inventions the exploitation of which is contrary to 'ordre public' or morality under **Art.53(a)** or methods for medical treatment under **Art.53(c)**. An undisclosed disclaimer may be used to exclude this subject-matter. Since the disclaimer is not related to the technical teaching of the invention and merely excludes subject-matter for legal reasons, its insertion is allowable. An example of such a disclaimer is the exclusion of human beings in a claim related to a method for avoiding economically undesirable offspring. (**G1/03** hn.II.1, r.2.4; **G1/16** r.37 and r.45)

5 A claim covers non-working embodiments. A disclaimer may not be used to excise non-disclosed, non-working embodiments. If there are a large number of conceivable alternatives falling within the claim and the disclosure enables the skilled person to find appropriate alternatives without undue effort, the inclusion of non-working embodiments in a claim is of no harm (see **T238/88**, **T292/85** and **T301/87**). Therefore, a disclaimer is neither necessary nor appropriate. If this is not the case and the claimed invention lacks reproducibility, there are two possibilities. First, if the claim expresses an effect, there is lack of sufficient disclosure (**Art.83**). A lack of sufficiency cannot be remedied during proceedings before the EPO (**T170/87** and **T313/86** not to be followed). Secondly, if the claim does not express the effect, but the effect is part of the problem to be solved, there is lack of inventive step across the scope of the claim (see **T939/92**). A disclaimer cannot help in supporting inventive step. (**G1/03** r.2.5; see also **G2/10** r.3.5-9; F-III,5.1)

If the limitation of a claim by an undisclosed disclaimer later turns out to have technical relevance (**T323/97** r.3), it will be found to contribute a new technical teaching and add subject-matter within the meaning of **Art.123(2)**; hence, the disclaimer will be considered unallowable retrospectively (**G1/03** hn.II.3, r.2.6). Addition of an undisclosed disclaimer having effects which go beyond the purpose set out in the above points 1, 2 or 4 is not allowable (**G1/03** r.2.6.5). The evaluation of inventive step has to be carried out disregarding the undisclosed disclaimer. In this way, any unallowable modification of the original technical teaching in the assessment of inventive step is avoided (**G1/16** r.46.4).

Even though **G2/10** r.4.5.1 states that all amendments must comply with the disclosure test (the 'gold standard'), **G1/16** decided that the disclosure test should not be applied to an amendment that introduces an undisclosed disclaimer, even though such an amendment does introduce technical subject-matter. Instead, an undisclosed disclaimer must comply with the above criteria of **G1/03**. Additionally, an undisclosed disclaimer may not change the identity of the invention as originally filed, and it may not become relevant for the assessment of inventive step or for the question of sufficiency of disclosure. (**G1/16** hn, r.42, 44, 47)

An undisclosed disclaimer is not permitted if the subject-matter of the claim under examination is in part not entitled to the priority date and the disclaimer excludes the part lacking priority in order to restore novelty over a cited document which represents prior art under **Art.54(2)** for the part lacking priority and which is not an accidental disclosure. Even if the cited document represents a prior European right under **Art.54(3)** for the part of the claim entitled to priority, the disclaimer is not permitted (**T1222/11**; followed by **T88/21**). The priority was partially invalid in those cases due to a still earlier application of the same applicant (see **Art.87(1):6**).

2.4.4 *Undisclosed disclaimer, formal issues*

An undisclosed disclaimer should not remove more than is necessary either to restore novelty or to disclaim subject-matter excluded from patentability for non-technical reasons (**G1/03** hn.II.2). The insertion of a necessary disclaimer is not on opportunity for the applicants to reshape their claims arbitrarily. To maintain transparency, the specification should mention the prior art on which the disclaimer is based and the relation between the prior art and the disclaimer should be shown. (**G1/03** r.3)

The requirement that no more than necessary may be disclaimed may be difficult to comply with where the prior art discloses the subject-matter to be disclaimed in several, possibly speculative or insufficiently disclosed variants; if the disclaimer is too narrow, the claim is not novel; if the disclaimer is too broad, the amendment violates **Art.123(2)**. The first and second requirement together may make it impossible to define an undisclosed disclaimer. According to **T2130/11** hn it is allowable to remove more than strictly necessary to restore novelty, without arbitrary reshaping the claim, in order to satisfy the clarity requirement of **Art.84**. A safer solution may be not to use an undisclosed disclaimer but to define the claim in terms of sub-ranges or sub-groups disclosed in the application, which may result in a patent which is narrower in scope but easier to defend.

The requirements relating to undisclosed disclaimer tend to make the claim more complex. However, the claim must remain clear under **Art.84**. These requirements are often incompatible, making it impossible to include an allowable undisclosed disclaimer. The solution is again to narrow the claim using sub-ranges or sub-groups disclosed in the application. See **T2130/11** as an example.

Inserting a disclaimer disclosed in neither the application as filed nor a novelty-destroying prior art document contravenes **Art.123(2)** (**T596/96** r.2; **T597/92** r.3).

G1/03 r.4, referring to **G2/98**, holds that the insertion of an undisclosed disclaimer not providing a technical contribution to the invention does not change the identity of the invention within the meaning of **Art.87(1)**, and, therefore, does not affect the right to priority from a first application not containing the disclaimer.

3 Amendment of the description

The description may need to be amended to acknowledge the state of the art (**T11/82**).

A closer prior art may be acknowledged in the description; such an amendment may only consist of features that follow directly and unequivocally from the prior art (**T11/82** r.20-22). However, if the incorporation of the reference to the prior art expressly or implicitly extends the subject-matter for which protection is sought, then **Art.123(2)** will be contravened (**T11/82** r.23; F-II,4.3; H-IV,2.1).

A claim which does not include a feature which is described in the description as essential, is not supported by the description according to **Art.84**. An amendment of the description making the feature unessential is not allowed, because it extends the subject-matter of the application. (**T133/85**)

Common general knowledge or what is implied by the description may indicate that a described feature not mentioned in an independent claim is essential for the invention. The EPO will request the insertion of the feature into the claim. However, an applicant or proprietor may retain the unamended claim if it is possible to convince the EPO that the feature is in fact not essential. (F-IV,4.3(ii))

An additional explanation of the functioning of a sufficiently disclosed technical feature is allowed if the functioning can be derived from the original application by a skilled person (T37/82).

A clarification of a technical effect of a feature may be added without contravening **Art.123(2)**, provided the effect can be deduced without difficulty by a person skilled in the art from the application as filed (H-V,2.1).

Later filed examples that support the validity of a broad claim cannot usually be added to the description. Such examples are carefully assessed by the examining division for extension of the subject-matter, because these examples could provide indications for the skilled person which were not evident from the original application, even when taking into account subject-matter not expressly mentioned but read into it by the skilled person (H-V,2.2).

The same applies to the inclusion of additional advantages in support of inventive step. For example, if the description mentions that a fluid is useful for cleaning woollen products it is not possible to amend the description by adding the information that the fluid also protects against moth damage. Such later filed examples or new effects, even if not allowed into the application, may be taken into account by the examiner as evidence in support of the patentability of the claimed invention (H-V,2.2).

Such supplementary technical information is put in the file and becomes available to the public together with the other contents of the file. Attention is drawn to this additional information which was submitted after the filing of the application and not included in the specification by a notice on the front page of the patent specification (H-V,2.3).

Art. 123(3) The European patent may not be amended in such a way as to extend the protection it confers.

1 Prohibition to extend protection during opposition

According to **Art.123(3)**, a European patent (i.e. the claims, description and drawings, if any) may not be amended in such a way as to extend the protection it confers (see **T1149/97**). This principle is applicable in all proceedings before the EPO, including limitation and opposition proceedings, as well as in national proceedings. (OJ 2007 se4 EN p.144)

The provision gives legal security to the public: the protection conferred by the patent as granted cannot be extended in post-grant proceedings. An amendment extending the protection of a patent is not allowable because it does not comply with **Art.123(3)**. Extension of protection is a ground for revocation in a national revocation procedure (**Art.138(1)(d)**).

The provision applies to both amendment of the granted claims and the addition of new claims. The scope of the claims may be influenced by the content of the description (Protocol on the interpretation of **Art.69**). Hence, changes in the description must also be considered when assessing compliance with **Art.123(3)** (**T1149/97** hn. II; **T142/05** hn). Reinstatement in the patent of subject-matter deleted from the application or indicated as no longer relating to the invention before the grant, is as a rule not admissible under **Art.123(3)**; the grant has a cut-off effect, in that it restricts the original disclosure to subject-matter relating to the invention for which a patent is granted and retained in the patent specification (**T1149/97** hn. III).

The limitation of a claim by restricting the number of components in a composition may have the undesired effect of extending the protection it confers. For example, consider a granted claim that defines 'a composition having 1-10% halogens by weight'. When the claim is limited in opposition proceedings to '1-10% chlorine by weight', the amount of fluorine is no longer defined and may be more than 10%, which is an unallowable extension of the protection. (H-IV,3.4; **T2017/07** hn)

2 **Change of claim category**

A change in the category of a claim by way of amendment after a patent has been granted will only be allowed on condition that the amendment is necessitated by a ground of opposition (**R.80**). Such a change in claim category is not open to objection under **Art.123(3)** if it does not result in extension of the protection conferred by the claim (**G2/88** hn. I). Examples of allowable amendments changing the category of a claim of a patent include the following:

1 A product claim may be amended to a claim to a particular use of the product. The use must define the use of a physical entity to achieve an effect and may not define such a use to produce a product. Since a product claim confers protection upon the product for all uses, the use claim confers less protection. Hence, the amendment does not violate **Art.123(3)**. (**G2/88** hn. II; H-V,7.1)

2 A product claim may be amended to a claim directed to a method for producing the product, provided that the method only results in the product previously claimed. As it is a fundamental principle of the EPC that the protection conferred by a product claim covers all methods for manufacturing the product, the limitation to one of these methods cannot extend the protection conferred originally. Note, that a process claim confers protection to all products directly obtained by the process according to **Art.64(2)**. (**T5/90**; **T54/90**; H-V,7.2)

3 A claim relating to a method of operating a device may be replaced by a claim relating to the device itself if the method claim is merely a definition of the device in terms of the function of its components (**T426/89**; **T378/86** r.3.1). However, such an amendment is not allowed if the method claim protects a device when in use and the device claim includes only technical features protecting the device whether or not it is in use (**T82/93** r.2.5, cardiac pacer). The summary of these cases in H-V,7.3 is unclear. Note, that a change of category from a method in which an apparatus is used to the apparatus itself is not allowable (**T86/90**). (H-V,7.3)

4 An amendment of a claim from a method in which a certain product is used to the use of the product in performing that same method is allowable (**T332/94**). However, a claim to a process for the preparation of a product may not be amended to the use of the product for a purpose other than previously claimed (**T98/85**; **T194/85**). (H-V,7.4)

On the other hand, under **Art.123(2)**, a method claim can serve as the basis for a claim directed to a system (apparatus) if the method claim sets out a system in terms of all its essential features, even while the method claim only defines a method of using or operating the system (**T2310/22** r.4).

3 Art.123(2)-(3) trap

An amendment made during the grant procedure, introducing a limiting feature in a claim that adds subject-matter but is approved by the examining division, must be removed in opposition proceedings if an objection is made under **Art.100(c)**. However, such an amendment violates **Art.123(3)**. Hence, with or without amendment, the proprietor loses the patent. The Enlarged Board of Appeal (**G1/93**) has indicated the cases in which an escape from this trap is possible. The EBoA distinguished the following four cases:

1 The added feature can be replaced by another feature disclosed in the application without violating **Art.123(3)**, and the patent can be maintained in amended form (**G1/93** hn.I, r.11, 13). For example, an added feature 'alcohol' can be replaced by its disclosed species 'ethanol'.

2 The added feature does not limit the scope of the claim, which allows the added matter to be removed without violating **Art.123(3)**, and the patent to be maintained in amended form (**G1/93** r.11). For example, the term 'flat' added to define an unspecified torsion spring was regarded as lacking an unambiguous and useful technical meaning, and did therefore not limit the scope of a claim comprising a flat torsion spring (**T231/89** hn.II, r.3.3). In other words, it is permissible under **Art.123(3)** to delete a feature from a claim if the feature is without any technical significance (**G1/93** r.4, **T2624/22**).

3 The added feature limits the scope of protection and provides a technical contribution to the subject-matter of the claimed invention; the amendment gives an unwarranted advantage to the proprietor, contrary to the purpose of **Art.123(2)**. Hence, the patent must be revoked. An example is the case where the limiting feature creates an inventive selection not disclosed in the application as filed. Such an added feature may not be removed, and the claim is not allowable (**G1/93** hn.I, r.16). An added feature is regarded as providing a technical contribution to the invention as claimed if it interacts with the remaining features of the claim such that it influences the solution of the technical problem (**T384/91** hn.II, added feature of absence of striae in an optical membrane influences process parameters for making the membrane).

4 The added feature limits the scope of protection by merely excluding protection for part of the subject-matter of the application as filed and does not provide a technical contribution to the subject-matter of the claimed invention. Such a feature need not be removed since it does not violate **Art.123(2)**. An example of an added feature not violating **Art.123(2)** is an undisclosed disclaimer that complies with **G1/03** (**Art.123(2)**:2.4). (**G1/93** hn.II, r.16) Decision **G1/93** departs from the strict interpretation of **Art.123(2)** as laid down in the disclosure test by allowing the addition of an undisclosed feature that merely excludes protection for part of the subject-matter of a claimed invention without providing a technical contribution, for legal reasons, i.e. to avoid the trap. The decision distinguishes between added features providing a technical contribution to the subject-matter of the claimed invention and features that do not provide such a contribution. The latter feature is unrelated to the teaching of the claimed invention, and its addition does not contravene **Art.123(2)** because it does not give an unwarranted advantage to the proprietor, nor does it adversely affect the interests of third parties (**G1/93** r.16). In an analogous manner, such a feature does not render the priority invalid (**T175/03**). Undisclosed features are only rarely found to be allowable on this ground (**T110/20** lists examples from the caselaw). The board in **T768/20** speculated that the only kind of amendment that might satisfy the conditions of **G1/93** is an undisclosed disclaimer that is in accordance

with **G1/03** (r.2.2.1). Generally, this part of **G1/93** is difficult to reconcile with **G2/10**.

National courts may take a stricter view on the addition of an undisclosed feature and still revoke a patent with an added feature on the grounds of **Art.138(1)(c)** even if the feature is allowable under **G1/93**. On the other hand, German courts interpret **Art.123** differently from the EPO and do not consider the deletion of an undisclosed feature from a granted claim as an extension of protection (OJ 1998 p.617). They neither require a patent to be revoked if a claim contains an undisclosed feature, provided the feature narrows the protection and does not lead to another teaching (OJ 2015 A78).

Art. 124 Information on prior art

1 **General**

This provision requires the applicant to provide information on prior art relevant to a European patent application when invited to do so by the EPO. The information provided allows the EPO to examine the application more thoroughly and makes the grant procedure faster and more efficient.

The EPO invites the applicant to provide information concerning the prior art cited during the examination of corresponding national and regional patent applications and patents and a failure to provide this information results in deemed withdrawal of the European patent application. The EPC does not oblige an applicant to disclose all relevant prior art known to it, in contrast with, for example, US patent law.

Invitations under **Art.124** are of limited value to the EPO since the examining division already has at its disposal prior art identified by the European search, and made available by work sharing between patent offices and the worldwide public data retrieval systems, which have made it easy to obtain information about national and regional patent applications. Moreover, the EPO can request information on prior art from other patent offices under **Art.130(1)**.

Art. 124(1) The European Patent Office may, in accordance with the Implementing Regulations, invite the applicant to provide information on prior art taken into consideration in national or regional patent proceedings and concerning an invention to which the European patent application relates.

Implemented by:
R.70b Invitation to file search results
R.141 Procedure for requesting information on prior art

1 **Information on corresponding applications**

Each applicant claiming priority must provide the results of any search carried out by the office of first filing on the priority application (**R.141(1)**). If not provided voluntarily on filing or regional phase entry, the EPO will request these search results under **R.70b**.

The EPO may also invite an applicant to provide information on prior art taken into account in corresponding national and regional patent proceedings (**R.141(3)**). Such an invitation may extend to corresponding utility models and utility certificates filed in EPC contracting states (**Art.140** referring to **Art.124**). Espacenet shows the documents cited in respect of family members.

The EPO may not request information other than prior art taken into consideration. Hence, the applicant need not forward communications and decisions from national authorities to the EPO. Similarly, Art.42 PCT forbids elected Offices from requiring the applicant to furnish copies of such documents relating to the same international application in any other elected Office.

Art. 124(2) If the applicant fails to reply in due time to an invitation under paragraph 1, the European patent application shall be deemed to be withdrawn.

1 **Failure to provide information**
If the applicant does not respond to an invitation under **Art.124(1)** within the specified period, the application will be deemed withdrawn and the EPO will notify the applicant under **R.112(1)**. The applicant can request an appealable decision according to **R.112(2)**. The non-observance of the period can be remedied with further processing (**Art.121**).

Note that there is no sanction for not providing information on all relevant prior art.

Art. 125 Reference to general principles

In the absence of procedural provisions in this Convention, the European Patent Office shall take into account the principles of procedural law generally recognised in the Contracting States.

1 **Procedural law of the EPC**
Since the EPC is an independent system based on the legal systems of the contracting states, any gaps in the procedural law of the EPC must be closed by taking account of the procedural principles generally recognised in the contracting states. These principles are often based on maxims of Roman Law, as these have proved themselves in practice over many centuries (**T167/93**, r.2.3). Not much use has been made of this provision. In most cases procedural gaps have been regarded as open questions which could be answered by a further development of the EPC in line with the generally accepted legal principles. The provisions of the EPC are by necessity formulated in a generalised and abstract way. Hence, an apparent procedural gap on application of a provision to a specific case can often be filled by interpretation of the provision concerned (**J6/86** hn. II). The reference to impartiality as a general principle of law in **G5/91** r.3 can be regarded as an application of **Art.125**.

The provision applies in principle only to procedural law, not to substantive patent law (**J15/86** hn. IV). However, a provision falling under **Art.125** may well cover issues which touch upon substantive matters, such as the scope of claimed subject-matter (**G4/19**, r.27). The Enlarged Board found that a European patent application is to be refused in certain cases under **Art.97(2)** and **Art.125** on the ground of impermissible double patenting (**G4/19**; see **Art.97(2):2**).

1.1 EXAMPLES OF PROCEDURAL GAPS THAT HAVE BEEN CLOSED

- An accompanying person may plead at oral proceedings only with permission of the EPO and under the supervision of the responsible representative. See **Art.134(1):2**.
- Errors in documents include missing indications (**J8/80**).

- An applicant has the right to withdraw a European patent application at any time. However, due to the mandatory publication of applications after eighteen months and the technical preparations that must be undertaken, applicants have no right to demand that publication must be prevented when withdrawing the application after those technical preparations are complete. Although publication cannot necessarily be prevented when the application is withdrawn after completion of the technical preparations, the EPO must nevertheless make an effort to prevent such publication. (**J5/81**)
- If changing circumstances deprive an appeal of its purpose (here the appellant was requesting file inspection before publication and the application was published in the meantime), the procedure will not be continued, in accordance with general principles of procedural law (**J27/87**).
- The designation of the inventor can be rectified without the consent of already correctly designated inventors even though this matter is dealt with differently in the various contracting states (**J8/82**).

1.2 GENERALLY RECOGNISED LEGAL PRINCIPLES

An example of a principle of procedural law recognised in the contracting states is the principle that all parties to proceedings before a court must be accorded the same procedural rights. This is the basis of the decision **G1/86** which decided that an appellant, being an opponent, has the right to re-establishment when not having observed the time limit for filing grounds of appeal. Likewise, the applicant of a Euro-PCT application has the same rights as the applicant of a direct European application (**J8/83** r.8). Other generally recognised legal principles are the narrow interpretation of provisions that exclude subject-matter from patentability (**G5/83** r.22) and the principle of good faith, as set out below.

In many such cases the legal principle concerned can be developed by considering the relevant EPC provision in light of the goal of the EPC as a whole.

1.3 EXAMPLES OF EPO'S OWN PROCEDURAL PRINCIPLES

- A withdrawal will only be recognised if it is unconditional and unequivocal (**J11/80**).
- The withdrawal of a European patent application cannot be revoked, once published, in order to protect third party interests (**J15/86**).
- A notice withdrawing a European patent application need not be phrased in specific terms (**J7/87**), but must be clear, and the circumstances must make clear that it expresses the true intention of the applicant (**J11/87**).
- A decision of a board of appeal in grant proceedings has no binding effect in subsequent first instance opposition proceedings or on appeal therefrom. The explicit provisions of the EPC regarding the assessment of patentability in grant and opposition proceedings precludes that a decision of the board of appeal in grant proceedings is regarded as an estoppel per rem judicatam in subsequent opposition proceedings. (**T167/93**)

2 Good faith

According to **Art.31(1)** of the Vienna Convention treaties shall be interpreted in good faith. Since the rules of the Vienna Convention are also applicable to the EPC (see Preamble 2.2), the EPC must be interpreted in good faith, even though the EPC does not explicitly refer to the principle. The relationship between the EPO and a party is based on the EPC and, therefore, is likewise governed by the principle of good faith. The principle of good faith, also referred to as the principle of protection of legitimate expectations, is generally recognised among the contracting states and is well established in European Union law. (**G5/88** r.3.2)

The principle of good faith may necessitate the provision of a remedy for a loss of rights in cases which might otherwise be irremediable. However, the principle also causes uncertainty for parties in that its applicability is not well defined. The application of the principle by the EPO, as derived from case law, allows two cases to be distinguished, a first case in which the EPO deviates from the course expected by a party and a second case in which a party deviates from the course expected by the EPO.

2.1 DEVIATION BY EPO

The most common deviations by the EPO are unexpected changes in procedure and erroneous or ambiguous notifications. The application of the principle of good faith to procedures before the EPO requires that measures taken by the EPO should not violate the reasonable expectations of parties (**G5/88** r.3.2).

A party may legitimately expect that a department of first instance will not deviate from the established case law if this case law has become part of the consistent practice of that department, in particular if this practice has been published in the Guidelines or a notice from the EPO. In such a situation, an applicant may legitimately expect that a practice allowing or even recommending a certain procedural conduct will not be changed without appropriate advance warning. (**J27/94** r.5; **J2/08** r.6)

If there is doubt whether an established practice exists, a party must seek clarification by means of an enquiry to the EPO (**J25/95**). See also **R.103(1):2** in which a deviation from a procedure set out in the Guidelines is regarded as a substantial procedural violation.

A party relying on a lenient practice of the EPO must obtain the legitimately expected result. However, parties should not stretch the practice to their advantage. If the practice is unclear, a party should seek clarification from the EPO and not jump to conclusions. (**T905/90** r.6, 7)

A party who embarked in good faith on proceedings, e.g. a self-opposition, which cannot adversely affect the rights of any third party, can continue such proceedings if the interpretation of the EPC changes after initiation of the proceedings, e.g. by forbidding self-opposition (**G9/93** r.6.1).

The applicant can, on the basis of the principle of good faith, rely on information from the EPO concerning procedural matters (**J10/84**). If an applicant acts wrongly because of an erroneous message or request from the EPO, the true nature of which is uncertain, and subsequently lose a European patent application, then the acts of the applicant and the EPO are totally null and void. If good faith requires it, adverse consequences provided for by the EPC will be disregarded: an erroneous or ambiguous message from the EPO shall not be detrimental to the applicant (**J2/87**; **J3/87**; **J15/92**). The ambiguous message may be a courtesy service, a message in writing or an oral communication (**J27/92**). Note, that no claim may be based on an omitted courtesy service (**J12/84**). Note also that **J19/10** r.8 held that a professional representative could not rely on an allegedly misleading statement in an examination report that was contradicted by established, published case law.

In contrast with the above examples of procedural errors by the EPO, the amendment of an application or patent following a proposal made by the EPO cannot be corrected by relying on good faith, even if it results in a final refusal of the application or revocation of the patent (see e.g. **Art.123(3):3**). The ultimate responsibility for any amendment of an application or patent always remains with the applicant or the proprietor (**G1/93** r.13). Hence, in such matters, a party cannot rely on advice from the EPO: the principle of good faith does *not* apply.

2.2 DEVIATION BY PARTY

The most common deviation from the expected course by a party is the filing of a deficient request. The request may be a request for further processing, a notice of opposition or appeal. The deficiency may be an incomplete written request or an omitted payment. The application of the principle of good faith to such cases does not require that the EPO always warns the party in time. This would take the principle of good faith too far. It is incumbent on both the EPO and a party to act in good faith (**J12/94**). A party cannot shift its own responsibility for complying with the provisions of the EPC to the EPO (**J41/92**). The following balance between the responsibility of the EPO and that of a party has been confirmed by the Enlarged Board of Appeal (**G2/97**).

A party can expect a warning from the EPO in good faith, if the deficiency in the request is readily identifiable for the EPO and can be remedied within the period for filing the request (**T14/89**; **J13/90**; **J12/94**). In the case of a request whose true nature is uncertain, the EPO should clarify the matter by asking the requester (**J15/92**). The EPO should, for example, draw the appellant's attention to missing grounds and facts in an application for re-establishment (**T14/89**).

Since payments are often made in a way which is not apparent from the letter containing the request (cf. **Rfees5(1)**), a request without accompanying payment does not contain a readily identifiable deficiency. The EPO can often only establish whether a specific fee has been paid after the expiry of the time limit, when it disposes of the complete data on all payments made during the relevant period. Hence, in general, a warning in respect of a missing payment should not be expected. (**J41/92**; **G2/97** hn, r.3.3, 3.4)

However, the EPO will warn a party in respect of a payment if the request contains erroneous information concerning the payment and the party would, without warning, inadvertently miss the time limit (**G2/97**). This is the case where a letter refers to an enclosed payment which is in fact missing (**T128/87**), or it is clear from a letter that a party is in error with regard to the need to pay a fee within a certain period (**J13/90**). The EPO is also obliged to give prompt, reliable information in response to a specific question (**J27/92**).

In **J15/90** hn. it was held that a period of 18 days is sufficient to remedy a deficient payment; in **J13/90** r.8 nine days were sufficient to warn a party of an omitted act under **R.136(2)**. In **T923/95** a period of one week was regarded as too long for the EPO to remain inactive after it had received an underpayment for the appeal fee; in contrast, **T161/96** r.8 held that the labour-intensive processing of payments by the EPO excluded the issuance of a warning within seven days from receipt of an underpaid opposition fee.

2.3 COMPLAINTS

Anyone may make a complaint when dissatisfied with a service provided by the EPO. The complaint should preferably be filed online (https://www.epo.org/en/service-support/contact-us; OJ 2013 p.608). The department DQMS, handling the complaint, aims to reply within 30 days. See for more information chapter 8 of the 'Handbook of Quality procedures before the EPO', available on the EPO website.

When the complaint relates to the behaviour of a specific examiner, for example where an improper procedure has been applied or an unsatisfactory response has been received, a party may, before launching an official complaint, contact the director of the examiner. No complaint should be raised about lack of progress in examination; instead, a request for acceleration should be filed.

Correspondence relating to complaints is normally not available in the public file. However, if it has a substantive and/or procedural bearing on an opposition, the EPO must exceptionally add it to the public file. (**T1691/15** r.3; E-VI,4)

A total of 214 complaints were registered in 2023 (Quality Report 2023).

In 2024, the EPO launched a Quality Dashboard (https://www.epo.org/en/about-us/services-and-activities/quality/quality-dashboard) presenting key performance indicators (KPIs) in quality.

Art. 126 (deleted)

Chapter II *Information to the public or to official authorities*

1 General

The EPO provides information to the public concerning European patent applications and patents, exchanges such information with the patent offices of contracting states and publishes information of a general character that may be of interest to users of the European patent system. The provisions in this chapter deal with the keeping of and inspection of the European Patent Register and the files relating to European patent applications and patents (**Art.127, 128**), the public availability of information (**Art.128, 129**) and the exchange of information between the EPO and other authorities (**Art.130-132**).

2 Information relating to patents and patent applications

The EPO publishes patent applications as prescribed in **Art.93**, making new technical knowledge available to the public. The publication of applications also informs the public of the property rights that are being sought. The publication of granted patents under **Art.98** and patents amended in opposition proceedings under **Art.103** informs the public similarly of the rights actually obtained.

The legislator regarded the possibility of accessing information about patent applications by file inspection as insufficient and therefore provided for their publication (Empel §421). European patent applications used to be published in paper form but are now available via the internet on a publication server at 'https://data.epo.org/publication-server', which is the sole legally authoritative publication medium for European A and B patent documents (OJ 2005 p.126). The search report is also published under **Art.92** on the publication server. The publication server provides a link to the Register entry for each patent document. The website also has a translation service for patent documents.

The EPO records data about grant and opposition proceedings in the European Patent Register (**Art.127**) in order to inform third parties and users of the EPC. Some of this data is published in the Bulletin under **Art.129(a)**. The Bulletin was formerly published in paper form but is now only available online through the EPO website. The Register can be inspected online at 'https://register.epo.org'; each page of the Register has a link to the file of the application or patent.

Documents in the EPO files relating to published European applications and patents are available for on-line inspection under **Art.128**. The complete patent documents of several patent offices can be found on 'http://worldwide.espacenet.com'. European patent documents retrieved from this site contain a link to the Register, which in turn has a link to the file.

3 Other information

The main entry to the EPO website is through www.epo.org. The website contains links to the publication server, Register and search engines, and discloses decisions and information of a general nature. The EPO website is publicly accessible and free of charge. The EPO does not guarantee the completeness and accuracy of the data and information available on the website, in contrast to information on the publication server, in the files, in the Register and in the Bulletin (see Terms of Use §4 on the website). Updates of the website are published on 'https://www.epo.org/en/service-support/website-updates' (OJ 1999 p.133).

Information of a general character issued by the EPO, such as selected decisions of the Boards of Appeal, is published in the Official Journal on the EPO website (see **Art.129(b)**). The publication of the paper version of the Official Journal was discontinued on 01.01.2014 (Not. EPO OJ 2013 p.93).

Users of the European patent system can find information for contacting the EPO on the customer services page 'https://www.epo.org/en/service-support/contact-us'. The EPO provides assistance by telephone free of charge; international freephone numbers are available for the EPC contracting states. (OJ 2013 p.91)

The EPO publishes each fortnight an e-mail newsletter providing announcements and recent news (https://www.epo.org/en/service-support/subscription-centre).

The list of professional representatives is kept up to date by the Legal Division (**Art.20**, **Art.134(1)**). The list is open for public inspection on the EPO website under the same conditions as the files, i.e. **R.145** and **R.146** (OJ 1985 p.42). The EPC has no provisions for the keeping and inspection of the list of professional representatives.

An overview of forms and publications available from the EPO and a price list is published on the EPO website.

Art. 127 European Patent Register

The European Patent Office shall keep a European Patent Register, in which the particulars specified in the Implementing Regulations shall be recorded. No entry shall be made in the European Patent Register before the publication of the European patent application. The European Patent Register shall be open to public inspection.

Implemented by:
R.143 Entries in the European Patent Register

1 **Entries in the European Patent Register**
Entries in the Register are made in the three official EPO languages (**Art.14(8)**) and are the responsibility of the Legal Division (**Art.20(1)**). A request to the Legal Division for amendment of an entry aimed at the revision of a final decision of a board of appeal must be refused (**G1/97** hn.IV).

On the filing of a European application, particulars concerning the application are entered in a non-public shadow register. When the application is published, the content of the shadow register is transferred to the public Register. Entries in the Register are generally made up until the expiry of the opposition period or the termination of opposition proceedings, including entries relating to transfers (**R.143(1)(w)** and **R.22**) in view of **R.85**, which refers to **R.22**. On the other hand, entries relating to licences (**R.143(1)(w)** and **R.23**) are entered only up until the grant of the patent, because **R.85** does not refer to **R.23**. Entries made in the Register are subsequently published in the European Patent Bulletin (**Art.129(a)**).

See **R.143(1):2** for the means of inspecting the Register.

Art. 128 Inspection of files

Art. 128(1) Files relating to European patent applications which have not yet been published shall not be made available for inspection without the consent of the applicant.

1 **Files not available for inspection**
Art.128(1) is the counterpart of **Art.127**, second sentence, and prohibits public access to the file of an unpublished European patent application. As a result, the application does not become part of the state of the art before its publication under **Art.93**, allowing the applicant to withdraw the application and, where appropriate, re-file it in amended or unamended form.

A file may only be inspected before publication with consent of the applicant (**Art.128(1)**). If the consent of the applicant is not provided together with a request for inspection, the EPO will ask the applicant for consent (A-XI,2.5). An applicant may inspect the unpublished files it owns and a professional representative files for which they are registered representative using MyEPO (Dec. Pres. 2024 OJ A20).

When an application has been withdrawn but is nevertheless published under **Art.93**, e.g. when it has been withdrawn after the termination of the technical preparations of **R.67** but before publication takes place, its file will not be available for public inspection.

The prohibition in **Art.128(1)** is not in fact absolute and the phrase 'unless otherwise provided' should probably have been added. The following provisions enable certain persons or authorities to inspect the file of an unpublished application without consent of the applicant:

- **Art.128(2)** allows access to a person against whom rights under the application have been invoked;
- **Art.128(3)** allows access to anybody, after a divisional application or a new application has been published;
- **Art.130** allows access to national industrial property offices; and
- **Art.131** allows access to courts and authorities of the contracting states.

Applicants can access the files of their own applications before publication (see **R.145(2):1**).

Art. 128(2) Any person who can prove that the applicant has invoked the rights under the European patent application against him may obtain inspection of the files before the publication of that application and without the consent of the applicant.

1 **Inspection after invocation of rights under application**
A person may inspect the file of an unpublished application without the consent of the applicant, if the applicant has invoked the rights under the application against that person. Such an invocation by an applicant can be an early warning to users of the invention of the rights that the applicant may assert against them under **Art.67** after publication of the application or under **Art.64** after grant. The rights within the meaning of **Art.128(2)** are also invoked when the invocation of rights has been made in respect of a first filing in a contracting state, provided the subsequent European application is mentioned at the same time (**J14/91** hn. I). The procedure for inspection is set out in A-XI,2.5.

Art. 128(3) Where a European divisional application or a new European patent application filed under Article 61, paragraph 1, is published, any person may obtain inspection of the files of the earlier application before the publication of that application and without the consent of the applicant.

Art.61(1) European patent applications filed by non-entitled persons

1 **Inspection of file of parent application**
Art.128(3) allows a third person to establish the basis on which a divisional or new application has been filed and to assess any possible extension of subject-matter immediately on publication of the divisional or new application. The need for such inspection may arise in cases where, after the filing of the divisional application, the parent application is withdrawn before publication. Without **Art.128(3)**, the file of this parent application would remain closed. The same applies in the case that a new application is filed under **Art.61(1)(b)** following an entitlement dispute.

Art. 128(4) After the publication of the European patent application, the files relating to the application and the resulting European patent may be inspected on request, subject to the restrictions laid down in the Implementing Regulations.

Implemented by:
R.144 Parts of the file excluded from inspection
R.145 Procedure for the inspection of files
R.146 Communication of information contained in the files
R.147 Maintenance of files

1 **Inspection of file of published application**
The content of the file of an application becomes public upon publication of the application. This allows a third person to make a proper determination of what rights are likely to be granted. A file can now be inspected online without making a formal request; the use of the word 'request' in **Art.128(4)** is a consequence of the fact that files used to be inspected by requesting paper copies of documents.

The restrictions mentioned in **Art.128(4)** relate to the parts of the file not available for inspection under **R.144** and to the limited time during which the files are kept according to **R.147**. The procedure for inspecting the files is set out in **R.145**, **R.146** and A-XI,2.

Art. 128(5) Even before the publication of the European patent application, the European Patent Office may communicate to third parties or publish the particulars specified in the Implementing Regulations.

1 **Communication by EPO of data prior to publication**
An example of the publication of particulars under **Art.128(5)** is the entry in the Register of the application number of the corresponding parent application on publication of a divisional application in the rare case where the parent is withdrawn before its publication (e.g. EP application 89100942.5).

The EPO publishes on its publication server the publication number of any application which was not actually published, even though the publication of the application and/or search report was announced in the Bulletin. Possible reasons for the lack of publication include the withdrawal of the application by the applicant and the non-fulfilment of formal requirements. (A-XI,2.6)

Art. 129 Periodical publications

The European Patent Office shall periodically publish:
(a) a European Patent Bulletin containing the particulars the publication of which is prescribed by this Convention, the Implementing Regulations or the President of the European Patent Office;

(b) an Official Journal containing notices and information of a general character issued by the President of the European Patent Office, as well as any other information relevant to this Convention or its implementation.

1 **European Patent Bulletin (Art.129(a))**
The Bulletin contains bibliographic data relating to and information on the procedural status of published applications and patents, as prescribed by the EPC or the President, e.g. in **Art.97(3), 105b(3), 112a(6), 122(5), 153(3), R.21(2)**. The Bulletin contains only part of the information contained in the Register. The legal provisions relating to the Register are found in **Art.127** and **R.143**. In the pre-internet era the Bulletin (which was then published in paper form) was the primary source of data concerning applications and patents.

The Bulletin is published weekly on Wednesday, even if the EPO is closed on that day. The Bulletin is published in digital form in the three official languages of the EPO (**Art.14(7)(a)**) and is available on the EPO website free of charge.

2 **Official Journal (Art.129(b))**
The Official Journal of the European Patent Office (OJ) publishes decisions of the President of the EPO, decisions of the Administrative Council amending the Implementing Regulations, decisions of the Enlarged Board of Appeal, Notices from the EPO relevant to the EPC and its implementation and other useful information. The OJ is published on the EPO website (OJ 2013 p.444, p.606).

Decisions of technical boards of appeal were published more frequently in the OJ in the past. Such decisions are published in all three official languages. In such cases the official text in the language of the proceedings (**T952/92** hn.V, r.2.2) remains the authentic text. Occasionally, a board of appeal decision is initially drafted in another EPO language if the rapporteur of the board is less competent in the language of the proceedings, and then translated into the language of the proceedings by the EPO (Art.5(6) RPBA; **J18/90** r.1.1; **G4/08** r.4.8). If such a decision is then published in the Official Journal, the German 'translation' of the decision, for which the language of proceedings is English, having been written by the rapporteur, may be more intelligible than the text in the language of proceedings, which is actually an EPO translation.

Art. 130 Exchange of information

Art. 130(1) Unless this Convention or national laws provide otherwise, the European Patent Office and the central industrial property office of any Contracting State shall, on request, communicate to each other any useful information regarding European or national patent applications and patents and any proceedings concerning them.

1 **Exchange of information with patent offices of contracting states**
The EPO and the central industrial property offices of the contracting states share with each other, when requested, useful information not only regarding European and national patent applications, but also regarding European and national patents. Such an exchange of information takes place unless the EPC or applicable national law provides otherwise. (OJ 2007 se4 EN p.152)

Art. 130(2) Paragraph 1 shall apply to the communication of information by virtue of working agreements between the European Patent Office and
(a) the central industrial property offices of other States;
(b) any intergovernmental organisation entrusted with the task of granting patents;
(c) any other organisation.

1 **Exchange of information with other patent offices**
Examples of offices with which EPO exchanges information include:
(a) the patent offices of the US, Japan and the extension states under **Art.130(2)(a)**;
(b) the OAPI patent office under **Art.130(2)(b)**;
(c) the International Bureau of the WIPO under **Art.130(2)(c)**.

Art. 130(3) Communications under paragraphs 1 and 2(a) and (b) shall not be subject to the restrictions laid down in Article 128. The Administrative Council may decide that communications under paragraph 2(c) shall not be subject to such restrictions, provided that the organisation concerned treats the information communicated as confidential until the European patent application has been published.

Art.128 Inspection of files

1 **Restrictions to information exchange**
The restrictions laid down in **Art.128** prevent the disclosure of information before publication of the application, as mirrored in the last sentence of **Art.130(3)**. The parts of the file excluded from inspection under **R.144** are not included in the exchange of information, because they relate to matter which is not useful (**Art.130(1)**).

Art. 131 Administrative and legal co-operation

Art. 131(1) Unless this Convention or national laws provide otherwise, the European Patent Office and the courts or authorities of Contracting States shall on request give assistance to each other by communicating information or opening files for inspection. Where the European Patent Office makes files available for inspection by courts, Public Prosecutors' Offices or central industrial property offices, the inspection shall not be subject to the restrictions laid down in Article 128.

Art.128 Inspection of files
Implemented by:
R.148 Communication between EPO and national authorities
R.149 Inspection of files by courts or national authorities

1 **Exchange of information between EPO and other authorities**
If an authority listed in **Art.131(1)**, second sentence, such as a court, requests information held in an EPO file, the restrictions relating to the non-disclosure of informaton prior to publication of the application and the exclusion of parts of the file from inspection (**R.144**) do not apply (**Art.131(1)**, second sentence). A request from any authority not listed in the second sentence, e.g. a tax authority, is subject to the restrictions of **Art.128**. Since **Art.131(1)** specifies authorities, private individuals and firms cannot use this provision to gain access to information (OJ 1993 p.588).

Under **Art.131(1)** the EPO may request information held in the file of a national patent office pertaining to a patent attorney (**J5/99** r.3.2) or request information concerning national law (**J18/99** r.3.1).

Art. 131(2) At the request of the European Patent Office, the courts or other competent authorities of Contracting States shall undertake, on behalf of the Office and within the limits of their jurisdiction, any necessary enquiries or other legal measures.

Implemented by:
R.150 Procedure for letters rogatory
Consistent with this provision, it is possible under **R.120** for the EPO to ask a competent national court to take evidence from a party, witness or expert who has been summoned before the EPO. This is more expicitly indicated in the German text of **Art.131(2)**.

Art. 132 Exchange of publications

Art. 132(1) The European Patent Office and the central industrial property offices of the Contracting States shall despatch to each other on request and for their own use one or more copies of their respective publications free of charge.

1 **Publications exchanged**
The publications referred to in this article include the Official Journal, the Patent Bulletin, and the published specifications of applications and patents. This exchange of information has benefited the EPO by providing it with a comprehensive collection of prior art documents to search.

Art. 132(2) The European Patent Office may conclude agreements relating to the exchange or supply of publications.

1 **Competence to conclude agreements**
The President is competent to make such agreements according to **Art.33(4)**.

Chapter III *Representation*

Art. 133 General principles of representation

1 General

Art.133 contains the general principles governing representation with respect to proceedings under the Convention.

In general, a person (e.g. applicant, proprietor, opponent) need not be represented in proceedings before the EPO (**Art.133(1)**). As an exception, a person not having a residence or place of business in a contracting state must be represented (**Art.133(2)**). Although not required by law, representation is also recommended for a person having a residence or place of business in a contracting state. Professional handling of the case is in the interest of both the person and the EPO, ensuring that the person achieves the desired goal and the procedure before the EPO is conducted efficiently. Representation may only be undertaken by a person on the list of professional representatives before the EPO (**Art.134(1)**) and, exceptionally, by an employee (**Art.133(3)**) or a legal practitioner (**Art.134(8)**). A party choosing to act in oral proceedings through a person not entitled to represent is equivalent to not appearing at all at the oral proceedings (**T927/05** r.2).

2 Appointment and authorisation of representative

Due representation before the EPO comprises the two separate procedural acts of appointment and authorisation (A-VIII,1.1; **J17/98** r.4.2, 4.3).

2.1 APPOINTMENT OF A REPRESENTATIVE

The appointment informs the EPO of the representative that will act before the EPO on behalf of the applicant, proprietor or opponent.

In each case where a party wishes or is obliged to be represented, an appointment must be filed in which the EPO is informed of the fact and of the name of the representative who will handle the case. Representatives are normally appointed by entering their name in the Request for Grant form (**R.41(2)(d)**) or in the notice of opposition (**R.76(2)(d)**). The proprietor in opposition and the parties in appeal are already known to the EPO and it is assumed that they will act through any already appointed representative unless it is indicated otherwise.

Either the party or the representative must sign the Request for Grant form. In the latter case, the representative must be identified as the appointed representative. Similarly, in the case of several applicants, each one of them or their representative must sign.

A party may appoint several representatives (**R.152(10)**). The name of the representative to whom the EPO will notify all communications must be entered in the form followed by the words 'et al' (see also **R.130(2)**); the names of the further representatives must be given on an additional sheet. In the case of a general authorisation previously registered with the EPO, only one representative and the registration number of the authorisation must be entered in the form; the names of the further representatives need not be given. (OJ 2013 p.535 section II)

A group of representatives can be registered with the EPO as an association, allowing appointment of all of them by merely entering the name of the association and the registration number in the same box of the form (see **R.152(11)**:1).

Several parties acting jointly may each appoint a representative, but they must act through a common representative (**R.41(3)**, **R.151**). See **R.41(3):1** for the appointment of the common representative.

2.2 **AUTHORISATION OF A REPRESENTATIVE**
The second procedural act for representation is the filing of an authorisation, which serves the purpose of establishing whether a representative acting before the EPO on behalf of a party has indeed been engaged by the party to do so. An authorisation or letter of engagement may be filed in respect of a single case or in respect of all transactions of a party with the EPO (general authorisation, **R.152(5)(b)**).

R.152(1) establishes the exceptional cases where the EPO requires the filing of an authorisation. In such cases the first act of a party before the EPO should refer to a (general) authorisation filed together with the first act or to a previously filed general authorisation of a single representative or an association of representatives (**R.152(11)**). Note, that the filing of a general authorisation without a link between a case and the authorisation does not imply the appointment of a representative for that case (**J17/98** hn. I). Since, as a rule, representatives are not obliged to file an authorisation, they are deemed to be entitled to act in the name of the respective party, unless they fail to file an authorisation in due time if invited to do so (**G2/04** r.1.1.2).

A party may authorise one or more representatives by means of an individual authorisation in respect of one or more individually mentioned cases of the party, preferably using Form 1003.

A party may instead use a general authorisation in respect of all cases of the party. A general authorisation, preferably using Form 1004, must be filed with the Legal Division, who will register it and issue a registration number. The registration number can be used when appointing a representative for a case. (OJ 2013 p.535 section II)

3 **Authorisation under PCT**
Representation before an international authority according to the PCT (receiving Office, ISA, IPEA) is governed by the law of the receiving Office where the international application is filed (Art.49, R.83 PCT). If the EPO is receiving Office, **Art.133** and **134** EPC apply (Art.27(7) PCT). However, a non-resident applicant (**Art.133(2)** EPC) may initiate processing of the application by the EPO as designated or elected Office without being represented (E-IX,2.3.1). The processing starts the day following that on which the procedural steps of Art.22(1) or 39(1)(a) PCT in conjunction with **Art.153(5)** and **R.159(1)** EPC are taken. The representative of a non-resident applicant in the international phase, who is not entitled to act before the EPO, is not allowed to act on the applicant's behalf before the EPO as designated or elected Office; the representative may not even initiate the regional European phase. Under Art.49 PCT the representative is not entitled to practice before the EPO as designated or elected Office. Any procedural steps the representative nonetheless takes (apart from payments) have no effect (**R.152(6)**).

If a national office is receiving Office, the national law determines the requirements for the representation in the entire international phase. If an international application is filed in the USA by a US patent attorney, the US patent attorney may act before the EPO as ISA and IPEA. However, when entering the EPO regional phase, the US patent attorney must give way to a representative complying with **Art.134** EPC, because representation before a designated or elected Office follows the national law of that office. This makes sense, as the international application is regarded in the national phase as a European application when the EPO is designated or elected Office (a Euro-PCT application).

4 **Authorisation in proceedings relating to UP**
A representative can be appointed to represent the applicant in the proceedings relating to the unitary patent (UP) (**UPR.6(2)(c)**). However, authorisation to represent in proceedings before the EPO does not automatically translate to a valid authorisation in UP proceedings. If an authorisation is needed, it must specifically indicate representation in UP proceedings (**UPR.20(1)**).

Art. 133(1) Subject to paragraph 2, no person shall be compelled to be represented by a professional representative in proceedings established by this Convention.

1 **Non-compulsory representation**
A person need not be represented in proceedings before the EPO. However, a person without residence or place of business in a contracting state must, according to paragraph 2, be represented. A person not requiring representation under **Art.133(1)** and **(2)** may still need to have documents signed on their behalf if they are not legally competent to act.

Art. 133(2) Natural or legal persons not having their residence or principal place of business in a Contracting State shall be represented by a professional representative and act through him in all proceedings established by this Convention, other than in filing a European patent application; the Implementing Regulations may permit other exceptions.

1 **Compulsory representation**
The compulsory representation of persons without residence or place of business in a contracting state stems from the desire to run the procedure before the EPO efficiently, requiring the familiarity of a party with the legal system and the avoidance of postal delays. Increased use of electronic filing and the EPO's online Mailbox service have made the latter point less relevant than at the time of drafting of the Convention. Whereas both the residence and the nationality of the party are important for use of an admissible non-EPO language when filing further documents (**Art.14(4)**), only the residence or principal place of business of the party matters for representation. Note that extension states and validation states are not contracting states.

A legal person must be represented unless it has its principal place of business in a contracting state, and not merely a branch or subsidiary located in one (travaux préparatoires EPC1973, Art.133, BR/169/72). On the other hand, a subsidiary having its place of business in a contracting state and duly registered as a legal person in that state may act itself as a party without representation under **Art.133(3)**; any control by a parent company is irrelevant (see also Singer Art.133, note 9). The subsidiary may not act as a representative for the parent company (**Art.134(1)**).

The adjective 'principal' for the place of business in **Art.133(2)** is not well-defined. The French and German versions of the provision instead use 'siège' and 'Sitz' respectively, terms that usually refer to the seat of a legal entity, i.e. the registered address.

The Administrative Council has hitherto not created any exceptions to the compulsory representation under **Art.133(2)**.

2 **Allowed acts**

Art.133(2) excludes the filing of a European patent application from the compulsory representation. Hence, persons not having their residence or place of business within a contracting state may file a European patent application without being represented. The filing includes all acts leading to the accordance of a date of filing (A-VIII,1.1 and **R.55**). Only after a date of filing has been accorded, i.e. during the formalities check of **Art.90(3)** and **R.57(h)**, will the EPO check the requirement of representation.

In the case of compulsory representation, the EPO requires a representative for all acts following the accordance of a date of filing, such as the appointment of a representative under **R.57(h)** and **R.58**. Note that payments may be made by any person including those obliged to be represented (**Rfees6(1):1**).

3 **Assessment and sanction**

Compliance with the requirement of compulsory representation is assessed when a party initiates proceedings before the EPO. The sanction for non-compliance is adapted to the particular proceedings concerned and included in the part of the EPC dealing with those proceedings.

In grant proceedings the assessment is carried out during the formal examination under **R.57(h)**. The procedure for correcting any deficiencies is given in **R.57:9**. If the lack of representation is not duly rectified, the application will be refused according to **Art.90(5)**. On the other hand, should a representative withdraw during the examination phase and this is not rectified within an extendable two-month time limit, the application will be deemed withdrawn according to **Art. 94(4)** (A-VIII,1.8).

On entry in the European phase, the EPO checks compliance with the requirements of **Art.133(2)** for an international application. If a lack of representation is not corrected following an invitation under **R.163(5)**, the application is refused under **R.163(6)**.

At the start of opposition proceedings the EPO assesses whether the opponent requires representation. The sanction when necessary representation is lacking is created in the Guidelines in D-IV,1.2.2.2(iv) by making non-compliance a deficiency under the 'cover-all' provision **R.77(2)**, causing the opposition to be inadmissible if the deficiency is not duly corrected.

There are no provisions provided for the assessment of representation and any corresponding sanction at the appeal stage, because normally no new parties enter the proceedings. Neither does the EPC have any expressly stated sanction in the case of an unrepresented party who enters opposition proceedings through intervention under **Art.105**.

Art. 133(3) Natural or legal persons having their residence or principal place of business in a Contracting State may be represented in proceedings established by this Convention by an employee, who need not be a professional representative but who shall be authorised in accordance with the Implementing Regulations. The Implementing Regulations may provide whether and under what conditions an employee of a legal person may also represent other legal persons which have their principal place of business in a Contracting State and which have economic connections with the first legal person.

1 **Representation by employee**
The representation of an enterprise by an employee is restricted to enterprises having a place of business in a contracting state according to **Art.133(3)**, first sentence. The employee need not be a professional representative. The employee is not regarded as a true representative but as a person through whom the party acts, as is clear from the distinction made between 'vertreten' versus 'handeln durch' in the German version and 'représenter' versus 'agir par' in the French version of **Art.133(2)**, **(3)** and **134**; the distinction is lost in the English version.

Directors of a company represent the company, as they express the will of the company; they need not be authorised. An employee, on the other hand, must be authorised (**R.152**). There is no provision in the Rules allowing an employee to act on behalf of another legal person, even when economically connected. Hence, an employee is not allowed to act for economically connected companies (see e.g. **T298/97** hn. II).

Art. 133(4) The Implementing Regulations may lay down special provisions concerning the common representation of parties acting in common.

Implemented by:
R.151 Appointment of a common representative

Art. 134 Representation before the European Patent Office

1 **General**
Art.134 deals with issues of professional representation, determining who may represent persons in proceedings established under the Convention and in particular, the conditions under which a person may be entered on the list of professional representatives. Furthermore, it deals with the entitlement of national representatives of a state acceding to the EPC to be entered on that list.

Representation in proceedings before the EPO may only be undertaken by persons whose names appear on the list of professional representatives of **Art.134(1)** or by certain legal practitioners under **Art.134(8)**. The purpose of this arrangement is to create a corpus of professional representatives with a monopoly status who possess the necessary qualification for their work. This is designed to protect the parties that have to rely on the services of a professional representative and to ensure the efficient conduct of proceedings before the EPO. (**G3/97** r.4.2.1)

Art. 134(1) Representation of natural or legal persons in proceedings established by this Convention may only be undertaken by professional representatives whose names appear on a list maintained for this purpose by the European Patent Office.

Implemented by:
R.152 Authorisations
R.154 Amendment of the list of professional representatives

1 **List of representatives**
All representation before the EPO must be undertaken exclusively by professional representatives entered on the list, employees according to **Art.133(3)** or by legal practitioners according to **Art.134(8)**.

The EPO makes available the list of professional representatives acting before the EPO in the form of a searchable database on its website. The database serves the purpose of providing the public with access to information concerning representatives, including their telecommunication details, and can be searched free of charge. The database contains the following mandatory information for each representative: last and first names; representative number; full postal address of place of business or employment; date of entry or re-entry; and the date of the relevant decision. The database also includes telecommunication data (e.g. telephone number, email address, web address) to the extent that a representative has made this information available to the EPO and consented to its publication. When a representative is deleted from the list (**R.154**), that representative's entry on the list will continue to be accessible for a period of five years from the date of the relevant decision. (Dec. Pres. OJ 2024 A107 and Not. EPO. OJ 2024 A109)

The Legal Division is responsible for adding representatives to the list and deleting them from it (**Art.20(1)**) and requests for entry, deletion and re-entry must be sent in writing to the Legal Division of the EPO (OJ 2015 A55). Representatives can also request deletion from the list and amend any telecommunication details they have provided using MyEPO Portfolio (Dec. Pres. OJ 2024 A20 and Not. EPO OJ 2024 A21). A person fulfilling the requirements of **Art.134(2)** will be entered on the list on request. A person will be deleted from the list on request or on account of **R.154**.

2 **Submissions by accompanying person during oral proceedings**

A person not entitled to represent parties before the EPO and accompanying a professional representative during oral proceedings has a limited opportunity to take part in the proceedings. The accompanying person is not entitled to make formal requests, such as requests relating to patentability (see e.g. **T1178/04** r.33). The accompanying person may make submissions during oral proceedings on specific legal or technical issues (**G2/94** hn. I; **G4/95** hn. I). The submissions may relate to facts, evidence or arguments (**G4/95** r.8). Note, that the admissibility of facts and evidence filed at a late stage in proceedings is always a matter of discretion for the EPO (**Art.114(2)**; E-VI,2.2).

The submissions must be made under the continuing responsibility and control of the professional representative and only in addition to the complete presentation of the case of the professional representative (**G4/95** hn. I, II(b) (iv)). Submissions may be made during oral proceedings in ex parte and inter partes proceedings, at both first and second instance (**G2/94** hn. I, emphasis on grant appeal proceedings; **G4/95** hn. I, emphasis on opposition proceedings).

Submissions by a non-entitled person cannot be made as a matter of right, but only with the permission of the EPO (**G2/94** hn. II(a), **G4/95** hn. II(a)). The professional representative must request permission for the submissions to be made, stating the name and qualifications of the accompanying person, specifying the subject-matter of the proposed submissions, and stating that the submissions will be made under the continuing responsibility and control of the professional representative (**G4/95** hn. II; E-III,8.5). The request must be filed on or before the date fixed for written submissions in the summons for the oral proceedings according to **R.116(1)**; a late filed request will only be allowed in exceptional circumstances or if all other parties agree to the making of the submissions (**G4/95** hn. II(b)(ii); E-III,8.5).

Decisions **G2/94** and **G4/95** do not state the meaning of the 'subject-matter' of the proposed submission to be specified in the request. In the context of the decisions it is reasonable to assume that the subject-matter comprises facts and evidence but does not include arguments.

Parties are not accompanying persons in the sense of **G4/95** (**T621/98** r.2). They have the right to make submissions in oral proceedings by virtue of their status as party to the proceedings. (E-III,8.5)

A non-entitled person cannot use the taking of evidence under **Art.117** as a basis for entitlement to make oral submissions involving the presentation of facts and evidence (**G4/95** r.8(a)).

Additional provisions specific for ex parte and inter partes proceedings are given below.

2.1 EX PARTE PROCEEDINGS

An accompanying person may be allowed to make oral submissions on legal and technical issues during oral proceedings in ex parte appeal proceedings. The request must be made in advance of the day of the oral proceedings. The Board must be informed of all relevant matters before deciding on the request. (**G2/94** hn. I, II(a), r.2)

2.2 INTER PARTES PROCEEDINGS

An accompanying person may be allowed to make oral submissions on legal and technical issues, other than under **Art.117**, during oral proceedings in opposition or opposition appeal. The request must be made sufficiently early so that all parties are able to prepare themselves properly in relation to the proposed submissions. A request made shortly before or at the oral proceedings will normally be refused, unless all parties agree to the making of the oral submissions. (**G4/95** hn. I, II)

2.3 FORMER MEMBER OF BOA

The EPO will normally refuse permission for former members of the boards of appeal to make oral submissions during oral appeal proceedings either ex parte or inter partes, unless at least three years have elapsed following termination of their appointment to the boards. After three years have elapsed, the EPO will grant permission, except in very exceptional circumstances. In this way, the boards cannot reasonably be suspected of partiality. (**G2/94** hn. II(b))

Art. 134(2) Any natural person who

(a) is a national of a Contracting State,

(b) has his place of business or employment in a Contracting State and

(c) has passed the European qualifying examination

may be entered on the list of professional representatives.

1 Conditions for entry on the list

During a transitional period a person not having passed the qualifying examination may be entered on the list (**Art.134(3)**).

See **Art.134a(1)(b)** for the European qualifying examination.

Art. 134(3) During a period of one year from the date on which the accession of a State to this Convention takes effect, entry on that list may also be requested by any natural person who

(a) is a national of a Contracting State,

(b) has his place of business or employment in the State having acceded to the Convention and

(c) **is entitled to represent natural or legal persons in patent matters before the central industrial property office of that State. Where such entitlement is not conditional upon the requirement of special professional qualifications, the person shall have regularly so acted in that State for at least five years.**

1 **Legacy clause**
The provision allows a representative allowed to act in patent matters under the national law of a contracting state acceding to the EPC to be entered on the list of European professional representatives without the requirement to pass the European qualifying examination within one year from the date of accession.

Art. 134(4) Entry shall be effected upon request, accompanied by certificates indicating that the conditions laid down in paragraph 2 or 3 are fulfilled.

Art. 134(5) Persons whose names appear on the list of professional representatives shall be entitled to act in all proceedings established by this Convention.

Art. 134(6) For the purpose of acting as a professional representative, any person whose name appears on the list of professional representatives shall be entitled to establish a place of business in any Contracting State in which proceedings established by this Convention may be conducted, having regard to the Protocol on Centralisation annexed to this Convention. The authorities of such State may remove that entitlement in individual cases only in application of legal provisions adopted for the purpose of protecting public security and law and order. Before such action is taken, the President of the European Patent Office shall be consulted.

1 **Place of business in Germany or the Netherlands**
Proceedings established by the EPC are conducted in Germany and the Netherlands. Hence, this provision allows non-German representatives to set up their business in Germany and non-Dutch representatives to set up their business in the Netherlands. See **Art.164(1):2** for the Protocol on Centralisation.

Art. 134(7) The President of the European Patent Office may grant exemption from:

(a) **the requirement of paragraphs 2(a) or 3(a) in special circumstances;**

(b) **the requirement of paragraph 3(c), second sentence, if the applicant furnishes proof that he has acquired the requisite qualification in another way.**

1 **Exemption from nationality requirement**
The President has delegated the power to grant exemptions to the Vice-President of DG5 (OJ 2012 p.13). An exemption under paragraph (a) is usually granted if the person has lived for at least four years in an EPC contracting state, is employed by a patent law firm or works in the patent department of a company, and has shown a real intention to stay there on a permanent basis and practice as a European patent attorney. Proof of the intention must be provided.

Art. 134(8) Representation in proceedings established by this Convention may also be undertaken, in the same way as by a professional representative, by any legal practitioner qualified in a Contracting State and having his place of business in that State, to the extent that he is entitled in that State to act as a professional representative in patent matters. Paragraph 6 shall apply mutatis mutandis.

1 **Representation by legal practitioner**

Art.134(8) is a special rule limited in scope to legal practitioners qualified in a contracting state that can act as a representative in patent matters. 'Legal practitioner' covers the profession Rechtsanwalt in Germany and solicitor and barrister in England. A patent attorney under national law cannot be regarded as such a 'legal practitioner' (**J19/89**). **Art.134(8)** allows legal practitioners to act before the EPO as professional representatives to the extent that they are entitled to act as such in their contracting state in patent matters. Legal practitioners entitled to act as representatives before the EPO are registered in an internal database administered by the Legal Division (OJ 2013 p.600); they are not entered on the list of professional representatives (**J18/99**; A-VIII,1.3).

The EPC draws a distinction between professional representatives and legal practitioners because of the professional representative's closer connection with the EPO:

- professional representatives are subject to the disciplinary authority of the epi or the EPO (**Art.134a(1)(c)**), whereas legal practitioners are subject to disciplinary authority under national law;
- professional representatives' entitlement to act can be ascertained by consulting the list of **Art.134**, whereas legal practitioners' entitlement is much harder to establish, as it is based on their qualification in a contracting state, their place of business and the right to act as professional representatives in patent matters in that state;
- professional representatives are always technically qualified, whereas legal practitioners may not be.

The requirement for legal practitioners to always submit an authorisation (see **R.152(1):1**) creates transparency for clients whether they are being represented by a professional representative or a legal practitioner (**J8/10** r.2.3, 8, 9).

Art. 134a Institute of Professional Representatives before the European Patent Office

1 **General**

Art.134a anchors the existence of the epi in the Convention and sets forth the powers of the Administrative Council to adopt provisions governing the standards for admission as a professional representative, the conducting of qualifying examinations and the disciplinary powers to be exercised by that institute or the EPO.

Art.134a(1)(d) confers on the Administrative Council the competence to create an evidentiary exception modelled on the US attorney-client privilege, applying solely to proceedings before the EPO (see **R.153**).

Art.134a(2) anchors in the Convention the principle clearly formulated in Article 5(1) of the Regulation on the Establishment of the Institute, to the effect that any person entered on the list of professional representatives shall be a member of the epi. (OJ 2007 se4 EN p.162)

Art. 134a(1) The Administrative Council shall be competent to adopt and amend provisions governing:

(a) the Institute of Professional Representatives before the European Patent Office, hereinafter referred to as the Institute;

(b) the qualifications and training required of a person for admission to the European qualifying examination and the conduct of such examination;

(c) the disciplinary power exercised by the Institute or the European Patent Office in respect of professional representatives;

(d) the obligation of confidentiality on the professional representative and the privilege from disclosure in proceedings before the European Patent Office in respect of communications between a professional representative and his client or any other person.

Implemented by:
R.153 Attorney evidentiary privilege

1 **epi (Art.134a(1)(a))**
The institute of professional representatives has been established and is called 'The Institute of Professional Representatives before the EPO' (*epi*). See OJ 2024 sp1 p.132 for the Regulation on establishment of the institute. Membership is compulsory for professional representatives (Regulation, Art.5(1)).

Membership requires payment of an annual fee (Regulation, Art.6(1)), which may be paid through standard banking procedure or by direct debiting mandate (see ADA.16). If the fee is not paid in due time, the entry of the professional representative will be deleted from the EPO list of professional representatives (R.154(1)).

Starting from 01.06.2024, entry and re-entry on the list may be requested via a corresponding feature in MyEPO. Changes to the list including deletion from it can also be requested in the dedicated representative area within MyEPO. (OJ 2024 A57)

2 **European qualifying examination (Art.134a(1)(b))**
The Regulation on the European qualifying examination (REE) mentioned in **Art.134a(1)(b)** has been amended by decision of the Administrative Council on 14.12.2023 and published in OJ 2024 A4 and OJ 2024 sp3 p.1. It has entered into force on 01.01.2025. The Implementing provisions to the Regulation on the European qualifying examination (IPREE) have been amended by decision of the Supervisory Board, and the new version, which entered into force on 01.01.2025 for modules F-M4, was published in OJ 2024 A25 and OJ 2024 sp3 p.20. The previous version of the REE (REE2009) was published in OJ 2019 sp2, p.2. The previous version of the IPREE (IPREE2018) was published in OJ 2019 sp2, p.18 and will continue to apply to papers governed by REE2009. In the following, when the article of REE or rule of IPREE is referred to, and its number is the same in both the current version and the new version, only the new number is given.

The EQE tests the candidate's knowledge of the law and its interpretation as valid on 31 October of the year prior to the examination in question (R.2 IPREE). The examination is an open-book examination (Instructions to candidates concerning the conduct of the EQE, published yearly on the EPO website). Candidates should not use any special knowledge they may have of a technical field which is the subject of a paper (R.22(3) IPREE2018, R.21(3) IPREE).

The present European qualifying examination (EQE) consists of a pre-examination and a main examination (Art.1(7) REE2009, R.10(1) IPREE2018). The last pre-examination took place in 2024 and the last main examination is set to take place in 2026. A pass grade in the pre-examination (if one is held) is required for admission to the main examination (Art.11(7) REE2009). The pre-examination consisted of one paper with multiple-choice legal and claim analysis questions (R.10 IPREE2018). The main examination consists of four papers, A, B, C and D, which assess candidates on drafting claims, responding to an EPO communication, drafting a notice of opposition, and answering legal questions (R.21 to 26 IPREE2018).

Due to the COVID-19 pandemic, the EQE has been held online (e-EQE) since 2021. Additional information is provided on the EPO website under 'EQE FAQ'. The new EQE has now been reformed in a modular format in order to be more suitable as an online examination and to minimise the required amount of screen time.

The new EQE consists of a foundation paper F and four main examination papers M1, M2, M3 and M4 (Art.1(5) REE). The papers of the new EQE are designed to test whether the candidates are 'qualified to practise' before the EPO. Paper F, roughly corresponding to an easier version of the pre-examination of the present EQE, assesses basic legal knowledge of the EPC and the PCT. Paper M1 tests the candidates' ability to understand and act upon instructions from a client and consider the relevance of prior art to a given invention, presumably at a level that is slightly higher than that of paper F. Paper M2, roughly corresponding to part DI of paper D of the present EQE, tests advanced knowledge of procedural and substantive patent law of the EPC and the PCT. Paper M3, roughly corresponding to papers A, B and C of the present EQE, comprises three parts: drafting claims, defending and attacking a patent application/patent. Note that unlike Art.1(4) REE2009, which refers to notice of opposition, Art.1(4) REE refers to challenging a European patent, European patent application or Euro-PCT application. It can be presumed that this may include drafting the grounds of appeal or responding to third party observations. Candidates will need to pass all three parts of M3 in a single year to achieve a pass in this paper. This requirement is due to the modular concept of the new EQE, i.e. that certain legal issues will only be tested in one part of paper M3, instead of potentially appearing in all three present EQE papers A, B and C. Paper M4, roughly corresponding to part DII of paper D of the present EQE, assesses candidates' ability to provide a detailed legal opinion to a client. (Art.1(5) REE)

During a transitional period, set to end with EQE 2026, the present and the new EQE are, to an extent, running concurrently. For example, the first paper F took place in 2025, together with papers A, B, C and D of the present EQE. Transitional provisions apply to candidates who passed a selection of the old EQE papers (Art.25 REE), see **Art.134a(1):2.3** for details.

2.1 ELIGIBILITY, REGISTRATION AND ENROLMENT

To be eligible to sit the EQE, candidates must possess a university-level scientific or technical qualification (Art.11(1)(a) REE). To sit the present EQE, candidates are additionally required to have completed – by the date of the examination in question – at least two years full time training for the pre-examination and three years full time training for the main examination (Art.11(2) and 11(7) REE2009). A reduction of the training period is possible in the circumstances listed in R.16 IPREE (see also OJ 2022 A12 II §2.2, likely to be updated). Candidates must have been trained under the supervision of a professional representative or must have represented their employer before the EPO in the sense of **Art.133(3)**. Work as an EPO examiner is also accepted as training. Training under the supervision of a legal practitioner entitled under **Art.134(8)** to act before the EPO does not count, because legal practitioners 'do not normally possess the scientific or technical knowledge required with a view to activities pertaining to European patent applications and patents' (**D14/93** hn, r.2.2).

To be eligible to sit Paper F of the new EQE, candidates need at least one year of professional activities as defined in Art.11(2)(b) REE. Papers M1 and M2 can be sat after at least two years, and papers M3 and M4 after at least three years of professional activities (Art.11(2)(a) REE). The required training times are the same for EPO examiners as for other candidates under the new REE.

Candidates must register with the Examination Secretariat on commencing their training (Art.11(1) REE). Registration is only possible online as described in OJ 2017 A24. Candidates need only register once, prior to enrolling for their first examination; re-registration is not required to enrol for examination re-sittings or the subsequent examination papers. Candidates must be registered by 28.05.2025 to be able to enrol for paper F in 2026 (OJ 2025 A9).

The EQE is held annually, typically in March; dates of the EQE 2026 and its enrolment times are given in OJ 2025 A9, with the latter running roughly from July until September. Registered candidates must enrol online to sit the foundation paper or the main examination. The fee for sitting the EQE depends on the number of papers for which the candidate enrols and the number of times a paper is re-taken (R.8 IPREE; OJ 2018 A108 §4).

2.2 PREPARING FOR THE EQE

Candidates are expected to be familiar with a number of documents related to the EPC, the PCT and the UP listed under R.22(1) IPREE2018, R.21(1) IPREE.

Instructions to candidates are published in OJ 2022 A20. Starting from EQE 2017, the duration of each of the main examination papers was increased by half an hour to 4 hours for paper A, 3.5 hours for paper B, and 5.5 hours for each of papers C and D (OJ 2019 sp2 p.41). For the e-EQE starting from 2021, additional time was provided for the pre-examination and papers C and D, and enforced breaks were defined during all papers. Duration of the new EQE papers can be variable, see R.22-26 IPREE.

Copies of past examination papers and examiners' reports are available on the EPO website. Details of the marking of papers can be found in the decision of the Disciplinary Board of Appeal **D7/05** r.4, 5. Information about the CEIPI training courses is available on the website www.ceipi.edu and in the OJ (OJ 2024 A46 and A47). For epi tutorials see the website www.patentepi.com. The European Patent Academy (see **Art.4(2):3**) also provides training in the form of seminars and in-house training (OJ 2017 A99). A guide for preparation for the EQE is published on the EPO website on a yearly basis (https://link.epo.org/elearning/EQE_study_guide.pdf).

2.3 TRANSITIONAL PROVISIONS

Transitional provisions apply to candidates that have passed some of the present EQE papers before the entry into force of the new REE (Art.25 REE). Candidates that would have been eligible for pre-examination in 2025 are exempted from it and may directly write papers A-D in 2026 (Art.25(6) REE). Candidates that passed the pre-examination are exempted from papers F and M1 (Art.25(2)(a) REE). Candidates that passed any of the papers A, B and C are exempted from sitting parts 1, 2 and 3 of paper M3 respectively (Art.25(2)(b),(c),(d) REE). Passing paper D exempts candidates from sitting papers M2 and M4 (Art.25(2)(e) REE). In 2026, candidates may sit part 1 of paper D instead of paper M2 (Art.27(2)(c) REE). Candidates that passed all present EQE papers but did not yet fulfil all requirements of Art.14(2) REE2009 are exempted from all new EQE papers (Art.25(2)(h) REE). Note that compensable fails in any present EQE papers cannot be used for the transitional provisions.

Once a candidate uses a transitional provision, they will have five years to qualify under an exemption (Art.25(4) REE). Candidates having enrolled for any paper of the new EQE may no longer enrol for any old EQE papers.

2.4 FURTHER FEATURES OF THE NEW EQE

The amended REE and IPREE changed several principles of the examination. One key change is a shift from a static passing grade requirement to a dynamic one, to be set by the Examination Board (R.6(6) IPREE). This means that the EQE will be marked on a curve, allowing balancing out the years where some papers are too easy or too difficult. This provision will be re-evaluated once three sessions of all examination papers have been completed, presumably in 2029 (R.6(6)(c) IPREE). The passing thresholds are to be set at 50-75% of total marks for papers F and M1, and at 30-60% of total marks for papers M2, M3 and M4 (R.6(6)(a)(i) and (ii) IPREE).

Compensable fail grade will no longer be available, neither for the papers of the new EQE nor as part of transitional provisions.

Candidates will have the option to skip paper F and sit all four main papers of the new EQE after three years of training (R.10(3) IPREE). This "intensive examination" track is meant for candidates that prefer to attempt all parts of the EQE in one year and to avoid studying for 2-3 years in a row. Candidates who select the intensive examination track will need to at least pass papers M1 and M2 or M2 and M3 to stay on it, or they will need to sit paper F.

Complaints about the conduct of the examination (including technical problems) must be submitted at the latest on the day following the examination paper in question (R.19(3) IPREE), contrary to at the latest by the end of the day on which the examination took place for the present EQE (OJ 2022 A20 I.8).

3 Discipline (Art.134a(1)(c))

The purpose of disciplinary proceedings is to serve the public interest in the orderly and proper exercise of professional representation before the EPO, not for individuals to pursue their interests vis-à-vis others. Claims of individuals arising from a representative's contravention of the rules of professional conduct are a matter for national courts under civil, criminal or administrative law. (**D25/05** r.3)

The disciplinary power extends to all activities related to the EPC. These activities include the acts of filing translations and the payment of renewal fees for European patents before national authorities. (**D25/05** r.4)

The disciplinary power is exercised by the Disciplinary Committee of the epi, the Disciplinary Board of the EPO and the Disciplinary Board of Appeal of the EPO (**R.12b(6)**; Art.5 Regulation on Discipline for professional representatives (RDR)). The epi Code of Conduct for Professional Representatives is published in OJ 2024 A111, and the RDR is published in OJ 2024 sp1 p.145. Point 2 of the Code sets rules for advertising by professional representatives (see e.g. **D12/88**). Additional Rules of Procedure of the Disciplinary Committee, the Disciplinary Board, and the Disciplinary Board of Appeal are published in OJ 2024 sp1 p.156, p.166 and p.70.

The Disciplinary Committee, consisting of professional representatives, considers breaches of the Code of Conduct and can dismiss a case, warn a representative or refer the case to the Disciplinary Board (Art.6(2) RDR). The Disciplinary Board and the Disciplinary Board of Appeal, both consisting of legally qualified members of the EPO and professional representatives (Art.9 and 10 RDR), may impose a fine or delete the name of a professional representative from the list of professional representatives. See e.g. **DB3/15** (OJ 2019 A40) where a fine was imposed, and **DB2/92** (OJ 1994 p.750) and **D11/91** Summ.I where a deletion for an indefinite period was imposed.

Below are two examples of breaching the Rules of Professional Conduct as set out in the RDR:

- An epi member posting on a social network announcing that they just acquired a new client and identifying this client without first asking them for permission (point 2(b)(1) in conjunction with point 1(b) of the Code of Conduct).

- An epi member advising two clients that are in direct competition with each other provided that the advice concerns a specific matter common to both clients (Art.3(2) RDR).

If such breaches are referred to the Disciplinary Committee (e.g. by the clients themselves), they may impose a disciplinary measure according to Art.4 RDR.

4 **Confidentiality and attorney client privilege** (**Art.134a(1)(d)**)

The Administrative Council may adopt provisions governing the obligation of confidentiality on the professional representative. It may also adopt provisions on the privilege from disclosure in proceedings before the European Patent Office in respect of communications between professional representative and their clients or any other person. The provision on privilege from disclosure as laid down in **R.153** is in response to the US practice of requiring disclosure of documents to all parties in discovery proceedings.

Art. 134a(2) Any person entered on the list of professional representatives referred to in Article 134, paragraph 1, shall be a member of the Institute.

Art.134(1) Representation before the European Patent Office

PART VIII IMPACT ON NATIONAL LAW

Chapter I *Conversion into a national patent application*

Art. 135 Request for conversion

Art. 135(1) The central industrial property office of a designated Contracting State shall, at the request of the applicant for or proprietor of a European patent, apply the procedure for the grant of a national patent in the following circumstances:
(a) where the European patent application is deemed to be withdrawn under Article 77, paragraph 3;
(b) in such other cases as are provided for by the national law, in which the European patent application is refused or withdrawn or deemed to be withdrawn, or the European patent is revoked under this Convention.

Art.77(3) Forwarding of European patent applications
Implemented by:
R.155 Filing and transmission of the request for conversion
R.156 Information to the public in the event of conversion

1 **General**
A European patent application not leading to a European patent can be converted, in two specific cases, into one or more national applications.

The basis for conversion is **Art.66,** which states that a validly filed European patent application is regarded as being equivalent to a national application with the same filing date (and where appropriate priority date). A converted national application therefore retains the filing date and any priority date enjoyed by the European application from which it derives if the requirements for conversion laid down in **Art.135** and **137** are fulfilled.

A European patent application or patent can also be converted into a national utility model or utility certificate in those contracting states that provide for such rights (**Art.140,** referring to **Art.135** and **137**).

2 **Conversion in case of filing with national authority** (**Art.135(1)(a)**)
All contracting states must provide for conversion if a European patent application is deemed to be withdrawn under **Art.77(3)**, i.e. if the application is filed with a national patent office (**Art.75(1)(b)**) but not forwarded by the national office to the EPO in good time (**Art.77(1); R.37(2)**).

3 **Conversion in other cases (Art.135(1)(b))**

The EPC permits contracting states to provide for conversion if a European patent application is refused, withdrawn or deemed to be withdrawn or if a European patent is revoked. However, conversion is not provided for when the application is still pending. The contracting states are free to set the conditions, if any, under which conversion is allowed.

Excessive use of this provision could seriously reduce the importance of the centralised grant procedure of the EPC but the contracting states have generally made limited use of it. The possibility of conversion is allowed under national law in the following situations (see NatLaw table VII, cols. 1 and 5):

3.1 MISSING TRANSLATION

Several states allow conversion if an application filed in a non-EPO language is deemed to be withdrawn because the translation in an official language of the EPO (**Art.14(2)**) was not filed in due time (**R.6(1)**).

3.2 WITHDRAWAL, REFUSAL OR REVOCATION

A few states allow conversion if a European patent application is withdrawn, deemed withdrawn or refused and if a European patent is revoked in opposition.

3.3 UTILITY MODEL

In general, the contracting states which provide in their national law for a utility model allow the conversion of a failed European patent application into a national utility model. Hence, several states allow conversion into a national utility model for European patent applications deemed withdrawn under **Art.77(3)**. Other states allow conversion into a national utility model for European patent applications deemed withdrawn because a translation in the language of the proceedings was not filed in time (**Art.14(2)**). Some states allow conversion into a national utility model of a European patent application withdrawn, deemed withdrawn or refused by the EPO. Conversion into a utility model is also allowed in Italy for European patents revoked for Italy.

Furthermore, Germany allows for the filing of a 'branching-off' (or 'splitting-off') utility model application from a pending European patent application or an opposed European patent. The utility model application can be filed even during a short period after the grant procedure before the EPO is concluded (by withdrawal, deemed withdrawal, refusal, or grant) or any opposition proceedings are completed. Branching-off is possible until ten years from the filing date of the European patent application (see OJ 1987 p.175). Austria also provides for branching-off utility model applications (NatLaw, table VII). The filing of a branching-off utility model application is not governed by **Art.135**.

Art. 135(2) In the case referred to in paragraph 1(a), the request for conversion shall be filed with the central industrial property office with which the European patent application has been filed. That office shall, subject to the provisions governing national security, transmit the request directly to the central industrial property offices of the Contracting States specified therein.

Implemented by:

R.155(1),(2) Filing and transmission of the request for conversion

1 **Submitting the request with a national office**
A European application that is filed with a national office (**Art.75(1)(b)**) but that is not forwarded by the national office to the EPO within fourteen months after the date of filing or priority is deemed to be withdrawn (**Art.77(3)**, **R.37(2)**); the period can be extended under **R.134(2)** in case of a general dislocation in the delivery of mail. The EPO can monitor the fourteen-month period because it is informed about the filing of the application even if the application documents are not forwarded to it (**R.35(3)**, A-II,3.2).

A request for conversion under **Art.135(1)(a)** must be filed with the national office within three months of the notification of the communication that the application is deemed to be withdrawn (**R.155(1)**), calculated using the EPC rules (**Art.120**). The request may be for conversion of the European patent application into a national patent application in the state in which the application was filed and/or in one or more other contracting states. Some national offices levy a fee for a request for conversion (NatLaw table VII).

The national office will forward a timely filed request for conversion together with a copy of the application's file to the national offices of any other states specified in the request unless national security regulations prohibit it from doing so (**R.155(2)**). The office may forward the request and a copy of the patent application under secrecy, e.g. on the basis of the 'NATO Agreement for the mutual safeguarding of secrecy of inventions relating to defence and for which applications for patents have been made' of 1960 or on the basis of a bilateral agreement. The procedure before the national offices that receive the request is set out in **Art.137**.

The converted application retains the priority and filing date of the spawning European application unless the effect under **Art.66** has lapsed (see national decision in OJ 1982 p.66). That effect lapses if the national office does not transmit the request within the twenty months from the filing date of the application or from the priority date (**R.155(3)**; **Art.135(4)**). Because the twenty-month period of **R.155(3)** must be observed by the national patent office, applicants must seek remedies under national law. The effect under **Art.66** also lapses if the three-month period for filing the request of **R.155(1)** is missed (**R.155(1)**, second sentence); again applicants must seek remedies under national law.

Art. 135(3) In the cases referred to in paragraph 1(b), the request for conversion shall be submitted to the European Patent Office in accordance with the Implementing Regulations. It shall not be deemed to be filed until the conversion fee has been paid. The European Patent Office shall transmit the request to the central industrial property offices of the Contracting States specified therein.

Implemented by:
R.155(1) Filing and transmission of the request for conversion

1 **Submitting the request with EPO**
In the case of **Art.135(1)(b)**, the applicant or proprietor must submit the request for conversion to the EPO and pay the conversion fee (**Rfees2(1)14**) within three months of withdrawal of the application or of the notification of a communication that the application is deemed to be withdrawn, or of a decision refusing the application or revoking the patent (**R.155(1)**). The EPO forwards a duly submitted request and the file of the application or patent to the national offices of the states specified in the request (**R.155(2)**). There is no period within which the EPO must forward the request. The procedure before the national offices that receive the request is specified in **Art.137**.

If the request is filed late by the applicant or proprietor, re-establishment should be available (**Art.122**). Further processing is likely not possible because **Art.121** refers to further processing of the European patent application and because the end of the period of **R.135(1)** would be undefined as no notification of the loss of rights is sent; on the other hand, **R.155** is not explicitly excluded by **Art.121(4)** and **R.135(2)**, and further processing is not reserved exclusively to the case of loss of the patent application (see **R.53(3)**).

The national application resulting from the conversion retains the priority and filing date of the spawning European application unless the effect under **Art.66** has lapsed (see national decision in OJ 1982 p.66). The effect under **Art.66** lapses if the request is not filed within the three-month period (**R.155(1)**).

Art. 135(4) The effect of the European patent application referred to in Article 66 shall lapse if the request for conversion is not submitted in due time.

Art.66 A European application with a filing date is equivalent to a regular national filing
Implemented by:
R.155(3) Period for transmission of the request for conversion

1 **Transmitting the request**

Art.135(4) concerns the case where a request under **Art.135(1)(a)** is not timely transmitted by the national office where the application was filed, as is clear from the German and French versions of the provision. The effect referred to in **Art.66** is that the converted application retains the priority and filing date of the spawning European application (see national decision in OJ 1982 p.66). **R.155(1)** provides for the lapse of the effect if the request for conversion is not filed in time by the applicant or proprietor.

Art. 136 (deleted)

Art. 137 Formal requirements for conversion

1 **General**

This provision allows national authorities to levy a filing fee and request a translation of the application. The documents accompanying the transmitted request for conversion, i.e. the copy of the file held by the office where the application was filed, are opened for public inspection in accordance with the national law of the office that receives the transmitted request (**R.156**), allowing the public to know the origin of the application.

Art. 137(1) A European patent application transmitted in accordance with Article 135, paragraph 2 or 3, shall not be subjected to formal requirements of national law which are different from or additional to those provided for in this Convention.

Art.135(2) Request for conversion where application is deemed withdrawn under Art.77(3)
Art.135(3) Request for conversion in other cases

Art. 137(2) Any central industrial property office to which the European patent application is transmitted may require that the applicant shall, within a period of not less than two months:

(a) pay the national application fee; and

(b) file a translation of the original text of the European patent application in an official language of the State in question and, where appropriate, of the text as amended during proceedings before the European Patent Office which the applicant wishes to use as the basis for the national procedure.

1 **Period for paying fee and filing translation**

The period of at least two months runs from receipt of the request by the national office.

Chapter II *Revocation and prior rights*

1 **Revocation and prior rights in national proceedings**
Art.138 and **Art.139** of this chapter contain provisions for the further existence of the uniform and centrally granted European patent in the contracting states and the mutual effects of European and national patents and patent applications.

A European patent can be revoked in central opposition proceedings (**Art.99** ff.), started within nine months after publication of the grant, which may lead to a revocation with effect for all designated states. The patent can also be revoked centrally by the revocation procedure of **Art.105a**. The other possibility to revoke a patent is in a revocation procedure before a court of a contracting state, leading to a revocation with effect only in that state.

The question of revocation often arises in national infringement procedures. Some states (e.g. DE, AT) start from the principle of the validity of the patent; a revocation must be requested in a special revocation procedure. In other states (e.g. NL) a revocation can be requested as a counterclaim in an infringement procedure. When requested in an infringement procedure, the decision of courts in some states (CH, IT) is only effective between the parties (inter partes), without automatic effect for everybody (erga omnes). A mixed form is also possible (FR), where apart from the nullity inter partes a court can also pronounce the nullity for the entire state.

The purpose of **Art.138** is to harmonise the national revocation and limitation procedures by imposing minimum rights for the proprietor. Proprietors have the right to limit their patent in view of grounds for revocation during national revocation proceedings; they also has the right of self-limitation. The essential parts of the revocation are thus bound by the EPC, which is an exception to the fact that the European patent is subject to the conditions applicable to national patents (**Art.2(2)**). These measures increase the legal certainty of the proprietors and leads to a further harmonisation of the legal effect of a European patent.

Whether or not a revocation procedure started within the opposition period is allowed, depends on national law. For instance, Germany does not allow it, Austria allows it if the party is not opposing the patent.

Art. 138 Revocation of European patents

Art. 138(1) Subject to Article 139, a European patent may be revoked with effect for a Contracting State only on the grounds that:

- **(a) the subject-matter of the European patent is not patentable under Articles 52 to 57;**
- **(b) the European patent does not disclose the invention in a manner sufficiently clear and complete for it to be carried out by a person skilled in the art;**
- **(c) the subject-matter of the European patent extends beyond the content of the application as filed or, if the patent was granted on a divisional application or on a new application filed under Article 61, beyond the content of the earlier application as filed;**
- **(d) the protection conferred by the European patent has been extended; or**
- **(e) the proprietor of the European patent is not entitled under Article 60, paragraph 1.**

Art.52 Patentable inventions

Art.53 Exceptions to patentability
Art.54 Novelty
Art.55 Non-prejudicial disclosures
Art.56 Inventive step
Art.57 Industrial applications
Art.60(1) Right to a European patent
Art.61 European patent application filed by non-entitled person
Art.139 Prior rights and rights arising on the same date

1 **Grounds for national revocation**

Art.138(1) provides an exhaustive list of grounds for revocation of a European patent in national proceedings. Since the provision does not refer to national law, it is clear that **Art.138** does not make national revocation of European patents conditional on the adoption of special national provisions (OJ 2007 se4 EN p.168).

Art.138 limits the number of possible grounds on which a national court may revoke a European patent. This gives legal certainty to the proprietor: a patent granted by the EPO may only be revoked in a national procedure on the grounds of **Art.138**, furthermore taking into account **Art.139**. The only allowed additional ground was the revocation of a patent claiming subject-matter falling under a reservation according to Art.167(2) EPC1973. The EPC does not compel the contracting states to use all five grounds for revocation.

Grounds (a) - (c) are equivalent to the opposition grounds of **Art.100(a)-(c)**. The additional ground (d) relates to the case where the patent has been maintained in opposition proceedings (**Art.101(3)(a)**) or amended in a limitation procedure (**Art.105b**), but the scope of protection has been extended, contrary to **Art.123(3)**.

Ground (e) covers the case where the proprietor is not entitled to the patent. If proof is provided that the proprietor is not entitled, the court of a state may revoke the patent for that state. National law may provide that only the person entitled to the patent can invoke the ground (as is the case in e.g. DE).

2 **National prior rights**

In a revocation procedure, the court has to consider the compulsory provision of **Art.139(2)** on the effect of national prior rights against a European patent. Hence, national prior rights are also considered in a revocation procedure before courts, including national utility models as national prior rights (**Art.140**). Furthermore, national law may prohibit the granting of a national and a European patent for the same invention and having the same effective date and applicant (**Art.139(3)**).

Art. 138(2) If the grounds for revocation affect the European patent only in part, the patent shall be limited by a corresponding amendment of the claims and revoked in part.

1 **Revocation in part**

The wording of **Art.138(2)** makes it clear that limitation and partial revocation of a European patent are always to take the form of a corresponding amendment to the patent claims. This does away with the possibility, formerly provided in the EPC1973, to partially revoke a patent by amending the description or drawings (OJ 2007 se4 EN p.168).

The provision does not refer to national law, thereby making it in principle directly applicable without a need for provisions in national law.

As in European opposition proceedings and in accordance with the limitation procedure (see **Art.105a ff.**), the effect of limiting or revoking a European patent in national revocation proceedings is retroactive. Therefore, **Art.68** refers to national revocation proceedings. (OJ 2007 se4 EN p.168)

Art. 138(3) In proceedings before the competent court or authority relating to the validity of the European patent, the proprietor of the patent shall have the right to limit the patent by amending the claims. The patent as thus limited shall form the basis for the proceedings.

1 **Right to limitation of patent**

Art.138(3) establishes the right to self-limitation of the patent by the proprietor and is binding in national proceedings relating to the validity of European patents, thereby extending the degree of harmonisation.

It is designed to give the patent proprietors the right in such proceedings to submit an amended, i.e. limited, version of the claims that, in the proprietor's view, meets the objections to the validity of the patent. This limited version of the patent must then form the basis for subsequent proceedings. If the court or authority dealing with the case considers that the proprietor's limitation is insufficient, it may further limit the patent or revoke it in full.

Art. 139 Prior rights and rights arising on the same date

1 **Conflicting European and national applications**

The situation addressed by **Art.54(3)** of two conflicting European patent applications can also occur between a European application or patent and a national application or patent. **Art.139(1)** addresses the case where the European application or patent has the earlier filing or priority date, **Art.139(2)** the case where the national application or patent has the earlier date. **Art.139(3)** deals with the case of a European patent application and national patent application having the same effective date and being directed to the same invention. **Art.139(2)** and (3) constitute an exception to the exhaustive list of grounds for revocation of **Art.138**.

Art.139(1) and (2) do not state a substantive rule but refer to national law (in line with **Art.2(2)**). The historical reason is that Switzerland and Liechtenstein used the so-called 'prior claim' approach for prior rights until 2008. Under this approach, the prior right effect was determined by the claims of the granted patent, which were not allowed to overlap. **Art.139** accommodates this historical difference between the contracting states. For the same reason, **Art.139(1)** refers to the prior right effect of not only a European patent application but also of a European patent (see further G1/03 r.2.1.1 for the historical background).

See **Art.97(2):2** for double patenting between two European applications with the same effective date.

1.1 EXTENSION STATES AND VALIDATION STATES

The prior right effect in extension states (**Art.169:2**) is governed by Art.7 of the Extension Ordinance, which corresponds to **Art.139(1)** and (2) (OJ 1994 p.84). An earlier European application has the same prior right effect in an extension state against a later filed national application in that state as a national application, provided that the extension fee for that state was paid. A national application in an extension state has the same prior right effect against a subsequent European application extended to that state as it has against a later national patent application in that state. Where an extended European patent and a national patent in an extension state have the same effective date and have been granted to the same person or successor in title, the national patent ceases to have an effect, to the extent that it covers the same invention, as from the day of expiry of the opposition period or conclusion of any opposition proceedings (Art.8 Extension Ordinance, cf. **Art.139(3)**).

Similarly, a European application validated in a validation state (**Art.169:6**) has the same prior right effect against a later national application as a national application. However, it only has this effect if the validation fee has been paid to the EPO. The same applies if an earlier national application or patent is prejudicial to a later European patent validated in the validation state (e.g. OJ 2016 A5 §16 for Morocco).

See **Art.140:1** for the effect of national prior utility models and utility certificates.

Art. 139(1) In any designated Contracting State a European patent application and a European patent shall have with regard to a national patent application and a national patent the same prior right effect as a national patent application and a national patent.

1 **Prior right effect of European application and patent**

A European patent application constitutes a prior right against a national patent application in a designated state if the effective date (filing date or priority date) of the European application is earlier than the effective date of the national application and the publication date of the European application is on or after the effective date of the national application. If this is the case, the courts and patent office of the designated state must apply the same rules (of national law) as when a national patent application constitutes the prior right (**Art.139(1)**). Since 2008, all contracting states have specified in their national law the same rule as in **Art.54(3)**: the entire content of the earlier application is considered for novelty only.

The provision is also to be applied in the case of a national utility model application (**Art.140**).

A not-regularly published European application does not have a national prior right effect, just as it does not have a European prior right effect (**J5/81** r.3).

Art. 139(2) A national patent application and a national patent in a Contracting State shall have with regard to a European patent designating that Contracting State the same prior right effect as if the European patent were a national patent.

1 **Prior right effect of national application and patent**

A national patent application filed in a designated state constitutes a prior right against a European patent in that state if the effective date (filing date or priority date) of the national application is before the effective date of the European patent while the publication date of the national application is on or after the effective date of the European patent. If this is the case, a court examining the validity of the European patent over the national prior right must treat the European patent as a national patent and apply the rules of national law regarding the validity of national patents in view of national prior rights.

Since 2008, all contracting states have specified in their national law the same rule as in **Art.54(3)**: the entire content of the earlier application is considered for novelty only. The prior right effect of the national patent application is, however, confined to the state where it was filed.

The provision is also to be applied when a national utility model application forms a prior right against a European patent in a designated state (**Art.140**).

National patent applications as prior rights are never comprised in the state of the art considered by the EPO for patentability. Consequently, the existence of a national prior right is neither an obstacle to patentability under **Art.52-Art.57** nor a ground for opposition under **Art.100**. During the search carried out for the European application, national prior rights are not specifically looked for. However, if found, the applicant is informed accordingly (B-VI,4.2). The EPO carries out a top-up search to find relevant national prior rights at the end of the grant proceedings and informs the applicant of any found national prior rights in the **R.71(3)** communication (C-IV,7.2).

During substantive examination, the applicant may file a separate set of claims and a separate description and drawings for a designated state in view of a national prior right that exists in that state after the EPO has evaluated the prior right (**R.138**; G-IV,6; H-III,4.4). A proprietor can do the same in opposition (H-III,4.4). After grant, national prior rights can be considered in limitation proceedings (D-X,10.1) and asserted by third parties in national revocation proceedings (**Art.138**).

Art. 139(3) Any Contracting State may prescribe whether and on what terms an invention disclosed in both a European patent application or patent and a national application or patent having the same date of filing or, where priority is claimed, the same date of priority, may be protected simultaneously by both applications or patents.

1 **Protection through single route and double protection**

The purpose of **Art.139(3)** is to avoid that both a European and a national patent are granted for a single invention. The provision was intended as a first step in abolishing national patents (travaux préparatoires 1962, 3076/IV/62-D, p.114a). After the decision to restrict the EPC to a system for granting patents only, it was left to the contracting states whether or not to allow an invention to be protected through both the national route and the European route.

Contracting states can use the faculty given by **Art.139(3)** to include in their national law a provision prohibiting double patenting where a European application and a national application having the same applicant and the same date of filing both proceed to grant. They may also regulate national utility models on the same terms (**Art.140**).

The provision assumes that the European patent application or patent and the national application or patent have the same applicant or proprietor.

The provision does not cover, probably unintentionally, the typical case where a European application claims priority of a national application and designates the state in which the national application was filed. The phrase 'having the same date of filing ... of priority' should read 'having the same effective date'.

Some contracting states allow the protection of an invention by both a European patent and a national patent having the same effective date (see NatLaw table X, note 1). Other contracting states prioritise the European patent, generally by stipulating that the national patent ceases to have an effect to the extent that it protects the same invention. The date on which the national patent ceases to have an effect differs for most states: see NatLaw table X, note 1. Germany allows simultaneous protection only for (national) utility models, not for national patent applications or patents

(NatLaw table X). See also **Art.65:1** for the consequences of automatic validation of European patents.

Double patenting between a European patent application and a granted European patent is not covered by **Art.139(3)**. Instead, it is a ground for refusal of the European patent application by the EPO (**G4/19**, see **Art.97(2):2**).

Chapter III *Miscellaneous effects*

Art. 140 National utility models and utility certificates

Articles 66, 124, 135, 137 and 139 shall apply to utility models and utility certificates and to applications for utility models and utility certificates registered or deposited in the Contracting States whose laws make provision for such models or certificates.

Art.66 Equivalence of European filing with national filing
Art.124 Information concerning national patent applications
Art.135 Request for the application of national procedure
Art.137 Formal requirements for conversion
Art.139 Rights of earlier date or the same date

1 **General**

The national law of several contracting states provides protection for utility models, the national law of France for utility certificates (see NatLaw table VII, note 5).

According to **Art.66**, a European filing is regarded as a valid national filing for a utility model or certificate in the designated states giving protection for them.

The applicability of **Art.124** entails that applicants on request by the EPO must mention the contracting states in which they have filed utility models or certificates. Beware, **Art.124** requires an applicant to mention all states, i.e. not only contracting states, in which they have filed corresponding patent applications.

Art.135 and **137** allow a European patent application to be converted into a national utility model or certificate where the application is filed with a national office and not forwarded to the EPO in a timely manner and in such other situations as are allowed under national law. See **Art.135(1):3** and NatLaw table VII for the states that make use of the latter possibility.

The applicability of **Art.139(1)** means that a European patent application or patent has the same prior right effect in regard of utility models and certificates as national patent applications and patents. All contracting states use the 'whole contents' approach. The prior rights are only taken into account for assessing novelty, not for inventive step of the utility model and certificate.

The applicability of **Art.139(2)** means that national filings of utility models and certificates are effective as prior rights for European patents in the same way as they are effective as prior rights for national patents. Hence, prior utility models and certificates filed in a contracting state may be prejudicial to later filed European patent applications designating such a state. A utility model in Germany is not prejudicial for a later filed European patent designating Germany, but the rights of the patent may not be exercised until the lapse of the utility model.

The applicability of **Art.139(3)** means that it is up to national law to arrange for double protection. In Germany, for instance, simultaneous protection by a patent and utility model is allowed (NatLaw table X).

Art. 141 Renewal fees for European patents

1 **Transition of payment**
While the renewal fees for a European patent application are to be paid to the EPO, the renewal fees for the granted patent are to be paid to the national patent offices. **Art.141** lays down the transition of the obligation to pay. See NatLaw table VI. The renewal fees for a patent are payable to the national office to allow national offices to levy the fees according to their own scales of fees.

The national patent offices pay their expenses mainly from the renewal fees of granted European patents. The national offices must transfer 50% of the renewal fees paid for European patents to the EPO as decided by the Administrative Council (OJ 1984 p.296 and **Art.39(1)**).

Renewal fees for unitary patents and any additional fees must be paid to the EPO (**UPR.13(1)**). The EPO deducts its share of 50% firstly and secondly the costs incurred by it for carrying out the tasks under the UPR and distributes the remaining sum to the participating member states according to a distribution key which is not public (Decision Select Committee OJ 2016 A41 Art.3).

Art. 141(1) Renewal fees for a European patent may only be imposed for the years which follow that referred to in Article 86, paragraph 2.

Art.86(2) Termination of the obligation to pay renewal fees to the EPO

1 **Example of renewal fee payment**
The patent application is filed on 02.06.1978; the patent year then ends on 02.06.1979, the next patent year begins on 03.06.1979. A possible priority right has no influence on these dates. When the mention of the grant is published on 02.06.1980, no renewal fees need be paid to the EPO anymore, but instead from the third year onwards renewal fees must be paid to the national offices of the contracting states where the patent is to be kept in force, or to the EPO for a unitary patent (A-X,5.2.4). When the mention is published on 03.06.1980, the renewal fee in respect of the third year must still be paid to the EPO and is due 30.06.1980 (this will not happen in practice, see **Art.86(2):2**), while the renewal fees in respect of the fourth and following years must be paid to the national offices according to their national rules.

2 **National law**
NatLaw table VI indicates the national requirements for the payment of renewal fees, such as the amount of the renewal fees, due date, grace period and the requirement to appoint a representative. The minimum period for payment with a surcharge is six months (article 5bis(1) Paris Convention), national law may set a longer period. Particulars about the bank accounts of the national offices are given in NatLaw table VIII. The moment a patent lapses if a due renewal fee is not paid to a national office is governed by national law and is not stated in NatLaw.

Art. 141(2) Any renewal fees falling due within two months of the publication in the European Patent Bulletin of the mention of the grant of the European patent shall be deemed to have been validly paid if they are paid within that period. Any additional fee provided for under national law shall not be charged.

1 **Two-month period before national office**
The two months period is a safe period to allow for different rules in different states. If the renewal fees are paid within this period, they must be regarded as paid timely, irrespective of national law. See **Art.65:1** for the concurrence of the two-month period and the period of **Art.65(1)** for filing a translation of the patent.

PART IX SPECIAL AGREEMENTS

Art. 142 Unitary patents

Art. 142(1) Any group of Contracting States, which has provided by a special agreement that a European patent granted for those States has a unitary character throughout their territories, may provide that a European patent may only be granted jointly in respect of all those States.

1 **Unitary patent**
Art.142(1) provides the legal basis for a European patent to benefit from unitary effect according to EU regulation 1257/2012. Indeed, Art.1(2) of that regulation specifically states that it constitutes a special agreement within the meaning of **Art.142.** The EU regulation applies as of 01.06.2023 along with the Unified Patent Court Agreement (UPCA). See **Ante UPR:1** for the status of ratification of the UPCA.

Switzerland and Liechtenstein have concluded a treaty, which is a special agreement in the sense of **Art.142(1)**, providing that a European patent granted for Switzerland and Liechtenstein is a unitary patent and can only be granted jointly for those States. The treaty is published in OJ 1980 p.407.

Art. 142(2) Where any group of Contracting States has availed itself of the authorisation given in paragraph 1, the provisions of this Part shall apply.

Art. 143 Special departments of the European Patent Office

Art. 143(1) The group of Contracting States may give additional tasks to the European Patent Office.

Art. 143(2) Special departments common to the Contracting States in the group may be set up within the European Patent Office in order to carry out the additional tasks. The President of the European Patent Office shall direct such special departments; Article 10, paragraphs 2 and 3, shall apply mutatis mutandis.

Art.10(2) Functions and powers of the President
Art.10(3) Replacement of President by Vice-President

1 **Special departments**
According to **UPR.4**, a Unitary Patent Protection Division is established within the EPO as a special department within the meaning of **Art.143(2)**. This division is managed by the President of the EPO who is responsible for its activities to the Select Committee of the Administrative Council (**UPR.3**).

Art. 144 Representation before special departments

The group of Contracting States may lay down special provisions to govern representation of parties before the departments referred to in Article 143, paragraph 2.

Art.143(2) Special departments of the European Patent Office

1 **Representation**
The rules relating to representation and authorisation when acting before the Unitary Patent Protection Division of the EPO are the same as those applying to other departments of the EPO (**UPR.20(1)** and **UPR.20(2)**).

Art. 145 Select committee of the Administrative Council

Art. 145(1) The group of Contracting States may set up a select committee of the Administrative Council for the purpose of supervising the activities of the special departments set up under Article 143, paragraph 2; the European Patent Office shall place at its disposal such staff, premises and equipment as may be necessary for the performance of its duties. The President of the European Patent Office shall be responsible for the activities of the special departments to the select committee of the Administrative Council.

Art.143(2) Special departments of the European Patent Office

Art. 145(2) The composition, powers and functions of the select committee shall be determined by the group of Contracting States.

1 **Select committee for the unitary patent**
In preparation for the entry into force of the unitary patent under EU regulation 1257/2012, the participating member states set up a Select Committee of the Administrative Council. See OJ 2016 A41 and OJ 2022 A41-A42 for three published decisions of the Select Committee relating to the unitary patent.

Art. 146 Cover for expenditure for carrying out special tasks

Where additional tasks have been given to the European Patent Office under Article 143, the group of Contracting States shall bear the expenses incurred by the Organisation in carrying out these tasks. Where special departments have been set up in the European Patent Office to carry out these additional tasks, the group shall bear the expenditure on staff, premises and equipment chargeable in respect of these departments. Article 39, paragraphs 3 and 4, Article 41 and Article 47 shall apply mutatis mutandis.

Art.39(3), (4) Payments by the Contracting States in respect of renewal fees for European patents
Art.41 Advances
Art.47 Provisional budget
Art.143 Special departments of the European Patent Office

1 **Expenditure**
According to Art.10 of EU regulation 1257/2012, the expenses incurred by the EPO in carrying out its additional tasks relating to the Unitary Patent will be covered by the fees generated by the European patent with unitary effect, i.e. the renewal fees payable to the EPO according to **UPR.13**.

Art. 147 Payments in respect of renewal fees for unitary patents

If the group of Contracting States has fixed a common scale of renewal fees in respect of European patents, the proportion referred to in Article 39, paragraph 1, shall be calculated on the basis of the common scale; the minimum amount referred to in Article 39, paragraph 1, shall apply to the unitary patent. Article 39, paragraphs 3 and 4, shall apply mutatis mutandis.

Art.39(1) The part of the renewal fees to be paid to the EPO
Art.39(3), (4) Payments by the Contracting States in respect of renewal fees for European patents

1 **Renewal fees for Switzerland and Liechtenstein**
Switzerland and Liechtenstein have made use of **Art.147** and a single annual renewal fee is due for those states after grant. (OJ 1980 p.407).

2 **Renewal fees for the unitary patent**
A single renewal fee is payable annually to the EPO for a European patent with unitary effect (**UPR.13** and **RfeesUPP.2(1)**).

Art. 148 The European patent application as an object of property

Art. 148(1) Article 74 shall apply unless the group of Contracting States has specified otherwise.

Art.74 Application of national law to a European patent application as an object of property

Art. 148(2) The group of Contracting States may provide that a European patent application for which these Contracting States are designated may only be transferred, mortgaged or subjected to any legal means of execution in respect of all the Contracting States of the group and in accordance with the provisions of the special agreement.

1 **Unitary Patent as an object of property**
No use has been made of the provision for applications resulting in unitary patents: Art.3(2) of EU regulation 1257/2012 only relates to unitary patents after grant (see **Ante UPR:4**).

Art. 149 Joint designation

Art. 149(1) The group of Contracting States may provide that these States may only be designated jointly, and that the designation of one or some only of such States shall be deemed to constitute the designation of all the States of the group.

1 **Joint designation of states**
Switzerland and Liechtenstein have made use of this possibility, so that both states can only be designated together (OJ 1980 p.407, Art.2). Because under **Art.79** all contracting states are automatically deemed to be designated, paragraph 1 means in practice that the designations of Switzerland and Liechtenstein can only be withdrawn simultaneously.

Art. 149(2) Where the European Patent Office acts as a designated Office under Article 153, paragraph 1, paragraph 1 shall apply if the applicant has indicated in the international application that he wishes to obtain a European patent for one or more of the designated States of the group. The same shall apply if the applicant designates in the international application one of the Contracting States in the group, whose national law provides that the designation of that State shall have the effect of the application being for a European patent.

Art.153(1) PCT applications

1 **Liechtenstein-Switzerland designation**
Because all contracting states are automatically designated in a PCT application for both national and regional patent protection (R.4.9(a) PCT), a PCT application can be continued in the regional phase procedure before the EPO with joint designation of Liechtenstein or Switzerland and also in the national phase procedure before the Swiss Patent Office in order to obtain a national patent for these two states, granted by the Swiss Patent Office (PCT Applicant's Guide, National Chapter for CH).

Art. 149a Other agreements between the Contracting States

1 **General**
Art.149a was added in EPC2000 to create a legal basis for any further agreements between the EPC contracting states concerning such matters as translation requirements or litigation concerning European patents.

Art. 149a(1) Nothing in this Convention shall be construed as limiting the right of some or all of the Contracting States to conclude special agreements on any matters concerning European patent applications or European patents which under this Convention are subject to and governed by national law, such as, in particular
(a) an agreement establishing a European patent court common to the Contracting States party to it;
(b) an agreement establishing an entity common to the Contracting States party to it to deliver, at the request of national courts or quasi-judicial authorities, opinions on issues of European or harmonised national patent law;

(c) an agreement under which the Contracting States party to it dispense fully or in part with translations of European patents under Article 65;

(d) an agreement under which the Contracting States party to it provide that translations of European patents as required under Article 65 may be filed with, and published by, the European Patent Office.

Art.65 Translation of the European patent

1 **Special agreements on patent court and translation regime**
Art.149a(1) expressly underlines that the Convention does not prevent any contracting state from concluding with other contracting states agreements on any matters which under the EPC are governed by national law, in particular **Art.2, 64(2)** and **65** (OJ 2007 se4). Sub-paragraph (a) covers the Unified Patent Court Agreement. Sub-paragraph (c) covers the 'London Agreement' on translations, which has meanwhile entered into force (see **Art.65(1):2**).

Art. 149a(2) The Administrative Council shall be competent to decide that:

(a) the members of the Boards of Appeal or the Enlarged Board of Appeal may serve on a European patent court or a common entity and take part in proceedings before that court or entity in accordance with any such agreement;

(b) the European Patent Office shall provide a common entity with such support staff, premises and equipment as may be necessary for the performance of its duties, and the expenses incurred by that entity shall be borne fully or in part by the Organisation.

1 **Support of the EPO staff**
Art.149a(2) addresses the involvement of the European Patent Organisation once an agreement under paragraph (1)(a) or (b) has been concluded and entered into force (OJ 2007 se4). It is not envisaged that **Art.149a(2)(a)** is used for the Unified Patent Court.

PART X INTERNATIONAL APPLICATIONS UNDER THE PATENT COOPERATION TREATY

Art. 150 Application of the Patent Cooperation Treaty

1 **Relationship between PCT and EPC**
This article lays down the principles governing the interaction between the EPC and PCT, i.e. the prevalence rule for the provisions of the PCT over those of the EPC.

Art. 150(1) The Patent Cooperation Treaty of 19 June 1970, hereinafter referred to as the PCT, shall be applied in accordance with the provisions of this Part.

'This Part' refers to Part X of the EPC and appertaining implementing regulations, i.e. **Art.150-153** and **R.157-165**.

Art. 150(2) International applications filed under the PCT may be the subject of proceedings before the European Patent Office. In such proceedings, the provisions of the PCT and its Regulations shall be applied, supplemented by the provisions of this Convention. In case of conflict, the provisions of the PCT or its Regulations shall prevail.

1 **General**
This provision expressly refers to the PCT Regulations, as the PCT itself lacks a provision corresponding to **Art.164(1)** EPC declaring the PCT Regulations to be an integral part of the Treaty. (OJ 2007 se4 EN p.178)

2 **Prevalence of the PCT**
An international application may be subject to proceedings before the EPO, both in the international phase with the EPO acting as receiving Office (rO, **Art.151**), International Searching Authority or International Preliminary Examining Authority (ISA or IPEA, **Art.152**), and in the regional phase with the EPO acting as designated Office or elected Office (**Art.153**) (E-IX,1).

In both phases the EPO must apply the provisions of the PCT, supplemented by those of the EPC (**Art.150(2)**, second sentence).

In the international phase the EPO applies the PCT for both procedural and substantive issues, supplemented by a few procedural provisions of the EPC, e.g. **Art.75, 151, R.157-158** and Rfees for payments to the EPO. The EPO uses the provisions of the PCT for substantive issues, such as for priority (Art.8 PCT and, hence, Art.4 Paris Convention), search (Art.15 PCT) and examination (Art.33 PCT). The EPO boards of appeal held that they have no jurisdiction in the international phase unless the PCT or EPC explicitly states so (**J20/89; J14/98** r.2.1).

The entry of a Euro-PCT application into the European phase is governed by Art.22 and 39 PCT, supplemented by **R.159-165** EPC. Art.23 PCT prohibits the EPO to process the application under its regional procedure before entry. On the other hand, the regional procedure requires, among other things, payment of certain fees before entry. The conflict is solved by giving prevalence to the provisions of the PCT, as required by **Art.150(2)**, last sentence: **R.159(1)** extends the periods for payment until the date of entry. The EPC requirements for form and content may not be used to supplement those of the PCT (Art.27(1) PCT). Hence, an international application complying with the PCT requirements regarding form and content may not be objected to because of different requirements of the EPC after entry.

The processing of the Euro-PCT application by the EPO as designated and elected office after it has entered the regional phase is governed by the procedural provisions of the EPC, because the PCT has no procedural provisions for the period after entry into the regional phase.

Art.27(5) PCT allows a PCT contracting state to apply national law in respect of patentability of an invention claimed in an international application. The EPO as designated and elected office makes use of this provision and applies its own substantive requirements. Since the validity of a claimed priority has a direct effect on the patentability, the EPO applies the provisions of the EPC for determining the validity of a priority claim of a Euro-PCT application in the European phase. However, the filing of the declaration of priority for the international application follows the provisions of the PCT, because the filing is a purely formal requirement to be fulfilled before the receiving Office. (**T577/11** r.6.2 and 6.5.8; see also **Ante Art.87:1**)

Art. 151 The European Patent Office as a receiving Office

The European Patent Office shall act as a receiving Office within the meaning of the PCT, in accordance with the Implementing Regulations. Article 75, paragraph 2, shall apply.

Art.75(2) Compulsory national filing because of national law relating to secrecy and national security
Implemented by:
R.157 The EPO as receiving Office

1 **EPO acting as receiving Office**

Art.151 deals with the role of the EPO as a PCT receiving Office (rO) and the regulations for the filing and transmittal of international applications (GL/PCT-EPO A).

2 **Filing and transmittal of the international application**

The EPO acts as a receiving Office in accordance with the provisions of **R.157**. These provisions permit residents and nationals of EPC contracting states to file international applications with the EPO as receiving Office. The reference to **Art.75(2)** in **Art.151** allows national law to prescribe filing of international applications with its national office, e.g. for reasons of national security, which national office will transmit the applications to the EPO as receiving Office.

Certain EPC contracting states prescribe that residents must always file the 'first' application with their national office, for example residents of France may file directly with the EPO or the IB only if claiming priority from an earlier application filed in France at the INPI. (AG-General Information, Annex B1; **Art.75(2)** EPC)

The Guidelines (E-IX,1) do not provide information about the EPO acting as receiving Office and instead refer to the GL/PCT-EPO. See **R.157** for the implementation.

Art. 152 The European Patent Office as an International Searching Authority or International Preliminary Examining Authority

The European Patent Office shall act as an International Searching Authority and International Preliminary Examining Authority within the meaning of the PCT, in accordance with an agreement between the Organisation and the International Bureau of the World Intellectual Property Organization, for applicants who are residents or nationals of a State party to this Convention. This agreement may provide that the European Patent Office shall also act for other applicants.

Implemented by:
R.158 Non-unity before EPO as ISA or IPEA

1 **EPO acting as ISA**

Art.152 governs the operation of the EPO as international searching authority (ISA) and as international preliminary examining authority (IPEA) under the PCT. Detailed information about the EPO as ISA can be found in the GL/PCT-EPO part B, and PCT Applicant's Guide Annex D(EP).

The agreement mentioned in **Art.152** is the agreement pursuant to Art.16(3) PCT and Art.32(2) PCT ('EPO-WIPO Agreement'). The current EPO-WIPO Agreement is published in OJ 2017 A115, with amendments published in OJ 2018 A24, OJ 2020 A35, OJ 2020 A68, OJ 2022 A37, OJ 2023 A37 and OJ 2024 A29. A consolidated version is published on the WIPO website.

The EPO has made use of the second sentence of **Art.152** in Art.3(1) and Annex A, item (i), of the EPO-WIPO Agreement; hence each rO can specify the EPO as competent for the searching of international applications filed with it (R.35 PCT). Most rO's have specified the EPO as competent ISA, including the rO's of the EPC contracting states (see GL/PCT-EPO B-II,1.1 and PCT Applicant's Guide Annex C). The EPO as ISA accepts English, French, and German as search languages, and Dutch if the rO is the patent office of the Netherlands (Annex A, item (ii), of the EPO-WIPO Agreement). If the application is filed in a different language and the EPO is to carry out the international search, an invitation under R.12.3 PCT is sent by the rO to file a translation.

If the EPO acts as ISA, the applicant must pay a search fee to rO for the benefit of the EPO (R.16.1 PCT, see **Rfees2(1)2** for the amount). See OJ 2025 A26 for details about a refund of the international search fee when the EPO as ISA can make use of an earlier search and **Rfees2(1):17** for the reduction of the international search fee for applicants from certain states. Details about the use of the international search report in the procedure before the EPO as designated Office are given in **Art.153(6)-(7)** (see also **R.164(2)**).

See **R.158(1)** and **R.158(3)** and section 4 below for the procedure in the event of a non-unity finding by the EPO acting as ISA.

2 **EPO acting as SISA**

The EPO can also act as an International Searching Authority competent to carry out supplementary international searches (SISA) according to R.45bis PCT (Art.3(4) EPO-WIPO Agreement). Details can be found in GL/PCT-EPO B-XII, and AG-IP Annex SISA(EP).

The fee for a supplementary international search carried out by the EPO is set at the same level as the fee for an international search (**Rfees2(1)2**). This fee, along with the supplementary international search handling fee, should be paid to the IB (not the EPO). The scope of a supplementary international search by the EPO is the same as the scope of an international search by the EPO. Although no separate written opinion is established, the EPO will provide explanations under R.45bis.7(e) PCT that are of equal value to a written opinion established by the EPO as ISA. (OJ 2017 A115, Art.3(4))

3 **EPO acting as IPEA**

The EPO can act as International Preliminary Examination Authority (IPEA) under Art.32(3) PCT (Art.3(2) EPO-WIPO Agreement). Detailed information about the EPO as IPEA can be found in GL/PCT-EPO part C, and AG-IP Annex E(EP).

The purpose of the international preliminary examination is to provide in the international phase a notice for the offices elected by the applicant, containing non-binding advice on the patentability of the claimed invention (Art.33(1) PCT). The advice relieves the burden on the grant procedure in the respective states. Details of the examination procedure are given in Art.34 PCT and R.66 PCT. The amount of the preliminary examination fee of R.58 PCT if the EPO acts as IPEA is specified in **Rfees2(1)19**. See **Rfees2(1):17** for a reduction of the fee.

See **R.158(2)-(3)** EPC and section 4 below for the procedure following a non-unity finding by the EPO acting as IPEA.

The EPO may act as an IPEA according to Art.32 PCT for all rO's for which it can act as ISA (**Art.152**, second sentence, Annex A of the EPO-WIPO Agreement, GL/PCT-EPO C-II,2). However, the EPO is only competent to act as IPEA for a patent application if the international search report was established by the EPO or by an ISA located in and operating for an EPC contracting state (see EPO-WIPO Agreement, Annex A). The EPO will therefore only act as IPEA if the international search was carried out by the EPO or by the Austrian, Finnish, Spanish, Swedish or Turkish patent office or the Nordic Patent Institute or the Visegrad Patent Institute (GL/PCT-EPO C-II,2). See **Rfees2(1):6.1** for a reduction of the supplementary European search fee in the regional phase if the international search was carried out by one of these other European ISA's.

The examination fee before the EPO as elected Office is reduced if the EPO acted as IPEA (**Rfees14(2)**).

4 **Non-unity**

The provision for payment of an additional fee in the case of a non-unity finding by the ISA is given in Art.17(3)(a) PCT and R.40 PCT. R.16.1 PCT allows an ISA to request a fee for carrying out the international search and other tasks such as additional searches in the case of non-unity.

The EPO levies a search fee for additional international searches according to **R.158(1)** EPC and **Rfees2(1)2**.

In the case of a non-unity finding by the EPO acting as IPEA, the applicant will be requested to restrict the claims or to pay an additional fee for a further examination (Art.34(3)(a) PCT, R.68 PCT). The EPO levies a fee for each additional invention examined according to **R.158(2)** EPC, see **Rfees2(1)19**.

When the EPO acts as ISA or IPEA, the additional fees may be paid under protest (R.40.2(c-e) PCT, R.68.3(c-e) PCT). A protest fee must be paid (**R.158(3)**, **Rfees2(1):16**). The EPO is obliged to examine the protest (OJ 2010 p.322).

Non-unity can also occur if the EPO acts as SISA; a protest procedure is available (R.45bis.6 PCT; **Rfees2(1):16**; OJ 2010 p.316, 320). At the supplementary search stage there is no opportunity for the applicant to have further inventions searched upon payment of additional search fees (OJ 2010 p.316, §9).

Art. 153 The European Patent Office as designated Office or elected Office

Implemented by:
R.159 The EPO as a designated or elected Office - Requirements for entry into the European phase
R.160 Consequences of non-fulfilment of certain requirements
R.161 Amendment of the application
R.162 Claims incurring fees
R.163 Examination of certain formal requirements by the EPO
R.164 Unity of invention and further searches of a Euro-PCT application
R.165 The Euro-PCT application as conflicting application under Art.54(3)

1 **General**
The requirements for entry into the regional phase before the EPO are set out in **R.159(1)** EPC; see also E-IX,2.

Art. 153(1) The European Patent Office shall be
(a) a designated Office for any State party to this Convention in respect of which the PCT is in force, which is designated in the international application and for which the applicant wishes to obtain a European patent, and
(b) an elected Office, if the applicant has elected a State designated pursuant to letter (a).

1 **Designation**
An international application designates all states which are contracting states of the PCT on the international filing date for a national patent and, if available, also for a regional patent (R.4.9(a)(i),(iii) PCT). Because every contracting state of the EPC is also a contracting state of the PCT, an international application automatically designates all EPC contracting states for the grant of a European patent under the all-inclusive designation system of R.4.9 PCT. The EPO is hence a designated Office for every international application, except for the rare case that the applicant expressly withdraws the designations of the EPC contracting states for a European patent (R.90bis.2 PCT).

Historically, the applicant had to write out the designated states in the PCT Request, indicating expressly for which states the designation was for a European patent, and pay a designation fee in the international phase (Art.2(1)(ii),(2) PCT). The requirements were gradually simplified until the current all-inclusive designation system of R.4.9 PCT was introduced in 2004.

The EPO is an elected Office if a Demand is filed (R.53.7 PCT).

Art. 153(2) An international application for which the European Patent Office is a designated or elected Office, and which has been accorded an international date of filing, shall be equivalent to a regular European application (Euro-PCT application).

1 **Euro-PCT applications**
This provision governs the conditions under which an international application has the effect of a European application (implementing Art.11(3) PCT) and defines the term 'Euro-PCT application'.

When an international application has been accorded an international filing date (Art.11(3) PCT), it is regarded as a regular national application and also as a regular application for a European patent (Art.2(vi) and Art.45 PCT). This is similar to **Art.66** EPC providing for the equivalence of a European application with a national application. Because the EPO is a designated or elected Office for every international application, each international application is formally also a Euro-PCT application, even before entry into the regional phase before the EPO (**Art.153(1)**; R.4.9 PCT). In daily practice, the term 'Euro-PCT application' is mainly used for international applications that entered the regional phase before the EPO.

Art. 153(3) The international publication of a Euro-PCT application in an official language of the European Patent Office shall take the place of the publication of the European patent application and shall be mentioned in the European Patent Bulletin.

1 **International publication**
Art.153(3) and **Art.153(4)** are closely related and deal with two different situations.

Art.153(3) deals with an international application that was published in the international phase (Art.21 PCT) in English, French or German. In this situation, the effects of the international publication take effect immediately at the time of the international publication, for instance, provisional protection in the EPC contracting states under **Art.67(1)**, subject to any national requirements set under **Art.67(3)** (Art.29 PCT).

Art.153(4) deals with the situation that the international publication was published in a language other than English, French or German. Upon entry into the European regional phase, the applicant has to furnish to the EPO a translation into English, French or German, which is subsequently published by the EPO. In line with Art.29(2) PCT, the provisional protection in the EPC contracting states only starts when the EPO publishes the translation, provided that any national requirements under **Art.67(3)** EPC are fulfilled.

Note that **Art.153(3)** does not define the start of the provisional protection when the international application is published in an official EPO language; on the other hand, **Art.153(4)** does not define which publication will take the place of the publication of the European patent application when the international publication is not in an official EPO language.

2 **Effect of international publication**
Art.153(3) specifies that the publication of an international application under Art.21 PCT in an official language of the EPO takes the place of the publication of the European patent application. This is of special importance for the start of provisional protection. Since the provisional protection laid down in **Art.67** starts at the date of publication of the European patent application, it starts at the date of the publication under Art.21 PCT for an international application published in an official EPO language, subject to

the possible need to file translated claims in a national language under **Art.67(3)**.

The accuracy of any translation made in the international phase is not checked by the EPO; it forms the basis of the grant procedure before the EPO. Correction of errors in the translation is allowed under Art.26 and 28 PCT.

See **Art.153(5)** and **R.165** for the prior right effect of an international application.

Art. 153(4) If the Euro-PCT application is published in another language, a translation into one of the official languages shall be filed with the European Patent Office, which shall publish it. Subject to Article 67, paragraph 3, the provisional protection under Article 67, paragraphs 1 and 2, shall be effective from the date of that publication.

Art.67(1) Rights conferred by a European patent application after publication
Art.67(2) Minimum rights conferred by application
Art.67(3) National requirements for publication and communication

1 **Publication of translation and provisional protection**
An international application published in a non-EPO language in the international phase will be re-published by the EPO in an official EPO language after entry into the European regional phase. The publication of the translated application includes all documents that were part of the international publication, including the claims as originally filed and any claims as amended under Art.19 PCT; any amendments filed on or after entry into the European phase are not published (E-IX,2.5.1).

Although not explicitly mentioned in **Art.153(4)**, payment of the 'national fee' (Art.22(1) PCT) equal to the 'filing fee' (**Rfees2(1)1**) is one of the requirements for entry into the regional phase before the EPO (see also **R.159(1)(c)**; **R.165**; E-IX,2.1.5.1). The EPO may only act and proceed to publish the translated application after entry into the European regional phase (Art.23(1) PCT). The provisional protection will be effective from the date of that publication (**Art.153(4)**, second sentence), provided any national requirements under **Art.67(3)** to file or submit translated claims have been met.

The EPO has not published guidance on the time of publication of the translation. In practice, the translation of the international application including the international search report will be published approximately 6 weeks after entry into the European phase; however, occasionally the publication may be up to 12 weeks after regional entry.

Art. 153(5) The Euro-PCT application shall be treated as a European patent application and shall be considered as comprised in the state of the art under Article 54, paragraph 3, if the conditions laid down in paragraph 3 or 4 and in the Implementing Regulations are fulfilled.

Art.54(3) European prior right
Implemented by:
R.159(1) Requirements for entry into European regional phase
R.165 Euro-PCT as conflicting application

1 **Treatment as European application**
This provision deals with two separate matters : one the hand the conditions for entry into the European phase, implemented in **R.159(1)**, and on the other hand the conditions for the Euro-PCT application to be treated as a prior right under **Art.54(3)**, implemented in **R.165**.

Since the travaux préparatoires EPC2000 state that this provision gives the conditions for entry into the European phase and those for considering a Euro-PCT application as a European prior right, it must be concluded that the word 'treated' refers to 'processed' and 'examined' in the sense of Art.23 PCT. Since this processing and examining is independent of the publication of the Euro-PCT application dealt with by **Art.153(3)** and **(4)**, the reference to these two paragraphs in **Art.153(5)** should be interpreted as pertaining only to the conditions for considering a Euro-PCT application as a prior right under **Art.54(3)**. The requirements for entry into the European phase are provided in **R.159(1)**.

Art. 153(6) The international search report drawn up in respect of a Euro-PCT application or the declaration replacing it, and their international publication, shall take the place of the European search report and the mention of its publication in the European Patent Bulletin.

1 **International search report takes place of European search report**
Concerning the designation fee, **Art.153(6)** is implemented by **R.159(1)(d)** which provides that the designation fee must be paid before expiry of the period of 31 months from the priority date, or from the filing date if no priority is claimed, unless the period of **R.39** has not yet expired. The six-month period starts to run from the publication of the international search report (in the international phase) for Euro-PCT applications by the effect of **Art.153(6)**.

For the request for examination including the examination fee, **Art.153(6)** is implemented by **R.159(1)(f)** which provides that the request for examination must be filed before the expiry of the 31-month period (including payment of the examination fee) unless the six-month period of **R.70(1)** has not yet expired. This six-month period also starts to run from the publication of the international search report (in the international phase) for Euro-PCT applications by the effect of **Art.153(6)**.

These two six-month periods are not yet expired by the end of the 31-month period in the event that the publication of the international search report is delayed until after 25 months from the priority date, or from the filing date if no priority is claimed. Such a delay of the international search is however rare. Note that the international search report can be published separately after the publication of the international application (R.48.2(g) PCT).

The drawing up of a supplementary European search report pursuant to **Art.153(7)** or the publication of the translation by the EPO pursuant to **Art.153(4)** does not affect the six-month period for payment of the designation and examination fees. A supplementary European search report entitles an applicant to the invitation of **R.70(2)** to indicate whether the applicant wishes to proceed further (E-IX,2.5.3).

The declaration mentioned in **Art.153(6)** is the declaration that the ISA issues if it finds that no meaningful search can be made (Art.17(2)(a) PCT). The declaration is published (Art.21(3) PCT); the publication takes the place of the mention of the publication of the European search report.

Art. 153(7) A supplementary European search report shall be drawn up in respect of any Euro-PCT application under paragraph 5. The Administrative Council may decide that the supplementary search report is to be dispensed with or that the search fee is to be reduced.

1 **Supplementary European search report**

Although **Art.153(6)** states that the international search report takes the place of the European search report, a supplementary European search report is drawn up by the EPO for any international application that enters the European phase unless the EPO as ISA drew up the international search report or the EPO drew up a supplementary international search report in the international phase (**Art.153(7)** and the implementing Decision of the Administrative Council of OJ 2009 p.594; see also Not. EPO OJ 2024 A33 §3(a)).

A search fee is payable for the supplementary European search (**R.159(1)(c)**). Details of the procedure in case of lack of unity of invention during the supplementary European search are given in **R.164(1)**.

No time limit has been set for completing the supplementary search report; in the past, it could take more than six years after regional entry, e.g., as in EP1120644. Under current practice, the EPO always accelerates the supplementary European search (OJ 2015 A93).

The supplementary European search report is not published as such, although its establishment is mentioned in the Bulletin. However, the supplementary search report is available from file inspection and is marked as 'A4'. (B-X,4)

Supplementary European search reports are accompanied by a search opinion in which the search division gives an opinion on whether the application and the invention to which it relates seem to satisfy the requirements of the EPC (**R.62(1)**; B-X, 1). A response to a negative opinion is mandatory (**R.70a(2)**).

2 **Search fee for the supplementary European search**

The search fee for the supplementary European search report is, in principle, equal to the usual European search fee (**Rfees2(1)2**; **R.159(1)(c)**) but is reduced in certain cases. See **Art.153(7):4** for details of the reduction. See **Rfees9(1)** for a possible refund of the search fee in respect of the supplementary European search.

If a supplementary European search report is to be drawn up (see **Art.153(7):3** below), the search fee must be paid within 31 months from the priority date (**R.159(1)(e)**). If not paid in due time, the application is deemed to be withdrawn (**R.160(1)**). Further processing is available (**Art.121** and **R.135**).

3 **No supplementary European search required**

No supplementary European search report will be drawn up for an international application entering the European phase for which an international search report has been drawn up by the EPO as ISA or for which the EPO has drawn up a supplementary international search report under R.45bis.7 PCT. Hence, no search fee under **R.159(1)(c)** needs to be paid in those cases. (Dec. Administrative Council OJ 2009 p.594; Not. EPO OJ 2024 A33 §3(a))

The supplementary European search report is also dispensed with if the EPO as ISA issued a declaration that no search was possible under Art.17(2)(a) PCT (**Art.153(6)**; E-IX,3.2).

4 **Reduction of search fee for the supplementary European search**
The amount of the search fee for the supplementary European search report is set out in **Rfees2(1)2**.

If an ISA of a contracting state of the EPC (the Austrian, Finnish, Spanish, Swedish or Turkish Patent Office, or the Nordic or Visegrad Patent Institute) has carried out the international search or a supplementary international search under R.45bis PCT, the amount of the search fee for the supplementary European search will be reduced significantly (see Dec. AC OJ 2024 A3 Art.4(1)).

Art. 154 (deleted)

Art. 155 (deleted)

Art. 156 (deleted)

Art. 157 (deleted)

Art. 158 (deleted)

PART XI TRANSITIONAL PROVISIONS (DELETED)

PART XII FINAL PROVISIONS

Art. 164 Implementing Regulations and Protocols

Art. 164(1) The Implementing Regulations, the Protocol on Recognition, the Protocol on Privileges and Immunities, the Protocol on Centralisation, the Protocol on the Interpretation of Article 69 and the Protocol on Staff Complement shall be integral parts of this Convention.

1 **Parts of the Convention**

The Implementing Regulations and the Protocols have the same legal effect as the EPC; the rules for their validity, revision, languages, etc. are the ones given in the EPC (see **Art.164(2)** and notes).

The Rules relating to Fees do not form part of the Convention and were added after the Munich Diplomatic Conference. **Art.51(4)** contains a reference to the Rules relating to Fees.

The text of the Protocols on Recognition and on the Interpretation of **Art.69** are included in this book. The Protocol on Centralisation is discussed in section 2 below. The text of the Protocol on Privileges and Immunities of the European Patent Organisation (Protocol on Privileges and Immunities) and the text of the Protocol on the Staff Complement of the European Patent Office at The Hague (Protocol on Staff Complement) are available on the website of the EPO and were published in OJ 2001 se4. These Protocols deal with organisational matters and do not directly affect parties to patent proceedings.

2 **Protocol on Centralisation**

The Protocol on the Centralisation of the European Patent System and on its Introduction (Protocol on Centralisation) essentially contains organisational provisions about how the national patent offices of the EPC contracting states had to adapt to accommodate the EPO when it was created. The text of the Protocol can be found in OJ 2001 se4 and also on the EPO website. Only a few provisions are still of practical relevance. Section I(1) of the Protocol provides the historical background to the creation of the branch of the EPO in The Hague (**Art.6(2)**). The sub-office of the EPO in Berlin is based on Section I(3)(a); see **Art.6(2):2**.

Section I(2) and II provide that national offices of EPC contracting states may not act as ISA or IPEA under the PCT. By way of exception, under Section III(1) a patent office of an EPC contracting state in which the official language is not an EPO language may act as ISA and IPEA for international applications filed by nationals or residents of that state and adjacent states. In addition, the national office of Austria acts as ISA based on a separate agreement with the EPO (OJ 1979 p.249). See also **Art.152**.

Art. 164(2) In case of conflict between the provisions of this Convention and those of the Implementing Regulations, the provisions of this Convention shall prevail.

1 **Priority rules**
The provisions of most protocols prevail over any contradictory provisions of the Convention (see e.g. section VII of the Protocol on Centralisation and Article 11 of the Protocol on Recognition).
Rules of priority for provisions:
1 the PCT has priority over the EPC (**Art.150(2)** EPC, second sentence);
2 the Protocol on Recognition has priority over the EPC (**Prot. Rec. Art.11**);
3 the Protocol on Centralisation has priority over the EPC (Section VII);
4 the Articles of the EPC have priority over the Rules of the EPC (**Art.164(2)** EPC).

2 **Conflict and ambiguity**
Despite frequent allegations by parties, there have been only few instances in which a board of appeal found a conflict between the Articles and the Rules of the EPC. In **T1063/18**, **R.28(2)** was considered to be in conflict with **Art.53(b)**. Having regard to **Art.164(2)**, **Art.53(b)** prevailed and **R.28(2)** was held to be invalid; note that **R.28(2)** was in effect reinstated by **G3/19**. In **T2558/18** hn it was decided that **R.71(6)** does not apply if a board remits a case to an examining division with an order to grant a patent with the claims, description and drawings as specified by the board, because of a conflict with **Art.111**.
See **Art.23(4):1** for conflicts between the Implementing Regulations and the Rules of Procedure of the BoA.

Art. 165 Signature – Ratification

Art. 165(1) This Convention shall be open for signature until 5 April 1974 by the States which took part in the Inter-Governmental Conference for the setting up of a European System for the Grant of Patents or were informed of the holding of that conference and offered the option of taking part therein.

1 **Signatory, participating and invited states**
The following states signed the Convention by 05.041974: Belgium, Denmark, France, Federal Republic of Germany, Greece, Ireland, Italy, Liechtenstein, Luxembourg, Netherlands, Norway, Sweden, Switzerland and the United Kingdom.
The following states only took part in the negotiations: Austria, Finland, Monaco, Portugal, Spain, Türkiye and Yugoslavia.
The following states were invited but did not take part in the negotiations: Cyprus and Iceland.

Art. 165(2) This Convention shall be subject to ratification; instruments of ratification shall be deposited with the Government of the Federal Republic of Germany.

Art. 166 Accession

Art. 166(1) This Convention shall be open to accession by:
(a) the States referred to in Article 165, paragraph 1;

(b) any other European State at the invitation of the Administrative Council.

Art.165(1) States which took part in the Inter-Governmental Conference for setting up the EPC or were offered the option of taking part

Art. 166(2) Any State which has been a party to the Convention and has ceased to be so as a result of the application of Article 172, paragraph 4, may again become a party to the Convention by acceding to it.

Art.172(4) States which cease to be a party after not ratifying a revised text of the EPC

Art. 166(3) Instruments of accession shall be deposited with the Government of the Federal Republic of Germany.

Art. 167 (deleted)

1 **Reservations for pending patent applications**
Art.167 offered contracting states the possibility of making certain reservations regarding the implementation of the EPC, for a limited period of time. Only three contracting states made reservations and all of them have now expired. Since newly acceding contracting states cannot make further reservations, **Art.167** is now otiose and has been deleted in EPC2000. However, **Art.167(5)** remains applicable to European patents granted in respect of European patent applications filed during the period in which any reservation was effective. (OJ 2007 se4)

The reservation for Spain that European patents are ineffective in Spain in so far as they confer protection on chemical or pharmaceutical products as such is still effective for applications filed before 08.10.1992 and divisional applications having an effective date of filing before said date and still pending before the EPO (OJ 1992 p.301).

Since 01.01.1996 Spain has been bound by the TRIPS agreement, which permits patents for any inventions, whether products or processes, without discrimination as to the field of technology. In spite of the fact that Spain has not yet withdrawn the reservation, the EPO recommends not to maintain a separate set of restricted claims for Spain. If applicants maintain the separate set of claims, they will not enjoy protection for chemical or pharmaceutical products as such in Spain. (OJ 2007 p.258 and p.439)

The reservation for Greece is still applicable. (OJ 2007 p.258)

Validation states may also make reservations for a limited period when concluding a bilateral validation agreement with the EPO (see e.g. **Art.169:6**).

Art. 168 Territorial field of application

Art. 168(1) Any Contracting State may declare in its instrument of ratification or accession, or may inform the Government of the Federal Republic of Germany by written notification at any time thereafter, that this Convention shall be applicable to one or more of the territories for the external relations of which it is responsible. European patents granted for that Contracting State shall also have effect in the territories for which such a declaration has taken effect.

1 **Territorial extent**

NatLaw table X, note 2 states the territorial field of application of the EPC. A few special cases are listed below.

The EPC is applicable to New Caledonia (FR), French Polynesia (FR), the Southern and Antarctic territories (FR), Wallis (FR), Département St-Pierre-et-Miquelon (FR), Mayotte (FR) and the Isle of Man (UK). The territory of the Federal Republic of Germany includes the territory of the former DDR for applications filed since 03.10.1990. A European patent granted for the Netherlands will also be valid for Bonaire, Sint Eustatius and Saba as part of the Netherlands and for Curaçao and Sint Maarten.

The EPC is *not* applicable to Greenland (DK), the Faroe Islands (DK) and Aruba (NL). A European patent granted in respect of the UK may be registered in overseas states and territories as indicated in OJ 2018 A97. The procedure to extend a European patent designating GB to Hong Kong is set out in OJ 2009 p.546.

Art. 168(2) If the declaration referred to in paragraph 1 is contained in the instrument of ratification or accession, it shall take effect on the same date as the ratification or accession; if the declaration is notified after the deposit of the instrument of ratification or accession, such notification shall take effect six months after the date of its receipt by the Government of the Federal Republic of Germany.

Art. 168(3) Any Contracting State may at any time declare that the Convention shall cease to apply to some or to all of the territories in respect of which it has given notification pursuant to paragraph 1. Such declaration shall take effect one year after the date on which the Government of the Federal Republic of Germany received notification thereof.

Art. 169 Entry into force

1 **Contracting states EPC**

1.1 LIST

The contracting states of the EPC and the date of entry into force of the EPC for each state are listed below.

Additionally, membership of the European Union (EU) is specified. A * indicates that the EU member state does not participate in EU Regulation 1257/2012 (note, UPR.5(2)(a) refers only to the participating EU member states).

Participation in the London Agreement (LA) is also shown. This agreement reduces the translation requirements for validating the European patent after grant (see **Art.65(1):2**) and OJ 2020 A55).

Finally, the states for which the UPCA is in force are shown (UP). Unitary patents have effect in these states (Art.18(2) EU Regulation 1257/2012). Situation on 01.04.2025.

Albania	AL	01.05.2010		LA	
Austria	AT	01.05.1979	EU		UP
Belgium	BE	07.10.1977	EU	LA	UP
Bulgaria	BG	01.07.2002	EU		UP
Croatia	HR	01.01.2008	EU*	LA	
Cyprus	CY	01.04.1998	EU		
Czech Republic	CZ	01.07.2002	EU		
Denmark	DK	01.01.1990	EU	LA	UP
Estonia	EE	01.07.2002	EU		UP

Finland	FI	01.03.1996	EU	LA	UP
France	FR	07.10.1977	EU	LA	UP
Germany	DE	07.10.1977	EU	LA	UP
Greece	GR	01.10.1986	EU		
Hungary	HU	01.01.2003	EU	LA	
Iceland	IS	01.11.2004		LA	
Ireland	IE	01.08.1992	EU	LA	
Italy	IT	01.12.1978	EU		UP
Latvia	LV	01.07.2005	EU	LA	UP
Liechtenstein	LI	01.04.1980		LA	
Lithuania	LT	01.12.2004	EU	LA	UP
Luxembourg	LU	07.10.1977	EU	LA	UP
Macedonia, North	MK	01.01.2009		LA	
Malta	MT	01.03.2007	EU		UP
Monaco	MC	01.12.1991		LA	
Montenegro	ME	01.10.2022			
Netherlands, the	NL	07.10.1977	EU	LA	UP
Norway	NO	01.01.2008		LA	
Poland	PL	01.03.2004	EU		
Portugal	PT	01.01.1992	EU		UP
Romania	RO	01.03.2003	EU		UP
San Marino	SM	01.07.2009			
Serbia	RS	01.10.2010			
Slovakia	SK	01.07.2002	EU		
Slovenia	SI	01.12.2002	EU	LA	UP
Spain	ES	01.10.1986	EU*		
Sweden	SE	01.05.1978	EU	LA	UP
Switzerland	CH	07.10.1977		LA	
Türkiye	TR	01.11.2000			
United Kingdom	GB	07.10.1977		LA	

1.2 TRANSITIONAL PROVISION

A state for which the EPC enters into force after the filing date of a European application cannot be designated in that application (**J14/90**). Similarly, the EPO can only act under the PCT as designated Office for states designated in an international application in respect of which the EPC was in force on the date on which the international application was filed (**J30/90**).

A state for which the EPC entered into force, for example, Montenegro on 01.10.2022, can be designated in a European application filed on or after the date of entry into force of the EPC for that state, i.e. 01.10.2022 for Montenegro. From that date, such a state is included in the designation of the EPC contracting states in the Request for Grant form. To allow Montenegro to be designated, the EPO accorded a European patent application filed in September 2022 the filing date of 01.10.2022 if the applicant expressly requested that filing date when filing the application. (OJ 2022 A78 §2)

Nationals, residents and legal persons having their place of business in such a state may file international applications with the EPO as receiving Office as from the date of entry into force of the EPC for that state, i.e. from 01.10.2022 for Montenegro. No European patents for Montenegro can be granted on the basis of international applications with a filing date prior to 01.10.2022. Euro-PCT applications entering the European phase with an international filing date prior to 01.10.2022 will not include the designation of Montenegro as an EPC contracting state (**Art.153(1)(a)**). (OJ 2022 A78 §3)

1.3 **BREXIT**

The UK withdrew from the EU on 31.01.2020. As the European Patent Organisation is independent of the EU, the withdrawal has no impact on the UK's status within the European Patent Organisation. Proceedings before the European Patent Office including examination, opposition, appeal, limitation and revocation are thus not affected by the withdrawal. The UK also remains a signatory to the London Agreement (see **Art.65(1):2**), which dispenses with translation requirements. (OJ 2020 A19)

The principles governing representation before the EPO are similarly unaffected by the withdrawal. UK-based professional representatives under **Art.134(2)** and legal practitioners under **Art.134(8)** continue to be fully entitled to represent parties in proceedings before the EPO. (OJ 2020 A19)

2 Extension Agreement

Since 1994 several states, not being contracting states, have concluded an Extension Agreement with the European Patent Organisation. The president of the EPO is authorised by the Administrative council to conclude such agreements under **Art.33(4)**. The agreements provide European patent applicants a cost-effective way of obtaining protection in those states. The rules under national law governing the extension of European patents to an extension state are set out in an Extension Ordinance for that state. See OJ 1994 p.75 for the complete text of an Extension Ordinance. The extension states are not contracting states, and have therefore no right to vote in the Administrative Council (**Art.34(1)**).

The extension of a European patent to such a state is not based on a direct application of the EPC but on national law modelled on the EPC. The extension procedure and the legal effects of the extension are governed solely by national law. Only those provisions of the Convention, Implementing Regulations and Rules relating to Fees which are referred to in the Extension Ordinance apply. The provisions referred to relate only to time limits and arrangements for paying the extension fee. Thus, EPC provisions concerning the legal remedies available to an applicant and the right to appeal do not apply in respect of actions taken by the EPO under the extension procedure. The principle of good faith is only applicable when the EPO is acting within the framework of the EPC; hence, the principle does not apply to acts carried out under an Extension Agreement (**J14/00** r.1.4). The EPO merely assists the extension states by undertaking the administrative task of collecting extension fees and passing on the greater part of them (**J14/00** r.1.2.2).

3 Extension system

An extension for a state can be requested for any European patent application filed on or after the Extension Agreement has entered into force for that state. The request for extension is automatically deemed to be made for any application filed on or after the entry into force of the Extension Agreement. The request may be indicated on the Request for Grant form, which indication is merely for information purposes.

By paying an extension fee for each extension state in which protection is desired (see **Rfees3(1)**), comparable to paying the designation fee for contracting states, applicants maintain the extension of their application. The extension fee must be paid to the EPO within the period of **R.39(1)** or **R.159(1)(d)**; see **Art.79(2):2.1**; Ext. Agr. and **J14/00** for remedies. The Rules relating to Fees apply mutatis mutandis. When extension fees are paid, the states for which they are intended must be specified. The amount of the extension fee for each extension state is EUR 102 as laid down in Art.3 of the Extension Ordinance (OJ 1994 p.82 n.b. the original DEM 200 converts to

EUR 102 at the exchange rate fixed when the Deutsche Mark was replaced by the Euro; see also Schedule of fees OJ 2024 sp4 p.27).

Any adverse decision of the Receiving Section in relation to the extension of a European patent application or payment of the extension fee is not open to appeal under **Art.106**, but a remedy can be sought under the national jurisdiction of the extension state (**J14/00** r.1.3.4).

The request for extension is deemed withdrawn if the extension fee is not paid in due time, or the application is refused, withdrawn or deemed withdrawn. Extension fees are not refunded. A divisional application may be extended to the same states to which the earlier application is extended.

A Euro-PCT application can also be extended to a PCT contracting state which has concluded an Extension Agreement, provided that both the EPO and that state are designated. An application can be extended to a state irrespective of whether the national phase before the patent office of that state has already been commenced or not. The extension fee must be paid to the EPO in the same way as the designation fee specified by **R.159(1)(d)**.

Renewal fees are payable to the national offices of extension states for the years following that in which the mention of the grant is published.

A flow chart of the Euro-direct and Euro-PCT extension procedure is published in OJ 1994 p.86 and 87.

4 Effects of extension

A European patent application for which extension has been requested is equivalent to a duly filed national application, and after publication confers a provisional protection corresponding to that of **Art.67**. The granted European patent has the same effect as a national patent, provided that, if the state prescribes so, a translation of the specification or claims is filed and a publication fee is paid equivalent to **Art.65**. National law may provide for rules covering cases of collision between and double protection arising from European and national patents or applications, similar to **Art.139(1)** and **(2)**. The specific requirements for each extension state are provided in NatLaw.

The provisional protection is lost ab initio if the request for extension subsequently lapses. Similarly, to the extent that the patent is revoked in EPO opposition proceedings, the provisional protection and other effects of the patent are again lost ab initio.

The extension states publish in their national register data of European applications and patents extending to their territory (A-III,12.5).

Detailed information about the extension system is published in OJ 1994 p.75; A-III,12 gives a summary. NatLaw Introduction and Tables contain details of the extension system for each extension state.

5 Extension states

States having concluded an Extension Agreement with the EPO and the date of entry into force of the Agreement for each state:

Bosnia and Herzegovina	BA	01.12.2004

The Extension Agreements of Albania, Croatia, North Macedonia and Serbia terminated with the entry into force of the EPC in these countries. As from the date of entry into force of the EPC, European patent applications and patents can no longer be extended to these countries. The extension system continues to apply to all European and international applications filed prior to that date as well as to all European patents granted in respect of such applications. (OJ 2007 p.638 §4; OJ 2008 p.507 §4; OJ 2010 p.96 §4; 394 §4).

On 01.11.2004 an Extension Agreement entered into force for the union of Serbia and Montenegro (OJ 2004 p.563). After the declaration of independence of Montenegro on 03.06.2006 the Extension Agreement did not apply anymore to the country (OJ 2007 p.406).

On 01.03.2010 a new Extension Agreement entered into force for Montenegro (OJ 2010 p.10). The Extension Agreement of Montenegro terminated on 30.09.2022 with the entry into force of the EPC for Montenegro. The extension system will, however, continue to apply to all European and international applications with a filing date prior to 01.10.2022, to divisional applications derived from earlier applications with a filing date prior to 01.10.2022 (Article 76(1) EPC) and to all European patents granted in respect of such applications.

6 **Validation Agreement**

The EPO can conclude a bilateral international agreement with a state not being an EPC contracting state that European patent applications and patents can be validated for that state and will confer essentially the same protection as patents granted by the EPO for the EPC contracting states.

Validation for such a state is deemed requested for any European patent application filed on or after entry into force of the agreement and for any Euro-PCT application designating both the EPO and the validation state and having an international filing date on or after the entry into force. Validation is not available for applications filed prior to that date or for any European patents resulting from such applications. The request is deemed withdrawn if the validation fee is not paid in due time. (**Art.79(2):2.3**; A-III,12)

The following table gives the states that can be validated and the date of entry into force:

Cambodia	KH	01.03.2018	(OJ 2018 A16)
Georgia	GE	15.01.2024	(OJ 2023 A105)
Lao People's Democratic Republic	LA	01.04.2025	(OJ 2025 A22)
Moldova	MD	01.11.2015	(OJ 2015 A85)
Morocco	MA	01.03.2015	(OJ 2015 A20)
Tunisia	TN	01.12.2017	(OJ 2017 A85)

See **Art.79(2):2.2** for validation fees for each validation state.

Specific requirements for each validation state are provided in NatLaw. Note that Cambodia excludes pharmaceutical products from patent protection until at least 2033, thereby benefitting from a World Trade Organisation waiver (OJ 2018 A16).

The procedure for extension and validation is the same. The distinction between them is mainly geographical. Validation Agreements are not limited to Europe and can be concluded with European and non-European states, even though non-European states have no prospect of acceding to the EPC (**Art.166**).

The unfortunate choice of the word 'validation' for this type of extension may cause confusion with the validation of a European patent after grant to obtain a valid patent in a contracting state (see **Art.65:1**).

Art. 169(1) This Convention shall enter into force three months after the deposit of the last instrument of ratification or accession by six States on whose territory the total number of patent applications filed in 1970 amounted to at least 180 000 for all the said States.

1 **Entry into force of EPC**
The condition of this paragraph was fulfilled on 07.10.1977. The EPC entered into force on this date for Belgium, France, Federal Republic of Germany, Luxembourg, Netherlands, Switzerland, and the United Kingdom. The EPO opened on 01.06.1978.

Art. 169(2) Any ratification or accession after the entry into force of this Convention shall take effect on the first day of the third month after the deposit of the instrument of ratification or accession.

Art. 170 Initial contribution

Art. 170(1) Any State which ratifies or accedes to this Convention after its entry into force shall pay to the Organisation an initial contribution, which shall not be refunded.

Art. 170(2) The initial contribution shall be 5% of an amount calculated by applying the percentage obtained for the State in question, on the date on which ratification or accession takes effect, in accordance with the scale provided for in Article 40, paragraphs 3 and 4, to the sum of the special financial contributions due from the other Contracting States in respect of the accounting periods preceding the date referred to above.

Art.40(3), (4) Level of fees and payments-Special financial contributions

Art. 170(3) In the event that special financial contributions were not required in respect of the accounting period immediately preceding the date referred to in paragraph 2, the scale of contributions referred to in that paragraph shall be the scale that would have been applicable to the State concerned in respect of the last year for which financial contributions were required.

Art. 171 Duration of the Convention

The present Convention shall be of unlimited duration.

Art. 172 Revision

Art. 172(1) This Convention may be revised by a Conference of the Contracting States.

1 **Revision of Art.63**
A Diplomatic Conference of the contracting states on 17.12.1991 in its competence according to **Art.172(1)** drew up an act revising **Art.63** relating to extension of the term of a European patent. This first revision of the EPC entered into force on 04.07.1997.

2 **Overall revision of the EPC (EPC2000)**

A first Diplomatic Conference for the overall revision of the EPC convened in November 2000 and adopted on 29.11.2000 a revised text of the EPC, referred to as EPC2000. The Act revising the Convention has been printed in OJ 2001 se4 pp.1-53 and is also available on the EPO website (OJ 1999 p.54; OJ 2000 p.173). The aim of the revision was (1) to take into account developments in international law, in particular the TRIPS Agreement and the Patent Law Treaty 2000, (2) to introduce a limitation procedure (Art.105a-c) and the possibility to have a board of appeal decision reviewed (Art.112a), both at the request of the user community, and (3) to transfer procedural detail to the Implementing Regulations to enhance flexibility.

A Conference Resolution expresses the need for another diplomatic conference to deal with subjects not dealt with in the first Diplomatic Conference, such as provisions on software and biotechnological inventions and the Community patent (OJ 2001 se4 p.52).

The travaux préparatoires to the Diplomatic Conference are available on the EPO web site here: https://www.epo.org/en/legal/epc/archive/documentation-epc-revision-2000/travaux-preparatoires.

The Diplomatic Conference authorised the Administrative Council (Art.3 of the Act revising the Convention) to draw up a new text of the revised EPC, including the amendments adopted by the Diplomatic Conference, to align its wording in the three languages, and to draw up transitional provisions. The Administrative Council made minor amendments to the text adopted by the Diplomatic Conference and adopted the new text and the transitional provisions by its decision of 28.06.2001 (OJ 2001 se4 pp.54-140). The complete text of the Articles of EPC2000 as adopted by the decision of the Administrative Council on 28.06.2001, the Implementing Regulations as adopted by decision of the Administrative Council of 12.12.2002 and explanatory remarks about the amendment of the Rules and the transitional provisions have been reproduced in OJ 2003 se1 pp.1-208. A trilingual version of the Articles and the Implementing Regulations is published in OJ 2007 se1. OJ 2007 se4 EN synoptically presents EPC1973 and EPC2000, showing the changes with explanatory remarks and detailed transitional provisions. Gaps in the transitional provisions are being closed by case law; see e.g. **J10/07** r.1 and **T616/08** r.5-17.

The Diplomatic Conference was convened before the anticipated accession of several new contracting states. The new member states that joined the EPC after 2002 had to ratify EPC2000. Since 11 new states joined, the minimum of 15 states to start the procedure for entry into force was already achieved on 13.12.2005.

EPC2000 entered into force on 13.12.2007. All contracting state had ratified EPC2000 at that date.

Art. 172(2) The Conference shall be prepared and convened by the Administrative Council. The Conference shall not be validly constituted unless at least three-quarters of the Contracting States are represented at it. Adoption of the revised text shall require a majority of three-quarters of the Contracting States represented and voting at the Conference. Abstentions shall not be considered as votes.

Art. 172(3) The revised text shall enter into force when it has been ratified or acceded to by the number of Contracting States specified by the Conference, and at the time specified by that Conference.

Art. 172(4) Such States as have not ratified or acceded to the revised text of the Convention at the time of its entry into force shall cease to be parties to this Convention as from that time.

1 **No ratification or accession**
The severe punishment for not ratifying or acceding to a revised text aims at keeping the text of the Convention identical for all contracting states. A state which has ceased to be party may accede again to the Convention according to **Art.166(2)**. See **Art.175** and **176** for the consequences of ceasing to be a party to the EPC.

Art. 173 Disputes between Contracting States

Art. 173(1) Any dispute between Contracting States concerning the interpretation or application of the present Convention which is not settled by negotiation shall be submitted, at the request of one of the States concerned, to the Administrative Council, which shall endeavour to bring about agreement between the States concerned.

1 **Dispute resolution**
If the contracting states cannot reach agreement on interpretation of the EPC, a contracting state may submit the issue to the Administrative Council, which will endeavour to bring about agreement.

An example of an issue about which the contracting states have not been able to reach agreement on is the definition of the patent term (see **Art.63(1):1**). Since the contracting states could not reach agreement on the definition during preparatory discussions in epi committees, it is unlikely that the same contracting states will reach agreement in the Administrative Council.

If after six months the Administrative Council has not reached agreement, a contracting state may submit the dispute to the International Court of Justice under **Art.173(2)** for a binding decision.

Art.173 thus provides a method for forced resolution of disputes on the interpretation of the EPC. Such a resolution requires that at least one contracting state is willing to submit the dispute to the Administrative Council and to the International Court of Justice.

Art. 173(2) If such agreement is not reached within six months from the date when the dispute was referred to the Administrative Council, any one of the States concerned may submit the dispute to the International Court of Justice for a binding decision.

Art. 174 Denunciation

Any Contracting State may at any time denounce this Convention. Denunciation shall be notified to the Government of the Federal Republic of Germany. It shall take effect one year after the date of receipt of such notification.

Art. 175 Preservation of acquired rights

Art. 175(1) In the event of a State ceasing to be party to this Convention in accordance with Article 172, paragraph 4, or Article 174, rights already acquired pursuant to this Convention shall not be impaired.

Art.172(4) Revision
Art.174 Denunciation

Art. 175(2) A European patent application which is pending when a designated State ceases to be party to the Convention shall be processed by the European Patent Office, as far as that State is concerned, as if the Convention in force thereafter were applicable to that State.

Art. 175(3) Paragraph 2 shall apply to European patents in respect of which, on the date mentioned in that paragraph, an opposition is pending or the opposition period has not expired.

Art. 175(4) Nothing in this Article shall affect the right of any State that has ceased to be a party to this Convention to treat any European patent in accordance with the text to which it was a party.

Art. 176 Financial rights and obligations of former Contracting States

Art. 176(1) Any State which has ceased to be a party to this Convention in accordance with Article 172, paragraph 4, or Article 174 shall have the special financial contributions which it has paid pursuant to Article 40, paragraph 2, refunded to it by the Organisation only at the time when and under the conditions whereby the Organisation refunds special financial contributions paid by other States during the same accounting period.

Art.40(2) Level of fees and payments-Special financial contributions
Art.172(4) Revision
Art.174 Denunciation

Art. 176(2) The State referred to in paragraph 1 shall, even after ceasing to be a party to this Convention, continue to pay the proportion pursuant to Article 39 of renewal fees in respect of European patents remaining in force in that State, at the rate current on the date on which it ceased to be a party.

Art.39 Payments by the Contracting States in respect of renewal fees for European patents

Art. 177 Languages of the Convention

The provision determines the languages in which the Convention is drawn up and the mutual relation of the three language versions of the Convention.

Art. 177(1) This Convention, drawn up in a single original, in the English, French and German languages, shall be deposited in the archives of the Government of the Federal Republic of Germany, the three texts being equally authentic.

1 **Three languages of the EPC**
The authentic text of the EPC is the text as set out in the hard-copy edition of the EPC as published by the EPO (see e.g. OJ 2008 p.1 and 'Terms and conditions of use for the website of the EPO', section 4.4). See OJ 2018 A98 for the html and pdf versions of the EPC.

All three texts are equally authentic. None of the three texts is a translation. The three texts can help to find the clear, well-defined will of the legislator. According to **Art.33(3)** of the Vienna Convention, all terms in each of the three texts should have the same meaning. If there is a discrepancy between the texts, the term should be interpreted in line with the goal of the EPC. Therefore, the Boards of Appeal often refer to the other texts to find the correct interpretation. A few examples:

A combination product comprising two sequentially administered medications can be seen as a product, especially a composition according to **Art.53(c)** and **Art.54(4)**, and, hence, can be protected as a product for use in therapy (first medical indication). The German term 'Stoffgemische' does not cover such a kit of parts, but the wider English and French term 'composition' does. (**T9/81**)

A substantial procedural violation is required for reimbursement of the appeal fee (**R.103**). The German text of the provision is clearer than the English and French texts: 'wesentlicher Verfahrensmangel' indicates an objective deficiency affecting the entire proceedings. (**J7/83**)

Proprietors can file an opposition against their own patent, as decided on the ground of text comparison (**G1/84**). If there were a difference between 'any person' and 'any third person' the text would have made that clear. Note that self-opposition is not allowed anymore after **G9/93**.

Art. 177(2) The texts of this Convention drawn up in official languages of Contracting States other than those specified in paragraph 1 shall, if they have been approved by the Administrative Council, be considered as official texts. In the event of disagreement on the interpretation of the various texts, the texts referred to in paragraph 1 shall be authentic.

There are no official texts yet in other languages.

Art. 178 Transmission and notifications

Art. 178(1) The Government of the Federal Republic of Germany shall draw up certified true copies of this Convention and shall transmit them to the Governments of all signatory or acceding States.

Art. 178(2) The Government of the Federal Republic of Germany shall notify to the Governments of the States referred to in paragraph 1:
(a) the deposit of any instrument of ratification or accession;
(b) any declaration or notification received pursuant to Article 168;
(c) any denunciation received pursuant to Article 174 and the date on which such denunciation comes into force.

Art.168 Territorial field of application

Art.174 Denunciation of Convention by contracting state

Art. 178(3) The Government of the Federal Republic of Germany shall register this Convention with the Secretariat of the United Nations.

IN WITNESS WHEREOF, the Plenipotentiaries authorised thereto, having presented their Full Powers, found to be in good and due form, have signed this Convention.

Done at Munich this fifth day of October one thousand nine hundred and seventy-three

Implementing Regulations to the Convention on the Grant of European Patents

of 5 October 1973
as adopted by decision of the Administrative Council of the European Patent Organisation of 7 December 2006 and
as last amended by decision of the Administrative Council of the European Patent Organisation of 10 December 2024
as in force as from 1 April 2025
Any references to persons made in the EPC Implementing Regulations are to be understood as being gender-neutral.

PART I IMPLEMENTING REGULATIONS TO PART I OF THE CONVENTION

Chapter I *General Provisions*

R. 1 Written proceedings

Amended by decision of the Administrative Council of 14.12.2023, which entered into force on 01.04.2024 (OJ 2024 A16; CA/D 26/23). The final words of the rule 'on paper' were deleted by the amendment.

In written proceedings before the European Patent Office, the requirement to use the written form shall be satisfied if the content of the documents can be reproduced in a legible form.

1 **General**
R.1 provides the possibility of electronic filing and all-electronic two-way communication. It specifies what documents fulfil the requirement to use the written form. (OJ 2003 se1 p.159)

2 **Form of written documents**
In written proceedings a document is regarded as being a written document if it can be reproduced in a legible form (**R.1**). Hence, an electronic file that can be processed by a computer program to produce a legible document is considered to be a written document.

Further requirements relating to the physical properties and the layout of the documents making up the patent application are governed by **R.49**. **Requirements relating to** documents filed after the application are specified in **R.50**.

The means by which written documents may be filed are set out in **R.2**.

R. 2 Filing of and formal requirements for documents

R. 2(1) In proceedings before the European Patent Office, documents may be filed by delivery by hand, by postal services or by means of electronic communication. The President of the European Patent Office shall lay down the details and conditions and, where appropriate, any special formal or technical requirements for the filing of documents. In particular, the President of the European Patent Office may specify that confirmation must be supplied. If such confirmation is not supplied in due time, the European patent application shall be refused; documents filed subsequently shall be deemed not to have been received.

Amended, in force since 01.04.2015 (OJ 2015 A17, A36 §1, 5).

Amended by decision of the Administrative Council of 10.12.2024, which entered into force on 01.04.2025 (OJ 2025 A16). The amendment was introduction of gender-neutral language.

1 **Filing of documents**

The President of the EPO is responsible for deciding the means by which documents fulfilling the requirement to use the written form (**R.2(1)**) may be filed at the EPO.

The Decisions of the President give an exhaustive list of the methods by which European patent applications and further documents may be filed. An application filed in another way, such as by telegram, telex or similar means, will be considered not to have been received (Dec. Pres. OJ 2019 A18 Art.1(3); see also **R.40(1):1.1**). The same applies to further documents (A-VIII,2.5). In general, e-mail cannot be used to perform a procedural act (OJ 2000 p.458; A-VIII,2.5); for exceptions see **R.2(1):9** below. As of 01.07.2024, fax is no longer a valid method of filing patent applications and other documents with the EPO (Dec. Pres. OJ 2024 A41 and Not. EPO OJ 2024 A42). European patent applications may still be filed by fax with the national authorities of the contracting states that allow it (A-II,1.1.2, Not. EPO OJ 2024 A42).

The President may specify that a confirmation copy must be supplied in certain circumstances (**R.2(1)**).

Recommended practice for filing requests with the EPO, in particular the forms that should be used and the formal requirements that apply, is given in Not. EPO OJ 2019 A79 section I.

Whereas **R.2** relates to the means that a party may use when communicating with the EPO, **R.125** governs the means by which the EPO may notify a party.

2 **Bulk requests**

The EPO permits the filing of a bulk request, i.e. a single request that concerns more than one application or patent (OJ 2019 A79). A bulk request may be used, for example, when multiple applications are being simultaneously transferred or when an applicant who has filed multiple applications changes address.

The relevant request should be filed only for the first application or patent concerned, indicating its full application number. The request should then clearly indicate that it concerns more than one application or patent and a separate sheet with the further application numbers should be included. The request should preferably be filed electronically using one of the EPO bulk request forms. Having filed the request, the requester should preferably send a complete list of all the application numbers as an Excel file by e-mail to facilitate processing by the EPO. (OJ 2019 A79 §17-20)

If the request is unclear or incomplete, the EPO will ask for clarification (OJ 2019 A79 §23). See **Rfees5(2):2.1** for payments in respect of multiple applications.

3 **Acknowledgement of receipt**

The EPO or national authority will always acknowledge receipt of a patent application (see **R.35(2)** and A-II,3.1 for European applications and **R.157(1):3** for international applications). The receipt of any document filed by electronic means is automatically acknowledged during the submission (see Dec. Pres. OJ 2024 A88, Art.11). However, for documents filed on paper (excluding new applications), the EPO's former practice of offering users the possibility of receiving acknowledgement of receipt was abolished as of 01.02.2024 (Not. EPO OJ 2023 A108). From this date, documents filed after the filing of an application may be accompanied by Form 1038 (letter accompanying subsequently filed items) but a copy will not be returned to the user. Instead, the EPO will indicate the date and location of receipt of the document concerned and upload the form to the electronic file.

4 Paper filing

R.2(1) allows European patent applications and further documents to be filed as a paper version delivered by hand or by post to the EPO or a national authority under **Art.75**. The mail addresses of the EPO filing offices are given in Not. EPO OJ 2018 A18, those of the national authorities in NatLaw Table II, note 1. In Munich and Berlin, the EPO and the German Patent Office are located in neighbouring buildings. The filing date of documents intended for the EPO but received by the German Patent Office and forwarded to the EPO will be the date of their actual receipt at the EPO (OJ 2005 p.444).

Debit orders may only be filed electronically (ADA.7.1.2); see ADA.12.1 for an exception if an application is filed with a national authority under **Art.75** (A-II,1.6).

For delivery by hand, the application documents may be handed over personally at one of the EPO filing offices during office hours. The date of filing accorded will be the date of handing over. See Not. EPO OJ 2018 A18 for the applicable EPO office hours.

Automated mailboxes provided by the EPO in Munich (Zollstrasse) and Berlin are available at any time. The other buildings in Munich and the office in the Hague have no automated mailbox; outside office hours, documents may be handed to the porter. (Dec. Pres. OJ 2017 A11 Art.1(3))

Filing by post includes both a state postal service and private delivery services, e.g. courier services (CA/47/14 §11, 16). Filing by post and by using certain courier services benefits from the protection under **R.133** for missing time limits in case of delays in the transmission. The date of filing accorded to an application filed with the EPO by post is the date of receipt at an EPO filing office (Not. EPO OJ 2005 p.44 §5.5). The date of filing accorded to an application filed with a national authority under **Art.75** is the date of receipt by the national authority (**Art.75(1)(b)**, last sentence).

5 Electronic filing

Documents including European patent applications may be filed electronically with the EPO as set out in Dec. Pres. OJ 2024 A88. The EPO encourages the online filing of applications by charging a reduced filing fee (see **Rfees2(1)1**).

European patent applications may also be filed electronically with the national authorities of those contracting states which so permit (**Art.75(1)(b)**; Dec. Pres. OJ 2024 A88 Art.2(2)). See e.g. Not. EPO OJ 2007 se3 A.6 for the electronic filing of European patent applications with the German patent office.

The EPO provides four different methods for electronic filing, each having different software requirements and each differing in terms of the documents that can be filed. The methods are Online Filing using the internet (OLF), Online Filing using a data carrier (OLF), Online Filing 2.0 and EPO Contingency Upload Service. All of these methods use the internet to transmit documents to the EPO, except Online Filing using a data carrier.

Where required, documents can be signed using a facsimile signature, i.e. an image of a handwritten signature, a text string between two forward slashes, or, when using OLF, an enhanced electronic signature. (Dec. Pres. OJ 2024 A88 Art.10)

Sequence listings must be filed electronically in xml format complying with WIPO Standard ST.26. If such a format is not available on filing, a sequence listing can first be submitted in pdf format and then subsequently filed in the correct format along with the payment of a late furnishing fee (see **R.30(3)**). See Dec. Pres. OJ 2021 A96 and A97 as well as Dec. Pres. OJ 2024 A54 and A55 and the user guides for electronic filing for details.

Electronic filing, with the exception of the EPO Contingency Upload Service, allows the filing of a pre-conversion archive in addition to the filed documents. The pre-conversion archive may contain original documents, i.e. before conversion into pdf or xml, in the format in which they were created, e.g. docx format. The original documents may be helpful in the event that quality issues arise and where colour is used. They do not become publicly available. (Dec. Pres. OJ 2024 A88 Art.9 and user guides)

The date of receipt of a document filed electronically is the date the document is received at the EPO or national authority (OJ 2018 A46 §2).

If a document filed electronically contains a part that is illegible or incomplete, that part will be deemed not to have been received. If the document is infected with a computer virus or contains other malicious software, it will be deemed to be illegible and therefore not to have been received. If a document is filed electronically using a method that is not allowed for the filing of such a document (e.g. if a priority document is filed using the EPO Contingency Upload Service), the document will be deemed not to have been received. In all these cases, the EPO notifies the sender without delay. (Dec. Pres. OJ 2024 A88 Art.12, Art.3)

The provisions for electronic filing apply not only to the filing of European patent applications and further documents but also to the filing of international applications and further documents filed with the EPO in the international phase (Dec. Pres. OJ 2024 A88 Art.2(1)).

Third parties can use a special method for the electronic filing of observations as set out in **Art.115:1.**

5.1 ONLINE FILING USING THE INTERNET (OLF)

Documents to be filed online with OLF are packaged on a local computer and submitted by the sender in encrypted form to a secure server at the EPO (Dec. Pres. OJ 2024 A88 Art.6(1)). The software to be used on the local computer can be downloaded free of charge from the EPO website, and regular software updates are made available to add functionality and update forms and fees. Currently, the earliest software version accepted by the EPO is set out in OJ 2024 A89 (in force since 01.01.2025).

Until the end of 2024, filing using OLF could be carried out using an activated smart card and certificates issued or accepted by the EPO. The EPO stopped issuing smart cards at the end of 2023 (Not. EPO OJ 2023 A97). Their use has been discontinued as of 01.01.2025 (Not. EPO OJ 2024 A90). Instead of using smart cards, the EPO now offers two-factor authentication methods to access EPO online services such as OLF (Not. EPO OJ 2023 A50, Not. EPO OJ 2023 A97, Not. EPO OJ 2024 A90).

OLF can be used for the filing of any document in all proceedings under the EPC, including opposition proceedings, limitation and revocation proceedings, appeal proceedings and proceedings for review under **Art.112a** (Dec. Pres. OJ 2024 A88 Art.2(1)). However, OLF can only be used for the filing of priority documents if they have been digitally signed by the issuing authority and the EPO accepts the signature (Dec. Pres. OJ 2024 A88 Art.3(1); see **R.53(1):2**). A priority document that is not duly signed is deemed not to have been received and the EPO informs the sender without delay (Dec. Pres. OJ 2024 A88 Art.3(3)).

The format of the documents to be filed must be xml or pdf or, for sequence listings, xml format complying with WIPO Standard ST.26 (Dec. Pres. OJ 2024 A88 Art.8(1), Art.4, and user guide OLF). The EPO will send an invitation to refile any document that does not comply with the specified format. Consequences of non-compliance vary – in the case of a European patent application, a refusal is issued (Dec. Pres. OJ 2024 A88 Art.8(3)). The EPO provides software to generate documents in xml format and to convert documents to pdf format with embedded fonts. The EPO provides an acknowledgement of receipt within the submission session (Dec. Pres. OJ 2024 A88 Art.11(1)(a)).

The EPO has announced the decommissioning of the online filing with OLF by end of 2025 on their website, but it has not yet (01.04.2025) been published in the OJ.

5.2 ONLINE FILING USING A DATA CARRIER (OLF)

Documents can be filed electronically with the EPO using a data carrier (Dec. Pres. OJ 2024 A88 Art.1(2)). A data carrier can be used for the filing of documents in all proceedings under the EPC. The documents and formats permitted are the same as those permitted when using Online Filing using the internet (see section 5.1 above).

Documents are prepared, signed where required, and packaged by the sender on a local computer using the same software applicable to Online Filing using the internet (OLF). The packaged file must be stored on a data carrier of the CD-R or a DVD±R type (Dec. Pres. OJ 2024 A88 Art. 1(2)).

The data carrier must be accompanied by a paper document identifying the applicant and/or the representative and containing an address for correspondence and a listing of the files stored. (Dec. Pres. OJ 2024 A88 Art.6(2))

The data carrier and the document must be filed with the EPO by hand, delivery service or post (Dec. Pres. OJ 2024 A88 Art.11(6)).

OLF is a misnomer when referring to the use of a data carrier, and this likely stems from the use of the OLF software for preparing the documents.

5.3 ONLINE FILING 2.0

Online Filing 2.0 was launched on 01.04.2021. The use of Online Filing 2.0 requires an EPO account registered for Online Filing 2.0 and a two-factor authentication (Dec. Pres. OJ 2024 A88 Art.5(2), OJ 2023 A50 II). Online Filing 2.0 is a secure web-based application that requires no local software other than an authenticator software if it is used for two-factor authentication. Online Filing 2.0 covers all proceedings before the EPO, including proceedings before the boards of appeal. Online Filing 2.0 also integrates WIPO's ePCT service for the filing and management of PCT applications. (Dec. Pres. OJ 2024 A88 Art.7)

After the launch of Online Filing 2.0, the pilot project has been maintained for the purpose of testing the filing of application documents in docx format (EPO website 'Continuation of the Online Filing 2.0 pilot project for DOCX filing'). Currently, docx appears to be available only for filings in one of the official EPO languages, as the required section headings of the application documents are given only in these languages, although the information on the EPO website mentions the filing of translations of application documents. Note also that the docx standard used, ISO/IEC 29500-1:2008, is outdated. (OJ 2020 A44, A45)

As of 01.04.2026, submitted documents and drafts will be stored in Online Filing 2.0 for a maximum of five years (OJ 2024 A32).

5.4 **EPO CONTINGENCY UPLOAD SERVICE**

A further online filing means, EPO Contingency Upload Service, was introduced on 01.07.2023. It has fully replaced Web-Form Filing as of 01.01.2025 (Not. EPO OJ 2023 A50, Not. EPO OJ 2024 A90) and is to be used in case the filing is urgent and the other EPO online filing services are unavailable. Priority documents cannot be filed through it (Dec. Pres. OJ 2024 A88 Art.3(2)). The documents must be in pdf, with the exception of sequence listings (Dec. Pres. OJ 2024 A88 Art.8(2) and Art.4). Debit orders may be filed through it exceptionally if other methods for filing debit orders are unavailable and it is the last day of the period for paying the fee (A-X,4.2.3, see **Rfees5(2):2.1**). The service can be accessed with an EPO account or via a link sent per email (Dec. Pres. OJ 2024 A88 Art.5(3)).

The receipt of documents is acknowledged within the service itself. A separate acknowledgement is sent only for new applications, as for paper filings (see **R.2(1):3**) (Dec. Pres. OJ 2024 A88 Art.11(5)).

5.5 **MYEPO**

The EPO has an online tool called MyEPO (previously MyEPO Portfolio), which is a secure, web-based online service for parties to proceedings before the EPO (including proceedings relating to European patents with unitary effect). Users are able to receive electronic notifications from the EPO via Mailbox, file documents electronically, inspect files (including unpublished files belonging to the party concerned), share documents informally with the EPO during consultations and use a representative area to administer entries in the list of representatives. (Dec. Pres. OJ 2024 A20 and Not. EPO OJ 2024 A21; Dec. Pres. OJ 2024 A19)

Electronic filing using MyEPO must generally comply with the requirements of Dec. Pres. OJ 2024 A88 (concerning the electronic filing of documents) unless otherwise provided in Dec. Pres. OJ 2024 A20 (concerning MyEPO). Users may respond to a communication from the EPO and file requests or notifications, together with accompanying documents, to the extent that such a response, request or notification is provided for in MyEPO and included in a list published on the EPO website or in any other suitable form. Accompanying documents must currently be filed in pdf or tiff format (with the exception of sequence listings for which xml format is required; Dec. Pres. OJ 2021 A96) and, for documents other than evidence, must comply with the pdf and tiff formats specified in the PCT Administrative Instructions (Part 7 and Annex F). Receipt is acknowledged electronically by the EPO within the submission session.

At present, MyEPO can be used to reply to a communication under **R.71(3)** or **Art.94(3)** EPC (with or without further processing), file a response to the extended European search report under **R.70a** (with or without further processing), request the correction of bibliographic information at the allowance stage and reply to subsequent communications from the examining division concerning such requests or concerning inconsistencies in the claim translations and reply to an invitation to indicate subject matter for search under **R.62a** or **R.63**. MyEPO may also currently be used to request the correction of the applicant's bibliographic data (including the rectification of the designation of an inventor under **R.21**), to withdraw an application, to reply to a communication under **R.161(1)** or **R.162** on entry into the European phase, to request the registration of the transfer of an application or patent or the registration or cancellation of a license or other right (**R.22. R.23. R.24. R.85** or **UPR.20(2)(b)**) without administrative fee (Dec. Pres. OJ 2024 sp4 p.18), to request a certified copy of a document without administrative fee (Dec. Pres. OJ 2024 sp4 p.18), to notify the EPO of changes in representation and to administer entries in the list of professional representatives.

When performing a procedural action using MyEPO, a signature in the form of a text string is required (A-VIII,3.3). The use of MyEPO requires authentication by any means allowed by the EPO (Dec. Pres. OJ 2024 A20). Currently, identification is possible via a two-step authentication.

6 E-mail

E-mail has no legal force in proceedings under the EPC and PCT and thus cannot generally be used to validly perform any procedural act and in particular to comply with time limits (OJ 2000 p.458).

6.1 E-MAIL DURING VIDEOCONFERENCES AND CONSULTATIONS

As an exception, e-mail must be used for the filing of documents, including authorisations, during consultations with examiners and oral proceedings by videoconference. The EPO will provide an e-mail address to which the documents referred to in **R.50** are to be sent. (Dec. Pres. OJ 2020 A71, C-VII,3; E-III,8.5.2)

Amended application documents must be attached in pdf format. Other attachments may be sent in any format that can be opened by the EPO and reproduced in a legible form. No confirmation on paper is necessary. Where a signature is required, this may be included in the attachment or in the e-mail. Documents that do not comply with these requirements are deemed not to have been filed. Documents or parts thereof which are illegible or incomplete, are also deemed not filed. (Dec. Pres. OJ 2020 A71)

The documents submitted by e-mail, other than documents excluded from file inspection under **R.144**, are added to the file. A routine confidentiality statement in an e-mail is not considered to be a request to exclude the e-mail from file inspection. (Dec. Pres. OJ 2020 A71)

6.2 OTHER USE OF E-MAIL

The Guidelines allow the use of e-mail for arranging a date for a consultation, informally communicating amendments during the consultation, and providing the examining division with amended claims shortly before oral proceedings in addition to an official submission, e.g. by OLF (C-VII,3.1).

Information may only be exchanged by e-mail if there is prior agreement between the examiner and the applicant to do so, e.g. as the result of a telephone call. An e-mail relating to procedural or substantive matters received by the examiner without prior agreement is added to the file (see **T599/06** r.4.2) and the applicant is invited to resubmit its contents using permitted means. (C-VII,3.1)

R. 2(2) Where the Convention provides that a document must be signed, the authenticity of the document may be confirmed by handwritten signature or other appropriate means the use of which has been permitted by the President of the European Patent Office. A document authenticated by such other means shall be deemed to meet the legal requirements of signature in the same way as a document bearing a handwritten signature which has been filed in paper form.

1 Signature on document

The EPC provides that the Request for Grant form (**R.41(2)(h)**) and further documents (**R.50(3)**) must be signed. Furthermore, the EPC explicitly states that the assignment of an application (**Art.72**), a designation of the inventor (**R.19(1)**) and an authorisation (**R.152(1)**) must be signed.

R.2(2) indicates how a document is to be validly signed. Paper documents that must be signed require a handwritten signature (**R.2(2)**). Documents filed in electronic form may be signed using a text string signature or an enhanced electronic signature (when using OLF) or their authenticity may be confirmed by a facsimile signature (Dec. Pres. OJ 2024 A88 Art.10; OJ 2016 A21).

The use of electronic signatures for authorisations (**R.152**), proof of transfers (**R.22, R.85**) and proof of licenses (**R.23, R.24**) has recently been expanded. For more details on signature requirements for authorisations, see the discussion under **R.152:1**. Signature requirements for agreements serving as proof of transfers and licenses are discussed in **R.22(1):1**.

2 **Incorrect or missing signature**

R.2(2) and the decisions of the President do not state the legal consequences that should ensue if a document is not properly signed. The following consequences can be derived from the EPC.

The EPO will request under **R.57(b)** and **R.58** the correction of a Request for Grant form not signed in accordance with **R.41(2)(h)**. The request should be signed by each applicant or their representative. The sanction on failure to correct after invitation in accordance with **R.58** is refusal of the application under **Art.90(5)**.

If a further document, filed after the filing of the application, is not signed, the EPO will invite the party to resubmit the document with a signature; if the invitation is not complied with, the document will be deemed not to have been filed (**R.50(3)**). The same applies to the designation of the inventor according to **R.19(1)**. A signature not complying with **R.2(2)** should probably be regarded as a missing signature for the purpose of **R.50(3)**.

R. 3 Language in written proceedings

Implementation of **Art.14(3)**

R. 3(1) In written proceedings before the European Patent Office, any party may use any official language of the European Patent Office. The translation referred to in Article 14, paragraph 4, may be filed in any official language of the European Patent Office.

Art.14(4) Translation of further document filed in admitted non-EPO language

1 **Derogation from language of proceedings by party**

The written submissions of parties are usually filed in the language of the proceedings (**Art.14(3)**). However, **R.3(1)** allows parties to file their documents, except those mentioned in **R.3(2)**, in an official EPO language (**Art.14(1)**) other than the language of proceedings, without a requirement to file a translation into the language of the proceedings. This situation occurs most often in opposition proceedings, where an opponent might prefer an official EPO language other than the language of the proceedings. Since **R.3(1)** refers to **Art.14(4)**, an entitled party may file a document to be filed within a time limit in an admissible non-EPO language. They must file a translation in an official EPO language under **R.3(1)**, not necessarily being the language of proceedings. The translation must normally be filed within one month of the filing of the document (**R.6(2)**).

Note that a request for unitary effect can only be made in the language of the proceedings (**UPR.6(2)**).

2 **Derogation from language of proceedings by EPO**
In written proceedings, the EPO will only use the language of the proceedings as determined by **Art.14(3)** (**G4/08** r.3.11; A-VII,2). Written decisions taken by the examining or opposition divisions may only deviate from the language of the proceedings in exceptional cases, such as in the case of witness statements. Arguments of parties in another official language must be summarised in the language of proceedings. (E-X 2.3).

R. 3(2) Amendments to a European patent application or European patent shall be filed in the language of the proceedings.

1 **Language of amendments**
Any amendment of the application or patent must be filed in the language of the proceedings according to **R.3(2)**.

However, since **Art.14(4)** takes precedence over **R.3(2)**, an amendment in response to a communication of the EPO, which has to be filed within a specified period, may be filed by an entitled party in an admissible non-EPO language within that time limit. Such an amendment must be translated in the language of the proceedings (**Art.14(4)** and **R.3(2)**) and be filed within one month of the filing of the amendment (**R.6(2)**). During further proceedings, the amendment must be discussed with reference to the text in the language of the proceedings. (**J18/90** r.1.2, 1.3)

Art.14(4) does not apply to an amendment not to be filed within a specified period. Hence, such an amendment must be filed in the language of proceedings.

R. 3(3) Documentary evidence and, in particular, publications may be filed in any language. The European Patent Office may, however, require that a translation in one of its official languages be filed, within a period to be specified. If a required translation is not filed in due time, the European Patent Office may disregard the document in question.

1 **Documents used as evidence**
A document used as evidence may be filed in any language (**R.3(3)**). The EPO often requests a translation into an official EPO language, for which it may set a period between two and six months depending on the language and the length of the document. The EPO may disregard the document if the translation is not filed in due time. (A-VII,3.4)

R. 4 Language in oral proceedings

Amended by decision of the Administrative Council of 10.12.2024, which entered into force on 01.04.2025 (OJ 2025 A16). The amendments were in paragraphs (1) and (3) to gender-neutral language.
Implementation of **Art.14(3)**

R. 4(1) Any party to oral proceedings before the European Patent Office may use an official language of the European Patent Office other than the language of the proceedings, if such party gives notice to the European Patent Office at least one month before the date of such oral proceedings or provides for interpretation into the language of the proceedings. Any party may use an official language of a Contracting State, if they provide for interpretation into the language of the proceedings. The European Patent Office may permit derogations from these provisions.

1 **Language in oral proceedings**
In oral proceedings the EPO will use the language of proceedings as determined by **Art.14(3)**. A derogation is provided in **R.4(2)**.

R.4(1) allows a party to use an official EPO language other than the language of the proceedings. In such a case the EPO will make provision for interpretation into the language of proceedings when the party gives the EPO at least one month notice (**R.4(5)**); otherwise the party itself must make provision for interpretation. If all parties have indicated that they will use another official language, an opposition division may depart from the language of proceedings to manage with fewer or no interpreters (E-V,1). The EPO will send a notice to parties when arranging a date for oral proceedings in an opposition procedure, requesting them to minimise the amount of interpretation required in view of the costs (OJ 1994 p.583).

A party in oral proceedings may use any official language of any contracting state, because in **R.4(1)** the use of such languages is not limited by the residence and nationality of the party as it is in **Art.14(4)**. The party in this case must always provide interpretation into the language of the proceedings. See E-V,3 for possible postponement of oral proceedings if a party is unable to arrange for translation.

If a party uses an official EPO language which is not the language of the proceedings in oral proceedings before a department of first instance, the party is only allowed to use this language again in subsequent oral proceedings before a department of second instance after filing a new request for use of this language, because the proceedings before the second instance are not a continuation of, but wholly separate and independent from the first instance proceedings (OJ 2007 p.118; **T34/90**).

R. 4(2) In the course of oral proceedings, employees of the European Patent Office may use an official language of the European Patent Office other than the language of the proceedings.

1 **Change to other official EPO language**
The employees of the EPO will normally use the language of proceedings during oral proceedings. By way of exception, **R.4(2)** allows the use of another EPO language. However, the EPO should not depart from the use of the language of the proceedings without good reason. The parties need not agree to such a departure. The EPO informs them prior to oral proceedings, unless they have equally requested to use the other EPO language. If parties are not competent in that language, the EPO will provide for interpretation into the language of proceedings under **R.4(5)** at its own expense. (E-V,5)

R. 4(3) Where evidence is taken, any parties, witnesses or experts to be heard who are unable to express themselves adequately in an official language of the European Patent Office or of a Contracting State may use another language. Where evidence is taken upon request of a party, parties, witnesses or experts expressing themselves in a language other than an official language of the European Patent Office shall be heard only if that party provides for interpretation into the language of the proceedings. The European Patent Office may, however, permit interpretation into one of its other official languages.

R. 4(4) If the parties and the European Patent Office agree, any language may be used.

There will be no interpretation or prior notice (E-V,2).

R. 4(5) The European Patent Office shall, if necessary, provide at its own expense interpretation into the language of the proceedings, or, where appropriate, into its other official languages, unless such interpretation is the responsibility of one of the parties.

R. 4(6) Statements by employees of the European Patent Office, parties, witnesses or experts, made in an official language of the European Patent Office, shall be entered in the minutes in that language. Statements made in any other language shall be entered in the official language into which they are translated. Amendments to a European patent application or European patent shall be entered in the minutes in the language of the proceedings.

See **R.124** for drawing up of the minutes and E-V,6 for language used.

R. 5 Certification of translations

Where the translation of a document is required, the European Patent Office may require that a certificate that the translation corresponds to the original text be filed within a period to be specified. If the certificate is not filed in due time, such document shall be deemed not to have been filed, unless otherwise provided.

Implementation of **Art.14**

1 **General**
The EPO will only require a certificate of translation if it has serious doubts as to the accuracy of the translation of a document. If the certificate is not filed in the period specified, the document will be deemed not to have been received (**R.5**, second sentence). This partial loss of rights can be remedied with further processing (**Art.121**). (A-VII,7)

R. 6 Filing of translations

Amended by decision of the Administrative Council of 14.12.2023, which entered into force on 01.04.2024 (OJ 2024 A3). The amendment concerned the removal of reduction of fees from the title and the deletion of paragraphs 3 to 7, which concerned said fee reductions. The provisions of those paragraphs (reduction of fees and the corresponding eligibility) are now covered under R.7a and 7b.
Implementation of **Art.14**

R. 6(1) A translation under Article 14, paragraph 2, shall be filed within two months of filing the European patent application.

Art.14(2) Translation of an application

1 **Period for filing translation of application**
A translation of an application must be filed within two months from filing the application. Note, that the period is triggered by the filing of the application, not by the date of filing (see **Art.80:4**). Hence, a re-dating of the application, e.g. due to late filing of drawings under **R.56(2)**, does not change the start of the period.

The filing of the translation is checked under **Art.90(3)** and **R.57(a)**. If the two-month period of **R.6(1)** is not observed, the EPO will issue an invitation under **R.58** to correct the omission within two months. The final time limit for filing the translation may be about five months from filing. The periods of **R.6(1)** and **R.58** are excluded from further processing under **R.135(2)** but re-establishment under **Art.122** is available, provided all due care can be proven. See also **Art.14(2):3**.

R. 6(2) A translation under Article 14, paragraph 4, shall be filed within one month of filing the document. This shall also apply to requests under Article 105a. Where the document is a notice of opposition or appeal, or a statement of grounds of appeal, or a petition for review, the translation may be filed within the period for filing such a notice or statement or petition, if that period expires later.

Art.14(4) Further documents in admitted non-EPO language
Art.105a Request for limitation or revocation

1 **Period for filing translation of further document**
A translation of a further document filed in an admissible non-EPO language under Art.14(4) into an official EPO language must be filed within one month of filing the document (**R.6(2)**, first sentence). Where the document is a notice of opposition or appeal, a statement of grounds of appeal or a petition for review, the translation may be filed within the period for filing such document if that expires later than the one-month period (**R.6(2)**, third sentence).

The reference to the request for limitation and revocation under **Art.105a** in **R.6(2)** is a lex specialis allowing the request to be filed in another language, provided a translation is filed (CA/PL/29/06 Add.1), even though the request need not be filed within a time limit as required by **Art.14(4)**. It should be noted that the Guidelines limit the languages of the request to those of **Art.14(4)**, i.e. admissible non-EPO languages (D-X,2.1(iv)), but it is not stated that the person filing the request must comply with the requirements of **Art.14(4)**. Hence, it appears to allow a Uruguayan party to file such a request in Spanish, although this is probably not intended.

If the time limit is not observed in grant proceedings, further processing (**Art.121** and **R.135**) may be requested. Re-establishment is excluded under **R.136(3)**. In opposition, further processing is not available (**Art.121(1)**). An opponent has no remedy for the late filing of a translation, because neither further processing nor re-establishment is available for an opponent in opposition proceedings (see **Art.122(1):1**).

R. 7 Legal authenticity of the translation of the European patent application

Unless evidence is provided to the contrary, the European Patent Office shall assume, for the purpose of determining whether the subject-matter of the European patent application or European patent extends beyond the content of the application as filed, that the translation filed under Article 14, paragraph 2, or Rule 40, paragraph 3, is in conformity with the original text of the application.

Art.14(2) Language and translation of application
R.40(3) Filing of translation of previously filed application
Implementation of **Art.14(2), 70(2)**

1 **Incorrect translation**
The EPO assumes that a translation of a European patent application is in conformity with the original text of the application, unless proof to the contrary is given (**R.7**). The proof may be provided by an opponent during opposition proceedings or by a third party after file inspection according to **Art.128**. The correction of a translation during opposition proceedings is permitted under **Art.14(2)**, provided the correction does not extend the scope of the claims of the patent (**Art.123(3)**).

R. 7a Reduction of fees

Inserted by decision of the Administrative Council of 14.12.2023, which entered into force on 01.04.2024 (OJ 2024 A3; preparatory document CA/63/23). Implementation of **Art.14** and **Art.51**.

1 **Reduction of fees**
R.7a was inserted, following a reassessment by the EPO of its fee structure, in order to assist smaller innovative entities in accessing the European patent system. The first two paragraphs of the rule are partly based on **R.6(3)** and **R.6(4)** as in force until 31.03.2024 (now deleted) and the fifth paragraph is partly based on **R.6(7)** as in force until 31.03.2024 (also now deleted). These parts of the new rule provide an ongoing system of compensation, based on a reduction of the filing and examination fees, for certain applicants that use an official language of a contracting state other than English, French or German. Paragraphs 3 and 4 provide a new system of compensation for 'micro-entities' that file relatively few European patent applications, based on a reduction of the filing, search, examination, designation, grant and renewal fees. Paragraph 6 specifies the point in time at which eligibility for both of these systems of compensation is to be assessed. The new rule applies to payments made on or after 01.04.2024, irrespective of the filing date of the application concerned. (CA/63/23; Not. EPO OJ 2024 A8)

The EPC has various fee reductions for which only certain parties are eligible, depending on nationality, residence, and/or size: these include the language reduction provided by **R.7a(1)**, the reduction for micro-entities provided by **R.7a(3)** and the reduction of the appeal fee provided by **Rfees2(1)11**. In addition, a cost rebate is available for certain proprietors of unitary patents under the compensation scheme of **UPR.8** and some fee reductions for PCT applications in the international phase are available to certain applicants (**Rfees2(1):17**). The criteria are different for each fee reduction.

R. 7a(1) Where a person referred to in Article 14, paragraph 4, files a European patent application or a request for examination in a language admitted in that provision, the filing fee or examination fee shall be reduced in accordance with the Rules relating to Fees.

1 **Reduction of the filing fee and examination fee when using an official language of a contracting state**
The provision provides financial compensation for the translation costs incurred by certain entities using an admissible non-EPO language, i.e. an official language of an EPC contracting state other than English, French or German.

The amount of the reduction is fixed in **Rfees14(1)** at 30 %.

Each of the following requirements must be complied with in order for the applicant to be entitled to the reduction:

- The applicant must be an **Art.14(4)** person, i.e. a natural or legal person having a residence or principal place of business within a contracting state having a language other than English, French or German as an official language or a national of such a state resident abroad.
- The applicant must use that official language when carrying out the essential element (see below) involved in filing the application (in order to benefit from a reduction in the filing fee) or involved in requesting examination (in order to benefit from a reduction in the examination fee).
- The translation of this essential element into one of the official languages of the EPO must be filed no earlier than simultaneously with the filing of the essential element in an official language of a contracting state (**G6/91** hn.1; A-X,9.3.1, 9.3.3). If the essential element is filed first in the language of the proceedings and subsequently in an admissible non-EPO language, the reduction is not available.
- The applicant must fulfil the requirements of **R.7a(2)** (must be an eligible person) and must make an appropriate declaration to that effect, at the latest when the reduced payment is made (**R.7b(1)**).

Because the applicant must be an **Art.14(4)** person in order to take advantage of the reduction, it is not available to a person having a residence (in the case of a natural person) or place of business (in the case of a legal person) outside the contracting states who is furthermore (in the case of a natural person) not a national of a contracting state, e.g. a Brazilian person resident in Brazil using Portuguese. Nor is the reduction available to a person who has the relevant residence or nationality but uses the official language of a different contracting state or the official language of a non-contracting state (see A-X,9.3.1).

The requirements relating to joint applicants are discussed below under **R.7a(5)**).

A declaration of entitlement must be filed, at the latest, when the reduced fee is paid (**R.7b(1)**). No evidence of entitlement need be provided unless such evidence is requested by the EPO (**R.7b(3)**). An applicant having doubts concerning entitlement to the reduction should pay the full fee as a precaution and request a refund of the 30% reduction (see **Rfees14:1**).

If the EPO establishes that a non-entitled person has wrongly paid a fee at a reduced rate, the application is deemed withdrawn (see **R.7b(4):1**).

Only the filing fee and the examination fee are reduced under this provision. The persons specified in **R.7a(2)** are also entitled to a reduction of the appeal fee (**Rfees2(1)11**), but this reduction is independent of nationality or residence and independent of the language in which the notice of appeal is filed.

The requirements relating to a request for compensation in respect of translation costs incurred in connection with a unitary patent are different (**UPR.8**).

2 Filing fee

The essential element involved in filing a European patent application is the description (J4/88 together with **G6/91** r.18-22, adapted to EPC2000 in A-X,9.3.2). Neither of the other two elements of **R.40(1)** are considered essential for these purposes and claims are not required for a filing date. The filing fee is therefore reduced if at least the description is filed in an admissible non-EPO language and a translation of that description into an official EPO language is filed at the earliest at the same time as the application.

The reduction also applies where an application is filed by reference under **R.40(1)(c)** to an application having a description in an admissible non-EPO language (A-X,9.3.2).

The description must be filed in a non-EPO language specified for the applicant in **Art.14(4)**, even though EPC2000 no longer limits the languages in which patent applications can be filed (**Art.14(2)**; A-X,9.3.1).

Since the additional fee for the 36th and each subsequent page is a part of the filing fee according to **R.38(2)**, the page fee will also be reduced (Not. EPO OJ 2024 A8 §10; A-III,13.2; A-X,9.3.2).

The fee for divisional application which is itself divided from a divisional application is also a part of the filing fee according to **R.38(4)**; hence, the divisional fee is also reduced (Not EPO OJ 2024 A8 §10; A-X,9.3.2).

Note that the reduction of the filing fee under **R.7a(1)** does not apply to the fee paid under **R.159(1)(c)** for a Euro-PCT application since **R.7a(1)** refers only to a person that 'files a European patent application'. Both the filing fee paid under **R.38(1)** and the filing fee paid under **R.159(1)(c)** are reduced under **R.7a(3)**.

3 **Examination fee**

The essential element involved in requesting examination is the written request for examination. The examination fee is reduced if the written request for examination is filed in an admissible non-EPO language. The request for grant form contains a pre-printed request for examination in the three official EPO languages and a box for entering the request for examination in an admissible non-EPO language. If this box is used, no translation of the request needs to be filed because of the pre-printed request for examination in English, French and German. Examples of the appropriate wording for the request in an admissible non-EPO language can be found on the EPO website under 'Forms'. (A-X,9.3.3)

Because the request for examination is not deemed filed until the examination fee is paid (**Art.94(1)**), the applicant may in any case take advantage of the reduction by filing the request for examination in an admissible non-EPO language at any time until the fee is paid, provided a translation of the request in an official EPO language is filed no earlier than simultaneously with the request and within the period of **R.6(2)**. Note that even if the pre-printed request for examination in the official languages is already on file as part of the request for grant form, a further translation into English, French or German is required in this case (A-X,9.3.3; **G6/91** r.12).

To benefit from the reduction, it is not necessary to file subsequent documents during the examination procedure in an admissible non-EPO language; only the language of the request for examination is relevant (A-X,9.3.3; see **G6/91**).

R. 7a(2) The reduction of fees referred to in paragraph 1 shall be available for:

(a) microenterprises;
(b) small and medium-sized enterprises;
(c) natural persons;
(d) non-profit organisations, universities or public research organisations.

1 **Kind of person entitled to reduction**

In order to take advantage of the reduction of the filing and examination fees, the applicant must be a 'micro-entity' or a small or medium-sized enterprise (SME). A 'micro-entity' is a micro-enterprise, a natural person, a non-profit organisation, a university or a public research organisation (OJ 2024 A8 §6).

A microenterprise is defined in Art.2(3) of European Commission recommendation 2003/361 of 06.05.2003 as an enterprise which employs fewer than 10 persons and whose annual turnover and/or annual balance sheet total does not exceed EUR 2 million. The definition of an SME is also provided by this Commission recommendation. An SME is an enterprise employing fewer than 250 persons, which has an annual turnover not exceeding EUR 50 million and/or an annual balance sheet total not exceeding EUR 43 million. (A-X,9.3.1)

The definitions of 'non-profit organisation', 'university' and 'public research organisation' are given in Not. EPO OJ 2024 A8 §8.

The status of the applicant when paying the relevant fee is decisive in determining whether the reduction applies or not (**R.7a(6)**) and a declaration of entitlement must be filed when paying the fee or earlier (**R.7b(1)**). A change in the status of the applicant which occurs later will not have a retroactive effect on the validity of a fee reduction (Not. EPO OJ 2024 A8 §16). If reasonable doubt arises as to the veracity of the declaration of the applicant, the EPO may request appropriate evidence (**R.7b(3)**).

R. 7a(3) Where a microenterprise, natural person, non-profit organisation, university or public research organisation files a European patent application or, in respect of an international application, performs the acts referred to in Rule 159, the following fees shall be reduced in accordance with the Rules relating to Fees:

(a) filing fee;
(b) fee for a European or supplementary European search;
(c) examination fee, and in addition the previously paid international search fee where the European Patent Office acted as International Searching Authority;
(d) designation fee;
(e) fee for grant;
(f) renewal fees for the European patent application.

1 **Reduction of multiple fees for micro-entities**

Irrespective of whether an applicant qualifies for a reduction of the filing and examination fee under **R.7a(1)**, an applicant that is a micro-entity also qualifies for a reduction of all the major procedural fees under the EPC (filing fee, search fee, examination fee, designation fee, fee for grant and renewal fees). A micro-entity is a microenterprise, a natural person, a non-profit organisation, a university or a public research organisation (but not a small or medium-sized enterprise). For the definition of these terms, see **R.7a(2):1**. In order to take advantage of this reduction, neither the nationality or residence of the applicant nor the language used is relevant. However, the reduction is only available if the micro-entity concerned files relatively few European and Euro-PCT patent applications (**R.7a(4)**). (A-X,9.4.1)

The amount of the reduction is fixed in **Rfees14(1)** as 30%.

A declaration of entitlement must be filed, at the latest, when the reduced fee is paid (**R.7b(1)**). No evidence of entitlement need be provided unless such evidence is requested by the EPO (**R.7b(3)**). It is the status of the applicant at the time each fee is paid that determines eligibility – if the application is transferred to a new applicant that does not qualify for a reduction then past payments at the lower rate are not invalidated. If applicant has doubts about their entitlement to the reduction, they should pay the full fee as a precaution and request a refund of the 30% reduction (see **Rfees14:1**). The EPO carries out checks concerning the entitlement of the applicant to the reduction on a random basis as well as requiring evidence in specific cases where reasonable doubts arise. (A-X,9.4.1, 9.4.3)

If the EPO establishes that a non-entitled person has wrongly paid a fee at a reduced rate, the application is deemed withdrawn (see **R.7b(4):1**).

2 **Filing fee**

The filing fee that qualifies for reduction is the fee paid under **R.38(1)** for a direct European patent application and the fee paid under **R.159(1)(c)** for a Euro-PCT application. The additional parts of the filing fee that apply under **R.38(2)** (due to the number of pages) and **R.38(4)** (in the case of certain divisional applications) are also reduced. Note that the reduction of the filing fee under **R.7a(1)** does not apply to the fee paid under **R.159(1)(c)** since that rule refers only to a person that 'files a European patent application' and not to a person that 'performs the acts referred to in **R.159**'.

3 **Search fee**

The search fee that qualifies for reduction is the fee paid under **R.38(1)** for a direct European patent application.

In the case of a Euro-PCT application, a supplementary European search is carried out by the EPO on regional phase entry if the EPO has not performed a search in the international phase as International Searching Authority or Supplementary International Searching Authority. In this case, it is the supplementary search fee paid under **R.159(1)(e)** that qualifies for the reduction.

In the case where the EPO acted as International Searching Authority, there is no supplementary European search on entry into the European regional phase. It is not possible in this case for the EPO to reduce any search fee since the international search fee is collected by the receiving Office under the PCT and no search fee is payable on regional phase entry. A further reduction of the examination fee is therefore provided in this case, equivalent to 30% of the international search fee that was paid (see Not. EPO OJ 2024 A8 and CA/63/23 §18).

In the case where the EPO acted as Supplementary International Searching Authority, no supplementary European search is carried out on regional phase entry and the supplementary search fee is collected by the International Bureau. It is not clear in this case whether a corresponding reduction of the examination fee applies or not.

In the case where a supplementary European search fee must be paid for a Euro-PCT application and an international search report or a supplementary international search report was drawn up by the Austrian Patent Office, the Finnish Patent and Registration Office, the Spanish Patent and Trademark Office, the Swedish Intellectual Property Office, the Turkish Patent and Trademark Office, the Nordic Patent Institute or the Visegrad Patent Institute, the supplementary European search fee is reduced by a fixed amount (OJ 2024 A3 Art.4; see **Art.153(7):4**). It is not clear whether the percentage-based reduction under **R.7a(3)** is to be applied before or after this fixed reduction is applied.

4 **Examination fee**

The examination fee that qualifies for reduction is the fee paid under **Art.94(1)** for both direct European patent applications and Euro-PCT applications.

As mentioned above (**R.7a(3):3**), the examination fee for a Euro-PCT application may also be reduced by an amount equal to 30% of the international search fee in certain cases. In such a case, according to Not. EPO OJ 2024 A8 §12 and CA/63/23 §18, the examination fee is first reduced by 30% and then by an amount equal to 30% of the actual international search fee paid (i.e. the international search fee net of refunds and reductions). This further refund based on the international search fee applies to any examination fee paid on or after 01.04.2024 regardless of whether the international search fee was paid earlier than that date.

It should be noted that the examination fee may also be reduced by a further 30% under **R.7a(1)** (**Rfees14(3)**). It is not clear at which point this reduction should be applied vis-à-vis the two possible reductions under **R.7a(3)**. Furthermore, the examination fee for a Euro-PCT application may also be reduced by 75% under **Rfees14(2)** and it is not clear at which point this reduction should be applied vis-à-vis the two possible reductions under **R.7a(3)** and the possible reduction under **R.7a(1)**. Since the reduction based on the international search fee is a fixed amount rather than a percentage reduction, the order in which these reductions are applied makes a difference and could potentially result in a negative amount. However, a negative amount cannot be offset against other fees paid (A-X,9.5.2).

5 **Designation fee**

The designation fee that qualifies for reduction is the fee paid under **R.39(1)** for a direct European patent application and the fee paid under **R.159(1)(d)** for a Euro-PCT application.

6 **Fee for grant**

The fee for grant that qualifies for reduction is the fee paid under **R.71(3)** for both direct European patent applications and Euro-PCT applications.

7 **Renewal fees**

The renewal fees that qualify for reduction are those that fall due for both direct European patent applications and Euro-PCT applications under **Art.86(1)**. Renewal fees payable to national offices after grant or to the EPO in respect of a European patent with unitary effect do not benefit from the reduction.

8 **Multiple reductions of the same fee sequentially**

It is possible for the same applicant to qualify for a reduction under both **R.7a(1)** and **R.7a(3)** and in this case the filing or examination fee is reduced twice by 30% sequentially (**Rfees14(3)**, A-X,9.2). As noted above, certain fees benefit from other separate reductions unrelated to **R.7a**.

R. 7a(4) The reduction of fees referred to in paragraph 3 shall not be available where the same person has filed five or more European patent applications or Euro-PCT applications within a period of five years preceding

- **the date of filing of the European patent application concerned or**
- **the date of entry into the European phase of the Euro-PCT application concerned.**

The relevant date for previous applications shall be the date of filing in the case of a European patent application or the date of entry into the European phase in the case of a Euro-PCT application.

1 **Reduction for micro-entity only available for infrequent filers**
The fee reductions of R.7a(3) are for the purpose of encouraging certain entities to use the European patent system more frequently. They are therefore only available to entities that have filed fewer than five European patent applications or Euro-PCT applications in the five years preceding the filing of the application for which fees are due. The 'filing' of the application in this sense is the date of filing for a direct European patent application and the date of regional phase entry in the case of a Euro-PCT application. For a divisional application, the relevant date is the date on which the divisional itself is filed. When assessing how many applications have been filed in the five-year window it is again the date of filing of each previous European patent application and the date of regional phase entry of each previous Euro-PCT application that counts. It is not clear whether divisional applications are to be regarded as separate applications or not. If multiple applications are filed on the same day and the fee reduction cannot apply to all of them as a result of the five-application cap being reached, they will be considered in order of their filing numbers. When an application is transferred to a new applicant, the cap is calculated in respect of future fee reductions on the basis of the number of applications filed by the new applicant. Ownership of the new application may limit the eligibility of the new applicant's other applications for fee reductions from the date on which the transfer is registered. Note that once an application has been filed, or has entered the EPO regional phase, it counts towards the cap regardless of its subsequent fate; the later withdrawal of the application, for example, does not remove it from the count. (Not. EPO OJ 2024 A8 §21-26, A-X,9.4.1)

The EPO is responsible for checking whether the condition of R.7a(4) is met or not in each case and no declaration from the applicant is required. The EPO carries out systematic checks (A-X,9.4.3).

According to Not. EPO OJ 2024 A8 §26, if a reduced fee is paid and the applicant is not entitled to the reduction because the cap has been exceeded, there is no automatic loss of rights. Rather, the EPO will invite the applicant to pay the missing amount within a period of two months. Only if the missing amount is not paid will the application be deemed to be withdrawn. However, in the case of a renewal fee, no such separate invitation will be issued and the applicant will have to pay the renewal fee late with surcharge (i.e. pay the missing amount plus 50% of the unreduced fee). If the grace period has expired by the time that the underpayment comes to light then it seems that it would be necessary to request re-establishment. (A-X,9.4.3)

R. 7a(5) In the case of multiple persons filing a European patent application or a Euro-PCT application, the reduction under paragraph 1 or 3 shall be available only if each applicant fulfils the applicable eligibility criteria.

1 **Entitlement of joint applicants**
If there are multiple applicants, each one must be a person within the meaning of R.7a(2) in order to qualify for the reduction of R.7a(1) and each one must be a person within the meaning of R.7a(3) in order to qualify for the reduction of R.7a(3). In the latter case, each applicant must additionally fulfil the requirements of R.7a(4) (A-X,9.4.1).

However, only one of them must comply with the language and nationality/residence requirements of **Art.14(4)** in order to benefit from the reduction of **R.7a(1)** (**J4/18** r.3.3, applied by analogy). Although **R.7a(5)** refers to 'eligibility criteria' as a whole, and could be taken to mean both entity status and **Art.14(4)** status, whereas corresponding **R.6(7)** in force on 31.03.2024, under which **J4/18** was decided, refers specifically to entity status, Not. EPO OJ 2024 A8 §15 seems to confirm that it is only the entity status which is relevant. This is confirmed in the Guidelines (A-X,9.3.1).

For example, the examination fee will be reduced when a request for examination is filed in Dutch by two applicants, an SME with place of business in the Netherlands and an SME with place of business in Germany, even though the German co-applicant may not file a document in Dutch under **Art.14(4)**.

In another example, reduction under **R.7a(1)** is available for two natural persons, one Italian, one Japanese, living in Japan and filing an application in Italian. Both applicants fulfil the eligibility criteria of **R.7a(2)** and the Italian applicant is eligible for the reduction under **R.7a(1)**. Note that **R.7a(3)** reduction may also be available in this case, provided that both applicants satisfy **R.7a(4)**, since both applicants fulfil eligibility criteria of **R.7a(3)**.

In a third example, reduction under **R.7a(1)** is not available for a natural person living in Slovenia and filing an application in Slovenian together with a Slovenian company employing over 1000 people. In this case, the large company does not fulfil the eligibility criteria of **R.7a(2)**, and therefore the reduction is not available for joint applicants. Note that **R.7a(3)** reduction is also not available because the large Slovenian company does not satisfy the eligibility criteria of **R.7a(3)**.

In a final example, reduction under **R.7a(1)** is not available to a French university filing a joint patent application with a Mexican microenterprise in Spanish. Despite both applicants fulfilling eligibility criteria of **R.7a(2)**, neither is entitled to **R.7a(1)** reduction, because France does not have Spanish as an official language and Mexico is not a contracting state. Note that **R.7a(3)** reduction may be available in this case, provided that both applicants satisfy **R.7a(4)**, since both applicants fulfil the eligibility criteria of **R.7a(3)**.

R. 7a(6) The eligibility criteria laid down in paragraphs 1 to 3 shall be fulfilled on the date of the payment of the fee concerned.

R. 7b Declaration of eligibility for a reduction of fees

Inserted by decision of the Administrative Council of 14.12.2023, which entered into force on 01.04.2024 (OJ 2024 A3; preparatory document CA/63/23). Implementation of **Art.14** and **Art.51**.

1 **Eligibility for fee reduction**

R.7b specifies an important procedural step that the applicant must take in order to benefit from one of the fee reductions available under **R.7a**: a declaration of eligibility must be timely filed and updated as necessary. **R7b(4)** also specifies the consequences of a non-entitled party paying a fee at a reduced rate. The first and third paragraphs of the rule are partly based on the first and second sentences, respectively, of **R.6(6)** as in force until 31.03.2024.

R. 7b(1) Applicants wishing to benefit from a reduction of fees under Rule 7a, paragraph 1 or 3, shall declare themselves to be a person within the meaning of Rule 7a, paragraph 2 or 3, at the latest when the first reduced payment is made.

1 **Declaration**
The declaration can be made by ticking the appropriate box provided in the relevant EPO form (Request for Grant form 1001 or Entry into European phase form 1200). Alternatively, the declaration may be made separately in a letter or using EPO form 1011. In either case, the declaration must be filed no later than the relevant reduced fee is paid. No reduction will be applied in the absence of a declaration, meaning that the EPO will not debit a reduced fee from a deposit account in the absence of a declaration. It is of course possible for an applicant to pay a reduced fee by other means without filing a declaration, in which case see **R.7b(4)**. (Not. EPO OJ 2024 A8 §18)

2 **Additional further processing fee**
When an applicant has failed to pay a fee and is making good the loss of rights using further processing, the omitted act must be completed by paying the fee concerned as well as a further processing fee (50% of the unpaid fee). It may be that the fee is to be paid at a reduced rate according to **R.7a**(1) or (3). In such a case, the declaration under **R.7b**(1), assuming it has not already been filed, is also an omitted act, and another further processing fee under **R.135**(1) needs to be paid for it to be considered validly filed (**J14/21**).

R. 7b(2) Applicants shall inform the European Patent Office of any change of status affecting eligibility for a reduction of fees at the latest when the fee concerned is paid.

1 **Change in status**
Changes in the status of an entity do not have any retrospective effect on fees paid before the change occurred. A change in status may occur as the result of the growth of the entity concerned or as a result of the transfer of the application to a new applicant. In the former case, the applicant should withdraw the previously filed declaration in order to ensure fees are not debited by the EPO at the reduced rate which no longer applies. In the latter case, the new applicant must file a new declaration in order to take advantage of a fee reduction. (Not. EPO OJ 2024 A8 §16)

R. 7b(3) In the event of reasonable doubt as to the veracity of the declaration within the meaning of paragraph 1 or, subsequently, as to the applicant's eligibility for a reduction of fees, the European Patent Office may request evidence.

1 **Request for evidence**
The EPO carries our random checks regarding the status of applicants and, if one of these checks gives rise to doubts concerning the declared status of the applicant, a request for evidence may be made (Not. EPO OJ 2024 A8 §17).

R. 7b(4) Should it become apparent that an incorrect declaration has been filed or the European Patent Office has not been informed of a change of status in accordance with paragraph 2 and a reduced payment is made, the fee shall be deemed not to have been paid and the application shall be deemed to be withdrawn.

1 **Consequences of reduced fee being paid by ineligible person**

It may be that a declaration is incorrect because the applicant is not actually a person specified by **R.7a(2)** or **R.7a(3)**. Alternatively, the applicant's status may have changed as a result of the growth of the entity concerned and the EPO may have wrongly debited the reduced amount or there may have been a change in the applicant's status as the result of the transfer of the application and a new updated declaration may not have been filed. In any of these cases, the fee is underpaid and the EPO will regard the fee as a whole as unpaid (**R.7b(4)**).

Although not covered by the literal wording of **R.7b(4)**, it must be assumed that the same consequence (fee deemed not paid) will arise in other circumstances in which the applicant is not entitled to the reduction, e.g. when evidence requested under **R.7b(3)** is not filed or is not convincing, or when a declaration is not filed or is filed too late. However, according to Not. EPO OJ 2024 A8 §26, if the applicant is ineligible as a result of the 5 application cap of **R.7a(4)**, the EPO sends an invitation to pay the missing amount rather than considering the fee unpaid.

As a consequence, in the case of the filing fee, search fee, examination fee, designation fee and fee for grant and publishing, the application will be deemed withdrawn. The legal basis for the deemed withdrawal will depend on the fee that is considered not to have been paid, i.e. **Art.78(2)** in the case of the filing or search fee, **Art.94(2)** in the case of the examination fee, **R.39(2)** in the case of the designation fee and **R.71(7)** in the case of the fee for grant and publishing. The EPO will issue a loss of rights communication under **R.112(1)** noting the deemed withdrawal. As a remedy, further processing (**Art.121**) can be requested. Further processing must be requested within two months of notification of the loss of rights communication by paying the deficit (in order to complete the omitted act) and the further processing fee. Since the omitted act is the payment of the fee concerned (fee deemed not paid in view of deficit), the further processing fee will amount to 50% of the full fee.

In the case of a renewal fee, the immediate consequence of the non-payment of the fee is that the applicant must pay the fee with surcharge within the six-month grace period of **R.51(2)**. Only if this further opportunity to pay the renewal fee validly is not taken advantage of will the application be deemed withdrawn (**Art.86(1)** and **R.51(2)**). Of course, it may also be the case that the underpayment only comes to light after the expiry of the grace period. In the case where the application is deemed withdrawn, only re-establishment is available since the period of **R.51(2)** is excluded from further processing (**R.135(2)**). Re-establishment must be requested within the relevant time limit of **R.136(1)** by completing the omitted act (payment of the deficit in the renewal fee and the 50% surcharge on the full fee), paying the fee for re-establishment and explaining how all due care was taken. Note that the 50% surcharge of **Rfees2(1)(5)** amounts to 50% of the 'belated renewal fee' and therefore applies to the full fee and not just the deficit.

If the applicant considers that there are in fact no good grounds for the deemed withdrawal, a decision under **R.112(2)** can be requested and the matter will be reviewed (A-X,9.3.4, 9.4.3). If the decision confirms the deemed withdrawal then the matter can be further reviewed by a board of appeal by filing an appeal against the decision.

Chapter II *Organisation of the European Patent Office*

R. 8 Patent classification

The European Patent Office shall use the classification referred to in Article 1 of the Strasbourg Agreement concerning the International Patent Classification of 24 March 1971, hereinafter referred to as the international classification.

1 **Strasbourg Agreement on classification**
See B-V on the classification of the application. Other references to classification: **R.11(1)**: assignment of duties to departments of first instance; **R.61(6)**: mention of the classification in the search report; and **R.143(1)(d)**: entry in the Register.

The complete International Patent Classification (IPC) is available on https://www.wipo.int/en/web/classification-ipc.

Since 01.01.2013 the EPO uses the Cooperative Patent Classification (CPC) system, developed jointly with the US Patent Office (USPTO) and compliant with the IPC (see www.cooperativepatentclassification.org). The USPTO uses the CPC since 01.01.2013 and the Chinese Patent Office (CNIPA) since 01.01.2014.

R. 9 Administrative structure of the European Patent Office

Amended, in force since 01.07.2016 (OJ 2016 A100).
Implementation of **Art.15**

R. 9(1) The European Patent Office shall be divided administratively into Directorates-General, to which the departments specified in Article 15(a) to (e), and the services set up to deal with legal matters and the internal administration of the Office, shall be assigned.

R. 9(2) Each Directorate-General shall be directed by a Vice-President. The assignment of a Vice-President to a Directorate-General shall be decided by the Administrative Council, after the President of the European Patent Office has been consulted.

R. 10 Responsibility of the Receiving Section and the Examining Division

Implementation of **Art.16**

1 **General**
R.10 delimits the period of the Receiving Section's responsibility for examination on filing and as to formal requirements and lays down the rules on the transition of responsibility to the examining divisions.

To avoid parallel responsibility, paragraph 1 provides that the Receiving Section ceases to be responsible when the examining division's responsibility begins.

Under **Art.94(1)**, the EPO examines, on request and in accordance with the Implementing Regulations, whether the application and the invention to which it relates meet the requirements of the EPC. The request is deemed not to have been filed until the examination fee has been paid. Therefore, the examining division becomes responsible once a request for examination has been filed (paragraph 2), with exceptions as provided in paragraphs 3 and 4.

In the event that the request for examination is filed before the European search report has been transmitted to the applicant, paragraph 3 provides that the examining division becomes responsible once the applicant indicates that they wish to proceed further with the application (**R.70(2)**). The EPO interprets the phrase 'the European search report has been transmitted to the applicant' as the day the search report is sent to the applicant (C-II,1). For search reports sent by post, this means the day on which the European search report is handed over to the EPO internal postal service; this moment is three days before the date stamped on the communication (see **G12/91** r.9.1). For search reports sent using the mailbox in MyEPO Portfolio, presumably the day on which the search report is made available in that mailbox is decisive.

Paragraph 4 is a separate provision governing cases where the applicant has waived the right under **R.70(2)**. The responsibility provisions are entirely consistent with the practice under EPC1973. (CA/PL17/06)

R.10 allows an examining division, after assuming responsibility, to check compliance with formal requirements, such as checking the payment of fees.

See **Rfees11** for the refund of the examination fee.

R. 10(1) The Receiving Section shall be responsible for the examination on filing and the examination as to formal requirements of a European patent application up to the time when the Examining Division becomes responsible for the examination of the European patent application under Article 94, paragraph 1.

Art.94(1) Examination of the European patent application

R. 10(2) Subject to paragraphs 3 and 4, the Examining Division shall be responsible for the examination of a European patent application under Article 94, paragraph 1, from the time when a request for examination is filed.

Art.94(1) Examination of the European patent application

R. 10(3) If a request for examination is filed before the European search report has been transmitted to the applicant, the Examining Division shall, subject to paragraph 4, be responsible from the time when the European Patent Office receives the indication under Rule 70, paragraph 2.

R.70(2) Invitation to proceed after early request for examination

R. 10(4) If a request for examination is filed before the European search report has been transmitted to the applicant, and if the applicant has waived the right under Rule 70, paragraph 2, the Examining Division shall be responsible from the time when the search report is transmitted to the applicant.

R.70(2) Invitation to proceed after early request for examination

R. 11 Allocation of duties to the departments of first instance

Implementation of **Art.15**

1 **General**
R.11 reflects the administrative grouping into directorates of the departments involved in the grant procedure – i.e. the search divisions, examining divisions and opposition divisions, made up of technically qualified examiners.

R. 11(1) Technically qualified examiners acting as members of Search, Examining or Opposition Divisions shall be assigned to Directorates. The President of the European Patent Office shall allocate duties to these Directorates by reference to the international classification.

R. 11(2) The President of the European Patent Office may allocate further duties to the Receiving Section, the Search, Examining and Opposition Divisions, and the Legal Division, in addition to the responsibilities vested in them under the Convention.

See **Art.20** for the allocation of duties to the Legal Division.

R. 11(3) The President of the European Patent Office may entrust to employees who are not technically or legally qualified examiners the execution of duties falling to the Search, Examining or Opposition Divisions and involving no technical or legal difficulties.

1 **Formalities officers**
Certain duties normally the responsibility of the examining or opposition division have been entrusted to non-examining staff for operational efficiency (Dec. Pres. OJ 2014 A6; Not. EPO OJ 2014 A32; Dec. Pres. OJ 2015 A104; Dec. Pres. OJ 2020 A80).

The employees of the non-examining staff are called formalities officers, allocated to the Receiving Section, examining and opposition divisions and boards of appeal. Formalities officers may take decisions concerning matters not involving legal or technical difficulties, such as concerning the inadmissibility of an opposition (**G1/02** hn). It is a substantial procedural violation in the sense of **R.103** if formalities officers take decisions not within their competence; such a decision will be set aside (see e.g. **T178/01**).

The competence of the Boards of Appeal to hear appeals is not affected by the entrustment of duties to formalities officers (**G2/90** hn. II). Hence, an appeal of a decision taken by a formalities officer of an examining or opposition division must be heard by a board of appeal competent under **Art.21** to hear the appeal had the decision been taken by the division itself. See **Art.20(1):1** for an exception regarding delegated duties normally the responsibility of the Legal Division.

R. 12 (deleted)

R. 12a Organisation and management of the Boards of Appeal Unit and President of the Boards of Appeal

Inserted, in force since 01.07.2016 (OJ 2016 A100).

Implementation of **Art.21**

1 **Reform of the boards of appeal and their independence**

The boards of appeal were reformed in 2016 following decision **R19/12**, which objected to the chair of the EBoA for suspected partiality because of the chair's connection as vice-president of Directorate-General 3 with the management of the EPO. The reform intends to increase the managerial autonomy, perception of independence and the efficiency of the boards by:

- Changing the boards from a directorate-general headed by a vice-president (**R.9**) to a BoA unit headed by a president of the boards of appeal, who is also the chair of the EBoA (**R.12a(1)**), thereby separating the administrative head of the boards of appeal from the President of the EPO. The president of the boards of appeal is hierarchically independent of the President of the EPO and responsible only to the Administrative Council.
- Delegation of powers of the President of the EPO relating to the management of the BoA Unit to the president of the boards of appeal (**R.12a(2)**).
- Creation of a BoA Committee as a subsidiary body of the Administrative Council (AC) which advises the Council (**R.12c**) and the President of the boards of appeal on the management of the boards of appeal.
- Relocating the boards to a separate building (see **Art.6:3**).

2 **Independence of BoA members**

The reform does not guarantee the envisaged independence of members of the boards under **Art.23** for several reasons.

Firstly, since the reform, re-appointment of a member after a five-year term requires under **R.12d(3)** a positive opinion of the President of the boards of appeal on his performance, which is a subjective criterion. The President of the boards of appeal may only propose a member for re-appointment (**R.12d(2)**); the decision is taken by the AC (**Art.11(3)**). Hence, re-appointment depends on the AC, an organ that is not part of the Boards of Appeal Unit and whose willingness to abide with the rule of law is not guaranteed (see notes to **Art.23(1)** for incidents). Further, a member needs a positive opinion from the President of the boards of appeal on performance to be promoted to the next grade at the time of re-appointment.

Secondly, in disciplinary proceedings against a board of appeal member, the AC can suspend a member indefinitely without a proposal from the EBoA for removal as required by **Art.23(1)** (see **Art.23(1):3**).

Thirdly, the AC and the President of the EPO can still exert influence on the boards through denying re-appointment of the President of the boards of appeal (**R.12a(1):1**); adopting the rules of procedure of the boards through a subsidiary body (**R.12c(2)**); influencing the above performance criteria (**R.12d(3)**); and the possibility that the President of the EPO revokes the delegation of powers to the President of the boards of appeal (**R.12a(2):1**).

Users of the EPC cannot ascertain the independence of the BoA members, because the AC does not usually publish their (re-)appointment and accompanying grounds. The lack of transparency makes it impossible to check whether the AC has applied the rule of law when denying a member re-appointment.

It appears that the independence of the board members can only be guaranteed by deletion of the five-year term in **Art.23(1)**, requiring a diplomatic conference under **Art.172**, which is unlikely to be convened in the short term.

R. 12a(1) The Boards of Appeal and the enlarged Board of appeal, including their registries and support services, shall be organised as a separate unit (the "Boards of Appeal Unit") and be directed by the President of the Boards of Appeal. The Chair of the Enlarged Board of Appeal shall act as President of the Boards of Appeal. The President of the Boards of Appeal shall be appointed by the Administrative Council on a joint proposal made by the Committee established under Rule 12c, paragraph 1, and the President of the European Patent Office. If the President of the Boards of Appeal is absent or indisposed, they shall be replaced by one of the members of the Enlarged Board of Appeal in accordance with the procedure laid down by the Administrative Council.

1 **President of the boards of appeal**

R.12a(1) lays down that the President of the boards of appeal is appointed by the AC on a joint proposal by the President of the EPO and the Boards of Appeal Committee, established by the AC under **R.12c(1)**. Note that **R.12a(1)** governs only the appointment of the President of the BoA, not re-appointment.

The term of the President of the boards of appeal is five years (**Art.23(1)**). Each five years the AC may re-appoint the President of the boards of appeal under **Art.11(3)** after consultation with the President of the EPO (see Annex 1 of CA/43/16 Rev. 1e, in particular Annex 3, §5 and Art.3(c) of the Act of Delegation). The five-yearly re-appointment makes the President of the boards of appeal dependent on the President of the EPO and the AC, in contradiction to the independence expected under **Art.23**.

The President of the boards of appeal also acts as chair of the EBoA following a long and successful tradition; the involvement of the administrative head in judicial activities reinforces the expertise and standing of the President of the boards of appeal (CA/43/16 Rev. 1, Annex 1, §5 and Annex 3 §5; see also **R.12d(1)**). In 2016 the AC appointed the first President of the boards of appeal (OJ 2017 A1) and the President of the boards of appeal appointed a deputy (OJ 2017 A70).

If the President of the boards of appeal is absent or indisposed, a deputy shall take the place of the President (**R.12a(1)**, fourth sentence). The president of the boards of appeal has the power to designate the deputy (see OJ 2018 A85).

R. 12a(2) The President of the Boards of Appeal shall manage the Boards of Appeal Unit and, to this end, have the functions and powers delegated by the President of the European Patent Office. In exercising the delegated functions and powers, the President of the Boards of Appeal shall be responsible solely to the Administrative Council and shall be subject to its hierarchical and disciplinary authority.

1 **Delegation of powers**

The President of the EPO delegates some functions and powers to the President of the boards of appeal to allow the latter to manage the BoA Unit. The President of the EPO may also revoke the delegation of these functions and powers.

According to OJ 2017 A19 the President of the EPO signed the act of delegation on 14.02.2017, which entered into force on 01.03.2017. The text of the signed act has not been published but the proposal for the text is available in CA/43/16 Rev. 1e, Annex 3, Part II.

On 01.07.2018 the next President of the EPO also signed an act of delegation (OJ 2018 A63), which also entered into force on 01.03.2017. It is not clear why the delegation was made twice.

R. 12a(3) Without prejudice to Article 10, paragraph 2(d), and Article 46, the President of the Boards of Appeal shall prepare a substantiated budget request for the Boards of Appeal Unit. This request shall be examined and discussed with the relevant departments of the European Patent Office, and be presented by the President of the Boards of Appeal to the Committee established under Rule 12c, paragraph 1, for opinion, before being forwarded to the President of the European Patent Office for consideration for the yearly draft budget. The President of the European Patent Office shall provide the President of the Boards of Appeal with the necessary resources, as set out in the adopted budget.

Art.10(2)(d) Power of President EPO to prepare and implement the budget
Art.46 Preparation and adoption of the budget

R. 12a(4) The President of the European Patent Office shall make the services mentioned in Rule 9, paragraph 1, available to the President of the Boards of Appeal as far as necessary and within the limits of the adopted budget.

R.9(1) Services dealing with legal matters and internal administration

R. 12b Presidium of the Boards of Appeal and business distribution scheme for the Boards of Appeal

Amended and number changed from R.12 to R.12b, in force since 01.07.2016 (OJ 2016 A100). Amended by decision of the Administrative Council of 10.12.2024, which entered into force on 01.04.2025 (OJ 2025 A16). The amendments were in paragraphs (1)-(5) to gender-neutral language.
Implementation of **Art.21**

1 **General**

The members of the boards of appeal are appointed by the Administrative Council (**Art.11(3)**). They elect from their ranks the Presidium of the boards of appeal, consisting of a chair and twelve members (**R.12b(1)**). The chair is the President of the boards of appeal.

The Presidium advises the President of the boards of appeal on the Rules of Procedure of the boards of appeal and the Enlarged Board of Appeal (**R.12b(3)(c)**), which are to be adopted by the BoA Committee (**R.12c**) and then approved by the AC. The Presidium designates the members of the boards of appeal and allocates their duties within the business distribution scheme (**R.12b(4)**). The composition of the Presidium and the boards of appeal is published annually in the OJ (see for example OJ 2025 A12-A15).

R. 12b(1) The autonomous authority within the Boards of Appeal Unit (the "Presidium of the Boards of Appeal") shall consist of the President of the Boards of Appeal, who shall act as Chair, and twelve members of the Boards of Appeal, six being Chairs and six being other members.

R. 12b(2) All members of the Presidium shall be elected by the Chairs and members of the Boards of Appeal for two working years. If the full composition of the Presidium cannot be reached, the vacancies shall be filled by designating the most senior Chairs and members.

R. 12b(3) The Presidium shall

(a) adopt the Rules of Procedure for the election and designation of its members;

(b) adopt, without prejudice to regulations adopted in accordance with Article 10, paragraph 2(c), and Article 33, paragraph 2(b), a Code of Conduct for the members and Chairs of the Boards of Appeal and of the Enlarged Board of Appeal, which shall be subject to the approval of the Administrative Council;

(c) advise the President of the Boards of Appeal on proposals for amendments to the Rules of Procedure of the Boards of Appeal and of the Enlarged Board of Appeal;

(d) advise the President of the Boards of Appeal on matters concerning the functioning of the Boards of Appeal Unit in general.

Art.10(2)(c) Power of President EPO to propose regulations
Art.33(2)(b) Competence of Administrative Council to adopt Service Regulations

1 **Code of Conduct for the BoA and EBoA members**

The Presidium of the Boards of Appeal adopted the new Code of Conduct on 23 November 2021 after extensive review of similar documents (e.g., the Code of Conduct of the CJEU) and consultation with the Boards of Appeal Committee (BOAC). It replaces the previous Code of Conduct, which was limited to the external activities of board members. The Code of Conduct includes articles on its framework (Art.1), scope (Art.2), principles (Art.3), independency and integrity (Art.4), impartiality (Art.5), loyalty and diligence (Art.6), discretion (Art.7), external activities (Art.8), application of the Code of Conduct and Advisory Committee (Art.9), freedom of expression (Art.10), and duties of the members after ceasing to hold office (Art.11).

The Code of Conduct was approved by the Administrative Council on 14 December 2021 (CA/D 21/21) and entered into force on 1 July 2022. Full text of the Code of Conduct and the explanatory remarks thereto can be found in CA/68/21.

R. 12b(4) Before the beginning of each working year, the Presidium, extended to include all Chairs, shall allocate duties to the Boards of Appeal. In the same composition, it shall decide on conflicts regarding the allocation of duties between two or more Boards of Appeal. The extended Presidium shall designate the regular and alternate members of the various Boards of Appeal. Any member of a Board of Appeal may be designated as a member of more than one Board of Appeal. These measures may, where necessary, be amended during the course of the working year in question.

R. 12b(5) The Presidium may only take a decision if at least five of its members are present; these must include the President of the Boards of Appeal or their deputy, and the Chairs of two Boards of Appeal. Where the tasks mentioned in paragraph 4 are concerned, nine members must be present, including the President of the Boards of Appeal or their deputy, and the Chairs of three Boards of Appeal. Decisions shall be taken by a majority vote; in the event of parity of votes, the Chair or their deputy shall have the casting vote. Abstentions shall not be considered as votes.

R. 12b(6) The Administrative Council may allocate duties under Article 134a, paragraph 1(c), to the Boards of Appeal.

Art.134a(1)(c) Disciplinary power over professional representatives

R. 12c Boards of Appeal Committee and procedure for adoption of the Rules of Procedure of the Boards of Appeal and of the Enlarged Board of Appeal

Inserted, in force since 01.07.2016 (OJ 2016 A100).
Implementation of **Art.21** and 23(4)

R. 12c(1) The Administrative Council shall set up a committee (the "Boards of Appeal Committee") to advise it and the President of the Boards of Appeal on the Boards of Appeal Unit in general and to adopt the Rules of Procedure of the Boards of Appeal and of the Enlarged Board of Appeal. The committee shall be composed of six members appointed by the Administrative Council, three from among the delegations of the Contracting States within the meaning of Article 26, and three from among serving or former judges of international or European courts or of national courts of the Contracting States. The President of the European Patent Office and the President of the Boards of Appeal shall have the right to attend the Committee's meetings. Further details, in particular as to the Committee's composition, alternate members, working arrangements and functions in advising the Boards of Appeal Unit, shall be determined by the Administrative Council in the decision setting up the Committee.

Art.26 Composition of the Administrative Council

1 **Boards of Appeal Committee**
The Boards of Appeal Committee is a subsidiary body of the Administrative Council and advises the Administrative Council and the President of the boards of appeal on the Boards of Appeal Unit in general and, since the reform of the boards of appeal in 2016, adopts the Rules of Procedure of both the boards of appeal and the Enlarged Board of Appeal. The Committee is one body that monitors the independence of the Boards of Appeal Unit, a corner stone of the rule of law, and provides guidance on criteria for performance evaluation. (OJ 2016 A101)

The Committee has six members, not being members of the boards of appeal, appointed by the Administrative Council. The President of the boards of appeal and the President of the EPO may participate in all meetings of the Committee. The advisory and supervisory functions of the Committee are limited to a general level; the day-to-day functioning of the boards of appeal is the responsibility of the President of the boards of appeal (R.12a(2)).

It should be noted that the Administrative Council and the President of the EPO have a decisive role in a committee that monitors the independence of the boards, whereas both have shown on several occasions to have other priorities than the rule of law (see e.g. **Art.23(1):2** and 3).

R. 12c(2) On a proposal from the President of the Boards of Appeal and after the President of the European Patent Office has been given the opportunity to comment, the Committee set up under paragraph 1 shall adopt the Rules of Procedure of the Boards of Appeal and of the Enlarged Board of Appeal.

1 **Amendments to the Rules of Procedure of Boards of Appeal**
The Boards of Appeal Committee adopts (amendments to) the Rules of Procedure of the Boards of Appeal (RPBA) on a proposal from the President of the BoA and after the President of the EPO has been given the opportunity to comment (see also **Art.23(4)** and **R.12c(1)**). The decision of the Committee is subject to the approval of the Administrative Council (**Art.23(4)**). The Presidium advises the President of the Boards of Appeal on proposals for amendments (**R.12b(3)(b)**). The same procedure is followed for amending the Rules of Procedure of the Enlarged Board of Appeal (RPEBA).

The Rules of Procedure of the Boards of Appeal are discussed in **Art.110:1**, the latest version is published in OJ 2024 A15. The Rules of Procedure of the Enlarged Board of Appeal are discussed in **Art.112:1**.

R. 12d Appointment and re-appointment of the members, including the Chairs, of the Boards of Appeal and of the Enlarged Board of Appeal

Inserted, in force since 01.07.2016 (OJ 2016 A100). Amended by decision of the Administrative Council of 10.12.2024, which entered into force on 01.04.2025 (OJ 2025 A16). The amendments were to gender-neutral language.
Implementation of **Art.21**

1 **General**
R.12d deals with the appointment and re-appointment of the members of the EBoA and the chair and members of the boards of appeal. The appointment of the chair of the EBoA, who is also the President of the Boards of Appeal, is not governed by **R.12d** but by **R.12a(1)**; re-appointment is governed by **Art.11(3)** (see **R.12a(1):1**).

R. 12d(1) The Chair of the Enlarged Board of Appeal shall, on appointment, also be appointed as a legally qualified member of the Boards of Appeal.

R. 12d(2) Upon delegation from the President of the European Patent Office, the President of the Boards of Appeal shall exercise the right to propose the members, including the Chairs, of the Boards of Appeal and the members of the Enlarged Board of Appeal for appointment by the Administrative Council, and the right to be consulted on their re-appointment (Article 11, paragraph 3) and on the appointment and re-appointment of external legally qualified members (Article 11, paragraph 5).

1 **Proposal for chair and members of boards**
The President of the Boards of Appeal may propose the chair and members of the boards of appeal and the members of the Enlarged Board of Appeal for appointment by the Administrative Council and the President of the Boards is consulted on their re-appointment (**R.12d(2)**). The President of the EPO may propose the chair of the Enlarged Board of Appeal and is consulted on re-appointment (CA43/16 Rev.1 en, Annex 3, §5).

R. 12d(3) The President of the Boards of Appeal shall exercise the right under paragraph 2 to be consulted on re-appointments by submitting a reasoned opinion, including an evaluation of the member's or Chair's performance, to the Administrative Council. The criteria for evaluating performance shall be set by the President of the Boards of Appeal in consultation with the Committee established under Rule 12c, paragraph 1. Subject to a positive opinion and performance evaluation and the number of posts under Article 11, paragraph 3, available in the adopted budget for the Boards of Appeal Unit, the members, including the Chairs, of the Boards of Appeal and the members of the Enlarged Board of Appeal shall be re-appointed at the end of their five-year term under Article 23, paragraph 1.

Art.11(3) Appointment of board of appeal members by the Administrative Council
Art.23(1) Term of board of appeal members

R. 13 Business distribution scheme for the Enlarged Board of Appeal

Before the beginning of each working year, the members of the Enlarged Board of Appeal appointed under Article 11, paragraph 3, shall designate the regular and alternate members of the Enlarged Board of Appeal in proceedings under Article 22, paragraph 1(a) and (b), and the regular and alternate members in proceedings under Article 22, paragraph 1(c). Decisions may only be taken if at least five members are present, including the Chair or deputy Chair of the Enlarged Board of Appeal; in the event of parity of votes, the Chair or deputy Chair shall have the casting vote. Abstentions shall not be considered as votes.

Amended, in force since 01.07.2016. The amendment deleted paragraph 2 and combined paragraphs 1 and 3. (OJ 2016 A100) Further amended by decision of the Administrative Council of 10.12.2024, which entered into force on 01.04.2025 (OJ 2025 A16). The amendment was to gender-neutral language.
Art.11(3) Appointment by the Administrative Council
Art.22(1)(a) Referral by board of appeal
Art.22(1)(b) Referral by the President of the EPO
Art.22(1)(c) Petition for review of a decision of a board of appeal
Implementation of **Art.22**

1 **Members of the Enlarged Board of Appeal**
The members of the Enlarged Board of Appeal are appointed by the Administrative Council (**Art.11(3)**) on a proposal from the President of the Boards of Appeal (**R.12d(2)**).

R.13 allows to designate specifically members for the proceedings under **Art.112**, i.e. referrals to the Enlarged Board of Appeal, and for the proceedings under **Art.112a**, i.e. petitions for review, to enable more members to work regularly on petitions for review. (OJ 2007 se5)

The composition of the Enlarged Board of Appeal is published annually in Supplementary Publication 1 of the OJ.

PART II IMPLEMENTING REGULATIONS TO PART II OF THE CONVENTION

Chapter I *Procedure where the applicant is not entitled*

R. 14 Stay of proceedings

Implementation of **Art.61**

1 **General**
A stay of proceedings before the EPO while entitlement is being contested secures the rights of a third party pending the decision of a national court of a contracting state (**J6/03** r.2). After the court's decision has become final, the third party has three months to take advantage of one of the remedies mentioned in **Art.61(1)**. The Legal Division is competent in procedures relating to the entitlement of the applicant or proprietor to the grant of a European patent (**Art.61(1), 99(5), R.14, R.15, R.18**) (OJ 2013 p.600).

Whereas **R.14-R.18** concern an applicant who is not entitled, **R.78** applies to a patent proprietor who is not entitled.

R. 14(1) If a third party provides evidence that they have instituted proceedings against the applicant seeking a decision within the meaning of Article 61, paragraph 1, the proceedings for grant shall be stayed unless the third party communicates to the European Patent Office in writing their consent to the continuation of such proceedings. Such consent shall be irrevocable. However, proceedings for grant shall not be stayed before the publication of the European patent application.

Art. 61(1) European patent application filed by non-entitled person
Amended by decision of the Administrative Council of 10.12.2024, which entered into force on 01.04.2025 (OJ 2025 A16). The amendment was introduction of gender-neutral language.

1 **Procedure for requesting stay of grant proceedings**
If third parties provide satisfactory evidence to the EPO that they have instituted entitlement proceedings at a national court and the conditions of **R.14(1)** are met, the EPO will stay the proceedings ex officio to safeguard the rights of the third party (A-IV,2.2.3). The stay takes effect on the date an allowable request is filed and is generally pronounced retroactively (**J9/12** r.11; **J15/06** r.14). If, exceptionally, the third party consents in writing to the continuation of the proceedings, the proceedings will not be stayed (**R.14(1)**). The meaning of 'institution of proceedings' is determined by national law (**J7/00** r.3).

The EPO does not have to give the applicant an opportunity to comment or take a formal decision. The applicant is simply informed of the stay. The applicant can then request the lifting of the stay by providing arguments and evidence, upon which the EPO will take a decision. The decision can be appealed by the adversely affected party. (**J28/94** r.2.2.1; **J18/06** r.2; A-IV,2.2.3)

The EPO will reject a request for a stay of proceedings if e.g. the grant proceedings are terminated or the conditions of **R.14(1)** are not met. The rejection is in the form of a formal decision. The third party can appeal the decision, the applicant becoming a party as of right. (**J28/94** r.2.2)

An immediate stay of proceedings makes it impossible for the applicant to withdraw the application (**R.15**), securing the rights of the third party (**J15/06** r.7). During the stay, a transfer of the application may not be recorded in the Register (**J17/12** hn) and no divisional application may be filed (**J9/12** r.5).

However, if the proceedings continue on express request of the third party, the applicant cannot be prevented from withdrawing the application (**R.15**), giving rise to an insecure situation for the third party. Withdrawal of the request for a stay is interpreted as consent to a continuation of the proceedings (**J1/06** r.3).

Grant proceedings can be stayed if the request for a stay and the required evidence are filed before the date of the publication of the mention of the grant in the Bulletin according to **Art.97(3)**, even if the request is filed after the decision to grant has been taken (**J7/96** hn, r.9; **J14/19** hn.1).

For direct EP applications, proceedings can only be stayed after publication (**R.14(1)**, last sentence). For Euro-PCT applications, **R.14(1)** becomes applicable after expiry of the time limit for entry into the European regional phase (A-IV,2.2); not all acts necessary for entry need to have been fulfilled (see EP 2 620 282 A1, decision dated 22.12.2011).

R. 14(2) Where evidence is provided that a final decision within the meaning of Article 61, paragraph 1, has been taken, the European Patent Office shall inform the applicant and any other party that the proceedings for grant shall be resumed as from the date stated in the communication, unless a new European patent application under Article 61, paragraph 1(b), has been filed for all the designated Contracting States. If the decision is in favour of the third party, the proceedings may not be resumed earlier than three months after the decision has become final, unless the third party requests the resumption.

Art. 61(1)(b) New European patent application filed by entitled person

R. 14(3) Upon staying the proceedings for grant, or thereafter, the European Patent Office may set a date on which it intends to resume the proceedings for grant, regardless of the stage reached in the national proceedings instituted under paragraph 1. It shall communicate this date to the third party, the applicant and any other party. If no evidence has been provided by that date that a final decision has been taken, the European Patent Office may resume proceedings.

1 **Date of resumption of the proceedings**

The EPO communicates the date of resumption of the proceedings to the third party and the applicant (A-IV,2.2.5). The date is chosen with due regard to the interests of the parties (see A-IV,2.2.5). If at the date set a judgement is expected soon, there will be a further stay. The proceedings will be resumed if the third party is suspected of employing delaying tactics. The decision to resume is appealable (see e.g. **J33/03** r.1).

The parties may request a change of date or an end to the stay (**T146/82**).

R. 14(4) All periods other than those for the payment of renewal fees, running at the date of the stay of proceedings, shall be interrupted by such stay. The time which has not yet elapsed shall begin to run from the date on which proceedings are resumed. However, the time still to run after such resumption shall not be less than two months.

1 **Interruption of periods**

All periods running at the date the proceedings are stayed are interrupted, except for any period relating to the payment of renewal fees, with or without surcharge (A-IV,2.2.4). Therefore, the third party must make sure that renewal fees continue to be paid. Note that any automatic debit order ceases to be effective if the proceedings are stayed; after resumption a new order must be filed if automatic debiting is to be used again (AAD.11.1(c)).

The phrase 'from the date' in **R.14(4)** is interpreted such that the date of resumption of proceedings is included in the time still to run; for example, a date of resumption of 5 January and a non-elapsed period of two months result in a time limit of 4 March.

A stay of proceedings under **R.14(4)** has a different effect on pending time limits than an interruption of the proceedings under **R.142**: on the resumption of proceedings following a stay, only the part of the period that had not yet elapsed when proceedings were stayed remains whereas when proceedings are resumed after an interruption, the whole period starts again in most cases.

2 **Example interruption of periods**

The six-month period of **R.70(1)** is triggered by the mention of the publication of the search report on 28.06.2017; thus, the computation of the period (**R.131(2)**) starts on 29.06.2017 and would normally have ended 28.12.2017. Proceedings are stayed on 22.09.2017 and resumed on 03.08.2018. The last day of the elapsed period is 21.09.2017. The non-elapsed period thus runs from 22 September to 28 December. The length of this period is 7 days (from 22 September, which is the first day of the period, to 28 September), plus 3 months (from 28 September to 28 December), making 3 months and 7 days in total. This non-elapsed period begins on 03.08.2018, which is already the first day of the period (**R.14(4)**: 'from the date'), and thus ends on 9.11.2018. (A-IV,2.2.4; see D-VII,4.3 for another example)

It is not clear whether an extension under **R.134(1)** should be included in the length of the non-elapsed period, since neither the EPC nor the Guidelines provide any relevant information. In the above case it would mean that the expiry of the extended, non-interrupted period on 02.01.2018 would result in a non-elapsed period of 3 months and 11 days instead of 3 months and 7 days, and thus expiry of the non-elapsed period on 13.11.2018.

Moreover, neither the EPC nor the Guidelines state definitively how the duration of the non-elapsed period should be calculated: first days and then weeks, first days and then months, first months and then days or any other combination. Since the length of the period depends on the manner of calculation, its length is indeterminate. In practice, the EPO determines the expiry of a time limit after the resumption of proceedings using the longest non-elapsed period that can be calculated.

R. 15 Limitation on withdrawals

From the date on which a third party provides evidence that they have instituted national proceedings under Rule 14, paragraph 1, and up to the date on which the proceedings for grant are resumed, neither the European patent application nor the designation of any Contracting State may be withdrawn.

R.14(1) Entitlement suit
Implementation of **Art.61**

1 **Prohibition to withdraw**
R.15 implements **Art.61**, securing the rights of the third party. Note, however, that **R.15** applies only if the third party has provided proof to the EPO of the initiation of entitlement proceedings and has not consented to continuation of the grant proceedings; if there is no stay of proceedings, the original applicant may still withdraw the application or the designation of a contracting state. The prohibition on withdrawal becomes effective on the day the EPO receives the evidence required under **R.14(1)** (**R.15**); there is no retroactive effect (A-IV,2.3).

R. 16 Procedure under Article 61, paragraph 1

Implementation of **Art.61**

R. 16(1) A person entitled to the grant of a European patent may only have recourse to the remedies under Article 61, paragraph 1, if:
(a) they do so no later than three months after the decision recognising their entitlement has become final, and
(b) the European patent has not yet been granted.

Amended by decision of the Administrative Council of 10.12.2024, which entered into force on 01.04.2025 (OJ 2025 A16). The amendment was introduction of gender-neutral language.

1 **Period for requesting remedy under Art.61(1)**
R.135(2) excludes the three-month period under **R.16(1)(a)** from further processing. Re-establishment is available, even though the entitled person is not the applicant, because the exclusion in **R.135(2)** implicitly recognises that, in principle, the entitled person under **Art.61(1)** has access to the remedies provided by the EPC to deal with a failure to observe a time limit. (OJ 2003 se1 p.159)

The 'European patent has not yet been granted' in **R.16(1)(b)** probably means that the remedies are available before publication of the mention of the grant (see **Art.97(3)**).

2 **Required actions and pendency of the original usurping application**
If the entitled person wishes to prosecute the European patent application in place of the applicant, a written declaration to this effect must be filed with the EPO. The entitled person will then take the place of the original applicant. (A-IV,2.4)

The case where the entitled person wishes to file a new European patent application in respect of the same invention is governed by **R.17**.

Alternatively, the person entitled to the grant of a European patent may request that the European patent application be refused, and the EPO must accede to this request. The decision to refuse the application is open to appeal. (A-IV,2.6)

In **G3/92** hn the Enlarged Board of Appeal decided, based on EPC1973, that the entitled person may file a new European patent application even if the original application is no longer pending. In such a case, this is the only remedy available to the entitled person (**G3/92** r.5.8; A-IV,2.1). The right of the entitled person to a patent outweighs the rights of third parties to legal certainty. A third party, having commenced infringing commercial activities after the lapse of the original application and before the filing of the new application, may defend itself in an infringement procedure before a national court by requesting the application of **Art.122(5)** mutatis mutandis. (**G3/92** r.6)

A minority of the members of the Enlarged Board in the above case dissented, considering that the words 'not yet' in Art.61(1) EPC1973 imply that the original application must still be subject to grant proceedings, and that the article is not applicable to non-pending applications. This would have given more legal security to third parties (likewise **T146/82**). Decision **G3/92** seems equally applicable under EPC2000 since the same terminology (the European patent 'not yet' being granted) is now found in **R.16(1)(b)**.

R. 16(2) Such remedies shall only apply in respect of Contracting States designated in the European patent application in which the decision has been taken or recognised or must be recognised on the basis of the Protocol on Recognition.

1 **Protocol on Recognition**

The Protocol on Recognition specifies in Art.1(1) that the courts of the contracting states have jurisdiction to decide on entitlement claims. It also provides in Art.9(1) that a final decision of a court of a contracting state must be recognised in all other contracting states. A first exception is that a decision of a court of a contracting state recognising a decision on entitlement taken by a court in a non-EPC state based on a bilateral agreement need not be recognised in the other EPC contracting states (Art.11(2)). Further exceptions are specified in Art.10 of the Protocol.

The Protocol on Recognition is an integral part of the EPC according to **Art.164(1)**. Before 07.10.1987, it was possible for states acceding to the EPC to exclude being bound by the Protocol on Recognition under Art.167(2)(d) EPC1973. This avoided delaying the accession of states to the EPC for reasons unrelated to patent law, such as constitutional objections to the recognition of decisions of foreign courts. All contracting states are bound by the Protocol under EPC2000. Therefore, normally, decisions must be recognised in all EPC contracting states, and any remedy under **Art.61(1)** will apply in respect of all contracting states, unless one of the exceptions mentioned in Art.10 and 11 of the Protocol applies.

R. 17 Filing of a new European patent application by the entitled person

Implementation of **Art.61**

1 **General**

A new application according to **Art.61(1)(b)** has many of the characteristics of a divisional application (see **Art.61(2)**; A-IV,2.5).

R. 17(1) Where the person adjudged by a final decision to be entitled to the grant of the European patent files a new European patent application under Article 61, paragraph 1(b), the original application shall be deemed to be withdrawn on the date of filing the new application for the Contracting States designated therein in which the decision has been taken or recognised or must be recognised on the basis of the Protocol on Recognition.

Art.61(1)(b) Filing of a new application by the entitled person

1 **Original application deemed to be withdrawn**
All contracting states have to recognise an entitlement decision taken by a court of a contracting state (Art.9 Protocol on Recognition) because the reservations on recognition pursuant to Art.167 EPC1973 have expired. An exception exists for decisions recognising judgments from non-EPC states (Art.9 Protocol on Recognition).

R. 17(2) The filing fee and search fee shall be paid within one month of filing the new application. If the filing fee or search fee is not paid in due time, the application shall be deemed to be withdrawn.

1 **Filing fee and search fee for new application**
The amount of the filing fee and the amount of the search fee are fixed in **Rfees2(1)1** and **Rfees2(1)2**, respectively.

If the filing fee and the search fee are not paid within one month of filing the new application, the application is deemed withdrawn (**R.17(2)**). The EPO sends the applicant a notification of loss of rights according to **R.112(1)**. The applicant may request further processing under **Art.121** and **R.135** within two months from notification of the communication.

The search fee for the new application must always be paid, even if a search fee has already been paid for the earlier application in respect of the same invention (A-IV,2.5(iii) and A-IV,1.4.1). The search fee for the new application will be refunded fully or in part if the search report can be based on the search report drawn up in respect of the earlier application (**Rfees9(2)**).

A page fee as part of the filing fee and claims fees may be payable. See **R.38** and **R.45**.

R. 17(3) The designation fee shall be paid within six months of the date on which the European Patent Bulletin mentions the publication of the European search report drawn up in respect of the new application. Rule 39, paragraphs 2 and 3, shall apply.

Amended, in force since 01.04.2009 (OJ 2008 p.513; OJ 2009 p.118 footnote 1).
R.39(2) Non-payment of the designation fee
R.39(3) Non-refundability of the designation fee

1 **Designation fee for new application**
For new applications filed on or after 01.04.2009 a flat designation fee must be paid within six months of the date on which the Bulletin mentions the publication of the search report for the new application (**R.17(3)**). If the fee is not paid in time, the procedure is the same as for a normal application because of the references to **R.39** in the provision.

Thus, if the designation fee is not paid in due time, the new application will be deemed withdrawn under **R.39(2)**. The loss of rights will be communicated to the applicant under **R.112(1)** and further processing under **Art.121** and **R.135** can be requested within two months from notification of the communication. The loss of rights takes effect upon expiry of the six-month period, not upon expiry of the period for further processing (**G4/98** hn. II, r.7.2 mutatis mutandis; A-III,11.2.3)). See **Art.92** for the publication of the search report.

2 **Other fees for new application**

The examination fee is to be paid at the latest within six months of the mention of the publication of the search report (**R.70(1)1**). Renewal fees are only due for the years following the year of the filing of the new application (**R.51(6)**).

R. 18 Partial transfer of the right to the European patent

Implementation of **Art.61**

1 **General**

The partial transfer of the right to a European patent may relate to the transfer of a part of the subject-matter of an application to the entitled party (**R.18(1)**), e.g. to only specific embodiments.

R. 18(1) If a final decision determines that a third party is entitled to the grant of a European patent in respect of only part of the subject-matter disclosed in the original European patent application, Article 61 and Rules 16 and 17 shall apply to such part.

Art.61 Application filed by non-entitled person
R.16 Procedure for entitled person
R.17 Filing of new application by entitled person

1 **Options for partially entitled person**

R.18(1) applies **Art.61** and **R.17**, which normally relate to the entire application, to parts of the subject-matter of an application. It follows that a new application can be filed for a part of the subject matter of an original application, e.g. for one or more embodiments.

Third parties that are adjudged to be entitled to only part of the subject-matter do not have the option of taking over the prosecution of the application under **Art.61(1)(a)**. They may file a new application under **Art.61(1)(b)** only for that part of the original subject-matter to which they have become entitled, e.g. for specific embodiments. The original application must then be restricted to the subject-matter to which the original applicant remains entitled (see the travaux préparatoires BR/144 e/71 §52). (C-IX,2.3)

The third party may also request under **Art.61(1)(c)** that the application be refused if the applicant does not excise the subject-matter to which the third party is entitled (Singer, Art.61, note 27).

If the entitled third party files a new application and the original application is confined to the subject-matter to which the original applicant remains entitled, a disclaimer can be used to disclaim originally disclosed embodiments provided that the requirements of **Art.123(2)** are met (**G2/10** r.4.6).

For the case that a third party is entitled to be a co-applicant, see **Art.61(1):2.**

R. 18(2) Where appropriate, the original European patent application shall contain, for the designated Contracting States in which the decision was taken or recognised or must be recognised on the basis of the Protocol on Recognition, claims, a description and drawings which are different from those for the other designated Contracting States.

1 **Different applications for different states**
If a decision that a third party is entitled to a part of the subject-matter exceptionally has effect in some but not all designated states (**R.16(2)**) and a new application is filed under **Art.61(1)(b)**, the original application must be restricted to the subject-matter to which the original applicant remains entitled only for the designated states in which the decision has effect. For the other designated states, a different set of claims can be kept directed to all subject-matter as an exception to **Art.118.**

Chapter II *Mention of the inventor*

R. 19 Designation of the inventor

Amended, in force since 01.04.2021 (OJ 2021 A3). The amendment replaced the requirement in R.19(1) to provide the inventor's full address by the requirement to provide the country and place of residence of the inventor. The amendment also deleted R.19(3) and (4).
Implementation of **Art.81**

R. 19(1) The request for grant of a European patent shall contain the designation of the inventor. However, if the applicant is not the inventor or is not the sole inventor, the designation shall be filed in a separate document. The designation shall state the family name, given names and country and place of residence of the inventor, contain the statement referred to in Article 81 and bear the signature of the applicant or their representative.

Art.81 Statement indicating the origin of the right to the patent
Also amended by decision of the Administrative Council of 10.12.2024, which entered into force on 01.04.2025 (OJ 2025 A16). The amendment was introduction of gender-neutral language.

1 **Designation**
The designation of the inventor must be signed by the applicant or the appointed representative, or, in the case of several applicants, by each applicant or the respective representative. However, if a common representative has been appointed, the signature of said common representative suffices (see also A-VIII,1.5). A signature is also required if the designation is filed as a separate document annexed to the request for grant (exception to the 'exception of annexed documents' in **R.50(3)**).

Prior to 01.04.2021, the designation of the inventor had to include the full address of the inventor. As of 01.04.2021, only the inventor's country and place of residence are required. This applies to any designation of the inventor filed or rectified on or after 01.04.2021, as well as to any international application entering the European phase on or after that date. The place of residence is the municipality, including the postal code if available, in which the inventor permanently resides. The EPO also accepts the country and place of residence of the inventor's employer (A-III,5.3). If the full address is filed on or after 01.04.2021, it will be included in the public part of the file. As of 01.11.2021, the EPO no longer publishes inventors' addresses in the Register (see **R.143(1)(g)**). (OJ 2021 A3, A12)

The 'statement referred to in Article 81', i.e. the statement indicating the origin of the applicant's right to the patent, can be short. In the case of a transfer, it need only state: 'by agreement of...'. In the case of employment it suffices to state that the inventor is an employee of the applicant. In the case of inheritance, a statement that the applicant is the heir of the inventor is sufficient.

In case of multiple inventors, the order in which they are listed can be changed by submitting an appropriate request while the application is pending (A-III, 5.6).

See **R.21** and **R.57(f)** for rectification of a missing or deficient designation of the inventor.

R. 19(2) The European Patent Office shall not verify the accuracy of the designation of the inventor.

1 **Correction of designation**
An error in a designation can be corrected under **R.21**, e.g. by deleting, changing or adding a name. The EPO informs the applicant of a missing designation under **R.60**.

R. 20 Publication of the mention of the inventor

Amended by decision of the Administrative Council of 10.12.2024, which entered into force on 01.04.2025 (OJ 2025 A16). Paragraphs (1) and (2) were amended by introducing gender-neutral language.
Implementation of **Art.81**

R. 20(1) The designated inventor shall be mentioned in the published European patent application and the European patent specification, unless they inform the European Patent Office in writing that they have waived their right to be thus mentioned.

1 **Mention of inventor in application and patent**
The waiver by an inventor of the right to be mentioned in the published application and patent under **R.20(1)** does not affect the status of that person as an inventor.

After a waiver of the right to be mentioned is received, the name of the inventor is excluded from the published European patent application and patent, an entry in the European Patent Register under **R.143(1)(g)** is not made, and the designation of the inventor in the file of the application is excluded from file inspection (**R.144(c)**). If a waiver is received after the publication of the European patent application, the mention of the inventor is removed from the Register. (A-III,5.2)

R. 20(2) Paragraph 1 shall apply where a third party files with the European Patent Office a final decision determining that the applicant for or proprietor of a European patent is required to designate them as an inventor.

1 **Inventor dispute**
The EPO assumes that the correct inventor has been designated and does not verify the accuracy of the designation (**R.19(2)**). The EPC has no provisions relating to the resolution of a dispute concerning the status of a person as an inventor. Any dispute must therefore be decided under national law. A court decision is not an absolute requirement since other national authorities may also have jurisdiction (**Prot.Rec.Art.1(2)**). The EPO will apply **R.20(1)** if it receives a decision that a third party must be designated as inventor (**R.20(2)**) and will mention the inventor in the patent application and specification, unless the inventor has waived this right.

R. 21 Rectification of the designation of an inventor

Implementation of **Art.81**

R. 21(1) An incorrect designation of an inventor shall be rectified upon request and only with the consent of the wrongly designated person and, where such a request is filed by a third party, the consent of the applicant for or proprietor of the patent. Rule 19 shall apply mutatis mutandis.

R.19 Designation of the inventor

1 **Rectification of the designation of inventor**

The meaning of this provision can be elucidated using case law and the Guidelines as set out below.

A designation of the inventor is incorrect if an inventor is wrongly named, the name of an inventor is omitted or data concerning an inventor is incorrect. See **R.60** for the subsequent designation of the inventor where a designation is not filed with the application.

The designation may be rectified voluntarily under **R.21** or mandatorily upon invitation under **R.60** if the EPO has noticed a deficiency under **R.57(f)** during the examination as to formalities. A voluntary rectification may be made at any time, even after termination of the proceedings before the EPO, e.g. after the grant of a patent (A-III,5.5). Mandatory rectification must be made within the period specified in **R.60(1)**.

A wrongly designated inventor will be removed from the designation of the inventor upon request, provided the request contains the consent of the wrongly designated inventor and, where the request is filed by a third party, the consent of the applicant or proprietor (**R.21(1)**, first sentence; A-III,5.5).

An inventor can also be added to the designation upon request. The addition of an inventor does not require the consent of any already named inventor, because an already named inventor is not 'wrongly designated' (J8/82 hn.I). The request must contain the required details concerning the added inventor and must be duly signed as required by **R.19(1)** (see reference to **R.19** in the provision). (A-III,5.5)

A request to correct data concerning an inventor can be filed at any time under **R.21(1)**.

R. 21(2) Where an incorrect designation of the inventor has been recorded in the European Patent Register or published in the European Patent Bulletin, its rectification or cancellation shall also be recorded or published therein.

Chapter III *Registration of transfers, licences and other rights*

R. 22 Registration of transfers

Implementation of **Art.71** and **73**

1 **General**

In order to ensure that the parties to the proceedings are properly identified, the EPO registers transfers of applications and patents up to the expiry of the opposition period or opposition procedure (**R.85**), including any subsequent appeal (**R.100(1)**) (**J17/91**). The EPO will regard a person as a party to the proceedings only if that person is duly recorded as such. A successor in title will therefore only be recognised by the EPO when the necessary formalities for recording the transfer have been completed. In the case of an applicant or proprietor the formalities are laid down by **R.22**. The requirement for any transfer to be registered allows the EPO to precisely and simply determine the identity of the parties, thereby avoiding complicated investigations into the relationship between an original party and a would-be successor (**T656/98** r.1.1). The EPO has no jurisdiction to decide entitlement disputes, for which reason **Art.60(3)** defines the person entitled to be granted a patent as the applicant of record.

The Legal Division is competent to take decisions in respect of entries in the Register (**Art.20**). However, routine requests relating to the entry of data in the Register and the correction of entries already made, i.e. requests which are not in dispute, are handled by the Receiving Section or the examining division depending on the stage of the grant procedure. The same applies to decisions taken under **R.21** (rectification of the designation of the inventor). (**J18/84**)

In order to validly transfer an application before the EPO, a written request to register the transfer must be filed along with proof of the transfer, and a fee must be paid. The transfer can be entered in the Register only after publication of the application (**Art.127**, second sentence). See also E-XIII. The corresponding PCT provisions can be found in R.92bis PCT.

A mere change of name on the part of the applicant, not involving any change in legal identity, will be registered upon request and production of relevant documentary evidence and is free of charge (E-XIV,5).

2 **Time of transfer**

A transfer effected before publication of the application is entered in a shadow Register and recorded in the public Register only after publication (in line with **Art.127**).

The EPO records the transfer of applications and patents that are or may become subject to proceedings before the EPO. If an application or patent can no longer be the subject of proceedings, there is no legal justification for recording any transfer. Hence, the EPO will still record the transfer of an application that is (deemed) withdrawn or refused as long as procedural rights are pending. Furthermore, the EPO will record the transfer of a granted patent during the nine-month opposition period and while opposition proceedings are pending.

An example of such a procedural right is the right to claim priority during a period of twelve months from filing. The transfer of a priority application that is deemed withdrawn during the priority year will therefore be recorded, which can be helpful when claiming priority for a subsequent application filed with another patent office.

Another example of a procedural right is the right to further processing during a period of two months from the notification of a loss of rights or re-establishment while the two-month and one-year periods of **R.136(1)** are pending. However, the EPO will only record the transfer of an application in these cases if the successor in title has taken remedial steps, such as requesting further processing and/or re-establishment. These steps should be taken at the latest when filing the request to record the transfer in order to safeguard legal certainty. (**J10/93** hn and r.4)

R. 22(1) The transfer of a European patent application shall be recorded in the European Patent Register at the request of an interested party, upon production of documents providing evidence of such transfer. Rule 2, paragraph 2, shall apply mutatis mutandis to the signature of the parties to the contract.

Amended by decision of the Administrative Council of 14.12.2023, which entered into force on 01.04.2024 (OJ 2024 A16; CA/D 26/23). The amendment added a reference to R.2(2).

1 **Request for transfer**

The request must be filed in one of the official languages of the EPO (**R.3(1)**). Evidence of the transfer, on the other hand, can be filed in any language (**R.3(3)**). The EPO can ask for a translation of such evidence.

It is not necessary to file a formal assignment complying with **Art.72**; any written evidence of the transfer is admissible, provided that the documents bear the name and signature of persons able to act on behalf of the parties. National law applies in determining who can sign on behalf of a legal person and an indication of the signatory's entitlement to sign must be given. A scanned copy of a properly executed assignment is sufficient (**J5/23**). If the evidence is unsatisfactory, the EPO will invite the parties to remedy the deficiency and specify a time limit for doing so. (E-XIV,3)

In **J5/23**, the Legal Board concluded, in the absence of any clarification in the Implementing Regulations, that an assignment under **Art.72** must bear the handwritten signatures of the parties, i.e. be on paper. The Legal Board found the Notice of the EPO that stated that certain electronic signatures could be used in documents filed as evidence under **R.22(1)** (OJ 2021 A86, now superseded) was not compatible with **Art.72**. In response, **R.22(1)** was amended by the Administrative Council (as of 01.04.2024) in order to add a reference to **R.2(2)**, asserting the right of the President to decide what kind of signature is permitted (E-XIV,3). The President has decided (OJ 2024 A17) that contracts and declarations submitted as evidence in support of a transfer of rights may be authenticated by a handwritten signature, a facsimile signature, a text string signature or a digital signature under the conditions specified by the EPO. A facsimile signature, as explained in Art.12(2) of Dec. Pres. OJ 2023 A48 concerning the electronic filing of documents, is a reproduction of a person's signature. A text-string signature, as explained in Art.12(3) of the same decision, is a string of characters, preceded and followed by a forward slash (/), selected by the signatory to prove their identity and their intent to sign. Documents bearing a facsimile signature or a text string signature may be filed either on paper or electronically. A digital signature is accepted if it is contained in a document that is filed electronically, is legible, is not infected with a computer virus and does not contain other malicious software. An example of an acceptable electronic signature is one that uses Public Key Infrastructure (PKI) technology (such as an advanced and qualified electronic signature within the meaning of the EU's eIDAS Regulation). The EPO will only require clarification and/or further evidence if it has specific doubts concerning the authenticity of a signature. When a natural person signs on behalf of a legal person, the position of the natural person within the legal person must be expressly indicated but the EPO will not require any further evidence. (Not. EPO OJ 2024 A22 concerning amended **R.22**)

The request may be filed by any interested party, i.e. not only by the applicant but also by the assignee (**R.22(1)**). The request is preferably filed using form 5050; further recommendations are given in OJ 2019 A79. Multiple transfers can be made in a single batch request; the multiple fees for transfer can be paid using a batch payment (OJ 2019 A79 §21; **R.2(1):2**). A decision to refuse the registration can be appealed (see **J5/23**).

R. 22(2) Registration of the transfer may be subject to the payment of an administrative fee under the conditions laid down by the President of the European Patent Office. Where a fee is due, the request shall not be deemed to have been filed until the administrative fee has been paid. It may be rejected only if paragraph 1 has not been complied with.

Amended by decision of the Administrative Council of 14.12.2023, which entered into force on 01.04.2024 (OJ 2024 A16; CA/D 26/23). The amendment added that the President decides when a fee is required.

1 **Fee for transfer**
Until 01.04.2024, it was always necessary to pay a fee in order to record a transfer in the Register. As a result of the amendment of **R.22(2)** coming into force on that date, the President now decides whether a fee must be paid (E-XIV,3). The fee is fixed by the President under **Rfees3(1)**. The fee is waived if the request to record a transfer is filed using MyEPO but is payable in other cases (Dec. Pres. OJ 2024 A5; Not. EPO OJ 2024 A22). If a request for transfer relates to multiple applications and the fee is not waived, it is due for each one. Batch payment is possible only via the corresponding function in Central Fee Payment (E-XIV,3).

R. 22(3) A transfer shall have effect vis-à-vis the European Patent Office only at the date when and to the extent that the documents referred to in paragraph 1 have been produced.

1 **Effective date of the transfer**
A transfer becomes effective before the EPO only when all of the registration formalities are complete, i.e. a duly substantiated request has been filed and the fee has been paid. The express wording 'only when' of **R.22(3)** makes any earlier date mentioned in the text of an assignment and effective between the parties to the assignment irrelevant for the EPO. Hence, a new owner is only entitled to file an appeal when the transfer has been recorded with the EPO. (**T656/98** r.3.5, 4.1; **G1/12** r.45.1)

R.22(3) does not apply to a universal succession in law as the result of which a party ceases to exist, e.g. in the case of a death or merger. When parties cease to exist, they lose party status. Since in general the authorisation of a representative does not terminate (**R.152(9)**), the proceedings are not interrupted (**R.142(1)(a)**) and the representative immediately represents the successor in law and can continue to act in proceedings (**T15/01** r.11). The successor in law automatically becomes a party before the EPO. In appeal proceedings, the change in name of a party may be corrected under **R.101(2)** (**T15/01** r.14).

2 **No reversal of registration of transfer**
There may be a dispute between parties as to whether an assignment of a patent application is valid (e.g. because of the alleged lack of an authorisation). If the assignment was registered under **R.22**, this registration cannot be undone by the EPO at the request of a party. Only national courts can decide whether an assignment is valid. If a dispute on this matter is pending in a contracting state, proceedings may be stayed by applying, possibly by analogy, **R.14** for applications and **R.78** for patents during opposition. (**J16/14**; E-XIV,3)

R. 23 Registration of licences and other rights

Implementation of **Art.71** and **Art.73**

1 **General**
To validly register a licence or other right in the European Patent Register (**R.143(1)(w)**), it is necessary to file a signed, written request (**R.23(1)**, **R.22**, and **R.50(3)**) and provide evidence that the license or right exists (**R.23(1)**). The President decides whether a fee is payable or not (**R.23(1)** and **R.22(2)**). The amount of the fee is fixed by the President under **Rfees3(1)**. At present, the fee is waived if the request to register a license or other right is filed using MyEPO (OJ 2024 A5). As is the case for the registration of a transfer under **R.22**, the evidence may be authenticated by a handwritten signature, a facsimile signature, a text string signature or a digital signature under the conditions specified by the EPO (see **R.22(1):1**).

A request for the registration of a licence can be filed by any interested party (**R.22(1)** with **R.23(1)**). However, the registration of an exclusive licence must be requested by both the applicant and the licensee (**R.24(a)**).

Licences and other rights cannot be registered after the publication of the mention of the grant (**Art.97(3)**) because **R.85** (transfer of the patent) does not refer to **R.23** and **24**, and there are no other applicable provisions in the EPC (**Art.73** only mentions applications).

A security interest (lien) is an example of a right other than a license that can be registered.

R. 23(1) Rule 22, paragraphs 1 and 2, shall apply mutatis mutandis to the registration of the grant or transfer of a licence, the establishment or transfer of a right in rem in respect of a European patent application and any legal means of execution affecting such an application.

R.22 Registering a transfer

R. 23(2) A registration under paragraph 1 shall be cancelled upon request, supported by documents providing evidence that the right has lapsed, or by the written consent of the proprietor of the right to the cancellation of the registration. Rule 22, paragraph 2, shall apply mutatis mutandis.

R.22(2) Payment of fee

1 **Cancellation of registration**
The fee for cancelling a registration is fixed by the President under **Rfees3(1)**.

R. 24 Special entries for licence registrations

A licence in respect of a European patent application shall be recorded
(a) as an exclusive licence if the applicant and the licensee so request;
(b) as a sub-licence where it is granted by a licensee whose licence is recorded in the European Patent Register.

Implementation of **Art.73**

1 **Types of licences**
An exclusive licence confers on the licensee a right in respect of an application or a patent to the exclusion of all other persons, including the licensor, i.e. the applicant or proprietor. Multiple exclusive licences may be granted under a single application or patent for distinct rights (such as the right to manufacture, the right to distribute and the right to use) for different territories (see **Art.73**), for different embodiments or for the use of the same embodiment in different fields of application. A non-exclusive licence places no restriction on the grant of further licences for the same right to different parties.

A sole licence confers on the licensee a right to the exclusion of all persons other than the licensor; the licensor may continue to use the licensed invention.

A licence may authorise the licensee to grant sub-licences to a third party without reference to the licensor. Such a sub-licence can be recorded in the Register, provided the licence is also recorded.

Chapter IV *Certificate of exhibition*

R. 25 Certificate of exhibition

Within four months of filing the European patent application, the applicant shall file the certificate referred to in Article 55, paragraph 2, which:

(a) is issued at the exhibition by the authority responsible for the protection of industrial property at that exhibition;
(b) states that the invention was in fact displayed there;
(c) states the opening date of the exhibition and, where the invention was disclosed later than on that date, the date on which the invention was first disclosed; and
(d) is accompanied by an identification of the invention, duly authenticated by the above-mentioned authority.

Art.55(2) Non-prejudicial disclosures
Implementation of **Art.55(2)**

1 **Certificate and identification**
If an applicant that has displayed an invention at an international exhibition files a statement under **Art.55(2)** on filing a patent application for the invention, a supporting certificate must be provided within four months of filing. The certificate must include an authenticated identification of the invention. The four-month period is calculated from the filing of the application, which is not necessarily the same as the date of filing accorded under **Art.80** (see **Art.80:4**). See **Art.55(2):1** for the procedure.

R.159(1)(h) governs the filing of the certificate for a Euro-PCT application.

Chapter V *Biotechnological inventions*

R. 26 General and definitions

Implementation of **Art.53(b)**

R. 26(1) For European patent applications and patents concerning biotechnological inventions, the relevant provisions of the Convention shall be applied and interpreted in accordance with the provisions of this Chapter. Directive 98/44/EC of 6 July 1998 on the legal protection of biotechnological inventions shall be used as a supplementary means of interpretation.

1 **EU Biotechnology Directive**

Chapter V of the EPC, containing **R.26** to **29**, was inserted (as Chapter VI, R.23b to 23e EPC1973) by a decision of the Administrative Council of 16.06.1999, which entered into force on 01.09.1999 (OJ 1999 p.437). The Chapter implements EU Directive 98/44/EC on the legal protection of biotechnological inventions (see OJ 1999 p.101 for the text of the Directive and OJ 1999 p.573 for an EPO notice concerning its implementation). **R.28(2)** was added in 2017 (OJ 2017 A56).

The EU Directive was adopted in 1998 to harmonise the protection of biotechnological inventions within the EU. Even though at that time, the relevant provisions of national law were most often taken from the EPC, the different interpretations of these provisions that were possible could have given rise to divergent national practices prejudicial to the proper operation of the internal market of the EU. The EU chose to harmonise national law by means of a Directive and the EPC was then also brought into conformity with these changes to EU national law, even though there are a number of EPC contracting states that are not EU member states. (Decision of the Court of Justice of the EU of 09.10.2001, C-377/98, r.2, 16, 22)

According to **R.26(1)**, the provisions in **R.26** to **29** have a common purpose in regulating the application and interpretation of pre-existing EPC provisions in the specific field of biotechnological inventions (in particular **Art.53(a)** and **Art.53(b)**). These provisions of **R.26** to **29** were not therefore intended, for example, to introduce completely new rules for the patentability of inventions directed to animals. (**T315/03** r.5.1)

The reference to the Directive aims to ensure that the recitals preceding the provisions of the Directive are also taken into account and to promote a uniform, Europe-wide interpretation of provisions relating to the patentability of biotech inventions. The text of the Directive is reproduced in OJ 1999 p.101. (OJ 1999 p.573)

Although **R.26** to **29** are intended to implement the EU Directive, the EBoA held in **G2/06** r.2-11 that there was no mechanism under the EPC whereby questions relating to the interpretation of the Rules, and hence the Directive, could be referred to the Court of Justice of the EU.

Provisions R.26 to R.29 are applicable not only to cases filed on or after the date the rules took effect but also to cases pending on that date (**T315/03** hn.I; **G2/06**). However, for **R.28(2)**, see **G3/19** hn.

R. 26(2) "Biotechnological inventions" are inventions which concern a product consisting of or containing biological material or a process by means of which biological material is produced, processed or used.

R. 26(3) "Biological material" means any material containing genetic information and capable of reproducing itself or being reproduced in a biological system.

1 **Biological material**
An animal, consisting of a material containing genetic information and capable of reproduction, is a product consisting of biological material in accordance with **R.26(3)** (**T315/03** r.5.2).

R. 26(4) "Plant variety" means any plant grouping within a single botanical taxon of the lowest known rank, which grouping, irrespective of whether the conditions for the grant of a plant variety right are fully met, can be:
(a) defined by the expression of the characteristics that results from a given genotype or combination of genotypes,
(b) distinguished from any other plant grouping by the expression of at least one of the said characteristics, and
(c) considered as a unit with regard to its suitability for being propagated unchanged.

R. 26(5) A process for the production of plants or animals is essentially biological if it consists entirely of natural phenomena such as crossing or selection.

1 **Essentially biological processes**
R.26(5) provides a definition of the term 'essentially biological' in **Art.53(b)**. However, the provision is self-contradictory in stating that crossing and selection are examples of natural phenomena, because crossing and selection in the context of processes for the production of plants (**Art.53(b)**) are not natural phenomena but method steps generally involving human intervention. **R.26(5)** and the legislative history of the Biotech Directive do not therefore provide any useful guidance in the interpretation of **Art.53(b)**. (**G2/07** r.4, 5)

Selfing (i.e. self-pollination) of transgenic plants is also excluded from patentability, as selfing, like crossing, is the mixing of entire genomes (G-II,5.4.2). See **Art.53:2.2** for the correct interpretation of the term 'essentially biological'.

R. 26(6) "Microbiological process" means any process involving or performed upon or resulting in microbiological material.

R. 27 Patentable biotechnological inventions

Biotechnological inventions shall also be patentable if they concern:
(a) biological material which is isolated from its natural environment or produced by means of a technical process even if it previously occurred in nature;
(b) without prejudice to Rule 28, paragraph 2, plants or animals if the technical feasibility of the invention is not confined to a particular plant or animal variety;
(c) a microbiological or other technical process, or a product obtained by means of such a process other than a plant or animal variety.

Inserted, in force since 01.09.1999 (OJ 1999 p.437, p.573). Amended, in force since 01.07.2017 (OJ 2017 A56).

R.28(2) exception for products obtained by essentially biological process
Implementation of **Art.53(b)**

1 **Patentable inventions**
The list of items in **R.27** that are explicitly considered patentable is not exhaustive (G-II,5.2).

R.27(b) reflects the principle that plants, plant material, animals and animal material other than plant and animal varieties are generally eligible for patent protection. The reference to **R.28(2)** makes it clear that the principle set forth in **R.27(b)** does not override the exclusion from patentability of plants and animals obtained by means of an essentially biological process (see **Art.53:2.2**).

The proviso in **R.27(c)** confirms, in line with **Art.53(b)**, that a product claim directed to a plant or animal variety is excluded from patentability even if the variety concerned is produced by means of a microbiological process or another technical process. Such a variety will nevertheless enjoy protection under **Art.64(2)** as the direct product of a patented microbiological or other technical process. (OJ 1999 p.573).

R. 28 Exceptions to patentability

Amended by decision of the Administrative Council of 29.06.2017, which entered into force on 01.07.2017 (OJ 2017 A56). The amendment inserted a new paragraph (2).
Implementation of **Art.53(a)**

R. 28(1) Under Article 53(a), European patents shall not be granted in respect of biotechnological inventions which, in particular, concern the following:
(a) processes for cloning human beings;
(b) processes for modifying the germ line genetic identity of human beings;
(c) uses of human embryos for industrial or commercial purposes;
(d) processes for modifying the genetic identity of animals which are likely to cause them suffering without any substantial medical benefit to humans or animals, and also animals resulting from such processes.

Art.53(a) Inventions contrary to morality
Also amended by decision of the Administrative Council of 10.12.2024, which entered into force on 01.04.2025 (OJ 2025 A16). Paragraph (1)(d) was amended by introducing gender-neutral language.

1 **Exclusion from patentability**
The provision contains four categories of inventions in the field of biotechnology that must be excluded from patentability under **Art.53(a)**. The words 'in particular' in **R.28(1)** indicate that the rule is not intended to provide an exhaustive list of inventions excluded from patentability. A case falling within one of the four categories (a) - (d) must necessarily be denied a patent under **Art.53(a)** and there is no need to consider that article further; a case not falling within one of those categories must be considered further under **Art.53(a)** (T315/03 hn.II.1). See **Art.53:1.2** and notes below for examples of excluded subject matter. In **T1553/22**, the board was considering an invention concerning the use of pluripotent cells to make a human-animal chi-

mera. It established that such an invention was not explicitly excluded by any of **R.28(1)(a)-(d)**, nor by Recital 38 of the EU Biotechnology directive which should be used to interpret **R.28** (see **R.26(1):1**). However, the board found that such an invention should also be excluded from patentability under **Art.53(a)** and **R.28(1)** since the rational underlying Recital 38 was also applicable to the claimed invention, adding a further case to the non-exhaustive list of **R.28(1)**.

2 **Use of human embryos (R.28(1)(c))**

R.28(1)(c) forbids the patenting of a claim directed to a human embryonic stem cell culture which - as described in the application - could only be prepared at the filing date by a method which necessarily involves the destruction of the human embryos from which the culture is derived, even if that method is not part of the claim. A later development allowing the invention to be practised without the destruction of any human embryos is of no significance; the applicability of **R.28(1)(c)** must be assessed at the filing date of the application. To do otherwise would reduce legal certainty and might be to the detriment of a third party who later provides an innocuous way of carrying out the invention. (**G2/06** hn.2; r.33; see also later decision C-34/10 of the CJEU)

The exact wording of the claims is not relevant; it is the manner in which the invention is carried out which is the critical issue. To restrict the application of **R.28(1)(c)** to what an applicant chooses to explicitly claim would have the undesirable consequence that skilful drafting would be sufficient to avoid the prohibition. (**G2/06** r.22)

As a consequence of **G2/06**, a method claim including the step of destroying a human embryo is not patentable. The point in time at which such destruction takes place is irrelevant (**T2221/10** r.37; G-II,5.2(ii)). However, if the invention is of broader applicability, the use of human embryos may be excluded by way of a disclaimer, even if the disclaimer has no basis in the application as filed. (**T329/06** r.2-8)

3 **Modification of genetic identity (R.28(1)(d))**

A claim directed to genetically modified animals or to processes for genetically modifying animals needs to meet the requirements of both **R.28(1)(d)** and **Art. 53(a)** (G-II,5.3(iv)). Under **R.28(1)(d)**, only three issues need to be considered: animal suffering, medical benefit and the necessary correspondence between the two in terms of the animals in question (**T315/03** hn.V.1). The three issues must be considered on the basis of evidence (**T315/03** r.9.5). The level of proof of suffering and of substantial benefit required for **R.28(1)(d)** is not more than 'likelihood' (**T315/03** r.6.2, r.9.3). The criteria must be assessed on the effective date of the patent application or patent, as with all criteria for the assessment of patentability (**T315/03** r.8.2).

The criterion 'substantial medical benefit to man or animal' constitutes a sub-range of benefits that fall completely within the broader range 'usefulness to mankind' in the test of **T19/90** (see **Art.53:1.2**). Hence, if the former criterion is established, the latter is necessarily established (**T315/03** r.7.1).

The provision requires that the benefit is obtained for all animals likely to suffer within the scope of the claim. Hence, a claim must be excluded from patentability if one animal covered by the claim is likely to suffer without evidence of substantial medical benefit (**T315/03** r.12.2.2-3). See also **T606/03**; here claims were allowed to animals that would not be expected to suffer, regardless of the potential medical benefit.

R. 28(2) Under Article 53(b), European patents shall not be granted in respect of plants or animals exclusively obtained by means of an essentially biological process.

Art.53(b) varieties and essentially biological processes

1 **Products of essentially biological processes**
The exclusion from patentability of claims directed to essentially biological processes in **Art.53(b)** also applies to product claims and product-by-process claims directed to plants, plant material or animals, if the claimed product is exclusively obtained by means of an essentially biological process or if the claimed process features define an essentially biological process (**G3/19** hn). See also **Art.53:2.2**.

R.28(2) is not applicable to applications and patents having a filing date before 01.07.2017, in view of **G3/19** (**T2796/18**).

Note that the exclusion as defined in **G3/19** appears to be broader than in **R.28(2)** by also excluding plant material.

If a claimed plant or animal to which **R.28(2)** applies might be the result of either a technical process or an essentially biological process, a disclaimer is required in order to limit the claim to the plant or animal when made by technical means (G-II,5.4). If the claimed plant or animal can only be produced by technical means (e.g. by using a transgene) then no disclaimer is necessary.

R. 29 The human body and its elements

Implementation of **Art.53(a)**, **(b)**

R. 29(1) The human body, at the various stages of its formation and development, and the simple discovery of one of its elements, including the sequence or partial sequence of a gene, cannot constitute patentable inventions.

R. 29(2) An element isolated from the human body or otherwise produced by means of a technical process, including the sequence or partial sequence of a gene, may constitute a patentable invention, even if the structure of that element is identical to that of a natural element.

R. 29(3) The industrial application of a sequence or a partial sequence of a gene must be disclosed in the patent application.

1 **Industrial application of sequence or gene**
Whereas industrial applicability, required by **Art.57**, is self-evident for most inventions and needs no clarification in the description (see **R.42(1)(f)**), the industrial applicability of a gene sequence is not obvious and, according to **R.29(3)**, must be stated explicitly in the application.

In particular, the disclosure must indicate the function performed by the sequence and the protein built from it (OJ 1999 p.573 §27). The function of a protein may be described in terms of its molecular function, its cellular function or its biological function in a broad sense – all are equally satisfactory for the purposes of **R.29(3)** insofar as a practical application (i.e. a profitable use) is derivable therefrom (**T898/05** hn.3).

Some disclosure of the function performed by the protein that a claimed gene encodes may also be necessary in order to demonstrate an inventive step. **T1329/04** r.11-12 notes that while post-published evidence may be taken into consideration, it may not serve as the sole basis used to establish that a claimed sequence solves the objective technical problem posed. This must be derivable in the sense of **G2/21** from the application itself.

R. 30 Requirements of European patent applications relating to nucleotide and amino acid sequences

Implementation of **Art.78(1)(b)**

1 **Filing of sequence listings**
An application disclosing a nucleotide or amino acid sequence must contain a sequence listing in an annex to the description, complying with the requirements of **R.30**. The EPO has adopted WIPO Standard ST.26 for the format of sequence listings.

For European patent applications and international patent applications having a date of filing on or after 01.07.2022, sequence listings must be filed electronically in xml format complying with WIPO Standard ST.26 according to Dec. Pres. OJ 2021 A96 (see Not. EPO OJ 2021 A97 and Not. EPO OJ 2022 A60). The current version of WIPO Standard ST.26 to be used is specified in Dec. Pres. OJ 2024 A54.

For European patent applications and international patent applications having a date of filing prior to 01.07.2022, sequence listings must be filed electronically in txt format complying with WIPO Standard ST.25 according to Dec. Pres. OJ 2011 p.372 and Not. EPO OJ 2013 p.542.

Sequence listings in the prescribed format are exempted from the page fee of **Rfees2(1)1a**. However, the EPO will charge the page fee for sequence listings not filed in the prescribed format (see **Rfees2(1):4.2.1**).

When filing a divisional application, the sequence listing must be filed again for the divisional (Not. EPO OJ 2021 A97 §16-18; A-IV,5.4). The format required is the one that applies on the date of filing (receipt) of the divisional. If a compliant sequence listing has been filed for the parent, the EPO will, on request, add it to the file of the divisional application for search purposes, i.e. not as part of the description. Any sequence listing which is to form part of the description of the divisional application as filed must be filed by the applicant. See A-IV,5.1 for sequence listings inserted as a missing part under **R.56**, and A-IV,5.3 for sequence listings filed by reference to a previous application under **R.40(1)(c)**. The EPO also allows filing the parent application's sequence listing compliant with WIPO Standard ST.25 in pdf format in the divisional application as a safeguard. Under certain conditions, these pages are not taken into account in the calculation of the page fee. (Not. EPO OJ 2023 A98)

A sequence listing may be corrected under **R.139** or amended under **Art.123(2)**. In these cases, a complete replacement sequence listing must be filed with the corrections or amendments (H-IV,2.2.5). The corrected or amended sequence listing must comply with the applicable WIPO standard, which depends on the application's date of filing (A-IV,5). See **J7/11** for an example of a correction of a sequence listing.

R. 30(1) If nucleotide or amino acid sequences are disclosed in the European patent application, the description shall contain a sequence listing conforming to the rules laid down by the President of the European Patent Office for the standardised representation of nucleotide and amino acid sequences.

1 **Obligation to include sequence listing**

The rule covers disclosures of nucleic acid sequences and amino acid sequences, regardless of whether such sequences are claimed in the application. Sequences which belong to the prior art and are publicly available in a database need not be listed in the application if they have been identified as set out in Not. EPO OJ 2021 A97 §7.

The rules for the standard representation of sequence listings and details of the procedure for filing them are laid down in Dec. Pres. OJ 2011 p.372 for applications with a filing date before 01.07.2022 and in Dec. Pres. OJ 2021 A96 for applications with a filing date on or after 01.07.2022. The sequence listing must be in electronic format and comply with the WIPO Standard ST.25 in the former case (txt format) and WIPO Standard ST.26 in the latter case (xml format). The sequence listing can be prepared using a tool called 'WIPO Sequence' (GL/PCT-EPO A-IV,3).

The EPO discourages the filing of sequence listings on paper and in pdf format. Where a sequence listing in the prescribed format is filed or corrected after the filing date, the applicant must submit a statement that it does not include subject-matter going beyond the content of the application as filed. (A-IV,5)

R. 30(2) A sequence listing filed after the date of filing shall not form part of the description.

1 **Late-filed sequence listing**

A sequence listing may be filed after the date of filing of the application for use in the search. Such a late-filed sequence listing will not be part of the description and the disclosure of the application and will not be published with the application (Not. EPO OJ 2021 A97 §15).

R. 30(3) Where the applicant has not filed a sequence listing complying with the requirements under paragraph 1 at the date of filing, the European Patent Office shall invite the applicant to furnish such a sequence listing and pay the late furnishing fee. If the applicant does not furnish the required sequence listing and pay the required late furnishing fee within a period of two months after such an invitation, the application shall be refused.

1 **Late filing of sequence listing**

Applicants have three opportunities to file a sequence listing. Firstly, on filing the application documents, they may file a sequence listing. If a sequence listing is not included when filing the application, they may file a sequence listing of their own volition up to the time the EPO invites them to do so under R.30(3); no late furnishing fee is due (A-IV,5). If the applicant has not provided a (standard-compliant) sequence listing by the time the Receiving Section examines formal requirements, the EPO invites the applicant to file a sequence listing in the prescribed format together with payment of the late furnishing fee within a two-month period from notification of the invitation (R.30(3); R.57(j)).

A sequence listing filed later than the filing date must be accompanied by a statement that the sequence listing does not extend the subject-matter of the application as filed (Dec. Pres. OJ 2021 A96 Art. 2(2)).

The amount of the fee for late furnishing is fixed in **Rfees2(1)14a.** The late furnishing fee is intended to cover the additional administrative costs entailed and to encourage applicants to supply a listing conforming to the relevant standard as quickly as possible.

The sanction for failure to meet the two-month period is the refusal of the application under **R.30(3).** Further processing under **Art.121** and **R.135** is available (Not. EPO OJ 2021 A97 §13): it is necessary to file the sequence listing, pay the late furnishing fee, file a statement that the sequence listing does not extend the subject-matter of the application as filed, and pay the further processing fee. A further processing fee is payable for each omitted act: a fixed fee for late submission of the sequence listing and 50% of the late furnishing fee (**Rfees2(1)12**).

Where a sequence listing is missing or does not comply with the required standard, the search will be postponed until a correction has been filed (A-IV,5). A sequence listing filed after the filing date will be used for the search but will not be published together with the application or specification because it does not form part of the description (**R.30(2), 68(1), 73**). Where a sequence listing is included as a missing part under **R.56,** it will be considered to be an integral part of the description on the date of filing (which may or may not have changed because of the inclusion) (A-IV,5.1).

R.30(2) and **(3)** also apply to Euro-PCT applications (see **R.163(3)**).

R. 31 Deposit of biological material

Implementation of **Art.78(1)(b)**

1 **Requirement for deposition of biological material**

Deposit of a sample of biological material under **R.31** for compliance with the disclosure requirement of **Art.83** is only required if the biological material to which the application relates is not available to the public and cannot be described in the application in an enabling manner. The requirements of **R.31** are satisfied for an application filed by reference if the application referred to already satisfied these requirements.

A consolidated notice on disclosure and deposition of biological material is published in OJ 2010 p.498. The requirements for deposition of biological material in **R.31-33** apply to direct European applications. See §5-13 of said notice for Euro-PCT applications.

2 **Availability of deposited material**

The material must be available as from the date of filing of the application (OJ 2010 p.498 §3.6). Access of the public is controlled by **R.33(1).**

The disclosure of the invention is considered to be insufficient if repeated requests to the depositary institution are necessary, and techniques considerably more sophisticated than those recommended by the depositary institution must be applied (**T418/89**).

R. 31(1) If an invention involves the use of or concerns biological material which is not available to the public and which cannot be described in the European patent application in such a manner as to enable the invention to be carried out by a person skilled in the art, the invention shall only be regarded as being disclosed as prescribed in Article 83 if:

(a) a sample of the biological material has been deposited with a recognised depositary institution on the same terms as those laid down in the Budapest Treaty on the International Recognition of the Deposit of Microorganisms for the Purposes of Patent Procedure of 28 April 1977 not later than the date of filing of the application;

(b) the application as filed gives such relevant information as is available to the applicant on the characteristics of the biological material;

(c) the depositary institution and the accession number of the deposited biological material are stated in the application, and

(d) where the biological material has been deposited by a person other than the applicant, the name and address of the depositor are stated in the application and a document is submitted to the European Patent Office providing evidence that the depositor has authorised the applicant to refer to the deposited biological material in the application and has given his unreserved and irrevocable consent to the deposited material being made available to the public in accordance with Rule 33.

Art.83 Disclosure of the invention
R.33 Availability of biological material

1 Deposition of biological material

1.1 PRIORITY (R.31(1)(A))

The depositary institution must be an international authority under the Budapest Treaty or a depositary institution recognised by the EPO by virtue of a bilateral agreement. The recognised institutions are published in the OJ.

A priority claimed by an application relating to deposited biological material is valid only if the priority application has a sufficient disclosure of the invention by referring to a deposition of the material made no later than the priority date. (OJ 2010 p.498 §1.4)

1.2 RELEVANT INFORMATION (R.31(1)(B)-(D))

The application as filed must disclose relevant information on the characteristics of the biological material (**R.31(1)(b)**), such as classification of the material, morphological or physiological characteristics relevant for recognition, and propagation of the material if it cannot replicate itself (F-III,6.3(i)). An accession number alone without a written description of a micro-organism does not provide a sufficient disclosure in the sense of **Art.83** (**T418/89**).

If biological material is deposited as part of the disclosure of an application, the application must state the depositary institution and the accession number of the deposit (**R.31(1)(c)**). If this information is provided after the date of filing as allowed by **R.31(2)**, the application must contain at the date of filing a reference that enables the deposit to be related to the later filed accession number. It is recommended to file the deposit receipt issued by the depositary institution, if available, already at the date of filing. (A-IV,4.1; F-III,6.3(ii); OJ 2010 p.498 §3.3, 3.11)

Communication of the information on the depositary institution, the accession number and, where applicable, details of a depositor other than the applicant to the EPO is considered as consent of the applicant to the biological material being made publicly available under **R.33** (**R.31(2)**, last sentence).

See OJ 2010 p.498 §3.7-3.9 for a deposit made by a person other than the applicant.

1.3 INFORMATION OF DEPOSIT

The Receiving Section checks, during the examination of formal requirements under **Art.90(3)**, whether the requirements of **R.31(1)(c)** are fulfilled. It notifies the applicant of any deficiencies and points out that the requirements must be fulfilled by the end of the period specified in **R.31(2)** (see **R.57:16**).

R. 31(2) The information referred to in paragraph 1(c) and (d) may be submitted

(a) within sixteen months after the date of filing of the application or, if priority has been claimed, after the priority date, this period being deemed to have been observed if the information is communicated before completion of the technical preparations for publication of the European patent application;

(b) up to the date of submission of a request under Article 93, paragraph 1(b);

(c) within one month after the European Patent Office has communicated to the applicant that the right to inspect the files under Article 128, paragraph 2, exists.

The ruling period shall be the one which is the first to expire. The communication of this information shall be considered as constituting the unreserved and irrevocable consent of the applicant to the deposited biological material being made available to the public in accordance with Rule 33.

Art.93(1)(b) Early publication of the application at applicant's request
Art.128(2) Inspection of files after invocation of rights
R.33 Availability of biological material

1 **Period for submission of information on deposition**

The information concerning the accession number of the deposited material according to **R.31(1)(c)** and, if applicable, the name, address and authorisation of the depositor according to **R.31(1)(d)** may not be submitted after expiry of the time limit set out in **R.31(2)(a)**, because of their relevance for the disclosure of the application (**G2/93**). For Euro-PCT cases, the relevant time limit is that of publication of the PCT application (**T328/04**).

2 **Consequence of failure to provide information on deposition**

Where the requirements of **R.31(1)(c)** or (d) and 31(2) are not fulfilled, the biological material is not regarded as disclosed under **Art.83** by reference to the deposit. (F-III,6.3)

The period of **R.31(2)** is excluded from further processing by **R.135(2)**. Re-establishment is available according to **T227/97** hn. However, OJ 2010 p.498 §3.10 holds that re-establishment is not possible (A-IV,4.1), based on an interpretation of **G2/93** that was disapproved of by **T227/97**, published before the notice; moreover, this interpretation also appears to violate the EPC (**Art.122(4)** and **R.136(3)**).

It is recommended that an applicant completes sections 34-37 of the Request for Grant form in order to allow the EPO to draw the applicant's attention to any deficiencies before expiry of the period of **R.31(2)**. (OJ 2010 p.498 §3.11)

R. 32 Expert solution

Amended, in force since 01.04.2025 (OJ 2025 A16). For an earlier amendment, see OJ 2017 A55 and Not. EPO OJ 2017 A61.
Implementation of **Art.78(1)(b)**

1 **Expert solution**
A third party can work a biological invention by requesting a sample from the biological material deposited under **R.31** and growing the sample according to the instructions given in the application. An applicant wishing to avoid a competitor catching up using the deposited material can restrict its availability until the grant of the patent by opting for the so-called 'expert solution'. In that case, a sample of the material is not made available to the requester but only to an expert nominated by the requester. A third party must request the EPO under **R.33** to make a sample available to an expert recognised by the EPO under **R.32(2)**; the requester can ask the expert to perform specific experiments on the sample and report the results.

The expert solution means that part of the disclosure of an application is not available to the public, as an exception to **Art.83**.

Details of the expert solution are set out in OJ 2010 p.498 §4 and A-IV,4.3.

R. 32(1) Until completion of the technical preparations for publication of the European patent application, the applicant may inform the European Patent Office that,
(a) until the publication of the mention of the grant of the European patent or, where applicable,
(b) for twenty years from the date of filing, if the application is refused or withdrawn or deemed to be withdrawn,
the availability referred to in Rule 33 shall be effected only by the issue of a sample to an independent expert nominated by the requester.

R.33 Availability of biological material

1 **Indicating expert solution and period of applicability**
Applicants must, according to **R.32(1)**, notify the EPO of their choice of the expert solution before completion of the technical preparations for publication (see **R.67**). Applicants can indicate their choice in the Request for Grant form. The fact that said solution has been chosen will be mentioned on the front page of the published application. If the EPO is not notified in time, the material will be available as provided for in **R.33** without an expert acting as an intermediary (OJ 2010 p.498, §4.4).

The expert solution applies until publication of the mention of the grant or, where applicable, twenty years from the date of filing if the application is refused, withdrawn or deemed to be withdrawn (**R.32(1)**).

R. 32(2) Any natural person may be nominated as an expert, provided that they comply with the requirements and obligations laid down by the President of the European Patent Office. The nomination shall be accompanied by a declaration from the expert that they undertake to comply with the aforementioned requirements and obligations and that they know of no circumstances which might give rise to justified doubts as to their independence or which might conflict in any other way with their function as expert. The nomination shall also be accompanied by a declaration from the expert vis-à-vis the applicant in which they enter into the undertaking given under Rule 33 until either the date on which the patent expires in all the designated States or, where the application is refused, withdrawn or deemed to be withdrawn, the date referred to in paragraph 1(b), the requester being regarded as a third party.

R.33 Availability of biological material
Amended by decision of the Administrative Council of 10.12.2024, which entered into force on 01.04.2025 (OJ 2025 A16). The amendments made the text gender-neutral.

1 **Recognition of experts**
A third party may nominate any natural person as an expert to whom deposited biological material may be made available under **R.33**. The request for nomination must be sent to the EPO accompanied by two declarations. Natural persons must declare to the EPO that they will comply with the requirements and obligations laid down in Dec. Pres. OJ 2017 A60 and declare to the applicant that they enter into the undertaking given under **R.33** (**R.32(2)**, second and third sentence). The requirements relate, among others, to knowledge, availability of facilities and independence and impartiality. Only in cases of reasonable doubts as to independence would the EPO turn to the requester before certifying the request (OJ 2017 A61 §7). The third party can use forms on the EPO website for the request and the declarations (OJ 2017 A61 §8).

The third party does not need the consent of the applicant for the use of the nominated expert. If an applicant could withhold consent, deposited material would not be available, contrary to **Art.83** (sufficiency of disclosure).

R. 33 Availability of biological material

Implementation of **Art.78(1)(b)** and **Art.83**

1 **General**
The depositary institution will store deposited material for a period of at least five years after the most recent request for the issue of a sample was received by the institution and, in any case, for a period of at least 30 years after the date of the deposit; the depositor may not withdraw the material before the expiry of this period. (Budapest Treaty)

The availability of the material is not affected by refusal or withdrawal of the application nor by lapse of the patent or expiry of the patent term (OJ 2010 p.498 §16). The issue of a sample may be restricted to an expert if the declaration under **R.32(1)** has been made, which restriction is mentioned on the front page of the published application.

Prescribed forms for requesting samples are available on the EPO website. The request must be submitted to the EPO (R.33(4)), who forwards it to the depositary institution (R.33(5)). The EPO's certification of the request signals to the depositary institution that it may issue a sample of the biological material to the requester or the expert (A-IV,4.4). The EPO does not charge a fee for the request, but the depositary institution may request a fee. The requester must also file a declaration agreeing to restrict the use of the biological material during the pendency of the application and patent as set out in R.33(2). See OJ 2010 p.498 §26 and A-IV,4.4 for the handling of the request within the EPO. The sample will be issued to the requester or, if the applicant has chosen the expert option of R.32, to the expert. The EPO is exempted from verifying and assessing the expert's suitability and independence (OJ 2017 A60).

Details of the availability of deposited biological material and requests for the issue of samples are given in OJ 2010 p.498 §14-27.

R. 33(1) Biological material deposited in accordance with Rule 31 shall be available upon request to any person from the date of publication of the European patent application and to any person having the right to inspect the files under Article 128, paragraph 2, prior to that date. Subject to Rule 32, such availability shall be effected by the issue of a sample of the biological material to the person making the request (hereinafter referred to as "the requester").

R.31 Deposit of biological material
R.32 Expert solution
Art.128(2) Inspection of files before publication

R. 33(2) Said issue shall be made only if the requester has undertaken vis-à-vis the applicant for or proprietor of the patent not to make the biological material or any biological material derived therefrom available to any third party and to use that material for experimental purposes only, until such time as the patent application is refused or withdrawn or deemed to be withdrawn, or before the European patent has expired in all the designated States, unless the applicant for or proprietor of the patent expressly waives such an undertaking. The undertaking to use the biological material for experimental purposes only shall not apply in so far as the requester is using that material under a compulsory licence. The term "compulsory licence" shall be construed as including ex officio licences and the right to use patented inventions in the public interest.

R. 33(3) For the purposes of paragraph 2, derived biological material shall mean any material which still exhibits those characteristics of the deposited material which are essential to carrying out the invention. The undertaking under paragraph 2 shall not impede any deposit of derived biological material necessary for the purpose of patent procedure.

R. 33(4) The request referred to in paragraph 1 shall be submitted to the European Patent Office on a form recognised by that Office. The European Patent Office shall certify on the form that a European patent application referring to the deposit of the biological material has been filed, and that the requester or the expert nominated by them under Rule 32 is entitled to the issue of a sample of that material. After grant of

the European patent, the request shall also be submitted to the European Patent Office.

R.32 Expert solution
Amended by decision of the Administrative Council of 10.12.2024, which entered into force on 01.04.2025 (OJ 2025 A16). The amendment was introduction of gender-neutral language.

R. 33(5) The European Patent Office shall transmit a copy of the request, with the certification provided for in paragraph 4, to the depositary institution and to the applicant for or the proprietor of the patent.

R. 33(6) The European Patent Office shall publish in its Official Journal the list of depositary institutions recognised for the purpose of Rules 31, 33 and 34.

Amended, in force since 01.10.2017 (OJ 2017 A55).
R.31 Deposit of biological material
R.33 Availability of biological material
R.34 New deposit of biological material
See OJ issue 4 of each year under *International Treaties*

R. 34 New deposit of biological material

If biological material deposited in accordance with Rule 31 ceases to be available from the recognised depositary institution, an interruption in availability shall be deemed not to have occurred if a new deposit of that material is made with a recognised depositary institution on the same terms as those laid down in the Budapest Treaty on the International Recognition of the Deposit of Microorganisms for the Purposes of Patent Procedure of 28 April 1977, and if a copy of the receipt of the new deposit issued by the depositary institution is forwarded to the European Patent Office within four months of the date of the new deposit, stating the number of the European patent application or of the European patent.

R.31 Deposit of biological material
Implementation of Art.78(1)(b)

1 **Biological material no longer available**
Deposited biological material ceases to be available if the material has degraded or the depositary institution no longer qualifies for that kind of material. In this case the applicant must make a new deposition under R.34 as set out in A-IV,4.1.1.

PART III IMPLEMENTING REGULATIONS TO PART III OF THE CONVENTION

Chapter I *Filing of the European patent application*

R. 35 General provisions

Implementation of **Art.75(1)**

R. 35(1) European patent applications may be filed in writing with the European Patent Office in Munich, The Hague or Berlin, or the authorities referred to in Article 75, paragraph 1(b).

Art.75(1)(b) Filing of a European patent application

1 **Filing offices**
European patent applications may be filed on paper with a filing office of the EPO or a national authority that allows such filing under **Art.75** (see NatLaw table II, note 1; **Art.75(1)(b)**). The filing offices of the EPO are in Munich (Isar and PschorrHöfe buildings), The Hague and Berlin (**R.35(1)**). Details of the EPO filing offices are given in OJ 2017 A11; OJ 2018 A18; A75 and **R.2(1):4**. Divisional applications must be filed directly with the EPO (**Art.76(1)**). For the filing of PCT applications with the EPO as receiving office, see **R.157**.

The EPO sub-office in Vienna is not a filing office for the purpose of **Art.75(1)(a)** and applications filed there will be forwarded to one of the filing offices and will only be accorded a filing date on receipt by the latter (OJ 2017 A11 Art.1(2)). Although not explicitly foreseen in OJ 2017 A11, this procedure is also applied to applications filed at the liaison bureau in Brussels and the building of the Boards of Appeal in Haar (confirmed by EPO Directorate Patent Law).

Similarly, paper documents intended for the EPO but filed with the German Patent Office, located in neighbouring buildings both in Berlin and in Munich, will be forwarded to the EPO and receive as filing date the date of their actual receipt at the EPO (OJ 2005 p.444).

The EPO filing offices can also receive subsequent documents (see **R.50:2**).

The means for communication with the EPO filing offices is governed by **R.2**. If a national authority allows means of communication not allowed by the EPO and an applicant uses such means to file a European application at that office, the EPO will accord the application a date of filing under **Art.75(1)(b)**, second sentence (J20/84).

R. 35(2) The authority with which the European patent application is filed shall mark the documents making up the application with the date of their receipt, and issue without delay a receipt to the applicant including at least the application number and the nature, number and date of receipt of the documents.

1 **Acknowledgement of receipt**
The authority with which the application is filed may be a filing office of the EPO or a national authority under **Art.75(1)(b)**. The same authority that receives the application must issue a receipt to the applicant (**R.35(2)**). The receipt must be issued without delay and includes at least the application number, the nature and number of the documents, the date of their receipt, and the applicant's or representative's file reference number (A-II,3.1). A range of application numbers is reserved for each place of receipt (A-II,1.7.2).

Receipt of applications filed online with the EPO is acknowledged electronically during the submission session (A-II,3.1). For applications filed other than by electronic means, the applicant may fill in the receipt page of the Form 1001 and provide this page, in original with two or three copies, together with the other application documents to the competent filing office. The filing office checks the nature and number of documents received and returns, by post, one of the copies of the receipt page stamped with the date of receipt as an acknowledgement of receipt. (OJ 2019 A18 Art.8, unaffected by Not. EPO OJ 2023 A108; Notes to Form 1001).

On receipt the EPO does not check the number of sheets, does not confirm the presence of drawings when the applicant has not indicated their presence on the receipt form, and does not check whether the titles in the Request for Grant form and at the beginning of the description match. This is examined later under **Art.90(3)**. The returned receipt page only serves to communicate the application number, the nature and number of the documents and the date of receipt. Therefore, no conclusions regarding the content of the documents received on the filing date can be drawn from a lack of a notification by the filing office in response to deficiencies (**J21/94** r.1 and note in Section 47 of the Request for Grant form, page 'Receipt for documents').

Confirmation of receipt does not imply that a filing date is accorded.

R. 35(3) If the European patent application is filed with an authority referred to in Article 75, paragraph 1(b), such authority shall without delay inform the European Patent Office of the receipt of the application, and, in particular, of the nature and date of receipt of the documents, the application number and any priority date claimed.

Art.75(1)(b) Filing of a European patent application

R. 35(4) Upon receipt of a European patent application forwarded by the central industrial property office of a Contracting State, the European Patent Office shall inform the applicant accordingly, indicating the date of its receipt.

1 **Confirmation of receipt of nationally filed application**
When the EPO has received an application which has been forwarded by a competent national authority under **Art.77**, the EPO issues a **R.35(4)** communication to the applicant confirming receipt of the application.

After receipt of the communication the applicant must file all further documents directly with the EPO and not with the national authority (A-II,3.2). Documents erroneously filed with the national authority may be forwarded to the EPO, but the date of receipt will be the date of receipt by the EPO.

R. 36 European divisional applications

Implementation of **Art.76(1)**

R. 36(1) The applicant may file a divisional application relating to any pending earlier European patent application.

Inserted, in force since 01.04.2014. The amended provision applies to divisional applications filed on or after 01.04.2014 (OJ 2013 p.501; OJ 2014 A22).

1 **Divisional application**
An applicant may file a divisional application based on a Euro-direct application, a Euro-PCT application pending before the EPO as designated or elected office, or a divisional European application. **G1/06** r.10.2 has accepted the validity of sequences of divisional applications. The word 'any' in **R.36(1)** clarifies that it is irrelevant what kind of application the earlier application is (A-IV,1.1; OJ 2002 p.112). The divisional application and the parent application may have overlapping claims; however no claim of the divisional application may be directed to the same subject-matter as a claim granted in the parent application, or vice versa (**G4/19**).

The term 'earlier application' in the provision refers to the immediate parent application on which the divisional application is based. (A-IV,1.1)

2 **Opportunity for filing**
An applicant may file a divisional application relating to a European application after the date of filing of this application and during its subsequent pendency. A divisional application filed on the same day as its parent is not considered validly filed (A-IV,1.1).

A Euro-PCT application is pending in the sense of **R.36(1)** only if the requirements for entering the European phase have been fulfilled, e.g. by an effective request for early processing (**J18/09** hn; **G1/09** r.3.2.5; E-IX,2.4.1; see also **R.159:3**).

R.14 prevents the filing of a divisional if the proceedings for the earlier application are stayed (**J9/12** r.3-5).

The following sub-sections set out the situations in which the earlier application ceases to be pending, and a divisional may no longer be filed. See **R.36(1):3** for possible remedies if the divisional is filed too late.

2.1 PENDING EARLIER APPLICATION
According to **R.36(1)**, the divisional application may only be filed when the earlier application is pending. In the case the earlier application is itself a divisional application, it is sufficient that this divisional is still pending at the filing date of the second divisional (A-IV,1.1.1). Pendency of still earlier applications is not required. During opposition proceedings and related appeal proceedings, the filing of a divisional application is not possible, as there is only a granted patent.

G1/09 r.3 distinguishes between a pending application and pending proceedings, which need not coincide in time. For example, opposition proceedings can only be pending after grant of the patent, i.e. when the patent application is no longer pending. According to **R.36(1)** the pendency of the application rather than the proceedings is relevant for the right to file a divisional application. An (earlier) application is pending as long as substantive rights deriving therefrom are still in existence. Examples of substantive rights which the applicant is entitled to exercise are provisional protection and the right to file a divisional application. The EPC lays down in **Art.67(4)** when provisional protection exists and, hence, when the application is pending. The Enlarged Board decided that the right to file a divisional application exists as long as provisional protection exists. Using this rule, the decision sets out the pendency of the application in the case of grant and refusal.

2.1.1 *Filing divisional and grant of earlier application*

The provisional protection of a patent application is in existence until the date of publication in the Bulletin of the mention of the grant under **Art.97(3)** (consequence of **Art.64(1)**). Since a substantive right for the application is in existence until the publication of the mention of the grant, the application is pending up to but not including the day the mention of the grant is published. The substantive right of filing a divisional application therefore exists up to but not including the day of publication of the mention of the grant of the earlier application. (**G1/09** r.4.3; A-IV,1.1.1)

The actual date the decision to grant is taken is not relevant, only the date the mention of the grant is published (cf. **J7/96** hn). The EPO informs the applicant of the intended date of publication of the mention of the grant (see **Art.97(1):4**).

Since **R.36(1)** does not lay down a period of predetermined duration within which a certain act must be carried out but rather a condition that must be complied with when filing a divisional, provisions of the EPC relating to periods are not applicable to the determination of the last day of validly filing a divisional. Such provisions include **R.133** for late receipt of documents and **R.134** for extension of periods (**J24/03** hn.III; **J19/10** r.5-7). Hence, the divisional must be filed at the latest on the last day before the publication of the mention of the grant on which the EPO is open for receipt of documents filed by the particular method of **R.2(1)** chosen by the applicant. (A-IV,1.1.1)

For example, if the mention of the grant is published in the Bulletin on Wednesday 04.10.2017, a divisional can be filed electronically at the latest on 03.10.2017; by post or delivery service to EPO Munich or Berlin at the latest on 02.10.2017 (03.10.2017 being a national holiday in DE) and to EPO The Hague at the latest on 03.10.2017. Filing by depositing the application in the automated mailbox in Munich or delivery by hand to the porter of EPO The Hague, Munich or Berlin can be made at the latest on 03.10.2017 (see **R.2(1):4** for acceptance of deliveries). The Bulletin is always published on a Wednesday.

An appeal by the applicant against a decision to grant a patent is usually found to be inadmissible since an applicant is rarely adversely affected by a decision to grant a patent (see **Art.107:2**). Therefore, according to **J28/03** r.11, 15, such an appeal does not automatically give rise to the possibility of filing a divisional application during the appeal procedure. According to this decision, it is only possible to file a divisional if the appeal is actually allowed (r.16). The Legal Board in **J1/24**, however, held that this reasoning of the board in **J28/03** (i.e. that the outcome of the appeal was determinative of whether a divisional could be filed or not) was 'not convincing' and that the suspensive effect of a decision is the same whether the decision is to grant a patent or to refuse an application. For the board in this decision, what is decisive is whether substantive rights still derive from the application or not. According to **G1/09** r.4.3.2, substantive rights under the EPC no longer derive from an application when the mention of grant is published. The board in **J1/24** concluded, based on this, that when the mention of grant is deleted because an appeal has been filed, the application is effectively pending again and a divisional may be validly filed until the mention of grant is republished (r.10.4). This was the case even though the appeal against the grant was withdrawn by the applicant before a decision was taken. It therefore seems to be the case that the validity of a divisional filed after the mention of grant of a patent has been published depends on whether the mention of grant is deleted as the result of an appeal being filed. The Legal Board also stated that the EPC has no provision restricting appeals of the applicant against the grant of a patent; such an appeal cannot therefore be seen as clearly inadmissible and lacking suspensive effect under **G2/19**.

2.1.2 *Filing divisional and refusal of the earlier application*

The substantive right of provisional protection conferred by an application may continue to exist until the application is finally refused, according to **Art.67(4)**. The application is finally refused upon expiry of the period for filing an appeal if no appeal is filed. Hence, an application which the examining division has refused is still pending until the expiry of the period for filing an appeal and, on the day after, is no longer pending if no appeal is filed. This applies both where the decision to refuse is given in written proceedings and where it is pronounced in oral proceedings. (**G1/09** r.4.2, overruling OJ 2002 p.112)

Hence, the last day for filing a divisional application is the expiry of the two-month period of **Art.108** for filing an appeal, triggered by the notification of the written decision of the examining division refusing the earlier application. It is not necessary to appeal a refusal to be able to file a divisional after the decision (**G1/09** r.4.3.3).

Additional time for filing a divisional application can be obtained by appealing the refusal; see e.g. **J23/13** r.8. If the notice of appeal is deemed not to have been filed (see **Art.110:1**), then no additional time is obtained. If the notice of appeal is validly filed but the grounds of appeal are not filed, the pendency of the application ends on the expiry of the period for filing the grounds according to **J23/13** r.8.3, or perhaps on the day before the date of the decision of the board rejecting the appeal as inadmissible. An application will be pending until the end of the appeal proceedings in the case of an admissible appeal against a refusal decision if the board subsequently confirms the refusal of the parent application and even longer if the case is remitted (A-IV,1.1.1).

A decision in appeal enters into force on pronouncement in oral proceedings or on the day of the notification in written proceedings (**G12/91** r.2, 3). Therefore, following **G1/09** r.4.2.1, in an appeal following the refusal of an application, the application is pending until pronouncement or notification of the decision of the board of appeal.

An applicant fearing a refusal at oral proceedings in appeal should file a divisional before the decision in oral proceedings and pay the fees for the divisional after the oral proceedings (but within the period of **R.36(3)**) only if the decision is not satisfactory. An unsatisfactory decision in first instance is less problematic since a divisional can be filed at any time during the period for filing an appeal.

2.1.3 *Filing divisional and deemed withdrawal*

Where the application is deemed withdrawn due to non-observance of a period (e.g. **Art.94(4)**), the deemed withdrawal takes effect at the expiry of the non-observed period (**G4/98** r.7; A-IV,1.1.1), i.e. the application is pending until midnight at the end of the last day of the non-observed period. Where the application is deemed withdrawn because of non-payment of a renewal fee, the application is pending until the expiry of the six-month period of **R.51(2)** (A-IV,1.1.1).

When the applicant receives the communication of the loss of rights under **R.112(1)**, the application is already no longer pending. A mere filing of a request for further processing or re-establishment does not make the application pending again. The application will only become pending, retroactively from the expiry of the non-observed period, if the request is granted, possibly only in appeal. Hence, a divisional filed after an application has been deemed withdrawn will only be validly filed if a remedy is applied successfully (**J4/11** hn, relating to re-establishment; extended in A-IV,1.1.1 to cover further processing).

2.1.4 *Filing divisional and withdrawal of parent*

The withdrawal of an application takes effect the moment the EPO receives a notice of withdrawal in writing or the withdrawal is communicated orally in oral proceedings. According to the Guidelines, a divisional application can be filed up to and including the date on which the declaration of withdrawal is received (A-IV,1.1.1). However, the case law tends to suggest that this would not be the case if the withdrawal was received first and the divisional was filed later on the same day and the order of events could be clearly established (**T517/97** r.4 mutatis mutandis). The late filing of the divisional may be remedied by reviving the withdrawn parent application by retracting the withdrawal, which may exceptionally be allowed as set out in **R.139:3.2**.

3 **Remedy for late filing**

If the EPO considers that the divisional application is filed too late, the divisional will not be accorded the date of filing (and priority) of the earlier application (**Art.76(1)**). Furthermore, it cannot be treated as a regular European patent application and accorded its own date of filing (**G1/05**, r.11.1). If applicable, a remedy is to ask for an appealable decision under **R.112(2)** within two months after the notification of loss of rights and provide proof that filing of the divisional did in fact occur in due time.

If a divisional is filed when the earlier application is no longer pending, **R.133** and **R.134** cannot be invoked, because these provisions apply only to periods and not to conditions such as the pendency of **R.36(1)**. Further processing cannot be used, because the loss of rights does not relate to failure to observe a time limit. Re-establishment can neither be used because the pendency in **R.36(1)** does not lay down a time limit within the meaning of **Art.122(1)** (**J24/03** hn.III; **J10/01** r.15). Remedies relating to pendency of the earlier application are indicated in the above sub-sections.

R. 36(2) A divisional application shall be filed in the language of the proceedings for the earlier application. If the latter was not in an official language of the European Patent Office, the divisional application may be filed in the language of the earlier application; a translation into the language of the proceedings for the earlier application shall then be filed within two months of the filing of the divisional application. The divisional application shall be filed with the European Patent Office in Munich, The Hague or Berlin.

Amended, in force since 01.04.2010. Amended **R.36(2)** applies to divisional applications filed on or after that date. (OJ 2009 p.296)

1 **Language of divisional application**
A divisional application may be filed in the language of the proceedings of the earlier application (**R.36(2)**, first sentence). It may also be filed in the language of the earlier application if this application was not filed in an official EPO language and translated into the language of proceedings of the earlier application. (**R.36(2)**, second sentence)

When filing the divisional in a non-EPO language, the applicant has the possibility of **Art.14(2)**, second sentence, to bring the translation into conformity with the divisional in the non-EPO language at any stage of the procedure. The language reduction of **R.7a(1)** may apply for the filing fee, divisional fee, page fee, and examination fee; after grant the compensation under **UPR.8** may apply. The micro-entity reduction of **R.7a(3)** may also apply, irrespective of the language.

When filing a divisional application by reference to a previous application following **R.40(1)(c)**, the previous application must be the parent application. The parent may be in a non-EPO language. If the previous application was a direct European application or an international application filed with the EPO as receiving Office, no copy of the previous application need be filed under **R.40(3)**. If the previous application was an international application not filed with the EPO as receiving Office, a certified copy must be filed. (A-II,4.1.3.1)

If a divisional is not filed in an admissible language specified in **R.36(2)**, it will not be dealt with as a European patent application, applying **Art.90(2)** by analogy (J13/14). A loss of rights communication will be sent under **R.112(1)**. If the applicant nevertheless considers the language used to be admissible, a decision under **R.112(2)** should be requested. A remedy is to re-file the divisional in an admissible language, heeding the pendency requirement of **R.36(1)**.

2 **Translation of divisional application**
R.36(2), second sentence, requires that a translation of the divisional into the language of the proceedings must be filed within two months of the filing of the divisional if the divisional was filed in the non-EPO language of the earlier application.

The filing of the translation is checked under **R.57(a)** and if not yet filed, an invitation will be sent under **R.58** to file the translation within two months. If not filed, the application will be deemed withdrawn according to **Art.14(2)**. Further processing is excluded for the period in **R.58** (**R.135(2)**); only re-establishment is available. (A-III,14)

Where the divisional is filed by reference to the parent under **R.40(1)(c)** and a translation of the parent is available, no translation need be filed and the EPO will include a copy of the translation of the parent in the file of the divisional (OJ 2009 p.486 §4; A-II,4.1.3.1). As admitted by the EPO, its publications on the requirement to file a translation in this situation are ambiguous (compare the previous two references with OJ 2009 p.481 §II and A-IV,1.3.3).

3 **Filing offices for divisional application**
A divisional application must be filed with the EPO. If it is filed on paper, it must be filed with the EPO filing office in Munich, The Hague or Berlin (**R.36(2)**, last sentence). See **R.35(1):1** for details of the EPO filing offices.

A divisional filed with a national office has no legal effect. The national office may, as a courtesy, forward the divisional to the EPO. The divisional is only deemed filed when it is received by the EPO. (A-IV,1.3.1)

R. 36(3) The filing fee and search fee shall be paid within one month of filing the divisional application. If the filing fee or search fee is not paid in due time, the application shall be deemed to be withdrawn.

1 **Payment of filing fee and search fee**
The amount of the filing fee and search fee is fixed in **Rfees2(1)1** and **Rfees2(1)2**, respectively.

The requirements, including the fees, for filing a divisional application are similar to those for filing a first application.

The filing and search fees must be paid within one month after filing of the divisional (**R.36(3)**; A-III,13.1). The search fee must always be paid, even when a search fee has already been paid for the same invention in the parent application. The search fee will be refunded fully or in part if the search report is based entirely or partly on the earlier search report drawn up for the parent application (**Rfees9(2)**).

If the filing fee or search fee is not paid, the divisional will be deemed withdrawn (**R.36(3)**, second sentence) upon expiry of the one-month period. The EPO informs the applicant of the loss of rights using the communication of **R.112(1)**. The applicant may request further processing under **Art.121** and **R.135** within two months of the notification of the communication.

If there are more than 15 claims, claims fees must also be paid within one month after filing (**R.45(1)** and **Rfees2(1)15**), even if claims fees have already been paid for the same claims in the parent application (A-IV,1.4.2).

If the application comprises more than 35 pages, the filing fee will include a page fee (see **R.38(2)** and **Rfees2(1)1a**).

If the earlier application is a divisional application, i.e. the divisional is of the second or subsequent generation, the filing fee will include a divisional fee (see **R.38(4)** and **Rfees2(1)1b**).

The above sanction and remedy for not paying the filing fee are also applicable to non-payment of a page fee or a divisional fee.

See **R.7a(1)** for a reduction of the filing, page and divisional fees if the divisional application is filed in a non-EPO language. (A-X,9.3.2) See **R.7a(3)** for a reduction of these fees and other fees for certain applicants.

See **R.51(3)** and **Rfees2(1)4** for renewal fees payable for a divisional application.

Any fees paid for the divisional will be refunded if the application is not accepted as a divisional, i.e. if it does not have the benefit of the date of filing and priority, if any, of the earlier application (**J11/91** hn.4).

R. 36(4) The designation fee shall be paid within six months of the date on which the European Patent Bulletin mentions the publication of the European search report drawn up in respect of the divisional application. Rule 39, paragraphs 2 and 3, shall apply.

Amended, in force since 01.04.2009 (OJ 2008 p.513; OJ 2009 p.118 footnote 1).
R.39(2) Non-payment of the designation fee
R.39(3) Non-refundability of the designation fee

1 **Payment of designation fee**
A designation fee, covering all contracting states, must be paid for a divisional application, the amount of which is fixed in **Rfees2(1)3**.

The designation fee must be paid within six months of the publication date of the search report drawn up in respect of the divisional application according to **R.36(4)**. If the designation fee is not paid in due time, the application will be deemed withdrawn (**R.39(2)**).

The EPO will inform the applicant of the loss of rights using the communication of **R.112(1)**. Further processing under **Art.121** and **R.135** is available. The withdrawal takes effect upon the expiry of the six-month period, not upon the expiry of the two-month period for requesting further processing (**G4/98** hn. II). See **R.39(3):1** for a possible refund of the designation fee.

Within the same six-month period, the request for examination (**R.70**) and a response to the search opinion (**R.70a**) must be filed, and any extension and validation fees must be paid.

R. 36(5) Rule 39, paragraph 2a, shall apply.

Amended, in force as of 16.12.2024 and applicable to divisional applications received on or after 25.06.2024 (Decision Administrative Council OJ 2024 A105 Art.2(c)). Note that this amendment is not present in the full English version of the amended Implementing Regulations annexed to the decision of the same date, concerning the amendments to gender-neutral language. **R.39(2a)** Deemed withdrawal designations in case of Russian applicant

1 **Deemed withdrawal of designations**
The provision applies to divisional applications received on or after 25.06.2024 (OJ 2024 A105, Art. 2(c)). The provision appears somewhat duplicative: for those divisional applications, the designation of the EU states was deemed to be withdrawn in the parent application as of 25.06.2024 under **R.39(2a)**. However, **R.36(5)** may be used if the applicant of the divisional application changes.

R. 37 Forwarding of European patent applications

Implementation of **Art.77**

1 **General**
R.37 contains details about how a European patent application that was filed with the central industrial property office of a Contracting State is forwarded to the EPO.

R. 37(1) The central industrial property office of a Contracting State shall forward European patent applications to the European Patent Office in the shortest time compatible with its national law relating to the secrecy of inventions in the interests of the State, and shall take all appropriate steps to ensure such forwarding within:
(a) six weeks of filing, where the subject of the application is evidently not liable to secrecy under the national law; or
(b) four months of filing or, if priority has been claimed, fourteen months of the date of priority, where the application requires further examination as to its liability to secrecy.

1 **Forwarding of applications under national security**
There are no sanctions if the 6-week or 4-month periods in paragraph 1 are not met (A-II,1.7). Hence, these periods will often be extended to the fourteen-month period of paragraph 2.

R. 37(2) A European patent application not received by the European Patent Office within fourteen months of filing or, if priority has been claimed, of the date of priority, shall be deemed to be withdrawn. Any fees paid in respect of this application shall be refunded.

1 **Failed forwarding**
If the EPO does not receive the application within fourteen months from filing or priority, the application will be deemed withdrawn and all fees will be refunded. The term 'fees' includes any additional fees or surcharges which may have been paid (OJ 2007 se5 EN p.60). See **R.134(2)** for the extension of the period in case of a general dislocation in the delivery or transmission of mail in the contracting state.

R. 38 Filing fee and search fee

Amended, in force since 01.04.2009. Amended **R.38** applies to European applications filed on or after that date and international applications that entered the regional phase on or after that date. The amendment introduced the page fee to be paid on filing the application. (OJ 2008 p.513)
Implementation of **Art.78(2)**

R. 38(1) The filing fee and search fee shall be paid within one month of filing the European patent application.

1 **Period for payment of filing and search fee**
The filing and search fee must be paid within one month of filing the application (**R.38(1)**; A-III,13.1). The EPO does not send an invitation to pay within the one-month period. See also **Art.78(2):1**.

Since the one-month period in **R.38(1)** is triggered by 'filing the application' and not 'the date of filing', the period does not change if the date of filing changes, for example due to late filing of drawings under **R.56(2)** (see **Art.80:4**).

The amount of the filing fee is fixed in **Rfees2(1)1**. The amount of the filing fee is reduced if the application documents are filed online (**Rfees2(1):3**) and also in certain cases if the application is filed in a non-EPO language (**R.7a(1)**). The amount of the search fee is fixed in **Rfees2(1)2**.

A (further) reduction of the filing and search fees for certain applicants is also possible, see **R.7a(3),(4)**.

R. 38(2) The Rules relating to Fees may provide for an additional fee as part of the filing fee if the application comprises more than 35 pages.

1 **Page fee**
The purpose of the additional fee, which is also known as the page fee, is to keep the number of pages of patent applications low.

The amount of the additional fee is fixed in **Rfees2(1)1a** and must be paid for applications comprising more than 35 pages. The way of counting pages is set out in **Rfees2(1):4**. The period for payment is set by **R.38(3)**. The additional fee is reduced in certain cases if the application is filed in a non-EPO language (**R.7a(1)**; A-X,9.3.2), as well as for certain applicants (**R.7a(3)**).

Note that the term 'additional fee' is also used in the EPC for the surcharge for belated payment of a renewal fee (**Rfees2(1)5** and for the surcharge for filing a divisional based on a divisional (**R.38(4)**). Therefore, the additional fee of **R.38(2)** is referred to in this book as the 'page fee'; see also A-III,13.2.

R. 38(3) The additional fee referred to in paragraph 2 shall be paid within one month of filing the European patent application or one month of filing the first set of claims or one month of filing the certified copy referred to in Rule 40, paragraph 3, whichever period expires last.

R.40(3) filing copy of previously filed application

1 **Payment of page fee**
The page fee is not included in the filing fee, because it would then be payable within one month of filing and at that time the number of pages of the application will not be known if the claims are filed later or the application is filed by reference to a not yet available previously filed application under **R.40(1)(c)**. Hence, the page fee is separate from the fixed part of the filing fee and must be paid within the later of one month of filing the application, the first set of claims, or the certified copy of the previously filed application (**R.38(3)**).

The page fee for a Euro-PCT application must be paid on entry into the European phase (**R.159(1):4.1**).

Since the page fee is part of the filing fee according to **R.38(2)**, non-payment of the page fee will result in the application being deemed withdrawn (**Art.78(2)**, **R.160(1)**). Failure to meet the one-month period can be remedied using further processing under **Art.121** and **R.135**. (A-III,13.2)

R. 38(4) The Rules relating to Fees may provide for an additional fee as part of the filing fee in the case of a divisional application filed in respect of any earlier application which is itself a divisional application.

Inserted, in force since 01.04.2014. Inserted **R.38(4)** applies to divisional applications filed on or after 01.04.2014 (OJ 2013 p.501; OJ 2014 A22).

1 **Divisional fee**
The additional fee is a surcharge on the filing fee levied for divisional applications that are filed in respect of an earlier divisional application. The additional fee tries to discourage the filing of sequences of divisional applications. The amount of the additional fee is fixed in **Rfees2(1)1b**. The additional fee is reduced in certain cases if the application is filed in a non-EPO language (**R.7a(1)**; **R.36(2)**; A-X,9.3.2), as well as for certain applicants (**R.7a(3)**).

The fee must be paid as part of the filing fee within one month of filing the divisional application (**R.36(3)**). If not paid in due time, the EPO will notify the applicant under **R.112(1)** that the application is deemed withdrawn (**R.36(3)**); further processing is available as a remedy.

Since the term 'additional fee' is used for several other fees, the additional fee of **R.38(4)** is referred to in this book as 'divisional fee'.

R. 39 Designation fees and deemed withdrawal

Amended, in force since 01.04.2009. Amended **R.39** applies to European applications filed on or after that date and international applications that entered the European phase on or after that date. The term 'designation fees' has been replaced by 'designation fee', implementing the switch from payment per designated state to a flat designation fee (see **Art.79**). For applications filed before 01.04.2009, see **Rfees2(2)**. (OJ 2008 p.513)

The Administrative Council has not yet amended the provision's title to reflect the fee's singular character.
Implementation of **Art.79(2)**, **(3)**

1 **General**
Explanatory notes to **R.39** are given under **Art.79(2)**.

R. 39(1) The designation fee shall be paid within six months of the date on which the European Patent Bulletin mentions the publication of the European search report.

1 **Designation fee**
The amount of the designation fee is fixed in **Rfees2(1)3** for applications filed on or after 01.04.2009 and in **Rfees2(2)** for applications filed before that date. A reduction is available for certain applicants (**R.7a(3),(4)**).

The search report is formally published (**Art.92**), i.e. on the publication server of the EPO; in addition, it will be visible in the public online file. The Bulletin mentions the date of the publication of the search report (**Art.129**). The date of the Bulletin (i.e. the date of publication of the Bulletin) starts the period for paying the designation fee.

R. 39(2) Where the designation fee is not paid in due time or the designations of all the Contracting States are withdrawn, the European patent application shall be deemed to be withdrawn.

R. 39(2a) Having regard to Article 5s(3) of amended Regulation (EU) No 833/2014, where the applicant or one of the applicants is a Russian national, a natural person residing in Russia or a legal person, entity or body established in Russia, the designation of those Contracting States that are Member States of the European Union shall be deemed withdrawn. This provision shall not apply to nationals of a Contracting State or to natural persons having a permanent or temporary residence permit in one of the Contracting States.

Inserted, in force since 16.12.2024 and applicable to European patent applications filed on or after 25.06.2024 and to Euro-PCT applications entering the European phase on or after 25.06.2024 (OJ 2024 A105, Not EPO OJ 2024 A106). Note that this amendment is not present in the full English version of the amended Implementing Regulations annexed to the decision of the same date, concerning the amendments to gender-neutral language.

1 **Sanctions against Russian applicants**
The designation of the EPC contracting states that are also EU member states shall be deemed to be withdrawn if the applicant or a co-applicant is a person as defined in the provision. The European patent will then not be granted for those states (see **Art.79:1**). As a result, registration of unitary effect will be impossible (**UPR.5(2)(a)**).

The designation of the other EPC contracting states is not affected. The designation fee must still be paid.

The EPO will first inform the applicant and give the applicant an opportunity to comment. If, thereafter, the EPO considers that the provision applies to the patent application, it will issue a communication under **R.112(1)** on the loss of rights. The applicant may request an appealable decision (**R.112(2)**) (OJ 2024 A106). Whether the rule is compatible with **Art.58** may therefore have to be decided by a board of appeal.

The rule specifies an exception for nationals of an EPC contracting state and natural persons having a residence permit in one of the EPC contracting states.

The provision also applies to divisional applications received on or after 25.06.2024, according to **R.36(5)** (OJ 2024 A105 Art.2). The rule that a divisional application only designates the contracting states that are designated in the parent application on the date of receipt of the divisional application (**Art.76(2)**) gives the same result.

See also **UPR.5(2)(b)** for the refusal of the registration of unitary effect in the case of a Russian patent proprietor. In that rule, the exception is limited to nationals of EU member states and certain other states.

R. 39(3) Without prejudice to Rule 37, paragraph 2, second sentence, the designation fee shall not be refunded.

R.37(2) Non-forwarded application deemed withdrawn

1 **Non-refund of designation fee**
If a European application is filed with a national authority and this authority does not forward the application to the EPO in due time, the application is deemed to be withdrawn, and the designation fee is refunded (**R.37(2)**; first half-sentence of **R.39(3)**).

The EPO refunds the designation fee in two further cases, notwithstanding **R.39(3)**. The first case is where the designation fee is paid on filing and the application is not dealt with as a European patent application because the requirements of **R.40** are not complied with or because a divisional application is not dealt with as such (**J11/91** r.4.3).

The second case is where the designation fee is paid, and the application is subsequently (deemed) withdrawn or refused before the mention of the publication of the search report. Because the designation fee falls due on the date of the mention of the publication of the search report (**Rfees4(1):1**; A-X,5.2.2), a payment before that date has no legal basis and should be refunded (see **Rfees9:1**). The EPO, however, retains the payment of the designation fee if paid before the due date. The payment will only be considered valid as from the due date, provided that the amount paid corresponds to the amount payable on the date of payment (A-X,5.2.2) and provided that the application is still pending on that date (A-X,10.1.1). Accordingly, if the designation fee is paid before the date on which the mention of the search report is published, the EPO will refund the designation fee if the application is no longer pending on said date (A-X,10.1.1; A-III,11.2.4).

R.39(3) corresponds to Art.79(3) EPC1973 and, accordingly, can be best understood in the historical context of applicants having to pay a designation fee for each designated state (see **Art.79:1** and **Art.79(3)**).

R. 40 Date of filing

Implementation of **Art.80**

1 **General**
R.40 specifies the requirements for a date of filing. The wording of **R.40(1)** follows the model of Art.5(1) and (7) of the Patent Law Treaty (PLT).

Under Art.5(7) and R.2(5)(a) PLT, contracting parties are obliged to accept a reference to a single, previously filed application instead of a description and any drawings, provided that the previously filed application is properly identified. These requirements are found in **R.40(2)**.

In such a case, **R.40(3)** requires the filing of a copy of the previously filed application (R.2(5)(b) PLT) – unless such a copy is already available to the EPO (R.4(3) PLT) – and, where appropriate, of a translation of that application. (OJ 2003 se1 p.159)

See **Art.90:2** for a discussion of the different options for filing an application allowed under **R.40**. The application of **R.40** when filing a divisional application is set out in **Art.76(1):1**.

R. 40(1) The date of filing of a European patent application shall be the date on which the documents filed by the applicant contain:
(a) an indication that a European patent is sought;
(b) information identifying the applicant or allowing the applicant to be contacted; and
(c) a description or reference to a previously filed application.

1 **Requirements for according date of filing**

Documents filed by the applicant will be accorded a date of filing if they contain the items listed under **R.40**. The word 'filed' in **R.40** must be interpreted as duly filed in the sense of **Art.75** with an office allowed by **Art.75** and **R.35(1)**, using a method of filing permitted by **R.2(1)**. Hence, the minimum requirements for according a European patent application a date of filing are given explicitly in **R.40** and implicitly in **Art.75**, **R.35(1)** and **R.2(1)**. No fees need to be paid to obtain a filing date.

The examination for according a date of filing is carried out under **Art.90(1)** and the procedure for correcting deficiencies is specified in **Art.90(4)**. The consequences of non-compliance with the requirements of **R.40** and any re-dating of the application are dealt with by **Art.90(2)** and **R.55**.

1.1 PLACE AND MEANS OF FILING (ART.75, R.35 AND R.2)

The place where the application is filed and the means used for communicating the application are important for according a date of filing and must therefore be regarded as requirements for according a date of filing, even though they are not mentioned in **R.40**.

A determining factor for according the date of filing of a patent application is the date of receipt of the application documents at a filing office of the EPO according to **Art.75(1)(a)** and **R.35(1)** or at a competent national authority according to **Art.75(1)(b)** and (2). Application documents filed with another office, e.g. the EPO sub-office in Vienna or the Dutch national authority, will be forwarded to a competent filing office as a courtesy service and the date of receipt at the competent filing office determines the date of filing.

The application must be filed using a means of communication permitted under **R.2(1)**, where appropriate with written confirmation. Application documents transmitted by other means, such as telex or telegram, will be deemed not to have been received (Dec. Pres. OJ 2019 A18 Art.1(3)) and cannot be accorded a date of filing. Where a national filing office allows means of communication not allowed by the EPO and an applicant uses such means to file a European patent application at that office under **Art.75(1)(b)**, the EPO will accord the application a date of filing (J20/84).

1.2 **INDICATION THAT A EUROPEAN PATENT IS SOUGHT (R.40(1)(A))**

The indication that a patent is sought need be in no particular form to obtain a date of filing (A-III,4.1). The EPO Request for Grant form (**R.41(1)**) contains a statement that a European patent is sought. Use of the form is not required to obtain a date of filing but then the statement must be provided in the application documents in another way. If a filing date is accorded, the completed Request for Grant form must be provided at a later stage, or the application will be refused according to **Art.90(3)**, **R.57(b)**, **R.41(1)** and **Art.90(5)**.

If the EPO receives a document that appears to be a patent application, but the indication is not provided, the EPO will send a **R.55** communication, requesting the applicant to correct the deficiency within two months. If corrected, the application will be redated to the date of receipt of the correction. If not corrected, the application will not be dealt with as a European patent application (**Art.90(2)**, **R.55**). (A-II,4.1.4 and 4.1.5)

If the EPO cannot read the language of the application documents, it will probably keep the documents and defer the examination on filing until a translation has been provided.

1.3 **INFORMATION IDENTIFYING THE APPLICANT (R.40(1)(B))**

R.40(1)(b) requires that information is provided to identify the applicant or allow the applicant to be contacted. If there are multiple applicants, the information must be provided for at least one of them (A-II,4.1.2). The EPO will take into account all data contained in the documents filed to determine whether this requirement is met (**J25/86** r.3). Any kind of information which allows the applicant to be contacted will be considered to fulfil the requirement of **R.40(1)(b)**, in particular the name and address of the applicant's representative, a PO box number or a phone number (A-II,4.1.2).

As **R.40(1)** does not mention representation and **Art.133(1)** and (2) allow the filing of applications without compulsory representation, representation is not required for an application to be accorded a date of filing. Therefore, the information need not be sufficient to determine whether the applicant must be represented under **Art.133(2)** (A-II,4.1.2).

A signature of the applicant or the applicant's representative is not required for according a date of filing. If the signature is not provided in response to an invitation to correct, the application will be refused according to **Art.90(3)**, **R.57(b)**, **R.41(2)(h)** and **Art.90(5)** (see e.g. **J19/13**).

Since there is no language requirement, the EPO may receive applications from which it cannot deduce the applicant's contact details. In such cases the EPO will probably keep the documents and wait for the applicant to approach the EPO. There is no legal basis for not treating the filing as a European patent application. Note that the procedure for correcting deficient information set out in A-II,4.1.4 is not applicable in this case, since there is no deficiency. In this case the invitation under **R.58** to file a translation cannot be notified publicly under **R.129**, even though this may be in conflict with **Art.128**.

According to A-II,4.1.4 there is a deficiency under **R.40(1)(b)** if no information concerning the applicant is provided or if the information provided does not enable the EPO to contact the applicant. This appears to be intended for the case where the address is deficient such that it does not enable the EPO to contact the applicant, and not to the case where the EPO is merely unable to read the address.

Since **R.55** does not refer to **R.40(1)(b)**, no invitation for correction will be sent under **R.55** if the contact information for the applicant is missing or insufficient. However, if the deficiency is corrected of the applicant's own motion within two months from the date of receipt of the original documents, then the date of filing is the date on which the requirements of **R.40** are regarded as met. If not corrected by the end of the two month-period, the application will not be dealt with as a European patent application (**Art.90(2)**). (A-II,4.1.4)

Note that the EPC does not provide a legal basis for the two-month period, although the period is similar to the one mentioned in **R.40(3)**.

1.4 DESCRIPTION (R.40(1)(C))

The application documents must contain a description or a reference to a previously filed application.

The description does not require close scrutiny at this stage of examination. It is sufficient to identify a document which appears to include a description of an invention (A-II,4.1.3).

If no description is provided, the EPO will send a **R.55** communication, requesting the applicant to correct the deficiency within two months. If corrected, the application will be redated to the date of receipt of the description. If not corrected, the application will not be dealt with as a European patent application (**Art.90(2)**, **R.55**). (A-II,4.1.4 and 4.1.5)

1.5 REFERENCE TO A PREVIOUSLY FILED APPLICATION (R.40(1)(C))

Instead of a description, the filing documents may contain a reference to a previously filed application. The previously filed application may be a priority application (A-II,4.1.3.1) or a parent application (A-IV,1.3.1).

The reference must comply with the requirements of **R.40(2)** and a certified copy of the previously filed application must be supplied under **R.40(3)**. More detail is provided in the notes to these provisions.

R.40(1)(c) specifies a 'reference to *a* previously filed application' and it is the intention that the reference is to a *single* previously filed application (OJ 2003 se1 p.168); accordingly Section 26.1 of the Request for Grant form allows entry of details for only one previously filed application.

When filing by reference using the Request for Grant form, the description and drawings of the previously filed application replace the description and any drawings. Optionally, the applicant can indicate on the filing date that the claims of the previously filed application take the place of claims in the application as filed. If no reference is made to the claims of the previously filed application, the claims may be filed as part of the application documents or filed later; the claims of the previously filed application are then not part of the application filed by reference (**T1195/18**). If the claims are filed later (**R.58**), they must have basis in the application as filed by reference, i.e. in the original description and drawings of the previously filed application (**Art.123(2)**; H-IV,2.3.1). It is not permitted to refer to a previously filed application and also include a description in the application documents. Similarly, no additional set of claims may be filed, nor can amended claims be submitted before receipt of the search report, if reference is made to the claims of the previously filed application; in such a case the claims of the previously filed application will serve as the basis for the search. (A-II,4.1.3.1)

The PLT has not defined the words 'previous' and 'application'. The EPO may use the definition of Art.2 PCT for an application, corresponding to that used in **Art.87(1)**. It is recommended to use one of the kinds of application mentioned in **Art.87(1)** as previously filed application, for which the certified copy required under **R.40(3)** can also be obtained. The application need not necessarily claim the priority of the previously filed application it refers to.

If the Request for Grant form is not used, it is recommended to indicate clearly what is referred to. For example, a reference to the description alone does not include a reference to the drawings and claims. Each referenced item must be specifically stated.

2 Issues irrelevant for according date of filing

2.1 LANGUAGE OF THE APPLICATION

R.40 does not contain any requirement as to the language of the application, which implies that the language of the application is not relevant for according a date of filing, as required by the PLT (A-VII,1.1). **Art.14(2)**, relating to the examination as to formalities, implies that an application may be filed in any language. The indication that a European patent is sought and the information identifying the applicant or allowing the applicant to be contacted may also be filed in any language. The PLT did not want to define 'language'. A minimum condition should be the ability to make a reliable translation, requiring the availability of a dictionary. For online filing there must be an ISO code for the characters of the language, because the EPO uses ISO codes.

It is not possible to file the application documents in the wrong language. The EPO does not require that these documents are all in the same language for obtaining a date of filing, but does view the use of more than one language a deficiency that needs to be remedied (A-VII,1.1).

The language requirements provided in **Art.14(2)** are examined in the formalities examination under Art.90(3) and **R.57(a)**, i.e. after the examination for according a date of filing. If the application is not filed in one of the official languages of the EPO, i.e. English, German or French (**Art.14(1)**), a translation into one of these languages must be provided under **Art.14(2)**.

2.2 CLAIMS

The presence of one or more claims is not a requirement for according a date of filing. If no claims are present on filing, the EPO will invite the applicant to file claims under **R.58**. Applicants may file the claims of their own volition before being so invited (A-III,15). As a formal requirement, at least one claim (**Art.78(1)(c)**) must be on file at the time of the formalities examination under **Art.90(3)** and **R.57(c)**. Note that the application is not re-dated on receipt of late-filed claims. The EPO always publishes the application with the claims.

Claims filed after the filing date are regarded as amendments under **Art.123(2)** and must have basis in the application as filed, i.e. in the description and drawings if the application is filed without claims (A-III,15). It is, therefore, advisable to include claim-like clauses in the description on filing to have basis for the desired claims.

The EPO may request the applicant under **R.137(4)** to indicate the basis for the late-filed claims in the application as filed since late-filed claims are regarded as an amendment (H-III,2.1.1(i)).

The applicant may indicate on filing that the claims of a referenced previous application take the place of claims in the application as filed. The indication can be made in Section 26 of the Request for Grant form. If such an indication is made, the claims of the previous application will form the basis of the search and examination (A-II,4.1.3.1).

Claims filed after the date of filing of the application are regarded as an amendment to the application and must comply with **R.3(2)**, i.e. they must be filed in the language of the proceedings. When the claims are filed before the translation of the application under **R.6(1)** has been filed, the language of the claims must be the language in which the application will be translated, as the application must be in one language.

2.3 FORM OF THE APPLICATION

R.40 does not give requirements for the form of the application. Hence, an identifiable description suffices for the purpose of according a filing date, even if it deviates from EPC requirements. The documents making up the application must be sufficiently legible to enable the information to be discerned (A-II,4.1). Note that the documents as filed also determine the content of the application beyond which extension is not allowed during subsequent proceedings (**Art.123(2)**).

2.4 DESIGNATION OF CONTRACTING STATES

On filing, no contracting states need be explicitly designated. All contracting states are automatically designated under **Art.79(1)**. See **Art.79(3):1** for withdrawing designations during the grant procedure.

2.5 FEES

Payment of fees is not necessary for according a date of filing, which makes a European patent application an economical way of securing a filing date for a priority document. If the filing fee and search fee are not paid within one month after filing, the application will be deemed to be withdrawn (**Art.78(2)**). The withdrawal does not affect the right to claim the priority of the application (**Art.87(2)** and **(3)**).

2.6 MISSING PARTS OF DESCRIPTION AND MISSING DRAWINGS

The EPO will check during the examination on filing whether any parts of the description or any drawings appear to be missing. Where such items are missing but the requirements of **R.40(1)** have been fulfilled, the application documents will initially be accorded a date of filing corresponding to the date they were received; any addition of missing parts may change this date.

Applicants may file missing parts of their own motion or on invitation by the EPO. The application will be re-dated to the date of receipt of the missing parts. However, the application will retain the original date of filing if a missing part of the description or a missing drawing is contained in an application from which priority is claimed. See **R.56** and notes thereto for details. The applicant may also replace erroneously filed parts under **R.56a**.

R. 40(2) A reference to a previously filed application under paragraph 1(c) shall state the filing date and number of that application and the Office with which it was filed. Such reference shall indicate that it replaces the description and any drawings.

1 **Reference to a previous application**
When a reference to a previously filed application is filed instead of a description, the following information must be provided according to **R.40(2)** for accordance of a date of filing (A-II,4.1.3.1):
1 the filing date of the previous application;
2 its file number, i.e. the application number;
3 the office where it was filed; and
4 an indication that this reference replaces the description and any drawings.
It is possible to indicate in the Request for Grant form, Section 26, that the reference also replaces the claims (see **R.57(c)**).

The previous application is normally a patent application but can also be an application for a utility model (A-II,4.1.3.1).

2 **Late filing of data of previous application**
The required indications concerning the previous application must be provided when filing the application. Their presence is a requirement for according a date of filing to an application filed by reference.

If any of the indications is not included in the application documents, the EPO will invite the applicant to provide it as a correction within two months of invitation (**R.55**, first sentence). If not provided, the application will not be dealt with as a European patent application (**R.55**, first sentence). If provided in due time, the EPO will redate the application to the date of receipt of the additional information and inform the applicant of the date of filing (**R.55**, second sentence). (A-II,4.1.4)

If either the filing date or the filing number is incorrect, correction under **R.139**, second sentence, may be possible since mistakes in the request do not have to be obvious (correction of the date or number of any priority application is similarly possible). On the other hand, a correction which amounts to the replacement of the description and drawings with a new text, would seem to be prohibited by **G2/95**. This decision, however, was taken under EPC1973 when filing by reference was not possible and may not be applicable. The procedure of **R.56a** regarding erroneously filed parts seems neither applicable. If a later date of filing is acceptable, the applicant can simply refile the application.

R. 40(3) Where the application contains a reference under paragraph 2, a certified copy of the previously filed application shall be filed within two months of filing the application. Where the previously filed application is not in an official language of the European Patent Office, a translation thereof in one of these languages shall be filed within the same period. Rule 53, paragraph 2, shall apply mutatis mutandis.

R.53(2) Copy previous document in EPO file

1 **Copy of previous application**
Where the application refers to a previously filed application under **R.40(1)(c)**, the applicant must file a certified copy of this previous application (**R.40(3)**, first sentence). A certified copy rather than a normal copy is required, since the previously filed application is not necessarily published. The copy of the previously filed application must be certified as a true copy by the authority with which that application was filed. If the application also claims the priority of the previously filed application, only one certified copy needs to be filed in order to satisfy both **R.40(3)**, first sentence and **R.53(1)**. (A-II,4.1.3.1)

According to **R.40(3)**, last sentence, the requirement to file a copy is dispensed with if the previous application is already available to the EPO. The previous application is only available where it is a European patent application or an international application filed with the EPO as receiving Office (OJ 2009 p.486). Hence, a divisional application referring e.g. to a Euro-PCT application that was not filed with the EPO as receiving Office, requires filing of a certified copy of the international application as originally filed with the receiving Office. (A-II,4.1.3.1 and A-IV,1.3.1)

Since it can be difficult to obtain a certified copy of an application from a patent office within the relatively short period of **R.40(3)**, it is recommended to use filing by reference only where the certified copy is available on filing or where the EPO will include the copy in the file.

2 **Period for filing copy of previous application**

A copy of the previously filed application must be filed within two months of filing the application (**R.40(3)**; see **Art.80:4**). If the copy is filed before the expiry of the two-month period, the application will retain its original date of filing. Note, that the provision of the certified copy is a requirement for according a date of filing that need not be complied with at the date of filing, but only two months later.

If the copy is not filed within two months of filing the application, the applicant will receive a communication setting a time limit of a further two months under **R.55**. If the copy is supplied within that period, the original filing date will be retained (A-II,4.1.5). If no copy is available by expiry of the further period, no filing date will be accorded and the application will not be dealt with as a European patent application (**R.55**, first sentence). (A-II,4.1.4)

The EPO has an interest in receiving the copy of the previous application and, where applicable, the translation, as early as possible for the purpose of publishing the application, particularly if the European application is filed towards the end of the priority period. Therefore, the two-month periods in **R.40(3)** and **R.55** for filing the copy are excluded from further processing under **R.135(2)**. However, re-establishment is available for the latter period.

3 **Translation of previous application**

If the previous application is not in an official EPO language, a translation in English, French or German must be filed in addition to the certified copy of the application (**R.40(3)**, second sentence). The translation must be presented in the same form as the application documents (**R.49(1)**). If the translation is already available to the EPO, it need not be filed again (**R.40(3)**, last sentence) and the EPO will include a copy in its file (A-II,4.1.3.1).

The provision of a translation is not a requirement for according a date of filing (A-II,4.1.4, last sentence). The mention of furnishing a translation in a provision concerning the requirements for according a date of filing is therefore incongruous. The legislator has allegedly included the requirement in this provision to reduce the amount of law text.

When the previous application is in an admissible non-EPO language according to **Art.14(4)**, the applicant may be entitled to a reduction of the filing fee (see **R.7a(1)**).

The translation may subsequently be brought into conformity with the previously filed application (A-VII,7; **Art.14(2)**, second sentence). It should be noted that, in contrast to **R.6(1)**, **R.40(3)** does not refer to **Art.14(2)**; however, **Art.14(2)** is regarded as applicable to all rules relating to translations of the application.

4 **Period for filing translation of previous application**

A translation of the previously filed application must be filed within two months of filing the application (**R.40(3)**, second sentence; see **Art.80:4**). This period is the same as the period for filing a translation under **R.6(1)**.

If the translation is not filed in time, the EPO will, as part of the formalities examination under **R.57**, invite the applicant under **R.58** to supply the translation within two months. If the translation is not filed in response to this invitation, the application will be deemed withdrawn under **Art.14(2)**, last sentence (A-III,16.2). However, the application retains its date of filing. The grant procedure is accelerated if the translation is filed as early as possibly, preferably within the period of **R.40(3)**.

The two-month periods of **R.40(3)** and **R.58** are excluded from further processing (**R.135(2)**) but the latter is open to re-establishment under **Art.122**.

Chapter II *Provisions governing the application*

R. 41 Request for grant

Implementation of **Art.78(1)(a)**

R. 41(1) The request for grant of a European patent shall be filed on a form drawn up by the European Patent Office.

1 **Request for Grant form**
Use of the Request for Grant form (Form 1001) is a compulsory formal requirement for filing a European patent application (**R.57(b)**). If the Form is not used on filing and not supplied after invitation, the application will be refused (**Art.90(5)**). However, use of the Form is not a requirement for according a date of filing (**R.40(1)(a)**). Use of the EPO Request for Grant form is not applicable to Euro-PCT applications (R.49.4 PCT).

The Request for Grant form can be downloaded from the EPO website, and an electronic version of the Form is included in OLF and Online Filing 2.0 (see **R.2(1)**:5; A-III,4.1).

R. 41(2) The request shall contain:

(a) a petition for the grant of a European patent;

(b) the title of the invention, which shall clearly and concisely state the technical designation of the invention and shall exclude all fancy names;

(c) the name, address and nationality of the applicant and the State in which their residence or principal place of business is located. Names of natural persons shall be indicated by the person's family name, followed by their given names. Names of legal persons, as well as of bodies equivalent to legal persons under the law governing them, shall be indicated by their official designations. Addresses shall be indicated in accordance with applicable customary requirements for prompt postal delivery and shall comprise all the relevant administrative units, including the house number, if any. It is recommended that the telephone numbers be indicated;

(d) the representative's name and the address of their place of business as prescribed in sub-paragraph (c) if the applicant has appointed a representative;

(e) where appropriate, an indication that the application constitutes a divisional application and the number of the earlier European patent application;

(f) in cases covered by Article 61, paragraph 1(b), the number of the original European patent application;

(g) where applicable, a declaration claiming the priority of an earlier application and indicating the date on which and the country in or for which the earlier application was filed;

(h) the signature of the applicant or their representative;

(i) a list of the documents accompanying the request. This list shall also indicate the number of sheets of the description, claims, drawings and abstract filed with the request;

(j) the designation of the inventor, where the applicant is the inventor.

Amended by decision of the Administrative Council of 14.12.2023, which entered into force on 01.04.2024 (OJ 2024 A16, CA/D 26/23). The amendments were in point (c) deletion of mention of fax number, and in points (c), (d) and (h) amendment to gender-neutral language.
Art.61(1)(b) Filing new application by entitled person

1 **Examination of the request for grant**
See the notes to **R.57(b)** for the examination of compliance with the requirements of **R.41(2)** during the examination of formal requirements of the application under **Art.90(3)**.

2 **Information on the applicant (R.41(2)(c))**
Applicants who may act without a representative may indicate an address for correspondence in a contracting state other than their address of residence or principal business (A-III,4.2.1).

Where an application is filed by multiple applicants, the information of **R.41(2)(c)** must be provided for each applicant (A-III,4.2.1).

R. 41(3) If there is more than one applicant, the request shall preferably contain the appointment of one applicant or representative as common representative.

1 **Appointment of common representative**
A professional representative (or legal practitioner, or association of professional representatives) can be appointed as the common representative by entering the details of the representative in section 15 of the Request for Grant form. If one of the applicants is named as the common representative, this should be done on a signed additional sheet instead (see points 14 and 15 of the Notes to the Request for Grant form).

If the form mentions several applicants but does not appoint a common representative, a common representative is appointed by the EPO according to **R.151**.

A representative authorised to the act for all the applicants can sign the form. If all the applicants sign the form, the form itself is a basis for their entitlement to act. An authorisation need be filed only on request by the EPO (**R.152(1)**). See also **Art.133:2** for appointment and authorisation.

R. 42 Content of the description

Implementation of **Art.78(1)(b)** and **Art.83**

1 **General**
The purpose of this rule is to ensure that there is enough technical information in the application for the skilled person to put the invention into practice as required by **Art.83**, and to enable a reader to understand the contribution that the invention makes to the art. The description must therefore disclose:
- the technical field (paragraph (1)(a));
- the prior art (paragraph (1)(b));
- a disclosure of the invention facilitating the identification of the problem and the solution to said problem (paragraph (1)(c));
- a brief description of the drawings (paragraph (1)(d));
- an embodiment (paragraph (1)(e));

- a way of exploiting the invention in industry, if necessary (paragraph (1)(f)).

R. 42(1) The description shall:
(a) specify the technical field to which the invention relates;
(b) indicate the background art which, as far as is known to the applicant, can be regarded as useful to understand the invention, draw up the European search report and examine the European patent application, and, preferably, cite the documents reflecting such art;
(c) disclose the invention, as claimed, in such terms that the technical problem, even if not expressly stated as such, and its solution can be understood, and state any advantageous effects of the invention with reference to the background art;
(d) briefly describe the figures in the drawings, if any;
(e) describe in detail at least one way of carrying out the invention claimed, using examples where appropriate and referring to the drawings, if any;
(f) indicate explicitly, when it is not obvious from the description or nature of the invention, the way in which the invention is industrially applicable.

1 **Prior art (R.42(1)(b))**
The term 'background art' in **R.42(1)(b)** and **(c)** has the same meaning as 'prior art' (**T11/82** hn.II).

Only the most appropriate prior art need be mentioned (F-II,4.4).

A prior right document must be clearly identified as such, and it should be indicated if said document is not relevant for the assessment of inventive step. Adding references to prior art documents after filing of the application does not extend the subject-matter in the sense of **Art.123(2)**. Later-added prior art references must be purely factual. The subject-matter of the application is understood to consist of those features which relate to the invention, starting off from the prior art. (F-II,4.3)

A reference to a priority document is not allowed.

A reference to a document giving information necessary to understand the invention must be contained in the application as filed. The later inclusion of such a reference introduces new matter. If such a document is not available to the public at the date of filing, a copy must be furnished to the EPO on or before the date of filing, and the document must be published before or on the date of publication of the application. (F-III,8 and H-V,2.5)

If the application refers to knowledge in the state of the art which cannot be classified as being in a relevant field, that knowledge cannot be used to the applicant's disadvantage as being in a neighbouring field merely on account of that reference. The link to said field is the inventor's internal state of the art. (**T28/87**)

The relevant content of a document referred to in the application as filed is regarded as forming part of the application when considering the effect of the application as prior right (**Art.54(3)**) against later applications. (F-III,8)

If necessary to put the contribution to the art made by the invention into proper perspective, the EPO may request that references to documents from the search report are cited (**T11/82**). Although the indication of prior art in the description is not specified in **R.42(1)(b)** as a requirement, it becomes mandatory if the EPO has indicated the prior art to be acknowledged (**T11/82** r.17, 25). If the applicant or proprietor does not follow the invitation to amend the references to the prior art, the application will be refused (**Art.97(2)** and **R.42(1)**) or the patent revoked (**Art.101(2)** and **R.42(1)**).

2 **Disclosure of the invention (R.42(1)(c))**
The description must disclose the invention as claimed, making the technical problem and its solution understandable; it may state any advantages in view of the state of the art (**R.42(1)(c)**). If the subject-matter of a dependent claim is self-explanatory, no additional explanation is necessary. If the invention resides in the recognition of a problem, i.e. the invention is a so-called problem invention, this should be indicated. Advantageous effects must not be presented in a way disparaging the products or processes of a third party or the validity of third party patent rights (**R.48(1)(b)**. If an independent claim defines a patentable invention, the underlying problem must be derivable from the application; only then is the requirement of **R.42(1)(c)** fulfilled (**T26/81**; F-II,4.6).

R.42(1)(c) is not a separate formal criterion independent of **Art.52**. The EPC does not require that an invention must have an advantageous effect to be patentable; it may provide a mere alternative to the prior art (G-VII,5.2). However, generally, no technical problem is solved by the claimed subject-matter if **R.42(1)(c)** is not complied with and inventive step is accordingly to be denied (**T1520/19**).

If the description describes subject-matter that is excluded from patentability under **Art.53**, such subject-matter must be prominently marked as not being according to the claimed invention (G-II,4.2; G-II,5.3). Alternatively, the discussion of the subject-matter can be deleted or reworded such that it does not fall under the exceptions to patentability.

3 **Description of an embodiment (R.42(1)(e))**
Details of well-known features need not be given, as the reader is assumed to be skilled in the art. The required number of embodiments depends on how broad the claimed field is. Normally a single embodiment renders it obvious how to put the invention into practice, but where the claims cover a broad field, a series of embodiments or variants extending over the field is necessary to satisfy **Art.83**. (F-III,1)

The requirements of sufficient disclosure of the invention (**Art.83**) and support of the claims by the description (**Art.84**) are based on the same legal principle that the patent monopoly should be justified by the technical contribution to the art. Therefore, the extent to which an invention is sufficiently disclosed is also highly relevant to the question of support. (**T409/91**)

In order to clarify the invention, it should be described not only in structural terms, but also in functional terms, unless the function of the elements is immediately clear. In some fields, e.g. computers, a functional description is often clearer than a structural one. (F-III,1)

4 **Industrial application (R.42(1)(f))**
In most cases the way in which an invention can be exploited in industry is self-evident, and needs no further clarification in the description. Since the industrial application of certain biotechnological inventions, i.e. sequences and partial sequences of genes, is not self-evident, the industrial application of such sequences must be disclosed in the application according to **R.29(3)**. (F-II,4.9 and G-III,4)

R. 42(2) The description shall be presented in the manner and order specified in paragraph 1, unless, owing to the nature of the invention, a different presentation would afford a better understanding or be more concise.

1 **Departure from R.42(1)**
The clarity of the description is the responsibility of the applicant. Hence, an examiner should not be too strict when the applicant requests amendments departing from R.42(1). (F-II,4.10)

R. 43 Form and content of claims

Implementation of Art.78(1)(c) and Art.84

R. 43(1) The claims shall define the matter for which protection is sought in terms of the technical features of the invention. Wherever appropriate, claims shall contain:
(a) a statement indicating the designation of the subject-matter of the invention and those technical features which are necessary for the definition of the claimed subject-matter but which, in combination, form part of the prior art;
(b) a characterising portion, beginning with the expression "characterised in that" or "characterised by" and specifying the technical features for which, in combination with the features stated under sub-paragraph (a), protection is sought.

1 **Form and content of claims**
Specifying a result to be achieved, i.e. a statement of purpose, is allowed if it helps in defining the invention. Functional features are allowed as long as a skilled person does not have to exercise inventive skills to provide means for performing the function in question. Claims to the use of an invention, in the sense of the technical application thereof, are allowed. (F-IV,2.1)

R.43(1)(a) applies only to independent claims and not to dependent claims. Only relevant features of the prior art have to be mentioned. If one or more features in the characterising part of a claim are known in combination with the features of the preamble of the claim (i.e. the first part reciting the prior art) and, in that combination, have the same effect as in the full combination of the invention, those features must be transferred to the preamble. (F-IV,2.2)

The two-part form need not be used, if this gives a misleading picture of the contribution made to the art. Examples are where the invention lies solely in the combination of known elements of equal status; modification of a known process by omitting a substance or substituting a substance for another one; a complex system of interrelated parts, the invention residing in changes in several of these parts or in their inter-relationships. A two-part claim should be avoided if the prior art is a prior right (F-IV,2.3). If a one-part claim is used, the description should clearly identify the prior art (T170/84).

Although not prescribed by the EPC, claims are normally drafted as a single sentence. Claims comprising more than one sentence are exceptional (see as an example EP 0 293 769 B1, Claim 1).

R. 43(2) Without prejudice to Article 82, a European patent application may contain more than one independent claim in the same category (product, process, apparatus or use) only if the subject-matter of the application involves one of the following:
(a) a plurality of interrelated products,
(b) different uses of a product or apparatus,
(c) alternative solutions to a particular problem, where it is inappropriate to cover these alternatives by a single claim.

Art.82 Unity of invention

1 **One independent claim per category**

The intention of **R.43(2)** is to limit the number of independent claims in an application. It legally defines the principle of 'one independent claim per category'. The only admissible exceptions to this principle are explicitly stated. The rule allows an examiner to object to a large number of independent claims without lengthy substantive argumentation. An applicant wishing to have more than one independent claim in the same category to obtain the desired scope of protection for the invention must, if the EPO objects, convincingly demonstrate that all the additional independent claims come under one of the exceptions explicitly given in the rule. So, the onus is on the applicant. (OJ 2002 p.112)

The EPO can raise an objection to multiple independent claims in the same category at the search stage under **R.62a** or during substantive examination (F-IV,3.3).

T263/05 r.5.19 regards **R.43(2)** as an administrative provision designed to facilitate the straightforward refusal of applications contravening **Art.82** and **84**; therefore, the rule is not applicable in opposition proceedings.

When, after an objection under **R.43(2)**, an applicant maintains a plurality of independent claims without providing convincing arguments that one of the three situations in the provision applies, the application may be refused under **Art.97(2)** (F-IV,3.3).

The provision aims at reducing the amount of work spent on the substantial number of applications drafted in the so-called US style, containing an excessive number of independent claims, which do not comply with the requirement of conciseness (**Art.84**). A proliferation of dependent claims is counteracted by **R.43(5)** (see also F-IV,5).

R.43(2) allows in principle one independent claim in each of the following four categories: product, process, apparatus and use. Basically, there are only two different claim types: physical entities (product, apparatus) and activities (process and use) (F-IV,3.1; **G6/88** r.2.2)). The use of different claim categories may help in obtaining full protection for the invention (F-IV,3.1). Note that a claim directed to a method and a claim directed to an apparatus using the method are independent claims (see also **R.43(4):1**).

R.43(2) acts as a filter that allows applications that comprise a plurality of independent claims in the same category to move forward to the search division only if these claims are covered by the three cases defined in the rule. The reference to Art.82 makes clear that, once past the filter, these claims also have to meet the requirement of unity. (F-V,3.2.1)

2 **Several independent claims per category**

In three specific cases R.43(2) allows an application to have two or more independent claims in the same category (see F-IV,3.2 for the examples):

1 A plurality of inter-related products having the same inventive concept, e.g. plug and socket, transmitter and receiver, intermediate and final product, gene - gene construct - host - protein - medicament.

The 'interrelated products' must relate to different objects that complement each other or work together; it does not cover different embodiments of essentially the same object (**T56/01** r.4.1).

Note, that **R.43(2)(a)** should cover interrelated methods, although they are not mentioned; for example a method for coding data and a method for decoding data.

2 Different uses of a product or apparatus, e.g. a substance disclosed for a number of distinct cosmetic or medical uses (second and further medical indication).

3 Alternative solutions to a particular problem based on the same inventive concept, where it is not appropriate to cover these alternatives by a single claim, e.g. where the invention resides in a group of new chemical compounds or in a number of processes for the manufacture of such compounds.

When two independent claims have a considerable overlap, they may be regarded as not relating to alternative solutions and it is appropriate to cover them by a single claim (**T56/01** r.4.3). Combining two independent claims relating to alternative solutions in one more general claim is not appropriate if it might cause extension of subject-matter or loss of priority (**T525/03** r.4.5).

When an objection under **R.43(2)** arises, the burden of proof that multiple independent claims can be maintained is on the applicant (**T56/01** r.5).

Examples of sets of claims for a computer-implemented invention complying with **R.43(2)** are given in F-IV,3.9.

R. 43(3) Any claim stating the essential features of an invention may be followed by one or more claims concerning particular embodiments of that invention.

R. 43(4) Any claim which includes all the features of any other claim (dependent claim) shall contain, if possible at the beginning, a reference to the other claim and then state the additional features. A dependent claim directly referring to another dependent claim shall also be admissible. All dependent claims referring back to a single previous claim, and all dependent claims referring back to several previous claims, shall be grouped together to the extent and in the most appropriate way possible.

1 **Independent and dependent claims**

According to **R.43(4)** a claim is dependent if it includes all the features of any other claim. Some special cases are given below.

A claim without a reference to another claim is only independent if it does not include all features of another claim. In the case where Claim 1 relates to a device and Claim 2 to the device including feature A without a reference to Claim 1, Claim 2 is a dependent claim, because it includes all features of Claim 1. The EPO will raise a clarity objection against Claim 2 and request compliance with the requirement of **R.43(4)** that the claim contain a reference to Claim 1.

A claim referring only to another claim of a different category is independent. First example: Claim 1 for a process and Claim 2 for an apparatus for carrying out the process of claim 1. Second example: Claim 1 for a product and Claim 2 for a process for the manufacture of the product of claim 1. Third example: Claim 1 for a product and Claim 2 for a use of the product of claim 1. See also F-IV,3.8.

A claim referring to another claim but not including all the features of the other claim is independent. First example: Claim 1 for a machine having part X and Claim 2 for the machine according to claim 1 modified in that X is replaced by Y. Here the reference between the claims is used for claiming alternative features (see F-IV,3.7). Second example: Claim 1 for a device including element A and Claim 2 for element B adapted for cooperation with element A of claim 1. It has to be carefully considered which elements of the claim referred to are necessarily comprised in the subject-matter of the referring claim and which are not.

If a product claim is patentable, an independent process claim for obtaining the product is also patentable, provided all features of the product result from the process (**T169/88**). Similarly, the patentability of a product claim implies the patentability of a claim for the use of the product, the use relating to the claimed features of the product (**T642/94**). In all other circumstances, the patentability of the independent claim referred to does not necessarily imply the patentability of the independent claim containing the reference. (F-IV,3.8)

2 **Form of dependent claims**

The phrases 'characterised in that' or 'characterised by' are not necessary in dependent claims, but are permissible (F-IV,3.4). Where the two-part form is used for the independent claim(s), dependent claims may relate to further details of features not only of the characterising portion but also of the preamble (F-IV,3.6). A dependent claim may refer back to one or more independent claims, dependent claims or to a combination thereof (F-IV,3.4). A claim can include a number of alternatives which can fairly be substituted one for another, as long as the number and presentation of alternatives in a single claim does not make the claim obscure or difficult to construe (F-IV,3.7).

3 **Use of dependent claims**

Dependent claims are useful during the grant and opposition procedure, because they define embodiments that can be used as fallback positions when the scope of an independent claim must be limited, e.g. in view of prior art discovered after the filing of the application. In the absence of such dependent claims, a fallback position would have to be created by adding one or more features from embodiments in the disclosure to the independent claim. The EPO may object to the inclusion of isolated features from an embodiment on the grounds that it results in an inadmissible intermediate generalisation (see **Art.123(2):2.3**).

The extent of protection conferred by a patent is defined mainly by the independent claims. However, dependent claims in a patent may be used to define specific embodiments covered by the independent claim, thereby avoiding any ambiguity in the meaning of features in an independent claim.

Dependent claims may also be useful in a patent as fallback position during national limitation proceedings, where national law does not allow post-grant limitation by including features from the description (see **Art.138(3)**).

It should be noted that the EPO makes an effort to reduce the number of dependent claims to decrease their workload, in spite of the usefulness of dependent claims to the applicant and proprietor. An important step was the introduction of the two-tier system for claims fees in 2009 (see **Rfees2(1)15**). See also the response of applicants in **R.45(1):2**.

R. 43(5) The number of claims shall be reasonable with regard to the nature of the invention claimed. The claims shall be numbered consecutively in Arabic numerals.

1 **Number of dependent claims**

A multiplicity of trivial claims will be objected to (F-IV,5). A large number of claims gives rise to the expense of paying a large number of claims fees (**R.45(1)**).

R. 43(6) Except where absolutely necessary, claims shall not rely on references to the description or drawings in specifying the technical features of the invention. In particular, they shall not contain such expressions as "as described in part ... of the description", or "as illustrated in figure ... of the drawings".

1 **Reference to description and drawing in claim**

An omnibus claim, i.e. a claim relying on references to the description or drawings for all its technical features, is not allowed (F-IV,4.17).

The applicant must show that a reference in a claim to the description or drawings is absolutely necessary (**T150/82**). Such an exceptional case can be a reference to a peculiar shape, illustrated in a drawing, an item hard to define in words or formulae, or a chemical product defined with reference to a graph or diagram.

A method of measuring a claimed parameter must appear completely in the claim itself (see **Art.84:1.5**). If explicit inclusion of the measurement method would make the claim unclear through complexity or lack of conciseness, a reference to the description may instead be made. (F-IV,4.11)

Examples of accepted references in claims:

- reference to a US patent for a measuring technique (EP 0 187 491 B1, Claim 7);
- reference to a diagram in a Figure of the specification for a chemical composition (EP 0 503 901 B1, Claim 3);
- reference to an international standard for a measurement procedure (EP 0 432 501 B1, Claim 1).

R. 43(7) Where the European patent application contains drawings including reference signs, the technical features specified in the claims shall preferably be followed by such reference signs relating to these features, placed in parentheses, if the intelligibility of the claim can thereby be increased. These reference signs shall not be construed as limiting the claim.

1 **Reference signs**

Reference signs are an aid to understanding the claim and may not be construed as limiting the scope of the claim; a comment to that effect in the description is acceptable (**T237/84**). A claim requiring reference signs for intelligibility may be refused, if reference signs are not inserted after a request to this effect by the EPO (**T237/84** r.6). However, the requirement to insert reference signs may be avoided if the applicant convincingly argues that if the claims without reference signs are clear in the sense of **Art.84** they must also be intelligible and emphasises that the insertion of reference signs is not obligatory but only preferable according to **R.43(7)**.

If there is a large number of embodiments, only the reference signs of the most important embodiment need be incorporated in the independent claim(s). Reference signs should be inserted both in the preamble and the characterising part of a two-part claim. (F-IV,4.18)

R. 44 Unity of invention

Implementation of **Art.82**

R. 44(1) Where a group of inventions is claimed in a European patent application, the requirement of unity of invention under Article 82 shall be fulfilled only when there is a technical relationship among those inventions involving one or more of the same or corresponding special technical features. The expression "special technical features" shall mean those features which define a contribution which each of the claimed inventions considered as a whole makes over the prior art.

1 Unity of invention

A group of inventions is unitary according to **Art.82** if they are so linked as to form a single general inventive concept. A single general inventive concept linking a group of inventions is a technical relationship among those inventions involving one or more of the same or corresponding special technical features (consequence of **R.44(1)**, first sentence, implementing **Art.82**).

1.1 SPECIAL TECHNICAL FEATURES

A special technical feature defines a contribution over the prior art (**R.44(1)**, second sentence); hence, it is a novel technical feature. The prior art is the prior art 'at hand' at the time of the assessment of unity, which may vary depending on the stage of proceedings. For example, before the search, the only prior art at hand may be the background art mentioned in the application and any common general knowledge of the skilled person. (F-V,2)

According to case law, a special technical feature must also contribute to the inventive step (**W6/90** r.3.3), briefly called 'an inventive feature'. Since an invention is defined by an independent claim, there is a single general inventive concept and, hence, unity of invention, only if a group of independent claims have a technical relationship involving one or more of the same or corresponding novel and inventive technical features. Since **R.44(1)** uses the word 'only', a unity argument must refer to special technical features; a unity argument for example based on a single general inventive step not mentioning special technical features therefore lacks legal basis.

There is a technical relationship between claims if:

- One or more special technical features of the claims are the same. 'Same' means identical wording (**W2/95** r.6.3).
- One or more special technical features of the claims have the same technical effect (**W11/99** r.2.7). Features have the same effect if, for example, they solve the same problem in a different way (**W17/03** r.2.4) or if they are alternatives of a similar nature, such as in a Markush claim (**W3/92** r.10).
- One or more special technical features of the claims have a causal relation. For example, a particular step in a manufacturing process causes a structural feature in the product (**W6/90** r.3.2), or different uses of a product have their basis in a particular structural feature of the product.
- One or more special technical features of the claims are interrelated to achieve a certain technical effect. The interrelation may be that the features complement each other or that they co-operate (F-V,2). For example, a specially formed prong of a plug co-operates with a slot of a socket to form an electrically conductive connection, or a special algorithm in a coding method complements an inverse algorithm in a corresponding de-coding method.

The first example in the above list relates to the presence in the claims of the 'same special technical features' in **R.44(1)**, the subsequent examples relate to the 'corresponding special technical features' in **R.44(1)**. The technical relationship among the claims with corresponding special technical features may be for example a same technical effect, a causal relation or an interrelation causing a technical effect.

1.2 ASSESSMENT OF UNITY

A substantive assessment of unity involves (F-V,3):

i) Determining any common matter between the claims of the different claimed inventions. Common matter may be present in features that are either the same, or which provide a common technical effect or a solution to a common technical problem. Any single general inventive concept must reside in the common matter.

ii) Comparing the common matter with the prior art at hand. If the common matter makes a non-obvious contribution over the prior art at hand, it comprises 'special technical features' within the meaning of **R.44(1)** and there is a single general inventive concept linking the claims. If the common matter is known or obvious in light of the prior art at hand, then the claims lack unity.

iii) If the claims lack unity, analysing any remaining technical features which are not part of the common matter to identify one or more groups of inventions in the claims, each group solving the same technical problem (see F-V,3.2).

The comparison at step (ii) with the prior art before the search is called an a priori assessment. During the search other prior art may be revealed, which may be taken into account in an a posteriori assessment of the unity. Since the prior art may change during the proceedings, the assessment of unity may also change.

2 Inventions in the same category

An application may comprise a plurality of independent claims in the same category, provided that these claims comply with the requirement of **R.43(2)**. The phrase 'without prejudice to **Art.82**' in that rule makes clear that the plurality of inventions must also meet the requirement of unity of **R.44(1)**. (F-V,3.2.1)

Examples of a group of unitary inventions of the same category are a group of different products all of which include the same special technical feature, and a group of different products having different special technical features that solve the same problem.

The group of inventions may be claimed in separate claims or as alternatives within a single claim (**R.44(2)**).

3 Inventions in different categories

An application may comprise independent claims in different categories. **R.44(1)** should be construed as permitting the inclusion of any one of the following combinations of claims of different categories in the same application: (i) an independent claim for a given product, an independent claim for a process specially adapted for the manufacture of said product and an independent claim for a use of said product; or (ii) an independent claim for a given process, an independent claim for an apparatus or means specifically designed for carrying out said process; or (iii) an independent claim for a given product, an independent claim for a process specially adapted for the manufacture of said product and an independent claim for an apparatus or means specifically designed for carrying out said process. A single set of independent claims according to any one of the combinations (i), (ii) or (iii) above is always permissible under **R.44(1)** and **R.43(2)**, while a plurality of such set of independent claims may be permitted only in certain cases (F-IV,3.1).

The EPO thereby continues the historical practice under R.30 EPC1973 which specified the three permitted sets of independent claims in the version before the amendment in 1991.

A group of inventions in different categories, for example including a product, a process specially adapted for the manufacture of the product and a use of the product, is only unitary if the inventions are linked by one or more of the same or corresponding technical features. An expression in the claim such as 'specially adapted' or 'specifically designed' does not necessarily imply that a single general inventive concept is present (F-V,3.2.2).

4 **Special inventions**
The Guidelines give the specific requirements for unity of Markush claims (F-V,3.2.5), and intermediate and final product claims (F-V,3.2.7).

Since these requirements do not take into account the special technical features of the claims, the unity reasoning for these claims is not based on **R.44(1)** and therefore lacks proper legal basis. The same applies to case law on unity not discussing the special technical features of the inventions; such case law should be regarded as overruled by said amendment in 1991.

R. 44(2) The determination whether a group of inventions is so linked as to form a single general inventive concept shall be made without regard to whether the inventions are claimed in separate claims or as alternatives within a single claim.

1 **Grouping of inventions**
A group of inventions may be claimed in separate independent claims, each claim defining an invention, or as alternatives within a single claim. The way of claiming does not affect the assessment of unity of the invention. (**R.44(2)**)

Whether or not a plurality of inventions can be claimed as alternatives in a single claim is a matter of clarity under **Art.84**. The number and presentation of alternatives should not make the claim obscure or difficult to construe. Non-unitary inventions may not be presented as alternatives in a single claim. (F-IV,3.7)

R. 45 Claims incurring fees

Implementation of **Art.78(2)**

1 **General**
The purpose of requiring payment of claims fees (**R.45(1)**) is not primarily fiscal but to keep the number of claims within reasonable limits (cf. **R.43(5)**), particularly for the purposes of the European search (**J9/84**; **J6/12** r.10).

R. 45(1) Any European patent application comprising more than fifteen claims shall, in respect of the sixteenth and each subsequent claim, incur payment of claims fees as laid down in the Rules relating to Fees.

Amended, in force since 01.04.2008 (OJ 2008 p.124).

1 **Amount due**
The amount of the claims fee is fixed in **Rfees2(1)15**.

Claims fees are due for 'any' European patent application, i.e. for Euro-direct applications, divisional applications, new applications (**Art.61**) and Euro-PCT applications. The claims fee must be paid for the sixteenth and each subsequent claim. Claims fees are also due for the claims of a divisional application, even if they have already been paid for the corresponding claims of the parent application (A-IV,1.4.2). When there are several sets of claims, the fees are payable only for the set with the highest number of claims (A-III,9).

If an application contains what can clearly be seen to be claims, especially in a section identified as such, then these claims contain the matter for which the applicant wants protection. All other matter, even in the form of a list of numbered clauses, is not regarded as claims for the purpose of determining the number of claims fees to be paid under **R.45** (J15/88). However, if the applicant indicates an intention to regard the clauses as claims, they will be regarded as claims for the purpose of **R.45** (J5/87).

2 **Reduction of claims fees**

The increases in claims fees in 2008 and 2009 has resulted in a reduction of the number of claims in applications filed with the EPO. However, dependent claims form necessary fallback positions both during and after the grant procedure (see **R.43(4):3**).

Due to the high cost of claims fees, applicants tend to obtain simultaneously a reduction in claims fees and the maintenance of fallback positions by including alternatives in a single claim, by adding features for dependent claims as preferred options in a main claim (using expressions such as 'preferably', 'for example'; see **Art.84:1.4**), and by adding claim-like passages to the description of the figures from which claims may be derived if required. These passages must be deleted prior to grant (F-IV,4.4) or rewritten to remove their claim-like character. It is also possible to file multiple applications each with a smaller number of claims; however, the total cost of these applications over their term should be balanced with the reduction in claims fees. Alternatively, the EPO may be bypassed by filing national applications.

Note that when the number of claims in a Euro-PCT application is reduced in response to the **R.161** invitation, i.e. after entry into the European regional phase, excess claims fees paid on national entry are refunded (**R.162(3)**).

R. 45(2) The claims fees shall be paid within one month of filing the first set of claims. If the claims fees have not been paid in due time, they may still be paid within one month of a communication concerning the failure to observe the time limit.

1 **Period**

The fees must be paid within one month of filing the first set of claims (**R.45(2)**). When the claims are filed together with the application documents, the claims fees have to be paid within the same period as the filing and search fee under **Art.78(2)**. This applies also to divisional applications and new applications. See **R.162** for Euro-PCT applications.

2 **Insufficient payment**

In the event that the amount of the claims fees paid is insufficient to cover all claims for which fees are due and no indication has been given as to which claims have been paid for, then the applicant will be invited to clarify the matter (**Rfees6(2)**). Since only the claims numbered 1 to 15 as filed are exempt from claims fee, it is not possible to transfer the fee exemption to a claim numbered 16 or higher (J9/84 r.2). If an application (particularly from the USA) contains a series of 'clauses' resembling claims, but not referred to as such, then no claims fees need be paid for them, and the subject-matter in them is not regarded as abandoned if no claims fees are paid for the clauses (T490/90, J15/88). If the claims fees for an application comprising several sets of claims are not paid, the claims numbered 16 and higher of each set are deemed to be abandoned under **R.45(3)**.

3 **Sanction on non-payment and remedy**
If the claims fees have not been paid within one month of filing the first set of claims, the EPO will send the applicant a communication pointing out the failure and invite payment of the claims fees without surcharge within a grace period of one month from notification of the communication (**R.45(2)**). If the claims fees are not paid within the one-month grace period, the claims concerned are deemed abandoned (**R.45(3)**).

The applicant is notified of this loss of rights (**R.112(1)**). There are two remedies: if applicable, the applicant may prove that the claims fees were indeed paid in time (**R.112(2)**), or, within two months from notification of the loss of rights, the applicant may request further processing under **Art.121** and **R.135**, pay the further processing fee (equal to 50% of the missing claims fees) and pay the missing claims fees. (A-III,16.2)

R. 45(3) If a claims fee is not paid in due time, the claim concerned shall be deemed to be abandoned.

1 **Loss of rights**
Deemed abandonment of claims need not result in a loss of rights if their subject-matter can be found in the description and drawings. The abandoned claims can then be re-introduced in an amendment under **Art.123(1)**, as they do not extend the subject-matter of the application as filed (**J15/88** r.6; A-III,9). Even if there is no basis for an abandoned claim in the description and drawings, the subject-matter of this claim may still be pursued in a divisional application (A-III,9).

Abandoned claims will not be searched (B-III,3.4) and amendments may not relate to unsearched subject-matter (**R.137(5)**). Any claims fees for re-introduced claims will be levied under **R.71(4)** before the grant of the patent.

See **Art.93(1):1** for the effect of deemed claim abandonment on publication of the application.

R. 46 (deleted)

Deleted by decision of the Administrative Council of 13.10.2022, which entered into force on 01.02.2023 (OJ 2022 A101) and replaced by amended R.49(2) as of 01.02.2023.

R. 47 Form and content of the abstract

Implementation of **Art.78(1)(e)** and **Art.85**

1 **Examination of the abstract**
The Receiving Section checks for obvious errors in the abstract under **Art.90(3)** and **R.57(d)** (A-III,10.2). The search division checks compliance of the abstract with the requirements of **R.47** under **Art.92** and **R.66** (F-II,2.2).

R. 47(1) The abstract shall indicate the title of the invention.

R. 47(2) The abstract shall contain a concise summary of the disclosure as contained in the description, the claims and any drawings. The summary shall indicate the technical field to which the invention pertains, and shall be drafted in a manner allowing the clear understanding of the technical problem, the gist of the solution of that problem through the invention, and the principal use or uses of the invention. The abstract shall, where applicable, contain the chemical formula which, among those contained in the application, best characterises the invention. It shall not contain statements on the alleged merits or value of the invention or on speculative applications thereof.

R. 47(3) The abstract shall preferably not contain more than one hundred and fifty words.

R. 47(4) If the European patent application contains drawings, the applicant shall indicate the figure or, exceptionally, the figures of the drawings which should be published with the abstract. The European Patent Office may decide to publish one or more other figures if it considers that they better characterise the invention. Each essential feature mentioned in the abstract and illustrated by a drawing shall be followed by a reference sign placed in parentheses.

1 **Figure to accompany the abstract**
The figure must be chosen from the drawings accompanying the application; a special figure for the abstract, not contained in the drawings, is not allowed. If the application contains figures, and no figure for the abstract is indicated, the search division will decide on the figure to be used. (A-III,10.3, F-II,2.4)

R. 47(5) The abstract shall be drafted in such a manner as to constitute an efficient instrument for the purpose of searching in the particular technical field. In particular, it shall make it possible to assess whether consultation of the European patent application itself is necessary.

R. 48 Prohibited matter

Implementation of **Art.78(1)**

R. 48(1) The European patent application shall not contain:
(a) statements or other matter contrary to "ordre public" or morality;
(b) statements disparaging the products or processes of any third party or the merits or validity of the applications or patents of any such party. Mere comparisons with the prior art shall not be considered disparaging per se;
(c) any statement or other matter obviously irrelevant or unnecessary under the circumstances.

1 **Prohibited matter**
A mere comparison with prior art, as required by **R.42(1)(b), (c)**, is not regarded as disparaging. Advertising with trademarks or industrial designs or models falls under paragraph (c). Excision of non-unitary subject-matter from an application may also be requested under **R.48(1)(c)**. See A-III,8 and F-II,7 for more examples of prohibited matter.

R. 48(2) If the application contains matter prohibited under paragraph 1(a), the European Patent Office may omit such matter from the application as published, indicating the place and number of words or drawings omitted.

R. 48(3) If the application contains statements referred to in paragraph 1(b), the European Patent Office may omit them from the application as published, indicating the place and number of words omitted. Upon request, the European Patent Office shall furnish a copy of the passages omitted.

R. 49 Presentation of the application documents

Amended by decision of the Administrative Council of 13.10.2022, which entered into force on 01.02.2023 (OJ 2022 A101). The decision amended the title and paragraph (2) and deleted paragraphs (3)-(12). See also Not. EPO OJ 2022 A114.
Implementation of **Art.78(1)**

R. 49(1) Any translation filed under Article 14, paragraph 2, or Rule 40, paragraph 3, shall be deemed to be a document making up the European patent application.

Art.14(2) Application filed in non-EPO language
R.40(3) Previously filed application in a non-EPO language

1 **Presentation requirements for translations**
R.49(1) clarifies that the presentation requirements of **R.49(2)** also apply to translations of the application documents.

R. 49(2) The President of the European Patent Office shall determine the presentation requirements of documents making up the application.

Amended by decision of the Administrative Council of 13.10.2022, which entered into force on 01.02.2023 (OJ 2022 A101, see also Not. EPO OJ 2022 A114).

1 **Application documents**

1.1 **DECISION ON PRESENTATION REQUIREMENTS**
The presentation requirements for the application documents (request, description, claims, drawings, and abstract) are laid down in Dec. Pres. OJ 2022 A113 Art.2. This decision replaces former R.49(3)-(12), presently (April 2025) without substantive amendments. The decision provides as follows:

Article 2 Presentation of the application documents

(1) The documents making up the application shall be presented so as to allow electronic and direct reproduction, in particular by scanning, photography, electrostatic processes, photo offset and microfilming, in an unlimited number of copies. All sheets shall be free from cracks, creases and folds. Only one side of the sheet shall be used.

(2) The documents making up the application shall be on A4 paper (29.7 cm x 21 cm) which shall be pliable, strong, white, smooth, matt and durable. Subject to paragraph 8 and Article 1, paragraph 2(h), each sheet shall be used with its short sides at the top and bottom (upright position).

(3) Each of the documents making up the application (request, description, claims, drawings and abstract) shall commence on a new sheet. The sheets shall be connected in such a way that they can easily be turned over, separated and joined together again.

(4) Subject to Article 1, paragraph 1, the minimum margins shall be as follows: top 2 cm; left side 2.5 cm; right side 2 cm; bottom 2 cm;

The recommended maximum for the margins quoted above is as follows: top 4 cm; left side 4 cm; right side 3 cm; bottom 3 cm

(5) All the sheets contained in the application shall be numbered in consecutive Arabic numerals. These shall be centred at the top of the sheet, but not placed in the top margin.

(6) The lines of each sheet of the description and of the claims shall preferably be numbered in sets of five, the numbers appearing on the left side, to the right of the margin.

(7) The request for grant of a European patent, the description, the claims and the abstract shall be typed or printed. Only graphic symbols and characters and chemical or mathematical formulae may, if necessary, be drawn or written by hand. The typing shall be 1½ spaced. All text matter shall be in characters, the capital letters of which are not less than 0.21 cm high, and shall be in a dark, indelible colour.

(8) The request for grant of a European patent, the description, the claims and the abstract shall not contain drawings. The description, claims and abstract may contain chemical or mathematical formulae. The description and abstract may contain tables. The claims may contain tables only if their subject-matter makes the use of tables desirable. Tables and chemical or mathematical formulae may be placed sideways on the sheet if they cannot be presented satisfactorily in an upright position. Tables or chemical or mathematical formulae presented sideways shall be placed so that the tops of the tables or formulae are at the left-hand side of the sheet.

(9) Values shall be expressed in units conforming to international standards, wherever appropriate in terms of the metric system using SI units. Any data not meeting this requirement shall also be expressed in units conforming to international standards. Only the technical terms, formulae, signs and symbols generally accepted in the field in question shall be used.

(10) The terminology and the signs shall be consistent throughout the European patent application.

(11) Each sheet shall be reasonably free from erasures and shall be free from alterations. Non-compliance with this rule may be authorised if the authenticity of the content is not impugned and the requirements for good reproduction are not thereby jeopardised.

1.2 PRESENTATION REQUIREMENTS

The provision also applies to the translation of the application under **Art.14(2)** (**R.49(1)**).

Margins need not be completely blank; in practice text in margins, e.g. reference numbers is not objected to.

There shall, preferably, be three series of page numbers: one for the request, one for the description with the claims and the abstract, and one for the drawings. The last two series may be combined into one. (A-IX,4.2)

The numbering of lines is optional (**T3181/19**).

The minimum height of capital letters must be 0.21 cm according to Dec. Pres. OJ 2022 A113 Art.2(7). This corresponds to 8.5 point Times New Roman and 9.0 point Arial, two common fonts available in Windows computer operating systems. Note that conversion from text processor format to pdf may involve scaling of the text.

The text content of a page approximately doubles when going from 12.0 point Times New Roman, often used for filing patent applications, to 8.5 point font size. This should be born in mind when filing an application exceeding 35 pages in view of the page fee. (see **Rfees2(1):4.2.1**)

Formulae and tables may be grouped on a separate sheet (A-IX,1.1), each provided with a reference sign (A-IX,11.1). However, they are preferably integrated into the text (A-IX,11.1).

Computer program listings cannot be used as the sole disclosure. A description, preferably accompanied by flow diagrams, is required. (F-II,4.12)

An overview of the SI units can be found in F-II Annex 2. When the SI equivalent needs to be added to the description pursuant to Dec. Pres. OJ 2022 A113 Art.2(9), a decision needs to be made on the number of decimal places to be included. No guidance on this is provided in F-II,4.13. As long as the original value in the non-SI unit is retained as the primary value then it is unlikely that the addition of the SI unit would be seen to contravene **Art.123(2)**, whatever the number of decimal places used.

The fourth sentence of point 8 (tables in the claims) is examined by the examining division only, not by the Receiving Section (Dec. Pres. OJ 2022 A113 Art.4(2)). Points 9 and 10 (SI units and consistency) are similarly examined by the examining division only.

2 Drawings

2.1 DECISION ON PRESENTATION REQUIREMENTS FOR DRAWINGS

The presentation requirements for drawings (i.e. the requirements as to the form of the drawings) are laid down in Dec. Pres. OJ 2022 A113 Art.1. This decision replaces former **R.46**, presently (April 2025) without substantive amendments:

(1) On sheets containing drawings, the usable surface area shall not exceed 26.2 cm x 17 cm. The usable or used surface shall not be surrounded by frames. The minimum margins shall be as follows: top 2.5 cm; left side 2.5 cm; right side 1.5 cm; bottom 1 cm.

(2) Drawings shall be executed as follows:

(a) Drawings shall be executed without colourings in durable, black, sufficiently dense and dark, uniformly thick and well-defined lines and strokes.

(b) Cross-sections shall be indicated by hatching which should not impede the clear reading of the reference signs and leading lines.

(c) The scale of the drawings and their graphical execution shall be such that electronic or photographic reproduction with a linear reduction in size to two-thirds will allow all details to be distinguished without difficulty. If, exceptionally, the scale is given on a drawing, it shall be represented graphically.

(d) All numbers, letters, and reference signs appearing on the drawings shall be simple and clear. Brackets, circles or inverted commas shall not be used in association with numbers and letters.

(e) Generally, all lines in the drawings shall be drawn with the aid of drafting instruments.

(f) Elements of the same figure shall be proportional to one another, unless a difference in proportion is indispensable for the clarity of the figure.

(g) The height of the numbers and letters shall not be less than 0.32 cm. For the lettering of drawings, the Latin and, where customary, the Greek alphabets shall be used.

(h) The same sheet of drawings may contain several figures. Where figures drawn on two or more sheets are intended to form a single figure, the figures on the several sheets shall be so arranged that the whole figure can be assembled without concealing any part of the partial figures. The different figures shall be arranged without wasting space, preferably in an upright position, clearly separated from one another. Where the figures are not arranged in an upright position, they shall be presented sideways with the top of the figures at the left side of the sheet. The different figures shall be numbered consecutively in Arabic numerals, independently of the numbering of the sheets.

(i) Reference signs not mentioned in the description and claims shall not appear in the drawings, and vice versa. Reference signs to features shall be consistent throughout the application.

(j) The drawings shall not contain text matter. Where indispensable to understand the drawings, a few short keywords, such as "water", "steam", "open", "closed" or "section on AB", may be included. Any such keywords shall be placed in such a way that, if required, they can be replaced by their translations without interfering with any lines of the drawings.

(3) Flow sheets and diagrams shall be deemed to be drawings.

2.2 PHOTOGRAPHS

The EPC makes no express provision for photographs in applications; they are nevertheless allowed where it is impossible to present in a drawing what is to be shown and provided that they are in black and white, directly reproducible and fulfil the applicable requirements for drawings (e.g. paper size, margins, etc.). Colour photographs and drawings are acceptable but will be available in the file in black and white only. Information coded in colour only may be lost. (A-IX,1.2; A-IX,7.1; F-II,5.3)

T1544/08 hn.3 allowed a proprietor to base an amendment on colour information in a drawing of the application as filed, even though the published application did not show the information, because **Art.123(2)** refers to the application as filed and not as published. The opponent could not know the colour information, as all documents in the public files of the EPO are black and white. The use of colour information in **T1544/08** is detrimental to public certainty if applications are not published in colour: a published patent application may contain information only accessible to the applicant and the EPO. The only solution appears to be that the EPO makes the documents in the public online file visible in full colour and deletes the words 'without colourings' in Dec. Pres. OJ 2022 A113 Art.1(2)(a).

2.3 PRESENTATION REQUIREMENTS FOR DRAWINGS

No indications like 'actual size' are permitted, as this does not allow a reduction of the drawing (A-IX,7.4).

An apostrophe (') after a number is allowed under Dec. Pres. OJ 2022 A113 Art.1(2)(d) (A-IX,7.5).

If the description or claims are amended by completely deleting references to a feature in the drawings, the corresponding reference sign must be removed from the drawings. If the removal is tedious, the examiner should not be too strict in requiring this removal. The reverse situation, where reference signs used in the description do not appear in the drawings, can be addressed by deleting the reference signs. Including a key to the reference signs at the end of the description is recommended for complex subject-matter incorporating many drawings (A-IX,7.5.4).

If an invention has many variants with features with basically the same function, such a feature may be numbered with a reference sign common to the features, preceded by the number of the figure or the variant, e.g. 115, 215, 315, etc. (A-X,7.5.5).

Symbols and keywords in flow sheets and functional diagrams are often regarded as indispensable for understanding the drawing and are therefore allowed under Dec. Pres. OJ 2022 A113 Art. 1(2)(j) (A-IX,8; F-II,5.1).

The requirements of Dec. Pres. OJ 2022 A113 Art.1(2)(i) and (j) are not examined by the Receiving Section but by the examining division only (Dec. Pres. OJ 2022 A113 Art.4(3)).

2.4 INFORMAL DRAWINGS

If drawings which depart substantially from the presentation requirements are filed in order to establish a particular date of filing, the Receiving Section will request the filing of correct drawings (see note 3 below). Any correct drawings are seen as an amendment and must comply with **Art.123(2)**. Applicants should therefore take care that the originally filed drawings directly and unambiguously show all the features necessary to illustrate the invention. (A-IX,10)

If formal drawings are submitted by way of amendment, any technical information provided by these formal drawings that cannot be derived directly and unambiguously from the original drawings (or description and claims as filed) will be a ground for invalidity of the patent under **Art.100(c)**. Returning to the original drawings after grant may sometimes violate **Art.123(3)** (see e.g. **T1360/13**).

The inclusion of the amended or replacement drawings in the published application merely signifies that the drawings have been accepted for publication, not that they comply with **Art.123(2)**. The final examination of the drawings is carried out by the substantive examiner (OJ 1987 p.123) and may be contested in opposition and revocation proceedings.

It may be possible to remedy drawings of low visual quality under **R.56a** if the drawings are of proper quality in the priority application (A-II,5.4.2).

3 Examination of presentation requirements

The examination of the presentation requirements for the application documents are laid down in Dec. Pres. OJ 2022 A113 Art.4, which implements **R.57(i)**:

Article 4 Examination as to formal requirements

*(1) The EPO shall examine, in accordance with **Art.90(3)** and **R.57(i)**, whether the requirements of Articles 1 and 2 of this decision have been complied with.*

(2) The Receiving Section shall examine whether the following requirements of this decision have been complied with: Article 1, paragraph 1 and paragraph 2(a) to (h), Article 2, paragraphs 1 to 7, Article 2, paragraph 8, sentences 1 to 3, 5 and 6 and Article 2, paragraph 11.

*(3) Any examination by the EPO of the requirements listed in paragraph 2 of this Article shall be limited to the extent necessary for the purpose of a satisfactory reproduction or a reasonably uniform publication of the application under **R.68(1)**.*

Art.4(3) of Dec. Pres. OJ 2022 A113 limits the extent of examination of the presentation requirements by the Receiving Section and examining division, in the sense that objections are only raised if necessary for reasonably uniform publication of the application (or for the reproduction). This limitation does not apply to the examination, only by the examining division, of the compliance with paragraph 8, fourth sentence (tables in claims), paragraph 9 (SI units) and paragraph 10 (consistency) of Art.2 of Dec. Pres. OJ 2022 A113, and for the drawings, paragraphs (2)(i) and (j) of Art.1 (reference signs and text matter) of Dec. Pres. OJ 2022 A113.

If the application documents do not comply with the presentation requirements examined under **R.57(i)**, the Receiving Section will invite the applicant under **R.58** to remedy the deficiencies within two months of invitation (A-III,16.1). Any correction may not extend the subject-matter of the application (H-IV,2.1). If the period is not observed, the application is refused under **Art.90(5)**. Further processing is excluded for the two-month period under **R.135(2)**; however, re-establishment is available according to **Art.122** and **R.136**. (A-III,3.2) An alternative remedy would be to file an appeal and correct the deficiency when filing the grounds (J11/20). In this case, interlocutory revision will be applied by the EPO (E-XII,7.4.4).

See A-III,3.2.2 for the examination of late-filed application documents, in particular inserted missing parts under **R.56** and correct parts under **R.56a.** Any deficiencies are only communicated when the complete application documents are on file.

Where the application is filed by reference to a previously filed application according to **R.40(1)(c)** and no translation is required, an invitation under **R.58** is issued if the certified copy of the previous application does not satisfy the presentation requirements. If the previous application has to be translated under **R.40(3)**, the translation must comply with the presentation requirements. (A-III,3.2.1)

Late-filed application documents, such as late-filed claims (**R.57(c)**), any inserted missing parts (**R.56**) and correct parts (**R.56a**), and amendments of the claims, description and drawings (**R.50(1)**) and translations of application documents (**R.49(1)**), must also comply with the presentation requirements (A-III,3.2; A-VIII,2.2).

R. 50 Documents filed subsequently

1 General

Documents filed after the filing of the patent application, also called 'further documents', may be filed in a form and by a method permitted by **R.2(1)**, relying on decisions of the President for details.

An applicant can file further documents in a single copy (OJ 2007 se5 EN p.86).

2 Filing office

All further documents should normally be filed with the EPO as mentioned in **R.35(1)** and not with a national patent office. There is no legal basis for this rule, with exception for the case is where the application has been filed with a national authority under **Art.75(1)(b)**. Further documents may then be filed with that authority until the applicant receives the EPO communication of **R.35(4)**, after which all further documents must be filed with the EPO (A-II,3.2). Documents nevertheless sent to a national authority may be forwarded by the authority as a courtesy service to the EPO; the EPO will give them a date equal to the date it has received the documents.

To expedite the procedure, paper documents relating to appeal proceedings should preferably be sent directly to Munich (OJ 2005 p.44 §2).

3 Form of documents

The only physical requirements for documents filed directly or by post are that they must be typewritten or printed and have 2.5 cm left margin (see **R.50(2)**). However, replacement pages of the patent application or patent must comply with the requirements for application documents (**R.50(1)**, **R.86**). The documents must be signed in accordance with **R.50(3)** and the language of the documents must comply with the provisions of **R.3.**

The EPC has no sanction for non-compliance with the layout requirements of **R.50(2)**. See **R.50(3)** for the sanction on failure to sign documents. A document which is not filed in the prescribed language or not translated in due time will be deemed not to have been filed (**Art.14(4)**).

R. 50(1) Rules 42, 43 and 47 to 49 shall apply to documents replacing documents making up the European patent application. Rule 49, paragraph 2, shall also apply to the translation of the claims referred to in Rule 71.

Amended by decision of the Administrative Council of 13.10.2022, which entered into force on 01.02.2023 (OJ 2022 A101), as a consequence of the deletion of **R.46** and amendment of **R.49** as of 01.02.2023.
R.42 Contents of the description
R.43 Form and content of claims
R.47 Form and content of the abstract
R.48 Prohibited matter
R.49 Presentation of the application documents
R.71 Examination procedure

1 **Replacements for application documents**
According to **R.50(1)**, documents filed after filing of the patent application and replacing documents of the patent application or patent or part of it are bound by the same formal requirements for content and form as the patent application itself. Hence, further documents replacing documents making up the application and relating to the description, claims and abstract must meet the same requirements as in the application documents (**R.42, 43, 47**). The replacement documents may not contain prohibited matter (**R.48**) and must have the same form as the application documents (**R.47, 49**).

Replacement document filed during opposition and appeal must comply with the same requirements (**R.86** and **R.100(1)**).

2 **Handwritten amendments**
Since the decision of the President taken under **R.49(2)** requires the description, claims and abstract to be typed or printed, any replacement document must also be typed or printed according to **R.50(1)**. Graphic symbols and characters and chemical and mathematical formulae may in exceptional cases be drawn or written by hand; however, it is recommended to type or print them (A-IX,11.1). The EPO enforces this rule strictly. Hence, any amendment of the description or claims must be typed or printed; handwritten amendments are deficiencies that must be corrected (A-III,3.2). (OJ 2013 p.603)

Amendments of an application should be filed with the EPO both as clean, typed replacement pages and as replacement pages with the amendments clearly marked. The amendments are preferably marked with a text editor but handwritten markings may be used (H-III,2.2).

Handwritten amendments will normally be accepted during oral proceedings before the examining division as a basis for discussion. A final decision granting a patent may be taken only on the basis of a typed or printed document. The EPO provides computers, pdf printers, copiers and internet access for preparing typed documents during oral proceedings. If a typed or printed document is not available during oral proceedings, the EPO will continue in writing and request to file a compliant document within two months. Where handwritten amendments are filed in examination proceedings, the EPO will request the submission of a typed or printed version if there is agreed patentable subject-matter. (E-III,8.7.2)

See **R.82(2)** for amendments filed in opposition.

3 **Form of translations**
The translation of the claims in the two official EPO languages other than the language of the proceedings to be filed in response to the **R.71(3)** communication must be presented as set out in **R.49**.

The translation under **Art.14(2)** or **R.40(3)** of a patent application is considered to be included in the 'documents making up the European patent application' (**R.49(1)**). Hence, the translation must also meet the requirements of **R.42, 43** and **47** to **49**.

R. 50(2) The President of the European Patent Office shall determine the presentation requirements of all documents other than those making up the application.

Amended by decision of the Administrative Council of 13.10.2022, which entered into force on 01.02.2023 (OJ 2022 A101).

1 **Form requirement subsequent documents**
Dec. Pres. OJ 2022 A113 Art.3 provides the following:
All documents other than those making up the application shall generally be typewritten or printed. There shall be a margin of about 2.5 cm on the left-hand side of each page.

R. 50(3) Documents filed after filing the application shall be signed, with the exception of annexed documents. If a document has not been signed, the European Patent Office shall invite the party concerned to do so within a time limit to be specified. If signed in due time, the document shall retain its original date of receipt; otherwise it shall be deemed not to have been filed.

1 **Signature on further documents**
Further documents filed with the EPO must be signed by a person authorised to act before the EPO, such as an applicant or proprietor who is not obliged to be represented under **Art.133(2)** or their representative (A-VIII,3.1). The name and position of that person must be clear from the signature. The EPO does not check entitlement of a person to sign on behalf of a legal person, except where it has reason to doubt the authority of the person (A-VIII,3.3). The reason for requiring a signature is to show clearly that the content of a document is authorised by the person who has filed it.

In general, an applicant obliged to be represented may only sign the application documents when filing a patent application (**Art.133(2)**) and may not sign further documents.

If there are several applicants, further documents need only be signed by the applicant or a representative who has been appointed as common representative in the Request for Grant form (**R.41(3)**), in a notice of opposition or in a separate notice of appointment, or who has been deemed to be a common representative by virtue of **R.151(1)**. (A-VIII,3.4)

All further documents except annexes must be signed (**R.50(3)**). As lex specialis, the following annexes must be signed: assignment of an application (**Art.72**), designation of the inventor (**R.19(1)**) and authorisation (**R.152(1)**).

Documents such as priority documents or translations should bear a note addressed to the EPO or be accompanied by a separate letter; the note or letter must be signed by a person authorised to act before the EPO. This also applies to a designation of the inventor signed by an applicant obliged to be represented (A-VIII,3.1).

Since the second sentence of **R.50(3)** refers to 'the party', the provision relates to documents submitted by parties; hence, observations filed by a third party under **Art.115** need not be signed (**T1336/09**, r.2.2; however, see **T146/07**, r.3).

The signature must comply with the requirements of R.2(2).

2 **Missing signature**
R.50(3) provides a remedy only for a missing signature. The signature of an unauthorised person, such as the assistant of an authorised representative or an applicant requiring representation, is regarded as a missing signature; this applies both to a handwritten signature (**T665/89** r.1.4; A-VIII,3.1) and to an electronic signature (**T1427/09** r.8). Similarly, any signature not complying with **R.2(2)** should probably be regarded as a missing signature, which can be corrected under **R.50(3)**.

The EPO informs a party of a missing signature on a further document and invites the party to supply a duly signed document within a period set by the EPO (**R.50(3)**). The period is fixed at two months as a rule, i.e. the same period as for correcting minor deficiencies (D-IV,1.2.1(ii) and E-VIII,1.2(i)). If signed in due time, the document retains its original date of receipt; otherwise it will be deemed not to have been filed (**R.50(3)**).

An applicant may remedy failure to meet the two-month period with further processing according to **Art.121** and **R.135**.

A missing signature on a patent application is not dealt with under **R.50(3)** but under **Art.90(3)**, **R.57(b)**, **R.41(2)(h)** and **Art.90(5)** (see **R.57(b):3**).

Chapter III *Renewal fees*

R. 51 Payment of renewal fees

Implementation of **Art.86**

R. 51(1) A renewal fee for the European patent application in respect of the coming year shall be due on the last day of the month containing the anniversary of the date of filing of the European patent application. The renewal fee in respect of the third year may not be validly paid more than six months before it falls due. All other renewal fees may not be validly paid more than three months before they fall due.

Amended, in force since 01.04.2018 (OJ 2018 A2).

1 **Payment of renewal fee**
A renewal fee of a European patent application must be paid on a due date (**R.51(1)**). Normally, a fee becomes due on the due date and may be paid within a fixed period following the due date. In contrast, the due date of a renewal fee is both the day on which a renewal fee becomes due and the last day on which it can be paid without an additional fee; it can be regarded as a period of zero days or no period at all. The EPC has provided flexibility for applicants by allowing valid payment of a renewal fee in a period before the due date.

The law distinguishes between a pre-payment period for the renewal fee in respect of the third year, i.e. the first renewal fee to be paid for a patent application, and for renewal fees in respect of all subsequent years. The EPO prefers a short pre-payment period of three months to reduce the opportunity for applicants to pay the smaller amount in the case of a fee increase (see OJ 1987 p.4). The law provides, exceptionally, a longer pre-payment period for the first renewal fee to simplify payment for a Euro-PCT application when entering into the European phase, by allowing payment of all fees necessary, including the first renewal fee, in one step on entry. A three-month pre-payment period would make it necessary to pay the first renewal fee in a second step if this period has not yet started when entering the European phase. That occurs if the Euro-PCT application claims priority and the last day of the calendar month containing the filing date lies more than nine months after the priority date. The beneficial longer pre-payment period is not only available for Euro-PCT applications but also for Euro-direct applications because of the principle of equal treatment (**Art.153(2)**).

Hence, the renewal fee in respect of the third year may be paid validly up to six months before the due date (**R.51(1)**, second sentence) and the renewal fee in respect of the fourth and following years may be paid validly up to three months before the due date (**R.51(1)**, third sentence). The Guidelines calculate the first day of the negative pre-payment period 'de ultimo ad ultimo' in the sense of **J4/91**, i.e. from the last day of the month to the last day of the month. For example, for the three-month pre-payment period, the first date for valid payment is 31 August if the due date is 30 November; the first date for valid payment is 28 February 2011 where the due date is 31 May 2011. (A-X,5.2.4)

A renewal fee paid up to one month before the start of the pre-payment period will, for practical reasons, be retained by the EPO, but the payment will not take effect until the first day of the pre-payment period (A-X,5.2.4; OJ 2009 p.118 §3.5).

The amount of the renewal fee is fixed in **Rfees2(1)4**. A reduction is available for certain applicants, see **R.7a(3)**.

2 **Due date falling on the last day of the month**
A renewal fee for a European patent application in respect of the coming year is due on the last day of the month containing the anniversary of the date of filing at the beginning of that year (**R.51(1)**). Hence, the first renewal fee payable for an application (for the third year, **Rfees2(1)**) is due on the last day of the month in which the second anniversary of the date of filing falls.

When the due date falls on a date the EPO cannot receive mail in the sense of **R.134(1)**, (2) or (4), the last day for valid payment is deferred to the first day the office is open and can receive mail again. However, the actual due date is not changed because the due date is not a 'period' which can be extended. (**J4/91** r.3.2; OJ 2020 A38 §5)

3 **Due date not falling on the last day of the month**
In some cases a renewal fee does not fall due on the last day of a month as defined in **R.51(1)**.

The first case is where the due date moves forward to a date on which a specific event takes place. A first example of such an event is the filing of a divisional application, where the renewal fees for the divisional application accrued before the date on which it is filed fall due on the filing date of the divisional (**R.51(3)**). A second example is the date of notification of a decision granting a request for re-establishment, where a renewal fee that would have fallen due between the loss of rights and said notification date falls due on the notification date (**R.51(4)**). A third example is the date of notification of the decision granting a petition for review and re-opening proceedings, where a renewal fee that would have fallen due between the decision of the board of appeal subject to the petition and said notification date also falls due on the notification date (**R.51(5)(a)**). A fourth example is the resumption of proceedings after an interruption under **R.142**, e.g. due to death of the applicant, where a renewal fee that would have fallen due during the period of interruption falls due on the date of resumption (**R.142(4)**, **J902/87**).

The due date does not shift to the first working day if it falls on a non-working day, because the due date is not the expiry of a period (**J4/91** r.3.2).

The second case is where the due date is deferred to the expiry of a period. This happens when the first renewal fee for a Euro-PCT application would have fallen due under **R.51(1)** earlier than the expiry of the 31-month period of **R.159(1)**, in which case the due date is deferred to the expiry of the 31-month period (**R.159(1)(g)**).

The 31-month period is extended under **R.134(1)** if it falls on a day on which one of the EPO filing offices is not open for business. In any event, the renewal fee falls due on the last day of the 31-month period.

Note that there are no special provisions for the payment of renewal fees for a new application filed under **Art.61(1)(b)**, because the new application is in effect a continuation of the usurped original application and takes over the obligation to pay renewal fees (see **R.51(6)**). In this case, no renewal fees that have already fallen due for the original application are payable on filing the replacement application.

R. 51(2) If a renewal fee is not paid on the due date under paragraph 1, the fee may still be paid within six months of the said date, provided that an additional fee is also paid within that period. The legal consequence laid down in Article 86, paragraph 1, shall ensue upon expiry of the six-month period.

Amended, in force since 01.01.2017 (OJ 2016 A102, A103). The amendment defines the date the sanction on non-payment takes effect, without changing the practice of the office. It removes the discrepancy noted in **T1402/13** between the previous text of the law and the practice of the office.
Art.86(1) Legal consequence of not paying renewal fee

1 **Six-month additional period where renewal fee is due on the last day of the month**

R.51(2), first sentence, provides for a six-month remedial period for payment of a renewal fee with additional fee if the renewal fee has not been paid on or before the due date. The additional fee is specified by **Rfees2(1)(5)** to be 50% of the belated renewal fee.

The six-month period starts on the due date, i.e. the last day of the month referred to in **R.51(1)**, even if the EPO cannot receive mail on that date because of holidays or other disruptions as set out in **R.134(1)**, (2), and (4). These circumstances do not postpone the due date for payment of renewal fees. Hence, the six-month period is not an aggregate period if the renewal fee falls due on the last day of the month. (**J4/91** hn. II; A-X,5.2.4)

The six-month period expires on the last day of the sixth month after the due date and not on the day of that month corresponding in number to the due date (i.e. it is not calculated in accordance with **R.131(4)**). **R.51(1)** and **R.51(2)** are regarded as a lex specialis of **R.131(4)**. Thus, the calculation must be made from the last day of the month to the last day of the month (de ultimo ad ultimo). If the due date is 28 February, then the end of the 6-month period is 31 August, and not 28 August. (**J4/91** hn. I, de ultimo ad ultimo)

R.134 may be applied to the expiry of the six-month period, extending the period of six months to the first date on which the EPO can again receive mail (**J4/91** r.3.2, last paragraph).

Notification of non-payment of a renewal fee, sanction and remedies are set out in **Art.86(1):3-5**.

First example:

15 December	filing date
31 December	due date for renewal fee
2 January	last day for payment without additional fee (**R.134(1)**)
30 June	expiry of 6-month period for payment with additional fee; if this is a Sunday, then under **R.134(1)**
1 July	last day for payment with additional fee.

Second example:

15 February	filing date
28/29 February	due date for renewal fee
31 August	expiry of 6-month period for payment with additional fee; if this is a Saturday, then under **R.134(1)**
2 September	last day for payment with additional fee.

2 **Six-month period in other cases**
Where the due date has moved to a date on which a specific event has taken place, i.e. the first case in **R.51(1):3**, the start of the six-month period is the due date (see e.g. **R.51(4)(b)**). The due date does not shift to the first working day if it falls on a non-working day (**J4/91** r.3.2). The expiry of the six-month period is not calculated 'de ultimo ad ultimo', but as a normal period using **R.131(4)** for the calculation of the duration of a period expressed in months. The six-month period may be extended on account of **R.134**. For the first three examples of the first case there is a four-month period running in parallel to the six-month period in which the renewal fee can be paid without surcharge. See **R.51(3):3** and **R.159(1):8** for examples.

Note that due dates for renewal fees falling due after the date on which the divisional is filed fall due under **R.51(1)** in the usual way and the 'de ultimo ad ultimo' calculation is used for the six-month period.

Where the due date has moved to the expiry of a period, i.e. the second case in **R.51(1):3**, the six-month period is calculated from the expiry of the period. The period concerned may have been extended under **R.134**. Hence, the six-month period is an aggregate time limit in such cases (**R.131(2):3**). The expiry of the six-month period is not calculated 'de ultimo ad ultimo', but as a normal period using **R.131(4)**. The six-month period may be extended on account of **R.134**. See **R.159(1):8.3** for an example.

3 **Start of the six-month period**
After the amendment of **R.51(2)** on 01.01.2017, the provision explicitly defines the period for payment with additional fee as six months of the due date stated in **R.51(1)**, i.e. six months of the last day of the month containing the anniversary of the date of filing of the European patent application. The purpose of this amendment was to clarify that a renewal fee can still be paid with additional fee if the renewal fee has not been paid on the due date under **R.51(1)** (CA/99/16 §32).

Whereas the amendment of the provision is appropriate for the normal due dates defined in **R.51(1)**, it does not take into account the alternative due dates discussed in **R.51(1):3**. Under the previous provision, the additional period for such an alternative due date was six months from the shifted due date and not from the normal due date as stipulated by the amended **R.51(2)**. Since the amendment was not intended to change the practice under the previous provision (OJ 2016 A103), the Guidelines apply the previous practice, despite now lacking a proper legal basis (A-X,5.2.4). The six-month periods in this book are based on the Guidelines.

R. 51(3) Renewal fees already due in respect of an earlier application at the date on which a divisional application is filed shall also be paid for the divisional application and shall be due on its filing. These fees and any renewal fee due within four months of filing the divisional application may be paid within that period without an additional fee. Paragraph 2 shall apply.

1 **Renewal fees for divisional application**
A divisional application is deemed filed on the filing date of the parent application (**Art.76(1)**). Renewal fees for the divisional application are therefore due in respect of the third year and subsequent years calculated from the filing date of the parent application (A-IV,1.4.3). The renewal fees that fell due before the filing of the divisional application are due on the filing of the divisional application (**R.51(3)**, first sentence). They may be paid without an additional fee within four months from the filing of the divisional application (**R.51(3)**, second sentence). If these renewal fees are not paid within

the four-month period, they may be validly paid within a six-month period from the filing of the divisional application, provided the additional fee is paid (**R.51(3)**, last sentence).

Since the due date for these renewal fees is the date on which the divisional application is filed, it does not usually fall on the last day of the month, as it does under **R.51(1)**. Because the due date is not the expiry of a period which can be extended under **R.134** (**J4/91** r.3.2), the due date does not shift to the first working day if it falls on a non-working day. The four- and six-month periods of **R.51(3)** run from the due date, irrespective of whether or not the due date is a non-working day. If the last day of either period is a non-working day, the extension under **R.134** may be applied. (**J4/91** r.3.2, last paragraph)

R.135(2) excludes the periods under **R.51(3)** from further processing. Re-establishment for the six-month period of **R.51(3)** is possible and must be requested within two months from removal of the cause of non-compliance (**R.136(1)**). The request must be filed at the latest within one year from the expiry of the six-month period. Although re-establishment is not ruled out in respect of the four-month period of **R.51(3)**, it is questionable whether it is available since no rights are lost as the direct consequence of the non-observance of this time limit. The application is only deemed withdrawn upon expiry of the six-month period (**R.51(2)**).

2 **Example of renewal fee payment for divisional application**

Example of the due dates for renewal fees for a parent and divisional application:

Parent application:	
03.02.2013	filing date of parent application
28.02.2015	due date renewal fee in respect of the 3rd year
02.03.2015	last day of valid payment (28.02.2015 Saturday)
31.08.2015	last day of 6-month period with additional fee for the 3rd year
29.02.2016	due date renewal fee in respect of the 4th year
31.08.2016	last day of 6-month period with additional fee for the 4th year.

Divisional application:	
13.02.2016	filing date of divisional application = due date for renewal fee in respect of 3rd year
29.02.2016	due date renewal fee in respect of the 4th year
13.06.2016	last day of 4-month period without additional fee for the 3rd and 4th year
16.08.2016	last day of 6-month period with additional fee for the 3rd year (13.08.2016 Saturday, 15.08.2016 holiday)
31.08.2016	last day of 6-month period with additional fee for the 4th year
16.08.2017	expiry of the one-year period for re-establishment in the 6-month period for the renewal fee in respect of the 3rd year
31.08.2017	expiry of the one-year period for re-establishment in the 6-month period for the renewal fee in respect of the 4th year.

R. 51(4) If a European patent application has been refused or deemed to be withdrawn as a result of non-observance of a time limit, and if the applicant's rights are re-established under Article 122, a renewal fee

(a) which would have fallen due under paragraph 1 in the period starting on the date on which the loss of rights occurred, up to and including the date of the notification of the decision re-establishing the rights shall be due on that latter date. This fee and any renewal fee due within four months from that latter date may still be paid within four months of that latter date without an additional fee. Paragraph 2 shall apply.

(b) which, on the date on which the loss of rights has occurred, was already due but the period provided for in paragraph 2 has not yet expired, may still be paid within six months from the date of the notification of the decision re-establishing the rights, provided that the additional fee pursuant to paragraph 2 is also paid within that period.

Art.122 Re-establishment of rights

1 **Renewal fees and re-establishment of rights**

R.51(4) concerns the case where an application has been refused or deemed withdrawn as a result of the failure to meet a time limit and renewal fees have fallen due in the period starting on the date on which the loss of rights has occurred and up to and including the date of notification of the decision granting the re-establishment of rights of the applicant under **Art.122**. Because of the retrospective effect of the re-establishment decision, these renewal fees will become due only on the date of notification (**R.51(4)(a)**, first sentence) and can still be paid without additional fee within a period of four months after that date (**R.51(4)(a)**, second sentence). If not paid within this period, **R.51(2)** applies, i.e. the fees can still be paid with an additional fee within a period of six months after the notification date (**R.51(4)(a)**, last sentence). (CA/PL17/06)

Where the loss of rights occurs during a pending six-month period, the renewal fee may still be paid within six months from the date of the notification of the decision. In other words, the six-month period will begin again as from the day of notification. The renewal fee can be validly paid in this deferred six-month period, provided the additional fee is also paid. (**R.51(4)(b)**)

This provision is applicable only if the whole application has been refused or deemed to be withdrawn because the time limit was not observed, as expressly stated in its introductory passage. It would not be appropriate in the case of so-called partial losses of rights, since a European patent application, for which renewal fees have to be paid at regular intervals, continues to be pending even if, for example, a priority right or the designation of a state is lost. (CA/PL29/06 Add.1)

R. 51(5) If the Enlarged Board of Appeal re-opens proceedings before the Board of Appeal under Article 112a, paragraph 5, second sentence, a renewal fee

(a) which would have fallen due under paragraph 1 in the period starting on the date when the decision of the Board of Appeal subject to the petition for review was taken, up to and including the date of the notification of the decision of the Enlarged Board of Appeal re-opening proceedings before the Board of Appeal, shall be due on that latter date. This fee and any renewal fee due within four months from that latter date may still be paid within four

months of that latter date without an additional fee. Paragraph 2 shall apply.

(b) which, on the day on which the decision of the Board of Appeal was taken, was already due but the period provided for in paragraph 2 has not yet expired, may still be paid within six months from the date of the notification of the decision of the Enlarged Board of Appeal re-opening proceedings before the Board of Appeal, provided that the additional fee pursuant to paragraph 2 is also paid within that period.

Art.112a(5) Petition for review by the Enlarged Board of Appeal

1 **Renewal fee and petition for review**
A situation analogous to **R.51(4)** exists where a petition for review under **Art.112a** is successful. Therefore **R.51(5)** likewise provides that the renewal fees, which need to be paid retrospectively because of the effect of the decision of the Enlarged Board of Appeal, become due only on the date of the notification of the decision of the Enlarged Board ordering re-opening of proceedings. (CA/PL17/06)

Note that the delayed payment of renewal fees to the EPO applies only to patent applications and not to granted patents. In the latter case the proprietor is advised to continue to pay any renewal fees due to the national offices if there are no provisions for delayed payment under national law.

R. 51(6) A renewal fee shall not be payable for a new European patent application filed under Article 61, paragraph 1(b), in respect of the year in which it was filed and any preceding year.

Art.61(1)(b) New application filed by entitled applicant

1 **Renewal fees for new application**
Renewal fees for a new application under **Art.61(1)(b)** need not be paid for the year in which it was filed and any preceding year. These previous renewal fees have already been paid for by the original applicant for the earlier application, deemed withdrawn according to **R.17(1)**.

Chapter IV *Priority*

R. 52 Declaration of priority

Implementation of **Art.88(1)**

1 **General**

In order to claim the priority of an earlier application, it is necessary to file a declaration of priority (**Art.88(1)**). The content of such a declaration is governed by **R.52(1)**.

R.52(2) imposes a time limit for the filing of a declaration of priority.

A declaration of priority may be corrected as set out in **R.52(3)**. A correction in this sense means an amendment to a declaration that has already been filed rather than the late filing of a declaration which should have been filed earlier (see OJ 2007 se5 p.96).

The possibility of adding or correcting a declaration of priority after the filing of an application is a requirement under the Patent Law Treaty (Art.13(1), R.14(1) and (3) PLT) and the time limit may not be less than that provided in the PCT regulations. Whereas the PCT deals with addition and correction of a declaration of priority in a singleprovision (R.26*bis*.1(a) PCT), the EPC deals with these matters separately (**R.52(1)** and **R.52(2)**). In certain cases, the addition or correction of a declaration of priority is also possible under **R.139**. Addition or correction under **R.139** is governed by case law: a request must generally be made in time for relevant information to be included in the published application and will only be successful in exceptional circumstances thereafter (see **R.139:3.1**).

R.52(4) prohibits the addition or correction of a declaration of priority after a request for early publication has been made under **Art.93(1)(b)** and **R.52(5)** requires the inclusion of the information in the declaration of priority in the published European patent application and patent.

R. 52(1) The declaration of priority referred to in Article 88, paragraph 1, shall indicate the date of the previous filing, the State party to the Paris Convention or Member of the World Trade Organization in or for which it was made and the file number. In the case referred to in Article 87, paragraph 5, the first sentence shall apply mutatis mutandis.

Art.87(5) First filing in recognised state not subject to Paris Convention or WTO
Art.88(1) Declaration of priority

1 **Formal requirements for declaration of priority**

The priority of a previous application is claimed by submitting a declaration stating the filing date of the previous application, the Paris Convention state or WTO member in or for which it was filed, and its application number. The priority declaration should preferably be made by completing the relevant section of the Request for Grant form when filing the application (**R.41(2)(g)**). Note that the state and the date are the mandatory components of the priority declaration – the number can be added later as the correction of a formal defect (see **R.52(2):2**).

There is no fee for making a declaration of priority.

Although **R.52(1)** refers to **Art.87(5)**, no use of this provision has yet been made.

R. 52(2) The declaration of priority shall preferably be made on filing the European patent application. It may still be made within sixteen months from the earliest priority date claimed.

1 **Period for making declaration of priority**
The declaration of priority is preferably made on filing the application but may in fact be made later. A declaration of priority may be made for the first time or an additional declaration may be added at any time before the expiry of sixteen months from the earliest priority date claimed (**R.52(2)**) provided that no request for early publication has been made (**R.52(4)**). The aim is to be able to publish European patent applications as soon as possible after the expiry of 18 months from the priority date (**Art.93(1)(a)**) along with any priority claim.

As an example, consider a European patent application filed on 06.02.2024 without a declaration of priority. An earlier national application with a filing date of 06.02.2023 is a first filing for the subject matter of the European patent application. The time limit for filing a declaration of priority is 06.06.2024.

Note that the time limit is calculated solely in relation to the earliest priority date and not in relation to the filing date (unlike **R.52(3)**). The period may expire earlier than 4 months from the filing date (if the priority period is extended under **R.134(1)** and the European application is filed on the last possible day) or later (if full use of the priority period is not made).

The 'earliest priority date claimed' includes the priority date that is being added in the relevant declaration.

Non-observance of the sixteen-month period may be remedied using re-establishment according to **Art.122** and **R.136** if all due care can be shown (further processing is excluded under **R.135(1)** in view of the desire to include the priority declaration in the published application (OJ 2003 se1 p.191).

In certain cases, a declaration of priority may also be made as a correction of the request under **R.139**, even after the expiry of the **R.52(2)** time limit, if the absence of a priority declaration in the request was the result of a mistake (the later decision to add the priority claim not being simply the result of a change of mind). The declaration must generally be made in time for relevant information to be included in the published application and will only be successful in exceptional circumstances thereafter (see **R.139:3.1.1**).

A certified copy of the previous application (priority document) has to be provided within the same sixteen-month period (**R.53(1)**).

2 **Consideration of the priority declaration by the Receiving Section**
The Receiving Section verifies whether the declaration of priority meets the requirements of **R.52** as part of its examination of formal matters under **R.57(g)** and the applicant may correct it by adding a missing file number in response to a communication under **R.59**, even if the time limit of **R.52(3)** has already expired. A missing indication concerning the date of the previous filing and the state in or for which it was filed cannot, however, be corrected under **R.59** and can only be corrected under **R.52(3)** or **R.139**.

The Receiving Section will not consider the validity of the priority claim other than by verifying that the European patent application was filed within the priority year and notifying the applicant if this is not the case (A-III,6.6). The applicant may react by correcting the priority declaration under **R.52(3)** or **R.139** or by filing a request for re-establishment of the priority period, as appropriate, if the relevant time limit has not expired or the relevant conditions are met.

3 **International applications**
When filing a declaration of priority based on a PCT application, it suffices to indicate only one of the states designated or elected in the PCT application.

The correction of a declaration of priority filed for a Euro-PCT application is possible under the same conditions as for a European application (J2/92, see **R.139:3.1**).

R. 52(3) The applicant may correct the declaration of priority within sixteen months from the earliest priority date claimed, or, where the correction would cause a change in the earliest priority date claimed, within sixteen months from the corrected earliest priority date, whichever sixteen-month period expires first, provided that such a correction may be submitted until the expiry of four months from the date of filing accorded to the European patent application.

1 **Period for correcting declaration of priority**
A declaration of priority may be corrected within sixteen months from the earliest priority date claimed, this period being calculated using the corrected priority date rather than the original priority date if the correction concerns the date and results in an earlier expiry of the sixteen-month period. However, a declaration of priority may also always be corrected within four months from the date of filing of the application if this period expires later (**R.52(3)**). As a caveat, correction is no longer possible after a request for early publication has been filed, even if one the two periods has not yet expired (**R.52(4)**). There are no further restrictions. The aim is to be able to publish European patent applications as soon as possible after the expiry of 18 months from the priority date (**Art.93(1)(a)**) along with a correct priority claim.

In certain cases, a declaration of priority may also be corrected under **R.139**, even after the expiry of the **R.52(3)** time limit. The correction must generally be made in time for relevant information to be included in the published application and will only be successful in exceptional circumstances thereafter (see **R.139:3.1.2**).

The wording of **R.52(3)** is apt to cause confusion. The effect of the provision is to ensure that an applicant may always request correction of a priority claim in the four months after filing the application, while a request for correction may be submitted even after this date in certain circumstances (A-III,6.5.2). The request for correction may be submitted by the later of:

1 four months from the date of filing the application; and
2 the earlier of
  (a) sixteen months from the originally-claimed earliest priority date; and
  (b) sixteen months from the corrected earliest priority date where the request for correction relates to the filing date of a priority application.

The sixteen-month and four-month periods for correcting a priority claim are excluded from further processing under **R.135(2)** for the same reason as the period under **R.52(2)**. Re-establishment according to **Art.122** and **R.136** is available.

2 **Examples**
- Filing date: 04.02.2025; priority claimed on filing: 13.03.2024; corrected priority date: 13.02.2024; time limit for requesting correction: 13.06.2025.

Sixteen months from the corrected priority date is 13.06.2025; this is the earlier of the two dates calculated from the priority dates. This is also later than 4 months from the filing date, and so it is the relevant time limit.

- Filing date: 13.02.2025; priority claimed on filing: 14.02.2024; corrected priority date: 15.03.2024; time limite for requesting correction: 18.06.2025.

  Sixteen months from original priority date is 14.06.2025, which is a Saturday, so extended to 16.06.2025. This is earlier than sixteen months from the corrected priority date, and later than 4 months from filing date, so it is the relevant time limit.
- Filing date: 06.02.2025; priority claimed on filing: 14.11.2024; corrected priority date: 13.12.2024; time limit for requesting correction: 14.03.2026.

  Sixteen months from original priority date is 14.03.2026, which is the earlier of the two dates calculated from the priority dates. This is also later than 4 months from the filing date, so it is the relevant time limit.

R. 52(4) However, a declaration of priority may not be made or corrected after a request under Article 93, paragraph 1(b), has been filed.

Art.93(1)(b) Request for early publication of application

1 **Addition or correction only before request for early publication**
This provision seeks to ensure that the priority data published with the application is complete and accurate.

R. 52(5) The particulars of the declaration of priority shall appear in the published European patent application and the European patent specification.

1 **Publication of priority data**
The priority data is published with the application under **R.68(2)** and with the granted patent under **R.73(2)**.

R. 53 Priority documents

Implementation of **Art.88(1)**

1 **Filing of priority document**
R.53 governs the filing of priority documents with the EPO when a European patent application claims the priority of a previous application. **R.54** governs the issuing of priority documents by the EPO for filing with other patent offices when the priority of a European patent application is claimed elsewhere.

The term 'priority document' is generally used to refer to a copy of a previous application which is issued by the authority with which it was filed and certified by that authority to be a true copy (A-III,6.7.1). According to **R.53(1)**, the date of filing of the priority document must also be certified as correct. The term 'previous application' is used in **Art.88** and **R.53** to refer to the priority application.

The applicant must file the priority document within sixteen months from the earliest priority date claimed (**R.53(1)**) or enable the EPO to retrieve the priority document itself from the WIPO Digital Access Service (DAS) by providing a DAS code. However, the applicant is relieved of this responsibility if the priority document is already available to the EPO under the conditions specified by the President (**R.53(2)**).

The disclosure of the priority document is not examined by the Receiving Section on filing. However, if it is immediately obvious that the wrong document has been filed, the applicant will be notified as a courtesy. (A-III,6.4)

R. 53(1) An applicant claiming priority shall file a copy of the previous application within sixteen months of the earliest priority date claimed. This copy and the date of filing of the previous application shall be certified as correct by the authority with which that application was filed.

1 **Period for filing priority document**

The period of sixteen months for filing the priority document is calculated from the earliest priority date claimed. The date of filing of the priority declaration (**R.52(2)**) and the filing date of the European patent application are not relevant (see **R.53(2):2** for divisional applications). If multiple priorities are claimed, all of the priority documents must be filed within sixteen months from the earliest claimed priority date (**Art.88(2)**). Any priority document timely filed under **R.53(1)** will therefore be part of the application file on publication of the European patent application and will enter the state of the art under **Art.54(2)** from that date as a result of the public availability of the file.

If a priority document is not provided within sixteen months of the earliest claimed priority date, the right of priority based on that document is not immediately lost. Instead, the EPO will invite the applicant to remedy the deficiency within a period to be specified (**R.59**). A two-month period is specified in practice (**R.132(2)**, A-III,6.7.2), as is usually the case for the correction of a formal deficiency (E-VIII,1.2). This period can be extended in line with **R.132(2)** by requesting an extension before the period expires. No reasons need to be given if the extension requested is no more than two months; however, the applicant will need to justify a longer extension (E-VIII,1.6.1). If the priority document is not filed within the period set under **R.59**, the priority right based on that document is lost pursuant to **Art.90(5)**. See **Art.54(3):2** for the effect of the loss of a priority right on the prior right effect of the application. The only possible remedy is re-establishment (**Art.122**). Further processing is excluded under **R.135(2)**.

Note the difference between failure to file the priority document and failure to observe the sixteen-month period for filing the designation of the inventor (**R.60(1)**; note that the period is deemed to have been observed if the designation is filed before the completion of the technical preparations for publication): the legal consequence in the latter case (the application is refused under **Art.90(5)**) follows directly on expiry of the relevant period. The omission of the designation of the inventor is a deficiency on the date of filing and is to be remedied within the period specified by **R.60(1)**. In contrast, the omission of the priority document becomes a deficiency only on the expiry of the period specified in **R.53(1)** and is to be remedied in a subsequent period to be specified by the EPO.

2 **Form of priority document and manner of filing**
According to **R.53(1)**, the copy of the priority application must be certified by the authority that issued it as being an exact copy of the previous application; that authority must also certify the date of filing of the previous application. The certification may be a separate document but is typically an integral part of the priority document itself (A-III,6.7.1). The priority document will typically also contain other information such as the applicant's name and the file number and an indication of whether any priority was claimed for the previous application.

The priority document may be a paper document issued by the authority with which the previous application was filed. Applicants must file the certified document issued by the relevant authority rather than a copy (A-III,6.7.1) and a priority document issued on paper must therefore be filed using a postal service or by hand. Where two European patent applications claim the priority of the same previous application, the applicant only needs to file one copy of the priority document, though it should be accompanied by separate letters relating to each of the applications (A-VIII,2.4).

Priority documents may also be issued by a relevant authority and filed at the EPO as an electronic file on a physical data carrier (e.g. a CD-R disc). In that case, as with a paper copy, the original data carrier must be filed using a postal service or by hand (A-III,6.7.1). The data carrier must come with a guarantee that its content cannot be undetectably altered.

Priority documents may also be issued by a relevant authority as an electronic file that can be filed electronically at the EPO. In this case, the priority document must be digitally signed by the issuing authority, and the document and signature must be in a format accepted by the EPO. An electronic priority document of this kind can be filed using OLF or Online Filing 2.0; the EPO Contingency Upload Service must not be used (Dec. Pres. OJ 2024 A88 Art.3). Such digitally signed electronic priority documents are currently issued by the patent offices of Austria, Brazil, Czech Republic, Greece, France, Italy, Poland, Portugal, Singapore and the USA (A-III,6.7.1).

There is no fee associated with the filing of a priority document. The priority document must be accompanied by a letter or note signed by the applicant if not filed simultaneously with the application (**R.50(3)**; A-VIII,3.1).

R. 53(2) The copy of the previous application shall be deemed to be duly filed if a copy of that application available to the European Patent Office is to be included in the file of the European patent application under the conditions determined by the President of the European Patent Office.

1 **Retrieval of priority document using DAS**
The WIPO Digital Access Service (DAS) is an electronic system allowing the exchange of priority documents between participating offices. The office with which the previous application is filed assigns a DAS access code to the application, informs the applicant of the access code, and makes the priority document available through DAS such that other participating patent offices can retrieve it using the access code provided by the applicant. The participating offices are listed on the WIPO website and include the IB, the EPO and the patent offices of CN, JP, KR, USA, and several EPC contracting states. The EPO does not charge any fee for the use of DAS, either for the issuance of a DAS code in respect of a European patent application (or international application filed with the EPO as receiving Office) or for the retrieval of an application filed elsewhere using a DAS code. (A-III,6.7.2)

When an applicant files a priority-claiming application with the EPO and requests the EPO to retrieve the priority document from DAS by providing the relevant access code, the EPO retrieves the priority document and includes the document in the file of the application (**R.53(2)**). The DAS access code can be specified in the Request for Grant form when filing a European patent application or filed separately. (Dec. Pres. OJ 2021 A83 Art.1(1); Not. EPO OJ 2019 A27)

If the EPO cannot retrieve the priority document via DAS, it is deemed not to have been filed. The applicant is informed accordingly and is given an opportunity to file the priority document subsequently under **R.53(1)** or **R.59** (Dec. Pres. OJ 2021 A83 Art.1(3) and Art.2).

The priority-claiming application may be a Euro-direct application or a Euro-PCT application entering the regional phase before the EPO as a designated or elected Office (**R.163(2)**; Dec. Pres. OJ 2021 A83 Art.3).

2 **Retrieval of priority document without DAS**

In some instances, the EPO will retrieve a copy of a priority document and add it to the file even if a DAS code is not provided. This is the case if the previous application is a European patent application or an international application filed with the EPO as receiving Office (Dec. Pres. OJ 2021 A83 Art.1(2)). There is no fee for this service.

For divisional applications, the EPO will also generally add a copy of the priority document to the file, free of charge and without being asked, provided that the priority document is already available in the file of the parent; the same applies for new patent applications filed under **Art.61(1)(b)** (Dec. Pres. OJ 2007 se3 B.2). If, at the date of filing of the divisional application, no priority document has been filed in respect of the parent application, the priority document must be filed in respect of both the divisional application and the parent application. Alternatively, the applicant can file the priority document in respect of the parent application and, in respect of the divisional application, request the EPO to add a copy to the divisional file. If the subject matter of a divisional application relates to only some of the priorities claimed for the parent, only the relevant priority documents need to be filed in respect of the divisional application. (A-IV,1.2.2)

R. 53(3) Where the previous application is not in an official language of the European Patent Office and the validity of the priority claim is relevant to the determination of the patentability of the invention concerned, the European Patent Office shall invite the applicant for or proprietor of the European patent to file a translation of that application into one of the official languages within a period to be specified. Alternatively, a declaration may be submitted that the European patent application is a complete translation of the previous application. Paragraph 2 shall apply mutatis mutandis. If a requested translation of a previous application is not filed in due time, the right of priority for the European patent application or for the European patent with respect to that application shall be lost. The applicant for or proprietor of the European patent shall be informed accordingly.

Amended, in force since 01.04.2013 (OJ 2012 p.442).

1 **Translation of priority document or declaration**

If the language of the priority document is not one of the official languages of the EPO, the EPO will invite the applicant or the proprietor to file a translation into one of the official languages of the EPO if the validity of the priority claim is relevant for determining the patentability of the invention (**R.53**(3), first sentence). A translation of the priority document is otherwise not required. Instead of filing a translation, the applicant or proprietor may declare that the European patent application being examined, or the European patent application that gave rise to the patent being considered in opposition proceedings, is a complete translation of the priority document (**R.53**(3), second sentence).

Even without a request from the EPO, an applicant may voluntarily file a translation (or a declaration) at any time (A-III,6.8.5).

If a translation is required, the applicant or proprietor will be invited to file it within a period specified by the EPO (**R.53**(3), see **R.53**(3):3 below). This requirement may arise during search, examination, opposition or appeal proceedings (A-III,6.8; F-VI,3.4; D-VII,2; see also Not. EPO OJ 2013 p.150 §1-3).

If a translation has already been filed for a European patent application when a divisional application is filed, no translation needs to be filed for the divisional application; the EPO automatically adds a copy to the divisional file. Otherwise, the EPO may request the filing of a translation for the divisional application in the usual manner. (A-IV,1.2.2; (**R.53**(3), third sentence; Dec. Pres. OJ 2007 se3 B.2)

Even if an applicant or proprietor considers that the validity of the priority claim is not or no longer relevant for patentability, e.g. because of an amendment to the claims and that the request for a translation is inappropriate, a translation of the previous application or corresponding declaration must still be filed within the time limit set. If, in response to the **R.53**(3) invitation, arguments are submitted instead of the requested translation/declaration, the right of priority will be lost (see **R.53**(3):4 below).

2 **Complete translation**

Instead of filing a translation, the applicant may declare that the European patent application claiming priority is a complete translation of the priority document (**R.53**(3), second sentence). The declaration can be made by crossing a box in the Request for Grant form, in the form for entry into the European phase, or by filing a separate letter.

An application is a 'complete' translation, in the sense of **R.53**(3), if the text of the description, the text of the claims and, where applicable, any text matter in the drawings of the application are all a complete translation of the corresponding parts of the priority document. If, however, the European patent application was filed without claims, then any claims in the priority document are not taken into account. The translation may not add or omit anything vis-à-vis the text of the priority document. The only tolerated differences are the simple rearrangement of two sections (e.g. transposition of the claims from the beginning to the end of the description) and the use of different reference numerals (e.g. Arabic rather than Roman numerals). Examples of impermissible changes are changing the order of the claims, adding reference signs, and making changes to a listing of components, a heading or words in the drawings. Where multiple priorities are claimed, it is to be expected that a declaration will only be appropriate for one of them. (A-III,6.8.6)

Where a declaration cannot be accepted for any of the above reasons, a complete translation must be filed (A-III,6.8.6). If the period of **R.53(3)** has expired when the deficiency concerning the declaration is appreciated, the translation will probably have to be filed using an appropriate remedy (see **R.53(3):5** below). It is unlikely that the EPO would issue a second invitation in these circumstances but it is not clear from the Guidelines what the actual EPO practice is.

3 **Period for filing translation or declaration**

The period for filing the translation is specified by the EPO in the invitation (**R.53(3)**, **R.132(2)**) and varies depending on the point at which the invitation is sent (A-III,6.8.1). The period can be extended under **R.132(2)**, by filing a request before expiry of the period, if the requirements set out in the Guidelines are met (E-VIII,1.6).

Where the search division finds that a translation of a priority document is necessary for a direct European application, the invitation will be issued at about the same time as the communication under **R.70a(1)** or **R.70(2)**. In both cases, the translation must be provided within the period for requesting examination or confirming a request for examination already filed, i.e. within six months from the date of mention of publication of the search report. The translation for a Euro-PCT application where a supplementary European search report is drawn up must be filed within six months from notification of the **R.70(2)** communication. Where the period between notification of the invitation and the expiry of the six-month period is less than two months, the period is extended to two months from notification in order to comply with **R.132(2)**. (A-III,6.8.1)

When the examining division or the opposition division requests the translation, an invitation setting a four-month period will be sent separately or together with a communication pursuant to **Art.94(3)** or **Art.101(1)**. For a Euro-PCT application, where the EPO acted as (S)ISA, the invitation may only be sent after the expiry of the six-month period of **R.161(1)**. If no translation is filed following a request from the examining division, no summons to oral proceedings will be issued until after the expiry of the period for further processing (see **R.53(3):5** below). (A-III,6.8.2; C-IV,3.1)

4 **Effect of missing translation or declaration**

If the EPO does not receive the requested translation or a corresponding declaration before the expiry of the period set, the right to priority is lost; the applicant is informed accordingly (**R.53(3)**, fourth and fifth sentence; **R.112(1)**). The effect is immediate and no further invitation is issued (A-III,6.8.3). In a case in which multiple priorities are claimed, priority is only lost for those priority claims in respect of which a translation was requested and no translation or declaration was filed. The intermediate documents which led to the validity of the priority claim being considered relevant to patentability will become prior art under **Art.54(2)** or (3) as applicable (A-III,6.8.3). See **Art.54(3):2** for the effect of the loss of a right to priority on the prior right effect of the application.

5 **Remedies**

The loss of rights resulting from non-compliance with an invitation pursuant to **R.53(3)** can be remedied during grant proceedings using further processing (**Art.121** and **R.135**). If the EPO requested a translation of more than one previous application, one further processing fee is due for each translation that is filed using further processing, even if the translations were requested in a single invitation (A-III,6.8.3).

During opposition proceedings, the loss of rights can potentially be remedied using re-establishment (**Art.122** and **R.136**).

Alternatively, in examination and opposition proceedings, a decision under **R.112(2)** may be requested if the notice of loss of rights is incorrect because the translation was actually filed in time (A-III,6.8.3). If a decision under **R.112(2)** is sought, it is prudent to nevertheless file a further copy of the translation (or declaration) along with a request for further processing or re-establishment as an auxiliary measure.

R. 54 Issuing priority documents

On request, the European Patent Office shall issue to the applicant a certified copy of the European patent application (priority document), under the conditions determined by the President of the European Patent Office, including the form of the priority document and the circumstances under which an administrative fee shall be paid.

Implementation of **Art.88(1)**

1 **Issuing priority documents on paper**

An applicant for a European patent may request that the EPO issues a copy of the application for use as a priority document. A written request is required. The EPO will issue a paper copy of the European patent application, certified as an exact copy, together with a certificate stating the date of filing. The President decides whether an administrative fee under **Rfees3(1)** must be paid (see Schedule of Fees, OJ 2024 sp4). A fee is payable in all cases unless the priority document is requested using MyEPO, in which case there is no charge (OJ 2024 A5). A priority document will only be issued to the applicant that filed the European patent application or that applicant's successor in title – no priority document will be issued to a third party. The applicant can furnish the priority document to a patent office where a priority-claiming application is filed (Art.4D(3) Paris Convention). (Dec. Pres. OJ 2020 A7, Dec. Pres. OJ 2019 A16, A-XI,5.2)

The priority document is a copy of the application as originally filed, not a copy of any translation in one of the official languages of the EPO filed under **Art.14(2)**. The content of the priority document corresponds to the application documents (i.e. description, and any claims and drawings) available on the filing date and contained in the electronic file, reproduced in black and white (A-XI,5.2). The priority document also states the name of the original applicant and whether any priority was claimed.

The EPO will issue a priority document directly to the International Bureau, following a request from the applicant, if the priority-claiming application is an international application for which the EPO acted as the receiving Office (R.17.1(b) PCT, GL/PCT-EPO A-III,4.4.1). An administrative fee must be paid for the benefit of the EPO. Note, however, that DAS can be used as an alternative and is free of charge (see **R.54:2** below).

The EPO also issues priority documents for international applications that it receives as receiving Office upon payment of an administrative fee (R.21.2 PCT, GL/PCT-EPO A-III,4.4.2).

2 **Issuing priority documents electronically**

Requests for the issuance of priority documents on paper are less common with the increasing use of the WIPO Digital Access Service (DAS) (see **R.53(2):1** for an explanation of DAS).

As a depositing office under DAS, the EPO automatically generates a DAS access code free of charge for each European application (other than a divisional application) as of 01.11.2018 and for each international application filed with it as receiving Office as of 01.04.2019 and notifies the applicant accordingly. The notification is included in the non-public part of the file. The EPO will also assign a DAS code to an application on request if one is not generated automatically. The code will only be valid once a filing date has been accorded. Once the code is assigned, the EPO makes a certified copy of the application (priority document) available in DAS. (OJ 2018 A79 IIA; OJ 2019 A27; A-XI,5.2)

The EPO has also begun to issue certified copies of European patent applications and international applications for which it acts as receiving Office in electronic format (Dec. Pres. OJ 2025 A3). Such electronic copies must be requested via MyEPO and are made available via the applicant's Mailbox. As with all requests for certified copies of priority documents filed via MyEPO (i.e. on paper or electronically), there is no charge (Not. EPO OJ 2025 A7). However, until further notice, electronic priority documents will only be available to MyEPO pilot participants. The electronic certified copy is issued as a single ZIP file comprising a substantive folder and a certification document. The substantive folder is a ZIP file comprising the certified copy in PDF format (front page, description, claims, drawings and abstract), a sequence listing (where applicable) in the originally filed format and a table of contents in XML format (Dec. Pres. OJ 2025 A8). The certification document is in PDF format and shows the application number and date of filing, a hash of the substantive folder ZIP file (calculated using SHA-256) and the timestamp of the advanced electronic seal based on a qualified certificate according to the eIDAS Regulation.

PART IV IMPLEMENTING REGULATIONS TO PART IV OF THE CONVENTION

Chapter I *Examination by the Receiving Section*

R. 55 Examination on filing

Amended by decision of the Administrative Council of 10.12.2024, which entered into force on 01.04.2025 (OJ 2025 A16). The amendments made the text gender-neutral.

If the examination under Article 90, paragraph 1, reveals that the application fails to meet the requirements laid down in Rule 40, paragraph 1(a) or (c), paragraph 2 or paragraph 3, first sentence, the European Patent Office shall inform the applicant of any deficiencies and advise them that the application will not be dealt with as a European patent application unless such deficiencies are remedied within two months. If the applicant does this, they shall be informed of the date of filing accorded by the Office.

Art.90(1) Examination on filing
R.40(1)(a) Indication that European patent is sought
R.40(1)(c) Description or reference to previously filed application
R.40(2) Filing date and number of previously filed application
R.40(3) Certified copy of previously filed application
Implementation of **Art.90(4)**

1 **Accordance of date of filing and re-dating**
R.55 deals with the examination under **Art.90(1)** as to whether the requirements for the accordance of a date of filing are fulfilled. If the examination reveals deficiencies relating to **R.40(1)(a)** or (c), **R.40(2)** or (3), the EPO will invite the applicant under **Art.90(4)** and **R.55** to correct the deficiencies within two months. If the deficiency relates to parts of the description or drawings that are missing, the EPO will follow the procedure of **R.56** instead of **R.55**.

When a correction is filed in response to the **R.55** invitation the filing date allocated to the application may be the date on which the correction is filed or the date on which the application was originally filed, depending on the deficiency corrected. The actual rules for according a date of filing after correction are not laid down in the EPC but only in the Guidelines.

If a deficiency relating to **R.40(1)(a)**, **(c)**, or **R.40(2)** is corrected in due time, the date of receipt of the correction will become the date of filing of the application. The applicant will be informed of this date under **R.55**, last sentence. (A-II,4.1.4)

If a deficiency relating to **R.40(3)**, first sentence, is corrected in due time, the original date of filing is retained (A-II,4.1.5).

See the notes to **R.40** for filing date requirements and the effect of specific corrections on the date of filing.

If the deficiencies are not remedied within two months of notification of the invitation, no date of filing will be accorded and the application will not be dealt with as a European patent application (**Art.90(2)**, **R.55**). The Receiving Section informs the applicant by means of a **R.112(1)** communication; if the applicant regards the communication as inaccurate, an appealable decision may be requested.

The two-month period of **R.55** is not extendable under **R.132**, because it is not an office time limit. **R.135(2)** excludes the two-month period from further processing. Re-establishment (**Art.122** and **R.136**) is possible. In the case that re-establishment is granted, and the deficiency relates to **R.40(3)**, first sentence, the original filing date is retained. In the case that re-establishment is granted, and the deficiency relates to **R.40(1)(a)**, **(c)**, or **R.40(2)**, the established practice of the Receiving Section is to accord a date of filing corresponding to the last day of the two-month period of **R.55**.

Instead of applying for re-establishment, the applicant may file a corrected application, provided the date of filing is not critical. This remedy is cheaper and more certain than re-establishment. Any fees paid in respect of the earlier application will be refunded as lacking legal basis (A-II,4.1.4).

R. 56 Missing parts of the description or missing drawings

Implementation of **Art.90(4)**

1 **Correction of missing parts by later filing**

The purpose of **R.56** is to allow the addition of parts of the description and drawings that are missing in the application as originally filed, e.g. as the result of an oversight when filing the application. It implements Art.5(6) of the Patent Law Treaty. The case of a patent application filed with incorrect drawings or claims, or an incorrect description, or incorrect parts thereof is dealt with separately in **R.56a**.

If, during the examination on filing, the EPO finds that a part of the description or a drawing appears to be missing, it will invite the applicant under **R.56(1)** to file the missing part(s) within two months from the invitation. Applicants may also file missing parts of their own motion within two months of the date of filing (**R.56(2)**). The application will be re-dated to the date of receipt of the missing part(s) (**R.56(2)**). Applicants may withdraw subsequently filed parts of the description and drawings in order to retain the original filing date (**R.56(6)**).

If the application claimed priority on the filing date and the missing part of the description or drawing was completely contained in the priority application, that missing part may be included in the application without loss of the original date of filing, provided the requirements of **R.56(3)** are met. (OJ 2003 se1 p.159)

R.56 refers only to missing parts of the description and missing drawings. Hence, the inclusion of one or more missing claims from a previous application using **R.56** is not permitted; **R.56a** can be used in case incorrect claims are filed. **R.56** cannot be used if the entire description is missing, see **R.40**. See A-IV,5.1 for a missing sequence listing.

R.56 cannot be used to amend or replace originally filed documents; it can only be used to supplement the originally filed documents with missing parts of the description and missing drawings (J15/12 r.4). However, **R.56a** can be used to amend an application filed with incorrect parts.

The 'content of the application as filed' for the purposes of **Art.123(2)** includes missing parts of the description and missing drawings incorporated under **R.56(3)** (H-IV,2.2.2).

Where the applicant has filed missing parts, the publication under **Art.93** contains the description, the claims and any drawings as originally filed (**R.68(1)**) and any late-filed missing parts of the description or drawings, provided that these were not subsequently withdrawn. Where the procedure under **R.56** is not finished at the point in time when the technical preparations for publication are completed, the application is republished as soon as the date of filing and content of the application are finally determined. (A-VI,1.3).

R.56 can, in principle, also be used for divisional applications (A-IV,1.1).

R. 56(1) If the examination under Article 90, paragraph 1, reveals that parts of the description, or drawings referred to in the description or in the claims, appear to be missing, the European Patent Office shall invite the applicant to file the missing parts within two months. The applicant may not invoke the omission of such a communication.

Art.90(1) Examination on filing

1 **Nomenclature**

R.56 refers to 'missing parts of the description' and 'missing drawings'.

A drawing means a single numbered figure. If part of a drawing is missing, the whole drawing will be regarded as completely missing for the purpose of **R.56**, and the EPO will invite the applicant to resubmit a complete drawing (A-II,5.3; CA/PL17/06). The EPO does not want to assemble a complete drawing by cutting and pasting.

A drawing of low visual quality is not considered a missing part and cannot be remedied under **R.56** (J12/14).

The missing parts of the description and the missing drawings are referred to together as 'missing parts' or, once filed with the EPO, as 'late-filed parts' (A-II,5).

2 **Missing parts and missing drawings noted by EPO**

During the examination on filing under **Art.90(1)** the EPO checks whether parts of the description or drawings referred to in the description or claims appear to be missing. If a missing part is noted, the applicant will be invited to file it within two months of notification of the invitation. The Receiving Section does not look for missing claims because the presence of claims is not a requirement for a date of filing (see **R.40(1):2.2**).

If the missing parts are filed in due time, the application will either be re-dated under **R.56(2)** or, where the missing parts are contained in a priority application and the criteria of **R.56(3)** are met, retain the original date of filing.

Failure to file the missing parts within the two-month period leads to the deletion of any references to the missing parts in the description and claims and no re-dating of the application (**R.56(4)(a)**).

3 **Period for filing**
The missing parts must be filed within two months of notification of the invitation. The two-month period is excluded from further processing by **R.135(2)**. Re-establishment under **Art.122** and **R.136** may be used as a remedy.

Re-filing the application with the correct description and drawings is also possible, and has the same effect as re-dating, although not all fees paid for the first application may be refunded (see **Rfees9(1)**).

R. 56(2) If missing parts of the description or missing drawings are filed later than the date of filing, but within two months of the date of filing or, if a communication is issued under paragraph 1 or under Rule 56a, paragraph 1, within two months of that communication, the application shall be re-dated to the date on which the missing parts of the description or missing drawings were filed. The European Patent Office shall inform the applicant accordingly.

Amended by decision of the Administrative Council of 14.12.2021, which entered into force on 01.11.2022 (OJ 2022 A3; Not. EPO OJ 2022 A71). The reference to **R.56a** is inserted. The amended text applies to applications filed on or after 01.11.2022.
R.56a Erroneously filed application documents or parts

1 **Missing parts and missing drawings noted by applicant**
Applicants may file missing parts of the description and missing drawings (not missing claims) of their own volition within two months of the date of filing (**R.56(2)**). However, if the EPO invites the applicant to file missing parts, the period under **R.56(1)** takes precedence (A-II,5.2), and the applicant may file any missing parts within two months from the invitation. The same applies to an invitation under **R.56a**.

The two-month period from the date of filing is excluded from further processing by **R.135(2)**. Re-establishment under **Art.122** and **R.136** is available. Alternatively, the applicant may re-file the application in the correct form.

It is advisable to file the missing parts as soon as possible because, in the case of re-dating, the application will be accorded the date of receipt of the missing parts as the date of filing. Moreover, if the EPO does not notice the absence of any missing parts and does not send the invitation under **R.56(1)**, the possibility to file the missing parts ends two months after the original date of filing (A-II,5.2).

The applicant may file a sequence listing as a missing part of the description where it is obvious from the description as a whole that the sequence listing is missing, for example, where the description mentions sequence identification numbers (A-IV,5.1). No late furnishing fee is incurred as a direct result since the sequence listing will form part of the application as of its date of filing. The procedure under **R.30** for the case of a sequence listing filed with incorrect formatting is unaffected.

2 **Re-dating of the application**
Where missing parts are filed, the EPO will re-date the application to the date on which the missing parts were filed (**R.56(2)**, first sentence) and inform the applicant of the new date of filing (**R.56(2)**, last sentence). See also **Art.80:4**.

However, there will be no re-dating when the special criteria of **R.56(3)** apply.

Re-dating an application need not result in a loss of rights if the new date of filing is still within the priority year of an earlier application from which it claims priority. If re-dating leads to a later effective date being allocated to the application, the applicant must balance, on the one hand, the risk of some pertinent prior art having been disclosed between the original effective date and a later effective date when the application is re-dated and, on the other hand, the risk of insufficiency of disclosure of the application (**Art.83**) if the later filed parts are withdrawn to retain the effective date (i.e. the priority date or the original filing date).

R. 56(3) If the missing parts of the description or missing drawings are filed within the period under paragraph 2, and the application claims priority of an earlier application on the date on which the requirements laid down in Rule 40, paragraph 1, were fulfilled, the date of filing shall, provided that the missing parts of the description or the missing drawings are completely contained in the earlier application, remain the date on which the requirements laid down in Rule 40, paragraph 1, were fulfilled, where the applicant so requests and files, within the period under paragraph 2:

(a) a copy of the earlier application, unless such copy is available to the European Patent Office under Rule 53, paragraph 2;

(b) where the earlier application is not in an official language of the European Patent Office, a translation thereof in one of these languages, unless such copy is available to the European Patent Office under Rule 53, paragraph 3; and

(c) an indication as to where the missing parts of the description or the missing drawings are completely contained in the earlier application and, where applicable, in the translation thereof.

Amended by decision of the Administrative Council of 14.12.2021 which entered into force on 01.11.2022 (OJ 2022 A3; Not. EPO OJ 2022 A71) to insert the requirement 'on the date on which the requirements laid down in Rule 40, paragraph 1, were fulfilled'.
R.40(1) Requirements for according date of filing
R.53(3) Application or translation available in EPO file

1 **Missing parts based on priority**
The application will not be re-dated and will retain the original date of filing if the missing parts are contained in an earlier application from which priority is claimed and the following criteria are satisfied within the period of **R.56(2)** (A-II,5.4):

i) the missing parts of the description or the missing drawings have been filed;
ii) the application claims the priority of the earlier application; for applications filed on or after 01.11.2022, the application must claim said priority on the filing date (OJ 2022 A3 Art.3);
iii) a request has been filed that the missing parts of the description or missing drawings be based on the earlier application to avoid redating;

iv) the missing parts of the description or missing drawings are 'completely contained' in the earlier application;
v) a copy of the earlier application has been filed unless such copy is already available to the EPO under **R.53(2)**;
vi) a translation of the earlier application in one of the official EPO languages has been filed if the earlier application is not in one of these languages unless such translation is already available to the EPO under **R.53(3)**;
vii) an indication is given as to where the missing parts of the description or missing drawings are 'completely contained' in the earlier application and, where applicable, in the translation thereof.

1.1 PRIORITY CLAIM (ITEM II)

The priority claim in question must have been in existence no later than the filing of the request under iii) above for applications filed before 01.11.2022 and on the filing date for applications filed on or after 01.11.2022.

The following applies for applications filed before 01.11.2022: the missing parts may also be based on a priority added after the original date of filing. The priority may not be added after the filing of the request in iii) above. An added priority claim must be filed within the period of **R.52(2)**, i.e. sixteen months from the earliest priority date. (see also A-II,5.4.1)

R.56(3) uses the term 'earlier application' intentionally to ensure that the paragraph only covers the case of a missing part contained in a priority application and not in any previously filed application (CA/PL17/06).

1.2 COMPLETELY CONTAINED IN EARLIER APPLICATION (ITEM IV)

The requirement of **R.56(3)** that the missing part be 'completely contained in the earlier application' is met only if the parts of the earlier application identified according to **R.56(3)(c)** contain the same drawings, with the same annotations or, for missing parts of the description, contain the same text. The missing part must be inserted in the description in a manner that does not add technical content. (A-II,5.4.2)

If a translation of the earlier application is required under **R.56(3)(b)**, the missing parts must be completely contained in the translation. (A-II,5.4.2)

The assessment of 'completely contained' is a formal matter that can be carried out by formalities staff attached to the Receiving Section (A-I,2). The EPO may require photographic identity.

Lawyers in the EPO have suggested that a missing part added to the description of an application must be taken from the description of the priority application, not from the claims of the priority application.

1.3 COPY AND TRANSLATION OF EARLIER APPLICATION (ITEM III, VI)

If no copy of the priority application is available to the EPO under **R.53(2)**, the applicant must furnish a copy (**R.56(3)(a)**), which need not be certified (A-II,5.4.3).

Where the priority application is not in an official language of the EPO (i.e. English, French or German), the applicant must file a translation into one of these languages unless such a translation is already available under **R.53(3)** (**R.56(3)(b)**).

Where the priority application is an official language of the EPO and the European application is a different official language of the EPO, no translation is necessary according to **R.56(3)(b)**. However, in order to show that the 'completely contained' is met, the applicant must nevertheless either file a declaration that the late-filed missing parts of the description, or drawings, are an exact translation of the identified parts of the priority application or else file a translation of the identified parts of the priority application in the language of the European patent application. (A-II,5.4.4)

At this stage, the language of the proceedings may not be known; hence, the EPO cannot require the filing of the translation in the language of the proceedings and instead allows the filing of the translation in any of the official languages. In the unlikely case that the applicant translates the priority application into an official language other than the language which later becomes the language of the proceedings, the EPO will probably apply A-II,5.4.4 mutatis mutandis.

1.4 INDICATION OF MISSING PARTS (ITEM VII)

The indication facilitates the processing of the missing parts of the description and the missing drawings by the EPO (CA/PL17/06).

2 **Effect of non-compliance**

Where criterion i) is not complied with, i.e. the missing parts have been filed after the expiry of either of the two-month periods of **R.56(2)**, the missing parts are deemed not to have been filed, and any references to these missing parts will be deemed deleted according to **R.56(4)(a)**. The application will not be re-dated, and the missing parts will not be introduced into the application.

Non-compliance with one or more of the criteria ii)-iv) leads to redating of the application to the date on which the missing parts were filed under **R.56(2)**.

Non-compliance with one or more of the criteria v)-vii) results also in redating to the date on which the missing parts were filed, but in this case under **R.56(5)**.

The EPO will inform the applicant of the non-compliance and the consequences under **R.56(4)(a)**, (2) or (5), whichever applies.

3 **Decision on late-filed missing parts**

The Receiving Section will inform the applicant of its decision on late-filed parts, in particular its decision concerning the requirement that the missing parts are 'completely contained' in the priority application. The decision will be reviewed by the search division (B-XI,2.1) and the examining division (C-III,1.1), who may also check any translation of the priority application, which may result in a change of the date of filing. An opposition division is possibly also entitled to review the 'completely contained' requirement if the change in filing date would lead to a change in the state of the art relevant to novelty or inventive step (**Art.100**). As of yet, there is no case law on this issue.

A decision of the Receiving Section to re-date the application can be reconsidered by the examining division if the examining division considers that the requirements of **R.56(3)** are met unless the examining division is bound by a decision of the board of appeal (B-XI,2.1).

The page fee is calculated on the basis of the documents present at the expiry of the one-month period of R.38(3) (A-III,13.2).

R. 56(4) If the applicant:

(a) fails to file the missing parts of the description or the missing drawings within the period under paragraph 1 or 2, or

(b) withdraws under paragraph 6 any missing part of the description or missing drawing filed under paragraph 2,

any references referred to in paragraph 1 shall be deemed to be deleted, and any filing of the missing parts of the description or missing drawings shall be deemed not to have been made. The European Patent Office shall inform the applicant accordingly.

1 **Late filing or withdrawal of missing parts**
The missing parts are deemed not to have been filed if the applicant files the missing parts after the expiry of two months from invitation under **R.56(1)** or from the date of filing under **R.56(2)**, or if the applicant withdraws any missing part under **R.56(6)** after a notification under **R.56(2)** or **R.56(5)** (A-II,5.5). In that case any references in the description or claims to these parts will be deemed to be deleted. The references are also deemed to be deleted if no missing parts are filed in response to the invitation under **R.56(1)**.

When a reference to a missing figure is deemed to be deleted, then reference signs referring to that figure are also deemed to be deleted. Technical information that is still meaningful without the reference will be retained. (A-II,5.5)

R. 56(5) If the applicant fails to comply with the requirements referred to in paragraph 3(a) to (c) within the period under paragraph 2, the application shall be re-dated to the date on which the missing parts of the description or missing drawings were filed. The European Patent Office shall inform the applicant accordingly.

1 **Non-compliance with requirements of R.56(3)**
R.56(5) provides for the sanctions applicable where the requirements referred to in paragraph (3)(a) to (c) are not complied with in due time. In such a case, the application will be re-dated to the date on which the missing parts of the description or missing drawings were filed. Alternatively, the applicant can withdraw the missing parts of the description or missing drawings under **R.56(6)** so as to avoid any modification of the filing date. (CA/PL17/06)

R. 56(6) Within one month of the notification referred to in paragraph 2 or 5, last sentence, the applicant may withdraw the missing parts of the description or the missing drawings filed, in which case the re-dating shall be deemed not to have been made. The European Patent Office shall inform the applicant accordingly.

1 **Withdrawal of missing parts or missing drawings**
Where an applicant files missing parts of the description or missing drawings under **R.56(2)** and **R.56(3)** does not apply or where one of the criteria of **R.56(3)(a), (b)** or **(c)** are not met, the EPO sends a communication informing the applicant of the new date of filing. The applicant may reconsider the filing of the missing parts of the description or missing drawings and withdraw the late-filed parts within one month of the notification of the communication. As a result, the re-dating is deemed not to have been made according to **R.56(6)** and the applicant is informed accordingly. (A-II,5.5)

Compliance with the 'completely contained' criterion may be reviewed in later proceedings (see **R.56(3):3** and the applicant may be notified of a change of filing date as the result of such a review. Thereafter, the applicant can still withdraw the added missing parts or drawings under **R.56(6)** within two months from the communication. (C-III 1.1.1)

The publication under **Art.93** does not contain any late-filed missing parts of the description or drawings that have already been withdrawn under **R.56(6)** (A-VI,1.3).

R. 56a Erroneously filed application documents or parts

Inserted by decision of the Administrative Council of 14.12.2021, which entered into force on 01.11.2022 (OJ 2022 A3; Not. EPO OJ 2022 A71; preparatory document CA/4/21). The provision applies to all applications filed on or after 01.11.2022 (OJ 2022 A3 Art.3).
Implementation of **Art.80** and **Art.90**(4)

1 **Treatment of erroneously filed application documents or parts**
R.56a is inserted as of 01.11.2022 to align the EPC with R.20.5bis PCT (which entered into force 01.07.2020) and allows the correction of erroneously filed application documents in EPC procedures. The EPO thus withdrew its notification of incompatibility with R.20.5bis PCT (OJ 2022 A71 §3; OJ 2020 A81). The provision provides remedies in cases where applicants, in particular when using online filing tools, have erroneously attached incorrect documents, for instance, a description belonging to another invention or a draft version of the description. (CA/4/21)

The application is published with the documents determined to be part of the application as filed under **R.56a** if the procedure is finalised in time. If, for instance, correct documents are added under **R.56a**(4), the publication will include both the correct documents and the erroneously filed application documents. Where the procedure under **R.56a** is not finalised at the point in time when the technical preparations for publication are terminated, the application is republished as soon as the date of filing and content of the application are finally determined (A-VI,1.3).

The documents determined to be part of the application as filed under **R.56a** are hence part of the application as filed under **Art.123**(2) (H-IV,2.2.3) and, by the same token, **Art.54**(3), including any erroneous parts that remain in the application under R.56a(4) (G-IV,5.1.2).

All application documents and parts that have been filed with the EPO are part of the public file, irrespective of whether or not they are considered to form part of the application as filed under **R.56a**. Upon reasoned request of the applicant, erroneously filed documents which are not considered to form part of the application as filed may be excluded from file inspection (OJ 2022 A71 §15). If the application is not published, the file is as a rule not public, with some exceptions (**Art.128**).

For international applications filed between 01.07.2020 and 31.10.2022, incorporations by reference allowed by the receiving Office under R.20.5bis(d) PCT, i.e. without changing the filing date, are not effective in proceedings before the EPO as designated/elected Office, irrespective of the date of entry into the European phase (OJ 2020 A81). For international applications filed on or after 01.11.2022, the EPO fully applies R.20.5bis PCT. Hence incorporation by reference by the receiving Office under R.20.5bis(d) PCT, i.e. without changing the filing date, are also effective before the EPO as designated or elected Office for international applications filed on or after 01.11.2022. (OJ 2022 A71 §23)

R.56a can in principle also be used for divisional applications (A-IV,1.1).

R. 56a(1) If the examination under Article 90, paragraph 1, reveals that the description, claims or drawings, or parts of those application documents, appear to have been erroneously filed, the European Patent Office shall invite the applicant to file the correct application documents or parts within two months. The applicant may not invoke the omission of such a communication.

Art.90(1) Examination on filing

1 **Invitation to file correct documents**
If, during the examination on filing, the EPO establishes that the description, claims or drawings (or parts of them) appear to have been filed erroneously, e.g. the drawings pertain to a different invention than the description, it will invite the applicant to file the correct documents (A-II,6). The applicant cannot oblige EPO to issue such an invitation later in the procedure, not even by pointing out that the application contains incorrect parts because the applicant cannot invoke the omission of the invitation. Filing a response is optional. Generally, the provision corresponds to **R.56(1)**, and the notes to **R.56(1)** apply mutatis mutandis.

R. 56a(2) If correct application documents or parts referred to in paragraph 1 are filed on or before the date of filing so as to correct the application, those correct application documents or parts shall be included in the application and the erroneously filed application documents or parts shall be deemed not to have been filed. The European Patent Office shall inform the applicant accordingly.

1 **Same-day corrections**
The provision codifies the EPO's practice to allow corrections of the received application documents on the filing date. Applicants thus do not need to file a second application and pay the corresponding fees if they realise on the filing date that they erroneously filed incorrect application documents. Note that if the first application is withdrawn on the filing date, all fees paid will be refunded except the filing fee, page fee, divisional fee and claims fees. The provision can also be applied in the rare case that the requirements of **R.40** are not met and no filing date is accorded. (A-II,6.6)

R. 56a(3) If correct application documents or parts referred to in paragraph 1 are filed later than the date of filing, but within two months of the date of filing or, if a communication is issued under paragraph 1 or under Rule 56, paragraph 1, within two months of that communication, the application shall be re-dated to the date on which the correct application documents or parts were filed. The correct application documents or parts shall be included in the application and the erroneously filed application documents or parts shall be deemed not to have been filed. The European Patent Office shall inform the applicant accordingly.

R.56(1) Missing parts of the description or missing drawings

1 **Filing corrections with change of filing date**
R.56a(3) allow applicants to correct the description, claims and drawings (or parts of them) within two months from the notification regarding missing parts (**R.56(1)**) or incorrect parts (**R.56a(1)**), or within two months from the filing date of the applicant's own volition. The erroneously filed application documents will be removed from the application, and the correct documents will be added.

However, the filing date will be changed to the date of receipt of the correct application documents (or parts); this may result in a loss of the priority date. Applicants will, therefore, often strongly prefer the procedure of **R.56a(4)**.

The two-month period is excluded from further processing (**R.135(2)**).

Generally, the provision corresponds to **R.56(2)**, and the notes to **R.56(2)** apply mutatis mutandis (OJ 2022 A71 §9).

Whether documents were erroneously filed, as required under **R.56a(1)**, will depend only on the applicant's statement of what was intended. No further evidence will be required by the EPO, even if the correct documents are filed of the applicant's own volition (OJ 2022 A71 §8). Accordingly, neither an error in the sense of **R.139** first sentence in the erroneously filed documents is required nor meeting the requirements for a correction under **R.139**, first sentence. Note, however, that this policy of the EPO does not bind national courts in nullity proceedings (see **Art.138(1)(c)**).

R. 56a(4) If the correct application documents or parts are filed within the period under paragraph 3, and the application claims priority of an earlier application on the date on which the requirements laid down in Rule 40, paragraph 1, were fulfilled, the date of filing shall, provided that the correct application documents or parts are completely contained in the earlier application, remain the date on which the requirements laid down in Rule 40, paragraph 1, were fulfilled, where the applicant so requests and files, within the period under paragraph 3:

(a) a copy of the earlier application, unless such copy is available to the European Patent Office under Rule 53, paragraph 2;

(b) where the earlier application is not in an official language of the European Patent Office, a translation thereof in one of these languages, unless such copy is available to the European Patent Office under Rule 53, paragraph 3;

and

(c) an indication as to where the correct application documents or parts are completely contained in the earlier application and, where applicable, in the translation thereof.

If these requirements are fulfilled, the correct application documents or parts shall be included in the application and the erroneously filed application documents or parts shall remain in the application.

R.40(1) Filing date requirements
R.53(2) Priority document deemed to have been filed
R.53(3) Translation of priority document

1 **Filing corrections keeping original filing date**

If the correct application documents (or parts) are completely contained in the priority document, **R.56a(4)** allows applicants to maintain the initial filing date when adding those documents (or parts). For legal certainty, the priority right must have been claimed on the filing date. The correct documents will be added to the application (A-II,6.4).

The erroneously filed application documents will remain in the application and may only be removed by amending the application under **Art.123(2)** in the further procedure (A-II,6.4). The page fee is based on the documents present at the expiry of the one-month period of **R.38(3)** (A-III,13.2). Where correct claims are filed under **R.56a**, the claims fee is calculated on the basis of the set of claims first filed.

Note that it would have been more logical if the erroneously filed application documents were replaced. The EPO, however, follows R.20.5bis(d) PCT, which specifies that the erroneous documents remain in the application, in addition to the incorporated correct parts, because some designated offices may have excluded that rule's application (PCT/WG/12/9 p.3). This is, however, no valid concern in the context of the EPC (see Mulder and Van Woudenberg in epi Information 3/2022).

The provision generally corresponds to **R.56(3)**, and the notes to **R.56(3)** apply mutatis mutandis.

Whether documents were erroneously filed depends only on the applicant's statement of what was intended to be filed. No further evidence is required (OJ 2022 A71 §8). There is no requirement that the erroneously filed documents contain an error in the sense of **R.139**; nor any requirement for due care when the documents were filed. The correct description, drawings and claims can be filed in their entirety or in part.

The correction must be filed within two months of the filing date or from the notification regarding missing parts (**R.56(1)**) or incorrect parts (**R.56a(1)**). In the same period, the applicant must (1) file a copy of the priority application, which need not be certified, unless such copy is already available to the EPO under **R.53(2)**, e.g. through DAS, (2) file a translation of the priority document, unless available under **R.53(3)** and, (3) file an indication as to where the correct application documents or parts are completely contained in the earlier application and, where applicable, in the translation thereof, which is in particular relevant if correct parts of the description are filed. The period is excluded from further processing (**R.135(2)**). If any of the requirements (a) –(c) is not met, the application is re-dated (**R.56a(6)**) unless the applicant withdraws the correction within one month of the notification of the re-date (**R.56a(7)**).

R. 56a(5) If the applicant:

(a) fails to file the correct application documents or parts within the period under paragraph 1 or 3,

or

(b) withdraws under paragraph 7 any correct application documents or parts filed under paragraph 3,

any filing of the correct application documents or parts shall be deemed not to have been made and the erroneously filed application documents or parts shall remain in the application or be restored to the application. The European Patent Office shall inform the applicant accordingly.

1 **Filing of corrections deemed not to have been made**

The provision generally corresponds to **R.56(4)** and the notes to **R.56(4)** apply mutatis mutandis. Paragraph (a) applies if the correct documents are filed late. Paragraph (b) applies if an applicant retracts correct documents to avoid a shift of the filing date.

R. 56a(6) If the applicant fails to comply with the requirements referred to in paragraph 4(a) to (c) within the period under paragraph 3, the application shall be re-dated to the date on which the correct application documents or parts were filed. The filing of the erroneously filed application documents or parts shall be deemed not to have been made. The European Patent Office shall inform the applicant accordingly.

R. 56a(7) Within one month of the notification referred to in paragraph 3 or 6, last sentence, the applicant may withdraw the correct application documents or parts filed, in which case the re-dating shall be deemed not to have been made. The European Patent Office shall inform the applicant accordingly.

1 **Period for withdrawing corrections**
The provision generally corresponds to **R.56(6)**. The notes to **R.56(6)** apply mutatis mutandis. In cases where the filing date would shift by a correction, the applicant may withdraw the correction to maintain the initial filing date within one month from the notification regarding the re-date. The period is excluded from further processing (**R.135(2)**). Re-establishment is available. See **R.56a(5)** for the effect of the withdrawal of the correct parts. (A-II,6.5)

R. 56a(8) If the applicant files correct application documents or parts under paragraph 3 or 4 after the European Patent Office has begun to draw up the search report, the European Patent Office shall invite the applicant to pay a further search fee within one month. If the search fee is not paid in due time, the application shall be deemed to be withdrawn.

1 **Additional search fee after filing corrections**
The fee amount is specified in **Rfees2(1)2**, first indent, and is equal to the search fee for a direct European application. Further processing is available if the fee is not paid in time. (A-II,6.7). Automatic debiting is neither available for the fee of **R.56a(8)** nor for the corresponding further processing fee (AAD 3.2(l), OJ 2024 sp2 Annex A.1).

R. 57 Examination as to formal requirements

If the European patent application has been accorded a date of filing, the European Patent Office shall examine, in accordance with Article 90, paragraph 3, whether:
(a) a translation of the application required under Article 14, paragraph 2, under Rule 36, paragraph 2, second sentence, or under Rule 40, paragraph 3, second sentence, has been filed in due time;
(b) the request for grant of a European patent satisfies the requirements of Rule 41;
(c) the application contains one or more claims in accordance with Article 78, paragraph 1(c), or a reference to a previously filed application in accordance with Rule 40, paragraphs 1(c), 2 and 3, indicating that it replaces also the claims;
(d) the application contains an abstract in accordance with Article 78, paragraph 1(e);
(e) the filing fee and the search fee have been paid in accordance with Rule 17, paragraph 2, Rule 36, paragraph 3, or Rule 38;
(f) the designation of the inventor has been made in accordance with Rule 19, paragraph 1;
(g) where appropriate, the requirements laid down in Rules 52 and 53 concerning the claim to priority have been satisfied;
(h) where appropriate, the requirements of Article 133, paragraph 2, have been satisfied;
(i) the application meets the requirements laid down in Rule 49, paragraph 1, and the applicable requirements prescribed by the President of the European Patent Office under Rule 49, paragraph 2;
(j) the application meets the requirements laid down in Rule 30.

Amended by decision of the Administrative Council of 13.10.2022, which entered into force on 01.02.2023 (OJ 2022 A101, see also Not. EPO OJ 2022 A114). Previous amendments in OJ 2008 p.513 and OJ 2009 p.296.

Art.14(2) Application filed in non-EPO language
Art.78(1) Requirements for application
Art.90(3) Examination as to formal requirements
Art.133(2) Compulsory representation
R.17(2) Period for paying filing and search fee for new application
R.19(1) Content of designation of the inventor
R.30 Requirements of application relating to nucleotide and amino acid sequences
R.36(2) Language of divisional application
R.36(3) Period for paying filing and search fee for divisional application
R.38 Period for paying filing and search fee for application
R.40(1)(c) Replacement of application by previous application
R.40(2) Bibliographic data of previous application
R.40(3) Translation of previous application
R.41 Content of request for grant
R.49 Presentation of the application documents
R.52 Declaration of priority
R.53 Priority documents
Implementation of **Art.90(3)**

1 **Formalities examination**

Examination as to formal requirements under **R.57** concerns the formalities examination to be conducted under **Art.90(3)** after a date of filing has been accorded.

In addition to the ten requirements listed in **R.57**, the Receiving Section also checks (A-III,1.2; A-III,8):

i) clarity and conciseness of the title (**R.41(2)(b)**), preliminary check;
ii) payment of claims fees under **R.45(1)** where appropriate;
iii) matter prohibited by **R.48**, preliminary check;
iv) the certificate of exhibition under **R.25** where the invention has been displayed under **Art.55(1)(b)**;
v) whether the information pursuant to **R.31(1)(c)** and (d) is complete where the application relates to biological material.

Verifying payment of the designation fee and extension fees is also part of the formalities examination. This examination can only be carried out after the expiry of the period for payment of these fees, i.e. six months after publication of the search report.

The examination set out below applies to direct European patent applications, including divisional and new applications. Euro-PCT applications are examined on entry into the European phase for compliance with **R.159** instead of **R.57**.

Where the EPO notices non-compliance with one of the requirements of **R.57(a)** to (d), (**h**) and (i), it will send an invitation under **R.58** to correct the deficiency, the sanction on non-compliance being refusal of the application unless an alternative sanction is specifically provided (**Art.90(5)**). There are special provisions for an invitation to correct and a sanction for non-compliance with each one of the requirements of **R.57(e)** to (g), (j) and the above further requirements i to v, as set out in the sections below.

See **Art.90(5):2** for the point at which a sanction takes effect.

2 **Translation of application (R.57(a))**

Where an application is not filed in one of the official EPO languages, a translation into such a language must be provided according to **Art.14(2)** within two months of filing the application (**R.6(1)**). Where a divisional application is filed in the language of the earlier application and this language is not an official EPO language, a translation must be provided within two months of filing the divisional application (**R.36(2)**). Where the application is filed by reference to a previously filed application, as allowed by **R.40(1)(c)**, and the previous application is not in an official EPO language, a translation into one of these languages must be filed within two months of filing the application, unless the translation is already available to the EPO, according to **R.40(3)**.

The EPO will check under **R.57(a)** whether the translation has been filed on the expiry of the two-month period; if not, it will invite the applicant to rectify the deficiency under **R.58** within a further period of two months (A-III,14).

Non-compliance results in the application being deemed withdrawn under **Art.14(2)**, last sentence.

The EPO will notify the applicant of the loss of rights according to **R.112(1)**. Where applicable, the applicant can ask for a decision on the deemed withdrawal within two months of the notification and show that the translation was filed in due time and the loss of rights finding is incorrect (**R.112(2)**).

The **R.58** period is excluded from further processing by **R.135(2)**. Re-establishment is possible under **Art.122** and **R.136**. It may also be possible to convert the European application to a national application in some contracting states under **Art.135(1)(b)**. Although re-establishment is not ruled out in respect of the two-month periods of **R.6(1)** and **R.40(3)**, it is questionable whether it is available since no rights are lost as a direct consequence of the non-observance of these time limits. The application is only deemed withdrawn upon expiry of the two-month period of **R.58**.

See also A-III,16 and **Art.14(2):3**.

3 **Request for grant (R.57(b))**

The Receiving Section examines whether the Request for Grant form complies with the requirements of **R.41**, several of which are dealt with below (A-III,4.2).

Use of the appropriate Request for Grant form is mandatory (**R.41(1)**). The form already contains a preprinted petition for the grant of a European patent, which is required under **R.41(2)(a)**.

The Request must contain the title of the invention (**R.41(2)(b)**). See the separate section below on the examination of the title.

The Request must properly identify the name, address and nationality of the applicant (**R.41(2)(I)**), and, if a representative has been appointed, the name and address of the representative (**R.41(2)(d)**, see also **R.57(h)**). When there are several applicants, the name, address and nationality of each of them must be given (A-III,4.2.1).

Where applicable, the Request must indicate that it relates to a divisional application and state the number of the earlier application (**R.41(2)(e)**). The same applies to a new application under **Art.61(1)(b)** (**R.41(2)(f)**).

The Request must be signed (**R.41(2)(h)**). The description, claims and drawings are not stated as requiring a signature; hence, they need not be signed separately. Other application documents requiring a signature are a separately filed designation of the inventor (**R.19(1)**) and an authorisation (**R.152**). The documents, with the exception of the authorisation of a representative, may be signed by an appointed representative instead of the applicant. (A-VIII,3.2)

If there is more than one applicant, each applicant (or representative of the applicant) must sign the request for grant and, where applicable, the appointment of a common representative. This also applies if one of the applicants is considered as the common representative under **R.151(1)**, first sentence. The common representative may sign the designation of the inventor and all further documents. An authorisation on behalf of more than one applicant must be signed by all the applicants. (A-VIII,3.4)

The Request must identify the documents annexed to the application (**R.41(2)(i)**).

The Request must contain the designation of the inventor where the applicant is the inventor (**R.41(2)(j)**). Otherwise, the designation must be filed in a separate document according to **R.19(1)**, which document must be signed by the applicant or the applicant's representative. The examination of the designation of the inventor is laid down in **R.57(f)**.

If the Receiving Section notes that the Request for Grant form has not been filed or notes any error in the Request for Grant form (with some exceptions, see **R.57:7**, **R.57:8** and **R.57:12**), it will invite the applicant under **R.58** to remedy the deficiency within two months of invitation. Non-compliance will result in the application being refused under **Art.90(5)**. Further processing is excluded by **R.135(2)**; however, re-establishment is available (**Art.122** and **R.136**). An alternative remedy would be to file an appeal and correct the deficiency when filing grounds (J11/20). In this case, interlocutory revision should be applied (E-XII,7.4.4).

Applicants may request correction of the Request for Grant form of their own volition under **R.139**, first sentence.

4 **Claims (R.57(c))**

Since the presence of one or more claims in the application is not a prerequisite for according a filing date to the application, the presence of claims is not verified on filing but in the subsequent formal examination (see A-III,15).

Applicants have three opportunities to file claims. Firstly, on filing the application documents they may include claims, either by supplying a set of claims or referring to claims in a previous document if incorporation by reference is being used to obtain a filing date. Secondly, if no claims are provided on filing the application, applicants may file claims of their own volition until the EPO invites them to do so under **R.58**. Thirdly, they may be provided within the two-month period set under **R.58**. (A-III,15)

The applicant can use only one of the three opportunities for filing claims. The filing of a second set of claims before receipt of the search report is not permitted under **R.137(1)**. Claims can only be filed by reference to a previous document on the date of filing; later filing of claims by reference is not allowed (A-II,4.1.3.1).

Claims filed after the date of filing must have a basis in the application as filed in order not to extend subject-matter in the sense of **Art.123(2)** (A-III,15). Such claims are an amendment of the application and must be filed in the language of the proceedings (see **R.3(2):1**).

During the formalities examination, it is verified that the application contains at least one claim, as required by **Art.78(1)(c)**. If not, the EPO will invite the applicant under **R.58** to remedy the deficiency within two months of the invitation. Failure to do so will result in refusal of the application according to **Art.90(5)**.

The EPO will notify the applicant of the decision. The two-month period of **R.58** is excluded from further processing according to **R.135(2)**. Re-establishment under **Art.122** and **R.136** is available. An alternative remedy would be to file an appeal and correct the deficiency when filing grounds (**J11/20**). In this case, interlocutory revision will be applied (E-XII,7.4.4).

5 **Abstract (R.57(d))**

Where the abstract, required under **Art.78(1)(e)**, is missing or obviously inappropriate, the Receiving Section will invite the applicant to correct the deficiency under **R.58** (A-III,10.2). If the application contains drawings, and the applicant has not indicated the drawing to accompany the abstract (**R.47(4)**), the search division will decide which figure to publish (A-III,10.3).

Non-compliance will result in refusal of the application under **Art.90(5)** (A-III,16.2). No further processing is possible for the two-month period of **R.58** (**R.135(2)**); however, re-establishment under **Art.122** and **R.136** is available. An alternative remedy would be to file an appeal and correct the deficiency when filing grounds (**J11/20**). In this case, interlocutory revision will be applied (E-XII,7.4.4).

The definitive content of the abstract is the responsibility of the search division (**R.66**) which checks compliance with all requirements of **R.47**.

6 **Filing fee, page fee, divisional fee and search fee (R.57(e))**

The Receiving Section checks whether the filing and search fees as required by **Art.78(2)** have been paid before expiry of one month from the filing of the application (**R.38(1)**). The filing fee is reduced in certain cases if a non-EPO language is used (**R.7a(1)**) (A-XI,9.2.2) and for certain applicants, see **R.7a(3)**. See **Rfees9** for refund of search fees.

For a divisional application under **Art.76(1)** or a new application under **Art.61(1)(b)** the filing and search fees must also be paid within one month of filing the application (**R.36(3)** and **R.17(2)**, respectively). For a divisional of second or higher generation an additional part of the filing fee must also be paid (**R.38(4)**).

A page fee as part of the filing fee may also be required and must be paid within the later of one month of filing the application, the first set of claims or the certified copy of **R.40(3)** (**R.38(3)**).

The EPO does not issue an invitation to pay the filing, page, divisional and search fees. Note that **R.58** does not refer to **R.57(e)**.

If any of these fees is not paid in due time, the application is deemed withdrawn according to **Art.78(2)**. The EPO will notify the applicant of the loss of rights under **R.112(1)**. Further processing according to **Art.121** and **R.135** may be requested for the one-month time limit within two months of the notification of the loss of rights. The further processing fee is equal to 50% of the missing fee(s) (**Rfees2(1)12**).

7 **Designation of inventor (R.57(f))**
An application must designate the inventor according to **Art.81**. The EPO does not verify the accuracy of the designation (**R.19(2)**); it only checks whether the designation conforms to **R.19(1)**. According to **Art.81** the designation must contain a statement indicating the origin of the applicant's right to be granted a patent if the applicant is not the inventor. The entitlement is not verified (**Art.60(3)** and **R.19(2)**). Applicants can request correction of the designation under **R.139** of their own volition during the proceedings before the EPO. A designation of an incorrect inventor may be corrected according to **R.21(1)**. A rectification of an incorrect designation already entered in the Register will be published in the Bulletin (**R.21(2)**). See also A-III,5.

A deficient designation is no ground for opposition (**Art.100**) or revocation (**Art.138**).

If the designation is missing or does not comply with **R.19(1)** (e.g. inventor's name or the signature of the applicant is missing), the EPO will follow the procedure under **R.60**.

8 **Priority claim (R.57(g))**
When claiming the priority of an earlier application, the Request for Grant form must indicate so and state the date and state of filing of the earlier application (**R.41(2)(g)**). See **Art.87**, **Art.88**, **R.52**, **R.53** and **R.139** for the requirements for claiming priority and the addition or correction of a priority claim of the applicant's own volition.

The Receiving Section need not examine the content of the priority document. However, where the document obviously relates to subject-matter different from the application, the applicant should be informed that the priority document does not appear to be the relevant document. (A-III,6.4)

Where a priority right is lost because deficiencies have not been corrected in due time, the applicant is notified. Periods calculated from the priority date that have not yet expired will be recalculated, but the loss of a priority right has no effect on a period that has already expired. (A-III,6.11)

8.1 DECLARATION OF PRIORITY
The declaration of priority is preferably made when filing the application (**R.52(2)**). The declaration should be included in the Request for Grant form (**R.41(2)(g)**); this form may be included with the application or filed later. If the declaration is not included in the Request for Grant form, then the Receiving Section may make a formal objection under **R.57(b)** and request correction under **R.58**. If the priority declaration is not submitted when filing the application, the declaration may still be made within sixteen months from the earliest priority date claimed (**R.52(2)**). In this case, the Receiving Section will not ask for the filing of a new Request for Grant form including the priority declaration (A-III,6.5). For claiming priority, the filing date of the previous application and the state in or for which it was filed must be filed within the sixteen-month period. If one of these indications is missing, then the priority declaration has not been filed, and re-establishment is the appropriate remedy since further processing is excluded for the time limit of **R.52(2)** by **R.135(2)**. The file number of the previous application can be indicated later, as explained below.

The date and state may be corrected voluntarily within the sixteen- / four-month period of **R.52(3)**. The period of **R.52(3)** is excluded from further processing (**R.135(2)**), but re-establishment under **Art.122** and **R.136** is available. (A-III,6.5.3)

If a missing file number is not provided within the sixteen- / four-month period of **R.52(3)**, the EPO will invite the applicant to file it within a period to be specified (**R.59**). The period is specified as two months (A-III,6.5.3). Non-observance of the period of **R.59** results in the loss of the priority right under **Art.90(5)**, last sentence. The period of **R.59** is excluded from further processing according to **R.135(2)**. Re-establishment under **Art.122** and **R.136** is available for this period. See also **R.59:1**; A-III, 6.5.3 and 16.2.

An incorrect or missing file number may also be corrected under **R.139** (A-III,6.5.3), but usually only if the correction is filed in time for a warning to be included in the publication of the application (CLBA IV.A.8.2.2).

8.2 **PRIORITY PERIOD**

Where the date of filing of the application falls after the expiry of the priority period, the EPO may invite the applicant to either correct the priority date within the sixteen- / four-month period of **R.52(3)** or request re-establishment of the priority period within two months of the expiry of the priority period according to **Art.122** and **R.136(1)**. The priority period is extended if **R.134** applies and the late filing of the application outside the priority period may be excused under **R.133** in appropriate cases. (A-III,6.6 and 6.9(i)(a), (b))

8.3 **PRIORITY DOCUMENT**

Before the expiry of sixteen months from the earliest priority date, a certified copy of the previous application (priority document) must be filed (**R.53(1)**) unless one of the exceptions of **R.53(2)** applies.

If no priority document is filed within the sixteen-month period, the EPO will invite the applicant to file the priority document within a two-month period (**R.59**; A-III,6.7.2). The period can be extended under **R.132(2)**. Non-observance of the period results in loss of the priority right under **Art.90(5)**, last sentence. The period of **R.59** is excluded from further processing according to **R.135(2)**. Re-establishment under **Art.122** and **R.136** is available for this period. See also **R.59:1**; A-III,6.7 and A-III,16.2.

8.4 **TRANSLATION OF PRIORITY DOCUMENT**

The EPO will request a translation into an official EPO language of a priority document in a non-EPO language only where the validity of the priority claimed is relevant to the assessment of the patentability of the invention concerned (**R.53(3)**). This invitation is usually sent during the examination or opposition procedure but may sometimes be sent by the search division whilst the examination as to formal requirements is ongoing (A-III,6.8.1). Applicants or proprietors may also send the translation of their own motion (A-III,6.8). Instead of a translation, the applicant or proprietor may file a declaration that the application is a complete translation of the priority document (**R.53(3)**). The EPO will include a copy of the translation in the file if the translation is already available to the EPO (**R.53(3)**, **R.53(2)**).

The translation must be filed within a period specified in the invitation (**R.53(3)**; A-III,6.8). The period can be extended under **R.132(2)**. If no translation is provided before the expiry of the period, the priority right is lost according to **R.53(3)**, 4th sentence. During grant proceedings, further processing under **Art.121** and **R.135** is available; during opposition proceedings, only re-establishment under **Art.122** and **R.136** can be used as a remedy.

9 **Compulsory representation (R.57(h))**

Applicants who do not have a residence or place of business in a contracting state must be represented by a professional representative, according to **Art.133(2)**. They may only file the application themselves; subsequent acts must be carried out by a duly appointed professional representative (**Art.133(2)**). If there are several applicants, each one of them has to comply with **Art.133(2)**.

During the examination of formal requirements under **Art.90(3)**, the Receiving Section checks whether the applicants have complied with the requirements relating to representation as set out in **Art.133(2)**. If they lack necessary representation, the EPO will send an invitation according to **Art.90(4)** and **R.58** to appoint a representative within a period of two months (**R.58**). The first communication of the Receiving Section to the applicant should cover this deficiency, besides other obvious deficiencies (A-III,16.1).

In special cases, the Receiving Section will also request the applicant to file a signed authorisation according to **R.152(1)** within the same period as for appointing a representative (**R.152(3)**). If the authorisation is not filed in time, any act performed by the representative other than the filing of a European patent application or entry into the EPO regional phase within the 31 month time limit is void (**R.152(6)**). (A-VIII,1.9)

If the representative is not appointed within two month period of **R.58**, the application is refused (**Art.90(5)**). Further processing is excluded by **R.135(2)**. Re-establishment under **Art.122** and **R.136** is available. An alternative remedy would be to file an appeal and correct the deficiency when filing grounds (J11/20). In this case, interlocutory revision will be applied (E-XII,7.4.4).

In case of multiple applicants, one applicant or representative must be appointed as the common representative, either by the applicants in the Request for Grant form (**R.41(3)**) or later. Otherwise, the EPO identifies the common representative under **R.151(1)**.

10 **Presentation requirements to be satisfied (R.57(i))**

The Receiving Section checks under **R.57(i)** whether the application documents comply with the presentation requirements of **R.49(2)**. For details of the procedure, see **R.49(2):3**.

11 **Sequence listing (R.57(j))**

Where a sequence listing is required, it must comply with the requirements of **R.30**. See **R.30(3):1** for late filing of a sequence listing. See A-IV,5.1 for sequence listings inserted as a missing part under **R.56**.

12 **Title**

The Receiving Section makes a preliminary check that the title of the invention which will appear in the published application is in general accord with the requirements of **R.41(2)(b)**, i.e. that it clearly and concisely states the technical designation of the invention and excludes fancy names (A-III,7.1). The EPO will make appropriate amendments to the title of its own motion, informing the applicant upon transmission of the search report (A-III,7.2). The communication announcing the forthcoming publication will inform the applicant of the wording of the title in the three official EPO languages. The ultimate responsibility for ensuring that the title conforms to the rules rests with the examining division (A-III,7.2).

A missing title, which is not specified in the Request for Grant form according to **R.41(2)(b)**, will result in a request for correction under **R.58** following the identification of a deficiency under **R.57(b)**.

13 **Claims fees**

An application comprising more than fifteen claims incurs payment of a claims fee in respect of each claim over and above that number (**R.45(1)**).

The claims fees must be paid within one month of filing the first set of claims (**R.45(2)**, first sentence). If not paid within the one-month period, the EPO will invite the applicant to pay claims fees within a further one month from invitation (**R.45(2)**, second sentence) without surcharge.

Where the application was filed by reference to a previous application under **R.40(1)(c)** and it is indicated that the claims of the previous application take the place of claims in the application as filed, the claims fee are due within one month of the date of filing. However, the EPO will send the invitation under **R.45(2)**, second sentence, only after receipt of the copy of the previous application, when it can check how many claims fees are due. (A-III,9)

If a claims fee is not paid within the period of grace, the claim concerned is deemed abandoned (**R.45(3)**) and the applicant is notified to that effect (A-III,9). Further processing under **Art.121** and **R.135** can be used as a remedy.

14 **Prohibited matter**

The application may not contain matter prohibited in the sense of **R.48(1)**.

The Receiving Section will carry out a cursory examination to ensure that the application does not contain such matter (A-III,8). The search division may also inform the Receiving Section of the existence of prohibited matter in the application (A-III,8.1 and 8.2). The examining division also examines whether prohibited matter is present (F-II,7.5).

The Receiving Section may take action to prevent publication of such matter under **R.48(3)**, notifying the applicant of the omitted matter (A-III,8).

15 **Certificate of exhibition**

The certificate of exhibition, accompanied by an identification of the invention, must comply with the requirements of **R.25**. The certificate and identification must be filed within four months of filing the application (**R.25**).

The Receiving Section acknowledges receipt of the certificate and identification of the invention (A-IV,3.2). The Receiving Section draws the applicant's attention to any manifest defects in the certificate or the identification in case it is possible to rectify the deficiencies within the four-month period allowed (A-III,1.2(iii); A-IV,3.2). If not rectified in due time, **Art.55(1)(b)** will not apply to the display at the exhibition (**Art.55(2)**) and the display will be regarded as belonging to the state of the art.

The applicant is notified according to **R.112(1)** if the certificate or identification is not furnished within the time allowed. The applicant may request further processing in respect of this loss of rights according to **Art.121** and **R.135**. (A-IV,3.2)

16 **Deposit of biological material**

Where an application relates to biological material and the material has been deposited, the information pursuant to **R.31(1)(c)** (the depositary institution and the accession number of the deposit) and, where applicable, **R.31(1)(d)** (details of depositor other than the applicant) must be provided within the time limit of **R.31(2)**. Where information pursuant to **R.31(1)(c)** is missing on the date of filing, the accession number must be traceable without ambiguity from the application as filed (see A-IV,4.2).

Where the application refers to a previous application under **R.40(1)(c)** and the previous application does not provide the information of **R.31(1)(c)**, the deficiency must still be rectified in the time limit of **R.31(2)**, even though the EPO can invite the applicant only after receipt of the copy of the previous application or its translation (A-IV,4.1.2).

The examining division assesses whether the available information sufficiently discloses the biological material to make it available to the public (F-III,6.2). If the information is insufficient, the biological material will not be considered disclosed pursuant to **Art.83** (F-III,6.2).

17 **Designation fee**
The designation fee must be paid within six months of the mention of the publication of the search report (**Art.79; R.39(1)**), i.e. within the same time limit in which the request for examination must be filed (**R.70(1)**).

18 **Extension fees and validation fees**
Extension fees and validation fees (for extending to or validating in a non-contracting state) must be paid within the same period as the designation fee. If not paid in due time, the request for extension or validation is deemed withdrawn for the state at issue. A communication of loss of rights will only be issued if a communication of loss of rights is issued in respect of an unpaid designation fee. Only in this case further processing (**Art.121** and **R.135**) is available for payment of the extension and validation fees. A grace period of two months from the expiry of the basic period is available in all cases according to which an extension fee or validation fee can be paid with a 50% surcharge (see OJ 2009 p.603 in respect of extension fees). Re-establishment is not possible. (see **Art.79(2):2.3**; A-III,12.2)

R. 58 Correction of deficiencies in the application documents

Amended by decision of the Administrative Council of 10.12.2024, which entered into force on 01.04.2025 (OJ 2025 A16). The amendment made the text gender-neutral.

If the European patent application does not comply with the requirements of Rule 57(a) to (d), (h) and (i), the European Patent Office shall inform the applicant accordingly and invite them to correct the deficiencies noted within two months. The description, claims and drawings may be amended only to an extent sufficient to remedy such deficiencies.

R.57 Examination as to formal requirements
Implementation of **Art.90(4)**

1 **Invitation to correct deficiencies in the application**
Where the formalities examination under **Art.90(3)** reveals that the application does not comply with the requirement of **R.57(a)** to (d), (**h**) and (**i**), the EPO will invite the applicant to correct them within two months of notification of the invitation (**R.58**). The two-month period of R.58 is not extendable (A-III,16.2). See the notes to **R.57** for the invitation in the cases where the requirements of **R.57(e)** to (g) and (j) are not complied with. **R.135(2)** excludes the two-month period of **R.58** from further processing. Hence, re-establishment according to **Art.122** and **R.136** is available.

The sanction for failure to meet the period of R.58 is the refusal of the application unless another sanction is provided (**Art.90(5)**). The notes to **R.57** mention the specific sanctions provided for not meeting the requirements and any remedies.

If the sanction is refusal, an appeal may be filed as a remedy, correcting the deficiency when filing the statement of grounds; the Receiving Section will grant interlocutory revision (E-XII,7.4.4; **J11/20**). In contrast, if the sanction is deemed withdrawal of the application and a decision under **R.112(2)** is requested, an appeal against a negative decision will merely be a re-examination of the loss of rights communication. The communication will only be regarded as inaccurate if the act was performed in due time. Hence, in such a case, an appeal cannot be used to correct a deficiency (**J11/20** r.16.1).

2 **Amendment of the application documents**

Prior to receipt of the search report, applicants may amend their application only if the Receiving Section has invited them under **R.58** to remedy particular deficiencies (see **R.137(1)**).

After receipt of the search report and before receipt of the first communication from the examining division, applicants may amend the application of their own volition (**Art.123(1)** and **R.137(2)**, A-V,2.1). Any voluntary amendments must be filed together with the response to the communication under **R.70a(1)**, (2) or **R.161(1)** (see **R.137(2)**:1).

Applicants may correct any errors in the application of their own volition by filing a request according to **R.139** (A-V,3).

R. 59 Deficiencies in claiming priority

Amended by decision of the Administrative Council of 10.12.2024, which entered into force on 01.04.2025 (OJ 2025 A16). The amendments made the text gender-neutral.

If the file number of the previous application under Rule 52, paragraph 1, or the copy of that application under Rule 53, paragraph 1, has not been filed in due time, the European Patent Office shall inform the applicant accordingly and invite them to file that file number or copy within a period to be specified.

R.52(1) Content of declaration of priority
R.53(1) Priority document
Implementation of **Art.90(4)**

1 **Correction of file number or filing copy of priority document**

Under **R.59** the applicant will be invited to indicate the file number of the previous application and to file a certified copy thereof if this has not already been done within the sixteen-month period under **R.52(2)** and **R.53(1)** unless one of the exceptions under **R.53(2)** for filing the certified copy applies. In accordance with **Art.90(5)**, the right of priority will be lost if the deficiencies noted in the invitation are not corrected within the period specified. (OJ 2003 se1 p.159)

The EPO specifies a period of two months for responding to the invitation (A-III,6.5.3 for the file number; A-III,6.7.2 for the copy).

Since the period for response is specified by the office, it can be extended by filing a request under **R.132(2)** before the expiry of the period. **R.135(2)** excludes the period of **R.59** from further processing. Re-establishment of rights is available as a legal remedy (**Art.122, R.136**).

See **R.57:8** for more detail.

R. 60 Subsequent designation of the inventor

Implementation of **Art.90(4)**

1 **Omission of the designation of inventor**
If it is difficult to complete a full inventorship determination within sixteen months from the date of filing or priority, at least one person considered most likely to be an inventor may be designated within the relevant time limit in order to avoid the more expensive remedies stated below. After the inventorship determination has been completed, the designation can be rectified under **R.21** if necessary. Note, that a change in designation of inventor may require an oath of inventorship for a corresponding patent application filed in the US.

R. 60(1) If the designation of the inventor has not been made in accordance with Rule 19, the European Patent Office shall inform the applicant that the European patent application will be refused unless the designation is made within sixteen months of the date of filing of the application or, if priority is claimed, of the date of priority, this period being deemed to have been observed if the information is communicated before completion of the technical preparations for the publication of the European patent application.

1 **Invitation to correct designation of the inventor**
The application must designate the inventor according to **Art.81**. Compliance of the designation with the requirements of **R.19(1)** or **R.41(2)(j)** is verified during the formalities examination under **Art.90(3)** and **R.57(f)**. The applicant will be informed of a missing or incorrect designation in accordance with **R.60(1)**. See **R.57:7** for the content of the designation.

2 **Period for filing designation of inventor**
The designation of inventor must be submitted on the date of filing. There is a deficiency if it is not filed together with the application documents or the designation is not correct. In that case the EPO will invite the applicant to file the designation or correction within sixteen months of the date of filing or, if priority is claimed, of the date of priority (**R.60(1)**). The period is deemed to have been observed according to **R.60(1)** if the deficiency is remedied before the completion of the technical preparations for publication of the application (see **R.67(1):1**). The timing of the remedy allows the EPO to mention the designation in the published application as required by **R.20(1)**.

If the designation is not filed before completion of the technical preparations, the application will be published without the designation; since the EPO can check compliance with **R.60(1)** only after said completion, the publication cannot be prevented. After the publication the EPO will subsequently issue a decision to refuse the application under **Art.90(5)**. The refusal can be remedied using further processing under **Art.121** and **R.135**, in spite of the fact that the sixteen-month period has a remedial character (see **R.135(2):1**).

In the case of an early publication of the application, at the request of the applicant or because of an early decision to grant (**Art.93(1)**, **(2)**), the sixteen-month period is not shortened and the applicant may file the designation after the publication of the application if this is still within the period. The application will not be re-published with designation; the designation will be published in the Bulletin and will be available in the Register (reason 3.2; not republishing appears to be in conflict with **R.20(1)**). (**J1/10** r.1-3; A-III,5.4)

The quasi-extension of the sixteen-month period, modelled on the PCT, was included in the provision to give the applicant more time; however, it obfuscates the expiry of the period and complicates the procedure.

R. 60(2) Where, in a divisional application or a new application under Article 61, paragraph 1(b), the designation of the inventor has not been made in accordance with Rule 19, the European Patent Office shall invite the applicant to make the designation within a period to be specified.

Art.61(1)(b) Application filed by non-entitled person
R.19 Content of designation of the inventor

1 **Designation of inventor for divisional and new application**
The designation of inventor for a divisional application and a new application under **Art.61(1)(b)** is also due on filing. If the designation is not made on filing the application, the EPO will invite the applicant to file it within a period to be specified, which is at least two months (**R.132(2)**).

Chapter II *European search report*

R. 61 Content of the European search report

Implementation of **Art.92**

1 **Contents**

The search report transmitted to the applicant contains the search report proper, mentioning the prior art documents retrieved in the search (**R.61**), the search strategy used for retrieving the documents (**R.61(1):2**), and the search opinion, giving an opinion on the patentability of the invention in view of the prior art (**R.62**). The search report is published under **Art.92** and **R.68**. The publication includes the search report proper. Neither the search strategy (OJ 2017 A106 §4(d)) nor the search opinion (**R.62(2)**) are published; they are available via file inspection.

R. 61(1) The European search report shall mention those documents, available to the European Patent Office at the time of drawing up the report, which may be taken into consideration in deciding whether the invention to which the European patent application relates is new and involves an inventive step.

1 **Cited documents**

The search report cites only those prior art documents which are present in the search documentation or to which the search division has access in another way (B-VI,6.1). Although the report usually cites written documents, it may also cite video and audio media fragments available on the internet (B-X,11.6). Instead of a document published before the filing date in an inconvenient language, the search examiner may cite a translation published after the filing date, such as another member of the same patent family (B-VI,6.2).

Apart from the documents mentioned in paragraph 1, the search report could also mention (B-X,8):

- claims not searched because a claims fee was not paid (**R.45(3)**);
- lack of unity: identification of groups of claims searched (**R.64(1)**);
- claims for which no meaningful search could be made (**R.63**), together with reason, e.g. lack of patentability (**Art.52(2)**, **Art.53**), lack of clarity (**Art.84**).

2 **Search strategy**

The search examiner uses a search strategy as set out in B-IV,2 for retrieving relevant prior art documents. Details of the strategy useful for applicants and third parties, such as the databases consulted and keywords used, are included in an information sheet that is attached to each search report drawn up by the EPO. The information sheet is sent to the applicant together with the search report (B-X,3.4). The information sheet is not published but is available via file inspection. (OJ 2017 A106)

R. 61(2) Each citation shall be referred to the claims to which it relates. Where appropriate, relevant parts of the documents cited shall be identified.

R. 61(3) The European search report shall distinguish between cited documents published before the date of priority claimed, between such date of priority and the date of filing, and on or after the date of filing.

1 **Documents published before and after priority and filing date**

The date of filing is the date when documents have been received complying with the requirements of **Art.80**; this date can be later than the date of receipt of the first documents filed if these are insufficient to accord a date of filing.

Only European applications can be regarded as prior rights under **Art.54(3)**. Under the PCT, international, European and national prior rights will be mentioned in the international search report and the international preliminary examination report (R.33.1(c) and R.64.3 PCT), but will not be considered prior art for the international preliminary examination (R.64.3 PCT). The PCT has no equivalent of **Art.55** EPC, i.e. it has no provisions for non-prejudicial disclosure.

If the claimed priority dates cannot be verified, uncertainty will exist as regards their validity and the search will be extended to all published patent applications with an earliest priority date up to the filing date (not the claimed priority date) of the application under consideration (B-VI,3). The search takes into account not only documents published before the earliest priority date, but also intermediate documents, published between the earliest priority date and the filing date of the application under consideration (B-VI,5.2). Since it is the examining division's responsibility to assess the validity of the priority claim, the search division does not conduct a thorough analysis. However, documents pointing to an invalid priority claim are indicated, e.g. an earlier filing for the same invention by the same applicant from which no priority has been claimed, or a USA continuation in part (CIP) of which the priority is claimed but where the priority of the parent of the CIP has not been claimed (B-VI,5.3).

2 **Categories of documents in search report**

The search report uses the following categories to distinguish between the cited documents (B-X,9.2):

X: particularly relevant document when taken alone;
Y: particularly relevant document when taken in combination with another document classified as Y;
A: document defining the general state of the art and not particularly relevant ('A' of German allgemein = general);
O: non-written disclosure ('O' of oral);
P: intermediate document published in the priority interval or on the date of priority (|'P' of priority);
T: document published after the filing or priority date and cited for the principle or theory underlying the invention ('T' of theory);
E: potentially conflicting patent document (prior right) published after the filing date of the application searched but having a filing or priority date earlier than that date; also a patent document having the same priority date ('E' of the German älteres Recht = prior right).
D: document cited in the application searched ('D' of description);
L: document throwing doubt on a priority claim, establishing the publication date of another citation or relevant for double patenting.

The Register also uses the category 'I' to indicate a document which, taken alone, casts doubt on inventive step.

R. 61(4) Any document which refers to an oral disclosure, a use or any other means of disclosure which took place before the date of filing of the European patent application shall be mentioned in the European search report, together with an indication of the date of publication, if any, of the document and the date of the non-written disclosure.

1 **Oral disclosure**
The search mentions a non-written disclosure only if there is a written confirmation or if the searcher is convinced that the facts can be proved. **Art.54** does consider a public oral description as prior art (B-VI,2). The PCT only recognises this as prior art if it is substantiated by a written disclosure.

R. 61(5) The European search report shall be drawn up in the language of the proceedings.

R. 61(6) The European search report shall contain the classification of the subject-matter of the European patent application in accordance with the international classification.

1 **Classification of documents in search report**
The code is the IPC (International Patent Classification) code (**R.8**).
A classification is given for each invention when the application lacks unity (B-V,3.3).

R. 62 Extended European search report

Implementation of **Art.92**

1 **Opinion on patentability**
To increase its efficiency the EPO issues the search report and the first opinion on patentability together. The measure helps to streamline the granting procedure, reduce the time applications are pending, and encourage early withdrawals. Since the BEST project (see **Art.15:1**) the search examiner is also the primary substantive examiner and it increases efficiency if the examiner prepares an opinion on patentability already at the search stage. As the opinion will cause more amendments to be filed upon entering substantive examination, it also helps to reduce the average time for granting a patent to the desired 36 months.

Since the Convention does not provide for integration of the search and substantive examination, the EPO has introduced the extended European search report (EESR) as an interim solution. The EESR contains the European search report and a non-binding opinion on whether the application and the invention to which it relates seem to meet the requirements of the Convention. Although the opinion is prepared in the context of the search, it is not part of the search report drawn up under **Art.92** and it is independent of the subsequent substantive examination under **Art.94**. The opinion may be used by applicants to assess the patentability of their invention and decide whether to continue prosecution or not.

Search and examination have been further integrated by making a response to an opinion that notes deficiencies compulsory. The response is to be filed before expiry of the period for requesting examination (**R.70a**). The contents of the opinion and the compulsory response make the search opinion effectively a first **Art.94(3)** communication. However, since it is drawn up during search and not during substantive examination, it is, in a legal sense, not an **Art.94(3)** communication and it is therefore called an opinion.

Moreover, the opinion does not bind the EPO, as emphasised by the word 'seem' in **R.62(1)**. (OJ 2005 p.435 §I.1)

R. 62(1) The European search report shall be accompanied by an opinion on whether the application and the invention to which it relates seem to meet the requirements of this Convention, unless a communication under Rule 71, paragraph 1 or 3, can be issued.

R.71(1) Communication of the Examining Division
R.71(3) Invitation to approve text for grant

1 **Extended European search report**
The EPO will draft an opinion on patentability, also called 'search opinion', to accompany the search report for European applications and Euro-PCT applications for which a supplementary search report must be drawn up under **Art.153(7)**. The opinion may include objections, suggestions to overcome the objections and positive statements about patentability (B-XI,3).

The 'unless' in the provision refers to the case where the examination fee has been paid before the search report is transmitted to the applicant and the right to the communication under **R.70(2)** has been waived (**R.10(4)**). In this special case substantive examination can start immediately after completion of the search report and no opinion is sent. Instead, a first communication of the examining division under **R.71(1)** or **R.71(3)** is sent. The **R.71(1)** communication is issued as soon as possible after completion of the search report if the application does not meet the requirements of the EPC (C-VI,3). This communication is legally binding, in contrast with the search opinion. A **R.71(3)** communication will be issued if the application is ready for grant and a final search does not reveal additional prior rights (C-VI,3). In all other cases the search report is accompanied by the opinion on patentability.

If the EESR contains a positive opinion, the applicant can pay the examination fee in the usual way. The applicant will then receive a **R.71(3)** communication, provided the top-up search carried out about eighteen months after the filing date (**Art.92:6**) does not reveal additional prior art under **Art.54(3)** and the examining division concurs with the opinion. (B-XI,3.9)

If the EESR contains objections to patentability, the applicant must comment on the objections within six months from publication of the search report (**R.70a**). The applicant may file voluntary amendments in the same period (**R.137(2)**). Substantive examination starts after completion of the requirements set out in **R.70**.

R. 62(2) The opinion under paragraph 1 shall not be published together with the search report.

1 **Transmittal and non-publication of opinion**
When the EPO transmits the search report to the applicant under **R.65**, it includes the opinion on patentability (B-X,12).

The opinion is not published together with the search report under **Art.92**, because it is not part of the search report. However, it is accessible to the public. Once the EESR is despatched to the applicant, it is part of the file and becomes available for inspection under **Art.128(4)** after publication of the application. (A-VI,1.3)

R. 62a Applications containing a plurality of independent claims

Inserted, in force since 01.04.2010 (OJ 2009 p.299).
Implementation of **Art.92**

1 **General**
The purpose of **R.62a** is to reduce the number of independent claims in the same category to within the scope of **R.43(2)** and define the invention more clearly at the start of the search stage, thereby reducing the problems of multiple independent claims in the same category during search and examination and providing legal certainty for the public about the scope of the application at an early stage. **R.62a** makes **R.43(2)** enforceable already at the search stage.

R.62a also applies to supplementary Europeans searches under **R.164(1)** and to searches under **R.164(2)** (**R.164(2)(c)**; B-VIII,4.5).

R. 62a(1) If the European Patent Office considers that the claims as filed do not comply with Rule 43, paragraph 2, it shall invite the applicant to indicate, within a period of two months, the claims complying with Rule 43, paragraph 2, on the basis of which the search is to be carried out. If the applicant fails to provide such an indication in due time, the search shall be carried out on the basis of the first claim in each category.

R.43(2) Several independent claims in one category

1 **Multiple independent claims during search**
If a search division considers that an application contains multiple independent claims in the same category that do not comply with **R.43(2)**, it will invite the applicant to indicate claims complying with **R.43(2)** on which to base the search. The invitation need not be reasoned. The applicant may respond by indicating claims complying with **R.43(2)** to be searched. These claims must be pending and must not have been deemed abandoned because of non-payment of claims fees (B-VIII,4.4). Claims dependent on an unsearched independent claim will likewise not be searched (B-VIII,4.6).

Alternatively, the applicant may contest the opinion of the search examiner, arguing that the independent claims do comply with the law or that apparently independent claims are in fact dependent. See **R.43(4):1** for the definition of an independent claim. If the search examiner is persuaded that the objection was not justified, all claims will be searched. If the applicant's arguments are not convincing, the search will be based on the first independent claim in each category (B-VIII,4.2.2). At this stage of the prosecution, amendments to the application are not yet admitted (**R.137(1)**).

The period for response to the invitation is two months (**R.62a(1)**, first sentence). If no response is filed in time, the search will be based on the first independent claim in each category (**R.62a(1)**, second sentence). Further processing is ruled out by **R.135(2)** to allow the search report to be established before the publication of the application; re-establishment is available.

2 **Multiple independent claims and non-unity**
The EPC does not provide for payment of a further search fee in respect of claims not complying with **R.43(2)**. Such further search fees are only provided for non-unitary inventions (**R.64**).

When an application to be searched has two non-unitary independent claims in the same category, the search examiner can choose between (1) objecting to multiple independent claims and sending the applicant an invitation under **R.62a(1)** to indicate the claims to be searched and (2) issuing a non-unity objection and inviting the applicant under **R.64** to pay further search fees. The first option does not provide an opportunity to have both claims searched. The choice of the examiner depends on the specific application being searched. Where both procedures must be applied, the EPO sends the invitation under **R.62a(1)** first. (B-VIII,4.5).

R. 62a(2) The Examining Division shall invite the applicant to restrict the claims to the subject-matter searched unless it finds that the objection under paragraph 1 was not justified.

1 **Restriction of claims during examination**
In case of multiple independent claims in the same category, the examining division will consider whether one of the exceptions under **R.43(2)** applies and raise an objection if not. Any amended claims filed in response may not pertain to subject-matter that was not searched in accordance with **R.62a(2)** (**R.137(5)**, second sentence). The examining division therefore invites the applicant under **R.62a(2)** to restrict the claims to the searched subject-matter together with the **R.43(2)** objection if an invitation under **R.62a(1)** was sent during the search. (F-IV,3.3)

The applicant may respond to the invitation under **R.62a(2)** by arguing that the objection under **R.43(2)** is not justified. If the examiner agrees, the invitation will be withdrawn and an additional search will be carried out (C-IV,7.3). If the applicant does not convince the examiner and the applicant does not restrict the claims as requested, the application may be refused under **Art.97(2)** for not meeting the requirement of **R.43(2)** (F-IV,3.3).

Subject-matter covered by claims not searched on account of a justified invitation under **R.62a(1)** may not be used for amending claims (**R.137(5)**, second sentence). Protection for such subject-matter can only be obtained by filing a divisional application. If the application is amended to provide a set of claims complying with **R.43(2)** but containing one or more claims directed to subject-matter excluded from the search in accordance with **R.62a(2)**, an objection under **R.137(5)**, second sentence, arises and such amendments will not be admitted. However, before such a decision can be taken, the applicant will be allowed to comment on the underlying issue of whether or not the claims in respect of which the invitation under **R.62a(2)** was sent did in fact comply with **R.43(2)**. (F-IV,3.3)

R. 63 Incomplete search

Amended, in force since 01.04.2010. Amended **R.63** applies to applications for which the search report or the supplementary search report is drawn up on or after 01.04.2010. (OJ 2009 p.299)
Implementation of **Art.84** and **Art.92**

1 **Unsearchable subject-matter**
R.63 provides an exception to the EPO's obligation to carry out a search for each application. The EPO will not search claims that are not properly drafted or relate to unpatentable subject-matter. In such cases it will invite the applicant to indicate the subject-matter to be searched. The indication, to be submitted before the search, should improve the quality of the search. If the applicant does not respond or the indicated subject-matter does not over-

come the deficiency, the EPO will issue a partial search report or a declaration that no search could be carried out. Unsearched subject-matter cannot be used anymore for amending the claims.

R.63 should induce applicants to comply with the clarity requirement of **Art.84** already at the search stage and avoid additional searches during the substantive examination.

R. 63(1) If the European Patent Office considers that the European patent application fails to such an extent to comply with this Convention that it is impossible to carry out a meaningful search regarding the state of the art on the basis of all or some of the subject-matter claimed, it shall invite the applicant to file, within a period of two months, a statement indicating the subject-matter to be searched.

1 **Reasons for incomplete search**

According to **R.63** the search division will not search applications or parts thereof that do not comply with the requirements of the EPC to such an extent that no meaningful search can be made. Important requirements are that the subject-matter must have technical character (**Art.52(2)**), not be excluded from patentability (**Art.53**) and be susceptible of industrial application (**Art.57**), and be disclosed in the application in a manner sufficiently clear and complete for it to be carried out (**Art.83**), and that the claims are clear, concise and supported by the description (**Art.84**), . As an example, a claim having eight independent numerical parameters was regarded unclear and therefore unsearchable (EP1540227).

R.63 may also be applied where the claims extend the subject-matter of the application as filed (**Art.123(2)**) or of the parent application (**Art.76(1)**, B-VIII,3(iv)). Non-compliance may also occur for only some of the claims or for part of a claim (B-VIII,1).

The search division determines what is or is not 'meaningful' as a question of fact. **R.63** should not be invoked because a search is difficult. **T1242/04** held that **R.63** relates only to the practicability of a search and not to the potential relevance of its results in subsequent substantive examination (see hn. I, r.8.5). B-VIII,3 gives examples where **R.63** may be applied.

R.63 constitutes an exception to the EPO's obligation to carry out a search as an essential element of the grant procedure and as such must be interpreted narrowly (**T1242/04** r.8.2). Hence, a declaration under **R.63** may be issued only in exceptional cases in which the claimed subject-matter, i.e. the entire set of claims including all independent and dependent claims, clearly has no technical character (**T1242/04** hn. II).

If the application refers to a document not available to the search division, it issues an invitation under **R.63** if the document appears essential for understanding the invention. The applicant can either submit the document or argue it is not essential. (B-IV,1.3)

1.1 SUBJECT-MATTER LACKING TECHNICAL CHARACTER UNDER ART.52(2) AND (3)

The search division will not search subject-matter excluded from patentability because it lacks technical character (**Art.52(2), (3)**).

A feature that is non-technical when taken in isolation may nonetheless contribute to the technical character if in the context of the invention it contributes to produce a technical effect. Claimed features must therefore be analysed in the light of the description and drawings to determine if they produce a technical effect and form part of a technical solution of a technical problem. The search opinion must indicate which claimed features do not contribute to the technical character of the invention. (B-VIII,2.2)

Hence, a claim merely relating to no more than a method of doing business will not be searched. A declaration under **R.63** to this effect will take the place of the search report. Where the claimed subject-matter involves technical means, a search report or partial search report will be issued. When the technical means are notorious knowledge, i.e. so conventional that they were widely available to everyone at the date of filing and no documentary evidence is considered required because of their notoriety, such as a standard computer, the search report will state so and will not cite any document (Not. EPO, OJ 2007 p.592; **T1411/08** r.4.1, 4.2). A search report not citing any document can only be issued for computer-implemented business methods (B-VIII,2.2.1).

The existence of notorious knowledge cannot be reasonably disputed. This should be distinguished from common general knowledge, which can in general be reasonably questioned (B-VIII,2.2.1; **Art.56:2.3**). The examining division must provide documentary evidence if the notoriety of the knowledge is challenged (**T2467/09** r.7-10).

1.2 SUBJECT-MATTER EXCLUDED FROM PATENTABILITY UNDER ART.53

The EPO will not search subject-matter excluded from patentability because its commercial exploitation contravenes morality (**Art.53(a)**), it relates to a plant or animal variety or a biological method for the production of plants or animals (**Art.53(b)**), or it relates to a method for medical treatment or diagnosis (**Art.53(c)**).

A claim relating to a medical method should be searched in the case that the determining technical feature is the effect of a substance, which can be searched (B-VIII,2.1).

1.3 SUBJECT-MATTER NOT COMPLYING WITH ART.83 AND 84

Important requirements are those for sufficiency of disclosure (**Art.83**), clarity and conciseness of the claims and support by the description (**Art.84**) (see also OJ 2000 p.228). Non-compliance with **Art.83** and **84** often occurs as a direct result of the applicant's drafting style. The following four examples clarify the problems posed by this non-compliance.

A broad claim supported by a limited disclosure covering a small part of the scope of the claim may lack support and sufficient disclosure. Such a claim may be searched only on the basis of the narrower, disclosed invention or even disclosed examples (B-III,3.6; B-VIII,3(i)). Search examiners may base their search on what they consider to be the extent to which the claims are defensible in a subsequent substantive examination.

A large number of claims or possibilities within a claim is not concise. The large number may make it burdensome to determine the subject-matter for which protection is sought and make a complete search de facto impossible or useless in view of the indefensibility of the claims or claim (B-VIII,3(ii); see example **T1873/06**). See also **R.62a** for a restriction on the number of independent claims.

A claim defined in terms of desiderata may violate **Art.83** and/or **Art.84**, leading to an incomplete search (OJ 2000 p.228).

The definition of a claim in terms of a particular parameter may make a meaningful search impossible, e.g. because the prior art does not use the parameter; in such a case a partial search may be made for the disclosed examples or the way in which the parameter is obtained (B-VIII,3(iii)).

2 **Statement indicating subject-matter to be searched**
If the search division is of the opinion that a normal search cannot be carried out, it will invite the applicant to file a statement more clearly defining the subject-matter to be searched (**R.63(1)**). The invitation is reasoned (B-VIII,3.1). The statement may (Not. EPO OJ 2009 p.533 §3.2; B-VIII,3.2):
- indicate that part of the description, e.g. a specific embodiment, which can be used for interpreting the claims; or
- consist of an explanation in the form of an improved claim wording; the amended claims will only become a formal amendment if requested so in the response to the extended European search report.

Note, that a search based on the statement may conflict with the EPC, because amendment of claims at this stage is prohibited by **R.137(1)**, **R.63** not qualifying as an exception (see also OJ 2009 p.533 §7.1 and the excuse in B-VIII,3.2.2), and the search must be based on the claims and not on a part of the description according to **Art.92**.

The applicant may, instead of indicating subject-matter to be searched, argue that the claimed subject-matter is searchable (B-VIII,3.2).

Any improvement of the claims during the substantive examination to improve compliance with **Art.53, 83** and **84** will very likely introduce unsearched subject-matter and will not be admissible under **R.137(5)**. Hence, the statement filed before the search will probably limit the scope of the claims, without a possibility to enlarge the scope later-on during substantive examination.

Any further interaction with the search examiner after filing the statement is not provided for in the EPC and Guidelines.

R. 63(2) If the statement under paragraph 1 is not filed in due time, or if it is not sufficient to overcome the deficiency noted under paragraph 1, the European Patent Office shall either issue a reasoned declaration stating that the European patent application fails to such an extent to comply with this Convention that it is impossible to carry out a meaningful search regarding the state of the art on the basis of all or some of the subject-matter claimed or, as far as is practicable, draw up a partial search report. The reasoned declaration or the partial search report shall be considered, for the purposes of subsequent proceedings, as the European search report.

1 **Procedure before search division**
The applicant must file the statement indicating the subject-matter to be searched within two months from invitation (**R.63(1)**). Further processing is not possible according to **R.135(2)** to allow publication of the search report together with the application; however, re-establishment is available.

If the statement is not filed within two months from invitation, if it is not sufficient to overcome the deficiencies, or if the arguments that the claimed subject-matter is searchable are not regarded convincing, the EPO will issue either a declaration that no meaningful search could be carried out or a partial search report covering only some of the subject-matter claimed. A statement may be insufficient if it refers to subject-matter without basis in the application as filed.

The declaration that no search could be carried out must be reasoned according to **R.63(2)**, first sentence, i.e. the search division must state why it regards the claims as not searchable. The partial search report must also give the reasons for restricting the search (B-X,8(iii)). The applicant cannot contest the opinion of the search division at the search stage; however, the applicant may argue against the reasoning of the search division during substantive examination (see **R.63(3)**).

If a document cited in the application appears to be essential for the search and the document is not available at the EPO, the search division will ask the applicant to file a copy of it. If the applicant fails to comply, a partial search may result or a declaration that no meaningful search could be made. (B-IV,1.3)

2 **Additional searches**
The EPO can carry out an additional search because of, e.g., amendments to the claims (but see **R.137(5)**), clarification of obscurities (**R.63**), reversal of the provisional opinion of the search division on unity (**R.64**) or exclusion from patentability, or imperfections in the initial search. (B-II,4.2; C-IV,7.3;). A search during examination can also be carried out for Euro-PCT applications under **R.164(2)** and supplementary European searches are carried out for certain Euro-PCT applications under **Art.153(6)**.

In the exceptional case where a **R.63** declaration has been issued, it is not always necessary to carry out an additional search. An objection of lack of inventive step may be raised without documented prior art, e.g. if the claimed subject-matter is obvious from the common general knowledge. However, if the claim features do not form part of the common general knowledge and the applicant does not acknowledge them to be known, an additional search must be carried out. (T1242/04 r.9.2)

R. 63(3) When a partial search report has been drawn up, the Examining Division shall invite the applicant to restrict the claims to the subject-matter searched unless it finds that the objection under paragraph 1 was not justified.

1 **Procedure before examining division**
If the search division has issued a partial search report, the examining division will raise the underlying objection, e.g. under **Art.52(2)** and invite the applicant to restrict the claims to the subject-matter searched, unless the examining division finds that the restriction of the search was not justified (**R.63(3)**) or the applicant addressed the objection by amendments filed in response to the search opinion. The applicant, may in response, contest the restricted search. If the argument convinces the examiner, no restriction of the claims is necessary (**R.63(3)**) and an additional search may be carried out (B-VIII,3.2; C-IV,7.3). The applicant may also file amended claims, these may however not relate to subject-matter not searched pursuant to a justified invitation under **R.63** (**R.137(5)**, second sentence; H-IV,4.1.1)).

If the applicant does not convince the examiner and does not restrict the claims as requested, the application will not meet the requirements of the EPC and may be refused under **Art.97(2)**.

Since **R.137(5)** does not allow amended claims to relate to subject-matter not searched pursuant to a justified invitation under **R.63**, protection for such subject-matter can only by pursued in a divisional application.

If a declaration that no search could be carried has been issued, no invitation under **R.63(3)** is issued. However, if the applicant successfully refutes the underlying objections during examination an additional search will be carried out (C-IV,7.3(i)).

R. 64 European search report where the invention lacks unity

Implementation of **Art.82** and **Art.92**

R. 64(1) If the European Patent Office considers that the European patent application does not comply with the requirement of unity of invention, it shall draw up a partial search report on those parts of the application which relate to the invention, or the group of inventions within the meaning of Article 82, first mentioned in the claims. It shall inform the applicant that, for the European search report to cover the other inventions, a further search fee must be paid, in respect of each invention involved, within a period of two months. The European search report shall be drawn up for the parts of the application relating to inventions in respect of which search fees have been paid.

Amended, in force since 01.04.2010 (OJ 2009 p.299).
Art.82 Unity of invention

1 **Non-unity opinion**

The search division assesses whether the application complies with the unity requirement of **Art.82**, i.e. whether the application relates to one invention or a linked group of inventions. See **R.44** for the definition of unity of invention. The search division considers unity using the prior art at hand, which may vary depending on the stage of proceedings. For example, where the assessment is carried out before the search, i.e. *a priori* assessment, it may be evident from the information contained in the application and the common general knowledge of the skilled person that different claims solve different problems and so do not relate to a single general inventive concept. The search may reveal prior art which discloses or renders obvious the solution to the unifying technical problem between the claims which thus do not relate to a single general inventive concept, i.e. *a posteriori* assessment. (F-V,3)

The opinion of the EPO on unity may change during prosecution of the application in the light of new facts and evidence (B-VII,1.4). Hence, a non-unity objection may be raised for the first time by the examining division.

2 **Procedure before search division**

If the search division considers that the application does not comply with the unity requirement, it will draw up a partial search report for the invention first mentioned in the claims (**R.64(1)**, first sentence). It will send the applicant a communication including the partial search report and a provisional opinion on the patentability of the invention first mentioned in the claims, a specification of the separate inventions, and the reasoning for the finding of non-unity (OJ 2017 A20; B-VII,1.1, 1.2; B-XI,5; F-V, 4.1). When raising a non-unity objection, the search division must provide the minimum reasoning set out in F-V,3.3.1. The opinion and the reasoning allow applicants to assess their chances of success in overcoming the objection. No reply is required and, if filed, will not be considered by the search division.

The communication also invites the applicant to pay a further search fee equal to the search fee (**Rfees2(1)2**) for each further invention to be searched. The period for paying further search fees is two months from the invitation (**R.64(1)**, second sentence; B-VII,1.2). For payment of further search fees, see **R.64(1):2.1** below.

After completion of the search, the search division issues the extended European search report consisting of a search report and an opinion covering the first invention and any further invention(s) for which the search fee has been paid (**R.64(1)**, third sentence; B-XI,5). The search opinion also contains the non-unity objection and the reasoning for it.

If the search can be extended to all inventions of a non-unitary application without much effort, e.g. in case of unity a posteriori and/or conceptually very close inventions, the search division will not ask for further search fees to be paid and will issue a complete search report and search opinion including the non-unity opinion (B-VII,2.2). The non-unity opinion cannot be contested in the search stage; this can only be done during the substantive examination (see **R.64(2):1**).

2.1 FURTHER SEARCH FEES

The period for paying further search fees is two months from invitation (**R.64(1)**, second sentence).

There is no obligation for applicants to pay any further search fees (F-V,4.2). If no further search fees are paid, the applicant is deemed to have elected the searched invention (C-III,3.2.1); no further inventions will be searched. Subject-matter that has not been searched will not be examined by the examining division (**G2/92**).

When applicants pay fewer further search fees than the number of further inventions, they must indicate to which further inventions the fees pertain. Without such an indication the purpose of the payment is not clear and the examiner will issue a communication under Rfees6(2) to establish the purpose.

If the automatic debiting procedure is used, applicants must inform the EPO within the two-month period if they do not want all or any of the further inventions to be searched. Otherwise all the further search fees will be debited automatically on the last day of the period (AAD.5.1; B-VII,1.2; **Rfees5(2):3**).

R.135(2) excludes the period for paying further search fees from further processing. Re-establishment under **Art.122** is available.

3 Procedure before examining division

The examining division is obliged to review the non-unity opinion of the search division (C-III,3.2; F-V,11.1; **T631/97** r.3.9.2). Decision **T631/97** interpreted an unclear paragraph in **G2/92** (r.3) relating to this obligation in the above sense. The examining division will also consider the question of unity even if the search division did not raise it (C-III,3.2). The examining division can, however, issue no invitation under **R.64** to pay further search fees.

Since the BEST project, the search examiner and the substantive examiner are the same person (see **Art.15:1**). Hence, an ex officio review of the non-unity opinion during the substantive examination appears unlikely. Instead, applicants who do not agree with the opinion should present their arguments in favour of unity in their response to the search opinion and request a review of the non-unity opinion.

If the examiner considers the opinion justified, the examination will proceed on the basis of the searched invention or, where several inventions have been searched, the searched invention selected by the applicant (C-III,3.2.2). Unless the non-unity opinion is withdrawn by the examiner, non-payment of further search fees deprives applicants of the right to choose which invention to pursue before the examining division; the applicant is limited to the searched invention (**G2/92** hn). The non-unity issue will not be the subject of an interlocutory decision. An applicant desiring a review of the unity objection by a board of appeal, should have the application refused in first instance on the ground of non-unity and appeal the refusal. Lack of substantiation of a non-unity decision may be regarded as a substantial procedural violation, justifying reimbursement of an appeal fee under **R.103** (**T708/00** r.20).

An applicant may not pursue an application for subject-matter for which the applicant paid no further search fees when requested to do so in a (justified) invitation under **R.64(1)** (**G2/92** hn). Hence, if the applicant amends the application to restrict the claims to one originally claimed invention, thereby complying with **Art.82**, but this claimed invention is unsearched because the applicant paid no further search fee for it in response to a justified invitation under **R.64(1)**, the application can be refused under **R.64** in line with **G2/92**. **R.137(5)** cannot be invoked. For Euro-PCT applications, **R.164(1)** respectively **R.164(2)(c)** can be cited instead of **R.64**. If no supplementary European search is carried out, the applicant must restrict to an invention that was searched by the EPO as ISA or SISA, or as part of the search under **R.164(2)(c)**; only limitations of the search on the ground of lack of unity can be invoked (H-II,6.2).

The prohibition of **G2/92** on pursuing an application for subject-matter for which no further search fees have been paid applies to inventions; it does not apply to features which are disclosed in the description in combination with the searched invention, even if one of the non-searched claims also specifies the feature (**T988/14**, r.2.2)

Any further search fee paid for a non-unitary invention gives entitlement to a refund under **Rfees9(2)** in respect of the search fee for a divisional application filed for this invention.

If the examiner considers the non-unity opinion unjustified, the examination will proceed on the basis of the unitary inventions, possibly supplemented by an additional search ordered by the examiner (B-II,4.2(iii)). Further search fees paid by the applicant will be refunded only if a refund has been requested under **R.64(2)**.

4 Basis of substantive examination

The EPO will only carry out the substantive examination of an invention if the invention has been searched (**G2/92** r.2). When a search fee has been paid for more than one invention, the applicant must inform the EPO on which searched invention the substantive examination is to be based (C-III,3.2.2). There are several opportunities for the applicant to inform the EPO of the invention to be examined.

If at the beginning of the substantive examination the examiner maintains the objection of lack of unity and the applicant has not yet stated on which one of several searched inventions the examination is to be based, the examiner will invite the applicant to do so and to limit the application by excising the parts belonging to the other inventions. The applicant may file divisional applications for the other inventions (C-III,3.2.2; 3.3; F-V,5.1). The applicant may also request an appealable decision on the set of claims that allegedly lacks unity of invention and appeal the refusal of the application.

Once the applicant has limited the claims to one searched invention, the examining division will refuse to admit amendments involving switching to a different searched invention under **R.137(3)** (C-III,3.5; H-II,6.1; **T158/12**).

During the examination, the applicant may request a refund of further search fees under **R.64(2)** if the examining division finds that the non-unity opinion of the Search Division was not justified.

The above procedure applies to a non-unitary direct European application. The procedure for a non-unitary Euro-PCT application is governed by **R.164**.

5 Period for paying further search fees

The period for paying further search fees is two months from invitation (**R.64(1)**, second sentence). **R.135(2)** excludes the period from further processing. Re-establishment under **Art.122** and **R.136** is available.

R. 64(2) Any fee paid under paragraph 1 shall be refunded if, during the examination of the European patent application, the applicant requests a refund and the Examining Division finds that the communication under paragraph 1 was not justified.

1 **Refund of further search fee**

If an applicant has paid further search fees under **R.64(1)** and considers that the application does comply with the requirement of unity, the applicant should request a refund of one or more of the further search fees paid under **R.64(2)**. The request will be dealt with by the examining division, not by the search division (**R.64(2)**). According to **T2703/18**, the examining division may complete the reasoning of the search division, but may not replace it by a new reasoning.

Since **R.64(2)** refers to the communication in **R.64(1)** expressing the non-unity opinion, the decision of the examining division need not deal with other objections such as an objection that the search report was not drawn up in accordance with the Guidelines. In such a case the examining division may arrange for an additional search if it considers a search report incomplete. (**J24/96** r.4)

If the request is to be refused, this will be communicated in an **Art.94(3)** communication giving the applicant a chance to comment before a decision on the matter is issued. (C-III,3.4)

A decision on the request for refund of further search fees is usually given in the form of an interlocutory decision. If the matter is decided early in the grant procedure, an interlocutory decision should be issued promptly. If a decision is reached near the end of the procedure, an interlocutory decision on the request should be issued with the **R.71(3)** communication or the decision on the request should be included in the decision refusing the application. (C-III,3.4)

The interlocutory decision on a request for refund is separately appealable (C-III,3.4). The appeal of such an interlocutory decision runs in parallel with the grant proceedings (**J21/09** r.11) and is usually decided well after grant of the patent. Hence, its outcome cannot affect the grant proceedings. If the board of appeal decides that the non-unity decision of the examining division is to be reversed and the further search fees refunded, the scope of the already granted claims complying with the non-unity decision of the examining division cannot be broadened anymore (see e.g. **J24/96**, where the decision of the board of appeal was issued three years after the decision to grant). If an applicant is not interested in broadening the scope of the claims but only in a refund of further search fees, the applicant should request an appealable interlocutory decision when requesting a refund of the further search fees.

If an applicant wishes to have the option of obtaining a patent covering all originally claimed subject-matter following a reversal of the non-unity decision in appeal, the applicant should request an appealable decision on the set of claims which allegedly lacks unity of invention and appeal the refusal of the application. Such a refusal is normally understood to implicitly or explicitly contain a refusal of the refund as well (**T1414/18**). If the refusal of the application is also based on other grounds, e.g. lack of novelty of the searched claims, the applicant should address these objections in the first instance proceedings by filing auxiliary requests where appropriate, in view of Art.12 RPBA.

R. 65 Transmittal of the European search report

Immediately after it has been drawn up, the European search report shall be transmitted to the applicant. The European Patent Office shall make available copies of any cited documents.

Amended by decision of the Administrative Council of 13.10.2022, which entered into force on 01.02.2023 (OJ 2022 A101, see also Not. EPO OJ 2022 A114). Implementation of Art.92

1 **Transmission of the search report**

Together with the search report, the EPO also forwards to the applicant:
- an annex to the search report listing the families of the patent documents cited in the search report (B-X,9; OJ 1999 p.90);
- information relating to the restriction of the subject of the search due to the non-payment of claims fees, a finding of non-unity or the impossibility of carrying out a meaningful or complete search (B-VIII.3.3; B-X,8);
- the translation of the title into the two other EPO languages (B-X,7);
- the definitive content of the abstract (B-X,7);
- the opinion on patentability (**R.62(1)**);
- an information sheet about the search strategy (B-X,3.4).

The annex listing the patent families of cited patent documents was helpful in finding equivalent publications in other languages when machine translation and easy online access to patent documents did not exist.

The EPO makes available the documents cited in search reports to the applicant through the Mailbox or by post, even if the documents are protected by copyright (Not. EPO OJ 2022 A114 §10). A machine translation of Korean and Japanese application documents is also made available. As of 01.10.2024, paper copies of patent documents are no longer sent by mail, but will need to be obtained from Espacenet (OJ 2024 A68).

Additional copies of the cited documents may be ordered from the EPO at a charge fixed under **Rfees3**.

Video and/or audio media fragments available on the internet are converted into a non-patent literature citation. The bibliographic data, as stated in the search report, contains the URL of the original location on the internet. If the cited disclosure ceases to be available on the internet, a copy will be made available to the applicant on request (B-X,11.6).

It may happen that, after completing a search report, the examiner discovers further relevant documents (e.g. in a later search for a related application). Such documents may be used in the examination (B-IV,3.2).

R. 66 Definitive content of the abstract

Upon drawing up the European search report, the European Patent Office shall determine the definitive content of the abstract and transmit it to the applicant together with the search report.

Implementation of **Art.85** and **Art.92**

1 **Purpose and content of abstract**

The sole purpose of the abstract is to provide information to the public (**Art.85**). The dissemination of information is the responsibility of the EPO. Hence, the EPO assesses the contents of the abstract. The search division examines the abstract, checking that it constitutes an efficient instrument for searching (F-II,2.2). After the search division has approved or modified the abstract, the EPO will transmit the definitive abstract to the applicant together with the search report (F-II,2.6).

Chapter III *Publication of the European patent application*

R. 67 Technical preparations for publication

Implementation of **Art.93(1)**

R. 67(1) The President of the European Patent Office shall determine when the technical preparations for publication of the European patent application are deemed to have been completed.

1 **Completion of technical preparation**
The preparations are deemed to have been completed at the end of the day that comes five weeks before expiry of the eighteenth month from the day of filing or, if priority is claimed, from the earliest date of priority (Dec. Pres. OJ 2007 se3 D.1).

Example: priority date: Tuesday 18.04.2017, expiry of the eighteen months for publication under **Art.93(1)**: Thursday 18.10.2018, 5 weeks before that date: Thursday 13.09.2018. The preparations are deemed to have been completed at the end of Thursday 13.09.2018 (adapted from **J11/80**, Summary of facts and submissions I and II).

Beware, **R.134** for extension of periods due to holidays does not apply to the eighteen-month period and the 5-week period.

After completion of the technical preparations, the application will be published. The publication is always on a Wednesday (OJ 1997 p.542).

Note, that the technical preparations for PCT applications are completed by the 15th day prior to the date of publication (AG-IP §9.013) and the publication date is a Thursday.

R. 67(2) The application shall not be published if it has been finally refused or withdrawn or is deemed to be withdrawn before the termination of the technical preparations for publication.

1 **Non-publication of application**
The application will not be published if it has been finally refused, withdrawn or deemed withdrawn before the completion of the technical preparations as set out in paragraph 1. In the case illustrated above, it would be necessary to withdraw the application before the end of Thursday 13.09.2018 to guarantee non-publication.

The EPO is not obliged to prevent publication of an application which is withdrawn after the completion of the technical preparations as set out in **R.67(1)**. The EPO endeavours to prevent publication in such cases as well, provided the actual circumstances still so permit. This is checked on a case-by-case basis. The EPO cannot guarantee non-publication (**J5/81**). In practice, publication can often be prevented if the declaration of withdrawal is received by the Receiving Section at the latest two weeks before the scheduled date of publication (Not. EPO OJ 2006 p.406 §3). If the scheduled date of publication in the above case is Wednesday 17.10.2018, then the withdrawal must have been received at the latest on Wednesday 03.10.2018.

The courtesy communication 'Notification of European publication number and information on the application of Article 67(3) EPC' informing the applicant of the date on which the technical preparations are completed, the publication number and the intended publication date of the application (A-VI,1.1), issued about four weeks before the scheduled date of publication, can be regarded as a final notification or warning of the date of publication (OJ 2006 p.406 §3).

To ensure immediate recognition of a declaration of withdrawal intended to prevent publication, the applicant should send the declaration to the EPO separately, not combined with other documents, clearly indicating the intention of preventing the forthcoming publication. (Not. EPO OJ 2006 p.406) Note that this notice mentions fax filing, which is no longer possible as of 01.07.2024 (Dec. Pres. OJ 2024 A41).

See **Art.93(1):3** for deferred publication after abandonment of a priority claim.

2 **Invalid publication**

An invalid publication, i.e. the publication of an application withdrawn before publication, is not a publication under **Art.93** and does not give rise to a prior right effect under **Art.54(3)**, but only under **Art.54(2)** (G-IV,5.1.1). Moreover, it gives no provisional protection under **Art.67(1)**. See also **Art.93(1):4**.

If the publication of the application according to **Art.93(1)** can still be prevented, it might be possible that the publication of the mention thereof in the Bulletin according to **Art.129(a)** can no longer be prevented. In that case, the erroneous mention will be revoked by a subsequently published announcement in the Bulletin, thereby avoiding the file being opened for inspection (**Art.128(4)**).

3 **Conditional and unconditional withdrawal**

The application can only be withdrawn by a clear, signed declaration; if the request of the withdrawal is ambiguous, the Receiving Section must invite applicants to clarify the request (J11/80). Use of EPO form 1018 is recommended (A-VI,1.2). Applicants are bound by the request to withdraw. The only exception is withdrawal by mistake, for instance as the result of a wrong file number being provided, in which case **R.139** may be applicable (J4/97) if legal certainty for third parties is not compromised.

A withdrawal can be made on condition of non-publication. This takes into account the procedural peculiarity that applicants who make their declaration of withdrawal later than five weeks before expiry of the eighteen-month period cannot know whether publication can still be prevented. (A-VI,1.2)

When requesting the EPO to withdraw an application to avoid publication, any pending priority application should also be withdrawn, because otherwise the subject-matter might still be published.

R. 68 Form of the publication of European patent applications and European search reports

Implementation of **Art.93(1)** and **Art.92**

R. 68(1) The publication of the European patent application shall contain the description, the claims and any drawings as filed, and the abstract, or, if these documents making up the application were not filed in an official language of the European Patent Office, a translation in the language of the proceedings, and, in an annex, the European search report, where it is available before the termination of the technical preparations for publication. If the search report or the abstract is not published at the same time as the application, it shall be published separately.

1 **Contents of publication**
The description, claims and drawings of an application are published as filed, according to **R.68(1)**. The abstract, possibly amended by the EPO under **R.66**, is included in the publication. Any sequence listing filed at the date of filing of the application will also be published with the application (Not. EPO OJ 2021 A97 §15).

If the application was not filed in an official EPO language, the text in the language of filing is the 'application as filed' (**Art.70(2)**). However, **Art.14(5)** stipulates that the application must be published in an official EPO language. Therefore, the lex specialis in the second half of the first sentence of **R.68(1)** makes it clear that in such a case the translation into the language of the proceedings will be published. The provisions of **Art.14(2)**, second sentence and **Art.70(2)** are unaffected. (CA/PL29/06 Add.1)

Where application documents (in particular, drawings) do not meet the presentation requirements laid down in the Implementing Regulations and replacement documents have been filed, it is the latter replacement documents that are published. Replacement documents are not used where the original application documents are of such bad quality that any improvement would result in an extension of subject-matter. (A-VI,1.3)

If the search report is available in time, it will be included in the publication; otherwise it will be published separately (**R.68(1)**). A partial search report, drawn up when there is a lack of unity (**R.64(1)**), is not published but is available in the file in the European Patent Register. Only the final search report covering all inventions for which fees are paid is published. (B-X,1)

R. 68(2) The President of the European Patent Office shall determine the form of the publication of the application and the data to be included. The same shall apply where the European search report and the abstract are published separately.

1 **Form of publication**
European patent applications, European search reports and European patent specifications are published in electronic form only by means of a publication server from which they can be downloaded (Dec. Pres. OJ 2007 se3 D.3 Art.1(1)). Publication on paper has been discontinued (OJ 2005 p.126).

The publication server at the EPO website 'https://data.epo.org/publication-server' provides free access to European patent applications and patents downloadable in sgml/xml and pdf formats. The site gives also direct access to the Register entries of the selected patent document (OJ 2005 p.126 §I.1). The server is available 24 hours a day, 7 days a week.

A list of patent and non-patent literature cited in the description will be included at the end of applications and specifications published as from 13.09.2006. The list is made by the EPO and is for information only and does not form part of the application or specification. (Dec. Pres. OJ 2007 se3 D.4)

2 **Identification of the publication**
The published application is given a serial publication number and an identification of the type of publication it corresponds to (A-VI,1.3; OJ 2001 p.117). The publication numbers are consecutive numbers given according to the order of publication of the applications; the patent number is the same as the publication number.

The EPO uses the following publication document codes:

A1 Patent application, front page with abstract (as approved or determined by search division) and search report

A2 Patent application and front page with abstract (as approved or determined by search division) without search report

A3 Search report and front page with abstract (as approved or determined by search division)

A4 Supplementary search report

A8 Corrected title page of an A document

A9 Complete reprint of a corrected A document

B1 Patent specification

B2 Patent specification as amended in opposition

B3 Patent specification as amended after limitation

B8 Corrected title page of a B document

B9 Complete reprint of a corrected B document

Applications are given an application number already before the publication; this number is hence different from the publication number. As of 01.01.2002, the serial number of an application reflects the filing year in its first two positions. The remaining digits form a serial number taken from the range assigned to the place where the application is filed. Separate ranges are assigned to each place of filing such as EPO Munich or The Hague for applications filed on paper, to all national patent offices under **Art.75(1)(b)**, and to online filing and Euro-PCT applications (OJ 2001 p.465). In all proceedings before the EPO, the application and the possible patent are customarily identified by the application number.

The EPO additionally uses the code A0 (A zero) in certain databases to identify Euro-PCT applications that have entered the European phase for which no translation had to be filed under **R.159(1)(a)** and which are hence not published by the EPO as the designated office (see **Art.153(3)**). These applications are also visible as 'A1' entries in Espacenet and are also included, as a front page only, on the EPO Publication Server (e.g. EP3068804A1). The code C0 (C zero) is used for unitary patents (see **UPR.16**).

R. 68(3) The designated Contracting States shall be indicated in the published application.

1 **Designations in published application**
The publication of the application indicates all contracting states party to the EPC on the date of filing of the application (A-VI,1.3). The publication also indicates all extension states. See **Art.79:1** for changes in the designation system.

R. 68(4) If the claims were not filed on the date of filing of the application, this shall be indicated when the application is published. If, before the termination of the technical preparations for publication of the application, the claims have been amended under Rule 137, paragraph 2, the new or amended claims shall be included in the publication in addition to the claims as filed.

Amended, in force since 01.04.2009. The amendment deleted the superfluous word 'patent'. (OJ 2008 p.513)
R.137(2) Voluntary amendment of application

1 **Publication of late-filed claims**
The first sentence in **R.68(4)** concerns cases where a European patent application is accorded a date of filing in accordance with **R.40(1)**, but the claims are only filed later. Since this later filing of claims may result in extension of subject-matter within the meaning of **Art.123(2)**, the fact that the claims were only filed after the date of filing is pointed out when the application is published. (CA/PL29/06, A-VI,1.3)

The publication of the amended claims is important, especially if the amended claims are broader than the original claims, because of the provisional protection afforded by the published application (**Art.67**).

R. 69 Information about publication

Amended, in force since 01.04.2010 (OJ 2009 p.299).
Implementation of **Art.92**

R. 69(1) The European Patent Office shall inform the applicant of the date on which the European Patent Bulletin mentions the publication of the European search report and shall draw their attention to Rule 70, paragraph 1, Article 94, paragraph 2, and Rule 70a, paragraph 1.

Amended by decision of the Administrative Council of 10.12.2024, which entered into force on 01.04.2025 (OJ 2025 A16). The amendment introduced gender-neutral language.
Art.94(2) Sanction on not filing request for examination
R.70(1) Request for examination
R.70a(1) Compulsory response to opinion attached to search report

1 **Information about publication of search report**
The communication under **R.69(1)** informs applicants of the date on which the Bulletin (**Art.129**) was published that mentions the search report and, to avoid a loss of rights, draws their attention to the period of six months from that date for filing the request for examination and paying the examination fee (**R.70(1)**) and to the consequences of not filing the request in due time (**Art.94(2)**). It reminds applicants of the requirement of **R.70a(1)** to respond to a negative search opinion within the same six-month period. The communication also draws the applicant's attention to the period of **R.39(1)** for the payment of designation, extension and validation fees (A-VI,2.1).

The communication is normally dispatched a few days, typically one week, after the actual date of publication of the search report, both for A1 and A3 publications.

R. 69(2) If a date of publication is specified in the communication under paragraph 1 which is later than the actual date of publication, that later date shall be the decisive date as regards the periods referred to in Rule 70, paragraph 1, and Rule 70a, paragraph 1, unless the error is obvious.

R.70(1) Request for examination
R.70a(1) Compulsory response to opinion attached to search report

1 **Erroneous date in communication**
The six-month period for filing the request for examination normally runs from the actual date of publication of the search report (**R.70(1)**). However, if the communication under **R.69(1)** erroneously mentions a later date of publication, this date will be the trigger for the six-month period for filing the request for examination and the response to the search opinion, unless the error in the date of publication is obvious (**R.69(2)**, second sentence). Although not stated explicitly, the later date should also be the trigger for the six-month period for payment of the designation and extension fees.

R. 70 Request for examination

Implementation of **Art.94(1)**

R. 70(1) The applicant may request examination of the European patent application up to six months after the date on which the European Patent Bulletin mentions the publication of the European search report. The request may not be withdrawn.

1 **Period for filing request for examination**
According to **Art.94(1)**, requesting examination includes filing a request for examination and payment of the examination fee (**Rfees2(6)**). Usually the request for examination is made on filing of the application, because it is pre-printed on the Request for Grant form. The completion of the request is then determined by the payment of the examination fee.

The examination fee may be paid at any time between the filing of the request for examination (the due date, A-X,5.2.2) and six months of publication of the search report (**R.70(1)**). The communication of **R.69(1)**, informing the applicant of the date of publication of the search report, draws the attention of the applicant to the time limit for payment of the examination fee (**R.70(1)**). Although the time limit for filing the request for examination and filing the mandatory response under **R.70a(1)** is the same, both acts need not be carried out simultaneously.

The applicant has to observe the six-month period without any further reminder from the EPO. An early request for examination and payment of the examination fee, e.g. on filing the application, has the advantage that the six-month time limit need not be monitored and any fee increases may be avoided. **R.70(2)**, along with **Rfees11**, provides for the refund of the examination fee where payment has been made before transmission of the search report and the application is withdrawn or deemed withdrawn after the transmission, e.g. because of prejudicial prior art mentioned in the search report. Payment near the end of the six-month period may have financial advantages for the applicant and the payment can be made contingent on the contents of the search report.

If the applicant has filed an automatic debit order, the examination fee will usually be debited on the last day of the six-month period (AAD.5.1(a)). According to AAD.5.1(c), however, the examination fee will be debited earlier on the date of receipt of any waiver for the invitation under **R.70(2)**, which may be made in the Request for Grant form, and on the date of receipt of any request for accelerated examination under the PACE programme (see OJ 2015 A93).

The six-month period usually expires about 24 months from the date of filing, or, if priority has been claimed, from the date of priority, because the search report is normally published immediately after eighteen months from priority or filing (**Art.93(1)**). A delay in the publication of the search report results in a later expiry of the period for filing the examination. Where the applicant requests an early publication under **Art.93(1)(b)**, i.e. before eighteen months from priority or filing, the search report might also be published early, resulting in an earlier expiry of the period for filing the request for examination and also an earlier start to substantive examination.

The six-month period for requesting examination for a divisional application is triggered by the mention of the publication of the search report for the divisional application (A-IV,1.8; see **Art.76(1):6**).

The period may be extended on account of non-working days (**R.134(1)**) or mail interruption (**R.134(2), (5)**). The period may be interrupted when the proceedings are stayed because a third party has opened entitlement proceedings (**R.14(1)**) or when the proceedings are interrupted on account of death or legal incapacity of the applicant or the representative (**R.142(3)**).

If applicants do not desire to proceed further with the application after receipt of the search report, they need not take any action and the application will be deemed withdrawn under **Art.94(2)**. Only if they have paid the examination fee early and waived the invitation under **R.70(2)** should they withdraw the application to receive a partial refund of the examination fee under **Rfees11(b)** if the search report is issued together with the first examining communication (as mentioned in OJ 2015 A94).

2 **Effect of non-payment and remedies**

If the examination fee is not paid within the six-month period, the application will be deemed withdrawn under **Art.94(2)**. The EPO will notify the loss of rights according to **R.112(1)** (A-VI,2.3). The applicant can request further processing under **Art.121** and **R.135** by paying the examination fee and the further processing fee within two months of notification of the loss of rights. The further processing fee is 50% of the examination fee (**Rfees2(1)12**). Re-establishment is not available for the six-month period for requesting examination but it is available for the two-month period for requesting further processing (**R.136(3)**).

See **Art.94(2):1** for the moment in time the loss of rights ensues.

3 **Prohibition to withdraw request for examination**

The prohibition in the last sentence of **R.70(1)** to withdraw the request for examination provides legal certainty, as it avoids problems about the conditions of withdrawal and the possibility of subsequently filing a new request. Nevertheless, the applicant can still terminate the grant procedure after having filed the request for examination by withdrawing the application (**Art.67(4)**), not filing a response to a communication (**Art.94(4)**) or not paying a renewal fee (**Art.86(1)**).

R. 70(2) If the request for examination has been filed before the European search report has been transmitted to the applicant, the European Patent Office shall invite the applicant to indicate, within a period to be specified, whether they wish to proceed further with the application, and shall give them the opportunity to comment on the search report and to amend, where appropriate, the description, claims and drawings.

Amended by decision of the Administrative Council of 10.12.2024, which entered into force on 01.04.2025 (OJ 2025 A16). The amendment was introduction of gender-neutral language.

1 **Confirmation of request for examination**

R.70(2) relates to the case where the applicant has filed the request for examination, i.e. filed the written request and paid the examination fee, before receipt of the search report. It obliges the EPO to invite applicants after transmission of the search report to indicate whether it is desired to continue with the application, because the content of the search report may have changed the applicant's opinion about continuing with grant proceedings.

The **R.70(2)** communication also gives the applicant an opportunity to comment on the search report and, where appropriate, amend the application in view of the prior art cited in the search report, as allowed under **Art.123(1)** and **R.137(2)** (**R.70(2)**). If the opinion attached to the search report is negative, the applicant is invited to respond by filing comments and/or amendments together with the indication to proceed further (**R.70a(2)**).

The relevant date for determining whether an invitation pursuant to **R.70(2)** is required or not is, according to **R.70(2)**, 'the transmission of the search report' to the applicant under **R.65**. Although the EPO has not provided guidance, this date is presumably the date of despatch rather than the date of notification of the search report since the word 'transmission' implies an action on the part of the EPO.

R.70(2) is applied to all Euro-PCT applications for which a supplementary search report is drawn up. For such applications the request for examination must be filed on entry into the European phase, which is before receipt of the supplementary search report. (E-IX,2.5.3)

2 **Procedure, withdrawal and refund**

The EPO specifies the period in which the applicant must file the indication whether to proceed (**R.70(2)**). It sets the period as six months from the publication of the search report (E-VIII,1.2), giving the same expiry date as the six-month period of **R.70(1)**, meaning that this period is not triggered by a notification of a communication. Hence, the examination can start at the latest on the same date for both routes.

For Euro-PCT applications where a supplementary search report is drawn up, the period for filing the indication whether to proceed is six months from the notification of the invitation under **R.70(2)** (E-IX,2.5.3). Since the supplementary search report is not published, the publication date cannot be used to trigger the period for response. The invitation is usually sent a few weeks after notification of the supplementary search report.

On receipt of the applicants' indication that they desire to proceed further, the Receiving Section transfers its responsibility to an examining division for the substantive examination of the application (**R.10(3)**). If the applicant withdraws the application, the examination fee will be refunded at a rate depending on the date of withdrawal (see **Rfees11**). The withdrawal may be made conditional on the refund (E-VIII,7.3).

An applicant's response to the search opinion is interpreted as the confirmation required by **R.70(2)**, even where not explicitly expressed as such (C-II,1.1).

If applicants desire not to continue, e.g. in view of prejudicial prior art mentioned in the search report, they can actively withdraw the application. Alternatively, the applicant can omit to respond to the invitation according to **R.70(2)**; after expiry of the six-month period the EPO will deem the application to be withdrawn under **R.70(3)** and notify the applicant according to **R.112(1)** of the loss of rights. Since the substantive examination has not yet begun, the examination fee is refunded in full (**Rfees11(a)**).

Failure to file the indication within the period of **R.70(2)** may be remedied by further processing according to **Art.121** and **R.135**. If no response has been filed to the **R.70a(2)** communication either, two further processing fees have to be paid, both at the fixed fee level (**Rfees2(1)12**), one fee for late filing the indication to proceed further and one fee for late filing the response to the search opinion. If the response to the search opinion cannot be prepared in time, it is therefore recommended that the indication is still filed within the six-month period to reduce the total further processing costs.

3 **Waiver of invitation**

The early payment of the examination fee may be made unconditional by waiving the right to an invitation pursuant to **R.70(2)**. A waiver has been preprinted on the Request for Grant form and can be put into effect by placing a cross in the relevant place. The waiver relieves the applicant from observing the six-month period of **R.70(2)** and accelerates the procedure, because the examining division need not wait for the applicant's reply to the **R.70(2)** invitation but can assume responsibility the day the search report is transmitted to the applicant (**R.10(4)**). The search report is issued together with a first communication under **Art.94(3)** and **R.71(1)** instead of the search opinion of **R.62**, or together with a communication under **R.71(3)** if there are no objections (**R.62(1)**, OJ 2015 A94).

If applicants desire to proceed further with the application after having taken cognisance of the search report, they need not take any action when a waiver has been filed. If, instead, they want to withdraw the application, they should withdraw the application before expiry of the period for replying to the communication under **Art.94(3)** that was issued together with the search report in order to obtain a 50% refund of the examination fee (see **Rfees11(b)**).

R. 70(3) If the applicant fails to reply in due time to the invitation under paragraph 2, the application shall be deemed to be withdrawn.

Chapter IV *Examination by the Examining Division*

R. 70a Response to the extended European search report

Inserted, in force since 01.04.2010. **R.70a** applies to applications for which the search report or the supplementary search report is drawn up on or after 01.04.2010. (OJ 2009 p.299)

Amended by decision of the Administrative Council of 10.12.2024, which entered into force on 01.04.2025 (OJ 2025 A16). Paragraphs (1) and (2) were amended by introducing gender-neutral language.

Implementation of **Art.94**

1 **Compulsory response to opinion**

R.70a obliges the applicant to respond to a negative opinion of the search division within six months from publication of the search report, i.e. within the period for requesting examination under **R.70(1)**. Note, that both acts need not be carried out simultaneously. The mandatory response should speed up the examination procedure, because the EPO does not have to issue a first communication under **Art.94(3)** identical to the opinion in the case the applicant has not responded to the opinion, as was common under previous practice. The requirement to respond effectively makes the opinion a communication under **Art.94(3)** as far as the applicant is concerned, although legally it is not. Hence, the EPO cannot directly refuse the application following the response.

The EPO may refuse an application if the response to a first communication from the examining division under **Art.94(3)** does not bring the application closer to grant. This can be avoided by including a conditional request for oral proceedings in the response (see **Art.94(3):5**; C-III,4).

See **Art.94(3):4** in case the first communication is a summons to oral proceedings.

It should be noted that **R.70a** appears to violate **Art.94. Art.94(3)** obliges the EPO to invite the applicant to file observations and to amend the application if substantive examination reveals deficiencies. This examination can only be started after the request for examination has been filed according to **Art.94(1). R.70a** compels applicants to correct deficiencies at the same time they file their request for examination. Hence, the EPO carries out a substantive examination of the application before the applicant has filed the request for examination and the applicant must file a first response before the EPO can start the actual examination.

This legal problem has arisen because the diplomatic revision conference in 2000 did not have sufficient time to amend **Art.15, 92** and **94** and merge the search and examination. Note, that in 1999 one of the triggers for the revision was to give a sound legal basis to the BEST project (see **Art.15:1**) (OJ 1999 p.545 §5).

R. 70a(1) In the opinion accompanying the European search report the European Patent Office shall give the applicant the opportunity to comment on the extended European search report and, where appropriate, invite them to correct any deficiencies noted in the opinion accompanying the European search report and to amend the description, claims and drawings within the period referred to in Rule 70, paragraph 1.

R.70(1) Request for examination

1 **Invitation to comment on opinion**
According to current EPO practice, the invitation under **R.70a(1)** is not actually included in the opinion accompanying the European search report but in a later communication. When the EPO sends the applicant the extended search report (comprising the search report and search opinion), it merely draws attention to the requirements of **R.70a**. The invitation under **R.70a(1)** is included in a separate communication pursuant to **R.69** informing the applicant of the date on which the European Patent Bulletin mentioned the publication of the European search report. In this communication the applicant's attention is drawn to the six-month period for paying the designation fee, filing a request for examination and paying the examination fee, commenting on the objections raised in the search opinion and filing amendments to the description, claims and drawings correcting deficiencies noted in the search opinion.

A response to the search opinion is not required if either the opinion is positive because there are no deficiencies and the examining division can issue the **R.71(3)** communication, or the opinion is negative but there are only minor deficiencies which the examining division will correct in the **R.71(3)** communication. A response to the search opinion is required if the opinion is negative and there are deficiencies which the applicant must correct.

The mandatory response to the invitation and any voluntary amendment must both be filed within the period of **R.70(1)**, i.e. within six months from publication of the search report. The consequence of not responding to the invitation is given in **R.70a(3)**. Admission of any voluntary amendment filed after expiry of this period is at the discretion of the examiner (**R.137(3)**).

R. 70a(2) In the case referred to in Rule 70, paragraph 2, or if a supplementary European search report is drawn up on a Euro-PCT-application, the European Patent Office shall give the applicant the opportunity to comment on the extended European search report and, where appropriate, invite them to correct any deficiencies noted in the opinion accompanying the European search report and to amend the description, claims and drawings within the period specified for indicating whether they wish to proceed further with the application.

R.70(2) Confirmation of early filed request for examination

1 **Invitation where request for examination was filed early**
If the request for examination has been filed before transmission of the search report by early payment of the examination fee (**R.70(2)**), the period to respond to the opinion and to file any voluntary amendment will be equal to the period specified in the **R.70(2)** communication for indicating whether the applicant wishes to proceed further with the application. The Guidelines specify this period as six months from publication of the search report (E-VIII,1.2). This period is extendible only exceptionally (E-VIII,1.6.1).

When the EPO has drawn up a supplementary search report and opinion for a Euro-PCT application, it will also invite the applicant to respond to deficiencies noted in the opinion and file any voluntary amendment (**R.70a(2)**; E-IX,2.5.3). The response must be filed in the period for confirming that the prosecution of the application is to be continued (**R.70a(2)**), i.e. within six months from notification of the invitation pursuant to **R.70(2)** and **R.70a(2)** (E-IX,2.5.3; Not. EPO OJ 2009 p.533 §5.1.5). See also **R.159(1):6**.

If the applicant files the request for examination early and waives the right to a **R.70(2)** communication, no search opinion and no **R.70a** communication is issued. Instead, an **Art.94(3)** communication is issued in the case where deficiencies exist and a **R.71(3)** communication is issued in the alternative.

R. 70a(3) If the applicant neither complies with nor comments on an invitation in accordance with paragraph 1 or 2, the application shall be deemed to be withdrawn.

1 **Sanction on not responding to invitation**
If the applicant does not file comments or amendments in response to an invitation within the period of **R.70a(1)** or (2), the application will be deemed withdrawn. Further processing under **Art.121** and **R.135** is available.

Since a positive opinion does not include an invitation, a response to the opinion is voluntary in this case.

R. 70b Request for a copy of search results

Inserted, in force since 01.01.2011. **R.70b** applies to all European applications and international applications filed on or after 01.01.2011. (OJ 2009 p.585)
Implementation of **Art.124(1)**

1 **Prior art information of priority application**
R.70b implements part of the procedure under **Art.124(1)** and **R.141(1)**, (2) in which the applicant must provide a copy of the search results drawn up in respect of a priority application. The complete procedure is set out in **R.141(1):2**.

R. 70b(1) Where the European Patent Office notes, at the time the Examining Division assumes responsibility, that a copy referred to in Rule 141, paragraph 1, has not been filed by the applicant and is not deemed to be duly filed under Rule 141, paragraph 2, it shall invite the applicant to file, within a period of two months, the copy or a statement that the results of the search referred to in Rule 141, paragraph 1, are not available to them.

R.141(1) Request for search results of priority application
Amended by decision of the Administrative Council of 10.12.2024, which entered into force on 01.04.2025 (OJ 2025 A16). The amendment was introduction of gender-neutral language.

1 **Invitation to provide search results**
Applicants must file with the EPO a copy of search results drawn up in respect of any priority application (**R.141(1)**). They should do so when filing a direct European application or on entering the EP regional phase with a Euro-PCT application. No copy which is already available to the EPO needs to be filed (see **R.141(2)**).

The EPO checks for compliance when the examining division assumes responsibility under **R.10**. If neither the applicant has filed a copy nor the EPO has included a copy in the file, the EPO will invite the applicant to file a copy or a statement that no search results are available (**R.70b(1)**).

The applicant must respond to the invitation within two months (**R.70b(1)**). If no response is filed, the application will be deemed withdrawn (**R.70b(2)**). Further processing under **Art.121** is available as a remedy.

A response to the **R.70b** invitation for a divisional application is not required if the search results have already been filed for the parent application (OJ 2010 p.410 §3.2).

R. 70b(2) If the applicant fails to reply in due time to the invitation under paragraph 1, the European patent application shall be deemed to be withdrawn.

R. 71 Examination procedure

Amended by decision of the Administrative Council of 10.12.2024, which entered into force on 01.04.2025 (OJ 2025 A16). The amendments were in paragraphs (5) and (6) to gender-neutral language.
Paragraphs (1) and (2) are an implementation of **Art.94(3)**;
Paragraphs (3) to (7) of **Art.97(1)**.

R. 71(1) In any communication under Article 94, paragraph 3, the Examining Division shall, where appropriate, invite the applicant to correct any deficiencies noted and to amend the description, claims and drawings within a period to be specified.

Art.94(3) Examination of the European patent application
Implementation of **Art.94(3)**

1 **Invitation to correct deficiencies**
Where the examiner notes any deficiencies in the application, i.e. notes that the application does not meet one or more requirements of the EPC, the examiner invites the applicant to correct them and amend the application. The invitation has a compulsory character: the applicant either amends the application or convinces the examiner that the application already meets the requirements of the EPC. If the applicant's response neither amends nor convinces, the application will be refused, provided that the requirements of **Art.113(1)** and **Art.116** are met.

The invitation will only be sent 'where appropriate', i.e. where the examiner expects a positive reaction. If no positive reaction is expected, no invitation will be sent and the application will be refused, provided that the requirements of **Art.113(1)** and **Art.116** are met (C-IV,3).

The applicant must reply within a period to be specified. The duration of the period, consequences of non-observance and remedies are dealt with in the notes to **Art.94(4)**.

The applicant must file a first substantive response to the search opinion if the opinion notes deficiencies (**R.70a**; **R.161(1)**). The response should include any voluntary amendment the applicant wishes to make (**R.137(2)**).

R. 71(2) Any communication under Article 94, paragraph 3, shall contain a reasoned statement covering, where appropriate, all the grounds against the grant of the European patent.

Art.94(3) Examination of the European patent application
Implementation of **Art.94(3)**

1 **Reasoned statement in communication**
An **Art.94(3)** communication must contain reasoned objections against the grant of a patent. The burden of proof that the adduced facts and evidence support the objections lies initially with the examining division. Accordingly, prior art documents must be cited in such a way that the applicant can check the conclusions without difficulty. (C-III,4.1.1)

The 'where appropriate' in the rule makes the extent to which the grounds are covered in a communication a matter of procedural expediency, at the examiner's discretion (**J32/95** r.3.2). If, for example, the claims are not clear, the first communication should cover the ground of clarity and, after the meaning of all features in the claims has been made clear, the second communication should cover the grounds of novelty and inventive step.

The examiner must give a reasoned statement of the grounds of objection under **R.71(2)** in view of the applicant's right to be heard under **Art.113(1)**. A communication under **Art.94(3)** must not merely state the examiner's finding that a requirement of the EPC is not met but also set out the essential legal and factual reasoning leading to that finding because, otherwise, a refusal of the application based on that finding contravenes **Art.113(1)** unless another communication issued in the procedure gave the reasoning (**T951/92** hn.II).

R. 71(3) Before the Examining Division decides to grant the European patent, it shall inform the applicant of the text in which it intends to grant it and of the related bibliographic data. In this communication the Examining Division shall invite the applicant to pay the fee for grant and publishing and to file a translation of the claims in the two official languages of the European Patent Office other than the language of the proceedings within four months.

Amended, in force since 01.04.2012 (OJ 2010 p.637).
Implementation of **Art.97(1)**

1 **Amendment of grant procedure**
The decision of the Administrative Council of 26.10.2010 amended **R.71** and inserted **R.71a**. The amendment defines the procedure involving amendments and/or corrections following a **R.71(3)** communication and postpones the formal requirements of payment of fees and filing translations until after agreement has been reached on the text of the patent to be granted. It simplifies the procedure and reduces delays.

2 **General**
R.71(3) to (7) are an implementation of **Art.97(1)** and provide details of the procedure from the moment the examining division intends to grant the patent to the approval of the text to be granted. An overview of the procedure is given in Not. EPO OJ 2012 p.52.

When the EPO considers that a patent can be granted on an application, it sends the applicant a **R.71(3)** communication in which it informs the applicant of the text it intends to grant and the bibliographic data and invites the applicant to pay the fee for grant and publishing and to file translations of the claims. The communication will also inform the applicant if any claims fees are due (**R.71(4)**). The applicant can approve of the text by paying the fees and filing the translations (**R.71(5)**), after which the decision to grant will be taken (**Art.97(1)** and **R.71a**) and the patent will be published (**Art.98**).

If the applicant does not agree with the proposed text, the applicant can request a grant based on a different text in response to the **R.71(3)** communication (**R.71(6)**); in that case neither fees need be paid nor translations filed. The EPO may send a new **R.71(3)** communication if it approves the different text. If it disapproves, the examination will be resumed (**R.71(6)**), which may involve an immediate refusal.

The sanction for non-payment of the fees or not filing the translation is set out in **R.71(7)**.

3 R.71(3) communication

When the examining division is of the opinion that the application is ready for grant, it must obtain the applicant's approval of the text to comply with **Art.113(2)** before it can take a decision. The approval is obtained by the procedure set out in **R.71(3)-(7)**.

3.1 TEXT INTENDED FOR GRANT

In the **R.71(3)** communication the examining division informs the applicant of the text in which it intends to grant the patent. The 'text' the provision refers to corresponds to the documents making up the 'Druckexemplar', i.e. the description, claims and drawings (**T1003/19** r.2.4.4). The transmission of the complete text allows the applicant to check the text without the need to assemble the text from previous communications, as is customary with some national patent offices. It also informs the applicant of the related bibliographic data.

The text intended for grant may include amendments and corrections made by the examining division on its own initiative. The examining division can make the amendments without consulting the applicant if the applicant can reasonably be expected to accept them. Examples are corrections of minor errors but also amendments which, although changing the scope of an independent claim, would very clearly have to be made. The examiner should contact the applicant, e.g. by telephone, if the examiner wants to make more substantial amendments, such as an amendment that can be made in different ways and that significantly changes the scope of a claim, or the deletion or combination of claims. (C-V,1.1)

The EPO prepares the Druckexemplar electronically, optionally by converting the text submitted by the applicant by OCR from a scanned filed paper version or directly from a filed pdf version to xml format. The examining division marks any amendments to the text with standard marks using in-house software (C-V,1.1 and C-V, Annex).

Applicants must also make their amendments to the Druckexemplar electronically; handwritten amendments are not allowed unless they relate to graphic symbols and characters and formulae (C-V,1.1).

The approved text of the Druckexemplar will be the text of the granted patent. Corrections of the text after grant are not possible (**R.140:3.1**). Hence, the review of the Druckexemplar is the last opportunity for the applicant to correct any errors. This includes any errors introduced by the EPO in the conversion and amendment of the text of the Druckexemplar. The way in which the pdf editing tool used by the EPO adds drafting symbols and line breaks can make it burdensome to check insertions proposed by the examining division. A full text comparison of the Druckexemplar with the application and any amendments as filed is recommended. When the EPO has introduced full electronic processing, the conversion will be made on filing of the application, giving the applicant more opportunities during the procedure for correcting errors.

3.2 ACTS TO BE COMPLETED

The **R.71(3)** communication invites the applicant to perform the following acts:

1 Pay the fee for grant and publishing within the period of R.71(3). The amount of the fee is set in **Rfees2(1)7**, or in **Rfees2(2)7** for applications filed before 01.04.2009. (C-V,1.2) A reduction is available for certain applicants (**R.7a(3)**).

2 File a translation of the claims in the two official EPO languages other than the language of the proceedings, as required by **Art.14(6)**. Where the application contains different sets of claims for different contracting states, a translation of all sets must be filed (C-V,1.3). The translations must be filed within the period of **R.71(3)**.

3 Pay any claims fees (**R.71(4)**, **Rfees2(1)15**) within the period of **R.71(3)** (C-V,1.4).

4 Pay the designation fee (**Rfees2(1)3**) under **R.71a(3)** within the period of **R.39(1)** if the period expires after the **R.71(3)** communication (C-V,2).

5 Pay any renewal fee under **R.71a(4)** before the due date of **R.51(1)** if the due date falls after the **R.71(3)** communication (C-V,2).

6 Correct any errors in documents other than the application documents, such as the bibliographic data and the designation of inventor (see **R.71(3):5.2**).

7 Instead of the first six acts, request grant based on a different text (**R.71(6)**).

3.3 FURTHER INFORMATION IN THE R.71(3) COMMUNICATION

The **R.71(3)** communication must inform the applicant of the different options to approve the text, to amend the text and, where an auxiliary request is regarded allowable, to disapprove the text of this request and maintain a higher-ranking request (**T1255/04** r.3.1). Note, that although **R.71** does not explicitly mention disapproval as a response, the applicant may not be deprived of this option (**T1255/04** r.3.1).

The **R.71(3)** communication informs the applicant also of the requirement of contracting states and extension states to file a translation of (part of) the specification under **Art.65**.

The payment of fees and filing of translations under **R.71(3)** as a prerequisite for the issuance of a decision to grant has as a consequence that oral proceedings in the grant procedure cannot be closed with a decision to grant the patent, but only with the prospect of a grant. In the subsequent written continuation of the procedure the fees can be paid and the translations filed, after which the decision to grant will be taken.

Any sanctions on non-performance of these acts have been set out in the following notes and in the provisions referred to.

4 **Period for response**

The response to the **R.71(3)** communication must be filed within a period of four months of notification of the communication. The period will be extended under **R.134** if it expires on a non-working day or in case of dislocation of mail; the period cannot be extended on request under **R.132(2)** (C-V,1.1).

For sanction on non-response and remedies, see R.71(7):1.

5 **Response to R.71(3) communication**

The applicant can respond to the **R.71(3)** communication in one of the following four ways.

5.1 APPROVAL

If the applicant agrees to the text to be granted and the bibliographic data, the applicant must pay the fee for grant and publishing and any claims fees and file a translation of the claims in the two EPO languages other than the language of the proceedings within four months of the **R.71(3)** communication (**R.71(3)**). Compliance with these requirements is regarded as an implicit approval of the text, including any amendments and corrections made by the examiner, and verification of the bibliographic data (**R.71(5)**). The approval of the text is not binding on the EPO or the applicant; see **R.71a(2)**.

The requirement to pay a designation fee or renewal fee after the four-month period will not affect the approval of the text to be granted but will delay issuance of the decision to grant and publication of the grant until payment of the fees has been made (see **R.71a(3)** and (4)). If the designation fee or renewal fee is not paid in due time (**R.39(1)**; **R.51**), the application will be deemed withdrawn (**R.39(2)**; **Art.86(1)**).

If the text intended for grant is based on an auxiliary request, the **R.71(3)** communication will include the reasons why the higher-ranking requests are not allowable. Payment of the fees and filing of the translations is regarded as approval of the text of the auxiliary request and abandonment of all higher-ranking requests (C-V,2).

When the acts required in the **R.71(3)** communication have been carried out, the procedure for grant continues as set out in the notes to **Art.97(1)**.

See **Art.97(1):2** for acceleration of the grant procedure.

5.2 DIFFERENT TEXT

If the applicant desires a grant based on a text different from the one included in the **R.71(3)** communication, the applicant must request so within the four-month period of **R.71(3)**. This occurs in about 15% of all responses to the **R.71(3)** communication. The procedure is set out in **R.71(6)**.

The filing of the request removes the obligation to pay the fee for grant and publishing and any claims fees and to file the translations within the four months of **R.71(3)**. It interrupts the grant procedure and the procedure is continued as set out in **R.71(6)**. Note, that **R.71** does not explicitly state that compliance with **R.71(3)** requires either payment of the fees and filing of translations *or* filing of amendments and corrections to the text; it is only clearly stated in C-V,4.1.

In the event amendments and corrections relate to the text to be granted, no fees need be paid and no translations filed within the four-month period of **R.71(3)** (C-V,4). If the filed amendments or corrections relate solely to other documents, such as the bibliographic data or the designation of inventor, the fees must be paid and the translations filed, otherwise the application will be deemed withdrawn under **R.71(7)**.

When requesting grant based on a different text, it is allowed, although not required, to pay the fees in response to the **R.71(3)** communication. The voluntary paid fees will be credited towards the amount due in response to the second **R.71(3)** communication (**R.71a(5)**) or may be refunded (**R.71a(6)**). See also **R.71(6):3**.

5.3 DELAY

If an applicant needs more time for preparing the response to the **R.71(3)** communication, the applicant can delay the procedure by not responding to the communication, i.e. not paying the fees and not filing any translations, amendments or corrections. Consequently, the application will be deemed withdrawn under **R.71(7)**. Using further processing under **Art.121**, the applicant may gain about three months' time.

Note, that the four-month period of **R.71(3)** cannot be extended on request under **R.132(2)** because it is not a period specified by the EPO.

5.4 NO GRANT

If, exceptionally, the applicant does not want the application to grant, the applicant can end the procedure in two ways. The first one is not to respond to the **R.71(3)** communication and let the application be deemed withdrawn under **R.71(7)**.

The second way is to inform the EPO of the disapproval of the text and not to pay any fees or file translations. The application will be refused under **Art.97(2)** for failure to comply with **Art.113(2)**, because there is no text agreed to by the applicant, provided that (i) the examining division did not propose any amendments or corrections under **R.71(3)**, (ii) the text was based on a main request, and (iii) the applicant did not file amendments or corrections together with the disapproval of the text. If amendments were proposed by the examining division, the disapproval is interpreted as a rejection of the proposal, and the procedure of **R.71(6)** will be followed. The same applies if the **R.71(3)** communication was based on an auxiliary request, in which case the disapproval is interpreted as a request for a higher-ranking request to be the basis for grant. (C-V,4.9)

The refusal of the application is appealable. The sanction of deemed withdrawn would deprive the applicant of the possibility to appeal the rejection of the application. (**T1181/04** r.3.3)

Note, that the sanction of refusal in the present case appears to be contrary to **Art.97(2)**, since **R.71(7)** provides in this case for the different sanction of deemed withdrawn.

R. 71(4) If the European patent application in the text intended for grant comprises more than fifteen claims, the Examining Division shall invite the applicant to pay claims fees in respect of the sixteenth and each subsequent claim within the period under paragraph 3 unless the said fees have already been paid under Rule 45 or Rule 162.

Amended, in force since 01.04.2012 (OJ 2010 p.637).
R.45 Claims fees on filing of direct European application
R.162 Claims fees on entry into the European phase
Implementation of **Art.97(1)**

1 **Claims fees**

If the number of claims in the allowable text is larger than fifteen, **R.71(4)** obliges the applicant to pay claims fees (**Rfees2(1)15**) for claims numbered 16 and higher, unless the claims fees for these claims have already been paid on filing of the application (**R.45**) or on entry into the European phase (**R.162**). If the text to be granted contains fewer claims than on filing or entry, no claims fees will be refunded. (C-V,1.4)

Where the allowed text is based on an auxiliary request, the claims fees are due only for the claims of the allowed text (C-V,1.4).

If the response to the **R.71(3)** communication does not amend the text to be granted, the claims fees must be paid within the four-month period of **R.71(3)**. Non-payment of the claims fees leads to the entire application being deemed withdrawn according to **R.71(7)**. The remedy has been set out in **R.71(7):1**.

If in response to the R.71(3) communication the applicant requests a grant based on a different text, the claims fees need not be paid within this period; instead, payment can be deferred to the four-month period of the second R.71(3) communication (C-V,4.1). However, if the applicant pays the claims fee voluntarily in response to the first R.71(3) communication, the amount paid will be credited to the payment of claims fees for a second R.71(3) communication (R.71a(5), C-V,4.2, 4.8.1). The onerous rules for the crediting are given in A-X,11.2 and C-V,4.2.

Note, that non-payment of the claims fees on filing or entry in the European phase results in abandonment of the claims for which no fees are paid (R.45(3)). The aggravation of the sanction on non-payment in the grant phase is necessary to avoid the legal complication of an abandonment of claims in an already approved application.

R. 71(5) If the applicant, within the period laid down in paragraph 3, pays the fees under paragraph 3 and, where applicable, paragraph 4 and files the translations under paragraph 3, they shall be deemed to have approved the text communicated to them under paragraph 3 and verified the bibliographic data.

Amended, in force since 01.04.2012 (OJ 2010 p.637).
Implementation of **Art.97(1)**

1 **Implicit approval**

If the applicant pays the fees and files the translations in due time in response to the R.71(3) communication, the applicant is deemed to have approved the text intended for grant and verified the bibliographic data (**R.71(5)**). Hence, the approval of the text intended for grant is given implicitly. The approval is not binding (see **R.71a(2):1**).

However, if the response to the **R.71(3)** communication additionally includes amendments or corrections, no approval is given (implied by C-V,4.2) and the procedure under **R.71(6)** is followed. The voluntarily paid fees may be credited to a second **R.71(3)** communication (**R.71a(5)**).

R. 71(6) If the applicant, within the period under paragraph 3, requests reasoned amendments or corrections to the communicated text or keeps to the latest text submitted by them, the Examining Division shall issue a new communication under paragraph 3 if it gives its consent; otherwise it shall resume the examination proceedings.

Amended, in force since 01.04.2012 (OJ 2010 p.637).
Implementation of **Art.97(1)**

1 **Different text for grant**

If the applicant desires a grant based on a text different from the one proposed by the examining division in the **R.71(3)** communication, the applicant must request so within the four-month period of **R.71(3)**. The following three cases can be distinguished:

1 Applicant no longer approves the latest text submitted and allowed by the examining division and wants to change the text. The applicant must submit amendments and/or corrections in response to the **R.71(3)** communication. The amendments or corrections must be reasoned (**R.71(6)**), i.e. the response must indicate why the amended documents comply with the EPC or why the corrections are evident in accordance with **R.139** (C-V,4.3). The basis for amendments in the application as filed must be indicated (H-II,2.5.5). If the amendments or corrections concern

the claims, it is recommended to provide at the same time any corresponding amendments to the description to avoid delay in the procedure (C-V,4.5).

The amendments to the application must be typed or printed. Handwritten amendments are not accepted, unless they relate to graphic symbols and characters and formulae (C-V,1.1; see also **R.71(3):3.1** and **R.50(1):2**).

2 The allowed text is an auxiliary request and the applicant desires grant of a higher-ranking request. The applicant must disapprove the communicated text and request grant of a higher-ranking request. The request must be reasoned (**R.71(6)**).

This possibility is not explicitly mentioned in **R.71(6)**, but can be regarded as a special case of amendment (see **T1255/04** r.4.1). See **R.71(6):5** below for more details.

3 Applicant does not approve the amendments and/or corrections proposed by the examining division in the text intended for grant. The applicant must reject the communicated text and request grant of the latest text submitted. Although **R.71(6)** does not require so, it is recommended to provide reasons for keeping to the latest text (C-V,4.6.1).

This case is explicitly mentioned in **R.71(6)** to provide a legal basis for the practice of the examining division to make amendments and/or corrections on its own initiative.

In these three cases, no fees need be paid nor translations filed within the four-month period of **R.71(3)** (see **R.71(3):5.2**). All three options can be combined with a PACE request to accelerate the further procedure (**Art.94(1):4.1**).

The request for amendment or correction or rejection of the examiner's amendments must be filed within four months from notification of the **R.71(3)** communication. If no response has been filed in the four-month period, the application will be deemed withdrawn under **R.71(7)** because the fees have not been paid and the translations have not been filed. This can be remedied using further processing by paying the further processing fee and completing the omitted act (requesting amendment).

If the examining division gives its consent, it issues a new **R.71(3)** communication. If the examining division does not consent, it resumes the examination proceedings.

R.71(6) does not apply if the **R.71(3)** communication is issued by the examining division after a decision of a board of appeal to remit a case with an order to grant a patent with the text as specified in the decision. In such a case, the application is deemed to be withdrawn under **R.71(7)** if the applicant submits amendments (**T2558/18**).

2 Admissibility of amendments and corrections

R.71(6) allows the applicant to submit a different text for grant in response to the invitation under **R.71(3)**. However, the admissibility of the submission depends on the circumstances of the case.

The examining division will exercise its discretion in accordance with **R.137(3)** in admitting amendments filed in response to the **R.71(3)** communication, taking into account the late stage of the proceedings at which the substantive examination has already been completed and the applicant has already had at least one opportunity to amend the application. At this stage the outcome of the earlier procedure should not be called into question; allowance of a request for amendment will be an exception rather than the rule. Only amendments which do not appreciably delay the preparations for grant will be admitted. However, the filing of separate sets of claims for states for which national prior rights exist or for which Art.167(2) EPC1973 applies is always admissible. (**G7/93**, also applicable to the amended **R.71** according to **T1064/04** and H-II,2.5.1).

Where the **R.71(3)** communication includes amendments to the claims carried out by the examining division on which the applicant has not yet had an opportunity to comment, any comment of the applicant relating to such amendments must be admitted under **Art.113(1)**. (C-V,4.6.1 and 4.7.1)

In the exceptional case that receipt of the **R.71(3)** communication triggers the opportunity to file voluntary amendments under **R.137(3)** as valid until 01.04.2010, amendments filed in response to the communication are always admissible under **R.137(2)** (C-V,4.4; H-II,2.5.4). This is also the case where no search opinion is drawn up and the first communication from the examining division is pursuant to **R.71(3)** EPC.

R.71(6) mentions corrections of errors under **R.139** separately from amendments under **R.137(3)**. As a consequence, the admissibility of corrections is not at the discretion of the EPO. Corrections are possible up to the decision to grant (H-VI,2.1; **J42/92**).

3 **Second R.71(3) communication**

If the request for grant based on a different text filed in response to the **R.71(3)** communication is admissible and allowable, the examining division will issue a second **R.71(3)** communication including the text based thereon (**R.71(6)**, C-V,4.6). The examining division may propose amendments of its own volition in this second **R.71(3)** communication (C-V,4.6.3).

Applicants can indicate their approval of the text by paying the fee for grant and publishing and any claims fees and filing the translations of the claims (see **R.71(3)**:3). Alternatively, applicants can again submit a different text in response to the second **R.71(3)** communication. If applicants make repeated requests for amendments in response to the second or a further **R.71(3)** communication, the examining division may not admit the amendments (R.137(3)). In this case, the application will be returned to examination proceedings and the applicant may be summoned to oral proceedings. (C-V,4.10)

4 **Resumption of examination proceedings**

If the request for grant based on a different text is not admissible or allowable, e.g. because the argumentation or evidence provided by the applicant in the response to the **R.71(3)** communication is not convincing, the examining division will resume the examination proceedings (**R.71(6)**; C-V,4.7).

Where the grounds and/or evidence for the non-admissibility or non-allowability have not yet been dealt with in examination proceedings, the examining division will issue an **Art.94(3)** communication setting out its findings. Oral proceedings may have to be appointed before taking a decision (see C-V,4.7.1). If agreement is reached on the text, a second **R.71(3)** communication will be sent, based on the agreed text (C-V,4.7.2). If no agreement can be reached, the application will be refused (C-V,4.7.3).

The application may be refused directly after receipt of the response to the **R.71(3)** communication if 1) the grounds and evidence for the non-admittance or non-allowance have already been dealt with in examination proceedings (**Art.113(1)**), 2) at least one **Art.94(3)** communication has been issued, and 3) the applicant's right to oral proceedings has been respected (**Art.116(1)**) (C-V,4.7.1).

5 Auxiliary requests

During grant proceedings the applicant may file one set of claims as a main request and one or more alternative sets of claims as auxiliary requests as set out in **Art.94(3):6**. When the examining division regards an auxiliary request allowable, it issues the **R.71(3)** communication in regard of that set of claims, stating the reasons why the higher-ranking requests are not considered allowable (**T1255/04** r.3.2; C-V,1.1). Applicants can proceed in one of the following ways:

- Agree to the opinion expressed in the communication and express their approval of the text to be granted by paying the fees and filing the translations under **R.71(3)**, thereby making the allowable set their sole request and abandoning the higher-ranking requests (C-V,2). This option deprives the applicant of the possibility to appeal the rejection of higher-ranking requests. Hence, an applicant wanting to maintain the option of appeal should not yield to a request of the examining division to make the allowable request their sole request.
- Refuse to approve the text regarded allowable and maintain a higher-ranking request in the response under **R.71(6)**. The application will usually be refused under **Art.97(2)** (see **Art.97(2):1**) in the resumed examination proceedings. The application may be directly refused, provided the applicant's right to be heard has been respected and the **R.71(3)** communication has provided sufficient information about the objections, to allow the applicant to comment on them (C-V,4.7.1.1). The decision refusing the application should state the reasons why the higher-ranking requests were considered not allowable. However, if arguments of the applicant in the response to the **R.71(3)** communication convince the examining division that the higher-ranking request meets the requirements of the EPC, a new **R.71(3)** communication will be issued. (C-V,4.6.2)
- File amendments to the claims of the request regarded allowable as permitted under **R.71(6)**, without paying the fee for grant and publishing and without filing the translations of the claims. If the examining division agrees, it will issue a new **R.71(3)** communication. If the examining division does not agree, it will resume the examination proceedings under **R.71(6)**.

An applicant may, on request, obtain an immediate decision on the non-patentability of the higher-ranking requests before the **R.71(3)** communication is issued. In that case the examining division issues the appealable final decision refusing the application immediately. (C-V,15)

If the applicant appeals the decision refusing the application and requests grant on the basis of the set of claims considered to be allowable, the examining division will rectify its decision by interlocutory revision under **Art.109**. Otherwise, the case will be remitted to the board of appeal without comments as to its merits; the board is not bound by the examining division's positive assessment of an auxiliary request.

R. 71(7) If the fee for grant and publishing or the claims fees are not paid in due time, or if the translations are not filed in due time, the European patent application shall be deemed to be withdrawn.

Amended, in force since 01.04.2012 (OJ 2010 p.637).
Implementation of Art.97(1)

1 **Sanction on non-compliance and remedies**

The application will be deemed withdrawn under **R.71(7)** if the fee for grant and publishing or any claims fees are not paid or the translations of the claims are not filed within four months from notification of the **R.71(3)** communication. If a different text is proposed under **R.71(6)** in response to the **R.71(3)** communication, no fees need be paid or translations submitted and the sanction does not apply (C-V,3). See **R.71(3):5.4** for a refusal following non-compliance with the requirements of **R.71(3)**.

The loss of rights is notified according to **R.112(1)** and can be remedied using further processing under **Art.121**. The omitted act must be completed and a further processing fee paid within two months from the notification of the loss of rights. The nature of the omitted act is determined by the desired course of action of the applicant. If the applicant wants the application to grant, the omitted act is the payment of fees and the filing of translations of the claims. The further processing fee is the fixed fee for late performance of acts under **R.71(3)** and 50% of any unpaid claims fees (**Rfees2(1)12**) (E-VIII,2). If only the claims fees were not paid in due time, the fee for further processing is 50% of the claims fees. Alternatively, if the applicant wants a different text for grant, the omitted act is filing amendments and/or corrections, filing a rejection of the amendments proposed by the examining division, or filing a request for grant of a higher-ranking request than the allowed auxiliary request (C-V,8). The further processing fee in this case is the fee 'other cases' in **Rfees2(1)12**.

If the applicant did perform the required acts in time, the applicant should request a decision under **R.112(2)** as main request and further processing as auxiliary request. Re-establishment is not available for the four-month period of **R.71(3)** but it is available for the two-month period of **R.112(2)** and **R.135(1)**.

Note that non-payment of a fee or not filing a translation results in a loss of the application without an appealable decision being taken. In that case a fee for grant and publishing paid in response to the **R.71(3)** communication will be refunded under **R.71a(6)**. Any paid claims fees may be refunded (**R.71a(6):1**).

See **R.71a(3):1** and **(4):1** for the consequences of non-payment of the designation fee and renewal fee.

R. 71a Conclusion of the grant procedure

Inserted, in force since 01.04.2012. **R.71a** applies to applications for which a **R.71(3)** communication is despatched on or after 01.04.2012. (OJ 2010 p.637)
See **R.71(3):2** for a summary of the revised grant procedure.
Implementation of **Art.97(1)** and (3).

R. 71a(1) The decision to grant the European patent shall be issued if all fees have been paid, a translation of the claims in the two official languages of the European Patent Office other than the language of the proceedings has been filed and there is agreement as to the text to be granted. It shall state which text of the European patent application forms the basis for the decision.

Implementation of **Art.97(1)**

1 **Decision to grant**

Once the applicant has approved the text intended for grant by paying the fees and filing the translations of the claims in response to the **R.71(3)** communication, the EPO will issue the decision to grant the patent (**R.71a(1)**). The decision to grant is usually taken between two and three weeks after the EPO has received the approval of the text according to **R.71(5)**, provided no further requests are filed together with or after the approval.

Issue of the decision will be delayed if designation or renewal fees have to be paid after notification of the **R.71(3)** communication (**R.71a(3)** and (4)).

The decision does not include the text of the application forming the basis of the decision but refers to the text included in the **R.71(3)** communication that has been approved by the applicant. The decision is not reasoned because it does not adversely affect the party (**R.111(2):1**).

See **R.140:2** for correction of errors in the decision and **R.140:3** for errors in the publication of the patent specification.

R. 71a(2) Until the decision to grant the European patent, the Examining Division may resume the examination proceedings at any time.

Implementation of **Art.97(1)**

1 **Resumption of examination**

After approval of the text according to **R.71(3)**, the examining division may resume the examination procedure at any time up to the moment the decision to grant is handed over to the EPO's internal postal service for transmittal to the applicant (**G12/91** hn; C-V,6.1). This date is indicated at the bottom of the decision to grant (**T2573/11**).

An approval of the text notified under **R.71(3)** does not bind an applicant (**G7/93** hn. I). The approval is considered withdrawn if applicants file an amendment to the text of the application after their approval and before the issue of the decision to grant (**G10/92** r.5, 7). The examining division has a discretion under **R.137(3)** whether or not to allow such an amendment and resume the examination proceedings. According to **T646/20**, however, the examining division does not have to wait until the expiry of the four-month period set under **R.71(3)** before taking a decision to grant if the applicant has approved the text.

In view of the late stage in the granting procedure, resumption of the proceedings will be an exception (**G7/93** hn. I, II) but may be justified if the applicant or a third party informs the EPO of very relevant prior art or the applicant requests amendments or corrections (C-V,6.1). Although the two G-decisions relate to an earlier version of **R.71(3)** and (6), they appear also applicable to the present version of these provisions.

Resumption of the proceedings cancels the previous approval of the text and a new **R.71(3)** communication will be issued if a new text is regarded as allowable (C-V,6.2).

R. 71a(3) If the designation fee becomes due after the communication under Rule 71, paragraph 3, the mention of the grant of the European patent shall not be published until the designation fee has been paid. The applicant shall be informed accordingly.

Implementation of **Art.97(3)**

1 **Designation fee**
The period for payment of the designation fee as provided in **R.39(1)** is six months from the publication of the search report. In the rare case that the expiry of the six-month period falls after notification of the **R.71(3)** communication, the decision to grant and the publication of the mention of the grant will be postponed until the designation fee has been paid (**R.71a(3)**). The applicant is informed accordingly (C-V,2).

If the designation fee is not paid within the six-month period, the application will be deemed withdrawn (**R.39(2)**) and the mention of the grant will not be published. Further processing according to **Art.121** and **R.135** can be used as remedy.

Note, that the word 'due' in the provision refers to the expiry of the period for payment of the fee. This is different from the meaning of the term in **Rfees4(1)**.

Application of **R.71a(3)** is infrequent because a **R.71(3)** communication is issued only after the search report is established and a top-up search is carried out; the top-up search is carried out no earlier than 18 months from the filing date (C-VI,3; C-IV,7.1). By that time, the search report will normally have been published already. However, if the claims as filed are allowable, examination has been requested before the search report is transmitted, and a PACE request for examination is filed, the top-up search may be performed quickly, and the **R.71(3)** communication may be issued within six months from the publication of the search report.

R. 71a(4) If a renewal fee becomes due after the communication under Rule 71, paragraph 3, and before the next possible date for publication of the mention of the grant of the European patent, the mention shall not be published until the renewal fee has been paid. The applicant shall be informed accordingly.

Implementation of **Art.97(3)**

1 **Renewal fee**
Art.86(2) provides that the renewal fee in respect of the patent year in which the mention of the grant is published must be paid to the EPO. Since the sanction in **Art.86(1)**, last sentence, that the application is deemed withdrawn on failure to pay the renewal fees is not applicable anymore after the grant of the patent, the EPC has to secure payment of the renewal fees due before grant by deferring the grant until they have been paid.

R.71a(4) relates to the case where the due date of a renewal fee falls between notification of the **R.71(3)** communication and the next possible date for publication of the mention of the grant. The decision to grant and the publication of the mention of the grant will be postponed until the renewal fee has been paid. The mention of the grant is published only once the renewal fees and any additional fees due by the planned publication date have been paid (European Patent Guide 5.4.014). The applicant is informed accordingly (C-V,2). The renewal fee must be paid before or on the due date or, with additional fee, within six months from the due date (**R.51(2)**). If the renewal fee is not paid in due time, the application will be deemed withdrawn under **Art.86(1)**, last sentence, and the mention of the grant will never be published. Further processing is excluded by **R.135(2)**, but re-establishment according to **Art.122** and **R.136** is available.

The case where the due date for payment of the renewal fee falls before the **R.71(3)** communication and the expiry of the six-month period of **R.51(2)** after that communication is not addressed by the wording of **R.71a(4)**, whereas it was covered by Art.97(2)(c) EPC1973. In practice, the mention of the grant is published only once the renewal fees and any additional fees due by the planned publication date have been paid (European Patent Guide 5.4.014).

R.71a(4) does not apply to the case where the anniversary of the date of filing and a subsequent publication of the mention of the grant would fall within the same month. In practice, the EPO avoids this by delaying the issue of the decision to grant (see **Art.86(2):2**).

R. 71a(5) If, in response to an invitation under Rule 71, paragraph 3, the applicant has already paid the fee for grant and publishing or the claims fees, the paid amount shall be credited if a further such invitation is issued.

Implementation of **Art.97(1)**

1 **Crediting of fees paid**

The EPO expects many applicants to pay the fees in response to the **R.71(3)** communication when amendments are filed. If the EPO were to refund the fees as having no legal basis, the refund and the obligation to pay the fees in response to a quickly issued second **R.71(3)** communication could cross, causing a confusing situation for the applicant. **R.71a(5)** avoids this situation by regarding the fees paid in response to the first **R.71(3)** communication as voluntarily paid and by not refunding the fees but crediting them to the fees to be paid in response to a further **R.71(3)** communication.

The EPO distinguishes two cases for crediting fees:

i) If an applicant responds to the **R.71(3)** communication by requesting a grant based on a different text, no approval of the text for grant is given and the fee for grant and publishing and the claims fees need not be paid within the four-month period of **R.71(3)** (C-V,4.1). If the fees are paid voluntarily, they will be credited to the fees to be paid for the second **R.71(3)** communication (**R.71a(5)**, C-V,4.2).

   The EPO will accept such voluntarily paid fees, in spite of the principle that fees lacking a legal basis are to be refunded (**Rfees9:1**; A-X,10.1.1(ii)).

ii) Similarly, if an applicant approves the text to be granted by paying the fee for grant and publishing and the claims fees and subsequently the examination is resumed (see **R.71a(2)**), the approval is withdrawn, but the fees were validly paid. The mandatory paid fee for grant and publishing and the claims fees are also credited to the fees to be paid for the second **R.71(3)** communication (**R.71a(5)**, C-V,6.3).

If in cases i. and ii. the fee for grant and publishing for the second **R.71(3)** communication is different, e.g. because of amendment of the fee rates, a shortfall has to be paid and an excess will be refunded (A-X,11.1, 11.2; C-V,4.2).

If in cases i. and ii. the claims fees for the second **R.71(3)** communication are higher, e.g. because of an increased number of claims, the shortfall must be paid (A-X,11.2).

If in case i. the claims fees for the second **R.71(3)** communication are lower, an excess will be refunded (C-V,4.2). However, if in case ii. the claims fees for the second R.71(3) communication are lower, an excess will *not* be refunded (A-X,11.2).

See **R.71a(6)** for refund of fees in the event that the application ceases to exist.

R. 71a(6) If the European patent application is refused, withdrawn prior to notification of the decision on the grant of a European patent or, at that time, deemed to be withdrawn, the fee for grant and publishing shall be refunded.

Implementation of **Art.97(1)**

1 **Refund of fees**

The fee for grant and publishing will be refunded under **R.71a(6)** if the application is refused, withdrawn or deemed to be withdrawn prior to notification of the decision to grant (C-V,4.2).

In such a situation, the claims fees will be refunded if they have been paid voluntarily (**R.71a(5):1** case i.). However, if the claims fees have been paid mandatory (**R.71a(5):1** case ii.), they will *not* be refunded (A-X,10.2.5).

R. 72 Grant of the European patent to different applicants

Where different persons are recorded in the European Patent Register as applicants in respect of different Contracting States, the European Patent Office shall grant the European patent for each Contracting State accordingly.

Implementation of **Art.97(1)**

Chapter V *The European patent specification*

R. 73 Content and form of the specification

Implementation of **Art.98**

R. 73(1) The specification of the European patent shall include the description, the claims and any drawings. It shall also indicate the period for opposing the European patent.

1 **Content of the specification**
The contents of the specification are governed by **R.73(1)**. The specification is published in the language of the proceedings (**Art.14(6)**), and contains the description, claims (in the three EPO languages (**Art.14(7)**) and any drawings (**R.73(1)**, first sentence). The text in the language of the proceedings is the authentic text in any subsequent proceedings (**Art.70(1)**). The specification may contain different descriptions, drawings and sets of claims for different designated contracting states due to the existence of different national prior rights (**R.138**).

R. 73(2) The President of the European Patent Office shall determine the form of the publication of the specification and the data to be included.

1 **Publication of the specification**
Under **R.73(2)** the President has prescribed that the specifications of European patents are published in electronic form only and are available by means of downloading from a publication server (Dec. Pres. OJ 2007 se3 D.3). See **R.68** for the publication server.

The publication of the specification takes place as soon as possible after the publication of the mention of the grant (**Art.98**).

See **R.140:3.2** for errors in the published specification.

2 **Withdrawal before publication**
Withdrawal of the application before publication of the specification follows the same principles as withdrawal of the application before publication under **R.67(2)**, in particular the avoidance of publication by withdrawing the application before the termination of the technical preparations for publication (C-V,11). In practice, publication can often be prevented if withdrawal is received at least two weeks before the scheduled date of publication. See **R.67(2):3** for the binding nature of the declaration of withdrawal and the limited possibility to retract it under **R.139**.

The technical preparations for publication are completed five weeks before the scheduled date of publication of the specification (OJ 2006 p.409). The completion is about one week before the internal decision to grant is taken (OJ 2006 p.409). The written decision, notified to the applicant when the technical preparations have been completed, states the date of publication of the mention of the grant in the Bulletin (C-V,10); this date is four weeks after the decision to grant was taken (OJ 2006 p.409). The patent specification is published as soon as possible after the publication of the mention of the grant (**Art.98**) (C-V,10).

3 **Data in specification**

The front page of the published specification shows the title and the designated contracting states (see **R.73(3)**). Information on the surrender or lapse of the patent in the contracting states can be obtained from the Register (see **R.143(1):1**) and the national patent offices. The front page mentions the same serial number as the front page of the published application and an identification of the kind of publication document (see **R.68(2):2**).

The front page of the specification will mention the presence of supplementary technical information in the file that has been introduced after the application has been filed. Such information may have been taken into account by the examiner as evidence in support of the patentability of the invention but could not be included in the application by way of amendment because of **Art.123(2)**. The information is contained in the part of the file that is open to public inspection (**Art.128(4)**), unless access is excluded under **R.144(d)** (H-V,2.3). Although the possibility of exclusion from the file is explicitly mentioned in the Guidelines, it is difficult to understand the circumstances in which this could occur since, according to **R.144(d)**, such exclusion is only possible when the document concerned does not serve the purpose of informing the public about the European patent application or patent.

A list of patent and non-patent literature cited in the description will be included at the end of applications and specifications published as from 13.09.2006. The list is made by the EPO and is for information only and does not form part of the application or specification. (Dec. Pres. OJ 2007 se3 D.4).

R. 73(3) The designated Contracting States shall be indicated in the specification.

1 **Designations published**

The publication of an application under **Art.93** mentions all designated EPC contracting states (**R.68(3)**); likewise the specification of the corresponding patent. States for which the designation has been withdrawn under **Art.79(3)** before completion of the technical preparations for publication of the application or patent are not mentioned.

R. 74 Certificate for a European patent

As soon as the specification of the European patent has been published, the European Patent Office shall issue to the proprietor of the patent a certificate for a European patent. The President of the European Patent Office shall prescribe the content, form and means of communication of the certificate and determine the circumstances in which an administrative fee is payable.

Implementation of **Art.98**

1 **Form of certificate**

The certificate for patent is communicated to the proprietor or each proprietor if there are several. The certificate is issued as a digital file for download from the Mailbox of the proprietor or the proprietor's representative where such a Mailbox is activated. If this is impossible, the certificate is issued on paper and delivered to the proprietor or representative by postal services. The certificate states the patent number, the name and address of the patent proprietor, the title of the invention and the date of publication of the mention of the grant in the European Patent Bulletin. If there is more than one proprietor, the certificate mentions each by name. The certificate also certifies that the patent has been granted, in respect of the invention described and the states designated in the patent specification, to the person(s) named in the certificate. (Dec. Pres. OJ 2021 A94 and Not. EPO OJ 2021 A95)

A certified copy of the certificate with the patent specification annexed will be issued in paper format to the proprietor only upon request and payment of an administrative fee as fixed under **Rfees3(1)**. (Dec. Pres. OJ 2021 A94 and Not. EPO OJ 2021 A95)

These provisions apply equally to issuing a new certificate for a patent amended in opposition proceedings (**R.87**) and a patent limited in limitation proceedings (**R.96**).

PART V IMPLEMENTING REGULATIONS TO PART V OF THE CONVENTION

Chapter I *Opposition procedure*

R. 75 Surrender or lapse of the patent

An opposition may be filed even if the European patent has been surrendered in all the designated Contracting States or has lapsed in all those States.

Implementation of **Art.99(1)**

1 **Opposition to surrendered or lapsed patent**
An opposition against a surrendered or lapsed patent may be useful, because revocation of the patent by the EPO has an effect ex tunc (**Art.68**), thereby changing rights previously established under **Art.64** and **Art.67**. In contrast, a lapse of the patent in a designated state usually has, depending on national law, an effect ex nunc (not changing previously established rights). The effect of the surrender of patent in a designated state is also a matter of national law and may be ex tunc or ex nunc.

Proprietors may inform a national office of a state that they surrender their European patent for that state. Lapse of a European patent for a state occurs most often by non-payment of a renewal fee to a national patent office. See **R.84(1)** for continuation of opposition proceedings after lapse or surrender of the patent.

R. 76 Form and content of the opposition

Implementation of **Art.99(1)**

R. 76(1) Notice of opposition shall be filed in a written reasoned statement.

1 **Written reasoned statement**
The term 'written' in this provision excludes the filing of oppositions orally, but does not exclude electronic filing (OJ 2007 se5 EN p.128). See the notes to **R.2(1)** for permitted methods of filing.

The phrase 'reasoned statement' in **R.76(1)** implies the requirement of providing arguments in the notice of opposition (D-III,6). The arguments must present the reasoning why the grounds for opposition have been raised against the patent in suit and show how the facts and evidence submitted under **R.76(2)(c)** support these grounds.

R. 76(2) The notice of opposition shall contain:
(a) particulars of the opponent as provided in Rule 41, paragraph 2(c);
(b) the number of the European patent against which opposition is filed, the name of the proprietor of the patent and the title of the invention;
(c) a statement of the extent to which the European patent is opposed and of the grounds on which the opposition is based, as well as an indication of the facts and evidence presented in support of these grounds;
(d) if the opponent has appointed a representative, particulars as provided in Rule 41, paragraph 2(d).

R.41(2)(c) Particulars of applicant
R.41(2)(d) Particulars of representative

1 **General**
R.76 gives requirements for entry of a second party in a procedure before the EPO; it resembles **R.41** for filing an application. EPO Form 2300 can be used as check list for the information to be provided for an opposition. Use of Form 2300 is advisable, but not mandatory.

If the requirements are not complied with, **Art.101(1)** and **R.77** will be applied for the correction and sanction. Any deficiency of **R.76** to which **R.77(1)** refers must be corrected before expiry of the opposition period. Deficiencies in other items can be corrected after the opposition period on invitation by the EPO (**R.77(2)**). Failure to correct in due time results in inadmissibility of the opposition (**R.77(1), (2)**).

2 **Identity of the opponent** (**R.76(2)(a)**)
2.1 REQUIREMENT
At the start of the opposition proceedings the identity of the opponent or opponents must be known and verifiable to both the EPO and the proprietor, because the opposition proceedings started with **Art.99(1)** are new proceedings with new parties, the identity of which must be known from the start. Hence, at the end of the opposition period the identity of the opponent(s) must be known, as they become parties to the proceedings. From this it is possible to establish which languages are permissible (**R.3(1)**), whether a representative is required (**Art.133(2), (3)**), and whether the general requirements as to the person's legal capacity have been met. (**T25/85** r.6)

2.2 ERROR IN IDENTITY
An error in details of the identity of the opponent can be corrected according to **R.76(2)(a)** in conjunction with **R.77(2)**, even after the end of the opposition period. The identity may be corrected if the correction does not involve a change of mind and the identity was clear at the expiry of the opposition period (**G1/12** r.11, 30; **T615/14** r.1.6). This interpretation of **R.76(2)(a)** with **R.77(2)** is equal to the interpretation of **R.40(1)(b)** with **Art.90(4)**: an applicant must be identified on filing, whereas details about the applicant as required under **R.41(2)(c)** may be provided subsequently under **Art.90(4)**. The same applies to the appeal proceedings: note the similar wording of

R.99(1)(a) and **R.101(2)** for appeal on the one hand and **R.76(2)(a)** and **R.77(2)** for opposition on the other hand.

A correction of the identity of the opponent under **R.139**, first sentence, is also possible, even where the identity was not clear at expiry of the opposition period (**G1/12** r.37; **T615/14** r.1.4, 1.5; see also **R.139:3**). The true intention may be demonstrated using evidence filed after the opposition period (**T615/14** r.1.7). The correction has retroactive effect, making the opponent deemed known at the end of the opposition period. The same possibility for correction applies to the applicant in the case of **R.40(1)(b)** or an appellant in the case of **Art.106(1)**, **107** and **108**. **R.76(2)(a)** and **R.77(2)** do not form a lex specialis in respect of **R.139** for the opponent (reversal of **T25/85**). **R.139** is of general applicability and other rules relating to remedying deficiencies are simply complementary to **R.139**. An invitation to remedy under **R.77(2)** has merely to be responded to, whereas a voluntary correction of a mistake under **R.139** may involve proving that an error was made, what the error was and what the correction should be. (**T219/86**; see also **T590/93**)

See **Art.99(1):2.2** for the entitlement of a straw person to oppose and **Art.99(1):2.4** for transfer of opposition.

3 Patent opposed (R.76(2)(b))

The sole purpose of **R.76(2)(b)** is to make a correct identification of the opposed patent possible (**T317/86**). The identification of the patent may be corrected under **R.77(2)**, even after expiry of the opposition period, because **R.77(1)** does not refer to **R.76(2)(b)** (**T344/88**).

4 Extent of opposition, grounds, facts and evidence (R.76(2)(c))

4.1 GENERAL

R.76(2)(c) has the double function of governing (together with other provisions) the admissibility of the opposition and of establishing at the same time the legal and factual framework within which the substantive examination of the opposition in principle shall be conducted. The latter function is of particular importance in that it gives proprietors a fair chance to consider their position at an early stage of the proceedings. (**G9/91** r.6)

The facts and evidence must be supplemented by arguments showing how they support the grounds for opposition (D-IV,1.2.2.1(v)).

4.2 STATEMENT OF THE EXTENT OF THE OPPOSITION

The extent of opposition refers to whether the opposition is directed to all subject-matter of the patent or only a part, i.e. whether all claims are opposed or only some. In the unusual case where an opposition is limited to a part of the subject-matter of the patent, the investigation must also be limited to the opposed part (**G9/91** r.9). For example, in case of a patent with two independent claims, the opponent may indicate that only one independent claim is opposed.

Subject-matter not covered by the extent of opposition is not subject to opposition, both in the opposition proceedings and in a possible appeal. Such subject-matter is not subject to any opposition in the sense of **Art.101**, nor are there any proceedings in the sense of **Art.114** and **Art.115**. (**G9/91** r.10, confirming **T9/87**). The patent may be maintained on the basis of the unopposed claims, irrespective of whether the proprietor has filed an explicit request for this during the proceedings, provided the requirements of **R.82** are met (**T809/21**).

However, if the opposition is explicitly directed only to an independent claim, then any associated dependent claims are considered as being implicitly covered by the extent and may be examined, provided their validity is *prima facie* in doubt on the basis of already available information (**G9/91** r.11, confirming **T293/88**).

The extent of opposition does not pertain to which grounds of opposition are invoked (**Art.100**).

4.3 STATEMENT OF THE GROUNDS

The statement of grounds in the notice of opposition gives the legal framework for the attack on the patent. The possible grounds are given in **Art.100**. An opposition is often based on a lack of novelty (**Art.54**) or a lack of inventive step (**Art.56**).

4.3.1 *Added grounds in first instance*

In principle, the opposition division should examine only those grounds which have been properly submitted by the opponent (**G10/91** hn.2). However, since it is the aim of the first instance opposition procedure to avoid invalid patents, the opposition division may of its own motion raise a ground for opposition not covered by the indication of the grounds (**Art.114(1)** is applicable to opposition proceedings (see also D-V,2.2)) or consider such a ground raised by the opponent or a third party (**Art.115**) during the opposition proceedings. This deviation from the indicated grounds should only take place where, *prima facie*, the grounds are believed to be relevant (**G10/91** hn.2). This case law is codified in **R.81(1)**.

The opposition division may not disregard a new ground without examination of its relevance (**T736/95**). A late-submitted ground disregarded by the opposition division may be considered by the board of appeal if the board considers that the division was wrong in this respect (**T986/93** hn). Grounds should not be excluded merely for being late; the division should at least consider whether the grounds *prima facie* prejudice the maintenance of the patent (**T798/05**). A new ground against foreseeable amendments to the claims is regarded as late filed (E-VI,2.1). A limitation to a dependent claim is a foreseeable amendment; a limitation by including a feature from the description is not (E-VI,2.1).

A ground will only be admitted if the ground is substantiated (**T222/85**). A ground is substantiated if the requirement of **R.76(2)(c)** is met, i.e. an indication of the facts, evidence and arguments presented in support of these grounds is given (see the following sections). The substantiation requirement of **R.76(2)(c)** is not affected by the patent proprietor's later submissions (**T2037/18** r.13).

A ground indicated as being relied upon in the notice of opposition, or on EPO Form 2300, but not substantiated, is not considered part of the proceedings (**R2/08**). An opposition division need not consider a ground substantiated in the notice of opposition but subsequently not maintained during the opposition, unless the ground is likely to prejudice the maintenance of the patent (**T274/95** hn. I). Such a ground is not regarded as a fresh ground of opposition and may be re-introduced during appeal proceedings without agreement of the proprietor, at the discretion of the board of appeal (**T274/95** hn. II). However, a ground withdrawn at oral proceedings is considered a fresh ground if reintroduced on appeal (**T376/04**).

Opponents may substantiate a ground of opposition against a single claim of each request on file. If they succeed in establishing that a claim of each request is not allowable, the patent will be revoked. Thus, an opponent is under no obligation to 'overkill' requests put forward by the proprietor by substantiating grounds for opposition against more than one claim of each request. (**T926/93** hn)

4.3.2 *Added grounds in second instance*

The aim of the opposition appeal is to give the losing party the opportunity to contest the opposition division's decision. Issues outside the subject-matter of the decision under appeal are not part of the appeal (**G1/99** r.6.1). Hence, during opposition appeal, in principle only the grounds considered in the first instance proceedings are considered. A fresh ground filed during appeal is allowed very exceptionally if it is *prima facie* highly likely to prejudice the maintenance of the patent and if the proprietor agrees to its introduction (**G10/91** hn.3). If such a fresh ground is admitted, the case should be remitted to the first instance (see **G9/91** r.16, 18). Following these decisions, **T1007/95** held an appeal to be inadmissible because the appeal was based on the new ground of lack of novelty in view of a new document, whereas the appealed decision of the opposition division was based only on lack of inventive step, the appeal therefore amounting to a new opposition; in this case the proprietor did not consent to consideration of novelty in appeal.

In case of amendments of the claims or other parts of a patent in the course of opposition or opposition appeal proceedings, such amendments are to be fully examined as to their compatibility with the requirements of the EPC, e.g. **Art.123(2)** and (3), even if **Art.100(c)** would be an inadmissible fresh ground of opposition (**G9/91** r.19); this only applies to amendments made in the course of the opposition proceedings and not to those made before grant (**T693/98**).

Decision **G10/91** overrules on the one hand **T122/84**, **T9/87** and **T182/89**, which restricted the grounds to those put forward in the notice of opposition because of speed of procedure and legal certainty, and on the other hand **T227/88** and **T493/88**, which allowed fresh grounds in order to deliver a sound patent in the interest of the public.

4.3.3 *Separate grounds*

The grounds of **Art.100(b)** and (**c**) each are single, separate grounds for opposition (**G1/95** r.4.2). The ground of unpatentable subject-matter according to **Art.52(2)** is separate ground from novelty and inventive step (**G1/95** hn). Likewise, novelty and inventive step are also separate grounds for opposition (**G7/95** hn). However, a novelty analysis vis-à-vis the closest prior art is a necessary preliminary step in the problem-solution approach and if such an analysis finds a lack of novelty then the ground of lack of inventive step may be upheld against the patent in opposition appeal proceedings where lack of novelty would have been a new ground(**G7/95** hn). In a case where a patent has been opposed on the ground of novelty and inventive step and only the ground of novelty has been substantiated in view of a prior art document, lack of inventive step in view of the same prior art document is not a fresh ground in appeal and can consequently be examined without the agreement of the proprietor (**T131/01** hn). Since the assessment of inventive step requires that an invention is novel, a simultaneous substantiation of lack of novelty and lack of inventive step in view of the same document is contradictory (**T131/01** hn, r.3.1).

4.4 INDICATION OF FACTS

The notice must give an indication of the facts presented in support of the grounds for opposition (**R.76(2)(c)**). Opponents have to make clear how these facts support the mentioned grounds. They must indicate how the facts, in particular when not taken from published documents, have been made available (**T328/87**).

The facts provided in the notice must be sufficient to make it objectively clear to a skilled person how the opposition is based on the grounds presented. A poor quality formulation can lead to inadmissibility. An opponent cannot ask the opposition division to find the facts itself (**T222/85** r.4 to 6: 16 patents filed by opponent as facts without indicating specific passages).

If the facts are not logical, the opposition may still be admissible (**T234/86**).

If one ground of opposition, i.e. attack, is sufficiently substantiated, **R.76(2)(c)** is complied with; there is no concept of partial admissibility of an opposition (**T212/97** r.3.1).

Facts and evidence filed after the expiry of the opposition period are in principle late-filed and will be admitted into the proceedings at the discretion of the opposition division (**Art.114(2)**). Such discretion is exercised taking into account their relevance to the decision to be taken, the state of the procedure and the reasons for late submission (E-VI,2). The first of these criteria is the most important – if new facts or evidence are prima facie relevant then they should always be taken into consideration. These principle are derived from the case law according to which new facts and evidence should be exceptionally admitted if they appear *prima facie* to prejudice the maintenance of the patent (**T1002/92** hn.I). A late submitted document may be taken into account in view of an amendment of the contested patent (**T501/94** r.2.7). No final decision on the opposition can be taken until the relevance of late filed facts and evidence has been considered (**T156/84** hn.2). The decision must provide reasons why the late submissions were or were not admitted (**T1855/13** r.1.8; CLBA IV.C.4.2). Late filed facts submitted without good reason and causing extra cost to other parties for oral proceedings or taking of evidence, may be taken into account in an apportionment of costs under **Art.104**.

During appeal, new facts, evidence and related arguments in support of the grounds on which the opposition is based are only very exceptionally admitted if they are *prima facie* highly relevant in the sense that they highly likely prejudice the maintenance of the patent; other relevant factors are possible objections of the proprietor to the admission and added procedural complications. (**T1002/92** hn.II). Discretion on the part of the board of appeal will be exercised in accordance with the RPBA and the relevant criteria vary according to the stage of the appeal procedure at which the new facts and evidence are presented. For instance, new facts and evidence filed with the grounds of appeal will not be admitted if they should have been submitted during the first instance proceedings before the opposition division (Art.12(6) RPBA) but any amendment of a party's appeal case after notification of a summons to oral proceedings will, in principle, not be taken into account unless there are exceptional circumstances which have been justified with cogent reasons (Art.13(2) RPBA).

4.5 **INDICATION OF EVIDENCE**

The notice of opposition must contain at least an indication of evidence that supports the asserted grounds of opposition (**R.76(2)(c)**). The evidence itself ('Beweismittel' in the German version of the law) should preferably be filed with the notice of opposition to expedite the opposition proceedings. Otherwise, if the opposition is admissible, the EPO will invite the opponent under **R.83** to file it, as a rule within two months. (D-IV,1.2.2.1(v))

The opposition division will assess the evidence only after it has formed an opinion on the admissibility of the opposition. It checks whether a priority claim is justified, whether the cited documents have been published before the priority date, and whether the documents support the arguments of the opponent (**T234/86**).

It does not suffice to provide only facts and evidence in a notice of opposition; a logical connection must be made between them. The 'reasoned statement' in **R.76(1)** implies the arguments that provide the required 'logical connection'. (D-IV,1.2.2.1(v); **T222/85** r.6, based on **R.55(c) EPC1973**, which mentioned 'arguments')

For written evidence the opponent must indicate the date of publication of the document and the relevant technical subject-matter.

If a document provided as evidence is not in an official EPO language, the EPO may request a translation in an official EPO language (**R.3(3)**; A-VII,3.4); in practice the opponent will always be requested to file a translation. The document may be disregarded if the requested translation is not filed (**R.3(3)**).

The prior art taken into account by the examining division is not automatically subject-matter in the opposition procedure, because the opposition procedure is a special procedure, and not a continuation of the grant procedure (**T198/88** hn.1). However, the document quoted in the patent as the closest prior art does form part of the opposition (**T536/88** hn.II; D-V,2.2). For oral evidence the witnesses must be identified with their testimony, date of publication and the group of people attending the disclosure. The same applies to public prior use.

See **Art.54(2):3.6** on public prior use. If an opposition is based only on an alleged public prior use, **R.76(2)(c)** is complied with only if the notice of opposition indicates, within the opposition period, all the facts which make it possible to determine the date of prior use, what has been used, and the circumstances relating to the alleged use. The notice of opposition must also indicate the evidence; the evidence itself can be filed later (**T328/87**).

An expert opinion according to **Art.117(1)(e)** is not often used in opposition proceedings. The technical knowledge of the members of the Division is generally sufficient. However, use is often made of sworn statements under **Art.117(1)(g)**.

5 **Identity of the representative (R.76(2)(d))**

If parties are represented, the parties are the opponents, not their representative. The authorisation of the representative must be filed on request only (**R.101(1)**).

If professional representatives act as a straw person, as permitted by **G3/97**, r.2.1, they should be indicated as opponent under **R.76(2)(a)** in the notice of opposition; such a straw person opponent can appoint a representative under **R.76(2)(d)**.

R. 76(3) Part III of the Implementing Regulations shall apply mutatis mutandis to the notice of opposition.

1 **Applicability of Part III of the Rules**
R.76(3) clarifies that also in opposition proceedings the general provisions on proceedings before the EPO and the provisions of Part III of the Implementing Regulations (**R.35-54**) shall apply mutatis mutandis. (CA/PL17/06)

Close analysis shows that numerous provisions in Part III of the Implementing Regulations can play an important role in these proceedings. In cases where Part III is generally to be applied mutatis mutandis, it will be necessary to establish whether and how a rule is actually applicable to a particular set of circumstances. Consequently, it will not matter if the reference is irrelevant in the case of one or the other provision. (CA/PL29/06)

R. 77 Rejection of the opposition as inadmissible

Implementation of **Art.101(1)**

1 **Assessment of admissibility**
After the examination upon receipt of the notice of opposition whether the opposition is regarded as filed (see **Art.101(1):1** and **Art.99(1):4**), the formalities officer assesses the opposition for admissibility. Major deficiencies must be remedied before expiry of the opposition period on penalty of inadmissibility. Minor deficiencies must be remedied within a period to be specified (usually a two-month period), also on penalty of inadmissibility.

Note that a failure to pay the opposition fee is not a deficiency under **R.77** but a deficiency under **Art.99(1)**, causing the notice of opposition deemed not to have been filed.

2 **Procedure for corrigible deficiencies**
When a notice of opposition which is deemed to have been filed reveals serious deficiencies under **R.77(1)**, the EPO will notify the opponent of the deficiencies if it is still possible to correct the deficiencies before the expiry of the opposition period. Since the EPO is not obliged to issue the notification, the opponent can seek no remedy against failure to issue it. (D-IV,1.3.3)

Minor deficiencies under **R.77(2)** must be remedied within a time limit set by the EPO, which may expire later than the expiry of the opposition period. The EPO is obliged to issue an invitation to correct such deficiencies (**R.77(2)**). If the invitation is inadvertently omitted, opponents may remedy deficiencies at their own initiative, at any time, without suffering adverse legal consequences. (D-IV,1.3.3)

Failure to meet the period of **R.77(2)** for correction cannot be remedied: it is not a time limit that the applicant failed to observe (**Art.121(1)**) or a time limit that the applicant or proprietor filed to observe (**Art.122**). The period may be extended on request under **R.132**.

3 **Procedure for incorrigible deficiencies**
If there are deficiencies which can no longer be remedied and which have not been communicated to the opponent because the opposition period has expired, the formalities officer notifies the deficiencies to the opponent, as required under **Art.113(1)**, allowing the opponent in general two months to submit comments, and points out that the notice of opposition is likely to be rejected as inadmissible. On expiry of the period for filing comments or of the period for remedying a deficiency, a decision is taken to reject the opposition as inadmissible and this decision is communicated to the parties (**R.77(3)**). (D-IV,1.4)

4 **Inadmissibility**

The EPO examines the admissibility of the opposition of its own motion throughout the proceedings (D-IV,5.1). Particularly, adequate substantiation of the notice of opposition is examined (D-IV 1.2.2.1(v)). The decision that the opposition is admissible is generally taken together with the final decision of the proceedings. This procedure is followed because the opposition can become inadmissible during the proceedings. This is not ruled out by a communication indicating the admissibility according to **R.79(1)** (**T222/85**). (D-IV,5.5)

When the opposition is inadmissible, the opposition fee is not refunded.

R. 77(1) If the Opposition Division notes that the notice of opposition does not comply with Article 99, paragraph 1, or Rule 76, paragraph 2(c), or does not sufficiently identify the patent against which opposition has been filed, it shall reject the opposition as inadmissible, unless these deficiencies have been remedied before expiry of the opposition period.

Amended, in force since 01.04.2009 (OJ 2008 p.513).
Art.99(1) Opposition
R.76(2)(c) Statement of extent of opposition

1 **Deficiencies to be corrected before expiry of the opposition period**

1.1 ART.99(1) NON-COMPLIANCE

The identity of the opponent is not known at the end of the opposition period (D-IV,1.2.2.1(vi), **T590/94** r.1.2.2; **Art.99(1):2.1** and **R.76(2):2**). See **R.76(2):2.2** for correction possibilities.

The notice is not filed with an EPO office in Munich, The Hague or Berlin. (D-IV,1.2.2.1(i))

The notice is not in writing. **R.86** requires that all documents must comply with Part III of the Rules (35-54), in which **R.50(2)**, applying also to opposition documents, states that it shall generally be typewritten or printed. Hence, the notice may be handwritten.

If the opposition fee is not paid or paid late, the opposition is deemed to not have been filed rather than inadmissible (**Art.99(1):3.3**).

1.2 R.76(2)(C) NON-COMPLIANCE

The notice does not state the extent of the opposition. If no indication of the extent of the opposition has been given, it suffices when the extent is clear from the notice in its entirety. See **R.76(2):4.2**. (D-IV,1.2.2.1(iii))

The notice does not give the grounds of opposition. If non-patentability is given as ground, the statement must at least implicitly indicate which conditions for patentability (**Art.52 - 57**) are considered not fulfilled. If the facts and evidence do not support the grounds, for example because they relate only to national prior rights, the opposition will be inadmissible (**T550/88**).

The notice does not indicate the facts and evidence to support the grounds of opposition (D-IV,1.2.2.1(v)). Abstracts of European prior rights cannot be used as facts (**Art.85**). On invitation under **R.83**, the evidence can be filed later within a term of usually two months. The evidence for prior use in an opposition need not be filed together with the facts and arguments, provided that the information on the prior use given in the facts and arguments is comprehensible enough for its merits to be examined (**T538/89**). If the indication of facts, evidence and arguments is not beyond any shadow of doubt, the public interest may lie in the examination of the opposition on its merits; thus, the benefit of the doubt as regards admissibility of the opposition should be given to the opponent (**T925/91** r.2.2 and **G1/84** r.3).

1.3 INSUFFICIENT IDENTIFICATION OF THE OPPOSED PATENT
This requirement is less strict than the requirement under **R.76(2)(b)**. It is complied with if the particulars available to the EPO are together sufficient to identify the patent easily and without doubt, i.e. either the publication number or application number normally suffices (**T317/86**). The indication of only the name of a large company does not suffice. However, a mere number suffices, provided no conflicting information is given, e.g. an inconsistent name of the proprietor (D-IV,1.2.2.1(ii)).

R. 77(2) If the Opposition Division notes that the notice of opposition does not comply with provisions other than those referred to in paragraph 1, it shall communicate this to the opponent and shall invite them to remedy the deficiencies noted within a period to be specified. If the deficiencies are not remedied in due time, the Opposition Division shall reject the opposition as inadmissible.

Amended by decision of the Administrative Council of 10.12.2024, which entered into force on 01.04.2025 (OJ 2025 A16). The amendment was introduction of gender-neutral language.

1 **Deficiencies to be corrected in an office time limit**
Examples of deficiencies under **R.77(2)** are (D-IV,1.2.2.2):
- Incomplete name or address and state of residence or business of opponent (**R.76(2)(a)** and **R.41(2)(c)**; **T25/85**).
- Incorrect identity of opponent (see **R.76(2):2.2**).
- Incomplete number, name of proprietor or title of opposed patent (**R.76(2)(b)**). If the particulars available to the EPO are together sufficient to identify the patent easily and without doubt, no deficiency exists within the meaning of **R.77(2)** with regard to the title (**T317/86**).
- Incomplete name or address of representative (**R.76(2)(d)** and **R.41(2)(d)**).
- The opponent must be represented according to **Art.133(2)**, but has not appointed a representative. The opponent will be invited to appoint a representative and arrange for the signature or approval of the notice of opposition by the representative. (D-IV,1.2.2.2(iv))

Another deficiency is the omission of the signature of the opponent or the opponent's representative. When the omission is not rectified on invitation, the opposition is regarded as not filed (**R.50(3)** is lex specialis); the opposition is not regarded as inadmissible. Hence, the signature is checked before the application of **R.77** (D-IV,1.2.1(ii); see **Art.99(1):4**).

Failure to correct the deficiencies in the notice of opposition in time cannot be redressed by further processing, because the failure does not relate to an application, neither by re-establishment because that remedy is in principle not open for opponents. (D-IV,1.4.2)

R. 77(3) The decision to reject an opposition as inadmissible shall be communicated to the proprietor of the patent, together with a copy of the notice of opposition.

1 **Communication of inadmissibility**
The decision to reject a notice of opposition can be taken without the participation of the proprietor. Proprietors are not asked for comments, and, if no other notices of opposition have been filed, amendments filed by them are not taken into consideration by the EPO, because there is no opposition procedure (D-IV,1.4.1; see e.g. **T550/88**). Without **R.77(3)**, the EPO would not have been obliged to inform the proprietor.

R. 78 Procedure where the proprietor of the patent is not entitled

Implementation of **Art.99(4)**

1 **General**
R.78 deals with the procedure to be followed where the registered proprietor of a patent was not entitled to the grant of the patent (D-VII,4).

R. 78(1) If a third party provides evidence, during opposition proceedings or during the opposition period, that they have instituted proceedings against the proprietor of the European patent, seeking a decision within the meaning of Article 61, paragraph 1, opposition proceedings shall be stayed unless the third party communicates to the European Patent Office in writing their consent to the continuation of such proceedings. Such consent shall be irrevocable. However, proceedings shall not be stayed until the Opposition Division has deemed the opposition admissible. Rule 14, paragraphs 2 to 4, shall apply mutatis mutandis.

Amended by decision of the Administrative Council of 10.12.2024, which entered into force on 01.04.2025 (OJ 2025 A16). The amendment was introduction of gender-neutral language.
Art.61(1) European patent application filed by non-entitled person
R.14(2)-(4) Resumption of proceedings

1 **Procedure for requesting stay of opposition proceedings**
R.78(1) provides for staying opposition proceedings when a third party starts national proceedings contesting entitlement to the patent, in the same way that **R.14(1)** provides for staying grant proceedings. During the stay, the third party can await the final decision on entitlement to the patent taken by a national court, without the risk of steps detrimental to the third party being taken by the proprietor. The Legal Division is responsible for the stay and resumption of the opposition procedure (OJ 2013 p.600; D-VII,4.4). **R.78(1)** refers to **Art.61(1)**, which, however, does not apply to granted patents; entitlement decisions for granted patents are dealt with in **Art.99(4)**.

The clause 'proceedings shall not be stayed until the Opposition Division has deemed the opposition admissible' means that the preliminary examination of admissibility shall not be stayed, i.e. the formalities officer or the opposition division can reject the opposition as inadmissible in the first stage of the procedure under **R.77**, without the proprietor being involved yet (see **Art.101(1):2**).

R.78(1) provides that **R.14** (2)-(4) applies by analogy. Hence, the opposition is resumed when evidence is provided that a final decision in the national proceedings has been taken. If the decision on entitlement is in favour of the third party, the opposition may not be resumed earlier than three months after the decision has become final, unless the third party requests resumption (D-VII,4.2.1). Upon staying the proceedings and thereafter, the Legal Division can set a date for the resumption of the opposition regardless of the stage reached in the national proceedings.

R. 78(2) Where a third party has, in accordance with Article 99, paragraph 4, replaced the previous proprietor for one or some of the designated Contracting States, the patent as maintained in opposition proceedings may, for these States, contain claims, a description and drawings different from those for the other designated States.

Art.99(4) Replacement of non-entitled proprietor

1 **Different patents for different states**
A third party who is entitled to the patent can replace the proprietor in the opposition procedure for one or more designated states (see **Art.99(4):1** for the requirements). If the third party replaces the proprietor for some but not all states, there are two proprietors. If these proprietors do not request to become joint proprietors, no common representative needs to be appointed (**R.151**), and the proprietors can act independently in the procedure (D-I,6). The opposition proceedings involving the different patent proprietors are to be conducted separately, and the outcomes can be different (D-VII,3.2). Accordingly, **R.78(2)** specifies that the patent may be maintained in different forms for the different states, as an exception to **Art.118**.

R. 79 Preparation of the examination of the opposition

Implementation of **Art.101(1)**

1 **Communication of documents**
R.79 provides for the distribution of documents between parties and for inviting them to submit observations and any amendments.

The opposition division will transmit a notice of opposition it has received to the proprietor of the patent in suit (**R.79(1)**). If several notices of opposition have been filed, the opposition division will also send a copy of each notice of opposition to the other opponents (**R.79(2)**). Any observations and amendments filed by the proprietor will be sent to the opponents (**R.79(3)**).

To reduce the number of documents transmitted by the EPO to the parties, the opposition division does not transmit to the parties copies of any documents annexed to notices of opposition or to letters which are available for inspection and for download in the Register (see **R.143(1):1**); paper copies are available only upon request (Not. EPO OJ 2022 A28). The EPO assigns reference numbers to documents cited in an opposition, labels each cited document in the Register with its reference number, and provides a consolidated list of the reference numbers (OJ 2020 A31). Parties are advised to inspect the Register before oral proceedings to ensure they have all relevant documents.

R. 79(1) The Opposition Division shall communicate the notice of opposition to the proprietor of the patent and shall give them the opportunity to file observations and to amend, where appropriate, the description, claims and drawings within a period to be specified.

Amended by decision of the Administrative Council of 10.12.2024, which entered into force on 01.04.2025 (OJ 2025 A16). The amendment was introduction of gender-neutral language.

1 **Communication of opposition to proprietor**
After the opposition period, any period for remedying deficiencies under **R.77(2)**, and any period for presenting evidence, the formalities officer invites the proprietor to file observations and to amend the patent within a four-month period (**R.79(1)**; D-IV,5.2), unless the opposition is already finally rejected as inadmissible under **R.77(3)**. The proprietor should submit a full response to the opposition. An extension of the period will only be granted in exceptional cases and only on the basis of a duly substantiated request (OJ 2016 A42). However, if the request for extension is denied by the opposition division, reasons for the denial should be provided (**T2120/18**, r.4.4).

There is no automatic sanction for the late filing of submissions and requests. If they are received before a decision is issued, they are regarded as received in due time (**G12/91**); any late filed facts and evidence are, however, to be treated as not filed in due time (**Art.114(2)**) (E-VIII,1.8). Such facts and evidence will be disregarded, unless they are prima facie relevant, i.e. they would affect the outcome of the decision to be taken (OJ 2016 A42 §5).

If there are several opponents, the formalities officer will send the notices of opposition also to the other opponents (**R.79(2)**).

The opposition division cannot revoke the patent without establishing that the proprietor had received the communication under **R.79(1)** or at least the correct notification thereof in order to safeguard the right to be heard of the proprietor (**T1529/20**).

R. 79(2) If several notices of opposition have been filed, the Opposition Division shall communicate them to the other opponents at the same time as the communication under paragraph 1.

R. 79(3) The Opposition Division shall communicate any observations and amendments filed by the proprietor of the patent to the other parties, and shall invite them, if it considers this expedient, to reply within a period to be specified.

1 **Communication with opponent**
The formalities officer will communicate observations of any of the parties immediately to the other parties for information. The opposition division can issue a separate invitation, usually setting a period of four months for filing a reply, if it considers that further submissions are necessary for the procedure (D-IV,5.4). In most cases, however, the opposition division will issue summons to oral proceedings directly after receiving the proprietors reply under **R.79(1)** (OJ 2016 A42 §3).

An opponent has no obligation to respond, and non-response has no legal consequences. However, an opponent who does not respond, runs the danger that later filed facts and evidence may be disregarded under **Art.114(2)** (E-VIII,1.8).

In the case of oral proceedings, the first substantive communication of the opposition division is annexed to the summons (D-VI,3.2).

R. 79(4) In the case of an intervention under Article 105, the Opposition Division may dispense with the application of paragraphs 1 to 3.

1 **Limited communication with intervener**
The application of the provisions in paragraphs 1 to 3 to a late-filed intervention (**Art.105**) might slow down the procedure too much. Therefore, the intervener is normally notified of all communications so far in the proceedings, and from then on the intervener participates as an opponent in the proceedings. (**G1/94** r.8)

R. 80 Amendment of the European patent

Without prejudice to Rule 138, the description, claims and drawings may be amended, provided that the amendments are occasioned by a ground for opposition under Article 100, even if that ground has not been invoked by the opponent.

Art.100 Grounds for opposition
R.138 Different claims, description and drawings for different states
Implementation of **Art.101(1)**

1 **Amendment of patent in opposition**
R.80 addresses substantive requirements for the admissibility of amendments made in opposition. The amendments must be occasioned by a ground for opposition, which ground need not have been invoked by the opponent (H-II,3.1). For example, in opposition proceedings admissibly opened on grounds of lack of novelty, the proprietor could also make amendments to remove added subject-matter. (Not. EPO OJ 1995 p.416)

Hence, the right to amend in opposition proceedings cannot be used merely to tidy up and improve the disclosure of the patent (**T127/85**). The mere addition of new claims to the claims as granted is inadmissible because such an amendment is neither appropriate nor necessary to meet a ground for opposition (**T674/96** r.3.10). However, replacing one independent claim as granted with multiple independent claims, each directed to a respective specific embodiment of the independent claim as granted, is admissible if the replacement is occasioned by a ground for opposition (**T223/97**, H-II,3.1). Furthermore, if an independent claim is amended, further consequential amendments of other claims and the description comply with **R.80** (H-II,3.2).

The amended claims must comply with the requirements of **Art.123(2)** and (3). The amendments themselves must also comply with the requirement of clarity under **Art.84** (see **G3/14**). Where amended claims do not comply with **Art.84** due to a lack of support in the description, and this deficiency already existed in the patent as granted, amending the description is neither necessary nor required (**T447/22**).

Amended claims in opposition need not comply with the requirement of unity of invention under **Art.82** (see **Art.82:3**) and neither with the limitation of the number of independent claims of **R.43(2)** (**T263/05** hn. II).

Hence, an amendment replacing a single independent claim with a plurality of independent claims is generally not objectionable under **R.80** (**T123/22** r.3.8). It is, in principle, legitimate for the proprietor to try to cover parts of the contested independent claim in order to overcome a ground of opposition, possibly by means of two or more independent claims (**T431/22** r.1). The number of independent claims is restricted by the requirement that 'the amendment is a necessary and appropriate response to a ground of opposition' (**T263/05** hn. I; r.5.19).

As indicated by its wording, **R.80** does not limit the application of **R.138**. Hence, amendments occasioned by national prior rights are also admissible during opposition proceedings (H-II,3.3).

Where a patent has been granted with different sets of claims for different contracting states (**R.138**), the proprietor may apply a limitation of one set to another set or file a single set for all contracting states (H-III,4.5).

R.80 is a lex specialis and prevails over **R.79(1)**. It gives proprietors the right to amend of their own volition. Amendments not related to the grounds of opposition, e.g. corrections or clarifications, will be taken into consideration up to the pronouncement of the decision in oral proceedings or until the date the decision taken in written proceedings is handed over to the EPO's internal postal service (H-II,3.2; **G12/91**).

2 **Correction of patent in opposition**

A correction of the patent under **R.140** is not possible (**G1/10**). This means that if the proprietor is requesting maintenance of the patent as granted, it is not possible to request the correction of obvious errors in the granted text since this would amount to a correction under **R.140** (**T657/11** hn; r.3; **T914/18** r.4.2.3). If, however, the proprietor is requesting that the patent be maintained in amended form under **Art.101(3)(a)**, the correction of obvious errors under **R.139** is possible (H-VI,2.1.1.1).

3 **Non-binding character of limitation of claim in opposition**

A proprietor who has reduced the scope of protection during opposition proceedings can enlarge the scope again later-on during the proceedings (**T123/85**). A limitation to meet objections does not irrevocably abandon subject-matter no longer covered by the limited claim (**T123/85** r.3.1.5). See **G1/99** for a redress in appeal of an inadmissible amendment held allowable by the opposition division in the case where the opponent is the sole appellant.

4 **Extension of protection and shift to unsearched subject-matter**

The opposition division and the board of appeal have the discretion to allow amendments in opposition (appeal) and may refuse them if filed at a late stage or if neither appropriate nor necessary (**T406/86**; D-VI,4.2). An amendment of the claims may not extend the protection conferred (see **Art.123(3)** and notes). An amendment during appeal proceedings enlarging the scope of protection as maintained in the first-instance proceedings is only allowed if the proprietor is the appellant and not merely a party as of right (see **Art.107:3**).

If the claims have been limited to subject-matter of a dependent claim, or to elements previously not set out in the claims, an additional search may be required (D-VI,5).

R. 81 Examination of opposition

Implementation of **Art.101(1)**

1 **General**

R.81 gives the details of the examination during the opposition procedure. **R.81(1)** governs which grounds of opposition the opposition division must examine. How the opposition division is to communicate with the parties is the subject of **R.81(2)**. According to **R.81(3)** the proprietor must, where necessary, be given an opportunity to amend the patent; a communication may contain a reasoned statement covering the grounds against maintenance of the patent.

Any party can request oral proceedings during the opposition procedure (**Art.116(1)**). The summons for oral proceedings is accompanied by a review of the items to be discussed and, usually, a non-binding opinion of the opposition division on the issues to be decided (D-VI,3.2).

The opposition division will not grant a request to stay opposition proceedings if the request is solely based on pending appeal or opposition proceedings in a related case (D-VI,8).

R. 81(1) The Opposition Division shall examine those grounds for opposition which are invoked in the opponent's statement under Rule 76, paragraph 2(c). Grounds for opposition not invoked by the opponent may be examined by the Opposition Division of its own motion if they would prejudice the maintenance of the European patent.

R.76(2)(c) Grounds of opposition

1 **Examination of grounds for opposition**

Paragraph 1 incorporates the principles established by the Enlarged Board of Appeal regarding the examination of grounds for opposition by the opposition division (see **G10/91**; OJ 1993 p.420; D-V,2.2). (OJ 2003 se1, p.159)

The extent of examination by the opposition division of its own motion is restricted by case law, as set out in **Art.114(1):1**.

R. 81(2) Communications under Article 101, paragraph 1, second sentence, and all replies thereto shall be sent to all parties. If the opposition division considers this expedient, it shall invite the parties to reply within a period to be specified.

Art.101(1) Examination of the opposition

1 **Information to all parties**

In view of **R.81(2)**, the EPO does not allow informal personal interviews and telephone conversations in opposition proceedings in which more than one party is involved. An exception is, for example, proceedings concerning the inadmissibility of a notice of opposition (see **R.77(3):1**). (E-III,1.1)

R. 81(3) In any communication under Article 101, paragraph 1, second sentence, the proprietor of the European patent shall, where necessary, be given the opportunity to amend, where appropriate, the description, claims and drawings. Where necessary, the communication shall contain a reasoned statement covering the grounds against the maintenance of the European patent.

Art.101(1) Examination of the opposition-Revocation or maintenance of the European patent

1 **Auxiliary requests**

The proprietor can file a main request in the form of the set of claims as granted or a new set of claims, and one or more auxiliary requests each in the form of an alternative set of claims. The auxiliary requests must be presented in order of preference. If the opposition division decides to revoke the patent or maintain the patent in amended form based on an auxiliary request, the decision includes the reasons for rejecting the main request and any (higher ranking) auxiliary requests. For comments on adaptation of description, see **Art.84:1.1.**

The proprietor may appeal the decision to reject the higher ranking requests. However, the admissibility of new claim requests in appeal is restricted, even if included with the grounds of appeal or reply (see **Art.114(2):2**). In particular, proprietors should not withdraw or withhold any claim requests in first instance proceedings that they may want to defend in appeal; requests not maintained in first instance are inadmissible in second instance under Art.12(6) RPBA (see also **T23/10**).

The number of requests should not be excessive (**T907/91**). The most broadly worded claims should be filed as main request and more limited claims as auxiliary request.

The opposition division examines the main and auxiliary requests as submitted by the proprietor and in the order indicated by the proprietor up to and including the highest-ranking allowable request, if any. If the opposition division considers a request allowable, and all parties have had an opportunity to comment as required by **Art.113(1)**, the opposition division immediately issues an interlocutory decision stating that the patent in amended form according to that request meets the requirements of the EPC and giving the reasons why the request is allowable and the higher ranking requests are not allowable. The decision is separately appealable under **Art.106(2)**. Any requests lower ranking than the allowable request will not be examined.

T926/93 holds that opponents need only substantiate a ground of opposition against a single claim of each request. If they succeed in establishing that a claim of each request is not allowable, the patent will be revoked.

Before issuing a decision revoking a patent solely on the basis of a proprietor's main request, the opposition division must ensure that the proprietor has expressly withdrawn all auxiliary requests (**T5/89**).

Both proprietor and opponent may appeal against an (interlocutory) decision to maintain the patent in amended form based on an auxiliary request, since both are adversely affected: the proprietor in that the main request has not been allowed, the opponent in that the patent has not been revoked (assuming full revocation has been requested).

R. 82 Maintenance of the European patent in amended form

Implementation of **Art.101(3)**

1 **General**

R.82 concerns the maintenance of the European patent in amended form. The legal consequences of failure to file the translation in due time are set out in paragraph 3.

R. 82(1) Before the Opposition Division decides to maintain the European patent as amended, it shall inform the parties of the text in which it intends to maintain the patent, and shall invite them to file their observations within two months if they disapprove of that text.

1 **EPO practice of interlocutory decision**

Provisions **R.82(1)** and **R.82(2)**, first sentence, are rarely used, particularly since the opposition division usually comes to a conclusion on whether the patent can be maintained in amended form at oral proceedings rather than in the written proceedings. The normal practice of the EPO in opposition proceedings is set out in the following paragraphs. The current practice was introduced by Not. EPO OJ 1989 p.393 in view of **G1/88**. It is unclear why **R.82** has not yet been brought into line with current practice.

If the opposition division considers that the patent can be maintained in amended form, whether in written proceedings or oral proceedings, it issues an interlocutory decision (see **Art.106(2)**) stating that, taking into consideration the amendments made, the patent and the invention to which it relates meet the requirements of the EPC. This is not yet the final decision of the opposition division according to **Art.101(3)(a)** to maintain the patent in amended form. The interlocutory decision is appealable. (D-VI,7.2.2.)

If no appeal is filed, the opposition division issues the invitation of **R.82(2)**, second sentence, to file the translations of the amended claims in the two other official languages of EPO, and in case of handwritten amendments, to file a typed text under **R.82(2)**, third sentence (D-VI,7.2.3). Once these formal requirements are met, the opposition division takes the final decision to maintain the patent in amended form of **Art.101(3)(a)** and **R.82(4)**. A mention of the decision is published in the Bulletin (**Art.103**), which starts the period for filing translations of the amended patent with national patent offices under **Art.65(1)** (D-VIII,1.4.1). No new translation needs to be filed to the EPO in connection with a unitary patent. Furthermore, a new patent specification is published (**Art.103** and **R.87**).

If the interlocutory decision is appealed, a board will review the interlocutory decision. The board may decide to maintain the patent in amended form based on the interlocutory decision or based on another specified text, reject the opposition as inadmissible, reject the opposition and maintain the patent unamended, or revoke the patent. If the Board maintains the patent in amended form, it will remit the case to the opposition division, which will issue the invitation of **R.82(2)**, second sentence, and proceed as in the previous paragraph. Usually, however, the Board will only decide on an allowable set of claims and will remit the matter back to the opposition division for adaptation of the description, which will then result in a further interlocutory decision being taken on the complete text of the amended patent. This further decision can also be appealed.

The interlocutory decision closes the debate before the opposition division on the issues decided in it and the opposition division has thereafter no power to consider those issues anymore (**T390/86** hn.2). Since the interlocutory decision is made separately appealable, any matters decided in it can no longer be challenged later in an appeal against the final decision under **R.82(4)**. The final decision is only appealable as far as it relates to issues occurring before the opposition division after the appealable interlocutory decision (see e.g. **T91/08** r.1).

2 **Remaining use of R.82(1)**

If an opposition division proposes amendments of its own motion in written proceedings, it can issue an invitation under **R.82(1)** to the parties to comment (D-VI,7.2.1). If the proprietor objects to the amendments, the examination of the opposition must be resumed (**Art.113(2)**); if the opponent has objections, the examination is resumed if the opposition division agrees with them (D-VI,7.2.1). If the examination is not resumed, the opposition division issues the invitation under **R.82(2)**, second sentence. An opponent who has not replied to the **R.82(1)** invitation can still appeal the decision to maintain the patent in amended form (**G1/88**).

The invitation of **R.82(1)** is not often used, even in written opposition proceedings. The reason is that the prerequisites for an interlocutory decision to maintain the patent in amended form are: 1) that the patent proprietor has submitted the new text (as main or auxiliary request) or has approved the new text in case of amendments by the opposition division (**Art.113(2)**), and 2) that the opponent has had sufficient opportunity to comment on the proposed new text in view of **Art.113(1)**. In written proceedings, a communication under **Art.101(1)** can be used to meet both prerequisites by giving the opponent the opportunity to comment and inviting the proprietor to approve the text in case of amendments by the opposition division. Once these requirements have been met, a separate communication under **R.82(1)** is neither necessary nor appropriate (**G1/88**).

R. 82(2) If a party disapproves of the text communicated by the Opposition Division, examination of the opposition may be continued. Otherwise, the Opposition Division shall, on expiry of the period under paragraph 1, invite the proprietor of the patent to file a translation of any amended claims in the official languages of the European Patent Office other than the language of the proceedings, within a period of three months. Where, in oral proceedings, decisions under Article 106, paragraph 2, or Article 111, paragraph 2, have been based on documents not complying with the applicable requirements prescribed by the President of the European Patent Office under Rule 49, paragraph 2, the proprietor of the patent shall be invited to file the amended text in a form compliant with those requirements within the three-month period.

Amended by decision of the Administrative Council of 14.12.2023, which entered into force on 01.04.2024 (OJ 2024 A3). The amendment removed the former fee for publishing. Earlier amendments can be found in OJ 2022 A101 and OJ 2015 A82.
Art.65(1) Translation of patent required by a contracting state
Art.106(2) Interlocutory decision in first instance
Art.111(2) Remittal of case to first instance
R.49(8) Requirement of typed version of text

1 **Procedure around interlocutory decision**

The first sentence of **R.82(2)** is hardly used; see **R.82(1):1**. If an opposition division considers that a patent can be maintained in amended form according to a certain text and **Art.113** is complied with, an appealable interlocutory decision is issued to that effect. Once the interlocutory decision can no longer be impugned and becomes '*res judicata*', i.e. after expiry of the appeal period or after the appeal procedure, the opposition division issues the invitation of **R.82(2)**, second sentence (**G1/88 r.7**). Hence, the word 'otherwise' in **R.82(2)**, second sentence, does not mean that the invitation of **R.82(1)** must be issued first, but that the examination of the opposition is closed.

2 **Translations**

The **R.82(2)** communication includes an invitation to file translations of the amended claims in the two EPO languages other than the language of the proceedings. The invitation is also sent if the amendments consist of deleting one or more claims.

Contracting states may prescribe that a translation of the amended patent specification is filed with the national patent office within three months from the publication of the patent in amended form (**Art.65(1)**).

3 **Typed version of amended text**
During oral proceedings in opposition and opposition appeal the proprietor may file handwritten amendments in documents replacing parts of the patent (see **R.50(1):2**). This can be useful in the case of oral proceedings held on the premises of the EPO. The documents with the handwritten amendments can serve as the basis of the interlocutory decision or the appeal decision. In such cases, the **R.82(2)** invitation includes a request to file a version of the amended text passages that is compliant with the applicable requirements prescribed by the President under **R.49(2)** in Dec. Pres. OJ 2022 A113, i.e. as typed text, for preparing the 'Druckexemplar' for publication (**R.82(2)**, third sentence). The formally deficient document with handwritten amendments remains the authentic text of the patent maintained in amended form. (OJ 2016 A22; D-VI,7.2.3; E-III,8.7.3).

The decision of the President (OJ 2022 A113) provides in Art.5 that: "*The applicable requirements under Rule 82(2), third sentence, EPC shall be the requirements of Article 2, paragraph 7, of this decision.*"

Art.2(7) of the decision provides that: "*The request for grant of a European patent, the description, the claims and the abstract shall be typed or printed. Only graphic symbols and characters and chemical or mathematical formulae may, if necessary, be drawn or written by hand. The typing shall be 1½ spaced. All text matter shall be in characters, the capital letters of which are not less than 0.21 cm high, and shall be in a dark, indelible colour.*"

The claims, description and drawings, as amended in opposition, must comply with all presentation requirements as provided under **R.49(2)** (**R.50(1)**); only the compliance with the requirement of typed text may be postponed under Art.5 of Dec. Pres. OJ 2022 A113. Making handwritten amendments on printed copies of the claims was often faster during oral proceedings held in person on the premises of the EPO, as amended claims were filed on paper and the available printers were less reliable than the photocopiers.

R. 82(3) If the acts required under paragraph 2 are not performed in due time, they may still be performed within two months of a communication concerning the failure to observe the time limit. Otherwise, the patent shall be revoked.

Amended by decision of the Administrative Council of 14.12.2023, which entered into force on 01.04.2024 (OJ 2024 A3). The amendment removed the surcharge of the former fee.

1 **Grace period for filing of translations and typed text**
If the filing of the translations of amended claims or, where necessary, the filing a typed version of the amended text has not been carried out within the three-month period of **R.82(2)**, the opposition division will invite the proprietor under **R.82(3)** to complete the omitted act(s) within two months. A divergence between a document with handwritten amendments and a typed version of the document submitted under **R.82(2)** will also trigger the communication under **R.82(3)** (OJ 2016 A22 §12).

In case the **R.82(3)** communication was not justified, the proprietor may provide proof that the acts required under **R.82(2)** had been carried out in time, and, if required, on an auxiliary basis, carry out the acts. Further processing is excluded for **R.82(3)**, because the failure does not relate to a patent application but to a patent.

If the requested acts have not been carried out on expiry of the two-month period, the patent will be revoked (**R.82(3)**, last sentence; **G1/90** hn). The proprietor may appeal the decision if e.g. the facts or the interpretation of the law is disputed (**G1/90** r.13). A proprietor that has missed the two-month period may apply for re-establishment, even if the decision to revoke has not yet been delivered (**G1/90** r.14). This must be done within two months from removal of the cause of non-compliance and at the latest within one year following the expiry of the two-month period. The proprietor must complete the omitted acts, request re-establishment, pay the fee for re-establishment and prove compliance with the all-due-care criterion. Alternatively, the proprietor can file an appeal and file the documents required under **R.82(2)** together with the grounds of appeal. This would remove the cause for revocation under **R.82(3)** and allow the decision to revoke the patent to be set aside (**J18/08** by analogy).

R. 82(4) The decision to maintain the European patent as amended shall state which text of the patent forms the basis for the decision.

R. 83 Request for documents

Documents referred to by a party to opposition proceedings shall be filed together with the notice of opposition or the written submissions. If such documents are neither enclosed nor filed in due time upon invitation by the European Patent Office, it may decide not to take into account any arguments based on them.

Implementation of **Art.101(1)**

1 **Documents filed in opposition**
In opposition proceedings, documents should be filed in a single copy (D-III,6(iii); D-IV,1.2.2.1(v)). If cited documents are not submitted within the opposition period, the EPO will request the party to file them as a rule within two months (D-IV,1.2.2.1).

R. 84 Continuation of the opposition proceedings by the European Patent Office of its own motion

Implementation of **Art.101(1)**

R. 84(1) If the European patent has been surrendered in all the designated Contracting States or has lapsed in all those States, the opposition proceedings may be continued at the request of the opponent filed within two months of a communication from the European Patent Office informing them of the surrender or lapse.

Amended by decision of the Administrative Council of 10.12.2024, which entered into force on 01.04.2025 (OJ 2025 A16). The amendment was introduction of gender-neutral language.

1 **Continuation of proceedings after surrender or lapse of patent**
The EPO requests the opponent to notify it within a period of two months whether the opponent wants to continue the opposition. The patent may lapse by non-payment of the renewal fees for the designated states or by expiry. The lapse or surrender must be proven to the EPO by means of excerpts from the national patent registers unless the EPO is already aware of the lapse or surrender.

If the proprietor renounces rights under the patent ex tunc or no request for continuation is filed by the opponent, the opposition proceedings will be terminated, and the parties informed accordingly. **R.84(1)** also applies in appeal proceedings through **R.100(1)** (see e.g. **T870/92** of 20.07.1999). Note that if the proprietor is an appellant in opposition appeal proceedings, then the proprietor also has the right to continue the proceedings, applying R.84(1) mutatis mutandis.

R. 84(2) In the event of the death or legal incapacity of an opponent, the opposition proceedings may be continued by the European Patent Office of its own motion, even without the participation of the heirs or legal representatives. The same shall apply where the opposition is withdrawn.

1 **Continuation of proceedings after death of opponent**
The opposition division has a discretion to continue the opposition proceedings after withdrawal of the opposition or in the event of the death or legal incapacity of the opponent. A continuation without heirs of the deceased opponent provides the possibility to continue the opposition speedily, even if the heirs take a long time to settle their affairs.

The opposition division will continue the proceedings if these are likely to result in limitation or revocation of the patent and it can do so without the assistance of the opponent and without too much effort. Otherwise, the proceedings are closed by issuing a decision. (D-VII,5)

If a notice according to **R.82(1)** has been issued, the opposition division should always continue the opposition in the public interest (**T197/88**).

The decision to terminate the proceedings is appealable (**T197/88**, Sum. F and S IV).

In spite of the general reference in **R.100(1)** to **R.84(2)**, relating to first instance proceedings, **R.84(2)** is not applicable to appeal proceedings in opposition because of the different legal nature of the two proceedings (**G7/91** r.7). Hence, withdrawal of the appeal by the opponent as sole appellant terminates the appeal proceedings in so far as the substantive issues settled by the contested decision at first instance are concerned (**G7/91** hn). The termination of the appeal is irrespective of whether the proprietor agrees to the termination or whether the patent satisfies the requirements of the EPC (**G8/93** hn).

R. 85 Transfer of the European patent

Rule 22 shall apply to any transfer of the European patent made during the opposition period or during opposition proceedings.

R.22 Registration of transfers
Implementation of **Art.71** and **Art.101(1)**

1 **Registering a transfer of the patent**
R.22 allows the transfer of a European patent application to be recorded in the European Patent Register. **R.85** makes this rule also applicable to the transfer of a European patent during the opposition period and during opposition proceedings. The new proprietor of the patent only becomes a party to opposition proceedings when the transfer has been registered. The transfer becomes effective when the EPO has received documents verifying the transfer and, where required, the associated fee has been paid (see **R.22(1):1**). A new proprietor takes the place of the previous proprietor both in the opposition and the appeal proceedings. The new proprietor's entitlement may not be questioned in these proceedings, as the legal fiction of **Art.60(3)** applies. The Legal Division is competent as it is responsible for the entry of transfers in the Register (**Art.20(1)**). (**T553/90**)

If and under what conditions the registration of a transfer of a patent with the EPO is recognised by a contracting state is determined by national law (see NatLaw table IX, note 6). If a transfer does not automatically take effect in a designated state, the transfer must also be registered in that state for the new proprietor to sue an infringer in such a state.

R.85 does not cover the transfer of licences (**R.23**) during opposition period or procedure. Hence, the EPO no longer registers licences once a patent is granted (**J17/91**).

R. 86 Documents in opposition proceedings

Part III of the Implementing Regulations shall apply mutatis mutandis to documents filed in opposition proceedings.

Implementation of **Art.101(1)**

1 **Applicability of Part III of Rules**
According to **R.86**, the provisions of Part III of the Implementing Regulations (**R.35-54**) are to be applied mutatis mutandis in opposition proceedings.

Close analysis shows that numerous provisions in the third part of the Implementing Regulations can play an important role in these proceedings. In cases where Part III is generally to be applied mutatis mutandis, it will be necessary to establish whether and how a rule is actually applicable to a particular set of circumstances. Consequently, it will not matter if the reference is irrelevant in the case of one or the other provision. (CA/PL29/06)

The mutatis mutandis in **R.86** is interpreted to mean that the provision can only be taken to refer to those requirements which it would still be reasonable to demand of the new documents relating to the amended patent (**G1/91** r.3.2). See also **T263/05** r.5.6-5.20, which decided that **R.43(2)** is not applicable in opposition.

R. 87 Content and form of the new specification of the European patent

The new specification of the European patent shall include the description, claims and drawings as amended. Rule 73, paragraphs 2 and 3, and Rule 74 shall apply.

R.73(2) Form of the specification
R.73(3) Indication of designated contracting states

R.74 Certificate for a European patent
Implementation of **Art.103**

R. 88 Costs

Implementation of **Art.104(2)**

R. 88(1) The apportionment of costs shall be dealt with in the decision on the opposition. Such apportionment shall only take into consideration the expenses necessary to assure proper protection of the rights involved. The costs shall include the remuneration of the representatives of the parties.

1 **Apportionable costs**
A cost apportionment takes into consideration only the expenses that were necessary to assure proper protection of the rights involved (**R.88(1)**). The costs shall be limited to expenses that are necessarily and reasonably incurred (see Art.16(2) RPBA). See **Art.104(2):1** for the procedure.

Generally, the costs to be paid are the expenses incurred by the receiving parties and caused by the culpable conduct of the party against whom the cost apportionment is ordered. Unlike Art.104 EPC1973, the costs are not limited to expenses incurred during the taking of evidence or in oral proceedings. Examples of such expenses are given in D-IX,1.3 and **T930/92** hn.III.

R. 88(2) The Opposition Division shall, on request, fix the amount of costs to be paid under a final decision apportioning them. A bill of costs, with supporting evidence, shall be attached to the request. Costs may be fixed once their credibility is established.

1 **Fixing the amount of costs**
The costs may only be fixed on the basis of a final decision apportioning them (**R.88(2)**, first sentence), i.e. after a decision in appeal (however, see **R.97(1)**) or an unavailed appeal period. See **Art.104(2):1** for the procedure of fixing the costs.

R. 88(3) A request for a decision by the Opposition Division may be filed within one month of the communication on the fixing of costs under paragraph 2. The request shall be filed in writing and state the grounds on which it is based. It shall not be deemed to be filed until the prescribed fee has been paid.

Rfees2(1)16 Fee for the awarding of costs

R. 88(4) The Opposition Division shall decide on the request under paragraph 3 without oral proceedings.

R. 89 Intervention of the assumed infringer

Implementation of **Art.105(1)**

R. 89(1) Notice of intervention shall be filed within three months of the date on which proceedings referred to in Article 105 are instituted.

Art.105 Intervention of the assumed infringer

R. 89(2) Notice of intervention shall be filed in a written reasoned statement; Rules 76 and 77 shall apply mutatis mutandis. The notice of intervention shall not be deemed to have been filed until the opposition fee has been paid.

R.76 Form and content of the opposition
R.77 Rejection of the opposition as inadmissible

1 **Notice of intervention**

The reference in paragraph 2 to **R.76** makes it clear that on filing a notice of intervention, particulars must be given corresponding to a complete notice of opposition. The provisions of the Implementing Regulations governing opposition, in particular **R.76** and **R.77**, shall equally apply to the admissibility of the intervention. (CA/PL17/06; CA/PL29/06)

The requirements for the notice of intervention have been set out in **Art.105(2):1.**

Chapter II *Procedure for limitation or revocation*

R. 90 Subject of proceedings

The subject of limitation or revocation proceedings under Article 105a shall be the European patent as granted or as amended in opposition or limitation proceedings before the European Patent Office.

Implementation of **Art.105a(1)**

1 **Subject of proceedings**
R.90 defines the subject of the centralised limitation or revocation procedure before the EPO. The provision makes it explicit that only the European patent as granted or amended by the EPO is to be the subject of such proceedings (OJ 2003 se1 p.159). Where previous limitations have been made before the EPO, the patent as limited will be the subject of future proceedings.

A country may have legal provisions for limiting a European patent before national authorities, which has effect for that country only. Amendments made before such national authorities are not taken into account in proceedings before the EPO. However, the proprietor may submit in limitation proceedings before the EPO the same amendments as made earlier in national proceedings.

R. 91 Responsibility for proceedings

Decisions on requests for limitation or revocation of the European patent under Article 105a shall be taken by the Examining Division. Article 18, paragraph 2, shall apply mutatis mutandis.

Art.18(2) Composition of examining division
Implementation of **Art.105a(1)**

1 **Competence of the examining division**
According to **R.91** the examining division is responsible for deciding on requests for limitation and revocation (as already implied in **Art.21(3)(a)**; OJ 2003 se1 p.159). The examining division is entrusted with limitation and revocation proceedings because amended claims in limitation proceedings are examined under **R.95(2)** for their compliance with both formal and substantive requirements, e.g. clarity (**Art.84**).

The formalities examination is entrusted to a formalities officer (Dec. Pres. OJ 2014 A6, Art.1 items 25 and 26). Substantive examination of the request up to the point where a decision is ready to be taken is as a rule entrusted to one examiner (**Art.18(2)** mutatis mutandis).

R. 92 Requirements of the request

Implementation of **Art.105a(1)**

1 **General**
R.92 sets out details of the requirements to be met by a request for limitation or revocation of a European patent.

R. 92(1) The request for limitation or revocation of a European patent shall be filed in writing in one of the official languages of the European Patent Office. It may also be filed in an official language of a Contracting State, provided that a translation is filed in one of the official languages of the European Patent Office within the period specified in Rule 6, paragraph 2. Part III of the Implementing Regulations shall apply mutatis mutandis to documents filed in limitation or revocation proceedings.

Amended, in force since 01.04.2009 (OJ 2008 p.513).

1 **Procedure for filing request**

R.92(1) requires that the request be filed in writing in one of the official languages of the EPO or in an official language of a contracting state. Although not stated in the provision, the Guidelines imply that the latter language must comply with **Art.14(4)**, i.e. it must be an official language of the contracting state of which the proprietor is a resident or national (D-X,2.1(iv)). A translation of the request into an official EPO language must be filed within one month of filing the request (**R.6(2)**). In accordance with **R.3(2)**, the text of the amended claims and, as the case may be, the amended description must be filed in the language of the proceedings in which the patent was granted.

R.92(1) refers to Part III of the Implementing Regulations (**R.35-R.54**). This means that the provisions of Part III are to be applied mutatis mutandis in limitation and revocation proceedings. Since the reference is to Part III in general, it is necessary to establish whether and how a provision of Part III is actually applicable to a particular set of circumstances. Consequently, it does not matter if the reference is irrelevant in the case of one or more provisions. (CA/PL29/06 Add.1)

The request must indicate whether limitation or revocation is sought. Under **Art.105a(1)**, the request is only deemed to be filed when the limitation or revocation fee has been paid. The amount of the appropriate fee is laid down in **Rfees2(1)10a**.

The request does not have to be accompanied by a statement of reasons, but this can be expedient where, for example, the limiting effect of the requested amendment of the claims is not unambiguously apparent from the request itself. (OJ 2003 se1 p.159) The reasons underlying the request need not be given, and are not relevant to the allowability of the request (D-X,4.2).

R. 92(2) The request shall contain:

(a) particulars of the proprietor of the European patent making the request (the requester) as provided in Rule 41, paragraph 2(c), and an indication of the Contracting States for which the requester is the proprietor of the patent;

(b) the number of the patent whose limitation or revocation is requested, and a list of the Contracting States in which the patent has taken effect;

(c) where appropriate, the names and addresses of the proprietors of the patent for those Contracting States in which the requester is not the proprietor of the patent, and evidence that the requester is entitled to act on their behalf in the proceedings;

(d) where limitation of the patent is requested, the complete version of the amended claims and, as the case may be, of the amended description and drawings;

(e) where the requester has appointed a representative, particulars as provided in Rule 41, paragraph 2(d).

R.41(2)(c) Particulars of applicant
R.41(2)(d) Particulars of representative

1 **Contents of request**
R.92(2) specifies the information and documents which the request must contain. Sub-paragraphs (a), (b) and (e) deal with the identification of the requester and, where appropriate, the representative, as well as the patent to which the request relates and correspond to provisions in **R.76(2) for a notice of opposition.**

R.92(2)(c) refers to cases in which the requester is not the patent proprietor for all the contracting states in which the European patent has taken effect (i.e. those designated states in which the patent has been validated and not revoked). In these cases, the requester must indicate the further patent proprietor(s) concerned and demonstrate entitlement to act on their behalf in the limitation or revocation proceedings. In view of the ex tunc effect of limitation and revocation under **Art.68**, this requirement also applies to patent proprietors in states where the European patent has lapsed. The EPO must rely on the information provided by the proprietor, because changes in ownership are not recorded in the Register.

Limitation of the European patent under **Art.105a(1)** is only possible by an amendment of the claims. **R.92(2)(d)** prescribes accordingly that the request must contain the complete text of the amended claims. The limitation of a dependent claim without any limitation of the associated independent claim is acceptable (D-X,4.3.1). A separate set of claims for a particular Contracting State may also be presented pursuant to **R.138** in view of a prior national right (see **Art.105b(3):1**).

The filing of a description modified in accordance with the amended text of the claims may or may not be required, depending on the nature of the amendments made to the claims. The same applies in respect of the drawings.

In accordance with **R.3(2)**, the text of the amended claims and, where appropriate, of the description must be filed in the language of the proceedings in which the patent was granted. All amended documents must comply with the general provisions concerning the form of documents filed with the EPO (**R.50**). (OJ 2003 se1 p.159)

R. 93 Precedence of opposition proceedings

Implementation of **Art.105a(2)**

1 **General**
An overview of the relation between limitation and revocation proceedings, opposition proceedings and national procedures is given in Art.105a(2):1. **R.93** governs the precedence of opposition proceedings over limitation and revocation proceedings.

R. 93(1) The request for limitation or revocation shall be deemed not to have been filed if opposition proceedings in respect of the patent are pending at the time of filing the request.

1 **Request for limitation or revocation while opposition is pending**
R.93(1) governs the situation where, at the time of filing the request for limitation or revocation, opposition proceedings relating to the patent are pending. **Art.105a(2)** stipulates that the request may not be filed while opposition proceedings are pending. **R.93(1)** clarifies that in such a case the request will be deemed not to have been filed. Accordingly, the fee for limitation or revocation is reimbursed. (OJ 2003 se1 p.179)

The EPC does not define when opposition proceedings are pending. It appears reasonable that they are regarded as pending after the valid filing of the notice of opposition and payment of the opposition fee; the effect of manifest inadmissibility on the pendency of an opposition is not clear. Opposition proceedings are no longer pending once the opposition division has taken a decision terminating the procedure, unless the decision is appealed (**G4/91** r.7). A limitation or revocation request filed during the two month appeal period is hence validly filed if an appeal is not filed (see also **Art.105(1):1.2**).

R. 93(2) If, at the time of filing an opposition to a European patent, limitation proceedings in respect of that patent are pending, the Examining Division shall terminate the limitation proceedings and order the reimbursement of the limitation fee. The reimbursement shall also be ordered in respect of the fee referred to in Rule 95, paragraph 3, first sentence, if the requester has already paid this fee.

R.95(3) Fee for publishing limited specification

1 **Filing opposition while limitation proceedings are pending**
R.93(2) provides that, if an opposition is filed against the European patent while limitation proceedings are already pending for that patent, the limitation proceedings are terminated by the EPO of its own motion. The limitation fee is reimbursed. This is in line with the principle of the precedence of opposition proceedings as laid down in **Art.105a(2)**. (OJ 2003 se1 p.179)

R.93(2) does not apply where an opposition is filed during a pending revocation procedure. In this case, the revocation proceedings will continue, leading to revocation of the patent, which makes the opposition pointless. Opposition proceedings will only start if the request for revocation is withdrawn or rejected.

The prescribed fee required by **R.95(3)** was abolished as of 01.04.2024 (OJ 2024 A3). However, **R.93(2)** still refers to this fee in order to provide a legal basis for the reimbursement of any fee paid before the amendment to **R.95(3)** came into force.

R. 94 Rejection of the request as inadmissible

If the Examining Division finds that the request for limitation or revocation fails to comply with the requirements of Rule 92, it shall invite the requester to correct the deficiencies noted, within a period to be specified. If the deficiencies are not corrected in due time, the Examining Division shall reject the request as inadmissible.

R.92 Requirements of the request
Implementation of **Art.105b(1)**

1 **Inadmissible request**

R.94 concerns the examination as to admissibility of requests under **Art.105a**. Prior to this examination, the request may already be rejected as deemed not filed in light of formal deficiencies (**R.92**), the precedence of opposition proceedings (**R.93**), or the non-payment of the appropriate fee (**Art.105a(1)**). **R.94** is analogous to **R.77(2)** which applies in opposition proceedings.

Non-observance of the period set for correcting deficiencies cannot be remedied using further processing, because further processing is only available during grant proceedings. Re-establishment of rights under **Art.122** is available but the request can in any case simply be refiled. The decision rejecting the request as inadmissible is open to appeal (D-X,2.2).

R. 95 Decision on the request

Implementation of **Art.105b(2)**

R. 95(1) If a request for revocation is admissible, the Examining Division shall revoke the patent and communicate this to the requester.

1 **Revocation of patent**

R.95(1) deals with the way in which a request for revocation is examined by the EPO. If the request for revocation is admissible, the examining division takes a decision to revoke the patent and communicates this to the requester (D-X,3). The decision takes effect on the date the mention of the decision is published in the Bulletin (**Art.105b(3)**); the revocation of the patent is effective ab initio.

R. 95(2) If a request for limitation is admissible, the Examining Division shall examine whether the amended claims constitute a limitation vis-à-vis the claims as granted or amended in opposition or limitation proceedings and comply with Article 84 and Article 123, paragraphs 2 and 3. If the request does not comply with these requirements, the Examining Division shall give the requester one opportunity to correct any deficiencies noted, and to amend the claims and, where appropriate, the description and drawings, within a period to be specified.

Art.84 Requirements for claims
Art.123(2), (3) Amendments

1 **Limitation**

R.95(2) deals with the way in which a request for limitation is examined by the EPO and requires that the amendment requested constitutes a limitation vis-à-vis the claims before limitation, i.e. a reduction in extent of protection conferred. An amendment for the sake of clarification only is not a limitation in the sense of **R.95(2)** (D-X,4.3.1). Furthermore, an amendment to a narrower subject matter which falls outside the scope of the claims of the patent is not an allowable limitation (**Art.123(3)**) – the limited claims must fall entirely within the scope of protection of the patent before limitation (D-X,4.3.2).

A limitation must reduce the extent of protection conferred by one of the claims. The limitation of a dependent claim only, without any independent claim being limited, is acceptable. However, it is not permissible to introduce non-limiting amendments in the description or claims that are not the direct consequence of a permissible limitation of the claims (e.g. for the purpose of improving clarity or correcting grammatical mistakes). Adding dependent claims is not permissible if not directly caused by the limitation of the claims. (D-X,4.3.1)

The claims before limitation are the most recent claims. Hence, if claims are restricted in a first limitation procedure, the claims cannot be broadened beyond the scope of this first limitation in a second limitation procedure (as this would be contrary to **Art.123(3)**). Once a first limitation procedure is complete, the claims of the patent as originally granted are no longer relevant.

2 Examination of other requirements

The amended claims must comply with certain substantive requirements. It must be established whether the requirements of **Art.84** and **Art.123(2)** and (3) have been met, and, where appropriate, whether consequent amendments to the description and the drawings comply with these requirements. This examination is carried out on the basis of the amended claims and any amended description submitted by the requester in accordance with **R.92(2)(d)**.

In principle, there should be no examination as to whether the subject-matter of the limited patent is patentable under **Art.52** to **57** or whether the supposed aim of the limitation – e.g. delimitation with respect to particular piece of prior art – is actually achieved by the requested amendment of the claims (OJ 2003 se1 p.181). However, a prima facie non-compliance with the patentability criteria will be addressed by the examining division. For example, limiting a generic plant to a specific plant variety in a claim would lead to a claim contravening **Art.53(b)** – such an amendment will not be allowed by the examining division. (D-X,4.3.4)

An amendment of the claims need not necessarily be accompanied by a corresponding amendment of the description; only the requirements of **Art.84** and **Art.123** must be met. Should an amendment lead to inconsistencies between the claims and the description, the patent proprietor must rectify this by further amending one or the other (D-X,4.3.3).

3 Opportunity to correct deficiencies

If the request does not comply with the requirements set out above, the examining division will give the requester only one opportunity to amend the claims and the description, within a period specified by the EPO which is usually a two-month period. The period specified is extendable, but only in exceptional circumstances (D-X,4.4). If the response gives rise to new objections, a further communication is issued giving the requester an opportunity to comment; normally no further amendments may be made in reply to that second communication (D-X,4.4). Errors of transcription or obvious mistakes can be rectified on request or by the EPO of its own motion (D-X,4.4). Since the request for limitation can be filed again at any time, restricting the requester to one round of amendments during a limitation procedure does not seem unreasonably harsh.

A request for oral proceedings according to **Art.116** must be granted if the request for limitation is not allowable. No further amendments may be submitted during oral proceedings if the opportunity to make amendments has already been taken. (D-X,4.4).

4 **Observations by third persons during limitation proceedings**
Third persons may file observations under **Art.115** during limitation and revocation proceedings. Such observations must relate to patentability, which is interpreted to include **Art.84** and **Art.123(2)**. The EPO forwards the observations to the proprietor, who may take them into account and introduce further limitations in response to the invitation under **R.95(2)**, or, if there is no such invitation, by filing another request for limitation. (D-X,4.5)

R. 95(3) If a request for limitation is allowable under paragraph 2, the Examining Division shall communicate this to the requester and invite them to file a translation of the amended claims in the official languages of the European Patent Office other than the language of the proceedings, within a period of three months; Rule 82, paragraph 3, first sentence, shall apply mutatis mutandis. If the requester performs these acts in due time, the Examining Division shall limit the patent.

Amended, in force since 01.04.2012 (OJ 2010 p.637). Amended by decision of the Administrative Council of 14.12.2023, which entered into force on 01.04.2024 (OJ 2024 A3). The amendment removed the prescribed fee. Further amended by decision of the Administrative Council of 10.12.2024, which entered into force on 01.04.2025 (OJ 2025 A16). The amendment was introduction of gender-neutral language.
Art.65(1) Translation of patent required by contracting state
R.82(3) Two-month grace period after notification

1 **Allowance of request for limitation**
If a request for the limitation of a European patent is to be allowed, the requester must file with the EPO a translation of the amended claims in the two other official languages. Before 01.04.2024, it was also necessary to pay a prescribed fee for publishing the amended patent specification but this is no longer required. Once the claim translations are filed, a decision to limit the patent is taken. (OJ 2003 se1 p.182)

A contracting state may require that a translation of the patent as limited into the national language of that state be filed under **Art.65**. If such a requirement is not complied with, the patent can be deemed to be void ab initio (**Art.65(3)**). See NatLaw Table IV.

If the claim translations are not filed within the three-month period, the EPO will send a communication concerning this failure to the proprietor and invite the proprietor to remedy the deficiency within a period of two months of the communication. Before 01.04.2024, it was also necessary to pay a surcharge within this two-month period but this is no longer required. (**R.95(3)**, with reference to **R.82(3)**)

Non-observance of the three-month period for filing the claim translations cannot be remedied using further processing, since further processing is restricted to grant proceedings (**Art.121(1)**); the same applies to the two-month period providing a second chance to file the claim translations. Re-establishment according to **Art.122** and **R.136** is available with respect to the latter period but the request for limitation can, in any case, simply be filed again.

R. 95(4) If the requester does not respond in due time to the communication issued under paragraph 2, or if the request for limitation is not allowable, or if the requester fails to perform the acts required under paragraph 3 in due time, the Examining Division shall reject the request.

1 **Rejection of request for limitation**
Under paragraph 4, a request for limitation of a European patent is rejected if the request is not allowable, or if the requester does not respond to a communication under paragraph 2 or fails to perform the acts required under paragraph 3 in due time. (OJ 2003 se1 p.182)

The decision to reject the request is appealable. However, since the appeal fee is more expensive than the limitation fee, it is cheaper to file a new request for limitation. If an appeal is filed, the competence of the board of appeal is limited to that of the examining division in limitation proceedings (see **R.95(2)**).

R. 96 Content and form of the amended European patent specification

The amended European patent specification shall include the description, claims and drawings as amended. Rule 73, paragraphs 2 and 3, and Rule 74 shall apply.

R.73(2) Form of the specification
R.73(3) Indication of designated contracting states
R.74 Certificate for a patent
Implementation of **Art.105c**

1 **Content of specification after limitation**
The specification of a European patent following limitation, as set out in **R.96**, has the same content as the specification of a European patent following opposition, which is governed by **R.87**. A certificate is issued after publication of the amended specification (**R.74**).

PART VI IMPLEMENTING REGULATIONS TO PART VI OF THE CONVENTION

Chapter I *Appeals procedure*

R. 97 Appeal against apportionment and fixing of costs

Implementation of **Art.106(3)**

R. 97(1) The apportionment of costs of opposition proceedings cannot be the sole subject of an appeal.

R. 97(2) A decision fixing the amount of costs of opposition proceedings cannot be appealed unless the amount exceeds that of the fee for appeal.

1 **Decision fixing costs**
A first instance decision fixing the amount of costs is a decision taken following a review by the opposition division of the costs which is has already fixed, i.e. deemed payable (**R.88(4)**). According to **R.97(2)**, the amount of costs fixed in the decision must be in excess of the appeal fee for an appeal to be admissible. See **Art.104(2):1** for the procedure.

R. 98 Surrender or lapse of the patent

The decision of an Opposition Division may be appealed even if the European patent has been surrendered in all the designated Contracting States or has lapsed in all those States.

Implementation of **Art.106(1)**

1 **Decision relating to lapsed or surrendered patent**
This provision allows the filing of an appeal following opposition proceedings even when the patent has lapsed or been surrendered, in the same way that **R.75** allows the filing of an opposition in such circumstances. These provisions are important because revocation and surrender or lapse have different legal consequences: revocation has effect ex tunc (**Art.68**), while lapse has effect ex nunc and surrender has effect ex nunc in many contracting states. See **Art.67(2), (4)**.

R. 99 Content of the notice of appeal and the statement of grounds

Implementation of **Art.108**

R. 99(1) The notice of appeal shall contain:
(a) the name and the address of the appellant as provided in Rule 41, paragraph 2(c);
(b) an indication of the decision impugned; and
(c) a request defining the subject of the appeal.

R.41(2)(c) Particulars of applicant

1 **Name and address (R.99(1)(a))**
The name and address of the appellant must be indicated in the same manner that the name and address of the applicant is indicated in the request form during grant proceedings (**R.41(2)(c)**). These details may be corrected under **R.101(2)** in response to a communication from the board or under **R.139** at the appellant's own initiative. Since the transfer of an opposition may cause uncertainty as to which legal entity is entitled to appeal (see **Art.99(1):2.4**), it is possible to file the appeal in the name of a first person and, as an auxiliary request, in the name of a second person (**G2/04** hn. II).

The requirement of **R.99(1)(a)** is satisfied if the appellant can be identified. Hence, an address is not always required. (**T662/09** r.1.2)

If the notice of appeal is filed on paper, EPO Form 3002 may be used. The form assists parties in formulating a correct notice of appeal.

2 **Impugned decision (R.99(1)(b))**
The notice of appeal must identify the impugned decision. The board may be able to identify the contested decision from the file (**T925/91** r.1.1). However, the notice of appeal must contain an explicit and unequivocal statement of a definite intention to contest an appealable decision (**T460/95** hn). Hence, a purported notice of appeal accompanying the payment of the appeal fee that merely states 'payment of the appeal fee relating to the aforementioned application' leaves the aim of the appeal unclear, and does not comply with **R.99(1)(b)** (**T460/95** r.5).

The extent of the appeal need no longer be stated expressly in or be implied by the wording of the notice of appeal, contrary to the position under EPC1973 (**T7/81** hn, **T32/81** r.1), and must instead be clear from the statement of grounds (see **R.99(2)**).

3 **Request (R.99(1)(c))**
The appellant's initial request, according to **G9/92** r.1 (=**G4/93**) and **G1/99** r.6.2, defines the subject of the appeal and thereby the framework of the appeal proceedings. **R.99(1)(c)** is satisfied if the notice of appeal contains a request, which may be implicit, to set aside the decision as a whole or (where appropriate) only partially. In the case of an appeal by an applicant or proprietor, it is not necessary that the notice of appeal also contains a request for maintenance of the patent in any particular form. (**T358/08** hn, r.4.11).

R. 99(2) In the statement of grounds of appeal the appellant shall indicate the reasons for setting aside the decision impugned, or the extent to which it is to be amended, and the facts and evidence on which the appeal is based.

1 **Statement of grounds**

The statement of grounds must state the legal and factual reasons why the decision should be set aside. It does not suffice that the statement asserts that the impugned decision is incorrect: **Art.108** requires that the appellant specifies the legal and factual grounds in light of which the decision should be set aside. A mere presentation of facts is not sufficient; what can be inferred from these facts must be made adequately clear (**T220/83**). If a decision declares an opposition inadmissible because of insufficient substantiation, and the grounds for appeal discuss merely patentability, not the admissibility of the opposition, then the appeal is inadmissible because of a lack of adequate substantiation (**T213/85**). An appeal may be based on a newly asserted fact that is crucial to the maintenance of the decision (**J902/87**); an appeal based on such a new fact can be admissible but the new factual assertion can be held inadmissible (Art.12(4) and Art.12(6) RPBA).

The statement of grounds must enable the board to immediately understand why the appealed decision is incorrect; the board should not be expected to have to make further investigation (**T809/06**).

The request in the notice of appeal may indicate whether the decision under appeal is contested as a whole or only partially (though this is not a requirement). Appellants are not necessarily obliged to align with any such indication in their statement of grounds. Any requirement for appellants to argue for claims they no longer want simply in order to validate the notice of appeal would be unhelpful. The grounds of appeal may therefore be more limited in extent than any initial indication in the notice of appeal (**R.99(1):3** and **T642/05**).

If the admissibility requirements of **Art.108** are fulfilled in respect of at least one claim request (assuming that an applicant or proprietor proposes a main request and one or more auxiliary requests), the appeal as a whole is admissible. It is not an absolute requirement for the admissibility of an appeal filed by an applicant or proprietor that the appellant should attack the contested decision as flawed. Where amended claims are filed, an appeal may also be admissible if sufficient reasons are given in the statement of grounds why the amendments are considered apt to remedy the deficiencies identified by the first instance department. Generally, whether the appellant's arguments are convincing or likely to be successful is irrelevant for the purposes of determining the admissibility of the appeal. (**T1320/19** summarising established case law)

The question of admissibility of the appeal does not depend on whether amended claims filed with the statement of grounds are subsequently admitted into the proceedings by the board; in the case at hand the amended claims were held inadmissible under Art.12(6) RPBA (**T2558/16**).

If there are several independent reasons in a decision for refusing an application (e.g. lack of clarity and lack of inventive step) and at least one of those reasons is not addressed in the statement of grounds, then the requirements of **R.99(2)** are not met (**T1045/02**).

An appeal of an opponent on the other hand is sufficiently reasoned if it contains a substantiated case relating to at least one objection or ground of opposition (**T767/14**). The reason is that if one attack against the claims held allowable by the opposition division is successful, the patent cannot be maintained in that form and the impugned decision must be set aside. Moreover, the admissibility of an appeal can only be assessed as a whole, there can be no partial admissibility of an appeal under **R.99(2)** (**T1311/13**).

The statement of grounds should also comply with Art.12 RPBA (**Art.108:7**).

R. 99(3) Part III of the Implementing Regulations shall apply mutatis mutandis to the notice of appeal, the statement of grounds and the documents filed in appeal proceedings.

1 **Procedural provisions**
R.99(3) refers to Part III of the Implementing Regulations (**R.35-R.54**). This means that the provisions of Part III are to be applied mutatis mutandis in appeal proceedings. Close analysis shows that numerous provisions in the third part of the Implementing Regulations can potentially play an important role in appeal proceedings. In cases where Part III needs to be applied mutatis mutandis, it is necessary to establish whether and how a rule is actually applicable to the particular set of circumstances being addressed. Consequently, it does not matter if one or more provisions of Part III is/are irrelevant. (CA/PL29/06)

R. 100 Examination of appeals

Implementation of **Art.110**

R. 100(1) Unless otherwise provided, the provisions relating to proceedings before the department which has taken the decision impugned shall apply to appeal proceedings.

1 **Applicability of first-instance provisions**
Examples of the applicability of provisions relating to proceedings before the department of first instance in appeal proceedings are given in the notes to **Art.110**.

Examples of provisions which are 'otherwise provided' according to **R.100(1)** are provisions in the EPC specifically relating to the appeal procedure (**Art.106-112, R.97-103**) and the Rules of Procedure of the Boards of Appeal (see **Art.110:1**).

R. 100(2) In the examination of the appeal, the Board of Appeal shall invite the parties, as often as necessary, to file observations, within a period to be specified, on communications issued by itself or observations submitted by another party.

1 **Communication of submissions**
In inter partes appeal proceedings, the board communicates each party's submissions (e.g. the notice of appeal, grounds of appeal and any response to the grounds of appeal) to the other parties. It also communicates any third party observations to all the parties. However, copies of documents cited by a party or a third party (including patent and non-patent literature) and attached documents containing amendments (such as an amended set of claims) are generally not forwarded and should instead be retrieved from the online file. They are, nevertheless, provided free of charge on request. Parties are informed of the filing of any item, such as a non-scannable object, which is not available for inspection in the online file. Parties are advised to check the online file in advance of oral proceedings to ensure that they are in possession of all relevant documents. (OJ 2022 A57)

The board may assign a reference number to each document cited by the parties for the first time during the appeal proceedings, and create a consolidated list of these documents which can be retrieved from the online file. Parties are recommended to adopt these reference numbers in further submissions (OJ 2020 A131 §1).

2 **Response to grounds of appeal**

In cases where there is more than one party, the board will invite the party or parties other than the appellant to file observations on the grounds of appeal, setting a period of four months for doing so (Art.12(1)(c) RPBA). This will occur in opposition proceedings, for example, if the patent has been revoked (proprietor is appellant and opponent is invited to comment on the grounds of appeal), the patent has been maintained as granted (opponent is appellant and proprietor is invited to comment on the grounds of appeal) or the patent has been maintained in amended form (both opponent and proprietor are potentially appellants and will be invited to comment on each other's grounds of appeal).

R. 100(3) If the applicant fails to reply in due time to an invitation under paragraph 2, the European patent application shall be deemed to be withdrawn, unless the decision impugned was taken by the Legal Division.

1 **No response from applicant**

This provision has the purpose of avoiding inappropriate delays in the prosecution of an application during appeal proceedings and corresponds to **Art.94(4)** which applies during first instance grant proceedings. The provision does not apply to proprietors and opponents, because it mentions only the 'applicant', and is therefore only applicable in grant proceedings. The provision itself states that it is also not applicable to appeals against a decision taken by the Legal Division, such decisions relating in general to the transfer of rights and not to the grant or refusal of an application. (**J29/94** r.1.2)

Applicants are notified of any loss of rights in the appeal procedure (**R.112(1)**); they can apply for a formal decision under **R.112(2)**, but they have no right to appeal that decision. The legal consequence of **R.100(3)** can be overcome by requesting further processing under **Art.121**. The sanction of deemed withdrawal of the entire application also applies where the appealed decision does not concern the refusal of the application but relates only to a request to add the designation of a contracting state (**J29/94** hn).

The only sanction for a party other than an applicant that does not reply to an invitation is that late-filed observations will in principle not be taken into account unless there are exceptional circumstances (see Art.13(1) and Art.13(2) RPBA). Such a party cannot use further processing because that remedy is only available to applicants. When a respondent in opposition appeal proceedings does not file a request or a response to the grounds of appeal, the board of appeal may not immediately allow the appeal, but must nevertheless examine the grounds of appeal and decide whether the appeal is allowable (**T501/92** hn.IV). Where a board allows an opponent's appeal and the respondent (proprietor) has not had the opportunity to comment on the grounds of appeal, this is a fundamental violation of the right to be heard (**R7/09**). The same would apply if the board allowed a proprietor's appeal without the opponent having had a chance to comment on the grounds of appeal.

R. 101 Rejection of the appeal as inadmissible

Implementation of **Art.110**

R. 101(1) If the appeal does not comply with Articles 106 to 108, Rule 97 or Rule 99, paragraph 1(b) or (c) or paragraph 2, the Board of Appeal shall reject it as inadmissible, unless any deficiency has been remedied before the relevant period under Article 108 has expired.

Art.106 Decisions subject to appeal
Art.107 Persons entitled to appeal and to be parties to appeal proceedings
Art.108 Period and form of notice of appeal
R.97 Appeal against apportionment and fixing of costs
R.99 Content of the notice of appeal and the statement of grounds

1 **Deficiencies resulting in inadmissibility of the appeal**
Once the board is of the opinion that the appeal has been validly filed, i.e. the notice has been filed and the appeal fee has been paid within the two-month period, it will assess the admissibility of the appeal (see **Art.110:3**). The following deficiencies will result in the appeal being rejected as inadmissible under **R.101(1)**.

1.1 ART.106 AND R.97: APPEALABLE DECISION
An appeal lying from a non-appealable decision is inadmissible. Examples of non-appealable decisions:
- a decision taken by a department not mentioned in **Art.106(1)**, e.g. by a search division or the President;
- an interlocutory decision which does not allow for separate appeal (**Art.106(2)**);
- a decision relating only to the apportionment of costs in opposition proceedings (**Art.106(3)**, **R.97(1)**);
- a decision fixing costs where the costs do not exceed the required amount (**R.97(2)**).

1.2 ART.107: ENTITLEMENT OF PARTY
An appeal filed by a party not entitled to appeal will be inadmissible. Examples of non-entitled parties:
- A party that is not adversely affected, e.g. a proprietor that appeals a decision taken by an opposition division to maintain the patent according the proprietor's main request.
- A party that was not a party to the first instance proceedings but a third party, e.g. a person who filed observations under **Art.115** during the first instance proceedings (**G2/19**).
- A party that has not been identified by the end of the appeal period (**T25/85** r.10). Deficiencies in the name and address may be corrected under **R.101(2)** and **R.139**, first sentence (**G1/12**).

1.3 ART.108: FILING FORMALITIES
Non-compliance with filing formalities generally results in an inadmissible appeal. Examples of filing deficiencies:
- The appeal is conditional, for example an appeal is filed as a subsidiary request conditional on the main request not being allowed (**J16/94** hn; **T254/03** r.1.3).
- The grounds are not filed at all or are filed after the four-month period (**T13/82**). A notice of appeal not giving any legal or factual reasons why the impugned decision should be set aside, but merely stating that the importance of a warning from the EPO was not recognised and an omitted act would be completed, is not regarded as a valid statement of grounds (**T22/88**).

1.4 R.99: IDENTIFICATION OF DECISION, REQUEST, REASONS AND FACTS

An appeal is inadmissible if the notice of appeal does not indicate the decision impugned (**R.99(1)(b)**) or if the notice does not include a request defining the subject of the appeal (**R.99(1)(c)**).

An appeal is also inadmissible if the statement of grounds does not indicate the reasons for setting aside the decision impugned or the extent to which it is to be amended, or does not indicate the facts and evidence on which the appeal is based (**R.99(2)**). A mere reference in general terms to passages in the literature showing the state of the art and to the Guidelines without any relevant factual and legal reasoning will not suffice as grounds. Lack of such reasoning will cause the appeal to be inadmissible according to **R.101(1)** (**T220/83**).

2 Deficiencies resulting in the appeal being deemed not filed

If the notice of appeal is filed after the expiry of the two month period of **Art.108** or if the appeal fee is paid later than the expiry of that period then the appeal is deemed not to have been filed (**Art.108**, **G1/18**, hn.1). The appeal fee is reimbursed (**G1/18**, hn.2)

The EPC provides the same sanction in respect of the following deficiencies:

- The notice of appeal bears no signature (**R.99(3)** in conjunction with **R.50(3)**) and the signature is not provided in due time following an invitation to correct, causing the notice of appeal to be deemed not to have been filed. If the invitation to correct is complied with, the notice retains its date of filing. The signature on the notice of appeal should be assessed analogously to the signature on a notice of opposition. If a notice of appeal is signed by a person who is not the appellant, or the appellant's representative, the notice is regarded as not being signed, and the appellant is requested to sign the notice correctly according to **R.50(3)** (analogous to **T665/89** r.1.4 relating to a notice of opposition).
- A translation of the notice of appeal required under **Art.14(4)** is not filed within the longer of one month after filing the notice or the end of the two-month appeal period (**R.6(2)**); the document is deemed not to have been filed (**Art.14(4)**). (**T323/87**)
- The notice of appeal is not in an admissible EPO language or an admissible language of a contracting state, e.g. the notice of appeal is filed in Japanese. The notice is deemed not to have been filed (**R.3(1)**, **Art.14(1)** and **Art.14(4)**).
- The notice of appeal is filed in an admissible official language of a contracting state, but the appellant is not entitled to use that language, e.g. a German person living in Munich files a notice of appeal in Italian. The notice is deemed not to have been filed (**R.3(1)** and **Art.14(4)**).

The above cases in which a notice of appeal is deemed not to have been filed apply mutatis mutandis to the statement of grounds. A case in which the statement of grounds is deemed not to have been filed is dealt with as a case in which the statement of grounds has not been filed at all. Hence, if the statement of grounds is deemed not to have been filed, the appeal is inadmissible (**T13/82** hn.1) and the appeal fee will not be reimbursed.

3 **Correction of deficiencies**
Any deficiency that would lead to inadmissibility under **R.101(1)** must be rectified before the end of the two-month or, where appropriate, the four-month period of **Art.108** (**R.101(1)**). If there is time to correct any such deficiency, the registry of the boards of appeal will invite the appellant to do so. If there is not sufficient time for correction, then before taking a decision to dismiss an appeal as inadmissible, the appellant is invited to file observations on the findings of the EPO (**Art.113(1)**). The appeal fee is not refunded if the appeal is inadmissible (**T89/84**).

Failure to meet the two- or four-month period can be remedied with re-establishment under **Art.122**, if the appellant is an applicant or proprietor, or, as an exception for the four-month period only, if the appellant is an opponent that did not file the grounds in time (**G1/86**).

R. 101(2) If the Board of Appeal notes that the appeal does not comply with Rule 99, paragraph 1(a), it shall communicate this to the appellant and shall invite them to remedy the deficiencies noted within a period to be specified. If the deficiencies are not remedied in due time, the Board of Appeal shall reject the appeal as inadmissible.

Amended by decision of the Administrative Council of 10.12.2024, which entered into force on 01.04.2025 (OJ 2025 A16). The amendment was introduction of gender-neutral language.
R.99(1)(a) Indication of name and address appellant

1 **Correction of name and address of appellant**
Deficiencies in the name or address of the appellant may be corrected under **R.101(2)** following an invitation from the board or under **R.139** on a party's own initiative. The deficiency may be an incorrect designation of the appellant (**T97/98**, correction under **R.101(2)**; **T814/98**, correction under **R.139**) including the case where joint applicants file an appeal and only one of them is named as appellant (**T1303/19**, correction under **R.101(2)**).

The nature of the deficiency is not relevant, because **R.99(1)(a)** and **R.101(2)** do not make a distinction in this respect. A correction under **R.101(2)** must comply with two requirements. In the first place the deficiency must be a genuine error. The correction may not reflect a later change of mind as to whom the appellant should be, but on the contrary, may only express what was intended when filing the appeal (confirmed by **G2/04** r.3.1). The true, original intention must be shown when making the correction, for which data in the file relating to the first instance proceedings may be useful. In the second place, the appellant must be identifiable at the expiry of the period for filing the notice of appeal (requirement of **R.101(1)**), even though the correction may be made after that point in time. Only then is it possible to determine whether or not the appeal was filed by a person entitled to appeal in accordance with **Art.107**. It suffices therefore that it is possible to derive from the information in the appeal, if necessary with the help of other information on file, with a sufficient degree of probability by whom the appeal should be considered to have been filed. (**T97/98** r.1.4, endorsed by **G1/12** r.26-29; **T124/10**). Free evaluation of evidence must be used (**G1/12** r.31).

The identity of the appellant may also be corrected using the general procedure for correcting errors under **R.139**, first sentence, by filing the request without delay and providing proof of the original intention (**G1/12** r.32-40; **T445/08**). A request for correction under **R.139** may be filed after the expiry of the period for filing the notice of appeal. See also **R.139:3**.

The EBoA has decided that 'true intention' can be used, and not only objective criteria, to establish deficiency of an identification in the sense of **R.101(2)** (**G1/12**).

A request for a change of the name of the appellant is not allowable if the name first provided was in conformity with the true intentions of the person filing the appeal; in such a situation there is no deficiency which may be remedied in accordance with **R.99(1)(a)** in conjunction with **R.101(2)** (**G2/04** r.3.1).

Examples of allowed corrections: supplying a missing address (**T613/91**), correction of the name of the appellant (**T1/97**), substitution of the named appellant for another natural or legal person if evidence is provided this was the true intention (**T97/98** hn), substitution of the named appellant for a universal successor in law (**T15/01** r.14). Example of a correction that was not allowed: substitution of the named appellant for another natural or legal person without evidence of transfer of the related business assets (**T298/97** hn. III).

The use of a previous and therefore incorrect name does not have the consequence that party status is to be denied or that procedural acts have to be regarded as invalid, as long as the identity of a legal person is not at issue (**T15/01** r.3).

R. 102 Form of decision of the Board of Appeal

Amended by decision of the Administrative Council of 10.12.2024, which entered into force on 01.04.2025 (OJ 2025 A16). The amendment introduced gender-neutral language.

The decision shall be authenticated by the Chair of the Board of Appeal and by the competent employee of the registry of the Board of Appeal, either by their signature or by any other appropriate means. The decision shall contain:

(a) a statement that it was delivered by the Board of Appeal;
(b) the date when the decision was taken;
(c) the names of the Chair and of the other members of the Board of Appeal taking part;
(d) the names of the parties and their representatives;
(e) the requests of the parties;
(f) a summary of the facts;
(g) the reasons;
(h) the order of the Board of Appeal, including, where appropriate, a decision on costs.

Implementation of **Art.111(1)**

1 **Authentication of decision**

Decisions of boards of appeal are usually authenticated under **R.102** by electronic means rather than by signature, and this is indicated on the decision directly below the names of the chair and the competent employee of the registry (OJ 2012 p.14). However, the manner in which the decision has been authenticated by electronic means is not clear from the decision itself, which does not bear any kind of signature, electronic or otherwise.

R. 103 Reimbursement of appeal fees

Amended by decision of the Administrative Council of 12.12.2019, which entered into force 01.04.2020, and applies to appeals pending on or filed after that date (OJ 2020 A5).The decision changed the previous paragraphs 2 and 3 to 3 and 6 respectively and inserted new paragraphs 2 and 4, which extend the possibilities for refund of the appeal fee.
Implementation of **Art.111(1)**

1 **Reimbursement of appeal fees**
R.103 provides for full and partial reimbursement of the appeal fee.

A full reimbursement is possible either in the event of a substantial procedural violation (**R.103(1)(a)**) or following withdrawal of the appeal before filing of the statement of grounds of appeal (**R.103(1)(b)**).

Possibilities for partial reimbursement are provided at different stages of the appeal proceedings as an incentive for appellants to consider whether they still have an interest in the appeal and/or reconsider their strategy and requests. The rule distinguishes the following possibilities (see CA/80/19 par. 57-86):

- withdrawal of the appeal before the start of substantive examination (75% reimbursement, **R.103(2)**);
- withdrawal of the appeal during examination (50% reimbursement, **R.103(3)**);
- withdrawal of the appeal in the decision phase (25% reimbursement, **R.103(4)(a), (b)**);
- withdrawal of a request for oral proceedings (25% reimbursement, **R.103(4)(c)**).

The reimbursement applies to the amount of the appeal fee actually paid by the appellant (T370/11). Periods specified in **R.103** are extended if **R.134** applies (T777/15).

If, following the lapse of a patent in opposition appeal proceedings, a party agrees to the termination of the appeal proceedings following a communication under **R.84(1)**, this is to be regarded as equivalent to the withdrawal of the appeal and a reimbursement under **R.103** is possible (T1548/15).

R. 103(1) The appeal fee shall be reimbursed in full

(a) in the event of interlocutory revision or where the Board of Appeal deems an appeal to be allowable, if such reimbursement is equitable by reason of a substantial procedural violation, or

(b) if the appeal is withdrawn before the filing of the statement of grounds of appeal and before the period for filing that statement has expired.

1 **Conditions for full reimbursement on procedural violation**
The reimbursement of the appeal fee in full by reason of a substantial procedural violation can only take place if all three conditions below are met (OJ 1996 p.342 §1.1.5):

- the appeal must be allowable, i.e. the board of appeal or, in the case of interlocutory revision, the department of first instance, in substance at least, follows the relief sought by the appellant, and allows the appellant's requests;
- there must be a substantial procedural violation; and
- the reimbursement must be equitable in light of this violation.

The department of first instance can grant reimbursement in case of interlocutory revision (**R.103(6)**) but is not competent to refuse it (**G3/03**). The board of appeal remains competent to decide on reimbursement of the appeal fee, even after the appeal has been withdrawn (**T41/82**).

Since **R.103(1)(a)** requires that the appeal is allowable as a condition for reimbursement, the appeal fee will not be reimbursed in full if the appeal is rejected as inadmissible or as unallowable (**T13/82**).

An appealed decision is normally set aside if a substantial procedural violation has occurred; the case is then remitted to the department of first instance without further substantive examination of the appeal and the appeal fee is reimbursed (Art.11 RPBA, second sentence; see **Art.111(1):2**).

Reimbursement is not equitable if a party can at least in part be blamed for the procedural violation, e.g. where a division overlooks a party's request for oral proceedings filed very late in the proceedings (**T1544/06** r.5.2; see also **J18/96** r.5). Neither is reimbursement equitable when there is no causal link between the procedural violation and the filing of the appeal (**T388/09**).

2 **Substantial procedural violation**

A substantial procedural violation is an objective deficiency affecting the entire proceedings (**J7/83**). A procedural violation occurs when the rules of procedure prescribed by the EPC have not been properly applied and also occurs if the EPO gives incorrect information which leads to the same consequences as the incorrect application of those rules (**J6/79** r.8).

A procedural violation which does not affect the decision taken is not considered substantial (CLBA V.A.11.6.2). A procedural violation which does not adversely affect a party cannot be considered substantial; the seriousness of a procedural violation derives from its adverse effects (**T682/91** r.4.2). An error which does not have any consequences for the outcome of the proceedings is therefore not a substantial procedural violation (**T49/13**). An incorrect composition of the department of first instance, however, is always a substantial procedural violation (**T382/92**).

A few examples of substantial procedural violations: a lack of sufficient reasoning in the first instance decision; unjustly disregarding a relevant document; the lack of an opportunity for a party to comment on the facts and evidence underlying the decision; giving parties insufficient time to study new amended claims before oral proceedings (**T783/89**); the loss of a letter by the EPO, so its content is not taken into account (**T205/89**); contradictory statements in a decision (**T616/08** r.4).

Substantial procedural violations were acknowledged in the case of a delay of three years between oral proceedings and the issue of the written decision (**T900/02** r.3), a delay of ten years in opposition proceedings (**T315/03** r.15.6), and a procedure lasting fourteen years from the filing of a patent application to its refusal (**T2707/16** r.34).

An extensive list of substantial procedural errors is given in Singer Art.111, note 54 ff.

On the other hand, an erroneous assessment of patentability cannot lead to reimbursement (**T153/84**). Neither is an incorrect interpretation of the prior art or a letter filed by the applicant a procedural error (**J3/87**).

Non-observance of a procedure set out in the Guidelines, which do not constitute legal provisions, is not a substantial procedural error if, at the same time, the EPC is not violated (**T42/84**). Where the EPC or established case law does not lay down unambiguously the procedure to be followed in a given situation, the use of an incorrect procedure does not constitute a substantial procedural violation (**T234/86** hn.3).

3 **Full reimbursement on early withdrawal of appeal**
R.103(1)(b) partly compensates for the lack of a cross-appeal facility in the EPC. An appeal filed as a precaution can be withdrawn if the other party does not file an appeal. If the appeal is withdrawn before the filing of the statement of grounds and before the expiry of the period for filing the statement of grounds, the paid appeal fee is reimbursed in full. (OJ 2007 se5 EN p.160)

The appellant must withdraw the appeal actively and unambiguously (T193/20). Terminating the appeal by not filing a statement of grounds in a timely manner causes the appeal to be rejected as inadmissible without reimbursement.

R. 103(2) The appeal fee shall be reimbursed at 75% if, in response to a communication from the Board of Appeal indicating its intention to start substantive examination of the appeal, the appeal is withdrawn within two months of notification of that communication.

1 **Partial reimbursement before substantive examination**
In long-pending appeal cases, the board will, as a rule, issue a communication informing the parties of the intended start of the substantive examination of the appeal and drawing attention to the possibility of withdrawing the appeal within two months of notification and receiving a partial reimbursement of the appeal fee of 75%. A board may decide to dispense with such a communication if the proceedings progress swiftly or if the board intends to promptly issue a summons to oral proceedings or a substantive communication. (CA/80/19 §66)

The purpose of such reimbursement is to provide an extra incentive for appellants to withdraw their appeal, thereby reducing the workload of the boards. The two-month period cannot be extended on request (CA/80/19 §67).

A **R.103(2)** communication and the annually published list of upcoming cases pursuant to Art.1(2) RPBA both inform the appellant that a board will take up a case in the near future. However, the list is not notified to parties and hence does not trigger the period of **R.103(2)**.

The 75% reimbursement rate only applies to a withdrawal in response to a **R.103(2)** communication; if the appeal is withdrawn after the expiry of the period of **R.103(1)(b)** and before such a communication is issued or in the absence of such a communication being issued, the 50% reimbursement of **R.103(4)** is applicable instead (T853/16).

R. 103(3) The appeal fee shall be reimbursed at 50% if the appeal is withdrawn after expiry of the period under paragraph 1(b), provided withdrawal occurs:
(a) if a date for oral proceedings has been set, within one month of notification of a communication issued by the Board of Appeal in preparation for these oral proceedings;
(b) if no date for oral proceedings has been set, and the Board of Appeal has issued a communication inviting the appellant to file observations, before expiry of the period set by the Board for filing observations;
(c) in all other cases, before the decision is issued.

1 **Partial reimbursement during examination of appeal**
If the period for filing the statement of grounds has already expired, and if no communication under **R.103(2)** was issued yet or the period of two months from such a communication has expired already, the appeal fee can still be reimbursed at 50% of the paid amount if the appeal is timely withdrawn.

If a date for oral proceedings has been set, the withdrawal must be made within one month of notification of a communication under Art.15(1) RPBA. Originally this referred to the mandatory communication under Art.15(1) RPBA, third sentence (referring to Art.15(1) RPBA in force from 01.01.2024; OJ 2023 A103), which often includes the board's preliminary opinion and at least draws attention to matters that seem to be of particular significance for the decision to be taken (CA/80/19 §74). However, **R.103(3)(a)** does not specify any particular criteria that a communication has to comply with for it to trigger a possible reimbursement, other than it must have been issued by the board in preparation for the oral proceedings. Hence, a communication concerning technical and organisational aspects of the scheduled oral proceedings can trigger the period (**T1730/16** by analogy).

The communication can be sent together with the summons or separately. The summons alone is probably not a communication in the sense of **R.103(3)(a)**.

A second or further communication starts a new period (**T1730/16**).

The 50% reimbursement is also possible if the appeal is withdrawn between the scheduling of oral proceedings and the notification of a communication under Art.15(1) RPBA (**T2361/18**).

If no date for oral proceedings has been set and the board has issued a communication inviting the appellant to file observations (e.g. under **R.100(2)**), the withdrawal must be made before the expiry of the period set for filing the observations in order to benefit from the refund under **R.103(3)(b)**; any second and further communication under **R.100(2)** also opens the possibility for reimbursement (**T265/14**). Note that if the appeal concerns the refusal of a patent application, failure to respond timely causes the application to be deemed to be withdrawn under **R.100(3)** and the termination of the appeal proceedings without any reimbursement.

R.103(3)(c) concerns appeals wherein at the date of withdrawal of the appeal, neither a date for oral proceedings has been set nor a communication under **R.100(2)** issued. In such cases, the appeal fee is reimbursed at 50% unless the decision has already been issued. Note that **R.103(4)** specifies further cases wherein the appeal fee is partially reimbursed upon withdrawal of an appeal.

Because **R.103(3)** is available after the expiry of the period under **R.103(1)(b)**, it is also available before and during the period of **R.103(2)**. Where more than one rate of reimbursement applies, reimbursement is at the higher rate (**R.103(5)**).

R. 103(4) The appeal fee shall be reimbursed at 25%

(a) if the appeal is withdrawn after expiry of the period under paragraph 3(a) but before the decision is announced at oral proceedings;

(b) if the appeal is withdrawn after expiry of the period under paragraph 3(b) but before the decision is issued;

(c) if any request for oral proceedings is withdrawn within one month of notification of the communication issued by the Board of Appeal in preparation for the oral proceedings, and no oral proceedings take place.

1 **Partial reimbursement on later withdrawal of appeal**

R.103(4)(a) provides for a 25% reimbursement of the appeal fee paid if an appeal is withdrawn by the appellant after the expiry of the one-month period under **R.103(3)(a)** but before the board announces a decision in oral proceedings. The decision on the appeal is usually announced just before the oral proceedings are closed (Art.15(6) RPBA) and typically after the board has come to a conclusion on all pending requests. The appeal fee can hence be partially reimbursed after the board has indicated that the appeal is not allowable during oral proceedings (see e.g. **T2415/16**). A withdrawal after the board has announced the decision during oral proceedings, but before the written decision is issued, has no effect and does not lead to reimbursement (**T2264/18**).

In appeal proceedings with multiple appellants, the appeal fee can also be partially reimbursed under **R.103(4)(a)** if the board gives a decision in writing, namely in cases wherein one appellant withdraws its appeal after the one-month period has expired, the oral proceedings are cancelled and the decision on the other appeals is issued in writing (**T833/17** r.7). The 50% reimbursement of **R.103(3)(c)** is not applicable in such cases (**T73/17**).

R.103(4)(b) concerns cases where, at the time an appellant withdraws its appeal, the period for replying to a communication under **R.100(2)** has expired, no decision has yet been taken, and no oral proceedings are scheduled.

2 **Withdrawal of request for oral proceedings**

R.103(4)(c) provides for a 25% reimbursement of the appeal fee paid if an appellant timely withdraws a request for oral proceedings, but not the appeal itself, provided that oral proceedings do not take place. The period expires at the same time as the period under **R.103(3)(a)**. Reimbursement is also possible if the appellant withdraws a request for oral proceedings between the notification of the summons and the communication issued in preparation of the oral proceedings (**T2361/18**). The withdrawal can be conditional, e.g. on the condition that the board allows a particular auxiliary request (**T2141/16**) or remits the case (**T2285/19**).

A board orders the reimbursement of its own motion if the requirements of **R.103(4)(c)** are met; no request from the appellant is necessary (**T277/17** r.7.2). Nonetheless, it is recommended to request a partial reimbursement when withdrawing the request for oral proceedings.

If a party announces within the one-month period of **R.103(4)(c)** that it will not attend scheduled oral proceedings but does not expressly withdraw its request for oral proceedings, and the oral proceedings are cancelled, the appeal fee will be partially reimbursed according to most decisions (e.g. **T517/17**, **T1563/21**). However, decisions **T2698/17** and **T73/17** (see r.9.3) come to the opposite conclusion, i.e. that the appeal fee should not be partially reimbursed without an express withdrawal of the request for oral proceedings.

In inter partes proceedings, a partial reimbursement is granted if an appellant withdraws its own request within the prescribed period and no oral proceedings take place, even if another party withdraws its request for oral proceedings only after the expiry of the period and the oral proceedings could only then be cancelled (**T1610/15** r.7.2). According to **T488/18** and **T598/19**, partial reimbursement of the appellant's appeal fee can also be based on the withdrawal of a request for oral proceedings by another party to the appeal proceedings (e.g. a respondent) because **R.103(4)(c)** refers to 'any request'. However, **T777/15** and **T795/19** have come to the opposite conclusion, i.e. that the appellant must have timely withdrawn its own request for oral proceedings to benefit from partial reimbursement.

The one-month period of **R.103(4)(c)** starts from notification of the same kind of communications as specified in **R.103(3)(a)**. However, **R.103(4)(c)** does not expressly require that the request is withdrawn after a date for oral proceedings has been set. Therefore, the 25% reimbursement is available for withdrawal of the request made at any time up to one month from notification of a communication issued in preparation for the oral proceedings under Art.15(1) RPBA (CA/80/19 §84, **T2361/18**). A further communication under Art.15(1) RPBA triggers a new one-month period under **R.103(4)(c)** (**T1730/16**).

Reimbursement is not applicable if oral proceedings are cancelled only because the appellant's main request is allowable (**T795/19**).

If an appellant withdraws both the appeal and the request for oral proceedings, **R.103(5)** provides that only the higher reimbursement rate applies. Hence, an accumulation of reimbursements is not possible.

R.103(4)(c) does not provide for reimbursement if oral proceedings are never requested. Note that oral proceedings can be requested at any stage of the procedure (**T556/95**). However, **T2249/18** applied the rule by analogy and gave a 25% reimbursement when oral proceedings, scheduled by the board at its own motion, were cancelled after the appellant filed a request that overcame all objections raised by the board.

R. 103(5) The appeal fee shall be reimbursed under only one of the above provisions. Where more than one rate of reimbursement applies, reimbursement shall be at the higher rate.

1 **No accumulation of reimbursements**

R.103(5) avoids the possibility of cumulative reimbursement under different provisions of **R.103**, e.g. by withdrawing a request for oral proceedings and then withdrawing the appeal.

R. 103(6) The department whose decision is impugned shall order the reimbursement if it revises its decision and considers reimbursement equitable by reason of a substantial procedural violation. In all other cases, matters of reimbursement shall be decided by the Board of Appeal.

1 **Department competent to reimburse**

In case interlocutory revision under **Art.109** is granted by the department of first instance, the department of first instance should order the reimbursement of the appeal fee if it considers the reimbursement equitable by reason of a substantial procedural violation. However, this department may not refuse a request for reimbursement in interlocutory revision; in such a case only the board of appeal is competent to decide on the request (**G3/03** hn.1). Hence, if interlocutory revision is granted by the department of first instance but a request for reimbursement is not granted, the request for reimbursement is forwarded to the board to decide on. The board of appeal which would have been competent under **Art.21** to deal with the substantive issues of the appeal if no interlocutory revision had been granted is competent to decide on the request for reimbursement (**G3/03** hn.2).

The appeal fee is not (partially) reimbursed if the appeal is withdrawn after the grant of interlocutory revision (**T683/14**).

Chapter II *Petitions for review by the Enlarged Board of Appeal*

R. 104 Further fundamental procedural defects

A fundamental procedural defect under Article 112a, paragraph 2(d), may have occurred where the Board of Appeal,

(a) contrary to Article 116, failed to arrange for the holding of oral proceedings requested by the petitioner, or

(b) decided on the appeal without deciding on a request relevant to that decision.

Art.112a(2)(d) Review because of any other fundamental procedural defect
Art.116 Obligation to arrange oral proceedings
Implementation of **Art.112a(2)(d)**

1 **Further fundamental procedural defects**
The right to oral proceedings, addressed in **R.104(a)**, is an important aspect of the 'right to be heard'. Ignoring a request for oral proceedings may therefore constitute a fundamental procedural defect, which in proceedings under **Art.112a** merits the same treatment as the cases covered by **Art.112a(2)** **(a)** to **(c)**. It is up to the Enlarged Board of Appeal to assess the seriousness of the procedural defect. Only the non-appointment of oral proceedings which are provided as of right under **Art.116** would be a reason for re-opening appeal proceedings.

The seriousness of the fundamental procedural defect addressed in **R.104(b)** is also to be assessed by the Enlarged Board of Appeal, which must interpret the terms 'fundamental' and 'relevant' to this end. The assumption is that only requests submitted in writing or recorded in the minutes of oral proceedings will fall within the ambit of the provision. Furthermore, the wording of **R.104(b)** implies that the fundamental procedural defect must have occurred with respect to the substantive aspects of the appeal. Therefore, requests relating to the apportionment of costs, the reimbursement of the appeal fee and other requests concerning collateral issues are probably not relevant. A partial re-opening of appeal proceedings with respect to collateral issues is not desirable. (OJ 2003 se1 p.159)

R. 105 Criminal acts

A petition for review may be based on Article 112a, paragraph 2(e), if a competent court or authority has finally established that the criminal act occurred; a conviction is not necessary.

Art.112a(2)(e) Review because of criminal act
Implementation of **Art.112a(2)(e)**

1 **Criminal acts**
R.105 provides that only a criminal act finally established by a competent court or authority can serve as the basis for proceedings under **Art.112a(2)(e)**. The act may be 'finally established' in any of the following ways:
- by a final judgment under (criminal) law;
- by another final decision of a competent court;

- by a final decision of a competent authority (e.g. under administrative criminal law, to the extent that such a breach of law is able to influence the decision of the Board of Appeal).

The operative criterion is not whether the (criminal) court or authority has passed sentence, as this would leave out cases where, for example, the perpetrator dies before sentence can be pronounced, or where a finding of diminished capacity makes sentencing impossible. Instead, the crucial issue is whether an act constituting a criminal offence has actually occurred, and whether the fact of its having occurred has been definitely established by a competent court or authority. (OJ 2003 se1 p.159)

Examples of acts that may be regarded as criminal acts are: forging or manipulating prior art documents, bribery, intimidating or threatening a board member and perjury by a witness. Under most national laws there is always perjury if a witness gives false evidence under oath but perjury may also occur even in the absence of an oath. The EPO cannot hear witnesses under oath, but it can ask for witnesses to give testimony under oath before a national court (**R.120**).

R. 106 Obligation to raise objections

A petition under Article 112a, paragraph 2(a) to (d), is only admissible where an objection in respect of the procedural defect was raised during the appeal proceedings and dismissed by the Board of Appeal, except where such objection could not be raised during the appeal proceedings.

Art.112a(2) Grounds for review
Implementation of **Art.112a(2)**

1 **Raising of objections**

R.106 establishes the obligation to raise any procedural objections on which a petition is based during the appeal proceedings, in so far as the party adversely affected by the procedural defect is – or should be – aware of it. It is up to the Enlarged Board of Appeal to interpret the term 'could not be raised' and to develop an appropriate standard for assessment. (OJ 2003 se1 p.159; see also comments on **R1/08** in **Art.112a(2):1**).

Objections under **R.106** need to comply with two criteria. First, the form of the objection must be such that the board of appeal can immediately and without a doubt recognise that an objection under R.106 (i.e. not a different objection) has been made. Second, the objection must be specific and must indicate which defect of **Art.112a**, paragraphs 2(a) to (d) it intends to rely on. (**R9/22**)

Where a decision is based on grounds that the petitioner was unaware of, it is apparent that no objection could have been raised during the appeal proceedings (**R1/08**, **R2/08**).

If no objection was raised during appeal proceedings, although it could have been raised (for example, where the petitioner responded to the alleged defect by proceeding with the appeal), then the petition is not admissible (**R3/08**).

Where an objection is raised during the appeal proceedings, it is necessary that it be dismissed by the board of appeal for there to be a defect (**R3/08**, **R4/08**).

It is recommended that parties raise objections arising during oral proceedings in writing and request that the objection be included in the minutes, indicating clearly that it is an objection under **R.106**.

Where a suspicion of partiality only arises after the board of appeal has taken its decision, the petition will probably be admissible.

R. 107 Contents of the petition for review

Implementation of **Art.112a(4)**

1 **Petition for review**
R.107 implements **Art.112a(4)**, first sentence, particularly in respect of the petitioners' duty to substantiate allegations. The 'reasoned statement' prescribed in **Art.112a(4)**, first sentence has to be filed within the relevant time limit laid down in **Art.112a(4)**, second or third sentence. Its contents must meet the requirements laid down in **R.107**. **R.107(3)** clarifies that the general provisions relating to proceedings before the EPO under Part III of the Implementing Regulations apply mutatis mutandis. (OJ 2003 se1 p.159)

The petition must present the petitioner's complete case. The indication of the decision to be reviewed, and the reasons, facts and evidence must all be filed within the relevant period of **Art.112a(4)**, i.e. two months from notification of the decision for a petition that is not based on a criminal act. There is some flexibility in that the EBoA may consider further submissions under Art.12(1) of the Rules of Procedure of the EBoA.

R. 107(1) The petition shall contain:
(a) the name and the address of the petitioner as provided in Rule 41, paragraph 2(c);
(b) an indication of the decision to be reviewed.

R.41(2)(c) Particulars of applicant

R. 107(2) The petition shall indicate the reasons for setting aside the decision of the Board of Appeal, and the facts and evidence on which the petition is based.

1 **Content of the petition**
Note that the petition does not need to contain any formal request; it only needs to specify the decision of the board of appeal that is to be set aside (R5/08). It must however be clear from the petition why the decision in question suffers from a fundamental procedural defect.

R. 107(3) Part III of the Implementing Regulations shall apply mutatis mutandis to the petition for review and the documents filed in the proceedings.

R. 108 Examination of the petition

Implementation of **Art.112a(5)**

R. 108(1) If the petition does not comply with Article 112a, paragraphs 1, 2 or 4, Rule 106 or Rule 107, paragraph 1(b) or 2, the Enlarged Board of Appeal shall reject it as inadmissible, unless any defect has been remedied before the relevant period under Article 112a, paragraph 4, expires.

Art.112a(1) Person entitled to file petition for review

Art.112a(2) Grounds for review
Art.112a(4) Form of review, period for filing, fee
R.106 Obligation to raise objections
R.107 Contents of the petition for review

1 **Examination of admissibility of petition**
R.108(1) lists the major admissibility requirements to be met by a petition for review. Any defect of the petition relating to these requirements must be remedied within the two-month or five-year period specified in **Art.112a(4)**. If not remedied in due time, the petition will be rejected as inadmissible (**R.108(1)**).

R. 108(2) If the Enlarged Board of Appeal notes that the petition does not comply with Rule 107, paragraph 1(a), it shall communicate this to the petitioner and shall invite them to remedy the deficiencies noted within a period to be specified. If the deficiencies are not remedied in due time, the Enlarged Board of Appeal shall reject the petition as inadmissible.

Amended by decision of the Administrative Council of 10.12.2024, which entered into force on 01.04.2025 (OJ 2025 A16). The amendment was introduction of gender-neutral language.
R.107(1)(a) Name and address of petitioner

1 **Remedy of deficiencies in petition**
R.108(2) is drafted in a manner corresponding to **R.101(2)**, which applies in appeal proceedings. Any deficiency relating to the name or address of the petitioner may be corrected following an invitation from the Enlarged Board in order to avoid the petition being rejected as inadmissible.

R. 108(3) If the petition is allowable, the Enlarged Board of Appeal shall set aside the decision of the Board of Appeal and order the re-opening of the proceedings before the Board of Appeal responsible under Rule 12b, paragraph 4. The Enlarged Board of Appeal may order that members of the Board of Appeal who participated in taking the decision set aside shall be replaced.

R.12b(4) Allocation of duties to boards of appeal by Presidium
The original reference to R.12 has changed to **R.12b**, in force since 01.07.2016 (OJ 2016 A100).

1 **Allowable petition**
Paragraph 3 concerns the decision of the Enlarged Board of Appeal if the petition is allowable. In accordance with the legal character of the petition as a special remedy, the Enlarged Board will set aside the decision of the Board of Appeal and order that the appeal proceedings be re-opened (the Enlarged Board cannot put itself in the position of the board of appeal and take any decision on the merits of the appeal). There is no discretionary element to this part of the remedy and a request to this end is therefore unnecessary. The consequence of an allowable petition is as defined: the proceedings are re-opened before the Board of Appeal responsible under the business distribution scheme enacted under **R.12b(4)**. The Enlarged Board of Appeal also has the discretionary authority to order that members of the board be replaced.

R. 109 Procedure in dealing with petitions for review

Implementation of **Art.112a(5)**

R. 109(1) In proceedings under Article 112a, the provisions relating to proceedings before the Boards of Appeal shall apply, unless otherwise provided. Rule 115, paragraph 1, second sentence, Rule 118, paragraph 2, first sentence, and Rule 132, paragraph 2, shall not apply. The Enlarged Board of Appeal may specify a period deviating from Rule 4, paragraph 1, first sentence.

Art.112a Petition for review by the Enlarged Board of Appeal
R.4(1) One month notice to use other language in oral proceedings
R.115(1) Two months' notice of summons oral proceedings
R.118(2) Two months' notice of summons to give evidence
R.132(2) Duration of office periods

1 **Procedure in dealing with petition**
Paragraph 1 is the parallel provision to **R.100(1) which applies provisions relating to first instance proceedings in appeal proceedings.** The corresponding provisions relating to appeal proceedings that apply in petition proceedings apply most particularly to proceedings before the Enlarged Board of Appeal in the five-member composition under paragraph 2(b). There are special rules that apply to proceedings before the Enlarged Board in the three-member composition of **R.109(2)(a)** which no longer apply if the Enlarged Board of Appeal has to decide in the composition provided in **R.109(2)(b)**. (OJ 2003 se1, p.159)

In the interest of procedural efficiency, the EBoA may shorten the following periods under **R.109(1)**, second sentence:

- the minimum period of two months for the summons to oral proceedings (**R.115(1)**, second sentence);
- the minimum of two months for periods specified by the EPO (**R.132(2)**);
- the period for a notice of summons to give evidence issued to a party, witness or expert (**R.118(2)**, first sentence);
- the period for requesting interpretation into the language of proceedings (R.4(1), first sentence). (OJ 2007 se5 EN p.166)

R. 109(2) The Enlarged Board of Appeal
(a) consisting of two legally qualified members and one technically qualified member shall examine all petitions for review and shall reject those which are clearly inadmissible or unallowable; such decision shall require unanimity;
(b) consisting of four legally qualified members and one technically qualified member shall decide on any petition not rejected under sub-paragraph (a).

1 **Composition of Enlarged Board of Appeal**
According to Art.3(2) of the Rules of Procedure of the EBoA the board constituted according to **R.109(2)(b)** will consist of the three members of the board allocated under **R.109(2)(a)** and two additional members.

The initial examination of a petition is carried out in an expedited manner by a three-member panel of the EBoA. If the petition is not rejected as clearly inadmissible or clearly unallowable by a unanimous decision of the three-member panel, the EBoA in five-member composition will examine the petition in full. The unanimity requirement applies only to the EBoA in the three-member composition. (OJ 2007 se5 EN p.168)

R. 109(3) The Enlarged Board of Appeal composed according to paragraph 2(a) shall decide without the involvement of other parties and on the basis of the petition.

1 **Rejection of petition as clearly inadmissible or unallowable**
The petition for review is assessed in a two-stage procedure before the EBoA. The first stage (**R.109(2)(a)**) filters out cases which are clearly inadmissible or clearly unallowable. In the second stage (**R.109(2)(b)**) the petition for review is allowed or rejected.

In the first stage, proceedings are conducted in accordance with paragraph 3; in the interests of legal certainty, review proceedings which clearly have no chance of succeeding are rapidly terminated. Proceedings under paragraph 3 are therefore conducted without involving the other parties (R5/08). The involvement of other parties is not necessary at this stage, because the three-member panel cannot allow a petition. If the petition is rejected as clearly inadmissible or clearly unallowable, the other parties are not adversely affected, as petition proceedings are terminated and the legal situation remains as decided by the Board of Appeal.

If the three-member panel intends to reject a petition, the petitioner will be invited to attend oral proceedings if such proceedings have been requested, or if the Enlarged Board of Appeal considers such proceedings to be expedient. If necessary, the period to be observed for issuing the invitation may be shortened. At the end of the oral proceedings (or otherwise in written proceedings), the three-member panel will either reject the petition for review as clearly inadmissible or clearly unallowable, or forward the petition to the five-member panel. If the petition is forwarded, the petition is examined by the EBoA in the five-member composition under **R.109(2)(b)** with the involvement of the other parties. The three-member panel decides 'on the basis of the petition', i.e. on the basis of the reasons, facts and evidence submitted within the period laid down in **Art.112a(4)**.

All decisions of the EBoA must be reasoned, in accordance with general principles.

From **Art.106** and **112a** it follows that there is no further right of appeal against a decision of the Enlarged Board of Appeal concerning a petition for review. (OJ 2003 se1 p.159)

R. 110 Reimbursement of the fee for petitions for review

The Enlarged Board of Appeal shall order the reimbursement of the fee for a petition for review if the proceedings before the Boards of Appeal are reopened.

Implementation of **Art.112a(5)**

PART VII IMPLEMENTING REGULATIONS TO PART VII OF THE CONVENTION

Chapter I *Decisions and communications of the European Patent Office*

R. 111 Form of decisions

Implementation of **Art.113**

R. 111(1) Where oral proceedings are held before the European Patent Office, the decision may be given orally. The decision shall subsequently be put in writing and notified to the parties.

1 **Effect of final decision**
A final decision closes the proceedings. The decision enters into force at the moment in time a party can take cognizance of it. A party cannot file submissions up to this moment because the decision-making department must be able to take all submissions into account when coming to a decision. The last moment in time for filing or making submissions depends on the type of proceedings, as indicated below. That last moment may only become known to a party after a decision has been taken. All documents filed after a decision has been taken serve no purpose. The notification of a decision in writing to a party does not end the proceedings; it might trigger a period, e.g. for filing an appeal.

See **R.36(1):2.1** for the relationship between the date of a decision and the pendency of an application.

2 **Decision in oral proceedings**
In oral proceedings, a party can make submissions up to the closing of the debate. Any subsequent reopening of the debate, allowing further submissions, is at the Division or Board's discretion (**T595/90**).

A decision taken at the end of oral proceedings enters into force the moment it is pronounced (**G12/91** r.2, 3). Such a decision is not, in general, reasoned and merely states whether a request is allowed or not. After conclusion of the oral proceedings the decision is written up in the form prescribed in **R.111(2)**, with the addition of reasons, and notified in written form to the party or parties. The written decision is usually notified under **R.111(1)** a few months after the oral proceedings.

The two-month period of **Art.108** for filing an appeal is triggered by the notification of the written decision in first instance proceedings and not by the pronouncement of the decision during oral proceedings, because the 'notification' in **Art.108** refers to the notification of the written decision in **R.111(1)** (**T390/86** r.2). See also **Art.116** on the procedure for oral proceedings.

3 **Decision in written proceedings of second instance**
In written proceedings before the second instance, a party can make submissions up to the date of the decision. This date is communicated in the written decision according to **R.102(b)**. The decision enters into force the date it is notified (**G12/91** r.2).

4 **Decision in written proceedings of first instance**
In contrast, the EPC does not specify that the date of a decision taken in first instance (the date it is signed) must be included in the decision. The legislator did therefore not intend to bind the division to its decision from the date of signature and prevent it from taking account of important developments occurring after this date but before the decision leaves its hands. (**G12/91** r.7.4)

After a first instance decision has been taken, the formalities section postdates the decision by at least 3 working days and hands the paper decision over to the EPO's internal postal service. The decision is thereby removed from the power of the department that issued it, completing the proceedings. The EPO postal service then despatches the decision on the notification date stamped on it. In respect of decisions to grant or refuse an application, it seems that the current practice of the EPO is to hand the decision to the internal postal service on a Friday and dispatch it on the following Thursday (four working days later). Both dates are indicated on the decision.

Therefore, in first instance written proceedings, the department concerned can take submissions into account and amend the decision taken up to a few days prior to the notification date stamped on the decision, i.e. up to the date on which the decision is handed to the EPO postal service. This date on which the decision is handed over corresponds to the closing of the debate in oral proceedings. The date is easy to ascertain by a party, albeit only once the decision has been notified, which provides legal certainty. (**G12/91** r.9)

As an example, taken from the case law, a first instance decision was stamped 06.03.1996 (Wednesday) and handed over to the EPO postal service three working days prior to that date, i.e. on 01.03.1996 (Friday); therefore, a party could only expect account to be taken of a submission filed before 01.03.1996 (**T394/96** r.4).

The decision taken in written proceedings enters into force when notified (**G12/91** r.2).

R. 111(2) Decisions of the European Patent Office which are open to appeal shall be reasoned and shall be accompanied by a communication pointing out the possibility of appeal and drawing the attention of the parties to Articles 106 to 108, the text of which shall be attached. The parties may not invoke the omission of the communication.

Art.106 Decisions subject to appeal
Art.107 Persons entitled to appeal and to be parties to appeal proceedings
Art.108 Time limit and of notice of appeal

1 **Form of written decision**

The EPC does not prescribe a particular form for a decision; **R.111(2)** requires only the presence of reasons and a written communication drawing attention to the possibility of appeal and referring to **Art.106-108**. The Guidelines set out the required contents of the written decision in E-X,1.3.

A decision open to appeal must give reasons why any not withdrawn request is inadmissible, allowable or rejected (**R.111(2)**; E-X,2.6). In the case of several subordinate requests (main request and auxiliary requests) reasons must be provided why each request of higher ranking than the allowed request is not allowed (**T406/86**). Since **R.111(2)** refers to 'decisions open to appeal', a decision not open to appeal, e.g. a decision that does not adversely affect a party, such as the grant of a patent, need not comply with **R.111(2)** and, hence, need not be reasoned. **R.111(2)** does not apply to a decision of a board of appeal because of lex specialis **R.102(g)**, which requires that such a decision must be reasoned, in spite of the fact that it is not open to appeal on account of **Art.106(1)**.

The reasons must contain the logical chain of facts and reasons on which the decision is based and at least some motivation on crucial points of dispute in this line of argumentation, in so far as this is not immediately apparent from the reasons given, in order to give the parties concerned a fair idea of why their submissions were not considered convincing (see a.o. **T740/93**, r.5.4). Other case law holds that **R.111(2)** has sufficiently been complied with when some reasons, even if incomplete and inadequate, were given (see a.o. **T856/91**, r.6.2). A decision not reasoned in conformity with **R.111(2)**, e.g. because the reasoning is not intelligible, amounts to a substantial procedural violation and may result in reimbursement of the appeal fee under **R.103** (see e.g. **T755/96** r.5.5, **T278/00** hn.3; **T2467/09** r.6, 13).

A party may not invoke the omission of the written communication stating the possibility of appeal and referring to **Art.106-108** according to the last sentence of **R.111(2)**. It may neither invoke failure of the EPO to attach the text of the articles to the communication (**T42/84** hn. II).

2 **Decision versus communication**

The EPC makes a clear distinction between a decision and a communication, as is apparent from **R.111** and **R.113(1)**; this distinction is not always apparent from the form in which the EPO sends them to parties. The EPC and case law do not prescribe a specific form for a decision. A decision may appear as a communication and vice versa without affecting its legal status. Case law has confirmed the freedom as to the form of decisions and communications.

The distinction between a communication and a decision is important because only decisions can be appealed (**Art.106**). An appealable decision must contain a reasoning but it need not state the possibility of appeal nor provide the text of **Art.106-108** (see previous section). A document providing the contents of a decision is not merely a communication when the requirements of **R.111(2)** are not fully complied with (**J8/81** r.2). A decision may be sent as a simple letter (**T713/02** r.2.1.4), contravening the prescribed form of notification in **R.126(1)**.

Whether a document issued by the EPO constitutes a decision or a communication depends on the substance of its contents, not upon its form (**J8/81**, hn. I). The decisive question is whether the document at issue, when objectively interpreted in its context, can be understood by its addressee as a final, i.e. not merely preliminary, and binding determination of substantive or procedural issues by the department of the EPO which has jurisdiction; even a document issued by a department of the EPO that does not have jurisdiction may constitute a decision (**J12/19**). The boards of appeal decide whether an appeal is allowable and, hence, whether the document is a decision. However, sometimes it can take a longer time for a first instance department to forward an appeal to the boards if the department considers that there is no appealable decision (see **J12/19**).

A communication may express a preliminary view or opinion of the EPO, in particular the communication that gives the party an opportunity to comment on a view of the EPO as required by **Art.113(1)** before the EPO takes a decision. Such a view or opinion is not binding. In contrast, a decision always closes the discussion on an issue and binds the department that issues it and can only be challenged by way of appeal (**T222/85**, r.3). Even the use of the word 'decision' does not make a document a decision in the sense of the EPC (**T713/02** r.2.1.4).

See **R.112(1):2** and **3** for the difference between a decision incurring a loss of rights and a communication under **R.112(1)** informing a party of a loss of rights arisen without a decision.

R. 112 Noting of loss of rights

Implementation of **Art.113**

R. 112(1) If the European Patent Office notes that a loss of rights has occurred, without any decision concerning the refusal of the European patent application or the grant, revocation or maintenance of the European patent, or the taking of evidence, it shall communicate this to the party concerned.

1 **Loss of rights**

Under the EPC a loss of rights can arise with or without a decision, depending on the phrasing of the law. The following sections indicate the cases where a decision is taken and where not and the differences in procedure between the two cases.

2 **Loss of rights with a decision**

A loss of rights will be based on a decision if the law states that the EPO will 'decide' or take a 'decision'. Examples of decisions that (may) incur a loss of rights are maintenance of a patent as amended (**Art.101(3)(a)**), apportionment of costs in opposition proceedings (**Art.104(1)**), a decision on an appeal (**Art.111(1)**), a decision on a request for further processing (**R.135(3)**) or on a request for re-establishment (**R.136(4)**; **G1/90**, r.14), a decision to take evidence (**R.117**). The grant of a patent according to **Art.97(1)** will be a loss of rights if the scope of the patent is less broad than desired. Note that a refusal, rejection or revocation implies a decision, which is also clear from the wording of **R.112(1)** (see also **G1/90**, r.5, 7). Examples are a refusal of an application (**Art.90(5)** and **Art.97(2)**), a rejection of a notice of opposition or appeal as inadmissible (**R.77(1)**, **R.101(1)**), a revocation of a patent (**Art.101(2)**, first sentence), a rejection of an opposition (**Art.101(2)**, second sentence).

In general, a decision is taken in cases where the EPO has to carry out an examination, often substantive in nature. After the examination the EPO informs the party of its view and gives the party an opportunity to comment under **Art.113(1)**. Subsequently the EPO takes a decision, which is notified to those concerned under **Art.119** and **R.126**.

A party adversely affected by a decision taken in first instance may appeal (**Art.107**). The appeal can be used as a re-examination of the grounds of the first instance decision, but also as a procedure to correct the deficiency that caused the loss of rights. If an application was refused for a formal deficiency under **Art.90(5)**, the deficiency can be remedied when filing the statement of grounds (**J11/20**). Such a correction in appeal is not possible if the decision appealed was taken under **R.112(2)** (see below).

If the notice of appeal is not filed within the period of **Art.108**, the decision cannot be contested anymore and becomes final. As soon as a decision is final, it is entered in the Register and published in the Bulletin, provided the patent application concerned has been published (**Art.127, 128**). The public can rely on the loss of rights as published. In the event of a change in legal position caused by re-establishment, a third party is protected by the right of continued use under **Art.122(5)**.

3 Loss of rights without a decision

The legislator has introduced the concept of 'loss of rights without a decision' to settle clear-cut cases and relieve the EPO from the task of writing a reasoned decision as required by **R.111(2)**. In such cases the loss of rights occurs automatically by operation of law (**G1/90**, r.6). The loss of rights is in general noted by a formalities officer simply by establishing the facts of the case and applying the law (E-VIII,1.9.2), without a need for issuing a preceding communication under **Art.113(1)**. A loss of rights without a decision arises in all cases where no decision is taken. Such cases are in general expressed in the EPC by the standard phrase 'deemed to be ... ' (**G1/90**, r.4). See the above section for the cases where a decision is taken. The list of decisions in **R.112(1)** should be regarded as examples of decisions, not as an exhaustive list.

The loss of rights must result from the Convention. A loss of rights caused by failing the time limit of **Art.65(1)** for filing a translation of a European patent in a contracting state is not a loss under **R.112(1)**, because the time limit and the loss are determined by national law (see **Art.65(3)**; **J43/92**, r.6). The loss of rights may be total, e.g. the application is deemed withdrawn, or partial, e.g. the right of priority is lost.

The most common cause of a clear-cut loss of rights is failure to meet a time limit resulting in a 'deemed to be withdrawn'. Most instances of **R.112(1)** relate to the grant procedure. Examples are the deemed withdrawn of the patent application (**Art.86(1)**, **Art.94(4)**, **R.37(2)**, **R.70(3)**, **R.71(7)**, **R.100(3)**, **R.160(1)**), loss of the right of priority (**Art.90(5)**; A-III,6.10), the deemed not filed of the notice of opposition (**Art.99(1)**), of the notice of appeal (**Art.108**, e.g. **G2/97**, Summ.II) and of a document (**Art.14(4)**, **R.5**, **R.2(1)**, **R.50(3)**), the application not being dealt with as a European patent application (**Art.90(2)**), procedural steps deemed not to have been taken (**R.152(6)**).

4 Communication of the loss of rights

The EPO notifies its finding about the loss of rights to the person concerned as a communication under **Art.119**. The communication is notified under R.125(2). In contrast with decisions, the communication of the loss of rights is not preceded by an invitation to comment on the view of the EPO under **Art.113(1)**.

The EPC does not prescribe the form of the communication distinguishing it from a decision, other communication or notice from the EPO. Normally the communication indicates that it refers to a noting of loss of rights pursuant to **R.112(1)**. If this indication is not provided, the content of the communication will be decisive; the content has at least to indicate which of the person's rights is concerned by a loss (**J43/92**, r.4).

Since the communication is not a decision but merely an opinion of the EPO about the effect of the operation of the law, it is not directly open to appeal, first a request for a decision under **R.112(2)** must be filed (see also J13/83, r.4).

The procedure under **R.112(1)** is an efficient way to conclude proceedings of an application in which the applicant has lost interest: the applicant simply refrains from responding to a communication from the EPO and the EPO need not formulate a decision but merely sends a communication under **R.112(1)**. In case the communication under **R.112(1)** is inaccurate or the loss of rights is not desired, a party can ask for a review under **R.112(2)** or apply a legal remedy to retract the legal consequences of the loss of rights, respectively.

5 **Remedies**

A loss of right resulting from the EPC and communicated under **R.112(1)** can be remedied in several ways, depending on the type of loss:

- If the finding of the EPO causing the loss of rights is inaccurate, a review of the finding should be requested by applying for a decision under **R.112(2)**. Such a request is preferably accompanied by requesting one or more remedies in auxiliary requests in case the EPO upholds its finding. Examples of multiple requests are given in **R.112(2):3**.
- The loss may be remedied using further processing under **Art.121** and **R.135**, provided the conditions for further processing have been complied with.
- If further processing is not available, re-establishment under **Art.122** and **R.136** may be used, provided the conditions for re-establishment have been met.
- No remedy is necessary if the loss of rights is intentional. For example, when a PCT application designates the EPO and the applicant decides not to enter into the European phase, the EPO will send a **R.112(1)** communication (see **R.159(1):1.3**).

R. 112(2) If the party concerned considers that the finding of the European Patent Office is inaccurate, it may, within two months of the communication under paragraph 1, apply for a decision on the matter. The European Patent Office shall take such decision only if it does not share the opinion of the party requesting it; otherwise, it shall inform that party.

1 **Application for a decision**

If the person affected by the loss of rights considers that the finding of the EPO is inaccurate, the person may apply for a decision under **R.112(2)** (E-VIII,1.9.3). A good overview of the procedure is given in Legal Advice **L16/85**, OJ 1985 p.141 (cancelled by Dec. Pres. OJ 2012 p.446). Possible inaccuracies of the EPO may be an incorrect calculation of a period or not applying provisions for late receipt such as **R.133, Rfees7(3)**, ADA.7.5. The person must state the facts and arguments contesting the finding of the EPO in the request and provide evidence where necessary.

The application for a decision under **R.112(2)** must be filed within two months from notification of the loss of rights under **R.112(1)**. Failure to meet the two-month period makes the finding of loss of rights incontestable, unless the person concerned successfully applies for re-establishment according to **Art.122** and **R.136** (E-VIII,1.9.3). **R.135(2)** excludes the two-month period of **R.112(2)** from further processing.

The decision is in general taken by the same formalities officer that noted the loss of rights (see e.g. **G1/02**, Summary of proc. I). According to **R.112(2)**, second sentence, the EPO will give a decision only if it does not share the opinion of the person requesting it; in cases where the EPO accepts the arguments of the requester, it will not issue a decision but inform the requester that the communication under **R.112(1)** will be set aside and the proceedings will continue. The possibility to 'apply for a decision on the matter' in **R.112(2)** is in fact to 'request a review of the communication under **R.112(1)**'.

An adverse decision, reasoned in accordance with **R.112(2)**, is open to appeal, provided the decision was taken by a department of first instance. The two- and four-months periods of **Art.108** for filing the appeal are triggered by the notification of the decision. The board of appeal will only re-examine the finding in the loss of rights communication under **R.112(1)**; the deficiency that caused the loss of rights cannot be corrected during the appeal procedure (**J11/20** r.16.1).

2 **Remedies and R.112(2)**

If the person concerned regards the communication under **R.112(1)** accurate but the resulting loss of rights undesirable, an application for a decision under **R.112(2)** is not useful. The decision will merely confirm the accuracy of the communication but it will not retract the legal consequences of the loss of rights. Instead, such a person must apply a legal remedy appropriate for the loss. Possible remedies are: further processing (**Art.121**), re-establishment (**Art.122**), invoking the principle of good faith in exceptional cases (e.g. **J14/94**; see **Art.125:2**). The period for requesting further processing is triggered by the notification of the **R.112(1)** communication (**R.135(1)**). The period for requesting re-establishment is triggered by the event that makes the party aware of the loss of rights (**R.136(1)**). This event may be the actual receipt of the **R.112(1)** communication.

When the person regards the **R.112(1)** communication inaccurate and applies for a decision under **R.112(2)**, the person will be informed of the result only several months after filing the request for a decision. If the result is a justified adverse decision, an appeal will not retract the loss of rights. Since the periods for requesting remedies of the loss of rights run parallel to the two months of **R.112(2)**, these will normally have expired by the time the party receives the decision under **R.112(2)**. Therefore, the party should apply for any remedy together with the application for a decision in the form of a main and auxiliary requests. The requests should be in order of increasing cost.

3 **Example of requests under R.112(2)**

The form of the requests will be clarified in the following example, where applicants pay the examination fee for their European patent application by giving an order to their bank in New York one day before the expiry of the period of **R.70(1)**. Subsequently the EPO sends a **R.112(1)** communication to the applicant's representative, pointing out that the fee was actually entered in the bank account held by the EPO after expiry of the period and that the application is deemed withdrawn under **Art.94(2)**. The representative files the following series of requests:

- main request: application for a decision under **R.112(2)** arguing that the time limit was considered to have been observed because the order for payment was given to the bank within the period within which the payment should have been made (**Rfees7(3)**);

- first auxiliary request: request re-establishment under **Art.122** and **R.136**, pay the fee for re-establishment, arguing that the delay in transfer of the payment was exceptionally long;
- second auxiliary request: request further processing under **Art.121** and **R.135** and payment of the further processing fee equal to 50% of the examination fee.

The EPO takes one decision, dealing with all requests in the order presented by the representative. The EPO will respond as follows:

- the main request is not allowed, because **Rfees7(3)** does not apply to payments from outside the contracting states;
- the first auxiliary request is not allowed, because **R.136(3)** and **R.135** excludes the period of **R.70(1)** from re-establishment;
- the second auxiliary request is allowed.

The fee for re-establishment and the fee for further processing are kept by the EPO. The representative can appeal the decision within two months from notification of the decision.

If the order of the first and second auxiliary request had been reversed, the fee for re-establishment would have been refunded as having no legal basis: the second auxiliary request would not have been dealt with because the higher-ranking request for further processing was allowable. Had the EPO allowed the main request, the fees for re-establishment and further processing would both have been refunded.

R. 113 Signature, name, seal

Implementation of **Art.113**

R. 113(1) Any decisions, summonses, notices and communications from the European Patent Office shall be signed by, and state the name of, the employee responsible.

1 **Missing signature**

All decisions issued by the EPO must be signed. If one or more members of the examining division or opposition division cannot sign the decision for serious reasons (e.g. resignation, illness, death), another member can sign on the missing member's behalf. The decision must include a brief written explanation of the reason for signing on behalf of another member. The substitute signature and explanation must both be included when the decision is issued and cannot be added later. (**T2348/19**, **T572/19**, E-X,2.3)

The requirement that decisions must be signed by and state the name of the employee responsible is not just a mere formality but an essential procedural step in the decision-making process. The name and the signature identify the decision's authors and express that they assume responsibility for its content; it aims to prevent arbitrariness and abuse. A violation of the requirement is a substantial procedural violation (**J16/17**).

R. 113(2) Where a document referred to in paragraph 1 is produced by the employee responsible using a computer, a seal may replace the signature. Where the document is produced automatically by a computer, the employee's name may also be dispensed with. The same shall apply to pre-printed notices and communications.

1 **Electronic seal and electronic authentication**

The EPO may replace handwritten signatures on decisions, summonses, notices and communications with a seal. The EPO may also electronically authenticate such documents by just mentioning the names of the employees responsible with an indication that the document has been electronically authenticated, to dispense with the handwritten signatures (OJ 2020 A37).

The names of the employees responsible for a decision can only be dispensed with if the decision is produced entirely automatically by a computer and not individually reasoned (**J16/17**).

Chapter II *Observations by third parties*

R. 114 Observations by third parties

Implementation of **Art.115**

R. 114(1) Any observations by a third party shall be filed in writing in an official language of the European Patent Office and state the grounds on which they are based. Rule 3, paragraph 3, shall apply.

1 **Method of filing and language of observation**
Observations by a third party in accordance with **Art.115** may be filed by any means permitted under **R.2(1)**, but preferably by electronic means (E-VI,3).

R.114 stipulates that observations must be filed in an official language of the EPO. If filed in another language, the EPO will request a translation from a non-anonymous third party. The reference to **R.3(3)** makes clear that the third party can file documentary evidence and, in particular, publications in any language. The Office may request a non-anonymous third party to supply a translation of the document and may disregard it if the translation is not filed in due time. (Not. EPO OJ 2017 A86 §3; A-VII,3.5)

R. 114(2) Any such observations shall be communicated to the applicant for or proprietor of the patent, who may comment on them.

1 **Procedure for observations**
The EPO places a received third-party observation in the public part of the file and forwards it to the applicant or proprietor for comment (**R.114(2)**). Any annexes to the observation are available only in the Register (Not. EPO OJ 2022 A28).

The EPO does not send communications in the procedure to the third party other than an acknowledgement of receipt and any request for translation under **R.114(1)**, as the third party is not a party to the proceedings. The EPO must give its opinion on the observations either in the next substantive communication or as a substantive comment in the Register. Both are available through file inspection (**Art.128(4)**), where an e-mail alert service may be used.

The examining or opposition division must consider the observation and comment on its relevance in the next substantive communication to the parties. If an observation received close to or after issue of the **R.71(3)** communication is regarded not relevant, the EPO will not issue a substantive communication but put a substantive comment in the Register. If an observation received close to or after issue of the **R.71(3)** communication is regarded relevant, the EPO will continue the examination and issue a substantive communication. (OJ 2017 A86 §4)

The EPO will make every effort to issue the next communication within three months of the receipt of the observation, provided the observation is substantiated and not filed anonymously. A non-anonymous filing allows the EPO to check that the person filing the observation is not the applicant or proprietor. (OJ 2017 A86 §5)

A third-party observation filed in the international phase of a Euro-PCT application will be taken into account after entry into the EP phase. The EPO will make every effort to issue the next substantive communication within three months after expiry of the **R.161** period if the third party filed the observation non-anonymously and expressly requested expedited issue of the next communication. The express request is not necessary if the observation is (re-)filed after entry. (OJ 2017 A86 §5)

If applicants or proprietors do not respond to the substantive communication by filing their comments under **Art.94(3)**, **Art.101(1)** or **R.100(2)**, the application is regarded as withdrawn (**Art.94(4)**, **R.100(3)**) or the patent may be revoked if the observations are prejudicial to the maintenance of the patent (**Art.101(2)**).

Chapter III *Oral proceedings and taking of evidence*

R. 115 Summons to oral proceedings

Implementation of **Art.116**

1 **General**
It is one of the goals of oral proceedings to make a case ready for decision at the end of the oral proceedings (see inter alia Art.15(6) RPBA). The summons inviting the party allows the parties to prepare for the proceedings by setting out the points to be discussed.

R. 115(1) The parties shall be summoned to oral proceedings under Article 116, drawing their attention to paragraph 2 of this Rule. At least two months' notice of the summons shall be given, unless the parties agree to a shorter period.

1 **Summons to oral proceedings**
The EPO invites a party to oral proceedings by means of a summons. The summons states the date, time and location of the oral proceedings. The summons normally gives parties at least four months' notice in examination and six months in opposition. Only in specific circumstances two to four months' notice can be given without preliminary agreement with the parties. Less than two months' notice always requires agreement with the parties (**R.115(1)**, second sentence). (E-III,6; OJ 2016 A42 §8)

The summons indicates the consequences of not appearing (**R.115(2)**) and the points to be discussed (**R.116(1)**). It is usually accompanied by the provisional and non-binding opinion of the Division. It sets a date, normally two months before the oral proceedings, for filing written submissions (**R.116(1)**). In this way, attention during the oral proceedings may be concentrated on the essential issues. (E-III,6; OJ 2016 A42 §8)

In appeal proceedings, the board endeavours to give the parties at least four-months' notice (Art.15(1) RPBA as in force from 01.01.2024; OJ 2023, A103). In a case relating to the right to inspect a file prior to publication of the application, a 20-day notice was regarded sufficient to allow the parties to prepare themselves properly. In this case the board regarded the urgency of the case more important than the lack of agreement of all parties and invoked **Art.164(2)** (**J14/91** r.2).

2 **Date of oral proceedings and postponement**
The practice for fixing and postponing the date of oral proceedings before departments of first instance is published in Not. EPO OJ 2009 p.68. The more restrictive practice of the boards of appeal is laid down in Art.15(2) RPBA.

The EPO fixes a single date for oral proceedings without prior consultation with a party. However, the EPO will ask a party for agreement with a notice of less than two months, and in first instance ex parte proceedings a party may be contacted by the examining division. The date may be any working day on which the relevant EPO office is open (E-III,6). The EPO will subsequently despatch the summons for oral proceedings according to **R.126**, both before the departments of first instance and before the boards of appeal, which informs the party of this date.

Another date will be fixed only if:

- parties concerned file a request as soon as possible after the grounds preventing them from attending the oral proceedings have arisen; and
- the request advances serious reasons, sufficiently substantiated in a written statement, which justify the fixing of a new date.

A statement why another representative cannot substitute the representative prevented from attending the oral proceedings need not be filed. However, if submissions were made by several representatives of a firm during written proceedings, an indication must be given why none of those who previously made such submissions can attend the oral proceedings. (E-III,7.1.1)

Any other parties to the proceedings should be consulted about their availability.

A board of appeal or the Enlarged Board of Appeal will only exceptionally allow a change of date (Art.15(2) RPBA; Art.14(3) RPEBA).

Acceptable reasons for postponement are ones beyond the control of the party, e.g.:

- previously notified summons to oral proceedings of the same party in other proceedings before the EPO, a national office, the UPC or a national court for the same day, for the preceding or following day, or for at least one of the two preceding or following days where the participation requires travelling to or from a geographically distant location;
- serious illness;
- death within the family;
- marriage of a person whose attendance in oral proceedings is relevant;
- military service or other obligatory civic duties;
- business trips or holidays firmly booked before notification of the summons; where holidays have been scheduled but not yet booked, the reason preventing rescheduling, such as school holidays, must be stated.

Of these reasons, the boards of appeal and the Enlarged Board of Appeal do not regard the following as acceptable: other proceedings on the one or two preceding or following days, and holidays only scheduled. The Board will however consider all the circumstances; for example, it may also consider that oral proceedings in another case have already been scheduled for the previous or following day at a different location (Explanatory Remark to Art.15(2) RPBA).

In first instance, the reasons only apply to participants whose presence is essential. A stricter approach may be applied in opposition proceedings to prevent a series of postponements (E-III,7.1.1). In appeal proceedings, if the party is represented, the reasons must relate to the representative (Art.15(2) RPBA).

Unacceptable reasons for postponement are: excessive work pressure; a summons to oral proceedings before the EPO or a national court notified after the summons in the relevant proceedings; and need to travel during the weekend (E-III,7.1.1). Departments of first instance will try, when requested, to enable parties to travel on the same day. Additional unacceptable reasons in appeal include: filing of new requests or submissions; unavailability of a represented party or accompanying person; and change of representative (Art.15(2)(c) RPBA).

The illness of a represented proprietor is not sufficient reason for adjournment of oral proceedings, even if the proprietor were to take part in the oral proceedings. Illness of an unrepresented party, a representative or an important witness is a good reason to request a change of the date of the oral proceedings. (T275/89)

R. 115(2) If a party duly summoned to oral proceedings before the European Patent Office does not appear as summoned, the proceedings may continue without that party.

1 **Absence at oral proceedings**

If the party was not duly summoned, the oral proceedings must be postponed. If a duly summoned party files a request for postponement with proper reasoning that the need for postponement was not the party's error, a new date must be fixed. If the need for postponement is due to carelessness of a party, the proceedings may still be postponed, but a decision on the costs will have to be taken. (E-III,8.3.3.1)

A notice of applicants in grant proceedings that they will not attend oral proceedings is normally treated by the EPO as a withdrawal of the request for oral proceedings, causing the examining division to take a decision on the file as it is (CLBA III.C.4.3.2; E-III,7.2.2). A request for a decision according to the state of the file is also considered a withdrawal of the request for oral proceedings (C-V,15.1). (OJ 2020 A124 §1)

If a party fails to connect to an oral proceedings by videoconference for reasons other than technical problems, the proceedings may continue in the party's absence. However, if technical problems prevent the oral proceedings by videoconference from being conducted, the division will issue a new summons to oral proceedings (Dec. Pres. OJ 2022 A103 Art.4).

In inter partes proceedings, if a duly summoned party fails to attend oral proceedings without notifying the EPO in advance, an apportionment of costs in favour of another attending party may be justified (**T930/92** hn. II, **T212/07** r.6).

A decision against a party who has been duly summoned but who fails to appear at oral proceedings may not be based on facts put forward for the first time during those oral proceedings. The late submission of new facts is worse procedural practice than non-attendance at oral proceedings; hence, the basic right of **Art.113(1)** is not forfeited by non-attendance. If the EPO decides not to disregard these facts but to examine them under **Art.114(1)**, the absent party must be given an opportunity to comment in accordance with **Art.113(1)**. The party who submitted the new facts is in principle responsible for any additional costs caused by a delay which is the result of the late submission. Evidence submitted for the first time during oral proceedings but notified previously, and which merely supports previous assertions of the party who submits them, may be used to support the reasons for the decision insofar as the relevant facts were already known to the other parties. New arguments not changing the grounds of the decision do not require an opportunity to comment by a non-attending party, since arguments do not constitute grounds or evidence in the sense of **Art.113(1)**. (**G4/92**, following **T484/90**, distinguishing **T574/89**)

A decision in oral proceedings may be based on a ground, e.g. extension under **Art.123(3)**, put forward for the first time during the oral proceedings, at least if the stage reached in the case was such that the absent proprietor could have expected the ground to be discussed (**T341/92** hn. I). Similarly, adding a clarifying restriction to a claim and removing formal deficiencies will not take an absent opponent by surprise, in interference of **Art.113(1)**, because the opponent had to expect that the proprietor would try to overcome any objections (**T202/92** r.6).

A party notifying the EPO in response to a proposal for a date for oral proceedings that it will 'take no further part in the proceedings' voluntarily surrenders its rights under **Art.113(1)** and a decision in oral proceedings may be based on any facts, grounds or evidence (**T892/94** r.2.5). During oral proceedings where the proprietor has decided to be absent the EPO does not have an opportunity to make any final amendment, however small, to make the patent maintainable; since the proprietor's consent is required under **Art.113(2)**, the EPO can only revoke the patent if such a final amendment is necessary (**T986/00** hn).

In examination, the examining division may decide to maintain the oral proceedings on the scheduled date, giving a decision orally at the end of the oral proceedings. Oral proceedings are typically maintained if amended claims have been filed in reply to the summons. The examining division may also decide to cancel the oral proceedings and to issue a written decision, even before the final date under R.116(1). (OJ 2020 A124)

R. 116 Preparation of oral proceedings

Implementation of **Art.116**

1 **General**

Implementation of **Art.114(2)** and **Art.116.** See also E-III,5 and 6.

R.116 aims at preparing the ground for oral proceedings such that a decision can be reached closing the proceedings. In general, the EPO states its opinion when issuing the summons, thereby providing the parties an opportunity to present their comments required by **Art.113(1)**. Written submissions from a party must reach the EPO and the other parties in time for them to be able to comment on their substance at the oral proceedings. Documents handed in during or just before oral proceedings do not fulfil this requirement and often lead instead to complaints from other parties that they have been taken off guard and are not prepared to discuss new points raised. Therefore, **R.116** sets a time limit for filing written submissions providing new facts or evidence (**R.116(1)**) or providing new requests in the form of amendments (**R.116(2)**). (OJ 1995 pp.418-419; **T755/96**, r.2-4)

R. 116(1) When issuing the summons, the European Patent Office shall draw attention to the points which in its opinion need to be discussed for the purposes of the decision to be taken. At the same time a final date for making written submissions in preparation for the oral proceedings shall be fixed. Rule 132 shall not apply. New facts and evidence presented after that date need not be considered, unless admitted on the grounds that the subject of the proceedings has changed.

Implementation of Art.114(2)
R.132 Extension of period on request

1 **Opinion of EPO and opportunity to file submissions**

Together with the summons the EPO communicates points to be discussed in the oral proceedings. It also sets a final date for written submissions to be taken into account.

The provision implements the EPO's discretion under **Art.114(2)** to accept or refuse late filed new facts and evidence. It thus supplements the line already developed by the Boards of Appeal to deal with abuses of the procedure, i.e. to refuse to consider facts or evidence put forward late without good reason. **R.116** should not be construed as an invitation to file new evidence or facts departing from the legal and factual framework of the case prior to the hearing (**T39/93** hn. I). The EPO will first consider the relevance of the late filed facts or evidence or the allowability of the late filed amendments on a prima facie basis. If not relevant or allowable, the submissions will not be admitted. Before admitting the submissions, the EPO will next consider procedural expediency (does it cause a prolonged adjournment of the proceedings), the possibility of abuse of the procedure (e.g. has the party already had sufficient opportunity to address the issues, is there a proliferation of auxiliary requests) and the question whether the parties can reasonably be expected to familiarise themselves in the time available with the new facts, evidence or amendments. (E-VI,2.2; H-II,2.7)

New facts and evidence may be filed late if the subject of the proceedings has changed (**R.116(1)**, last sentence). Examples of a change in the subject of the proceedings, which allow late filing of facts and evidence, are the bringing forward of new material by other parties in their own preparatory papers or the filing of amendments by the proprietor which have the result that a new document becomes relevant, or the introduction of a pertinent new document by the examining division during oral proceedings (**T951/97** hn). Documents may acquire relevance through an amendment of claims, making such documents admissible (**T366/11** r.3.5.6; E-VI,2.2).

In examination proceedings, an applicant may file submissions in response to the summons to bring the application closer to grant, which could lead to oral proceedings being cancelled. Such submissions can be discussed with the first member in an informal consultation (**Art.116:2**; C-IV,8). If parties consider that their submission overcomes the objections of the examining division and makes oral proceedings pointless, they should not wait for a response but telephone the first member about cancellation of the oral proceedings (see e.g. **T1183/02**). The division informs the applicant whether or not oral proceedings are cancelled following such submissions (E-III,7.2.1).

A computer-generated slideshow presentation may facilitate the understanding of a submission. It is in essence the presentation of written material and may contain such a quantity of information that parties must be provided with copies before the oral proceedings under **R.116(1)** (**T1122/01** r.2; **T1110/03** r.3, followed by **T555/06** r.1; E-III,8.5.1.1). A projection screen should be available in most meeting rooms; however, the EPO does not provide a computer or projector (E-III,8.5.1).

2 **Period for filing submissions**

Normally the EPO sets the final date for submissions two months before the date of the oral proceedings (D-VI,3.2). Although the period for this final date is set by the office, it cannot be extended on request under **R.132** (**R.116(1)**, third sentence).

The extensions of **R.134** do not apply to the period for filing submissions (E-VIII,1.6.2.3). See also **R.134:2**.

3 **Opinion of boards of appeal and opportunity to file submissions**

R.116(1) does not apply to the Boards of Appeal and is regarded as an example of the 'unless otherwise provided' in **R.100(1)**.

However, according to the RPBA, a board must issue a communication in which it draws attention to points to be discussed during the oral proceedings (Art.15(1) RPBA). The communication does not have to be issued with the summons to oral proceedings. In most cases, the communication will also give a preliminary opinion, and may invite a party to file observations within a period. The board endeavours to issue the communication at least four months in advance of the oral proceedings. Further, if more than one party is involved, the board must not send the communication until at least one month has elapsed from the receipt by the board of the written reply of any other party to the grounds of appeal under Art.12(1)(c) RPBA. Any amendment of a party's case filed after notification of the communication is not admitted unless there are exceptional circumstances (Art.13(2) RPBA).

R. 116(2) If the applicant or patent proprietor has been notified of the grounds prejudicing the grant or maintenance of the patent, they may be invited to submit, by the date specified in paragraph 1, second sentence, documents which meet the requirements of the Convention. Paragraph 1, third and fourth sentences, shall apply mutatis mutandis.

Amended by decision of the Administrative Council of 10.12.2024, which entered into force on 01.04.2025 (OJ 2025 A16). The amendment was introduction of gender-neutral language.

1 **Invitation to submit amendments**

This paragraph, like the previous one, is also designed to speed up the procedure and to prevent parties being unfairly confronted with new requests in oral proceedings. If applicants or proprietors have been informed beforehand that refusal or revocation is likely (and why), then they can reasonably be expected to react if the EPO gives them adequate time to do so. The discretionary power to refuse new requests for amendment filed after the specified date is governed by **Art.123, R.137(3)** and **R.80** and in the exercise of this power the EPO must balance the applicant's interest in obtaining a proper patent protection and the EPO's interest in concluding the procedure by the issue of a decision (**G7/93** r.2.2 and 2.5; **T755/96** r.4.2).

New requests filed in response to a summons in first instance proceedings will normally be discussed at the oral proceedings (C-IV,8).

A refusal must be adequately reasoned in conformity with **R.111(2)** and should comprise the balancing of interests; a mere ground that it was filed too late is not adequate (**T755/96** r.5).

R. 117 Decision on taking of evidence

Implementation of **Art.117(2)**

Where the European Patent Office considers it necessary to hear a party, witness or expert, or to carry out an inspection, it shall take a decision to this end, setting out the investigation which it intends to carry out, relevant facts to be proved and the date, time and place of the investigation and whether it will be conducted by videoconference. If the hearing of a witness or expert is requested by a party, the decision shall specify the period within which the requester must make known the name and address of any witness or expert concerned.

Amended, in force since 01.01.2021 (OJ 2020 A132). The decision enables evidence to be taken by videoconference. For more details, see OJ 2020 A135.

1 **Period for making witnesses known**
The period is between two and four months according to **R.132** (E-IV,1.4).

R. 118 Summons to give evidence before the European Patent Office

Implementation of **Art.117(2)**

R. 118(1) A summons to give evidence before the European Patent Office shall be issued to the parties, witnesses or experts concerned.

R. 118(2) At least two months' notice of a summons issued to a party, witness or expert to testify shall be given, unless they agree to a shorter period. The summons shall contain:
(a) an extract from the decision under Rule 117, indicating the date, time and place of the investigation ordered, specifying whether it will be conducted by videoconference and stating the facts in respect of which parties, witnesses or experts are to be heard;
(b) the names of the parties and particulars of the rights which the witnesses or experts may invoke under Rule 122, paragraphs 2 to 4;
(c) an indication that a party, witness or expert who has been summoned to appear before the European Patent Office on its premises may, on request, be heard by videoconference;
(d) an indication that the party, witness or expert may request to be heard by a competent court of their country of residence under Rule 120, and an invitation to inform the European Patent Office, within a period to be specified, whether they are prepared to appear before it.

Amended, by decision of the Administrative Council of 15.12.2020, which entered into force on 01.01.2021 (OJ 2020 A132). The decision enables evidence to be taken by videoconference. For more details, see OJ 2020 A135. Further amended by decision of the Administrative Council of 10.12.2024, which entered into force on 01.04.2025 (OJ 2025 A16). The amendment was introduction of gender-neutral language.
R.117 Taking of evidence by the EPO
R.120 Hearing by a competent national court
R.122(2)-(4) Reimbursement of witnesses or experts

R. 119 Examination of evidence before the European Patent Office

Implementation of **Art.117(2)**

R. 119(1) The Examining Division, Opposition Division or Board of Appeal may commission one of its members to examine the evidence adduced.

R. 119(2) Before parties, witnesses or experts may be heard, they shall be informed that the European Patent Office may request the competent court in their country of residence to re-examine their testimony under oath or in an equally binding form.

Amended by decision of the Administrative Council of 10.12.2024, which entered into force on 01.04.2025 (OJ 2025 A16). The amendment was introduction of gender-neutral language.

1 **Request for re-examination under oath**
The option to request a national court to hear a witness under oath is an instrument to put pressure on the person to be heard to speak the truth. See **R.120(2)**.

R. 119(3) The parties may attend an investigation and may put relevant questions to the testifying party, witness or expert.

R. 120 Hearing by a competent national court

Amended by decision of the Administrative Council of 10.12.2024, which entered into force on 01.04.2025 (OJ 2025 A16). Paragraphs (1) and (2) were amended by introducing gender-neutral language.
Implementation of **Art.117(2)**

R. 120(1) A party, witness or expert who is summoned before the European Patent Office may request the latter to allow them to be heard by a competent court in their country of residence. If this is requested, or if no reply is received within the period specified in the summons, the European Patent Office may, in accordance with Article 131, paragraph 2, request the competent court to hear the person concerned.

Art.131(2) Administrative and legal co-operation
The countries are restricted to contracting states.

R. 120(2) If a party, witness or expert has been heard by the European Patent Office, the latter may, if it considers it advisable for the testimony to be given under oath or in an equally binding form, issue a request under Article 131, paragraph 2, to the competent court in the country of residence of the person concerned to re-examine the testimony under such conditions.

Art.131(2) Administrative and legal co-operation

1 **Taking of evidence by national court**
The purpose of this provision is to obtain a new taking of the evidence and a statement under oath, on which possible penal sanctions can be based.

The EPO cannot take hearings under oath, as it does not have the power to enforce legal sanctions in the case of perjury. However, it can put pressure on a witness to tell the truth by threatening application of **R.120(2)**. The national court will cooperate because of **Art.131(2)**.

R. 120(3) When the European Patent Office requests a competent court to take evidence, it may request the court to take the evidence under oath or in an equally binding form and to permit a member of the department concerned to attend the hearing and question the party, witness or expert, either through the intermediary of the court or directly.

R. 121 Commissioning of experts

Implementation of **Art.117(2)**

R. 121(1) The European Patent Office shall decide in what form the opinion of an expert whom it appoints shall be submitted.

R. 121(2) The terms of reference of the expert shall include:
(a) a precise description of the task;
(b) the period specified for the submission of the opinion;
(c) the names of the parties to the proceedings;
(d) particulars of the rights which the expert may invoke under Rule 122, paragraphs 2 to 4.

Amended by decision of the Administrative Council of 10.12.2024, which entered into force on 01.04.2025 (OJ 2025 A16). The amendment was introduction of gender-neutral language.
R.122(2) Expenses for travel and subsistence of witnesses or experts
R.122(3) Compensation for loss of earnings of witnesses and fees for experts
R.122(4) Payment of cost by EPO

R. 121(3) A copy of any written opinion shall be submitted to the parties.

R. 121(4) The parties may object to an expert. The department of the European Patent Office concerned shall decide on the objection.

R. 122 Costs of taking of evidence

Implementation of **Art.117(2)**

R. 122(1) The taking of evidence by the European Patent Office may be made conditional upon deposit with it, by the party requesting the evidence to be taken, of an amount to be fixed by reference to an estimate of the costs.

1 **Deposit of estimate of cost**
The estimate of the cost is based on salary scales of the EPO.

R. 122(2) Witnesses or experts who are summoned by and appear before the European Patent Office shall be entitled to appropriate reimbursement of expenses for travel and subsistence. An advance for these expenses may be granted to them. This shall also apply to persons who appear before the European Patent Office without being summoned by it and are heard as witnesses or experts.

1 **Reimbursement of expenses**
An overview of compensation and fees payable to witnesses and experts is published in OJ 1983 p.100.

As a rule, the party requesting evidence meets the costs of the witness or expert. However, in opposition proceedings the EPO may fix a different apportionment for reasons of equity. The EPO may make the taking of evidence conditional upon deposit with the EPO by the party who requested the evidence of an advance for reimbursement of expenses of witnesses or experts. (E-IV,1.9).

Persons not being summoned are only reimbursed if a party or the EPO requests taking their evidence, and the competent department decides to grant the request (E-IV,1.6.2). There is of course no reimbursement if the inventor or another employee accompanying the representative is allowed to give a clarification of facts, without being heard as witness.

R. 122(3) Witnesses entitled to reimbursement under paragraph 2 shall also be entitled to appropriate compensation for loss of earnings, and experts to fees for their work. These payments shall be made to the witnesses and experts after they have fulfilled their duties or tasks.

R. 122(4) The Administrative Council shall lay down the details implementing paragraphs 2 and 3. Any amounts due under these provisions shall be paid by the European Patent Office.

R. 123 Conservation of evidence

Amended by decision of the Administrative Council of 14.12.2023, which entered into force on 01.04.2024 (OJ 2024 A3). The amendment deleted R.123(3), abolishing the fee for conservation of evidence. R.123(4) became R.123(3). Implementation of **Art.117(2)**

1 **General**

Implementation of **Art.117**.

The provision is a precautionary measure taken before the start of a procedure or earlier than requested in a procedure, and stemming from the probatio ad perpetuam rei memoriam. It aims at conserving evidence of facts liable to affect a decision which may later be difficult or impossible to submit, e.g. evidence from a witness about to emigrate or evidence of public prior use in the form of perishable matter.

The procedure involves (E-IV,2.2):

- filing a request according to **R.123(2)**;
- indication of facts which are important for a decision probably to be taken later;
- reasons why the taking of evidence will be difficult or impossible at the later point of time.

R. 123(1) On request, the European Patent Office may, without delay, take measures to conserve evidence of facts liable to affect a decision which it may be called upon to take with regard to a European patent application or a European patent, where there is reason to fear that it might subsequently become more difficult or even impossible to take evidence. The date on which the measures are to be taken shall be communicated to the applicant for or proprietor of the patent in sufficient time to allow them to attend. They may ask relevant questions.

Amended by decision of the Administrative Council of 10.12.2024, which entered into force on 01.04.2025 (OJ 2025 A16). The amendment was introduction of gender-neutral language.

1 **Date for taking evidence**
There is no at least two months' notice of a summons as for the normal taking of evidence under R.118(2), because of the urgency of the case.

R. 123(2) The request shall contain:
(a) particulars of the requester as provided in Rule 41, paragraph 2(c);
(b) sufficient identification of the European patent application or European patent in question;
(c) an indication of the facts in respect of which evidence is to be taken;
(d) particulars of the means of giving or obtaining evidence;
(e) a statement establishing a prima facie case for fearing that it might subsequently become more difficult or impossible to take evidence.

R.41(2)(c) Particulars of applicant

R. 123(3) The decision on the request and any resulting taking of evidence shall be incumbent upon the department of the European Patent Office which would have to take the decision liable to be affected by the facts to be established. The provisions with regard to the taking of evidence in proceedings before the European Patent Office shall apply.

1 **Competence of EPO departments**
Up to the decision to grant the examining division is competent, then the opposition division, thereafter the board of appeal (E-IV,2.3). After a refusal of the examining division the board of appeal should be competent.

R. 124 Minutes of oral proceedings and of taking of evidence

Implementation of Art.117(2)

R. 124(1) Minutes of oral proceedings and of the taking of evidence shall be drawn up, containing the essentials of the oral proceedings or of the taking of evidence, the relevant statements made by the parties, the testimony of the parties, witnesses or experts and the result of any inspection.

1 **Drawing up of the minutes**
See E-III,10 for the procedure relating to the drawing up of the minutes and R.4(6) for the language of the minutes. The minutes are sent to the parties (R.124(4)).

Only EPO employees are allowed to use any kind of sound recording device in the hearing room at oral proceedings (Not. Vice-Pres. OJ 1986 p.63 and OJ 2007 se3 p.117). According to E-III,10.1, sound recording can only be used for taking of evidence. A verbatim record of the proceedings can only be obtained by parties by hiring a shorthand writer. Parties may use laptops, but they cannot be used for sound recording. Use of portable computers is allowed in second instance oral proceedings, provided they do not disturb participants and are not used for recording (OJ 2014 A21).

The minutes of oral proceedings in first instance proceedings should record arguments of parties relevant for the decision, any new requests of parties, comments of the division relevant for the decision, and an indication of the decision. (E-III,10.3)

The minutes of oral proceedings in appeal should record the requests of the parties on which a decision of the board is required, such as allowability of the appeal, and statements which have an impact on the definition of the subject-matter, such as a statement of surrender of subject-matter. Arguments of parties should not be recorded, as being neither essential nor relevant. (**T263/05** hn.IV)

R. 124(2) The minutes of the testimony of a witness, expert or party shall be read out, submitted to them, so that they may examine them or, where they are recorded by technical means, played back to them, unless they waive this right. It shall be noted in the minutes that this formality has been carried out and that the person who gave the testimony approved the minutes. If approval is not given, the objections shall be noted. It is not necessary to play back the minutes or to obtain approval of them if the testimony has been recorded verbatim and directly using technical means.

Amended by decision of the Administrative Council of 10.12.2024, which entered into force on 01.04.2025 (OJ 2025 A16). The amendment was introduction of gender-neutral language.

1 **Minutes of taking of evidence**
According to current practice, the evidence of the person testifying is as a rule summarised section by section by the legal member and dictated in this form onto a voice recording device. The person being examined has the opportunity to raise objections immediately to the dictated text, so that it can be corrected at once.

The first sentence of **R.124(2)**, gives persons the right to have the whole of their testimony played back to them afterwards, unless they waive this right. Normally the person waives this right.

In order to enhance the authenticity of the minutes and to simplify and accelerate the taking of evidence, it could in certain cases make sense to produce the minutes verbatim using technical means instead of summarising the evidence. The requirements in **R.124(2)** of playing back the recording and obtaining approval would be impractical in this case. Therefore, the fourth sentence of **R.124(2)** provides that in the case of verbatim recording no playback or approval is necessary. (OJ 2007 se5 EN p.189)

R. 124(3) The minutes shall be authenticated by the employee responsible for drawing them up and by the employee who conducted the oral proceedings or taking of evidence, either by their signature or by any other appropriate means.

Amended, in force since 01.04.2015 (OJ 2015 A17, A36 §4).

R. 124(4) The parties shall be provided with a copy of the minutes.

1 **Correction of the minutes**
Parties receive a copy of the minutes and may file a request for correction of any perceived deficiencies (E-III,10.4). The minutes should be checked carefully and immediately on receipt and any correction should be requested promptly (**T2241/15**). The minutes are considered to correctly reflect the course of the oral proceedings if no correction is requested (**T690/09**). Only the department before which the oral proceedings took place is competent to decide on a request for correction of the minutes, even if an appeal has been filed (**T1198/97** hn.2). The minutes are corrected if, for example, essen-

tial submissions, requests or important procedural statements are missing or incorrectly reflected in the minutes (E-III,10.4; **T642/97**, r.9.3).

Chapter IV *Notifications*

R. 125 General provisions

Implementation of **Art.119**

R. 125(1) The European Patent Office shall, as a matter of course, notify those concerned of decisions and summonses, and of any notice or other communication from which a time limit is reckoned, or of which those concerned must be notified under the Convention, or of which notification has been ordered by the President of the European Patent Office. Any notification to be made shall take the form of the original document, a copy thereof certified by or bearing the seal of the European Patent Office, a computer print-out bearing such seal or an electronic document containing such seal or otherwise certified. Copies of documents emanating from the parties themselves shall not require such certification.

Amended, in force since 01.04.2015 (OJ 2015 A17, A36 §2, 5).

1 **Documents to be notified**
Notification of a document by the EPO is the act of making it available to a party. The possible ways in which a document can be notified are set out in **R.125(2)**.

The EPO notifies all communications from which a time limit is calculated and those communications which must be notified under the EPC or by order of the President. The EPO does not formally notify other communications.

R. 125(2) Notification shall be made:
- **(a) by postal services in accordance with Rule 126;**
- **(b) by means of electronic communication in accordance with Rule 127;**
- **(c) by delivery on the premises of the European Patent Office in accordance with Rule 128; or**
- **(d) by public notice in accordance with Rule 129.**

Amended, in force since 01.04.2015 (OJ 2015 A17, A36 §2, 5).
R.126 Notification by postal service
R.127 Notification by means of electronic communication
R.128 Notification by delivery by hand
R.129 Public notification

R. 125(3) Notification through the central industrial property office of a Contracting State shall be made in accordance with the law applicable to that office in national proceedings.

R. 125(4) Where a document has reached the addressee, if the European Patent Office is unable to prove that it has been duly notified, or if provisions relating to its notification have not been observed, the document shall be deemed to have been notified on the date established by the European Patent Office as the date of receipt.

1 **Irregular notification**

Where a period starts from a notification, the period starts from the date of the deemed receipt of the document notified unless otherwise provided (**R.131(1)**). For notification by postal service and electronic means of communication, the date of notification is specified in **R.126(2)**, respectively **R.127(2)**.

The EPO must be able to prove that a party failed to comply with a time limit. Therefore, it must be able to establish the date of notification of the document that triggered the non-observed period. In case the delivery of notifications by registered letter or electronic means of communication is delayed and takes more than seven days, the date of notification is still the date the document bears, but the period is extended, as specified by **R.126(2)** and **R.127(2)**.

Where the notification of a document is irregular, i.e. the party receives the document but not in the prescribed manner, the date of receipt, which the EPO can establish (i.e. can prove), will be regarded as the date of notification (**R.125(4)**). This can be e.g. the date of an email sent by the EPO to the party (**T1529/20**). The date of actual receipt can be the date given by the addressee or, if not provided, the date of any letter filed in response to the notification. (E-II,2.6; see e.g. **J9/99**)

The EPO will attempt to notify a letter twice. If the second attempt also fails, a note is made in the Register of an upcoming public notification in the Bulletin. The public notification under **R.129** by publication of a notice in the Bulletin takes place about one month after the EPO has received the second non-delivery notice; the date of publication of the public notice is entered in the Register. The letter is deemed notified to the addressee one month after the public notification (**R.129(2):1**). If the one-month period expires on a day the EPO is closed, the period is not extended to the next working day. The EPO uses the fictitious date of notification to determine the expiry of the period for responding to the letter.

Where a document that triggers a time limit is notified simultaneously to two parties (e.g. a written decision in opposition proceedings triggering the time limit for filing a notice of appeal) and the document is notified on different days, the time limit may expire on a different day for each party (**T1596/14**).

R. 126 Notification by postal services

Implementation of **Art.119**

1 **General**

The EPO may notify documents using a postal service (E-II,2.4). Other means of notification (e.g. notification by means of electronic communication, **R.127**) are also available. The postal service used by the EPO may be the traditional postal authority, commonly called 'the post', a courier service or any other service the EPO regards suitable (CA/47/14 §11, 16). Note, that the 'postal service' is the means of transmission and the 'postal service provider' is the operator of the service.

Communications from the EPO are sent to the address of the party or, if the party is represented, to the address of the representative (**R.130(1)**). The address used is the one specified in the Request for Grant form or the notice of opposition. Non-represented applicants having their residence or place of business in a contracting state may indicate in the Request for Grant form an address for correspondence different from the official address that will be indicated in the European Patent Register and in the publication of the application (e.g. the address of a firm's patent department which is different from the address of the firm's head office). (Not. EPO OJ 2014 A99)

R. 126(1) All notifications by postal services shall be by registered letter.

Amended by decision of the Administrative Council of 28.03.2019, which entered into force on 01.11.2019. The amendment removed the obligation for the EPO to send certain communications with advice of delivery. With advice of delivery, the postal service provider provides confirmation to the sender that delivery to the addressee has taken place. It had proved to be an unreliable service. (OJ 2019 A31, A57; CA/D 2/19)

1 **Registered letter**
Any notification sent by the EPO using a postal service is sent as a registered letter.

As of 01.01.2024, the EPO no longer requests parties to acknowledge the receipt of important documents such as summonses and decisions (OJ 2023 A108). This does not affect the duty of the EPO to establish the date of receipt of a document in the case of a dispute (**R.126(2)**) but reflects the fact that the majority of these documents are now notified by the EPO electronically.

See E-II,2.6 for procedure in the case of an irregular delivery where the EPO cannot establish the actual date of notification.

R. 126(2) Where notification is effected in accordance with paragraph 1, the document shall be deemed to be delivered to the addressee on the date it bears, unless it has failed to reach the addressee. In the event of any dispute concerning the delivery of the document, it shall be incumbent on the European Patent Office to establish that the document has reached its destination and to establish the date on which the document was delivered to the addressee. If the European Patent Office establishes that the document was delivered to the addressee more than seven days after the date it bears, a period for which the deemed receipt of that document is the relevant event under Rule 131, paragraph 2, shall expire later by the number of days by which the seven days were exceeded.

Amended by decision of the Administrative Council of 13.10.2022, which entered into force on 01.11.2023 and applies to documents notified by the EPO on or after that date (i.e. dated 01.11.2023 or later, Not. EPO OJ 2023 A29). The amendment abolished the ten-day deemed notification period according to which a document sent by postal services was deemed to be notified on the tenth day following its handover to the postal service provider. A document is now deemed to be delivered on the date it bears. The amendment also introduced a seven-day rule in order to compensate for postal service delays. (OJ 2022 A101; CA/D 10/22)
R.131(2) Calculation of periods

1 **Notification on date document bears and seven-day rule**
For documents to be notified by the EPO pursuant to **R.126(1)** on or after 01.11.2023, a legal fiction applies according to which the document is deemed notified to the addressee on the date that it bears (OJ 2022 A101; Not. EPO OJ 2022 A114; Not. EPO OJ 2023 A29). The EPO is therefore relieved of the need to establish the actual date on which the document was delivered to the addressee in each case; periods are calculated from the date of the document itself rather than the date of delivery.

The date stamped on the document to be notified is the date the EPO handed over the document to the postal service provider. It is this date stamped on the document which is the date of deemed notification and not any other date stamped on the envelope by the postal service provider.

This legal fiction (replacing the previously applicable ten-day legal fiction) was introduced as part of the ongoing digital transformation of the grant procedure, specifically in view of the fact that the EPO notifies almost all of its documents instantaneously by electronic means to the applicant's or representative's Mailbox.

In order to compensate for delays in the postal system, **R.126(2)** provides a seven-day rule that mirrors the seven-day rule of R.80.6 PCT. Accordingly, if a document is delivered to the addressee more than seven days from the date it bears (i.e. if actual notification occurs more than seven days from the date of deemed notification), any period that is calculated from the date of notification will be extended to compensate for the delay in notification. The extension is equal to the number of days by which the seven days were exceeded. So, for example, if a communication pursuant to **Art.94(3)** EPC is delivered to the applicant on 21.11.2023, setting a four month time limit for responding, and is dated 10.11.2023, the four month time limit will expire on 14.03.2024 (four days added to the end of the four month period calculated from the date of the document). Where days are to be added to the end of the period under both **R.126(2)** (to compensate for postal delays) and under **R.134(1)** (in view of the period ending on day on which an EPO filing office was closed) they should be added in that order since the total length of the period must first be established under **R.126(2)** before it can be established whether that period expires on a day on which one of the filing offices is not open for the receipt of documents. Thus, in the above example, if the communication is delivered only on 23.11.2023, the four month time limit will expire on 18.03.2024 (with six days added to the end of the four month period calculated from the date of the document), 16.03.2024 being a Saturday.

The EPO bears the burden of establishing that a document has been delivered to the addressee and, if it has been delivered, the date on which it was delivered. Accordingly, registered letters are used for notifications on paper since the postal service provider keeps a register of such letters, and the EPO can initiate a postal investigation concerning the delivery of the letter (see e.g. **T1529/20**).

If the party timely disputes the delivery of the letter in a substantiated way and the EPO is unable to prove that a document was delivered, then any period linked to the notification of the document will not be considered to have started and the EPO will attempt to notify the document again (**T247/98**).

The current text of **R.126(2)** applies to documents "to be notified by the European Patent Office on or after 1 November 2023" (Art.3 of the Decision of the Administrative Council of 13.10.2022). According to Not. EPO OJ 2023 A29, the relevant event is the sending of the document by the EPO and the new rule therefore applies to any document bearing a date of 01.11.2023 or later.

2 Ten-day rule for notification (applicable until 31.10.2023)

The previous text of **R.126(2)** established a different legal fiction according to which a document notified by postal services was deemed notified on the tenth day following its handover to the postal service provider. No seven-day rule was provided.

If a registered letter was received after the tenth day from the date printed on the document, the fiction did not apply, and the date of notification was the actual date of delivery. In the event of a dispute, the burden was on the EPO to prove the date of delivery (**R.126(2)**).

R. 126(3) Notification in accordance with paragraph 1 shall be deemed to have been effected even if acceptance of the letter has been refused.

1 **Acceptance of letter**
A letter is regarded as received even if acceptance is refused (**R.126(3)**). National postal law governs whether a person, e.g. an adult belonging to the family, is competent to refuse a letter (**R.126(4)**).

R. 126(4) To the extent that notification by postal services is not covered by paragraphs 1 to 3, the law of the State in which the notification is made shall apply.

R. 127 Notification by means of electronic communication

Implementation of **Art.119**

R. 127(1) Notification may be effected by means of electronic communication as determined by and under the conditions laid down by the President of the European Patent Office.

Amended, in force since 01.04.2015 (OJ 2015 A17, A36 §3, 5). Further amended by decision of the Administrative Council of 10.12.2024, which entered into force on 01.04.2025 (OJ 2025 A16). The amendment was introduction of gender-neutral language.

1 **Online notification**
By virtue of **R.127**, the EPO is able to notify documents electronically. A party to proceedings before the EPO may also file documents electronically, see **R.2(1):5**.

A party can elect to receive electronic notifications from the EPO by activating the Mailbox service (Dec. Pres. OJ 2015 A28 §9; OJ 2021 A5 for individuals other than professional representatives; Dec. Pres. OJ 2024 A20 for access via MyEPO; Dec. Pres. OJ 2024 A19 for proceedings relating to European patents with unitary effect). No paper copies are sent when this option is chosen.

Almost all communications in examination and opposition proceedings (as of 01.04.2021), communications in appeal proceedings (as of 01.06.2021) and communications relating to requests for unitary effect (as of 01.06.2023) can be notified electronically (OJ 2021 A5, A37; OJ 2023 sp3 p.7-8). As of 01.02.2025, communications in proceedings before the Enlarged Board of Appeal can also be notified via the Mailbox (OJ 2025 A11). A full list of communications which can be notified electronically via the Mailbox is available at https://www.epo.org/en/applying/myepo-services/interact/mailbox/updates.

R. 127(2) Where notification is effected by means of electronic communication, the electronic document shall be deemed to be delivered to the addressee on the date it bears, unless it has failed to reach its destination. In the event of any dispute concerning the delivery of the electronic document, it shall be incumbent on the European Patent Office to establish that the document has reached its destination and to establish the date on which it reached its destination. If the European Patent Office establishes that the electronic document has reached its destination more than seven days after the date it bears, a period for which the deemed receipt of that document is the relevant event under Rule 131, paragraph 2, shall expire later by the number of days by which the seven days were exceeded.

Amended by decision of the Administrative Council of 13.10.2022, which entered into force on 01.11.2023 and applies to documents notified by the EPO on or after that date (i.e. dated 01.11.2023 or later, Not. EPO OJ 2023 A29). The amendment abolished the ten-day deemed notification period according to which a document sent electronically was deemed to be notified on the tenth day following its transmission. A document is now deemed to be delivered on the date it bears. The amendment also introduced a seven-day rule in order to compensate for delays in transmission. (OJ 2022 A101; CA/D 10/22)

R.131(2) Calculation of periods

1 **Notification on date electronic document bears and seven-day rule (applicable from 01.11.2023)**

For electronic documents to be notified by the EPO on or after 01.11.2023, a legal fiction applies according to which the document is deemed notified to the addressee on the date that it bears (OJ 2022 A101; Not. EPO OJ 2022 A114; Not. EPO OJ 2023 A29). The EPO is therefore relieved of the need to establish the actual date on which the document was delivered to the addressee in each case; periods are calculated from the date of the document itself rather than the date of delivery.

The date recorded on the document to be electronically notified is usually the date the EPO transmits the document electronically to the addressee's Mailbox. However, as was the case before 01.11.2023, the date of the document is decisive in determining the deemed notification date even if the document is actually available to the addressee in the addressee's Mailbox on an earlier date (E-II,2.3).

This legal fiction (replacing the previously applicable ten-day legal fiction) was introduced as part of the ongoing digital transformation of the grant procedure, specifically in view of the fact that the EPO notifies almost all of its documents instantaneously by electronic means to the applicant's or representative's Mailbox.

Delays in electronic notification are much rarer than delays in transmission by postal services. However, since there is no longer a ten-day deemed notification period to compensate for any delay, the EPO has introduced a new seven-day rule that mirrors the seven-day rule of R.80.6 PCT. Accordingly, if an electronic document is delivered to the addressee more than seven days from the date it bears (i.e. if actual notification occurs more than seven days from the date of deemed notification), any period that is calculated from the date of notification will be extended to compensate for the delay in notification. The extension is equal to the number of days by which the seven days were exceeded. So, for example, if a communication pursuant to **Art.94(3)** EPC is delivered electronically to the applicant's Mailbox on 20.11.2023, setting a four month time limit for responding, and is dated

10.11.2023, the four-month time limit will expire on 13.03.2024 (three days added to the end of the four-month period calculated from the date of the document). Where days are to be added to the end of the period under both **R.127(2)** (to compensate for postal delays) and under **R.134(1)** (in view of the period ending on a day on which an EPO filing office was closed) they should be added in that order since the total length of the period must first be established under **R.127(2)** before it can be established whether that period expires on a day on which one of the filing offices is not open for the receipt of documents.

The EPO bears the burden of establishing that an electronic document has been delivered to the addressee's Mailbox and, if it has been delivered, the date on which it was delivered. If the party disputes the delivery in a substantiated way and the EPO is unable to prove that the document was delivered, any period linked to the notification of the document will not be considered to have started, and the EPO will attempt to notify the document again.

The current text of **R.127(2)** applies to documents "to be notified by the European Patent Office on or after 1 November 2023" (Art.3 of the Decision of the Administrative Council of 13.10.2022). According to Not. EPO OJ 2023 A29, the relevant event is the transmission of the document by the EPO, and the new rule therefore applies to any document bearing a date of 01.11.2023 or later.

2 **Ten-day rule for notification of an electronic document (applicable until 31.10.2023)**

The previous text of **R.127(2)** established a different legal fiction according to which a document notified electronically was deemed notified on the tenth day following its transmission. No seven-day rule was provided. Any period triggered by the notification of the document under **R.131(2)** was, in principle, calculated from this fictitious date. However, for the legal situation to be fully appreciated it was also important to bear in mind the date of the document, i.e. the date printed on the document, the date of transmission by the EPO and the date of actual receipt, i.e. the date the document is made available to the recipient. The date of transmission was the date indicated on the document, provided that the addressee could access it in the Mailbox by that date.

The notification of an electronic document was actually governed by two legal fictions. The first one was laid down in **R.127(2)**, according to which the notification of an electronic document was deemed to have been effected on the tenth day after transmission of the document to the Mailbox of the recipient. This legal fiction did not apply when the document failed to reach its destination or reached its destination at a later date (**R.127(2)**). The second legal fiction was established by a Decision of the President (OJ 2015 A28 Art.9(4)), which stated that when the document was already available in the Mailbox before the date of the document, the transmission was still deemed to have occurred on the date of the document; hence, the tenth day was calculated from the date of the document in the case of a transmission on a day before the date of the document.

These two legal fictions had the following consequences for the notification of an electronically communicated document:

- When the document became available in the Mailbox on or before the date of the document, both legal fictions applied and the date of the document triggered the ten-day period. Hence, the document was deemed notified on the tenth day following the date it bore (OJ 2015 A36 §3.3.1-2).

- When the document was not yet available in the Mailbox on the date of the document, the second legal fiction did not apply and the date on which the document actually became available was the date of transmission. If the EPO disputed the date of transmission according to the recipient, it had to establish the date on which the communication reached its destination (**R.127(2)**; OJ 2015 A36 §3.3.3). The document was deemed notified on the tenth day following the date it actually became available.
- When the document was not yet available in the Mailbox on the tenth day following the date of the document, neither the first legal fiction, i.e. the ten-day rule, nor the second legal fiction applied. The notification date of the document was the date the document actually became available. If the EPO disputed the date of transmission according to the recipient, it had to establish the date on which the communication reached its destination (**R.127(2)**).
- When the document failed to reach its destination, neither legal fiction applied. The recipient received a notice of loss of rights, in response to which the recipient could argue under **R.112(2)** that it never received the document. In such a case the EPO had to establish that the electronic document had reached its destination (**R.127(2)**).

The previous text of **R.127(2)** was similar to the previous text of **R.126(2)** governing the notification of registered letters, with the exception of the flexible character of the date of transmission. Since an electronic communication is not delivered to a physical person but to a destination, such as a mailbox or portal, the phrase 'delivered to the addressee' in **R.126(2)** was replaced by 'reached its destination' (CA/47/14).

R. 128 Notification by delivery by hand

Notification may be effected on the premises of the European Patent Office by delivery by hand of the document to the addressee, who shall on delivery acknowledge its receipt. Notification shall be deemed to have been effected even if the addressee refuses to accept the document or to acknowledge receipt thereof.

Implementation of **Art.119**

1 **Delivery by hand**
Delivery by hand is sometimes used to avoid postal delays. This method of notification may only be used on the premises of the EPO according to **R.128** and is mainly used during oral proceedings.

R. 129 Public notification

Implementation of **Art.119**

R. 129(1) If the address of the addressee cannot be established, or if notification in accordance with Rule 126, paragraph 1, has proved to be impossible even after a second attempt, notification shall be effected by public notice.

R.126(1) Notification by registered letter

1 **Public notification**
Public notification is used only as a last resort and there can be no assumption that a party notified in this way will actually become aware of the notified document. It is primarily used to notify a loss of rights following an applicant's failure to enter the European phase with a Euro-PCT application. Public notification allows the EPO to close the file if no request for further processing is received in time. See also **R.125(4):1**.

R. 129(2) The President of the European Patent Office shall determine how the public notice is to be given and the beginning of the period of one month on expiry of which the document shall be deemed to have been notified.

1 **Method of public notification**
Notification under **R.129** is achieved by publication of relevant information in the European Patent Bulletin. The document is deemed to have been notified one month after the date of publication in the Bulletin. (Dec. Pres. OJ 2007 se3 p.127). See **R.125(4):1** for more information.

R. 130 Notification to representatives

Implementation of **Art.119**

1 **General**
The provisions of the EPC state that communications, e.g. containing information or an invitation, must be sent to the appropriate party to the proceedings (e.g. applicant, proprietor or opponent). **R.130** is a lex specialis for these provisions: if a representative has been appointed, communications must be sent to the representative rather than the party. As most parties are represented in proceedings before the EPO, the EPO will normally send a communication to a party's representative pursuant to **R.130**.

R. 130(1) If a representative has been appointed, notifications shall be addressed to that representative.

Amended by decision of the Administrative Council of 10.12.2024, which entered into force on 01.04.2025 (OJ 2025 A16). The amendment was introduction of gender-neutral language.

1 **Notification to representative**
The rule of mandatory notification (**R.130(1)**: 'shall') applies to professional representatives (**Art.134(1)** and (8)) only. Hence, if the applicant acts through an employee (**Art.133(3)**), notification is effected at the address of the applicant, and not that of the employee.

Since **R.130(1)** mentions 'appointed', the EPO should notify representatives as from their appointment, not from receipt of any authorisation under **R.152(1)**.

If, contrary to **R.130(1)**, the EPO sends a communication to a party instead of to the duly appointed representative, the notification is not effective; the communication is regarded as notified only on the date the communication is received by the representative (**T703/92**).

R.130(1) implies that in the case a party has not appointed a representative, notifications will be addressed to the party.

R. 130(2) If several representatives have been appointed for a single party, notification to any one of them shall be sufficient.

R. 130(3) If several parties have a common representative, notification to the common representative shall be sufficient.

1 **Notification to common representative**
Two or more parties may act in common under the EPC, e.g. as joint applicants or joint opponents. In general the EPO sends one document (**Art.119**) to the common representative appointed according to **R.41(3)** or **R.151** (E-II,2.5); the other person or persons acting jointly do not receive a copy of the document unless the common representative notifies them.

Chapter V *Time limits*

R. 131 Calculation of periods

Implementation of **Art.120**

1 **General**
The EPC distinguishes two classes of periods. The first class contains the periods of a legally indicated length fixed for carrying out a particular procedural act, the second class contains periods within which a party need not perform an act before the EPO and internal periods of the EPO (see **Art.120:3** for examples).

Failing other provisions for calculating periods, the EPO uses the calculation of **R.131** for all periods in the EPC, including 'negative periods', such as the pre-payment period of **R.51(1)** for advance payment of a renewal fee. There is no unanimity about the method for calculating the term of a patent (see **Art.63(1):1**).

A period is triggered by an event as defined in **R.131(2)**. The expiry of the period is defined by **R.131(3)**, **(4)**, **(5)** and **(2)** for periods laid down in terms of full years, months, weeks or days, respectively. The expiry of a period is the last day on which an act to be performed within the period can still be validly performed.

R. 131(1) Periods shall be laid down in terms of full years, months, weeks or days.

R. 131(2) Computation shall start on the day following the day on which the relevant event occurred, the event being either a procedural step or the expiry of another period. Where the procedural step is a notification, the relevant event shall be the deemed receipt of the document notified, unless otherwise provided.

Amended by decision of the Administrative Council of 13.10.2022, which entered into force on 01.11.2023 (OJ 2022 A101; preparatory document CA/30/22 rev.2). The word 'deemed' was inserted (OJ 2022 A114 §16).

1 **Computation of periods**
R.131(2) governs the triggering of a period and its computation. It also defines the calculation of periods expressed as a certain number of days.

2 **Triggering of period by a procedural step**
According to **R.131(2)**, first sentence, a period is triggered by the day following the day on which a relevant event occurs. This allows a period of one or more months to generally expire on the day having the same number as the day on which the event occurred (**R.131(4)**) and has a similar effect for periods expressed in years or weeks.

The meaning of 'relevant event' is clear from the German and French text of the provision: the event on the basis of which the start of the period is fixed. The relevant event may be a procedural step. The procedural step may be taken by the applicant. For example, the filing of an application triggers the one-month period of **R.38(1)** for payment of the filing and search fee, and the removal of the cause of non-compliance triggers the two-month period of **R.136(1)** for filing the application for re-establishment. The procedural step can also be taken by the EPO. For example, the publication of the search report triggers the six-month period of **R.70(1)** for filing the request for examination, the notification of a communication under **Art.94(3)** triggers a period for filing a reply. The event can also be the expiry of another period (see below).

Since 01.11.2023, **R.131(2)** provides that if a period starts from a notification, the relevant event is the *deemed* receipt of the document notified unless otherwise provided; the word 'deemed' was added. The rule applies to documents notified by the EPO on or after that date (OJ 2022 A114 §17). The deemed receipt of the document must be understood as the deemed delivery of a document under **R.126(2)** in case of notification by post and the deemed delivery under **R.127(2)** in case of electronic notification, i.e. the date the document bears. Note that **R.126(2)** and **R.127(2)** both provide for an extension of the period in case of delays in the transmission of the document.

In the rare case of delivery by hand (**R.128**), the actual date of receipt should be the relevant event, even though this is not expressly provided. In case of notification through the central industrial property office of a contracting state, the national law of the state concerned governs the notification (**R.125(3)**). In case of notification by publication in the Bulletin the document is deemed to have been notified one month after the publication (**R.129**).

R.131(2), second sentence (as it was in force until 31.10.2023), stated that in the case of notification, the relevant event was the receipt of the document notified (receipt theory, see **Art.119:2**). Starting from 01.11.2023, the document is deemed notified to the addressee on the date that it bears. This amendment of **R.131(2)** introduced a new notification fiction, and is motivated by the prevalence of notification by means of electronic communication. Retaining the notification fiction in a new form allows the EPO to continue avoiding establishing an actual date of receipt of each document for the purpose of calculating the relevant event. Various safeguards continue to apply in case of non-receipt or exceptionally late receipt of documents by the users. Notably, the EPO has introduced a new seven-day rule (see new **R.126(2)** and **R.127(2)**) that mirrors the seven-day rule of R.80.6 PCT. See also discussion and examples under **R.127(2):2**. (Not. EPO OJ 2023 A29)

Where the Rules specify a period to be observed following an invitation or communication from the EPO, the period always starts with the notification of such communication, since all decisions, notices and communications have to be notified to the parties (**Art.119, R.125**). Therefore, the provisions concerned do not expressly refer to the requirement of notification (see e.g. **R.55, 56, 58**).

3 **Triggering of a period by expiry of another period**

The relevant event in **R.131(2)** triggering a period may also be the expiry of another period. The two linked periods result in a so-called aggregate or composite period.

When the principles of aggregate periods under EPC1973 are applied to EPC2000, EPC2000 has probably four aggregate periods: 1) the one-year period for filing a request for re-establishment of **R.136(1)** triggered by the expiry of the unobserved period, 2) the two-month period for requesting re-establishment in the priority period and for filing a petition for review of **R.136(1)** triggered by the expiry of the unobserved period, 3) the six-month additional period for paying renewal fees with surcharge for a Euro-PCT application in a special case of **R.159(1)(g)** and triggered by the expiry of the 31-month period of **R.159(1)** and 4) the two-month grace period for payment of the extension fee triggered by the expiry of the basic period for paying the designation fee (see to **Art.79(2):2.3**). The aggregate character of these periods has not yet been confirmed by the EPO. The EPO tries to reduce the number of aggregate periods in the EPC because its calculation is liable to mistakes.

The expiry of an aggregate period is calculated as follows: the expiry of the first period is calculated according to **R.131** and **R.134**, i.e. including extensions due to non-working days of the EPO and reductions due to missing days at the end of a month; from that expiry the next period is calculated, again taking into account the extensions due to closure of the EPO and reductions due to missing days at the end of a month (the best explanation of the calculation can be found in Legal Advice **L5/93** rev. OJ 1993 p.229, cancelled by Dec. Pres. OJ 2012 p.446; other sources are **J1/89** hn.II and A-X,5.2.4). See for examples of aggregate period calculations **R.51(3):3** and **R.159(1)(g)**. Note that the above calculation is not applied to the six-month additional period in **R.51(2)** for payment of renewal fees (**J4/91** r.3.3).

4 **Computation of periods**
The computation of a period starts on the day following the day on which the relevant event occurred (**R.131(2)**, first sentence). The expiry of the period is determined by **R.131(3)-(5)**, depending on whether the period is a certain number of years, months or weeks. For example, the computation of a period of one week triggered by a relevant event on 1 June starts on 2 June according to **R.131(2)** and the period expires on 8 June according to **R.131(5)**. The duration of the period from 2 June to and including 8 June is seven days, which is equal to the one week. The start of a period is in particular relevant for the determination of the patent year in which the mention of the grant is published (see **Art.86(1):1**).

The start of the computation of a period on the day following the day on which the relevant event occurred, as stated in **R.131(2)**, first sentence, does not mean that a day is added for the computation of periods expressed in weeks, months or years as specified in **R.131(3) – (5)** (**J14/86** hn.). The manner of computation specified in **R.131(3) – (5)** already takes into account **R.131(2)**.

5 **Period expressed in days**
When a period is expressed as a certain number of days, computation shall start on the day following the day on which the relevant event occurred, and the period shall expire on the day on which the last day of the count has been reached (based on **R.131(2)**). For example, the computation of a period of seven days triggered by an event on a Monday starts on the following day, Tuesday, as the first day and expires on the next Monday as the seventh day.

R. 131(3) When a period is expressed as one year or a certain number of years, it shall expire in the relevant subsequent year in the month having the same name and on the day having the same number as the month and the day on which the said event occurred; if the relevant subsequent month has no day with the same number, the period shall expire on the last day of that month.

1 **Period expressed in years**
The last part of the provision takes account of leap-days. Examples of periods expressed in years can be found in **Art.63(1)** (term of the patent), **R.136(1)** (re-establishment), **Art.174** (denunciation of the convention) and **R.147(4)** (keeping of files). Note that the priority period in **Art.87(1)** is not expressed in terms of one year but twelve months.

R. 131(4) When a period is expressed as one month or a certain number of months, it shall expire in the relevant subsequent month on the day which has the same number as the day on which the said event occurred; if the relevant subsequent month has no day with the same number, the period shall expire on the last day of that month.

1 **Period expressed in months**
A deviation from this rule following **J4/91** hn.I occurs in the pre-payment period of R.51(1) and the six-month additional period of **R.51(2)** for renewal fees.

R. 131(5) When a period is expressed as one week or a certain number of weeks, it shall expire in the relevant subsequent week on the day having the same name as the day on which the said event occurred.

1 **Period expressed in weeks**
An example of a period expressed in weeks is the period of five weeks in the decision of the President under **R.67(1)** determining the date of completion of the technical preparations for publication.

R. 132 Periods specified by the European Patent Office

Implementation of **Art.120**

R. 132(1) Where the Convention or these Implementing Regulations refer to "a period to be specified", this period shall be specified by the European Patent Office.

R. 132(2) Unless otherwise provided, a period specified by the European Patent Office shall be neither less than two months nor more than four months; in certain circumstances it may be up to six months. In special cases, the period may be extended upon request, presented before the expiry of such period.

1 **Duration of periods**
The Convention specifies periods or time limits to be specified by the EPO, the so-called office periods or office time limits. They have the procedural advantage that an applicant may request extension of the period under **R.132(2)**.

The Guidelines (E-VIII,1.2) give general directives for determining the duration of the periods to be set by the EPO in the interest of a uniform period calculation. The duration of the period is often based on the amount of work to be performed.

R.132(2) specifies a duration of two to four months for an office period. A two-month period is generally used for correcting formal or small deficiencies, for example the subsequent filing under **R.83** of documents referred to by a party. The upper limit of four months in **R.132(2)** is generally used for communications from examining or opposition divisions under **Art.94(3)** containing substantive objections to the application or patent. The six-month period for special circumstances may be used for exceptionally complicated cases. It is also used for indicating whether to proceed with the application after receipt of the search report in the event that the request for examination has been filed before receipt of the search report (**R.70(2)**; E-VIII,1.2).

The 'unless otherwise provided' in **R.132(2)** allows that a provision in the EPC permits the EPO to set the duration of an office period shorter than the minimum duration of two months in **R.132(2)**. Since the amendment of **R.64(1)** of 01.04.2010 deleted the period to be specified between 2 to 6 weeks, the EPC has no such provisions anymore.

2 **Request for extension of a period**

An office period may be extended on request (**R.132(2)**, second sentence). The request must be filed before expiry of the period. Multiple extensions can be requested (E-VIII,1.6.1).

Extension is only possible for a period in which a party must take an action before the EPO. Other periods, e.g. the twelve-months priority period of **Art.87(1)(b)**, cannot be extended. An office period may be excluded explicitly from extension under **R.132**.

The extension of a period does not result in an aggregate period but in a unitary period. For example: the date of notification of a communication stipulating a two-month period within which a deficiency is to be rectified is 30 December. The expiry date is 28 February. If the period is extended with one month, the unitary three-month period expires 30 March, and not as aggregate period of 2+1 month on 28 March. (see Legal Advice **L5/93** rev. point III, OJ 1993 p.229; cancelled by Dec. Pres. OJ 2012 p.446)

A request for extension removes an application from the PACE programme (**Art.94(1):5**).

3 **Extension of periods in specific procedural stages**

The possibilities to extend a period depend on the procedure before the EPO.

Periods set by the EPO in the procedure up to grant may be extended on request. A request for extension, even if filed without reasons, is normally allowed if the total period does not exceed six months, in spite of the 'in special cases' in **R.132(2)**. A short period can normally be extended by two months. A request for extension to a total period of more than six months may only be granted if the subject-matter of the application or patent is exceptionally complicated. Such a request must be reasoned, referring to exceptional circumstances such as illness or extensive biological research, but not to foreseeable or avoidable circumstances such as high workload (this is normal) or leave. (OJ 1989 p.180-181; E-VIII,1.6)

A request for extension of a period in opposition proceedings will only be granted in exceptional, duly substantiated cases. A granted extension automatically applies to all parties. (E-VIII,1.6.1)

Extension of a period set by a board of appeal requires a reasoned request (Art.12(7) RPBA).

4 **Decision on request for extension**

A decision by the examining division rejecting a request filed in due time for an extension of for example a period set for filing observations to a communication under **Art.94(3)** to more than six months or for a second extension cannot be appealed, because such a decision does not terminate proceedings (**Art.106(2)**). The decision will normally be notified after expiry of the non-extended period. The ensuing loss of rights under **Art.94(4)** will be notified under **R.112(1)** and can be overcome only by filing a request for further processing under **Art.121** and **R.135**, paying the fee for further processing and filing a response to the communication.

If parties consider the rejection unjust, they should at the same time file a secondary request for reimbursement of the fee for further processing. The two requests must be filed within two months from the notification of the loss of rights. The secondary request will be decided on in connection with the final decision granting the patent or refusing the application. The decision on the secondary request may be appealed together with the final decision (**Art.106(2)**) when the final decision on the application is adverse, or separately when the final decision is not adverse. The latter separate appeal does not make much sense because the appeal fee is much higher than the amount to be reimbursed. If there is no final decision, e.g. because of withdrawal of the application, the department of first instance may decide on the rejection itself in response to the request for reimbursement, the decision on which may again be appealed. (**J37/89**)

R. 133 Late receipt of documents

Implementation of **Art.120**

1 **General**
R.133 is modelled on R.82.1 PCT and provides a remedy for all periods to be observed before the EPO or national offices (see **R.133(2)**), including the priority period, and missed due to a delay in the mail delivery. It supplements the remedies for failed time limits (further processing, re-establishment) and the extension and legal fiction in the case of disruption of mail delivery (**R.134(2)** and **R.134(5)**).

The application of **R.133** must be requested for each individual case; it provides a legal fiction of valid filing for a late received document. The provision cannot be used for documents lost in the post. **R.133** is one of the instances where the EPO uses the despatch theory instead of the receipt theory (see also **Art.119:2**). (OJ 1999 p.301 §22-32) Note that nowadays, most documents are filed electronically (with the exception of for example paper copies of priority documents) and money transfers at least within the EPC contracting states take place either the same or the following day.

In the case where **R.133** does not provide a remedy, even applying **R.134**, recourse may be had to remedies such as further processing or re-establishment.

2 **Late receipt of payments**
R.133 does not apply to fee payments, for which **Rfees7(3)** (bank transfers) and ADA.7.1 (debit orders) are *leges speciales* (OJ 1999 p.301 §25). Hence, documents and payments have different fail-safe provisions, with documents having to be despatched at least five calendar days before expiry of the period and payments having to be made before expiry of the period. If, for example, the act of payment and filing a written request for re-establishment must be completed at the latest on 12.02.2020, a letter containing the request must be posted at the latest on 07.02.2020 for **R.133** to be applicable and a bank transfer must be effected at the latest on 12.02.2020 within a contracting state for **Rfees7(3)** to be applicable.

R. 133(1) A document received late at the European Patent Office shall be deemed to have been received in due time if it was delivered to a recognised postal service provider in due time before expiry of the period in accordance with the conditions laid down by the President of the European Patent Office, unless the document was received later than three months after expiry of the period.

Amended, in force since 01.04.2015 (OJ 2015 A17, A36 §1).

1 **Document received late and deemed delivered in time**

A document sent to the EPO is deemed to have been delivered in due time if it was delivered to a recognised postal service provider in due time before expiry of the relevant period (**R.133(1)** and Dec. Pres. 2015 A29).

The longer time for the actual delivery is not an extension of the period in the sense of **R.134** but a legal fiction concerning observance of the period to file a particular document, similar to the fiction of **Rfees7(3)** for late receipt of a particular fee. Despite this legal fiction that the time limit has been observed, the filing date of the document remains the day on which it was actually received (E-VIII,1.7). This is in particular relevant for the priority period, where the date of filing of the priority-claiming application triggers several periods.

A document is deemed to have been received by the EPO in due time, only if the following conditions are fulfilled (Dec. Pres. OJ 2015 A29; E-VIII,1.7):

- The document is despatched at least five calendar days before the expiry of the relevant period. Note, that the 'at least' is intended by the EPO (E-VIII,1.7) but not included in the Decision of the President.

  Where the relevant period is extended under **R.134(1)** or (2), the expiry of the extended period must be used for the calculation of the last day for the application of **R.133**.
- The document is sent by a recognised postal service provider mentioned in the Decision of the President. The recognised postal service providers include the postal authority of a country, commonly called 'the post'. The Decision also mentions several courier service providers.
- The document must be sent as registered letter or equivalent. The 'equivalent' covers evidence of receipt other than the advice of delivery common for a postal authority.
- The document must be sent by airmail if posted outside Europe. Note that a definition of Europe of the purpose of **R.133** was removed E-VIII,1.7 in 2019.

At the request of the EPO, confirmation of the registration by the post office or of receipt by the delivery service provider must be supplied as evidence that the document was despatched in due time.

The remedy of **R.133(1)** is, unlike R.82.1(b) PCT, not applicable to documents received by the EPO later than three months after expiry of the time limit (**R.133(1)**). A loss of rights due to mail received later or lost should be remedied by further processing, re-establishment or a remedy for interruption in the delivery of the mail under **R.134(2)** or **R.134(5)**, whichever is applicable.

2 **Example of late receipt in case of priority claim**

As an example, a first patent application was filed on 17.11.2017. A subsequent European patent application was posted by registered letter in Sweden on 12.11.2018, i.e. seven days before expiry of the priority year on 19.11.2018 (17.11 is a Saturday), and received at the EPO on 26.11.2018. According to **R.133(1)** the subsequent application will be deemed to have been filed within the priority year and may validly claim the priority of the first application. Periods that run from the filing date (not the priority date) of the application will be calculated from the actual filing date and not from the expiry of the priority year (see E-VIII,1.7). Hence, the one-month period for payment of the filing fee and search fee (**R.38(1)**) expires on 02.01.2019 (26.12.2018 until and including 01.01.2019 are non-working days).

R. 133(2) Paragraph 1 shall apply mutatis mutandis to any period where transactions are carried out with the competent authority in accordance with Article 75, paragraphs 1(b) or 2(b).

Art.75(1)(b) Voluntary filing of a European patent application with a national authority
Art.75(2)(b) Compulsory filing of a European patent application with a national authority

1 **R. 134 Extension of periods**
Implementation of **Art.120**

2 **General**
R.134 deals with automatic extension of periods in which a party has to complete an act before the EPO, both convention periods and office periods. Whereas an extension of a period under **R.132** must be requested by a party for an individual case and for a particular period, an extension under **R.134** occurs usually by operation of law for all parties.

Under **R.134**, periods to be observed before the EPO are extended on account of an obstacle to receive documents. The obstacle may be an inability to receive documents lying within the responsibility of the EPO, such as closure of an EPO filing office because of non-working days or defective means of communication in an EPO office (**R.134(1)**). The obstacle may also be external to the EPO, for example general dislocation of mail (**R.134(2)**). The EPO publishes the duration of general dislocations (**R.134(4)**). The extensions of **R.134(1)** and (2) also apply to periods to be observed before national patent offices, i.e. to the priority period within which a European application can be filed with a national office (**R.134(3)**).

The extension of a period results in a longer period within which the required act may be validly completed. The extension does not lead to a legal fiction in the sense of **R.133**, where an act carried out late is deemed to have been completed in due time.

Whereas **R.134(2)** relates to delay in delivery due to a general dislocation of mail in a contracting state, **R.134(5)** relates to delay due to a local interruption of communication in any state. **R.134(5)** does not fit in the system of **R.134**, because it does not give rise to an extension of a period (see title of rule) but to a legal fiction of the period being deemed to have been observed. The provision is in fact similar to **R.133** but restricted to a dislocation due to exceptional occurrences.

Although the extension of a period under **R.134** is in general automatic and does not require a request, a party should inform the EPO of any relevant event under **R.134(1)**, second sentence (such as an unannounced outage), and **R.134(2)**, so that the EPO may investigate the event further. Application of the legal fiction of **R.134(5)** must always be requested.

Where a late receipt cannot be remedied by the extension of a period under **R.134**, a party may resort to other remedies, such as the legal fiction of timely receipt under **R.133**, possibly combined with an extension under **R.134**, further processing under **Art.121**, re-establishment under **Art.122** or a grace period such as the six-month period for late payment of a renewal fee under **R.51(2)**.

3 **Periods extended**
The extension under **R.134** applies to all periods provided in the EPC, i.e. periods having a well-defined start and end within which a procedural act vis-à-vis the EPO has to be completed, including the period for filing an opposition and for performing the acts of **R.159(1)** (E-VIII,1.1; E-VIII,1.6.2.3).

The extension does not apply to acts which do not have to be performed within a period but, instead, must be performed in accordance with specific conditions, such as filing of a divisional application while the parent application is pending and filing a first application at the latest on the day the invention is being published.

An extension under **R.134** also does not apply to procedural acts to be performed by a specific date. Hence, the date on which a request under **R.22** (request for registration of a transfer) or **R.54** (request for a certified priority document) is deemed to be filed does not change because of an extension. (E-VIII,1.6.2.3)

Similarly, the final date for making written submissions prior to oral proceedings fixed under **R.116** is not extended by virtue of **R.134**. However, examining and opposition divisions may take a general dislocation in the mail or an exceptional occurrence under **R.134(5)** into account at their discretion. (E-VIII,1.6.2.3)

Although **R.134(1)** refers only to periods within which a document must be filed with the EPO, it also applies to periods for payment (**J1/81** r.6; E-VIII,1.6.2.3). See **R.134(1):1** and **R.134(1):3.3** below for the extension of periods for payment under the first and second sentence of **R.134(1)**.

R. 134(1) If a period expires on a day on which one of the filing offices of the European Patent Office under Rule 35, paragraph 1, is not open for receipt of documents or on which, for reasons other than those referred to in paragraph 2, mail is not delivered there, the period shall extend to the first day thereafter on which all the filing offices are open for receipt of documents and on which mail is delivered. The first sentence shall apply mutatis mutandis if documents filed by one of the means of electronic communication permitted by the President of the European Patent Office under Rule 2, paragraph 1, cannot be received.

Amended, in force since 01.04.2015 (OJ 2015 A17, A36 §5).
R.2(1) Filing of and formal requirements for documents
R.35(1) EPO filing offices for filing patent applications
R.134(2) Reasons for dislocation of mail not within responsibility EPO

1 **Extension of period if EPO cannot receive documents**

R.134(1) sets out if and how the EPO will extend a period if on the day of expiry of the period a means of filing documents with an EPO filing office is not available. The rule distinguishes two different cases: unavailability because an office is not open or cannot receive mail (**R.134(1)**, first sentence) and unavailability because of an outage of electronic communication (**R.134(1)**, second sentence).

2 **EPO not open or unable to receive documents (R.134(1), first sentence)**

R.134(1), first sentence, governs the situation where a period expires on a day on which at least one of the filing offices of the EPO in Munich, The Hague and Berlin is not open for receipt of documents, or on which mail cannot be delivered there.

The 'reasons other than those referred to in paragraph 2' in the provision relate to exceptional internal obstacles to receiving documents, such as a natural disaster or strike that affects the functioning of the EPO.

R.134(1), first sentence is generally used in respect of those days on which a filing office is closed, i.e. non-working days, including all Saturdays and Sundays. The list of non-working days is regularly published in the OJ (for 2025, see OJ 2024 A91) and on the EPO website. The offices are closed from Christmas Eve until and including New Year's Day.

Any day on which at least one of the filing offices is closed causes the extension of a period expiring on that day for all filing offices. Such a period is extended to the first day on which all the filing offices are open again (**R.134(1)**, first sentence). For example, any period expiring on Friday 03.10.2025 (Day of German Unity in Berlin and Munich) is extended to Monday 06.10.2025 for all filing offices, including The Hague.

The extension under **R.134(1)**, first sentence, applies to any method of filing documents with the EPO permitted under **R.2(1)**, including filing by post and electronic filing. Hence, even if electronic communication is available during the weekend, periods will be extended until the first day on which all filing offices are open. For example, if a period for filing a document expires on a Saturday, a party may file the document on Monday using electronic communication, in spite of the fact that electronic filing had been available all weekend.

The extension applies not only to periods for filing documents but also to periods for making payments (E-VIII,1.6.2.3; ADA.11). When an EPO office is closed on the day a period for payment expires but the bank is open, the period will be extended, in spite of the possibility to pay within the non-extended period (J1/81 hn.II). In the opposite case, i.e. the EPO is open but the bank is closed, e.g. because of a national holiday, the period is not extended. In such a case another method of payment should be used, e.g. debit order, credit card, asking someone in another country to make the payment, or applying a legal remedy, such as further processing or re-establishment, where appropriate. See **R.51(1):2** for extension of periods relating to renewal fees.

3 Outage of electronic communication (R.134(1), second sentence)

The second sentence of **R.134(1)** is a special provision for extension of a period for filing a document where a means of electronic communication permitted under **R.2(1)** is not available. The 'mutatis mutandis' in the provision has allowed the EPO to set up a special set of rules for outages of electronic communication. The average number of outages of electronic communication is one a week, often during weekends (see EPO website, 'Outages of Online Filing and fee payment services').

The EPO Notice OJ 2020 A120 sets out the implementation of **R.134(1)**, second sentence. The terminology of the Notice can be reconciled with that of the law by equating 'means of electronic filing' in the Notice with the means of electronic communication under **R.2(1)** for filing documents in that rule. The effects of an outage on filing a document and making a payment have been covered separately in the sections below because of a few special characteristics of making payments.

The sections below discuss the effect of outages on the procedure before the EPO acting under the EPC. See OJ 2020 A120 §23-29, 35-36 and 42, as well as GL/PCT-EPO E-IV,2 for the EPO acting in the international phase under the PCT.

3.1 OUTAGE OF MEANS OF ELECTRONIC FILING

The permitted means for the electronic filing of documents with the EPO are OLF, Online Filing 2.0 and the Contingency Upload Service (Dec. Pres. OJ 2024 A88). The permitted means for the electronic filing of documents with the EPO as receiving Office under the PCT are given in **R.157(1):1**.

If one of the means of electronic filing documents is not available on a working day, a period expiring on that day will be extended to the first working day on which all means of electronic filing are available again (OJ 2020 A120 §12). If on said first working day not all filing offices are open, the period will be further extended to the first day that all filing offices are open (**R.134(1)**, first sentence).

For example, if a party wants to file a document on the last day of a period using OLF and notices that Online Filing 2.0 is not available that day, the period will be extended, even though OLF is available. An extension due to an unavailable means of electronic filing probably does not give rise to an extension for other means of filing, such as filing by hand or post, as these means are not covered by **R.134(1)**, second sentence. Hence, a document submitted in an extension of a period due to an outage of electronic filing must probably be filed using electronic filing.

Where an outage of electronic filing occurs on a non-working day, any period expiring on that day will be extended under **R.134(1)**, first sentence, irrespective of the outage, to the first working day where all filing offices are open, provided that the outage does not extend to that working day. In such a situation there is no need to request the EPO an extension and to provide evidence that the outage was attributable to the EPO.

The EPO draws a distinction between planned and unplanned outages.

3.1.1 *Planned outage of means of electronic filing*

The EPO plans outages for carrying out maintenance work on or improvements to a service. A planned outage of a means of electronic filing will be announced at least two working days in advance on the EPO website (search for 'Outages of Online Filing and fee payment services'). Wherever possible, planned outages will be during a weekend, starting after midnight at the end of Friday. (OJ 2020 A120 §7, 10)

Where a planned outage of at least one of the means of electronic filing lasts for four hours or more on a single working day (in the Central European Time zone), **R.134(1)**, second sentence, applies and all periods that expired on that day will be extended for all users. If the planned outage is less than four hours and is announced at least two working days in advance, **R.134(1)**, second sentence, does not apply and periods will not be extended. (OJ 2020 A120 §20, 22)

The four hours strikes a balance between the interest of the public, in that any short outage will not give rise to a general extension, and the interest of a party not having to wait unreasonably long for the means to be in operation again (OJ 2018 A25 §4). This means that, for example, a party in a contracting state two hours ahead of CET need not wait until past midnight local time for filing a document if a four hour outage starts 18:00 CET, because the period will be extended under **R.134(1)**, second sentence, and the document can be filed the next day. If a planned outage lasts less than four hours on one working day, the EPO expects users to adapt their working schedule accordingly (OJ 2020 A120 §20).

Where the EPO despatches a notice of loss of rights despite a planned outage having occurred, a party is advised to quote the reference number of the announcement when replying. It is not necessary to submit evidence of the outage. (OJ 2020 A120 §16)

3.1.2 *Unplanned outage of means of electronic filing*

Unplanned outages may occur due to malfunctions or other exceptional circumstances. They will be announced on the EPO website as soon as possible upon discovery; the announcement will be updated regularly until the service is restored (OJ 2020 A120 §7). Where an unplanned outage affects all users, periods will be extended for all users and the announcement will be updated accordingly (OJ 2020 A120 §14). The conditions for what 'affects all users' have not been published. Up until 11.02.2024, there has only been one instance where a general extension was provided via the announcement (technical fault references nos. 1279522 and 1279907). The outage took place from 08:00 CET on 26.11.2020 until 11:00 CET on 27.11.2020, and affected CMS (a retired means of online filing). All time limits expiring on 26.11.2020 and 27.11.2020 were extended until the following working day, i.e. 30.11.2020.

Users who are unable to file a document should contact the EPO's Customer Services. If the EPO confirms that the unavailability of the service is attributable to the EPO, said users will not suffer any adverse consequences. The duration of the unplanned outage is irrelevant. (OJ 2020 A120 §32)

Users concerned about a possible loss of rights due to a failed filing, for example where there is uncertainty as to whether the failure is attributable to an outage of an EPO system or to issues on the user's side, should request a legal remedy on an auxiliary basis (OJ 2020 A120 §18).

Users may additionally request the EPO to apply **R.134(1)**, second sentence, providing evidence that the outage affected them and prevented them from filing in due time via that means (OJ 2020 A120 §17, 33).

If the outage has not yet been published, users should also provide evidence about the outage (OJ 2020 A120 §17). If the outage has been published, they must quote the reference number of the announcement; they need not provide evidence that the outage was attributable to the EPO (OJ 2020 A120 §16).

The actions a user affected by an unplanned outage should take and the way the EPO takes care that the user does not suffer any adverse consequences is not completely clear from OJ 2020 A120 and the Guidelines.

3.2 OUTAGE OF MEANS OF MAKING PAYMENT

The accepted means of making payment to the EPO electronically are Online Filing 2.0 and OLF for filing debit orders, and the Central Fee Payment (CFP) for making payments via credit card. CFP is the preferred means for preparing a payment by bank transfer. Since methods of payment by deposit account are not part of the EPC procedures (**T170/83** r.8) and are therefore not covered by **R.134**, a legal basis for any extension of periods for filing debit orders is provided separately in ADA.11.

An outage of one of these means for making payment on the day of expiry of a period for payment will be extended to the first working day thereafter on which all such means are available (OJ 2020 A120 §37; ADA.11). There is no minimum duration of the outage and it seems that the party does not need to prove the outage prevented the payment, unlike for filing of documents (where an outage of three hours for example may cause an extension if the party can prove the outage prevented filing of the document). However, payment periods are not extended if the outage of a means of making payment is planned, announced at least two days in advance, and lasts for less than four hours (OJ 2020 A120 §41).

Since the Central Fee Payment service for making payments via credit card serves exclusively for making payments, outages affecting this service cannot be invoked for periods relating to filing of documents (OJ 2020 A120 §39, which predates the Central Fee Payment service, but it is assumed that information about the previous Online Fee Payment service also applies to Central Fee Payment service).

R. 134(2) If a period expires on a day on which there is a general dislocation in the delivery or transmission of mail in a Contracting State, the period shall extend to the first day following the end of the interval of dislocation for parties which are resident in the State concerned or have appointed representatives with a place of business in that State. Where the State concerned is the State in which the European Patent Office is located, this provision shall apply to all parties and their representatives. This paragraph shall apply mutatis mutandis to the period referred to in Rule 37, paragraph 2.

R.37(2) Forwarding of European patent applications

1 **Dislocation of mail**

Whereas **R.134(1)** concerns internal obstacles in the EPO to the receipt of documents, **R.134(2)** relates to external dislocations of mail delivery or transmission. In this context, mail transmission covers the filing of documents using the technical means of communication permitted by the President of the EPO. (OJ 2007 se5 EN p.200)

There is a general dislocation if the public in general is affected by it, i.e. also in the case of a local postal strike, but not in the case of a strike in a factory. In other words: 'general' is not restricted to 'nation-wide' (**J3/90** r.10). Whether there is a 'general dislocation' is to be decided by the facts and any credible information, especially from national patent offices, not only by a notice of the President. In case of doubt, the EPO will enquire of its own motion (**Art.114(1)**) whether or not a dislocation qualifies as a general dislocation within the meaning of **R.134(2)** (**J11/88** applied mutatis mutandis).

Individual cases where mail is delayed do not give rise to extension of the period under **R.134(2)** (**J4/87**). However, if the requirements of **R.133** have been met, the delay in an individual case may be excused.

The general dislocation must occur in an EPC contracting state, according to **R.134(2)**. The legislator took the view that only for the contracting states could the EPO be sure of obtaining the information necessary to enable the President to announce a general interruption or dislocation. Hence, it was decided not to extend **R.134(2)** to postal interruptions outside those states and to introduce paragraph 5, which places the burden of proof on the party. (**J13/05** r.3.2)

The extension is applicable to parties whose residence or place of business is in the contracting state concerned or who have appointed representatives with a place of business in that state (**R.134(2)**). The second sentence of **R.134(2)** is generally interpreted to refer to 'a state in which a filing office of the EPO is located'. It has the effect that a general dislocation in the Netherlands or Germany causes an extension of the periods applicable to all parties, because any mail or payment may be sent to either Munich, The Hague or Berlin, irrespective of the type of proceedings. Note, that the EPO offices in Vienna and Brussels are not filing offices.

Note that the extension only applies to periods and does not cover acts for which no period is specified, see **R.134:2**.

2 **Extension on account of general interruption of mail**
The duration of a dislocation in postal services in a contracting state and the resulting extension of periods are published in the OJ. The EPO publishes the date of commencement and end of any dislocation (**R.134(4)**). The extension occurs automatically by operation of law, without a request from a party.

The earthquakes in Türkiye and Syria in February 2023 resulted in time limits expiring in the period from 06.02.2023 to 06.04.2023 being extended to 07.04.2023 for parties having their domicile or principal place of business in Türkiye or having appointed representatives with their place of business in Türkiye. Since Syria is not a contracting state, the safeguard of **R.134(2)** does not apply (see **R.134(5):1** for an applicable safeguard). (OJ 2023 A14)

The COVID-19 pandemic caused a general dislocation of mail in Germany. Hence, according to **R.134(2)**, second sentence, all periods expiring on or after 15.03.2020 (including payment of fees) were extended to 02.06.2020 for all parties and their representatives. Thereafter, parties and representatives in countries where the coronavirus continued to cause a dislocation in delivery or transmission of mail had to provide evidence of the dislocation under **R.134(5)**. (OJ 2020 A29, A43, A60, A74 and A123)

In cases such as **J10/20 and T1640/22**, where a party has been told by the EPO that **R.134(2)** applies, it has been recognised that the principle of legitimate expectations may be relied upon and that the rights of a party taking advantage of the extension must be upheld.

The period for filing an opposition may be extended under **R.134(2)**, even though the opponent is not a party to proceedings before the opposition is filed (**T1640/22**).

According to the last sentence of **R.134(2)**, the fourteen-month period within which a national office must forward a European application filed with it to the EPO under **R.37(2)** is also extended in the case of a general dislocation of mail.

The extension of the period is effective not only for delays in filing caused directly by the delayed mail service, but for all delays, even non-observance of the period, e.g. a reply to a communication filed late by post from a state affected by the general dislocation.

R. 134(3) Paragraphs 1 and 2 shall apply mutatis mutandis where acts are performed with the competent authority in accordance with Article 75, paragraphs 1(b) or 2(b).

Art.75(1)(b) Voluntary filing of a European patent application with a national authority
Art.75(2)(b) Compulsory filing of a European patent application with a national authority

1 **Extension on account of closed national office**
Periods under the EPC to be observed before a national office will be extended similar to periods to be observed before the EPO (**R.134(3)**). A party requiring an extension under this provision because of a failed electronic filing, must provide evidence that the filing failed because an electronic filing means of the national office was down (OJ 2020 A120 §19).

The only act under the EPC to be performed before a national office within a period is the filing of a priority claiming European application within the priority period of twelve months. If the priority period expires on a day the national office is closed or the mail is dislocated, the priority year will be extended to the first day the national office can again receive mail. Thus, the application claiming priority can be filed with the national office on that first working day without losing the priority claim.

An extension of the priority period in a contracting state other than Germany or The Netherlands does not extend the priority period before the EPO. Hence, a European application for which the unavailed priority period expired on 14.07.2017 (Quatorze Juillet, Friday) can be filed at the latest on 17.07.2017 with the French national office but not with an EPO filing office.

This provision does not apply to periods within which other documents must be filed, because a national office does not give such documents a date of receipt but only forwards them to the EPO as a courtesy service.

R. 134(4) The date of commencement and the end of any dislocation under paragraph 2 shall be published by the European Patent Office.

1 **Publication of dislocation**

The extension of periods under **R.134(1)** to (3) occurs automatically by operation of law if the requirements are fulfilled. For reasons of clarity and in line with the current practice of the Office **R.134(4)** expressly provides that the EPO publishes a notice informing on the commencement and the end of the dislocation under **R.134(2)**. (OJ 2007 se5 EN p.200)

R. 134(5) Without prejudice to paragraphs 1 to 4, a party concerned may produce evidence that on any of the ten days preceding the day of expiry of a period the delivery or transmission of mail was dislocated due to an exceptional occurrence such as a natural disaster, war, civil disorder, a general breakdown in any of the means of electronic communication permitted by the President of the European Patent Office under Rule 2, paragraph 1, or other like reasons affecting the locality where the party or their representative resides or has their place of business. If the evidence produced satisfies the European Patent Office, a document received late shall be deemed to have been received in due time, provided that the mailing or the transmission was effected at the latest on the fifth day after the end of the dislocation.

Amended, in force since 01.04.2015 (OJ 2015 A17, A36 §5). Further amended by decision of the Administrative Council of 10.12.2024, which entered into force on 01.04.2025 (OJ 2025 A16). The amendment was introduction of gender-neutral language.

R.2(1) Filing of and formal requirements for documents

1 **Fiction of timely receipt in case of interruption of mail**

Whereas **R.134(2)** covers only general dislocations in the delivery of mail inside EPC contracting states, **R.134(5)** has a broader applicability and covers dislocations of mail of a smaller scale inside and outside EPC contracting states due to an exceptional occurrence. Paragraph 5 was created to cover the 9/11 terror attacks.

A document received late will be deemed to have been received in due time under **R.134(5)** if all of the following requirements are met:

- The delivery or transmission of mail was dislocated. Since **R.134(5)** supplements **R.134(2)**, the dislocation must similarly be 'general', in the sense that more than one person using the mail service has been or could have been affected, even if the dislocation was merely minor or geographically limited (**J13/05** r.3.2). The decision held that loss of a mail bag was not a general dislocation. **R.133** should be used for individual dislocations.
- The dislocation was due to an exceptional occurrence. Examples of such occurrences are a natural disaster, war, civil disorder, or other like reasons.
- The occurrence must have affected the locality of the party's or representative's residence or place of business (**R.134(5)**); i.e. the locality of despatch, not the locality of receipt. Hence, the provision does not apply to a local dislocation in Munich affecting mail sent from Cologne to the EPO (**J13/05** r.3.2). Occurrences affecting the locality of receipt should be dealt with under **R.134(1)**, **(2)** or **R.133**.
- The dislocation must have existed on any of the ten days preceding the expiry of the period (**R.134(5)** first sentence).
- The mail must have been sent at the latest on the fifth day after the end of the dislocation (**R.134(5)** second sentence).
- The party must provide satisfactory evidence of all of the above facts.

If the EPO knows the circumstances of the dislocation and has published them, parties using **R.134(5)** need only submit proof that they sent the document in time; the EPO will assume compliance with the other requirements (OJ 2015 A61 §2). For example, applicants, parties to proceedings, and their representatives affected by the earthquake in Japan on 01.01.2024 may invoke the safeguard of **R.134(5)** in case of non-observance of a time limit, since it applies to natural disasters (OJ 2024 A11)).The earthquake in Syria in February 2023 is another such example (OJ 2023 A14). In contrast with **R.134(2)**, which applies to contracting states, the period is not extended under **R.134(5)**, but the document received late is deemed received in due time. Moreover, this legal fiction is not applied automatically but requires the filing of a reasoned request. Where the EPO has issued a loss of rights communication and a request for correction under **R.134(5)** is filed, the remedy of further processing or re-establishment where appropriate may be added as an auxiliary request.

2 **Fiction of timely receipt in case of interruption of payment**

Although the wording of the provision appears to imply that it is applicable to filing of documents only, the EPO applies it also to making payments in the case where the failure to observe a period for payment is the result of exceptional circumstances beyond the control of the party concerned. Examples of such circumstances are closure of banks and ban on cross-border payments. Evidence must be provided that on any of the ten days (l'un quelconque de dix jours) prior to expiry of the period payment could not be made and that the payment was ordered within five days after banks resumed business. (OJ 2015 A61; OJ 2019 A88 §2)

Note, that if the payment was made within a contracting state, the failsafe arrangement of **Rfees7(3)** can also be used to remedy a late payment due to delay by the bank. Use of **Rfees7(3)** or **R.134(5)** both require the submission of evidence. A correction of a payment under **R.134(5)** or a request under **Rfees7(3)** can be filed as a main request, and a request for further processing or re-establishment as an auxiliary request.

R. 135 Further processing

R. 135(1) Further processing under Article 121, paragraph 1, shall be requested by payment of the prescribed fee within two months of the communication concerning either the failure to observe a time limit or a loss of rights. The omitted act shall be completed within the period for making the request.

Art.121(1) Further processing of an application
Implementation of **Art.121(2)**

1 **Fee for further processing**
R.135(1) requires that a fee be paid for further processing within two months from the notification of the communication concerning the failure to observe a time limit. The amount of the fee is given in **Rfees2(1)12** and depends on the nature of the omitted act and the period failed.

The fee for further processing for a failed payment is 50% of the late paid fee and a fixed amount for a failed filing of a document. If several acts have been omitted, the fee for further processing is the sum of the fees for each act. If for example a corrected sequence listing is not filed and the late furnishing fee is not paid within two months from invitation under **R.30(3)**, the fee for further processing is the fixed fee for late submitting the corrected listing plus 50% of the late furnishing fee. As an exception, the fee for further processing for all acts required under **R.71(3)** is only the fixed fee. (E-VIII,2)

Since no request in writing is necessary, the request can be made simply by payment of the further processing fee, thereby facilitating further processing after failure to meet a time limit for payment of fees. No reasoning need be provided why the time limit was not observed.

Since payment of the further processing fee is the only act that marks a remedy as further processing, the omission of the payment will be regarded as omission of a request for further processing.

Where a request for automatic debiting has been filed, the further processing fee will be debited automatically when a response to a communication is filed late within the further processing period.

2 **Period for requesting further processing**
According to **R.135(1)** the request must be filed within two months of notification under **R.126(2)** of the communication concerning either the failure to observe a time limit or a loss of rights. It is not clear why the provision expressly refers to a communication concerning a loss of rights. Since a failure to observe a time limit is a necessary condition according to **Art.121(1)** for the application of further processing, the 'loss of rights' in **R.135(1)** is superfluous as further processing is not available for cases without failure to observe a time limit. The EPO may improve the wording of the provision in the next review of the Implementing Regulations.

For legal reasons the two-month time limit has been fixed so as to provide the same length of time for filing a request for further processing as for filing a notice of appeal under **Art.108** or a request for a decision following the noting of loss of rights under **R.112(2)**.

The date of notification of the communication of loss of rights is not a starting point for a period in which the request may be filed but simply a reference point for calculating the expiry of the two months. Hence, a request filed between the expiry of the non-observed period and notification of the communication is permissible (E-VIII,2).

Failure to meet the two-month time limit can be remedied using re-establishment (as a consequence of **R.136(3)**). Further processing of the two-month time limit is excluded by **Art.121(4)**, first sentence.

3 **Completion of the omitted act**

R.135(1) also requires that the omitted act that brought about the failure to observe the time limit and the loss of rights, must be completed within the two-month period of the request.

The request for further processing is inadmissible if the omitted act is not completed within the two-month period. If a communication under **Art.94(3)** has not been replied to in due time, a response must be submitted together with the request for further processing; a request for an extension of the already expired period is not a completion of the omitted act. If a request for extension, filed just before expiry of the period, is refused, further processing is an adequate remedy to obtain an extension of approximately three months (see **R.132(2):4**).

4 **Procedure**

The procedure of further processing is triggered by payment of the further processing fee following a loss of rights with or without a decision.

If an application is refused following failure to meet a period, e.g. not filing the designation of the inventor after an invitation under **R.60(1)**, the decision will be notified to the applicant. The applicant can request further processing within two months from the date of notification of the decision. Since the loss of rights results from a decision, it is in principle possible to file an appeal against the decision. However, an appeal should only be lodged if the legality of the decision is to be clarified. If the applicant considers the reply to be in due time, the applicant may file an appeal and simultaneously an auxiliary request for further processing, which allows further processing in case the appeal is inadmissible or not allowable. If the decision to refuse is well-founded, an appeal only will be of no avail and the grant proceedings will not continue.

If an application is deemed to be withdrawn, the applicant will be notified according to **R.112(1)** of the loss of rights. Within two months of the date of notification the applicant must request further processing. If the applicant regards the notice under **R.112(1)** erroneous, the applicant must apply for a decision under **R.112(2)** simultaneously with the request for further processing. If the EPO agrees, it will set aside the **R.112(1)** communication and refund the fee for further processing. Had the applicant requested further processing only after notification of the decision under **R.112(2)**, the applicant would have risked non-observance of the two-month period for requesting further processing, making the request inadmissible. In that case the applicant could try and request re-establishment in the two-month period of **R.112(2)**. See also **R.112(2):1**.

After receipt of the request for further processing the competent department of the EPO takes a decision. If the decision is positive, the legal consequences of the refusal or withdrawal will be deemed not to have ensued (**Art.121(3)**) and the proceedings will continue. A negative decision, usually closing the proceedings, is appealable.

An example of the procedure for further processing. The unavailed period for paying the search fee under **R.38(1)** expires on 01.02.2018. The communication under **R.112(1)** concerning the failure to observe the period and the deemed withdrawal under **Art.78(2)** is dated 19.03.2018 and is deemed notified under **R.126(2)** on the same date, 19.03.2018. The two-month period for filing the request for further processing expires on 19.05.2018 (Saturday), extended to 22.05.2018 (21.05.2018 is Whit Monday) under **R.134(1)**. The applicant must pay the fee for further processing, equal to 50% of the search fee (**Rfees2(1)12**), and the search fee (**Rfees2(1)2**) at the latest on 22.05.2018. The applicant may pay these fees as from 02.02.2018.

R. 135(2) Further processing shall be ruled out in respect of the periods referred to in Article 121, paragraph 4, and of the periods under Rule 6, paragraph 1, Rule 16, paragraph 1(a), Rule 31, paragraph 2, Rule 36, paragraph 2, Rule 40, paragraph 3, Rule 51, paragraphs 2 to 5, Rule 52, paragraphs 2 and 3, Rules 55, 56, 56a paragraphs 1 and 3-7, 58, 59, 62a, 63,64, Rule 112, paragraph 2, and Rule 164, paragraphs 1 and 2.

Amended, in force since 01.04.2014. The amendment deleted **R.36(1)(a)** and (**b**) from the provision. The amended provision applies to divisional applications filed on or after 01.04.2014. (OJ 2013 p.501) Amended to include **R.164(1)** and (**2**) starting from 01.11.2014 (OJ 2013 p.503).

Amended by decision of the Administrative Council of 14.12.2021 which entered into force on 01.11.2022 (OJ 2022 A3; explanatory remarks in CA/4/21). Rule 56a paragraphs 1 and 3-7 are included in the exclusions of R.135(2) as of this date.

Art.121(4) Excluded periods
R.6(1) Period for filing translation of application
R.16(1)(a) Period for action for entitled applicant
R.31(2) Period for filing information on deposition of biological material
R.36(2) Period for filing translation of divisional
R.40(3) Period for filing copy and translation of previous application
R.51(2) Period for payment of renewal fee with additional fee
R.51(3) Period for payment of renewal fee for divisional
R.51(4) Period for payment of renewal fee in case of reestablishment of rights
R.51(5) Period for payment of renewal fee in case of petition for review
R.52(2) Period for filing declaration of priority
R.52(3) Period for correcting declaration of priority
R.55 Period for correcting deficiencies to obtain date of filing
R.56 Period for filing missing parts of description or drawings
R.56a(1) Period for filing correct application documents or parts
R.56a(3) Re-dating the application in case of corrected documents or parts
R.56a(4) Effect of a priority claim to the filing date
R.56a(5) Cases in which corrected documents or parts are not taken into account
R.56a(6) Re-dating the application
R.56a(7) Effect of withdrawal of corrected documents or parts.
R.58 Period for correcting deficiencies regarding formal requirements
R.59 Period for correcting priority claim
R.62a Period for indicating independent claims for search
R.63 Period for filing statement with subject-matter to be searched
R.64 Period for payment of further search fees
R.112(2) Period for applying for decision on loss of rights
R.164(1) Period for paying further search fees for non-unitary inventions
R.164(2) Period for paying search fees for non-searched inventions
Implementation of **Art.121(4)**

1 **Periods excluded from further processing**

Although further processing has been set up as the standard legal remedy in cases of failure to observe time limits in the grant procedure, several periods have been excluded from further processing for various reasons. The present list of exclusions is the result of bargaining in the Administrative Council without a clear philosophy at the time of preparing EPC2000.

Art.121(4) excludes the priority period of **Art.87(1)**, the periods for filing an appeal in **Art.108**, the period for filing a petition for review under **Art.112a(4)** and the period for requesting further processing in **R.135(1)** and re-establishment in **R.136(1)**. The reasons for these exclusions have been set out in **Art.121(4):1**.

Several exclusions in **R.135(2)** are based on the ground that further processing should not be available if another adequate legal remedy has already been provided (MR/24/00 Art.121). The periods in **R.6(1)** for filing the translation of **Art.14(2)**, in **R.36(2)** for filing the translation of a divisional, and in **R.40(3)** for filing of a copy of the previously filed application to which reference is made and a translation thereof are excluded because these time limits may be remedied under **R.58, 55** and **58**, respectively (OJ 2003 se1 p.159).

The periods under **R.51(3)** relating to the payment of renewal fees for divisional applications are excluded from further processing on the same ground. If the four-months period in **R.51(3)** for the payment of renewal fees without a surcharge expires and the renewal fees have not been paid, the remedy is already provided for in **R.51(3)**, last sentence, namely the payment with surcharge within six months as of filing the divisional application. Similarly, the four-month periods in **R.51(4)** and (5) are excluded. (CA/PL17/06)

Further processing should neither be applicable to periods that have a remedial character. Hence, the six-month period of **R.51(2)** for payment of renewal fees is a period of grace (see Art.5*bis* of the Paris Convention – period of grace for payment of fees) (OJ 2003 se1 p.159). The six-month period of **R.51(3)** is excluded like the period under **R.51(2)**, as clarified by the reference in **R.135(2)** to the whole paragraph 3 of **R.51**. Similarly, the six-month periods in **R.51(4)** and (5) are excluded (CA/PL14/06). The exclusion of the periods in **R.55, 56, 56a paragraphs 1 and 3-7, 58** and **59** is based in particular on the fact that the procedure under these Rules is a form of legal remedy (OJ 2003 se1 p.159).

Some periods are excluded because failure to observe them does not result in a communication of the EPO. Thus, the necessary procedural calculating point for further processing period is lacking. The three-month period under **R.16(1)(a)** for enforcement of rights under **Art.61** is excluded from further processing because it is not monitored by the EPO and no communication can be issued if it is missed. Similarly, if the two-month period under **R.112(2)**, which allows for an administrative review of any loss of rights resulting from the Convention, is missed, the loss of rights becomes final without any further decision or communication being issued by the EPO. As the procedure under **R.112** already has a remedial character, further processing also has to be ruled out on substantive grounds (OJ 2003 se1 p.159). The period for paying additional search fees when there is a lack of unity of invention provided for in **R.64** is excluded, because this preserves the legal situation of EPC1973 and avoids complex procedural problems in a case where the Office is not aware of any real need for further processing (CA/PL17/06). Similarly, the periods in **R.164(1)** and (2) are excluded.

A period may be excluded from further processing to avoid procrastinating the procedure. The periods under **R.31(2)** for providing information on the deposition of biological material are excluded from further processing, because non-compliance would cause the invention to be regarded as not disclosed under **R.31**. Legal certainty requires that the information is available in due time before publication of the application (CA/PL17/06). Also in view of the publication of the application, the periods for late declaration of priority under **R.52(2)** and for correcting it under **R.52(3)** do not permit further processing (OJ 2003 se1 p.159). The periods in **R.62a** and **R.63** for responding to an invitation from the search examiner have been excluded to allow the search report to be published together with the application. It should be noted that, even though a re-establishment case causes a considerably longer procedural delay than further processing, the average delay in the proceedings is less for re-establishment because re-establishment is used ten times less frequently than further processing.

The list of exclusions in **R.135(2)** could have included a few more periods that have a remedial character (e.g. second one-month period in **R.45(2)**; **R.163**) or where another legal remedy has been provided (e.g. first one-month period in **R.45(2)**).

R. 135(3) The department competent to decide on the omitted act shall decide on the request for further processing.

Implementation of **Art.121(2)**

1 **Department competent to decide**

If the competent department decides not to allow further processing, the applicant can appeal the decision (**Art.106(1)**), provided the department that took the decision is not a board of appeal. When in the meantime responsibility has been transferred to the next department, e.g. from the Receiving Section to the examining division, the Receiving Section remains competent.

R. 136 Re-establishment of rights

R. 136(1) Any request for re-establishment of rights under Article 122, paragraph 1, shall be filed in writing within two months of the removal of the cause of non-compliance with the period, but at the latest within one year of expiry of the unobserved time limit. However, a request for re-establishment of rights in respect of any of the periods specified in Article 87, paragraph 1, and in Article 112a, paragraph 4, shall be filed within two months of expiry of that period. The request for re-establishment of rights shall not be deemed to have been filed until the prescribed fee has been paid.

Art.87(1) Priority period
Art.112a(4) Period for filing petition for review
Art.122(1) Re-establishment of rights
Implementation of **Art.122(2)**

1 **Request for re-establishment**

R.136(1) lays down that a request for re-establishment must include the filing of a written request and payment of a fee. Paragraph 2 adds the requirement of completion of the omitted act. The period for carrying out the acts is specified in the provision.

The written request must be filed in a way complying with **R.50**. The request must state the grounds on which it is based, and set out the facts on which it relies (**R.136(2)**). **R.136(2):2** sets out the requirements for the omitted act.

R.136(1) defines two situations for filing a request for re-establishment, a general situation and a special situation for re-establishment in the priority period or the periods for filing a petition for review.

2 General situation for requesting re-establishment

The general situation provides a two-month period for requesting re-establishment from the removal of the cause of non-compliance with the unobserved period. Within this two-month period the written request must be filed, the payment made and the omitted act completed.

Where parties miss several periods expiring independently of one another and each resulting in a loss of rights, they must apply for re-establishment and pay the fee for re-establishment in respect of each unobserved period. It is irrelevant whether the requests are filed in the same letter or in different letters and whether they are based on the same or different grounds. (**J26/95**)

2.1 REMOVAL OF THE CAUSE OF NON-COMPLIANCE

The two-month period of **R.136(1)** is triggered by the removal of the cause of non-compliance, i.e. by the event through which the party became aware why a loss of rights had ensued. The following items are pertinent to the establishment of removal of the cause of non-compliance: how is the loss of rights notified, who must be notified and when is it notified. No request for re-establishment is necessary if the EPO could have warned the party timely of the non-compliance. In that event the loss of rights must be remedied under good faith (see **Art.125:2**).

The principle of good faith requires the EPO to warn the requester of any impending loss of rights if such a warning can be expected in all good faith. A warning can be expected if the deficiency, e.g. not completing the omitted act together with the request for re-establishment, is readily identifiable for the EPO and the requester can still correct it within the time limit (**T14/89**; **J13/90** r.7). If a warning can be expected but is not issued to the applicant within the time limit to be observed, the EPO must set a period in which the applicant can correct the deficiency and perform the procedural act in time. (**J13/90**)

The cause of non-compliance is removed when the party concerned is made aware of the loss of rights. If the party is represented by a duly appointed professional representative, then a notification of the loss of rights to the representative removes the cause of non-compliance (**J27/90** hn1). This also applies where the professional representative is instructed via a national patent attorney (**J27/90** hn1). The date of notification is the date at which the representative sees the document, not the day a secretary sees it: the cause of non-compliance is only removed if the representative is aware of the facts, as the representative is responsible for the decision whether or not to request re-establishment (**T191/82**). An independent renewal fee payment agency does not take away the responsibility of the representative: the representative is the person to act on the notification according to **R.112(1)** (**J27/90** hn2). In the case of an applicant from a contracting state without a representative, the date of removal of the cause of non-compliance is the date the applicant did become aware of the non-compliance, not when they ought to have become aware of it. Thus, the knowledge of patent law of the person responsible for the application vis-à-vis the EPO is also taken into account. (**J1/20**)

In the absence of circumstances to the contrary, the receipt of the **R.112(1)** notice triggers the two-month time limit of **R.136(1)**, as the notice ought to remove the cause of non-compliance (**J27/90** hn1). This is often the case, in particular where a time limit is missed through ignorance or inadvertence.

2.2 ONE-YEAR PERIOD

Re-establishment is no longer possible if the request for re-establishment has not been filed and the omitted act completed within one year from the expiry of the unobserved period according to **R.136(1)**, first sentence, and **R.136(2)**, in order to guarantee legal certainty for the public (**J35/03** r.6). After the one-year period has lapsed, a third party may safely assume that the application or patent will not be revived. The option to file the grounds and complete the omitted act after expiry of the one-year period as allowed by **J6/90** is probably no longer possible under EPC2000.

Exceptionally, a refused or (deemed) withdrawn application may yet give rise to protective rights after the expiry of the one-year period if a new application in the sense of **Art.61** is filed by an entitled applicant after the expiry of the one-year period (**G3/92**).

The six-month period of grace under **R.51(2)** for payment of the renewal fee plus additional fee is not to be deducted from the one-year period, as was the case under the old law, Art.122(2), fourth sentence, EPC1973. Now the one-year period begins on expiry of the six-month period. Since a **R.112(1)** communication will be sent to the applicant within two months from the due date after not paying the renewal fee, re-establishment will in practice be invoked seldom and the de facto extension of the six-month period does not put third parties at an unreasonable disadvantage (OJ 2003 se1 p.159).

The similar nature and purpose of the four-month period in **R.51(3)** for payment of renewal fees for a divisional application warrant equal treatment with respect to the one-year period. Hence, the one-year period for re-establishment in the four-month period should run from the expiry of the four-month period.

The EPO will regard the one-year period as an aggregate period because it is triggered by the expiry of the unobserved period. See A-IV,1.4.3 for an example; **R.131(2):3** for the calculation).

The one-year period is not applicable for requesting re-establishment in the priority period and the period for filing a petition for review, as is clear from the wording of **R.136(1)**.

3 Special situation for requesting re-establishment

R.136(1) defines that the request for re-establishment of rights for the priority period under **Art.87(1)** and the periods for filing a petition for review under **Art.112a(4)** must be filed within two months of the expiry of those periods. This short period for filing the request for re-establishment in the priority period is the minimum period fixed by the Patent Law Treaty, chosen because of the urgent need for clarity in view of the valid claiming of priority. The same period is chosen for re-establishment in the period for filing the petition for review in view of the overriding need for legal certainty in this late procedural stage (CA/PL 17/06, OJ 2007 se5 EN p.208).

The EPO regards the two-month period from the expiry of the non-observed period as an aggregate period. The calculation of aggregate periods is set out in **R.131(2):3**. For example, a priority application is filed on 30.03.2017. The priority period expires on 30.03.2018 (Good Friday), extended under **R.134(1)** to 03.04.2018. The two-month period for filing the request for re-establishment and filing the priority claiming application expires on Sunday 03.06.2018, again extended under **R.134(1)** to 04.06.2018.

4 **Concurrence of re-establishment and R.112(2) decision**
The two-month period to apply for a decision according to **R.112(2)** starts on the date the **R.112(1)** communication of loss of rights by the EPO bears (**R.126(2)**). If parties are of the opinion that the EPO made a mistake with the communication under **R.112(1)**, they must request an appealable decision under **R.112(2)** and, if further processing is not possible, at the same time apply for re-establishment and pay the fee for re-establishment as an auxiliary request. Both requests must be filed within the shorter of two months after notification of the **R.112(1)** communication and two months of the removal of the cause of non-compliance. The removal is normally the actual receipt of the **R.112(1)** communication. The EPO will assess the correctness of the communication. If it decides the communication was erroneous, the party is notified and the procedure is continued. The fee for re-establishment will be refunded because the request for re-establishment is in that case without grounds. If the EPO decides the communication was correct, it will consider the request for re-establishment and issue an appealable decision on both the correctness of the communication and the request for re-establishment (**J23/96** r.3).

5 **Fee for re-establishment**
The fee for re-establishment is fixed in **Rfees2(1)13**.

Loss of rights due to a late payment of the fee for re-establishment can be appealed after a communication of loss of rights under **R.112(1)** and a decision under **R.112(2)**. Re-establishment is excluded by **Art.122(4)**. The fee is refunded if it has been paid late or if there is no failure to meet a time limit. Payment without a written request is not regarded as a valid request for re-establishment, even if the payment indicated 're-establishment fee' and mentioned the relevant application (**J19/90**).

R. 136(2) The request shall state the grounds on which it is based and shall set out the facts on which it relies. The omitted act shall be completed within the relevant period for filing the request according to paragraph 1.

Implementation of **Art.122(2)**

1 **Grounds and facts**
The English and French texts of **R.136(2)** require the grounds and facts to be filed within two months, whereas the German text requires additionally that the substantiation of the facts ('glaubhaft machen') is filed within the same time limit. The broadest text should be used to interpret the EPC, i.e. the English and French text in this case. Hence, the request for re-establishment must contain the grounds and facts (**R.136(2)**); the facts may be substantiated later by providing means by which those facts are supported, e.g. medical certificates, sworn statements and the like. (**T324/90**)

Filing facts only with the statement of grounds of appeal in an appeal against a decision rejecting a request for re-establishment is too late: the parties have not complied with their burden of allegation and proof for re-establishment (**J18/98**).

A broad statement such as a claim that 96% of the mail is delivered on the next working day does in general not reflect what happens in individual cases (**T777/98** r.2.2.2.2). See **Art.117** (taking of evidence) for means to make the facts credible ('glaubhaft' in the German version of **R.136(2)**).

2 **Omitted act**

The completion of the omitted act implies that the act meets the requirements of the EPC for admissibility. As an example, if a statement of grounds of appeal, filed as completion of an omitted act, is inadmissible for the purpose of **Art.108**, the request for re-establishment itself is inadmissible. (T167/97 hn). In case the omitted act is the payment of one or more fees and the request for re-establishment is refused or withdrawn, any fees paid to complete the omitted act are reimbursed (**T555/08, T1426/14; T2093/22**).

R. 136(3) Re-establishment of rights shall be ruled out in respect of any period for which further processing under Article 121 is available and in respect of the period for requesting re-establishment of rights.

Art.121 Further processing of the patent application
Implementation of **Art.122(4)**

1 **Periods excluded from re-establishment**

R.136(3) rules out the re-establishment of rights in respect of any periods for which further processing is available. Either further processing or re-establishment of rights may be requested if a specific time limit has been missed. During the grant procedure only further processing will normally be available; re-establishment of rights thus only comes into play where further processing is excluded with regard to a specific period. The limitation of the possibility of re-establishment of rights during the grant procedure will, however, be offset to some extent by the fact that re-establishment of rights with regard to the period for further processing will continue to be possible. (OJ 2003 se1 p.159)

The exclusion of the period for requesting re-establishment from re-establishment in **R.136(3)** is a repetition of **Art.122(4)**, first sentence.

R. 136(4) The department competent to decide on the omitted act shall decide on the request for re-establishment of rights.

Implementation of **Art.122(2)**

1 **Department competent to decide**

The department competent to decide on the omitted act also decides on the request for re-establishment.

Where the re-establishment is in respect of an unobserved time limit for appeal when the conditions for granting interlocutory revision are fulfilled, the department that took the contested decision will consider the re-establishment only if it can grant re-establishment within the three-month period of **Art.109(2)**; in all other cases the board of appeal will decide on the request for re-establishment (see e.g. **T65/11**, where the conditions for granting were not fulfilled). (E-VIII, 3.3)

If the department of first instance rejects a request for re-establishment and, after an appeal has been lodged, does not apply interlocutory revision according to **Art.109**, the board of appeal decides on the allowability of the request for re-establishment (**J22/86**).

Chapter VI *Amendments and corrections*

R. 137 Amendment of the European patent application

Amended, in force since 01.04.2010 (OJ 2009 p.299).
Implementation of **Art.123(1)**

1 **General**
The provision limits the opportunities during the grant procedure for the applicant to amend the application as of right, making the proceedings more efficient. The allowability of amendments in terms of substance is restricted by **Art.123(2)** and **R.137(5)**.

R.80 is the corollary to **R.137** for the amendment of a patent during opposition proceedings.

R. 137(1) Before receiving the European search report, the applicant may not amend the description, claims or drawings of a European patent application unless otherwise provided.

1 **No amendment before receipt of search report**
The purpose of the prohibition of **R.137(1)** is to prevent the applicant from disrupting the search by changing the invention to which the application is directed.

The 'otherwise provided' allows exceptions where necessary. The major exceptions are:

- **R.56** late filing of missing drawings or missing parts of the description;
- **R.56a** late filing of corrections in the case that a part of the application was erroneously filed;
- **R.58** late filing of missing claims, correction of deficiencies noted under **R.57**;
- **R.139**, second sentence: correction of obvious errors in the patent application.

Amendments filed under **R.58** should not extend beyond what is necessary to remedy the deficiencies noted by the Receiving Section (**R.57**).

This prohibition does not extend to parts of the application other than the description, claims and drawings: it is nevertheless possible, for example, to amend the abstract (**R.47**), the Request for Grant form (**R.41**), the designation of the inventor (**R.19**), a priority claim (**R.52**), or an authorisation (**R.152**) (see **R.139**, first sentence).

R. 137(2) Together with any comments, corrections or amendments made in response to communications by the European Patent Office under Rule 70a, paragraph 1 or 2, or Rule 161, paragraph 1, the applicant may amend the description, claims and drawings of their own volition.

R.70a(1) invitation to respond within period for filing request for examination
R.70a(2) invitation to respond within period for confirming request for examination
R.161(1) invitation to respond to PCT written opinion or examination report
Amended by decision of the Administrative Council of 10.12.2024, which entered into force on 01.04.2025 (OJ 2025 A16). The amendment made the text gender-neutral.

1 **Voluntary amendment of the application**

Before the substantive examination of the application by the examining division commences, the applicant has an opportunity to amend the application as of right, as provided by **Art.123(1)**. **R.137(2)** specifies that this voluntary amendment is to be made together with the response to the communication issued by the EPO under **R.70a(1)**, (2) or **R.161(1)**.

Any further amendment will only be admitted with the consent of the examining division (**R.137(3)**). The combined effect of **R.137(2)** and (3) is that the applicant has only one chance to file voluntary amendments that the Office must admit.

However, the EPO does not interpret the word 'together' in **R.137(2)** as meaning that the voluntary amendment and the response must be provided in one submission but as meaning that the voluntary amendment must be filed within the same period as the period for filing the response. Hence, a voluntary amendment may also be filed before or after the response.

R.137(2) mentions the following three opportunities for filing voluntary amendments:

- the communication under **R.70a(1)** gives an opportunity to comment on the search report and opinion within the period for filing the request for examination.
- the communication under **R.70a(2)** allows an applicant to comment on the search report and opinion where the request for examination has already been filed, or on the extended supplementary search report and opinion, within the period for indicating whether the applicant wishes to proceed further with the application.
- the communication under **R.161(1)** invites the applicant of a Euro-PCT application to comment on the written opinion or the preliminary examination report drawn up by the EPO as ISA or IPEA.

If the opinion notes deficiencies in the application, a response to any of the three communications is mandatory, in which case any voluntary amendment must be filed in addition to a response. If the opinion is positive, a response is not required, but a voluntary amendment may nevertheless be filed within the stated period. (B-XI,8)

In cases where no search opinion is prepared, e.g. where the examination fee has been paid early and the **R.70(2)** communication has been waived, the applicant must file any voluntary amendments together with the response to the first communication from the examining division (H-II,2.2; note that this possibility for filing voluntary amendments is not covered by **R.137(2)** but must be provided anyway in view of **Art.123(1)**, second sentence).

A fourth opportunity is provided with the **R.161(2)** communication, allowing the applicant to voluntarily amend a Euro-PCT application before the start of a supplementary search and within six months from notification of the communication.

The EPC and the Guidelines appear not to address the situation where the applicant wants to file voluntary amendments after having waived his right to the **R.161(1)** communication. In such a case the restrictions on filing voluntary amendments in **R.137(2)** might not apply and the applicant may be allowed to file voluntary amendments in response to the first communication from the examining division.

A fifth opportunity for voluntary amendment is following a search on a Euro-PCT application under **R.164(2)(b)**. (OJ 2014 A70 §16)

The voluntary amendment may be accompanied by comments and corrections. When an amendment of the claims is received before the termination of the technical preparation for the publication of the application, the amended claims are included in the publication in addition to the original claims (**R.68(4)**).

Any amendments submitted under **R.70a** or **R.164(2)(b)** must comply with **R.137(5)**.

R. 137(3) No further amendment may be made without the consent of the Examining Division.

1 **Voluntary amendment after first response**
After the response to the communication mentioned in **R.137(2)**, no further amendments may be made without the consent of the examining division (**R.137(3)**). As an exception, **R.164(2)** provides for a further right to amend voluntarily the application (**R.164(2):2.4**).

The examining division will admit amendments to the extent that they are necessary to correct deficiencies noted in one of its communications; such amendments are mandatory. Voluntary amendments filed after said response are admitted only at the examiner's discretion. The use of this discretion must strike a balance between the applicant's interest in obtaining an optimal patent and the EPO's interest in bringing the procedure swiftly to a close (H-II,2.3). See H-II,2.3.1 for examples of the exercise of discretion.

If amended claims are not admitted into the procedure, the EPO must send the applicant the reasons underlying the inadmissibility (**Art.113(1)**; E-X,2.11; H-II,2.6). In such a situation, where there are no other requests on file, the EPO has no text to examine and decide upon, and the refusal of the application is to be expected (E-X,2.11).

The examining division has a discretion to admit voluntary amendments until the decision to grant is handed over to the EPO's internal postal service (C-V,6.1) or a decision is pronounced in oral proceedings (E-III,9) (**G7/93** hn.1, **G12/91**, H-II,2.6). The admittance of an amendment filed after the communication under **R.71(3)** will be exceptional (**G7/93** hn.2). However, such an amendment must be admitted if the **R.71(3)** communication is the first communication from the examining division and the applicant has not yet had a chance to file voluntary amendments (C-V,4.4). See also **R.71(6):2**. During opposition proceedings proprietors may also amend the patent, but they are restricted, in particular, by **Art.123(3)** and **R.80** .

R. 137(4) When filing any amendments referred to in paragraphs 1 to 3, the applicant shall identify them and indicate the basis for them in the application as filed. If the Examining Division notes a failure to meet either requirement, it may request the correction of this deficiency within a period of one month.

1 **Identification and indication of basis for amendments**
When amending the description, claims or drawings, the applicant must identify the amendments made and indicate the basis for them in the application as filed (**R.137(4)**, first sentence). The purpose of this provision is to make it easier for the EPO to assess the allowability of the amendments, particularly when there is no literal basis. Whether basis has been provided and whether the amendments comply with **Art.123(2)** are assessed independently (H-III,2.1).

Amendments may conveniently be identified by using a 'track changes' tool or by using handwritten annotations. In both cases, clean copies of the amended pages must also be provided. (H-III,2.2)

The basis for the amendments is preferably indicated by listing the amendments made and their basis in the originally filed documents. Where necessary, the applicant should explain why **Art.123(2)** is complied with (H-III,2.2). The indication must be specific and vague statements such as 'see the description as filed' should be avoided. An indication is sufficient if, on consulting those parts of the application indicated, it is not necessary to look further (H-III,2.1).

2 **Applicability of R.137(4)**

The requirement to indicate basis applies to any amendment filed before grant of the patent. It therefore applies to both voluntary and mandatory amendments, and also to a first set of claims filed after the date of filing under **R.58**. For Euro-PCT applications, the requirement also applies to any amendment made in the international phase that is maintained on entry into the European phase and to any amendments made on entry (H-III,2.1.1).

A **R.137(4)** communication will not be sent in respect of amendments filed during oral proceedings or in response to the summons thereto. In these cases, the basis must be provided during the oral proceedings. If not provided, the amendments may be rejected as inadmissible under **R.137(3)**. (H-III,2.1.3)

Since **R.137(4)** applies to applications only, it does not apply to granted patents and its requirements need not be complied with during opposition proceedings and any opposition appeal proceedings. However, if the basis for an amendment is not specified then this may have negative consequences when the admissibility of the amendment is being considered, particularly in appeal proceedings.

Note that the requirement of **R.137(4)** does not apply to applications for which the search report was drawn up before 01.04.2010 (transitional provision of the amendment, OJ 2009 p.299 Art.2). As a consequence, its requirements need not be complied with when amending such applications. (H-III,2.1.4)

3 **Missing identification of amendments**

If the applicant files amendments without identifying them or indicating the basis of them, the examining division may request correction of this deficiency within a non-extendible period of one month from notification (**R.137(4)**, second sentence). The 'may' in the provision allows the examiner to exercise discretion in deciding whether to issue such a request. In some cases it may be more efficient for the examiner to identify the basis directly rather than issuing an invitation under **R.137(4)**. The examiner may also reject an amendment without basis as inadmissible. (H-III,3.3.1)

If the applicant does not respond in time to the invitation, the application will be deemed withdrawn under **Art.94(4)**. Further processing is available (**Art.121**).

R. 137(5) Amended claims may not relate to unsearched subject-matter which does not combine with the originally claimed invention or group of inventions to form a single general inventive concept. Nor may they relate to subject-matter not searched in accordance with Rule 62a or Rule 63.

R.62a Plurality of independent claims
R.63 Incomplete search due to unsearchable subject-matter

1 **Features taken from the description**

R.137(5), first sentence, concerns amendments based on subject-matter that is taken from the description and that result in the claiming of a different invention compared to the one originally claimed.

The provision was introduced in 1995 as an addition to the rule, which was formulated in **G2/92**, that amended claims may not relate to an invention for which the applicant paid no additional search fee in reply to an invitation to do so under **R.64** (see H-II,6.2). The EPO was concerned that applicants could circumvent this rule by disclosing inventions in the description rather than claiming them. In particular, because the search is carried out on the basis of the claims (**Art.92**), the EPO issues no invitations under **R.64** for unclaimed inventions that are only mentioned in the description, and no such invitations can be issued later during the substantive examination, even if the claims are amended (OJ 1995 p.409). Accordingly, the provision prohibits amendments based on subject-matter extracted from the description that result in the claiming of a separate invention compared to the invention(s) originally claimed, i.e. the invention(s) that were claimed when the search was carried out. If the subject-matter resulting from the amendment is not a separate invention, but e.g. is a foreseeable limitation of the original claims, the amendment cannot be objected to. In principle, the search should have covered the subject-matter resulting from any such foreseeable limitation (B-III,3.5); if this is not the case, an additional search (free of charge) may have to be carried out by the EPO during the examination of the amended claims (see B-II,4.2). On the other hand, if the search division voluntarily extends the search to cover a separate invention found in the description, an amendment directed to this searched subject-matter cannot be objected to under **R.137(5)**.

For these reasons, the provision only permits amendments that result in the claiming of subject-matter which (i) has unity of invention with any of the original claims or (ii) was (voluntarily) searched by the EPO. If the amended claim meets either requirement (or both), no objection can be raised against it under **R.137(5)**, first sentence.

The question to be asked for condition (i) is whether adding the amended claim to the original set of claims would have caused an objection of lack of unity of invention under **Art.82** (**T708/00**; H-IV,4.1.2). This is not the case if the amended claim has unity of invention with at least one of the original claims; no objection under **R.137(5)** can be raised in such a case (**T708/00**). The comparison is with all original claims, irrespective of whether they were searched under **R.64** (H-IV,4.1.2).

An amendment would typically lead to an objection of lack of unity of invention under (i) if the amendment involves replacing a technical feature of the claim with another technical feature that is taken from the description, said alternative feature having an effect unrelated to the effect(s) of the features of the originally claimed invention(s) (H-IV,4.1.2).

Any lack of unity that already existed in the original set of claims is not relevant under **R.137(5)**. However, the amended claim can be objected to under **G2/92** (rather than **R.137(5)**) if it relates to an originally claimed invention for which the search division issued an invitation under **R.64** (or **R.164**) and the applicant did not pay the additional search fee requested in that invitation (H-II,6.2).

R.137(5) does not give the examining division a discretionary power, unlike **R.137(3)**, and requires an in-depth analysis rather than a prima facie analysis. The objection must be reasoned. (H-IV,4.1). If a claim does not comply with the provision, the claim is unallowable, not inadmissible (**T2431/19** r.2.2.3; H-IV,4). The rejection of a claim on this ground is accordingly subject to a full review in appeal proceedings following a decision to refuse the application.

If only condition (i) is met, the amendment cannot be objected to and a further search directed to the amended subject-matter is to be carried out during examination (free of charge).

Any amendments submitted under **R.70a** or **R.164(2)(b)** must comply with **R.137(5)** even though they are not subject to **R.137(3)**.

If a claim amendment is not allowable under **R.137(5)**, the subject-matter of the claim can only be prosecuted in a divisional application. For direct European applications, the absence of the amended subject-matter from the original claims cannot therefore be remedied during the prosecution of the application. The applicant should include the amended subject-matter in the set of claims filed as part of the divisional (or in the set of claims filed later under **R.58**) to ensure that it is searched by the EPO.

Because optional (e.g. preferred) features of a claim are non-limiting, and may not be searched by the EPO, an amendment based on an optional feature of a claim should be treated in the same way as a feature taken from the description (see also Y. Robin in epi Information 4/2016).

1.1 EURO-PCT APPLICATIONS

R.137(5), first sentence, aims to ensure that applicants include all subject-matter for which protection may be sought in the set of claims that the EPO searches (such that the EPO can request the payment of an appropriate number of additional search fees).

The condition (ii) above is therefore only met if the subject-matter of the amended claim was searched by the EPO; any search carried out by a different patent office in the international phase is irrelevant.

If a supplementary European search is carried out by the EPO under **R.164(1)**, condition (i) is met if the amended claim has unity of invention with at least one claim in the set of claims that is pending at the time of the supplementary European search (**T1871/14**). If the amended subject-matter is directed to an invention for which the applicant refused to pay an additional search fee when requested by the EPO under **R.164(1)**, an objection is raised under **R.164(1)(c)** in accordance with **G2/92** (see H-II,6).

For Euro-PCT applications in respect of which the EPO was ISA, condition (i) is met if the amended claim has unity of invention either with a claim in the set of claims pending at the time of the search by the EPO as ISA or with a claim in the set of claims pending at the time of the check for unsearched subject-matter carried out by the examining division under **R.164(2)(a)**. Condition (ii) is met if the subject-matter of the amended claim was searched by the EPO as ISA or under **R.164(2)**.

If the amendment is directed to an invention which was searched neither by the EPO as ISA nor under **R.164(2)** and for which the applicant refused to pay a search fee when requested by the EPO under **R.164(2)**, an objection is raised under **R.164(2)(c)** in accordance with **G2/92** (H-II,6). If the amended claim is directed to an invention for which the applicant refused to pay an additional search fee when requested by the EPO as ISA, and which was not present in the claims at the time of the check for unsearched claims under **R.164(2)(a)**, an objection can be raised applying **G2/92** by analogy (H-II,6.4.1; E-IX,4.2).

For Euro-PCT applications where the EPO was SISA, i.e., carried out a supplementary international search (R.45bis PCT), the same principles apply. However, it should be taken into account that no additional search fee can be requested as part of a supplementary international search. Hence, **G2/92** cannot be simply applied by analogy.

R.137(5) does not apply to amendments filed on entry into the European phase under **R.159(1)(b)** or during the period set under **R.161** because the EPO can request the payment of an additional search fee under **R.164** where appropriate (OJ 2014 A70 §13; C-III,3.1.).

2 **Multiple independent claims**

Under **R.62a**, applicants must select the independent claims they want to be searched if there are multiple independent claims in one category that do not comply with **R.43(2)**. The subject-matter of the independent claims that are not selected and of any claims dependent on them will not be searched. Amended claims may not relate to such subject-matter (**R.137(5)**, second sentence).

R.137(5), second sentence, also applies to Euro-PCT applications if the supplementary European search (**R.164(1)**) is limited under **R.62a** or if the search under **R.164(2)** was limited on the same ground (**R.164(3)**).

If the applicant shows that the objection of the search division was unjustified because the independent claims complied with one of the exceptions of **R.43(2)**, the amended claim cannot be objected to and an additional search may be necessary; such a search is free of charge (C-IV,7.3).

R.137(5), second sentence, does not apply to applications for which the search report was drawn up before **R.62a** came into effect, i.e. before 01.04.2010 (OJ 2009 p.299 Art.2).

3 **Unsearchable subject-matter**

If the EPO cannot carry out a meaningful search because the claims are severely deficient, e.g. due to a severe lack of clarity, it will invite the applicant to submit a statement under **R.63(1)** indicating the subject-matter to be searched. If the statement does not resolve the matter satisfactorily, the EPO may issue a declaration that no search could be carried out or draw up a partial search report (**R.63(2)**). Amended claims may not relate to subject-matter not covered by the partial search report (**R.137(5)**, second sentence).

R.137(5), second sentence, also applies to Euro-PCT applications if the supplementary European search (**R.164(1)**) is limited under **R.63** or if the search under **R.164(2)** was limited on the same ground (**R.164(3)**).

Where the EPO has issued a partial search report or a declaration that no search was possible under **R.63**, the applicant can refute the deficiencies with arguments or amend the claims before the examining division. Provided the amendments overcome the issues raised, a new search may be carried out and the amendment is not to be considered to relate to unsearched subject-matter (C-IV,7.3(ii)).

R.137(5), second sentence, does not apply to applications for which the search report was drawn up before **R.62a** came into effect, i.e. before 01.04.2010 (OJ 2009 p.299 Art.2).

R. 138 Different claims, description and drawings for different States

If the European Patent Office is informed of the existence of a prior right under Article 139, paragraph 2, the European patent application or European patent may, for such State or States, contain claims and, where appropriate, a description and drawings which are different from those for the other designated States.

Art.139(2) National prior right
Implementation of **Art.118**

1 **Amendment on account of national prior rights**
National prior rights are not comprised in the state of the art as defined in **Art.54(2)** and (3) and are not taken into account when assessing the patentability of an invention under the EPC. Furthermore, the requirement for unity of the application laid down in **Art.118** prevents the applicant from pursuing different claims in respect of different contracting states. However, **R.138** provides an exception to this principle by allowing different claims, a different description and different drawings for different states where national prior rights exist so as to ensure that the patent remains valid after grant in those contracting states where the national prior rights are effective.

It is not possible to file an application with different claims for different states in order to take into account national prior rights since the Receiving Section is not competent to decide whether the filing of such claims is justified. Moreover, it is not always possible for applicants to know of the existence of third-party prior rights when filing a European patent application, since they often remain unpublished at this point. The first opportunity to file different claims for different states is therefore during the examination procedure. (**J21/82**)

According to **R.138**, the EPO must be 'informed' of the existence of the national prior rights. This means it must evaluate the need to file an additional set of claims (**J21/82 r.6**). The applicant should file a copy of the national prior right in order for the EPO to assess whether a deviation from the requirements of **Art.118** is justified (H-III,4.4). The EPO will not itself suggest that the applicant takes into account prior national rights (H-III,4.5) but will carry out a search for such rights and include the results in the communication pursuant to **R.71(3)** in order to help the applicant decide whether unitary effect should be requested on grant. An additional set of claims must be filed before the decision of the examining division is handed over to the EPO internal post services to be taken into account in the grant procedure (**G12/91**).

The examining division will check that the separate claims, description and drawings comply with **Art.123(2)** and meet the other requirements of the EPC (H-III,4.5, **J21/82**). The examining division will not, however, verify whether the claims have been limited to the extent necessary to restore novelty over the national prior right (H-III,4.4).

Claims fees (**R.45**) are calculated on the basis of the set of claims having the highest number of claims (A-III,9). All claim sets must be translated into the two official EPO languages other than the language of the proceedings under **R.71(3)**.

A similar procedure is possible in opposition (D-I,3; H-III,4.4) and in limitation proceedings (**Art.105b(3):1**).

It is not possible to have different texts in respect of extension states (H-III,4).

Note that unitary effect can only be registered if the European patent is granted with the same text for all participating Member States (**UPR.5(2)**).

2 **Amendment on account of European prior rights**
R.138 does not allow different texts of the application where a European prior rights exists since under EPC2000 a prior European right applies to all designated states. However, the prior art for applications filed before the entry into force of EPC2000 (13.12.2007) includes European prior rights only for those contracting states that are commonly designated. Such an application may therefore contain different claims, a different description and different drawings for states for which the European prior right is effective if it is only effective for some designated states (R.87 EPC1973; see **Art.54(3):3**).

R. 139 Correction of errors in documents filed with the European Patent Office

Linguistic errors, errors of transcription and mistakes in any document filed with the European Patent Office may be corrected on request. However, if the request for such correction concerns the description, claims or drawings, the correction must be obvious in the sense that it is immediately evident that nothing else would have been intended than what is offered as the correction.

Implementation of **Art.123(1)**

1 **General**
R.139 allows a party to request the correction of errors in documents filed with the EPO. An error exists in a document if the document does not express the true intention of the person on whose behalf it was filed (**J8/80** r.4; **J6/91** r.2.2). The correction restores the document to the form in which the party intended to file it. The request may be filed at any time during pending grant, opposition or limitation proceedings (**J42/92**; H-VI,2.1; see **R.80:2** for opposition).

The department handling the procedure is competent to decide on a request for correction. If the correction concerns the description, drawings or claims, and the request is filed in an early stage, the Receiving Section may decide to pass on the request to the examining division if it involves technical considerations (**J4/85**). A formalities officer acting on behalf of an examining division or opposition division is not competent to decide on a request for correction under **R.139** that concerns the description, claims or drawings (Dec. Pres. OJ 2014 A6).

If, upon termination of the technical preparations for publication of the application, a request for correction is still pending and third party rights could be jeopardised by the proposed correction, a reference to the request must be made on the front page of the publication (A-VI,1.3).

The EPC does not define the meaning of the term 'amendment' and how an 'amendment' relates to a 'correction'. On the one hand, it is the practice of the EPO to treat corrections differently from amendments and to allow correction at any point during grant proceedings, without applying the restrictions relating to amendments found in **R.137**. On the other hand, **G3/89** has made **R.139**, second sentence, dependent on **Art.123(2)**, such that a correction under **R.139**, second sentence may not extend the subject-matter of the application, implying that a correction is a particular kind of amendment.

This decision was based on the dependency of articles and rules in view of their order in the EPC and the importance of extension of subject-matter in opposition and revocation proceedings, where it is irrelevant whether the extension results from a correction under **R.139** or an amendment under **R.137**.

2 Conditions for correction

The general principles according to which a request for correction must be assessed, as developed in the case law, are summarised in **G1/12**:

(a) The correction must introduce what was originally intended and cannot be used to effect a change of mind or the development of plans. It is the relevant party's actual intention which must be considered.

(b) Where the original intention is not immediately apparent, the requester bears the burden of proof, which must be a heavy one.

(c) The error to be remedied may be an incorrect statement or an omission.

(d) The request for correction must be filed without delay.

The provision does not restrict the right to request correction to certain persons; hence, any party and any third person may correct documents filed by itself or in its name. The most frequent users of **R.139** are applicants and, to a lesser degree, proprietors.

Since **R.139** does not contain an explicit limitation to specific procedures or points in time, a request for correction may be filed at any stage of grant, opposition or limitation proceedings. The proceedings must be pending, otherwise the EPO has no jurisdiction (**J42/92** r.4-6). Even the approval of the text to be granted under **R.71(3)** does not stop the applicant from correcting an error under **R.139** (**T200/89** r.2.2, H-II,2.6). During examination proceedings a request for correction will be considered if it is filed before a decision has been handed over to the EPO's internal postal service for transmission to the applicant in written proceedings (date at the bottom of the decision to grant form 2006A), or has been pronounced in oral proceedings (**G12/91**; H-VI,2.1). As set out below, however, the requirement for third parties to have legal certainty may restrict the ability of the applicant to correct some errors beyond a certain point in the grant procedure.

The correction of an error is not a right that belongs to any party. The word 'may' in **R.139** indicates that the allowance of a correction is at the discretion of the EPO (**J6/91** r.5.3). The criteria to be applied when exercising discretion have been developed in the case law, balancing the interests of parties and the public. A correction may not compromise legal certainty by changing information that the public should be able to rely on. Hence, a correction is normally only allowable if it is both compatible with legal certainty and compliant with the requirements of **R.139**. The following sections first set out the general requirements applicable to all types of corrections and then add the additional requirements specific to corrections under either the first or second sentence of **R.139**.

2.1 LEGAL CERTAINTY

A correction under **R.139** should not compromise legal certainty. **T824/00** r.6 derives this from the fact that the provision for correcting errors in documents is framed as a rule rather than as an article, which is evidence that the discretionary power under **R.139** is subordinate to other considerations, e.g. the principle of legal certainty (see also **J4/82**, r.2). This is in line with the restrictions that apply to re-establishment (**Art.122**), which may allow the true intention of a party to prevail over procedural certainty when a loss of rights results from the non-observance of certain time limits – with specific exclusions listed in **Art.122(4)** and third party protection provided for in **Art.122(5)**.

Legal certainty requires that the EPO can rely on certain statements made by a party to the proceedings, limiting the extent to which a party's true intention may be taken into account (**J10/87** r.10). Hence, a statement can only be corrected under **R.139** before it is relied on in a formal juridical act (**T824/00** r.8). Examples of juridical acts are an entry in the Register, a publication in the Bulletin and the posting of a decision. Re-establishment in the period before the juridical act is excluded, because this period is not a time limit in the sense of **Art.122(1)** (**J7/90** r.3).

Corrections affecting information to be published must be made before its publication in the Bulletin or entry in the Register, because third parties must be able to rely on the information provided by the EPO. As an exception, a correction after publication may be allowed if the correction was obvious for the public. Examples of corrections relating to the withdrawal of a patent application, the withdrawal of the designation of a contracting state and changes in priority data are given below.

A request for correction must be made without undue delay after the error was discovered (**G1/12** r.37; **J16/08** r.13; H-VI,2.1).

A **R.139** correction may not breach the principle of procedural legal certainty. A request for correction of a document cannot reverse the effect of a decision already taken on the basis of the uncorrected document (**J3/01**, r.7). The correction of a request in written proceedings filed after a decision based on the uncorrected request has been handed over to the EPO's internal postal service should not be allowed because this would be incompatible with legal procedural certainty (**T824/00**, hn.I; **J3/01** r.10). In oral proceedings, a request for correction should be submitted before the closure of the debate and prior to the pronouncement of the decision (see notes prior to **R.111**).

Similarly, **R.139** cannot be used to re-open a procedural phase already terminated or a time-limit already expired (**J3/01** r.7). In **J27/96** the applicant requested the addition of an erroneously omitted designation of a contracting state after expiry of the grace period for payment of the designation fee, with the aim of re-opening the grace period for payment of the fee. The Board refused the correction. Even if it is accepted that the correction by addition of a designation could have retroactive effect in the sense that the corrected designation is deemed to have been made as from the filing date of the application, that does not mean that applicants can thereby reinstate the procedural phase when designations have to be made and fees have to be paid with the consequence that the procedural opportunities associated with that phase become available to them again. Correction of a mistake is an isolated procedural measure and does not allow the re-establishment of a defined procedural phase as a whole. **J21/84**, r.9 decided similarly.

2.2 TYPE OF DOCUMENT

R.139 restricts correction to documents filed with the EPO. This includes documents filed in appeal (**G1/12** r.35). A failed payment cannot be corrected using **R.139**, because a failure to pay is not an error in a document (**T152/85** r.2). This applies to payments by bank transfer and by credit card (A-X,7.1.1).

However, a validly filed debit order (**Rfees5(2):2**) can be corrected, provided the principles of **G1/12** are followed. As an example, in case the debit order lacks the indication of the method of payment, but a letter accompanying it states that the payment is made from a deposit account and its number is given, correction is allowed (**T317/19**). In **T1000/19**, correction was even allowed without the number of the deposit account. If the fee code is correct but the amount is not, the EPO should correct the amount of its own motion (A-X,4.2.3). In **T1146/20**, correction of electronically filed form 1038E (letter accompanying subsequently filed items) was allowed in order to introduce instructions for debiting the opposition fee from a deposit account. These instructions had originally been given in the notice of opposition itself rather than in electronically processable xml format. In **T1678/21** the board also allowed the correction of a Form 1038 in which the applicant had mistakenly indicated that a reduced appeal fee should be paid rather than the full amount. Since there were sufficient funds in the applicant's deposit account when the form was filed, the full fee was deemed to have been paid retroactively on the basis of the correction.

The first sentence of **R.139** contains conditions applying to the correction of errors in any document. The second sentence of **R.139** contains an additional condition applying to the correction of errors in the description, claims and drawings, namely that the correction must be obvious (see below for an extensive discussion). The provisions for the application itself (**R.139**, second sentence) are stricter than for other documents because of the prohibition of extension of subject-matter under **Art.123(2)**. It is clear from the language of **R.139** that the correction of errors in documents other than the description, claims and drawings need not be obvious in the sense defined in the second sentence of **R.139** (**J8/80**, r.3).

2.3 NATURE OF ERROR

According to **R.139**, the correction of errors falling in three different categories is possible: linguistic errors, errors of transcription and mistakes. A linguistic error is an error in the language, e.g. a missing article before a noun, transposed words, a garbled sentence (**T565/97; T658/94; T609/95**). An error of transcription is a typing error, e.g. an erroneous application number, incorrect priority data, transposed digits in a parameter value, an omitted feature in a claim retyped for a request (**J3/91; J2/92; T712/91**). A mistake may be said to exist in a document if the document does not express the true intention of the person on whose behalf it was filed. No mistake exists where the document did express the true intention and a change of mind gave rise to the request for correction.

The mistake may be an incorrect statement or an omission (**J8/80**, r.4), e.g. a missing designation, an omitted priority claim, an erroneous withdrawal of the designation of a contracting state or of a patent application, the naming of the wrong applicant in the Request for Grant form, an erroneous request in opposition proceedings, giving an incorrect name for a compound, specifying the wrong value for a parameter or an incorrect reference in the description (**J21/92, J8/01, J11/89, J10/87, J4/97, J18/93, T824/00, T955/92, T581/91, T417/87**). The definitions of 'error of transcription' and 'mistake' overlap where they relate to incorrect statements.

3 Corrections under R.139, first sentence

Correction of errors in documents other than the description, claims and drawings is briefly called 'correction under **R.139**, first sentence', even though the first sentence applies equally to correction of the description, claims and drawings. An allowed correction restores the document to the form originally intended by the party and has retroactive effect (**T219/86** r.5).

Case law relating to the correction of the designation of states and priority declarations has established general principles for correction under **R.139**, first sentence, as summarised in **J6/91** r.2 and endorsed by **G1/12**, which should be applied in addition to the conditions set out in **R.139:2** above:

- The correction under **R.139** may not be used to implement a change of mind or subsequent development of plans. To avoid such abuse the EPO checks if a mistake was made, what the mistake was, and what the correction should be (**J8/80**). A mistake made as a result of confusing the instructions of different clients is in principle correctable (**J8/80** r.8). However, correction of a declaration filed by a representative without consulting the client is not allowable if the declaration corresponds to the representative's intention at the time; the client has a duty to inform the representative in time of any change of mind or development of plans and the representative has a duty to consult the client before taking action (**T309/03** r.2.4).
- If the correction is not self-evident, the burden of proof is a heavy one, and lies on the party. A mere statement of the intention to proceed in a certain manner, unsupported by evidence, is almost certain to be insufficient. There should be no reasonable doubt concerning the true intention of the person on whose behalf the error was made. (**J8/80**)
- When the error concerns items third persons might expect to be able to take at face value, so that their rights would be jeopardised by the correction (e.g. of the priority claim), the correction must be made promptly and in time for inclusion in the publication of the application, or at least in time for a warning to be included in the publication (A-V,3; **J21/84**), excepting special circumstances.

The same general rules apply to Euro-PCT applications. In the international phase only obvious errors may be corrected, regardless of whether they are in the description, claims and drawings or elsewhere (R.91.1(a) PCT, GL/PCT-EPO H-IV,2). Normally such a correction must be authorised by an international authority; in the case of errors in the Request form (R.4 PCT), the rectification is authorised by the receiving Office (R.91.1(e)(i) PCT). A refused request for rectification may be published together with the application (see GL/PCT-EPO H-IV,2.2). In order to take advantage of the more lenient EPO approach to correction of the request, not accepted by an international authority, the request for correction must be made again before the EPO as designated Office (after entry into the regional phase). Since the publication of the PCT application takes the place of the European publication (Art.29 PCT, **Art.93** and **Art.153**(3) EPC), the warning has been duly published. When a correction is requested for the first time in the regional phase before the EPO, it is not possible any more to include a warning in the publication of the patent application, which publication has already taken place in the international phase. (**J6/91** r.2.4)

Most corrections under **R.139**, first sentence relate to data in the Request for Grant form. The rule provides a possibility for applicants to correct any errors of their own volition. When the EPO notes any errors in the form, it will invite applicants to correct them under **Art.90**(4). In that case, correction is compulsory, but applicants need not provide proof that a mistake was made, what the mistake was, and what the correction should be; they only need to show that the correction does not implement a change of mind.

3.1 CORRECTION AND ADDING OF PRIORITY DECLARATION

Correction under **R.139**, first sentence, of errors associated with priority claims may be allowable. However, under lex specialis **R.52(2)** an applicant may add a priority claim and under **R.52(3)** correct an existing priority claim without the restrictions of **R.139**. This option is available until the expiry of the sixteen- / four-month period defined in **R.52(2)** and **(3)**. Correction after this period is governed by **R.139** (A-V,3), and different conditions exist for correction before and after publication of the application.

The conditions developed in case law for correction of priority data under **R.139** are summarised in **J6/91** r.3. A correction must meet all conditions listed in **R.139:2** and **R.139:3** above: the EPO must be satisfied that an error was made, the applicant must be able to prove what the error was and what the correction should be, and the request must be filed promptly and, except in exceptional circumstances, sufficiently early for a warning to be included in the publication of the application.

Correction of a priority declaration without a warning in the publication has, exceptionally, been allowed where one or both of the following additional special circumstances existed:

1 the EPO was partly responsible for the fact that no warning was published (**J11/89**);
2 the interest of the public was not seriously affected, for example the mistake was obvious on the face of the published application, or the public was otherwise informed about the full scope of protection sought by the applicant. (**J6/91** r.3)

3.1.1 Correction of omitted priority claim

An omitted first and only priority claim can be corrected under **R.139** in those cases where the conditions listed in **R.139:3.1** above have been fulfilled, and the application can still be published eighteen months after the corrected priority date. (**J3/82**)

The omission of a priority declaration will, in nearly every case, be an error, and, in general, the applicant need not provide special evidence such as affidavits to prove that a mistake has been made and that the request for correction was not due to a change of mind (**J9/91** r.5).

The correction of a missing priority claim without a warning in the published application has exceptionally been allowed where the mistake was apparent on the face of the published application, e.g. if a third party would be expected to inspect the file to obtain the correct information (A-III,6.5.2). For examples of apparent discrepancies see **J6/91** r.5.5, **J3/91** r.4.3, **J2/92** r.5.2.2 and **J11/92**.

The addition of a priority under **R.139** where an earlier priority has already been claimed is allowed, provided that the request is made sufficiently early for a warning to be included in the publication of the application (**J4/82**). In **J7/94** the addition of a second priority of later date without warning in the publication of the application was refused, because the addition was relevant for the evaluation of the state of the art (**J14/82** and **J11/89** not followed). Note that addition of a priority claim within sixteen months from the earliest priority date is not governed by **R.139** but by **R.52(2)**.

Since **R.139** has no express provisions protecting third parties comparable to the provisions of **Art.122(5)**, the solution of any problem regarding third party rights must be left to the national courts applying **Art.122(5)** mutatis mutandis (**J12/80** and **J10/87**).

3.1.2 *Correction of date, state and file number in priority declaration*

An error in the indication of the date and/or state of the previous filing in the Request for Grant form may be corrected under **R.139** in those cases where the conditions listed in **R.139:3.1** above have been fulfilled (**J14/82**, **J3/91** r.3; A-III,6.5.3).

An erroneous file number for a priority document may be corrected without the restrictions listed in **R.139:3.1** above (**J3/91** r.5). An applicant who has provided no file number will be invited by the EPO to provide it under **R.59**. (A-III,6.5.3)

3.2 CORRECTION OF WITHDRAWAL OF A PATENT APPLICATION

A retraction of the withdrawal of an application as a whole may be allowable under **R.139** if, according to **J5/19**:

- the withdrawal did not reflect the true intention of the applicant;
- there was no undue delay in seeking correction; and
- third parties who might have taken note of the withdrawal by inspection of the file would have had reason to suspect that the withdrawal was erroneous.

The board in this case decided that a further criterion proposed in previous cases (that the error was an excusable oversight) no longer applied in view of **G1/12** and the lack of textual basis for this requirement.

Publication of the withdrawal in the Register (**J4/97** r.6; **J25/03** r.9) and in the Bulletin (**J15/86** hn.III) both amount to officially notifying the public, preventing retraction of the withdrawal. A withdrawal that is only apparent from an inspection of the file is treated differently from a withdrawal that has been officially published (see the last item of the above list), because legal certainty for third parties is of greater importance after official publication by the EPO (**J10/87** r.10).

3.3 CORRECTION OF OTHER ERRORS UNDER R.139, FIRST SENTENCE

A request for retraction of the withdrawal of the designation of a contracting state may be allowable if the withdrawal has not yet been officially published, the error is excusable, the correction does not cause too much delay in the procedure and third persons are sufficiently protected (**J10/87**).

The EPC contains special rules for the correction of errors in a translation of a patent application in **Art.14(2)** and for correction of the designation of an inventor in **R.21**.

An error in the indication of the applicant is correctable (**J7/80**). A correction substituting the name of the applicant is allowable under **R.139**, first sentence, provided there is sufficient evidence to support the request for correction (**J18/93** hn).

The identity of an opponent or appellant may be corrected under **R.139**, first sentence, provided the requirements listed in **R.139:3** above have been complied with. The correction has a retrospective effect, and the correct identity will be regarded as provided within the 9-month opposition period or the 2-month appeal period (**G1/12** r.37). See also **R.77(1):1.3** and **R.101(2):1**.

The correction of errors in the designation of the inventor is dealt with in **R.57:7**.

R.140 governs the correction of errors in decisions.

4 **Correction under R.139, second sentence**

The second sentence of **R.139** governs the correction of an error in a description, claims or drawings, i.e. the parts of the application or patent relating to the disclosure. Such a correction must comply with the requirements of **R.139**, both the first sentence and the second sentence. The first sentence restricts the type of errors that can be corrected (see **R.139:2.3** above) and demands that a request be filed. The second sentence requires that the correction must be obvious in the sense that it is immediately evident that nothing else would have been intended than what is offered as the correction.

The error in the application or patent must be obvious such that a skilled person is in no doubt that this information is incorrect. If it is doubtful whether any information at all is incorrect, then a correction is ruled out. The same applies if incorrect information only becomes apparent in the light of the proposed correction. (**G3/89 r.5**)

The correction of the error must be obvious in that it is immediately evident for a skilled person that nothing else would have been intended than what is offered as the correction. The whole disclosure must allow a skilled person – using the common general knowledge on the date of filing – directly and unequivocally to ascertain the precise content of the information the person making the request for correction actually meant to give, instead of the incorrect particulars, on the date of filing or when making an amendment under **Art.123**. If there is any doubt that nothing else would have been intended than what is offered as the correction, a correction cannot be made. (**G3/89 r.6**)

The above content of the information must be derived from the application as originally filed and any document which reflects the common general knowledge on the date of filing. The prohibition on extending subject matter under **Art.123(2)** means that other documents, such as the abstract or a priority document, may not be used to justify a correction, even if they were filed together with the patent application. (**G3/89 r.7**)

The application as originally filed includes any late-filed missing parts of the description and missing drawings filed according to **R.56**, and any correction of an erroneously filed part under **R.56a**, regardless of whether this resulted in a change of the date of filing. However, claims filed after the date of filing in response to an invitation under **R.58** cannot be used in assessing the allowability of a request for correction. (A-V,3)

Where the application is filed in electronic form and the application documents are attached on the filing date in the original data format in an admissible manner (OJ 2024 A88 Art.9), the latter documents may also be used to determine the allowability of the request for correction (A-V,3).

The corrected information merely expresses what a skilled person would already derive from the application and, therefore, does not change the contents as filed. Thus, the correction cannot be said to have a retroactive effect. Since such a correction is of a declaratory nature only, it does not contravene **Art.123(2)**. (**G3/89 r.4**)

In opposition proceedings, if an amendment occasioned by a ground of opposition is filed, it is then also possible to correct obvious errors under **R.139**, second sentence (H-VI,2.1.1.1; **R.80:2**).

Applicants may not replace under **R.139** the complete documents forming a patent application, that is the description, claims and drawings, by other documents they had intended to file with the request for grant. Such a replacement constitutes an extension of subject matter, violating **Art.123(2)** to which **R.139** is bound. A part of the application may only be replaced under **R.56a**. (**G2/95**) A part of the application may be replaced under **R.56a** since 2022.

A missing drawing or a missing part of the description cannot be added under **R.139** (**G2/95**) but may be added under **R.56**. On the other hand, an obvious error in a drawing or a part of the description may be corrected under **R.139**.

More examples of errors are given in **R.139:2.3** above and in H-VI,2.1.

R. 140 Correction of errors in decisions

In decisions of the European Patent Office, only linguistic errors, errors of transcription and obvious mistakes may be corrected.

Implementation of **Art.123(1)** and **Art.97(1)**

1 **Procedure for correction**

The purpose of **R.140** is to correct an obvious clerical mistake in a decision that does not express the manifest intention of the deciding body (**G8/95** r.3.2). The EPO makes the correction in the form of a decision, either of its own motion or in response to a reasoned request (H-VI,5; see e.g. **T150/89**). Such a request can be filed at any time, because **R.140** does not specify a time limit (**G1/10** r.15).

The body which is competent to make the correction is the body which has taken the decision. Hence, the examining division is competent to decide on a request to correct errors in the decision to grant. (**G8/95** r.3.4)

A decision refusing a request for correction is appealable (see e.g. **T850/95** and **T1093/05** which both concern requests to correct the text of a granted patent (see **R.140:3.1**)). In **T255/22**, however, the board found that it had no competence to correct or amend under **R.140** the reasons given by a first instance department in its decision, the opposition division having refused a request to correct its decision.

The person requesting correction must be given a chance to comment on the reasons for refusing the request before a decision is taken in order to comply with **Art.113(1)** (H-VI,3.1).

The correction of a decision under **R.140** has retrospective effect; as a result, the decision does not need to be cancelled and reissued. In any case, a body cannot generally cancel a decision it has issued. Instead, the relevant body issues a further decision allowing or refusing the correction. (**T212/88** r.1) Note that periods connected with the taking of a decision, such as the time limits for filing an opposition or an appeal, are not recalculated when the decision is corrected (H-VI,3).

2 **Errors in decisions**

According to **R.140**, only linguistic errors, errors of transcription and obvious mistakes in a decision may be corrected. In order to ensure legal certainty for third parties the error must be obvious, i.e. it must be clear not only that the deciding body did not intend to decide a matter in the form expressed by the decision, but also in what form it did intend to decide. The correct intention can usually be derived from the file of the case. (**T1093/05** r.7)

It should be noted that the correction of a decision under **R.140** is a remedy directed only against the form in which the decision is expressed, whereas an appeal against a decision under **Art.106** is directed against the substance of the decision (**T1093/05** r.10). An legal error associated with a substantive or procedural aspect of the decision cannot be corrected under **R.140** (**G1/97** r.2(c)). If the decision to be corrected has been taken by a first instance department of the EPO, a correction of this kind can be requested by filing an appeal according to **Art.106**, in so far as the decision adversely affects the appellant (**Art.107**). If the decision has been taken by a board of appeal then a procedural deficiency may be correctable by the filing of a petition for review according to **Art.112a.**

The correction may relate to allegedly incorrect reasoning in a decision, both at first and second instance (see e.g. **T867/96**) or to a mistake in signing the decision (**T212/88** r.1). The correction may also concern a priority claim which the EPO has erroneously omitted from the granted patent (e.g. case EP1800984).

In **T965/98** the board allowed a correction under **R.139** of an obvious error in claims submitted during oral proceedings, the request for correction being filed during the preparation of the written reasons. The decision of the board given during the oral proceedings was amended under **R.140** to take into account the correction.

3 Errors relating to grant

The published specification of a patent is normally the first complete expression of the decision to grant the proprietor receives. The decision itself merely consist of an electronically generated form which refers to the documents indicated in the communication pursuant to **R.71(3)**, stating that a patent is granted based on those documents (**T1093/05** r.2). The published specification allows the proprietor to verify whether the specification actually corresponds to the text of the application in the **R.71(3)** communication which was approved.

The text of the specification may diverge in two ways from what was intended: the decision to grant may be incorrect and refer to the wrong documents or the decision to grant may be correct but the published specification may not be consistent with the decision.

Correction of bibliographic data is possible, irrespective of the origin of the error; requests for such correction are dealt with by a formalities officer. For example, a spelling mistake in the name of the proprietor can be corrected, provided it does not cause the identity of the proprietor to be different from the applicant to whom the patent was intended to be granted. (H-VI,3.2)

3.1 CORRECTION OF THE GRANTED PATENT

Art.98 attaches no legal significance to the publication of the specification and the text of the published specification therefore has no binding character.

The description, claims and drawings of a European patent cannot be corrected using **R.140** (**G1/10** r.3, 5). A request to this effect is inadmissible (**G1/10** hn.1). This applies after grant of the patent, in opposition proceedings and in limitation proceedings (**G1/10** r.13). This prohibition ensures legal certainty for third parties and avoids other adverse effects, such as a delay in opposition proceedings, a change in the scope of a patent in opposition proceedings in the absence of any remedy for an opponent or a change in the scope of a patent after nine months from grant without an adversely affected party having the option of filing an opposition (**G1/10** r.7). (H-VI,3)

Applicants have an ample opportunity during grant proceedings to correct mistakes in documents they have filed, including the opportunity to correct misspelled or incorrect words under **R.139** and the opportunity to request amendment under **R.71(6)** in the final stages of examination. Applicants alone are therefore responsible for any errors remaining in the patent after a decision to grant has been taken, even if the error was introduced by the examining division. **R.140** cannot be used to tidy up the patent after grant. (**G1/10** r.9-11).

If the text specified in the decision to grant does not correspond to the text approved by the applicant, e.g. because the examining division has changed a claim after approval or disregarded amendments filed by the proprietor without allowing an opportunity to comment, a violation of **Art.113(2)** has occurred which can be remedied by filing an appeal. If the examining division considers the appeal to be allowable, it will carry out interlocutory revision and it may reimburse the appeal fee. (**G1/10** r.12; see also **G8/95** r.3.1; **T1093/05** r.10-12)

An obvious mistake in a patent will not adversely affect opponents or others, because they should read the patent as if corrected and an actual correction should not be necessary (**G1/10** r.8).

A proprietor also has the opportunity to correct any perceived error in the patent as an amendment under **Art.123** during opposition or limitation proceedings or as a secondary issue when such an amendment has been made (**G1/10** r.13). The correction of an error in the description, claims, or drawings is admissible in opposition proceedings under **R.139** if the correction is part of an amendment going beyond the mere removal of an error, namely part of an amendment complying with **R.80**, or is in addition to such an amendment, and is admissible in limitation proceedings if it is part of an amendment constituting a limitation in the sense of **R.95(2)**, or is in addition to such an amendment (H-VI,2.1.1.1; **T1111/19**).

Formatting and editing errors that have occurred during the preparation of the text intended for grant but are neither marked in said text nor indicated in the communication under **R.71(3)** (e.g. the unacknowledged deletion of text) may always be corrected by the EPO of its own motion or at the request of the patent proprietor, even after grant. Such correction does not influence the start of the opposition period. No correction is allowed after grant if an amendment listed in the communication under **R.71(3)** is in fact not present in the text intended for grant. (H-VI,4)

Note that **R.140** explicitly allows the correction of obvious mistakes in decisions and, hence, in the patent, because, as confirmed by **G1/10** r.3, the text of the patent is an integral part of the decision. By prohibiting correction of a patent using **R.140**, **G1/10** appears to prohibit what the legislator intended to permit.

G1/10 is limited to correction of the description, claims and drawings of a patent and does not relate to the correction of other matter, e.g. the bibliographic data referred to in **R.71(3)** (**G1/10** r.3; H-VI,3.2). A request for the correction of such matter under **R.140** during opposition proceedings is referred to the examining division (H-VI,3.3).

In exceptional cases it may be possible to correct a patent after grant by appealing the decision to grant within two months of notification of the date of the decision. If the documents intended for grant in the **R.71(3)** communication contain a significant amendment, e.g. missing drawings, that does not correspond to any request of the applicant nor to any amendment explicitly suggested by the examining division, the documents do not reflect the intention of either the applicant or the examining division. In such a case it may be considered that the applicant has not approved the granted text and is adversely affected by the decision to grant. **G1/10** r.12 specifically mentions such an appeal. (**T1003/19** hn.2, r.4)

3.2 CORRECTION OF THE PUBLISHED SPECIFICATION

If the decision to grant is correct but the published specification diverges from the decision, the applicant has been granted what was requested; however, an error has occurred in the preparation of the published specification.

Since **Art.98** attaches no legal significance to the publication of the specification, the text of the specification has no binding character and merely serves to make available to the public information concerning the patent. Mistakes in the published specification of the patent deviating from the decision to grant therefore have no effect on the content of the patent granted. Only the text the decision to grant refers to is relevant (**Art.97(1)** and **R.71a(1)**). This text, i.e. the description, claims and drawings, is in the language of the proceedings (**Art.70(1)**). (C-V,10; **J14/87** hn1)

If the published specification diverges from the granted text (see **R.71a(1)**), it may be corrected at any time. Since the specification should be consistent with the decision to grant, the EPO must correct any publication errors on request or of its own motion (**T150/89**). An example of such an error is where parts of the specification, e.g. one or more claims, have disappeared. See EP 0 326 761 B1 for an example of a patent having an incorrect set of claims. If necessary, the EPO republishes the patent specification. (C-V,10; H-VI,6)

3.3 CORRECTION OF TRANSLATION OF CLAIMS

Since the text of the patent in the language of proceedings is the authentic text (**Art.70(1)**), the translations of the claims are for information only and do not form part of the decision to grant. They cannot therefore be corrected under **R.140** (H-VI,5). Correction under **R.139** can only be requested during pending proceedings (**J42/92**). If a corrected version of a translation of the claims is received early enough, the EPO will use the corrected version instead of the original version in the published specification (H-VI,5).

An error in the claim translations has no legal effect. However, the proprietor should check the translations of the specification filed with the national offices of the designated contracting states under **Art.65(1)** for similar errors in view of the effect of **Art.70(3)**.

Amendment of the claim translations filed at the EPO is only possible when the patent is maintained in amended form in opposition proceedings (**R.82(2)**) or amended in limitation proceedings (**R.95(3)**). (H-VI,5)

Chapter VII *Information on prior art*

R. 141 Information on prior art

Amended, in force since 01.01.2011 (OJ 2009 p.585).
Implementation of **Art.124(1)**

R. 141(1) An applicant claiming priority within the meaning of Article 87 shall file a copy of the results of any search carried out by the authority with which the previous application was filed together with the European patent application, in the case of a Euro-PCT application on entry into the European phase, or without delay after such results have been made available to them.

Art.87 Priority right
Amended by decision of the Administrative Council of 10.12.2024, which entered into force on 01.04.2025 (OJ 2025 A16). The amendment made the text gender-neutral.

1 **Prior art information of priority application**
Any applicant claiming the priority of an earlier application must file a copy of any search results relating to the priority application and prepared by or for the patent office with which the priority application was filed (**R.141(1)**). Where multiple priorities are claimed, the obligation applies to all of the priority applications. The priority application may be an application for a patent, a utility model or a utility certificate, as allowed by **Art.87**. If the priority of an international application is claimed, the international search report must be filed.

The document filed must be a copy of an official document issued by the patent office. A translation of a document not drawn up in an EPO language is not required. Copies of documents cited in the search results need not be provided. (Not. EPO OJ 2010 p.410 §2.1)

The submission of such search results does not entitle the applicant to a reduction of the search fee, unless the conditions of **Rfees9** apply. If the applicant wants the EPO search report to be drawn up independently, uninfluenced by search results drawn up for a priority application, the applicant should file those search results after the completion of the EPO search in response to a **R.70b** invitation. Where **R.141(2)** applies, and it is desired that the EPO search be drawn up independently, the applicant should file two priority applications, one to be searched and the other (which will not be searched) only for claiming priority from.

2 **Procedure**
The copy of any search results available should, in principle, be filed together with a direct European application (A-III,6.12) or on entry into the regional phase with a Euro-PCT application (E-IX,2.3.5.2). If not available at the date of filing or the date of regional phase entry, applicants should supply the copy immediately after they have received the search results (**R.141(1)**). The EPO prefers to receive any search results before drawing up the European search report, although a more independent search can be expected if the search results are submitted later. The obligation to submit search results exists as long as the application is pending.

The applicant need not submit search results that are already available to the EPO; in that case the EPO will include a copy in the file (**R.141(2)**).

When the EPO notes at the start of the substantive examination that search results have not been filed and that the search results are not deemed to be filed under **R.141(2)**, it will send the applicant an invitation under **R.70b** to file them within a two-month period or else to confirm that they are not available. Search results may not yet have been sent to the applicant or else the priority application may not be subject to any search at all.

If the applicant states in response to the **R.70b** invitation that the search results are not yet available, the EPO may invite the applicant to file them again under **R.141(3)** at a later stage in the proceedings.

The EPO automatically issues a **R.70b** invitation for a divisional application that claims priority if neither search results nor a statement concerning their non-availability is provided on filing the divisional. If all relevant search results have already been filed for the parent, the applicant need not respond (as expressly indicated on the invitation). However, if the applicant has filed a statement of non-availability for the parent, a new statement of non-availability or a copy of the search results must be filed for the divisional. (OJ 2010 p.410 §3.2)

If the applicant does not respond to an invitation in time, the application will be deemed withdrawn under **R.70b(2)** or **Art.124(2)**. Further processing is available as a remedy.

R. 141(2) The copy referred to in paragraph 1 shall be deemed to be duly filed if it is available to the European Patent Office and to be included in the file of the European patent application under the conditions determined by the President of the European Patent Office.

1 **Prior art information available to EPO**

The applicant need not file a copy of the results of any search if a copy is available to the EPO since in this case a copy will be automatically included in the application file (**R.141(2)**; OJ 2010 p.410 §2.2; OJ 2013 p.217, A-III,6.12).

The EPO will include a copy of the search report drawn up in respect of a priority application if it has drawn up the search report itself. The search report may be a European search report, an international (type) search report or a search report drawn up by the EPO on behalf of a national office on a national application. (Dec. Pres. OJ 2010 p.600)

The EPO will also include a copy of the search results drawn up in respect of a priority application if that application was filed in AT, CH, CN, CZ, DK, ES, GB, JP, KR, SE or US (OJ 2022 A80).

Likewise, the EPO includes a copy of the search results drawn up in respect of a priority application in the file of a divisional application if the results have already been included in the file of the parent application (OJ 2010 p.410).

R. 141(3) Without prejudice to paragraphs 1 and 2, the European Patent Office may invite the applicant to provide, within a period of two months, information on prior art within the meaning of Article 124, paragraph 1.

1 **Other prior art information**

R.141(3), referring to **Art.124(1)**, allows the EPO to ask the applicant to provide information on prior art taken into consideration in national or regional proceedings concerning an invention to which the European patent application relates. This pertains in particular to applications whose priority is not being claimed. (C-III,6)

An invitation under **R.141(3)** is only issued during substantive examination and only in individual cases. An invitation under **R.141(3)** may be issued whether or not the provision of prior art under **R.141(1)** and (2) **in relation to a priority application is required.** The EPO may use such an invitation under **R.141(3)** to also request the provision of search results required under **R.141(1)** if they have not been provided in response to a **R.70b** invitation. (OJ 2010 p.410 §2.3)

The sanction for not responding to the invitation is provided in **Art.124(2).**

Chapter VIII *Interruption of proceedings*

R. 142 Interruption of proceedings

Implementation of **Art.120**

1 **General**

The EPO will interrupt proceedings in the three specific cases set out in R.142(1). An interruption provides a remedy for failed time limits due to medical and financial hardship of the applicant and proprietor (**R.142(1)(a)** and (**b**)) and of their professional representative (**c**). Note that the remedy does not apply to opponents or their representatives. See **R.84(2)** for the death or legal incapacity of an opponent.

Interruption is typically declared retroactively. In such a case, any non-observance of time limits during the retroactively declared interruption period is to be regarded as not having occurred. Thereby **R.142** provides for a remedy, next to **Art.121** and **122**. An interruption interrupts all periods, which start anew or continue to run after the resumption of the proceedings. Moreover, decisions taken during the period of interruption are void (**T1389/18** hn.2). Neither the EPO nor the parties can perform legal acts in the case during the interruption (**J10/19** r.8).

In principle, the EPO applies **R.142** ex officio, either because it learns of the relevant facts ex officio or because it is informed of these facts by a party to the proceedings or by a third party. However, in the case of **R.142(1)(a)**, last sentence, proceedings are interrupted on request only (E-VII,1.1). A party may request interruption on any of the grounds of **R.142**; a rejection of the request by the Legal Division can be appealed (**J7/20**). A board of appeal cannot set aside a declaration of interruption by the Legal Division with retroactive effect, not even if it was declared erroneously (**J9/21**).

The interruption has (retroactive) legal effect from the date of the occurrence of the event. However, if the proceedings are interrupted on request under **R.142(1)(a)**, last sentence, the interruption is effective from the date of receipt of the request. Communications and decisions of the EPO notified during the interruption are considered null and void and will be notified anew after the resumption of the proceedings. (E-VII,1.3, 1.4)

As an example, proceedings were interrupted retroactively in **T1389/18**, with the consequence that oral proceedings, held in the meantime, and the decision given during those oral proceedings, were retroactively non-existent. In another example, in EP 3 535 150, the period for requesting further processing of the acts to enter the European regional phase of a PCT application was retroactively interrupted.

The Legal Division is responsible for matters relating to the interruption and resumption of proceedings during first instance proceedings (**Art.20**; Dec. Pres. OJ 2013 p.600). A board of appeal does not have to await a decision on interruption by the Legal Division and may decide whether the circumstances of an interruption exist (**T854/12** r.1.2; **T54/17** r.1.4).

Annually, the proceedings of about 300 cases are interrupted.

R.142 is considered to be an implementation of **Art.125** on historical grounds (travaux préparatoires to Rule 90 EPC1973) but can also be seen as pertaining to **Art.120** (Münchner Gemeinschaftskommentar Art. 120, Rdn. 163)

R. 142(1) Proceedings before the European Patent Office shall be interrupted:

(a) in the event of the death or legal incapacity of the applicant for or proprietor of a European patent or of the person authorised by national law to act on their behalf. To the extent that the above events do not affect the authorisation of a representative appointed under Article 134, proceedings shall be interrupted only on application by such representative;

(b) in the event of the applicant for or proprietor of a patent, as a result of some action taken against their property, being prevented by legal reasons from continuing the proceedings;

(c) in the event of the death or legal incapacity of the representative of an applicant for or proprietor of a patent, or of their being prevented for legal reasons resulting from action taken against their property from continuing the proceedings.

Amended by decision of the Administrative Council of 10.12.2024, which entered into force on 01.04.2025 (OJ 2025 A16). The amendment was introduction of gender-neutral language.
Art.134 Representation before the European Patent Office

1 **Death or legal incapacity of applicant or proprietor (R.142(1)(a))**
The legal incapacity of applicants or proprietors to carry out legal transactions relating to their application or patent must be determined according to national law since their interest in the application or patent is an interest in property (cf. **Art.74** and 2(2)) (**J900/85** r.9). Legal incapacity may be recognised under national law, e.g. in case of severe mental illness (**J900/85** r.7).

R.142(1)(a) applies to applicants, proprietors and persons authorised to represent them by national law (e.g. a trustee or director). In the latter case, the applicant or proprietor can also be a company.

In general, the proceedings will be interrupted automatically and retroactively from the first day of the incapacity.

However, the proceedings are interrupted only on request if the unfortunate applicant or proprietor is represented and the authorisation of the professional representative is not affected by the events (**R.142(1)(a)**, second sentence). For example, the death of a party does not terminate an authorisation unless provided to the contrary (**R.152(9)**). In such circumstances, the representative must apply for interruption of the proceedings if an interruption is desired. The interruption will be effective from the date of receipt of the request.

2 **Action against property of applicant or proprietor (R.142(1)b))**
Bankruptcy is an example of an action taken against property, see e.g. **J7/83** and **J26/95**. Whether an action taken against the property of the applicant or proprietor qualifies for interruption of proceedings at the EPO depends on the national law. The decisive criterion for interruption is whether the action against the property is such as to make it legally impossible for the applicant or proprietor to continue the proceedings (**J26/95**).

3 **Death, legal incapacity, or bankruptcy of representative (R.142(1)(c))**
R.142(1)(c) deals with death, legal incapacity, bankruptcy, or other action taken against the property of the representative of the applicant or proprietor. For the actions taken against the property of the representative, the same conditions apply as for the applicant or proprietor; see **R.142(1):2**.

The test for the legal incapacity of representatives laid down by the EPO is: was the representative concerned in a fit mental state to do the work required of them at the material time, or did they lack the capacity to make rational decisions and to take necessary actions? (**J900/85** r.11)

The EPO must ex officio apply the interruption once it is clear that a situation under **R.142(1)(c)** exists. The EPO must establish when the representative was legally incapacitated and specify the time limits which are interrupted. (**J902/87** r.2.6)

R. 142(2) When, in the cases referred to in paragraph 1(a) or (b), the European Patent Office has been informed of the identity of the person authorised to continue the proceedings, it shall notify such person and, where applicable, any third party, that the proceedings will be resumed as from a specified date. If, three years after the publication of the date of interruption in the European Patent Bulletin, the European Patent Office has not been informed of the identity of the person authorised to continue the proceedings, it may set a date on which it intends to resume the proceedings of its own motion.

Amended, in force since 01.07.2020 (OJ 2020 A36).

1 **Resumption of proceedings**

Once the EPO has been informed that the original party or a new party is able to continue the proceedings, a date for resumption is set, and the party or parties are informed accordingly (**R.142(2)**, first sentence). Proceedings can only be resumed with ex nunc effect (**J10/19**); hence a future date is set for the resumption.

If the EPO does not receive the information within three years from the publication of the interruption, it may set a date for resumption (**R.142(2)**, second sentence). This prevents cases from being interrupted indefinitely if no such information is provided. Resumption of the proceedings may be postponed upon the filing of a reasoned request with supporting evidence, e.g. if legal proceedings for succession in title are still pending. (OJ 2020 A76)

R. 142(3) In the case referred to in paragraph 1(c), the proceedings shall be resumed when the European Patent Office has been informed of the appointment of a new representative of the applicant or when the Office has informed the other parties of the appointment of a new representative of the proprietor of the patent. If, three months after the beginning of the interruption of the proceedings, the European Patent Office has not been informed of the appointment of a new representative, it shall communicate to the applicant for or proprietor of the patent:

(a) where Article 133, paragraph 2, is applicable, that the European patent application will be deemed to be withdrawn or the European patent will be revoked if the information is not submitted within two months of this communication; or

(b) otherwise, that the proceedings will be resumed with the applicant for or proprietor of the patent as from the notification of this communication.

Art.133(2) Compulsory representation of non-EPC-state party

R. 142(4) Any periods, other than those for requesting examination and paying renewal fees, in force at the date of interruption of the proceedings, shall begin again as from the day on which the proceedings are resumed. If such date is less than two months before the end of the period within which the request for examination must be filed, such a request may be filed within two months of such date.

1 **Interruption of periods**

The purpose of **R.142(4)** is to specify how periods are to be calculated when the proceedings resume (J7/83 r.10). From the text of **R.142(1)**: 'proceedings ... shall be interrupted' it follows that all periods are interrupted (J7/83 r.8). On resumption of the proceedings, most periods begin to run again for their original duration.

As an exception, the period for filing the request for examination (including payment of the examination fee) and the period for paying the renewal fees (**R.142(4)**, first sentence) are suspended (E-VII,1.5; E-VIII,1.4). On resumption of the proceedings, these periods are resumed for the non-elapsed portion, with a minimum of two months for the period for requesting examination as prescribed by **R.142(4)**, second sentence (J7/83 hn).

The due date for paying renewal fees (**Art.86(1)**) is not a period in the normal sense. The EPC does not prescribe a period for payment of the renewal fee but simply states a date on which it must have been paid. Therefore, if the renewal fee falls due during the period of the interruption, **R.142(4)** must be interpreted as deferring the due date until the date the proceedings are resumed. In that case, the renewal fee can still validly be paid up to the day of the resumption, or within the following six months on payment of the additional fee (J902/87 hn.3; r.3.12, E-VII,1.5). For safety's sake, the fee should preferably be paid some time in advance of the resumption. As is clear from **R.142(4)** and also from **R.14(4)**, the time left for paying the renewal fee will not be extended by two months as it is for the request for examination.

The six-month period for paying the renewal fee with an additional fee (**R.51(2)**) is a period that will be suspended on the day of interruption and begins to run again for the remaining period on the date of resumption; the remaining period will not be extended to a minimum of two months as it is for the request for examination (E-VII,1.5; J902/87, r.3.6).

See **R.14(4):2** for an example of how the periods are calculated in the case of a stay of proceedings.

Chapter IX *Information to the public*

R. 143 Entries in the European Patent Register

Implementation of Art.127

R. 143(1) The European Patent Register shall contain the following entries:

(a) number of the European patent application;
(b) date of filing of the application;
(c) title of the invention;
(d) classification symbols assigned to the application;
(e) the Contracting States designated;
(f) particulars of the applicant for or proprietor of the patent as provided in Rule 41, paragraph 2(c);
(g) family name, given names and country and place of residence of the inventor designated by the applicant for or proprietor of the patent, unless the inventor has waived the right to be mentioned under Rule 20, paragraph 1;
(h) particulars of the representative of the applicant for or proprietor of the patent as provided in Rule 41, paragraph 2(d); in the case of several representatives only the particulars of the representative first named, followed by the words "and others" and, in the case of an association referred to in Rule 152, paragraph 11, only the name and address of the association;
(i) priority data (date, State and file number of the previous application);
(j) in the event of a division of the application, the numbers of all the divisional applications;
(k) in the case of a divisional application or a new application under Article 61, paragraph 1(b), the information referred to in sub-paragraphs (a), (b) and (i) with regard to the earlier application;
(l) date of publication of the application and, where appropriate, date of the separate publication of the European search report;
(m) date of filing of the request for examination;
(n) date on which the application is refused, withdrawn or deemed to be withdrawn;
(o) date of publication of the mention of the grant of the European patent;
(p) date of lapse of the European patent in a Contracting State during the opposition period and, where appropriate, pending a final decision on opposition;
(q) date of filing opposition;
(r) date and purport of the decision on opposition;
(s) dates of stay and resumption of proceedings in the cases referred to in Rules 14 and 78;
(t) dates of interruption and resumption of proceedings in the case referred to in Rule 142;
(u) date of re-establishment of rights where an entry has been made under sub-paragraphs (n) or (r);
(v) the filing of a request for conversion under Article 135, paragraph 3;

(w) rights and transfer of such rights relating to an application or a European patent where these Implementing Regulations provide that they shall be recorded;
(x) date and purport of the decision on the request for limitation or revocation of the European patent;
(y) date and purport of the decision of the Enlarged Board of Appeal on the petition for review.

Amended by decision of the Administrative Council of 10.12.2024, which entered into force on 01.04.2025 (OJ 2025 A16). The amendments made the text gender-neutral.

Amended, in force since 01.11.2021 (OJ 2021 A3, A12). The amendment concerned R.143(1)(g). Amended R.143(1)(g) applies to patent applications published in the European Patent Register on or after that date.

Art.61(1)(b) European patent applications non-entitled
Art.135(3) Further processing
R.14 Stay of proceedings
R.20(1) Publication of the mention of the inventor
R.41(2)(c) Particulars of applicant
R.41(2)(d) Particulars of representative
R.78 Procedure where the proprietor of the patent is not entitled
R.142 Interruption of proceedings
R.152(11) Authorisation of an association

1 **Additional entries in the Register**

The contracting states also communicate the date of lapse of a European patent when a renewal fee is not paid in order to inform the EPO that no further renewal fee payments under **Art.39(1)** need be expected. This data is entered in a special section of the Register under **R.143(1)(p)**, even if no opposition is pending. Some contracting states take a long time to inform the EPO but up-to-date information can be obtained from the national patent offices.

The EPO itself enters the date of lapse of a European patent with unitary effect in the Register if it occurs during the opposition period or while opposition proceedings are in existence (Dec. Pres OJ 2023 sp3 p.1). Such information is always entered in the Register for unitary patent protection (**UPR.16(1)(m)**).

The date of re-establishment of rights is only entered under **R.143(1)(u)** if there has been an actual loss of rights which has been entered in the Register.

Whether an appeal has been lodged can be derived from the file (see **R.145** and **R.146**) and by consulting the Register online, even though this information is not specified under **R.143(2)**.

The Register mentions the payment of renewal fees (important for **R.14(4)**).

2 **Register for unitary patent protection**

Entries in the Register are also made in respect of European patents with unitary effect (see **UPR.15(1):1**).

3 **Inspection of the Register**
Provisions relating to the inspection of the Register are consistent with the provisions in **R.145** (Procedures for the inspection of files) and **R.146** (Communication of information contained in the files). The Register can be freely inspected in one of the following ways (A-XI,4):
- Inspection of the European Patent Register can be carried out free of charge on the EPO website 'https://register.epo.org'.
- A register monitoring tool Register Alert is available on the website, providing e-mail alerts whenever a change occurs in the Register relating to an EP or Euro-PCT application of interest (OJ 2012 p.22 §3). The service is available nearly 24 hours a day, 7 days a week.
- The MyEPO permits users to organise their favourite files in folders and allows secure inspection of their own files prior to publication. (OJ 2006 p.535; 2007 p.142; 2012 p.22 §1)
- Information can be requested by telephone (see **Ante Art.127**).

R. 143(2) The President of the European Patent Office may decide that entries other than those referred to in paragraph 1 shall be made in the European Patent Register.

1 **Additional entries in the Register**
The following additional entries are made in the Register (Dec. Pres. OJ 2014 A86, Dec. Pres. OJ 2023 sp3 p.1):
1 'no opposition filed' after expiry of the opposition period without a notice of opposition having been filed;
2 'patent specification corrected on (date)' in the event of correction of errors;
3 date of despatch of supplementary European Search report;
4 date of despatch of first examination communication;
5 date of receipt of request for re-establishment of rights;
6 refusal of request for re-establishment of rights;
7 opponent's name, address and country of residence or principal place of business;
8 name and business address of the opponent's representative;
9 new documents coming to light after the European search report has been drawn up; this does not include documents introduced in opposition proceedings, for which reference should be made to the file;
10 for international applications for which the EPO acts as designated Office:
(a) the international filing number;
(b) the international publication number;
(c) the international publication date;
11 date of request for limitation or revocation of the European patent;
12 requester's name, address and country of residence or principal place of business;
13 date of petition for review by the Enlarged Board of Appeal;
14 petitioner's name, address and country of residence or principal place of business;
15 file number of the petition for review;
16 date of refusal, withdrawal or deemed withdrawal of divisional application, if this gives rise to the latter's non-publication;
17 date of despatch of examining division's first communication in the sense of **R.36(1)** as valid until 01.04.2014, where this communication was issued before 01.04.2014;
18 date of despatch examining division's communication with search results under **R.164(2)** annexed;

19 date of lapse of the European patent with unitary effect during the opposition period and, where appropriate, pending a final decision on opposition.

R. 144 Parts of the file excluded from inspection

Amended by decision of the Administrative Council of 10.12.2024, which entered into force on 01.04.2025 (OJ 2025 A16). The amendments made the text gender-neutral.

The parts of the file excluded from inspection under Article 128, paragraph 4, shall be:
(a) the documents relating to the exclusion of or objections to members of the Boards of Appeal or of the Enlarged Board of Appeal;
(b) draft decisions and notices, and all other documents, used for the preparation of decisions and notices, which are not communicated to the parties;
(c) the designation of the inventor, if they have waived the right to be mentioned under Rule 20, paragraph 1;
(d) any other document excluded from inspection by the President of the European Patent Office on the ground that such inspection would not serve the purpose of informing the public about the European patent application or the European patent.

Art.128(4) Inspection of files
R.20(1) Waiver of right to be mentioned as inventor
Implementation of **Art.128(4)**

1 **Exclusion from inspection under (a) and (d)**
The exclusion from inspection of documents relating to exclusion of members of boards of appeal and of the Enlarged Board of Appeal under **Art.24** should apply also to exclusion of members of departments of first instance.

By decision of the President, the following documents are also excluded from file inspection under **R.144(d)**: medical certificates, documents relating to the issue of priority documents, file-inspection proceedings or the communication of information from the files, requests for exclusion from inspection and requests for accelerated search and accelerated examination under the PACE programme (Dec. Pres. OJ 2007 se3 p.125 Art.1(1)). Statements in a patent application that are detrimental to public safety or which would offend public morality according to **R.48(1)(a)** are not published but are available in the file for inspection.

2 **Exclusion from inspection on request**
Documents other than those referred to in Art.1(1) of the above decision of the President may be excluded from inspection at the reasoned request of a party if their inspection would be prejudicial to the legitimate personal or economic interests of a natural or legal person (Art.1(2) of Dec. Pres). The EPO may also exclude such other documents of its own motion if their inspection would be prima facie prejudicial to the interest of a person other than a party. If a decision is taken to reject a request for exclusion, the document concerned will become open for inspection as soon as the decision becomes final. (Dec. Pres. OJ 2007 se3 p.125 Art.1(2); D-II,4.3)

A request for the exclusion of a document will be rejected if the document is filed as evidence of an inventive step, since the public must be aware of such information (**T516/89**).

Exceptionally, and following a substantiated request, documents filed as evidence may remain unconsidered in the proceedings and be returned to the party that filed them without having been laid open for public inspection. Such exceptional circumstances may arise if the interest of the party in having them returned unconsidered clearly prevails over the interests of the other party or parties and the public interest. This may be the case if the documents were filed in breach of a confidentiality agreement and if they did not belong to the state of the art but were third-party statements filed in response to an opposition, and if the other parties involved agree with the request. (T760/89)

A party may request the EPO to exclude an otherwise public non-patent document from file inspection for reasons of copyright. The EPO will usually grant the request if the requesting party does not own the copyright and the document is relatively easily retrievable, possibly against payment, and make only the cover page of the document available via file inspection, allowing the public to retrieve the entire document from another source. Such a document is not considered to be excluded from file inspection and can be used as evidence. (D-II,4.3)

In **T811/90** the opposition division did not inform the proprietor of the withdrawal of the opponent's request for oral proceedings and its forthcoming decision to maintain the patent as granted. The board decided that amendments to the patent filed by the proprietor in preparation for the oral proceedings should not be open for inspection and, since the amendments did not fall under **R.144**, they should be returned to the proprietor.

R. 145 Procedures for the inspection of files

Implementation of **Art.128(4)**

1 **General**

The file of a European patent application or patent can be inspected under **Art.128** on the website of the EPO or by requesting the provision of a copy . The file of an international application for which the EPO acts as a designated or elected Office can also be inspected. The means of inspection are governed by **R.145(1)**, the method of inspection by **R.145(2)**. An overview of the procedure is given in the Notice of the EPO published in OJ 2006 p.535.

The EPC has no provisions governing the inspection of the Register. However, the Register may also be inspected in more or less the same way as the files, and most methods of inspection are free of charge. Online inspection of the Register is possible on the EPO website (see **R.145(1):1**). See also **R.143(1):2** and **R.146**.

R. 145(1) Inspection of the files of European patent applications and patents shall either be of the original document, or of copies thereof, or of technical means of storage if the files are stored in this way.

1 **Means of file inspection**

The files may be inspected by the means specified in the Decision of the President, published in OJ 2019 A16.

The primary means of inspection is online (https://register.epo.org). Files not yet available in electronic form but existing only as paper file will as a rule be made available online within ten working days from entry of the relevant number in the online search engine, provided they have not yet been destroyed under **R.147**. Files or parts thereof that are not scannable are made available in their original form or as filed on the premises of the EPO. (Dec. Pres. OJ 2019 A16 Art.1)

Paper copies of documents in a file are provided only exceptionally and on request, see **R.145(2):1**.

R. 145(2) The President of the European Patent Office shall determine all file-inspection arrangements, including the circumstances in which an administrative fee is payable.

1 **Request for inspection**

Following the introduction of electronic files and free online inspection on the EPO website, the historical practice of inspection of paper files on the EPO premises is almost obsolete (Dec. Pres. OJ 2019 A16 Art.1(2); see also **R.143(1):2**).

In exceptional cases, file inspection by means of paper copies is made available following a duly substantiated request (OJ 2019 A16 Art.2(1); A15 §10). In such a case the EPO will furnish copies of documents on paper or, if the documents comprise more than 100 pages, on an electronic storage medium (OJ 2019 A15 §9, 10; A16 Art.2(2)). There is no charge for this service. The EPO will also issue a certified paper copy of documents in a file on request and on payment of a fee (**Rfees3(1):1**; A-XI,5). For the legalisation of the certified copies, see OJ 2020 A7. A request for ordering the certified copies is available on the EPO website, may be used (A-XI,2.2). The request for inspection itself is excluded from public file inspection (see **R.144:1**). For the issuing of priority documents by the EPO, see **R.54**.

Inspection of the files of non-published applications under **Art.128(1)**, **(2)** or **(3)** requires the filing of a request, grounds and proof. Applicants can inspect the file of their own applications prior to their publication online through MyEPO, a secure portal on the EPO website (OJ 2012 p.22 §1).

R. 146 Communication of information contained in the files

Amended by decision of the Administrative Council of 14.12.2023, which entered into force on 01.04.2024 (OJ 2024 A3). The amendment deleted the requirement of payment of an administrative fee.

Subject to the restrictions laid down in Article 128, paragraphs 1 to 4, and in Rule 144, the European Patent Office may, upon request, communicate information concerning any file relating to a European patent application or European patent. However, the European Patent Office may refer to the option of file inspection where it deems this to be appropriate in view of the quantity of information to be supplied.

Art.128(1) No inspection before publication
Art.128(2) Early inspection with approval of applicant
Art.128(3) Inspection of parent from publication divisional
Art.128(4) Inspection after publication
R.144 Parts of the file excluded from inspection
Implementation of **Art.128(4)**

1 **General**
Almost all of the useful information held by the EPO in its files can now be accessed by online file inspection. In the rare cases that additional information is sought, and subject to the restrictions on file inspection laid down in **Art.128** and **R.144**, the EPO will furnish the information on request. Before 01.04.2024, an administrative fee was payable for this service but the fee is no longer required (OJ 2024 A3). The applicant or proprietor is not notified of any request of this kind and relevant correspondence is not stored in the public part of the file. (A-XI,3)

R. 147 Constitution, maintenance and preservation of files

Amended, current version in force since 01.04.2024 (OJ 2015 A83; OJ 2016 A90; OJ 2024 A16). The latest amendment concerned paragraph (3) and mainly incorporated the legal basis for destroying data carriers.
Implementation of **Art.128(4)**

R. 147(1) The European Patent Office shall constitute, maintain and preserve files relating to all European patent applications and patents in electronic form.

R. 147(2) The President of the European Patent Office shall determine all necessary technical and administrative arrangements relating to the management of electronic files according to paragraph 1.

1 **Form of files**
The files of European patent applications and international applications for which the EPO acts under the PCT are created, maintained and processed in an electronic file system (Dec. Pres. OJ 2024 A31).

R. 147(3)
(a) Documents incorporated in an electronic file shall be considered to be originals.
(b) The initial version of such documents filed on paper or on a data carrier shall only be destroyed after expiry of at least five years. This preservation period starts at the end of the year in which the document was incorporated in the electronic file.

1 **Electronic files and paper documents**
For reasons of reliability and accessibility, EPO files are maintained in electronic format; the electronically stored documents are considered to be originals (**R.147(3)**, part (a)). Documents filed on paper are scanned as images upon receipt, checked for quality and stored in the electronic file.

The preservation periods for files specified in **R.147(4)** and (5) relate to the electronic files. **R.147(3)**, part (b), on the other hand, relates to the preservation of paper documents and data carriers. A paper document or data carrier is kept until five years from the end of the year in which the document was scanned and stored in the electronic file. The five-year period provides legal certainty and allows for the rescanning of a document where necessary. Providing a finite period, on the other hand, also allows the EPO to deal with paper documents and data carriers efficiently. (CA71/15e)

The five-year period does not apply to record copies of PCT applications filed with the EPO on paper and kept by the EPO on behalf of the International Bureau (OJ 2016 A90 §5).

R. 147(4) Any files shall be preserved for at least five years from the end of the year in which:
(a) the application is refused or withdrawn or is deemed to be withdrawn;
(b) the patent is revoked by the European Patent Office; or
(c) the patent or the corresponding protection under Article 63, paragraph 2, lapses in the last of the designated States.

Art.63(2) Extended term of the European patent

1 **Keeping of files**
The files in the EPO's electronic file system are preserved until the end of the appropriate period laid down in paragraph 4 or 5, i.e. at least five years after the application or patent ceases to exist.

The five-year period is extended when the term of the patent is extended under **Art.63(2)**, e.g. on account of war or as compensation for a lengthy authorisation procedure, as occurs in the pharmaceutical sector.

The electronic file relating to a case in which appeal or opposition proceedings have taken place is not destroyed before 25 years have elapsed from the date of filing (OJ 1990 p.365).

A patent often lapses due to the non-payment of a renewal fee. As these fees are paid before the year in respect of which they are due, the patent lapses about one year after the last renewal fee payment, dependent on national law. For example, if the last renewal fee is paid in 2018, the patent lapses in 2019, and the electronic file can be inspected until at least 31.12.2024.

The entries in the Register relating to the files of applications and patents that have been destroyed are not affected. (OJ 1990 p.365)

R. 147(5) Without prejudice to paragraph 4, files relating to applications which have given rise to divisional applications under Article 76 or new applications under Article 61, paragraph 1(b), shall be preserved for at least the same period as the files relating to any one of these last applications. The same shall apply to files relating to any resulting European patents.

Art.61(1)(b) Application filed by non-entitled person
Art.76 Divisional applications

1 **Keeping of files of earlier applications**
The file of the parent application is retained for at least as long as any divisional application exists in order to allow file inspection for the purpose of assessing a possible extension of subject-matter and various formal matters (**R.147(5)**).

Chapter X *Legal and administrative co-operation*

R. 148 Communications between the European Patent Office and the authorities of the Contracting States

Implementation of **Art.131**

R. 148(1) Communications between the European Patent Office and the central industrial property offices of the Contracting States which arise out of the application of this Convention shall be effected directly between these authorities. Communications between the European Patent Office and the courts or other authorities of the Contracting States may be effected through the intermediary of the said central industrial property offices.

R. 148(2) Expenditure in respect of communications under paragraph 1 shall be borne by the authority making the communications, which shall be exempt from fees.

R. 149 Inspection of files by or via courts or authorities of the Contracting States

Implementation of **Art.131**

R. 149(1) Inspection of the files of European patent applications or of European patents by courts or authorities of the Contracting States shall be of the original documents or of copies thereof; Rule 145 shall not apply.

R.145 Procedures for the inspection of files

R. 149(2) Courts or Public Prosecutors' offices of the Contracting States may, in the course of their proceedings, communicate to third parties files or copies thereof transmitted to them by the European Patent Office. Such communications shall be effected in accordance with Article 128 and shall not be subject to any fee.

Art.128 Inspection of files

R. 149(3) The European Patent Office shall, when transmitting the files, draw attention to the restrictions which may, under Article 128, paragraphs 1 and 4, apply to file inspection by third parties.

Art.128(1) No inspection before publication
Art.128(4) Inspection after publication

R. 150 Procedure for letters rogatory

Implementation of **Art.131(2)**
This provision indicates how requests from the EPO, e.g. for the taking of evidence before a national court under **Art.117**, are transmitted to the national courts.

R. 150(1) Each Contracting State shall designate a central authority to receive letters rogatory issued by the European Patent Office and to transmit them to the court or authority competent to execute them.

R. 150(2) The European Patent Office shall draw up letters rogatory in the language of the competent court or authority or shall attach to such letters rogatory a translation into that language.

R. 150(3) Subject to paragraphs 5 and 6, the competent court or authority shall apply national law as to the procedures to be followed in executing such requests and, in particular, as to the appropriate measures of compulsion.

R. 150(4) If the court or authority to which the letters rogatory are transmitted is not competent to execute them, the letters rogatory shall be sent forthwith to the central authority referred to in paragraph 1. That authority shall transmit the letters rogatory either to the competent court or authority in that State, or to the European Patent Office where no court or authority is competent in that State.

R. 150(5) The European Patent Office shall be informed of the time when, and the place where, the enquiry or other legal measure is to take place and shall inform the parties, witnesses and experts concerned.

R. 150(6) If so requested by the European Patent Office, the competent court or authority shall permit the attendance of members of the department concerned and allow them to question any person giving evidence either directly or through the competent court or authority.

R. 150(7) The execution of letters rogatory shall not give rise to any reimbursement of fees or costs of any nature. Nevertheless, the State in which letters rogatory are executed has the right to require the Organisation to reimburse any fees paid to experts or interpreters and the costs arising from the procedure under paragraph 6.

R. 150(8) If the law applied by the competent court or authority obliges the parties to secure evidence and the competent court or authority is not able itself to execute the letters rogatory, that court or authority may, with the consent of the European Patent Office, appoint a suitable person to do so. When seeking such consent, the competent court or authority shall indicate the approximate costs which would result from this procedure. If the European Patent Office gives its consent, the Organisation shall reimburse any costs incurred; otherwise, the Organisation shall not be liable for such costs.

Chapter XI *Representation*

R. 151 Appointment of a common representative

Implementation of **Art.133(4)**

1 **General**
The provision must be interpreted in light of the necessity for the EPO to have one person to address during proceedings. For **R.151** to apply, each party or the party's duly authorised representative must have signed the document (request for grant, notice of opposition, etc.) giving rise to the party's participation (A-VIII,1.5), and the parties must not have appointed a common representative themselves.

A communication sent by the EPO to the common representative is sufficient (**R.130(3)**); the other parties may not receive any communication from the EPO. The EPO assumes that all joint members are aware of a communication sent only to the common representative (**T1908/09** r.3.1). An opposition or appeal must be filed by the common representative mentioning all joint members (**Art.99(1):2.1, 2.5; Art.107:1**, respectively).

R. 151(1) If there is more than one applicant and the request for grant of a European patent does not name a common representative, the applicant first named in the request shall be deemed to be the common representative. However, if one of the applicants is obliged to appoint a professional representative, this representative shall be deemed to be the common representative, unless the applicant first named has appointed a professional representative. The same shall apply to third parties acting in common in filing a notice of opposition or intervention and to joint proprietors of a European patent.

1 **Appointment of common representative by EPO**
If there is more than one applicant, the Request for Grant form should preferably contain the appointment of a common representative (**R.41(3)**) to ensure unity of procedure as required under **Art.118**. The appointment of a common representative in the form is not compulsory. If there is more than one applicant and no common representative is appointed, the EPO applies **R.151(1)** to assign a common representative, because the EPO needs one address for correspondence. The same applies to joint proprietors and to parties acting in common in filing a notice of opposition or intervention (**R.151(1)**, last sentence and A-VIII,1.5), filing a request for limitation or revocation (**R.92** and **R.41(3)**) and petition proceedings (**R18/09** r.6).

R.151(1) is formulated in a knotty way and case law on its interpretation is scarce (see e.g. **T755/09** r.5, 6; **T1908/09** r.3.1). A possible interpretation is:

1 Is there more than one applicant?
   (a) No, then the EPO communicates with the applicant or the authorised representative.
   (b) Yes, then
2 Has an applicant or representative been appointed as common representative in the Request for Grant form (**R.41(3)**)?
   (a) Yes, then the appointed applicant or representative is the common representative.
   (b) No, then

3 Is one of the applicants obliged to be represented and has appointed a representative (**Art.133(2)**)?
(a) No, then the first-named applicant or the representative of the first-named applicant is the deemed common representative.
(b) Yes, then
4 Is the first-named applicant represented?
(a) Yes, then the representative of the first-named applicant is the deemed common representative.
(b) No, then the representative of the applicant obliged to be represented is the deemed common representative. If there is more than one applicant obliged to be represented, then the representative of the first-named* obliged applicant is the deemed common representative.

* Although **R.151(1)** does not mention the 'first-named' applicant obliged to be represented, it has been inserted to cover all possible cases of multiple applicants. The insertion is plausible on account of the application of the rule in the first sentence of **R.151(1)**: 'the first-named applicant not obliged to be represented is considered to be the common representative' to the case where multiple applicants are obliged to be represented (Singer Art.133, note 54).

The above rule has the following undesirable consequence. If an application has two applicants who are not obliged to be represented and only the second-named applicant has appointed a representative, the rule appoints the first-named, unrepresented applicant as the common representative instead of the representative of the applicant named second on the request. This is a downside, because the EPO would prefer the professional representative to be deemed the common representative for ease of communication. In other words, if none of the joint applicants are obliged to be represented, the order in which they appear on the request overrides representation status.

The rule also applies to joint proprietors, to joint opponents (persons filing a notice of opposition in common; **G3/99** r.10) and to parties acting in common in filing a notice of intervention (**R.151(1)**, last sentence and A-VII,1.5), filing a request for limitation or revocation (**R.92** and **R.41(3)**) and in petition for review proceedings (**R18/09** r.6). If a patent has multiple proprietors (e.g. in different contracting states), these are joint proprietors (with an exception relating to entitlement disputes in **Art.99(4)**).

2 **Acts by parties acting in common**
Parties acting in common, either applicants, proprietors or opponents, can only act through the common representative. If one of these parties, not being the common representative, carries out a procedural act, the EPO will not admit the act. E.g. an opponent not being the common representative who files a submission is regarded as a non-entitled person and the submission is treated as an act for which a signature is missing; the EPO will request a rectification under **R.50(3)** by having the common representative sign the submission (**G3/99** hn.2 and r.14 extended to all procedural acts).

R. 151(2) If the European patent application is transferred to more than one person, and such persons have not appointed a common representative, paragraph 1 shall apply mutatis mutandis. If such application is not possible, the European Patent Office shall invite such persons to appoint a common representative within a period to be specified. If this invitation is not complied with, the European Patent Office shall appoint the common representative.

1 **Appointment of common representative after transfer**
The appointment of a deemed common representative by the EPO according to **R.151(1)** applies equally to the transfer of the application, patent or opposition during grant, opposition or appeal proceedings to more than one person who have not appointed a common representative. The application of **R.151(1)** may be not be possible, if, e.g., heirs of an applicant cannot agree on representation. In such cases **R.151(2)** obliges the EPO to request the new applicants to appoint a common representative within two months; otherwise, the EPO will appoint the common representative itself.

R.151(2) does not cover all possibilities that can arise after a transfer, such as where the assets of the first named applicant are inherited by one person obliged to be represented but who has not appointed a representative. The EPO covers these cases by not limiting the application of the last two sentences of **R.151(2)** to the situation of the first sentence, i.e. to a transfer to more than one person, but extending it to all cases where the appointment of a common representative after a transfer is not provided for in the EPC (J35/92).

R. 152 Authorisations

Implementation of **Art.134(1)**

1 **General**
A professional representative acting before the EPO must file a signed authorisation only in the cases set down by the President (**R.152(1)**; A-VIII,1.6). As of 01.11.2024, the same conditions apply to legal practitioners entitled to act as representatives under **Art. 134(8)** (OJ 2024 A75 Art. 1(1), OJ 2024 A77 §3).

Authorisations can be signed by hand, with a facsimile or a text-string, as well as digitally, provided that the latter fulfils the conditions set out in OJ 2024 A77 §6-7. Authorisations signed with a facsimile or a text-string may be filed on paper or electronically (OJ 2024 A77 §5).

An authorisation on behalf of more than one applicant must be signed by all applicants (A-VIII,3.4).

A change of representative for more than one application or patent can be filed as a bulk request using the corresponding EPO form (OJ 2019 A79; **R.2(1):2**).

In case of change of representative, as of 01.11.2024, the EPO no longer sends the previous representative a copy of the new representative's authorisation, but rather simply informs them of the change of representative (OJ 2024 A75 Art. 1(2), OJ 2024 A77 §4).

See **Art.133:2** for details of authorisation.

R. 152(1) The President of the European Patent Office shall determine the cases in which a signed authorisation shall be filed by representatives acting before the European Patent Office.

1 **Compulsory filing of authorisation**
The President has determined the cases where an authorisation is to be filed (OJ 2024 A75). The first such case is a change of representative to one from a different firm without the original representative notifying the EPO (OJ 2024 A75 Art.1(2)). The second case is the presence of any doubt regarding the status of the representative such as their entitlement to act (OJ 2024 A75 Art.1(3)). In such cases, if a representative does not file an authorisation of

their own motion, the EPO will invite them to do so within a period of at least two months (**R.132(2)**).

Any individual authorisation submitted is placed on file even if it has not been requested (OJ 2024 A75 Art.1(1)). The issue of authorisation will in general be raised during the examination of formalities under **R.57(h)**. The procedure for correction is set out in **R.57:9**.

Note, that a withdrawal from representation does not automatically terminate an automatic debit order. Termination requires a separate revocation of the automatic debit order to be filed with the withdrawal (OJ 2022 sp3 Annex A.1 10.3). Parties are also advised to update their deposit account refund instructions if their representative changes or if rights are transferred (OJ 2024 A23; see **Rfees9:2**).

The EPO does not require an authorisation if a representative other than the appointed one, who is not a member of the same association or law firm, performs a procedural act on behalf of a party, provided that it is apparent from their submission that they are acting at the request of that party without the intention to take over representation. (A-VIII,1.6)

R.152(1) makes an exception to the general obligation to file an authorisation for professional representatives. As of 01.11.2024, legal practitioners of **Art.134(8)** are treated the same as professional representatives (OJ 2024 A75 Art. 1(1), OJ 2024 A77 §3). However, employees of **Art.133(3)** must file a signed authorisation or a reference to a general authorisation under **R.152(4)** that is already on file. If not filed together with their appointment, the EPO will request the employee to file an authorisation within a period to be specified. (OJ 2024 A75 Art.2; A-VIII,1.6) Authorisations filed with the EPO in the international phase of a Euro-PCT application do not automatically extend to the regional phase before the EPO unless this is explicitly stated (E-IX,2.3.1). Employee representatives are required to file an authorisation for the regional phase of a Euro-PCT application if their continued representation in this phase was not expressly stated in the original authorisation (A-VIII,1.6).

There is no requirement that the date of the signature on the authorisation is prior to the procedural act performed by the professional representative. Neither is it required that any procedural step taken by the representative before the signature's date be explicitly approved in the signed authorisation (**T924/17**).

When signing authorisations on behalf of a legal person, individuals authorised to do so via their position within the legal person should identify this position (OJ 2024 A77 §9).

2 **Authorisation for divisional application**

Representatives acting for a parent application are not automatically authorised to act for a divisional application. They will be validly authorised if a general authorisation covers divisionals, the authorisation for the parent application expressly states coverage of divisionals, or a separate authorisation covers the divisional.

R. 152(2) Where a representative fails to file such an authorisation, the European Patent Office shall invite them to do so within a period to be specified. The authorisation may cover one or more European patent applications or European patents.

Amended by decision of the Administrative Council of 14.12.2023, which entered into force on 01.04.2024 (OJ 2024 A16; CA/D 26/23). The amendment implemented gender-neutral language and removed reference to the number of copies of the authorisation to be filed.

R. 152(3) Where the requirements of Article 133, paragraph 2, have not been satisfied, the same period shall be specified for the appointment of a representative and the filing of the authorisation.

Art.133(2) Compulsory representation

1 **Authorisation of applicant from a non-contracting state**
Where the applicant has neither residence nor place of business in a contracting state and has not appointed a representative according to **Art.133(2)**, the request for appointment and authorisation will be sent to the applicant. A period of two months will normally be specified for filing both the appointment and the authorisation. The period may be extended according to **R.132**. Authorisations can also be filed by applicants, even if they are obliged to be represented under **Art.133(2)**, because fulfilling the requirement to be represented is not itself a procedural step requiring representation within the meaning of **Art.133(2)** (A-VIII,1.6). When the authorisation is not filed in due time, the sanction of **R.152(6)** follows.

R. 152(4) A general authorisation may be filed enabling a representative to act in respect of all the patent transactions of a party.

Amended by decision of the Administrative Council of 14.12.2023, which entered into force on 01.04.2024 (OJ 2024 A16; CA/D 26/23). The amendment removed reference to the number of copies of the authorisation to be filed.

1 **General authorisation**
A party can grant a general authorisation enabling a representative to represent it in any of its proceedings before the EPO. The EPO Form 1004 is recommended for this purpose. The original signed general authorisation must be filed. Once filed, the EPO will assign a number to the general authorisation; this number can, for example, be entered in the Request for Grant form on filing a patent application. The representative need not file a separate authorisation for each case and can simply quote the registration number of the general authorisation (A-VIII,1.6).

Even when a general authorisation is filed or referred to in a specific case, a representative still has to be appointed (**J17/98** hn.I). The EPO does not assume that the representative granted the general authorisation is appointed for all of the party's patent matters. (A-VIII,1.7)

A general authorisation can be used to enable an association of representatives in the sense of **R.152(11)** to act for a party. Note that legal practitioners are presently not covered by an authorisation of an association (see **R.152(11):1**). The Legal Division has authority to register general authorisations and to examine whether the persons mentioned in the authorisation are entitled under the EPC to represent the authorising party (**J9/99** r.1.5).

A general authorisation is also valid for acting before the EPO as designated or elected Office for a Euro-PCT application, but not automatically for acting before the EPO as receiving Office, ISA or IPEA. The authorisation must expressly give permission to act in the international phase.

R. 152(5) The President of the European Patent Office may determine the form and content of:
(a) an authorisation relating to the representation of persons under Article 133, paragraph 2;
(b) a general authorisation.

Art.133(2) Compulsory representation

(a) This has not yet been done
(b) EPO Form 1004 is recommended (R.152(4)).

R. 152(6) If a required authorisation is not filed in due time, any procedural steps taken by the representative, other than the filing of a European patent application, shall be deemed not to have been taken, without prejudice to any other legal consequences provided for by this Convention.

1 **Effect of not filing an authorisation**
The office period of **R.152(2)** for filing the authorisation can be extended (**R.132**). Failure to observe the period can be redressed by further processing. The EPO informs parties of the nullity of their procedural steps (A-VIII,1.9).

The phrase 'without prejudice' in the provision means that other legal consequences may follow the consequence set out in **R.152(6)**. For example, when a representative files an opposition for a party and, upon request of the board of appeal, fails to provide a signed original authorisation and copy in due time, the EPO will consider the opposition void and reimburse the opposition and appeal fees (**T1700/11** r.9-10).

2 **Invalid authorisation**
When the EPO is informed that a representative has acted before the EPO on behalf of a party without being instructed to do so and without filing a valid authorisation, it will consider the proceedings null and void and reimburse all fees paid to the EPO (**J12/88**).

R. 152(7) Paragraphs 2 and 4 shall apply to the withdrawal of an authorisation.

R. 152(8) A representative shall be deemed to be authorised until the termination of their authorisation has been communicated to the European Patent Office.

Amended by decision of the Administrative Council of 14.12.2023, which entered into force on 01.04.2024 (OJ 2024 A16; CA/D 26/23). The amendment implemented gender-neutral language.

1 **Communication of termination to EPO**
Sending a termination of an authorisation by a party to a representative is not effective before the EPO. The termination becomes effective before the EPO only on the date the EPO receives the termination. (**R4/15** r.3)

R. 152(9) Unless it expressly provides otherwise, an authorisation shall not terminate vis-à-vis the European Patent Office upon the death of the person who gave it.

R. 152(10) If a party appoints several representatives, they may act either jointly or singly, notwithstanding any provisions to the contrary in the communication of their appointment or in the authorisation.

R. 152(11) The authorisation of an association of representatives shall be deemed to be an authorisation of any representative who can provide evidence that they practise within that association.

Amended by decision of the Administrative Council of 14.12.2023, which entered into force on 01.04.2024 (OJ 2024 A16; CA/D 26/23). The amendment implemented gender-neutral language.

1 **Authorisation of an association**

The provision allows a party to authorise several representatives as an association instead of doing it one by one. The authorisation of an association is deemed to be an authorisation of any representative practising within that association; each individual member of the association is entitled to act before the EPO, not the association itself. An advantage is that changes in the composition of the association only require a single registration with the EPO instead of doing it separately for each file the firm is handling. The EPO keeps an internal list of representatives that have provided evidence that they practise within a given association. (J8/10 r.5, 7)

The authorisation covers only professional representatives. Legal practitioners are currently excluded from authorisation through an association (J8/10 r.11; see **Art.134(8):1**). Both private practice firms and in-house patent departments can form associations (J16/96 r.4 and OJ 2013 p.500).

2 **Registration and appointment of an association**

An association of representatives must be registered with the Legal Division to enable its use in appointments and authorisations. The use of EPO Form 52304 is recommended. The Legal Division informs the applicant of the registration number of the association. (OJ 2013 p.535 §I)

The association is appointed, for example, by entering its name and registration number in the same box of the Request for Grant form. The address in the form, which the EPO will use for notifying communications, may be different from the registered address. Documents submitted to the EPO can be signed by any member of the association; in addition to the signature, the name of the member and of the association and its registration number must be provided. (OJ 2013 p.535 §I)

The association may be cited in specific and general authorisations. The name and registration number of the association should be provided in the authorisation.

R. 153 Attorney-client evidentiary privilege

Amended, in force since 01.04.2009. (OJ 2008 p.513)
Implementation of **Art.134a(1)**

1 **General**

Art.134a(1)(d) bestows competence on the Administrative Council to adopt provisions governing the obligation of confidentiality of professional representatives and the privilege from disclosure in proceedings before the EPO in respect of communications between professional representatives and their clients or any other person.

The obligation of confidentiality binding professional representatives is provided for by Article 2 of the Regulation on discipline for professional representatives. As some legal systems distinguish between this obligation of confidentiality and an evidentiary privilege protecting the confidentiality of attorney-client communications, **R.153** entrenches such an evidentiary privilege for communications between professional representatives and their clients which are subject to the representative's professional obligation of confidentiality. **R.153(1)** draws its language from the definition of the evidentiary privilege in US law as cited from Wigmore's Evidence in the

Bristol- Myers Squibb v. Rhone Poulenc Rorer case (Southern District of New York, 19.04.1999).

It is clear that the word 'client' in **R.153(1)** encompasses any person for whom the representative may be acting, whether an individual or a corporation, the representative's employer, the associated or subsidiary company of the employer, etc.

The reference to Article 2 of the Regulation on discipline has been added to align the provision more closely with the US requirement that such communications should be of a confidential nature. The wording of the provision makes clear that only such communications subject to the representatives' obligation of secrecy are covered by the evidentiary privilege.

Article 2 of the Regulation on discipline reads:

'Professional secrecy. A professional representative shall be bound not to disclose information accepted by him in confidence in the exercise of his duties, unless he is released from this obligation.' (OJ 2003 se1 p.196)

2 **Extent of privilege**

National law of most EPC contracting states does not contain a provision on privilege. The provision in the disciplinary rules of the epi do not confer the equivalent of a privilege laid down in law. As a first step towards protecting correspondence between representatives and parties for US discovery the Administrative Council has made use of its power under **Art.134a(1)(d)** to include **R.153** on attorney evidentiary privilege. It is not certain whether US courts will accept a provision in international law for the privilege; they may require a basis in national law. EPC contracting states are therefore strongly advised to include the privilege in their national civil laws.

In US discovery procedures parties are obliged to grant other parties inspection of all documents in their possession relating to the case in suit. Only documents covered by attorney client privilege are excepted from inspection. US case law on which documents are covered by the privilege is not consistent.

A US court will probably invoke the privilege of **R.153** if the document is a communication between a European representative and a party relating to an advice sought by the client, which is kept confidential and relates to proceedings before the EPO. The privilege will probably not cover communications that do not relate to an advice, do not relate to proceedings before the EPO, or are not kept confidential. As a consequence, an opinion on infringement of a European patent will not be covered by the privilege in a US court, because it does not relate to proceedings before the EPO. Note, however, that the privilege under **R.153** is broader and does cover infringement opinions.

R. 153(1) Where advice is sought from a professional representative in their capacity as such, all communications between the professional representative and their client or any other person, relating to that purpose and falling under Article 2 of the Regulation on discipline for professional representatives, are permanently privileged from disclosure in proceedings before the European Patent Office, unless such privilege is expressly waived by the client.

Amended by decision of the Administrative Council of 10.12.2024, which entered into force on 01.04.2025 (OJ 2025 A16). The amendment was introduction of gender-neutral language.

1 **Privilege from disclosure**
The wording of the provision makes clear that the privilege from disclosure covers only correspondence between representatives and clients. Employees acting for their employer under **Art.133(3)** are not covered by the privilege. It is not yet clear whether a representative as employee, e.g. a representative in a patent department of a company, is protected by the privilege.

The privilege covers all communications between representatives and their clients in proceedings before the EPO, unless the privilege is waived by the client (**R.153(1)**). It does not relate to national proceedings, such as infringement proceedings. The protection of correspondence in these proceedings must be dealt with on a national level.

R. 153(2) Such privilege from disclosure shall apply, in particular, to any communication or document relating to:
(a) the assessment of the patentability of an invention;
(b) the preparation or prosecution of a European patent application;
(c) any opinion relating to the validity, scope of protection or infringement of a European patent or a European patent application.

1 **Documents covered by privilege**
The list of documents in **R.153(2)** that are covered by the privilege is non-exhaustive ('in particular').

R. 154 Amendment of the list of professional representatives

Amended by decision of the Administrative Council of 10.12.2024, which entered into force on 01.04.2025 (OJ 2025 A16). Paragraphs (1) and (2) were amended by introducing gender-neutral language.
Implementation of **Art.134(1)**

1 **The list of professional representatives**
A person appearing on the list of professional representatives must pay an annual subscription to the Institute of Professional Representatives (epi), established under **Art.134a(1)(a)**. See ADA.16 for the possibility to pay the subscription by debiting a deposit account of the EPO by direct debiting mandate.

R. 154(1) The entry of a professional representative shall be deleted from the list of professional representatives if they so request or if, despite a reminder, they fail to pay the applicable annual subscription to the Institute within five months from either:
(a) 1 January for members on the list at that date; or
(b) the date of entry for members entered on the list after 1 January of the year for which the subscription is due.

Amended, in force since 01.01.2019. (OJ 2018 A57)

1 **Deletion of entry because of non-payment of subscription**
Professional representatives must pay the annual subscription for a certain year to the epi at the latest on 31 May of that year or, if they were entered on the list after 1 January, within five months from the date of entry. They will receive a reminder before expiry of the period. If the subscription is paid during the last two months of this period, the amount due will be higher than if paid during the first three months (CA/46/18, Annex 1).

If not paid within five months, the Legal Division will send the representative an **Art.113** communication with the intention to remove their name from the list and an invitation to comment. Next, if a satisfactory response is not received, the EPO issues an appealable decision of deletion and removes the name from the list. Payment of the increased subscription before the period for filing an appeal has expired will close the procedure for removal and the representative will remain on the list.

The above procedure usually allows the deletion of representatives before the end of the year, so that the epi is not obliged to send them an invoice for the next year. (CA/46/18)

R. 154(2) Without prejudice to any disciplinary measures taken under Article 134a, paragraph 1(c), the entry of a professional representative may be deleted ex officio only:
(a) in the event of their death or legal incapacity;
(b) where they are no longer a national of one of the Contracting States, unless they were granted an exemption under Article 134, paragraph 7(a);
(c) where they no longer have their place of business or employment within one of the Contracting States.

Art.134(7)(a) National of a contracting state
Art.134a(1)(c) Disciplinary power of epi
'without prejudice' = 'without detriment (to existing right or claim)'

R. 154(3) Any person entered on the list of professional representatives under Article 134, paragraphs (2) or (3), whose entry has been deleted shall, upon request, be re-entered on that list if the conditions for deletion no longer exist.

Art.134(2) Entry on the list by passing EQE
Art.134(3) Entry on the list by legacy

PART VIII IMPLEMENTING REGULATIONS TO PART VIII OF THE CONVENTION

R. 155 Filing and transmission of the request for conversion

Implementation of **Art.135(1)**

R. 155(1) The request for conversion referred to in Article 135, paragraph 1(a) or (b), shall be filed within three months of the withdrawal of the European patent application, or of the communication that the application is deemed to be withdrawn, or of the decision refusing the application or revoking the European patent. The effect of the European patent application under Article 66 shall lapse if the request is not filed in due time.

Art.135(1)(a) Conversion if application deemed withdrawn under Art.77(3)
Art.135(1)(b) Conversion in other cases provided by national law
Art.66 Equivalence of European filing with national filing

1 **Procedure for requesting conversion**
See **Art.135(2):1** for the filing of a conversion request in cases wherein a European patent application filed with a national patent office is not forwarded in due time to the EPO and **Art.135(3):1** for the procedure in other cases in which the European application is refused, withdrawn, deemed to be withdrawn or the European patent is revoked.

R. 155(2) When transmitting the request for conversion to the central industrial property offices of the Contracting States specified in the request, the central industrial property office concerned or the European Patent Office shall attach to the request a copy of the file relating to the European patent application or European patent.

R. 155(3) Article 135, paragraph 4, shall apply if the request for conversion referred to in Article 135, paragraphs 1(a) and (2), is not transmitted before the expiry of a period of twenty months from the date of filing or, if priority has been claimed, the date of priority.

Amended, in force since 01.04.2009. The amendment replaced the word 'or' after '1(a)' by 'and'. (OJ 2008 p.513)
Art.135(1)(a) Conversion if application deemed withdrawn under Art.77(3)
Art.135(2) Filing of the request for conversion of par 1(a)
Art.135(4) Effect of request transmitted late

R. 156 Information to the public in the event of conversion

Implementation of **Art.135(1)**

1 **General**
The rule realises the right of the public to know the origin of the national application that originated from the conversion of a European application.

R. 156(1) The documents accompanying the request for conversion under Rule 155, paragraph 2, shall be made available to the public by the central industrial property office under the same conditions and to the same extent as documents relating to national proceedings.

R.155(2) Transmission of request for conversion to national office

1 **Obligation to publish documents**
The documents related to the conversion are open for public inspection according to **R.156(1)** and national law, not according to **Art.128**.

R. 156(2) The printed specification of the national patent resulting from the conversion of a European patent application shall mention that application.

PART IX IMPLEMENTING REGULATIONS TO PART X OF THE CONVENTION

R. 157 The European Patent Office as a receiving Office

Implementation of Art.151

R. 157(1) The European Patent Office shall be competent to act as a receiving Office within the meaning of the PCT if the applicant is a resident or national of a Contracting State to this Convention and to the PCT. Without prejudice to paragraph 3, if the applicant chooses the European Patent Office as a receiving Office, the international application shall be filed directly with the European Patent Office. Article 75, paragraph 2, shall apply mutatis mutandis.

Art.75(2) Requirement for compulsory filing at national office of contracting state
R.157(3) Time limit for forwarding an international application by contracting state

1 **EPO as receiving Office**
The requirements for filing an international application with the EPO as PCT receiving Office (rO) are set out in Not. EPO OJ 2014 A33.

R.157(1) sets out the competence of the EPO acting as a rO under the PCT. The EPO is a competent receiving Office for residents and nationals of EPC contracting states. The provision also states that an international application must be filed directly with the EPO if the applicant chooses the EPO as the rO. The reference to **R.157(3)** and **Art.75(2)** in **R.157(1)** provides an exception to the obligation to file directly with the EPO. **Art.75(2)** EPC prescribes that under national law, an international patent application may have to be filed nationally first, e.g. for reasons of national security (GL/PCT-EPO A-II,3.2). The national office will transmit the international application to the EPO as rO before the time limit prescribed in **R.157(3)** and the EPO will accord the date of receipt by the national office as the date of filing of the application (A-II,4.1.5(i)). An international application filed with a national office for transmittal to the EPO as rO but not complying with the national provisions mentioned in **Art.75(2)**, e.g. because the application turns out not to be prejudicial to national security, will be accorded the date of receipt with the national office as the date of filing.

The permitted methods of filing an international application with the EPO are governed by provisions of the PCT, decisions of the President and the Guidelines (see GL/PCT-EPO A-II,1.2 and Not. EPO OJ 2014 A33). The EPO as rO accepts international applications filed electronically using EPO Online Filing (OLF) Software, Online Filing 2.0, or the EPO Contingency Upload Service (Dec. Pres. OJ 2024 A88), or using ePCT (Dec. Pres. OJ 2014 A107). When filing using the Contingency Upload Service, fees must usually be paid separately (A-X,4.2.3, see **Rfees5(2):2.1**).

2 **Filing date requirements**

The EPO will respond differently when an applicant files a European patent application than when an applicant files an international application.

If the applicant files a direct European patent application, a date of filing is accorded when the requirements of **R.40(1)** EPC are met (see also **Art.80** EPC). Hence, no claims are required.

If the applicant files an international application with the EPO as rO, the filing date requirements are governed by Art.11 and R.20 PCT and the application must contain at least one claim. Note also that the PCT requirements for filing by reference are different from those under the EPC: only a previous application whose priority is claimed on filing can be used as a basis for incorporating the description, claims and drawings by reference under the PCT and the international application must contain, on filing, a statement reserving the right to later confirm the incorporation by reference of an element of the application (R.4.18 and R.20.3 PCT). Similarly, if an applicant subsequently wishes to file missing parts of the description or missing drawings, the applicant must realise that the requirements under the EPC (**R.56** EPC) also differ from those under the PCT (R.20.5 and R.20.6 PCT). The same differences are also evident when correcting an erroneously filed part (R.20.5*bis* PCT and **R.56a** EPC).

3 **Acknowledgement of receipt**

Although the EPO generally does not send postal acknowledgements of receipt as of 01.02.2024 (OJ 2023 A108), receipt of international applications filed on paper or on a physical electronic data carrier is still acknowledged via EPO Form 1031 sent by post. Applications filed electronically continue to receive an immediate and automatic acknowledgement of receipt within the submission session. (GL/PCT-EPO A-II 3.1)

The acknowledgement lists the various documents filed (PCT request, description, etc.) but does not verify the number of sheets of the documents, similar to the acknowledgement under **R.35(2)**.

R. 157(2) Where the European Patent Office acts as a receiving Office under the PCT, the international application shall be filed in English, French or German. The President of the European Patent Office may determine that the international application and any related item shall be filed in more than one copy.

1 **Language and number of copies**

R.157(2) implements the language provision R.12.1 PCT and states that the languages of the international application accepted by the EPO as rO are English, French and German. **Art.14(2)** is not applicable when filing an international application with the EPO, because PCT provisions prevail over EPC provisions according to **Art.150(2)**. Hence, an international application in Swedish filed with the EPO as rO does not comply with **Art.11(1)(ii)** PCT; hence, the remedy of R.19.4 PCT will be carried out, making the IB the rO instead (GL/PCT-EPO A-II,2). **R.157(2)** explicitly mentions the three languages, English, French and German, rather than referring to the languages of **Art.14(1)**, because **Art.14(1)** does not apply when filing an international application with the EPO.

An international application must be filed in one copy. (**R.157(2)**; Dec. Pres. OJ 2006 p.439).

R. 157(3) If an international application is filed with an authority of a Contracting State for transmittal to the European Patent Office as the receiving Office, the Contracting State shall ensure that the application reaches the European Patent Office not later than two weeks before the end of the thirteenth month from filing or, if priority is claimed, from the date of priority.

1 **Transmittal of international application to EPO as rO**

R.157(3) EPC requires that the national office of an EPC contracting state must ensure that an international application filed with it under **R.157(1)**, last sentence (national security), has been received by the EPO two weeks before the end of the 13th month from filing or, where appropriate, the priority date. There is no sanction for non-compliance under the EPC.

If an international application is filed through a national office as an intermediary and does not reach the International Bureau (IB) in the prescribed period, it will be considered withdrawn (Art.12(3) PCT). The period is three months (R.22.3 PCT) after the IB has notified the applicant that it has not received the record copy of the application within fourteen months of the priority date (R.22.1(c) PCT) or that the record copy has not been received after the applicant has become active (R.22.1(g) PCT). The notification allows the applicant to take action, thereby lessening the harshness of the fourteen-month period.

R. 157(4) The transmittal fee for the international application shall be paid within one month of filing the application.

1 **Transmittal fee**

The amount of the transmittal fee levied by the EPO under R.14.1 PCT for transmitting copies of the international application to other PCT authorities and for performing its tasks as rO is fixed in **Rfees2(1)18**. The transmittal fee must be paid within one month of filing the application (**R.157(4)**).

R. 158 The European Patent Office as an International Searching Authority or International Preliminary Examining Authority

Implementation of **Art.152**

R. 158(1) In the case of Article 17, paragraph 3(a) PCT, an additional international search fee shall be paid for each further invention for which an international search is to be carried out.

Art.17(3)(a) PCT Non-unity found during the search

1 **International search fee**

There is no specific basis in the Articles or Rules of the EPC for payment of the search fee in respect of an international search (R.16.1 PCT) when the EPO acts as ISA. However, this fee is referred to in **Rfees2(1)2**, which directly refers to the corresponding R.16.1 PCT. Note that **R.158(1)** only refers to *additional* international search fees, which become relevant upon a lack of unity finding.

Note also that there are some slight discrepancies between the terms used in the EPC and the PCT relating to international search. The term 'international search fee' used in **R.158(1)** EPC does not exist in the PCT; R.16.1 PCT refers to the 'search fee'. This is in contrast to the wording of **Rfees2(1)2** which more closely matches the term in the PCT. Moreover, the 'additional international search fee' in **R.158(1)** EPC should be the 'additional fee' according to R.40.1 PCT. R.40.2(a) PCT allows the ISA to determine the amount of the 'additional fee', the EPO having chosen the 'additional fee' to be equal to the 'search fee'.

The non-unity procedure before the EPO as ISA is given in GL/PCT-EPO B-VII,2.

During a supplementary international search, the EPO as SISA can raise a non-unity objection according to R.45bis.6 PCT, in which case the PCT procedure is followed (OJ 2010 p.316 §7).

R. 158(2) In the case of Article 34, paragraph 3(a) PCT, an additional fee for international preliminary examination shall be paid for each further invention for which the international preliminary examination is to be carried out.

Art.34(3)(a) PCT Non-unity found during the examination

1 **International preliminary examination fee**

There is no specific basis in the Articles or Rules of the EPC for payment of the preliminary examination fee (R.58.1 PCT) when the EPO acts as IPEA. However, this fee is referred to in **Rfees2(1)19**, which directly refers to the corresponding R.58 PCT. Note that **R.158(2)** only refers to *additional* international preliminary examination fees, which become relevant upon a lack of unity finding during international preliminary examination.

Note also that there are some slight discrepancies between the terms used in the EPC and the PCT relating to international preliminary examination. The term 'fee for international preliminary examination' used in **R.158(2)** EPC is referred to as the 'preliminary examination fee' in R.58 PCT. This is in contrast to the wording of **Rfees2(1)19** which more closely matches the term in the PCT.

The non-unity procedure before the EPO as IPEA is given in GL/PCT-EPO C-V.

R. 158(3) Where an additional fee has been paid under protest, the European Patent Office shall examine the protest in accordance with Rule 40.2(c) to (e) or Rule 68.3(c) to (e) PCT, subject to payment of the prescribed protest fee. Further details concerning the procedure shall be determined by the President of the European Patent Office.

R.40.2(c) PCT Non-unity procedure before ISA
R.68.3(c) PCT Non-unity procedure before IPEA

1 **Protest procedure**
The EPO, acting as ISA or IPEA, applies a protest procedure in accordance with R.40.2 and R.68.3 PCT, where an applicant, invited to pay additional international search or preliminary examination fees, wishes to do so 'under protest'. Review panels are responsible for examination of protests, each review panel being made up of three examiners (OJ 2015 A59). See Not. EPO OJ 2010 p.322 §5-7 for details of the protest procedure and protest fee payable upon filing the protest (see R.40.1(iii) / R.68.2(v) PCT ; **Rfees2(1)21**). See GL/PCT-EPO B-VII,7 for the protest procedure before the EPO as ISA (OJ 2010 p.316 §7 and p.322 §11-12).

R. 159 The European Patent Office as a designated or elected Office – Requirements for entry into the European phase

Implementation of **Art.153**

1 **Entry into the European phase**
An international application which has been accorded an international filing date and designates the EPO is equivalent to a regular European application and is referred to as a Euro-PCT application (**Art.153(2)**). The EPO may only process such an application after expiry of the 31-month period of **R.159(1)** (Art.23(1) PCT) or upon receipt of an express request at an earlier date (Art.23(2) PCT). Hence, a Euro-PCT application is a regular, pending European application as from its international filing date, but placed under a temporal processing prohibition. The EPO may only process the application once the prohibition has been lifted (**G1/09** r.3.2.5; see also **J18/09**).

In view of the above, the phrase 'entry into the European phase' does not mean that the international application becomes a European application only on entry. In fact, the international application has been a European patent application since the international filing date. The title of **R.159** might suggest that the 'entry' means 'start of processing the application'. However, the EPO has already started processing when assessing compliance with **R.159**, even when these requirements have not been fulfilled. The 'entry into the European phase' should probably be regarded as meaning the 'start of prosecution of the application by the EPO'.

The EPO may not require compliance of the form and content of the application with requirements of the EPC different from or additional to those of the PCT (Art.27(1) PCT). However, it may require acts to be carried out similar to those due for a direct European patent application, such as payment of fees and filing a request for examination, including acts for which the period has expired during the international phase. The EPO may not require that the applicant carries out these acts before the expiry of the 31-month period, because of the processing prohibition of Art.23(1) PCT. The possibility for a later execution is provided by **Art.150(2)** and implemented in **R.159(1)**: all periods for acts under the EPC that would have expired in the international phase are extended to the expiry of the period for entry into the European phase. Paragraphs (d), (f) and (g) of **R.159(1)** and **R.162** define the periods for requesting examination and paying the designation fee, renewal fees and claims fees as the longer of the period for entry into the European phase and the corresponding period for a direct European patent application.

2 **Procedure for entry into the European phase**
The procedure for entry into the regional phase before the EPO is set out in **R.159-R.162**. See also E-IX,2.1.

Prior to expiry of the period for entering the regional phase before the EPO, the EPO used to send the applicant of an international application an invitation (EPO Form 1201) to carry out the acts of **R.159** in due time as required for valid entry into the European phase. Informing the applicant is not regarded as 'processing' the application, therefore it does not violate the processing prohibition of Art.23(1) PCT. Starting from 01.11.2023, Form 1201 is no longer sent as a sustainability measure and in response to long-standing users' request. The EP application number is not required to enter the EP phase, the international application number is sufficient for appropriate identification of the application. The EP application number is indicated in the Register after publication of the PCT-application (or allocated upon entry in case of early entry before publication), and other information required for entry into European phase, presently in Form 1201, will be in a dedicated section at the EPO website. (Not. EPO OJ 2023 A66)

Since the EPO is aware of its designation or election from the notification by the IB under Art.20(1)(a) PCT and R.47.1(a) PCT or R.76.5 PCT and has received a copy of the international application from the IB under Art.20(1) PCT, it will start processing the international application automatically upon expiry of the 31-month period without request from the applicant (R.49.1(a-bis) PCT; E-IX, 2.1.3). As a consequence, when an international application designates the EPO and the applicant decides not to prosecute the application before the EPO, the EPO will send a loss of rights communication under **R.160(2)** and **R.112(1)**, even if the applicant has not carried out any act for national entry into the European phase. Since the EPO has not been informed of the appointment of a representative, it will send the communication to the applicant, not to an agent that may have acted in the international phase. See **R.160** for remedies.

Applicants are recommended to use 'Form 1200 for entry into the European phase' for the acts to be performed under **R.159(1)** and other required acts. Use of Form 1200 is not mandatory. Form 1200 contains a pre-printed 'written request for examination'. If, upon entry into the European regional phase, the applicant does not use Form 1200 and only pays the fee for examination, the Euro-PCT application is deemed to be withdrawn because the 'written request for examination' was not filed. See in particular the Notes attached to the form.

At expiry of the 31-month period, the EPO will start processing the application automatically, even if the applicant takes no action at all before the EPO as designated or elected office. The EPO will first assess whether the applicant has completed the acts required under **R.159(1)** and any additional acts before the expiry. If not complied with, the European application will be deemed withdrawn under **R.160(1)**. If complied with, the EPO will start processing the application by carrying out the supplementary European search (if applicable) and the substantive examination.

3 **Early entry into the European phase**

The EPO is prohibited from starting the processing of an international application before expiry of the 31-month period from priority of **R.159(1)** (Art.23(1); Art.40(1) PCT). However, an applicant may wish the EPO to start earlier, for example to have the patent granted early or to correct in the regional phase before the EPO an error that has occurred in the international phase using the review and excuse procedure (see **R.159(2):1**). The EPO will start processing early if the prohibition is lifted by an express request of the applicant (Art.23(2); Art.40(2) PCT). The procedure is set out in Not. EPO OJ 2013 p.156 and E-IX,2.8. The filing of a divisional application is only possible after entry into the regional phase before the EPO (E-IX,2.4.1).

3.1 REQUESTING EARLY PROCESSING

A request for early processing may be filed with the EPO at any time before expiry of the 31-month period. The request does not require a specific wording, but applicants must clearly express that they wish the processing of their application before the EPO as designated/elected Office to commence early under Art.23(2) PCT or Art.40(2) PCT. The request can be made by ticking a box in EPO Form 1200 (OJ 2017 A74). Automatic debiting can be used for payments to be made (OJ 2022 sp3 Annex A.1 point 5.1(c)).

For the request to be effective, the applicant must comply with the requirements stipulated in **R.159(1)** as if the 31-month period expired on the date the applicant requests early processing. Note that these necessary requirements to make a request effective have no basis in the EPC. The following requirements must be complied with to make a request effective:

- payment of the filing fee (including any additional fee if the application comprises more than 35 pages);
- filing of a translation (if a translation is required under **Art.153(4)**);
- specification of the application documents; and
- payment of the search fee (where a supplementary European search report has to be drawn up under **Art.153(7)**).

It depends on the date on which early processing is requested which other requirements stipulated in **R.159(1)** must be complied with, since the (regular) periods for paying the designation fee (**R.39(1)**) and the renewal fee (**R.51(1)**) and for filing the request for examination and paying the examination fee (**R.70(1)**) may not have expired on the date of filing of the request for early processing. (Not. EPO OJ 2013 p.156; E-IX,2.8)

Note that filing the certificate of exhibition (**R.159(1)(h)**) is not a necessary requirement (OJ 2013 p.156 §13). However, if applicants want to exclude a disclosure at an international exhibition from the prior art, they must take care that the certificate is filed at the latest on the day that the request becomes effective.

If an applicant desires early processing of the application and the IB has not yet sent the international application to the EPO under Art.20(1) PCT by that time, the applicant may, but does not have to, file a request with the IB to do so; if needed, the EPO will take care of this itself (R.44bis.2(b) and R.47.4 PCT; Not. EPO OJ 2013 p.156 §17). If proceedings should be accelerated, the applicant should file the application themselves.

3.2 EFFECTIVE REQUEST

If on the date that the request for early processing is filed all necessary requirements for entry into the European phase are complied with, the request is effective and the Euro-PCT application will as from that date be processed in the same way as a normal Euro-PCT application which has entered the European phase without a request for early processing having been filed. On that date, the international phase is regarded terminated in respect of the EPO as designated/elected Office. The EPO will issue the **R.161/162** communication directly after it has established that the request is effective. (OJ 2013 p.156 §10)

If a necessary requirement is not fulfilled when filing the request for early processing, the request will become effective only when this requirement is complied with. Fulfilment of a further requirement of **R.159(1)** for which the period has not yet expired when filing the request, e.g. payment of the designation fee or a renewal fee or filing the request for examination, does not affect the request becoming effective. Such further requirements must be complied with before expiry of the appropriate period, even if such a period expires before the end of the 31-month period. Since by filing an effective request for early processing the processing ban is lifted, as from that date it is no longer possible to delay acts until expiry of the 31-month period. (OJ 2013 p.156 §10, 18-22)

3.3 ACCELERATED PROSECUTION OF A EURO-PCT APPLICATION

An early entry does not automatically lead to accelerated processing in the European phase; this requires a separate PACE request (OJ 2015 A93 §13). If the **R.70(1)** period for requesting examination has not yet expired when entering the European phase early, the prosecution can be shortened by filing the request for examination together with the request for early entry (OJ 2013 p.156 §15). See also **R.161(1):3** for acceleration of Euro-PCT applications where the EPO was (S)ISA, and **R.161(2):2** for acceleration of Euro-PCT applications where the EPO was not (S)ISA.

4 Review and excuse procedure

The international phase of an international application will end prematurely if the international application is refused a filing date or is considered withdrawn. Nevertheless, the EPO as designated or elected Office may decide that the international application can proceed as a European application (Art. 25 PCT). To this end, the applicant must carry out the required acts for entering the European phase and start the review and excuse procedure. Since the European phase must be entered shortly after the loss of rights has occurred, the entry will usually be early as set out in the above section.

If the loss of rights in the international phase is caused by an erroneous decision of an international Office, the applicant may request the EPO to review the negative decision and rectify it. If, on the other hand, the loss of rights is caused by an error of the applicant, the applicant must request the EPO to excuse the error. Usually, an applicant will file a main request to review and rectify the decision and, in case the review confirms the decision, an auxiliary request to excuse the error. The procedure is similar to that of **R.112(2)**.

4.1 REVIEW PROCEDURE

An applicant can request a review under Art.25(2)(a) PCT with the EPO as designated (or elected) Office by paying the filing fee of **R.159(1)(c)**, filing any translation of **R.159(1)(a)** with the EPO, and request the IB to send copies of any document in its file to the EPO (Art.25(1)(a) PCT), all within two months from the date of the communication of the loss of rights by the rO or IB (R.51.1 PCT; R.51.3 PCT; E-IX,2.9.1). The EPO recommends performing the other required acts under **R.159(1)** at the same time, possibly with a request for early processing (E-IX,2.9.1).

If the EPO finds that the decision is the result of an error or omission on the part of the rO or IB, it will treat the international application as if no such error or omission had occurred and allow the application to proceed as a European application, if necessary taking as filing date the date of receipt of the international application by the rO. The formalities officer acting on behalf of the examining division decides on the request (OJ 2014 A6 Art.1(23)). A decision refusing the request is appealable.

4.2 EXCUSE PROCEDURE

Art.48(2)(a) PCT obliges the EPO as designated (or elected) Office to excuse any delay in meeting any PCT time limit for reasons admitted under the EPC (see GL/PCT-EPO E-IX,2.9.2). This provision is of fundamental importance for the legal security of the PCT route in the absence of comprehensive legal remedies in the international phase (OJ EPO 1984 p.565 r.3). Hence, further processing and re-establishment are available as remedies before the EPO as designated (or elected) Office for time limits missed in the international phase (R.82bis.2 PCT), provided that the conditions for further processing and re-establishment are fulfilled (**J5/80** r.12). The type of remedy available for the missed PCT time limit is determined by reference to the comparable time limit under the EPC (OJ EPO 1984 p.565 r.6).

Under Art.24(2) PCT, the EPO as designated (or elected) Office may maintain the effect of the international application as a European patent application accorded the international filing date, even if the international application is considered withdrawn. This provides the basis for entering the European phase with an international application that is considered withdrawn and for requesting a remedy using Art.48(2)(a) PCT or any other remedy available under the EPC, in case of a missed time limit.

Any time limit for filing a request for excuse under Art.24(2) PCT with the EPO is governed only by the EPC (**J19/16** hn). Hence, the periods of **R.135(1)** and **R.136(1)** are applicable for further processing and for re-establishment, respectively. If the period for further processing is missed, re-establishment of this period can be requested (E-VIII,3.1.1). A request for excuse under Art.24(2) PCT can also be based on the principle of protection of legitimate expectations (**J19/16** r.7, without time limit; **Art.125:2**), on a request for correction (**R.139**; **J17/99**), or on any remedy which is available for Euro-direct applications in a comparable situation (**J17/99** r.6), e.g. a retroactive interruption of proceedings (**R.142**), or by requesting a decision under **R.112(2)** on the ground that the issue leading to a deficiency under the PCT that causes the application to be considered withdrawn forms no deficiency under the EPC (cf. Art.27(4) PCT).

The formal requirements for filing a request for excuse are the same as for a request for review (see **R.159:4.1**), except that the two-month period under R.51.1 PCT does not apply (E-IX,2.9.2).

Note that the PCT Applicant's Guide, Introduction into the National Phase, §6.025, indicates different requirements. Namely, the applicant must perform all acts to enter the regional phase and request the EPO to apply a remedy within the period specified in the EPC for that remedy without the need to request the IB to send a copy of the file to the EPO.

4.3 REVIEW BY THE EPO OF OWN MOTION

The EPO as designated (or elected) Office reviews, of its own motion, whether a decision of the rO to accord the international filing date based on incorporation by reference of a missing part or element complies with some of the requirements for such a decision, including the requirement that the added part or element is completely contained in the priority document (R.82*ter*.1(b) PCT). If the EPO disagrees with the decision of the rO, the EPO informs the applicant that it intends to consider the date on which the missing part or element was furnished as the international filing date of the Euro-PCT application and invites the applicant to comment. The applicant may request that the EPO disregards the added parts, thereby avoiding a re-dating of the application (E-IX,2.9.3). If the rO considered correct application documents to be incorporated by reference under R.20.5bis(d) PCT, the EPO proceeds as described in **R.159:6** (E-IX,2.9.4). When the rO has granted a request to restore a right of priority, the EPO as designated (or elected) Office may also review, of its own motion, the decision if it has reasonable doubt that some of the requirements for such a decision, including showing 'due care', were met (R.49ter.1(c) PCT; E-IX,2.3.5.3).

5 Rectification of errors made by the receiving Office or the International Bureau

After a regular entry into the European phase, an applicant can ask the EPO to rectify certain errors made by the rO or the IB.

An applicant may request the EPO as designated Office under R.82ter.1(a) PCT to review an allegedly incorrect filing date accorded by the rO, e.g. in case of an unjustified re-dating under R.20.3 PCT, or a priority claim incorrectly considered void by the rO or IB (R.26bis.2(b) PCT). The EPO must rectify the error if it would rectify it under the EPC. (E-IX,2.9.3)

6 **Treatment of erroneously filed parts corrected during the international phase**

The following applies to a PCT application filed between 01.07.2020 and 31.10.2022. If the PCT application is filed with incorrect parts, the rO may decide to allow the incorporation by reference of the correct parts from the priority document without changing the filing date (R.20.5*bis*(d) PCT; not applied by the EPO as rO). However, the EPO as designated Office does not accept such a decision of the rO for the PCT application (as it is filed between 01.07.2020 and 31.10.2022; R.20.8(b-bis) PCT; OJ 2022 A71 §23). Instead, the EPO re-dates the filing date of the Euro-PCT application to the date of receipt by the rO of the correct parts. The EPO will then consider the application as filed to include the correct application parts but not the erroneously filed parts. The EPO informs the applicant of this in a communication issued before the communication under **R.161**, setting a two-month period for reply (C-III,1.3; E-IX,2.8 for the procedure in case of early processing; OJ 2020 A81). The applicant may request within the two-month period that the EPO disregards the parts that were incorporated by reference under R.20.5*bis*(d) PCT in order to maintain the original filing date (R.20.8(c) PCT and R.82*ter*.1(d) PCT). The proceedings before the EPO as designated Office will be based on the application documents as filed on the original filing date. Alternatively, the applicant may file observations within the two-month period (R.82*ter*.1(c) PCT); the EPO will then issue an interlocutory decision taking those observations into account. Applicants may also either renounce the parts incorporated by reference or agree with the re-dating in advance of the communication from the EPO. (C-III,1.3; OJ 2020 A81)

For PCT applications filed on or after 01.11.2022, the EPO fully applies Rule 20.5bis PCT. This means that an incorporation by reference by the rO under Rule 20.5bis(d) PCT, i.e. without changing the filing date, is also effective before the EPO as designated Office, subject to a review under R.82ter.1(b) PCT if the EPO as designated office considers the decision of the receiving Office to be incorrect (OJ 2022 A71 §23)).

Any translation under **R.159(1)(a)** must include a translation of both the erroneously filed parts of the application and the corrected parts incorporated by reference. If the translation of the erroneously filed part of the application is omitted, the EPO invites the applicant to file it within a two-month period. If the applicant does not comply with the invitation, the application is deemed to be withdrawn (E-IX,2.1.4). The translation is published with both the erroneously filed and the correct parts (E-IX,2.5.1).

See **Rfees2(1):4.2.2** for the calculation of the page fee in these cases.

If the EPO as designated Office disregards claims submitted with a correction under R.20.5bis(d) PCT, thereby reinstating the original claims, this may trigger an invitation to pay a search fee under **R.164(2)** if the EPO acted as ISA (as set out in GL/PCT-EPO B-III,2.3.3) (C-III,3.1).

R. 159(1) In respect of an international application under Article 153, the applicant shall perform the following acts within thirty-one months from the date of filing of the application or, if priority has been claimed, from the priority date:

(a) supply, where applicable, the translation of the international application required under Article 153, paragraph 4;

(b) specify the application documents, as originally filed or as amended, on which the European grant procedure is to be based;
(c) pay the filing fee provided for in Article 78, paragraph 2;
(d) pay the designation fee if the period under Rule 39 has expired earlier;
(e) pay the search fee, where a supplementary European search report has to be drawn up;
(f) file the request for examination provided for in Article 94, if the period under Rule 70, paragraph 1, has expired earlier;
(g) pay the renewal fee in respect of the third year provided for in Article 86, paragraph 1, if the fee has fallen due earlier under Rule 51, paragraph 1;
(h) file, where applicable, the certificate of exhibition referred to in Article 55, paragraph 2, and Rule 25.

Amended, in force since 01.04.2009 (OJ 2008 p.513).
Art.55(2) Formalities for non-prejudicial disclosure at an exhibition
Art.78(2) Payment of filing fee
Art.86(1) Renewal fees
Art.94 Examination of the European patent application
Art.153 The European Patent Office as designated Office or elected Office
Art.153(4) Translation of international application published in a non-EPO language
R.25 Certificate of exhibition
R.39 Designation fee
R.51(1) Payment of renewal fee on last day of month containing anniversary
R.70(1) Payment of examination fee up to six months after publication of the search report

1 Acts for entry into the European phase

1.1 ACTS MENTIONED IN R.159(1)

R.159(1) lists the acts an applicant must perform with the EPO on entry of the international application into the European regional phase. The period fixed in the provision is 31 months from the date of filing of the international application or, if it claims priority, from the earliest priority date. The EPO has made use of the option given under Art.22(3) [Art.39(1)(b)] PCT to fix a period for entry longer than the 30-month period of Art.22(1) [Art.39(1)(a)] PCT. Since the period is an EPC period (because the duration is fixed in **R.159(1)** EPC), it must be calculated using **R.131(4)** EPC and not R.80.2 PCT.

The acts of specifying the documents for the European procedure under **R.159(1)(b)** and the payment of the filing fee under **(c)** must be carried out within the 31-month period. In some cases the normal periods for payment of the designation fee **(d)** and the renewal fee in respect of the third patent year **(g)** and filing of the request for examination expire later than the 31-month period. These acts may then be completed after expiry of the 31-month period. The filing of the translation **(a)** and payment of a search fee in relation to a supplementary European search **(e)** are necessary in certain cases only. A certificate of exhibition **(h)** is only rarely to be filed. The specific conditions for each of the acts mentioned in **R.159(1)** are given in the notes below, including the consequences of not performing the act in due time and any available remedies.

1.2 ADDITIONAL ACTS FOR ENTRY INTO THE EUROPEAN PHASE

In addition to the acts mentioned in **R.159(1)**, the applicant may be required to or voluntary carry out additional acts, depending on the facts of the case. Details of the additional acts are given in the provisions referred to and in the notes below:

- pay the claims fees of **R.162(1)** within the period of **R.162(2)** if the international application, taking into account any amendment under **R.161**, has more than fifteen claims;
- provide, upon invitation, data concerning the inventor if not submitted in the international phase (**R.163(1)**);
- where priority is claimed, furnish, upon invitation, the number and copy of the priority application if not yet submitted (**R.163(2)**);
- where applicable, file, upon invitation, a sequence listing in the correct format if not yet submitted (**R.163(3)**);
- if not yet submitted, furnish, upon invitation, the applicant's address, nationality and state of residence or principal place of business (**R.163(4)**);
- appoint, upon invitation, a professional representative if the applicant does not have a residence or place of business within the territory of an EPC contracting state (**Art.133(2)**; **R.163(5)**);
- pay, upon invitation, additional search fees under **R.164** if any claims were not searched by the EPO as (S)ISA;
- provide any search results for a priority application under **R.141(1)**, possibly after an invitation under **R.141(3)**;
- pay extension fees for extension states within the same period as the designation fee if protection there is desired (see **R.159(1):5.3**);
- pay validation fees for non-contracting states within the same period as the designation fee if protection there is desired (see **R.159(1):5.4**);
- file a request for restoration of priority (see **R.159(1):10**).

See Not. EPO OJ 2010 p.498 §5-13 and E-IX,2.4.4 for the requirements the international application must comply with for validly referring to a deposited biological sample under **R.31**.

1.3 FAILURE TO CARRY OUT ACTS IN TIME

If the applicant has not performed acts a, c, d, e, or f of **R.159(1)** within the 31-month period, the EPO will communicate to the applicant the fact that the application has been deemed withdrawn (**R.160(2)** and **R.112(1)**). The EPO issues a loss of rights communication pursuant to **R.112(1)** which indicates that the Euro-PCT application is deemed to be withdrawn (**R.160(2)**) and also indicates the missing items. The applicant may use further processing according to **Art.121** and **R.135**. The two-month period for requesting further processing starts with the notification of the communication of loss of rights. The Euro-PCT application will be deemed withdrawn if not remedied in due time (**R.160(1)**).

Further processing can be used even if the applicant carried out no acts at all to enter the European phase before the end of the 31-month period. The EPO issues a loss of rights communication for all PCT applications that did not timely enter the European phase. In such a case, further processing must be carried out for each omitted act separately. The renewal fee for the third year may have to be paid with a surcharge, depending on the due date; further processing is not available for the renewal fee. If the applicant fails to take any action within the period for requesting further processing, re-establishment can still be requested and multiple re-establishment fees will be due according to the EPO (see Example 1 in E-VIII,3.1.3; note that the renewal fee is not considered therein).

Note that not all the acts of **R.159(1)** are mentioned in **R.160(1)**, which means that if, for example a renewal fee is not paid (**J1/08**) or if a certificate of an international exhibition is not filed upon entry into the EP regional phase, no communication of deemed withdrawal under **R.160(2)** will be issued.

Failure to carry out any of the above 'additional acts' results in a different response from the EPO depending on which act was missed. See for example **R.162(2)** for missed claims fees, **R.163(6)** for a number of formal requirements mentioned in **R.163**, and **R.30(3)** for a missing sequence listing.

The 31-month period for completing the acts may be deferred by abandoning a priority claim. An abandonment in the international phase must be made within 30 months from the priority date (R.90bis.3(a) PCT). The EPO will probably not process an abandonment filed with it before expiry of the 31-month period because of the processing prohibition of Art.23(1) PCT. An abandonment received after expiry of the 31 months will not affect the time limit (A-III,6.11).

2 Translation (R.159(1)(a))

2.1 FILING TRANSLATION

Where the language of the international application as published in the international phase is not German, English or French, the applicant must furnish a translation in one of these languages upon entry into the regional phase as required by **Art.153(4)**. The language of the translation becomes the language of the proceedings before the EPO.

If the international application is published in English, French or German, the applicant has 'chosen' the language of the proceedings. The applicant cannot then file a translation in one of the other official languages of the EPO (**G4/08** hn.1). Any translation which is nevertheless filed will be ignored.

Art.14(2) allows correction of a translation of direct European applications filed in a language other than English, German or French. The provision also applies by analogy to Euro-PCT applications, because Euro-PCT applications are equivalent to regular European applications (**Art.153(2)**). Hence, an English translation filed on entry into the European phase may be brought into conformity with an original Japanese PCT application throughout proceedings before the EPO. (**T1483/10** r.2.2; A-VII,7)

An overview of which parts of the application must be included in the translation is given in E-IX,2.1.4. The translation must always include the originally filed description and claims; at least these parts must be filed within the 31-month period to avoid the application becoming deemed to be withdrawn under **R.160(1)**. (E-IX,2.1.4(i)-(ii))

The translation must also include, where applicable, any text in the drawings as originally filed and the abstract as published, any published request for rectification under R.91.3(d) PCT, any free text in a sequence listing unless already available to the EPO in English or the langue of the proceedings (Not. EPO OJ 2021 A97 §31), and any separately furnished references to deposited biological material. If the translation lacks any of these parts, the EPO issues an invitation to furnish the missing parts within a two-month period from notification of the invitation. Failure to file the missing parts within the two-month period leads to the application being deemed to be withdrawn. (E-IX,2.1.4(iii)-(vii))

If the claims were amended under Art.19 PCT and these amended claims are to form the basis for the procedure before the EPO, a translation of the amended claims must also be filed together with a translation of any statement under Art.19(1) PCT and a translation of the accompanying letter under R.46.5(b) PCT. If the translation lacks any of these parts, the EPO issues an invitation to furnish the missing parts within a two-month period from notification of the invitation. Failure to file the missing translation of the amended claims within the two-month period leads to the amendment under Art.19 PCT being disregarded. If the translation of the statement or accompanying letter is not filed within the two-month period, the EPO will disregard that statement and letter and may proceed under **R.137(4)**. (E-IX,2.1.4(viii))

If the EPO acts as elected Office, translations of all annexes to the international preliminary examination report (IPER) must also be filed. These annexes include replacement sheets, in particular amended claims considered by the IPEA in the IPER, and any accompanying letter under R.70.16 PCT and R.46.5(b) PCT. A translation of the IPER itself is not required from the applicant; a translation into English is prepared by the IB (R.72 PCT). If the translation lacks any part of the annexes to the IPER, the EPO issues an invitation to furnish the missing parts within a two-month period from notification of the invitation. If the translation of the replacement sheets is not filed within the two-month period, the application is deemed to be withdrawn. If the translation of the accompanying letter is not filed within the two-month period, the EPO will disregard that letter and may proceed under **R.137(4)**. (E-IX,2.1.4(ix))

2.2 EFFECT OF LATE FILING AND REMEDIES

If the translation of the originally filed description and claims has not been filed within 31 months of the priority date (**R.159(1)(a)**), the application is deemed to be withdrawn (Art.24(1)(iii) [Art.39(2)] PCT, **R.160(1)** and **R.112(1)**; E-IX,2.1.4). If the translation lacks any of the other elements, the EPO issues an invitation to furnish the translation within a two-month period from notification of the invitation (as discussed above in **R.159:2.1**). If the applicant does not timely respond to the invitation, the application is deemed to be withdrawn unless the missing part of the translation is an accompanying letter or the statement under Art.19 PCT which are merely disregarded if not filed (E-IX,2.1.4).

If the application is deemed to be withdrawn, one remedy is further processing, which can be achieved by paying the further processing fee and completing the omitted act, i.e. filing the translation, within two months of notification (**Art.121, R.135** and **Rfees2(1)12**). Another remedy, if applicable, is to ask within two months of notification for a decision under **R.112(2)** and prove that the translation was filed in due time.

Reinstatement (i.e. re-establishment) of rights can be requested as remedy for not filing a translation of the international application; a reference to R.49.6(d)(i) PCT has been explicitly added to the entry for re-establishment of rights in **Rfees2(1)13** (OJ 2007 p.692, III; R.49.6 PCT). This leads to the rather strange situation that the applicant may request re-establishment in the period for filing the translation. The PCT overrules here **R.136(3)** EPC, which excludes re-establishment in periods for which further processing is available (**Art.150(2)** EPC, last sentence).

According to R.49.6 PCT, reinstatement is only possible 'after failure to perform the acts referred to in Art.22 PCT', i.e. for filing the translation and paying the national fee (i.e. the filing fee). Hence, reinstatement is not available for late payment of, for example, the designation fee or the examination fee. The acts which can be remedied pursuant to R.49.6 PCT are the same as those for creating a prior-right effect (**Art.54(3)**) of a Euro-PCT application under **R.165** and **Art.153(5)**.

Re-establishment is probably useful only if the applicant has not met the two-month period for requesting further processing, otherwise it is strongly recommended to use the remedy of further processing. However, if the applicant has missed the period for requesting further processing for excusable reasons and entry of the international application before the EPO is still desired, re-establishment in the period of further processing may be requested while proving all due care.

3 **Amendment and basis for the grant procedure (R.159(1)(b))**

The grant procedure before the EPO as designated Office is normally based on the application documents as published by the IB, including any claims amended under Art.19 PCT. The grant procedure before the EPO as elected Office is usually based on the documents on which the international preliminary examination report is based, including any annexes (Art.34 PCT; E-IX,4.3.2).

R.159(1)(b) implements Art.28 PCT and allows the filing of amendments of the application on entry as basis for the grant procedure. Art.28 PCT allows an applicant to amend the international application to comply with specific requirements regarding patentability or multiple dependencies of claims of national or regional offices (see R.6.4(a) PCT). Whereas multiple dependencies are usually removed for national entry in for example the US and KR, there is no need to remove them for the EP procedure.

The possibility of voluntary amendment on entry under **R.159(1)(b)** is a lex specialis alongside **R.137(2)**. Note that amendments on entry are made after receipt of the search report mentioned in **R.137(1)**, because the international search report has taken the place of the European search report (**Art.153(6)**).

Amendments to the description, claims or figures can be filed as replacement pages. The complete set of claims should be replaced, not individual claims (OJ 2009 p.338).

The applicant may indicate that any of the application documents are to be replaced for the grant procedure by amendments filed under Art.19 PCT, Art.34 PCT and/or filed for the first time on entry. Shortly after entry into the European phase, the EPO will give the applicant an additional opportunity to amend the application under **R.161**.

Since **R.160(1)** does not refer to **R.159(1)(b)**, there is no sanction on not specifying the documents on which the grant procedure is to be based. Rather, the international application as published as well as any amendments made in the international phase will be used for the procedure before the EPO as designated or elected Office. Any amended pages filed in the international phase are in these cases treated as additional pages for the calculation of the page fee of **R.159(1)(c)** (E-IX,2.1.2; **Rfees2(1):4**).

4 Filing fee (R.159(1)(c))

4.1 PAYMENT OF FILING FEE

Upon entry into the regional phase, a filing fee must be paid, which is equal to the filing fee of **Art.78(2)**, the amount of which is fixed in **Rfees2(1)1**, with a lower fee level if the documents are filed online. Moreover, a page fee must be paid as part of the filing fee for any international application containing over 35 pages (**Rfees2(1)1a**). The page fee is calculated as set out in **Rfees2(1):4**.

There is no language reduction of the filing fee under **R.7a(1)**, because R.7a(1) refers only to the filing of a European patent application and because the filing fee of **R.159(1)(c)** is not equivalent to the filing fee of **R.7a(1)**. Indeed, the filing fee of **R.159(1)(c)** corresponds to the "national fee" of Art.22(1) and 39(1) PCT (E-IX,2.1.5.1), and, as such, does not fall under **R.7a(1)**. The fee may be reduced under **R.7a(3)** if the applicant qualifies for the reduction. Note, that the page fee is based on the international application as published by the IB, regardless of the language of the publication, but taking into account amendments under **R.159(1)(b)** (A-III,13.2).

4.2 FAILURE TO PAY AND REMEDY

If the filing fee, including any page fee, is not paid within 31 months (**Art.78(2), R.159(1)(c)**), the Euro-PCT application is deemed to be withdrawn (**R.160(1)** and **R.112(1)**). Moreover, the application will not have a prior right effect (**Art.153(5), R.165, Art.54(3)**). A first possible remedy is to request further processing, pay the further processing fee (50% of the filing fee) and complete the omitted act, i.e. pay the filing fee, within two months of the notification (**Art.121, R.135, Rfees2(1)1** and **Rfees2(1)12**). A second remedy, applicable if the EPO has made a mistake, is to ask for a decision under **R.112(2)** and prove that the payment was made in time.

As discussed in **R.159(1):2.2** above, under R.49.6 PCT, the applicant may also request re-establishment (**Art.122, R.136**) for payment of the filing fee (which is deemed to be to the national fee of Art.22 PCT), despite further processing (**Art.121, R.135**) being available (**Rfees2(1)13**; OJ 2007 p.692, III).

5 Designation fee (R.159(1)(d))

5.1 DESIGNATION FEE

A flat designation fee covering all EPC contracting states must be paid on entering the regional phase (**Art.79**; A-III,11.2.5; see **Rfees2(1)3** for the amount). A reduction is available for certain applicants, see **R.7a(3),(4)**.

Since all PCT contracting states are designated in the international application and all EPC contracting states are PCT contracting states, all EPC contracting states are designated upon entering the European regional phase, provided these states acceded to the EPC on or before the international filing date. The applicant may expressly withdraw the designation of one or more contracting states at any time up to the grant of the patent (A-III,11.2.4).

For most international applications the designation fee must be paid within 31 months from the date of filing or, where applicable, the priority date (**R.159(1)**). In the exceptional circumstance that the international search report is published after 25 months from the date of filing or priority and the period of **R.39(1)** therefore expires later than the 31 months, **R.159(1)(d)** does not apply and the designation fee may be paid up to the expiry of the six-month period of **R.39(1)**. This may also occur upon early entry into the European phase (OJ 2013 p.156 §10, 18, 19). See notes to AAD.3 note I.3 in ADA Annex A.2 for the automatic debiting of the designation fee.

5.2 **FAILURE TO PAY AND REMEDY**

If the designation fee is not paid in due time (**R.159(1)(d)**), the Euro-PCT application is deemed to be withdrawn (**R.160(1)**) at the expiry of the normal period of **R.159(1)(d)** (**G4/98** hn.II applied mutatis mutandis, A-III,11.2.3). The EPO will send a communication notifying the loss of rights under **R.160(2)** and **R.112(1)**. (A-III,11.2.5).

The remedy after failure to pay the designation fee in due time is further processing, which can be achieved by paying the further processing fee (50% of the designation fee) and completing the omitted act, i.e. paying the designation fee, within two months of the notification (**Art.121, R.135, Rfees2(1)3** and **Rfees2(1)12**). No request in writing for further processing needs to be filed. Alternatively, if the applicant regards the payment as having been made in due time, the applicant can ask within two months of notification for a decision under **R.112(2)** and provide proof of timely payment.

5.3 **DESIGNATION OF EXTENSION STATES**

Extension fees for extension states (see A-III,12 and **Art.169:3**) designated in an international application must be paid within the same period as the designation fee (A-III,12.2).

If an extension fee is not paid within the applicable period, the request for extension is withdrawn. If the designation fee is paid such that the application is not deemed withdrawn under **R.39(2)** and one or more extension fees have not been paid, then no communication under **R.112(1)** will be issued notifying the applicant of the loss of rights. In this case, further processing under **Art.121, R.135** will not be possible in respect of extensions deemed withdrawn. However, if one or more extensions are deemed withdrawn due to non-payment of the extension fees and the application is deemed withdrawn due to non-payment of the designation fee, then a communication under **R.160(2)** and **R.112(1)** will be issued notifying the applicant of the loss of rights with respect to both the withdrawn application *and* the withdrawn extensions in question (provided the applicant has not actively withdrawn all designations and has not waived the right to receive a **R.112(1)** communication for the designations). In this case, further processing under **Art.121, R.135** is possible for both the deemed withdrawn application and deemed withdrawn extensions, with the further processing fee of **Rfees2(1)12** applying mutatis mutandis for extension fees. Re-establishment of rights according to **Art.122, R.136** is not possible for payment of extension fees. (A-III,12.2)

A grace period of two months is available from expiry of the period in which the designation fee is to be paid or two months from notification of the communication of loss of rights due to an omitted payment of the designation fee. Payments of extension fees within the grace period attract a 50% surcharge. (A-III,12.2; OJ 2009 p.603)

5.4 **VALIDATION OF NON-CONTRACTING STATE**

A validation fee for a non-contracting state can be paid on entry into the European phase. The procedure for validation is similar to that for designation of extension states, see the preceding note. See A-III,12.2, and **Art.79(2):2.2**.

6 Search fee for the supplementary European search (R.159(1)(e))

6.1 PAYMENT OF SUPPLEMENTARY EUROPEAN SEARCH FEE

In principle, a supplementary European search report is drawn up in respect of any Euro-PCT application (**Art.153(7)**). A search fee must be paid where a supplementary search report has to be drawn up (**R.159(1)(e)**). The amount of the search fee for the European supplementary search is set in **Rfees2(1)2**. No supplementary European search report will be drawn up and no search fee need be paid on entry for international applications for which the EPO as ISA has drawn up an (supplementary) international search report (**Art.153(7):3**). See **Art.153(7):4** for the cases for which a reduced search fee applies. A reduction is available for certain applicants, see **R.7a(3),(4)**.

If a supplementary European search report is drawn up, the EPO will send an invitation under **R.70(2)** after issuing said search report, thereby inviting applicants to indicate whether they want to proceed further with the application, unless the right to this invitation has been waived by the applicant. See **R.164(1):2** for details of the procedure of the supplementary search report.

See **Rfees9** for a possible refund of the search fee in respect of the supplementary European search.

6.2 FAILURE TO PAY AND REMEDY

Any search fee must be paid within 31 months from filing or, where applicable, priority (**R.159(1)(e)**). If a due search fee is not paid within the 31-month period, the Euro-PCT application is deemed to be withdrawn (**R.160(1)**). One remedy is further processing, which can be achieved by paying the further processing fee (50% of the search fee) and completing the omitted act, i.e. paying the search fee, within two months from notification of the communication (**R.160(2)**; **R.112(1)**) informing the applicant of the deemed withdrawal (**Art.121, R.135, Rfees2(1)2** and **Rfees2(1)12**). No request in writing for further processing need be filed; acts in relation to fees can be carried out electronically. In the event that the EPO has made an error, the situation may be remedied by asking for a decision under **R.112(2)** and proving that the search fees were paid on time.

7 Request for examination (R.159(1)(f))

7.1 PAYMENT OF EXAMINATION FEE

The request for examination of the international application under the EPC is based on **Art.94** EPC, and includes a written request and payment of an examination fee (**Art.94(1)**, **R.70(1)**). The written request is contained (pre-printed) in the form for Entry into the European phase (EPO form 1200).

The amount of the examination fee is fixed in **Rfees2(1)6**. The examination fee may be reduced by 30% under **R.7a(1)** EPC and **Rfees14(1)** for entitled persons using an admissible language for the written request for examination (see **R.7a(1):1**), if the written request for examination is filed in an admissible non-EPO language (A-X,9.3.3). The examination fee may be reduced also under **R.7a(3)** for certain applicants.

In addition, the examination fee may be reduced by 75% under **Rfees14(2)** if the EPO acted as IPEA in the international phase. If two of the above reductions apply (reduction under **R.7a(1)** or **R.7a(3)** and reduction under **Rfees14(2)**), the total reduction in the examination fee is 82.5% (A-X,9.5.2). If all the reductions apply, the total reduction in the examination fee is 87.75%. The examination fee may be further reduced by 30% of the previously paid international search fee in case the EPO was the ISA (see **R.7a(3):4**).

The amount of the examination fee is dependent on which international authorities acted as ISA, SISA and/or IPEA. If the EPO acted as ISA or SISA in the international phase, then the EPO does not draw up a supplementary European search report, whereas if the EPO did not act as ISA or SISA in the international phase, then the EPO will draw up a supplementary European search report (**Art.153(7)**). If a supplementary European search report is drawn up, applicants have a six-month period from a communication under **R.70(2)** and **R.70a(2)** to state whether they wants to continue with the prosecution of the Euro-PCT application and, if so, to correct any deficiencies in the opinion accompanying the supplementary European search report; failure to respond will result in the application being deemed withdrawn (OJ 2009 p.533 §5.1.5).

The examination fee must normally be paid within 31 months from the date of filing or, where applicable, priority (**R.159(1)**). In the exceptional circumstance that the international search report (which takes the place of the European search report (**Art.153(6)**)) is published after 25 months from the date of filing or priority and the period of **R.70(1)** will expire later than the 31 months, **R.159(1)(f)** does not apply and the request for examination may be filed up to the expiry of the six-month period of **R.70(1)**. This may also occur upon early entry into the European phase (OJ 2013 p.156 §10, 18, 19). The period for payment of the examination fee is independent of whether or not a supplementary European search report will be drawn up.

The above periods are not affected by a possible supplementary European search report drawn up by the EPO or by the publication of the translation of an international application earlier published in a language other than an official EPO language (**Art.153(4)**). If a supplementary European search report has to be drawn up, applicants will receive the communication of **R.70(2)** (E-IX,2.5.3), inviting them to indicate whether to proceed with the application.

See **R.159:4** for acceleration of prosecution before the EPO, and **Rfees11** for refund of the examination fee.

7.2 FAILURE TO PAY OR FILE REQUEST AND REMEDY

If the examination fee is not paid in due time, the Euro-PCT application is deemed to be withdrawn (**R.160(1)**). One remedy is further processing, which can be achieved by paying the further processing fee (50% of the examination fee) and completing the omitted act, i.e. paying the examination fee, within two months of the notification of the communication (**R.160(2)** and **R.112(1)**) informing the applicant of the deemed withdrawal (**Art.121, R.135, Rfees2(1)6** and **Rfees2(1)12**). No request in writing for further processing need be filed; acts in relation to fees can be carried out electronically. In the event that the EPO has made an error, the applicant may remedy the situation by asking for a decision under **R.112(2)** and proving that the examination fee was paid on time.

In the case where no form 1200 is used on entry into the EP phase and the written request for examination has not been filed, the loss of rights can be remedied using further processing by filing the written request for examination and paying the fixed further processing fee of **Rfees2(1)12**. Note, that in the case where none of the acts of **R.159(1)** have been completed, i.e. no steps have been taken to enter the EP phase, further processing can also be used as remedy.

8 Renewal fees (R.159(1)(g))

8.1 PAYMENT OF RENEWAL FEES

The amount of the renewal fees is fixed in **Rfees2(1)4**. The renewal fee for the third year can be validly paid until the later of the due date according to **R.51(1)** and the expiry of the 31-month period (**R.159(1)(g)**). This is a consequence of the fact that the PCT provisions prevail over the EPC provisions (**Art.150(2)** EPC, last sentence and Art.23, Art.40 PCT). A reduction is available for certain applicants, see **R.7a(3),(4)**.

8.2 FAILURE TO PAY AND REMEDY

If the renewal fee is not paid in due time, the EPO informs applicants as a courtesy that the renewal fee has not been paid and indicates that a six-month additional period applies in which they may still pay the renewal fee with a 50% additional fee (A-X,5.2.4; **R.51(2)**; **Rfees2(1)5**). The six-month period is triggered by the due date according to **R.51(1)** or the expiry of the 31-month period, depending on the case (**R.159(1)(g)**; see section 8.3 and 8.4 below).

If not paid at expiry of the six-month additional period, the Euro-PCT application is deemed to be withdrawn (**R.51(2)** last sentence).

The failure to pay cannot be remedied by further processing because the period of **R.51(2)** is excluded in **R.135(2)**. However, because of this exclusion, re-establishment is possible under **Art.122** and **R.136**, provided all due care can be proven. In the event that the EPO has made an error, the applicant may remedy the situation by asking for a decision under **R.112(2)** and proving that the renewal fee was paid in due time.

Note, that non-payment of renewal fees is not mentioned in **R.160(1)** as a ground for deemed withdrawal of a Euro-PCT application.

8.3 DUE DATE BEFORE EXPIRY OF THE 31-MONTH PERIOD

There are two different cases for calculation of the last day on which the renewal fee can validly be paid. The first case is where the due date falls before the expiry of the 31-month period. This happens when the application does not claim priority or was filed within approximately 7 months from the priority date. The date of expiry of the 31-month period becomes the deferred due date according to **R.159(1)(g)**. This date also forms the basis for calculating the additional aggregate six-month period of **R.51(2)** (**J1/89** r.4; A-X,5.2.4; E-IX,2.1.5.5). Any extension under **R.134** should be applied to both the expiry of the 31-month period and of the six-month additional period. An example of an aggregate period calculation:

11.01.2016	priority date, relevant event for start of 31-month period;
09.05.2016	international filing date, relevant event for renewal fee;
31.05.2018	due date renewal fee in respect of the 3rd year;
11.08.2018	(Saturday) expiry of 31-month period;
13.08.2018	(Monday) expiry of 31-month period, extended under **R.134(1)**; deferred due date;
13.02.2019	expiry of 6-month period of **R.51(2)**.

Note, that the deviating calculation of **J4/91** for the additional period (see **R.51(2):1**) and the comparable calculation of periods for renewal fees for divisional applications according to **R.51(3)** are not applicable in this situation. Since the deferred due date is the expiry of a period, the calculation of aggregate periods must be used (see **R.131(2):3**).

8.4 **DUE DATE AFTER EXPIRY OF THE 31-MONTH PERIOD**

The second case is where the due date falls after the expiry of the 31-month period. This happens when the application is filed after about seven months from the priority date. In the second case the due date is the last day of a month according to **R.51(1)** and the calculation of the six-month period follows the rules for a direct European application as given in **R.51(3):1.** Because the due date is not the expiry of a period which can be extended under **R.134** (**J4/91** r.3.2), the due date does not shift to the first working day if it falls on a non-working day. Only the payment of the renewal fee may validly be deferred to the next working day. The six-month additional period runs from the due date, irrespective of whether or not the due date is a non-working day, to the last day of the sixth month (**J4/91**, de ultimo ad ultimo). If that day is a non-working day, **R.134** should be applied.

An example of a calculation:

13.12.2015	priority date, relevant event for start of 31-month period;
12.12.2016	international filing date, relevant event for renewal fee;
13.07.2018	expiry of the 31-month period;
31.12.2018	(New Year's Eve) due date renewal fee in respect of the 3rd year;
02.01.2019	last day for valid payment without additional fee (**R.134(1)**);
30.06.2019	(Sunday) expiry of 6-month period (**R.51(2)**);
01.07.2019	(Monday) last day for valid payment with additional fee (**R.134(1)**).

Beware, the 31-month period runs from the priority date, whereas the third year for the renewal fee is calculated from the international filing date!

Since the renewal fee in respect of the third year may be paid up to six months before the due date, the applicant may include the renewal fee in the payments made on entry also in the second case (see **R.51(1):1**).

9 Certificate of exhibition (R.159(1)(h))

A disclosure at an international exhibition may be removed from the prior art of a direct European application, when on filing of the application a statement about the display at the exhibition is made (**Art.55(2)**) and within four months from filing a certificate providing facts about the exhibition is submitted (**R.25**).

For a Euro-PCT application **R.159(1)(h)** requires that only the certificate be filed within the 31-month period of **R.159(1)**. The applicant will be notified of any defects in the certificate (A-IV,3.2).

An applicant may anticipate any EPO requirement by including a declaration on non-prejudicial disclosures under R.4.17(v) PCT when filing the international application. If done so, and no certificate was filed on entry into the European phase, the EPO will notice the omission and send the applicant a loss of rights communication under **R.112(1)**, which allows further processing as remedy.

If the applicant did not include the declaration in the PCT filing, the EPO will not notice a missing certificate and will not issue a loss of rights communication (see however E-IX,2.4.3). In such a case further processing is not available because **R.135(1)** is not applicable where no loss of rights communication is issued. Re-establishment may be possible.

If the certificate has not been filed, there is no application of **Art.55(2)**.

10 **Restoration of priority**
If the PCT application was filed after the expiry of the priority period but within two months of that expiry, the applicant may file a request for restoration of priority with the EPO as designated (or elected) Office upon entry into the European phase under R.49ter.2 PCT (E-IX,2.3.5.3). The request must be reasoned; the EPO applies the 'due care' criterion of R.49ter.2(a)(i) PCT in accordance with its practice under **Art.122**. The fee of **Rfees2(1)13** must be paid within the same period (R.49ter.2(d) PCT). If the fee is not paid in due time, the request is deemed to not have been filed (**J8/18**).

The procedure can be used if restoration of priority is desired and no request for restoration of priority was filed with the rO in the international phase, or if such a request was filed with the rO but rejected by the rO, or if such a request was granted by the rO under the 'unintentional' criterion. The EPO as designated Office generally recognises decisions of the rO taken under R.26bis.3 PCT to grant the restoration of priority based on the 'due care' criterion (R.49ter.1(a) PCT; Not. EPO OJ 2007 p.694). Decisions of the rO to grant restoration based on the 'unintentional' criterion have no effect with the EPO as designated Office and a new restoration request must be filed with the EPO (**J13/16**). A request for restoration filed with the rO cannot be taken into account as a request in the proceedings before the EPO as designated Office (**J13/16**).

The period for filing the request is one month from the expiry of the 31-month period or from the effective date of early entry into the European phase (R.49ter.2(b)(i) PCT). If the application is deemed withdrawn under **R.160(1)** for failure to comply with a requirement under **R.159(1)**, the request for restoration of priority may still be filed together with a timely request for further processing in respect of the **R.159(1)** period or with a timely request for re-establishment for said further processing (E-IX,2.3.5.3). If the request for restoration is not filed with EPO as designated Office in due time, neither further processing is available as a remedy (**J8/18** r.3.11) nor re-establishment (**J13/16** hn.2, r.4.9).

If a request for restoration is rejected and the 31-month time limit running from the priority date has already expired prior to this rejection, this time limit will not be deferred. In other words, the change in the priority date does not restore any loss of rights that occurred before the loss of the priority date. (E-VIII,1.5)

R. 159(2) The Examining Division shall be competent to take decisions of the European Patent Office under Article 25, paragraph 2(a) PCT.

Art.25(2)(a) PCT Review procedure

1 **Review by EPO as designated office**
The EPO may decide, in accordance with the review procedure of Art.25 PCT, to allow an international application that is deemed to be withdrawn or not accorded a filing date, to proceed as a European application (see **R.159:4**). The examining division is competent to take decisions in relation to such applications, and the Receiving Section transfers copies of any documents received from the IB under the circumstances of Art.25(1)(a) PCT to the examining division.

R. 160 Consequences of non-fulfilment of certain requirements and deemed withdrawal

Amended, in force since 16.12.2024 (OJ 2024 A105, Not. EPO OJ 2024 A106).

Implementation of **Art.153**

R. 160(1) If either the translation of the international application or the request for examination is not filed in due time, or if the filing fee, the search fee or the designation fee is not paid in due time, the European patent application shall be deemed to be withdrawn.

1 **Effect of non-compliance**
A Euro-PCT application is deemed to be withdrawn according to **R.160(1)**, if within 31 months from the date of filing or, if priority has been claimed, from the priority date:
- a required translation has not been filed (**R.159(1)(a)**);
- the filing fee, including the page fee, has not been paid (**R.159(1)(c)**);
- the designation fee has not been paid unless the period of **R.39** has not yet expired (**R.159(1)(d)**),
- a required search fee in respect of the supplementary European search has not been paid (**R.159(1)(e)**); or
- the request for examination has not been filed or is deemed to not have been filed because the examination fee has not been paid, unless the period **R.70(1)** has not yet expired (**R.159(1)(f)**).

R. 160(2) If the European Patent Office notes that the application is deemed to be withdrawn under paragraph 1, it shall communicate this to the applicant. Rule 112, paragraph 2, shall apply mutatis mutandis.

R.112(2) Review of opinion regarding loss of rights

1 **Procedure for correction**
After expiry of the 31-month period of **R.159(1)**, the EPO automatically starts the processing of all international applications which designate the EPO, including those applications for which the applicant does not have the intention to obtain a patent under the EPC, for instance because of prejudicial prior art mentioned in the (supplementary) international search report. The EPO can only close the files of the latter applications after it has communicated the loss of rights to the applicant. If the EPO notes that the Euro-PCT application is deemed to be withdrawn, it shall communicate this to the applicant under **R.160(2)**, first sentence.

The standard remedy is further processing. However, the applicant may, within two months from the notification, request the EPO to review its opinion on the loss of rights under **R.112(2)**, if the applicant can prove that the periods were actually met (**R.160(2)**, second sentence). See **R.112(2):1** for the procedure. Any loss of rights ensues upon expiry of the normal period (**G4/98**).

Not all acts of **R.159(1)** are mentioned in **R.160(1)**; this means that if, for example a renewal fee is not paid or if the certificate of an international exhibition is not filed upon entry into the EP regional phase, no communication of deemed withdrawal under **R.160(2)** will be issued (see **R.159(1):8** for failure to pay the renewal fee).

2 **Further processing and re-establishment**
The normal period of **R.159(1)** for payment of the designation fee or search fee for the supplementary European search and for filing the request for examination is excluded from re-establishment because further processing is available as a remedy (**Art.121, Art.122, R.136(3)**. As discussed in **R.159(1):2.2**, since the EPO has withdrawn its reservation filed under R.49.6 PCT, the applicant may, in principle, request re-establishment (**Art.122, R.136**) for pay-

ment of the filing fee and filing of the translation, despite further processing (**Art.121**, **R.135**) being available.

R. 160(3) On entry of a Euro-PCT application into the European phase, the designation of those Contracting States that are Member States of the European Union shall be deemed to be withdrawn in accordance with Rule 39, paragraph 2a.

Inserted by decision of the Administrative Council and in force since 16.12.2024. R.160(3) is applicable to Euro-PCT applications entering the European phase on or after 25.06.2024 (OJ 2024 A105, Not. EPO OJ 2024 A106). Note that this amendment is not present in the full English version of the amended Implementing Regulations annexed to the decision of the same date, concerning the amendments to gender-neutral language.
R.39(2a) Deemed withdrawal designations in case of Russian applicant

1 **EU sanctions against Russia**
New **R.160(3)** implements the 14th package of EU sanctions against Russia for Euro-PCT applications. Once the processing by the EPO as designated or elected Office starts, the designation of any contracting states that are EU member states is deemed withdrawn (Not. EPO OJ 2024 A106 Art.7). If the information identifying any applicant is missing, the EPO will first send an invitation to provide it, and, if this is not done, will refuse the application (**R.163(4)** and **R.163(6)**). For further information, see **R.39(2a)**.

R. 161 Amendment of the application

Amended, in force since 01.05.2011 (OJ 2010 p.634; see also OJ 2009 p.582).
Implementation of **Art.153**

1 **Communication issued after entry into European phase**
Shortly after entry into the European phase the EPO issues a communication under **R.161**, which can have one of three forms. If the EPO was (S)ISA, it will issue a communication under **R.161(1)** and will not carry out a supplementary European search. There are two types of the **R.161(1)** communication: either the communication includes an invitation to correct deficiencies or the communication does not include such an invitation. Only in the first case is a response mandatory. The invitation is not included if the EPO did not note any deficiencies in the international phase or if the applicant has already filed a response dealing with the deficiencies. If the EPO was not (S)ISA, it will issue a communication under **R.161(2)**, providing an opportunity to amend voluntarily the application, and, subsequently, it will carry out a supplementary European search.

Both types of **R.161(1)** communication and the **R.161(2)** communication also give the applicant the opportunity to make voluntary amendments. Hence, the applicant's right to amend voluntarily the application before the EPO as designated or elected Office, based on Art.28(1), R.52.1 PCT and Art.41(1), R.78.1 PCT, is implemented by **R.137(2)** when the EPO has acted as (S)ISA, and by **R.161(2)** when the EPO has not acted as (S)ISA.

R. 161(1) If the European Patent Office has acted as the International Searching Authority and, where a demand under Article 31 PCT was filed, also as the International Preliminary Examining Authority for a Euro-PCT application, it shall give the applicant the opportunity to comment on the written opinion of the International Searching Authority or the International Preliminary Examination Report and, where appropriate, invite them to correct any deficiencies noted in the written opinion or in the International Preliminary Examination Report and to amend the description, claims and drawings within a period of six months from the respective communication. If the European Patent Office has drawn up a supplementary international search report, an invitation in accordance with the first sentence shall be issued in respect of the explanations given in accordance with Rule 45*bis*.7(e) PCT. If the applicant does not comply with or comment on an invitation in accordance with the first or second sentence, the application shall be deemed to be withdrawn.

Art.31 PCT Demand for international preliminary examination
R.45bis.7(e) PCT Explanations in supplementary international search report
Amended by decision of the Administrative Council of 10.12.2024, which entered into force on 01.04.2025 (OJ 2025 A16). The amendment was introduction of gender-neutral language.

1 **Response to written opinion drafted by EPO as (S)ISA or IPEA**
R.161(1) applies to Euro-PCT applications where the EPO has acted as ISA, SISA, or both as ISA and IPEA. The **R.161(1)** communication always gives the applicant an opportunity to comment on the results of the examination by the EPO in the international phase.

The communication includes 'where appropriate' an invitation to correct any deficiencies in the application and to amend the application. The invitation is 'appropriate' if deficiencies are noted in the written opinion prepared by the EPO as ISA, in the explanations that are part of the supplementary international search report prepared by the EPO as SISA, or in the IPER prepared by the EPO as IPEA. (OJ 2010 p.316; E-IX,3.2)

Where the communication contains an invitation to correct deficiencies, filing a response is mandatory and the application is deemed to be withdrawn if no response is filed in due time. The mandatory response can be a correction of the deficiencies or a comment on the invitation, i.e. a substantive rebuttal of the alleged deficiencies. A mere procedural request, such as for oral proceedings, is not a sufficient response (E-IX,3.3.1; B-XI,8).

The communication does not include an invitation to correct deficiencies if the EPO did not note any deficiencies and the written opinion or, where applicable, the IPER prepared by the EPO was positive (E-IX,3.3.2). The invitation is neither included if a response is already on file in the form of new amendments and/or comments filed upon entry of the regional phase before the EPO under **R.159(1)(b)**. The invitation is also omitted if amended claims were filed under Art.19 PCT or Art.34 PCT, provided that the EPO did not already consider the amendments as IPEA and these claims are maintained upon entry of the EP phase (OJ 2009 p.533 §5.2.3; E-IX,3.3.1). Filing a response is voluntary in the case of a **R.161(1)** communication without the invitation.

Under **R.137(2)** applicants may file amendments of their own volition within the **R.161(1)** period. These voluntary amendments may be filed during the entire period, as a separate letter or together with a mandatory response.

In the event that the receiving Office notifies the EPO as ISA of correct parts of the international application that are included in the application under R.20.5*bis* PCT, the EPO as ISA will in certain cases draw up an international search report and written opinion for the correct parts, as well as a non-official search report and written opinion for the application with the original incorrect parts (OJ 2020 A81 §6). The applicant has no obligation to respond to the non-official written opinion under **R.161(1)** (GL/PCT-EPO B-III,2.3.4).

2 **Period for filing response**

The **R.161(1)** communication is sent to the applicant shortly after the expiry of the 31-month period for entry into the European phase, typically after about two months. The period for filing a response is six months from the notification of the communication (**R.161(1)**, first sentence).

Where the communication contains an invitation to correct deficiencies, filing a response is mandatory and the application is deemed to be withdrawn if no response is filed in due time. (**R.161(1)**, last sentence). Further processing under **Art.121** and **R.135** is available. If voluntary amendments are filed after the expiry of the period, they can still be admitted at the discretion of the examining division (**R.137(3)**).

3 **Acceleration of processing**

The EPO will not start examining the Euro-PCT application upon receipt of the response under **R.161(1)**, but wait until expiry of the six-month period, because the applicant may file voluntary amendments during the entire period, either together with the mandatory response or by separate letter (see **R.137(2):1**). If applicants do not want the EPO to wait until the expiry of the six-month period, they may waive the remainder of the period. They can send the waiver together with or after the filing of the response. (OJ 2015 A94 §5)

Applicants can accelerate the processing of the application by waiving their right to the **R.161(1)** communication, either in Form 1200 or by separate letter. The EPO will not issue the **R.161** communication and start processing the application immediately only if the applicant has filed a waiver and, additionally, has complied with all requirements of **R.161** and **162** (OJ 2015 A94 §4). The requirements are payment of any claims fees and filing a mandatory response where required. If not complied with, the waiver will not be valid, a communication under **R.161(1)** will be issued and processing will start in principle only after the expiry of the six-month period, even if a PACE request has been filed (E-IX,3.2). Note, that claims fees cannot be paid using automatic debiting if the communication has been waived, because the six-month period of **R.162(2)** will not be triggered (see notes to AAD.3 note I.4 in ADA Annex A.2); payment should be made on entry by other means. If the **R.161(1)** communication is waived, voluntary amendments may be filed at any time during the grant procedure (see **R.137(2):1**).

The examination can be further accelerated by filing a PACE request. The requirements for such a request are set out in **Art.94(1):5**. The request can be filed at any time during the European phase if the EPO was (S)ISA, for example together with the Form 1200 or with the response to the **R.161(1)** communication (OJ 2015 A93 §13). The applicant can enquire about the status of the file as set out in **Art.94(1):6**.

R. 161(2) Where the European Patent Office draws up a supplementary European search report on a Euro-PCT application, the application may be amended once within a period of six months from a communication informing the applicant accordingly. The application as amended shall serve as the basis for the supplementary European search.

1 **Amendment of application for which EPO did not act as ISA or SISA**
A **R.161(2)** communication is issued for Euro-PCT applications for which the EPO will draw up a supplementary search report under **Art.153(7)**. This is the case where the EPO did not act as ISA or SISA (Dec. AC OJ 2009 p.594); hence also if the EPO was IPEA but another office was ISA (**Art.152:3**). The **R.161(2)** communication gives the applicant the opportunity to file voluntary amendments within a period of six months. Applicants may also comment on the written opinion or IPER but they are not required to. The provision of such an opportunity for amendment on entry into the regional phase is required by the PCT. The application as amended will serve as the basis for the subsequent supplementary European search (**R.161(2)**, last sentence). Any comments submitted will be taken into account. (E-IX,3.1)

Any voluntary comments and amendments must be filed within six months of the **R.161(2)** invitation. Failure to meet the period can probably not be remedied using further processing, because no communication of failure to observe the period as required by **R.135(1)** will be issued. After receipt of the supplementary European search report, the applicant will have a second opportunity to file a voluntary amendment within the period of **R.70a(2)**. (H-II,2.2; C-II,3.1)

2 **Acceleration of processing**
The EPO will only start the supplementary search after expiry of the six-month period of **R.161(2)**, even if the applicant replies earlier the communication under **R.161(2)**.

If applicants do not wish to use the entire six-month period, they can request an immediate start of the search in reply to the **R.161(2)** communication, thereby waiving the remaining part of the period. The request may be filed together with amendments. (OJ 2015 A94 §5)

The applicant can accelerate the start of the search by waiving the **R.161(2)** communication, either in the Form 1200 for entry into the European phase or by separate letter. A valid waiver requires payment of any claims fees under **R.162(1)** upon entry into the European phase. If the waiver is valid, no **R.161(2)** communication is issued (OJ 2015 A94, §4). See also **R.161(1):3**.

The EPO always accelerates the supplementary search; no PACE request for accelerated search is needed. The EPO strives to issue the supplementary search report within six months from expiry of the six-month period of **R.161(2)**, or, if the **R.161(2)** communication has been waived, from entry into the European phase (OJ 2015 A93 §6, 9, 10(iii)).

If the supplementary search report of PCT application has not been issued within six months from expiry of the period under **R.161(2)** and the applicant files an enquiry about the status of the file using Form 1012 (see **Art.94(1):6**), the EPO will issue the search report within one month from receipt of the enquiry. If the supplementary search report of an application filed before 01.06.2014 and claiming priority has not been issued yet and the applicant files an enquiry using Form 1012, the EPO will issue the search report within six months from receipt of the enquiry. (OJ 2016 A66 §6; E-VIII,7)

The prosecution can be accelerated further by waiving the **R.70(2)** communication normally issued after completion of the supplementary search (OJ 2015 A94 §1). The waiver can be made on the Form 1200 (E-IX,2.5.3).

A PACE request for accelerated examination can be filed once the examining division is responsible for the application (OJ 2015 A93 §12). The request can be filed at the earliest together with the confirmation required under **R.70(2)** or, if the **R.70(2)** communication is waived, together with the response to the first **Art.94(3)** communication (OJ 2015 A93 §12 and R.70a(2):1). The formal requirements for the request are set out in **Art.94(1):5**.

The grant can also be accelerated as set out in **Art.97(1):2**.

R. 162 Claims incurring fees

Implementation of **Art.153**

1 **General**

This rule provides the legal basis for levying claims fees for an international application in the European phase and is structured according to **R.45**. The claims fees are based on the number of claims present upon entry into the European phase (**R.162(1)**), or, if amended in response to the **R.161** communication, on the number of claims in the response. In the latter case, any claims fees overpaid in the period of **R.159(1)** are refunded (**R.162(3)**) or any underpaid claims fees are charged. (OJ 1999 p.660, 696)

Claims fees are payable for claims 16 and above (**Rfees2(1)15**). Applicants are advised to keep the number of claims to a maximum of fifteen if at all possible, or reduce the number of claims after European regional phase entry to a reasonable number using **R.161**, to avoid payment of the excess claims fees (see **R.45(1):2**).

R. 162(1) If the application documents on which the European grant procedure is to be based comprise more than fifteen claims, claims fees shall be paid for the sixteenth and each subsequent claim as laid down in the Rules relating to Fees within the period under Rule 159, paragraph 1.

Amended, in force since 01.04.2008 (OJ 2008 p.124).
R.159(1) Requirements for entry into the European phase

1 **Amount and period**

The amount of the claims fee is fixed in **Rfees2(1)15**. Claims fee are due only for those claims on which the grant procedure is to be based. In principle, the claims fees must be paid in the 31-month period of **R.159(1)** from the date of filing or, where applicable, date of priority.

R. 162(2) If the claims fees are not paid in due time, they may still be paid within the period under Rule 161, paragraph 1 or paragraph 2, as the case may be. If within this period amended claims are filed, the claims fees due shall be computed on the basis of such amended claims and shall be paid within this period.

Amended, in force since 01.01.2017. The amended rule applies to Euro-PCT applications for which the **R.161/162** communication had not been issued on 01.01.2017. (OJ 2016 A102, A103). The amendment is a response to **J11/12** and clarifies the unchanged practice of the office.
R.161(1) Invitation to respond to written opinion where EPO was ISA
R.161(2) Invitation to amend application where EPO was not ISA

1 **Effect of non-payment and further processing**
If the claims fees are not paid within the 31-month period they may still be paid within the six-month period of **R.161**, without a surcharge being payable (**R.162(2)**; E-IX,2.3.8).

The applicant may file amended claims in response to the **R.161** communication. The claims fees due shall be computed on the basis of such amended claims and shall be paid within this period.

If not paid by expiry of the **R.161** period, the excess claims are deemed abandoned (**R.162(4)**). The loss of rights may be remedied using further processing (**Art.121, R.135**), with the further processing fee being 50% of the unpaid claims fees. In the event the EPO has made an error, the applicant may ask, within two months after notification of the loss of rights, for a decision under **R.112(2)** and prove that the claims fees were timely paid.

2 **Special cases**
When automatic debiting is used, the claims fees are deemed paid on the last day of the six-month period of **R.162(2)** (AAD.5.1(a)). Where the communication under **R.161** and **162** is waived, any claims fees cannot be paid by automatic debiting and must be paid by another means of payment (notes to AAD.3 note I.4 in ADA Annex A.2).

If a mandatory response to the **R.161(1)** communication is not filed in the six-month period, the EPO will inform the applicant that the application is deemed withdrawn. The applicant may respond by requesting further processing and filing amended claims in the two-month period for further processing. Since the amended claims will form the basis for the grant procedure, any claims fees must, according to **R.162**, be paid for the amended set of claims. A further processing fee has to be paid being the total of the fixed fee for late filing the response, and 50% of the claims fee (which may be zero) (**Rfees2(1)12**). Any claims fees the EPO may already have debited using automatic debiting at expiry of the six-month period will be refunded and any claims fees due plus the further processing fee will be debited on the last day of the further processing period (notes to AAD. 3 note I.4 in ADA Annex A.2).

If a voluntary response to the **R.161** communication is not filed within the six-month period, the EPO will not send a loss-of-rights communication. The response is voluntary if the EPO was ISA and the IPER was positive, amendments were filed on entry into the EP phase, or the EPO was not ISA. If, in such a case, claims fees are due and are not paid within the six-month period, the EPO will send a loss-of-rights communication informing the applicant of the abandonment of the excess claims. In response, the applicant can pay the claims fees or leave the excess claims abandoned. However, the applicant also has the possibility to file an amended set of claims in the further processing period, e.g. with fewer claims, and pay any claims fees for the amended claims. A further processing fee has to be paid being 50% of the claims fee (which may be zero) (**Rfees2(1)12**).

R. 162(3) Any claims fees paid within the period under paragraph 1 and in excess of those due under paragraph 2, second sentence, shall be refunded.

1 **Automatic refund**
If a European patent attorney is asked, for example by a US patent attorney, at the last minute to enter the regional phase before the EPO for a US applicant with an international application comprising a large set of claims, the European patent attorney can enter the European regional phase with the large set of claims. There is no immediate sanction if the claims fees on the large set of claims are not paid. The number of claims can then be reduced in response to the **R.161** communication and any claims fees for the reduced set paid.

However, if the excess claims fees were paid on entry and the European patent attorney later, under **R.161**, reduces the number of claims to a 'reasonable' number, the excess claims fees will be automatically refunded, under **R.162(3)**.

R. 162(4) Where a claims fee is not paid in due time, the claim concerned shall be deemed to be abandoned.

1 **Forced abandonment**
The EPO applies the same rule for reinstatement of a claim deemed abandoned after non-payment of the claims fee for direct European applications and Euro-PCT applications. Features of a claim deemed to have been abandoned pursuant to **R.162(4)** and which are not otherwise to be found in the description or drawings cannot subsequently be reintroduced into the application and, in particular, into the claims (A-III,9 and E-IX,2.3.8). See also **R.45(3):1.**

Further processing can be used to remedy non-payment of claims fees, because **R.162** is not excluded in **R.135(2)**.

R. 163 Examination of certain formal requirements by the European Patent Office

Implementation of **Art.153**

R. 163(1) Where the designation of the inventor under Rule 19, paragraph 1, has not yet been made within the period under Rule 159, paragraph 1, the European Patent Office shall invite the applicant to make the designation within two months.

R.19(1) Designation of the inventor
R.159(1) 31-month period for entry into European phase

1 **Invitation to submit data of inventor**
The period in **R.159(1)** is the 31-month period from the date of filing or, where applicable, priority.

R.163(1) uses the possibility offered by the PCT to file the data concerning the inventor later if national law allows that they be furnished at a time later than that of filing of a national application (Art.4(1)(v), (4), Art.22(1) second sentence, (3), Art.39(1)(b) PCT).

If the data are not furnished upon entry into the European phase, the EPO invites the applicant to make the designation of inventor within two months of the notification of the invitation (**R.163(1)**). If not provided in due time, the Euro-PCT application will be refused (**R.163(6)**; E-IX,2.3.4). The loss of rights may be remedied with further processing (**Art.121, R.135**): within two months of notification of the communication, file the inventor's designation, and pay the fee (**Rfees2(1)12**). In the event the EPO has made an error, the applicant may ask, within two months of notification of the loss of rights, for a decision under **R.112(2)** EPC and prove that the data were filed in due time.

R. 163(2) Where the priority of an earlier application is claimed and the file number of the previous application or the copy thereof provided for in Rule 52, paragraph 1, and Rule 53 have not yet been submitted within the period under Rule 159, paragraph 1, the European Patent Office shall invite the applicant to furnish that number or copy within two months. Rule 53, paragraph 2, shall apply.

Amended, in force since 01.04.2009 (OJ 2008 p.513).
R.52(1) Declaration of priority
R.53 Priority documents
R.159(1) 31-month period for entry into European phase

1 **Invitation to submit data and copy of the previous application**
The IB typically transmits priority documents to the EPO as dO (R.17.2(a) PCT) once the applicant has submitted the priority document or once the priority document is available through the DAS library (R.17.1 PCT). In the exceptional case that the EPO does not have the file number and/or the priority document (certified copy of the previous application) by expiry of the 31-month period of **R.159(1)**, it will invite the applicant to furnish them within a two-month period (**R.163(2)**). However, in the following two cases the EPO will not request a priority document:

Firstly, because of the reference to **R.53(2)**, no priority document is requested under **R.163(2)** if the EPO can retrieve a copy using DAS or if the previous application is a European patent application or an international application filed with the EPO as receiving Office (see **R.53(2):1**).

Secondly, the EPO as dO may not ask the applicant to furnish a priority document, under R.17.2(a) PCT, second sentence (which prevails over **R.163(2)** under **Art.150(2)**) if the applicant has, in the international phase, submitted the priority document to the IB or the rO (R.17.1(a) PCT) or, when the rO has issued the priority document, asked the rO to transmit it to the IB (R.17.1(b) PCT), or has requested the IB to retrieve the priority document using DAS, if available (R.17.1(b-bis PCT; AG-IP 5.070). In such a case the EPO as dO requests the IB to transmit the priority document to the EPO (R.17.2(a) PCT, first sentence). If, despite the applicant complying with R.17.1(a), R.17.1(b) or R.17.1(b-bis) PCT, the IB does not transmit a copy of the priority document to the EPO as dO, the EPO may nevertheless proceed with the substantive examination of the application. However, no European patent may be granted until the priority document is on file. See also E-IX,2.3.5 and F-VI,2.1.

If the file number or the priority document is not filed in due time, the right of priority is lost for the application under **R.163(6)**. Further processing under **Art.121** and **R.135** is available.

2 **Translation of priority document**
The EPO will only request a translation of a priority application that is not in an official EPO language if the validity of the priority claim is relevant for the assessment of the patentability of the invention (**R.53(3)** EPC; R.51bis.1(e)(i) PCT).

R. 163(3) Where, at the expiry of the period under Rule 159, paragraph 1, a sequence listing complying with the standard provided for in the Administrative Instructions under the PCT is not available to the European Patent Office, the applicant shall be invited to file a sequence listing complying with the rules laid down by the President of the European Patent Office within two months. Rule 30, paragraphs 2 and 3, shall apply mutatis mutandis.

R.30(2) Late filed sequence listing not part of description
R.30(3) Invitation to file amended sequence listing
R.159(1) 31-month period for entry into the European phase

1 **Invitation to submit sequence listing**

The rule is based on R.5.2(a) PCT and R.13ter.3 PCT.

The EPO invites the applicant to furnish a sequence listing in electronic form in the prescribed format if such a sequence listing is not yet available to the EPO and has not been filed at the expiry of the 31-month time limit. A sequence listing in the prescribed format is available to EPO if it was contained in the international application under R.5.2 PCT, was filed with the EPO as ISA or IPEA, or is made available by WIPO. (E-IX,2.4.2)

A sequence listing late-furnished under **R.163(3)** will not form part of the description (**R.30(2)**). The late furnishing is subject to payment of a late furnishing fee (**R.30(3)**; **Rfees2(1)14a**). If the applicant does not furnish the prescribed sequence listing and pay the fee when invited to do so, the application will be refused in accordance with **R.30(3)**. Note that, as an exception, the sanction of non-compliance is not in **R.163(6)** but in **R.30(3)**. A refusal under **R.30(3)** can be remedied using further processing (see **R.30(3):1**). (E-IX,2.4.2; for international applications filed on or after 01.07.2022: Dec. Pres. OJ 2021 A96 and Not. EPO OJ 2021 A97; for international applications filed before 01.07.2022: OJ 2011 p.372 and OJ 2013 p.542)

R. 163(4) Where, at the expiry of the period under Rule 159, paragraph 1, the address, the nationality or the State in which their residence or principal place of business is located is missing in respect of any applicant, the European Patent Office shall invite the applicant to furnish these indications within two months.

R.159(1) 31-month period for entry into European phase
Amended by decision of the Administrative Council of 10.12.2024, which entered into force on 01.04.2025 (OJ 2025 A16). The amendment was introduction of gender-neutral language.

1 **Invitation to furnish nationality or state of residence**

R.4.5(a) PCT requires the name, address and nationality/residence of all applicants to be furnished to the rO. However, if these indications are not furnished for all applicants, this can be overlooked by the rO under R.26.2bis(b) PCT (see PCT §2.2.3). In the national phase, any designated Office may ask for the missing indications to be furnished under R.51bis.1(a)(vii) PCT; the EPO has made use of this option in **R.163(4)** EPC.

If the address, nationality or state of residence of any applicant is missing at the expiry of the period for entry into the European phase, the EPO invites the applicant to furnish these indications within two months of notification of the invitation (**R.163(4)**).

Failure to rectify this deficiency in due time leads to refusal of the application (**R.163(6)**). The applicant will be notified of this decision according to **R.126(1)**. Failure to file the indications in due time may be remedied by further processing (**Art.121**; **R.135**). (E-IX,2.3.1; R.4.5(a)(ii) and (iii) PCT; R.51bis.1(a)(vii) PCT; R.26.2bis(b) PCT)

2 **Signatures**
If an international application is not signed by all applicants in the international phase as required by R.4.15 PCT, this can be overlooked by a rO under R.26.2bis(a) PCT. In the national phase, any designated office may ask for missing signature(s) under R.51bis.1(a)(vi) PCT; the EPO has not implemented this possibility.

R. 163(5) Where, at the expiry of the period under Rule 159, paragraph 1, the requirements of Article 133, paragraph 2, have not been satisfied, the European Patent Office shall invite the applicant to appoint a professional representative within two months.

Art.133(2) Compulsory representation
R.159(1) 31-month period for entry into European phase

1 **Invitation to appoint a professional representative**
Art.27(7) PCT allows a designated Office to apply national law for representation after the processing of the international application before that Office has started. The EPO as designated Office applies **Art.133(2)** EPC via **Art.150(2)** EPC. The EPO starts processing the international application immediately after the expiry of the 31-month period. Hence, applicants who must be represented under **Art.133(2)** may themselves perform any action before the period expires, such as the acts of **R.159**. After the expiry, any procedural acts must be carried out by a professional representative entitled to practise before the EPO under **Art.134(1)**. (E-IX,2.3.1)

If representation is required and no representative has been appointed by the expiry of the 31-month period, the EPO will invite the applicant to appoint a representative within two months (**R.163(5)**; **Art.133(2)**; see also, A-III,16.2(i), applicable to Euro-PCT applications by the reference from E-IX,2.3.1 to A-III,2 to A-III,16). The sanction for non-compliance is the refusal of the application under **R.163(6)**. Further processing under **Art.121** and **R.135** is available. (E-IX,2.3.1)

An agent appointed for the international phase will not be automatically regarded as representative for the national/regional phase. Hence, a professional representative appointed as agent for the international phase must be re-appointed for the European phase on regional entry, unless the professional representative was appointed for the procedure before the EPO acting as rO, ISA or IPEA, and it is clear from the file that this appointment extends to the European phase. (E-IX,2.3.1)

R. 163(6) If the deficiencies noted under paragraphs 1, 4 or 5 are not corrected in due time, the European patent application shall be refused. If the deficiency noted under paragraph 2 is not corrected in due time, the right of priority shall be lost for the application.

1 **Sanctions on not correcting deficiencies**
If any of the periods in **R.163(1)**, (2), (4), or (5) is missed, further processing may be used as a remedy because **R.163** is not excluded from further processing under **Art.121(4)** or **R.135(2)**. See E-IX,2.3.4 for **R.163(1)**, E-IX,2.4.2 for **R.163(3)** referring to **R.30(3)** where **R.30(3)** is not excluded, and E-IX,2.3.1 for **R.163(4)** and (5). Further processing should, mutatis mutandis, be possible in the case of **R.163(2)**, although it is not mentioned explicitly in E-IX,2.3.5. Note that the sanction for not complying with **R.163(3)** is not in **R.163(6)** but in **R.30(3)**.

R. 164 Unity of invention and further searches

Amended, in force since 01.11.2014 (OJ 2013 p.503). See EPO document CA/91/13 and OJ 2014 A70 for explanatory remarks. The amendment broadens the possibility to have the EPO as designated or elected office search one or more inventions not searched in the international phase.
Implementation of **Art.153**

1 **General**
Under **R.164**, an applicant of a Euro-PCT application may, on entry into the European phase and upon payment of a search fee, obtain a search of any invention that was not searched by the EPO in the international phase. Such an invention may be a non-unitary invention claimed in the PCT application as filed and not searched in the international phase or an invention added to the claims on entry into the European phase.

There are two different procedures for the search, depending on the ISA that searched the application. **R.164(1)** provides for a procedure where the EPO did not act as ISA or SISA and in which a supplementary European search must be carried out. **R.164(2)** applies to the situation where the EPO acted as ISA or SISA and a supplementary European search is dispensed with under **Art.153(7)**. The provisions in **R.164(3)** and (4) clarify aspects of the procedure under **R.164(2)**, whereas **R.164(5)** provides for a refund of any search fee paid after an unjustified non-unity objection under **R.164(1)** or (2) in line with **R.64(2)** EPC.

If after the **R.164** procedure more than one invention has been searched by the EPO, the EPO will invite the applicant to select the invention to be prosecuted and restrict the application to this invention.

R.164 ensures that applicants of Euro-direct and Euro-PCT applications, irrespective of whether the EPO was (S)ISA or not, have equal rights regarding prosecution before the EPO, especially in the case of non-unity (OJ 2014 A70 §4). However, rights are not equal in that an applicant of a Euro-PCT application has two opportunities to have multiple inventions searched (in the international phase and in the European phase) whereas an applicant of a Euro-direct application has only one opportunity (see OJ 2007 se5 EN p.256). There is also a difference in treatment between applicants of an international application where the EPO was ISA and where the EPO was not ISA regarding the refund of the examination fee (see **R.164(1):2.5**).

2 **Basis of search**

An applicant has two opportunities to amend the Euro-PCT application voluntarily before the search under **R.164:** on entry when specifying the application documents on which the grant procedure is to be based under **R.159(1)(b)** (see **R.159(1):3**) and in response to the **R.161** communication, issued shortly after entry (see **R.161(1):1**). The claims as pending at expiry of the response period for the **R.161** communication are the basis of any searches under **R.164**.

The amendments may not extend the subject-matter of the application as filed (**Art.123(2)**). However, both amendments are not restricted by the requirement of **R.137(5)** (OJ 2014 A70 §13); hence, the amended claims need not combine with the originally claimed invention(s) to form a single general inventive concept.

The application on which the prosecution is to be based may be the application as filed or amended in the international phase, amended on entry or in response to the **R.161** communication. The amendments may add subject-matter from the description to the claims. The application may claim unsearched inventions, e.g. inventions for which no search fee was paid after a non-unity objection by the ISA. Note that the EPO as SISA searches only the invention first mentioned in the claims; no search fee can be paid for other claimed inventions, which the SISA will therefore not search.

R. 164(1) If the European Patent Office considers that the application documents which are to serve as the basis for the supplementary European search do not comply with the requirement of unity of invention, it shall:

(a) draw up a partial supplementary search report on those parts of the application which relate to the invention, or the group of inventions within the meaning of Article 82, first mentioned in the claims;

(b) inform the applicant that, for the supplementary European search report to cover the other inventions, a further search fee must be paid, in respect of each invention involved, within a period of two months; and

(c) draw up the supplementary European search report for the parts of the application relating to inventions in respect of which search fees have been paid.

Art.82 Unity of invention

Applicable to any application for which the supplementary European search report under **Art.153(7)** has not been drawn up on 01.11.2014 (note a different wording in OJ 2014 A70 §23).

1 **Further searches where the EPO was not (S)ISA**

R.164(1) applies to Euro-PCT applications for which the EPO did not act as ISA or as SISA and will draw up a supplementary search report. It provides that an applicant of a Euro-PCT application in the European phase, where the EPO opines that the application lacks unity of invention, is entitled to have further searches performed upon payment of further search fees. Furthermore, the applicant is entitled to select from among all inventions in the application documents which were searched by the EPO, the invention to be prosecuted in the European grant procedure.

The provision follows, where possible, the wording of **R.64** (non-unity). Accordingly, **R.62a** (plurality of independent claims) and **63** (no meaningful search possible) apply in the same way as to any supplementary search. (OJ 2014 A70 §7)

2 Procedure

2.1 ENTRY INTO EUROPEAN PHASE

When the EPO has not acted as ISA or SISA, the EPO will draw up a supplementary search report under **Art.153(7)**. The search fee for the supplementary search (**Rfees2(1)2**) must be paid under **R.159(1)(e)** within 31 months from filing or priority. The search fee will be reduced when the (S)ISA is one of the authorities mentioned in OJ 2011 p.616 and OJ 2012 p.584 (**Art.153(7)**).

The request for examination, which includes payment of the examination fee, must be filed within six months from the publication of the PCT search report (**R.70(1)** and **Art.153(6)**). If the six-month period expires before 31 months from filing or priority, which is usually the case, the request must be filed within 31 months from filing or priority (**R.159(1)(f)**).

Shortly after entry, the EPO despatches the **R.161(2)** communication, giving the applicant a six-month period to amend the application. A response to the communication is not mandatory; the applicant may of course file arguments or amendments in which the written opinion of the ISA other than the EPO is taken into account. The opportunity for amendment may be used to reduce the number of claims because the number of claims pending at the expiry of the six-month period determines the claims fees to be paid (**R.162(2)**).

2.2 SUPPLEMENTARY SEARCH

After expiry of the six-month period of **R.161(2)**, a search division will carry out a supplementary search under **Art.153(7)** based on the claims of the Euro-PCT application, possibly amended under **R.159(1)(b)** or **R.161(2)** (F-V,13.2).

The search examiner will assess the unity of the pending set of claims. If found to be unitary, the procedure under R.164(1) will not be applied, and the supplementary search will be carried out. When completed, the supplementary search report will be transmitted to the applicant together with the search opinion.

2.3 SEARCH OF NON-UNITARY INVENTIONS

If the search division considers that the claims lack unity, the search division will draw up a partial supplementary search report on the invention first mentioned in the claims (**R.164(1)(a)**). The report states the unity objection and gives a specification of the separate inventions. The report includes a provisional opinion on the patentability of the invention first mentioned in the claims (OJ 2017 A20; B-VII,2.3; B-XI,5). No reply is required to the provisional opinion and, if filed, will not be considered by the search division. The partial search report will be sent to the applicant together with an invitation to pay a further search fee for each non-unitary invention (**R.164(1)(b)**).

If an application has a plurality of independent claims in a claim category, the EPO will usually send first a request to indicate the independent claims to be searched under **R.62a(1)**, followed by the invitation to pay further search fees. (B-VIII,4.5)

If no meaningful search can be carried out, the EPO will usually send first a request to indicate the subject-matter to be searched under **R.63(1)** followed by the invitation to pay further search fees. (B-VIII,3.4; C-III,2.3)

The fee reduction mentioned in the above section **2.1** does not apply to the further search fees (A-X,9.5.1). It should be noted that the further search fee in the European phase is lower than the additional fee for a further search in the international phase (see **Rfees2(1)2**).

Any further search fee must be paid within two months (**R.164(1)(b)**). The period is excluded from further processing (**R.135(2)**), but re-establishment is available. If no further search fees are paid, the applicant is taken to have elected the first searched invention for prosecution (C-III,3.2.1). The further search fees will be debited automatically where an automatic debit order is on file; if applicants do not want this, they must inform the EPO before the expiry of the two-month period (OJ 2022 sp3 Annex A.2 point 3 note I.2).

If further search fees have been paid, the search division will draw up a supplementary search report relating to each invention for which a search fee has been paid (**R.164(1)(c)**). The supplementary search report together with a search opinion will be sent to the applicant; the search opinion contains the reasoning behind the lack of unity (B-XI,5). See **R.164(5)** for a refund of search fees.

2.4 END OF SEARCH PROCEDURE

At the end of the search procedure, the EPO invites applicants to respond to the search opinion if any objections to grant are noted (**R.70a(2)**) and to indicate whether they want to proceed with the application in view of the results of the search (**R.70(2)**; **R.70a(2)**). The response must be filed within six months (E-IX,2.5.3). After receipt of the indication to proceed, the responsibility for the application transfers from the search division to the examining division (**R.10(3)**) and the substantive examination under **Art.94** begins.

At the beginning of the examination, the applicant is invited to restrict the application to a single invention searched by the EPO for prosecution if not yet done so in response to the search opinion (**G2/92**; C-III,3.2.2; H-II,6.4.2). Note that the invitation is not mentioned in the law. If the application is not properly restricted to a searched invention, the application may be refused under **R.164(1)** in line with **G2/92** (H-II,6.2).

A divisional application may be filed for any invention not pursued in the application. If the EPO has already drawn up a search report for such an invention, the search fee paid for the divisional may be refunded under **Rfees9(2)**.

If no indication to proceed is filed within six months, the application is deemed withdrawn (**R.70(3)**). See **R.70(2):2** for remedies. Since the examining division has not yet assumed responsibility, the examination fee paid under **R.159(1)(f)** is refunded in full (**Rfees11(a)**; A-VI,2.2).

2.5 EXAMPLE

As an example, an ISA different from the EPO opines that inventions A and B claimed in a Euro-PCT application are non-unitary. The applicant does not pay a further search fee and the ISA searches only invention A that is first mentioned in the claims. On entry into the European phase, the applicant specifies inventions B, A and C for prosecution, where C has been taken from the description. No amendment is made under **R.161(2)**. The partial supplementary search report relates to invention B, raises a non-unity objection to inventions B, A and C, and invites the applicant to pay further search fees for inventions A and C. The applicant pays a further search fee for invention C. The supplementary search report will now cover inventions B and C. The applicant selects invention C for prosecution to grant and deletes inventions A and B. Inventions A and B can only be pursued in divisional applications.

R. 164(2) If the supplementary European search report is dispensed with and the Examining Division considers that in the application documents which are to serve as the basis for examination an invention, or a group of inventions within the meaning of Article 82, is claimed which was not searched by the European Patent Office in its capacity as International Searching Authority or Authority specified for supplementary international search, the Examining Division shall:

(a) inform the applicant that a search will be performed in respect of any such invention for which a search fee is paid within a period of two months;

(b) issue the results of any search performed in accordance with paragraph (a) together with:

- **a communication under Article 94, paragraph 3, and Rule 71, paragraphs 1 and 2, in which it shall give the applicant the opportunity to comment on these results and to amend the description, claims and drawings, or**
- **a communication under Rule 71, paragraph 3, and**

(c) where appropriate, in the communication issued under paragraph (b), invite the applicant to limit the application to one invention, or group of inventions within the meaning of Article 82, for which a search report was drawn up by the European Patent Office in its capacity either as International Searching Authority or as Authority specified for supplementary international search, or for which a search was performed in accordance with the procedure under paragraph (a).

Art.82 Unity of invention
Art.94(3) Examination of the European patent application
R.71(1), (2) Invitation to correct deficiencies
R.71(3) Invitation to approve text to be granted
Applicable to any application for which the first communication under **Art.94(3)** and **R.71(1)** and (2) or, as the case may be, **R.71(3)** has not been drawn up at 01.11.2014 (note a different wording in OJ 2014 A70 §24).

1 Further searches where the EPO was (S)ISA

R.164(2) applies to Euro-PCT applications for which the EPO acted as ISA or as SISA. It provides that an applicant of a Euro-PCT application in the European phase, where the EPO opines that the application includes a claimed invention that is not searched by the EPO as (S)ISA, is entitled to have this invention searched upon payment of a search fee. Furthermore, the applicant is entitled to select, from among all inventions in the application documents which were searched by the EPO, the invention to be prosecuted in the European grant procedure.

The focus in **R.164(2)** is on whether examination is requested for a non-searched invention, not on whether the application documents to be assessed by the examining division comply with the requirement of unity of invention (C-III,3.1).

2 Procedure

2.1 ENTRY INTO THE EUROPEAN PHASE

When the EPO has acted as ISA or SISA, the EPO will not draw up a supplementary search report under **Art.153(7)** and no search fee need be paid under **R.159(1)(e)** on entry into the European phase.

The request for examination, which includes payment of the examination fee, must be filed within six months from the publication of the PCT search report (**R.70(1)** and **Art.153(6)**). If the 6-month period expires before 31 months from filing or priority, which is usually the case, the request must be filed within 31 months from filing or priority (**R.159(1)(f)**).

Shortly after entry into the European phase the EPO issues a **R.161(1)** communication, giving a six-month period for response. The application of **R.161(1)** is independent of the procedure in **R.164(2)**. If an invention for which a negative written opinion or IPER was drawn up is specified for prosecution, the communication will invite to applicant to respond to the deficiencies noted in the written opinion or IPER. A response to a negative opinion is mandatory, even if the applicant wants to prosecute another invention than the one on which the written opinion or IPER is based. The applicant may respond by deleting the invention or addressing the deficiencies. (CA/91/13)

In response to the **R.161(1)** communication voluntary amendments may be filed. The opportunity for amendment may be used to reduce the number of claims, because the number of claims pending at expiry of the six-month period determines the claims fees to be paid (**R.162(2)**).

2.2 START OF EXAMINATION

After expiry of the six-month period for response to the **R.161(1)** communication, the examining division starts the substantive examination. See **R.164(4):1** for the competence of the examining division for the searches under **R.164(2)**.

As a first step, the examiner will assess under **R.164(2)** whether the application documents claim any invention that was not searched by the EPO acting as ISA or SISA (see AG-IP §8.045 for non-unity before SISA).

Neither **R.164(2)**, nor the Guidelines, nor OJ 2014 A70 §13 explain when the EPO as designated or elected office considers an invention not to have been searched by the EPO as (S)ISA. The EPO applies a test similar to the test used for **R.137(5)** (C-III,3.1): an invention is considered not searched by the EPO as (S)ISA if the invention lacks unity with each of the one or more searched inventions; if the invention is unitary with at least one searched invention, the invention is considered to have been searched.

If there are no unsearched inventions, the procedure under **R.164(2)** will not be carried out and the examiner will continue the examination procedure by issuing an **Art.94(3)** or a **R.71(3)** communication.

2.3 ADDITIONAL SEARCHES

If the examining division considers that the application claims one or more unsearched inventions, it will issue an invitation under **R.164(2)(a)** to pay a search fee for each unsearched invention. The communication may also invite the applicant to restrict the scope of the search under **R.62a(1)** (multiple independent claims) and/or **R.63(1)** (unsearchable claims) (C-III,3.2.3).

It should be noted that the further search fee in the European phase is lower than the additional fee for a further search in the international phase (see **Rfees2(1)2**). See **R.164(5)** for a refund of search fees.

Any search fee must be paid within two months (**R.164(2)(a)**). The period is excluded from further processing (**R.135(2)**), but re-establishment is available. The search fees will be debited automatically where an automatic debit order is on file; if applicants do not want this, they must inform the EPO before expiry of the two-month period (OJ 2022 sp3 Annex A.2 point 3 note I.2).

If no search fee is paid, the procedure under **R.164(2)** ends at expiry of the two-month period and the prosecution continues with a communication under **Art.94(3)** or **R.71(3)** (C-III,3.2.1), based on the first invention searched by the EPO in the international phase, and requesting the applicant to delete non-searched inventions from the claims.

If a search fee is paid, the examining division will search the corresponding invention. This search is neither a European search (see **R.164(4)**) nor a supplementary search, which latter term is reserved for searches under **Art.153(7)**. Rather, it is a 'search incident during substantive examination'. If amended claims are filed at the same time as paying the search fee, the search will in principle be carried out on the basis of the claims pending upon expiry of the **R.161** period; the amended claims may informally be taken into account (C-III,3.1).

If the claims are not sufficiently clear to identify a non-searched invention, the examining division will issue an **Art.94(3)** communication setting out the objection under **Art.84.** If after clarification claims relate to unsearched subject-matter, no invitation to pay a search fee under **R.164(2)** will be issued anymore and the claims can only be prosecuted in a divisional. (C-III,3.1)

If the invention to be searched has a plurality of independent claims in a claim category, the EPO will first send a request to indicate the independent claims to be searched under **R.62a(1)** before starting the search. (B-VIII,4.5)

If no meaningful search can be carried out on an invention to be searched, the EPO will send first a request to indicate the subject-matter to be searched under **R.63(1)** before starting the search. (B-VIII,3.4)

2.4 COMMUNICATION OF SEARCH RESULTS

The search results of each invention for which a search fee has been paid are communicated to the applicant in an annex to an **Art.94(3)** communication or a **R.71(3)** communication (**R.164(2)(b)**). The communication will also give the findings of the examining division (OJ 2014 A70 §16). The **Art.94(3)** communication invites applicants to comment on the search report and the findings and to amend the application of their own volition within a set period (OJ 2014 A70 §16). The amendments at this stage are subject to the requirements of **R.137(5)**, first sentence (C-III,3.1; 3.2.3) but are not subject to **R.137(3)** (H-II,2.3). The communication will also request the applicant to select a single invention for prosecution to grant from the inventions searched by the EPO both in the international and in the European phase (**R.164(2)(c)**). Other inventions in the application, searched and unsearched, can be pursued in a divisional.

The transmission of the **Art.94(3)** or **R.71(3)** communication to the applicant terminates the **R.164(2)** procedure.

If applicants do not want to pursue the application anymore in view of the search results, they can actively withdraw the application within the period for filing a reply to the **Art.94(3)** communication, resulting in a 50% refund of the examination fee (see **Rfees11**). The earlier communication under **R.164(2)(a)** does not trigger the period of **Rfees11(b)**; the communication under **R.164(2)(b)** and **Art.94(3)** is the first communication in the sense of **Rfees11(b)**. (A-VI,2.5)

If applicants do not want to pursue the application anymore in view of the search results, they can actively withdraw the application within the period for filing a reply to the **Art.94(3)** communication, resulting in a 50% refund of the examination fee (see **Rfees11**). The earlier communication under **R.164(2)(a)** does not trigger the period of **Rfees11(b)**; the communication under **R.164(2)(b)** and **Art.94(3)** is the first communication in the sense of **Rfees11(b)**. (A-VI,2.5)

Note that if a supplementary European search report is drawn up for a Euro-PCT application under **R.164(1)** and the applicant withdraws the application after receipt of that search report, the examination fee is refunded in full. The reason is that the search division is competent until a response to the **R.70(2)** invitation is received; hence the search division is responsible for the supplementary search and any further searches under **R.164(1)** and substantive examination can begin only after the response to the **R.70(2)** invitation (**R.10(3)**; F-V,13.2).

2.5 **EXAMPLE**
An example of the procedure under **R.164(2)** is as follows. The EPO as ISA opines that inventions A and B claimed in a Euro-PCT application are non-unitary. The applicant does not pay a further search fee and only invention A first mentioned in the claims is searched. On entry into the European phase, the applicant specifies inventions B, A and C for prosecution, where C has been taken from the description. No amendments are filed in response to the **R.161(1)** communication. The examining division invites the applicant to pay search fees for inventions B and C. The applicant pays a search fee for invention C. The **Art.94(3)** communication includes the search results for invention C, the findings of the examining division for invention A and C, and a request to limit the application to a single invention. The applicant selects invention C and deletes inventions A and B from the claims. Inventions A and B can only be pursued in divisional applications.

R. 164(3) In the procedure under paragraph 2(a), Rules 62a and 63 shall apply mutatis mutandis.

R.62a Plurality of independent claims
R.63 Unsearchable subject-matter

1 **Provisions applicable during search**
R.164(3) states explicitly, for reasons of clarity, that **R.62a** (plurality of independent claims) and **R.63** (unsearchable subject-matter) apply mutatis mutandis to the procedure under **R.164(2)(a)** (CA/91/13 §29).

The procedure in C-III,3.1 not to carry out the **R.164(2)** procedure if the claims are not sufficiently clear to identify a non-searched invention could be regarded as conflicting with **R.164(3)**, which obliges the EPO to carry out the **R.62a** procedure in case of lack of clarity during the **R.164(2)** procedure.

R. 164(4) Rule 62 and Rule 70, paragraph 2, shall not apply to the results of any search performed in accordance with paragraph 2.

R.62 Extended European search report
R.70(2) Confirmation of early filed request for examination

1 **Competence of the examining division for R.164(2) searches**
R.164(2) states that the examining division is responsible for the searches under this provision. **R.164(4)** accordingly specifies that the results of a search under **R.164(2)** will not be issued as an extended search report under **R.62**, i.e. as a search report and an opinion. The results will instead be set out in an annex to an **Art.94(3)** communication. **R.164(4)** also states that no invitation under **R.70(2)** to indicate whether the applicant wishes to proceed further will be issued.

R. 164(5) Any fee paid under paragraphs 1 or 2 shall be refunded if the applicant requests a refund and the Examining Division finds that the communication under paragraphs 1(b) or 2(a) was not justified.

1 **Refund of further search fee**
Applicants may request a refund of search fees if they regard the non-unity opinion (partly) unjustified under **R.164(1)** or (2). The examining division will refund the fees as under **R.64(2)** if it concurs with the applicant. A lack of sufficient justification of the non-unity opinion is also a ground for refund. (CA/91/13 §32; C-III,34)

A request filed during the search procedure under **R.164(1)** will only be dealt with after start of the examination, because only an examining division is competent to decide on the opinion. A request filed during the search procedure of **R.164(2)** can be dealt with immediately, because the examining division handles the search procedure (A-X,10.2.2). See **R.64(2):1** and C-III,3.4 for the refund procedure.

A search fee paid under **R.164** may be refunded if the search can be based on an earlier search according to **Rfees9(2)**. Accordingly, a search under **R.164** may give rise to a refund of a search fee paid for a later application, e.g. a divisional. (OJ 2014 A70 §22)

R. 165 The Euro-PCT application as conflicting application under Article 54, paragraph 3

A Euro-PCT application shall be considered as comprised in the state of the art under Article 54, paragraph 3, if in addition to the conditions laid down in Article 153, paragraph 3 or 4, the filing fee under Rule 159, paragraph 1(c) has been paid.

Art.54(3) European prior right
Art.153(3) Publication of Euro-PCT application
Art.153(4) Language of Euro-PCT application
R.159(1)(c) Filing fee for Euro-PCT application
Implementation of **Art.153(5)**

1 **General**
This provision explicitly states that once the publication and language requirements of **Art.153(3)** or (4) have been satisfied and the filing fee has been paid for the Euro-PCT application, the application is considered to form part of the state of the art according to **Art.54(3)** (OJ 2007 se5 EN p.256). The provision is an implementation of Art.27(5) PCT.

In concrete terms, if the filing fee of **R.159(1)(c)** has been paid to the EPO as designated or elected Office and either the international application has been published by the IB in German, French or English or the translation required under **Art.153(4)** has been filed with the EPO as designated or elected Office, the PCT application forms a prior right under **Art.54(3)**.

Accordingly, a Euro-PCT application does not need to fulfil all conditions of **R.159(1)** for entry into the European phase in order to be considered a prior right under **Art.54(3)** and the Euro-PCT application can form a prior right even if it is deemed to be withdrawn as of the expiry of the 31-month period (G-IV,5.2). In such cases a brief mention is published in the Bulletin under **Art.129(a)** since 25.08.2021 (Not. EPO OJ 2021 A51). Any translations filed for such applications are not published but are available in the public file of the EPO for the application.

See **Art.54(3):3** for the additional requirements for Euro-PCT applications to form prior rights for European and Euro-PCT applications filed under EPC1973.

2 **Remedies**

Both further processing (**Art.121, R.135**) and re-establishment (**Art.122, R.136**) are available as a remedy for failure to timely file the translation and for failure to timely pay the filing fee (see **R.159(1):2.2**). The payment of the filing fee after expiry of the applicable period of **R.159(1)(c)** is not valid unless a remedy is successfully applied (A-X,10.1.2).

Protocol on the Interpretation of Article 69

of 5 October 1973

as revised by the Act revising the EPC of 29 November 2000

Art. 1 General principles

Article 69 should not be interpreted as meaning that the extent of the protection conferred by a European patent is to be understood as that defined by the strict, literal meaning of the wording used in the claims, the description and drawings being employed only for the purpose of resolving an ambiguity found in the claims. Nor should it be taken to mean that the claims serve only as a guideline and that the actual protection conferred may extend to what, from a consideration of the description and drawings by a person skilled in the art, the patent proprietor has contemplated. On the contrary, it is to be interpreted as defining a position between these extremes which combines a fair protection for the patent proprietor with a reasonable degree of legal certainty for third parties.

1 **Object of the Protocol on Interpretation**
The revised text of the Protocol adopted by the Administrative Council in its decision of 28.06.2001 (OJ 2001 se4 p.55) has become an integral part of the Revision Act of 29.11.2000 under Art.3(2), second sentence of that act.

The Protocol on Interpretation of **Art.69** is an integral part of the Convention by the reference to it in **Art.164(1)**. It is intended to provide guidance on how **Art.69** should be applied with respect to determining the scope of protection of the granted European patent. The Protocol under EPC1973 included only the current **Art.1** Protocol; **Art.2** Protocol was added by the revisions of EPC2000.

The object of the Protocol is to avoid too much emphasis on the literal wording of the claims when considered in isolation from the remainder of the text of the patent in which they appear; and also to avoid too much emphasis upon the general inventive concept disclosed in the text of the patent as compared to the relevant prior art, without sufficient regard also to the wording of the claims as a means of definition. (G2/88 r.4 third paragraph)

This is intended to form a 'middle way' between the former extremes of adopting a purely literal approach to the claims, and adopting a broader approach which uses the claims merely as guidelines. However, as infringement is determined on a country-by-country basis, different countries have maintained somewhat divergent approaches to determining the combination of fair protection and legal certainty mandated by **Art.1** Protocol.

Art. 2 Equivalents

For the purpose of determining the extent of protection conferred by a European patent, due account shall be taken of any element which is equivalent to an element specified in the claims.

1 **Revision of the Protocol**
The provisions governing the extent of protection conferred by a European patent, i.e. **Art.69** and the Protocol on its interpretation, have turned out not to achieve, to the extent desired, the goal of ensuring as uniform an application and interpretation as possible. In particular, this is the case regarding the treatment of so-called equivalents and the importance of prior statements made by the applicant for or proprietor of a patent in the application or in the specification or during prosecution before the EPO or in proceedings concerning the validity of the patent.

The Diplomatic Conference revising the EPC discussed the incorporation of an explicit reference to equivalents into the Protocol, mainly to force UK courts to take equivalents into account, and the adoption of provisions on the use of the file history of the patent in determining the scope of protection, similar to the US. Several courts regard it as undesirable that a scope including equivalents increases with time when more equivalents are being developed over time.

There was no agreement on including provisions on the use of the file history (Dipl. Conf. document MR/24/00), nor on including an explicit definition of 'equivalents'; the intention being (as noted by the German delegation) to allow national courts sufficient latitude to apply the provisions to complex cases. (OJ 2007 se4 EN p.70)

2 **Transitional provision**

The revised Protocol on the Interpretation of **Art.69** is applicable to European patents already granted at the time of EPC2000 entry into force and to European patents granted on European patent applications pending at, or filed on or after that time. (OJ 2007 se4 EN p.70)

Although the Special Edition does not mention the 'or filed on or after', this must be included in view of **Art.7(1)**, first sentence of the Revision Act.

3 **Equivalents**

No definition of 'equivalents' is given in the Protocol or the EPC. The basic proposal by the WIPO from 1991 for the 'Treaty supplementing the Paris Convention as far as patents are concerned' extends the protection of a claim to cover not only all the elements as expressed in the claim but also equivalents. In **Art.21(2)(b)** it defines equivalents as:

An element ('the equivalent element') shall generally be considered as being equivalent to an element as expressed in a claim if, at the time of any alleged infringement, either of the following conditions is fulfilled in regard to the invention as claimed:

1 the equivalent element performs substantially the same function in substantially the same way and produces substantially the same result as the element as expressed in the claim, or

2 it is obvious to a person skilled in the art that the same result as that achieved by means of the element as expressed in the claim can be achieved by means of the equivalent element.

A similar definition was given in **T697/92**, using an equivalent in the assessment of inventive step.

The interpretation of equivalents in the contracting states has not yet been harmonised (see for example Singer Art.69, note 35 ff.).

Use of the term 'elements' in Art.2 Protocol conforms with the terminology of the Patent Law Treaty, and was considered during the Diplomatic Conference to be more precise than the proposed alternative 'means', as well as being more applicable to fields such as chemistry.

Protocol on Jurisdiction and the Recognition of Decisions in respect of the Right to the Grant of a European Patent

(PROTOCOL ON RECOGNITION)

of 5 October 1973

Art. 1(1) The courts of the Contracting States shall, in accordance with Articles 2 to 6, have jurisdiction to decide claims, against the applicant, to the right to the grant of a European patent in respect of one or more of the Contracting States designated in the European Patent application.

1 **Protocol on Recognition**
The Protocol on Recognition serves to realise the aims of **Art.61**. It governs the competence of the national courts and the recognition of their decisions. The Protocol applies only to European patent applications, not to granted patents. See **Art.99(4):1** for the recognition of court decisions in entitlement proceedings for granted patents. The Protocol is an integral part of the EPC according to **Art.164(1)**.

Art. 1(2) For the purposes of this Protocol, the term "courts" shall include authorities which, under the national law of a Contracting State, have jurisdiction to decide the claims referred to in paragraph 1. Any Contracting State shall notify the European Patent Office of the identity of any authority on which such a jurisdiction is conferred, and the European Patent Office shall inform the other Contracting States accordingly.

1 **Authority having jurisdiction on entitlement**
At present the second sentence of **Art.1(2)** applies only for the patent office in Great Britain.

Art. 1(3) For the purposes of this Protocol, the term "Contracting State" refers to a Contracting State which has not excluded application of this Protocol pursuant to Article 167 of the Convention.

1 **Reservations**
The reservations under **Art.167** have ended on 07.10.1992, apart from the rights still in force for applications filed before this date (see **Art.167:1**).
Since **Art.167** has been deleted in EPC2000, **Prot.Rec. Art.1(3)** should also have been deleted.

Art. 2

Subject to Articles 4 and 5, if an applicant for a European patent has his residence or principal place of business within one of the Contracting States, proceedings shall be brought against him in the courts of that Contracting State.

Art. 3

Subject to Articles 4 and 5, if an applicant for a European patent has his residence or principal place of business outside the Contracting States, and if the party claiming the right to the grant of the European patent has his residence or principal place of business within one of the Contracting States, the courts of the latter State shall have exclusive jurisdiction.

Art. 4

Subject to Article 5, if the subject-matter of a European patent application is the invention of an employee, the courts of the Contracting State, if any, whose law determines the right to the European patent pursuant to Article 60, paragraph 1, second sentence, of the Convention, shall have exclusive jurisdiction over proceedings between the employee and the employer.

Art. 5

Art. 5(1) If the parties to a dispute concerning the right to the grant of a European patent have concluded an agreement, either in writing or verbally with written confirmation, to the effect that a court or the courts of a particular Contracting State shall decide on such a dispute, the court or courts of that State shall have exclusive jurisdiction.

Art. 5(2) However, if the parties are an employee and his employer, paragraph 1 shall only apply in so far as the national law governing the contract of employment allows the agreement in question.

Art. 6

In cases where neither Articles 2 to 4 nor Article 5, paragraph 1, apply, the courts of the Federal Republic of Germany shall have exclusive jurisdiction.

1 **Jurisdiction**

The following points summarise the provisions in Art.2 to 6:

1 If there is an agreement between parties, the court in a contracting state both parties have agreed to is competent, provided national labour law allows the agreement (Art.5(1)).

If there is no agreement or a not-allowed agreement or if the court is not in a contracting state, then

2 If the patent application relates to an employee invention, the courts of that contracting state are exclusively competent whose law determines the right to the patent under **Art.60(1)** (Art.4). According to **Art.60(1)** it is the contracting state in which the employee is mainly employed; if that state cannot be determined, it is the state in which the employer has the place of business to which the employee is attached.

If it is not an employer-employee case, then

3 If the applicant lives or works within a contracting state, a court in that contracting state is competent (Art.2).

4 If the applicant lives or works outside the contracting states and the claiming party lives or works within a contracting state, the courts of the latter contracting state are competent (Art.3).

5 If none of the previous cases applies, e.g. the applicant and the claiming party both live and work outside the contracting states, the courts in Germany are competent (Art.6).

Art. 7

The courts of Contracting States before which claims referred to in Article 1 are brought shall of their own motion decide whether or not they have jurisdiction pursuant to Articles 2 to 6.

Art. 8

Art. 8(1) In the event of proceedings based on the same claim and between the same parties being brought before courts of different Contracting States, the court to which a later application is made shall of its own motion decline jurisdiction in favour of the court to which an earlier application was made.

1 **Priority in the case of several courts**
A third party can start proceedings in different states, or different parties living in different states can each start proceedings in their own state. This provision gives the priority between the several courts.

Art. 8(2) In the event of the jurisdiction of the court to which an earlier application is made being challenged, the court to which a later application is made shall stay the proceedings until the other court takes a final decision.

Art. 9

Art. 9(1) Subject to the provisions of Article 11, paragraph 2, final decisions given in any Contracting State on the right to the grant of a European patent in respect of one or more of the Contracting States designated in the European patent application shall be recognised without requiring special procedure in the other Contracting States.

1 **Recognition of decisions**
Decisions on entitlement given in a contracting state must be recognised in all contracting states. A first exception applies if it is a decision pursuant to Art.11(2) of the Protocol to recognise a judgment from a non-EPC state in a contracting state based on an agreement between those states (travaux préparatoires BR 219 §65). Such a decision need not be recognised under the Protocol. Two further exceptions are given in Art.10 of the Protocol.

Art. 9(2) The jurisdiction of the court whose decision is to be recognised and the validity of such decision may not be reviewed.

Art. 10

Article 9, paragraph 1, shall not be applicable where:

(a) an applicant for a European patent who has not contested a claim proves that the document initiating the proceedings was not notified to him regularly and sufficiently early for him to defend himself; or

(b) an applicant proves that the decision is incompatible with another decision given in a Contracting State in proceedings between the same parties which were started before those in which the decision to be recognised was given.

Art. 11

Art. 11(1) In relations between any Contracting States the provisions of this Protocol shall prevail over any conflicting provisions of other agreements on jurisdiction or the recognition of judgments.

Art. 11(2) This Protocol shall not affect the implementation of any agreement between a Contracting State and a State which is not bound by the Protocol.

Rules relating to Fees

of 20 October 1977
as adopted by decision of the Administrative Council of
the European Patent Organisation of 7 December 2006
and last amended by decision of the Administrative Council of
the European Patent Organisation of 14 December 2023

Rules relating to fees

THE ADMINISTRATIVE COUNCIL OF THE EUROPEAN PATENT ORGANISATION,

HAVING REGARD to the European Patent Convention and in particular Article 33, paragraph 2(d), thereof,

HAS ADOPTED THE FOLLOWING RULES RELATING TO FEES:

Rfees 1 General

The following shall be levied in accordance with the provisions contained in these Rules:

(a) fees due to be paid to the European Patent Office (hereinafter referred to as the Office) as provided for in the Convention and in the Implementing Regulations and the fees and expenses which the President of the Office lays down pursuant to Article 3, paragraph 1;

(b) fees and expenses pursuant to the Patent Cooperation Treaty (hereinafter referred to as the PCT), the amounts of which may be fixed by the Office.

1 **References to Rules relating to Fees**
The Rules relating to Fees (Rfees) fix the amount of the fees and how they must be paid. The obligation to pay and the period for payment are laid down in the Convention. Art.51 EPC provides the relation between the Rfees and the Convention. The Rfees are set by the Administrative Council (Art.33(2)(d)). A consolidated text of the Rfees is given in OJ 2023 sp2. A provision of the Rfees is called 'Article', not 'Rule'; i.e. **Rfees1** as used herein indicates Article 1 of the Rfees.

Rfees 2 Fees provided for in the Convention and in the Implementing Regulations

Amended by decision of the Administrative Council of 14.12.2023, which entered into force on 01.04.2024 (OJ 2024 A3). The amendment involved an increase of many fees, deletion of some fees and deletion of paragraphs (3) and (4) about special fee levels for documents filed in character-coded format. The fee levels of former paragraphs (3) and (4) were never applied in practice.

Rfees2(1) The fees due to be paid to the Office under Article 1, unless otherwise provided in paragraph 2, shall be as follows:

		EUR
1.	**Filing fee (Article 78, paragraph 2)**	
	(i) where the European patent application or, in the case of an international application, the form for entry into the European phase (EPO Form 1200) is filed online	**135**
	(ii) where the European patent application or, in the case of an international application, the form for entry into the European phase (EPO Form 1200) is not filed online	**285**

1a.	Additional fee for a European patent application comprising more than 35 pages (not counting pages forming part of a sequence listing) (Rule 38, paragraph 2)	plus EUR 17 for the 36th and each subsequent page
1b.	Additional fee in the case of a divisional application filed in respect of any earlier application which is itself a divisional application (Rule 38, paragraph 4)	
	- fee for a divisional application of second generation	235
	- fee for a divisional application of third generation	480
	- fee for a divisional application of fourth generation	715
	- fee for a divisional application of fifth or any subsequent generation	955
2.	Search fee in respect of	
	- a European or supplementary European search on an application filed on or after 1 July 2005 (Article 78, paragraph 2, Rule 62, Rule 64, paragraph 1, Rule 56a, paragraph 8, Article 153, paragraph 7, Rule 164, paragraphs 1 and 2)	1520
	- a European or supplementary European search on an application filed before 1 July 2005 (Article 78, paragraph 2, Rule 64, paragraph 1, Article 153, paragraph 7)	1040
	- an international search (Rule 16.1 PCT, Rule 40*bis* PCT in conjunction with Rule 20.5*bis* PCT, and Rule 158, paragraph 1).	1845
	- a supplementary international search (Rule 45*bis*.3(a) PCT)	1845
3.	Designation fee for one or more Contracting States (Article 79, paragraph 2) in respect of an application filed on or after 1 April 2009	685
4.	Renewal fees for the European patent application (Article 86, paragraph 1), calculated in each case from the date of filing of the application	
	- for the 3rd year	690
	- for the 4th year	845
	- for the 5th year	1000
	- for the 6th year	1155
	- for the 7th year	1310
	- for the 8th year	1465
	- for the 9th year	1620
	- for the 10th and each subsequent year	1775
5.	Additional fee for belated payment of a renewal fee for the European patent application (Rule 51, paragraph 2)	50% of the belated renewal fee
6.	Examination fee (Article 94, paragraph 1) in respect of	
	- an application filed before 1 July 2005	2135
	- an application filed on or after 1 July 2005	1915

	- an international application filed on or after 1 July 2005 for which no supplementary European search report is drawn up (Article 153, paragraph 7)	2135
7.	Fee for grant including fee for publication of the European patent specification (Rule 71, paragraph 3), in respect of an application filed on or after 1 April 2009	1080
8.	*deleted*	
9.	*deleted*	
10.	Opposition fee (Article 99, paragraph 1, Article 105, paragraph 2)	880
10a.	Limitation or revocation fee (Article 105a, paragraph 1)	
	- request for limitation	1355
	- request for revocation	615
11.	Fee for appeal (Article 108) for an appeal filed	
	- by any person referred to in Rule 7a, paragraph 2 (a) to (d)	2015
	- by any other person	2925
11a.	Fee for petition for review (Article 112a, paragraph 4)	3400
12.	Fee for further processing (Rule 135, paragraph 1)	
	- in the event of late payment of a fee	50% of the relevant fee
	- in the event of late performance of the acts required under Rule 71, paragraph 3	300
	- other cases	300
13.	Fee for re-establishment of rights/fee for requesting restoration/fee for reinstatement of rights (Rule 136, paragraph 1, Rule 26*bis*.3(d) PCT, Rule 49*ter*.2(d) PCT, Rule 49.6(d)(i) PCT)	750
14.	Conversion fee (Article 135, paragraph 3, Article 140)	0
14a.	Fee for late furnishing of a sequence listing (Rule 30, paragraph 3)	265
15.	Claims fee (Rule 45, paragraph 1, Rule 71, paragraph 4, and Rule 162, paragraph 1) in respect of an application filed on or after 1 April 2009	
	- for the 16th and each subsequent claim up to the limit of 50	275
	- for the 51st and each subsequent claim	685
16.	Fee for the awarding of costs (Rule 88, paragraph 3)	90
17.	*deleted*	
18.	Transmittal fee for an international application (Rule 157, paragraph 4)	150
19.	Fee for the preliminary examination of an international application (Rule 58 PCT and Rule 158, paragraph 2)	1915
20.	Fee for a technical opinion (Article 25)	4560
21.	Protest fee (Rule 158, paragraph 3, Rule 40.2(c) PCT and Rule 68.3(e) PCT)	1020
22.	Review fee (Rule 45*bis*.6(c) PCT)	1020

Amended by decision of the Administrative Council of 14.12.2023, which entered into force on 01.04.2024 (OJ 2024 A3).

1 **Publication of fees**

The EPO regularly publishes a 'Guidance for the payment of fees, expenses and prices' in the OJ (most recently in OJ 2024 A37). The document gives information concerning the fee levels, payment methods, refunds, and reductions for both European and international applications.

Current fee rates are included in the interactive 'Schedule of fees' on the EPO website. The current fee rates (as of 01.04.2024) were published in OJ 2024 sp4. This publication includes the current text of the Rfees and tables with the amounts of the fees of **Rfees2**, the administrative fees and the expenses for services under **Rfees3**, as well as certain miscellaneous fees (including validation fees), and the amounts of the fees for unitary patents. The amounts of the PCT fees fixed by WIPO that are payable to the EPO in the international phase were published in OJ 2024 A103.

Additional information about the payment of fees for unitary patents can be found in OJ 2023 sp3 p.26.

2 **Amendment of fee rates**

The amount of the fees is normally increased every two years as a compromise between regularly compensating for inflation and reducing the administrative effort of the fee changes. However, the fee rates were increased in 2022, 2023 and 2024.

In case of a change of a fee rate, the amount to be paid is generally the amount of the fee on the date of payment, not on the (earlier) due date (A-X, 5.1.2). As an exception, the date of receipt of a PCT application determines the amount of the transmittal fee, the international filing fee and the search fee (R.14.1(c) PCT; R.15.3 PCT; R.16.1(f) PCT). The amount of the handling fee and the preliminary examination fee is determined by the date of payment (R.57.3(d) PCT; R.58.1(b) PCT).

If the old amount of the fee is paid within six months of a fee increase, the fee will be regarded as validly paid if the deficit is paid within two months of an invitation from the EPO (OJ 2024 A3 Art.6(3)).

3 **Filing fee (Rfees2(1)1)**

The fee rate depends on whether the European application was filed online or not. For the filing fee paid on entry into the European phase under **R.159(1)(c)**, the fee rate depends on whether Form 1200 is filed online or not.

The language reduction applies to the filing fee of Euro-direct applications if the conditions of **R.7a(1)** and **R.7b** are met. The micro-entity reduction applies to the filing fee of Euro-direct applications and Euro-PCT applications if the conditions of **R.7a(3)** and **R.7b** are met.

4 **Page fee (Rfees2(1)1a and Rfees2(2)7)**

4.1 AMOUNT OF PAGE FEE

The term 'additional fee under R.38(2)' is replaced by 'page fee' in this book for reasons of clarity.

A page fee for excess pages is payable on filing (OJ 2008 p.10). The amount of the page fee defined in **R.38(2)** is fixed in **Rfees2(1)1a**. For a direct European application, the page fee must be paid within one month from filing the first set of claims or the copy of a previously filed application under **R.40(3)**, whichever period expires last (**R.38(3)**). For a Euro-PCT application, the page fee must be paid on entry into the European phase (**R.159(1)(c)**). The sanction on non-payment is given in **R.38(3):1**.

The manner of calculating the number of pages for the page fee under **Rfees2(1)1a** is set out in the Not. EPO, OJ 2009 p.118, section 3.2; see also A-III,13.2 and the summary below.

4.2 NUMBER OF PAGES OF APPLICATION

4.2.1 *Direct European applications*

For direct European applications, the calculation of the page fee is based on the number of pages of the description, claims, any drawings and one page for the abstract, in the language of filing. The pages of the Request for Grant form do not count. The language reduction and the micro-entity reduction apply to the page fee if the conditions of **R.7a** and **R.7b** are met. (A-III,13.2; A-X,9.3.2; Not. EPO OJ 2024 A8 §10)

A sequence listing filed as a separate part of the description as an xml file in the format of the ST.26 standard does not count for the page fee (**R.30(1)**; A-III,1.2). However, a sequence listing in a non-compliant format will be subject to the page fee (OJ 2021 A97). By way of exception, the page fee is not payable for a sequence listing in a divisional application that is the parent application's sequence listing in the former ST.25 format in pdf (OJ 2023 A98). (A-III,13.2)

Where an application is filed without claims, the first set of claims filed after the date of filing will be included in the page count.

In the case of filing by reference to an earlier application under **R.40(1)(c)**, the number of pages of the certified copy will be used, excluding the pages for the certification and bibliographic data, and excluding any pages for a sequence listing in the former ST.25 format (A-IV,5.3).

The page fee for an application filed with claims must be paid within one month of filing (**R.38(3)**). Since this month expires before the time limit for correcting formal deficiencies of the application under **R.57(i)** and **R.58**, the number of pages can only be determined on the documents as filed. In contrast, according to A-III,13.2, second paragraph, if there are formal deficiencies in the application, such as margins, line spacing and font size not complying with **R.49(5)** and (8), the EPO will use the number of pages after they have been corrected. However, there is no legal basis for requesting payment of the page fee after the one-month period of **R.38(3)**.

4.2.2 *Euro-PCT applications*

Since the page fee for a Euro-PCT application is payable on entry into the European phase, the number of pages is calculated based on the documents available on entry. Hence, amendments filed on entry are included in the calculation, and those filed later, e.g. in response to the **R.161** communication, are not. The date of the entry is the expiry of the 31-month period or the date of a valid request for early processing. Amendments that increase the number of pages should therefore preferably be filed after entry. Similarly, an amendment in response to the **R.161** communication reducing the number of pages will not result in a refund of an already paid page fee.

The micro-entity reduction applies to the page fee if the conditions of **R.7a** and **R.7b** are met.

The basis for the calculation is, in principle, the international application as published, i.e. the WO publication, even if published in a non-EPO language. However, see below for the case of amendments. The pages of the description, claims and drawings are counted, as well as one page for the abstract. It does not matter if the bibliographic data and the abstract extend to a second page of the publication. Form 1200 for entry into the European phase is not included in the calculation either. Any pages of a standard-compliant sequence listing are not counted. (OJ 2009 p.338; A-III,13.2)

Any amended claims under Art. 19 PCT are included in the WO publication as additional pages, and are counted as such, unless the applicant indicates that the procedure in the European phase is not to be based on them when entering the European phase (A-III,13.2). However, Box 6.1 of Form 1200 for entry into the European phase indicates that amended claims under Art.19 PCT replace the originally filed claims, with an option to indicate that further amendments are enclosed.

Moreover, any amendments under Art.34 PCT, i.e. filed in the course of international preliminary examination, will be taken into account as additional pages (A-III,13.2). However, Box 6.2 of Form 1200 indicates that proceedings before the EPO as elected office are based on the documents on which the IPER is based, including any annexes (i.e. the claims on which the IPER is based), with an option to indicate that further amendments are enclosed.

If the international application is published in an EPO language, any amended pages filed under **R.159(1)(b)** when entering the European phase replace the respective pages of the application as published. If the claims are amended at this stage, an entire set of claims must be submitted and the page fee is based on the entire set of claims as amended (A-III,13.2).

If the international application was published in a non-EPO language, and if no amendments are filed on entry into the European phase, the WO publication in the non-EPO language is taken as the basis for calculating the page fee. However, if pages are amended upon entry, the translation of the application as required under R.159(1)(a) is taken as the basis instead. If the description is amended, the translation of the description is taken as the basis for calculating the additional fee. In this case, the amended pages replace the respective pages of the description as translated. If the drawings are amended, the translated drawings are taken as the basis for calculating the additional fees and the amended pages of the drawings replace the respective pages. If only the claims are amended, the page fee is based on the description and drawings as published in the WO publication, plus the entire set of amended claims in the EPO language (A-III,13.2; OJ 2009 p.338).

If the applicant explicitly states that application documents filed on entry into the European phase have merely been reformatted to reduce the number of pages, the EPO disregards these reformatted application documents and does not accept them as the basis for calculation of the page fee (OJ 2009 p.118; A-III,13.2).

For Euro-PCT applications containing erroneously filed parts and correct parts incorporated by reference under R.20.5bis(d) PCT, the basis for calculating the number of pages is the international publication. If the applicant renounces either the erroneously filed parts or correct parts incorporated by reference when entering the European phase and before payment of the page fee (see **R.159:6**), the renouncement is considered an amendment of the application, and the amended text is taken as the basis for calculating the page fee. (A-III,13.2)

4.2.3 *Issues affecting number of pages*

If missing or correct parts are filed under **R.56** or **R.56a**, the page fee is calculated on the basis of the documents present at the expiry of the one-month period of **R.38(3)** (A-III,13.2).

Any amendments filed in reply to a communication under **R.161** are not taken into account in the calculation.

The amount of the fee for further processing for the page fee is calculated on the basis of the number of pages on file on expiry of the relevant period for which the page fee has not been paid; the basic filing fee is not taken into account (A-III,13.2; E-VIII,2).

5 Divisional fee (Rfees2(1)1b)

An additional fee must be paid for a divisional filed in respect of any earlier application which is itself a divisional (**R.38(4)**). The amount of the fee depends on the generation of the divisional. The generation of a divisional is equal to the number of divisionals in the sequence from the root application up to and including the divisional being filed. Hence, a first generation divisional is a divisional filed in respect of an earlier application that is not a divisional, i.e. in respect of a root application. (OJ 2014 A22; A-IV,1.1.2, 1.4.1.1)

Since the divisional fee is part of the filing fee according to **R.38(4)**, the language reduction and the micro-entity reduction apply to the page fee if the conditions of **R.7a** and **R.7b** are met (**Rfees14(1)**; A-IV,1.4.1.1; Not. EPO OJ 2024 A8 §10).

6 Search fee (Rfees2(1)2)

6.1 DIRECT EUROPEAN AND EURO-PCT APPLICATIONS

The amount of the search fee as fixed in **Rfees2(1)2**, first indent, is the same for:

- a search on a direct European application (**Art.78(2)**; **R.62**);
- a further search on a direct European application in case of lack of unity of invention (**R.64**);
- a further search on replacement of erroneously filed application documents or parts, when filed after the EPO has begun to draw up the search report (**R.56a(8)**, as of 01.11.2022);
- a supplementary search on a Euro-PCT application (**Art.153(7)**); and
- a further search on a Euro-PCT application in case of lack of unity of invention (**R.164**).

The search fee for applications filed before 01.07.2005, laid down in **Rfees2(1)2**, second indent, is lower because no search opinion is drafted (OJ 2005 p.7). The lower search fee is compensated by a higher examination fee.

The search fee covers about 30% of the actual costs of a search for the EPO. The other part is covered by the renewal fees.

See **Rfees9** for a refund of the search fee for a European search when the EPO can make use of an earlier search it has made.

The supplementary search fee (**Art.153(7)**) is substantially reduced if a (S) ISA of a contracting state of the EPC has carried out the (supplementary) international search, i.e. if the Austrian, Finnish, Spanish, Swedish or Turkish Patent Office, or the Nordic or Visegrad Patent Institute acted as (S)ISA (OJ 2024 A3 Art.4(1)). If one of these offices drew up the international search report and another carried out a supplementary international search, the reduction is given only once (OJ 2024 A3 Art.4(2)).

The reduction is given only for the supplementary search fee paid under **R.159(1)(e)**. It is not relevant whether the invention first mentioned in the claims pending at the time of the supplementary search was searched by the ISA in the international phase. The reduction does not apply to any further search fees to be paid under **R.164(1)** (A-X, 9.5.1).

The micro-entity reduction applies to the search fee if the conditions of **R.7a** and **R.7b** are met.

Further information concerning these search fees is given in Not. EPO OJ 2024 A33. This notice does not discuss the possible reductions of the fee under **R.7a**.

6.2 INTERNATIONAL APPLICATIONS

For international applications where the EPO acts as (S)ISA, the amount of the search fee as fixed in **Rfees2(1)2**, third and fourth indent, is the same for:

- an international search (R.16.1 PCT);

- an additional international search in case of lack of unity of invention (**R.158(1)** EPC);
- a supplementary international search (R.45bis.3 PCT); and
- an additional search in the event incorrect parts or elements of the application are corrected (R.40bis.1 PCT in conjunction with R.20.5bis PCT; OJ 2020 A81 §5).

See **Rfees2(1):17** for the reduction of the international search fee for applicants from certain states. See OJ 2025 A26 for details about a refund of the search fee for an international search when the EPO as ISA can make use of an earlier search report drawn up by the EPO on an application whose priority is claimed.

If the application enters the European phase and the micro-entity reduction applies, a reduction of the fees will be given equal to 30% of the fee for the international search if the EPO was the ISA, based on the amount of the fee for the international search fee effectively paid to the EPO (i.e. after any reductions and refunds), under **R.7a(3)(c)**.

7 Designation fee (Rfees2(1)3)

The micro-entity reduction applies to the designation fee if the conditions of **R.7a(3)** and **R.7b** are met.

For applications filed before 01.04.2009 and international applications entering the European phase before that date, the designation fee still depends on the number of designated states. The amount is fixed separately in **Rfees2(2)**.

8 Renewal fee (Rfees2(1)4)

The micro-entity reduction applies to the renewal fees for applications if the conditions of **R.7a(3)** and **R.7b** are met.

The amounts of the renewal fees for unitary patents are laid down in **RfeesUPP.2**, with a possible reduction under **UPR.12**.

9 Examination fee (Rfees2(1)6)

9.1 AMOUNT OF EXAMINATION FEE

An overview of the amounts of the examination fee is given in Not. EPO OJ 2024 A33. This notice does not discuss the possible reductions of the fee under **R.7a**.

For Euro-direct applications, the (lower) fee level of the second indent applies; the first indent is now practically obsolete (see OJ 2022 A29 §2).

For Euro-PCT applications, the higher fee level of the third indent applies if the EPO drew up the (supplementary) international search report in the international phase and, hence, no supplementary European search is drawn up after entering the European phase (**Art.153(7)**; OJ 2009 p.594). The lower fee level of the second indent applies if the EPO draws up a supplementary European search report; in such a case the search fee of **R.159(1)(e)** must be paid as well.

The higher examination fee of the third indent is justified because the written opinion prepared by the EPO as ISA for such a Euro-PCT application is not of the same quality as the search opinion drawn up by the EPO as designated/elected office (CA/138/04 §16).

9.2 REDUCTION AND REFUND OF EXAMINATION FEE

The language reduction and the micro-entity reduction apply to the examination fee if the conditions of **R.7a** and **R.7b** are met (**Rfees14(1)**). For the language reduction, the written request for examination must be filed in an admissible non-EPO language (see **Art.14(4)**), the applicant must be an entitled entity, and a declaration must be filed.

The examination fee for a Euro-PCT application (**R.159(1)(f)**) is reduced under **Rfees14(2)** when the EPO has drawn up an international preliminary examination report, i.e. if a Demand was filed in the international phase and the EPO acted as IPEA. This reduction can be combined with the language reduction and the micro-entity reduction.

The refund of the examination fee, e.g. in case of withdrawal of the application, is governed by **Rfees11.**

10 **Fee for grant (Rfees2(1)7)**

The micro-entity reduction applies to the grant fee if the conditions of **R.7a(3)** and **R.7b** are met.

The fee for grant of **Rfees2(1)7** applies to applications filed on or after 01.04.2009 and for international applications entering the European phase on or after that date. For applications filed or entered before 01.04.2009, the fee for grant and printing is fixed separately in **Rfees2(2)7**, the amount of the fee depending on the number of pages of the patent to be granted. Before 01.04.2009, no page fee was due on filing or entry; instead, the page fee was levied at grant.

11 **Appeal fee (Rfees2(1)11)**

The appeal fee is reduced for natural persons and for microenterprises, SME's, universities and the other types of persons referred to in **R.7a(2)** (see OJ 2018 A5 §6-8 for definitions). There are no restrictions on language of the appeal and on nationality and residence, because **Rfees2(1)11** refers specifically to the persons of items (a) to (d) of **R.7a(2)**, hence, the restrictions of **Art.14(4)** do not apply (**J8/18** mutatis mutandis). Note that the scope of eligible parties is broader than for the micro-entity reduction: small and medium-sized enterprises are eligible for the reduction of the appeal fee. The reduced appeal fee ensures that the access to the appeal procedure is not impeded for such appellants. (CA/43/16 Rev. 1 §60; CA/102/17 §70-80)

Appellants wishing to benefit from the reduced appeal fee must file a declaration showing their entitlement, preferably using EPO Form 1011bis, according to Not. EPO OJ 2018 A5. An incorrect or missing declaration may cause termination of the appeal procedure according to OJ 2018 A5 §9-11. However, the remark in OJ 2018 A5 about a declaration being required lacks legal basis because **Rfees2(1)11** does not refer to **R.7b** (**T225/19** r.2.4 mutatis mutandis). The Board may, however, require evidence that the appellant is a person referred to in **R.7a(2)**.

If the opponent who files an appeal is a strawman party, the strawman opponent must be a person under **R.7a(2)**, not the principal (**T84/19**).

An appeal fee can be paid in full with a request to grant the reduction under **Rfees2(1)11** as a partial reimbursement (**T1216/23**).

12 **Fee for further processing (Rfees2(1)12)**

The fee for further processing is a flat fee unless the missed act is the payment of a fee. In the event of belated payment of a fee, the fee for further processing is 50% of the fee. In case applicants request further processing because they had paid a fee only in part within a period, e.g. by incorrectly paying a reduced amount, they have to pay the missing amount of the fee as omitted act together with 50% of the full unpaid fee as the further processing fee (**Rfees8**; see also **R.7b(4)**). However, the further processing fee for the page fee is based on the number of pages for which the page fee was not paid (E-VIII,2).

Where several acts have the same legal basis and form a unitary procedural act to be carried out in the same period, further processing in respect of this period requires payment of a single fee, the amount of which depends on the number and character of the omitted acts. For example, the further processing fee for an omitted filing of the written request for examination and payment of the examination fee under **Art.94(1)** is the sum of the flat fee for the request and 50% of the examination fee. (E-VIII,2)

As an exception, the further processing fee for an omitted payment of the fee for grant and publishing and omitted filing of translations of the claims under **R.71(3)** is only one flat fee (**Rfees2(1)12**). If in addition claims fees due under **R.71(4)** were not paid in due time, the single fee for further processing amounts to the sum of the flat fee and 50% of the claims fees (E-VIII,2).

Where several acts do not form a unitary procedural act and are subject to independent periods, further processing requires payment of a fee for further processing for each unobserved period. (E-VIII,2)

13 **Fee for re-establishment (Rfees2(1)13)**

The relatively high fee for re-establishment reflects the exceptional nature of re-establishment compared to further processing.

The fee for requesting restoration of the priority right for PCT applications entering the European regional phase (R.49ter.2 PCT) and during the international phase if the EPO is the receiving Office (R.26bis.3 PCT) is set at the same level as the fee for re-establishment.

Where several independent procedural acts are omitted, each resulting in the application being deemed withdrawn, a fee for re-establishment is due for each omitted act. Accordingly, if none of the acts required for entry of an international application into the European phase is performed in the 31-month period, and the period for requesting further processing is missed as well, four or more fees for re-establishment may be due (for the filing fee, designation fee, search fee, and the written request for examination combined with the examination fee; each with further processing). (E-VIII,3.1.3)

However, **T1823/16** r.2 held that re-establishment of rights for failure to file a notice of appeal as well as a statement of grounds requires payment of only one fee for re-establishment if the non-observance of both periods is intrinsically linked to the same cause of non-compliance.

14 **Claims fees (Rfees2(1)15)**

Claims fees are payable on filing of the application (**R.45**) or entry into the European phase (**R.162**) and, if the number of claims at grant is larger than at filing, also at grant for the added claims (**R.71(4)**). They are due for the 16th claim and up.

The amount of the claims fees for applications filed before 01.04.2009 and international applications that entered the European phase before that date is still fixed separately in **Rfees2(2)15**.

See **R.45(1):2** for possibilities for reducing the claims fees.

15 **Transmittal fee (Rfees2(1)18)**

The transmittal fee must be paid if the EPO acts as the receiving Office for a PCT application. The date of receipt of the PCT application determines the amount of the transmittal fee, not the date of payment (R.14.1(c) PCT).

16 **Protest fee (Rfees2(1)21)**

Rfees2(1)21 relates to the amount of the protest fee for non-unity in the international search (R.40.2.e PCT) and in the international preliminary examination (R.68.3(c) PCT).

17 **Reduction of PCT fees**
The international filing fee for filing a PCT application with the EPO as rO is reduced by 90% for applicants who are natural persons from certain EPC contracting states (GL/PCT-EPO A-III,8.1.2); the same applies for the supplementary search handling fee and the handling fee (GL/PCT-EPO A-III,8.1.2). The international filing fee is also reduced if the application and the request are filed in pdf, the fee is further reduced if the request is filed in xml and even further reduced if the application documents are filed in xml (GL/PCT-EPO A-III,8.1.1). If both reductions apply, the electronic filing reduction is deducted first (GL/PCT-EPO A-III,8.1.2).

The search fee for a (supplementary) international search under **Rfees2(1)2** and the fee for the preliminary examination of an international application under **Rfees2(1)19** will be reduced by 75% if each applicant is a natural person who is a national *and* resident of a state which is not party to the EPC and which is classified as a low-income or lower-middle-income economy (OJ 2020 A4, A35; 2023 A67; GL/PCT-EPO A-III,8.2). These states are listed in OJ 2024 A69, Annex I. The reduction also applies if each applicant is a natural or legal person who is a national *and* resident of a state having a validation agreement with the EPO, irrespective of the state of the economy (OJ 2020 A4, A35; 2023 A67).

Rfees2(2) For European patent applications filed before 1 April 2009 and international applications which entered the regional phase before that date, the amount of the fees specified in Article 2, item 3, item 3a, item 7 and item 15 of the Rules relating to Fees as in force until 31 March 2009 shall be as follows:

3.	**Designation fee for each Contracting State designated (Article 79, paragraph 2), designation fees being deemed paid for all Contracting States upon payment of seven times the amount of this fee**	**120**
3a.	**Joint designation fee for the Swiss Confederation and the Principality of Liechtenstein**	**120**
7.	**Fee for grant including fee for printing the European patent specification (Rule 71, paragraph 3), where the application documents to be printed comprise:**	
7.1	**not more than 35 pages**	**1080**
7.2	**more than 35 pages**	**The amount of item 7.1 plus EUR 18 for the 36th and each subsequent page**
15.	**Claims fee for the sixteenth and each subsequent claim (Rule 45, paragraph 1, Rule 71, paragraph 4, and Rule 162, paragraph 1)**	**275**

Amended by decision of the Administrative Council of 14.12.2023, which entered into force on 01.04.2024 (OJ 2024 A3).

1 **Fees for applications filed or entered the European phase before 1 April 2009**
Rfees2(2) provides several fees for direct European applications filed before 1 April 2009 and international applications that entered the European phase before 1 April 2009. In particular, the designation fee payable depends on the number of designated states, the fee for grant includes a page fee, and the claims fees have no higher amount as from claim 51. The amounts of these fees are regularly increased together with the fees in **Rfees2(1)**. See **Rfees2(1)** for notes to the fees of **Rfees2(2)**. (OJ 2009 p.587)

Rfees 3 Fees, expenses and prices laid down by the President of the Office

Rfees3(1) The President of the Office shall lay down the amount of the administrative fees provided for in the Implementing Regulations and, where appropriate, the amount of the fees and expenses for any services rendered by the Office other than those specified in Article 2.

1 **Administrative fees and fees for services**
The amounts of the administrative fees and expenses of **Rfees3(1)** in force as of 01.04.2024 are published in OJ 2024 A5.

Examples of administrative fees are the fees for registering a transfer (**R.22(2)**) and issuing priority documents, i.e. certified copies of patent applications (**R.54**). In both cases, no fee is charged if the request is filed using MyEPO. A further example is the administrative fee for file inspection by means of certified copies.

An example of an expense for a service is the fee for an international-type search of a national patent application (OJ 2024 A5).

The extension fees and validation fees are not administrative fees under **Rfees3(1)**; see **Art.79(2):2**.

Rfees3(2) He shall also lay down the prices of the publications referred to in Articles 93, 98, 103 and 129 of the Convention.

Art.93 application
Art.98 specification
Art.103 new specification after opposition
Art.129 Official Journal and the Patent Bulletin

1 **Price list for publications**
Patent applications and patent specifications are published on the Publication Server on the EPO website. The Official Journal and the Patent Bulletin are also published on the EPO website. They can be downloaded free of charge. Certified copies of publications of patent applications and patent specifications are issued upon payment of a fee, and by exception without fee if requested using MyEPO. The amount of the fee is published in OJ 2024 A5.

Rfees3(3) The amounts of the fees provided for in Article 2 and of the fees and expenses laid down in accordance with paragraph 1 shall be published in the Official Journal and on the website of the European Patent Office.

1 **Publication of Schedule of fees**
The amounts of the administrative fees and expenses of **Rfees3(1)** are published in OJ 2024 A5 and in the Interactive schedule of fees on the EPO website.

Rfees 4 Due date for fees

1 **Due date of a fee**
The term 'due date of a fee payment' has a special meaning in the EPC, namely the first day on which payment can be validly made (A-X,5.1.1). The last day of valid payment is the day of expiry of the period pertaining to the fee (A-X,10.1.2). The due date is the date at which a legal ground comes into existence which forms the basis of the payment and causes the fee to become indebted.

Note, that, in contrast with the EPC, 'the due date of payment' in common English is the last date on which payment can be validly made. **R.51** and **R.71a(3)** use 'due' in the common English meaning.

The EPC does not provide for postponement of fee payments in support of applicants in need. When drafting the EPC, it was agreed that it is up to the individual contracting states to provide financial support for such applicants.

2 **Prepayment of a fee**
A payment made before the due date is not valid and will be refunded to avoid payers escaping an increase of fees by paying early (**G1/18** r.VIII; A-X,5.1.1). Instead of refunding the fee, the EPO may reject such a payment as invalid if paid by debit order using specific methods of filing debit orders (**Rfees5(2):2.1**). There are five exceptions to this principle of refunding or rejecting a prepayment:

- Renewal fees may be paid during a prepayment period of six months before the due date for the renewal fee in respect of the third year and of three months for all other renewal fees (**R.51(1)**; A-X,5.2.4).
- The due date for the designation fee is the publication of the search report. If the designation fee is paid before the due date, e.g. even as early as on filing of the application, the EPO will retain the payment; the payment will only be considered valid as from the due date, provided that the amount paid is the amount payable on the date of payment (A-X,5.2.2).
- A payment made shortly before the due date need not be refunded by the EPO but may be regarded as a payment taking effect only later on the due date (A-X,5.1.1). However, a payment of a renewal fee before the prepayment period of **R.51(1)** will always be rejected (A-X,5.2.4).
- Fees paid voluntarily together with amendments in response to a **R.71(3)** communication will be credited to the fees payable for a subsequent **R.71(3)** communication (**R.71a(5)**; A-X,5.1.1).
- Fees paid for a Euro-PCT application before expiry of the 31-month period where no early processing is requested will be retained; the EPO assumes that the applicant wishes to enter into the European phase by expiry of the period (A-X,5.2.1).

Rfees4(1) Fees in respect of which the due date is not specified in the provisions of the Convention or of the PCT or of the Implementing Regulations thereto shall be due on the date of receipt of the request for the service incurring the fee concerned.

1 **Due date of specific fees**
Examples of the due date for some fees in order of procedure (A-X,5.2):
- The filing fee and search fee are due on the day the application is filed.
- The designation fee is due on publication of the search report (A-X,5.2.2), not on the filing date. See **Rfees4:2** for payment before the due date.
- The examination fee is due when the written request for examination is filed. Since the request is contained in the Request for Grant form, the fee is due on the date of filing if the form is used on filing.
- Any claims fees are due upon filing of the first set of claims, which is the later of the date of filing of the application and the date of subsequent filing of the claims.
- The fee for grant and publishing falls due on notification of the communication of **R.71(3)**. Under **R.71(4)**, the same applies for the claims fees, unless they were already paid earlier under **R.45** or **R.162**.
- Renewal fees fall due on the last day of the month containing the anniversary of the date of filing. See **Rfees4:2** for payment before the due date.
- The opposition fee and appeal fee are due on the date of receipt of the notice of opposition and appeal, respectively (**G1/18** r.VIII and XI). Similarly, the fees for limitation, revocation and petition for review are due on the date the request or petition is filed (A-X,5.2.6).
- If a request incurs payment of a fee and no due date is specified, the fee is due on the date of receipt of the request (Rfees4(1); A-X,5.1.1). Payment of the fee makes the request effective (A-X,5.2.7).

Rfees4(2) The President of the Office may decide not to make services within the meaning of paragraph 1 dependent upon the advance payment of the corresponding fee.

Rfees 5 Payment of fees

1 **Online service for fee payments**
The EPO provides an online Central Fee Payment service (CFP), which enables fees to be paid by credit card, to prepare payments by bank transfer, and to claim refunds. CFP can also be used to pay from a deposit account (see **Rfees5(2):2.1**) with two-factor authentication. Deposit accounts can be managed via the Central Fee Payment (OJ 2022 A25, A81).

The Central Fee Payment service is required to pay fees by credit card (see **Rfees5(2):4**), and can be used to prepare payment by bank transfer (see **Rfees5(1):1**). The user selects the desired fees to be paid and indicates at the check-out stage whether the method of payment will be by deposit account, bank transfer or credit card. The check-out stage includes a validation functionality to automatically reject payment of fees that cannot be validly paid. (OJ 2022 A81)

Rfees5(1) The fees due to the Office shall be paid in euro by payment or transfer to a bank account held by the Office.

Amended, in force since 01.04.2008, applies to payments made from that date (OJ 2007 p.533).

1 **Payment to EPO bank account**
All payments to the EPO must be made to the EPO bank account in euros without charge to the payee. See OJ 2022 A81 for requirements for bank transfers and for the details of the EPO bank account (as footnote 9).

The CFP service can be used to make an order for payment by bank transfer for one or more applications. Once the order is confirmed, the service provides an order confirmation with a payment reference. The payment reference is to be used in the bank transfer and allows the EPO to associate the payment with the relevant applications. The payment reference is usable once and is valid for two months. (OJ 2022 A81)

A payment order cannot be cancelled or amended by the user. In the event of an underpayment where the money reaching the EPO bank account is less than the total amount in the order, the fees will be paid in ascending order of the application numbers, with PCT preceding EP, and in ascending order of fee codes. Any underpaid and unpaid fees will be indicated in the payment confirmation in the online service. A new order for payment is required to redress the underpayment. (OJ 2022 A81)

A bank transfer for a single application can also be made without using CFP by specifying the application number, fee code, and amount per fee code as the payment reference (OJ 2017 A100). The fee codes can be found in OJ 2024 sp4 under 'Description of fee codes'. However, it is strongly recommended to use the CFP service, even for payments for a single application.

If a renewal fee, or surcharge, is paid by bank transfer without using CFP and the fee is not due, the fee will be directly repaid to the bank account (OJ 2024 A82 §6). The same applies to renewal fees and surcharges for unitary patents (OJ 2024 A82 §67).

The term 'payment to a bank account' in **Rfees5(1)**, as an alternative to 'transfer to a bank account', refers to effecting payment by depositing cash at the counter of a bank. See, e.g., **J7/81.**

Rfees5(2) The President of the Office may allow other methods of paying fees than those set out in paragraph 1.

1 **Other methods of payment**

The President has allowed the following methods of paying fees other than payment and transfer to the EPO bank account: debiting a deposit account held with the EPO, either using a debit order or automatic debiting (ADA, OJ 2022 sp3) and payment by credit card (OJ 2017 A72). See OJ 2018 A32 for a summary. In addition, fees can be paid by requesting a re-allocation of a refund of an earlier payment (A-X,2; A-X,10.4; **R.71a(6)**).

The payment methods in **Rfees5(1)** and (2) are exhaustive. Other methods for paying fees in procedures are not allowed; any payment made by such a method will be regarded as not received (**R2/09** r.2.3). For example, a payment by cheque will not be accepted (OJ 2007 p.626).

2 **Deposit account**

The payment of fees by debiting a deposit account is governed by the Arrangements for Deposit Accounts (ADA). The version valid as of 01.04.2024 was published in OJ 2024 sp2, p.9, with an amendment effective on 07.10.2024 published in OJ 2024 A81 (Notice in OJ 2024 A82) and a further amendment which entered into force on 01.04.2025, published in OJ 2025 A17 (Notice in OJ 2025 A18).

Since the ADA is an administrative regulation falling outside the EPC, certain provisions of the EPC do not apply, in particular, **Art.14** on languages and **R.2** on filing methods.

A deposit account is an account kept by the EPO in the name of an account holder, such as a party or representative. The account is similar to a bank account, is kept in Euros and is for payment of fees to the EPO (ADA.1). Deposit accounts can only be used to pay fees payable to the EPO in connection with European and PCT proceedings and proceedings relating to European patents with unitary effect and annual subscriptions for epi (ADA.7). A person may open a deposit account under ADA.2. The account holder can effect payment of a fee by filing a debit order with the EPO, upon which the EPO debits the deposit account (ADA.7). Debit orders can only be filed electronically in a prescribed format (ADA.7.1.2). Alternatively, the account holder may authorise the EPO to automatically debit upcoming fees by filing an automatic debit order (ADA.14), see note 3 below. Account holders must make payments by bank transfer into the EPO bank account to replenish their deposit account to maintain sufficient funds (ADA.3).

The main advantage of payment through a deposit account is that payments can be made easily by filing a debit order by accepted means (**Rfees5(2):2.1**), possibly simultaneously with filing other documents, or by automatic debiting.

Account holders can inspect their pending orders, payment plan and transactions performed, download their statements and monitor their account balances via Central Fee Payment (ADA.6.2) (OJ 2022 A81).

A deposit account with no transaction in the last four years will ex officio be set to inactive if it shows a positive balance and be closed if it shows a zero balance (ADA.6.3). In both cases the EPO will notify the account holder.

2.1 DEBITING THE ACCOUNT

A debit order for paying one or more fees must be filed in the prescribed electronically processable format (xml) using either Online Filing (OLF), Online Filing 2.0, Central Fee Payment, or MyEPO. Additionally, ePCT may be used for fees pertaining to PCT applications where the EPO is the rO, ISA or IPEA. (ADA.7.1.2 with amendments effective on 07.10.2024 in OJ 2024 A81)

Debit orders filed in any other way, e.g., on paper, or using a different format such as a pdf attachment, or in the annotation field of the online forms, are invalid and will not be carried out (ADA.7.1.3). See section **2.1.2** below for an exceptionally permitted debit order on paper via national authority.

If a system breakdown occurs at the payer's end, another payment method should be used, such as a bank transfer or credit card, or the payment should be made by a person not affected by the breakdown. Exceptionally, a debit order can be filed through the Contingency Upload Service if the debit order is filed on the last day for paying the fee and the payer is affected by an unavailability, outage, or system malfunction meaning that any of the regular means of filing debit orders is unavailable, irrespective of the cause. The payer must provide evidence, e.g. screenshots. Moreover, the deposit account must have sufficient funds (ADA.7.1.4; A-X,4.2.3).

If a payment period expires on a day on which one of the accepted means of filing debit orders is not available at the EPO, i.e. is unavailable for reasons attributable to the EPO, the payment period is extended to the first day on which all such means are available again (ADA.11). The payer does not need to try using another payment method (**T480/21**). A period may also be extended under **R.134(5)** in case of a general breakdown of electronic communications services at the locality of the payer or other like reasons. (ADA.11)

The day of receipt of the debit order will be regarded as the date on which the payment is made, provided the account contains sufficient funds; debit orders may specify a payment date later than the date of submission (ADA.10.1, 10.2). Debit orders are processed upon their receipt, provided there are sufficient funds in the deposit account (ADA.7.2.1).

A debit order may be revoked as a whole or in part on its date of receipt by a written notice signed by the person making the payment and filed by email or as an attachment to an EPO online contact form (ADA.13.1). A debit order with a deferred payment date can be revoked via the Central Fee Payment at the latest the day preceding the specified payment date, or by a written notice filed by email or via the online contact form on the specified payment date (ADA.13.2). Debit orders with deferred payment date can be filed via Central Fee Payment (OJ 2022 A81).

Debit orders concerning multiple applications are processed in ascending order of application number, PCT preceding EP; EP preceding UP (for Euro-PCT applications and unitary patents, the EP application number is used). Individual fees are booked in ascending order of fee codes, with appeal fee and opposition fee taking precedence over other fees. The page fee for EP application is booked together with the filing fee, despite its fee code. (ADA.7.3). A list of the fee codes can be found in OJ 2023 sp2 under 'Description of fee codes'; with further fee codes for unitary patents in OJ 2023 sp3 p.26.

The Central Fee Payment (CFP) service allows to submit batch debit orders relating to multiple applications or patents by uploading batch order files in xml format or as csv files. See OJ 2022 A81 §13-14 for more information on batch payments.

The CFP service includes a validation function for debit orders, which rejects payments that are obviously invalid. For example, a debit order for payment of a renewal fee under **Art.86** that is not due (e.g. for a granted patent) is automatically rejected (also when included in a batch debit order). See ADA.9.1 and ADA.9.2 and A-X,4.2.3 for other examples of invalid payments that are rejected and exclusions from the validation. The automatic rejection relieves the EPO of the burden of refunding such payments. The EPO stores a message in the account history and in the file that the debit order could not be carried out (ADA.9.5 as amended, effective on 07.10.2024, OJ 2024 A81).

2.1.1 *Deficient debit order*

The software for filing debit orders prescribed in ADA.7.1.2 ensures that debit orders include all information necessary for automatic processing, such as the application number, amount, and fee code. A debit order can be corrected under **R.139** provided that the requirements of **G1/12** r.37 are met: (a) the correction must introduce what was originally intended; (b) where the original intention is not immediately apparent, the requester bears the burden of proof, which is a heavy one; (c) the error to be remedied may be an incorrect statement or an omission; and (d) the request for correction must be filed without delay (**J8/19, T3098/19**). An allowable correction has a retroactive effect (**G1/12** r.37).

Moreover, the EPO may overlook small amounts lacking (**Rfees8**).

A debit order is carried out notwithstanding incorrect information given in it, provided the intention of the person giving the order is clear (**T152/82**). If the amount of a fee indicated in a debit order does not correspond to the amount due for the type of fee on the date of receipt of the debit order, the EPO corrects the amount and debits the correct amount if there are sufficient funds in the deposit account. The party is informed of the correction and can object to it within a period of two months, in which case the correction is reversed, and the original amount indicated is debited. The EPO does not add any missing fees to a debit order, even if they are due on the date of receipt of the debit order. (A-X,4.2.3; A-X,7.1.1)

An evidently incorrect purpose of the payment is not prejudicial if the intended purpose can be established without difficulty from the remaining information; the inadvertent use of the payment by the EPO for a purpose different from the evidently intended purpose has no effect on the intended purpose (**J16/84**; A-X,7.1.2).

If a renewal fee that is not due is paid using a debit order submitted by means other than CFP (e.g. using Online Filing or Online Filing 2.0), the fee is automatically repaid directly to the deposit account used to make the payment (ADA 9.6 as amended by OJ 2024 A81; Not. EPO OJ 2024 A82).

2.1.2 *Debit order via national authority*

The fees for a European patent application filed with a national authority under **Art.75(1)(b)** can be paid by a debit order submitted online with the EPO (ADA.12; A-II,1.6).

If a European application is filed on paper with a national authority, the fees may be paid also on paper using the Form 1020 debit order included with the application. The debit order will be regarded as filed in due time, even if received after expiry of the period for payment, provided that evidence is provided that the debit order was filed with the national authority together with the application and that the account contained sufficient funds on the date on which the period expired. (ADA.12.1; 12.2)

2.1.3 *Shortfall of the account*

The account holder must ensure that sufficient funds are available in the account. The EPO will book the fees of automatic debit orders and any other debit orders to be executed on the same day in a specific order. If the account does not contain sufficient funds to cover all the fees indicated, the fees are booked in said order as long as the funds allow. Once a debit order cannot be executed in full due to insufficient funds, no other debit order is booked until the account is duly replenished. The holder is informed accordingly by e-mail or post. (ADA.7.4.1)

After the deposit account is duly replenished, the EPO processes any pending debit orders (automatic debit orders taking precedence over other debit orders, ADA.7.4.2) and the payment is considered to have been made on the date of replenishment, not on the date of receipt of the debit order or the decisive payment date in case of automatic debiting (ADA.7.4.3). The date of replenishment is the date the replenishment payment was actually entered in the EPO bank account (**Rfees7(1)**); and this will also be the date of payment of the fee by the debit order. However, the EPO will deem a period for paying a fee to have been observed if the bank transfer for the replenishment was ordered in a particular manner before expiry of the period (ADA.7.5; see below). Otherwise, a shortfall may cause debit orders to be processed after expiry of the relevant period for payment and remedies for late paid fees may have to be applied. Further processing under **Art.121** and **R.135** is available for most late paid fees; the fee for further processing is usually 50% of the late paid fee (**Rfees2(1)12**). Some late paid fees, such as appeal fee, renewal fee plus additional fee, renewal fee for divisional, further search fees, and any fee paid in the further-processing period require re-establishment under **Art.122** and **R.136** as remedy; the fee for re-establishment (**Rfees2(1)13**) must be paid and all due care proved (**Art.122(1):4**). There is no such remedy for a late paid fee for re-establishment (**Art.122(4)**).

A shortfall can be avoided by checking the upcoming payments in Central Fee Payment and replenishing the account accordingly. For example, check twice weekly the total amount of the fees due for the next 20 days and replenish the account to the total amount, correcting for incidental extra payments. The EPO debits the account at the end of the day of the decisive payment date of a fee that must be debited automatically or on the date of receipt of the debit order for any other fee (ADA.7.2.1).

Regarding replenishment of deposit accounts in case of a shortfall, a payment by debit order is deemed to have been made in time even if on the date of payment there were insufficient funds on the deposit account, provided that the debit account holder initiated a bank transfer payment to replenish the deposit account by ordering a SEPA credit transfer at least one day before or a SEPA instant credit transfer at least on the last day of the period for payment. For banks located in a contracting state not participating in the SEPA (Albania, Montenegro, Serbia and Türkiye), a bank payment order for replenishment of the deposit account given at least three days before the expiry of the period for payment is deemed sufficient (ADA.7.5). Note, the requirements for the fail-safe provision of ADA.7.5 are different from those of **Rfees7(3)**.

2.2 ANNUAL SUBSCRIPTIONS EPI

A professional representative can pay the annual subscription to the Institute of Professional Representatives before the European Patent Office (*epi*) by direct debiting of a deposit account held by the EPO on the basis of an agreement between the EPO and the *epi* (OJ 2022 sp3 Annex B.1 and B.2). The representative must thereto file a direct debiting mandate signed by the account holder with the *epi*, not with the EPO. The *epi* will transmit the debit orders to the EPO, upon which the EPO debits the accounts and pays the sum to the *epi*. (ADA.16)

3 Automatic debiting

An applicant or proprietor may file an automatic debit order according to the Arrangements for the Automatic Debiting procedure (AAD). The version of the AAD in force as of 01.04.2024 is published in OJ 2024 sp2 Annex A.1, with explanations given in OJ 2024 sp2 Annex A.2, and with an amendment effective 01.04.2025 published in OJ 2025 A17 (see Not. EPO OJ 2025 A18). The amendment of 01.04.2025 also changed a few points of the explanations in Annex A.2, see Art.3 of Dec. Pres. OJ 2025 A17.

An automatic debit order authorises the EPO to debit a deposit account for fees due for an application or patent automatically on the due date of the fee. An automatic debit order must be filed and revoked online (AAD.1.2 and 10); recommended practice for revoking an automatic debit order is given in the notes to AAD.10 (OJ 2024 sp2 Annex A.2). On closing a deposit account, the EPO revokes all pending automatic debit orders associated with the deposit account (AAD.10.4).

Applicants and proprietors can use the automatic debiting in all procedures for European patent applications and patents, and for PCT applications in the international phase where the EPO is receiving Office, ISA or IPEA and for PCT applications before the EPO as designated or elected office. Note that an automatic debit order filed for the international phase is not applicable in the regional EP phase; a separate automatic debit order must be filed for both proceedings (AAD.2.2). A new automatic debit order must be filed for European patents in limitation and revocation proceedings and any subsequent appeal or review proceedings, as well as for proceedings relating to unitary patents (AAD.2.3; for unitary patents: UP-3.1.3).

An opponent cannot pay the opposition fee using automatic debiting; other excluded fees are listed in AAD.3.3. These fees are also excluded if the debit order is of the 'for all fees' type.

The automatic debit order must be filed in xml in Online Filing or Online Filing 2.0 using one of the prescribed forms or via Central Fee Payment. Automatic debit orders relating to PCT applications for fees to be paid to the EPO must be filed using Online Filing, Online Filing 2.0, Central Fee Payment or ePCT, using the PCT fee calculation and payment feature. (AAD.1.2)

AAD.3 specifies the fees that are covered by the automatic debiting. The date of payment under automatic debiting, i.e. the decisive payment date, is usually the last day of the period for paying a fee (AAD.5.1(a)). The fee for further processing is paid on the last day of the period for requesting further processing where the omitted act was a payment, and on the date of completion of the omitted act where the omitted act was the non-performance of a procedural act other than payment of a fee (AAD.5.2). The fee for re-establishment, for limitation or revocation, for appeal and for petition for review is paid on the date of receipt of the request (AAD.5.1(c)). Automatic debit orders are processed at the end of the day of the date of payment (ADA.7.2.1, AAD.4.4). The order for processing the fees is the same as for debit orders, see note 2.1 above, with the exception of opposition fee, which cannot be paid by automatic debiting. In case there were not sufficient funds on the deposit account on the decisive payment date, automatic debit orders take precedence over debit orders once the account is replenished (ADA.7.4.2).

As of 01.04.2025, an automatic debit order for European patent grant proceedings can be given for renewal fees only, for all fees except renewal fees, or for all fees (which still does not cover the excluded fees of AAD.3.3). An automatic debit order given through OLF is always for all fees (Not. EPO OJ 2025 A18 §7). Until 01.04.2025, an automatic debit order was always for all fees; this remains the case for debit orders in PCT proceedings and in proceedings relating to unitary patents (Not. EPO OJ 2025 A18 §6). An automatic debit order for renewal fees and an automatic debit order for all other fees can be active simultaneously for an application (e.g. with different payers), other combinations are not possible (OJ 2025 A18 §8).

Under the automatic debiting procedure, all fees becoming due during the procedure will be paid automatically. Hence, the further search fees for all non-unitary inventions are automatically debited (OJ 2024 sp2, Annex A.2, Re point 3, note I.2); similarly, all claims fees are automatically debited (OJ 2024 sp2, Annex A.2, Re point 3, note I.4). If applicants do not want to pay one or more of these fees, they must inform the EPO accordingly or revoke the automatic debit order before expiry of the relevant period (OJ 2024 sp2, Annex A.2, point 3, notes I.2 and I.4). If a fee is paid by another means of payment and is received at least two days before the decisive payment date, the EPO will not carry out the automatic debit order in respect of that fee (AAD.9). Payment by another means can also be used to avoid a fee increase by paying early (OJ 2024 sp2, Annex A.2 notes to point 9).

In case not all automatic debit orders can be carried out due to insufficient funds, the priority of processing the orders will be the same as for normal debit orders (AAD.6 referring to AAD.4.5; see above **Rfees5:2.1.3**).

4 **Credit card**
Fees can also be paid by credit card in euros, using Central Fee Payment (OJ 2022 A81). The date of payment is the date in Central European Time on which the transaction is approved, which date is indicated in the confirmation made available to the payer. A transaction that failed before it was approved is considered not to have been made, even if the failure was not attributable to the payer. If a failure causes the payment to have been made after the expiry of the period for payment, the period will still be considered to have been observed if evidence is provided to the EPO that the payer received a confirmation of approval within the period. (Dec. Pres. OJ 2017 A72) Credit card payments can be made Central Fee Payment using American Express, Mastercard or Visa. The EPO will bear any transaction charges as long as the rules set by the EPO (including the daily limit for credit card payments) are followed. (Not. EPO OJ 2022 A18)

Any refund will not be made into the credit card account but will be paid into a deposit account with the EPO or, if not available, by bank transfer (A-X,10.3).

Rfees 6 Particulars concerning payments

Rfees6(1) Every payment must indicate the name of the person making the payment and must contain the necessary particulars to enable the Office to establish immediately the purpose of the payment.

1 **Person making the payment**
Since the Rules relating to Fees use the general term 'the person making the payment' instead of 'the party' as in the EPC, a payment can be made by any person; it is not restricted to parties or their representatives (A-X,1). Applicants who must be represented under **Art.133(2)** can nevertheless make payments (Legal Advice **L6/91** rev. §1, OJ 1991 p.573; cancelled by Dec. Pres. OJ 2012 p.446). However, any communication relating to the payment must be made by the party concerned or the representative.

2 **Particulars of payment**
For the efficient processing by the EPO of payments made by bank transfer, the payer should include the payment reference previously generated in Central Fee Payment service (OJ 2022 A81) in the payment-reference field of the (electronic) bank transfer, or include the application number and the fee code(s) (see **Rfees5(1):1**). See **Rfees6(2)** for unclear or incomplete payment details.

3 **Correction of payment**
An omitted payment cannot be corrected under **R.139**, because an omitted payment is not covered by **R.139**, first sentence (**J21/84** r.7,8; **T170/83** r.8, last paragraph). However, a validly filed debit order for a deposit account can be corrected, see **R.139:2.2**.

Rfees6(2) If the purpose of the payment cannot immediately be established, the Office shall require the person making the payment to notify it in writing of this purpose within such period as it may specify. If he does not comply with this request in due time the payment shall be considered not to have been made.

1 **Purpose of payment**
If the indicated purpose of the payment is obviously wrong, this deficiency is not prejudicial if the EPO can derive the intended purpose from the remaining information (**J16/84** hn.1).

If the intended purpose cannot be established immediately (taking into account all information), the EPO must ask the payer (**Rfees6(2)**). If the EPO requests the payer to specify the purpose of a payment and the payer responds in due time, the payment and the original payment date remain valid (A-X,7.1.2). If the payer does not reply to the request, the payment is considered not to have been made (**Rfees6**(2), last sentence) and is refunded to the payer (A-X,10.4).

The inadvertent use by the EPO of a payment for a purpose different from that evidently intended by the payer has no effect on the validity of the payment for the purpose intended by the payer. (**J16/84** hn.2, r.5,6)

Rfees 7 Date to be considered as the date on which payment is made

1 **Date of payment**
Rfees7 governs which date the EPO considers as the date on which a payment has been made. **Rfees7(1)** gives the general rule for payments into and transfers to the EPO bank account. Rules for other methods of payment are given by the President (**Rfees7(2)**). **Rfees7(3)** sets out the conditions under which a late payment may be regarded as having been made in due time; **Rfees7(4)** gives the corresponding procedure.

Rfees7(1) The date on which any payment shall be considered to have been made to the Office shall be the date on which the amount of the payment or of the transfer is actually entered in a bank account held by the Office.

Amended, in force since 25.10.2007 (OJ 2007 p.533).

1 **Date of payment for payments into the EPO bank account**
The EPO considers the date of payment as the date the amount paid is actually entered into the EPO account (**Rfees7(1)**). The EPO regards the amount as 'actually entered' on the date of issue of the bank statement that shows the amount. The bank statements for the EPO account are issued daily. The EPO disregards the value date of the payment, because that date can be changed retroactively by the bank, in contrast with the date of the bank statement, which cannot be changed. (see OJ 1997 p.217 §7)

Timely payment generally requires that the amount has been actually entered into the EPO account before expiry of the period for payment. As an exception, **Rfees7(3)** provides that the EPO considers an amount as timely paid if the payment is initiated in a contracting state before expiry of the period for payment but the amount actually enters into the EPO account after the expiry.

When a payment has to be made on the last day of a period from outside a contracting state, one should request the bank to make an urgent transfer on the same day, file a debit order, or make a credit card payment.

See **Rfees7(2):1** for the date of payment where another method of payment than payment into the EPO bank account is used.

Rfees7(2) Where the President of the Office allows, in accordance with the provisions of Article 5, paragraph 2, other methods of paying fees than those set out in Article 5, paragraph 1, he shall also lay down the date on which such payments shall be considered to have been made.

1 **Date of payment for debit order and automatic debiting**
The date of receipt by the EPO of a debit order is considered as the date of payment, provided the account has sufficient funds (ADA.10.1). Under the automatic debiting procedure, fees are in general debited from the deposit account on the last day of the relevant period (AAD.5.1(a)). See **Rfees5(2):2.1.3** for the date of payment in case of shortfall of the account.

2 **Date of payment for credit card payment**
A payment by credit card is deemed to have been made on the date on which the transaction is approved. This date is indicated in the transaction confirmation made available to the payer (Dec. Pres. OJ 2017 A72, Art.3). Where, due to a failure in the transaction process, payment of a fee is not considered to have been made until after the expiry of the period, it shall be considered that this period has been observed if evidence is provided to the EPO that, within this period, the payer has received a confirmation that the transaction was approved (OJ 2017 A72, Art.4(2)).

Rfees7(3) Where, under the provisions of paragraphs 1 and 2, payment of a fee is not considered to have been made until after the expiry of the period in which it should have been made, it shall be considered that this period has been observed if evidence is provided to the Office that the person who made the payment fulfilled one of the following conditions in a Contracting State within the period within which the payment should have been made:
(i) he effected the payment through a banking establishment;
(ii) he duly gave an order to a banking establishment to transfer the amount of the payment.

Amended, in force since 01.04.2020 (OJ 2020 A3 Art.2).

1 **Fail-safe arrangement for payments within a contracting state**
Rfees7(3) provides a 'fail-safe arrangement' for bank payments inside the EPC contracting states. Bank payments that are duly initiated before expiry of a period are considered to be timely paid, even if the paid amount actually enters the EPO bank account after the expiry of the period due to delays in the banking system. The amount payable is the amount applying on the date of payment, i.e. the date the amount was actually entered into the EPO account. Therefore, if the amount increases in the meantime, the difference must be made up (A-X,6.2.4).

The fail-safe arrangement applies only to bank payments that have duly been initiated within the period for payment, i.e. in the way prescribed by **Rfees7(3)**: effecting the payment through a bank or giving an order to a bank to transfer the payment. In addition, the payment must be initiated with a bank located in a contracting state according to **Rfees7(3)**, making this provision an exception where the EPO uses the despatch theory instead of the receipt theory (see **Art.119:2**). Hence, the arrangement does not apply to payments from outside the contracting states. Such payers should appoint a professional representative as soon as possible and effect payment through the representative.

The term 'banking establishment' in **Rfees7(3)** covers the banking services of post offices of contracting states for payment or transfer to the bank account held by the EPO. Paragraph (i) refers to cash payment at the premises of a bank (J7/81 r.5); paragraph (ii) covers effecting a payment e.g. through a bank's website or app.

See **R.134(5):2** for another remedy for a late payment caused by a delay in the banking system. A fail-safe system also exists for replenishment payments of deposit accounts (ADA.7.5) with requirements different from those of **Rfees7(3)**.

Rfees7(4) The Office may request the person who made the payment to produce evidence as to the date on which a condition according to paragraph 3 was fulfilled within a period to be specified by it. If he fails to comply with this request or if the evidence is insufficient, the period for payment shall be considered not to have been observed.

Amended, in force since 01.04.2020 (OJ 2020 A3 Art.2).

1 **Provision of evidence**
If a payment enters into the EPO bank account after expiry of the period for payment, the EPO will send a loss of rights communication to the applicant under **R.112(1)**. If applicants claim that the payment was duly initiated according to **Rfees7(3)** for a direct payment of a fee to the EPO, or to ADA.7.5 for a replenishment payment of a debit account, they must apply for a decision under **R.112(2)** and submit the requisite evidence for the claim. (A-X,6.2.5)

If the EPO accepts the evidence and the payment was initiated within the period for payment, the period is considered to have been observed (**Rfees7(3)**). If the evidence is not filed or is insufficient, the period for payment will be regarded as not observed (**Rfees7(4)**).

Rfees 8 Insufficiency of the amount paid

A time limit for payment shall in principle be deemed to have been observed only if the full amount of the fee has been paid in due time. If the fee is not paid in full, the amount which has been paid shall be refunded after the period for payment has expired. The Office may, however, in so far as this is possible within the time remaining before the end of the period, give the person making the payment the opportunity to pay the amount lacking. It may also, where this is considered justified, overlook any small amounts lacking without prejudice to the rights of the person making the payment.

Amended, in force since 01.04.2009 (OJ 2009 p.7).

1 **Insufficient payment**
A period for payment is considered to have been observed in principle if the full amount due has been paid before expiry of the period (**Rfees8**, first sentence). If the amount paid is insufficient, the EPO can respond in one of the following three ways:

- The EPO may send the payer an invitation to pay the amount lacking, provided there is sufficient time remaining until expiry of the period (**Rfees8**, third sentence).

- If there is not sufficient time, the EPO will refund the amount paid after expiry of the period (**Rfees8**, second sentence). Any legal consequence of non-payment may be reversed by applying a remedy, such as further processing.
- If the amount lacking is small, the EPO may overlook the small amount lacking (**Rfees8**, last sentence) and may deem the paid amount sufficient (A-X,7.1.1; D-IV,1.2.1(i)).

If a payment is entered in the EPO bank account within a period of six months after the date of increase of the rates but the old amount is paid, the payment will be regarded as valid if the payer pays the deficit within two months after a request by the EPO (OJ 2020 A3 Art.5(4)). The deficit must also be paid if the payment is entered in the EPO bank account on or after the date of the fee increase but the payer arranged the payment before the date of the increase; **Rfees7(3)** does not change this (J18/85).

2 **Small underpayment**

The purpose of **Rfees8**, last sentence, is to remedy underpayment by a small amount. The smallness of the amount must be assessed on purely arithmetical grounds in relation to the full amount. The provision is not intended as a remedy when a reduced fee has been paid without entitlement. (**T905/90** r.10)

The EPO may overlook a small amount, irrespective of whether a remedy is available to pay the amount lacking, such as further processing (**Art.121**), re-establishment of rights (**Art.122**) or late payment with surcharge (**J11/85**; **J27/92**). To 'overlook' means that the EPO accepts the payment of an insufficient amount without the payer being obliged to make good the shortfall (**T3023/18** r.15).

Underpayments in the order 10% or less were considered to be a small amount, 25% as not a small amount in **J11/85** (r.3). 20% of the opposition fee was considered to be a small amount (**T290/90** r.4b); 20% was considered as a small amount for a party misinformed by the EPO (**J27/92**). However, this case law is highly fact specific. The difference between full appeal fee and reduced appeal fee, 17%, was not considered to be a small amount when a non-entitled person paid the reduced appeal fee (**T3023/18**; **T2422/18**). Where several fees are paid together, the assessment of the small amount must be made in respect of the total amount (**J11/85** r.6).

Note that a debit order may be corrected in the event of underpayment, see **R.139:2.2**.

Rfees 9 Refund of search fees

1 **Reasons for refund of a fee, general**

A fee payment lacking a legal basis must be refunded. A legal basis is lacking if the payment relates to proceedings that are not pending, e.g. it relates to an application already deemed to be withdrawn. A legal basis is also lacking if the payment is made before the due date. If e.g. the payment is made before or on the due date and if no later than that date the legal basis ceases to exist (e.g. because the application is deemed to be withdrawn or is withdrawn), the amount paid is to be refunded. (A-X,10.1.1, listing two exceptions)

A payment made shortly before the due date may possibly not be returned by the EPO and be regarded as valid payment on the due date (A-X,5.1.1).

Fees which have not been validly paid must be refunded, e.g. filing, search or examination fee paid late without the further processing fee (A-XI,10.1.2). Depending on the method of payment, the EPO may reject the payment of such a fee when validating debit orders (**Rfees5(2):2.1**). A validly paid fee is not refunded unless there is a special provision for the refund. For example, a fee for further processing is not refunded if the request is inadmissible because an omitted act is not completed. (A-X,10.1)

An excess payment by an insignificant amount will not be refunded, unless the payer requests so (**Rfees12**). For example, a fee can paid in the full amount out of precaution with a request for a partial refund corresponding to an applicable fee reduction (e.g. **T1216/23**).

Fees paid on or after the due date are refunded only if there is a particular reason for a refund (A-X,10.2), for instance:

- The filing fee, any page fee and any divisional fee is refunded fully if the application is not dealt with as a European application (**Art.90(2)**) or if the national office does not forward the application filed with it to the EPO in due time (**R.37(2)**).
- The search fee is refunded fully if the application is not dealt with as a European patent application (**Art.90(2)**), if a national office does not forward the application filed with it to the EPO (**R.37(2)**), or if the application is withdrawn, refused or deemed to be withdrawn at a time the EPO has not yet begun to draw up the search report (**Rfees9(1)**). The search fee is refunded fully or in part if the EPO can make use of an earlier search as specified in **Rfees9(2)**. See GL/PCT-EPO A-III,9.2 for refund of the international search fee when the ISA can use an earlier search.
- An additional search fee paid in response to a non-unity communication of the search division will be refunded on request if the examining division finds no justification for charging the additional fee (**R.64(2)**).
- The designation fee may be refunded in the exceptional cases set out in **R.39(3):1**.
- Claims fees will be refunded if the application is filed with a national office and is deemed to be withdrawn pursuant to **R.37(2)**, and are also refunded if the number of claims of a Euro-PCT application is reduced after national entry into the European phase (**R.162(3)**). There is no refund if the number of claims at grant is smaller than on filing or on entry into the European phase.
- The examination fee will be refunded as specified in **Rfees11** if the examination is not carried out. Where the EPO has drawn up an international preliminary examination report under Chapter II PCT, the European examination fee will not be refunded but reduced (**Rfees14(2)**).
- The fee for grant and publishing is refunded if the application is withdrawn before notification of the decision to grant (**R.71a(6)**; see e.g. **J15/86** F and S IV).
- A renewal fee is refunded if the application is not anymore pending on the due date (see **Art.86(1):6**).
- All fees are refunded if no date of filing is accorded (A-II,4.1.4).
- Validly paid extension fees and validation fees are not refunded (A-III,12.3).
- An opposition fee is refunded if the notice of opposition is deemed not filed (see **Art.101(1):1**).
- An appeal fee is reimbursed if the notice of appeal is deemed not filed (see **Art.108:6**) and in the case of a substantial procedural violation or early withdrawal under **R.103**.
- An excess payment is refunded where the full amount of a fee has been paid and the applicant is entitled to a reduction under **Rfees14**.

2 **Refund procedure**
The EPO will make a refund to the deposit account that parties have indicated in their refund instructions. The deposit account may also be held by a third party. Refund instructions must be filed in an electronically processable format via OLF, Online Filing 2.0, or ePCT using one of the prescribed forms (ADA.15.2).

If a representative changes or rights are transferred, parties should update their refund instructions. If in such cases the EPO does not receive new refund instructions, it will delete ex officio obviously invalid instructions, such as making a refund to the deposit account of a withdrawn applicant. (Not EPO OJ 2024 A23)

If a renewal fee for a European patent application that is not due, a surcharge that is not due, or a fee for a unitary patent that is not due is paid by debit order, (which means that the debit order is submitted other than via Central Fee Payment), the amount will be repaid to the deposit account indicated in the debit order (ADA.9.6 OJ 2024 A81).

Refund instructions must be filed in an electronically processable format via OLF, Online Filing 2.0, or ePCT using one of the prescribed forms (ADA.15.2). For unitary patents, separate refund instructions must be provided; existing instructions for the European patent application do not automatically extend to the corresponding unitary patent (UP-3.1.6).

The EPO sends a communication to parties informing them of a pending refund and the deposit account to which the refund will be made (A-X,10.3.1). If the EPO cannot make the refund to a deposit account and the party to the proceedings or their authorised representative is a user of MyEPO, the refund can be claimed directly in Central Fee Payment. The EPO informs the party to the proceedings that a refund is pending and can be claimed in Central Fee Payment. In other cases, the EPO invites the party to the proceedings to claim the refund in Central Fee Payment with a refund code. When claiming the refund, the user can select whether the refund is to be made to a bank account or a deposit account (ADA 15.3; OJ 2024 A23; A-X,10.3.2).

Rfees9(1) The search fee paid for a European or supplementary European search shall be fully refunded if the European patent application is withdrawn or refused or deemed to be withdrawn at a time when the Office has not yet begun to draw up the search report.

1 **Refund of search fee for non-pending application**
According to **Rfees9(1)** the search fee will be fully refunded if the application is withdrawn, refused or deemed to be withdrawn before the start of the search (Not. EPO, OJ 2009 p.99).

The drawing up of the search report begins on the date the examiner carries out the first search task, i.e. triggering a pre-search algorithm generating a list of documents to be inspected. This date is recorded in the public part of the file. For applications not yet published, this information can be accessed using the MyEPO; the EPO will also provide the applicant with the relevant information upon request. (A-X,10.2.1)

Rfees9(2) Where the European search report is based on an earlier search report prepared by the Office on an application whose priority is claimed or an earlier application within the meaning of Article 76 of the Convention or of Rule 17 of the Convention, the Office shall refund to the applicant, in accordance with a decision of its President, an amount which shall depend on the type of earlier search and the extent to which the Office benefits from the earlier search report when carrying out the subsequent search.

Art.76 divisional application
R.17 new application filed by an entitled person

1 Conditions for refund of search fee

The search fee for a European search report or supplementary European search report will be refunded (Dec. Pres. OJ 2025 A25) if the search report can be based on an earlier search report prepared by the EPO for:

- an application whose priority is claimed; or
- an earlier application within the meaning of **Art.76** (parent application of the present divisional application); or
- an original application within the meaning of **R.17** (i.e. the present application is a new application under **Art.61**).

The earlier search report must have been prepared by the EPO (**J8/81**). That is the case e.g. for a (supplementary) European search report (**Art.92**; **R.164(1)**), for a (supplementary) international search report drawn up by the EPO as (S)ISA (Art.15 PCT), for a search made by EPO on behalf of a national office on a national application (see OJ 2025 A25 and A-III,6.12 for the relevant contracting states), and for an international-type search carried out by the EPO (Art.15(5) PCT). An international-type search can be carried out by the EPO on the request of the applicant for a national application filed in an EPC Contracting State if the law of that state provides for an international-type search (OJ 1999 p.300). At present (April 2025), this is the case for BE, BG, CH, DK, FI, HU, IS, LI, NL, NO, PL, SE and SK (PCT Applicant's Guide, Section B). See OJ 2025 A25 for further details of the refund.

Search results under **R.164(2)** are not mentioned in OJ 2025 A25 but can support a refund of a search fee paid in respect of a later application (e.g. a divisional application) (Not. EPO OJ 2014 A70 §22 third sentence).

The search fees that can be refunded are the European search fee (**Art.78(2)**), the further search fee (**R.64(1)**) and the fee for the supplementary European search (**Art.153(7)**), and also the search fees under **R.164(1)** and **R.164(2)** (Not. EPO OJ 2014 A70 §22). A search fee under **R.56a(8)** can likely also be refunded.

2 Amount of the refund

The amount of the refund is either a full refund or a partial refund of the search fee, depending on the extent to which the EPO can base its search report on the earlier search. The full refund is between 70% and 100% and the partial refund between 17.5% and 25%, depending on the type of earlier search (Dec. Pres. OJ 2025 A25).

The EPO informs the applicant of the amount of the refund in a separate communication and will make the refund. In the event of disagreement, the applicant may request an appealable decision to be issued by the Receiving Section or examining division (A-X,10.2.1).

3 Criteria for applicable refund rate

The criteria for determining the applicable refund level are given in OJ 2009 p.99. A full refund of the search fee applies where the search report can be completely based on the earlier search (i.e. no search needs to be carried out). This is the case, in particular, where the claims of the earlier and later application are identical or where the claims of the later application are limited by deleting alternative features from an independent claim or by moving a limiting feature from a dependent claim to the independent claim it refers to in the earlier application.

A partial refund applies where the search report can be based partly on the earlier search. This applies, in particular, where the claims of the later application are a further generalisation of the invention searched in the earlier application, or the claims are limited by a feature not disclosed in the earlier application but relating to the same invention as the searched earlier application.

No refund will be made where the subject-matter of the claims represents an invention different from that searched in the earlier application or where any of the conditions of given in OJ 2009 p.99 is not met (see **Rfees9(2):1**).

Rfees 10 Refund of the fee for a technical opinion

An amount of 75% of the fee for a technical opinion under Article 25 of the Convention shall be refunded if the request for a technical opinion is withdrawn at a time when the Office has not yet begun to draw up the technical opinion.

Rfees 11 Refund of examination fee

The examination fee provided for in Article 94, paragraph 1, of the Convention shall be refunded:

(a) in full if the European patent application is withdrawn, refused or deemed to be withdrawn before the substantive examination has begun;

(b) at a rate of 50% if the European patent application is withdrawn after substantive examination has begun and

- **before expiry of the time limit for replying to the first invitation under Article 94, paragraph 3, of the Convention issued by the Examining Division proper or,**
- **if no such invitation has been issued by the Examining Division, before the date of the communication under Rule 71, paragraph 3, of the Convention.**

Amended, in force since 01.07.2016 (OJ 2016 A48, see Not. OJ 2016 A49).
Art.94(1) request for examination
Art.94(3) invitation to file observations
R.71(3) communication of text to be granted

1 **Refund of the examination fee**

The EPO will refund the examination fee at a rate depending on the moment in time when the grant procedure terminates, either due to refusal by the EPO, being deemed withdrawn or active withdrawal by the applicant. A reason for the refund is that an applicant should not have to pay for a service the EPO does not deliver. Moreover, the refund provides an incentive for the applicant to withdraw an application they are no longer interested in; this frees examiner capacity which can be deployed to reduce the EPO's backlog in examination.

2 **Full refund**

If the procedure terminates before substantive examination by the examining division has begun, the entire examination fee will be refunded (**Rfees11(a)**). The termination may be a withdrawal, a refusal or the application becoming deemed to be withdrawn.

The substantive examination begins on the date the examiner carries out the first substantive task of the examining division, namely identifying the European prior rights that were not yet available when the search was carried out. The date is recorded in Form 2095 in the public part of the file to ensure it is verifiable. If Form 2095 is not on file, the substantive examination is deemed to have started on the date on which the first communication from the examining division proper is issued (see **Rfees11:3** below). For applications not yet published, only the applicant can access the information, either electronically using the MyEPO service or by requesting the information from the EPO (A-VI,2.5).

Applicants unsure whether substantive examination has begun and wanting to withdraw only if they receive the 100% refund may make the withdrawal contingent upon the refund (A-VI,2.5).

If the application is deemed to be withdrawn for failure to submit an indication of the wish to proceed further under **R.70(2)**, the substantive examination by the examining division does not begin (**R.10(3)**), and the examination fee is fully refunded.

3 Partial refund

If the application is actively withdrawn after the start of the substantive examination but before the expiry of the period for response to the first substantive communication of the examining division, 50% of the examination fee will be refunded (**Rfees11(b)**). There is no refund if the applicant withdraws the application later. A refusal or a deemed withdrawal does not give rise to a refund under **Rfees11(b)**. A withdrawal causes a clear end to the procedure without the possibility of reinstating the application through common remedies such as further processing.

In most cases, the withdrawal must be submitted before the expiry of the period for replying to the first **Art.94(3)** communication. If the period for response is extended upon request under **R.132(2)**, it is possible to submit the withdrawal until the expiry of the extended period (A-VI,2.5). If the first **Art.94(3)** communication is a summons for oral proceedings, the withdrawal can be made up to the last date for submitting written submissions set therein under **R.116**, according to EPO practice.

A few communications that are not issued under **Art.94(3)**, e.g. summons to oral proceedings to which a preliminary opinion is attached that fully sets out the issues, minutes of consultations accompanied by an invitation to remedy deficiencies, and communications relating to the 'completely contained' criterion of **R.56(3)** and **R.56a(4)**, are considered communications under **Art.94(3)** 'issued by the examining division proper' and are taken into account under **Rfees11(b)**. (A-VI,2.5)

A communication under **R.164(2)(a)** (additional search by examining division), **R.53(3)** (translation of priority document) or **Art.124** (request for information on prior art) are not taken into account under **Rfees11(b)**; note that the communication with the results of a search under **R.164(2)(b)** is taken into account (A-VI,2.5). The status of invitations under **R.137(4)** to indicate the basis for amended claims is not specified in A-VI,2.5.

Communications that are issued under **Art.94(3)** by formalities officers on behalf of examining divisions are not taken into account under **Rfees11(b)**.

If any of these communications that are not taken into account is sent as a first communication of (or for) the examining division, the applicant receives a 50% refund of the examination fee if the application is withdrawn during the period for replying to it, and also if the application is withdrawn later, namely up to the expiry of the period for replying to the (first) later communication that is taken into account under **Rfees11(b)**. If the communication that is not taken into account under **Rfees11(b)** is issued before the substantive examination has begun, the examination fee can be refunded still at 100%. (Not. EPO OJ 2016 A49)

In cases where the first communication of the examining division is a communication under **R.71(3)**, the withdrawal must be submitted at the latest on the day before the date printed on the communication for a 50% refund (Not. EPO OJ 2016 A49). Note that an applicant has no advance information about when the communication will be sent. A withdrawal may be made conditional on the 50% refund (Not. EPO OJ 2016 A49).

Rfees 12 Refund of insignificant amounts

Where too large a sum is paid to cover a fee, the excess shall not be refunded if the amount is insignificant and the party concerned has not expressly requested a refund. The President of the Office shall determine what constitutes an insignificant amount.

1 **Insignificant amount**
An insignificant amount is EUR 17 or less (Dec. Pres. OJ 2023 A27). Hence, an overpayment of more than EUR 17 is refunded without request, an overpayment of EUR 17 or less is refunded only on request. The request must be made before expiry of the period of **Rfees13(2)**. (A-X,10.1.3)

Rfees 13 Termination of financial obligations

Amended, in force since 13.12.2007 (OJ 2007 p.533).

1 **General**
The provision takes care of the extinction of financial claims that have become out-of-date. It avoids the situation that parties will experience difficulties in providing evidence when rights are not executed for a long time.

The provision is not very relevant anymore because reminders for payment and refunds are processed by computer and will nearly always be carried out well before expiry of the periods mentioned in the provision.

Rfees13(1) Rights of the Organisation to the payment of a fee to the European Patent Office shall be extinguished after four years from the end of the calendar year in which the fee was due.

1 **Right of Organisation to payment**
Rfees1 defines what fees are: fees to be paid to the EPO and provided for in the Articles and Rules, and fees fixed by the President for special services.

The EPO is not entitled to most of these fees; a party is free to pay them. If a party does not pay, certain intended acts will not become effective, e.g. the request for examination (**Art.94(1)**), the opposition (**Art.99(1)**), the appeal (**Art.108**). In other cases the application will be regarded as withdrawn, e.g. when the filing fee or the search fee is not paid in time (**Art.78(2)**).

In a few cases the EPO has a right to a payment, e.g. for subscriptions to patent information databases.

Rfees13(2) Rights against the Organisation for the refunding by the European Patent Office of fees or sums of money paid in excess of a fee shall be extinguished after four years from the end of the calendar year in which the right arose.

1 **Right of party to refund**
Examples of rights of parties to a refund of a fee are refund of renewal fees paid twice by different payers or refund of the fee for further processing or re-establishment when the remedies were requested on an auxiliary basis and the main request was granted. Other examples are full or partial refund of a search fee under **Rfees9**, and reimbursement of an appeal fee according to **R.103(1)**.

Rfees13(3) The period laid down in paragraphs 1 and 2 shall be interrupted in the case covered by paragraph 1 by a request for payment of the fee and in the case covered by paragraph 2 by a reasoned claim in writing. On interruption it shall begin again immediately and shall end at the latest six years after the end of the year in which it originally began, unless, in the meantime, judicial proceedings to enforce the right have begun; in this case the period shall end at the earliest one year after the judgment enters into force.

Rfees13(4) The President of the European Patent Office may waive action for the enforced recovery of any sum due if the sum to be recovered is minimal or if such recovery is too uncertain.

1 **Sum due**
A sum is due if the EPO has rendered a service or has delivered goods to be paid afterwards, such as for example the delivery of publications ordered (**Rfees3(2)**).

Rfees 14 Reduction of fees

1 **General**
Where a fee is reduced - in contrast to cases of fee refunds - the reduced rate may be paid instead of the full fee.

If there is doubt about entitlement to a reduction of a fee, the full fee should be paid as a precaution. When the reduced fee is applicable, the EPO will refund the excess payment. When the reduced fee has been paid without entitlement, the amount lacking is, in general, not a small amount in the sense of **Rfees8**, and the payment will be deemed not to have been made. (**T905/90** r.6, 10)

See **Art.153(7)** for the reduction of the supplementary European search fee.

Rfees14(1) The reduction laid down in Rule 7a, paragraphs 1 and 3, of the Convention shall be 30% of the relevant fee.

Amended, in force since 01.04.2024 (OJ 2024 A3). The amendment was a consequence of the amendment of R.6 and introduction of **R.7a**.
R.7a(1) Language reduction
R.7a(3) Micro-entity reduction

Rfees14(2) Where the European Patent Office has drawn up an international preliminary examination report, the examination fee shall be reduced by 75%. If the report was established on certain parts of the international application in accordance with Article 34, paragraph 3(c), PCT, the fee shall not be reduced if subject-matter not covered by the report is to be examined.

Amended, in force since 01.04.2018 (OJ 2018 A4).
Art.34(3)(c) International preliminary examination report in the case of non-unity

1 **Reduction of examination fee for Euro-PCT application**
Rfees14(2) provides for a reduction in the amount of the examination fee where the EPO has already drawn up an international preliminary examination report (IPER). If the IPER of a non-unitary application covers only certain parts of the international application, the reduction will only apply if the examination is on subject-matter completely covered by the IPER (**Rfees14(2)**, second sentence). The reduction does also not apply to a divisional application for whose parent application the EPO has drawn up the IPER (A-X,9.5.2).

Rfees14(3) If more than one reduction applies to the same fee for the same application, the reductions shall be calculated sequentially.

Newly inserted, in force since 01.04.2024 (OJ 2024 A3; explanations in OJ 2024 A8). The amendment codifies the established practice of the EPO.

1 **Combinations of reductions**
Where both reductions of **Rfees14(1)** and (2) apply to a fee, or if multiple reductions apply under **Rfees14(1)**, the reduction can be calculated by multiplication, e.g. [fee amount] x 0.7 x 0.7 if the reductions of **R.7a(1)** and **R.7a(3)** both apply to the filing fee or examination fee.

If the examination fee is reduced under both **Rfees14(2)** and **R.7a(1)** (or R.7a(3)), the full fee is first reduced by 75% and the resulting amount by 30%, i.e. a total reduction of 82.5% (A-X,9.5.2). Note that when combining only reductions expressed as percentages, the order of applying the reductions is not relevant.

Rfees 15 Entry into force

These Rules shall enter into force on 20 October 1977.

DONE at Munich, 20 October 1977 for the Administrative Council

The Chairman

Rules relating to Unitary Patent Protection

as adopted by decision of the Select Committee of the Administrative Council of the European Patent Organisation of 15 December 2015 and as last amended by decision of the Select Committee of the Administrative Council of 13 November 2024.

Rules relating to Regulation (EU) No 1257/2012 of the European Parliament and of the Council of 17 December 2012 implementing enhanced cooperation in the area of the creation of unitary patent protection and to Council Regulation (EU) No 1260/2012 of 17 December 2012 implementing enhanced cooperation in the area of the creation of unitary patent protection with regard to the applicable translation arrangements.

(hereinafter "Rules relating to Unitary Patent Protection")

1 **Setting up a unified patent system**
A unitary patent (UP) covering the member states of the EU, which is both granted and litigated in a single procedure, has long been sought in Europe. The legislative basis for such a unified patent system, which was finally agreed upon in 2011-2013, consists of two EU regulations creating the unitary patent (EU regulations 1257/2012 and 1260/2012) and the Unified Patent Court Agreement (UPCA) which establishes a new court to litigate both UPs and classical European patents for participating member states. The EU regulations were adopted under enhanced cooperation, which is a procedure under EU law that enables the adoption of EU regulations in which some EU member states participate, and others do not. Croatia and Spain are not participating member states in the enhanced cooperation on the unitary patent. All other EU member states are 'participating member states' in the sense of Art.1(a) of EU regulation 1257/2012.

A UP has unitary effect in those participating member states in which the UPCA has taken effect at the date of registration of unitary effect by the EPO (Art.18(2) of EU regulation 1257/2012), i.e. on the date communicated by the EPO under **UPR.7(1)**). The UPCA has effect in those EU member states that have ratified it. As of 01.04.2025, eighteen participating member states had ratified the UPCA, namely Austria, Belgium, Bulgaria, Denmark, Estonia, Finland, France, Germany, Italy, Latvia, Lithuania, Luxembourg, Malta, the Netherlands, Portugal, Romania, Slovenia, and Sweden. The UPCA took effect for Romania on 01.09.2024, while the date of entry into effect for the other countries was 01.06.2023. Hence, a UP has effect in Romania if the date of registration of unitary effect is on or after 01.09.2024. The date of publication of the mention of the grant is not relevant, because Romania was already a participating member state when it ratified the UPCA (Art.18(2) of EU regulation 1257/2012).

UPR.5 defines how the term 'participating member states' is to be interpreted. Indeed, in some instances, it means all 25 EU countries except Croatia and Spain, and in others, it means those countries where a granted EP patent with unitary effect is in force, i.e. countries for which the UPCA was in force when the unitary effect was registered.

For some further information about the UPC, see **Preamble:4.2** and **Art.64(3):2.**

EU regulation 1257/2012 of 17.12.2012 was published in OJ 2012 p.111, and establishes the UP, i.e. regulates the implementation of enhanced cooperation in the area of the creation of unitary patent protection. EU regulation 1260/2017 on the translation arrangements of the UP was published in OJ 2012 p.132 and separately specifies the language arrangements for the UP because only these provisions had to be adopted unanimously by the Council of the EU (see Art.118, second paragraph, of the Treaty on the Functioning of the European Union).

The EPO will administer the UP. Rules relating to Unitary Patent Protection (UPR) were adopted by a decision of the Select Committee of the Administrative Council of 15.12.2015 and first published with the official explanatory notes in OJ 2016 A39. Corresponding Rules relating to Fees for Unitary Patent Protection (RfeesUPP) were adopted at the same time, published with explanatory notes in OJ 2016 A40 and republished in OJ 2022 A41. The UPR were amended by a decision of the Select Committee on 16.12.2021 (OJ 2022 A39) and on 23.03.2022 (OJ 2022 A40). A consolidated version was published in OJ 2022 A41.

The EPO has also published UP Guidelines, which can be found on the website of the EPO.

2 A European patent with unitary effect

Details concerning a request for unitary effect and other aspects of the procedure under the UPR are provided in the following notes on the UPR and RfeesUPP. Some aspects of EU regulations which are not found in the UPR or RfeesUPP are discussed briefly below.

A European patent with unitary effect, also called UP (unitary patent), has a unitary character and provides uniform protection and has equal effect in all the participating member states. The booklet 'National measures relating to the Unitary Patent' published by the EPO contains information about national legislation accompanying the implementation of the UP and the territorial field of application of the UP in terms of overseas territories and areas.

Acts that the proprietor of a UP can forbid third parties to carry out based on a UP, are those defined in Art.25-29 of the UPCA (Art.5(3) of EU regulation 1257/2012 referring indirectly to the UPCA). Art.6 of EU regulation 1257/2012 defines the exhaustion of rights with respect to a UP.

A UP may be limited, transferred, revoked, or lapse only in respect of all the countries where it has taken effect. (Art.3(2) of EU regulation 1257/2012).

The unitary effect of UP applies only in those participating member states for which the UPCA is in force at the date of registration of the unitary effect (Art.18(2) of EU regulation 1257/2012). The geographical scope of a UP will not extend to any countries for which the UPCA comes into force after registration.

A UP takes effect in the participating member states on the date of publication of the mention of the grant, unless no unitary effect is registered. It is not allowed to have both a UP and a national EP validation in force for a given country. (Art.4 of EU regulation 1257/2012)

3 Translation during transitional period and in the event of dispute

A translation of the European patent in a single EU language is required when requesting unitary effect during a transitional period of at most 12 years (Art.6 of EU regulation 1260/2012, **UPR.6**(2)).

In the event of infringement proceedings relating to a UP, the alleged infringer can request the proprietor to provide a full translation of the UP into an official language of the participating member state where the alleged infringement took place, or the state in which the alleged infringer has its domicile. A court can also request the proprietor to provide a full translation into the language used in the proceedings in that court. The translation should not be a machine translation, and the cost of translation in both cases will be borne by the proprietor. (Art.4(1)-(3) of EU regulation 1260/2012)

In the event of a dispute concerning damages, where the alleged infringer is a SME, natural person, a non-profit organisation, a university or a public research organisation, the court will take into consideration whether the alleged infringer acted without knowing or without reasonable grounds for knowing that they were infringing the UP before receiving the translation (Art.4(4) of EU regulation 1260/2012).

4 UP as an object of property

A UP as an object of property is treated, for all participating member states, as a national patent of the participating member state in which the patent has effect and in which, according to the European Patent Register, the applicant was resident or had a principal place of business at the date of filing of the EP application. If this condition is not fulfilled, the UP is treated as a national patent of the participating member state in which the applicant had, according to the Register, a place of business at the time of filing of the application. Information on such a 'place of business on the date of filing' can be provided, voluntarily, but only together with the request for unitary effect (**UPR.16(1)(w)**). The law of the relevant participating member state will be applied to any proceedings relating to the UP as an object of property. (Art.7(1) of EU regulation 1257/2012)

In case of joint applicants, the residence or principal place of business of the first mentioned applicant that is in a participating member state will define the country of applicable law. In case none of the joint applicants had a residence or principal place of business in a participating member state at the filing date of the EP application, the second option of having a place of business within a participating member state is applied in the same manner. (Art.7(2) of EU regulation 1257/2012).

In case none of the above is applicable, the UP as an object of property will be dealt with according to German law (Art.7(3) of EU regulation 1257/2012).

According to Art.3(2) of EU regulation 1257/2012, a European patent with unitary effect may only be transferred in respect of all the participating member states. The EPO will register any transfer (**UPR.20(2)**). A UP can however be licensed also for only part of the participating member states.

5 Safety net

The booklet 'National measures relating to the Unitary Patent' contains information on the so-called safety net that can be implemented by participating member states. The safety net is a mechanism providing the possibility to validate a European patent where a request for unitary effect has been rejected either by the EPO or the UPC, or where the unitary effect has been revoked by the UPC at the time when deadlines for validating the European patent have already expired.

Most of the participating member states have implemented the mechanism; some states are planning to introduce it or are still considering it. So far, only Bulgaria and Italy have implemented the option of national validation after revocation by the UPC. The other countries are only allowing/ planning to allow national validation in case the request for unitary effect has been rejected.

6 Grounds for revocation

Art.65(2) UPCA provides that the UPC may revoke a unitary patent only on the grounds of **Art.138(1)** and **Art.139(2)** EPC. **Art.139(2)** EPC, however, provides no ground for revocation as such. Instead, it refers to national law as it provides that a national patent application has the same prior right effect against a European patent in a designated state as the national patent law of that state specifies for the case of a national patent application forming a prior right against a national patent. Hence, the national court must treat the European patent as a national patent and apply the rules of its national law regarding the validity of national patents in view of national prior rights. The UPC has, however, no national law of its own. It is therefore not entirely clear what the effect of a single anticipatory national prior right will be on the UP as a whole and whether the UP will need to be restricted as a whole to avoid revocation. It is equally unclear what will happen to a UP if the claims are amended in EPO opposition or limitation proceedings to take into account a prior national right in a single participating member state, which will mean that the UP no longer complies with Art.3(1) of EU regulation 1257/2012 and **UPR.5(2)**. The EPO carries out a top-up search to find possible novelty-destroying national prior rights at the end of the grant proceedings and informs the applicant of the results in the **R.71(3)** EPC communication.

PART I INSTITUTIONAL PROVISIONS

Chapter I *Subject Matter*

R. 1 Subject matter

(1) The participating Member States hereby entrust the European Patent Office with the tasks referred to in Article 9, paragraph 1, Regulation (EU) No 1257/2012. In carrying out these tasks, the European Patent Office shall apply the present Rules and shall be bound by decisions handed down by the Unified Patent Court in actions brought under Article 32, paragraph 1(i), Agreement on a Unified Patent Court.

1 **Participating member states**
The participating member states are defined in Art. 2 of EU regulation 1257/2012 as member states which participate in the enhanced cooperation, i.e. irrespective of whether the UPCA has taken effect in that state. The European patent with unitary effect can however only be granted and have a unitary character only in those participating member states where the UPC has exclusive jurisdiction with regard to European patents with unitary effect at the date of their registration (Art. 18(2) of EU regulation 1257/2012).

2 **The role of the UPC**
The actions mentioned in Art.32(1)(i) of the UPCA are appeals relating to decisions of the EPO in carrying out its administrative tasks relating to the UP (Art.9 of EU regulation 1257/2012). Thus, all appeals relating to decisions taken by the Unitary Patent Protection Division of the EPO in carrying out its tasks under the UPR must be filed at the UPC.

(2) In case of conflict between the provisions of the present Rules and Union law, including Regulation (EU) No 1257/2012 and Regulation (EU) No 1260/2012, the provisions of Union law shall prevail.

Chapter II *Select committee of the Administrative Council*

R. 2 Competences and duties

(1) The Select Committee of the Administrative Council shall be competent to amend
(a) the present Rules;
(b) the Rules relating to Fees for Unitary Patent Protection;
(c) other rules or decisions of a financial or budgetary nature;
(d) its Rules of Procedure.

1 **The Select Committee**
The Select Committee was set up in 2013 pursuant to Art.(9)(2) EU regulation 1257/2012. It consists of representatives of the participating member states, the President of the EPO, the Board of Auditors of the EPO and the EPO Staff Committee. The European Commission, the epi, Business Europe and non-participating as well as non-EU EPC contracting states are observers of the Select Committee.

Decisions of the Select Committee are taken with due regard for the position of the European Commission and in accordance with **Art.35(2)** EPC (Art.9(2) of EU regulation 1257/2012).

(2) The Select Committee of the Administrative Council shall ensure the governance and supervision of the activities related to the tasks entrusted to the European Patent Office in accordance with Rule 1, paragraph 1.

UPR.1 Subject matter

Chapter III *Functions and Powers of the President of the European Patent Office*

R. 3 Functions and Powers of the President of the European Patent Office

The Unitary Patent Protection Division referred to in Rule 4 shall be managed by the President of the European Patent Office, who shall be responsible for its activities to the Select Committee of the Administrative Council. To this end, Article 10, paragraphs 2 and 3, EPC shall apply mutatis mutandis.

Art.10 EPC Management

1 **Functions and powers of the president**
Art.10(2) EPC gives the President the power to, for example, adopt internal instructions and submit proposals for amending the convention (such as the Implementing Regulations) to the Administrative Council. In this context, the President therefore has the power to formulate internal guidelines governing the way in which the Unitary Patent Protection Division implements the UPR and submit proposals to the Select Committee of the Administrative Council relating to possible amendment of the UPR and RfeesUPP.

R. 4 Unitary Patent Protection Division

(1) A Unitary Patent Protection Division is hereby established within the European Patent Office as a special department within the meaning of Article 143, paragraph 2, EPC.

Art.143 EPC Special departments of the European Patent Office

1 **Unitary Patent Protection Division**
The President has decided to allocate the duties of the Unitary Patent Protection Division to members of the Legal Division (Dec. Pres. OJ 2022 A69, Part I).

(2) The tasks entrusted to the European Patent Office in accordance with Rule 1, paragraph 1, shall be carried out under the responsibility of the Unitary Patent Protection Division.

UPR.1 Subject matter

(3) Decisions of the Unitary Patent Protection Division shall be taken by one legally qualified member.

1 **Decisions that can only be taken by a legally qualified member**
Decisions involving no legal difficulties can be taken by a formalities officer (see **UPR.4(4):1**). Other decisions will be taken by a single legally qualified member. Decisions that must be taken by a legally qualified member include decisions on a request for registration of a transfer of rights filed after grant and before registration of unitary effect, decisions in cases where a request for unitary effect is filed by a person who is not the proprietor of the

patent, decisions in cases where the patent does not have the same set of claims in respect of all the participating member states, decisions where oral proceedings or the taking of evidence is needed to decide on a request for re-establishment, and decisions in cases where there are substantive deficiencies in any document relating to a transfer, license or other right to be registered. (Dec. Pres. OJ 2022 A69, Part II Art.2)

(4) The President of the European Patent Office may entrust to employees who are not legally qualified members the execution of duties falling to the Unitary Patent Protection Division and involving no legal difficulties.

1 **Duties entrusted to formalities officers**
Most duties of the Unitary Patent Protection Division have been entrusted to formalities officers (Dec. Pres. OJ 2022 A69 Part II Art.1), including the examination of requests for unitary effect and the registration of unitary effect in straightforward cases. Formalities officers are also responsible for communicating obvious deficiencies to the requester and rejecting the request for unitary effect if the request is filed late or if any of the requirements in **UPR.6(2)** is not met and not timely corrected upon invitation.

Formalities officers are furthermore responsible inter alia for taking decisions concerning the grant of compensation for translation costs, granting requests for the re-establishment of rights in straightforward cases, correcting certain errors in documents filed with the EPO (as in **R.139** EPC, first sentence), and registering the transfer of rights and changes of name where such requests can be granted directly.

PART II PROCEDURES TO BE CARRIED BY THE EUROPEAN PATENT OFFICE

Chapter I *The Request for Unitary Effect*

R. 5 General

(1) At the request of the proprietor of the European patent, unitary effect shall be registered by the European Patent Office in the Register for unitary patent protection.

1 **Requester of unitary effect**
Only the proprietor of the European patent can request unitary effect. If there are several proprietors, all proprietors must be mentioned in the request, except for those proprietors who are proprietors or co-proprietors only in an EPC contracting state that is not covered by the unitary effect (UP-2.2.2). The unitary effect covers neither the EPC states that are not participating member states (such as Switzerland) nor the participating member states where the UPCA has not taken effect. The latter exclusion is due to Art.18(2) of EU regulation 1257/2012, which indicates a derogation to Art.3(2) of the same regulation, i.e. indicates that no unitary effect can be registered for a state where the UPC does not have exclusive jurisdiction on European patents with unitary effect (see Luginbühl/Hütterman, Einheitspatentsystem, 2024, UPR.6 note 36).

The unitary effect can also be registered if the European patent is granted to different proprietors for different participating member states (UP-2.2.2).

(2) Unitary effect shall be registered only if
(a) the European patent has been granted with the same set of claims in respect of all the participating Member States, and
(b) the proprietor of the European patent is not subject to the restrictive measure laid down in Article 5s(2) of Regulation (EU) No 833/2014 as amended by Regulation (EU) 2024/1745, having regard to Article 5s(5) of that amended Regulation.

Amended as of 15.11.2024 (Dec. Select Committee OJ 2024 A96, Not. EPO OJ 2024 A97) to add subparagraph (b). This clause applies to requests for unitary effect pending on15.11.2024 and to requests filed on or after that day. For an earlier stay of the registration of unitary effect since 10.07.2024 in the same circumstances, see OJ 2024 A70.

1 **Granted with a single set of claims for all participating states**

According to Art.3(1) of EU regulation 1257/2012, second sentence, a European patent granted with different sets of claims for different participating member states cannot benefit from the unitary effect. According to the first sentence of that provision, the European patent must be granted in respect of all the participating member states.

The term 'participating member states' reflects the fact that EU regulation 1257/2012 is a special type of EU regulation in which the EU member states can choose to participate or not (so-called enhanced cooperation). At present, 25 of the 27 EU member states participate (see the list in **Art.169:1.1**). The requirement hence applies to the 25 EU member states that participate in the enhanced cooperation, even if the member state has not ratified the UPCA (UP-2.1). In particular, the requirement is not affected by the derogation in Art.18(2) of EU regulation 1257/2012 for participating member states that have not ratified the UPCA since the derogation relates solely to the unitary effect itself and not to the conditions under which unitary effect may be granted.

In practice, it is rare to have different claims for different contracting states. For the patent as granted, this is only allowed in case of a national prior right (**R.138** EPC).

Since the European patent must have been granted 'in respect of all the participating member states' for the unitary effect to be registered, it is not possible to obtain a unitary patent in the case where the designation of a participating member state has been withdrawn or is deemed to be withdrawn under **R.39(2a)**.

Furthermore, registering unitary effect is neither possible if the European patent concerned does not designate one of the participating member states because the patent has a filing date that is earlier than the accession of that state to the EPC. For example, a European patent application filed before 01.03.2007, when Malta acceded to the EPC, cannot benefit from unitary effect because it does not designate all the participating member states. This may cause a further problem in the future when a country joins the EU and wishes to participate in the unitary patent but has only recently acceded to the EPC unless Art.3(1) of EU regulation 1257/2012 is amended.

2 **Sanctions under EU regulation 833/2014**

EU regulation 833/2014, as amended on 24.06.2024, concerning restrictive measures in view of Russia's actions destabilising the situation in Ukraine, instructs in article 5s(2) the EU member states to ensure the refusal of requests for unitary effect that are filed by Russian nationals or natural persons residing in Russia, or by legal persons, entities or bodies established in Russia, or where such persons or legal persons are co-applicant.

Article 5s(5) of said regulation provides an exception for nationals of an EU member state, of a country that is a member of the European Economic Area, or of Switzerland (also in case of dual nationalities), and for natural persons having a temporary or permanent residence permit in an EU member state, in a country that is a member of the European Economic Area, or in Switzerland (see also Not. OJ 2024 A97).

The rejection decision can be appealed to the UPC (**UPR.20(1):2**). Because the provision implements EU law, the UPC will refer questions to the Court of Justice of the EU on its application when appropriate.

R. 6 Requirements of the request for unitary effect

(1) The request for unitary effect shall be filed with the European Patent Office no later than one month after publication of the mention of grant of the European patent in the European Patent Bulletin.

1 **Time limit for requesting unitary effect**
The period for requesting unitary effect is one month from the publication of the mention of the grant, i.e. shorter than the minimum period of three months for national validation of a European patent (**Art.65(1)** EPC). The period is prescribed in Art.9(1)(g) of EU regulation 1257/2012. Should the time limit for requesting unitary effect be missed, the proprietor may still be able to validate the European patent nationally. However, this will not help when the EPO rejects the request for unitary effect after the expiry of the three-month period for national validation. Some participating member states have established a safety net in case the request for unitary effect is rejected after the three-month period (**Ante UPR.5**).

The period cannot be extended. If it is not complied with, re-establishment may be used as a remedy if due care can be shown (**UPR.22(1)**). Re-establishment must be requested within two months of the missed time limit.

The EPO allows filing of an early request for unitary effect as soon as the decision to grant has been issued, i.e. before publication of the mention of the grant in the Bulletin. The request will only be processed once the mention of the grant is published (UP-2.2.1).

In case of a transfer of the patent between the filing of an early request for unitary effect and the publication of the mention of the grant, the UPP Division will ask the new proprietor to confirm the request for unitary effect (UP-2.2.1).

2 **Request to delay registration**
If a state accedes to the UPCA, a unitary patent only has effect in that state if the unitary effect is registered after the date on which the UPCA enters into force for that state (Art.18(2) of EU regulation 1257/2012). Furthermore, a state that accedes to the UPCA first deposits an instrument of accession, and the UPCA enters into force for that state on the first day of the fourth month thereafter (Art.86(4) UPCA and Art.89(2) UPCA). In order to allow proprietors to benefit from unitary patent protection also for the acceding state, the EPO allows patent proprietors to request a delay of the registration of unitary effect in the period between the deposit of the instrument of accession by a state and the entry into force of the UPCA for that state (UP-1.5.2).

The term 'ratification' refers to the UPCA entering into force for an EU member state that had already signed the UPCA at the time the treaty was concluded. The term 'accession' refers to the UPCA entering into force for other EU member states.

(2) The request for unitary effect shall be filed in writing in the language of the proceedings and shall contain:

(a) particulars of the proprietor of the European patent making the request (hereinafter "the requester") as provided for in Rule 41, paragraph 2(c), EPC;

(b) the number of the European patent to which unitary effect shall be attributed;

(c) where the requester has appointed a representative, particulars as provided for in Rule 41, paragraph 2(d), EPC;

(d) a translation of the European patent as required under Article 6, paragraph 1, Regulation (EU) No 1260/2012, as follows:
where the language of the proceedings is French or German, a full translation of the specification of the European patent into English; or where the language of the proceedings is English, a full translation of the specification of the European patent into any other official language of the European Union.

R.41 EPC Request for grant

1 **Requirements for the request**

This rule specifies the mandatory requirements for requests for unitary effect. The legal consequences for not fulfilling each of these requirements differ slightly, as explained in **UPR.7**.

The request must be filed in the language of the proceedings as defined in **Art.14(3)** EPC, i.e. the language of the grant procedure (Art.2(a) and Art.3(2) of EU regulation 1260/2012). This requirement differs from the general rule that all official languages of the EPO may be used for requests under the EPC (**R.3(1)**). It is, therefore, recommended to use EPO form 7000, as it has the necessary wording in all three official languages. The form can also be used when filing the request for unitary effect electronically using the EPO online filing software (OLF) or Online Filing 2.0. Use of the form is not mandatory.

The request must contain the name, address and nationality of the proprietor(s) making the request, as well as the proprietor's country of residence or principal place of business. If there are multiple proprietors, the request generally must be made by all proprietors. See **UPR.5(1):1** for an exception in the case of different proprietors for different states. The proprietors may be listed in a different order as in the European patent specification (UP-2.2.3; see also **R.151(1)**).

The request must also include the number of the European patent. While it is not mandatory to indicate the application number according to **UPR.6(2)**, there is a corresponding mandatory field to be completed in OLF and Online Filing 2.0. Including the application number also provides a safety net in case an incorrect patent number is specified.

In case a representative is appointed, the name and address of the representative must also be provided. The provisions of the EPC concerning representation before the EPO apply mutatis mutandis to any proceedings concerning unitary effect (**UPR.20(1)**). However, if an authorisation is needed, it must specifically indicate that it covers proceedings relating to unitary effect.

The request may optionally include an indication of the place of business of the original applicant as of the filing date of the European patent application (UP-2.2.6; see also **UPR.16(1)(w)**).

2 **Translation requirements**

During a transitional period, the request must also contain a translation of the complete patent specification. The transitional period is set to last at least six years, commencing from 01.06.2023, which is the date the UPCA entered into force (Art.6(3) of EU regulation 1260/2012). The transitional period can be extended for up to twelve years. (Art.6(3)-(5) of EU regulation 1260/2012). After the end of the transitional period, no translation will be required (Art.3(1) of EU regulation 1260/2012).

The translation is for information only and has no legal effect (Art.6(2) of EU regulation 1260/2012).

The language of the translation must be English if the language of proceedings (for the grant procedure of the patent) was French or German. If the language of proceedings was English, the language of the translation can be any official EU language. For example, a proprietor wishing to request unitary effect and additionally validate the patent in Spain or Poland can use the necessary translation of the patent into Spanish or Polish also for the request for unitary effect, provided the translation is available in time. Alternatively, in case the application was originally drafted in an official EU language different from French, German and English, or the patent family has an application in a country having a language in common with one of the EU countries (such as Brazil), those texts can be updated to correspond to the granted patent.

A translation of the description, claims, and any text in the drawings must be filed. Sequence listings typically do not require translation. If exceptionally a translation of a sequence listing is required, the UPP Division will issue an invitation to file such a translation (UP-2.2.7).

In cases where the claims and/or the description are amended in subsequent opposition or limitation proceedings, there is no requirement to file a further amended translation for a unitary patent (UP-2.2.7).

The form requirements for the translation are the same as for the translation of a European patent application (**R.50(2)**; UP-2.2.7.1).

3 **Withdrawal of the request**

The request for unitary effect can be withdrawn until the time the EPO registers the unitary effect under **UPR.7(1)**.

R. 7 Examination of the request by the European Patent Office

(1) If the requirements under Rule 5, paragraph 2, are met and the request for unitary effect complies with Rule 6, the European Patent Office shall register the unitary effect in the Register for unitary patent protection and communicate the date of this registration to the requester.

UPR.5 General

1 **Notification of registration; certificate**

The notification of the communication about the date of the registration may trigger a period for paying a renewal fee in certain cases (**UPR.13**(4) and (5). The communication does not indicate if this is the case or not.

The date of registration of the unitary effect is also decisive for the territorial scope of the unitary patent in the event a participating member state ratifies the UPCA (see **Ante UPR:1**).

The EPO sends a certificate to the proprietor once the unitary effect has been registered (UP-7.6.7).

(2) If the requirements under Rule 5, paragraph 2, are not met or the request for unitary effect does not comply with Rule 6, paragraph 1, the European Patent Office shall reject the request.

UPR.5 General

UPR.6 Requirements of the request for unitary effect

1 **Rejection of the request**

The request for unitary effect is rejected if the patent does not have the same set of claims for all 25 participating member states (**UPR.5(2)**) or if the request has not been filed within one month of publication of the mention of grant of the patent (**UPR.6(1)**). The EPO does not send an invitation to correct either of these deficiencies but must at least give the requester a chance to comment before taking a decision since **Art.113** EPC applies by virtue of **UPR.20(1)**. If the time limit is not complied with, re-establishment may be used as a remedy (**UPR.22(1)**). Re-establishment must be requested within two months of the missed time limit. If the deficiency concerns **UPR.5(2)**, and the EPO has not made a mistake, then no remedy is possible. Validation of the patent in the individual states is typically possible and may be performed simultaneously with a request for re-establishment (see also Table II Safety net in the EPO publication National measures relating to the Unitary Patent). Furthermore, the decision to reject the request can be appealed before the UPC (see **UPR.20(1):2**)

(3) If the requirements under Rule 5, paragraph 2, are met and the request for unitary effect complies with Rule 6, paragraph 1, but fails to comply with the requirements of Rule 6, paragraph 2, the European Patent Office shall invite the requester to correct the deficiencies noted within a non-extendable period of one month. If the deficiencies are not corrected in due time, the European Patent Office shall reject the request.

UPR.5 General
UPR.6 Requirements of the request for unitary effect

1 **Mistakes that can be remedied**

In the case that the request for unitary effect is filed in time and the granted patent has only one set of claims for all the participating member states, but the request does not comply with one of the requirements of **UPR.6(2)**, the EPO will send an invitation to correct these deficiencies, setting a one-month period. This time limit cannot be extended. Should the requester not correct the deficiencies, the request will be rejected.

The relevant correctable deficiencies are: (1) the request is filed in the wrong language; (2) the request does not contain the necessary particulars concerning the proprietor; (3) the number of the European patent is omitted; (4) particulars concerning an appointed representative are not included; and (5) the translation is not attached.

Having already drawn attention to the deficiency and thereby respecting the requester's right to be heard, the request can be rejected as soon as the one-month period for correcting deficiencies has expired. Re-establishment is excluded for this time limit, and no remedy is therefore available before the EPO (**UPR.22(6)**). However, validation of the patent in the individual states could be possible, also after the regular time limit; see also Table II (Safety net) in the EPO publication National measures relating to the Unitary Patent. Furthermore, the decision to reject the request can be appealed before the UPC (see **UPR.20(1):2**).

Other deficiencies, such as the need for representation or the lack of a signature, are dealt with in the same way as they would be in grant proceedings before the EPO (**UPR.20(1)** and (2)).

Chapter II *Compensation Scheme*

R. 8 Definition and beneficiaries

(1) Proprietors of European patents with unitary effect for which the European patent application was filed in an official language of the European Union other than English, French or German shall be entitled to compensation for translation costs if their residence or principal place of business is in a member state of the European Union and they are an entity or a natural person referred to in paragraph 2.

1 **Compensation for translation costs**

This provision provides a compensation scheme whereby certain proprietors who had to translate the European patent application into one of the official languages of the EPO are retrospectively given a fixed lump sum payment to help offset the translation costs incurred.

In order to qualify for the compensation, the proprietor must be resident in or have a principal place of business in an EU member state (which is not necessarily a member state participating in the unitary patent system). The nationality of the proprietor is unimportant. The proprietor must also be an entity as defined in **UPR.8(2)**.

Additionally, the application must have been originally filed in an official EU language other than English, French or German. There is no requirement that the language of filing is an official language of the state of residence or place of business of the applicant (Art.9(1)(f) of EU regulation 1257/2012 and Art.5 of EU regulation 1260/2012).

Note that the requirements under **UPR.8(1)** differ from those of the language reduction of the filing fee under **R.7a(1)**.

UPR.8(4) gives a special rule for the case the European patent application or patent was transferred between the filing date of the application and the filing of the request for compensation.

If the patent has multiple proprietors, compensation will be granted only if each proprietor fulfils these conditions (at the filing date of the application or at the date of filing the request for compensation, as the case may be) (**UPR.8(3)**; UP-3.2.1.3).

According to **UPR.8(5)**, the compensation also applies to Euro-PCT applications; there is no requirement that the EPO was the receiving Office. The language of filing the PCT application at the receiving Office is the relevant one, not the language of the WO publication (see UP-3.2.1.4).

The compensation must be expressly requested together with the request for unitary effect (**UPR.9**).

(2) Compensation for translation costs shall be granted, on request, to a patent proprietor falling within one of the following categories:

(a) small and medium-sized enterprises as defined in European Commission recommendation 2003/361/EC dated 6 May 2003;

(b) natural persons; or

(c) non-profit organisations as defined in Article 2, paragraph 1(14) of Regulation (EU) No 1290/2013, universities and public research organisations.

1 **Proprietors entitled to the compensation**
The categories are the same as those specified for the language reduction in R.7a(2), with the exception that non-profit organisations are defined by reference to an EU regulation and that European Commission recommendation 2003/361/EC is explicitly referred to.

The EPO applies the same definitions of universities and public research organisations as for R.7a(2) (see OJ 2024 A8 §8).

The category of SMEs under **UPR.8(2)(a)** includes the microenterprises in the sense of R.7a(2)(a).

Entities under **UPR.8(2)** must also meet the requirements of **UPR.8(1)** in terms of residence or principal place of business, which are different from those of R.7a(1).

(3) If the patent has multiple proprietors, compensation will be granted only if each proprietor fulfils the conditions referred to in paragraphs 1 and 2.

(4) If the European patent application or the European patent was transferred before a request for unitary effect was filed, compensation will be granted only if both the initial applicant and the proprietor of the patent fulfil the conditions referred to in paragraphs 1 and 2.

1 **Entity status of the proprietor in case of a transfer**
Where a request for compensation is submitted by a proprietor who was not the applicant at the filing date of the European application, e.g. because of a transfer of the patent application or patent, the compensation will be granted only if both the original applicant and the (new) proprietor fulfil the eligibility conditions of **UPR.8**, the original applicant at the filing date of the patent application and the new proprietor at the time of requesting compensation (UP-3.2.1.3).

Changes in the entity status and transfers of the UP after the compensation is granted have no retrospective effect on the compensation (**UPR.10(2)**).

(5) The compensation scheme provided for in paragraph 1 shall also apply to Euro-PCT applications originally filed at a receiving office in an official language of the European Union other than English, French or German.

R. 9 Request for compensation

(1) The proprietor of a European patent who wishes to benefit from compensation under Rule 8 shall file a request for it together with the request for unitary effect referred to in Rule 6.

UPR.6 Requirements of the request for unitary effect
UPR.8 Definition and beneficiaries

1 **Filing the request for compensation**
The proprietor must specifically request compensation, and this request must be filed together with the request for unitary effect. The form for requesting unitary effect contains a tick box to this effect.

(2) The request for compensation for translation costs shall contain a declaration that the proprietor of the European patent is an entity or a natural person referred to in Rule 8, paragraph 2.

UPR.8 Definition and beneficiaries

1 **Declaration**
The request must also contain a declaration as to entity status. The relevant declaration is also included in the form for requesting unitary effect and is made automatically when the tick box for requesting for compensation is crossed. A previous declaration under **R.7b(1)** EPC is not sufficient for obtaining compensation, even if the proprietor is the original applicant.

R. 10 Examination of the request and grant of compensation

(1) After the European Patent Office has registered the unitary effect of the European patent in the Register for unitary patent protection and has examined the request for compensation, it shall inform the patent proprietor whether that request has been granted or rejected.

1 **Grant or rejection of the request**
If the request for compensation is rejected, the proprietor can appeal by filing an action with the UPC (Art.32(1)(i) UPCA; UP-3.2.3.3; see **UPR.20(1):2**).

(2) Once granted, compensation shall not be rescinded, even if, as a result of changed circumstances, the proprietor no longer qualifies for it under Rule 8.

UPR.8 Definition and beneficiaries

1 **Change in the entity status**
Even if the entity status of the proprietor changes after the grant of the compensation or the UP is transferred to a party that would not have qualified for it, the compensation does not need to be reimbursed (UP-3.2.3.1).

(3) Should the Office have reason to doubt the veracity of the declaration filed under Rule 9, paragraph 2, it shall invite the patent proprietor to provide evidence that he fulfils the requirements of Rule 8, paragraph 2. Articles 113(1) and 114 EPC shall apply.

Art.113 EPC Right to be heard and basis of decisions
Art.114 EPC Examination by the European Patent Office of its own motion
UPR.8 Definition and beneficiaries
UPR.9 Request for compensation

1 **Doubts about the declaration**
The EPO may request evidence proving that the declaration is correct, of their own motion or, for example, because a third party has provided information casting doubt on the declaration. This information may, in the case of an SME, relate to the finances of the company, the number of employees and/or the ownership of the company. For non-profit organisations, universities and public research organisations, the information may, for example, concern their statutes.

(4) If the Office finds that the compensation was granted on the basis of a false declaration, it shall invite the patent proprietor to pay, together with the next renewal fee falling due, an additional fee composed of the amount of the compensation paid and an administrative fee as laid down in the Rules relating to Fees for Unitary Patent Protection. If this additional fee is not paid in due time, the European patent with unitary effect shall lapse under Rule 14.

1 **Administrative fee**
The amount of the administrative fee is defined in **RfeesUPP.4(2)**, and is 50% of the compensation.

R. 11 Level of compensation

Reimbursement of translation costs shall be made up to a ceiling and paid in the form of a lump sum, in accordance with the Rules relating to Fees for Unitary Patent Protection. The ceiling shall be fixed on the basis of the average length of a European patent and the average translation cost per page, taking account of the average reduction granted under Rule 6 EPC.

R.6 EPC Filing of translations and reduction of fees

1 **Level of compensation**
The amount of the compensation is defined in **RfeesUPP.4(1)**.

Chapter III *Licenses of Right*

R. 12 Filing of the statement by the patent proprietor

(1) The proprietor of a European patent with unitary effect may file a statement with the European Patent Office that he is prepared to allow any person to use the invention as a licensee in return for appropriate consideration. In that case, the renewal fees for the European patent with unitary effect which fall due after receipt of the statement shall be reduced; the amount of the reduction shall be fixed in the Rules relating to Fees for Unitary Patent Protection. The statement shall be entered in the Register for unitary patent protection.

1 **Availability of a licence**
A proprietor willing to grant a licence on their invention may file a statement to this effect at the EPO. Such licence is to be treated as a contractual licence (Art.8 of EU regulation 1257/2012). The statement is preferably filed using EPO form 7001. There is no fee for registering the statement.

Any renewal fees falling due after receipt of the statement are reduced (Art.11(3) of the EU regulation 1257/2012), the reduction being 15% (**RfeesUPP.3**). Any additional fee for late payment of the renewal fee is calculated based on the reduced fee.

Art.32(1)(h) UPCA provides that the UPC has jurisdiction in relation to disputes concerning compensation payable under licences on the basis of Art.8 of EU regulation 1257/2012.

(2) The statement referred to in paragraph 1 may be withdrawn at any time by a communication to this effect to the European Patent Office. Such withdrawal shall not take effect until the amount by which the renewal fees were reduced is paid to the European Patent Office.

1 **Withdrawal of the statement**
The statement can be withdrawn, and the withdrawal is preferably made using EPO form 7002. The amount by which renewal fees were reduced at the time during which the statement was effective must be paid to the EPO before the withdrawal is effective and it is recommended to make this payment at the same time as filing the withdrawal.

(3) The statement referred to in paragraph 1 may not be filed as long as an exclusive licence is recorded in the Register for unitary patent protection or a request for the recording of such a licence is pending before the European Patent Office.

(4) No request for recording an exclusive licence in the Register for unitary patent protection shall be admissible after the statement referred to in paragraph 1 has been filed, unless that statement is withdrawn.

Chapter IV *Renewal Fees*

R. 13 Payment of renewal fees for European patents with unitary effect

(1) Renewal fees for European patents with unitary effect and additional fees for their late payment shall be paid to the European Patent Office. Those fees shall be due in respect of the years following the year in which the mention of the grant of the European patent which benefits from unitary effect is published in the European Patent Bulletin.

1 **Payment of renewal fees**
Art.11 of the EU regulation 1257/2012 concerns renewal fees for European patents with unitary effect. Art.11(1) of this regulation states that renewal fees are to be paid by the patent proprietor. Considering that the EPO accepts renewal fee payments for European patent applications from parties other than the applicant, it is presumed that the same would apply to renewal fees falling due for a UP.

The 'year' in the provision refers to patent years, calculated from the anniversaries of the filing date. The renewal fee for the patent year in which the mention of the grant is published must be paid to the EPO under **Art.86** (see **Art.141**).

(2) A renewal fee for the European patent with unitary effect in respect of the coming year shall be due on the last day of the month containing the anniversary of the date of filing of the European patent application which led to the European patent with unitary effect. Renewal fees may not be validly paid more than three months before they fall due.

1 **Due dates for renewal fees**
The due date for a renewal fee of a unitary patent is treated by the EPO in the same manner as the due date for a renewal fee of a European patent application (UP-3.1.7.1). Thus, when a renewal fee for a unitary patent falls due on a day on which one of the filing offices of the EPO is closed, it is possible to pay the renewal fee without surcharge on the first day on which the EPO filing offices are open again, even though a due date of a renewal fee is not a time limit to be met (**J4/91**; formerly in UP Guide, 3rd edition 2024, §107).

Payments for unitary patents are accepted once the unitary effect has been registered.

If the unitary patent is granted on a divisional application, the filing date of the (root) parent application is the relevant date (**Art.76(1)** EPC; see A-IV,1.4.3)

(3) If a renewal fee is not paid in due time, the fee may still be paid within six months of the due date, provided that an additional fee is also paid within that period.

1 **Late payment**
The additional fee for late payment is 50% of the unpaid fee (**RfeesUPP.2(1).2**). If the renewal fee is not paid in due time, the EPO will send a reminder to the proprietor, as a courtesy service. The proprietor may thus not invoke the omission of this reminder. The six-month period for the payment of a renewal fee with the additional fee expires on the last day of the sixth month after the due date, in line with **J4/91** (UP-3.1.7.3; see the notes to

R.51(2) EPC for the calculation of the period). If the last day of the sixth month is not a working day, the last day for valid payment is the first working day thereafter (**R.134(1)** EPC in view of **UPR.20(2)(g)**).

2 **Consequence of non-payment and remedies**
If the renewal fee is not paid by the due date, or within the six-month grace period with surcharge, the UP will lapse (Art.11(2) of the EU regulation 1257/2012, **UPR.14(1)(b)**). The EPO will inform the proprietor by sending a notification of loss of rights. The lapse takes effect on the day the renewal fee was due (**UPR.14(2)**), not at the end of the six-month period as under **R.51(2)** EPC.

The failure to pay the renewal fee with surcharge within the additional period can be remedied with re-establishment (**UPR.22**). In case the finding of the EPO leading to the notice of loss of rights is erroneous, the proprietor can request a decision under **R.112(2)** EPC (**UPR.20(2)(d)**). This decision can then be appealed at the UPC (Art.32(1)(i) UPCA).

(4) A renewal fee in respect of a European patent with unitary effect falling due under paragraph 2 within three months of the notification of the communication referred to in Rule 7(1) may still be paid within that period without the additional fee referred to in paragraph 3.

UPR.7 Examination of the request by the European Patent Office

1 **Renewal fee due shortly after registration of unitary effect**
A renewal fee falling due within three months of the notification of registration of unitary effect can be validly paid within that three-month period without additional fee. It may be noted that this is more generous than the two-month period provided by **Art.141(2)** for payment of renewal fees to national offices shortly after grant. The six-month period for paying with a surcharge does not shift and is calculated from the original due date. The communication under **UPR.7** does not indicate if this provision applies or not. Payments for unitary patents are accepted once unitary effect has been registered.

Example:

20 October	publication of the mention of the grant
15 December	notification of registration of unitary effect
31 December	due date for renewal fee
15 March	last day for payment without additional fee
30 June	expiry of 6-month period for payment with additional fee

(5) A renewal fee for a European patent with unitary effect which would have fallen due under paragraph 2 in the period starting on the date of publication of the mention of the grant of the European patent in the European Patent Bulletin up to and including the date of the notification of the communication referred to in Rule 7(1) shall be due on that latter date. This fee may still be paid within three months of that latter date without the additional fee referred to in paragraph 3.

UPR.7 Examination of the request by the European Patent Office

1 **Renewal fee due before registration of unitary effect**
A renewal fee falling due in the normal way before the notification of registration of unitary effect is actually due on the date of notification and can be validly paid within three months of this notification date without additional fee. Payments for unitary patents are accepted by the EPO once unitary effect has been registered. The six-month period also starts on the shifted due date, i.e. the date of notification of registration of unitary effect. The communication under **UPR.7** does not indicate if this provision applies or not.

Example:

20 October	publication of the mention of the grant
31 December	original due date for renewal fee
5 January	notification of registration of unitary effect and new, postponed due date for renewal fee
5 April	last day for payment without additional fee
5 July	expiry of 6-month period for payment with additional fee

(6) Rule 51, paragraphs 4 and 5, EPC shall apply mutatis mutandis.

R.51 EPC Payment of renewal fees

1 **Renewal fees in certain cases**
R.51(4) concerns the payment of renewal fees in situations where a European patent application has been refused or deemed to be withdrawn because the applicant has not observed a time limit, and rights have thereafter been re-established. Applying this provision mutatis mutandis to a unitary patent, it will apply when the unitary patent lapses because a renewal fee is not paid with surcharge within the grace period, re-establishment is granted, and further renewal fees have fallen due in the meantime.

The application of **R.51(5)** by analogy concerns situations in which a European patent has been revoked by a board of appeal in opposition proceedings (or where the board rejects an appeal against a decision of the opposition division to revoke the patent) and the appeal decision is set aside by the Enlarged Board of Appeal as the result of a successful petition for review. The proprietor can pay the renewal fee for the unitary patent within a period after the notification of the decision of the Enlarged Board of Appeal as set out in **R.51(5)**.

Chapter V *Lapse*

R. 14 Lapse

(1) A European patent with unitary effect shall lapse:

(a) 20 years after the date of filing of the European patent application;

(b) if a renewal fee and, where applicable, any additional fee have not been paid in due time.

1 **Term of a UP**
A UP will lapse at the latest 20 years after the date of filing of the EP application. This terminology is clearer than the corresponding provision of **Art.63(1)** EPC, as it explicitly uses the term after. While the Convention should prevail over the present rules, it can be expected that the last day of validity of a UP will be the day that comes 20 years after the filing date, in the same month and on the day having the same number as the filing date, i.e. the last day of validity of a patent with a filing date of 20.06.2022 would be 20.06.2042.

(2) The lapse of a European patent with unitary effect for failure to pay a renewal fee and any additional fee within the due period shall be deemed to have occurred on the date on which the renewal fee was due.

1 **Lapse**
If the renewal fee and additional fee are not paid within the six-month period for paying the renewal fee with the additional fee of **UPR.13(2)**, the patent is deemed to have lapsed at the due date, not at the expiry of the six-month period as in **R.51(2) EPC**.

PART III INFORMATION TO THE PUBLIC

Chapter I *Register for Unitary Patent Protection*

R. 15 Establishment of the Register for unitary patent protection

(1) The Register for unitary patent protection provided for in Article 9, paragraph 1(b), Regulation (EU) No 1257/2012 is hereby established as a special part of the European Patent Register kept by the European Patent Office under Article 127 EPC.

Art.127 EPC European Patent Register

1 **Register for unitary patent protection**
According to Art.9(1)(b) of EU regulation 1257/2012, the EPO is responsible for setting up and maintaining a register for unitary patent protection within the European Patent Register. The entries to be made in this Register are specified in **UPR.16(1)**, but this list is not exhaustive (**UPR.16(2)**). The structure and functionalities of this Register are the same as that of EPO's Register, and information relating to UP can be found in the chapter 'Unitary Patent' under the panel view 'UP All documents'.

The EPO and UPC have signed an agreement on the exchange of data, thereby providing a legal basis for exchange of data between EPO's Register and UPC's Register. The agreement entered into force at the same time as the UPCA.

(2) Entries in the Register for unitary patent protection shall be made in the three official languages of the European Patent Office. In case of doubt, the entry in the language of the proceedings shall be authentic.

R. 16 Entries in the Register for unitary patent protection

(1) The Register for unitary patent protection shall contain the following entries:

- **(a) date of publication of the mention of the grant of the European patent;**
- **(b) date of filing of the request for unitary effect for the European patent;**

(c) particulars of the representative of the proprietor of the European patent as provided for in Rule 41, paragraph 2(d), EPC; in the case of several representatives, only the particulars of the representative first named, followed by the words "and others" and, in the case of an association referred to in Rule 152, paragraph 11, EPC, only the name and address of the association;
(d) date and purport of the decision on the registration of unitary effect for the European patent;
(e) date of registration of the unitary effect of the European patent;
(f) date of effect of the European patent with unitary effect pursuant to Article 4, paragraph 1, Regulation (EU) No 1257/2012;
(g) participating Member States in which the European patent with unitary effect has unitary effect pursuant to Article 18, paragraph 2, Regulation (EU) No 1257/2012;
(h) particulars of the proprietor of the European patent with unitary effect as provided for in Rule 41, paragraph 2(c), EPC;
(i) family name, given names and country and place of residence of the inventor designated by the applicant for or proprietor of the patent, unless he has waived his right to be mentioned under Rule 20, paragraph 1, EPC;
(j) rights and transfer of such rights relating to the European patent with unitary effect where the present Rules provide that they shall be recorded at the request of an interested party;
(k) licensing commitments undertaken by the proprietor of the European patent with unitary effect in international standardisation bodies pursuant to Article 9, paragraph 1(c), Regulation (EU) No 1257/2012, where the proprietor requested their registration;
(l) date of filing and date of withdrawal of the statement provided for in Rule 12;
(m) date of lapse of the European patent with unitary effect;
(n) data as to the payment of renewal fees for the European patent with unitary effect, including, where applicable, data on the payment of an additional fee pursuant to Rule 13, paragraph 3;
(o) a record of the information communicated to the European Patent Office concerning proceedings before the Unified Patent Court;
(p) a record of the information communicated to the European Patent Office by the central industrial property offices, courts and other competent authorities of the participating Member States;
(q) date and purport of the decision on the validity of a European patent with unitary effect taken by the Unified Patent Court;
(r) date of receipt of a request for re-establishment of rights;
(s) refusal of a request for re-establishment of rights;
(t) date of re-establishment of rights;
(u) dates of interruption and resumption of proceedings;
(v) date of issuance, date of expiry and date and purport of the decision on the validity of a supplementary protection certificate for a product protected by the European patent with unitary effect as well as the participating Member State issuing it;
(w) information regarding a place of business of the applicant on the date of filing of the application for the European patent pursuant to Article 7, paragraph 1(b), Regulation (EU) No 1257/2012, which may be provided by the proprietor of the European patent together with the request for unitary effect referred to in Rule 6.

(x) information regarding the residence or principal place of business of the applicant on the date of filing of the application for the European patent pursuant to Article 7, paragraph 1(a), Regulation (EU) No 1257/2012.

R.20 EPC Publication of the mention of the inventor
R.41 EPC Request for grant
R.152 EPC Authorisations
UPR.6 Requirements of the request for unitary effect
UPR.12 Filing the statement by the patent proprietor
UPR.13 Payment of renewal fees for European patents with unitary effect 01.06.2023 (and OJ 2022 A40).

1 **Register for UP**
The Register for unitary patent protection contains similar information to the European Patent Register (**R.143** EPC). It additionally contains information concerning licensing commitments made by the proprietor to international standardisation bodies (when requested by the proprietor) and information concerning supplementary protection certificates. It also contains information concerning any proceedings pending before the UPC as well as information on any decision taken by the UPC on the validity of the UP. For cases where the applicant, at the time of filing the EP application, did not have a residence or principal place of business in a participating member state, the UP Register may also contain information relating to a place of business of the applicant at the time of filing, within a participating member state. This information may be provided when filing the request for unitary effect. See **Ante UPR:4.**

European patents with unitary effect will be identifiable with the identifier C0 (C zero) and are visible as a 'publication' in Espacenet (e.g. EP4134005C0) even though there is no actual publication of the unitary patent, or of the submitted translation, in addition to the B1 publication of the patent specification.

(2) The President of the European Patent Office may decide that entries additional to those referred to in paragraph 1 shall be made in the Register for unitary patent protection.

Chapter II *Publications*

R. 17 European Patent Bulletin and Official Journal of the European Patent Office

(1) The European Patent Bulletin referred to in Article 129(a) EPC shall contain, as a special part, the particulars the publication of which is prescribed by the present Rules, the Chairperson of the Select Committee of the Administrative Council or the President of the European Patent Office.

Art.129 EPC Periodical publications

(2) The Official Journal referred to in Article 129(b) EPC shall contain, as a special part, notices and information of a general character issued by the Select Committee of the Administrative Council or by the President of the European Patent Office, as well as any other information relevant to the implementation of unitary patent protection.

Art.129 EPC Periodical publications

R. 18 Publication of translations

The President of the European Patent Office shall determine the form of the publication of the translations referred to in Rule 6, paragraph 2(d), and the data to be included.

UPR.6 Requirements of the request for unitary effect

1 **No publication of translations**
The President has not taken any decision on the publication of translations. The translation will therefore not be published but will be available via file inspection in the UP Register.

R. 19 Inclusion of decisions of the Unified Patent Court in the files

The European Patent Office shall include a copy of any decision of the Unified Patent Court forwarded to it by the Court and relating to European patents with unitary effect, including those decisions referred to in Rule 1, in the files relating to the European patent with unitary effect, where it shall be open to inspection.

UPR.1 Subject matter

PART IV COMMON PROVISIONS

R. 20 Common provisions governing procedure

(1) The following provisions of the EPC, as amended, shall apply mutatis mutandis: Article 14, paragraphs 1, 3 and 7; Article 113, paragraph 1; Articles 114, 117, 119, 120, 125; Article 128, paragraph 4; Articles 131, 133; Article 134, paragraphs 1, 5 and 8.

Art.14 EPC Languages of the European Patent Office, European patent applications and other documents
Art.113 EPC Right to be heard and basis of decisions
Art.114 EPC Examination by the European Patent Office of its own motion
Art.117 EPC Means and taking of evidence
Art.119 EPC Notifications
Art.120 EPC Time limits
Art.125 EPC Reference to general principles
Art.128 EPC Inspection of files
Art.131 EPC Administrative and legal co-operation
Art.133 EPC General principles of representation
Art.134 EPC Representation before the European Patent Office

1 **UP proceedings vs. EP proceedings**

Proceedings concerning unitary effect before the EPO have a similar character to proceedings concerning European patent applications and patents. However, there are some differences.

1.1 LANGUAGES

UPR.20(1) does not refer to **Art.14(4)** EPC, meaning that documents that have to be filed with the EPO within a time limit in the UP procedure cannot be filed in a language of a contracting state, but can only be filed in one of the official languages of the EPO (with the exception of the request for unitary effect, which must be filed in the language of the proceedings according to **UPR.6(2)**). Thus, for example, a request for re-establishment cannot be filed in Swedish by a Swedish proprietor, even if a translation into English, French or German is filed afterwards. (UP-7.4)

UPR.20(2)(a) specifies that **R.3(1)** EPC, first sentence applies unless otherwise provided, meaning that while the request for unitary effect must be filed in the language of the proceedings according to **UPR.6(2)**, further documents can be filed in any of the official languages of the EPO.

1.2 REPRESENTATION

The provisions on representation that apply to proceedings before the EPO in grant and opposition proceedings also apply to proceedings concerning the UP.

It is permitted to appoint a different professional representative for proceeding relating to the unitary patent from the one appointed for the European patent (e.g., representing the proprietor in any opposition procedure). The former will be entered in the Register for unitary patent protection, the latter in the European Patent Register (UP-7.2.1).

An authorisation to represent an applicant or proprietor before the EPO in proceedings established by the EPC does not automatically cover the proceedings relating to UP. The EPO forms 1003 (individual authorisation) and 1004 (general authorisation) therefore have a tick box for authorising representation in UP proceedings. The corresponding UP forms are 7003 and 7004. The requirements for signing and filing authorisations in proceedings before the Unitary Patent Protection Division are given in Dec. Pres. OJ 2024 A76. Authorisations may be authenticated by a handwritten signature, a facsimile signature, a text-string signature or a digital signature under the conditions specified by the EPO.

R.151 EPC applies by analogy (**UPR.20(2)(l)**). A common representative can be named in the request for unitary effect. If the request does not name a common representative, the proprietor first named in the request will be considered the common representative. The order of the proprietors in the request may differ from their order in the patent. However, if one of the proprietors named in the request is required to appoint a professional representative, the duly appointed professional representative will be considered the common representative acting on behalf of all proprietors, unless the proprietor first named in the request has appointed a professional representative, in which case that professional representative will be considered to be acting on behalf of all proprietors (UP-2.2.2).

1.3 EXTENSION OF PERIODS

UPR.20(2) does not refer to **R.132(2)** EPC about the extension of periods specified by the EPO. Most periods in proceedings before the Unitary Patent Protection Division are laid down in the applicable rules. However, there are some exceptions, such as the period for filing evidence on entitlement to compensation (**UPR.10(3)**). Arguably, the Unitary Patent Protection Division has the inherent power to extend periods not specified in the applicable rule if a party requests it before the expiry of the period, up to a total duration of four months (see **UPR.20(4)**; however, see also UP-7.5.1).

The reason for the separate provision on periods in **UPR.20(4)** is to shorten the minimum period to one month (OJ 2016 A39).

1.4 REGISTRATION OF TRANSFERS

The Unitary Patent Protection Division is competent to register a transfer of a unitary patent in the Register for unitary patent protection at the request of an interested party and on the production of documents satisfying the EPO that the transfer took place, as long as the patent is in force. If a request for registration of a transfer is refused, the requester can file an appeal to the UPC; possibly also if a transfer is registered and a natural or legal person is adversely affected by the registration (Art.32(1)(i) and Art.47(7) UPCA). The UPC has the power to rectify the Register for unitary patent protection (Art.66(1) UPCA), which implies the power to order that the registration of a transfer is undone (differently from the boards of appeal, see **R.22(3):2**).

2 Appeals against decisions of the UPP Division

Appeals against decisions of the UPP Division are to be filed with the UPC; the appeal is called an 'action' (Art.32(1)(i) UPCA; **UPR.1(1)**). The appellant is called the claimant. The central division of the UPC is competent (Art.33(9) UPCA). No representation is required (Art.48(7) UPCA), but only lawyers and European patent attorneys with appropriate qualifications, such as a European Patent Litigation Certificate, may act as a representative (Art.48(2) UPCA).

A decision taken under **UPR.20(2)(d)** and **R.112(2)** EPC after a notice of loss of rights can be appealed if the proprietor disagrees with the findings of the UPP Division, e.g. if the EPO considers that a renewal fee was not paid in time and the proprietor disagrees.

The details of the procedure can be found in the Rules of Procedure (RoP) of the UPC.

The following applies to appeals concerning decisions of the UPP Division, except for refusals of requests for unitary effect. The appellant must be adversely affected by the decision of the UPP Division but need not be the proprietor; moreover, there is no explicit requirement that only parties to the proceedings before the UPP Division can appeal (Art.47(7) UPCA; R.88.2.b RoP). The period for filing an appeal ('application to annul or alter a decision') and paying the fixed fee is two months (R.88.1 RoP), to be calculated using the provisions of the UPCA. A remedy of retrospective extension of the period may apply (R.9.3 RoP). The appeal must be filed in the language in which the patent was granted (R.88.1 RoP, i.e. the language specified in **Art.14(3)** EPC), include the grounds and the facts, evidence and arguments relied on, and include further information such as the name of the claimant (appellant) (R.88.2 RoP). The grounds are listed in R.87 RoP as (a) infringement of EU regulations 1257/2012 and 1260/2012, (b) infringement of the implementing rules, e.g. the UPR, (c) infringement of an essential procedural requirement, and (d) misuse of power. The appeal has a suspensive effect (R.86 RoP).

If an appeal is filed but a formal requirement is not met, or no appeal fee is paid, the Registry of the UPC issues a notification giving a 14-day period to remedy the deficiency (R.89 RoP). If the appeal is admissible (according to the UPC Registry), the appeal is forwarded to the EPO (R.90(d) RoP). The EPO grants interlocutory revision within two months if it considers the appeal to be well-founded (R.91 RoP, **UPR.24**). When granting interlocutory revision, the EPO must grant the order or remedy sought by the claimant (**UPR.24(a)**). If no interlocutory revision is granted, the appeal is heard by a three-member panel or by a single judge if the claimant requests so (R.92 RoP). An oral hearing takes place at the request of the claimant (R.85(1)(c) RoP).

Parties shall bear their own costs (Art.66(2) UPCA; R.98 RoP). The court fees may be reimbursed in part on reasoned request in certain cases (R.370(9)-(11) RoP).

The UPC may exercise any power of the UPP Division in such procedure, including the rectification of the Register for unitary patent protection (Art.66(1) UPCA; **UPR.15**).

An example is the proprietor's appeal against the premature registration of the unitary effect for EP3516914 (the unitary effect was registered shortly before Romania acceded). The EPO granted interlocutory revision.

In the event of a decision to reject a request for unitary effect, the proprietor may appeal. The procedure is governed by R.97 RoP. The period for filing the appeal ('application to annul or alter a decision') and paying the fixed appeal fee is three weeks (R.97.1 RoP), to be calculated using the provisions of the UPCA. A remedy of retrospective extension of the period may apply (R.9.3 RoP). The appeal must include the grounds, facts, evidence, and arguments relied upon. If the appeal does not comply with certain formal requirements or the appeal fee is not paid, the Registry of the UPC issues a notification giving a 14-day period to remedy the deficiency (R.97.2 RoP referring to R.89 RoP). Interlocutory revision by the EPO is not available (UP-7.7.2).

The standing judge decides within three weeks. Both the proprietor and the President of the EPO can appeal against the decision of the standing judge. The appeal is handled by the standing judge of the UPC Court of Appeal (R.97.5 RoP).

(2) The following provisions of the Implementing Regulations to the EPC, as amended, shall apply mutatis mutandis:
- **(a) Rules 1 and 2; unless otherwise provided Rule 3, paragraph 1, first sentence; Rule 3, paragraph 3; Rules 4 and 5;**
- **(b) Rules 22 to 24;**
- **(c) Rule 50, paragraphs 2 and 3;**
- **(d) Rule 111, paragraph 1; Rules 112 and 113;**
- **(e) Rule 115; Rule 116, paragraph 1; Rules 117 to 124;**
- **(f) Rules 125 to 130;**
- **(g) Rule 131; Rule 133, paragraph 1, subject to the proviso that the document referred to in that provision has been received no later than one month after expiry of the period; Rule 134;**
- **(h) Rule 139, first sentence, and Rule 140;**
- **(i) Rule 142;**
- **(j) Rules 144 to 147;**
- **(k) Rules 148 to 150;**
- **(l) Rules 151 to 153.**

R.1 EPC Written proceedings
R.2 EPC Filing of and formal requirements for documents
R.3 EPC Language in written proceedings
R.4 EPC Language in oral proceedings
R.5 EPC Certification of translations
R.22 EPC Registration of transfers
R.23 EPC Registration of licenses and other rights
R.24 EPC Special entries for license registrations
R.50 EPC Documents filed subsequently
R.111 EPC Form of decisions
R.112 EPC Noting of loss of rights
R.113 EPC Signature, name, seal
R.115 EPC Summons to oral proceedings
R.116 EPC Preparation of oral proceedings
R.117 EPC Decision on taking of evidence
R.118 EPC Summons to give evidence before the European Patent Office
R.119 EPC Examination of evidence before the European Patent Office
R.120 EPC Hearing by a competent national court
R.121 EPC Commissioning of experts
R.122 EPC Costs of taking of evidence
R.123 EPC Conservation of evidence
R.124 EPC Minutes of oral proceedings and the taking of evidence

R.125 EPC General provisions
R.126 EPC Notification by postal services
R.127 EPC Notification by means of electronic communication
R.128 EPC Notification by delivery by hand
R.129 EPC Public notification
R.130 EPC Notification to representative
R.131 EPC Calculation of periods
R.133 EPC Late receipt of documents
R.134 EPC Extension of periods
R.139 EPC Correction of errors in documents filed with the European Patent Office
R.140 EPC Correction of errors in decisions
R.142 EPC Interruption of proceedings
R.144 EPC Parts of the file excluded from inspection
R.145 EPC Procedures for the inspection of files
R.146 EPC Communication of information contained in the files
R.147 EPC Constitution, maintenance and preservation of files
R.148 EPC Communications between the European Patent Office and the authorities of the Contracting States
R.149 EPC Inspection of files by or via courts or authorities of the Contracting States
R.150 EPC Procedure for letters rogatory
R.151 EPC Appointment of a common representative
R.152 EPC Authorisations
R.153 EPC Attorney-client evidentiary privilege

(3) When applying the provisions referred to in paragraphs 1 and 2 mutatis mutandis, the term "Contracting States" shall be understood as meaning the Contracting States to the EPC, except in Article 125 EPC, where it shall be understood as meaning the participating Member States.

Art.125 EPC Reference to general principles

(4) Where the present Rules, including the provisions of the EPC applicable mutatis mutandis under the present Rules, refer to "a period to be specified", this period shall be specified by the European Patent Office. Unless otherwise provided, a period specified by the European Patent Office shall be neither less than one month nor more than four months.

R. 21 Oral proceedings

(1) Oral proceedings shall take place either at the instance of the European Patent Office if it considers this to be expedient or at the request of any party to the proceedings. However, the European Patent Office may reject a request for further oral proceedings where the parties and the subject of the proceedings are the same.

1 **Oral proceedings**
Oral proceedings that do not concern a request for unitary effect (see **UPR.21(2)**) must be arranged by the EPO at the request of a party, as long as they are not duplicative of oral proceedings already held. Such oral proceedings could concern, for example, a request for re-establishment following failure to pay a renewal fee with surcharge, or the registration of a transfer or a licence. Dec. Pres. OJ 2023 sp3 p.2-4 gives details on oral proceedings. In

particular, oral proceedings before the Unitary Patent Protection Division are normally held by video conference.

(2) Nevertheless, in the procedure concerning the request for unitary effect, oral proceedings shall take place before the Unitary Patent Protection Division at the request of the proprietor of the European patent only where the Unitary Patent Protection Division considers this to be expedient.

(3) Oral proceedings before the Unitary Patent Protection Division shall not be public.

R. 22 Re-establishment of rights

(1) A proprietor of a European patent or of a European patent with unitary effect who, in spite of all due care required by the circumstances having been taken, was unable to observe a time limit vis-à-vis the European Patent Office shall have his rights re-established upon request if the non-observance of this time limit has the direct consequence of causing the European patent with unitary effect to lapse according to Rule 14, paragraph 1(b), or the loss of any other right or means of redress.

UPR.14 Lapse

(2) Any request for re-establishment of rights under paragraph 1 shall be filed in writing within two months of the removal of the cause of non-compliance with the period, but at the latest within one year of expiry of the unobserved time limit. However, a request for re-establishment of rights in respect of the period specified in Rule 6, paragraph 1, shall be filed within two months of expiry of that period. The request for re-establishment of rights shall not be deemed to have been filed until the fee prescribed in the Rules relating to Fees for Unitary Patent Protection has been paid.

UPR.6 Requirements of the request for unitary effect

1 **Time limit for requesting re-establishment on requesting unitary effect**
The time limit for requesting re-establishment of rights following the failure to meet any time limit other than the time limit for filing the request for unitary effect is the same as that provided in **R.136(1)** EPC. A request for re-establishment of the period under **UPR.6(1)** for requesting unitary effect is, however, only two months from the expiry of the one-month period from the publication of the mention of the grant. This one-month period runs concurrently with the period of three months from the publication of the mention of the grant for requesting national validation. Therefore, unless the conditions that led to missing the period for filing the request for unitary effect are such that re-establishment is guaranteed, it would seem more secure to request validation nationally. It can be expected that the all due care criterion will be interpreted as strictly as it is in European grant and opposition proceedings.

(3) The request shall state the grounds on which it is based and shall set out the facts on which it relies. The omitted act shall be completed within the relevant period for filing the request according to paragraph 2.

(4) The European Patent Office shall grant the request, provided that the conditions laid down in the present Rule are met. Otherwise, it shall reject the request.

(5) If the request is granted, the legal consequences of the failure to observe the time limit shall be deemed not to have ensued.

(6) Re-establishment of rights shall be ruled out in respect of the time limit for requesting re-establishment of rights and in respect of the period referred to in Rule 7, paragraph 3.

UPR.7 Examination of the request by the European Patent Office

1 **Time limits excluded from re-establishment**
Re-establishment cannot be requested for missing the time limit for requesting re-establishment. It cannot either be requested when the EPO invites the requester to correct deficiencies in the request for unitary effect pursuant to UPR.7(3) and the requester fails to reply in time.

(7) Any person who, in one or several participating Member States, has in good faith used or made effective and serious preparations for using an invention which is the subject of a European patent with unitary effect in the period between the loss of rights referred to in paragraph 1 and publication in the Register for unitary patent protection of the mention of re-establishment of those rights, may without payment continue such use in the course of his business or for the needs thereof.

R. 23 Form of decisions

Decisions of the European Patent Office against which actions can be brought before the Unified Patent Court in accordance with Article 32, paragraph 1(i), Agreement on a Unified Patent Court shall be reasoned and shall be accompanied by a communication pointing out the possibility of bringing an action before the Unified Patent Court. The parties may not invoke the omission of the communication.

1 **Decisions of the EPO appealed to the UPC**
See UPR.20(1):2 for details of the procedure for appealing decisions of the Unitary Patent Protection Division.

R. 24 Interlocutory revision

If the European Patent Office is informed by the Unified Patent Court that an application to annul or alter a decision of the European Patent Office is admissible and if the European Patent Office considers that the application is well founded, it shall, within two months of the date of receipt of the application,

(a) rectify the contested decision in accordance with the order or remedy sought by the claimant and

(b) inform the Unified Patent Court that the decision has been rectified.

Rules relating to Fees for Unitary Patent Protection (RFeesUPP)

as adopted by decision of the Select Committee of the Administrative Council of the European Patent Organisation of 15 December 2015

Art. 1 General

The fees due to be paid to the European Patent Office, the compensation for translation costs to be paid to proprietors of a European patent with unitary effect by the European Patent Office, as provided for in the Rules relating to Unitary Patent Protection, and the fees and expenses which the President of the European Patent Office lays down pursuant to Article 5 shall be levied or paid in accordance with the provisions contained in Articles 2 to 6.

Art. 2 Fees provided for in the Rules relating to Unitary Patent Protection

(1) The fees due to be paid to the European Patent Office shall be as follows:

	EUR
1. Renewal fees for the European patent with unitary effect (Rule 13, paragraph 1, Rules relating to Unitary Patent Protection), calculated in each case from the date of filing of the application	
- for the 2nd year	35
- for the 3rd year	105
- for the 4th year	145
- for the 5th year	315
- for the 6th year	475
- for the 7th year	630
- for the 8th year	815
- for the 9th year	990
- for the 10th year	1 175
- for the 11th year	1 460
- for the 12th year	1 775
- for the 13th year	2 105
- for the 14th year	2 455
- for the 15th year	2 830
- for the 16th year	3 240
- for the 17th year	3 640
- for the 18th year	4 055
- for the 19th year	4 455
- for the 20th year	4 855
2. Additional fee for belated payment of a renewal fee (Rule 13, paragraph 3, relating to Unitary Patent Protection)	50% of the belated renewal fee

UPR.13 Payment of renewal fees for European patents with unitary effect

1 **Amount of the renewal fee**
The renewal fee for a unitary patent for a given year corresponds approximately to the total of the renewal fees payable in the four countries where European patents were most often validated in 2015. The criteria of four countries with the most EP validations was selected as it resulted in a renewal fee that was equivalent to the level of renewal fees paid for a European patent with an average geographical coverage at the time (Art.12(3)(a) of EU regulation 1257/2012). It is assumed that the fees will increase when the sys-

tem has been in force for at most five years, and every five years thereafter (see **RfeesUPP.7**), as renewal fees have increased since 2015.

Art.10 of EU regulation 1257/2012 expressly states that the expenses incurred by the EPO in relation to UPs are to be covered by the renewal fees. This can be understood as not allowing the EPO to levy a fee on the request for unitary effect as such.

The level of renewal fees needs to be such that it covers at least a majority of the costs of the EPO in administering the UPs, as well as allowing the EPO to distribute 50% of the renewal fees to the participating member states in accordance with Art.12 of EU regulation 1257/2012.

The renewal fees are reduced if the proprietor files a statement with the EPO indicating an intention to grant a licence to any person in return for a licence fee (**UPR.12, RfeesUPP.7**). No reduction is available on the ground that the proprietor is a micro-entity (different from **R.7a(3)**).

(2) The fee for re-establishment of rights (Rule 22, paragraph 2, relating to Unitary Patent Protection) shall be payable in the amount laid down in Article 2, paragraph 1, item 13, of the Rules relating to Fees under the EPC, as amended.

UPR.22 Re-establishment of rights
Rfees2 EPC Fees provided for in the Convention and in the Implementing Regulations

1 **Fee for re-establishment**
The amount of the fee for re-establishment of rights is the same as for EP cases. The provision expressly states that the amount will be the one in force at any particular moment ('as amended').

Art. 3 Reduction of renewal fees

The reduction of the renewal fees for the European patent with unitary effect laid down in Rule 12, paragraph 1, relating to Unitary Patent Protection shall be 15%.

UPR.12 Filing of the statement by the patent proprietor

1 **Reduction of renewal fees in case of interest of the proprietor to grant a license**
If the proprietor files a statement with the EPO indicating an intention to grant a license to any person in return for a license fee, the renewal fees are reduced by 15%. For more details, see **UPR.12**.

Art. 4 Compensation for translation costs

(1) The amount of the lump sum provided for in Rule 11 relating to Unitary Patent Protection shall be EUR 500.

UPR.11 Level of compensation

1 **Compensation for translation costs**
The UPR provide (in particular in **UPR.8**) that certain proprietors can, upon request, obtain compensation for translation costs incurred as a result of filing a European patent application in a non-EPO language. **UPR.9** defines how the compensation is requested, and **UPR.10** how the request is examined.

(2) The administrative fee provided for in Rule 10, paragraph 4, relating to Unitary Patent Protection shall be 50% of the lump sum referred to in paragraph 1.

UPR.10 Examination of the request and grant of compensation

Art. 5 Fees, expenses and prices laid down by the President of the European Patent Office

The administrative fees provided for in the Rules relating to Unitary Patent Protection and the fees and expenses charged for any services rendered by the European Patent Office other than those specified in the present Rules shall be payable in the amounts laid down by the President of the European Patent Office pursuant to Article 3 of the Rules relating to Fees under the EPC.

Rfees3 EPC Fees, expenses and prices laid down by the President of the Office

1 **Other fees payable to the EPO**
An examplc of such a fee is the administrative fee for registration of a transfer or license.

Art. 6 Common provisions governing procedure

The following provisions of the Rules relating to Fees under the EPC, as amended, shall apply mutatis mutandis: Articles 4 to 8, Article 12 and Article 13.

Rfees4 EPC Due dates for fees
Rfees5 EPC Payment of fees
Rfees6 EPC Particulars concerning payments
Rfees7 EPC Date to be considered as the date on which payment is made
Rfees8 EPC Insufficiency of the amount paid
Rfees12 EPC Refund of insignificant amounts
Rfees13 EPC Termination of financial obligations

1 **General issues about fees**
The RfeesUPP refer to the Rules relating to Fees as in force at any particular moment ('as amended') for any general matters concerning fee payment that is not specifically addressed in RfeesUPP.

2 **Repayments**
If a fee for a unitary patent is paid which is not due (which can happen if the payer does not use CFP for the payment; see **Rfees5:1**), the EPO will automatically repay the amount to the deposit account used for making the payment (ADA 9.6 as amended by OJ 2024 A81).

Art. 7 Review of renewal fee level and report on specific entities

No later than five years from the date of application of Regulation (EU) No 1257/2012, and every five years thereafter,

(a) the European Patent Office shall submit a report to the Select Committee of the Administrative Council assessing the financial impact of the European patent with unitary effect on the budget of the European Patent Organisation and on the renewal fee income of the participating Member States and, where necessary, make an appropriate proposal for adjusting the level of renewal fees;

(b) the European Patent Office shall, after consultation of the European Commission, submit a report to the Select Committee of the Administrative Council on the use of the European patent with unitary effect by specific entities, such as small and medium-sized enterprises, and, where necessary, make proposals with a view to improving their access to the European patent with unitary effect.

1 **Follow-up of the system and review of the amount of renewal fee**
Five years after entry into force of the unitary patent system, at the latest, the EPO must prepare a report on the use of the UP as well as on its financial impact on the European Patent Organisation. It can be expected that such a report will actually be prepared earlier. After an initial adjustment, the amount of the renewal fees can only be increased every five years.

The budgetary and financial rules were published in OJ 2016 A41.

Cross-reference index

EPC1973 - EPC2000

The list compares the provisions of EPC1973 with thematically corresponding provisions of EPC2000. The list is an amended version of the list published in Special edition 1 of OJ 2007, p. 210.

EPC1973	EPC2000
-	Art. 4a
Art. 16 (elmts)	R. 10
Art. 18(1)	R. 10
Art. 52(4)	Art. 53(c)
Art. 54(4)	-
Art. 54(5)	Art. 54(4)
-	Art. 54(5)
Art. 61(1) (elmts)	R. 16
Art. 77 (elmts)	R. 37
Art. 78(2) (elmts)	R. 38
Art. 79(2) (elmts)	R. 39(1)
Art. 79(3) (elmts)	R. 39(3), (4)
Art. 80 (elmts)	R. 40
Art. 88(1) (elmts)	R. 53(1), (3)
Art. 90(1)(a)	Art. 90(1)
Art. 90(1)(b)	R. 57(e)
Art. 90(1)(c)	R. 57(a)
Art. 90(2)	Art. 90(2), (4)
Art. 90(3)	Art. 78(2); Art. 14(2)
Art. 91(1)	Art. 90(3); R. 57
Art. 91(2)	Art. 90(4)
Art. 91(3)	Art. 90(5)
Art. 91(4)	R. 39(2)
Art. 91(5)	Art. 90(5); R. 60
Art. 91(6)	R. 56
Art. 92(2)	R. 65
Art. 93(1)	Art. 93(1), (2)
Art. 93(2)	R. 68(1)
Art. 94(2)	Art. 94(1); R. 70(1)
Art. 94(3)	Art. 94(2)
Art. 95	-
Art. 96(1)	R. 70(2)
Art. 96(2)	Art. 94(3)
Art.96(3)	Art.94(4); R. 70(3)
Art. 97(1), (2)	Art. 97(2), (1)
Art. 97(3)	R. 71(7)
Art. 97(4), (5)	-
Art. 99(3)	R. 75
Art. 99(4), (5)	Art. 99(3), (4)
Art. 101(2)	Art. 101(1)
Art. 102(1), (2)	Art. 101(2)
Art. 102(3)	Art. 101(3)(a)
-	Art. 101(3)(b)

EPC1973	EPC2000
Art. 102(4), (5)	R. 82(2), (3)
Art. 104(2) (elmts)	R. 88(1), (3)
Art. 105 (elmts)	R. 89
-	Art. 105a-c
Art. 106(2)	R. 98
Art. 106(3)	Art. 106(2)
Art. 106(4), (5)	Art. 106(3); R. 97
Art. 110(2), (3)	R. 100(2), (3)
-	Art. 112a
Art. 115(1) (elmts)	R. 114(1)
Art. 115(2)	R. 114(2)
Art. 117(2)	R. 119(1)
Art. 117(3)	R. 118
Art. 117(4) - (6)	R. 120
Art. 121(1) (elmts)	Art. 121(3)
Art. 121(2), (3)	R. 135(1), (3)
-	Art. 121(2), (4)
Art. 122(2) - (4)	R. 136(1), (2), (4)
Art. 122(5)	Art. 122(4); R. 136(3)
Art. 126	Rfees13(1), (2), (3)
Art. 134(3) - (7)	Art. 134(4) - (8)
Art. 134(8)	Art. 134a(1)
-	Art. 134a(2)
Art. 135(2)	Art. 135(4); R. 155(1)
Art. 136(1)	Art. 135(3); R. 155(2)
Art. 136(2)	Art. 135(2), (4); R. 155(3)
-	Art. 138(3)
-	Art. 149a
Art. 150(3)	Art. 153(2)
Art. 150(4)	Art. 150(2)
Art. 151(1) (elmts)	R. 157
Art. 151(2), (3)	-
Art. 152(1) - (3)	R. 157(1), (3), (4)
Art. 153(2)	R. 159(2)
Art. 154(1), (2)	Art. 152
Art. 154(3)	R. 158(3)
Art. 155(1), (2)	Art. 152
Art. 155(3)	R. 158(3)
Art. 156	Art. 153(1)
Art. 157(1) - (3)	Art. 153(6), (7)
Art. 158(1), (2)	Art. 153(3), (5)

EPC1973	EPC2000
Art. 158(3)	Art. 153(4)
Art. 159 - 162	-
Art. 163(1) - (4), (6)	Art. 134(3), (4), (7)
Art. 163(5), (7)	-
Art. 167	-
-	R. 1
-	R. 2
R. 1	R. 3
R. 2	R. 4
R. 4 (elmts)	R. 36(2)
R. 5	R. 5
R. 6	R. 6, 7a(1), (2), (5), (6)
R. 7	R. 7
R. 8	R. 8
-	R. 10
R. 9	R. 11
R. 10	R. 12
R. 11	R. 13
R. 12	R. 9
R. 13(1) - (5)	R. 14
R. 13(4)	R. 78(1)
R. 14	R. 15
-	R. 16
R. 15(1), (2)	R. 17
R. 15(3)	-
R. 16(1), (2)	R. 18
R. 16(3)	R. 78(2)
R. 17	R. 19
R. 18	R. 20
R. 19	R. 21
R. 20	R. 22
R. 21	R. 23
R. 22	R. 24
R. 23	R. 25
R. 23a	-
R. 23b	R. 26
R. 23c	R. 27
R. 23d	R. 28
R. 23e	R. 29
R. 24	R. 35
R. 25	R. 36
R. 26	R. 41
R. 27	R. 42
R. 27a(1), (4)	R. 30
R. 27a(2), (3)	-
R. 28(1), (2)	R. 31
R. 28(4), (5)	R. 32
R. 28(3), (6) - (9)	R. 33
R. 28a	R. 34
R. 29	R. 43
R. 30	R. 44
R. 31	R. 45

EPC1973	EPC2000
R. 32	R. 49
R. 33	R. 47
R. 34	R. 48
R. 35	R. 49
R. 36(1) - (3)	R. 50
R. 36(4)	-
R. 36(5)	R. 2(1)
R. 37	R. 51
R. 38(1), (2), (6)	R. 52
R. 38(3) - (5)	R. 53
R. 38a	R. 54
R. 39	R. 55
R. 40	R. 57
R. 41(1)	R. 58
R. 41(2), (3)	-
-	R. 59
R. 42	R. 60
R. 43	R. 56
R. 44	R. 61
R. 44a	R. 62
R. 45	R. 63
R. 46	R. 64
-	R. 65
R. 47	R. 66
R. 48	R. 67
R. 49	R. 68
R. 50	R. 69
R. 51(1)	R. 70(2)
R. 51(2) - (11)	R. 71, 71a
R. 52	R. 72
R. 53	R. 73
R. 54	R. 74
-	R. 75
R. 55	R. 76
R. 56	R. 77
-	R. 78
R. 57	R. 79
R. 57a	R. 80
R. 58(1) - (3)	R. 81
R. 58(4) - (8)	R. 82
R. 59	R. 83
R. 60	R. 84
R. 61	R. 85
R. 61a	R. 86
R. 62	R. 87
R. 62a	R. 87
R. 63	R. 88
-	R. 89 - 98
R. 64	R. 99
R. 65	R. 101
R. 66(1)	R. 100(1)
R. 66(2)	R. 102
R. 67	R. 103
-	R. 104 - 110

EPC1973	EPC2000	EPC1973	EPC2000
R. 68	R. 111	R. 87	R. 138
R. 69	R. 112	R. 88	R. 139
R. 70	R. 113	R. 89	R. 140
-	R. 114	R. 90	R. 142
R. 71	R. 115	R. 91	Rfees13(4)
R. 71a	R. 116	R. 92	R. 143
R. 72(1)	R. 117	R. 93	R. 144
R. 72(2)	R. 118	R. 94	R. 145
R. 72(3), (4)	R. 119	R. 95	R. 146
-	R. 120	R. 95a	R. 147
R. 73	R. 121	R. 96	-
R. 74	R. 122	R. 97	R. 148
R. 75	R. 123	R. 98	R. 149
R. 76	R. 124	R. 99	R. 150
R. 77	R. 125	R. 100	R. 151
R. 78	R. 126	R. 101	R. 152
-	R. 127	-	R. 153
R. 79	R. 128	R. 102	R. 154
R. 80	R. 129	-	R. 155
R. 81	R. 130	R. 103	R. 156
R. 82	R. 125(4)	R. 104	R. 157
R. 83	R. 131	R. 105	R. 158
R. 84	R. 132	R. 106	-
R. 84a	R. 133	R. 107	R. 159
R. 85	R. 134	R. 108	R. 160
R. 85a	-	R. 109	R. 161
R. 85b	-	R. 110	R. 162
-	R. 135	R. 111	R. 163
-	R. 136	R. 112	R. 164
R. 86	R. 137	-	R. 165

The list compares the provisions of the Implementing Regulations of EPC2000 with thematically corresponding provisions of the Implementing Regulations of EPC1973. The list is an amended version of the list published in Special edition 1 of OJ 2007, p.212.

EPC2000	EPC1973
R.1	-
R.2	-
R.3	R.1
R.4	R.2
R.5	R.5
R.6	R.6
R.7	R.7
R.7a(1), (2), (5), (6)	R.6(3)
R.7b	-
R.8	R.8
R.9	R.12
R.10	Art.16; Art.18(1)
R.11	R.9
R.12	R.10
R.12a	-
R.12b	R.10
R.12c	-
R.12d	-
R.13	R.11
R.14	R.13(1) - (3), (5)
R.15	R.14
R.16	Art.61(1)
R.17	R.15(1), (2)
R.18	R.16(1), (2)
R.19	R.17
R.21	R.19
R.22	R.20
R.23	R.21
R.24	R.22
R.25	R.23
R.26	R.23b
R.27	R.23c
R.28	R.23d
R.29	R.23e
R.30	R.27a(1), (4)
R.31	R.28(1), (2)
R.32	R.28(4), (5)
R.33	R.28(3), (6) - (9)
R.34	R.28a
R.35	R.24
R.36	R.4; R.25
R.37	Art.77
R.38	Art.78(2)
R.39	Art.79(2), (3)
R.40	Art.80
R.41	R.26
R.42	R.27

EPC2000	EPC1973
R.43	R.29
R.44	R.30
R.45	R.31
R.47	R.33
R.48	R.34
R.49	R.35
R.50	R.36
R.51	R.37
R.52	R.38(1), (2), (6)
R.53	R.38(3) - (5)
R.54	R.38a
R.55	R.39
R.56	R.43
R.57	Art.91(1); R.40; R.41
R.58	Art.91(1); R.40; R.41
R.59	-
R.60	R.42
R.61	R.44
R.62	R.44a
R.62a	-
R.63	R.45
R.64	R.46
R.65	Art.92(2)
R.66	R.47
R.67	R.48
R.68	Art.93(2); R.49
R.69	R.50
R.70	Art.94(2), (3); Art.96(1); R.51(1)
R.70b	-
R.71(1) - (3)	R.51(2) - (4)
R.71(4)	R.51(7)
R.71(5) - (6)	R.51(5) (elmts)
R.71(7)	R.51(8)
R.71a(1) (elmts)	R.51(11)
R.71a(2)	-
R.71a(3)	R.51(8a)
R.71a(4)	R.51(9)
R.71a(5)	-
R.71a(6)	R.51(6) (elmts)
R.72	R.52
R.73	R.53
R.74	R.54
R.75	Art.99(3)
R.76	R.55
R.77	R.56

EPC2000	EPC1973	EPC2000	EPC1973
R.78	R.13(4), R.16(3)	R.122	R.74
R.79	R.57	R.123	R.75
R.80	R.57a	R.124	R.76
R.81	R.58(1) - (3)	R.125	R.77, R.82
R.82	R.58(4) - (8)	R.126	R.78
R.83	R.59	R.127	-
R.84	R.60	R.128	R.79
R.85	R.61	R.129	R.80
R.87	R.62, R.62a	R.130	R.81
R.88	R.63	R.131	R.83
R.89	Art.105	R.132	R.84
R.90	-	R.133	R.84a
R.91	-	R.134	R.85
R.92	-	R.135	Art.121(2), (3)
R.93	-	R.136	Art.122(2) - (5)
R.94	-	R.137	R.86
R.95	-	R.139	R.88
R.96	-	R.140	R.89
R.97	Art.106(4), (5)	R.141	Art.124(1) (elmts)
R.98	Art.106(2)	R.142	R.90
R.99	R.64	R.143	R.92
R.100	Art.110(2), (3); R.66(1)	R.144	R.93
		R.145	R.94
R.101	R.65	R.146	R.95
R.102	R.66(2)	R.147	R.95a
R.103	R.67	R.148	R.97
R.104	-	R.149	R.98
R.105	-	R.150	R.99
R.106	-	R.151	R.100
R.107	-	R.152	R.101
R.108	-	R.153	-
R.109	-	R.154	R.102
R.110	-	R.155	Art.135(2); Art.136(1), (2)
R.111	R.68		
R.113	R.70	R.156	R.103
R.114	Art.115	R.157	Art.151(1); Art.152, R.104
R.115	R.71		
R.116	R.71a	R.158	R.105
R.117	R.72(1)	R.159	Art.153(2), R.107
R.118	R.72(2)	R.160	R.108
R.119	Art.117(2); R.72(3), (4)	R.161	R.109
		R.162	R.110
R.120	Art.117(4) - (6)	R.163	R.111
R.121	R.73	R.165	-

Case Law Table

The table gives the number of the decisions and references to the sections of the book.

A reference without a colon refers to the text of the law. A reference with a colon refers to the text of the notes to the law. Hence, Art.90(3) refers to Article 90(3) EPC, R.46(1):2 refers to note 2 of Rule 46(1) EPC. 'P' refers to the Preamble of the EPC and 'Ante' before a reference refers to the section preceding that reference.

Decisions of the Enlarged Board of Appeal

G1/83	Art.54(5):2.3, Art.112(3):4	Allowed the use of Swiss style second medical use claims which are no longer valid following G2/08; a use-limited compound/ composition claim is now allowed instead under Art.54(5) EPC2000.
G5/83	P:2.2, P:2.2.2, P:2.3, Art.52(1):1, Art.53:3, Art.54(4):2, Art.54(5):2.3, Art.112(3):4, Art.125:1.2	Consolidated with G1/83.
G6/83	Art.54(5):2.3, Art.112(3):4	Consolidated with G1/83.
G1/84	Art.99(1):2.1, Art.99(1):2.3, Art.112(3):1, Art.112(3):4, Art.177(1):1, R.77(1):1.2	Patent proprietor may file an opposition; reversed by G9/93.
G1/86	P:2.2.2, Art.108:6.4, Art.112a(4):1, Art.122(1):1, Art.122(1):2, Art.125:1.2, R.101(1):3	Art.122 is available for an opponent to file statement of grounds of appeal.
G1/88	Art.107:2, R.82(1):1, R.82(1):2, R.82(2):1	Opponent can appeal even when having made no comment on text intended for maintenance of the patent (R.58(4) EPC1973, R.82(1) EPC2000).
G2/88	Art.52(1):1, Art.52(2):2, Art.54(1):1, Art.54(1):5, Art.54(1):7.1, Art.54(1):7.2, Art.54(2):3.6.2, Art.84:1.3, Art.123(3):2, Art.1:1	Change of category of claim during opposition proceedings is allowable if protection is not extended. Claim to a compound can be amended to use of the compound. Technical effect underlying a new use of a known product is a functional technical feature of a claim to the new use, rendering it novel.
G4/88	Art.99(1):2.4	Opposition is transferable only with business assets to which the opposition relates.
G5/88	Art.5(3):1, Art.10:1, Art.125:2, Art.125:2.1	Agreement with German patent office relating to the filing of documents is not valid prior to opening of EPO Berlin office since the President had no power to sign (this agreement is no longer in force).
G6/88	Art.54(1):7.2, R.43(2):1	Consolidated with last point of G2/88.
G7/88	Art.10:1	Consolidated with G5/88.
G8/88	Art.10:1	Consolidated with G5/88.

G3/89	Art.123(2):1.2, R.139:1, R.139:4	Correction of description, claims and drawings of application under R.88 EPC1973 (R.139 EPC2000) is possible if skilled person would derive the correction directly and unambiguously, using common general knowledge, at the date of filing.
G1/90	Art.101(1):6, R.82(3):1, R.112(1):2, R.112(1):3	Revocation in opposition proceedings for (not paying the publishing fee, up to 01.04.2024, or) not filing translations of the amended claims requires a decision (Art.102(4) and (5) EPC1973, R.82(3) EPC2000).
G2/90	Art.21:2, Art.21(3):1.2, Art.21(4):1, R.11(3):1	Legal BoA is competent to hear appeals against decisions taken by a three-member examining division if decision does not concern refusal or grant.
G1/91	Art.56:3.4, Art.82:3, Art.101(3):1, R.86:1	Compliance with Art.82 (unity of invention) is not to be considered when patent is amended in opposition proceedings.
G2/91	Art.107:3.1, Art.108:1	Party as of right in appeal cannot continue if the sole appellant withdraws appeal.
G3/91	Art.112(3):4	Availability of re-establishment if time limits for paying fees under EPC1973 were not complied with. No longer has any relevance under EPC2000.
G4/91	Art.105(1):1.1, Art.105(1):1.2, R.93(1):1	Notice of intervention can be filed within the period for filing a notice of appeal contesting a decision of the opposition division, provided an appeal is also validly filed. Otherwise the intervention has no legal effect.
G5/91	Art.19(2):1, Art.24:2, Art.24(2):1, Art.106(1):2, Art.106(2):1, Art.125:1	The requirement for impartiality applies in principle to employees of the departments of the first instance of the EPO taking part in decision-making activities affecting the rights of any party.
G6/91	Art.14(2):1, Art.14(4):1, Art.14(4):6, Art.94(1):3, R.7a(1):1, R.7a(1):2, R.7a(1):3	Reduction of fees under (now) R.7a(1)) available only if the translation is filed no earlier than simultaneously (Art.14(2) EPC1973).
G7/91	Art.110:11, R.84(2):1	Appeal proceedings are terminated, in so far as substantive issues are concerned, when the sole appellant withdraws its appeal.
G8/91	Art.110:11, Art.114(1):3	Consolidated with G7/91.
G9/91	Art.101(3):1, Art.110:5, Art.111(1):1, Art.114(1):1, Art.114(1):3, R.76(2):4.1, R.76(2):4.2, R.76(2):4.3.2	Opposition division or BoA may not examine the validity of an independent claim in a patent if the validity of that claim is not contested by the opponent (R.55(c) EPC1973, R.76(2)(c) EPC2000), but if an opposed independent claim falls, the validity of claims dependent upon it may be considered (even if not explicitly opposed) if their validity is prima facie in doubt.

G10/91	Art.101(1):5, Art.101(2):1, Art.110:5, Art.110:8, Art.111(1):1, Art.114(1):3, Art.115:4, R.76(2):4.3.1, R.76(2):4.3.2, R.81(1):1	Opposition division is not obliged to consider grounds of opposition not invoked in notice of opposition (R.55(c) EPC1973, R.76(2)(c) EPC2000). In principle, only grounds substantiated in notice are considered; other grounds can exceptionally be considered by opposition division if they are prima facie prejudicial to the maintenance of the patent. Fresh grounds for opposition may be considered in appeal proceedings only with the approval of the proprietor.
G12/91	Art.101(1):6, Art.105(1):1.2, Art.110:9, Art.116(1):1, R.10:1, R.36(1):2.1.2, R.71a(2):1, R.79(1):1, R.80:1, R.111(1):2, R.111(1):3, R.111(1):4, R.137(3):1, R.138:1, R.139:2	Decision-making process in written proceedings is complete when the decision is handed to the postal service of the EPO.
G1/92	Art.54(1):1, Art.54(2):3.6.2	The chemical composition of product is state of the art if the product as such is available to the public and can be analysed and reproduced by a skilled person. Same principle applies mutatis mutandis to any other product.
G2/92	Art.92:4, R.64(1):2.1, R.64(1):3, R.64(1):4, R.137(5):1, R.137(5):1.1, R.164(1):2.4	If further search fees (R.46 EPC1973, R.64 EPC2000) are not paid where there is no unity of invention, the claims to be examined may not be directed to an unsearched invention.
G3/92	Art.60(1):1, Art.60(3):1, Art.61(2):1, Art.61(2):3, R.16(1):2, R.136(1):2.2	New application under Art.61(1)(b) may be filed even if original application is no longer pending.
G4/92	Art.113(1):1, R.115(2):1	A decision in inter partes oral proceedings against a party summoned but not present may not be based on facts advanced for the first time in those oral proceedings. New evidence may not be considered unless it has been previously notified and merely supports the submissions made. New arguments may always be used.
G5/92	Art.112(3):4	Availability of re-establishment under EPC1973. No longer relevant under EPC2000.
G6/92	Art.112(3):4	Consolidated with G5/92.
G9/92	Art.107:3.2, Art.107:3.2.1, Art.107:3.2.2, Art.111(1):1, R.99(1):3	Prohibition of reformatio in peius in an appeal against a decision to maintain a patent in amended form (sole appellant, whether proprietor or opponent, cannot be put in a worse position than if they had not appealed).
G10/92	R.71a(2):1	Availability of re-establishment under EPC1973. No longer relevant under EPC2000.
G1/93	Art.69(2):1, Ante Art. 87:1, Art.123(2):1, Art.123(2):1.2, Art.123(2):2.1, Art.123(2):2.4.3, Art.123(3):3, Art.125:2.1	Inescapable trap when a limiting amendment made during grant proceedings is challenged for non-compliance with Art.123(2) during opposition proceedings.

G2/93	R.31(2):1, R.31(2):2	The accession number of deposited biological material cannot be filed after the expiry of the time limit of R.28(2)(a) EPC1973 (R.31(2)(a) EPC2000).
G3/93	Art.88(4):3, Art.112(1):1	Document having same technical contents as priority document but published during the priority interval is Art.54(2) prior art against EP application claiming that priority to the extent that the priority is invalid. This may be the case where priority document and EP application concern different inventions and EP claims subject-matter not disclosed in priority document.
G4/93	Art.107:3.2, R.99(1):3	Consolidated with G9/92.
G5/93	Art.112(3):1	Availability of re-establishment under EPC1973. No longer relevant under EPC2000.
G7/93	Art.110:6, R.71(6):2, R.71a(2):1, R.116(2):1, R.137(3):1	A board should only overrule the way in which a first instance department has exercised its discretion if that department has not exercised its discretion in accordance with the right principles or in an unreasonable way (r.2.6) (headnotes no longer relevant under EPC2000).
G8/93	Art.110:11, R.84(2):1	If the opponent as sole appellant withdraws the opposition, the appeal proceedings are terminated.
G9/93	P:2.2.1, Art.99(1):2.3, Art.105a:1, Art.112(3):1, Art.112(3):4, Art.125:2.1, Art.177(1):1	The patent proprietor may not file an opposition.
G10/93	Art.97(2):1, Art.107:3.2, Art.110:5, Art.114(1):3	In appeal following the refusal of an application, the BoA has a right to consider whether all requirements of the EPC are met, even those the examining division did not consider or considered to be met.
G1/94	Art.105:1, Art.105(1):1.3, Art.107:1, R.79(4):1	Intervention of an assumed infringer admissible during pending appeal and may be based on any ground of opposition.
G2/94	Art.134(1):2, Art.134(1):2.1, Art.134(1):2.3	Accompanying persons may be allowed to speak during ex parte oral proceedings if certain requirements are met.
G1/95	R.76(2):4.3.3	Non-patentability under Art.52(2) is a fresh ground of opposition when raised in appeal (only novelty and inventive step having been raised at first instance) and cannot be introduced without consent of patentee.
G2/95	R.40(2):2, R.139:4	Complete documents of EP application cannot be replaced by way of correction under R.88 EPC1973 (R.139 EPC2000) by other documents. Now allowable to some extent under R.56a.
G3/95	Art.112(1):3	Requirement of 'different decisions' for admissibility of a referral to the EBoA.

G4/95	Art.117:1, Art.117(1):2, Art.134(1):2, Art.134(1):2.2	Accompanying persons may be allowed to speak during inter partes oral proceedings if certain requirements are met.
G6/95	Art.23(4):1, Art.110:1	R.71a EPC1973 (R.116 EPC2000) is not binding on the BoA (but see Art.15 RPBA which now requires a substantive communication from the board in advance of oral proceedings).
G7/95	R.76(2):4.3.3	Lack of novelty is a fresh ground of opposition, compared to lack of inventive step; a finding of lack of novelty over the closest prior art however leads to a lack of inventive step.
G8/95	Art.21(3):2, R.140:1, R.140:3.1	Appeal of decision taken by examining division to refuse to correct decision to grant under R.89 EPC1973 (R.140 EPC2000) to be heard by technical board of appeal. G1/10 also relevant.
G1/97	Art.21:1, Art.111(1):3, Art.112(3):4, Art.112a:1, Art.127:1, R.140:2	Decision of a BoA could not be reviewed under EPC1973. Petition for review now possible under EPC2000.
G2/97	Art.125:2.2, R.112(1):3	The EPO only has a good faith duty to inform a party of a missing fee (here appeal fee) if it could be inferred that the party would otherwise miss the time limit for paying the fee.
G3/97	Art.99(1):2.1, Art.99(1):2.2, Art.99(1):2.4, Art.117(1):4, Art.134:1, R.76(2):5	Oppositions filed by a strawman are not as such inadmissible.
G4/97	Art.99(1):2.2	Consolidated with G3/97.
G1/98	Art.53:2.1, Art.64(2):1, Art.64(2):2	A claim wherein specific plant varieties are not individually claimed is not excluded from patentability under Art.53(b) even though it may embrace plant varieties.
G2/98	Art.52(1):1, Ante Art. 87:1, Art.87(1):4, Art.88:1, Art.88(3):1, Art.88(3):2, Art.88(4):1, Art.88(4):2, Art.123(2):1.2, Art.123(2):2.1, Art.123(2):2.3, Art.123(2):2.4.4	Subject-matter of a claim only enjoys priority if the skilled person can derive the subject-matter directly and unambiguously, using common general knowledge, from the previous application as a whole.
G3/98	Art.55(1):1, Art.80:4, Art.112(1):3	The six-month period of Art.55(1) (evident abuse) is calculated from the filing date – any priority claimed is irrelevant.
G4/98	Art.76:2, Art.76(1):6, Art.76(2):1, Art.79(2):1.2, Art.86(1):4, Art.87(3):1, Art.90(5):2, Art.112(1):3, Art.121(2):2, Art.122(2):2, R.17(3):1, R.36(1):2.1.3, R.36(4):1, R.159(1):5.2, R.160(2):1	A loss of rights associated with the non-payment of a designation under EPC1973 occurred at the expiry of the normal time limit for paying the fee and had no retroactive effect.

G1/99	Art.107:2, Art.107:3.2.2, Art.114(1):1, R.76(2):4.3.2, R.80:3, R.99(1):3	Prohibition of Reformatio in peius in case of opponent as sole appellant and exceptions.
G2/99	Art.112(1):2	Consolidated with G3/98.
G3/99	Art.99(1):2.1, Art.99(1):2.5, Art.99(1):3.3, Art.107:1, Art.112(1):2, R.151(1):1, R.151(1):2	Joint opponents filing a single opposition in common need to pay only one opposition fee and must act through a common representative.
G1/02	Art.16:1, R.11(3):1, R.112(2):1	Delegation of the power to take decisions involving no technical or legal difficulties to formalities officers is possible.
G1/03	Art.53:3.2, Art.53:3.3.1, Art.54(1):6, Art.54(3):1, Art.83:2.1, Art.83:2.2, Art.83:3.1, Art.88(4):2, Art.115:2, Art.123(2):1.2, Art.123(2):2.4, Art.123(2):2.4.2, Art.123(2):2.4.3, Art.123(2):2.4.4, Art.123(3):3, Art.139:1	Undisclosed disclaimers are permitted in certain cases, e.g. to restore novelty over a prior right under Art.54(3), to delimit the claim against an accidental anticipation in a remote field under Art.54(2), and to disclaim non-technical subject-matter.
G2/03	Art.53:3.2, Art.123(2):2.4.3	Consolidated with G1/03.
G3/03	Art.109:1, Art.112(1):3, R.103(1):1, R.103(6):1	Competent department for deciding on reimbursement of appeal fee in case of interlocutory revision.
G4/03	Art.105(1):1.3	Terminated without decision.
G1/04	Art.52(1):1, Art.53:3, Art.53:3.1, Art.53:3.4.1, Art.53:3.4.2, Art.53:3.4.3, Art.84:1.2, Art.112(1):1, Art.112(1):3	Definition of diagnostic methods as excluded under Art.53(c). To be excluded, a claim must specify both the diagnosis for curative purposes stricto sensu (representing the deductive medical or veterinary decision phase as a purely intellectual exercise), and the steps necessary for making that diagnosis and the interactions of a technical nature with the human or animal body which take place during those steps.
G2/04	Art.99(1):2.4, Art.107:1, Art.112(1):1, Art.133:2.2, R.99(1):1, R.101(2):1	Opponent status in an opposition cannot be freely transferred.
G3/04	Art.105(1):1.1, Art.105(1):1.3, Art.105(2):1, Art.107:1	After withdrawal of the sole appeal, the proceedings may not be continued with a third party who intervened during the appeal proceedings.
G1/05	Art.24(1):1, Art.24(1):2, Art.24(2):1, Art.24(3):1, Art.76:2, Art.76(1):9, Art.106(2):1, Art.123(2):2.1, R.36(1):3	A divisional application containing subject-matter extending beyond the content of the parent application as filed can be amended later in the procedure in order to remedy this deficiency. Principle of the prohibition of double patenting recognised.

G1/06	Art.76:2, Art.76(1):1, Art.76(1):2, Art.76(1):6, Art.76(1):7, Art.76(1):8, Art.76(1):9, Art.123(2):1.2, Art.123(2):2.1, R.36(1):1	Sequence of divisionals. Each divisional application divided from a divisional itself can only include subject-matter that is directly and unambiguously derivable from the subject-matter of its direct parent application and each previous application in the sequence.
G2/06	Art.53:1.1, Art.53:1.2, R.26(1):1, R.28(1):2	R.28(1)(c) forbids the patenting of claims directed to products which - as described in the application - at the filing date, could only be prepared by a method which necessarily involved the destruction of the human embryos from which said products are derived, even if said method is not part of the claims.
G3/06	Art.76(1):9	Terminated without decision.
G1/07	Art.53:3.2, Art.53:3.3.1, Art.53:3.4.1, Art.53:3.4.2, Art.53:3.5, Art.53:3.6	A method, in which, when carried out, maintaining the life and health of the subject is important, and which comprises or encompasses an invasive step representing a substantial physical intervention on the body which requires professional medical expertise to be carried out and which entails a substantial health risk even when carried out with the required professional care and expertise, is excluded from patentability as a method for treatment of the human or animal body by surgery.
G2/07	Art.33(1):4, Art.52(1):1, Art.53:2.2, Art.111(2):1.2, R.26(5):1	A non-microbiological process for the production of plants which contains or consists of the steps of sexually crossing the whole genomes of plants and of subsequently selecting plants is in principle excluded from patentability as being 'essentially biological' within the meaning Art.53(b).
G1/08	Art.53:2.2	Consolidated with G2/07.
G2/08	Art.24:2, Art.24(3):1, Art.54(4):2, Art.54(5):2, Art.54(5):2.1, Art.54(5):2.2, Art.54(5):2.3, Art.112(3):1, Art.112(3):4	Swiss-type claims no longer allowed for applications with a priority/filing date later than 28.01.2011.
G3/08	Art.4(2):2, Art.24(3):1, Art.52(2):6, Art.112(1):1, Art.112(1):3	Referral inadmissible. Confirmed that a claim having a combination of technical and non-technical features is not excluded under Art.52(2); the non-technical features do not contribute to inventive step (r.10.13).
G4/08	Art.129:2, R.3(1):2, R.159(1):2.1	If an international patent application has been filed and published under the PCT in an official language of the EPO, it is not possible, on entry into the European phase, to file a translation of the application into another EPO official language in order to change the language of proceedings.

G1/09	Art.90(5):2, Art.106(1):3, R.36(1):2, R.36(1):2.1, R.36(1):2.1.1, R.36(1):2.1.2, R.159:1	A divisional application can validly be filed in the appeal period after a refusal of an application regardless of whether an appeal is filed or not.
G1/10	Art.21(3):2, R.80:2, R.140:1, R.140:3.1	R.140 is not available to correct the text of a patent.
G2/10	Art.54(1):1, Art.54(1):6.2, Art.54(2):4.1, Art.76(1):7, Art.76(1):8, Art.84:3, Art.87(1):4, Art.88(4):2, Art.97(2):2, Art.123(2):1, Art.123(2):1.2, Art.123(2):2.1, Art.123(2):2.4, Art.123(2):2.4.2, Art.123(2):2.4.3, Art.123(3):3, R.18(1):1	An amendment complies with Art.123(2) if the subject-matter of the amended claim is directly and unambiguously disclosed in the application as filed, be it explicitly or implicitly ('gold standard', r.4.3). This also applies to amendments disclaiming subject-matter disclosed in the application as filed (disclosed disclaimer).
G1/11	Art.21(3):1, Art.21(3):1.2	A technical board of appeal is competent to hear an appeal against a decision refusing a refund of a search fee.
G1/12	R.22(3):1, R.76(2):2.2, R.101(1):1.2, R.101(2):1, R.139:2, R.139:2.1, R.139:2.2, R.139:3, R.139:3.2, R.139:3.3, Rfees5(2):2.1.1	The erroneous identification of the appellant can be corrected. Proceedings before the EPO are conducted in accordance with the principle of free evaluation of evidence.
G2/12	P:2.2.2, Art.53:2.2, Art.112(3):4	Exclusion of essentially biological processes for the production of plants in Art.53(b) has no effect on the patentability of product claims. Reversed for applications filed on or after 01.07.2017 by G3/19 and R.28(2).
G1/13	Art.107:1	Where an opponent (company) ceases to exist and is subsequently retroactively restored under national law, party status is maintained retroactively.
G2/13	Art.53:2.2, Art.112(3):4	Consolidated with G2/12.
G3/14	Art.84:1, Art.84:4, Art.100:2, Art.101(3):1, R.80:1	Claims amended during opposition proceedings are examined for clarity under Art.84 only to the extent that the amendment introduces a lack of clarity.
G1/15	Art.87(1):4, Art.87(1):6.3, Art.88:3, Art.88(3):1, Art.88(3):2, Art.88(4):2	Partial priority of a claim encompassing alternative subject-matter is acknowledged, provided that said alternative subject-matter has been disclosed for the first time, directly, or at least implicitly, unambiguously and in an enabling manner in the priority document.
G1/16	Art.123(2):2.4.3	Confirms the validity of G1/03 allowing undisclosed disclaimers.
G2301/16	Art.23(1):2, Art.23(1):3	Pressure by the president of the EPO on EBoA jeopardises its judicial independence.

G1/18	Art.108:4, Art.108:6.1, Art.108:6.2, Art.110:3, R.101(1):2, Rfees4:2, Rfees4(1):1	If the appeal fee is not paid and/or the notice of appeal filed in time, the appeal is deemed not to have been filed and the appeal fee is reimbursed. If no notice of appeal is filed, the appeal fee is also reimbursed.
G1/19	Art.52(2):1, Art.52(2):6, Art.56:1, Art.56:3, Art.56:3.2, Art.56:4, Art.56:4.1, Art.56:4.3	Inventive step of computer-implemented simulations should be assessed within the existing framework for computer-implemented inventions (COMVIK approach). Basing the simulation on technical principles underlying the simulated system/process is not sufficient.
G2/19	Art.6(2):3, Art.106(1):3, Art.116:1, Art.116(1):1, R.101(1):1.2	Holding appeal oral proceedings in Haar does not violate the EPC; purported appeal filed against a decision to grant a patent by a person who filed third party observations during grant proceedings has no suspensive effect and does not give rise to a right to oral proceedings.
G3/19	P:2.2.2, Art.23(3):1, Art.53:2, Art.53:2.2, Art.112(3):1, Art.112(3):4, Art.164(2):2, R.26(1):1, R.28(2):1	R.28(2) is not applicable to applications and patents having a filing date before 01.07.2017.
G4/19	Art.54(3):1, Art.76(1):7, Art.97(2):2, Art.125:1, Art.139(3):1, R.36(1):1	Double patenting: an EP application can be refused if it claims the same subject-matter as a granted patent of the same applicant which does not form part of the state of the art pursuant to Art.54(2) and (3).
G1/21	Art.116:2.1	Oral proceedings by videoconference are compatible with the EPC during a general emergency having an effect on travel, even without the consent of the parties.
G2/21	Art.52(1):1, Art.54(5):2.2, Art.56:1, Art.56:3, Art.56:3.2, Art.117(1):2, Art.117(1):4, R.29(3):1	Plausibility: later filed and/or published evidence may be used to prove a technical effect, provided a skilled person would derive this effect as being encompassed by the teaching of the application as filed and as embodied by the same originally disclosed invention.
G1/22	Ante Art. 87:1, Art.87(1):3, Art.87(1):3.1, Art.112(3):2	Presumption that applicant is entitled to priority if priority is correctly claimed.
G2/22	Art.87(1):3, Art.112(3):2	Consolidated with G1/22.
G1/23	Art.54(2):3.6.2, Art.112(3):3	Availability to the public, pending.
G1/24	Art.54(1):5, Art.69:1, Art.84:1.1	Interpretation of claims for patentability, pending.
G2/24	Art.105(1):1.3	Status of an intervener, pending

Decisions on petitions for review

R1/08	Art.112a(2):1, R.106:1	**R3/08**	Art.112a(5):1, R.106:1
R2/08	Art.112a(2):1, R.76(2):4.3.1, R.106:1	**R4/08**	R.106:1

Decisions of the Legal Board of Appeal

J11/89	R.139:2.3, R.139:3.1, R.139:3.1.1
J19/89	Art.134(8):1
J20/89	Art.150(2):2
J32/89	Art.120:3
J37/89	Art.106(2):1, Art.106(2):2, R.132(2):4
J3/90	R.134(2):1
J6/90	R.136(1):2.2
J7/90	Art.3:1, Art.90(1):2, R.139:2.1
J13/90	Art.125:2.2, R.136(1):2.1
J14/90	Art.169:1.2
J15/90	Art.125:2.2
J16/90	Art.112(1):1
J18/90	Art.129:2, R.3(2):1
J19/90	R.136(1):5
J27/90	R.136(1):2.1
J30/90	Art.169:1.2
J3/91	R.139:2.3, R.139:3.1.1, R.139:3.1.2
J4/91	Art.86:1, R.51(1):1, R.51(1):2, R.51(1):3, R.51(2):1, R.51(2):2, R.51(3):1, R.131(2):3, R.131(4):1, R.159(1):8.3, R.159(1):8.4, (2):1, (3):1
J6/91	R.139:1, R.139:2, R.139:3, R.139:3.1, R.139:3.1.1
J9/91	R.139:3.1.1
J11/91	Art.33(1):4, R.36(3):1, R.39(3):1
J14/91	Art.112(1):1, Art.128(2):1, R.115(1):1
J17/91	R.22:1, R.85:1
J2/92	R.52(2):3, R.139:2.3, R.139:3.1.1
J11/92	R.139:3.1.1
J15/92	Art.125:2.1, Art.125:2.2
J21/92	R.139:2.3
J27/92	Art.125:2.1, Art.125:2.2, Rfees8:2
J35/92	R.151(2):1
J41/92	Art.122(1):4, Art.125:2.2
J42/92	R.71(6):2, R.139:1, R.139:2, R.140:3.3
J43/92	R.112(1):3, R.112(1):4
J47/92	Art.112(1):1
J10/93	R.22:2
J18/93	Art.60(3):1, R.139:2.3, R.139:3.3
J7/94	R.139:3.1.1
J12/94	Art.125:2.2
J14/94	R.112(2):2
J16/94	R.101(1):1.3
J21/94	R.35(2):1
J27/94	Art.111(2):1.2, Art.125:2.1
J28/94	R.14(1):1
J29/94	R.100(3):1
J22/95	Art.112(1):1
J25/95	Art.125:2.1
J26/95	R.136(1):2, R.142(1):2
J32/95	R.71(2):1
J7/96	Art.97(3):1, R.14(1):1, R.36(1):2.1.1
J16/96	Art.23(3):1, R.152(11):1
J18/96	Art.90(1):2, R.103(1):1
J23/96	R.136(1):4
J24/96	R.64(2):1
J27/96	R.139:2.1
J4/97	R.67(2):3, R.139:2.3, R.139:3.2
J8/98	Art.111(1):1
J14/98	Art.150(2):2
J15/98	Art.112(1):1, Art.112(1):3
J17/98	Art.133:2, Art.133:2.2, R.152(4):1
J18/98	R.136(2):1
J5/99	Art.131(1):1
J9/99	R.125(4):1, R.152(4):1
J17/99	R.159:4.2
J18/99	Art.131(1):1, Art.134(8):1
J7/00	R.14(1):1
J14/00	Art.169:2, Art.169:3
J2/01	Art.59:1, Art.60(3):1, Art.76(1):2, Art.76(1):3, Art.76(1):8
J3/01	R.139:2.1
J8/01	R.139:2.3
J9/01	Art.112(1):1
J10/01	R.36(1):3
J6/03	R.14:1
J22/03	Art.89:1, Art.90(1):3
J24/03	Art.120:3, Art.122(1):2, R.36(1):2.1.1, R.36(1):3
J25/03	R.139:3.2
J28/03	Art.106(1):3, R.36(1):2.1.1
J33/03	R.14(3):1
J35/03	R.136(1):2.2
J18/04	Art.120:2, Art.120:3, Art.122(1):2, Art.122(1):3
J13/05	Art.122:1, R.134(2):1, R.134(5):1
J16/05	Art.72:1
J1/06	R.14(1):1
J15/06	R.14(1):1
J18/06	R.14(1):1
J10/07	Art.80:2, Art.172(1):2
J1/08	R.159(1):1.3
J2/08	Art.125:2.1
J16/08	R.139:2.1
J18/08	Art.90(5):1, R.82(3):1
J18/09	R.36(1):2, R.159:1

Decisions of the technical boards of appeal

T299/89	Art.107:2
T300/89	Art.94(3):2, Art.94(3):5
T338/89	Art.105(1):1.3
T357/89	Art.110:11
T386/89	Art.56:3.2
T387/89	Art.114(1):2
T418/89	R.31:2, R.31(1):1.2
T426/89	Art.123(3):2
T454/89	Art.84:1.3
T482/89	Art.54(2):2.1, Art.54(2):2.3, Art.54(2):3.6.1, Art.117(1):2
T516/89	R.144:2
T534/89	Art.114(2):1.1, Art.114(2):3.1
T538/89	R.77(1):1.2
T552/89	Art.56:3.4
T560/89	Art.56:2.4, Art.56:3.3.2
T563/89	Art.99(1):2.4
T564/89	Art.56:3.3.1, Art.56:3.3.7
T574/89	R.115(2):1
T576/89	Art.107:3.2.2
T603/89	Art.52(3):1
T611/89	Art.83:2.1.2
T665/89	R.50(3):2, R.101(1):2
T666/89	Art.54(2):4.2
T695/89	Art.110:11
T702/89	Art.99(1):3.2, Art.99(1):3.3, Art.119:2
T760/89	R.144:2
T765/89	Art.104(1):1
T767/89	Art.56:3.3.2
T772/89	Art.56:2.3
T774/89	Art.53:3.1, Art.53:3.3.1, Art.53:3.3.2
T780/89	Art.53:3.3.2
T783/89	R.103(1):2
T789/89	Art.110:11
T5/90	Art.123(3):2
T19/90	Art.53:1.2, R.28(1):3
T34/90	R.4(1):1
T47/90	Art.109:1
T54/90	Art.123(3):2
T55/90	Art.106(2):2
T86/90	Art.123(3):2
T95/90	Art.56:3.3.2
T97/90	Art.114(1):2, Art.114(2):2, Art.114(2):3.2
T154/90	Art.104(2):1, Art.106(3):1
T156/90	Art.107:2
T182/90	Art.53:3.1, Art.53:3.2, Art.53:3.3.1, Art.53:3.4.3
T204/90	Art.84:1.6.2
T270/90	Art.117:1
T288/90	Art.54(1):3
T290/90	Rfees8:2
T324/90	R.136(2):1
T358/90	Art.56:3.3.2
T376/90	Art.106(2):1
T390/90	Art.105(1):1.3
T409/90	Art.88(4):2
T484/90	R.115(2):1
T490/90	R.45(2):2
T553/90	Art.21(4):1, R.85:1
T591/90	Art.56:8
T595/90	Art.56:3.3.1, Art.84:3.2, R.111(1):2
T664/90	Art.64(2):2
T689/90	Art.83:2.1.2, Art.123(2):1.1
T737/90	Art.83:2.1.2
T788/90	Art.112(3):1
T811/90	R.144:2
T830/90	Art.54(2):2.4
T845/90	Art.112(1):1
T854/90	Art.52(2):1, Art.52(2):8, Art.57:2
T877/90	Art.54(2):2.3
T893/90	Art.54(5):2.1
T905/90	Art.125:2.1, Rfees8:2, Rfees14:1
T17/91	Art.114(2):3.1
T24/91	Art.53:3, Art.53:3.1, Art.53:3.3.1, Art.53:3.4.3
T60/91	Art.107:3.2
T79/91	Art.109:1
T143/91	Art.112(1):1
T227/91	Art.84:1.5
T245/91	Art.123(2):2.4.1
T246/91	Art.56:3.2, Art.84:2
T255/91	Art.123(2):2.4.1
T267/91	Art.83:2.1.2
T289/91	Art.101(1):2
T369/91	Art.107:3.2.2
T384/91	Ante Art. 52:1, Art.123(3):3
T409/91	Art.83:2, Art.84:3, Art.84:3.1, Art.84:3.2, Art.84:4.1, Art.100:2, R.42(1):3
T412/91	Art.54(2):4.5
T435/91	Art.83:2.2, Art.84:4.1
T438/91	Art.53:3.3.2
T455/91	Art.56:2.1, Art.56:2.2
T473/91	Art.110:3, Art.110:4
T495/91	Art.56:3.1
T500/91	Art.56:2.1, Art.56:2.2
T506/91	Art.107:2
T525/91	Art.122(1):4
T581/91	R.139:2.3
T613/91	R.101(2):1
T623/91	Art.84:1.4
T677/91	Art.56:6.2
T682/91	R.103(1):2
T712/91	R.139:2.3
T766/91	Art.56:2.3

T843/91	Art.24(1):1, Art.24(4):1, Art.111(1):3, Art.111(2):1.1
T852/91	Art.56:5
T856/91	R.111(2):1
T857/91	Art.54(2):3.2
T891/91	Art.56:3.3.2
T907/91	Art.94(3):6, R.81(3):1
T925/91	Art.101(1):2, R.77(1):1.2, R.99(1):2
T934/91	Art.104(2):1
T951/91	Art.114(2):1.1
T1/92	Art.106(1):3
T92/92	Art.56:3.2
T104/92	Art.56:3.3.3
T111/92	Art.122(1):4
T160/92	Art.85:1, Art.116:3
T164/92	Art.56:2, Art.56:2.4
T189/92	Art.56:3.3.2
T202/92	R.115(2):1
T223/92	Art.56:2.1
T273/92	Art.56:3.1
T341/92	R.115(2):1
T372/92	Art.107:3.2.3
T382/92	Art.19(2):1, R.103(1):2
T406/92	Art.54(2):3.3
T422/92	Art.54(1):3
T432/92	Art.56:3.1
T436/92	Art.55(1):2
T441/92	Art.76(1):7, Art.76(1):8, Art.76(1):9, Art.123(2):1.1
T455/92	Art.84:1.9.1
T465/92	Art.56:3, Art.112(1):1, Art.112(1):3
T472/92	Art.54(2):3.6.1, Art.117:1
T501/92	R.100(3):1
T545/92	Art.76(1):7
T585/92	Art.55(1):2
T597/92	Art.123(2):2.4.4
T601/92	Art.112(1):1
T645/92	Art.56:3, Art.56:3.3.7
T655/92	Art.53:3.4.3
T667/92	Art.115:4
T675/92	Art.56:3.3.2
T694/92	Art.56:2.3, Art.83:2
T697/92	Art.2:3
T703/92	R.130(1):1
T802/92	Art.123(2):2.1
T804/92	Art.117(1):2
T820/92	Art.53:3.3.1, Art.53:3.3.2
T870/92	Art.99(1):2.4, R.84(1):1
T892/92	Art.113(1):1
T910/92	Art.76(1):8, Art.123(2):2.1
T920/92	Art.54(2):2.1, Art.83:2.1.2
T930/92	Art.104(2):1, R.88(1):1, R.115(2):1
T939/92	Art.56:2.2, Art.56:2.3, Art.56:3.1, Art.56:3.2, Art.56:3.3.4, Art.56:5, Art.84:3.1, Art.112(1):1, Art.123(2):2.4.3
T951/92	Art.116:3, R.71(2):1
T952/92	Art.54(2):3.6.2, Art.129:2
T955/92	R.139:2.3
T971/92	Art.56:7
T1000/92	Art.56:3.1
T1002/92	R.76(2):4.4
T1011/92	Art.105(2):1
T1055/92	Art.84:1.2
T1085/92	Art.54(2):3.4
T39/93	Art.56:2.1, R.116(1):1
T51/93	Art.54(5):2.1
T74/93	Art.53:3.3.1, Art.57:1
T82/93	Art.53:3.3.1, Art.53:3.3.2, Art.123(3):2
T85/93	Art.114(2):3.2
T149/93	Art.56:5
T167/93	Art.111(1):3, Art.111(2):1.1, Art.125:1, Art.125:1.3
T219/93	Art.109:1
T254/93	Art.54(5):2.1
T296/93	Art.56:5, Art.105(1):1
T356/93	Art.53:1.1, Art.53:1.2, Art.53:2.1, Art.53:2.2, Art.53:2.3
T412/93	Art.56:2
T422/93	Art.56:2.4
T433/93	Art.24:2
T583/93	Art.123(2):2.1
T588/93	Art.56:3.2
T590/93	R.76(2):2.2
T740/93	R.111(2):1
T798/93	Art.99(1):2.1, Art.99(1):2.2
T843/93	Art.54(1):5.1
T860/93	Art.84:1.3
T926/93	R.76(2):4.3.1, R.81(3):1
T977/93	Art.54(2):3.6.2
T986/93	R.76(2):4.3.1
T20/94	Art.84:1.8
T207/94	Art.56:5
T284/94	Art.123(2):2.2.1, Art.123(2):2.3
T303/94	Art.107:3.2.3
T329/94	Art.53:3.1, Art.53:3.4.2, Art.53:3.4.3
T332/94	Art.123(3):2
T400/94	Art.123(2):1
T464/94	Art.53:3.3.2
T469/94	Art.53:3.3.1
T501/94	R.76(2):4.4
T522/94	Art.101(1):2
T590/94	R.77(1):1.1

T1286/14	Art.110:5
T1426/14	Art.122(2):2, R.136(2):2
T1596/14	R.125(4):1
T1833/14	Art.54(2):3.6.2
T1871/14	R.137(5):1.1
T1931/14	Art.54(1):5.1, Art.84:1.9.2
T237/15	Art.56:3.3.3
T261/15	Art.54(1):6.2
T320/15	Art.56:3.1
T449/15	Art.111(1):3
T611/15	Art.107:2
T777/15	R.103:1, R.103(4):2
T1087/15	Art.56:3.3.7
T1148/15	Art.56:3.1, Art.56:3.3.1
T1519/15	Art.88(3):2
T1548/15	R.103:1
T1553/15	Art.53:1.2
T1610/15	R.103(4):2
T1691/15	Art.125:2.3
T1758/15	Art.54(4):2
T1807/15	Art.116:2.1
T1943/15	Art.54(2):3.2
T2241/15	R.124(4):1
T2321/15	Art.56:7
T395/16	Art.106(1):3
T419/16	Art.54(4):2, Art.123(2):2.2.1
T694/16	Art.54(5):2.1
T817/16	Art.56:4.3
T853/16	R.103(2):1
T1186/16	Art.54(5):2
T1252/16	Art.52(2):9
T1294/16	Art.110:8.2
T1730/16	R.103(3):1, R.103(4):2
T1823/16	Rfees2(1):13
T1966/16	Art.111(1):2
T2141/16	R.103(4):2
T2314/16	Art.56:4.2
T2415/16	R.103(4):1
T2558/16	R.99(2):1
T2704/16	Art.94(3):7
T2707/16	Art.110:10, R.103(1):2
T7/17	Art.99(1):2.4
T54/17	Art.20(1):1, R.142:1
T73/17	R.103(4):1, R.103(4):2
T277/17	R.103(4):2
T377/17	Art.83:2.2
T439/17	Art.105(1):1
T517/17	R.103(4):2
T697/17	Art.52(2):6
T731/17	Art.111(1):2
T752/17	Art.54(5):2.1, Art.54(5):2.2
T833/17	R.103(4):1
T882/17	Art.107:3.2.3
T890/17	Art.54(1):1
T924/17	R.152(1):1
T943/17	Art.97(2):2
T1011/17	Art.56:5
T1440/17	Art.110:8.2
T1525/17	Art.110:6
T1621/17	Art.111(1):2
T1705/17	Art.54(1):5
T1790/17	Art.110:8.2
T2526/17	Art.106(2):1
T2698/17	R.103(4):2
T2699/17	Art.53:3.2
T2766/17	Art.84:1.1
T116/18	Art.54(3):3, Art.110:6
T184/18	Art.110:8
T233/18	Art.113(1):1
T234/18	Art.99(1):2.4
T245/18	Art.116:2.1
T488/18	R.103(4):2
T494/18	Art.110:8
T505/18	Art.56:4.1
T521/18	Art.87(1):3
T844/18	Art.87(1):3
T908/18	Art.110:8.2
T914/18	R.80:2
T1024/18	Art.84:1.1
T1063/18	Art.110:10, Art.164(2):2
T1195/18	R.40(1):1.5
T1255/18	Art.123(2):1.2
T1389/18	R.142:1
T1414/18	R.64(2):1
T1599/18	Art.54(1):5
T1616/18	Art.111(1):2
T1968/18	Art.84:1.1
T1989/18	Art.84:1.1
T2037/18	Art.87(1):3, R.76(2):4.3.1
T2091/18	Art.110:8
T2117/18	Art.110:7, Art.110:8
T2120/18	R.79(1):1
T2243/18	Art.110:8
T2249/18	R.103(4):2
T2264/18	R.103(4):1
T2293/18	Art.84:1.1
T2361/18	R.103(3):1, R.103(4):2
T2422/18	Rfees8:2
T2558/18	Art.164(2):2, R.71(6):1
T2796/18	R.28(2):1
T2866/18	Art.110:8
T2920/18	Art.110:8.2
T2988/18	Art.110:6
T3023/18	Rfees8:2
T84/19	Rfees2(1):11
T98/19	Art.100:2
T225/19	Rfees2(1):11
T317/19	R.139:2.2
T351/19	Art.56:4.1
T438/19	Art.54(2):3.6.2, Art.112(3):3
T446/19	Art.110:6
T598/19	R.103(4):2

Decisions of the Disciplinary Board of Appeal

Index to the AEPC

www.ingramcontent.com/pod-product-compliance
Ingram Content Group UK Ltd.
Pitfield, Milton Keynes, MK11 3LW, UK
UKHW020129290926
15471UKWH00003B/365

9 789403 522999